1993 Novel & Short Story Writer's Market

1993

Novel & Short Story Writer's Market

Editor: Robin Gee

Writer's Digest Books

Cincinnati, Ohio

Distributed in Canada by McGraw-Hill Ryerson,
300 Water St.,
Whitby, Ontario L1N 9B6.
Distributed in Australia by Kirby Books, Private
Bag No. 19, P.O. Alexandria NSW 2015.
Distributed in New Zealand by David Bateman
Ltd., P.O. Box 100-242, North Shore Mail Cen-
tre, Auckland 10

Managing Editor, Market Books Department:
Constance J. Achabal; Supervisory Editor:
Michael Willins

International Standard Serial Number
ISSN 0897-9812
International Standard Book Number
0-89879-578-8

Cover illustration by Frank Ansley

Contents

Writing Techniques

Personal Views

Craft and Technique

Writing and Publishing

The Markets

From the Editor

Change. In the publishing industry it's the only constant. Every year publishers change policies and editors change jobs. With all the buy-outs, mergers and restructures it's hard to keep up with who owns whom, let alone who's publishing what. That's why, in terms of your writing career, the 1993 edition of *Novel & Short Story Writer's Market* is one of the most important purchases you'll make this year.

Every year we bring you the latest information on the publishing industry to help you target the best markets for your work. Our book is the tool you need to locate new markets, pinpoint trends and keep abreast of publishers' ever-changing needs and policies.

We've brought you this help for more than a decade and, as we look back, we notice our book has changed too. As we've learned more about the field and, especially, about your needs, we've changed the information we provide. Over the years, we've changed our format, our name, how our book is structured and even the questions we ask publishers.

This year we decided it was time to step back a bit and take a look at what we've done. We conducted extensive research, including a large reader survey, and discovered a wealth of information about you. This information helped us make the 1993 edition the most useful edition ever.

For the most part, our changes are subtle, more like refinements. We learned you need all the information we provide in the listings, but would like even more. Our most important change, therefore, is the inclusion of our editorial comments. Whenever possible we've added bulleted comments to the listings about awards and honors, how the markets treat writers and anything specific that could help your selection of the best markets for your work.

We've added handy section reference pages at the start of Writing Techniques, The Markets and Resources to help you locate these sections of interest with ease. Our Category Index now includes page numbers for quick reference. We've changed a few categories and added subcategories within listings to provide information on the specific needs of each listing.

Bringing you more of what you want

Because you want to hear from more editors, we've included interviews with several, including Michaela Hamilton, editorial director for NAL/Dutton's mass market line; Jean Cavelos, senior editor of Dell/Abyss; Dawn Raffel, fiction editor for *Redbook* and Clint McCown, editor of *Beloit Fiction Journal*.

You told us you are interested, too, in what other writers have to say about their experiences. We've included interviews with several established authors, including W. P. Kinsella, John Edgar Wideman and William Kennedy. Yet we've also added First Bylines, a special section in which we discuss first sales with newly published short story writers and novelists.

We've paid careful attention to our upfront article section this year to bring you a mix of articles for beginning and seasoned writers. Jack Bickham describes why strong story beginnings and endings are vital, while Monica Wood walks you through the pitfalls and pleasures of working with present tense. On more heady subjects, Matt Devens defends baroque word style and Diane Lefer tells you when it's okay to break the rules. These and other upfront authors reflect your diverse interests.

Refining information to fit your needs

Your feedback has led us to refine some of the information we've added in recent years. How to Get the Most Out of This Book, for example, has been reworked to include more specific details on using this book as a working tool and on developing your own market plan. Our report on publishing trends is back, but this year it's titled Commercial Fiction Trends Report. The new title reflects its expanded scope which includes trends in all areas of commercial fiction including children's, religious and other fiction markets, as well as genres such as romance and mystery.

You'll still find our helpful Business of Fiction, section introductions, Glossary and Markets Index. As in the past, we include cover illustrations with captions that explain a little about the philosophy of each magazine featured. Our Resource section is back, too, and the Conference and Workshops section is greatly expanded.

Although we've changed and refined many things this year, with your help we expect our book to continue to evolve. Feel free to contact us with your suggestions and concerns. Our commitment to helping you advance your writing career is one thing we will never change.

Robin Gee

Editor

How to Get the Most Out of This Book

We know a lot of work has gone into your writing even before you opened this book. Chances are you've been writing and rewriting every chance you get. Some of you have studied writing formally; others have received feedback on their work by sharing it with a writers' group. You are well-read in your particular writing interest and may already have some markets in mind. You've put a great deal of time into your writing and now it's time to share it with others.

The temptation with any book like this is to go straight to the listings and start sending out your work. Perhaps this is the fastest, but it is not the most efficient route to publication. Many successful writers start by spending almost as much time selecting markets for their work as they do perfecting their craft.

Finding the right market for your fiction requires careful research and planning. This book is designed as a tool to help you in your search by providing information on the publishing industry as well as detailed listings of magazine and book publishers looking for fiction submissions.

What you'll find here

Novel & Short Story Writer's Market is divided into three parts, each presenting a different type of information. The first is Writing Techniques. In this part we provide in-depth interviews with established authors, articles on the craft of writing and informational pieces on the business side of publishing. This is where you will find our Business of Fiction Writing and Commercial Fiction Trends Report, in addition to other articles on writing and publishing fiction.

Following Writing Techniques is Markets, offering magazine and book publisher listings. The heart of our book, Markets is divided into five sections. The largest is the Literary and Small Circulation Magazines section, which includes listings of literary journals of all sizes and smaller magazines whose circulations are under 10,000. Next is the Commercial Periodicals section containing magazines with commercial appeal and circulations of more than 10,000. After this section you'll find the Small Press section, which includes nonprofit and independent small presses and university publishers. The Commercial Publishers section includes listings of major publishers of both hardcover, trade paperback and mass market books. Finally, the Contests and Awards section includes listings for contests, awards and grants programs open to fiction writers.

Throughout the market section you'll find Close-up interviews. These are short interviews with editors, publishers and writers designed to give you a closer look at what specific publications and publishers are looking for, including their immediate needs, how to approach them and sell to them.

The last part is Resources. We like to refer to this as our "community" section because it offers listings of places where writers can make contact with other writers. This includes Conferences and Workshops, Retreats and Colonies, Organizations and Publications of Interest to Fiction Writers.

Developing your marketing plan

If you are not sure in what category your work fits or if you just want to explore the possibilities, start by reading the introductions and browsing through the sections to find markets that interest you. The browsing method also helps you get an idea of how many different types of markets there are and may lead you to a market you hadn't thought of before.

To help you with your search, use the Category Index in the back of the book. The Category Index is divided into sections corresponding to those in our Markets sections, each including a list of fiction subjects such as romance, mystery, religious, regional. Look for the subject that seems closest to your style and interest in writing. The subject headings are then followed by the names of listings interested in that topic.

To further narrow your list, determine the level of listing most likely to be interested in your work. Each listing is ranked with a Roman numeral code just after the listing's name. In the magazine and book publisher sections, these codes indicate the openness of the markets and what level of writing they will consider. Those ranked I, for example, are most open to new writers, while those ranked III are primarily interested in established writers. For more on the ranking codes, see the introductions to each section.

Listings new to our book are indicated by the double dagger symbol (‡). Many are newly established firms and are most open to the work of new writers. Some of the listings with double daggers are not new, but have recently decided to list with us because they have increased their fiction needs. In the book publisher sections, we use other symbols to indicate different types of publishers. Check the introductions to these sections for more information.

Reading the listings

Once you've narrowed the market, read the listings carefully. You will find you can streamline your list even further based on the market's philosophy, advice, specific needs, terms, payment and reputation.

After the name and contact information for each listing, you'll find a brief description of the philosophy and audience. Following this is a physical description of the magazine or the books published. Physical descriptions can tell you a lot about the market's budget and give you hints about its quality and prestige. Check also the establishment date, circulation or number of books or amount of fiction published.

Following the profile is the Needs section of the listing. In addition to a list or description of the type of work the market needs, you'll also find how much work the market receives from writers each year and how much it publishes. This will give you an idea of how competitive the market is. Also included are specifics on length and other requirements.

After the Needs section comes How to Contact. Here is where you'll find out how to approach the market and what material to include with your submission. We suggest you follow the requirements for submission carefully. For more information on submission, presentation and cover letters, see The Business of Fiction Writing on page 76.

Next in the listing comes the Terms and Payment sections. When possible, we've provided a range of payment, but note that many publications in the Literary and Small Circulation section pay only in copies or subscriptions. We also indicate when you will be paid. For magazines, if you are paid on acceptance, you'll receive payment once your story is accepted, but if you're paid on publication, you may have to wait up to one year.

Also in Terms, you'll find information on what type of rights the market buys. For more on rights, see the Business of Fiction Writing. Keep in mind the more rights you retain, the more chance you will have to make additional money on your work.

Remember your market research should begin with a careful study of the listings, but it should not end there. Whenever possible obtain a sample copy or catalog. Send a self-addressed, stamped envelope for writer's guidelines, if provided. For book publishers, check *Books in Print* at the library to find a publisher's titles and take a look at some of their books. The library also has publishing industry magazines such as *Publishers Weekly* as well as magazines for writers. Some of these magazines are listed in the Publications of Interest to Fiction Writers section located later in this book. These can help you keep informed of new publishers and changes in the field.

The next step

The next step, of course, is to send your work out. If you have any questions on how to present your work, see the Business of Fiction Writing. When in doubt, remember to make it as easy as possible for an editor to read your work. Because editors are very busy, they will not waste time reading a manuscript that is messy and difficult to read. It may be good writing, but the editor may never read it to find that out. If you show you care about your work, the editor will too.

Also keep careful records. We've asked our listings to indicate how long it will take them to report on a submission, but at times throughout the year the market may get behind. Keeping track of when you sent a manuscript will help you decide when it is time to check on the status of your submission.

About our policies

We occasionally receive letters asking why a certain magazine, book publisher or contest is not in the book. Sometimes when we contact a listing, the editor does not want to be listed because they: do not use very much fiction; are overwhelmed with submissions; are having financial difficulty or have been recently sold; use only solicited material; accept work from a select group of writers; do not have the staff or time for the many unsolicited submissions a listing may bring.

Some of the listings do not appear because we have chosen not to list them. We investigate complaints about misrepresentation by editors in the information they provide us or about unethical or unprofessional activities in a publisher's dealings with writers. If we find these reports to be true, after thorough investigation, we will delete a listing. See Important Listing Information for more on our listing policies.

If a listing appeared in our book the previous year but is no longer listed, we list them at the end of each section with an explanation, if provided. Sometimes the listing does not appear because the editor did not respond in time or it may not appear for any of the reasons mentioned above.

If you feel you have not been treated fairly by a market listed in our book, we advise you to take the following steps:

- First, try to contact the listing. Sometimes one phone call or letter can quickly clear up the matter.
- Be sure to document all your correspondence with the listing. When you write to us with a complaint, we will ask for the name of your manuscript, the date of your submission and the dates and nature of your subsequent correspondence.
- We will write to the publisher or editor and ask them to resolve the problem. We will enter your letter into our files.

● The number, frequency and severity of unresolved complaints will be considered in our decision whether to delete a listing from the book.

Listings appearing in *Novel & Short Story Writer's Market* are compiled from detailed questionnaires, phone interviews and information provided by editors, publishers and awards directors. The publishing industry is volatile and changes of address, editor, policies and needs happen frequently. To keep up with the changes we suggest you check the monthly Markets column in *Writer's Digest* magazine.

We also rely on our readers for information on new markets and changes in the markets listed in the book. Write us if you have any new information or if you have suggestions on how to improve our listings to better suit your writing needs.

Writing Techniques

An Interview with W.P. Kinsella

by Jack Neff

W.P. Kinsella creates characters who don't let reality stand in the way of a good fantasy. But realities stood in the way of Kinsella's own writing for years.

After he wrote his first stories as a child, Kinsella virtually gave up writing as a young adult. He worked as a civil servant, cab driver, bill collector and salesman to support his family. Only in his 30s could he afford to go to college and begin writing and publishing seriously. He was 47 when he published his first novel, *Shoeless Joe*. That allowed him to turn down an offer of tenure at the University of Calgary and become a fulltime writer for the first time.

Best known for his three baseball novels, Kinsella also has published 11 collections of short stories. He was first known in his native Canada for writing Indian stories, and his second novel, *The Iowa Baseball Confederacy* combined elements of his baseball and Indian fiction. His latest novel, *Box Socials*, published in 1992, combines baseball lore with the remote, impoverished setting of his childhood in Alberta, Canada.

Kinsella won the prestigious Houghton Mifflin Literary Fellowship Award for *Shoeless Joe*. And he's a former professor who earned his master's degree from and taught at Iowa Writer's Workshop. But he rejects the trappings of "serious" literature and academia.

He recalls taking Ballantine Books to task for not publishing a special edition of *Shoeless Joe* to capitalize on the film adaptation, *Field of Dreams* – something he was told they don't do with "literature." He says he makes his work more accessible than some writers who've influenced him, such as Gabriel Garcia Marquez and T.R. Pearson, because only academics read difficult works. "Ultimately," he says, "I'm in this business to make a living."

Though he may not have much to do with academia anymore, Kinsella shows here he still has plenty to teach.

JN: Why did you choose baseball as the setting for so much of your work?

WPK: Well, it comes about by accident, like everything else. When I wrote *Shoeless Joe*, I was living in Iowa City around 1977. I got the idea from thinking about some stories that my father had told me about Shoeless Joe Jackson, and what became of him after the Black Sox Scandal. They weren't necessarily true stories, but they were good stories. And I wondered what would happen if Joe Jackson came back to life in this time and place.

If it hadn't been successful, I don't think I would have done any more baseball writing. But I discovered there was a market out there for good baseball fiction, something that hasn't been exploited. You're always looking for some niche that hasn't been filled. There are 10 million mystery writers and sci-fi writers and middle-of-the-road fiction writers. And if you want to be successful, you have to find some niche that hasn't been filled yet. So I will try to continue writing baseball fiction as long as I have ideas and as long as there are people out there willing to read what I write.

Jack Neff *is a Cincinnati-based freelance writer and editor. He's also author of two books for Writer's Digest Books – and a big baseball fan.*

JN: Why do you think baseball provides such a good setting? Could any other sports provide such good settings?

WPK: I think baseball is conducive to fiction writing because of its open-endedness. The other sports are all twice enclosed, first by time limits and then by rigid playing boundaries. It doesn't matter how wonderful Michael Jordan or Wayne Gretzky are, they're still trapped on these tiny playing fields. In baseball, there's no time limit. And on the true baseball field, the foul lines diverge forever, eventually taking in a good part of the universe. That makes for myth and larger-than-life characters. I think that's why there's been a fair amount of good baseball writing done, and virtually nothing about the other sports.

JN: I read that you were working on another baseball novel, *If Wishes Were Horses*, and I wondered whatever happened to it.

WPK: I wrote it right after *The Iowa Baseball Confederacy*, but my editor didn't like it, and my agent didn't like it very much. Ordinarily, I would go ahead and submit it on my own. I did that with *The Alligator Report* [a collection of short stories] and it has sold all kinds of copies. But I had so many projects going, and I thought it probably does need a rewrite. I think the problem was, unlike *Shoeless Joe* and *The Iowa Baseball Confederacy*, the main character wasn't likeable. He was too much of a smart ass. I think I've got to change him.

JN: Your protagonists do usually seem likeable. And the story lines are usually positive. I was wondering why that seems to work best for you?

WPK: Well, I think ultimately we write the kind of stories we like to read, and those are the kinds of stories I like. I liked Richard Brautigan's works, where the guys were kinds of amiable people who sometimes didn't quite understand what was happening to them.

JN: What is the most important source of your stories? Where do the details, the characters and the ideas come from?

WPK: Details I create. I get a lot of ideas for stories from the newspaper. Wherever I am I read the local newspapers and *USA Today* from beginning to end every day. I may only get two or three ideas a year, but that's all you need.

JN: You've discounted the role of autobiographical material in your work, and in successful fiction in general. But it seems that *Box Socials* contains a lot of autobiographical material. Why does it work there?

WPK: It works because what I've used in *Box Socials* is the setting and the situation. Everything else is made up. There's nothing autobiographical in any of the characters. Our lives were absolutely uninteresting. Our neighbors were not interesting. We were not interesting. I've sort of made life there sound appealing in that book. It was anything but appealing. It was cold. It was miserable. We were poor. The land was awful. There were mosquitoes the size of cocker spaniels. It rained all the time. There was snow nine months a year. It flooded in the spring.

JN: I've read that you had a somewhat isolated time in early childhood, and I was wondering what effect that had on your becoming a writer. Did it help you develop the imagination you needed to be a writer?

WPK: I think it did. I had to create my own entertainment as a child. I'm sure that helped. Not having other playmates, I had to use my imagination more. And when I came to have other children to play with, I discovered that what I did by myself was much more interesting than what they did. Playing with other kids was pretty banal, I found. So, I have always enjoyed being by myself. So many people can't stand silence.

JN: How long was it after your first story was published in *The Alberta Civil Service Bulletin* in 1953 that you were able to make a living strictly as a writer?

WPK: I was able to make a living after 1982 when *Shoeless Joe* came out. You can't make a living writing in Canada, for one thing. You have to crack the U.S. and international markets, and *Shoeless Joe* did that for me. So, in 1982, I was able to tell the university where I was teaching to shove tenure where the sun doesn't shine. I decided I was going to make a living as a writer and I've done very well ever since.

One thing that really helps me out is that all 17 or 18 of my books are in print, and they all sell 1,000 to 3,000 copies a year. I'm certainly the best backlist author in Canada, and I think I'm not a bad backlist author in the U.S. either.

JN: You worked a wide variety of non-writing jobs. How did those influence your work, and do you think that kind of experience is valuable for writers?

WPK: I don't think so. I think it's much better to write. You'll get your life experience one way or another. I held a lot of mediocre jobs. I drove a cab, which isn't really very interesting. I've got two little stories I've written about cab driving, and they're not anywhere near my best. I wrote one story about teaching at a university, which is probably the angriest thing I've written. Imagination is so much more wonderful than anything that happens to you in real life.

I would have been just as well off if I could have made a living as a writer right from the start. And I think I could have if I had dedicated myself to it. I think I could have struggled by as a freelancer doing mainly articles and stuff, and occasional stories. I had a few friends who made precarious livings doing that. But I chose to take employment. And once I had my family and young children, I had no choice but to stay on in these evil jobs and write a little bit on the side.

JN: How much time were you able to devote to writing while you had those jobs?

WPK: Not very much. Most of my 20s, I didn't do anything. A little bit of journalism, and that was it. At about 30, I started doing more journalism and writing more stories, which weren't successful. And then, when I was 35, I was operating a business that was successful, and was able to take some time off to go to the university.

That was sort of the turning point in my writing. It came from reading. I had always been a voracious reader, but I had read essentially pop fiction. I had never read Flannery O'Connor or Ibsen or Scott Fitzgerald. I got a whole new education when I came to the university. It was in the fourth year that I started publishing seriously. And I've published almost everything I've written ever since.

JN: How important do you think formal writing instruction was for you and is for writers in general?

WPK: I don't think it was actually the creative writing courses I took. It was the reading, and analyzing the reading to see what in the world it was that other writers did that made people love their characters in a few pages.

And I was very lucky to have an instructor who was on the same wavelength as I was and then put me on the right track. He would take one of my stories and rip off the first page and rip off the last page and scissor off half of the second to last page and say: "There's your story. You warmed up for a page before you started it. Don't do that." I was smart enough that he only had to do that to me twice. And then I got five acceptances in one week and went from there.

JN: You certainly faced your share of rejections, like most writers. *The New Yorker* — Roger Angell — even rejected *Shoeless Joe* as too sentimental. I was wondering how you dealt with rejection?

WPK: It's just part of stamina. I always made a list of five places where I was going to send a story before I sent it out. When it came back, I just detached the rejection slip, attached a new bio and sent it out again.

I always say that writing involves ability, imagination, passion and stamina. Ability is being able to write complete sentences in clear straightforward standard English, which gets rid of almost everyone. Imagination, having stories to tell, eliminates the rest. And passion, being that nebulous thing that keeps you turning pages in the book and makes you love the characters, essentially can't be taught. Each of those combined are worth about 5 percent each, and stamina is about 85 percent.

Stamina is sending your stuff out in the mail 30 times. And stamina is sitting down to write your 50th short story, knowing that the previous 49 have been unsuccessful, knowing that the 50th one will also be unsuccessful, but will be 1 percent better than the previous 49.

Writing when you don't feel like it is the other part of stamina. I set a rigid quota and have stuck to it. Some days I'll do my quota in an hour. And some days it will take me 12 hours, and every word is like pulling a tooth. But when I go back to read the finished story, I can't tell which passages were like that and which flowed off the typewriter in an hour. So, it's a matter of working whether you feel like it or not and not waiting around for inspiration.

JN: You've been writing stories practically since you were old enough to write. But you never wrote a novel until Lawrence Kessenich, an editor at Houghton Mifflin, encouraged you to turn your short story, "Shoeless Joe Jackson Comes to Iowa," into one. Why did it take so long?

WPK: I always thought in terms of short fiction. I didn't feel I had enough story to write a novel, so I had never attempted one. I guess I wouldn't have, certainly not in the foreseeable future, until Larry wrote to me.

I actually had turned another short story of mine called "The Grecian Urn" into a novel before *Shoeless Joe*. It had been out in the mail a few times and nobody liked it very much. After *Shoeless Joe*, I rewrote it again and titled it *Honk If You Love Willie Nelson*, and nobody likes it yet. So, it's still sitting on the shelf.

JN: Your other novels also have started as short stories. Is this an approach you think would work for other writers?

WPK: I'm not sure about it working for other writers, because everyone is so different in their writing habits and where they get their ideas. But because I was a successful short fiction writer first, I can now look at things I wrote 15 years ago and find that there is so much material in my short stories that they can become novels.

JN: In transforming a short story into a novel — *Shoeless Joe*, for instance — what steps do you take?

WPK: When Larry wrote to me and suggested *Shoeless Joe* should be a novel, I thought about what I could add to it. I thought about what other short stories I intended to write.

I intended to write something about J.D. Salinger, because he makes himself conspicuous by hiding. I had admired his work. I knew he put himself through college working as an actor on a cruise ship, so he knew how to hold his audience. What other writer who hadn't published in 17 years still managed to stay in the limelight? I thought about how I could tie this guy into the story I already had. I thought, what if Ray is instructed to go off to Boston to kidnap J.D. Salinger and take him to a baseball game?

I knew I wanted to write something about Moonlight Graham, who I had discovered in the *Baseball Encyclopedia*. I wondered what that instant of playing major league ball had done to his life. Was he one of these American Legion drunks who sat around forever bragging about having played major league ball? I didn't know what I would do until I drove to Chisolm, Minnesota, and actually researched him. He turned out in real life to be a much more wonderful character than I could ever have invented. Virtually everything I wrote about him in the novel was true.

The odds of finding someone like Moonlight Graham are almost impossible. Most real people you would go and look up, their lives would be so dull that no one would be interested in them. I always tell my fiction writing students: Trust me, your life is not interesting; don't write about it. Nine out of ten of us have lives that are so dull that no one would be interested in them. And the tenth person, their life is so bizarre that no one would believe it. So you have to have little bits of the bizarre and tone it down and little bits of the mundane and tone it up.

My feeling is if you create wonderful characters and put them in an interesting situation, that something great can't help but happen. I had all these characters coming back to the magical baseball field.

JN: Having written novels, do you still prefer short stories?

WPK: I think I have enjoyed writing short stories more, and when I get a great idea for a short story, it is more fun. But certainly to make a living you have to write novels. And I'm working more and more toward novels all the time.

JN: Were you surprised that J.D. Salinger objected to the possibility of a movie portrayal, after not hearing anything about the book?

WPK: Actually, it was the other way around. He did hear about the book, but not the movie. Before the book came out, Robie Macauley, who was head honcho at Houghton Mifflin fiction, went and had lunch with Salinger's agent, not to discuss the book with her, but just to see what he was doing and what kind of mood he was in. Salinger is apparently still writing, and has a couple of novels at least, maybe more. But he isn't going to publish anything during his lifetime, because he doesn't want anything to do with the critics. After the book was published, Houghton Mifflin's lawyers got a grumbling letter from J.D. Salinger's lawyers, saying he was outraged and offended to be portrayed in the novel and would be very unhappy were it to be transferred to other media. They didn't say they would do anything, just that they would be very unhappy.

JN: You mentioned that you have an agent. Why do you think that's important?

WPK: The one advice I would give to aspiring writers—other than to read, read, read and read some more—is to never sign a contract without an agent. You can market your own book, up to the point that a publisher says they want to do it. Then, get an agent to read the contract. They will pay for themselves in gold many times.

It has cost me a lot of money not to have had an agent for my first books. Publishers are generally not dishonest. But they're businessmen, and they write contracts that favor themselves. I would have paid them to publish me when I was first accepted. So, I wasn't going to complain about the contract. I had a 50-50 split on movie and television rights on my first story collections. An agent would have just hacked that right out of the contract. Now, my first book has been optioned by Norman Jewison for 10 years, and I have to split all that with my publisher 50-50.

JN: I was wondering if achieving commercial success has changed you or your writing at all?

WPK: I don't think it's changed anything. I'm a mid-list author. So I'm not that successful. I'm no Stephen King or Danielle Steele. I'm way down on the mid-list. A successful book for me would be an abject failure for any top writer. My wife and I own a little condo in Palm Springs. And when we came out [to British Columbia] to teach, we traded it with a retired school teacher. She's living in Palm Springs for three months and we're living in her condo here so we can both save money. We drive a little car. The only extravagance we have is spending our winters in a warm place. I could live forever in a warm climate. If there were some way I could get some kind of decent medical insurance, we would live in the U.S. all the time. There are a great many pluses about living in the U.S., but there's one minus that negates all the pluses, and that is lack of medical insurance.

JN: You seem to have had good relations with editors. Larry Kessenich even played a very crucial role in your success. Why have the relations always been good?

WPK: They've always been pretty good, and one reason is that my work doesn't get edited very much. And I don't mind being edited. My feeling is that if you're publishing the book, take my manuscript and change it any way you need to change it and don't bother me. I don't care if I even see the changes. So many writers don't want a comma changed without their permission and will fight over commas. I couldn't care less. I would guess in a book like *Box Socials*, after it was copy edited, I complained about three changes in a 300-page novel. I said I think you changed the meaning by doing this. Those are the only changes that I argue about.

JN: You must be a fairly rigorous editor, since you have so few changes.

WPK: I don't edit much. But I think things out very carefully before I write them down. That stems back to the days when there were only typewriters. I'm a slow, awkward typist, and I never wanted to type anything more than twice. So, I would do the first draft in longhand, which I still do quite often, and then would revise it extensively as it went on the typewriter. I don't think I've ever typed anything more than three times.

I know colleagues who rewrite everything 30 times. I just don't have the temperament to do that. And I think that's one of the reasons I've been able to turn out a fairly large volume of work.

JN: Do you use a computer now?

WPK: Yes, I use a word processor now. But I don't edit very much on it. When I see a sentence at the end of the paragraph that would be better at the beginning of the paragraph, I change it. In the past, on the typed version, I would not have changed it.

JN: What is your work space like?

WPK: We used to have two condos in one building on the waterfront in British Columbia in White Rock. We had a two-bedroom unit overlooking the water that we used as an office. Then a year or so ago we bought a huge house with my oldest daughter, because we're away so much and she had to look after our places so often when we were gone. This house has a room about as big as what I was using before, over the garage and connected to the house. I have a big oak table that I use, and a big oak desk for my computer. And I have all my books around the walls, and posters and things like that.

JN: Do you have a work routine?

WPK: I try when I'm working to write two days on and one day off. And I try to do four pages of new material on the days when I work, or an amount of revision I honestly consider equal to four pages of new material.

My schedule in the last three or four years has gotten so busy that I sometimes have to try and cram work in when I can. And that means I work sometimes six or seven days in a row, trying to get as much done as I possibly can, because I know I have to go on tour for a week. I don't like that. I like to keep a schedule.

I'm also 57 now, and I find my sense of urgency is diminishing. I'm not keeping that schedule as much as I did. I used to always work when I traveled. I mean, what else is there to do on airplanes? If we were staying in hotels, having to check out by 11 o'clock is a great incentive to have your writing quota done by 11 o'clock. But I've gotten really lazy in the last couple of years. I didn't work at all on this last book tour. I still have more stories in my head than I could write in three lifetimes, but I'm not as fanatical about getting them down as I was ten years ago.

JN: It sounds like you've always got a lot of projects going at the same time.

WPK: That's one of the ways that I always keep working. I always have eight or ten projects going. If I can't stand the sight of one, then I can work on another. I'm never without something to do.

An Interview with John Edgar Wideman

by Christine Martin

"My fiction is often about the problematic line between fact and fiction," says author John Edgar Wideman, two-time winner of the PEN/Faulkner Award. "The older I get, the more I write, the freer I feel in crossing boundaries, ignoring everything from grammatical lines to genre lines, and trying to sing, trying to make something and let somebody else figure out what it is, let somebody else categorize it," he says.

At present, Wideman's work includes seven novels and three short story collections, the most recent titled *All Stories Are True*, a proverb from the Igbo of West Africa that Wideman finds particularly fitting. In most of these stories and much of his other work, he writes about the lives of families in and around Homewood, the ghetto district where he grew up in Pittsburgh, Pennsylvania.

Back then Wideman thought he wanted to be a professional basketball player, and he left Pittsburgh to attend the University of Pennsylvania on a Benjamin Franklin scholarship. Though he originally intended to major in psychology, "I got tired of counting the number of times the rat went up the shoot and either drank the cup of sugar water or didn't," he says. "Penn was a center of experimental, behavioral psychology, and, in my naivete, I thought we would be doing things like learning about Freud and Jung and those interesting areas of the study of the mind and what makes people work."

Disinterested in the psychology program, and with thoughts of playing professional basketball fading (though he was later inducted into the Philadelphia Big Five Basketball Hall of Fame), Wideman switched his major to English. The switch comes as little surprise when one listens to him recall how he loved "the time in the homeroom [in grade school] when we could have a little relaxation while the teacher went to the powder room and I'd get a chance to tell a story." Still, Wideman maintains the same kinds of interest in what makes people tick, and his work is often noted for its psychological insight.

In 1963, after studying at the University of Pennsylvania, Wideman received a Rhodes Scholarship to Oxford University. He was only the second black student ever selected for this honor; the first was Alain Locke in 1905. With such recognition also came a letter from Hiram Haydn, the man who would not only publish Wideman's first book, but also become a good friend.

"He wrote me right after I won the Rhodes Scholarship and asked me if I ever had a book published or if I had a piece of a book that I was interested in publishing that he could have a look at, and I was very sympatico with him," Wideman says of Haydn. "He was an older man, an established critic, a man who had published his own novels. He was very much, in some ways, an establishment figure. He also told great stories about the publishing world. With him I felt part of some tradition."

Wideman's relationship with Haydn resulted in the publication of his first novel, *A Glance Away*, in 1967, when he was 26, just a year after he returned from studying 18th-

Christine Martin is co-editor of Poet's Market, *former assistant editor of* Novel & Short Story Writer's Market *and a film reviewer for* Critic's Choice, *a national review syndicate.*

century literature at Oxford. The book describes the struggles of a drug addict the day he comes home from rehabilitation.

A stimulating environment

Prior to the book's release, Wideman spent a year as a Kent Fellow at the University of Iowa's Creative Writing Workshop. "Iowa was kind of culture shock, returning from Europe, the Continent, and then suddenly being in the middle of a cornfield," he says. "It was there that I met Jose Donoso, who's one of the best writers in the world. He became a mentor, if you will, somebody I learned a lot from and learned to respect. There were also other quite accomplished writers as well as lots of younger people who went on to publish quite successfully, so it was a stimulating environment for a writer."

Still Wideman considers attending a writer's workshop "a totally individual proposition." It can be quite tricky, he says, "because workshops are like greenhouses. They're an artificial environment, and they can make you lose your sense of reality. You spend a lot of time talking to other students and to teachers and that's kind of a captive audience. The danger is to become too provincial, too much of a hothouse group, a mutual admiration society."

Wideman, who currently teaches creative writing in a MFA program at the University of Massachusetts, is quick to point out, however, that there are many positive sides to workshop participation. "One of the best things is the other side of its danger and that is that you have a group of people in a workshop who are treating writing as something very, very important, who are reading books and critiquing one another's work. That's something that doesn't happen out in the real world very often," he says. "Commercial interests have taken over in publishing to such a degree that real honest constructive criticism and seriousness about books is rare, and I think a proper workshop atmosphere can create and sustain a concern about craft."

As far as Wideman's craft is concerned, critics have generally viewed his first two novels, *A Glance Away* and *Hurry Home*, a book about a black law school graduate's search for identity (published in 1970), as a reflection of his formal training. His third novel, however, *The Lynchers*, about four black men who plan the lynching of a white cop (published in 1973), is said to reflect his increased interest in uniquely American, black-oriented themes, myths and dialects, brought about, Wideman is noted as saying, by a growing awareness of other black authors.

It was in 1968, while he was teaching at the University of Pennsylvania, that a group of students asked Wideman to start a course in Afro-American literature. This prompted what he has referred to as his "second education," though he does not perceive his work as primarily influenced by any certain group.

The question of influence

When asked which writers have influenced him the most, Wideman says, "I read all the time, so I wouldn't even know where to begin. I'd rather talk in terms of a written tradition, which I'm very familiar with and very enamored of, the written tradition that includes everybody from Benjamin Franklin to Thomas Pynchon, everybody from Phillis Wheatley to Virginia Woolf. That's one part of influence.

"The other is oral tradition, the way people talk, the way people talked around me, what they talked about, storytellers in my family, in the barber shop, my friends as we grew up. I see the two things coming together, that kind of literate tradition and the oral tradition, and the play between those, the tension somehow between those, propels my writing," Wideman says.

By its very nature, perhaps, Wideman's writing about Homewood, the Pittsburgh neighborhood where he spent his childhood, includes more of his "oral tradition." The first stories, about the settling of Homewood, were gathered in *Damballah*, a book whose title refers to a voodoo god, "good serpent of the sky." That collection was published in 1981, the same year as Wideman's fourth novel, *Hiding Place*, which continues the story of some of the Homewood characters, namely Tommy and the sister of his great grandmother, Mama Bess, whom Tommy visits in an effort to hide after involvement in a robbery that ends in murder.

Wideman followed *Hiding Place* with another book set in Homewood, *Sent for You Yesterday*, about the ill-fated return of Albert Wilkes, a blues pianist, who is one of the book's multiple narrators. This novel, published in 1983, won Wideman the 1984 PEN/Faulkner Award, a true tribute from his peers, as the judges are also fiction writers.

All three of these books, *Damballah*, *Hiding Place* and *Sent for You Yesterday*, were released as paperback originals. It was a move which brought outcries from critics who believed Wideman was not receiving the hardcover attention he deserved. However, Wideman himself had requested the paperback format in order to make his work accessible to a wider readership, particularly to the people he was writing about. As he told Edwin McDowell in *The New York Times*, "I spend an enormous amount of time and energy writing and I want to write good books, but I also want people to read them." The three books were collected in a paperback edition and reissued in 1985 as *The Homewood Trilogy*.

Wideman's writing about Homewood has prompted comparisons to Faulkner's Yoknapatawpha County as well as many questions regarding how much of the work is based upon real characters. "There is a family tree at the front of the Homewood books, but it's fictional," he says. "It's there as much for my benefit as anybody else's, because I made it up. It doesn't follow any genealogical research. It's the family tree of the people who appear in the stories. If I paid somebody some money and they did make up a genealogical tree for my actual family, it probably would correspond in some ways and in other ways it would diverge completely."

Playing games

"I'm not intimidated by the prospect of writing about people's lives, the lives of people who are close to me. On the other hand, I observe my own set of rules so that I don't infringe. In a sense, I play games," says Wideman. "You have to start with the intent that when you write fiction you are literally making something up, and you make it up with freedom and the kind of playfulness and seriousness that a sculptor might mold clay. In my mind I may have the image of a horse that I hack out of clay and it may not look like a horse to anybody else, but to me that's a horse.

"The beauty of art is that, if it works, the object created doesn't need an introduction or any kind of documentation or a label on it that says 'Oh, this is important because this is the writer's grandmother' or 'This is important because it's what the writer thinks is important.' If the object has some interest and subtlety and form and ideas compressed into it, that's enough. That's all you need to know."

Yet Wideman has written directly about his own family in Homewood in a memoir titled *Brothers and Keepers*, published in 1984 and nominated for a National Book Award that same year. The book examines the relationship between Wideman and his younger brother Robby, who was involved in a robbery much like the one in which Wideman's character

Tommy finds himself in the novel *Hiding Place*. During the robbery, a man was shot and killed; and though Robby did not pull the trigger, he is now serving a life sentence without parole in a Pennsylvania prison.

When Wideman next wrote of Homewood, it was once again in a fictional sense. This time the novel was *Reuben*, published in 1987 and named for the character who serves as the common thread among the others, a man dispensing legal aid. After *Reuben*, however, Wideman temporarily abandoned his well-known Homewood setting for Philadelphia. In his second collection of short stories, *Fever*, published in 1989, the title story is about an 18th-century black doctor who treats Philadelphia's yellow fever victims. The book's other stories are set in the same city but the present century. "All the stories are about a kind of illness or trouble in the air," Wideman told Judith Rosen in *Publishers Weekly*. "These stories are also about ways of combating that malaise."

Unimaginable boldness

The collection, Rosen points out, served as a bridge to the novel that was to follow, *Philadelphia Fire*, published in 1990. The book is about the 1985 police bombing of the MOVE commune headquarters which ultimately destroyed an entire Philadelphia city block. It is also about a writer who lives in exile and returns to search for the boy seen running from the burning building. In the middle of this novel, Wideman addresses his own son, Jacob, lost to prison walls for murdering a companion on a camping trip at age 16. As Rosemary L. Bray writes in *The New York Times Book Review*, "It is an act of almost unimaginable boldness to take such personal sadness and to insert it into a novel." *Philadelphia Fire* brought further recognition from Wideman's peers with the 1991 PEN/ Faulkner Award.

Wideman's most recent book, *All Stories Are True*, published in 1992, begins with a new collection of short stories under the same title. These are followed by his two earlier collections, *Fever* and *Damballah*. In the ten new stories, some of which were previously published in periodicals, Wideman returns to Homewood once again. This time it's from the viewpoint of someone older.

When asked which form he enjoys more, the novel or the short story, he says, "I think, emotionally, I feel more at ease or more involved, of course, in a longer work. There's more at stake. But, in another way, I don't care. If I'm having fun, if there are challenges and demands and if I'm meeting some of them successfully, then it really doesn't matter. Narrative is narrative. And often, in fact, when I start a story, I don't know if it's going to be twelve pages or fifty pages or one page. When the work is going well, I'm writing. The product becomes determined by the process."

Though he has published 11 books, including *Brothers and Keepers*, Wideman finds that writing never gets easier. "Unfortunately, it's always difficult. That's just the nature of the process," he says, adding that he finds that writer's block must be broken through daily. "Just like for an athlete, the points that you've scored in the game before don't count for the game today. That's what's tough about writing or athletics. That's also the beauty of it.

The process of rewriting

"There are some few times when material just seems to be almost given," Wideman says, but even after that happens, there is the process of rewriting. "With Hiram Haydn I learned how to edit a book, how to get outside of it and rewrite, and the importance of rewriting. It's something that's been quite useful to me in my teaching as well.

"What I do is I read and read and read things over and over again. Each time I read the script, I'm doing something to it, either mentally making changes or scratching changes. I also write in pencil. A lot of times the first draft is in one of my notebooks and then they get so laden with notes and revisions and new writing and little pieces of yellow paper and paper clips and cross references, they get to be unintelligible basically. So then I have to write another draft and then another draft. At some point, the right point, I hope, I try to get a clean handwritten draft so that my wife or somebody else can do a typed draft. That's the first appearance in the world.

"I also like to read things to my wife. That's another important stage of composition: actually feeling both secure enough and that something is intelligible enough to be shared. Now that doesn't mean it's a final draft, but hearing it aloud, that's an important experience for me as I'm moving toward a more finished product. When I go to readings at colleges and whatnot, I'll often read something in progress for that same purpose of editing, hearing. But there's a stage before I go that public with it which is usually a one-on-one."

Wideman says his routine depends on the time of the year. "What might be typical is to get up pretty early in the morning. I like that time of day. It's uncluttered, my mind seems to work best, my memory is clearest. In the summertime, I like to work outdoors looking at a lake," he says. "Working on a book is a rather strange business. You don't punch a time clock and have hours—at least I don't—where I sit down for a certain time and work on it. When you're writing a book, I think you're always writing it. You might be writing it while you're dreaming, writing it while you're riding on a trolley car as well as when you're sitting at a desk."

Besides Faulkner's work, Wideman's writing has prompted comparisons with the works of Richard Wright, Ralph Ellison and Jean Toomer as well as James Joyce, T.S. Eliot and Shakespeare. His use of stylistic techniques, which include leaps in time, various points of view, interior monologues and lack of quotation marks (often all in the same work), has also prompted comments (some good, some bad) from critics. In *The Bloomsbury Review*, for instance, in reference to *Philadelphia Fire*, Mark Hummel writes, "Wideman freely mixes fiction and nonfiction, past and present, street rap and Shakespeare, which, carried to the reader through multiple narrators, conjure a novel of layered depth."

Yet Wideman views technique as "just a way of getting a job done. The most difficult thing is finding a subject that is important to you and allows you to express yourself. Style is a way to tackle that subject and is something that grows out of each project," he says. He also advises writers to "love the doing of it. It's a tough hustle and it never gets any easier. You can't control the prizes you win, the books you sell or the money you make."

Finally, says Wideman, "Everybody has a kind of primal language. By that I mean the language in which they first learn to feel. That's the language that writers should try to excavate from their conscious. That language has a lot to do with family, growing up, the stories you hear, the way people walk and talk and laugh. That's the one you have to learn to use, learn to share."

First Bylines

by Jenny Pfalzgraf

In this day and age, having a first work of fiction published is truly an accomplishment. Not only must writers give birth to brilliant prose, but they must also put on their helmets and prepare to toot their own horns. As unromantic as it may sound, writers have to market themselves today in order to be heard.

As the interviews with these new novelists and short story writers show, there are many different ways to obtain an added edge in the industry. Each, in his or her own unique way, has found a peephole, pushed through it, and sent a fresh, new voice into the world. They share their insights, frustrations and triumphs in this feature, and recount the steps that led to publication.

Ashley Curtis
"Anomalies of the Heart," *Alfred Hitchcock Mystery Magazine*

Ashley Curtis has traveled around the world and experienced a potpourri of countries and cultures. After spending much of his childhood in Italy and Switzerland, he returned to the United States to attend Yale. As an undergraduate, he studied Chinese and spent a summer in Taiwan. He also wrote his first short story—and discovered he loved writing.

After college he continued to write, but never sent anything off. "I guess I really didn't know how to approach publishers," he recalls. "I imagined that if I wrote something that was really good, it would magically get into print. Then when I turned thirty, I started feeling old and realized if I wanted to be published, I was going to have to do something about it."

But by the time Curtis came to this realization, he had returned to Switzerland to become a teacher. He was an ocean away from many of the markets he hoped to crack. "The fact that I was submitting from Switzerland added a little more uncertainty to the process," he recalls. "As I was taking my submissions to the post office in this little village, I found it hard to believe that some New York editor would actually receive my story, much less read it."

He began submitting work to American markets, and although he received many rejections, he also received several hand-written notes of encouragement from editors. "The first sign of encouragement I got was a penned note from Gordon Lish, the editor of *The Quarterly*," he recalls. "Even though he rejected my story, I was really excited that he had responded positively. So I continued to send things out regularly.

"Writers should know that people actually do read unsolicited manuscripts, and it seems to me that's really an amazing service for the price of a postage stamp—just to have someone read your stuff."

After two years of fruitless submissions, Curtis sent a new story, "Anomalies of the

Jenny Pfalzgraf, *editor of* Artist's Market, *was also assistant editor of the 1993* Writer's Market.

Heart," to *Alfred Hitchcock Mystery Magazine*. "I was hesitant to send it to *Alfred Hitchcock*," he says, "because it had already been rejected by *Ellery Queen's Mystery Magazine*, which is owned by the same company. But I did it anyway. Then it was away with them for a long time, five and one-half months, by which time I had given up on ever getting it back. But it finally did come back, with a contract for much more money than I ever imagined I'd get for something like that!" The story was published in July of 1992.

"Something that always helps me now is to realize that a rejection does not necessarily imply that your story is not good," he says. "Even supposing you have a great story, there's a huge element of chance happening. Are you going to hit, in your fairly random mailing, an editor who can afford to publish your story, has the right amount of space, and can deal with your subject matter? If a magazine has a theme issue coming out, are you going to hit it at the right time with the right theme? I think the odds are fairly heavily stacked against this, if you are only willing to send out your story once or twice. If you know it's good, send it out fifteen or twenty times, or more."

Curtis continues to write fiction, and his second story, "The Photographic Miracle," is forthcoming in *Alfred Hitchcock Mystery Magazine*. He also recently finished the first draft of a novel which takes place in Taiwan. "A lot of my stories take place in various places where I've lived," he says, "so a lot of the research is just having lived there and remembering what it's like."

Jody Jaffe
"Sunday," *Housewife-Writer's Forum*

As a journalist for the *Charlotte Observer*, Jody Jaffe developed skills as a researcher, communicator and wordsmith. She loved the exhilaration of seeing her name in print on a weekly basis and the myriad of experiences that came her way as a feature writer. But after 15 years, she was ready for a change.

"I switched from journalism to fiction for many reasons," she says. "One reason was to learn the truth. You might think that sounds kind of odd coming from a journalist, but I'm not so sure journalists deal in truth as much as they do in facts. For example, you could read five newspapers full of articles about the atrocities in South Africa, and walk away with a general knowledge (a cerebral term) of what happened there. Yet one Nadine Gordimer story can knock you off your feet and let you know what it's like to live in South Africa. She gives you truth and newspapers give you facts. She sends her stories out because she has something important to tell."

And Jaffe, too, had some stories she wanted to tell. For that reason, she left her newspaper job four years ago and started writing fiction. "The first thing I ever sent out was a story called 'Shilling for the Yeshiva,' " she recalls. "The book editor at the paper where I worked told me about a contest at the Writer's Workshop in North Carolina. So I sent my story, and it won second prize. And I think they had over one hundred entries, so it was really encouraging to win. That experience was enough to propel me on."

In spite of Jaffe's second-place finish, however, the story remained unpublished. When her subsequent submissions to magazines came back in the mail with few or no comments, she became frustrated. "For a while, I'd go on these spurts and send a bunch of stories to the biggies: *The New Yorker, The Atlantic.* And they would come right back. With second tier journals, I might get a nice note, but it was still a rejection. It got really discouraging. I was used to the community and the camaraderie of newspapers and having colleagues around. Fiction writing can be so lonely because you feel like you're in this vacuum. Your stories just bounce back with little or no human contact."

Then, Jaffe decided to send some of her stories to smaller circulation magazines. She selected a short short called "Sunday," that she had written as part of an assignment at a writing workshop, and sent it out. The story was accepted almost immediately by *Housewife-Writer's Forum* and appeared in the July/August 1992 issue. "*HWF* does something that's really great for beginning writers," she remarks. "The fiction editor writes a critique for each story that is published in the magazine. In fact, the critique he wrote for my story was longer than the actual story itself! He just talked about what made it work for him, and it was really wonderful for me to see that as the person who wrote the story. I think it's a very generous magazine in terms of what it does for the writer."

In hindsight now, Jaffe warns that it's not always a great idea to submit first to the most prestigious markets. "This business about starting at the top, I don't know if it's good advice," she says. "Because getting bombarded with rejection slips can sometimes be debilitating. I think all writers need some stroking sometimes."

Now, as a graduate student in the MFA creative writing program at the University of Maryland, Jaffe has once again found camaraderie in a community of writers. But she has also entered an environment that is very structured and demanding, and at times, somewhat foreign. "I'm having to break old habits from my days as a journalist," she explains. "When I wrote for the paper, I always had to whittle away everything to write tighter, more economical articles. But now, as a fiction writer, I have this problem of getting in and out of a story too quickly. The rule in journalism is that you have to hook them in the first paragraph, so I'm always afraid I'm going to lose the reader.

"My teacher, Howard Norman, said to me: 'You've got to assume a different reader—one who will stay with you.' That's the sort of dance that goes on between a reader and a fiction writer. And it's exhilarating to know that the reader is going to stay with you."

Jim Leightheiser
"Static," *Cimarron Review*

"I've learned that the only way to stay sane about the publishing business is to become schizophrenic," says Jim Leightheiser. "One personality has to be very pragmatic and unemotional in the face of all the staggering odds. The other personality has to be visionary, else you'd never dare to send your story into the ocean of submissions in the first place."

Leightheiser's first published story, "Static," appeared in the July 1992 issue of *Cimarron Review*. But the road to his success was rocky and at times, discouraging. " 'Static' was first written in November-December of 1989," he recalls, "and in its first incarnation it was rejected by four magazines in a year and a half. It was also returned unopened twice by magazines that had ceased operations. I imagined that editors viewed my curse-ridden manuscript as the 'kiss of death' for their publications."

Nevertheless, he continued to send the story out. "I had a yearning for outside validation," he says. "Although the story had survived the gauntlet of my friends' critiques, I wanted an unbiased opinion on whether my scribbles were worth anything."

In August of 1991, that substantiation came in a letter from Deborah Bransford at *Cimarron Review*. "She made some concrete suggestions for improvement and said she'd be happy to look at the story again if I made the changes," says Leightheiser. "Needless to say, her comments were very constructive and I resubmitted a fine-tuned version in November of 1991." A month later the story was accepted. It appeared in the magazine two and a half years after it was first written.

Although he never took any formal creative writing classes, Leightheiser experimented with several writing groups as he developed his own voice as a fiction writer. "I was in a writing workshop for two years and found both pluses and negatives," he recollects. "On the positive side, it was a forcing function for finishing stories and a ready-made source of criticism. It was also nice seeing patterns in the critiques. I had a tendency to rationalize weak areas in my stories, but when I saw ten critiques pointing to the same weakness, I knew I had to do something about it." He also remembers, however, that the workshop was very time-consuming. "I had to read three stories (twice) each week and provide meaningful critiques while still trying to find time for my own writing. I finally left the workshop because I felt that if I was ever going to become a 'real writer' I was going to have to impose my own deadlines and my own standards of quality."

Today, Leightheiser works at INDIVIDUAL, Inc., a company that produces customized electronic newspapers for business professionals. Although he does a fair amount of business writing at work, he still finds time to write fiction. "Often I'll see so many numbers in the course of a day that I can't wait to get home and take out the notebook—just to show myself that I still have a voice," he says. "I try to write for at least a half hour every day. I generally find an opening sentence and then see where it takes me.

"Often what motivates me is finishing and looking back at what's emerged. It's amazing sometimes to see what can bubble up from a mind you thought was too tired and frazzled to do anything. Writing can be excruciatingly painful. Having written is always a pleasure."

Tom Chiarella
Foley's Luck, Alfred A. Knopf

At first, Tom Chiarella had no plans to be a writer. As an undergraduate student at St. Lawrence University, he studied painting. In his senior year, he took a creative writing class, but never imagined that he would do anything with it. This soon changed however.

"At the end of the semester I looked at my paintings and thought they were really amateurish," he says. "I thought they really didn't show any flashes of anything. But my stories had something. It was more fun writing stories, too, frankly. Painting is so much suggestion. You have to capture everything in a glance or gesture. I found it to be less satisfying than stories, in which a series of gestures or a series of glances become part of a greater whole and that whole is changing with everything you add to it."

© Brian Ullem

Ultimately Chiarella reconsidered his strengths and chose to attend the University of

Alabama as a graduate student in creative writing. Once he made the switch, he started sending out stories right away. *"Mid-American Review* at Bowling Green University accepted my first story," he recalls. "And when that happened I finally felt credible. It was really life-sustaining. Being published just gave me this sense of being hooked into a larger body. When people asked to read my stories, I could hand them a magazine. It felt like something."

As a graduate student he continued to publish short stories (one was published in *Story* in 1991) and was eventually given the name of an agent to contact by a visiting writer. "It was tempting to send the agent some stories right away," he recalls, "but I decided not to write to her until I had a whole collection. So I kept her address for two years. In 1987, I turned in a collection of stories as my thesis, and then sent what I thought was a finished book to her."

After six months, he talked with the agent. She particularly liked several stories involving one protagonist (named Berard), and suggested he rework the book with Berard as its center. "I was kind of dejected," he admits, "but in the interim, it made me focus on this character. I decided what I'd do was include ten stories about Berard and then throw in another five stories."

But a year later when Chiarella sent the revised collection back to the agent, she asked him to eliminate the extra five stories. He reluctantly agreed, and went back to work on the book for two more frustrating years. "I'd send her stories and she would write back with critiques," he recalls. "There were times when I was really mad at her. But the great thing about having an agent was that I always knew she was attuned to what I was trying to do. She never deceived me. She never said, 'We can make a lot of money on this,' or 'This could be a great movie.' All she said was 'I like your work and your character is recognizable to me.' When she talked about my book, she talked in the same terms I did. So for me, finding an agent was the key to pulling the book together."

Although the book initially received some consideration from Norton, it was finally accepted and published by Alfred A. Knopf. "I can still remember every detail of my kitchen as I received that phone call," he recalls. "My agent had known someone at Knopf who she thought would like the work. That's the key—just getting it on the right desk. Finding the right editor is a big deal."

To Chiarella's surprise, however, the revisions were not over, even after the book was accepted. "They wanted me to change my main character's name," he explains, "because they thought too many people would be calling him Bernard, and they were afraid no one would realize that Berard was his last name. I really fought this tooth and nail. I sent them long letters about it and tore my hair out over it. Finally I capitulated and sent them a list of twenty names I'd gotten out of a phone book that I thought would work. After three months, we finally settled on the name Dan Foley."

And so Berard was transformed into Dan Foley, and Chiarella's collection, *Foley's Luck*, was released in September of 1992. "I definitely hold compromise close to my heart," says the author, "because I had to give up the name; I had to give up stories I liked; and I had to give up on my original vision of the book. But the book is successful and I've got to give credit to the people who helped me compromise."

The key to publishing is understanding editors and what they want, says Chiarella. "Each publishing house has its own aesthetic. You ought to feel a connection to a market before you submit a story to it. For example, if you love *The Atlantic*, then you read it. But not like a puzzle, thinking, 'How do I get in here?' You read it like something you're celebrating and trying to bring closer to you in some way."

Terri de la Pena
Margins, Seal Press

"I never really had any formal training as a writer," says Terri de la Pena. "I just went from playing dolls to writing. It was a natural progression for me. But being a minority kid, I never had much guidance. And I was shy. I never questioned the way things were done."

Consequently, de la Pena took a secretarial job and wrote only for herself, never sharing her writing. It wasn't until she enrolled in Santa Monica College (in her early thirties) that others received a glimpse of her talent as a writer. "At that time, I took two creative writing classes," she recalls, "and the instructor told me that in twenty-five years of teaching, he considered me one of his top ten writing students. This blew me away because it was the first time I'd ever shared any of my writing with anyone. He wanted me to start sending out stories, but I just didn't feel ready. I wanted to believe him, but I didn't quite believe him."

© Tee Corinne

Nevertheless, with this encouragement de la Pena joined a Latino writers' group and began to share her writing. At the suggestion of one of the women in the group, she entered the University of California at Irvine Chicano Literary Competition and won third prize in the short story category. "When I won," she recalls, "I had to give a reading, and it was the first time I'd ever read anything that personal in public. It was amazing to me. People laughed in the right places. It was a very positive response. Then I thought, maybe I actually have something here."

De la Pena went on to publish short stories in several lesbian/feminist magazines and small press anthologies. She also began working on a novel about a chicana lesbian and her changing relationship with her family. "I started my novel, *Margins,* in 1982," she recalls, "but I had to put it away for several years because I wasn't ready to deal with its subject matter yet. But then I got it out again when I was ready in 1987 and resumed work on it."

When the first draft of the novel was completed she applied to Flight of the Minds, an annual workshop in Oregon for women writers, and took her work with her for critique. "They were offering a scholarship for women of color, which I won. So I only had to pay half tuition," she remembers. "As part of the workshop, I read a chapter of *Margins.* Afterwards, one of the instructors, Evelyn White, approached me and said I ought to get the work published. A published writer herself, she had some connections with small presses and offered to submit my book to publishers for me, provided I finish it by the following summer. After that, she called me every two months to check on my progress."

In the summer of 1989, de la Pena returned to Flight of the Minds with a third draft of the book. "Evelyn took it and submitted it to Seal Press for me," she says. "Soon after that, I got a letter from Seal saying that they were interested in publishing it! I already knew their books (I had read quite a few) so I knew they published quality books. I was happy to go with them."

Seal asked de la Pena to do several rewrites before the book was approved for publication. "I ended up writing seven drafts of the novel," she groans, "but the editors were very tactful and talked a lot about the strengths of the work. At first I resisted taking their suggestions, but I'm glad I finally made the changes. I had to cut one character a great deal, and beef up some other ones, but I think it's a stronger book now." *Margins* was finally released in March of 1992, three years after it was first submitted.

"I feel a strong connection to all writers who are doing alternative things—feminist writers, gay and lesbian writers, Chicano writers, people of color. We're all doing the same thing, making ourselves visible in literature. There are so many negative stereotypes floating around. And we need positive role models for minority kids," she says.

A lot of small presses do theme anthologies, says de la Pena, and these are a great place to start out. "Beginning writers should be aware of these opportunities," she advises. "A lot of the stuff I got published was in response to those kinds of things, where it was a topic I probably wouldn't have written about if I hadn't seen the call for submissions. I call it reaction writing. But I think this kind of writing makes you more flexible. If you respond to something like this, it challenges you and forces you to step outside yourself."

Jim Lewis
Sister, Graywolf Press

Jim Lewis always knew that he would someday be a published writer. The son of a newsman and a librarian, he was imbued from the start by a passion to communicate. "I was born with a pen in my hand," he says. "I didn't so much decide to sell my work as assume, from the start, that one wrote in order to be read, which entails being published."

© Larry Clark

After graduating from Brown University in 1984, Lewis published several short stories in literary magazines, and then began working on a novel as he entered graduate school in philosophy at Columbia. He finished the novel two years later and began sending it to agents for consideration. "I was told— and I think it's true—that it's almost impossible to sell a book, especially a first 'literary' novel, without an agent," he says.

But Lewis's manuscript was rejected by 25 agents before it was finally picked up; and then, even with the boost of representation, it was rejected by nearly 30 publishers in a year. "I find the entire experience somewhat brutalizing," he admits, "and to be honest, I wouldn't recommend it . . . which I guess isn't going to stop anyone. It wouldn't have stopped me to have heard as much from someone else when I was starting out."

Indeed, such warnings didn't stop him. In spite of the rejections, he started a new novel, *Sister,* and searched for a new agent. At the same time, he began writing art criticism and travel pieces on a freelance basis. "That, and teaching a literature course at Columbia, enabled me to survive while I was finishing the second book," he recalls.

Finally, the Janklow & Nesbitt Literary Agency expressed an interest in *Sister.* With their assistance, the book was accepted in 1992 by Graywolf Press, a leading small press based in Saint Paul, Minnesota.

There have been many advantages to publishing through a small press, comments Lewis. "For one thing, they're very flexible and efficient. It's kind of like working with a SWAT team as opposed to an army. Also, the process is very personalized. You get more attention and you're very involved in the process. Graywolf even allowed me to pick the cover and typeface for my book."

As Lewis looks forward to the release of *Sister* in April of 1993, he is also preparing for several publicity tours. "I don't want to get blocked into the psychology of just having my first book out," he says. "I want to start another novel before this one comes out, if only to save me from getting stalled.

"I'm motivated by the same things that motivate most writers—love, fear, rage, affection, curiosity, the need to have an effect. I don't, on the other hand, write to express myself; I don't write for or about myself, except in the most attenuated way; I don't 'write about what I know.' I think writing should be, above all, unselfish.

"I think it's important to try to find the right story to tell, by which I mean, one that people are waiting to have told, one which they may or may not already know, in some vague form. I mean 'the right story' in the abstract—not just the right sequence of events, but also the right tone, the right language, the right metaphysic. When I wrote *Sister* I wanted to find that real story—it's a sweet and fierce one—and nail it down."

Trayce Primm
Michael's Wife, Harlequin

There are many different ways to become published, and Trayce Primm's success proves it. Her approach has been anything but traditional.

For example, she doesn't live in New York City. She is still one semester shy of a bachelor's degree. She uses no methods, no tactics, no rituals to get motivated. She works on two or three novels at a time, switching back and forth between genre and mainstream fiction. "I'm just not a linear person," she explains. "I'm interested in too much at once to move in a straight line."

© Shawn Northcutt

After attending Texas Tech University, Primm owned her own hair salon for 11 years, had children, and managed to schedule more schooling and writing around these commitments. She loved to write and was involved in several writing groups, but never tried to get any of her work published.

Then, while attending a Romance Writers of America conference in Seattle, Washington, with her writing group, she entered a contest sponsored by Harlequin. The challenge was to write a fantasy in five pages. "I placed in the top two," she recalls, "and Harlequin asked if I'd like to submit a book idea." With guidance from Romance Writers of America and several writing books, she put together a book proposal that included three sample chapters and an outline.

"I showed my proposal to my writing group before I sent it off," she says. "They liked the writing a lot, but they thought it was too different. It was a little more erotic than traditional romance novels." Nevertheless, the editors at Harlequin liked the proposal and called to ask whether the book was finished. "It was like a dream," says Primm. "The editor said it was the kind of proposal where, when she finished reading it, she couldn't wait to read the rest!"

Once the book was finished, however, it took two years before a contract was actually offered. "There was a lot of turnover at Harlequin—I went through four editors there—during the process," she recalls. "My book kept getting passed on to new editors and it took time for each one to read the manuscript. You have to expect delay. But after I signed the contract, everything went really fast. There were some revisions, but not many." The novel, *Michael's Wife*, was released in February of 1993, and the contract included an option on a second book.

As part of the contract Harlequin asked Primm to choose a pseudonym for her novels. She chose a name close to her own, Tracy Morgan. "I don't have a problem with the fact that Harlequin requires pseudonyms," she explains, "because I plan to do some other stuff that is more mainstream, and I'd like to keep the two types of writing separate with two separate identities. And in any case, I think that romance readers are pretty dedicated to authors they like. If they like your writing, they'll find out if you're writing under another name. They'll follow you."

In hindsight, muses Primm, the fact that *Michael's Wife* was unusual may have been the reason the book sold. "I think the romance market has changed significantly in the last five years or so," she contends. "The books are dealing much more with real subjects (such as alcoholism, for example), and publishers are more open to new ideas and techniques. Romance writers now have a lot more latitude on topics, vocabulary and style.

"Someday I'd like to get my degree in creative writing, but being a hairstylist is also a great education. Just working with the public and talking to people is one of the best educations a writer can have. It's my dream to some day fill out an IRS form, and under occupation, put writer. But you always have to think of yourself as a writer, even before you are published. What's important is who you are and not what you do.

"I've always been a big reader, and because of it, was always afraid that once I started writing I wouldn't have a voice that was distinct. I was afraid of echoing what I had read. But I have found my own voice and it is unique. Sometimes it is a little more lush than I would like, and I wish I could write more staccato like Hemingway. But I just don't write like that so I have to make the best of what I've got."

A Beginner's Guide to Present Tense

by Monica Wood

Present tense is a powerful storytelling tool that is misunderstood, burdened with unrealistic expectations and often misused by writers who don't fully appreciate its complexities. Used skillfully and in the proper context, present tense can contribute the exact tone you've been searching for, and at the same time enhance elements already contained in the story: character, plot, theme.

In oral storytelling, present tense is the most natural way to startle your listener into really *seeing* a story's action. In the daily dramas we relate to our friends, colleagues and spouses, we almost always slip into present tense, even if we've begun in past tense: "I didn't see Edward all day, then two minutes before closing he waltzes into my office to tell me there's a problem with my paycheck ... " Children, the most natural storytellers, use present tense to tell each other scary stories: " ... and the footsteps on the stairs go tap-tap-tap!" Lately even sportscasters have taken to present tense in their commentary: "If I'm Coach Ford right now, Bob, I've got to be wondering, should I take Parish out with four fouls and let Klein finish out the quarter?"

But oral storytelling is its own art; what works for a listener does not always work for a reader. As writers, we must give present tense its due, while acknowledging that it will not work for every story and that it comes with a unique set of problems.

The truth about present tense

Before you delve into the problems and rewards of present tense, you should know what it can and cannot do for you. Let's begin by examining some common misconceptions:

Misconception #1: Present tense is easy to use. You may be one of those writers with a natural facility with the present tense, but in general, present tense is more difficult to use than past tense. Oral storytelling may lend itself to present tense, but the written literary tradition has a long history of past tense. There is a reason for this: Past tense lends a story heft, giving the reader a sense that a story's events have already happened and have been deemed worth repeating. Past tense also has the comfort of the familiar: We are used to stories in past tense, beginning with the once-upon-a-times of fairy tales.

This venerable history of past tense poses a problem for the writer who chooses present tense. Present tense makes for a feeling of a story-in-progress; events are unfolding rather than being retold, and the writer must therefore find the story's "heft" from sources other than tense—from lovely prose, perhaps, or flawless pacing. Of course all stories benefit from these qualities, but with present tense you are bucking tradition and must consequently try harder to justify your choice.

Ironically, another feature of present tense that makes it harder to use is the *recent* trend of present-tense stories. Some readers equate the present tense with minimalism, that oft-maligned school of story writing that employs a stripped-down, sometimes staccato

Monica Wood's new novel, Secret Language *was published in January by Faber and Faber. Her fiction has appeared in numerous magazines including* Redbook, Yankee, North American Review *and* Fiction Network.

writing style. The best of these stories are real gems (writers like Raymond Carver, Ann Beattie and Amy Hempel penned some of the best examples), and many of them are written in present tense. Unfortunately, hoards of imitators have given minimalism, and therefore present tense, a bad name. If you care to "try this at home" you should be forewarned that your little story is vying for the interest of a reader (or editor) who may be ill-disposed toward present tense and expecting the worst. You must strive to make the present tense unobtrusive by combining it with fresh, original prose.

Misconception #2: Present tense will pick up the pace of a story by adding "immediacy." Although it is true that present tense, used skillfully, can add a sense of urgency, a "you-are-there" quality to a story, the only cure for a sluggish story is a ruthless edit. If your story suffers from slow pacing, don't blame tense or any other technique. Instead, ask yourself: Do I know what this story is about? Perhaps you have let your story wander in the hope that a character, theme or plot will eventually show itself through the thicket of words. All writers do this; meandering is important and necessary. It's what early drafts are for. If you have become impatient with wandering, however, don't look to present tense to correct the problem; look instead for a tighter focus, which comes not by fiddling with tense but by writing a fourth, eighth, tenth draft.

Let's dissect the following example. It is the problematic opening of a story written in past tense:

> Harry woke to a glorious morning, yet he couldn't seem to move out of bed. The monotonous chirping of the sparrows outside his window filled him with a curious dread. He turned to look at the bedside clock and saw that it read 6:30. It was past his usual rising time, and still he was tired. He rolled over in his tangled sheets and sighed. Perhaps the memory of Alicia was still weighting him, making him incapable of movement. Or perhaps it was something as innocent as jet lag. Harry looked again at the clock, and realized that a half hour had passed. It seemed to him that time had become an unreliable quantity, moving slowly, then quickly, then slowly again, ever since he first saw Alicia at the display table next to his at the entomology conference . . .

Et cetera et cetera. After an opening like this your reader won't be able to get out of bed, either. Let's say you've looked this over, realized that the opening is a bore, and decided you've identified the problem: wrong tense. You convince yourself that Harry's story demands to be told in the present. Here goes:

> Harry wakes to a glorious morning, yet he can't seem to move out of bed. The monotonous chirping of the sparrows outside his window fills him with a curious dread. He turns to look at the bedside clock and sees that it reads 6:30. It is past his usual rising time, and still he is tired. He rolls over in his tangled sheets and sighs. Perhaps the memory of Alicia is still weighting him, making him incapable of movement. Or perhaps it is something as innocent as jet lag. Harry looks again at the clock, and realizes that a half hour has passed . . .

Well, you get the picture. It's true that you can't make a silk purse out of a sow's ear. What this opening needs is a sense of forward motion that present tense alone cannot provide. If anything, the present tense makes this opening even more stultifying, for we have no sense, as we do in past tense, that Harry's waking up this way is anything more than a third-person stream of consciousness. The past-tense version has slightly more credibility, possessing the automatic "heft" mentioned earlier: Harry's waking up has already happened someplace in the past and therefore a forgiving reader may assume that the opening scene must be germane to whatever events will follow. In either tense, however, this opening is a woke-up-this-morning story that is a common beginner's mistake. We've got to get Harry out of bed and talking to someone.

Misconception #3: A past-tense story can easily be converted to present tense. Manipulating language is a complicated, frustrating, challenging proposition. Language is stubborn and uncooperative. This is the joy of writing. You simply cannot tell the same story in past tense that you can in present tense. Present-tense verbs are different from past-tense verbs in rhythm, sound, tone and intimation; these qualities affect a story's theme, pace, even plot. Changing tense transforms a story almost as profoundly as changing point of view or switching the gender of the main character. To believe otherwise will cause you hours of frustration; if you decide to change tense, be willing to rethink the entire story.

A short example can illustrate this point. Here is a snippet from a scene in which a man remembers how badly he misinterpreted the expression on his father's face just before his father told him that his mother had died in the night:

> *Past tense:* Papa listed forward, his face close to mine. He had a secret. His eyes glittered the way they did when the salmon were running, a mixture of awe and anticipation that I had long associated with miraculous events.
>
> *Present tense:* Papa lists forward, his face close to mine. He has a secret. His eyes glitter the way they do when the salmon are running, a mixture of awe and anticipation that I have long associated with miraculous events.

Notice how many elements of this passage are *profoundly* changed by converting to present tense. In the past-tense version, the narrator is an adult looking back with irony and longing; he understands the nature of his mistake because he has the wisdom that comes with time. In the present-tense version, the narrator is experiencing the moment first hand, and therefore cannot be an adult looking back — he must be a child. These words are not convincing from a child narrator, however. Similarly, the wistful tone is suddenly wrong: grown men are wistful, young boys are not. And the irony of the boy's associating "miraculous events" with fishing rather than dying is largely lost, because the narrator does not yet know, as he speaks in present tense, what his father's secret is.

Let's try another example that at first glance might seem easier to convert. The story is about a woman who is trying to decide whether to leave her husband:

> *Past tense:* Robin watched Geoff let himself into the house, right on time. He was reliable, she had to give him that. She imagined herself months from this day, lying on a beach in Aruba and casually glancing at her watch, knowing with unflinching certainty that Geoff would at that very moment be unlocking their front door with a sack of groceries tucked under one arm. It suddenly seemed easier to leave, being able to take with her this small comfort. She would always know where he was.
>
> *Present tense:* Robin watches Geoff let himself into the house, right on time. Geoff is reliable, Robin has to give him that. She imagines herself months from this day, lying on a beach in Aruba and casually glancing at her watch, knowing with unflinching certainty that Geoff would at that very moment be unlocking the front door with a sack of groceries tucked under one arm. It suddenly seems easier to leave, being able to take with her this small comfort. She will always know where he is.

The differences in this example are a little more subtle, but no less consequential. The main character and point of view are the same in both versions, but the *story* is different. The past-tense version of this story is about a *decision already made*; the present-tense version is about a *decision in the making*. This difference changes the way the writer presents the character to us.

In the first version, the reader presumes that Robin made her decision, one way or the other, in the recent or distant past. As a result, we perceive her as a calmer, more reliable, more reflective character than the present-tense Robin who has yet to decide. The writer must ask herself: Am I writing a story about how Robin *comes* to a decision, or a story about how she *remembers* a decision?

Making present tense work for you

Now that we have examined the three most common misconceptions about present tense, let's talk about some techniques that make present tense work to our best advantage. Often, present tense can have an unintended leaden quality, or sound too staccato. If you prefer more fluid, natural-sounding prose, the following guidelines will help.

Guideline #1: Avoid a string of one-syllable verbs. Consider the verbs in this passage: "Mavis *looks* out the window. She *sees* Brandon *cross* the street. He *squints* at the house. Mavis *sighs*." We'll get to what else is wrong with this short passage in a moment, but for now, let's look at the verbs. One verb per sentence, one syllable per verb. The result is rather wooden, don't you think? Let's try some minor surgery on this one: "Mavis *glances* out the window. She sees Brandon. He squints at the house. Mavis *shudders*." By replacing a couple of one-syllable verbs with two-syllable verbs, the prose is somewhat lightened. Let's move on to see what else we can do to improve this passage.

Guideline #2: Don't neglect the present progressive. Present progressive is a form of present tense that implies continuing action: "I *am sitting* in this chair"; "He *is living* in Seattle." The Mavis-Brandon passage can be further improved by inserting the progressive form of "squint": "Mavis glances out the window. She sees Brandon cross the street. He *is squinting* at the house. Mavis shudders." Do you see how this passage is beginning to take on a kind of rhythm? Although too much present progressive is as bad as too many one-syllable verbs (the word "is" in present progressive can get monotonous), it is invaluable for adding melody to a tuneless sentence.

Another tense form that you might use for variety is the *present perfect*, which implies a present action that has been going on for some time, as in "Brandon *has been squinting* at the house all morning." It may also describe an action that has already occurred at the time of speaking: "It seems to Mavis that she *has looked* out the window a hundred times today."

Guideline #3: Vary sentence structure. This guideline is critical for prose of any kind, but especially for stories in present tense. Present-tense stories that rely almost exclusively on the very basic sentence construction of subject-verb-complement can sound awfully dull, as we saw in the first Mavis-Brandon example. Instead of relying on a string of similarly constructed sentences, let's manipulate the constructions by blending sentences, throwing in some modifying phrases, beginning with something other than the subject. In other words, let's have some *fun* with the English language:

> Glancing out the window, Mavis catches sight of Brandon as he crosses the street. He is squinting at the house as if appraising it for a bank, his hands thrust deep in his pockets. Mavis sighs.

This version of Mavis and Brandon is far more interesting syntactically, which makes it more intriguing fictionally. We've blended the first two sentences and added an elliptical phrase and a modifying phrase to the next sentence. The last sentence reads as originally written—"Mavis sighs." This simple sentence, dull in its original context, has been transformed by the more complex sentences that precede it; instead of lying flat on the page, indistinguishable from the other, similar sentences, it now offers the final beat to this rhythmic passage.

If you insist on using basic sentence structure for your present-tense story (some stories may indeed demand it), beware of combining present tense with first person. Your protagonist may end up sounding like a character in a Humphrey Bogart movie:

"I get to my office at three in the morning. I'm in no mood for games. It's been a long night. I'm out of cigarettes and my wallet is missing. I fumble for my key. The door is already open . . . ."

This gets even worse in second person:

"You get to your office at three in the morning. You're in no mood for games. It's been a long night. . . ."

Most of these suggestions can be applied to prose of any kind, written in any tense. However, the present tense does pose unique linguistical dilemmas that can be both maddening and delightful. As you work more and more with present tense, you will undoubtedly form guidelines of your own to add to the list. Like writing itself, the present tense will offer you many successes, a few failures and the irreplaceable thrill of discovery.

Characters, Not People

by Johnny Payne

Insisting that a character has to be plausible is not the same thing as insisting that a character has to be realistic. Asking that a character engage our interest is not the same thing as asking that a character be likeable. These are two maxims I try to get my creative writing students to take to heart. Turning to fellow classmates like a jury of their peers, my students are often too quick to take each other to task for violating what they mistakenly consider to be cardinal "rules" of fiction: a character has to be realistic, a character has to be likeable.

Leecia, who dresses in flowing garb like a gypsy, all scarves and skirts and hoop earrings, has written a tale about a disaffected teenager at college who hasn't spoken to her parents in months. "That's not realistic," Jason objects, rapping his pencil on the table, taking the floor with the peremptory aplomb of a district attorney. He's in journalism, and doesn't hold any brief for outbursts of exaggerated emotion. "I talk to my parents at least once a week. And anyway, a girl who doesn't talk to her parents for months on end isn't very likeable. I rest my case." And he sits down, with a kind of Perry Mason air of finality about him. Sitting cross-legged in her chair in the corner, ringlets of raven hair spilling over her purple elastic headband like the tendrils of a jungle plant, Leecia glowers and doesn't say anything. She's as dark and brooding as the heroine of a gothic novel. I have a sneaking suspicion that Leecia's next story will be heavy with the perfume of mystery, a tale about a disaffected teenager who murders one of her classmates in a fit of passion.

Create characters truer than life

At this point, I feel duty-bound to remind Jason and his jury of peers of a couple of things. I ask them whether Heathcliff in *Wuthering Heights* is a believable character, banging his head against a tree in the howling night on the moors, making his forehead a mass of blood-knots, calling out Catherine's name. There's nothing remotely realistic about him, but there is something definitely plausible about his passion and his grief, something about the very exaggeration of it that takes a hold on our imagination and doesn't let go. Leecia agrees. Heathcliff is both plausible and sexy, she says; Jason sees the matter otherwise. Well then, what about Shakespeare, I suggest. Does anyone *like* Richard the Third? Would we invite him to share a hotel room on a spring break to Cancun? Doubtful, and yet, he is, to my mind, the most powerful character in all of Shakespeare.

Richard, in his opening monologue, speaks of himself as "I, that am curtail'd of this fair proportion, cheated of feature by dissembling nature, deform'd unfinish'd, sent before my time into this breathing world, scarce half made up, and that so lamely and unfashionable that dogs bark at me as I halt by them." He is gnarly, in the literal sense of the much-abused word. Richard, the most memorable of freaks, is a true and vivid character, but is he realistic, much less likeable? Even the dogs that bark at him as he passes seem reluctant to accept him as human. They know he's not a *person*. Nor should he be. With that uncanny

Johnny Payne *is assistant professor of fiction writing at Northwestern University. His book* Conquest of the New Word *is forthcoming from University of Texas Press. He has published stories in* Chicago Tribune Sunday Magazine, Southern Review *and elsewhere.*

sixth sense of theirs, dogs are sometimes quicker to make the essential, all-important distinction between characters and people than we humans are.

But Flannery O'Connor did once say that the reason Southern writers have so many freaks in their stories is because we still know how to recognize them. Two of the most memorable characters in modern fiction are Miss Amelia and Cousin Lyman in Carson McCullers' moving story "The Ballad of the Sad Cafe." Both of those characters are freakish, grotesque, extraordinary, and, in a deeper sense that has nothing whatsoever to do with *people*, both of them are absolutely true to life. Miss Amelia, dwelling in a dusty little hick burg in rural Georgia, runs a store that sells guano and snuff, and operates a still back in a swamp, making the best liquor in the county. "She was a dark, tall woman, with muscles and bone like a man . . . . There was about her sunburned face a tense, haggard quality. She might have been a handsome woman if, even then, she was not slightly cross-eyed." Miss Amelia, who shuns people in general and especially men, finally falls hard in love with a sorry-looking stranger who drifts into town one night. The object of her affection, who goes by the improbable name of Cousin Lyman, turns out to be a distant cousin not only to her, but to Richard the Third. That is to say, he's not the first of his kind. Like King Richard, Cousin Lyman is a hunchback; like Richard, he's shunned at first; and like Richard, he has in the end the capacity to stir powerful human emotions.

> He was scarcely more than four feet tall, and he wore a ragged, dusty coat that reached only to his knees. His crooked little legs seemed too thin to carry the weight of his great warped chest and the hump that sat on his shoulders. He had a very large head, with deep-set blue eyes and a sharp little mouth. His face was both soft and sassy — at the moment his pale skin was yellowed by dust and there were lavender shadows beneath his eyes.

Carson McCullers is masterful here at creating a character who is an unusual object of contemplation and, at the same time, rooting him in the kind of specific detail that makes him seem absolutely ordinary and familiar, even in all his oddness. The "crooked little legs" and the "great warped chest" are set squarely in our view before we ever get to the hump. By the time we do, Cousin Lyman has taken on enough flesh for us to believe in that strange appendage on his back. As a character, he compels our attention. It is easy for us to imagine dogs chasing him as they did Richard the Third, barking as they run after Cousin Lyman along that dusty Georgia road, while he drags his suitcase behind him. He may not be realistic, but he's certainly real enough. The fact that his face is "soft and sassy" prepares us for the weakness and impertinence that will cause him to take advantage of the reclusive Miss Amelia's sudden and uncharacteristic generosity toward him. We may not know any hunchbacks ourselves, but we begin to feel, as we read "The Ballad of the Sad Cafe," that we've known a Cousin Lyman or two along the way. He might even be us.

Select a character type

The first misstep that novice writers often make is failing to recognize that there are a limited number of human types to draw on in the creation of character. Strictly speaking, there are no new characters under the sun. Even Leecia and Jason, though it might sadden them to hear it, are not the first of their kind upon the face of the earth. As the novelist Wright Morris puts it, "What was once raw about American life has now been dealt with so many times that the material we begin with is a fiction." Our job as writers is to seize hold of the types that most appeal to us, and reshape and individuate them according to our tastes and passions, necessities and whims.

For a long time, I had it in mind to write a story based on a person who was very close to me, but I never could get a handle on exactly what angle of approach to take in the creation of this character on the page. I wanted to write a story about a middle-aged man who has lived a somewhat dissipated life, boozing and carousing, and who has never come to terms with his conflictual relationship with his father. His father dies just as the man is reaching a crisis of middle age, and he bitterly regrets never having made his peace with his father.

When the plot summary is given in this way, the story sounds trite. You may think to yourself, "I've read a hundred stories about midlife crisis, and a hundred more about generational conflict. I've even tried to write a couple myself." This was precisely my dilemma; how to retell a story that was personal to my experience, but also archetypal, an experience that had been shared and written about by many others before me. The solution, I found, lay not in trying to emphasize what was unique and individual about the man, but instead, finding the right character type for giving shape to his experience, and then embellishing on that.

Let me be more specific. Part of my heritage is Appalachian, and among my friends and relations from that part of the country, there's a lot of emphasis on verbal culture: jokes; anecdotes; lore; witty stories about preachers, backwoods lawyers, hunters, drunkards, farmers. Every story, short or long, seems to contain one or more of these human types; it's not uncommon for a joke to begin: "A preacher, a lawyer and a farmer were all on an airplane that was running out of fuel." Jokes are a form of verbal lore that we share with the rest of America, but even when the joke is one that also gets told in California, we Kentuckians add our own little artful touches to it, and thereby describe the peculiarities of the way that we live, think and behave. An anthropologist who wants to penetrate to the core of our existence might do well to begin by taking a sampling of our jokes. A short story writer would be well advised to do the same.

Reflecting on this verbal art, I decided that instead of blocking my creativity by thinking of the prototype of my character as middle-aged, in conflict with his father, etc., why not begin instead with the storytelling tradition that he's a part of, and see where that takes me? After all, what could be more in the tradition of American writing and the American character than oral tradition? Isn't the fact that the primordial American novel, *Huck Finn*, is made up of yarns and tall tales, a certain speaking voice, precisely what keeps us going back to it generation after generation? *Huck Finn* is a novel of *character*, but it's as much about the way he tells his life-story as it is about him. We can see ourselves and our culture accurately in the distorted mirror of his fabrications and exaggerations, and that's why they give us pleasure. Huck and those surrounding him—the Duke, the King, Jim—are *not* true to life—they're larger than life.

Embellish your character type

One of the things that had long defined the prototype of the character I wanted to write about was his fondness for drink, until he gave it up a decade ago. And Appalachian lore is full of jokes about men who drink too much. The man who fell into a barrel of whisky and drowned, but not before he got out three times to go to the bathroom. The man who was crawling along a railroad track, and complained that this was the longest set of stairs he'd ever climbed. The fact that I was trying to create a memorable character, and to write about serious matters such as death, alcoholism and the longing for one's lost parent, was all the more reason to use a joke as my point of departure. In my experience, humor is often the best and most appropriate means of dealing with serious subjects, and it is certainly the way my Kentuckians tend to deal with them. There's a joke that's told in many versions that goes more or less as follows: A drunk staggers out of a local bar and decides to take a shortcut home, so he goes through the cemetery. In the dark, he stumbles into a freshly dug grave, can't get out, and starts yelling. Another drunk from the bar hears him, goes to the edge of the grave, and asks what's the matter. The first drunk says, "I'm about to freeze down here!" The second one peers down into the grave and answers, "Why, no wonder! You done throwed all the dirt off you!"

It is, of course, a long way from this slight anecdote, and this bare-bones character type to a story that engages our emotion fully, in the way that stories should. This is precisely where the writer's imagination and personal sense of his or her character come into play. The title of my story is "Tall Tales." In making my character, Jean, the *first-person narrator* of the story, instead of just its object, I accomplished two things: I allowed him to be "larger than life," as he would be in a yarn, while at the same time allowing myself the necessary latitude for supplying what I knew of this man's habits, dreams, fears, secrets and idiosyncrasies.

In other words, I gave him the overt psychological complexity that is often lacking in jokes and folk tales. The resulting character was a marriage between folk legend and the "actual" person who I'd had in mind to write about for so many years. In choosing this intermediate path, I found that in the end, I captured his temperament more exactly than if I had striven for a more straightforward and "realistic" portrayal. The visit to the graveyard, instead of simply serving as a plot device, became the moment when Jean confronts his own mortality.

Using a larger-than-life character paradoxically gives me greater scope and freedom in letting him vent plausible human frustrations about his fear of death, his addiction to drink and his love for his dead father. Emotions that could seem excessive or overdrawn in a realistic setting are tempered here by having the pathos of the scene situated within the comic framework of a tall tale. Again, it doesn't have to be "realistic" in order for the emotional underpinnings to be *plausible*. The "punch line" of this episode, which is the same as it is in the old joke ("You done throwed all the dirt off you!") has a very different effect in the story, because it serves as an ironic comment on the character Jean's fear of loss and death.

Offer a bedrock of believability

I use this technique again in the story's climactic episode, when Jean is out near his rural birthplace fixing some plumbing for a cousin of his. He goes outdoors to sit down cross-legged in the leaves and to have a smoke, and at that moment the ghost of his dead father appears to him. I want to emphasize that the fantastical or tall tale elements of the story are always undercut by humor and mundane reality, in order to make the characters, including the ghost, continue to seem plausible. If you are going to ask readers to suspend their disbelief, that's all the more reason to offer them a bedrock of believability.

I looked up the other way and here came Bart, wading down the holler, up to his waist in leaves. He had on the makeshift Confederate-soldier costume he used to wear every year in the reenactment of the Battle of Richmond up at Indian Fort. I could see the flash of the black stripe in the leg of the steel-blue tuxedo pants as he shuffled along. The costume looked like it could stand to be dry-cleaned. Orange and yellow leaves clung to the brim of his hat. In his left hand, he was carrying his mandolin by the neck, letting it swing back and forth like it was maybe a bottle of corn whiskey he'd picked up on his way to a dance.

Bart, I whispered, not daring to move, or even exhale my smoke too fast. Is it you?

You know, Jean, he said, I've been hankering after some of Francine's soup beans with that good chow-chow she makes. I think about those damn things all the time, and it likes to drive me crazy.

The fake uniform that needs dry cleaning, the leaves on the hat, the mandolin, and Bart's memory of soup beans and chow-chow are all essential elements in the creation of his character. They give him weight, flesh, and make him believable, even though he is an "otherwordly" ghost. Without them, he would be as insubstantial as Jean's cigarette smoke. With them, he stands somewhere between this world and the next. What contemporary writers ought to strive for, in using the techniques of the tall tale for characterization, is the blending of exaggeration with realistic detail. The combination of the two makes for potent and memorable characters, and can actually give your characters more dimensionality than if you simply try to "draw from life" in an uncomplicated fashion.

Since writing "Tall Tales," I have given a number of public readings of it, and inevitably people come up to me afterward to tell me how the characters Jean and Bart, and the way they talk, remind them of such-and-such a person. Usually, the ones who say this are over 50, and they make a point of commenting favorably on the psychological accuracy of Jean's feelings about mid-life, and his conflictual relationship with his father. Those are the very qualities that I set out to portray, but I was only able to get to them by abandoning my ideas about being faithful to the "real" person I had in mind, and concentrating instead on finding the form and type that would best fit the character.

The writer Sherwood Anderson puts the matter well when he says "The interest in this lies in the figures that went before the eyes of the writer. They were all grotesques. All of the men and women the writer had ever known had become grotesques. The grotesques were not all horrible. Some were amusing, some almost beautiful." In writing short stories, you must keep in mind that you are dealing with characters, not people. If the oddities of the characters seem pronounced at times, so be it. It is in that transformation from people to characters that the art lies, and that the possibilities of humor and beauty in humans begin to emerge.

Beginnings and Endings

by Jack M. Bickham

Your story beginning and ending — often only a few lines or paragraphs out of many pages — may determine whether you sell it. That hardly seems fair, does it? But it's a fact.

The beginning of your story is crucial because it must hook your reader, catch her interest and keep her reading. The ending of your story is equally important because it will determine whether your reader finishes with a sense of pleasure and satisfaction.

For these reasons, writers worry endlessly about how to begin and end stories. "Should I begin with dialogue or description?" they may ask or "Must I provide a happy ending, or can it be downbeat?"

Every story is unique. No one can tell you what mode of narration, what tone or what specific dramatic tactic will always work for you. One story may demand a dialogue opening and a happy ending. The next may only "work" with an action beginning or an ending that states a theme. As many such possible variations as there are, however, your understanding of a few basic principles will help you start your next fiction project with more confidence and end it with greater dramatic finality.

Further, these principles should be discussed together because the opening of your story and its ending are inextricably connected, or should be.

What motivates a reader to turn the pages of your story? The answer: curiosity. Curiosity about what? The outcome, of course. But to be more specific, the reader reads your story with pleasantly tense concern *in order to learn the dramatic answer to the question you posed at the outset*.

Thus, while there may be countless different ways to set up and verbalize your story opening and ending, two essentials remain like bedrock beneath all the variations: (1) The opening must raise a worrisome question in the reader's mind; (2) The ending must answer that question.

Now, of course if there were no more to it than that, all of us could write successful stories without much worry. If the only story-opening requirement were the posing of a question, all we would have to do is list a question at the top of page one (such as: Will Brad solve the crime? *or*—; Can Sally find her true love? *or even*—; What is the meaning of life?) and readers would plunge into our yarns with fervent fascination. But since it's clear that the posing of such bald questions won't get the job done in terms of fascinating a reader, then obviously something more must be involved.

What's involved, in a nutshell is *viewpoint*, *threat* and *resolve*. When you combine them you provide your reader with the interest-elements which provide *drama*, and drama is the icing on the cake of "story question" that makes her worry and read — and love it.

Establish character viewpoint and add threat

The opening of your story should establish a viewpoint — a heart and mind and soul of a living, breathing story character from whose senses and thoughts the story is experienced. Discussion of viewpoint is beyond the scope of this short article except to point out that

Jack Bickham's novels include Breakfast at Wimbledon, Tiebreaker, Ariel *and many others. He is also author of* 38 Most Common Fiction Writing Mistakes (and How to Avoid Them) *(Writer's Digest Books) and a frequent contributor to* Writer's Digest *magazine.*

readers will identify with—and sympathize with—the person in your story who sees and hears all the action, the character from whose vantage point everything is presented.

To put this another way, once you establish a viewpoint character at the start of your story, you have provided the *possibility* of reader involvement and interest. So establishing your viewpoint character is vital to everything that follows. It may be done very briefly, such as *"Dave saw the storm approaching,"* or *"Jill was worried,"* but it must be done immediately in your story's opening.

Once your viewpoint character has been established in this way, you should show a threat to the happiness (or safety, or survival, or sanity or whatever) of that viewpoint character. Almost always, the threat should be an external happening that knocks your lead character for a loop. Often this is another character, an antagonist who does something that throws your lead off-stride. Other times, the opening threat might be a sudden snowstorm which strands your character on an isolated road at night . . . or a threatening letter . . . or an unexpected illness. This external cause—whatever or whoever it is—constitutes a clear and pressing danger to your viewpoint character. Your reader will begin to worry about that!

Thus you have a living, breathing story character, and you present her with a pressing story problem.

Give your character resolve

Even at this point, however, establishment of a powerful story opening is not complete. You must show your threatened viewpoint character forming a *resolve*.

What is resolve? It's a firm intention. A strong goal. Resoluteness. Plan and determination. In terms of story opening, it's *the viewpoint character's formation of a game plan—an action or series of maneuvers—which she believes will solve her story problem.*

This resolve in the viewpoint character needs to be directed toward a specific and possibly attainable goal, something with which the reader can identify. Further, your reader MUST know what the goal is. Any of the following might be legitimate story goals, stated as they might be stated in a story:

> "I'll never know I'm a man until I climb Mt. Blanc," Jim said. "I've got to climb that mountain!"
>
> Slade knew it was murder, and he knew it was up to him to find the killer before he struck again.
>
> Jennifer faced her father. "Forgive me. Please!"
>
> The HELP WANTED sign fired Rick with hope. Shoulders squared, he threw open the door of the employment office and strode in. "You have a job? I want it."

Now, it may be that your reaction to these samples was to begin thinking how story goal might be stated in less obvious terms. A dangerous misconception running rampant in the land is that writers should be subtle. Here subtlety is not what you want, for the moment your story makes clear the character's resolve in terms of a story goal, your reader will clutch it and form it into the *story question* she'll read and read in order to get answered.

I don't know why this is so. Perhaps it's just that we're all such curious creatures. Or perhaps generations of earlier fiction writers have trained readers (without the readers knowing it consciously) to seek out the stated viewpoint character goal, and turn it into a question. All I know is that readers will do it every time.

To say it differently: When you state a character's story goal, your reader *will make a question out of it.*

Thus, going back to the sample goal statements used earlier, the reader will form story questions as follows:

WILL Jim succeed in climbing the mountain?
CAN Slade find the killer before it's too late?
IS IT POSSIBLE for Jennifer to win her father's forgiveness?
DOES Rick get a job?

Having formed this question, your reader will worry and turn pages to get the answer.

Put it all together

One of your major challenges in writing good story beginnings is in finding ways to condense the opening elements, dramatize them, and present them in as brief and arresting a manner as possible. How brief is "brief?" Twenty words. Sixty. A hundred. Perhaps two hundred. In a short story, you should be uneasy if you require much more.

Of course in such a brief segment you won't be able to show everything you wish to show about the setting, the characters, the background and everything else you know about the opening situation. But you certainly can establish a viewpoint, a threat and a resolve that quickly. Remember, these are the aspects that your impatient modern reader is looking for as guide to your story and motivation for reading on. You get these things done first, and worry about adding more detail only after your reader has been hooked.

Getting that opening right is seldom easy. That's why so many writers toil day after day on just the first few paragraphs. But it's worth the effort; everything else depends on it.

As to effective endings: Once you realize that the ending must answer the story question posed at the outset, half the battle is already won. *If you answer the question you originally asked, reader satisfaction is virtually guaranteed.* If you don't answer the question, or answer some other question instead, reader disappointment and irritation are equally certain.

That's why you'll find many writers jotting down the story question on a 3×5 card or sheet of paper and tacking it over their computer. The plot is a record of the character's struggle to reach the goal and the ending must clearly say whether she did or didn't.

This simply means that the struggles along the way in your story must relate to the long-term goal, and have relevance to the story question, and the climax of the story must be designed to provide a final, dramatic confrontation, race, fight, argument or whatever, which will answer the question clearly, once and for all.

So, to go back to the earlier goal samples one last time:

The climax of Jim's story almost certainly will be a final desperate attempt to scale the last mountain slope, perhaps in a race with death, and at the very end he will either stand on the peak, triumphant, or reel back to the base camp, a shattered man.

In the climax to his story, Slade will uncover a crucial clue, then probably confront the killer.

Jennifer and her father will have an ultimate emotional confrontation, and either she will convince him to forgive her or she will fail.

Rick will either get the job or he won't.

You should strive to provide this answer to the story question through presentation of a final dramatic scene — an ultimate confrontation between your viewpoint character and the character or obstacle at the heart of the problem. "Realization endings" are seldom as gripping as on-stage action of some kind in which all the chips are stacked on the table and the answer to the story question must be decided *now*, win or lose, do or die.

Most readers tend to like "happy" endings. What they demand, however, is *endings that fit*. As the brief examples above may indicate, it doesn't seem to matter so much whether the answer is happy or sad. It just has to answer the question.

Perhaps much of this will become clearer if you try to think of story as the record of a quest. Something happens to cause your character unhappiness. Your character determines what she will try to accomplish in order to solve the problem and, like the knights of the Crusades, she launches into her journey. At the end, having struggled, she either finds her Holy Grail or doesn't . . . either wins or loses . . . answers the reader's question.

Stack the deck, but not too much

To assure strong forward movement and a dramatic ending, you should make this quest a difficult one. Just as a knight of the Middle Ages would not have mounted his noble steed in full armor to visit the local equivalent of a 7-Eleven, your character can't be pushed into an enthralling story climax if the problem all along has been routine, or the solution too easy or obvious. Nor can your reader be expected to be much interested. Big endings grow out of difficult quests, which grow out of *serious* threats posed at the outset.

Still, remember that the goal, while difficult, should not be impossible. I have seen stories which failed to fascinate because the problem was so overwhelming that there was *no* hope of character success, and therefore no credible goal or story question to worry about, no possible ending but failure. The so-called naturalistic writers of the early part of this century loved stories of doomed people. The style didn't make a hit with the readers. To get interested in the game, most fans must have a tough contest, but one that's *possibly* winnable for the home team. With the possible exception of games involving our recent Olympic "Dream Team," hopeless causes and runaway routs are equally uninteresting.

Finally, a word of warning about your endings. Obvious manipulation by the author is deadly. Getting the right characters in the right place and time, is sometimes a major plotting problem. You may find that you have to go back into earlier segments of your story to patch up character thinking and motivation in order to get the right people onstage for the climax. In addition, once you have the climax all set up, it's vital that you have things set up in such a way that the final conflict plays out as the characters would realistically do it and that *the characters work it out*, not you the intruding author.

Let me say that differently, if negatively. Never impose the solution on your characters— never have a miraculous storm or arrival by the cavalry or any other author-manipulated outside agency to the rescue. Having set up your question, devise a climax in which the answer comes from character interaction and struggle, *not* Roy Rogers galloping in on Trigger to save the day. In summary:

● An effective opening establishes a viewpoint, a threat and a resolve (goal orientation).

● Your reader will turn the goal statement into a story question and worry about it.

● The story's ending must dramatically answer the story question, thus rewarding and satisfying the reader.

● Story-opening problems should be tough, but not impossible.

● Story-ending solutions should grow out of the characters and plot, not out of the writer's grab-bag of tricks.

Beginning and ending . . . the one foreordaining the nature of the other . . . will give you direction and story unity. And with those firmly in place, your chances of fiction success will be much, much greater. I wish you luck.

Breaking the "Rules" of Story Structure

by Diane Lefer

Several years ago, I worked with a creative writing student who produced stylish, astute literary criticism but kept turning in conventionally plotted stories that clunked their way to pat conclusions. Finally I confronted him. "What happens to all your sophistication when you sit down to write fiction?" He explained he'd once been told to pack it away until he'd mastered the so called basics: "You have to learn to write a traditional story before you begin to experiment." To me that's like saying a musical person with great fingers but no breath control has to master the trumpet before trying the piano.

There's a mistaken premise here. The "basics" to me include attention to language, convincing characterizations, a sense of discovery and surprise, insights that make the reader stop and marvel, prose that lives and tells the truth.

Questioning the traditional story

There's nothing second-rate about a traditional story. Lots of people write great ones and millions of people love to read them. For some writers, though, the form itself may feel unnatural, not suited to portraying the complexities of a world marked by ambiguity and dislocations, chaos and incongruities, where answers are suspect and bizarre juxtapositions a part of daily life. Before beginning a story, you might ask yourself:

- Do I want to go beyond telling what happened and recreate the feeling?
- Am I as interested in inner life as in outward action?
- Am I as curious to find out what a character is going to say or think next as in the next turn of the plot?
- Do I take pleasure in what critics writing about Franz Kafka called "the mind reveling in its own keenness?"
- Do I pay attention to language itself and judge stories — including my own — not just on how they read on the page, but out loud?
- Do I often discover what I'm writing about only in the process of writing?
- Do I tend to order events by their emotional or psychological links rather than their chronology?
- Do I think we can best approach Truth through intuition, through hints and suggestions, that Truth flees at any direct approach?

If you answered yes to many of these questions, you probably find traditional structure confining, an obstacle to expression instead of a helpful guide. You're not alone. Consider some of the writers and readers who have questioned the premises many of us take for granted.

Diane Lefer has published several dozen stories in literary journals and magazines including The Kenyon Review, Redbook, Virginia Quarterly Review, and Vogue. A five-time winner of PEN Syndicated Fiction prizes, she has also received grants from the National Endowment for the Arts and the New York Foundation for the Arts. She teaches in the MFA Writing Program at Vermont College.

The traditional story revolves around a conflict. This is a requirement Ursula LeGuin disparages as the "gladiatorial view of fiction."

The movement of the story progresses from rising action to climax to the falling off of the denouement. Hmmm, say the feminist literary critics. Sounds suspiciously like male sexual response. Which is *not*, they note, the only way to satisfy a reader. (This doesn't mean for a moment that only women will reject the standard progression: Kafka began "The Metamorphosis" with the most dramatic moment: "As Gregor Samsa awoke one morning from uneasy dreams he found himself transformed in his bed into a gigantic insect." I can just imagine a modern-day workshop leader telling Kafka that this transformation is clearly the climactic moment and must happen near the *end*. But Kafka—like many contemporary writers who wonder how ordinary life goes on after great trauma—is not concerned with the hows and whys of the unthinkable cataclysmic event, but rather its aftermath.

In modern fiction, it's strange to talk about story climax anyway. These days, stories often end with a subtle realization or epiphany rather than rockets going off. As a result, the edgy juxtapositions and pulsing rhythms of an unconventional story may actually be more engaging to readers than the traditionally structured build-up to a quiet or inconclusive resolution.

A main character must undergo a change. (I like to imagine Kafka walking out of a workshop before starting to write "The Metamorphosis." "You want change?" he mutters. "All right, I'll give you change!") My objection is that life experience teaches us an equally dramatic (if frustrating) truth: In spite of conflict, confrontation and crisis people often don't, can't, or won't change.

Some alternative metaphors

Critics have compared Amy Hempel's stories to *mosaics*: she provides scenes and information in bits and pieces until the whole picture comes together. I would go further and say she strategically leaves a few key scenes out, so that the reader must participate in the creation. In her powerful story "In the Cemetery Where Al Jolson Is Buried," (from *Reasons To Live*, Alfred A. Knopf, 1985), the narrator recalls her visits to a dying friend and her inability to give all the desired support. We never see a confrontation between the two young women; though we know it happens, there's no account of the death; there's no funeral. Can't you just hear the workshop complaint: Amy, you're avoiding the emotion. Precisely! The reader must fill in the incidents too painful for the narrator to recount. The story ends with a series of memories and anecdotes that bring home an emotional understanding of the narrator's sense of threat, uncertainty, guilt and grief.

I've heard author William Least Heat-Moon use the metaphor of a *wheel* to describe Native American storytelling. The heart of the story is the hub of the wheel. The storyteller moves around the circumference a bit, then down one of the spokes to touch the hub, then back to the circumference, approaching the heart again and again from different points. As with Hempel's mosaic, the listener or reader shares in the effort of creation until all points on the circumference are connected, every spoke leads to the hub, the whole wheel is filled in.

A story that seems to work this way is "The Water-Faucet Vision" by Gish Jen, first published in *Nimrod*, reprinted in *Best American Short Stories 1988* (Houghton Mifflin) and later forming part of Jen's novel *Typical American* (Houghton Mifflin, 1991). The hub is a desire, the idea of seeking comfort for the pains of life. The circumference represents the narrator Callie's life history as she grows up in a turbulent Chinese-American family, attends Catholic school and longs to be a martyred miracle-working saint, reaches adulthood and mourns her mother's death. The narrative jumps around in time, i.e., all over the circumference of the wheel, but whatever its starting point, every anecdote and every memory becomes another spoke leading to the desire for comfort. Every moment re-counted connects to the hub, the heart which is the yearning for belief, for a time when — in the story's closing words — "one had only to direct the hand of the Almighty and say, just here, Lord, we hurt here — and here, and here and here."

More metaphors

A jazz musician may seem to go all over the place in a *musical improvisation.* but there's always an underlying structure to return to. The sense of liberating spontaneity is exhilarat-ing when matched by technical proficiency and control. That's the feeling I got from Sandra Cisneros' collection, *Woman Hollering Creek and Other Stories* (Random House, 1991), a series of Mexican-American vernacular solos of such spilling-forth immediacy they feel effortless though the careful crafting and choice of language and image make it clear they were not. In many of these short short stories — some no more than a page or two in length — Cisneros states an idea or image in the first sentence, flies away with it and returns to the same image (the way a musician returns to a chord) to ground the story in the end. One story opens and closes with language reminiscent of a nostalgic ballad; another reads like a *ranchera*-style love song written in paragraphs instead of stanzas. Some stories in the collection (the most self-conscious and least successful, I think) are longer, more tradi-tional, and more sustained; some are like overheard gossip sessions. The overall effect made me think of attending a concert in a plaza, walking into the church or movie theater, watching people and listening to their chatter in between songs. Cisneros even ends the book with a brass instrument flourish: "tanT ¡ tanT!"

Tim O'Brien's "How to Tell a True War Story" (from *The Things They Carried,* Houghton Mifflin/Seymour Lawrence, 1990) makes devastating use of *instant replay.* O'Brien holds up the memory of a terrible moment in Vietnam: A man is blown up by a landmine. At such times, O'Brien writes, "The angles of vision are skewed . . . . The pictures get jumbled; you tend to miss a lot," and so he tells it again and again, differently each time, obsessed by the incident and by trying to tell it truly. The story's unconventional structure (replay — authorial commentary — replay — commentary) forces the fascinated and horrified reader to face the relentless intensity and impossible-to-resolve contradic-tions of war.

Marlene Nourbese Philip's "Burn Sugar" (anthologized in *International Feminist Fiction,* Crossing Press, 1992) is a *process* story, focused not on what happens, but how. The action is simple: The narrator, a Caribbean-born woman now living in Canada, bakes a cake from a family recipe while remembering her mother's kitchen. She describes the beating hand, the batter stiffening in resistance, the disappearance and blending of ingredients. At the same time, the language of the narrative switches between Caribbean and Canadian En-glish. The very process of baking the cake is metaphoric on different levels, all having to do with cultural transformation and survival as well as the conflicted relationship between mother and daughter. The process bridges cultures, past and present, mother and daughter. This doesn't happen *in* the story, but rather *through* it.

If a story which rises to a climax and then falls off is "male," what sort of story would illustrate *female textual/sexual response?* Could it be a story which peaks again and again, in which waves of excitement and satisfaction are diffused throughout the text instead of being focused on a single moment near the end? Is it a story in which individual themes and incidents connect up in a sense of union or unity instead of resulting in a clear-cut choice or a change?

What "happens" in Kate Braverman's chillingly seductive story "Winter Blues" (*Squandering the Blue*, Fawcett Columbine, 1990) is deceptively simple. The protagonist, Erica, works on a college paper about contemporary American poets while her bored daughter demands attention. As far as plot goes, that's it. But what really happens is that Braverman weaves together several themes and makes them cohere into a frightening vision. The Chernobyl nuclear accident hangs like a threat over the story; the poets Erica writes about are suicidal and self-destructive; shocking memories of life with her drug-addicted husband surface as Erica tries to keep her young child distracted. The elements of the story are not related through logic or cause and effect but through image and incantatory almost hallucinogenic prose. Poets wear "their diseases like garlands," the blood of Los Angeles is "a red neon wash, a kind of sea of autistic traffic lights," the Hawaiian sky is the "pink of irradiated flamingos," and children are taught not to touch flame: "Then we touch it."

Why look for metaphor?

Obviously the alternative metaphors I've cited overlap and are not the only possibilities. But be forewarned. In reliance on metaphor, sound and rhythm, careful and evocative word choice, intuitive links, unexpected juxtapositions and suggestion instead of statement, the unconventional story uses many of the techniques of poetry, an art form many people in our society, alas, disdain. If you choose this route, you'll have to expect a specific kind of rejection on occasion: the stodgy editor who sniffs, "This isn't a story, it's a prose poem," as if poetic effect doesn't enrich a story but rather diminishes it!

Why do I look for metaphors and invent labels? Isn't that just as arbitrary and rule-bound as following conventional form?

Our brains are wired so that thinking often takes the path of least resistance, the most worn path. (I suspect that's one reason why we may end up with pat, predictable stories when we follow the most traditional structure. We may shunt our most original insights and deepest intuition off onto unused branch lines as we barrel down the familiar track.) Once alternative structures have been brought into conscious awareness—something metaphor can do in a suggestive rather than a dogmatic way—they become internalized, part of our psychic inventory. We can intuitively select the best form for our material without always falling back on the same old scheme.

It happens because it has to

I don't sit down and think I'm going to write a male story today, or a female story. (Anyway, I think most great stories are androgynous, with both "male" and "female" attributes. It's not a question of exclusion, but rather of emphasis.) An alternative structure usually appears naturally as a story develops—because it *has* to. I may not even recognize the controlling metaphor until I start revising. Then I'll use the model to help shape the story and make the elements cohere, to lessen the danger that an intuitively written story will end up too scattered or random and meaningless to anyone but the author. For example, in a mosaic story, each constituent piece has its own boundaries, its own shape. I'll try to see that each separate incident has a small but noticeable climactic moment. I'll alternate dramatic incidents with digressions, meditations or sections that explore the inner workings of a character's mind. All these separate pieces are held together because they are inside the same frame and—to mix a metaphor—because the same search or question or metaphor or symbol runs through all, like a thread through the hearts of many beads.

Continuity vs. change

Consider one of history's great transformations, when Saul, the persecutor of Christians became Paul, who practically created Christianity as an institution and church. But it's not unreasonable to interpret Paul's story this way: that he was vigorous, zealous and single-minded both before and after the transformative experience. So much for change!

Still, if fictional characters appear the same at beginning and end, they're likely to seem sculpted rather than alive, and that can make a story static. But if there has to be a turning point, why not make it a shift in the *reader*? What if the *reader* changes and comes to see a character or a situation in a new light?

One day, I shocked myself by joining in a conversation complaining about the younger generation. When I was an adolescent, I swore I'd never forget what it was like to be a kid and would never judge teenagers cruelly or put them down, but there I was, doing just that. I reacted to my treachery by writing "What She Stood For," (*The Literary Review*, Fall, 1991). I started out by intentionally repeating and illustrating all the common negative stereotypes I had attributed to today's teens, saddling my protagonist, Kendra, with her shallow shopping mall mentality, her lack of values, her flirtation with violence, her emotionally disconnected sexuality. But as I wrote, I tried to see her point of view, and found myself bringing her environment to life with all its contradictions and hypocrisy, its background of terrible but half-understood world events and troubled adults. In the course of the story, Kendra began to look almost heroic to me, striving and yearning for something better, sometimes choosing self-defeating paths because she hadn't yet been able to see any others. Kendra didn't so much change, as show her shifting shape—formed by the interplay of her own intrinsic qualities and outside forces—and her possibilities. I'd begun by dismissing, despising and satirizing her. I hope that readers changed their views as I did: first separating themselves from Kendra, laughing bitterly and shaking their heads with despair but eventually identifying with her struggle for self, fervently hoping she would not just survive but thrive.

Creating out of a personal vision

There's a serious omission in this discussion: no discussion of truly experimental writers, such as Nobel-laureate Samuel Beckett; Robert Kelly whose "Russian Tales" (in his collection, *Cat Scratch Fever*, McPherson & Company, 1991) are "experiments in telling," based on intuitive responses to a chart of Russian-language roots; Diane Williams with her postmodern broken disjunctions (*Some Sexual Success Stories and Other Stories in Which God Might Choose To Appear*, Grove Weidenfeld, 1992). The authors I used as examples may be unconventional, but they are also widely read—and not just by literary sophisticates. I chose them to emphasize a point: You can explore many possibilities in structure and form and still be entirely accessible.

Still, I won't deny that if you hope to be a popular author and even make money at it, you probably stand a better chance if you can write like Stephen King rather than Virginia Woolf. But I don't believe that's a matter of choice. Most writers create out of a personal vision; we each have a particular way of seeing the world.

I began this piece by telling of a student who kept struggling with traditional form. By trying to fit himself into some arbitrary category, this talented writer was unintentionally denying and deforming his gift. When he broke the "rules" for the first time and told his story as he felt it needed to be told, he produced a remarkable piece of fiction that was promptly accepted by a prestigious journal and nominated for a Pushcart Prize. Can the same happen to you? The only way to find out is to give yourself the freedom to try.

Going for Baroque: Overcoming Fear of Narrative

by Matt Devens

Diction becomes distinguished and non-prosaic by the use of unfamiliar terms, i.e., strange words, metaphors, lengthened forms, and everything that deviates from the ordinary modes of speech. —Aristotle, *Poetics*

Disclaimer

Despite the doctrinaire stance of the preceding epigraph and the stuffy reputation of its author, the following essay will strive *not* to be prescriptive or to dwell on rules (of thumb or otherwise). I am convinced such things do not exist when it comes to fiction, though if I'm mistaken, they do in that any successful piece of writing should evidence discipline and craft, and should meet every demand it makes of itself. In short, it should be good. I want simply to talk about possibilities, options, choices, and if as I'm doing so this piece emits the faint odor of literary autobiography, please bear with me. I don't presume to be more than what I am—a young(ish) writer in the midst of a long and arduous apprenticeship who would like to share some thoughts and experiences (hoping they're of some value) with others of like station in the literati.

—M.D.

Have you abandoned the idea of law school?

When I first arrived at the University of Alabama Writing Program nearly a decade ago, I half-expected the other M.F.A. students to lay palm fronds at my feet and feed me peeled grapes. My ego had been dangerously fattened by four years of writing workshops at tiny, bucolic Knox College, and the several recruitment valentines and fellowship offers from Alabama seemed to promise even more heaping portions of worship and adoration. During my brief initial visit with the program director, though, I was given my first taste of unsweetened criticism. He let me take a look at my application file and suggested I make note of the admission committee's responses to my writing sample. "This guy needs the baroque pummeled out of him," and "Maybe some Kaopectate would cure him of his adjective condition," are among the comments that still remain fresh in my memory. Well, I was stricken at the time; a few curt ink scrawls had lain the wood to my very *raison d'etre*. I pouted for a few days and seriously considered taking the LSAT; perhaps my wordlust would be best put to use writing circumlocutive legal briefs. But this funk passed. I finished my degree and have been working at fiction with some degree of success. And I've been writing (or at least *thinking* about writing) long enough to know that's what I'm going to be doing for a long time to come.

About the baroque thing, though. In French the word means literally "misshapen pearl," and over the years has come to connote artistic excess and extravagance. The early

Matt Devens' fiction has appeared in Story *magazine. He has taught English at the University of Alabama and the University of New Orleans. He and his wife live on the Indiana shore of Lake Michigan where he writes and does construction work.*

part of this century saw a large measure of hostility toward and rebellion against all things baroque. Architects Louis Sullivan and Frank Lloyd Wright thumbed their noses at the prevailing neo-classical idioms of their art and reinvented it by placing function before form. Henry James caused many writers and readers to impugn the validity of the omniscient, intrusive narrator, and Ernest Hemingway cast a suspicious eye on the sole medium of literature, *language*. For Hemingway, words were ideally vehicular; to allow them to upstage the truths and emotions they were meant to convey was to miss the mark as a writer. (It is ironic, though, that through his militant effacement of the word, Papa attracted so much attention and scrutiny to his prose.)

These people are visionaries, revolutionaries, though their careers did not mark the geneses of their respective art forms. While it's a young writer's prerogative, or perhaps even instinct, to hew to the aesthetic and absorb the influence of a particularly admired master or movement, it's necessarily ignorant to dismiss as irrelevant the great remainder of literary heritage. There's much in Raymond Carver's work that instructs and inspires, but don't George Eliot's books speak just as profoundly to our modern lives?

Different stories, different narrative

To get more to the point, I think it's quite unfortunate that so many fictioneers and their critics (particularly those in graduate writing programs) froth at the mouth when confronted by prose styles and narrative techniques that dare to ignore current, widely-accepted minimalist and utilitarian dicta. *Show, don't tell!*, for example. And, *Less is more and more is less*. Good advice, perhaps, for writers who haven't a clue. But for many workshop critics and journal editors, these phrases are as reflexive and irrepressible as a sneeze. Indeed, we have Hemingway on record as saying that a story is like an iceberg, whose integrity lay in the seven eighths of it unseen beneath the water. The Nobel laureate also insisted that truths are best rendered in fiction through action and drama rather than explicative narration. And yes, these proved to be considerations by which to write great literature—for *Hemingway*, that is, and some other writers with instincts akin to his.

Stand clear of the sparks, though, if you try to test a great many other works of fiction against the "show, don't tell rule." John Nordholm, the 19-year-old narrator of John Updike's lovely story "The Happiest I've Been," is unabashedly explicit and guileless in his ruminations on friendship, coming of age, romance and the future. If used by a lesser writer, such a narrative strategy might very well backfire, and come off as expedient and artless—offenses which would be difficult to pinpoint in Updike's work, even that of the early period of his career when this story was written. Rather than communicate his narrator's feelings of exhiliration, optimism and genuine good cheer through coy banter and an accumulation of "telling" gestures begging for interpretation, Updike lays his cards on the table. John Nordholm sees the events of the story (a New Year's Eve party and imminent road trip back to school) as the happiest time of his life and tells the reader why. In the story's final paragraph, John Nordholm goes so far as to explain the title (which is not ironic—a feat in itself during these cynical modern times) in deliberate, summary fashion and in doing so does not insult or condescend; rather, he elicits a sigh of satisfaction, at least from this reader. No jigsaw puzzle here. No bell diving to the base of an iceberg. Yet it is hardly a facile piece of fiction in that it challenges the reader to connect with an intelligent character who articulates a broad and complex range of emotions and insight.

The contemporary pantheon abounds with countless other writers who, to the anal retentive, might seem downright atavistic in their love for beefy, expatiating narrative. When Walker Percy wants to explain why his memorable protagonist Will Barrett is gripped by existential despair and keeps falling down on the golf course, he doesn't skimp on the philosophical noodlings. Although Percy's often cerebral, learned discourses-within-a-novel may chafe some, the serious, conscientious reader will spend the time and the intellectual and emotional energy necessary to distill every last soul-deep drop of satisfaction from them.

Saul Bellow is another writer who seems conspicuously resistant to minimalist trends, or *any* literary trend, for that matter. If anything, his writing is traditionally continental. From his early novel *The Adventures of Augie March*, for instance, the reader gets not only all eight eighths of the iceberg, but the kitchen sink as well. For the most part, Bellow is not suppliant to the tyranny of plot or expectations of economically packaged nuggets of theme; rather, novels like *Augie March* are discursive picaresques of the body, mind and soul. To be sure, long works dependent upon a single protagonist's responses to his every environmental stimulus run great risks. If a writer is not very interesting or insightful and can't compensate for such deficiencies with whirligigs of plot, he obviously is bound to produce a fairly boring book.

So far I've devoted a fair amount of space to emphasizing that there are no rules or restrictions when it comes to choosing a narrative strategy. And though I place many of the above examples in counterpoint to more economical, understated storytelling, I harbor no prejudice against the latter form. Much of the genius in, say, Willa Cather's *My Antonia*, lies in its reserved, often whispering voice. And Jake Barnes certainly wouldn't be the poignant, sympathetic character that he is had Hemingway invested him with the syntactical tics and volubility of, say, Howard Cosell. Whether a narrative be tight as a drum or meandering, cryptic or explicit, the writer must bring a method to and control over it.

In defense of erudite sudras

When I was a freshman in college I heard a political science professor deliver a talk called "Diction in Fiction." The professor was a tweedy, cuddly septagenarian who was as popular as college teachers come. The many file cabinets of unpublished novels he had written over the years evidently qualified him to speak of fiction with some authority, though by the end of the talk I realized, even at the tender age of 19, that he really didn't know much about the subject. The gist of his lecture was that too many contemporary writers spent too much time hunched and sweating over the smithy of language, forging extravagant prose quite unsuited for the subject matter that modern American experience offered them. Yes, he said, Shakespeare's florid verse was appropriate for tales of royalty and faeries, and Kate Chopin's purple prose seemed indigenous to the rarefied atmosphere in which her turn-of-the-century, blue-blooded New Orleanians flitted about. But when you write about "real people," he said, you have to use "real words." "In a story about a short garbage truck driver, are you going to refer to him as *homunculus*? Of course not!" Well, he lost me right there, and just about everyone else in the room as well. I guess he should have defined his terms. What are "real people?" Hominids who watch *Major Dad*? Sure. Why not? Just the same, aren't those who read and enjoy Susan Sontag "real people" too? And what about "real words"? *Short* and *guy* are "real words." They're both in the dictionary, as is *homunculus*.

He was essentially saying that the subject matter of, and the social, educational and cultural milieu of the principals in a story dictate the level of diction a writer should use. To that I say *Hooey*! These concerns should never inhibit a writer from using any of the only tools he can use in his job—*words*. Words are all we have to give shape to such abstractions as emotion, thought and feeling. They need to perform within a reader's brain the work of all five senses. There are 137 pounds of them in the latest edition of *Oxford English Dictionary*, and if my bathroom scale is correct, the compact edition (with magnifying glass) weighs in at about 28. If you are so inclined, learn them, love them, use them, despite the strange opposition you may encounter for doing so.

Let me give you an example. During my first semester in Tuscaloosa I submitted to the fiction workshop a story called "Elephant Delicacy," which is told from the first person point of view of an Asian Indian sudra (of the Hindu caste one step above the Untouchable) named Parbat. Parbat is a sweet fellow who is distraught over the dissolution throughout his village of traditional Hindu values. To make a long story short, he makes friends with a nearby herd of elephants and enlists their help in stampeding his village during the story's climax. Parbat also spoke with the mannered, erudite voice of an Oxford graduate. Several people in the workshop liked the piece very much, though the majority was a bit miffed by it. Would a rural Indian peasant *really* refer to his nemesis as a "citified upstart and minion of a ruling kshatriya class gone slack-souled and megalomaniacal"? If I were striving for social realism, I suppose not, he wouldn't be speaking in *English*, for that matter. I would have had the story translated into Sanskrit. The story's supporters and I were finally able to convince the hecklers that a story about mystical communion with pachyderms is necessarily fabular, and subsequently abides by a rather different set of rules.

First person: How much latitude?

What about more realistic stories, the ones whose success cannot rely on the reader's willing suspension of disbelief? Must the writer limit his diction so as not to put off his audience? Perhaps, depending on whether he uses a first or third person narrator. The first person obviously has fewer possibilities than the third. Let's go back to our short garbage truck driver. Would *homunculus*, or other such uncommon terms, seem right coming out of his mouth? Well, it depends on the multiplicity of variables that make him and every other fictional character tick. The writer must know the basic quiddity of a character before bringing him to life on the page. What's his educational background like? What are his interests? Does he read? What does he read? The answers to questions such as these will pretty much determine how the character speaks. If the writer decides his garbage truck driver conforms to a type, that is, reads *Hustler* if he reads anything, sits in his La-Z-Boy all evening drinking Schlitz and watching *Dukes of Hazzard* reruns, and is willfully ignorant and proud of it, then the reader might fairly wonder why *homunculus* slides so readily from his tongue. And unless the writer is a master of dramatic irony, the reader might fairly find the story hackneyed and pointless.

A writer usually does himself, the reader, and short garbage truck drivers an enormous favor by creating characters who confound common stereotypical perceptions. In doing so he raises the odds of producing an interesting story and grants himself greater latitude in choosing diction. For instance, our word-drunk garbage truck driver may come from a long line of renaissance garbage men who place a premium on self-education and appreciation of high art and culture. Perhaps he has an M.F.A. in Creative Writing and finds the salary and benefits offered by the local Department of Sanitation better than those offered by the local junior college.

There is a danger in freighting a first person narrator with such biographical circumstances. If they serve only to justify his unexpectedly high falutin diction, and don't inform his character or advance the story in any other way, the writer has merely given himself shabby fiat to commence the verbal pyrotechnics. I suggest you take a gander at Padgett Powell's *Edisto* to see how such pitfalls are masterfully avoided. This novel's pubescent narrator, Simons Everson Manigault, has a vocabulary and knack for metaphor that would seem precocious beyond belief had he not a mother to force-feed him the Canon from birth and encourage him to cultivate a picaroon writer's lifestyle during pre-adolescence.

Third person: Infinite possibilities

Now in third person fiction, the storytelling voice is a character entirely unto itself, whether it is limited to the point of view of a particular character or entirely omniscient. The amplitude of diction and sophistication of metaphor in this voice ought to be determined solely by the writer's instincts and narrative strategy. Although the infinite range of language possibilities afforded by the third person seems to me a given in fiction, any radical disparity between the voice of a particular character and the narrative voice which has created him is often met with resistance. Instructive examples of such disparity might readily be found in any book by contemporary American fiction's Crown Prince of Darkness, Cormac McCarthy. McCarthy's characters, to politely state the case, are often illiterate, inbred, unspeakably depraved hill trash who are nonetheless propelled by a narrative of, at times, psalmic eloquence and extravagance. Early on in the novel *Outer Dark*, mountain miscreant Culla Holme takes a last look back on the infant son/nephew he has left for dead in the woods:

> And as he lay there a far crack of lightning went bluely down the sky and bequeathed him in an embryonic bird's first fissured vision of the world and transpiring instant and outrageous from dark to dark a final view of the grotto and the shapeless white plasm struggling upon the rich and incunabular moss like a lank swamp hare. He would have taken it for some boneless cognate of his heart's dread had the child not cried.

This selection serves well to illustrate this essay's epigraph. The diction not only meets the Aristotlean criteria for distinction, but also replicates for the reader the primal chill curdling Culla's marrow.

Although McCarthy is a recent recipient of a MacArthur Foundation "genius grant," I suspect, from my experience, that prose such as that exemplified here might run into vehement criticism in any number of writing workshops and editorial offices. For one thing, it might be argued, the character of Culla Holme probably couldn't read his own name, let alone the book he appears in. If you accept what I've already stated as a given—that, in a third person narrative, the latitude to mould worlds and people with language that "deviates from the ordinary modes of speech" is intrinsic to the writer's business—then such criticism is patently specious.

There's another criticism I've encountered *ad nauseum* that warrants more extensive rebuttal. It arises from the elitist presumption that a man like Culla Holme could not possibly have the kind of intelligence and emotional depth with which the brilliant McCarthy's prose invests him. This would be a truism to someone who believes artists have a monopoly on acutely manifested fear, psychic pain, depression, dementia, joy, ecstasy, love and hate. I would submit, however, that despite the *de facto* existence of so many Tormented Artist Societies, the artist is no more "whole" a human being than the Rotarian. You would find as much alcoholism, family dysfunction, and emotional upheaval at the local electricians' union hall than you would at the Breadloaf Writers' Conference. As much as many writers would like to think so, they are not the "antennae of the race." Rather, they are reporters of and commentators on the human experience; they have chosen as theirs the business of giving symbolic and metaphorical dimension to that which any human can feel, intuit and apprehend intellectually, though to which he might not be able to give ready and clear expression.

I am not a dictionary! I am a human being!

While there are rudiments of logic underpinning many of the aforementioned critical fronts, I've often been mystified when journal editors and workshop critics dismiss some prose simply for its density and use of unfamiliar language. To be certain, a helpful critical reader is obliged to mark and comment on such substantive prose glitches as redundancy, evidence of tin ear, word inaccuracies and genuine verbosity. But for an otherwise intelligent reader/writer to say something like "This is a really great story, *but* there were too many ten dollar words. I'm not a goddamn dictionary" is patently self-indicting. I would be admitting to sloth, for instance, if I took offense at the use of *incunabular* in the preceding McCarthy passage. I'd be on firm critical ground if the word were misused, but it isn't in this case. I might argue that McCarthy could use a more recognizable term, but since there are few, if any, true synonyms in English, he would betray his intentions in doing so. I might argue that using such a term is an exercise in verbosity; however, if verbosity is the unnecessary accumulation of words when fewer would do, it would be more economical to use *incunabular* than its definition, "in the thing's early stages."

I think these hypothetical arguments illustrate one of the writer's most important considerations — audience. When a writer begins mixing theme, character, plot, language and other elements into his fiction stew, he is always mindful of audience. Whether he should or shouldn't be is a debatable point, but the fact remains every writer has as he composes a niggling concern about future audience response to his work. And he asks himself questions: Do I go full throttle and satisfy my artistic intentions and drives? or, Do I pull back for the sake of accessibility? Ultimately, these questions are a matter of conscience, and either answered in the extreme affirmative can produce egregious results — verbal masturbation or simple-minded slop. Ideally, one wishes to communicate through fiction. And, ideally, one wishes to reach as wide an audience as possible without compromising himself. This seems a difficult goal to achieve. Book sales are about the only empirical measure of how wide an audience a writer reaches, and these sales figures invariably indicate that the more sophisticated the language of work of fiction, the fewer people it reaches.

I suppose the best advice a writing teacher can give a young writer is something of a truism: "Tell a story *you* want to tell, and tell it the way *you* want to tell it. If you do so in a disciplined, careful manner, the audience question will take care of itself." And whether a young writer is inclined to write in a minimalist or a baroque vein, he should never turn his back on language and lose his lust for words. He should get drunk on them from time to time, discover the many he's never seen before and rediscover those he's known, and then, when he is sober, use them as he sees fit.

Eating Your Eggshells: What Writers Should Know about the Nitpicking of Editors

by J.C. Hendee

Market newsletters, both large and small, often have letters sections in which various problems and concerns on both sides of the writing/publishing industry get aired. Writers may complain about the butchering of their masterpieces, and editors sometimes berate the lack of quality in submissions. All in all, being both a writer and the editor of *Figment* magazine, I would have to say to writers that the editors might be getting the shorter end of the stick. They must walk the line between responsible publishing and the fearful (and sometimes misused) battle cry of "censorship" coupled with the flag of "artistic integrity." It would seem that the job of an editor is to dance delicately on eggshells, and when one of them breaks, to swallow the pieces. Actually, not every editor has ended up in this position. However, I've heard of it often enough that it amazes me so many people are unaware of market standards governing the editing of material for publication. As a writer, you should be aware of these standards to give yourself a better chance of avoiding the pitfalls in the publishing world, and to give yourself better ground for negotiation with editors.

I've heard it argued by some editors that no manuscript should be accepted unless it is publishable in its present format. And I have heard writers claim that their works are perfect just the way they are, and the editor should not need to change a thing. Both of these viewpoints are pure fallacy. Professional writers appreciate an editor with a judicious eye for solidifying the continuity of their prose, giving their work the added edge and aim it needs for a particular readership, and they realize that no one is perfect—perfection is subjective. Professional editors know that they are not "perfecting" a writer's prose when they ask for specific changes; they are merely adjusting the aim of the work to hit dead-center on the targeted market readership they are trying to reach with their publication. They handle the editing of manuscripts with care and due consideration for that element called "artistic integrity." And for writers, realizing these two facts of the situation can alleviate much of the tension and mixed feelings that can arise in the editing process.

There are resources available that cover the subject of what is acceptable in the editing process and how that process should be conducted. You should familiarize yourself with these definitive texts. One of my personal favorites, concise but perhaps not thoroughly encompassing, is *Webster's Standard American Style Manual*. This text has been helpful to me in developing the following basic guidelines for understanding the step-by-step process for the bare-bones aspects of editing manuscripts and for specifics *writers should pay attention to*! By taking these details into consideration before submitting a manuscript, you

J.C. Hendee's *short stories have appeared in* Pulphouse's Rats in the Soufflé *anthology, the* Banks Literary Award *anthology and in* Eldritch Tales, Leading Edge *and* Deathrealm. *He is editor and publisher of* Figment *magazine and* Fugue, *published by the University of Idaho.*

not only make your manuscript more "editor-proof," but through your work you will be presenting yourself as an attentive, professional writer due the respect of any editor.

Consistency and clarity

One of the first things checked for is *consistency*, something which you as a writer can take control of even before your manuscript gets in the editor's hands. The entire manuscript will be reviewed with regards to punctuation, capitalization, abbreviations, numeral and date formatting, hyphenation, m-dashes, etc. (all the technical format elements) to see if the pattern of use is consistent, if not syntactically correct. Editors give some consideration for stylistics; that is, if the use of one of the above does not conform to standard rules, then a check is made to see if the deviation is consistent throughout the work. If so, the editor will consider whether the writer has made a stylistic choice to emphasize some element of the work. If the deviation is inconsistent, then corrections are made or requested—and rightly so. Names or titles will be checked for proper format as well as spelling. You should be fully certain of all these details before submitting. And if an editor questions these elements of your work, it is only because an inconsistency has been found and corrections *must* be made.

The next thing usually checked for, and the detail which causes the most conflict between editor and writer, is *clarity*—of style as well as content. Any section of text which is unclear in content or focus should be changed to facilitate comprehension. This is a delicate subject and will be handled judiciously by a professional editor. The writer should be aware that the editor is only attempting to help the work reach its intended audience with a maximum impact. The editor may take one of two approaches for such a correction: The section may be edited by staff and submitted to the writer for consideration or approval or the writer may be contacted for a rewrite of specified sections of the work. Either is acceptable as described; the latter of course, is highly preferable. For in this manner, the writer is given majority control over the final content of the manuscript. Similar steps should be taken where the "style" (of narrative, dialogue, etc.) is concerned. I had to request a changed paragraph from Kristine Kathryn Rusch (now editor for *The Magazine of Fantasy & Science Fiction*) for her story "Light Through Mist" (in *Figment #4*) due to a character action that didn't seem to work right for us. She responded with a concise paragraph to fit the needs of the story, and because she handled the rewrite, she was able to consider the integrity of the story from her own perspective. Kristine has always deserved high marks in this business for her professionalism.

Professional editors know that every writer has a narrative/prose voice to be considered. If a section's style is incongruous with the rest of the text, a professional editor will contact the writer and request a rewrite. In the case of a style deviation where the intent is clear and subsequently creates a necessary effect in the story, then that deviation will be maintained. But if that is not the case, if the reason for the shift is not apparent to the editor, then something may be wrong, and the writer should not be upset over a requested change. Lack of clarity—or of intent—should be corrected in all such cases, without exception. If the writer disagrees with a proposed change in this area, he or she should be prepared to explain why. Editors are human, i.e., not perfect, of course, and maybe something was missed in review. An explication of the style/content element in question will help both sides come to agreement. Yet ultimately, if such an explanation doesn't solve the matter, the writer should be prepared to rewrite or try the original version with another editor or publication.

Sometimes the *text structure* must be considered with an eye to the publication's format. Once in a while a paragraph, indentation, word or sentence order and/or sequencing of clauses within a sentence may need to be altered to facilitate clarity, rhythm or accommodate the format of the publication – a rarity, but it can happen. The handling of dialogue, quotations and quote tags can be a sticky subject in this area as well. Once again, the writer must understand that the readership's needs take precedent. All these elements will be considered from the viewpoint of a readable and comprehensible text. I recently made some changes to the structuring of T. Jackson King's novelette "Tides of Fear," (*Figment #10*) to facilitate prose clarity. Tom was agreeable and understanding, and returned the proof sheets containing my changes, with a few changes of his own which were entered into the master copy. This kind of professionalism makes a writer well thought of by any editor, and you can be sure we have always looked forward to the chance to work with Tom again. As a writer, approaching such "fine-tuning" with an attitude of "teamwork" with an editor will take you far in this sometimes-crazy business of publishing.

Check and double-check

Verification will always be done in order to protect the writer, the editor and the publication, and is an element a writer should pay special attention to once a work is finished and being prepped for submission. Trademarks named in the text will be checked for correct spelling and capitalization. It is recommended, where it does not affect the plot, that generic names be used instead of trademarks. Facts will be verified when possible. Quoted passages, referenced sources and foreign terminology are always expected to be accurately represented. This should be checked by the writer before submitting, but it doesn't hurt to have the editor double-check. P.D. Cacek's story "Contract Incorporis" (*Figment #3*) originally had another Latin name. Upon investigation we could not find a legitimate translation for it after consulting two university professors in the classics. We compiled a list of alternative titles, along with translations representing accurate Romantic Latin, and she chose the one that was closest to her original concept. Everybody ended up happy with the result.

Any accidental misrepresentation is a potential embarrassment to both the writer and the editor, and no writer should take offense when an editor has a question concerning validity or accuracy. The editor is simply making sure neither of you ends up with egg on your face.

The occasional *bias* should be eliminated. Such can be found even in an otherwise excellent work. This refers to sections of the text which display sexual/racial/religious/etc. bias in the narrative approach to the work. This does not mean altering character or environmental elements which portray bias; such may be a contention point integral to the work's intent. But any section of text which is demeaning or slanderous according to sex, religion, race, etc., and is not a necessary trait of a character or premise of conflict in plot, should be cut or altered. No exceptions. If there is a potential misunderstanding of intention, talk it out with the editor. Perhaps there is a better way of portraying such an element that won't leave the reader believing it was a writer's viewpoint they read and not just an element of the story. This is a quintessential element of responsible editing and publishing – and writing – and no professional writer will object to this type of editing.

Legalities are an absolute must in final verification. You should not object to any attention to such details – you should *insist* upon it. Copyrights of previous publication should be checked and appropriately noted, and the writer should make sure such are correctly listed on the original manuscript. Potentially libelous passages should be verified, supported, possibly annotated and sources of facts supporting such statements archived for future defense (even so, it is better to simply edit such material out or have it rewritten appropriately). A specific and legal contract (or letter of agreement) should be signed and dated (by editor/publisher and the writer), and should include the creator's SSN (Social Security Number) if cash payment is made for the rights. The contract should include specific details pertaining to rights purchased, compensation and payment, date of payment, longevity of agreement, terms of reversion if the text is unused by the end of longevity, relevant options, and reversion rights after publication. Anything less is foolish for both the author and editor/publisher.

The last detail of the editorial process between acceptance and publication is the one which would eliminate half of the hostilities between editors and writers over the content of a published work: *Proof sheets* or *galley proofs*. After all alterations to a manuscript have been made by the editor, according to the writer's rewrites or the editor's notification of changes to the writer, proof sheets (rough copy) of the text should be sent to the author and returned *with approval* before publication. If you've worked with an editor before and have developed a comfortable relationship where you have confidence in an editor, you may not have to be concerned about it. Still, proof sheets are the standard *professional* practice in this business. Proof sheets protect your vested interest in your published work. Any editor who doesn't use them, ever, may eventually end up chewing on eggshells! Almost all professional publications use proof sheets, or some process which fulfills the same objective, and the writer has every right to insist on them.

In summary

These are only the basics. There are other details to be considered, but if you keep them in mind when composing and submitting, and remember them when it comes time to work with an editor on revisions, everyone will end up with a lot less calcium between their teeth. Not to mention the establishment of a truly professional reputation which will carry both the writer and editor into a prosperous future and specifically into the next acceptance and/or publication.

As a writer, you do have rights within the editing process, but you must be correctly aware of what those rights are according to market standards of operation. Adhere to them and professional editors will respect you for your knowledgable approach to the editing process.

Making a Living

by Laurie Henry

*For more than five years I maintained myself thus solely by the labor of my hands, and
I found that by working about six weeks in a year, I could meet all the expenses of living.* —
Henry David Thoreau, *Walden*.

I thought it would be a good idea to find a job where I could work about 10 hours a week
and earn around $25,000 a year. This would give me the writing time I needed to polish
up my two completed but unrevised novels and to finish my most recent and promising
one.

Over the past few years, however, I've found the high pay/low effort jobs relatively hard
to find, and those that do pay really well seem (unfairly!) to demand effort, concentration,
special training and/or natural ability.

Soon after turning my back, probably forever, on the "$100,000 a year guaranteed"
court-reporting jobs so tantalizingly advertised (though never actually offered to me) in
the court reporter's trade magazines, to return to a more traditional, less time-consuming
writer's job (part-time freshman composition teaching), I decided to find out how other
writers make a living. I sent questionnaires to 20 writers whose names I found in the 1991
edition of St. James Press' *Contemporary Novelists* and 41 to writers listed in Poets &
Writers' '91-'92 *Directory of American Poets and Fiction Writers*.

The *Contemporary Novelists* authors were people whose biographies suggested they had
worked at an unusual variety of jobs at some point in their lives. From *A Directory of
American Poets and Fiction Writers*, I tried to choose a fiction writer from each state (some
writers I wanted to contact had moved and left no forwarding address, perhaps an indication of the lot of writers in these trying times), who had published at least one book. I
wanted to find out how a wide variety of writers managed their lives from a financial and
logistical point of view. I was delighted to receive 24 responses, some as long as three
single-spaced pages.

Making a living from fiction writing

Although all 24 writers who responded had published one book, and some had published
many more, only eight said they earned their livings entirely from writing fiction. Some
writers do very well, of course; one whom I contacted said, "My income consists entirely
of interest earned on the investments purchased with a writer's income." And others mention that the sale of their work to places other than publishing companies has brought them
a measure of security: John Thorndike, whose most recent book is *The Potato Baron* (Villard, 1989), for example, writes that he has supported himself through writing during the
last few years "mainly because Hollywood has stepped in and they write bigger checks."
Ann McLaughlin, author of *The Balancing Pole* (John Daniel & Co., 1991), writes that,
although the income from her first novel did not bring her great wealth, "it was unusually
generous, owing in part to the fact that *The Reader's Digest* bought the novel for their
Condensed Books series."

Laurie Henry *holds graduate degrees in fiction writing from the Johns Hopkins University and the
University of Iowa Writers' Workshop. She has worked as a cotton mill weaver, legal and bilingual secretary,
editor, court reporter, and part-time college English instructor.*

Many writers agree with Barbara Corcoran, whose most recent books *Family Secrets* (Atheneum) and *The House on Blank Street* (Scholastic), were published within the last year. Corcoran supports herself through writing but says "it's very much 'feast or famine' — and one good year doesn't guarantee that future years will also be lucrative."

Dagoberto Gilb, whose most recent collection of stories is *Getting a Job in Dell City* (University of New Mexico Press, 1993), agrees. "A couple of years ago," he says, "I made money as a writer. Then there were two years I went back to nothing." This year, Gilb received an NEA fellowship, which has made things easier, although it has not allowed him to stop looking for non-writing-related work. Other writers, despite an impressive publication record, report more famine than feast: Doug Hornig, whose most recent novel is *Stinger* (NAL, 1990), left his job as a computer programmer after the publication of his second book. Hornig says his writing brings in his family's second income and would not be sufficient alone. "This is especially disappointing after seven published novels," he says.

Short story writers suggest that earning enough money from fiction writing to live may be harder now than ever. Kurt Vonnegut, interviewed on "Writers Workshop," a coproduction of the University of South Carolina and the South Carolina ETV Network, said that he had been able to become a fulltime writer after selling a story for several hundred dollars because "it was more than they were paying me at General Electric." But as Ellyn Bache, author of four books, including a novel, *Festival in Fire Season*, and a collection of stories, *The Value of Kindness*, both published in 1992, writes, there are fewer good paying markets for short stories than there were even 10 years ago.

"I've published more than 30 short stories in addition to my books," says Bache, "and it's distressing to me that the commercial short story market seems to be drying up. I had five stories in *McCall's* and was well paid for them in the '80s, but today *McCall's* doesn't publish fiction at all. *Mademoiselle*, a long-time good market for writers like me, also stopped."

Bache, whose story is typical, continues, "I've been publishing books since 1982 and feature stories since the mid-'70s, and I've *never* earned my living through writing, at least not enough of a living to support my family (husband, four kids)." Bache adds that the most she has ever earned from fiction "was not even from the book. It was from selling film options two years running for *Safe Passage*. I earn a few thousand dollars a year from fiction that we can count on, some years a lot more, but not reliably."

Retirement pay and social security were mentioned by some writers — including Harold Adams, whose book, *The Man Who Was Taller than God*, was published by Walker & Co. in 1992 and Milton Bass, who has two detective novels, *The Half-Hearted Detective* and *The Broken-Hearted Detective*, forthcoming from Pocket Books in 1993 — as a way they have found the money to write. Perhaps retirement writing time is a worthy incentive for middle-aged writers with "regular" jobs to contribute to their pension plans.

Of course, there are writers who say they would work at their non-writing professions even if it were possible for them to live on writing income alone. As Norman Lavers, whose book, *The Northwest Passage*, was published by the Fiction Collective in 1984, suggests, there may even be disadvantages to living on writing earnings alone: "I have known people who made their entire living from writing," he says, "and it seemed to me they were in a real rat race. They had little time for anything but writing, and they often had to compromise writing what they wanted to write because of market considerations."

Jobs that involve writing

Journalism and public relations have brought in a steady income for many writers, keeping them in touch with words and writing during the workday as well as before and after. Although writing-related professions generally require a lot of concentration and energy, some writers find them rewarding in themselves—and they usually pay better than mechanical, repetitive pursuits.

Kathy Acker, whose most recent book is *My Mother: Demonology*, published by Pantheon Books in 1993, says she has also worked at "miserable" jobs and definitely prefers earning a living from writing-related activities "such as journalism, performances, teaching gigs, anything that has to do with writing."

Fletcher Knebel, author of 14 books including *Sabotage* (Berkeley, 1989) and *Trespass* (Ace, 1987), worked as a newspaper reporter while completing his first three books and then became a fulltime novelist after their success. Although he feels reporting helped his writing because "a newspaper reporter covers all manner of stories and meets all manner of characters," he quit, "because I was working myself silly, working on the books nights and weekends for three years. Just recalling that much now makes my shoulders ache." Still, he advises writers that it's important to have some contact with the outside world, even if it isn't financially necessary. "It takes a Marcel Proust," he says, "to turn a cloistered life into ammunition for writing novels."

The writing in writing jobs is often not closely related to the writing a fiction writer does at home. Harold Adams, a writer for well over 30 years before publishing, worked for much of his life writing monthly bulletins, news releases and reports on businesses for the Minneapolis Better Business Bureau, later becoming executive director for the Minnesota Charities Review Council.

"Both the Bureau and Council provided useful background for my writing efforts," he says, "but I discovered I never could make really good use of the experiences until I stopped working at the jobs. I wasn't interested in writing about the Bureau when I worked there, since much of my time at the office was devoted to writing nonfiction on the subject, and I couldn't mix the two. Same with the Council."

Milton Bass, like Fletcher Knebel a journalist before retirement, writes that "working on a newspaper gets you in the habit of thinking and writing quickly," clearly an advantage for a writer. "This sometimes leads to superficiality," he warns, "but if one realizes this, it is controllable."

Jocelyn Riley, whose novels, *Crazy Quilt* and *Only My Mouth is Smiling*, were both published by Bantam in 1986, worked in the marketing department of a publishing house and later as a freelance editor and proofreader but does not recommend this kind of work. She continued for a while after her books' publication, but quit, "because I could never get ahead—too much work for too little money."

Riley now has her own company, Her Own Words! Woman's History and Literature Media, for which she writes, produces and distributes videotapes. She says that she loves her work and would recommend that others start their own businesses. "I suggest designing and manufacturing some sort of product that can be sold over and over again, such as videos or widgets," she says. "You can never get ahead if you have to start each project from scratch."

Some writers find that after spending a day writing, it's hard to go home and pick up a pen or sit down at the computer all over again. Gloria Goldreich, whose most recent novel is *Years of Dreams* (Little, Brown, 1992), formerly a public relations writer for an urban university, says, "the demands of a fulltime job were fatiguing, and writing had to be sandwiched in. I did my own work in the evening or on weekends. Not easy." Goldreich now supports herself solely through writing, but says "it took 25 years for this to happen."

Careers unrelated to writing

This category includes jobs that seem to involve so much intellectual or physical effort that much thought about fiction writing during the day would be impossible (unless you were really a goof-off).

Jose Yglesias, whose most recent books are *Tristan & the Hispanics* (Simon & Schuster, 1989) and *One German Dead* (Ballantine, 1989), supported his family by working for a pharmaceutical company before becoming a fulltime writer. He writes "when I quit, my boss tried to persuade me to stay by letting me write for three hours each day" on the job. No other writers report a similar arrangement, but some have found considerable satisfaction in non-writing related careers.

Irving Faust, whose third collection of stories will be published this year, worked as a high school guidance counselor and later became director of guidance and counseling in another public high school. Faust continued this work after the publication of his first book. He says, "I'm compulsive about my counseling work and *enjoy* it — so I give 100 percent — and it is a splendid counter-balance to the introspective action of writing fiction." He says he wouldn't change his lifestyle "even if I made a million-dollar movie sale."

Faust finds it helpful to remain "in the *real* world, not just a personal, angst-ridden world," and urges writers to "work in a field that has nothing to do with writing fiction. It's not for everyone, but it keeps you fresh, involved and controls the ego."

Dagoberto Gilb found work, after studying philosophy and religion in college, as a laborer at a construction site. "I worked regularly in the construction trades because I needed to make money (I became a father of two boys, and I couldn't find anything else)," Gilb says. "In 1988, a combination of my wife getting a job, my getting a fellowship from Texas (the Dobie-Paisano), and the construction work economy collapsing, gave me more time devoted, consciously, to the idea of me being a 'writer.' I try to take side-jobs (little jobs — hanging doors, fixing this or that) whenever they spring up, and I depend on that money . . . I go from pounding nails to pounding keys, until I feel guilty or broke, and I need to work again."

Writers who don't have the long summer vacations of the academic year and who don't "enjoy" the forced downtime of a construction worker — which at least leaves the writer with writing time — tend to be less satisfied with their non-writing-related careers. Barbara Milton, whose *A Small Cartoon* was published by Wordbeat Press in 1983, gave up teaching math after her book's publication and went back to school to study environmental sciences. Now, as educational coordinator for the Urban Resources Initiative, a program run out of the Yale School of Forestry and Environmental Studies, she writes, "The job is *too* consuming. I hope to resolve it by working parttime and forcing myself to use my free time to write. She finds "plenty of material — important material" at her job, "but no time for reflection, much less writing.

"I'd like to be less conflicted about how I spend my time," Milton admits. "I think my job is important; I yearn to write, and I have a 4-year-old-son I want to be a good mother to." Her advice is that writers work at "nothing too consuming, nothing that is open-ended."

Jobs that leave the mind free

The advantages of what Gloria Goldreich describes as "a job which is not draining emotionally and could be dismissed intellectually at the end of the day" are clear: no work to carry home, and if you don't want to define yourself by what you do during the day, maybe there's some extra incentive to work hard at what you do (write) after hours.

Sometimes this kind of job can be ideal. Norman Lavers writes that a mystery writer acquaintance of his "required absolute quiet for his writing, and therefore wrote at night, sleeping by day. He got a job as night watchman at a big warehouse, which was perfect. He got a salary while he sat in a big quiet empty building writing. His employers were happy, because his writing kept him awake all night. Those who had the job before him tended to fall asleep."

Kathy Acker writes that she has held "all sorts of miserable jobs, any job which did not take too much time. The best job was being ticket-taker at The Kitchen, a Manhattan nightspot; the worst, file clerk at Texaco Co." At age 30, when she left a job selling cookies in a bakery to try to make a living by writing, she worried that she was being "foolhardy and worse," but she now feels her decision was the correct one.

She adds, "I always hated holding any job that didn't concern writing and resented the time taken away from writing. Every job helped as far as material. Nevertheless, a miserable job is a miserable job." Her advice: "Avoid those jobs which robotize you, which vampirize you."

Both John Thorndike and Norman Lavers suggest driving as an occupation where the writer's mind could wander; Thorndike in particular urges the writer to find something removed "from words and fiction." Lavers hypothesizes that truck driving might provide "long hours alone with the mind free," and suggests that writers could learn to "dictate stories, etc., into a tape recorder," but points out that truck drivers don't enjoy the long, valuable vacations that teachers do.

Lavers, who delivered mail for a while, also suggests mail carrier as a healthier occupation than truck driving, because of the exercise, and adds, "You get wonderful insights into people from the mail they receive; you are alone most of the day, doing pleasant work (especially if you can find a place where mailmen still walk their routes)."

Teaching

Most teaching offers summers and holidays off, but two writers, Jay Neugeboren, whose memoir, *His Heart, My Sleeve*, has been set for publication by Doubleday in 1993, and Barbara Corcoran, specifically point out the difficulty of teaching outside the university setting: Neugeboren says he "found high school teaching tiring—not much energy left after a long day of teaching," and Corcoran agrees that teaching below the college level has "too many demands."

A number of writers specifically advise against teaching English or creative writing full time at a university, feeling that it's wrong for a writer to exist outside the "real world," primarily living one's life among other writers and students who hope to become writers. John Thorndike, Doug Hornig and Ellyn Bache all urge writers to stay out of academia. The objection of Thorndike, who quit his job doing "construction and magazine pieces on the side" after the publication of his first novel, is similar to those of writers who find other writing-relating jobs difficult because there are "too many words with teaching. I could build all day and write at night, but the teaching interrupted the flow."

Scott Russell Sanders, in an article published by the *AWP Chronicle* in September of 1992, "The Writer in the University," says he would advise students in the ideal college writing program to "learn a trade—farming or carpentry, welding or weaving, cooking or sewing or surveying." He advises writers to "settle somewhere," but warns, "if that somewhere happens to be a university, I would tell them, don't mistake it for the universe."

And Norman Lavers, who strongly recommends college teaching as a career, points out a potential problem: "My friends who teach in big prestigious writing programs find themselves under a great deal of pressure from demanding students who want every minute of their time to help them advance their careers."

Although Barbara Corcoran, who has worked with the WPA Writers Project, in typing/filing, in radio and department store copywriting positions, as manager of Celebrity Service in Hollywood, and as a college teacher, writes that "college teaching and the years at Celebrity Service were the easiest," she says college teaching isn't exactly effortless.

Still, despite the warnings against it, teaching is a career that writers continue to be drawn to for one reason or another. Kent Haruf, for example, who milked cows, worked in construction, shelved books, and taught high school English before the publication of his first book, took a job on a college campus afterwards. Dagoberto Gilb, whose primary ambition is not to teach, accepted an offer to teach at the University of Arizona, in part, he says, because he was offered the job at a time when he needed the money.

Other college-teacher/writers really love their jobs, though. Norman Lavers, who says that he would like to teach even if he weren't a writer, explains that teaching also helps his writing. "Since my living is taken care of by my teaching job," he says, "I can write what I want, even though that means I publish mainly in small literary magazines that do not pay very much (I usually get from $100 to $300 for a story or essay). I usually make around $1,500 a year directly from writing (with occasional windfalls from fellowships, etc.), but, as a college teacher, I make a good deal from my writing indirectly.

"A major advantage to college teaching, is the flexibility of time. I usually have a schedule where I only teach classes three mornings a week. Naturally I have papers to mark, and classes to prepare, but I do that at home and can pick the time when I work on that, saving prime time for my own writing. And of course, thanks to long summer and Christmas vacations, I only work eight months of the year." Because teaching doesn't pay "enormously," Lavers cautions, however, "some writers have to teach summer school to get by," which, of course, cuts into their writing time.

If you don't need much money, parttime teaching can be an attractive possibility: often parttimers are hired with only MAs and, except for the money and prestige, parttime teaching offers all the advantages that fulltime does.

Ann McLaughlin and Ellyn Bache say they find teaching writing workshops, parttime, stimulating. Bache adds that "these are great fun, but I feel lucky to have the freedom not to do them more often. Novel writing, for me at least, takes up great chunks of time." Parttime teaching *is* interesting to many writers, but, like most parttime jobs, it pays much less then fulltime work.

Children and family

I didn't ask about the effects of children and family on writing, but a number of writers brought up the subject. All agree that a working spouse can be a great help—can sometimes make fiction writing possible at all—but that having children can make it necessary to live a more stable lifestyle than a writer otherwise would choose. Dagoberto Gilb, for example, mentions that his children "are often pointing to their mouths and feet" while he's at the keyboard.

Certainly caring for small children takes a lot of time. Ellyn Bache, mother of four children, writes, "I didn't write a novel until the youngest was in school full time." A writer who avoids having children simply because children seem likely to eat into the writer's work-time is probably making the right decision for all concerned; for the rest of us, patience is probably the key. As John Thorndike, who found it difficult to write when his son, now 21, was younger, points out, "Time takes care of that."

Simplify, simplify

Norman Lavers advises all writers to read Thoreau. "*Walden* is really a tract on economics," he writes. "What he says is that there are two very opposite economic strategies you can follow. The first — the one most people follow — is to spend as many minutes of the day working as hard as you can so you can make enough money to buy everything you see advertised. Thoreau's approach, and the one I have tried to live by, is to limit the number of things you buy, and therefore you need less money, and therefore you don't need to work as many hours.

"We have a cheap house out in the country where living is cheap, and we live near a small city in the mid-south where the cost of living is low. I have never taught summer school, and when the occasional grants have come along, because we had low mortgage payments, because, except for the house, we save up and pay cash for everything, we had no debts, we were able to take a year off and go live in some foreign country."

Other writers agree that letting one's allegiance be to a lifestyle rather than to writing can be harmful. As Harold Adams attests, "If writing is your real goal and primary satisfaction, you can't let making money become so important it leaves no time for creative work. It is possible to make a great deal of money as a writer, but it is damned rare and unlikely for most of us."

John Robinson writes, "to support myself during the writing of my first novel, I sold my house and lived on the last nickels until it was completed." Robinson, who lived and traveled in Europe with very little money, continues, "In the beginning you can live the bohemian lifestyle and live on practically nothing."

Time

When I started this article, I had hoped the writers I contacted would know about secret writing times and techniques with which few people were acquainted, but there really are only 24 hours in a day, after all. Anne Tyler, who found writing after work difficult "because I have a 'morning' mind and yet my mornings were spent on the job," discovered that the only real solution was "just to do my best to write at night."

Among the most important attributes that a writer could possess seem to be what Jocelyn Riley describes as "sheer willpower" and what Doug Hornig describes as his most valuable talent: "the ability to pick work up where I left it off and continue without problems." Wallace Knight says that he started to accomplish things only when he decided to write every Tuesday evening, "no matter what else was going on." Another writer who, like Tyler, has a "morning" mind is Harold Adams, who eventually established a routine "of getting up at 4:45 a.m. to write until time to go to work at 8:00 a.m." He writes: "In 1988 I retired but made no change in my 4:45 schedule; I have now extended it until late morning." Adams now usually stops writing and takes an hour's walk before lunch, only rarely returning to novel writing after noon.

Not everyone can or wants to stick to this firm a routine, of course; Ellyn Bache writes that her friends "who worked fulltime could never also write fiction unless they took a year off."

Many writers have juggled other careers or jobs successfully along with writing, and the implication is that it's easier to do the other job than it is to write. It's a little refreshing to see a writer who disagrees with this viewpoint, as does John Irving, who says in a "Writer's Workshop" interview, "The people who keep writing are largely people who can't do anything but write. And I think the people who have more staying power at writing are the people who can't ever be seduced by the possibility that there is another life that could ever satisfy them or make them happy."

He continues, "It didn't bother me that I didn't have any money as a young writer. Young writers aren't supposed to have any money. But when I'd written three books, and I recognized among my classmates people who felt they had deserved, financially, their success as lawyers and doctors by their apprenticeships, and, when I was not only untenured but not even on tenure track, and living on less than an average assistant professor's salary while watching my hair grow grey, I resented the lack of success I had."

He explains, however, that the anger he felt was energizing, "and you need the energy, but I could never entertain the idea that I could do anything else."

Fodder for the fire

Dagoberto Gilb says, "I'm still not sure that being a writer is a good idea unless you're already rich, have some inheritance, or you don't mind living off a spouse, or you simply do not care for the ordinary pleasures of stability." Still, he and others continue to write, and unless you get lucky and sell your novel right away, life will continue to hold uncertainties, and no single job seems likely to satisfy every possible writer (although some would be more satisfying than others). And maybe employment doesn't even really matter anyway, since, as many of the writers I contacted mentioned (with more or less tact), a writer who really *wants* to write will do so no matter what the obstacles.

"Any kind of job that leaves one with enough energy to write the fiction nights and days off" is fine, Fletcher Knebel says. "If a writer has that impelling fire in the belly to write, any job and all experience will produce fodder for the fire." And, as Milton Bass observes, "If you really want to write, you will find the energy and make the time."

Commercial Fiction Trend Report

by Robin Gee

Hit hard by the recession, publishers have been cutting costs everywhere—firing staff, consolidating book lines, reducing the number of titles published and cutting back on print runs. At times this frantic downsizing seemed more like a panic than the "studied effort to promote growth through efficiency" that publishers purported it to be. Yet it appears the dust has settled, all is not doom and gloom, and recent reports even indicate a little growth in 1992.

According to most industry reports, sales in 1992 were up by more than 8% over the previous year and continued slow growth is expected. The number of book titles increased by about 3% overall from 1991 to 1992, according to a recent R.R. Bowker data services report featured in *Publishers Weekly*, the industry's leading trade journal. "Cautious optimism" may best describe the mood of most large commercial publishers. Careful not to hail the recent upswing as a full-fledged bounce back, Gordan Graham, editor of the 1992 *Book Industry Trends Report*, an annual report on the publishing industry, announced, "Finally, a slow but steady recovery."

Yet, Graham went on to say, "There are no such things in publishing as 'good' years and 'bad' years. A publishing house is like a garden. It takes years of work to develop and years of neglect to destroy. The weather merely causes temperature fluctuations in performance . . . The enemy of publishing is short-term thinking."

Graham echoes what so many writers and editors have said in recent years. There has been too much emphasis on the annual bottom-line and not enough on the development of good writers, editors and books. Although most writers would agree publishers have a long way to go, there's some evidence a handful of publishers have been listening.

Big-name authors continue to garner huge advances and generous terms, but publishers are more willing to sign books promising less sensational, but strong, steady sales. They have rediscovered the strength of their fiction midlist, those writers who may not be stars, but who turn out good quality fiction with moderate but solid sales.

Despite this, however, publishers are still unlikely to take any big risks this year and the market will remain about the same. Publishers will continue their reliance on agented authors and writers who already have proven sales records, but, at the same time, they will not give up their quest for new talent.

About market-watching

The most important thing to note about the market for fiction is that, while there are some definite trends, publishers buy books up to two years in advance. What is being published now may not necessarily reflect what publishers are currently interested in. On the other hand, the changes in book publishing tend to be gradual. It may take several years for a so-called trend to peak. If you are a savvy market watcher you can spot trends as they begin to take hold.

Robin Gee *is editor of* Novel & Short Story Writer's Market, *a freelance writer, regular contributor to* The Artist's Magazine *and film reviewer for* Critics Choice, *a national review syndicate.*

In addition, the commercial fiction market tends to be cyclical. A good example of this has been the resurgence of gothic novels. Almost entirely gone from most publishers' lists in the 1970s and most of the 1980s, this type of novel has made a steady comeback. In 1992 we predicted novels with gothic elements would be popular across different genres, and this year gothics have appeared in mystery, romance and horror categories. Fueled by the continued success of Anne Rice's novels and popular movies such as Francis Ford Coppola's "Dracula," this trend may continue for quite some time.

Watch out for saturation. Last year booksellers complained of the glut of serial killer novels. Indeed, less of this type has been published recently. Right now, thanks to the success of Scott Turow and John Grisham, you'll find bookstores brimming with courtroom-based crime novels. While many publishers are interested in these still, a few bookstore owners we spoke with said there were already too many on the market.

The market for fiction

Despite the aforementioned growth, the number of hardcover fiction titles decreased slightly from 1991 to 1992 and most experts predict the market will stay about the same. Last year readers spent an average of $23 to $25 a book for hardcover fiction. Some hardcovers priced at $30 or more met with buyer resistance. Industry experts concede few people are willing to spend more than $20 for a book and those who do are not likely to buy one every month.

Many publishers are turning to trade paperbacks as a midway solution between hardcover and mass market paperback. Trade paperbacks present a way for publishers to publish books with higher quality paper and printing, and a little more prestige, at a lower-than-cloth price. The amount of original fiction sold in this format has steadily increased over the years. Look for more opportunities here for new writers in the next year. Consolidations at Bantam, Doubleday and other publishers with mass market lines have led to a decrease in the number of mass market fiction titles published this year. On the other hand a few publishers, in particular Zebra and Silhouette, bucked the trend and have actually added mass market lines.

All in all it's been a tough year for publishers and, therefore, a tough year for writers. Yet there are a few bright spots. Certain areas of commercial fiction have done quite well.

Some specific growth areas

Before launching into a look at specific areas of fiction, it's worth mentioning some trends spotted last year are continuing this year. In particular is the growing audience for all types of popular fiction. No longer is science fiction, for example, the exclusive dominion of its hard-core fans. More and more mainstream fiction readers are buying category fiction, and quite a few genre novels have made it onto bestseller lists.

As the audience expands for various genres, the tendency for these books to crossover into mainstream and other areas increases. Romantic suspense, supernatural romances and historical mysteries continue to be popular, but even religious fiction novels are crossing over into secular mystery, romance and fantasy.

A number of religious publishers have introduced fiction lines. Many are experimenting with series fiction and offering religious westerns, mysteries and historical novels. Bethany House and Lion Publishing have historical series and both Crossway and Baker Book House introduced mystery series this year. One publisher, Thomas Nelson, even published a techno-thriller with religious roots, Larry Burkett's *The Illuminati*.

As with the children's publishing industry in general, fiction for young adults and chil-

dren continues to do well. Although many parents are still buying more classics than original fiction, according to *Children's Writer's & Illustrator's Market*, titles with multicultural
themes—featuring characters and issues from different races, cultures and backgrounds—
are in increased demand.

Environmental fiction is also a popular topic for children's books, marked last year by
a number of picture books including *Brother Eagle, Sister Sky*, published by Dial and featuring the words of Chief Seattle, and *A River Ran Wild*, by Lynne Cherry and published by
Harcourt Brace Jovanovich. In fact, HBJ recently launched an entire line of environmental
children's books under the name Gulliver Green.

For writers interested in the children's book market, check our sister publication *Children's Writer's & Illustrator's Market*. The title of this book reflects the close ties between
illustrators and writers in this field. Late in 1992 the leading organization for children's
book writers changed its name to include illustrators. The Society of Children's Book
Writers and Illustrators now addresses the needs of all creative people in the industry.
Several of this group's regional conferences are listed in the Conferences and Workshops
section of *Novel & Short Story Writer's Market*.

Children's audio is another area of growth and both children's and adult fiction are
slowly gaining ground in this area. Long a popular format for previously published fiction,
audio publishers are slowly beginning to buy original work. Last year we added our first
original fiction audio market, Books in Motion. Though not large enough yet to be considered a publishing trend, very slowly more fiction is being made available in different formats
such as audio tape, disk and online computer services. CD-ROM, electronic book players
and book disks have started the industry thinking about new technologies. Nineteen ninety-
two marked the first meeting of the Electronic Book Committee of the United States.
Although the first market for this type of technology appears to be in nonfiction and how-
to publishing, it won't be long before novels are available.

The need for more multicultural books is not restricted to children's publishing. Last
year was the second year in a row the American Booksellers Association annual convention
featured books by African American publishers and authors. Two new groups have been
formed to help African American book publishers and booksellers promote their books,
and a new sales-tracking service, Blackboard, offers a list of top sellers in African American
fiction and nonfiction. Asian and Latin American authors are also finding an expanded
audience with fiction readers and publishers.

Work from gay and lesbian writers is becoming more accepted in the mainstream, and
publishers devoted to these writers are doing very well. With the increased political and
social activity in this community, the growth of nonfiction books was expected, but the
tremendous growth in terms of both quality and quantity of fiction titles is a welcome
surprise. Last year was the fourth year for the Lambda Literary Awards, honoring both
fiction and nonfiction by gay and lesbian writers. St. Martin's and Penguin's NAL, Viking,
Dutton and Plume are commercial publishers who offer strong lists in this area, but almost
all major publishers include some books from writers in this community.

From the list of growth areas above, it's easy to see diversity as a trend. Small but solid
niche markets are beginning to make headway with larger audiences, and commercial
publishers are starting to pay attention. Last year we focused our report on a number of
traditional genres. This year we include the three largest categories.

In brief, however, western fiction remains strong and steady. Traditional westerns have
made a nice comeback, but frontier fiction is very strong. Bantam's publisher says it has
the most active list. Books with realistic portrayals of Native Americans were popular this
year especially in light of the 500-year Columbus anniversary. Watch for increased interest

in historical westerns sparked by a new ten-hour Ken Burns PBS documentary planned for 1996.

Horror seems to be doing a bit better this year, but the area of the most growth could be called dark fantasy. As mentioned earlier the latest Dracula movie will help the trend along. Vampire books are everywhere. In fact, one horror bookseller quoted in the September 21, 1992 issue of *Publishers Weekly* said so many have been published in the last three years they could represent their own category line. We wouldn't go that far, but the supernatural in a variety of forms is enjoying a modest comeback. At least one publisher has been breathing new life into the horror genre. Despite the odds, Dell launched the Abyss line in 1991 and it's doing very well. See our interview with Abyss Editor Jean Cavelos in the Commercial Publishers section.

Mystery

The market for mystery fiction remains as strong as ever. In fact, many mass market publishers who deal with a variety of genres say mystery seems to be the most recession-proof. Continuing many of the trends apparent over the last few years, mysteries are crossing over into mainstream lists at a dizzying rate and, despite some price resistance, the number of hardback mysteries has increased.

Another nice development in this field is the growth of mystery bookstores. Jim Huang, editor of *The Drood Review of Mysteries* and owner of the Deadly Passions bookstore in Kalamazoo, Michigan, estimated there are now about 70 mystery bookstores in the U.S. up from 40 or so only a few years ago.

Most commercial publishers already have large mystery lines, so in 1992 they continued to publish about the same number of books as before. St. Martin's, for example, regularly publishes 135 mysteries each year. In 1992 Berkley, however, doubled the size of its mystery line, while a few other publishers, feeling the pinch of the recession, cut back and consolidated lines. Ballantine reduced its line a bit and the Doubleday Crime Club downsized and reorganized, becoming Doubleday Perfect Crime.

Most of the trends noted last year remain. Exotic settings, complex protagonists, women writers and women sleuths still dominate the scene. What has changed over the last few years is the readership. Overwhelmingly, most mystery readers today are female. They're usually well-read and interested in the world around them.

Women writers have displayed "terrific strength" in the market, says Otto Penzler, owner of the Mysterious Book Shop and publisher of Mysterious Press. Female private eyes continue their hold on the hard-boiled detective subgenre, but the presence of women in mystery can be felt in all areas. Traditional male protagonists almost have become an endangered species. On the other hand, more personable, well-developed male characters are holding their own.

Cozies, mysteries featuring amateur sleuths, the powers of deduction and very little violence, play big roles in today's mystery market. In the past British authors and English settings were popular, but today the trend is in favor of American writers and settings. Look for small U.S. cities and towns, especially locations in the Pacific Northwest and the South in the next few years.

No subject is taboo in today's mystery market. Social issues, including child abuse, drugs and alcohol dependence, the environment, and care of the elderly have all been mystery book topics this year. Protagonists hold a variety of jobs, but books featuring female professionals are in demand.

"I'm starting to see a lot more historical mysteries, " says Kate Stein, editor of *Armchair*

Detective and associate editor at Mysterious Press. "I've seen every time period used as a setting—the Turn of the Century, Ancient Rome and Egypt, the Renaissance."

Huang agrees historical settings and protagonists with unusual interests or jobs are popular now and a good way to share a variety of cultural information, but he worries that these novels run the risk of losing the basic story. "I'm getting a little tired of special interests in mysteries. Too many writers are getting away from what the story is about—murder and detection can become secondary. Sometimes I feel impatient. I want to get to the story and more writers are drifting away from the central mystery. It seems writers are giving their characters too many quirks just to be different." He sees a return, at least for hard-core mystery fans, to an interest in "no frills, no gimmicks mysteries," such as those of Robert Crais.

Still, the growing audience for mysteries appears to like detail as long as it is done well. Stein says one writer who works extensive research into his work, but who does it in such a way that it's "evocative, rather than obtrusive," is Steven Saylor, whose books are set in ancient Rome.

No discussion of the current mystery field would be complete without mention of Patricia Cornwell's work. A forensic expert, her books, *Body of Evidence* and *All That Remains* display an apt blending of technical knowledge and social concerns. It seems writers such as Cornwell and Saylor have used their professional expertise in other areas to carve themselves a special niche.

This market is doing so well, new writers who write well have an excellent opportunity in this field. There's no one area to avoid, except to say in the vast array of female private investigator novels, there's only room for the very best to sell well now. While some experts said courtroom-based mysteries are doing quite well, thanks to Scott Turow and John Grisham, others fear we're approaching glut level. Two areas mentioned as under-represented were romantic suspense and, due to the changes in global politics, espionage thrillers.

Penzler mentioned many publishers are now doing mystery anthologies and are opening these to more original short fiction. He also went on to say that, speculation aside, his advice to the budding mystery writer is "to write the best book you can" regardless of trends.

Romance

Despite the recession, the romance market has been holding its own, says Agent Patricia Teal. "Royalty statements are looking very good," she says. In fact, some romance publishers have launched new lines this year. Harlequin, the giant of the industry, now has 13 different romance lines including it's newest Silhouette line, Shadows.

Besides the publication and success of *Scarlett*, the sequel to *Gone With the Wind*, one of the biggest news items in the romance field this year was the aborted sale of Zebra to Harlequin. After the death of legendary Zebra publisher and partner Roberta Bender Grossman, William Zacharius put Zebra up for sale. He was working a deal with Harlequin when he changed his mind. Romance writers, afraid that such a sale might silence a diverse voice in the field, issued a collective sigh of relief. Zacharius now says he plans to expand Zebra and has already launched a new line, Lucky in Love. He's also added to another fairly new line, To Love Again, aimed at readers over the age of 45.

The line between romance and what is known in the mainstream as women's fiction has blurred. Many more romances are being published in hardcover and promoted as mainstream novels—and many have made it onto bestseller lists. HarperCollins announced a new line of women's fiction in 1992, Harpermonogram, which includes contemporary fiction with romance elements. TOR Books, known as a leader in the science fiction field, also has plans to get into women's fiction publishing. Their new line will feature women's historicals, mysteries and westerns.

A number of unresolved issues continue to plague the romance industry. Romance Writers of America has been working with large publishers to address problems such as complex royalty statements and the ownership of pseudonyms. Within the organization, a group of published authors developed the Published Authors Network or PAN to specifically address the issues writers face after publication.

In keeping with their focus on improving relations with publishers and protecting the rights of romance authors, RWA developed the Industry Award a few years ago. The award honors people in the industry who not only have promoted the genre, but who also have supported fair treatment of writers. In 1992 the award went to Marilyn Black of Meteor, the publisher of Kismet romances. The publisher was chosen because of her policies, including quick contract turnaround, clear and fair quarterly royalty statements and author ownership of pseudonyms.

Romance book covers continued to make industry news this year. While you can still find many of the classic beefy-hero-embracing-swooning-heroine covers, some contemporary romances, especially those which may cross over into mainstream women's fiction, have appeared with no models. Instead these "softer" covers feature flowers, lace, jewels and fabrics. The step back cover is also becoming popular. This type of cover includes a softer, subtle overleaf with a cutout showing only a tiny part of a picture underneath. When exposed, the inside picture is as steamy as any on the racks.

Romance readers seem to like the steamy model covers, however, and a number of cover heroes have become stars. In addition to romance convention, talk-show and bookstore appearances, cover model Fabio has been banking on his success to build an acting career. Christmas 1992 even featured the first Fabio calendar in major bookstores.

Heroes in the last few years have become more realistic, more likeable and down to earth, says Katherine Orr, Harlequin's vice president of public relations. Fatherhood is in, as are men with regular jobs. Part of this softening of the hero may be related to the reaction against the materialistic 80s. While glitz is still popular with a number of large mainstream women's fiction lines, contemporary series romance seems to be giving more emphasis to salt-of-the-earth heroes rather than powerful CEOs. Children are becoming an integral part of many contemporary romances as are older women and romances between men and women over the age of 50.

Glitz may be waning just a little bit, but the market for contemporary romances remains strong. Most settings are acceptable, but Harlequin has had success with a number of small town settings. One recent series featured 12 books by different authors all set in the fictional town of Tylersville, Wisconsin. Another is planned for a Texas town and we predict there will be more set in rural and small town America.

Historicals and regency romances continue their popularity. Western themes and Native American characters seem to be doing well. Other popular settings include frontier novels and Civil War backgrounds. After the success of the romantic film version of the *Last of the Mohicans* and *Far and Away*, we expect more early American settings.

Gothics are big as are romantic suspense thrillers. Look for the return of the "dark hero," one with a mysterious past and possible supernatural ties. Like horror, vampires are popular. Lori Herter is the author to watch in this vein with her series of vampire romances for Berkley. Tanya Huff, a DAW author, introduced a series that ties romance, mystery and horror with a female detective whose partner is a vampire. Ghost romances sell well, too.

More romances are looking to the future for inspiration. The difference between a futuristic and a science fiction romance is subtle. Futuristic romances tend to be continuations of life as we know it and involve the same elements used in historical or other time period romances. Leisure Books has been a leader in publishing this type of romance and its line includes many examples of this subgenre including Jackie Castro's *The New Frontier* and Marilyn Campbell's *Pyramid of Dreams*.

Some science fiction publishers are doing books with strong romantic elements. DAW's Anne McCaffrey and newcomers Cheryl Franklin and Carole Nelson Douglas are some writers to watch.

Related to these subgenres is Time Travel romances. Again Leisure is a leader here. Publishers warn writers, however, to focus on the romance elements of the story and not to get too hung up on the technical aspects of time jumping.

Camelot and anything medieval is good fodder for fantasy romances. Magic is afoot and watch for some growth in this field as writers mine popular legends and myths. New Age romance incorporates many of the elements of fantasy and has a small, but solid following.

Science fiction and fantasy

The market for science fiction and fantasy was sluggish last year and seems to be bouncing back very slowly. Last year we discussed fantasy separately from science fiction and that division, at least in the industry, remains. Still, many publishers continue to publish and market these genres together. This year, too, the name of the leading organization for science fiction authors was changed to Science Fiction and Fantasy Writers of America to reflect this partnership.

One thing all experts agree on is the growing diversity of the market. "The fragmentation of the science fiction and fantasy audience is part and parcel a result of the genre's mainstreaming," says John Silbersack, editor-in-chief of Warner's Questar line. Science fiction is in a building mode, widening its audience. More science fiction is crossing over into mainstream lists and, even, a small amount into other genres. The broadening audience is more tolerant of eclecticism than the traditional core SF readers, says Silbersack.

Although mass market paperback is still the backbone format of the field, some established science fiction and fantasy authors are doing well in hardback. More authors also are being published in trade paperback, in keeping with this trend in all fiction areas.

Although things looked a little brighter for the industry last year than in 1991, it will be a year remembered with sadness. In spring 1992 we lost science fiction legend Isaac Asimov. Known for his tremendous talent and ability to write almost nonstop—he had more than 500 books published in all areas of fiction and nonfiction—Asimov, winner of five Hugo Awards and three Nebula Awards, is perhaps best remembered for his Foundation Trilogy and its sequels. Bantam books published the last of the sequels to this classic late last year.

The year brought a number of small market changes worth noting. In January 1992 Bantam/Doubleday/Dell purchased four Davis publications including *Isaac Asimov's Science Fiction Magazine* and *Analog Science Fiction & Fact*. Later the company redesigned each magazine, introduced new logos and dropped Asimov's first name from the one magazine's title. More changes in the coming year are expected.

A good sign of growing popularity, Walden Books recently launched a new science fiction newsletter, *Hailing Frequencies*, with former Ace Editor Peter Heck at the helm. Heck edited the bookseller's old SF newsletter, *Xignals*, before moving to Ace.

Del Rey introduced its new "Discovery" program. The publisher will select a small group of new authors to be part of the program. It was created to single out new authors for special promotion. Other changes at publishers involved line reductions and consolidations. Bantam, for example, underwent large cuts in many of its lines. Pulphouse also went through a painful downsizing and many of its projects were put on hold. Later in the year, however, this publisher launched a new science fiction magazine, *Tomorrow*.

The market for short fiction in science fiction and fantasy is fairly strong. Another new magazine market arrived late in 1992. *Science Fiction Age* touts the largest circulation of any science fiction publication to date. *Omni* magazine announced it will be available online and its book publishing division, Omni Books, planned two new anthologies. The anthologies include reprint and new material the publisher has on hand. Although closed to submissions for now, the publisher plans to expand the book line.

Keeping an eye on the market

There are numerous ways to keep an eye on the publishing industry. The writer's best friend can be his or her local bookseller. These are the people on the front lines. Not only are they painfully aware of what is not selling well or what seems to be flooding the market, they are also keen observers of what is growing in popularity. It's their business to know what readers want.

Other writers can be great sources of "insider" information. In addition to your local writing group, there are hundreds of regional and national writers' organizations throughout the U.S. and Canada. Some are open to all writers, while others are open to those who write a particular genre or fiction category. No matter what the focus of these groups, however, almost all publish some form of market newsletter.

Another way to meet writers, editors, agents and publishers is to attend a writers' conference. Most include panel discussions on various concerns (and trends!) within the industry. You'll find listings of writers' organizations and conferences in the Resource section of this book.

Writers' magazines and trade journals also can help you keep up with the market for fiction. *Writer's Digest* features a monthly markets column and smaller publications such as *Gila Queen's Guide to the Markets* are devoted entirely to sharing market information. For the industry, *Publishers Weekly* takes the lead with up-to-date news on publishing and bookselling.

It's good business to know your market and your competition, but keep in mind trends only go so far. Writers, editors, agents, publishers and booksellers all agree: If you write the book you believe in and take time to carefully craft your prose, by all means send it out. There's always room for well-done fiction regardless of trends.

The Business of Fiction Writing

by Robin Gee

It's true there's no substitute for talent and hard work. A writer's first concern must always be attention to craft. No matter how well presented, a poorly written story or novel has little chance of being published. Yet, on the other hand, a well-written piece may be equally hard to sell in today's competitive publishing market. Talent alone is just not enough.

To be successful, writers need to study the field and pay careful attention to finding the right market. While the hours spend perfecting your writing are usually hours spent alone, you're not alone when it comes to developing your marketing plan. *Novel & Short Story Writer's Market* provides you with detailed listings containing the essential information you'll need to locate and contact the markets most suitable for your work.

Yet once you've determined where to send your work, you must turn your attention to presentation. We can help here, too. Over the years we've made our listings as concise as possible in order to leave more space for new listings. In this effort, however, we took out some of the very basics of manuscript preparation. We've included these basics below, along with a compilation of information on submission procedures, approaching markets and the basics of manuscript mechanics – the "business" of fiction.

Approaching magazine markets: While it is essential for nonfiction markets, a query letter by itself is usually not needed by most magazine fiction editors. If you are approaching a magazine to find out if fiction is accepted, a query is fine, but editors looking for short fiction want to see *how* you write. A cover letter, however, can be useful as a letter of introduction, but it must be accompanied by the actual piece. Include basic information in your cover letter – name, address, a brief list of previous publications – if you have any – and two or three sentences about the piece (why you are sending it to *this* magazine or how your experience influenced your story). Keep it to one page and remember to include a self-addressed, stamped envelope for reply. See "Short Story Cover Letter" included on page 80.

Approaching book publishers: Some book publishers do ask for queries first, but most want a query plus sample chapters or an outline or, occasionally, the complete manuscript. Again, make your letter brief. Include the essentials about yourself – name, address, phone number and publishing experience. Include only the personal information related to your story. Show that you have researched the market with a few sentences about why you chose this publisher.

Book proposals: A book proposal is a package sent to a publisher that includes a cover letter and one or more of the following: sample chapters, outline, synopsis, author bio, publications list. When asked to send sample chapters, send up to three *consecutive* chapters. An outline covers the highlights of your book chapter by chapter. Be sure to include details on main characters, the plot and subplots. Outlines can run up to 30 pages, depending on the length of your novel. The object is to tell what happens in a concise, but clear, manner. A synopsis is a very brief description of what happens in the story. Keep it to two or three pages. The terms synopsis and outline are sometimes used interchangeably, so be sure to find out exactly what each publisher wants.

Agents: Agents are not usually needed for short fiction and most do not handle it unless they already have a working relationship with you. For novels, you may want to consider working with an agent, especially if marketing to publishers who do not look at unsolicited submissions. For more on approaching agents see *The Guide to Literary Agents & Art/Photo Reps* (Writer's Digest Books, 1507 Dana Ave., Cincinnati OH 45207).

Approaching markets outside your own country: When sending return postage to another country, do not send stamps. You must purchase International Reply Coupons (IRCs). The publisher can use the IRCs to buy stamps from his/her own country. IRCs cost 95 cents each and can be purchased at the main branch of your local post office. This rule applies between countries in North America—U.S. writers without access to Canadian postage (and vice versa) may use IRCs.

Main branches of local banks will cash foreign checks, but keep in mind payment quoted in our listings by publishers in other countries, is usually payment in their currency. Also note reporting time is longer in most overseas markets. To save time and money, you may want to include a return postcard (and IRC) with your submission and forego asking for a manuscript to be returned.

Some mailing tips: Manuscripts under five pages long can be folded into thirds and sent in a business-size (#10) envelope. For submissions of five pages or more, however, mail it flat in a 9×12 or 10×13 envelope. Your manuscript will look best if it is mailed in an envelope only slightly larger. For the return envelope, fold it in half, address it to yourself and add a stamp (or clip IRCs to it with a paper clip).

Mark both of your envelopes in all caps, FIRST CLASS MAIL or SPECIAL FOURTH CLASS MANUSCRIPT RATE. The second method is cheaper, but it is handled the same as Parcel Post (Third Class) and is only for manuscripts weighing more than one pound and mailed within the U.S. First Class mailing assures fastest delivery and better handling.

Book manuscripts should be mailed in a sturdy box (a ream-size typing paper box works well). Tape the box shut and tape corners to reinforce them. To ensure your manuscript's safe return, enclose a self-addressed and stamped insulated bag mailer. You may want to check with the United Parcel Service (UPS) or other mailing services for rates.

If you use an office or personal postage meter, do not date the return envelope—it could cause problems if the manuscript is held too long before being returned. First Class mail is forwarded or returned automatically. Mark Third or Fourth Class return envelopes with "Return Postage Guaranteed" to have them returned.

If you send a cover letter with a Fourth Class manuscript, you must indicate this on the envelope (FIRST CLASS LETTER ENCLOSED) and include First Class postage.

It is not necessary to insure or certify your submission. In fact, many publishers do not appreciate receiving unsolicited manuscripts in this manner. Your best insurance is to always keep a copy of all submissions and letters.

Manuscript mechanics: A professionally presented manuscript will not guarantee publication. Yet a sloppy, hard-to-read manuscript will not be read—publishers simply do not have the time. Here's a list of suggested submission techniques for polished manuscript presentation:

● Use white, 8½×11 bond paper, preferably 16 or 20 lb. weight. The paper should be heavy enough so that it will not show pages underneath it and strong enough to take handling by several people. Do not use onion skin or erasable paper.

● Type your manuscript on a typewriter with a dark ribbon. Make sure the letters are clean and crisp. You can also use a computer printer, but avoid hard-to-read dot matrix.

● Proofread carefully. An occasional white-out is okay, but don't send a marked up manuscript with many typos. Keep a dictionary, thesaurus and stylebook handy.

● Always double space and leave a 1¼ inch margin on all sides of the page. For a short story manuscript, your first page should include your name, address and phone number (single-spaced) in the upper left corner. In the upper right, indicate an approximate word count. Center the name of your story about one-third of the way down, skip two or three lines and center your byline (byline is optional). Skip three lines and begin your story.

● On subsequent pages, put last name and page number in the upper right hand corner.

● For book manuscripts, use a separate cover sheet. Put your name, address and phone number in the upper left corner and word count in the upper right. Some writers list their agent's name and address in the upper right (word count is then placed at the bottom of the page). Center your title and byline about halfway down the page. Start your first chapter on the next page. Center the chapter number and title (if there is one) one-third of the way down the page. Include your last name and page number in the upper right of this page and each page to follow. Start each chapter with a new page.

● There are a number of ways to count the number of words in your piece. One way is to count the number of words in five lines and divide that number by five to find an average. Then count the number of lines and multiply to find the total words. For long pieces, you may want to count exactly how many words in the first three pages, divide by three and multiply by the number of pages you have.

● Always keep a copy. Manuscripts do get lost. To avoid expensive mailing costs, send only what is required. If you are including artwork or photos, but you are not positive they will be used, send photocopies. Artwork is hard to replace.

● Most publishers do not expect you to provide artwork and some insist on selecting their own illustrators, but if you have suggestions, please let them know. Magazine publishers work in a very visual field and are usually open to ideas.

● If you want a reply or if you want your manuscript returned, enclose a self-addressed, stamped envelope (SASE). For most letters, a business-size (#10) envelope will do. Avoid using any envelope too small for an 8½ × 11 sheet of paper. For manuscripts, be sure to include enough postage and an envelope large enough to contain it. If you are requesting a magazine, send an envelope big enough to fit.

● When sending electronic (disk or modem) submissions, contact the publisher first for specific information and follow the directions carefully.

● Keep accurate records. This can be done in a number of ways, but be sure to keep track of where your stories are and how long they have been "out." Write down submission dates. If you do not hear about your submission for a long time—about three weeks to one month longer than the reporting time stated in the listing—you may want to contact the publisher. When you do, you will need an accurate record for reference.

Rights: Know what rights you are selling. The Copyright Law states that writers are selling one-time rights (in almost all cases) unless they and the publisher have agreed otherwise. Below is a list of various rights. Be sure you know exactly what rights you are selling before you agree to the sale.

● All Rights allow a publisher to use the manuscript anywhere and in any form, including movie and book club sales, without further payment to the writer.

● Copyright is the legal right to exclusive publication, sale or distribution of a literary work. This right is that of the writer or creator of the piece and you need simply to include your name, date and the copyright symbol © on your piece in order to copyright it. You can also register your copyright with the Copyright Office for additional protection. Request information and forms from the Copyright Office, Library of Congress, Washington DC 20559. Publications listed in *Novel & Short Story Writer's Market* are copyrighted *unless* otherwise stated. In the case of magazines that are not copyrighted, be sure to keep a copy with your notice printed on it.

- First Serial Rights mean that the publisher has the right to publish your work for the first time in any periodical.
- First North American Serial Rights are the same as First Serial, but they are only for publication on the North American Continent.
- One-time Rights allow a publisher to publish a story one time.
- Reprint Rights are permission to print a piece that was first published somewhere else.
- Second Serial Rights allow a publisher to print a piece in another periodical after it appeared for the first time in book form or in a magazine.
- Subsidiary Rights are all rights other than book publishing rights included in a book contract such as book club rights, movie rights and paperback rights.
- Work-for-hire is work that does not belong to the creator. If you do work-for-hire, you do not own the copyright and cannot sell any rights. For example, if you write a pamphlet for your company as an employee, generally the rights to that material do not belong to you. Writers doing work-for-hire are usually paid a flat fee for the work and do not collect royalties or other payments.

Samples

This year we're very pleased to repeat the sample cover letter by writer Don Feigert with his comments on why he feels the letter has worked well for him. He answered our call in the 1991 edition for sample cover letters from our readers. For more on formats see *The Writer's Digest Guide to Manuscript Formats*, by Dian Dincin Buchman and Seli Groves.

The sample letter is followed by postal charge charts for the US and Canada. A 7% Government Sales Tax is now required on postage in Canada. Since Canadian postage rates will be voted on in January (before this book is released), check for updated information from the Canada Post Corp. Customer Service Division office located in most cities in Canada.

Why this letter works

Don Feigert is a part-time freelance writer with nearly 50 publication credits. This letter format has worked for him several times. He explains why he feels it has been so successful:

> The first paragraph of this cover letter is characteristically brief. Writers should avoid "explaining" their stories. The significant thing here is the acknowledgement of the magazine's general theme.
>
> The second paragraph makes clear the writer has shown a serious interest in the press to which he is submitting. Without becoming obsequious, writers should relate that they respect their intended markets and that they are professional enough to subscribe or purchase sample copies and study them before submitting anything.
>
> The "bio note" paragraph is alway a problem. Published writers tend to boast about past successes, while unpublished writers fear their lack of credits disadvantage them. Generally, a few brief but relevant remarks will do. In the example case, my "bio" paragraph is longer than usual, because so much of my background relates to this particular magazine's outdoor, rural, Appalachian emphasis. I believe, however, that I received a quick acceptance here not because of past credits but because I sent the editors a very good story that was right up their thematic alley.

The Short Story Cover Letter

Don Feigert
Address
Phone

May 20, 199X

Ms. Carolyn Page, Co-Editor
Potato Eyes
Nightshade Press
Box 76
Troy, ME 04987

Dear Ms. Page:

Please consider the enclosed short story "Killing the Water-dog" for publication. I think it will fit in well with your Appalachian themes.

I first became aware of Nightshade Press when I purchased The Wild Trout by Walt Franklin. Later I received my contrib-utor's copy of Great Elm Press's Riveries and bought the 1991 edition of Novel and Short Story Writer's Market. You and Co-Editor Roy Zarucchi were featured in both. Finally, I sent for a sample copy of Potato Eyes and enjoyed it much. Hence this, my first submission to your magazine.

I am a lifelong outdoorsman, and I have spent twenty years in education, as a teacher and college recruiter. I write stories for outdoor magazines such as Gray's Sporting Jour-nal and Pennsylvania Game News and poems and stories for literary magazines such as Hiram Poetry Review and Samisdat. My first book, Visiting the Pig Farm, a collection of outdoor stories and poems, was published in December, 1989, by Old Hickory Press, Jackson, TN.

Thanks for your consideration,

Sincerely,

Don Feigert

U.S. Postage by the Page

by Carolyn Hardesty

Mailing costs can be an appreciable part of writing expenditures. The chart below can help save money as well as time by allowing you to figure the fees for sending your manuscripts to prospective publishers.

Postage rates are listed by numbers of pages (using 20 lb. paper) according to the most commonly used envelopes and their self-addressed, stamped envelopes (SASEs). While most writers prefer to send their work First Class, Third Class is becoming a choice for some. Third Class moves more slowly, but it costs less than First Class after the first 4 ounces. Also, it is permissible in Third Class to include a letter pertaining to the material inside.

First Class mail weighing more than 11 ounces is assessed according to weight plus geographical zone so it needs to be priced at the Post Office.

Postcards can be a bargain for writers. If the postage costs are higher than another computer printout or photocopied version of a manuscript, a postcard can be used for the editor's reply. The cost is 20¢.

For short manuscripts or long queries, use a #10 (business-size) envelope with a 29¢ stamp. Four pages is the limit if you are including a SASE. Another option is the 6×9 envelope. For 1-3 pages, postage is 29¢ in the U.S. For 1-7 pages with SASE, cost is 52¢ in the U.S.

Ounces	9×12 9×12 SASE number of pages	9×12 SASE (for return trips) number of pages	First Class Postage	Third Class Postage	Postage from U.S. to Canada
under 2	...	1 to 2	$ .39*	$ .39*	$ .63*
2	1 to 4	3 to 8	.52	.52	.73
3	5 to 10	9 to 12	.75	.75	.86
4	11 to 16	13 to 19	.98	.98	1.09
5	17 to 21	20 to 25	1.21	1.21	1.32
6	22 to 27	26 to 30	1.44	1.21	1.55
7	28 to 32	31 to 35	1.67	1.33	1.78
8	33 to 38	36 to 41	1.90	1.33	2.01
9	39 to 44	42 to 46	2.13	1.44	2.24
10	45 to 49	47 to 52	2.36	1.44	2.47
11	50 to 55	53 to 57	2.59	1.56	2.70

*This cost includes an assessment for oversized mail that is light in weight.

Carolyn Hardesty's *short fiction and essays have appeared in* Four Minute Fictions, The North American Review, Cream City, The Montana Review *and others.*

Canadian Postage by the Page

by Barbara Murrin

The following chart is for the convenience of Canadian writers sending domestic mail and American writers sending an envelope with International Reply Coupons (IRCs) or Canadian stamps for return of a manuscript from a Canadian publisher. Unfortunately these figures are approximate, because the Canadian Postal Service meets to determine new fees in January each year, after we go to press. Check your post office for changes.

Manuscripts returning from the U.S. to Canada will take a U.S. stamped envelope although the original manuscript was sent with Canadian postage. This applies to return envelopes sent by American writers to Canada, too, which must be accompanied with IRCs or Canadian postage.

In a #10 envelope, you can have up to five pages for 42¢ (on manuscripts within Canada) or 48¢ (on manuscripts going to the U.S.). If you enclose a SASE, four pages is the limit. If you use 10 × 13 envelopes, send one page less than indicated on the chart.

IRC's are worth 48¢ Canadian postage but cost 95¢ to buy in the U.S.

Canada Post designations for types of mail are:

Standard Letter Mail Minimum size: 9 × 14cm (3⅝ × 5½"); Maximum size: 15 × 24.5cm (5⅞ × 9⅝"); Maximum thickness: 5mm (³⁄₁₆")

Oversize Letter Mail Exceeds any measurement for standard; Maximum size: 27 × 38cm (10⅞ × 15"); Maximum thickness: 2cm (¹³⁄₁₆")

International Letter Mail Minimum size: 9 × 14cm (3⅝ × 5½"); Maximum size: Length + width + depth 90cm (36") Greatest dimension must not exceed 60cm (24")

Insurance: To U.S. — 45¢ for each $100 coverage to a maximum coverage of $1000. Within Canada $1 for first $100 coverage; 45¢ for each additional $100 coverage to a maximum of $1,000.

Registered Mail: $2.85 plus postage (air or surface — Canadian destination). Legal proof of mailing provided.

Weight up to	9 × 12 envelope, 9 × 12 SASE number of pages*	9 × 12 SASE (for return trips) number of pages	Canada Standard	Oversize	First Class to U.S. Standard	Oversize
30 g/1.07 oz.	. . .	1 to 3	$ .42	$ .84	$ .48	$ 1.08
50 g/1.78 oz.	1 to 4	4 to 7	.65	.84	.70	1.08
100 g/3.5 oz.	5 to 14	8 to 18	. . .	.84	. . .	1.08
200 g/7.1 oz.	15 to 46	19 to 49	. . .	1.30		2.05
300 g/10.7 oz.	47 to 57	50 to 61	. . .	1.90		3.50
400 g/14.2 oz.	58 to 79	62 to 82	. . .	1.90		3.50
500 g/17.8 oz.	80 to 101	83 to 104	. . .	1.90		3.50
1.0 kg/2.2 lbs.	102 to 208	105 to 212	**	**(air pkt.)		9.20

*Based on 20 lb. paper and 2 adhesive labels per envelope.
**For Canadian residents mailing parcels 1 kg. and over within Canada (domestic mail), rates vary according to destination. Ask your Post Master for the chart for your area.

Barbara Murrin owns and operates a desk-top publishing business in Williams Lake, British Columbia. She teaches music and business subjects at a nearby community college and, when there is time, writes romance. One of her short stories has been included in Insight's Most Unforgettable Stories, *a compilation of stories from 20 years of publication.*

The Markets

Important Listing Information

- *Listings are* not *advertisements. Although the information here is as accurate as possible, the listings are not endorsed or guaranteed by the editor of* Novel & Short Story Writer's Market.
- Novel & Short Story Writer's Market *reserves the right to exclude any listing that does not meet its requirements.*

Key to Symbols and Abbreviations

‡ *New listing in all sections*
* *Subsidy publisher in Small Press and Commercial Book Publishers sections*
■ *Book packager or producer*
ms — *manuscript;* mss-*manuscripts*
b&w — *black and white (photo)*
SASE — *self-addressed, stamped envelope*
SAE — *self-addressed envelope*
IRC — *International Reply Coupon, for use on reply mail from countries outside your own.*

(See Glossary for definitions of words and expressions used in writing/publishing.)

The Markets

Literary and Small Circulation Magazines

Despite the large investment in time, money and commitment involved in starting and running a small magazine or literary journal, this section remains the largest in our book and continues to grow each year. This year, for example, we've added more than 100 new magazines. For writers, this section offers a wide array of opportunities, especially for those more interested in exposure and experience than in monetary reward.

While a few of the more prestigious journals may offer several hundred dollars for a short story, many of the publications listed here pay in copies, subscriptions or small honorariums. Yet publication in these magazines can be the first step on the road to a successful writing career.

Publishing in small magazines helps new writers gain publication credits and experience submitting and dealing with editors. For more experienced writers, publication in literary journals can bring the added benefits of prestige and recognition. Book publishers, as well as the editors of the more lucrative commercial magazines, look to small and literary magazines for new talent. In other words, publication in small magazines and literary journals helps get you and your work noticed.

Hundreds of opportunities

We've outlined exactly what types of magazines are included in this section and how to come up with your own list of places to submit in How to Get the Most Out of This Book starting on page 3. See this and the Business of Fiction Writing for some general guidelines on submission procedures.

There are, indeed, hundreds of opportunities for writers in this section. You'll find prestigious journals such as *The Paris Review* and *The Georgia Review*, but you'll also find magazines devoted to promoting the work of beginning writers including *Gotta Write Network Litmag* and *The Oak*. You also will find several magazines devoted to particular subjects such as *Other Worlds* for science fiction and fantasy, or promoting certain regions such as *The Mountain Laurel* featuring writing about the Blue Ridge Mountains.

Basically, the magazines listed in this section can be divided by type. University and state-supported journals often feature the work of well-known writers along with work by talented newcomers. Fanzines or micro-press journals are usually one- or two-person operations and include more work by new writers. Some of these feature highly experimental work and graphics. In between are magazines devoted to almost every topic, every level of writing and every type of writer.

Making an informed choice

In addition to browsing through and reading the listings that catch your eye, using the Category Index will help you narrow your search. You will find the Category Index starting on page 616. How to use the Category Index is outlined in How to Get the Most Out of This Book. Mostly it will help those writers who can determine that their writing is of a particular type or about a certain subject. Check under a heading that best fits the type of work you do (such as experimental or mystery) and check those magazines listed under that heading.

If your writing cannot be categorized or if you'd rather submit to a broad range of publications, you may want to use our ranking system as your guide. Most of the publications listed in this section have a Roman numeral ranking code after their title. This code refers to the level of work accepted at the magazine. For an explanation of these codes see the end of this introduction.

Once you have a list of magazines you might like to try, you can further zero in on those most likely to be interested in your work by reading the listings carefully. In addition to a general, one-sentence description included just after the address and some helpful advice at the end of most listings, there is a lot of material included within the listing that will give you clues to the type, style and needs of each publication.

Read the listing

Much of the material within each listing carries clues that tell you more about the magazine. How to Get the Most Out of This Book describes in detail information common to all listings. Under the "Needs" subhead of listings in this section you will find a list of the types of fiction the magazine is most interested in. You also may find a sentence or two about what the magazine does *not* want to see. Starting last year we also included information on whether a magazine does theme issues or special editions and whether some sort of editorial calendar is available.

Although most magazines accept material year-round, if the magazine does not read manuscripts during a certain time of year, this too will be indicated. This happens a lot with university publications which may shut down for the summer.

Other information included in the "Needs" subhead can give you an indication of your competition. Check how many manuscripts (mss) the magazine receives each issue and compare that with how many actually are published. If a magazine publishes one story an issue and receives 100, your chances of publication may not be as good as one that publishes 10 for every 40. New writers, therefore, may want to opt for those that publish a higher percentage.

New to this edition

To let you know even more about the magazines listed, this year we've added our own editorial comments. These are indicated within the listing by a bullet (●) and they appear just before the "Needs" subhead. This allows us the opportunity to let you know if a magazine has received honors, awards or favorable comments by industry experts. It also allows us to explain more about the special interests or requirements of a publication and any information we've learned from our readers that we feel will help you choose wisely. We have checked several sources including the magazines themselves for information on awards and honors. Since this is new, we do not claim to include every award or every publication honored and hope to increase this information in the future.

To get a good feel for what is considered the best in short fiction today, take a look at one of the prize anthologies mentioned in the comments. If you see an award mentioned you'd like to find more about, check for more information at the library or ask the magazine to elaborate. Here's a list of a few awards publications frequently referred to in our editorial comments. Keep in mind these are not open to submission. They are award-winning collections of stories published in magazines the previous year.

● *Pushcart Prize: Best of the Small Presses*, published by Pushcart Press, Box 380, Wainscott NY 11975.

● *Prize Stories: The O. Henry Awards*, published by Doubleday/Anchor, 666 Fifth Ave., New York NY 10103.

● *Best American Short Stories*, published by Houghton Mifflin, One Beacon St., Boston MA 02108.

You may also want to take a look at the *Writer's Digest* Fiction 50, a list of magazines ranked best for writers by the editors of *Writer's Digest* and published annually in June.

Esquire is known for its thoughtful criticism of the current literary scene. The magazine published an article in the July 1992 issue to which we sometimes refer in our editorial comments. The article featured a short discussion accompanied by a drawing of a tree. The tree contained different magazines as leaves, branches, roots, etc. sympolizing their contribution to supporting writers and the literary community. When appropriate we've noted some publications *Esquire* listed as literary "roots" – good places for writers to start.

Since we have so many journals affiliated with universities, we've also indicated whether the editors of these magazines change each year. For many of these journals there is a whole new staff every school year. Where possible, we've asked for the editor or editors for the calendar year 1993 or an advisor or permanent editor to which material may be submitted. Yet if it is after 1993 and we indicate the editors change, you may want to check with the university for the name of the new editor.

In years past so few publications accepted simultaneous submissions that we only indicated if they did take them. This has changed because many editors now realize that writers just don't have the time to give them an exclusive review of a manuscript. Reporting time (the time it takes an editor to get back to you regarding submissions) is increasing every year. Since editors do not feel they can take less time, many are now agreeing to accept simultaneous submissions. We've decided to include the magazine's policy on this within the listing this year. Keep in mind, however, it is considered courteous to indicate if a submission is being sent to more than one editor for consideration. Establish your own criteria on what you will do if you receive more than one acceptance (many writers feel it is fairest to take the first response). No matter what you decide, remember to inform other editors of your acceptance.

Submitting your work

See The Business of Fiction Writing for the specific mechanics of manuscript submission. Above all, editors appreciate a professional presentation. Include a brief cover letter and, if you want your manuscript returned, be sure to send a large enough self-addressed stamped envelope (SASE). Some writers opt to send just a business-size SASE for a reply or even a reply postcard. When submitting to countries other than your own, you will need to send International Reply Coupons instead of stamps. These are available at the main branch of your post office. U.S. and Canadian publications are included in this section, followed by a special section for international literary and small circulation magazines.

If you are interested in learning more about literary and small circulation magazines, you may want to look at *The International Directory of Little Magazines and Small Presses* (Dustbooks, Box 100, Paradise CA 95967).

The following is the ranking system we have used to categorize the listings in this section:

I   **Publication encourages beginning writers or unpublished writers to submit work for consideration and publishes new writers regularly.**

II   **Publication accepts work by established writers and by new writers of exceptional talent.**

III   **Publication does not encourage beginning writers; prints mostly writers with previous publication credits; very few new writers.**

IV   **Special-interest or regional publication, open only to writers in certain genres or on certain subjects or from certain geographical areas.**

ABERATIONS, (II), Experiences Unlimited, 544 Ygnacio Valley Rd., #13, or (POB 8040), Walnut Creek CA 94596. (510)825-4434. Editor: Jon L. Herron. Fiction Editor: J. Moretz. Editors change each year. Magazine: Digest-sized, 5½ × 8½; 64 pages; 20 lb. bond; 80 lb. glossy cover; b&w illustrations and photographs. "Adult horror, science fiction and dark fantasy short stories and poems for an over-18 audience." Estab. 1992. Circ. 1,700.
- Fiction Editor J. Moretz was nominated for "Best New Editor" by the Small Press Writers and Artists Organization in 1992. *Aberations* was also rated #27 on the 1992 *Writer's Digest* Fiction 50 list.

Needs: Erotica, experimental, fantasy (dark), horror, humor/satire, prose poem, science fiction (hard science). No formula stories. Receives 200-300 unsolicited mss/month. Buys 10-12 mss/issue; 120 mss/year. Publishes ms "within 6 issues." Published work by Jeff Vandermeer, Kevin J. Anderson, Brad Boucher. Length: 4,000 words preferred; 500 words minimum; 9,000 words maximum. "Always" critiques rejected mss and recommends other markets.

How to Contact: Send complete ms with cover letter that includes Social Security number, telephone number and bio. Reports within 16 weeks. SASE. Simultaneous and electronic submissions (MicroSoft Word 5 or Word Perfect) OK. Sample copy for $3.50 and 4 first class stamps. Fiction guidelines for #10 SAE and 1 first class stamp.

Payment: Pays ¼¢/word, plus contributor's copy; extra contributor's copies for reduced charge. Maximum payment: $7.

Terms: Pays on acceptance for first North American serial rights or one-time rights. Sends galleys to author on request.

Advice: "With the advent of the personal computer the small press magazine market has boomed. I expect the market to continue growing into the next decade. We don't want erotica just for erotica sake, but we want good stories where the sex, gore, profanity is instrumental to the story not just thrown in for the sake of blood, guts, sex etc. We will print stories that other magazines might reject just because of the usage of certain words etc."

ABYSS MAGAZINE, "Games and the Imagination," (II, IV), Ragnarok Enterprises, P.O. Box 140333, Austin TX 78714-0333. (512)472-6535. FAX: (512)472-6220. Editor: David F. Nalle. Fiction Editor: Patricia Fitch. Magazine: 8½ × 11; 28 pages; bond paper; glossy cover; illustrations; photos. "Heroic fantasy fiction: some fantasy, horror, SF and adventure fiction, for college-age game players." Bimonthly. Plans special fiction issue. Estab. 1979. Circ. 1,500.
- *Abyss Magazine* is available through Internet online service as well as their own electronic bulletin board. The magazine has been a winner of the Sigma Award for "Best Periodical" in both 1988 and 1990.

Needs: Adventure, fantasy, horror, psychic/supernatural/occult, cyberpunk, science fiction, heroic fantasy, sword and sorcery. "Game-based stories are not specifically desired." Receives 20-30 unsolicited mss/month. Buys 1 ms/issue; 7 mss/year. Publishes ms 1-12 months after acceptance. Published work by Antoine Sadel, Kevin Anderson, Alan Blount; published new writers within the last year. Length: 2,000 words average; 1,000 words minimum; 4,000 words maximum. Publishes short shorts occasionally. Also publishes literary essays and literary criticism. Sometimes critiques rejected mss or recommends other markets.

How to Contact: Send for sample copy first. Reports in 1 month on queries; 2 months on mss. "Do send a cover letter, preferably entertaining. Include some biographical info and a precis of lengthy stories." SASE. Simultaneous submissions OK. Prefers electronic submissions by modem or network. "Call our BBS at (512)472-6905 for modem ASCII info." Sample copy and fiction guidelines $3. Reviews novels and short story collections (especially fantasy novels).
Payment: Pays 1-3¢/word or by arrangement, plus contributor's copies.
Terms: Pays on publication for first North American serial rights.
Advice: "We are particularly interested in new writers with mature and original style. Don't send us fiction which everyone else has sent back to you unless you think it has qualities which make it too strange for everyone else but which don't ruin the significance of the story. Make sure what you submit is appropriate to the magazine you send it to. More than half of what we get is completely inappropriate. We plan to include more and longer stories."

ACM, (ANOTHER CHICAGO MAGAZINE), (II), Left Field Press, 3709 N. Kenmore, Chicago IL 60613. (312)248-7665. Editor: Barry Silesky. Fiction Editor: Sharon Solwitz. Magazine: 5½ × 8½; 150-200 pages; "art folio each issue." Estab. 1977.
Needs: Contemporary, literary, experimental, feminist, gay/lesbian, ethnic, humor/satire, prose poem, translations and political/socio-historical. Receives 75-100 unsolicited fiction mss each month. Published work by David Michael Kaplan, Diane Wakoski, Gary Soto; published new writers in the last year. Also publishes literary essays. Sometimes recommends other markets.
How to Contact: Unsolicited mss acceptable with SASE. Publishes ms 6 months to 1 year after acceptance. Sample copies are available for $8 ppd. Reports in 2 months. Receives small press collections.
Payment: Small honorarium plus contributor's copy.
Terms: Acquires first North American serial rights.
Advice: "Get used to rejection slips, and don't get discouraged. Keep introductory letters short. Make sure ms has name and address on every page, and that it is clean, neat and proofread. We are looking for stories with freshness and originality in subject angle and style, and work that encounters the world and is not stuck in its own navel."

THE ACORN, (I,II), 1530 7th St., Rock Island IL 61201. (309)788-3980. Editor: Betty Mowery. Newsletter: 8½ × 11; 8-10 pages; illustrations. "Manuscripts of interest to K-12th grade audience or K-12th grade librarians and teachers." Bimonthly. Estab. 1989. Circ. 150.
Needs: Ethnic, juvenile, mainstream, mystery/suspense (young adult), prose poem, regional, religious/inspirational, romance (contemporary, historical, young adult), science fiction, young adult. "We use some adult manuscripts, if they are of interest to young people. No erotica or anything degrading to race or religion or background." Receives 50 unsolicited fiction mss/month. Accepts 10-12 mss/issue; 60-70 mss/year. Publishes ms within 2 months after acceptance. Length: 500 words preferred; 200 words minimum; 500 words maximum. Accepts short shorts. Length: 200 words. Sometimes critiques or comments on rejected mss and recommends other markets.
How to Contact: Send complete ms with cover letter. Reports in 1 week. SASE. Simultaneous submissions and reprints OK. Sample copy for $2. Fiction guidelines are contained in publication.
Payment: Pays in contributor's copies.
Terms: Acquires first rights.
Advice: Looks for "tight writing and a manuscript that has something to say and isn't preachy, but still gets the point across. I am open to all manuscripts from both published and unpublished writers. I'm eager to help a beginning author get into print. "

ADRIFT, Writing: Irish, Irish American and . . . , (II), #4D, 239 E. 5th St., New York NY 10003. Editor: Thomas McGonigle. Magazine: 8 × 11; 32 pages; 60 lb. paper stock; 65 lb. cover stock; illustrations; photos. "Irish-Irish American as a basis—though we are interested in advanced writing from anywhere." Semiannually. Estab. 1983. Circ. 1,000 +.

> *Market categories: (I) Open to new writers; (II) Open to both new and established writers; (III) Interested mostly in established writers; (IV) Open to writers whose work is specialized.*

Needs: Contemporary, erotica, ethnic, experimental, feminist, gay, lesbian, literary, translations. Receives 40 unsolicited mss/month. Buys 3 mss/issue. Recent issues have included work by Francis Stuart; published new writers within the last year. Length: open. Also publishes literary criticism. Sometimes critiques rejected mss and recommends other markets.
How to Contact: Send complete ms. Reports as soon as possible. SASE for ms. Sample copy $5. Reviews novels or short story collections.
Payment: Pays $7.50-300.
Terms: Pays on publication for first rights.
Advice: "The writing should argue with, among others, James Joyce, Flann O'Brien, Juan Goytisolo, Ingeborg Bachmann, E.M. Cioran, Max Stirner, Patrick Kavanagh."

THE ADVOCATE, (I, II), PKA Publications, 301A Rolling Hills Park, Prattsville NY 12468. (518)299-3103. Editor: Remington Wright. Tabloid: 11¼ × 13¾; 32 pages; newsprint paper; line drawings; b&w photographs. "Eclectic for a general audience." Bimonthly. Estab. 1987.
Needs: Adventure, contemporary, ethnic, experimental, fantasy, feminist, historical (general), humor/satire, juvenile (5-9 years), literary, mainstream, mystery/suspense, prose poem, regional, romance, science fiction, senior citizen/retirement, sports, western, young adult/teen (10-18 years). Nothing religious, pornographic, violent, erotic, pro-drug or anti-environment. Receives 24 unsolicited mss/month. Accepts 4-6 mss/issue; 30-40 mss/year. Publishes ms 2 months to 1 year after acceptance. Length: 1,000 words preferred; 2,500 words maximum. Sometimes critiques rejected mss and recommends other markets.
How to Contact: Send complete ms with cover letter. Reports in 2 weeks on queries; 2 months on mss. SASE. No simultaneous submissions. Sample copy for $2 (US currency for inside US; $4.25 US currency for Canada). Writers guidelines for SAE and 1 first class stamp.
Payment: Pays contributor's copies.
Terms: Acquires first rights.
Advice: "The highest criterion in selecting a work is its entertainment value. It must first be enjoyable reading. It must, of course, be original. To stand out, it must be thought provoking or strongly emotive, or very cleverly plotted. Will consider only previously unpublished works by writers who do not earn their living principally through writing."

AETHLON, (I,II,IV), East Tennessee State University Press, Johnson City TN 37614-0002. Editor: Don Johnson (615)929-6675. Fiction Editor: Fred Boe (615)265-5184. Magazine: 6 × 9; 180-240 pages; illustrations and photographs. "Theme: Literary treatment of sport. We publish articles on that theme, critical studies of author's treatment of sport and original fiction and poetry with sport themes. Most of our audience are academics." Semiannually. Plans "possible" special fiction issue. Estab. 1983. Circ. 800.
Needs: Sport. "Stories must have a sport-related theme and subject; otherwise, we're wide open." No personal experience memoirs. Receives 10-15 fiction mss/month. Accepts 4-8 fiction mss/issue; 10-15 fiction mss/year. Publishes ms "about 6 months" after acceptance. Length: 2,500-5,000 words average; 500 words minumum; 7,500 words maximum. Also publishes literary essays, literary criticism, poetry. Sometimes critiques rejected mss.
How to Contact: Send complete ms with cover letter. Reports in 6 months. SASE. No simultaneous submissions. Reprint submissions OK. Sample copy $12.50. Reviews novels and short story collections. Send books to Professor Brooke Horvath, Dept. of English, Kent State University, 6000 Frank Ave., Canton OH 44720.
Payment: Pays 1 contributor's copy and 5 offprints.
Terms: Sends pre-publication galleys to author. Publication copyrighted.
Advice: "Too many people with no talent are writing. Too many people think a clever idea or an unusual experience is all it takes to make a story. We are looking for well-written, insightful stories. Don't be afraid to be experimental."

AGNI, (II), Creative Writing Program, Boston University, 236 Bay State Rd., Boston MA 02215. (617)353-5389. Editor-in-Chief: Askold Melnyczuk. Magazine: 5½ × 8½; 320 pages; 55 lb. booktext paper; recycled cover stock; occasional art portfolios. "Eclectic literary magazine publishing first-rate poems and stories." Semiannually. Estab. 1972.
● Work from *Agni* has been selected regularly for inclusion in both *Pushcart Prize* and *Best American Short Stories* anthologies. *Esquire* magazine (July 1992) also called this publication one of America's "literary roots."

Needs: Stories, excerpted novels, prose poems and translations. Receives 200 unsolicited fiction mss/month. Buys 4-7 mss/issue, 8-12 mss/year. Reading period Oct. 1 to June 1 only. Published work by Joyce Carol Oates, Stephen Dixon, Andra Neiburga, Ha Jin. Rarely critiques rejected mss or recommends other markets.
How to Contact: Send complete ms with SASE and cover letter listing previous publications. Simultaneous submissions OK. Reports in 1-4 months. Sample copy $7.
Payment: Pays $10/page up to $150; 2 contributor's copies; one-year subscription.
Terms: Pays on publication for first North American serial rights. Sends galleys to author. Copyright reverts to author upon publication.
Advice: "Read *Agni* carefully to understand the kinds of stories we publish. Read—everything, classics, literary journals, bestsellers."

AGORA, The Magazine for Gifted Students, (IV), AG Publications, P.O. Box 10975, Raleigh NC 27605. (919)787-6832. Editors: Thomas E. Humble and Sally Humble. Magazine: 8½×11; 32 pages; illustrations and photographs. "We publish winners of our writing competitions for students in grades 7-12." Bimonthly (4 issues per school year). Estab. 1986. Circ. 3,200.
Needs: Ethnic, historical (general), humor/satire, literary, regional, religious, science fiction. Receives 2-4 unsolicited mss/month. Length: 450-1,500 words average. Publishes short shorts.
How to Contact: "Subscribe to magazine or attend a school that subscribes to a class set." Accepts electronic submissions via disk. Sample copy $4. Free fiction guidelines.

‡THE AGUILAR EXPRESSION, (II), P.O. Box 304, Webster PA 15087. Editor: Xavier F. Aguilar. Magazine: 8½×11; 10-16 pages; 20 lb. bond paper; illustrations. "We are open to all writers of a general theme—something that may appeal to everyone." Semiannually. Estab. 1989. Circ. 150.
Needs: Adventure, ethnic/multicultural, experimental, horror, mainstream/contemporary, mystery/suspense (romantic suspense), romance (contemporary). No religious or first-person stories. Will publish annual special fiction issue or anthology in the future. Receives 10 unsolicited mss/month. Acquires 1-2 mss/issue; 2-4 mss/year. Publishes ms 1 month to 1 year after acceptance. Recently published work by Aphrodite Mitsos, Linda Keegan, Loueva Smith. Length: 1,000 words average; 750 words minimum; 1,500 words maximum. Also publishes poetry.
How to Contact: Send complete ms with cover letter. Reports on queries in 1 week; mss in 1 month. SASE (or IRC) for a reply to a query or a disposable copy of the ms. No simultaneous submissions. Sample copy for $5. Fiction guidelines for #10 SAE and 52¢ postage.
Payment: Pays 1 contributor's copy. Additional copies at a reduced rate of $3.
Terms: Acquires one-time rights. Not copyrighted. Write to publication for details on contests, awards or grants.

ALABAMA LITERARY REVIEW, (II), Smith 253, Troy State University, Troy AL 36082. (205)670-3286, ext. 3307. Editor: Theron Montgomery. Fiction Editor: Jim Davis. Magazine: 6×11½; 100+ pages; top paper quality; some illustrations; photos. "National magazine for a broad range of the best contemporary fiction, poetry, essays, photography and drama that we can find." Semiannually. Estab. 1987.
  ● The Troy State University radio program featuring five-minute readings of poetry from *ALR* has ended for the time being. It's a very good chance, however, they'll start up again in Spring 1993. The program can be heard across the state.
Needs: Contemporary, erotica, ethnic, experimental, fantasy, feminist, historical (general), humor/satire, literary, mystery/suspense, prose poem, regional, science fiction, serialized/excerpted novel, translations. "Serious writing." Receives 50 unsolicited fiction mss/month. Acquires 2 fiction mss/issue. Publishes ms 5-6 months after acceptance. Recently published work by Manette Ansay, Ed Peaco, Pete Fromm, John Holman and Mary Sue Weston; published new writers within the last year. Length: 2,000-3,500 words average. Publishes short shorts of 1,000 words. Also publishes literary essays, literary criticism, poetry. Sometimes comments on rejected mss and recommends other markets.

 The double dagger before a listing indicates that the listing is new in this edition. New Markets are often the most receptive to submissions by new writers.

How to Contact: Send complete ms with cover letter or submit through agent. Reports on queries in 2 weeks; on mss in 2-4 weeks (except in summer). SASE. Simultaneous submissions OK. Sample copy for $4 plus 50¢ postage. Reviews novels or short story collections. Send to Steve Cooper.
Payment: Pays in contributor's copies.
Terms: First rights returned to author upon publication. Work published in *ALR* may be read on state-wide (nonprofit) public radio program.
Advice: "Read our publication first. Avoid negative qualities pertaining to gimmickry and a self-centered point of view. We are interested in any kind of writing if it is *serious* and *honest* in the sense of 'the human heart in conflict with itself.' "

ALASKA QUARTERLY REVIEW, (II), University of Alaska, Anchorage, 3211 Providence Dr., Anchorage AK 99508. (907)786-1327. Fiction Editor: Ronald Spatz. Magazine: 6×9; 146 pages; 60 lb. Glatfelter paper; 10 pt. C15 black ink varnish cover stock; photos on cover only. Magazine of "contemporary literary art and criticism for a general literary audience." Semiannually. Estab. 1982.
• Work appearing in the *Alaska Quarterly Review* has been selected for the *Pushcart Prize* and *Best American Short Stories* anthologies.
Needs: Contemporary, experimental, literary, prose poem and translations. Receives 100 unsolicited fiction mss/month. Accepts 5-11 mss/issue, 15-22 mss/year. Does not read mss May 15-August 15. Published new writers within the last year. Publishes short shorts. Occasionally critiques rejected mss.
How to Contact: Send complete ms with SASE. Simultaneous submissions "undesirable, but will accept if indicated." Reports in 2 months. Publishes ms 6 months to 1 year after acceptance. Sample copy $4.
Payment: Pays 1 contributor's copy and a year's subscription.
Terms: Acquires first rights.
Advice: "We have made a significant investment in fiction. The reason is quality; serious fiction *needs* a market. Try to have everything build to a singleness of effect."

Alaska Quarterly Review
LITERATURE • CRITICISM • PHILOSOPHY
Vol. 11 No. 1 & 2   Fall & Winter 1992

"All of our covers must be artistically distinct and depict a representational aspect of the Alaskan experience," says Alaska Quarterly Review *Executive Editor Ronald Spatz. "We hope each cover will draw the reader to the journal and invite a sampling of the literary contents inside. In this photograph, which depicts the small boat harbor in Homer, Alaska, the eye is attracted to the striking contrasts and vertical lines and then follows a fishing boat as it begins its journey to the bountiful waters of Kachemak Bay. Likewise on AQR's pages the reader will discover a rich and varied body of literary art by both familiar and new writers." The photographer, Sam Kimura, is a professor of art at the University of Alaska, Anchorage. (Photo, © 1992 Sam Kimura.)*

ALDEBARAN, (II), Roger Williams University, 1 Old Ferry Rd., Bristol RI 02809. (401)253-1040. Editor: Quantella Owens. Magazine: 6×9; 60-100 pages; illustrations; photos. Literary publication of prose and poetry for a general audience. Published annually or twice a year. Estab. 1970.
Needs: Will consider all fiction. Does not read mss between April 2 and September 1, and November 2 and February 1. Preferred length: 3,500 words or shorter.
How to Contact: Send complete ms with SASE and cover letter, which should include "information for possible contributor's notes—but cover letters will not influence decision on publication." No simultaneous submissions. Reports in 3 months. Sample copy $4 with SASE.

Payment: Pays 2 contributor's copies.
Terms: Copyright reverts to author on publication.
Advice: "We accept both traditional and innovative approaches and encourage submissions from all genres except pornography." Mss are rejected because of "incomplete stories, no live character, basic grammatical errors; seldom returned with suggestions for revision and character change."

ALPHA BEAT SOUP, (II, IV), 31 A Waterloo St., New Hope PA 18938. Editor: Dave Christy. Magazine: 7½ × 9; 95-125 pages; illustrations. "Beat and modern literature – prose, reviews and poetry." Semiannually. Estab. 1987. Circ. 475.
 • Work from *Alpha Beat Soup* appeared in the *Pushcart Prize* anthologies in 1988 and 1991.
 Alpha Beat Press (not listed in this book) publishes poetry chapbooks and supplements.
Needs: Erotica, experimental, literary and prose poem. Plans another magazine, supplementing *Alpha Beat Soup*, and an *ABC Anthology*. Recently published work by Charles Bukowski, Joy Walsh and Joan Reid; published new writers within the last year. Length: 600 words minimum; 1,000 words maximum. Also publishes literary essays, literary criticism, poetry. Sometimes recommends other markets.
How to Contact: Query first. Reports on queries within 2 weeks. SASE. Simultaneous and reprint submissions OK. Sample copy for $5. Reviews novels and short story collections.
Payment: Pays in contributor's copies.
Terms: Rights remain with author.
Advice: "*ABS* is the finest journal of its kind available today, having, with 9 issues, published the widest range of published and unpublished writers you'll find in the small press scene."

THE AMARANTH REVIEW, (I, II), Window Publications, P.O. Box 56235, Phoenix AZ 85079. Editor: Dana L. Yost. Magazine: 8½ × 11; 100-160 pages; 60 lb. offset paper; 90 lb. cover stock; illustrations and occasional photos. "Our theme is eclectic – we are interested in poetry and short fiction which deals with the human condition in its broadest possible expression. For an educated, thinking audience of those who enjoy quality poetry and fiction." Estab. 1989. Circ. 1,500.
Needs: Literary, contemporary, experimental, science fiction, western. "Fiction which takes some risks." Receives 100+ unsolicited mss/month. Buys 20+ mss/year. Publishes ms 2-6 months after acceptance. Recently published work by Cathryn Alpert, Clarinda Harriss Raymond and Daniela Kuper. Length: 10,000 maximum. Publishes short shorts. Also publishes literary essays, literary criticism, poetry. Sometimes critiques rejected mss and recommends other markets.
How to Contact: Send complete ms with cover letter. "Include how the writer heard about us – brief bio is also welcome." Reports in 2 weeks on queries; 1 month on ms. SASE. Simultaneous submissions OK. Accepts electronic submissions (IBM Word Perfect 5.0 only). Sample copy for $6.50. Writer's guidelines for #10 SAE and 1 first class stamp. Reviews novels and short story collections.
Payment: Pays cash. For current rate send for guidelines.
Terms: Buys first North American serial rights.
Advice: "The one basic requirement is that the piece be good, quality fiction. But more specifically, we look for the piece to deal with some basic condition of human existence, and we look for the piece to hit hard, to take some risks, to knock us into thinking – really thinking – about the issue or circumstances of the story. I also think that today's fiction writers need to take more chances – a lot of the stories we receive could have been written by a dozen other writers, and that almost always means that they will end up being rejected. We are now looking for stories that are longer (up to 10,000 words), and I think we are looking for stories that are taking some kind of risk – with form, content, whatever – it isn't really a conscious decision on our part, that just seems to be where the better fiction is headed right now."

AMATEUR WRITERS JOURNAL, Four Seasons Poetry Club Magazine, (I), R.V. Gill Publishing Co., 3653 Harrison St., Bellaire OH 43906. (614)676-0881. Editor: Rosalind Gill. Magazine: 8½ × 11; 38 pages; 20 lb. paper; illustrations. "Stories, articles, essays and poetry on all subjects. No avant-garde or porno-type manuscripts of any kind accepted. Poetry, when seasonal, published only in the season for which it is appropriate. Same rule applies to stories. For a family audience." Quarterly. Estab. 1967. Circ. 700 + .

Read the Business of Fiction Writing section to learn the correct way to prepare and submit a manuscript.

Needs: Adventure, contemporary, fantasy, humor/satire, mainstream, mystery/suspense, religious/inspirational, contemporary romance, science fiction, young adult/teen. Receives around 300 fiction mss/month. Accepts 8 fiction mss/issue; 48 mss/year. Publishes ms "within 3 months" after acceptance. Length: 1,200 words average; 1,500 words maximum. Also publishes literary essays, poetry. Sometimes critiques rejected mss and recommends other markets.

How to Contact: Send complete ms with cover letter. State whether you are offering first rights, or, if material has been published elsewhere, the name of the publication in which your work appeared. Reports on queries in 1 month; on mss in 1 week. SASE. No simultaneous submissions. Sample copy available for $1.85 and 3 first class stamps. Fiction guidelines for #10 SAE and 2 first class stamps.

Payment: No payment.

Terms: Acquires one-time rights.

Advice: "I believe that all fiction writers should have a showplace for their work, and my magazine readers prefer fiction to nonfiction, although I accept both."

AMBERGRIS, (II), Dept. N, P.O. Box 29919, Cincinnati OH 45229. Editor: Mark Kissling. Magazine: 5 × 8; 80-160 pages; illustrations; photographs. "*Ambergris* is a non-profit magazine dedicated to quality art and literature, and to fostering the emerging author and artist." Annual. Estab. 1987. Circ. 1,000.
- The editor tells me *Ambergris 10*, planned for November 1993, will be a special retrospective issue. For writers interested in finding out more about the magazine, Kissling says, this issue is a good place to start.

Needs: "We are looking for literary short stories, experimental short fiction, and literary essays (particularly essays with fictional elements — essays that read like fiction)." Simultaneous submissions OK (if noted). No poetry, no genre fiction, nothing strictly for children or young adults, and no novel excerpts (unless the excerpt is unpublished and completely self-contained). Also no scholarly articles or academic essays. Receives more than 1,000 mss/year. Buys 8-12 mss/year. Does not read in May, June and July. Publishes most mss within a year of acceptance, but "writers are notified on offer of acceptance if a ms is not to be published for more than a year." Recently published work by Mona Simpson, Nicole Cooley and Anne Panning. Length: 5,000 words maximum.

How to Contact: Send complete ms with cover letter which should include a three-line biographical sketch. One work of fiction per submission *only*. Please include computer disk specs and availability if applicable. Reports in 3 months, "longer if a ms is under serious consideration." Enclose sufficient SASE for return of ms, "or at least a #10 SASE for reply. Submissions without either will not be considered or returned." Current issue $4.95; sample copy $3.95. Fiction guidelines for #10 SASE.

Payment: Pays $5/published page, $50 maximum. Writers also receive 2 contributor's copies, extras available at a discount.

Terms: Buys first North American serial rights and the right to reprint.

Advice: "*Our reading period is August through April.* Manuscripts received at other times will be returned unread, and then only if SASE is enclosed. We attempt to foster the emerging author, but we strongly encourage beginning writers and others not familiar with our format to invest in and *read a sample copy* before submitting work. There is simply no other way to determine what kind of fiction and essays this or any other literary magazine publishes without first reading an issue. We also give special consideration to works by Ohio authors and about the Midwest in general."

AMELIA, (II), 329 E St., Bakersfield CA 93304. (805)323-4064. Editor-in-Chief: Frederick A. Raborg, Jr. Magazine: 5½ × 8½; 124-136 pages; perfect-bound; 60 lb. high-quality moistrite matte paper; kromekote cover; four-color covers; original illustrations; b&w photos. "A general review using fine fiction, poetry, criticism, belles lettres, one-act plays, fine pen-and-ink sketches and line drawings, sophisticated cartoons, book reviews and translations of both fiction and poetry for general readers with catholic tastes for quality writing." Quarterly. Plans special fiction issue each July. Estab. 1984. Circ. 1,250.
- The editor of this well-respected magazine also edits *Cicada* (devoted to Oriental-style writing) and *SPSM&H* (devoted to sonnets and sonnet-inspired work). The magazine also sponsors a long list of fiction awards. Listings for the other publications and for the *Amelia* Awards appear in this book. *Amelia* also ranks #28 on the 1992 *Writer's Digest* Fiction 50 list.

Needs: Adventure, contemporary, erotica, ethnic, experimental, fantasy, feminist, gay, historical (general), humor/satire, lesbian, literary, mainstream, mystery/suspense, prose poem, regional, science fiction, senior citizen/retirement, sports, translations, western. Nothing "obviously pornographic or patently religious." Receives 160-180 unsolicited mss/month. Buys up to 9 mss/issue; 25-36 mss/year. Published Judson Jerome, Jack Curtis, Maxine Kumin, Eugene Dubnov and Merrill Joan Gerber; published new writers within the last year. Length: 3,000 words average; 1,000 words minimum; 5,000 words maximum. Usually critiques rejected ms. Sometimes recommends other markets.

How to Contact: Send complete manuscript with cover letter with previous credits if applicable to *Amelia* and perhaps a brief personal comment to show personality and experience. Reports in 1 week on queries; 2 weeks-3 months on mss. SASE. Sample copy for $7.95. Fiction guidelines for #10 SAE and 1 first class stamp.

Payment: Pays $35-50 plus 2 contributor's copies; extras with 20% discount.

Terms: Pays on acceptance for first North American serial rights. Sends galleys to author "when deadline permits."

Advice: "Write carefully and well, but have a strong story to relate. I look for depth of plot and uniqueness, and strong characterization. Study manuscript mechanics and submission procedures. Neatness does count. There is a sameness—a cloning process—among most magazines today that tends to dull the senses. Magazines like *Amelia* will awaken those senses while offering stories and poems of lasting value."

AMERICAN DANE, (II, IV), The Danish Brotherhood in America, 3717 Harney, Omaha NE 68131-3844. (402)341-5049. Editor: Jennifer Denning-Kock. Magazine: 8¼ × 11; 20-28 pages; 40 lb. paper; slick cover; illustrations and photos. "*American Dane* is the official publication of the Danish Brotherhood. Corporate purpose of the Danish Brotherhood is to promote and perpetuate Danish culture and traditions and to provide fraternal benefits and family protection." Estab. 1916. Circ. 7,500.

Needs: Ethnic. "Danish!" Receives 4 unsolicited fiction mss/month. Buys 1 ms/issue; 12 mss/year. Reads mss during August and September only. Publishes ms up to one year after acceptance. Length: 1,000 words average; 3,000 words maximum. Also publishes literary essays, some literary criticism, poetry.

How to Contact: Query first. SASE. Simultaneous submissions OK. Sample copy for $1 and 9 × 12 SAE with 54¢ postage. Fiction guidelines for #10 SAE and 1 first class stamp. Reviews novels and short story collections.

Payment: Pays $15-50.

Terms: Pays on publication for first rights. Publication not copyrighted.

Advice: "Think Danish!"

AMERICAN LITERARY REVIEW, A National Journal of Poems and Stories, (II), University of North Texas, P.O. Box 13615, Denton TX 76203. (817)565-2127, 565-2124. Editor: James Ward Lee. Magazine: 7 × 10; 128 pages; 70 lb. Mohawk paper; 67 lb. Wausau Vellum cover. "Publishes poems and stories for a general audience." Semiannually. Estab. 1990. Circ. 200.

Needs: Mainstream and literary only. No genre works. Receives 25 unsolicited fiction mss/month. Accepts 7-10 mss/issue; 14-20 mss/year. Publishes ms within 2 years after acceptance. Published work by Gordon Weaver, Gerald Haslam and William Miller. Length: 3,500 words preferred; 5,000 words maximum. Often critiques or comments on rejected mss. Also accepts poetry.

How to Contact: Send complete ms with cover letter. Reports in 6-8 weeks. SASE. Simultaneous submissions OK. Sample copy for $5. Fiction guidelines free.

Payment: Pays in contributor's copies.

Terms: Acquires one-time rights. Sends pre-publication galleys to author.

Advice: "We want to publish poems and stories that reflect the kinds of writing being done in various regions of America. We are not looking for a 'style' or an aesthetic to make us distinctive." Looks for "literary quality and careful preparation."

‡AMERICAN SHORT FICTION, (II), University of Texas Press, English Dept., University of Texas at Austin, Austin TX 78712-1164. (512)471-1772. Editor: Laura Furman. Magazine: 5¾ × 9¼; 128 pages; 60 lb. natural paper; 8015 karma white cover. "*American Short Fiction* publishes fiction *only*, of all lengths, from short short to novella." Quarterly. Estab. 1990. Circ. 1,200.

Needs: Literary. "No romance, science fiction, erotica, mystery/suspense and religious." Receives 500 unsolicited mss/month. Acquires 6 mss/month; 25-30 mss/year. Does not read mss April 1-September 30. Publishes ms up to 1 year after acceptance. Agented fiction 20%. Recently published work by Reynold Price, Ursula K. Le Guin and Rick Bass. Length: open. Publishes short shorts. Length: under 500 words.

How to Contact: Send complete ms with cover letter. Reports in 3-4 months on mss. Send SASE (IRC) for reply, return of ms; or send disposable copy of the ms. Simultaneous submissions OK if informed. Sample copy for $7.95. Fiction guidelines for #10 SAE with 1 first class stamp.

Payment: Pays 2 contributor's copies; additional copies at 30% discount.
Terms: Acquires first rights. Sends galleys to author.
Advice: "We pick work for *American Short Fiction* along simple lines: Do we love it? Is this a story we will be happy reading four or five times? We comment only *rarely* on submissions because of the volume of work we receive."

‡THE AMERICAN VOICE, (II), 332 W. Broadway, #1215, Louisville KY 40202. (502)562-0045. Editor: Frederick Smock. Magazine: 6×9; 130 pages; photographs. "Avant-garde feminist literature." Triannually. Estab. 1985. Circ. 2,000.
• Work from *The American Voice* has appeared in the *Pushcart Prize* anthologies. The magazine is also a member of The Council of Literary Magazines and Small Presses.
Needs: Feminist, literary. Receives 200 unsolicited mss/month. Buys 5 mss/issue; 15/year. Publishes ms 6-12 months after acceptance. Agented fiction 5%. Recently published work by Susan Griffin, Michelle Cliff, Isabel Allende, Olga Brovmas. Publishes short shorts. Also publishes literary essays, literary criticism, poetry.
How to Contact: Send complete ms with cover letter. Should include bio and list of publications. Reports in 2 weeks on queries; 1 month on mss. Send SASE for reply, return of mss or send a disposable copy of the manuscript. Does not consider simultanous submissions, reprints or electronic submissions. Sample copy for $5.
Payment: Pays $400 maximum, free subscription to the magazine, 2 contributor's copies. Additional copies at a reduced rate, $2.50.
Terms: Pays on publication for first North American serial rights. Sends galleys to author.

THE AMERICAS REVIEW, A Review of Hispanic Literature and Art of the USA, (II, IV), Arte Publico Press, 4800 Calhoun, University of Houston, Houston TX 77204-2090. (713)743-2841. Editors: Dr. Julian Olivares and Evangelina Vigil-Pinon. Magazine: 5½×8½; 128 pages; illustrations and photographs. "*The Americas Review* publishes contemporary fiction written by U.S. Hispanics — Mexican Americans, Puerto Ricans, Cuban Americans, etc." Quarterly. Estab. 1972.
Needs: Contemporary, ethnic, literary, women's, hispanic literature. No novels. Receives 12-15 fiction mss/month. Buys 2-3 mss/issue; 8-12 mss/year. Publishes mss "6 months to 1 year" after acceptance. Length: 3,000-4,500 average number of words; 1,500 words minimum; 6,000 words maximum. Publishes short shorts. Sometimes critiques rejected mss and recommends other markets.
How to Contact: Send complete manuscript. Reports in 3 months. SASE. Accepts electronic submissions via IBM compatible disk. Sample copy $5; $10 double issue.
Payment: Pays $50-200; 5 contributor's copies.
Terms: Pays on acceptance for first rights, and rights to 40% of fees if story is reprinted. Sponsors award for fiction writers.
Advice: "There has been a noticeable increase in quality in U.S. Hispanic literature."

THE AMHERST REVIEW, (II, IV), Box 1811, Amherst College, Amherst MA 01002. (413)542-2000. Editor: Ismee Bartels. Magazine: 7½×8½; 60-70 pages; illustrations and photographs. "We are a college literary magazine publishing work by students, faculty and professionals. We seek submissions of poetry, fiction, and essay for the college community." Annually.
Needs: Adventure, confession, contemporary, ethnic, experimental, fantasy, feminist, gay, historical (general), horror, humor/satire, lesbian, mainstream, prose poem, psychic/supernatural/occult, regional, romance, science fiction, mystery/suspense, translations, western. "No sentimentality." Receives 10-20 unsolicited mss/month. Does not read mss March-August. Length: 4,500 words; 7,200 words maximum.
How to Contact: Send complete ms with cover letter. Reports in 4 months on mss. Sample copy for $5, SAE and $1 postage.
Payment: Pays 2 contributor's copies; $5 charge for extras.
Terms: Acquires first rights.

‡ANARCHY, A Journal of Desire Armed, (II, IV), C.A.L. Press, POB 1446, Columbia MO 65205-1446. (314)442-4352. Editors: Jason McQuinn, Toni Otter. Magazine: 8¼×10¾; 88 pages; Mando Brite paper; 50 lb. offset cover; illustrations and photos. "Libertarian/anarchist fiction — i.e. fiction which does not glorify or reinforce authority, but which demystifies or subverts it, though we also publish fiction which may explore any aspect of life." Quarterly. Estab. 1980. Circ. 5,000.
• *Utne Reader* nominated this magazine to receive an Alternative Press Award. *Anarchy* is a

member of COSMEP (an organization of independent publishers) and, of course, the Anarchist Media Network.

Needs: Erotica, ethnic/multicultural, experimental, feminist, gay, lesbian, literary, science fiction (soft/sociological). "No religious, inspirational, conventional, romance, uncritical material." Receives 2-4 mss/month. Acquires 1 mss/issue; 4 mss/year. Publishes ms 3-6 months after acceptance. Recently published work by Richard Kostelanetz, Paul Goodman, Nancy Bogen. Length: 2,000 words preferred; 500 minimum; 4,000 words maximum.

How to Contact: Send complete ms with cover letter. Reports in 2-3 months. Send SASE for reply, return of mss or send a disposable copy of the manuscript. Simultaneous, reprint and electronic submissions OK. Sample copy for $3.

Payment: Pays free subscription to the magazine, 5-6 contributor's copies; additional copies for $1.50.

Terms: Acquires one-time rights. Sends galleys to author. Not copyrighted.

ANSUDA MAGAZINE, (I, II), (formerly *The Pub*), Ansuda Publications, Box 158J, Harris IA 51345. Editor/Publisher: Daniel R. Betz. Magazine: 5½×8½; 72 pages; mimeo paper; heavy stock cover; illustrations on cover. "We prefer stories to have some sort of social impact within them, no matter how slight, so our fiction is different from what's published in most magazines. We aren't afraid to be different or publish something that might be objectionable to current thought. *Ansuda* is directed toward those people, from all walks of life, who are themselves 'different' and unique, who are interested in new ideas and forms of reasoning. Our readers enjoy *Ansuda* and believe in what we are doing." Published 2 times/year. Estab. 1979. Circ. 300.

Needs: Literary, psychic/supernatural/occult, fantasy, horror, mystery, adventure. "We are looking for honest, straightforward stories. No love stories or stories that ramble on for pages about nothing in particular." Accepts reprints. Accepts 4-6 mss/issue. Receives approximately 35-40 unsolicited fiction mss each month. Published new writers within the last year. Length: 8,000 words maximum. Also publishes poetry. Sometimes recommends other markets.

How to Contact: Send complete ms with SASE. Simultaneous submissions OK, if noted. Reports in 1 month. Publishes ms an average of 6 months after acceptance. Sample copy $3.75. Guidelines for #10 SASE.

Payment: Pays 2 contributor's copies. Cover price less special bulk discount for extras.

Terms: Acquires first North American serial rights and second serial rights on reprints.

Advice: "Read the magazine—that is *very* important. If you send a story close to what we're looking for, we'll try to help guide you to exactly what we want. We appreciate neat copy, and if photocopies are sent, we like to be able to read all of the story. Fiction seems to work for us—we are a literary magazine and have better luck with fiction than articles or poems."

ANTAEUS, (III), The Ecco Press, 100 West Broad St., Hopewell NJ 08525. (609)466-4748. Editor-in-Chief: Daniel Halpern. Managing Editor: Cathy Jewell. Magazine: 6½×9; 275 pages; Warren old style paper; some illustrations and photographs. "Literary magazine of fiction and poetry, literary documents, and occasional essays for those seriously interested in contemporary writing." Quarterly. Estab. 1970. Circ. 5,000.

● This prestigious literary journal is published by The Ecco Press, also listed in this book. *Antaeus* has been a past winner and finalist in the National Magazine Award for fiction and has some of the most beautiful covers I've ever seen (unfortunately, they don't reproduce well in black and white).

Needs: Contemporary, literary, prose poem, excerpted novel, and translations. No romance, science fiction. Receives 600 unsolicited fiction mss/month. Published fiction by Richard Ford, Donald Hall, Joyce Carol Oates; published new writers within the last year. Rarely critiques rejected mss. Also publishes poetry.

How to Contact: Send complete ms with SASE. No multiple submissions. Reports in 6-8 weeks. Sample copy $10 plus $1.50 postage. Fiction guidelines for SASE.

Payment: Pays $10/page and 2 contributor's copies, 40% discount for extras.

Terms: Pays on publication for first North American serial rights and right to reprint in any anthology consisting of 75% or more material from *Antaeus*.

Advice: "Read the magazine before submitting. Most mss are solicited, but we do actively search the unsolicited mss for suitable material. Unless stories are extremely short (2-3 pages), send only one. Do not be angry if you get only a printed rejection note; we *have* read the manuscript. Always include an SASE. Keep cover letters short, cordial and to the point."

ANTIETAM REVIEW, (II, IV), Washington County Arts Council, 82 W. Washington St., Hagerstown MD 21740. (301)791-3132. Editor: Susanne Kass. Magazine: 8½×11; 42 pages; photos. A literary journal of short fiction, poetry and black-and-white photographs. Annually. Estab. 1982. Circ. 1,000.
Needs: Contemporary, ethnic, experimental, feminist, literary and prose poem. "We read manuscripts from our region—Delaware, Maryland, Pennsylvania, Virginia, West Virginia and Washington D.C. only. We read from October 1 to March 1." Receives about 100 unsolicited mss/month. Buys 7-9 stories/year. Published work by Rachel Simon, Elisavietta Ritchie, Philip Bufithis; published new writers within the last year. Length: 3,000 words average.
How to Contact: "Send ms and SASE with a cover letter. Let us know if you have published before and where." Reports in 1 to 2 months. "If we hold a story, we let the writer know. Occasionally we critique returned ms or ask for rewrites." Sample copy $5. Back issue $3.
Payment: "We believe it is a matter of dignity that writers and poets be paid. We have been able to give $100 a story and $25 a poem, but this depends on funding. Also 2 copies." Prizes: "We offer a $100 annual literary award in addition to the $100, for the best story."
Terms: Buys first North American serial rights. Sends pre-publication galleys to author if requested.
Advice: "We look for well-crafted work that shows attention to clarity and precision of language. We like relevant detail but want to see significant emotional movement within the course of the story—something happening to the central character. This journal was started in response to the absence of fiction markets for emerging writers. Its purpose is to give exposure to fiction writers, poets and photographers of high artistic quality who might otherwise have difficulty placing their work."

THE ANTIGONISH REVIEW, (II), St. Francis Xavier University, Antigonish, Nova Scotia B2G 1C0 Canada. (902)867-3962. Editor: George Sanderson. Literary magazine for educated and creative readers. Quarterly. Estab. 1970. Circ. 800.
Needs: Literary, contemporary, prose poem and translations. No erotic or political material. Accepts 6 mss/issue. Receives 25 unsolicited fiction mss each month. Published work by Arnold Bloch, Richard Butts and Helen Barolini; published new writers within the last year. Length: 3,000-5,000 words. Sometimes comments briefly on rejected mss.
How to Contact: Send complete ms with cover letter. SASE or IRC. No simultaneous submissions. Accepts disk submissions compatible with Apple, Macintosh, WordPerfect (IBM) and Windows. Prefers hard copy with disk submission. Reports in 6 months. Publishes ms 3 months to 1 year after acceptance.
Payment: Pays 2 contributor's copies.
Terms: Authors retain copyright.
Advice: "Learn the fundamentals and do not deluge an editor."

ANTIOCH REVIEW, (II), Box 148, Yellow Springs OH 45387. (513)767-6389. Editor: Robert S. Fogarty. Associate Editor: Nolan Miller. Magazine: 6×9; 128 pages; 60 lb. book offset paper; coated cover stock; illustrations "seldom." "Literary and cultural review of contemporary issues in politics, American and international studies, and literature for general readership." Quarterly. Published special fiction issue last year; plans another. Estab. 1941. Circ. 4,000.
Needs: Literary, contemporary, translations and experimental. No children's, science fiction or popular market. Buys 3-4 mss/issue, 10-12 mss/year. Receives approximately 175 unsolicited fiction mss each month. Approximately 1-2% of fiction agented. Length: any length the story justifies.
How to Contact: Send complete ms with SASE, preferably mailed flat. Reports in 2 months. Publishes ms 6-9 months after acceptance. Sample copy $5; Guidelines for SASE.
Payment: Pays $15/page; 2 contributor's copies. $2.70 for extras.
Terms: Pays on publication for first and one-time rights (rights returned to author on request).
Advice: "Our best advice, always, is to *read* the *Antioch Review* to see what type of material we publish. Quality fiction requires an engagement of the reader's intellectual interest supported by mature emotional relevance, written in a style that is rich and rewarding without being freaky. The great number of stories submitted to us indicates that fiction apparently still has great appeal. We assume that if so many are writing fiction, many must be reading it."

ANYTHING THAT MOVES, Beyond The Myths of Bisexuality, (II, IV), Bay Area Bisexual Network, #24, 2404 California St., San Francisco CA 94115. (415)564-BABN. Editor: Karla Rossi. Fiction Editor: Marcy Sheiner. Magazine: 8½×11; 64 pages; newsprint paper; glossy cover; illustrations and photographs. "Of interest to bisexuals—priority given to bisexual writers and bisexual themes." Quarterly. Estab. 1991. Circ. 5,000.

Needs: Bisexual: erotica, ethnic, experimental, fantasy, feminist, gay, historical (general), humor/satire, lesbian, prose poem, psychic/supernatural/occult, science fiction. Upcoming themes: "Spirituality" (Winter 1993); "History" (Spring 1993); "Relationships & Family" (Summer 1993); Special Focus on Bisexuals of Color (Fall 1993). Receives 100 unsolicited mss/month. Accepts 3-5 mss/issue; 20 ms/year. Publishes ms up to 1 year after acceptance. Length: 2,500 words maximum. Publishes short shorts. Also accepts poetry.
How to Contact: Query with clips of published work. No simultaneous submissions. Reports in 2 weeks on queries; 6-8 weeks on mss. SASE. Sample copy for $6. Fiction guidelines for SAE and 1 first class stamps.
Payment: Pays contributor's copies.
Terms: Acquires first rights.
Advice: Looks for "especially strong beginning, tight, non-rambling plot and dialogue. We are especially interested in writers w/themes regarding controversial topics or traditionally censored writers and topics. Erotica considered, but graphic sex or pornography rejected. Erotica is not a priority with us."

APPALACHIAN HERITAGE, (I, II), Hutchins Library, Berea College, Berea KY 40404. (606)986-9341. Editor: Sidney Farr. Magazine: 6×9; 80 pages; 60 lb. stock; 10 pt. Warrenflo cover; drawings and b&w photos. "*Appalachian Heritage* is a southern Appalachian literary magazine. We try to keep a balance of fiction, poetry, essays, scholarly works, etc., for a general audience and/or those interested in the Appalachian mountains." Quarterly. Estab. 1973. Circ. 1,100.
Needs: Regional, literary, historical. Receives 20-25 unsolicited mss/month. Accepts 2 or 3 mss/issue; 10 or more mss/year. Published work by Robert Morgan, Richard Hague and James Still; published new writers within the last year. Length: 2,000-2,500 word average; 3,000 words maximum. Publishes short shorts. Length: 500 words. Occasionally critiques rejected mss and recommends other markets.
How to Contact: Send complete ms with cover letter. Reports in 1-2 weeks on queries; 3-4 weeks on mss. SASE for ms. Simultaneous submissions OK. Sample copy for $5.
Payment: Pays 3 contributor's copies; $5 charge for extras.
Terms: Acquires one-time rights. No reading fee, but "would prefer a subscription first."
Advice: "Trends in fiction change frequently. Right now the trend is toward slick, modern pieces with very little regional or ethnic material appearing in print. The pendulum will swing the other way again, and there will be a space for that kind of fiction. It seems to me there is always a chance to have really good writing published, somewhere. Keep writing and keep trying the markets. Diligent writing and rewriting can perfect your art. Be sure to study the market. Do not send me a slick piece of writing set in New York City, for example, with no idea on your part of the kinds of things I am interested in seeing. It is a waste of your time and money. Get a sample copy, or subscribe to the publication, study it carefully, then send your material."

ARARAT QUARTERLY, (IV), Ararat Press, AGBU., 585 Saddle River Rd., Saddle Brook NJ 07662. (201)797-7600. Editor: Dr. Leo Hamalian. Magazine: 8½×11; 72 pages; illustrations and b&w photographs. "*Ararat* is a forum for the literary and historical works of Armenian intellectuals or non-Armenian writers writing about Armenian subjects."
Needs: Condensed/excerpted novel, contemporary, historical (general), humor/satire, literary, religious/inspirational, translations. Publishes special fiction issue. Receives 25 unsolicited mss/month. Buys 5 mss/issue; 20 mss/year. Length: 1,000 words average. Publishes short shorts. Length: 500 words. Also publishes literary essays, literary criticism, poetry. Sometimes critiques rejected mss and recommends other markets.
How to Contact: Send complete ms with cover letter. Reports in 1 month on queries; 3 weeks on mss. SASE. Simultaneous and reprint submissions OK. Sample copy $7 and $1 postage. Free fiction guidelines. Reviews novels and short story collections.
Payment: Pays $40-75 plus 2 contributor's copies.
Terms: Pays on publication for one-time rights. Sends galleys to author.

ARCHAE, A Paleo-literary Review, (II), Cloud Mountain Press, 10 Troilus, Old Bridge NJ 08857-2724. (908)679-8373. Editor: Alan Davis Drake. Magazine: 7×8½; 50-70 pages; illustrations. "For a literary, anthropological, general audience." Semiannually. Estab. 1990. Circ. 425.
Needs: Contemporary, experimental, historical, humor/satire, literary, mainstream, prose poem, translations. "No confessional material." Receives 8-10 unsolicited fiction mss/week. Accepts 1-2 mss/issue; 2-4 mss/year. Publishes mss 2-3 months after acceptance. Length: 3,000-6,000 words preferred; 8,000 words maximum. Publishes short shorts. Length: 500 words. Also publishes literary essays, criti-

cism, poetry. Occasionally critiques or comments on rejected mss and recommends other markets.
How to Contact: Query first. Reports in 2 days on queries; in 1-2 weeks on mss. SASE. Simultaneous submissions OK. Accepts electronic submissions. Sample copy for $7, 8×9 SAE and 4 first-class stamps. Fiction guidelines for #10 SAE and 1 first-class stamp. Make checks payable to "Alan Drake." Reviews novels and short story collections.
Payment: Pays in contributor's copies.
Terms: Aquires first North American serial rights. Sends pre-publication galleys to author.

ARGONAUT, (II, IV), Box 4201, Austin TX 78765-4201. Editor: Michael Ambrose. Magazine: 5⅜×8½; 60 pages; 60 lb. paper; coated cover stock; illustrations. *"Argonaut* is primarily a science fiction magazine. Our readers want original, literate, unusual stories with a strong science fiction or weird element." Semi-annually. Estab. 1972. Circ. 500.
   ● The editor says he's now almost exclusively looking for science fiction—especially hard sf—as opposed to horror or fantasy.
Needs: Science fiction (especially hard science) and weird fantasy. Receives 40-50 unsolicited fiction mss each month. Acquires 5-8 mss/issue. Recently published work by John Alfred Taylor, Ardath Mayhar, Ken Wisman and Denis Tiani. Length: 2,500-7,500 words. Also publishes poetry. Sometimes recommends other markets.
How to Contact: Send complete ms with SASE. "Cover letter OK but not necessary." Reports in 1-2 months. "We do not consider simultaneous submissions or reprints." Sample copy for $4.95. Guidelines available for #10 SASE.
Payment: Pays 3 or more copies. Extras at 50% discount.
Terms: Acquires first North American serial rights.
Advice: "We are not interested in heroic or 'high' fantasy, horror, or media-derived stories. Our main focus is upon science fiction, particularly of the 'hard' variety, although we also publish weird fantasy of a highly original, unusual nature. We are looking above all for a *good story* with credible characters. Too often, a writer will forget these basics in building up the idea."

ARNAZELLA, (II), English Department, Bellevue Community College, Bellevue WA 98007. (206)641-2373. Advisor: Laura Burns Lewis. Editors change each year; contact advisor. Magazine: 5×6; 104 pages, 70 lb. paper; heavy coated cover; illustrations and photos. "For those interested in quality fiction." Annually. Estab. 1976. Circ. 500.
Needs: Adventure, contemporary, ethnic, experimental, fantasy, feminist, gay, historical, humor/satire, lesbian, literary, mainstream, prose poem, regional, suspense/mystery, translations. Submit in fall and winter for issue to be published in spring. Published new writers within the last year. Publishes short shorts. Also publishes literary essays and poetry. *Preference may be given to local contributors.*
How to Contact: Send complete ms with cover letter. Reports on mss in spring. "The months of June through October are very hard for us to read mss because we have no staff at that time. The best times to submit are October through January." SASE. No simultaneous submissions. Sample copy for $5. Guidelines for SASE.
Payment: Pays in contributor's copies.
Terms: Acquires first rights.
Advice: "Read this and similar magazines, reading critically and analytically."

ARTEMIS, An Art/Literary Publication from the Blue Ridge and Virginia, (IV), Box 8147, Roanoke VA 24014. (703)365-4326. Editor: Dan Gribbin. Magazine: 8×8; 85 pages; heavy/slick paper; colored cover stock; illustrations; photos. "We publish poetry, art and fiction of the highest quality and will consider any artist/writer who lives or has lived in the Blue Ridge or Virginia. General adult audience with literary interest." Annually. Estab. 1976. Circ. 2,000.
Needs: Literary. Wants to see "the best contemporary style." Receives 50 unsolicited fiction mss/year. Accepts 3-4 mss/issue. Does not read mss Jan.-Aug. Publishes ms 4-5 months after acceptance. Published works by Rosanne Coggeshall, Jeanne Larsen, Kurt Rheinheimer; published work by new writers within the last year. Length: 1,500 words average; 2,500 words maximum. Also publishes poetry.

Check the Category Indexes, located at the back of the book, for publishers interested in specific fiction subjects.

How to Contact: Submit 2 copies of unpublished ms between Sept. 15-Nov. 15, name, address and phone on title page only. Reports in 2 months. SASE for ms. No simultaneous submissions. Sample copy $6.50.
Payment: Pays 1 complimentary copy.
Terms: Acquires first rights.
Advice: "We look for polished quality work that holds interest, has imagination, energy, voice."

ARTFUL DODGE, (II), Department of English, College of Wooster, Wooster OH 44691. (216)263-2000. Editor-in-Chief: Daniel Bourne. Magazine: 150-200 pages; illustrations; photos. "There is no theme in this magazine, except literary power. We also have an ongoing interest in translations from Eastern Europe and elsewhere." Annually. Estab. 1979. Circ. 1,000.
Needs: Experimental, literary, prose poem, translations. "We judge by literary quality, not by genre. We are especially interested in fine English translations of significant contemporary prose writers." Receives 40 unsolicited fiction mss/month. Accepts 5 mss/year. Recently published fiction by Edward Klein Schmidt, Sesshu Foster and Zbigniew Herbert; and interviews with Tim O'Brien, Lee Smith and Stuart Dybek; published 2 new writers within the last year. Length: 10,000 words maximum; 2,500 words average. Also publishes literary essays, literary criticism, poetry. Occasionally critiques rejected mss.
How to Contact: Send complete ms with SASE. Do not send more than 30 pages at a time. Reports in 3-4 months. Sample copies of older, single issues are $2.75 or five issues for $5; recent issues are double issues, available for $5.75. Fiction guidelines for #10 SAE and 1 first class stamp.
Payment: Pays 2 contributor's copies and small honorarium.
Terms: Acquires first North American serial rights.
Advice: "If we take time to offer criticism, do not subsequently flood us with other stories no better than the first. If starting out, get as many readers, good ones, as possible. Above all, read contemporary fiction and the magazine you are trying to publish in."

ART:MAG, (II), P.O. Box 70896, Las Vegas NV 89170. (702)734-8121. Editor: Peter Magliocco. Magazine: 5½ × 8½; 60 pages; 20 lb. bond paper; b&w pen and ink illustrations and photographs. Publishes "irreverent, literary-minded work by committed writers," for "small press, 'quasi-art-oriented' " audience. Estab. 1984. Circ. under 500.
Needs: Condensed/excerpted novel, confession, contemporary, erotica, ethnic, experimental, fantasy, feminist, gay, historical (general), horror, humor/satire, lesbian, literary, mainstream, mystery/suspense, prose poem, psychic/supernatural/occult, regional, science fiction, translations and arts. No "slick-oriented stuff published by major magazines." Receives 1 plus ms/month. Accepts 1-2 mss/issue; 4-5 mss/year. Will read only between July and October. Publishes ms within 3-6 months of acceptance. Recently published work by James Purdy, Alan Catlin, and Robin Merle. "Collaborated with *Gypsy* magazine (90) to feature fiction from various authors; similar future projects are possible." Length: 2,000 words preferred; 250 words minimum; 3,000 words maximum. Also publishes literary essays "if relevant to aesthetic preferences," literary criticism "occasionally," poetry. Sometimes critiques rejected mss and recommends other markets.
How to Contact: Send complete ms with cover letter. Reports in 3 months. SASE for ms. Simultaneous submissions OK. Sample copy for $2.50, 6×9 SAE and 79¢ postage. Fiction guidelines for #10 SAE and first class stamp.
Payment: Pays contributor's copies.
Terms: Acquires one-time rights.
Advice: "Seeking more novel and quality-oriented work, usually from solicited authors. Magazine fiction today needs to be concerned with the issues of fiction writing itself—not just with a desire to publish or please the largest audience. Think about things in the fine art world as well as the literary one and keep the hard core of life in between."

ASYLUM ANNUAL, (II), (formerly *Asylum*), P.O. Box 6203, Santa Maria CA 93456. Editor: Greg Boyd. Magazine: 8½ × 11; 160 pages; 10 pt. C1S cover. "For a literary audience." Annually. Estab. 1985. Circ. 2,000.
Needs: Contemporary, erotica, experimental, literary, prose poem, translations. "We have published a 'best of' fiction collection entitled: *Unscheduled Departures: The Asylum Anthology of Short Fiction*." Receives 100 unsolicited mss/month. Accepts 25 mss/issue; 25 mss/year. Publishes ms 6-18 months after acceptance. Agented fiction 1%. Publishes short shorts. Also publishes literary criticism, poetry. Rarely critiques rejected mss or recommends other markets.

How to Contact: Send complete ms with cover letter. Reports in 1-4 weeks on queries; 1-4 months on mss. SASE. No simultaneous submissions. Sample copy for $8. Reviews a limited number of novels and short story collections each year.

Payment: Pays contributor's copies.

Terms: Acquires first rights. Sends galleys to author.

Advice: "Short, tightly written prose fiction and prose poems stand the best chance of gaining acceptance in *Asylum Annual*. Writers should read the magazine before submitting work."

‡**THE ASYMPTOTICAL WORLD (II)**, Box 1372, Williamsport PA 17703. Editor: Michael H. Gerardi. Magazine: 8½ × 11; 54 pages; glossy paper; illustrated cover; b&w illustrations. *"The Asymptotical World* is a *unique* collection of psychodramas, fantasies, poems and illustrations which elucidates the moods and sensations of the world created in the mind of men, for 18 year olds and older; those who enjoy work completed in style and mood similar to Poe." Annually. Estab. 1984. Circ. 1,300.

Needs: Experimental, fantasy, horror, psychic/supernatural/occult. Receives 30 unsolicited fiction mss/month. Buys 10 fiction mss/issue. Publishes ms 6 months to 1 year after acceptance. Length: 1,000 words minimum; 2,000 words maximum.

How to Contact: Query first. SASE. Reports in 1-2 months on queries; 1-2 months on mss. Simultaneous submissions OK. Sample copy $6.95 with SAE and 8 first class stamps. Fiction guidelines for 4x9 SAE and 1 first class stamp.

Payment: Pays $20-50.

Terms: Pays on publication. Buys first rights.

Advice: *"The Asymptotical World* is definitely unique. It is strongly suggested that a writer review a copy of the magazine to study the format of a psychodrama and the manner in which the plot is left 'open-ended.' The writer will need to study the atmosphere, mood and plot of published psychodramas before preparing a feature work."

ATALANTIK, (II, IV), 7630 Deer Creek Drive, Worthington OH 43085. (614)885-0550. Editor: Prabhat K. Dutta. Editors change each year. Magazine: 8½ × 11; approx. 80 pages; paper quality and cover stock vary; illustrations and photos. "The publication is bilingual: Indian (Bengali) and English language. This was started to keep the Indian language alive to the Indian immigrants. This contains short stories, poems, essays, sketches, book reviews, cultural news, children's pages, etc." Quarterly. Estab. 1980. Circ. 400.

Needs: Adventure, condensed novel, contemporary, ethnic, experimental, historical (general), humor/satire, juvenile (5-9 years), literary, mainstream, mystery/suspense, psychic/supernatural/occult, romance (romantic suspense), science fiction (hard science), translations, travelogue, especially to India. No politics and religion. Plans special issues, upcoming themes: "Family Values"; "India"; "Changing World"; "Education." Receives 15 unsolicited fiction mss/month. Publishes about 2-4 fiction mss/issue; about 20-50 mss/year. Publishes ms an average of at least 6 months after acceptance. Length: 2,000-5,000 words average. Publishes short shorts. Length: 1-2 pages. Also publishes literary essays, literary criticism, poetry. Sometimes comments on rejected mss and recommends other markets.

How to Contact: Query with clips of published work or send complete ms with cover letter; "author's bio data and a synopsis of the literary piece(s)." Reports on queries in 1 month; on mss in 4 months. SASE. Simultaneous submissions OK. Sample copy $6; fiction guidelines for #10 SASE. Reviews novels and short story collections.

Payment: Pays in contributor's copies; charge for extras.

Terms: Acquires all rights. Sponsors contests for fiction writers.

Advice: "A short story has to be short and should have a story too. A completely imaginative short story without any real life linkage is almost impossible. The language should be lucid and characters kept to a small number. A short story is not simply the description of an incident. It goes far beyond, far deeper. It should present the crisis of a single problem. Usually a successful short story contains a singular idea which is developed to its most probable conclusion in a uniquely charted path. A smaller version of *Atalantik* is managed by Keshab K. Dulta (36B, Bakul Bagan Rd., Calcutta 700025, India), for distribution in India and other Asian countries."

‡**THE ATAVACHRON AND ALL OUR YESTERDAYS, (IV)**, U.S.S. Resolution, Box 6501, Victoria, B.C. V8P 5M4 Canada. (604)721-0682. Editor: Alister Craig. Magazine: 8½ × 11; 60-120 pages; 20 lb. new paper; 20 lb. card stock cover; illustrations; photos. "For Star Trek fans of all ages." Quarterly (*The Atavachron*); Annually (*All Our Yesterdays*). Estab. 1985. Circ. 250.

Needs: Science fiction: Star Trek. "No gay or KS (Kirk and Spock) stories." Publishes annual special fiction issue. Receives 2 unsolicited mss/month. Accepts 3 mss/issue; 11 mss/year. Publishes ms 2-6 months after acceptance. Published work by John Herbert, Jeffrey Taylor, David Gordon-MacDonald. Length: 10,000 words average; 25,000 words maximum. Publishes short shorts. Sometimes critiques rejected mss and recommends other markets.
How to Contact: Send complete manuscript and cover letter with background on author. Reports in 3 weeks. SASE. Simultaneous and reprint submissions OK. Sample copy $1.50 for *Atavachron*, $5 (Canadian) for *All Our Yesterdays*. Fiction guidelines for $1 (Canadian).
Payment: Pays in contributor's copies.
Terms: Acquires one-time rights.

‡**ATHENA INCOGNITO MAGAZINE (II)**, 1442 Judah St., San Francisco CA 94122. (415)665-0219. Editor: Ronn Rosen. Magazine: 8½×11; approximately 30-40 pages; illustrations; Xeroxed photos. "Open-format magazine with emphasis on experimental and/or any type of quality writing. Emphasis on poetry and experimental artwork especially." Quarterly. Estab. 1980. Circ. 100.
Needs: Any subjects OK. Receives 15 unsolicited mss/month. Publishes ms usually 2-3 months after acceptance. Requires magazine subscription "to cover postage and expense of publication" of $4 (for 1 issue) before reading ms. Published new writers within the last year. Publishes short shorts. No long pieces over 2 pages. Sometimes critiques rejected mss.
How to Contact: Send complete ms with cover letter. Reports in 2 weeks to 1 month. SASE. Simultaneous and reprint submissions OK. Sample copy for $4; fiction guidelines for SAE and 1 first class stamp.
Payment: Pays in contributor's copies.
Terms: Acquires all rights. Publication not copyrighted.
Advice: "Experiment and practice eclecticism of all kinds! Discover! Pioneer! Dada lives!"

‡**THE ATLANTEAN PRESS REVIEW, (II)**, 354 Tramway Dr., Milpitas CA 95035. (408)262-8478. Editor: P. LeChevalier. Magazine: 7½×7½; 125 pages; book stock paper; 10 pt CIS cover; black and white illustrations and photographs. "*The Atlantean Press Review* publishes work in the school of Romantic-Realism: stories that are carefully plotted and have strong, heroic characters whose values drive the story." Annually. Estab. 1992. Circ. 300.
Needs: Adventure, literary, mainstream/contemporary, mystery/suspense (private eye/hard boiled, amateur sleuth), science fiction (if realistic), sports, translations, westerns. "Not interested in ethnic stories—we look for *universal* values." Receives 3 mss/month. Buys 8-10 mss/year. Does not read mss March-July. Publishes ms 5 months after acceptance. Recently published work by Edward Cline, Andrew Bernstein, Bill Bucko. Length: 5,000 words average; 2,000 words minimum; 10,000 words maximum. Also publishes literary essays, literary criticism, poetry. Often critiques rejected mss.
How to Contact: Query first. Should include estimated word count and one-page bio with submission. "Tell us your purpose and ambitions in writing." Reports in 3 weeks on queries; 2 months on mss. Send SASE (IRC) for reply, return of ms or send a disposable copy of the ms. Simultaneous, reprint and electronic submissions OK. Sample copy for $12, #10 SAE and 1 first class stamp or IRC.
Payment: Pays $15-100, plus 5 contributor's copies.
Terms: Pays on publication for first North American serial rights or one-time rights. Sends galleys to author.
Advice: Looks for "clarity, originality, logic, strong plot, heroic characters. It should be clear that you spent much longer *planning* the story than drafting it. Read *Atlas Shrugged*, *Quo Vadis*, *Shane* and Victor Hugo. Study a sample copy. Digest Rand's *The Romantic Manifesto*."

ATLANTIS, A Women's Studies Journal, (IV), Institute for the Study of Women, Mt. St. Vincent University, Halifax, Nova Scotia B3M 2J6 Canada. (902)457-6319. Editor: Deborah C. Poff. Some editors change every two years. Magazine: 7½×9½; 170-200 pages; recycled paper; glossy cover stock; b&w illustrations and photos. "Interdisciplinary women's studies journal, accepts original research and some fiction in French and English for academics and researchers interested in feminism." Semi-annually. Estab. 1975. Circ. 800.
   • This is a scholarly feminist journal with little space for fiction. Preference is given to Canadian authors.
Needs: Feminist research and creative work (short stories, poetry, etc.). Receives 10 unsolicited fiction mss/month. Accepts 1-2 mss/year. Publishes ms 3-6 months after acceptance. Publishes short shorts. Also publishes literary criticism, poetry. Critiques rejected mss.

How to Contact: Send complete ms with cover letter. No simultaneous submissions. Current issue for $10; back issue for $7.50 (Canadian). Occasionally reviews novels and short story collections. Send books to Managing Editor.
Payment: Pays 1 contributor's copy.
Advice: "We welcome and have published work by previously unpublished writers."

ATROCITY, Publication of the Absurd Sig of Mensa, (I), 2419 Greensburg Pike, Pittsburgh PA 15221. Editor: Hank Roll. Newsletter: 8½×11; 8 pages; offset 20 lb. paper and cover; illustrations; photographs occasionally. Humor and satire for "high IQ-Mensa" members. Monthly. Estab. 1976. Circ. 250.
Needs: Humor/satire. Liar's Club, parody, jokes, funny stories, comments on the absurdity of today's world. Receives 20 unsolicited mss/month. Accepts 2 mss/issue. Publishes ms 3-6 months after acceptance. Published new writers within the last year. Length: 50-150 words preferred; 650 words maximum.
How to Contact: Send complete ms. "No cover letter necessary if ms states what rights (e.g. first North American serial/reprint, etc.) are offered." Reports in 1 month. SASE. Simultaneous and reprint submissions OK. Sample copy for 50¢, #10 SAE and 2 first class stamps. Reviews novels and short story collections—"humor only."
Payment: Pays contributor's copies.
Terms: Acquires one-time rights.
Advice: Manuscript should be single-spaced, copy ready. Horizontal format to fit on one 8½×11 sheet. "Be funny."

AURA Literary/Arts Review, (II), University of Alabama at Birmingham, Box 76, University Center, Birmingham AL 35294. (205)934-3216. Editor: Zelda Harris. Magazine: 6×9; 150 pages; b&w illustrations and photos. "We publish various types of fiction with an emphasis on short stories. Our audience is college students, the university community and literary-minded adults, the arts community." Semiannually. Estab. 1974. Circ. 1,000.
Needs: Literary, contemporary, science fiction, regional, romance, men's, women's, feminist and ethnic. No mss longer than 7,000-8,000 words. Acquires 3-4 mss/issue. Receives 30-50 unsolicited fiction mss each month. Published works by Nickell Romjue, Josephine Marshall, Rodolfo Tomes; published new writers within the last year. Length: 2,000-8,000 words. Publishes short shorts; length according to editor's decision. Also publishes literary essays, literary criticism, poetry. Critiques rejected mss when there is time.
How to Contact: Send complete ms with SASE. No simultaneous submissions; please include biographical information. Reports in 3 months. Sample copy $2.50. "Occasionally" reviews novels and short story collections.
Payment: Pays 2 contributor's copies.
Terms: Acquires first North American serial rights.
Advice: "We welcome experimental or traditional literature on any subject."

THE AZOREAN EXPRESS, (I, IV), Seven Buffaloes Press, Box 249, Big Timber MT 59011. Editor: Art Cuelho. Magazine: 6¾×8¼; 32 pages; 60 lb. book paper; 3-6 illustrations/issue; photos rarely. "My overall theme is rural; I also focus on working people (the sweating professions); the American Indian and Hobo; the Dustbowl era; and I am also trying to expand with non-rural material. For rural and library and professor/student, blue collar workers, etc." Semiannually. Estab. 1985. Circ. 600.
 • *Azorean Express* is published by Art Cuelho of Seven Buffaloes. He also publishes *Black Jack Hill and Holler* and *Valley Grapevine* listed in this book. See also his listing for the press.
Needs: Contemporary, ethnic, experimental, humor/satire, literary, regional, western, rural, working people. Receives 10-20 unsolicited mss/month. Accepts 2-3 mss/issue; 4-6 mss/year. Publishes ms 1-6 months after acceptance. Length: 1,000-3,000 words. Also publishes short shorts, 500-1,000 words. "I take what I like; length sometimes does not matter, even when longer than usual. I'm flexible." Sometimes recommends other markets.
How to Contact: "Send cover letter with ms; general information, but it can be personal, more in line with the submitted story. Not long rambling letters." Reports in 1-4 weeks. SASE. Sample copy for $5.75. Fiction guidelines for SASE.

Payment: Pays in contributor's copies. "Depends on the amount of support author gives my press."
Terms: Acquires first North American serial rights. "If I decide to use material in anthology form later, I have that right." Sends pre-publication galleys to the author upon request.
Advice: "There would not be magazines like mine if I was not optimistic. But literary optimism is a two-way street. Without young fiction writers supporting fiction magazines the future is bleak, because the commercial magazines allow only formula or name writers within their pages. My own publications receive no grants. Sole support is from writers, libraries and individuals."

BABY SUE, (I), Box 1111, Decatur GA 30031-1111. (404)875-8951. Editor: Don W. Seven. Magazine: 8½×11; 20 pages; illustrations and photos. "*Baby Sue* is a collection of music reviews, poetry, short fiction and cartoons," for "anyone who can think and is not easily offended." Biannually. Plans special fiction issue. Estab. 1983. Circ. 1,500.
● Sometimes funny, very often perverse, this 'zine featuring mostly cartoons and "comix" definitely is not for the easily offended.
Needs: Erotica, experimental and humor/satire. Receives 5-10 mss/month. Accepts 3-4 mss/year. Publishes ms within 3 months of acceptance. Publishes short shorts. Length: 1-2 single-spaced pages.
How to Contact: Query with clips of published work. SASE. Simultaneous submissions OK.
Payment: Pays 1 contributor's copy.
Advice: "If no one will print your work, start your own publication—it's easy and cheap. It's also a great way to make contact with other people all over the world who are doing the same."

BAD HAIRCUT, (II), #4, 1055 Adams St. SE, Olympia WA 98501-1443. Editors: Ray Goforth, Kim Goforth. Magazine: 5½×8½; 30 pages; illustrations. Published irregularly. Estab. 1987. Circ. 1,000.
Needs: Experimental, humor/satire, prose poem, translations, political, world-conscious. Receives 20 fiction ms/month. Accepts 1-3 mss/issue; 4-12 mss/year. Publishes short shorts. Also publishes literary essays, poetry. Almost always critiques rejected mss and recommends other markets.
How to Contact: Query with or without clips of published work; send complete ms with cover letter; or "send by special messenger." Reports in 1 week on queries; 2 months on mss. SASE. Simultaneous and reprint submissions OK. Sample copy for $4. Fiction guidelines for #10 SAE and 1 first class stamp.
Payment: Pays subscription to magazine or contributor's copies; charge for extras. Payment "depends on our financial state."
Terms: Acquires first North American serial rights. Rights revert to author.
Advice: "We focus exclusively upon politics, human rights and environmental issues. Always include a nice cover letter describing who you are and why you're sending your stuff to us."

BAHLASTI PAPERS, The Newsletter of the Kali Lodge, O.T.O., (I), P.O. Box 15038, New Orleans LA 70115. (504)899-7439. Editor: Soror Chén. Newsletter: 8½×11; 12 pages; 20 lb. paper; 20 lb. cover; 2 illustrations; occasional photographs. "Occult, mythological, artistic, alternative and political material for the lunatic fringe." Monthly. Estab. 1986. Circ. 200.
Needs: Condensed/excerpted novel, erotica, ethnic, experimental, fantasy, feminist, gay, horror, humor/satire, lesbian, literary, psychic/supernatural/occult, science fiction, serialized novel, "however our emphasis is on the occult. We do not publish poetry." Plans special compilation issues. Receives 5 unsolicited mss/month. Accepts 2 mss/issue; 24 mss/year. Publishes mss approx. 1 month after acceptance. Recently published work by Nancy Collins, Steve Canon and Darius James. Publishes short shorts. Also publishes literary essays, literary criticism.
How to Contact: Send complete ms with cover letter telling "why author is interested in being published in *Bahlasti Papers*." Reports in 2 weeks on queries and 1 month on mss. SASE. Simultaneous and reprint submissions OK. Sample copy for $2.25 with #10 envelope and 2 first class stamps. Occasionally reviews novels and short story collections.
Payment: Pays subscription to magazine.
Terms: Publication not copyrighted.
Advice: "We look for the odd point-of-view; the individual; independence of thought; work which breaks down established archetypes and so liberates us from social programming."

BAKUNIN, P.O. Box 1853, Simi Valley CA 93062-1853. Editor: Jordan Jones. Magazine: 5½×8½; 96 pages; acid-free paper; b&w high contrast illustrations; half-tone photographs. "A magazine for the dead Russian anarchist in all of us. We are looking for well-written stories and do not pre-judge themes or styles. For a literary, counter-culture audience." Semiannually. Estab. 1990. Circ. 500.
● For a look at this publication, you may want to check out their special March 1993 issue on

the Los Angeles "uprising." *Bakunin* often includes works of social commentary.
Needs: Confession, erotica, ethnic, experimental, feminist, gay, lesbian, literary, prose poem, serialized novel, translations (translators must submit proof of their right to translate that author's work.) "No formula fiction." Receives 45 unsolicited mss/month. Accepts 6-8 mss/issue; 12-16 mss/year. Usually publishes ms within 6 months after acceptance. Published work of Harold Jaffe, Mark Wisniewski, Barbara Jamison. Length: 2,000 words or less preferred; 4,000 words maximum. Publishes short shorts. Sometimes critiques rejected mss and recommends other markets.
How to Contact: Send complete ms with cover letter. Cover letter should include short biographical note. Reports in 2 weeks to 3 months on mss. SASE. Simultaneous submissions (if noted) OK. Accepts electronic submissions via disk (IBM-DOS (high-density) or Macintosh format). Sample copy for $5. Fiction guidelines for #10 SAE and 1 first class stamp.
Payment: Pays 2 contributor's copies.
Terms: Acquires first North American serial rights.
Advice: "We are looking for well-written work. Much of the work we accept is humorous and/or anti-establishment."

BAMBOO RIDGE, The Hawaii Writers' Quarterly, (II, IV), P.O. Box 61781, Honolulu HI 96839-1781. (808)599-4823. Editors: Darrell Lum and Eric Chock. "Writing that reflects the multicultural diversity of Hawaii." Published 2-4 times/year. Estab. 1978.
● Devoted to featuring the work of Hawaiian writers, *Bamboo Ridge* also operates the Bamboo Ridge Press also listed in this book.
Needs: Ethnic, literary, Hawaii interest. "Writers need not be from Hawaii, but must reflect Hawaii's multicultural ethnic mix." Publishes annual special fiction and poetry issues (special collections by single authors). Publishes ms 6 months-1 year after acceptance. Length: up to 25 typed pages, double-spaced. Publishes short shorts.
How to Contact: Query first. Reports in 1 month on queries; 3-6 months on mss. SASE. Photocopied submissions OK. Fiction guidelines for #10 SAE and 1 first class stamp.
Payment: Pays 2 contributor's copies, small honorarium and 1 year subscription depending on grant money. Charges for extras (40% discount).
Terms: Pays on publication for first North American serial rights.

BARDIC RUNES, (IV), 424 Cambridge St, Ottawa, Ontario K1S 4H5 Canada. (613)231-4311. Editor: Michael McKenny. Magazine. Estab. 1990.
Needs: Fantasy. "Traditional or high fantasy. Story should be set in pre-industrial society either historical or of author's invention." Length: 3,500 words or less.
Payment: Pays ½¢/word.
Terms: Pays on acceptance.

‡THE BARRELHOUSE, An Excursion Into the Unknown, (I, IV), 1600 Oak Creek Dr., Edmond OK 73034. Editor: Doug Coulson. Magazine: 7×8½; 50-70 pages; 20 lb. white paper; 60 lb. gloss cover; 8-12 illustrations. "*The Barrelhouse*, essentially a science fiction, fantasy and horror magazine, also publishes existentialist works, experimentation, satire, speculative mainstream, as well as articles, others, to interest an intelligent audience seeking imaginative outlooks and alternative viewpoints. An artistic magazine." Quarterly. Estab. 1992. Circ. 500.
Needs: Adventure, erotica, ethnic/multicultural, experimental, fantasy (science fantasy, sword and sorcery), historical (general), horror, humor/satire, literary, mainstream/contemporary, mystery/suspense (private eye/hard-boiled, amateur sleuth, police procedural) psychic/supernatural/occult, science fiction (hard science, soft/sociological), translations. "Speculative mainstream is excellent, surrealism well-done always in demand, too. Intelligent plots. No romance, westerns, amateur fluff, overtly religious materials." List of upcoming themes available for SASE. Plans special fiction issues/anthologies in future. Receives 30-50 unsolicited mss/month. Buys 5-10 mss/issue; 25-30 mss/year. Publishes ms 6-12 months after acceptance. Agented fiction 2%. Recently published work by Darnbrook Colson, William Marden, D. Douglas Graham. Length: 2,000-3,000 words average. Publishes short shorts. Length: 200-500 words. Also publishes literary essays, literary criticism and poetry. Sometimes critiques or comments on rejected mss.
How to Contact: Send complete ms with a cover letter. Should include estimated word count, bio (20-50 words), Social Security number and list of publications. Reports in 1 month on queries; 3 months on mss. Send SASE for reply, return of ms or a disposable copy of ms. Simultaneous and reprint submissions OK. Accepts electronic (disk) submissions; ASCII formatted 3.5" discs. Sample

copy for $2.50; fiction guidelines for #10 SAE and 1 first class stamp. Reviews novels and short story collections.

Payment: Pays $2-25, 2 contributor's copies; additional copies at a reduced rate of $2.

Terms: Pays ½ on acceptance, ½ on publication. Buys first North American serial rights, one-time rights, reprint rights, second (serial). Not copyrighted. Sponsors contests. Request guidelines to contests with SASE.

Advice: "We use new and established writers, and are seeking well-written, strange manuscripts, with an intelligent sensibility to them. Originality always a must. Do not try to impress us with gratuitous sex, violence. We are especially interested in experimentation, speculative mainstream, surrealism, and sharp imagery within traditional genre contexts. New writers should study everything from classics to moderns, purchase sample copies of several top magazines that interest them, then submit. Never reveal plot in a cover note to a magazine market! Not only does it damage your chances at acceptance, it also damages an editor's ability to accurately judge and comment on a manuscript's merits. Interested especially in good, intelligent SCI FI, with a hard science orientation, also speculative mainstream (William Golding's *Lord of the Flies*, Joseph Conrad's *Heart of Darkness*, etc.) and quality satire in a context similar to Kurt Vonnegut, Jr., Anthony Burgess' *A Clockwork Orange*."

BEING, A Celebration of Spirit, Mind & Body, (I, II, IV), M. Talarico Publications, P.O. Box 417, Oceanside CA 92049-0417. (619)722-8829. Editor: Marjorie E. Talarico. Magazine: Digest-sized; 40-50 pages; "desk-top published;" vellum cover; black-and-white, pen-and-ink illustrations. "General and New Age short stories, poems and articles for those interested in the correlation of spirit, mind and body to the culmination of being." Bimonthly. Estab. 1989. Circ. 350.

Needs: New Age, reincarnation, pagan, homeopathic/holistic health, fantasy, horror, prose poem, psychic/supernatural/occult, religious/inspirational, shamanism. "Looking for New Age fairy tales/fantasy for children. Length: 500 to 2,500 words. Also need articles on tarot, astrology, magick for a better life, herbs, past and future lives, psychic/metaphysical/occult experiences. No AIDS, drugs or porno stories." Upcoming themes: "Soulmates/Pure Love Issue" (looking for short stories with "lovers throughout eternities"; up to 2,500 words; deadline May 1993); "Reincarnation Short Stories/Poems" with upbeat stories of incarnations; up to 3,500 words; deadline August 1993; "Angels Above & Below," poems about angels (guardian and otherwise); up to 2,500 words; deadline November 1993. Receives 100 unsolicited fiction mss/month. Accepts 6-10 mss/issue; 60 mss/year. Publishes mss 2-4 months after acceptance. Recently published work by Cleve Otis Hulsey, David Wooten, Debbie Bauman Rosenberg, Gurattan Khalsa. Length: 2,500 words preferred; 300 words minimum; 7,500 words maximum. Publishes short shorts. Length: 650 words. Also publishes literary essays, poetry. Sometimes critiques or comments on rejected mss and recommends other markets.

How to Contact: Send complete ms with cover letter. "I like to know a little bit about the author, credits (if any) and what prompted author to write this particular story." Reports in 10-12 weeks. SASE. Simultaneous and reprint submissions OK. Sample copy for $3.95, 7½ × 10¼ SAE. Fiction guidelines for #10 SAE and 1 first class stamp.

Payment: Pays in contributor's copies; charges for extras; ½ price for subscribers.

Terms: Acquires one-time rights.

Advice: Looks for "Originality! I like to see an author really bend their imagination and keep me wanting to turn the pages. (If there is artwork to go along, I would like to see it.)"

LA BELLA FIGURA, (I, II, IV), Box 411223, San Francisco CA 94141-1223. Editor: Rose Romano. Magazine: 8½ × 11; 10 pages. Publishes "work by Italian-American women, mostly about us. We now publish men also." Quarterly. Estab. 1988. Circ. 150.

Needs: Ethnic, feminist, lesbian, literary, prose poem, translations and Italian-American culture and heritage. "It is the purpose of *LBF* to provide a space for a much-neglected group of people. It is our space to share ourselves with each other and to help others understand us." Receives 10-15 mss/month. Accepts 1-2 mss/issue; 4-8 mss/year. Publishes ms within 3-6 months of acceptance. Published work by Maria Mazziotti Gillan, Rina Ferrarelli, Jennifer Lagier and Anna Bart. Length: about 5 double-spaced pages preferred. Publishes short shorts. Also publishes literary essays, poetry. Sometimes critiques rejected mss and recommends other markets.

How to Contact: Send complete ms with cover letter, which should include previous publications and any other credits. Reports within 4 months. SASE. No simultaneous submissions. Reprint submissions OK. Sample copy for $2. Reviews novels and short story collections.

Payment: Pays 3 contributor's copies; charge for extras.
Terms: Acquires one-time rights.
Advice: "There's not enough work by and about Italian-Americans published yet. The writer must find that space between stereotyped and assimilated. Although any good writing is considered, I'm most interested in work about Italian-American culture."

THE BELLETRIST REVIEW, (I, II), Marmarc Publications, Suite 290, 17 Farmington Ave., Plainville CT 06062. (203)793-9509. Editor: Marlene Dube. Fiction Editor: Marc Saegaert. Magazine: 8½×11; 50 pages; heavy paper; 90 lb. cover stock; illustrations. "We are interested in compelling, well-crafted short fiction in a variety of genres. Our title *Belletrist*, means 'lover of literature.' This magazine will appeal to an educated, adult audience that appreciates quality fiction." Semiannually.
• *The Belletrist Review* plans to offer a special fiction contest in September 1993. The award will be $200 – check with them for details.
Needs: Adventure, contemporary, erotica, horror (psychological), humor/satire, literary, mainstream, mystery/suspense, regional, science fiction (soft/sociological). "To give writers an idea of our eclectic tastes in fiction, we are inspired by the masters such as Poe, Chekhov, and O'Henry, and contemporary authors such as Richard Selzer, Ray Bradbury and Isaac Bashevis Singer." No fantasy, juvenile, westerns, or overblown horror or confessional pieces. Accepts 10-12 mss/issue; approximately 25 mss/year. Publishes ms within 1 year after acceptance. Length: 2,500-5,000 words preferred; 1,000 words minimum; 5,000 words maximum. Comments on or critiques rejected mss when time permits and recommends other markets on occasion.
How to Contact: Send complete ms with cover which should include brief biographical note and any previous publications. Reports in 1 month on queries; 2 months on mss. SASE. Simultaneous submissions OK. 1993 Fiction Contest Guidelines for SASE.
Payment: Pays contributor's copies.
Terms: Acquires one-time rights.
Advice: "In order to give your writing the consideration it deserves, please be sure your manuscript is neatly typed and professionally presented, and only submit one manuscript at a time. Don't tell us about the story or its merits in your cover letter; let us discover this for ourselves. Also, many submissions we receive tend to read more like a narration of an event than a story. Re-read your drafts aloud and cut, ruthlessly, anything that instead of furthering the plot, bogs it down with unnecessary detail."

BELLOWING ARK, A Literary Tabloid, (II), Box 45637, Seattle WA 98145. (206)545-8302. Editor: R.R. Ward. Tabloid: 11½×16; 28 pages; electro-brite paper and cover stock; illustrations; photos. "We publish material which we feel addresses the human situation in an affirmative way. We do not publish academic fiction." Bimonthly. Estab. 1984. Circ. 500.
• Work from *Bellowing Ark* appeared in the *Pushcart Prize* anthology in 1991. The editor says he's using much more short fiction these days. Remember he likes a traditional, narrative approach and "abhors" minimalist and post-modern work.
Needs: Contemporary, literary, mainstream, serialized/excerpted novel. "Anything we publish will be true." Receives 450-500 unsolicited fiction mss/year. Accepts 2-3 mss/issue; 12-18 mss/year. Time varies, but publishes ms not longer than 6 months after acceptance. Recently published work by Jon Remmerde, Shelly Uva and Robin Sterns; published new writers within the last year. Length: 3,000-5,000 words average. Publishes short shorts. Also publishes literary essays, literary criticism, poetry. Sometimes critiques rejected mss and recommends other markets.
How to Contact: No queries. Send complete ms with cover letter and short bio. "I always cringe when I see letters listing 'credits' and stating the 'rights' offered! Such delights indicate the impossible amateur. Many beginners address me by first name – few of my close friends do." No simultaneous submissions. Reports in 6 weeks on mss. SASE. Sample copy for $2, 9×12 SAE and 85¢ postage.
Payment: Pays in contributor's copies.
Terms: Acquires first rights.
Advice: "*Bellowing Ark* began as (and remains) an alternative to the despair and negativity of the Workshop/Academic poetry scene; we believe that life has meaning and is worth living – the work we publish reflects that belief. Learn how to tell a story before submitting. Avoid 'trick' endings – they have all been done before and better."

BELOIT FICTION JOURNAL, (II), Box 11, Beloit College WI 53511. (608)363-2308. Editor: Clint McCown. Magazine: 6×9; 130 pages; 60 lb. paper; 10 pt. C1S cover stock; illustrations and photos on cover. "We are interested in publishing the best contemporary fiction and are open to all themes except those involving pornographic, religiously dogmatic or politically propagandistic representations.

Close-up

Clint McCown
Editor
Beloit Fiction Journal

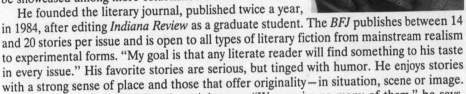

Clint McCown, editor of the *Beloit Fiction Journal*, feels the mission of his magazine is two-fold: to publish new writers and established ones who enjoy fewer outlets than ever in the commercial marketplace. "My heart lies in discovering new writers," says McCown, "but it's to their advantage to be showcased among more established talents."

He founded the literary journal, published twice a year, in 1984, after editing *Indiana Review* as a graduate student. The *BFJ* publishes between 14 and 20 stories per issue and is open to all types of literary fiction from mainstream realism to experimental forms. "My goal is that any literate reader will find something to his taste in every issue." His favorite stories are serious, but tinged with humor. He enjoys stories with a strong sense of place and those that offer originality—in situation, scene or image.

His least favorite? Childhood reminiscence. "We receive so many of them," he says, "and such stories usually sink under the weight of the author's nostalgia." Other pet peeves include stories that employ phonetic misspellings to suggest dialect and those written in sentence fragments. He also sees too many stories that suffer from "academic paper syndrome," meaning they are too neatly structured as introduction, body and conclusion. Too often, he finds writers summarizing and theorizing at the end of a story rather than trying to "strike the right note."

Though he publishes nearly 40 stories per year, McCown says the competition for space in the *BFJ* is very tough. He receives 50 stories per week. So a story might be better than 97 out of 100 and still not be taken. This situation is true at most literary magazines, but he feels writers should not give up. "The statistics might sound depressing, but an awareness of them can help the writer from feeling bad about piling up rejection slips," says McCown. "I've known of stories being rejected by 50 or more magazines before finally being snapped up by a first-rate publication. Most of the people we publish are people we've rejected on earlier occasions."

He advises writers to research the markets, to study the kinds of stories editors are publishing. "If you like what you see in a particular journal that might mean you share certain tastes with the editor, so send your stuff there first," he says.

Other than including an SASE, which he feels is crucial, McCown has few gripes or biases about the submission process. He doesn't even see the need for a cover letter as long as the writer includes name and address on the first page of the story. "I've never taken a story because of the cover letter, but I've been put off of stories by them," he says.

Even simultaneous submissions don't bother him. Writers can ill-afford to wait for a long time before a magazine responds. "My approach as an editor is that I'm on the side of the writer. I would rather see an editor lose a story than a writer lose a chance for publication."

—Jack Heffron

Our magazine is for general readership, though most of our readers will probably have a specific interest in literary magazines." Semiannually. Estab. 1985.

● Editor Clint McCown is featured as a Close-up in this book. Work first appearing in *Beloit Fiction Journal* has been reprinted in award-winning collections, including the *Flannery O'Connor* and the *Milkweed Fiction Prize* collections.

Needs: Contemporary, literary, mainstream, prose poem, spiritual and sports. No pornography, religious dogma, political propaganda. Receives 75 unsolicited fiction mss/month. Accepts 8-10 mss/issue; 16-20 mss/year. Replies take longer in summer. Publishes ms within 9 months after acceptance. Length: 5,000 words average; 250 words minimum; 10,000 words maximum. Sometimes critiques rejected mss and recommends other markets.

How to Contact: Send complete ms with cover letter. Reports in 1 week on queries; 1-6 weeks on mss. SASE for ms. Simultaneous submissions OK, if identified as such. Sample copy $5. Fiction guidelines for #10 envelope and 1 first class stamp.

Advice: "Many of our contributors are writers whose work we have previously rejected. Don't let one rejection slip turn you away from our—or any—magazine."

BEYOND . . . SCIENCE FICTION & FANTASY, (I, II, IV), Other Worlds Books, P.O. Box 136, New York NY 10024. (201)791-6721. Editor: Shirley Winston. Fiction Editor: Roberta Rogow. Magazine: 8½×11; 56 pages; illustrations. Science fiction and fantasy fiction, art and poetry. Audience is "mostly adults, some younger." Quarterly. Estab. 1985. Circ. 300.

Needs: Fantasy and science fiction (hard science, soft sociological). No pornography. Receives 100 unsolicited mss/month. Accepts 11 mss/issue; 44 mss/year. Publishes ms "up to 2 years after acceptance." Length: 5,000 words average; 500 words minimum; 12,000 words maximum. Publishes short shorts. Sometimes critiques rejected mss and recommends other markets.

How to Contact: Send complete ms with cover letter. Reports in 3-4 months. SASE. No simultaneous submissions. Sample copy for $4.50; fiction guidelines for SASE.

Payment: Pays ⅓¢ per word and contributor's copies.

Terms: Pays on publication for first North American serial rights.

BILINGUAL REVIEW, (II, IV), Hispanic Research Center, Arizona State University, Tempe AZ 85287. (602)965-3867. Editor-in-Chief: Gary D. Keller. Scholarly/literary journal of US Hispanic life: poetry, short stories, other prose and theater. Magazine: 7×10; 96 pages; 55 lb. acid-free paper; coated cover stock. Published 3 times/year. Estab. 1974. Circ. 2,000.

Needs: US Hispanic creative literature. "We accept material in English or Spanish. We publish original work only—no translations." US Hispanic themes only. Receives 50 unsolicited fiction mss/ month. Accepts 3 mss/issue; 9 mss/year. Publishes ms an average of 1 year after acceptance. Published work by Demetria Martínez, Alicia Gaspar de Alba, Tomás Rivera; published work of new writers within the last year. Also publishes literary criticism on US Hispanic themes and poetry. Often critiques rejected mss.

How to Contact: Send 2 copies of complete ms with SAE and loose stamps. Reports in 1 month. Simultaneous and high-quality photocopied submissions OK. Sample copy for $9. Reviews novels and short story collections.

Payment: Pays 2 contributor's copies. 30% discount for extras.

Terms: Acquires all rights (50% of reprint permission fee given to author as matter of policy).

Advice: "We do not publish literature about tourists in Latin America and their perceptions of the 'native culture.' We do not publish any fiction set in Latin America; we only publish works set in the United States."

‡THE BLACK HAMMOCK REVIEW, A Literary Quarterly, (I, II, IV), P.O. Box 1642, Oviedo FL 32765. (407)628-4014. Editor: Edward Anthony Nagel. Magazine: 8½×11; 40+ pages; 20 lb. paper; illustrations and photos. "*The Black Hammock Review* is published by Quantum Press, a Florida nonprofit cooperative. It was established to publish works which reflect rural motifs, for example, such settings as Oviedo, Geneva, Chuluota and the Black Hammock area in east-central Florida." Quarterly. Estab. 1992.

Needs: Ethnic/multicultural, experimental, fantasy (artistic), humor/satire, literary, mainstream/contemporary, psychic/supernatural/occult, regional, romance (contemporary), science fiction (soft/sociological), serialized novel, translations, "bucolic themes." Receives 10 unsolicited mss/month. Buys 4 mss/issue; 16+ mss/year. Publishes ms 3 months after acceptance. Length: 2,500 words preferred; 1,500 words minimum; 3,500 words maximum. Publishes short shorts. Length: 500 words. Also publishes literary essays, literary criticism and poetry. Always critiques or comments on returned mss.

How to Contact: Send complete ms with a cover letter. Should include bio (short), list of publications and brief statement of writer's artistic "goals." Reports in 2 weeks. Send SASE for reply, return of mss or a disposable copy of the ms. No simultaneous submissions. Sample copy for $4 and 8½ × 11 SAE. Reviews novels and short story collections.

Payment: *Charges membership fee $25 for individual; $50 for 3 writers.* Each member of the cooperative is assured publication of at least one carefully edited piece each year, subject to approval by our editors. Expenses not covered by the fees and subscriptions will be shared by the members, pro rata, not to exceed an amount fixed by the members, prior to the publication each quarter. Pays $50-75, subscription to the magazine and 6 contributor's copies. Additional copies at a reduced rate, $2.

Terms: Pays on publication for one-time rights.

Advice: Looks for "work that evokes in the reader's mind a vivid and continuous dream, vivid in that it has density, enough detail and the right detail, fresh with the author, and shows concern for the characters and the eternal verities. And continuous in that there are no distractions such as poor grammar, purple prose, diction shifts, or change in point of view. Short fiction that has a beginning, middle and end, organically speaking. Immerse yourself in the requested genre, format i.e., bucolic themes, work the piece over and over until it is 'right' for you, does what you want it to do; read the masters in your genre on a stylistic and technical level, begin to 'steal instead of borrow.' Transmute your emotions into the work and 'write short.' "

THE BLACK HOLE LITERARY REVIEW, (I), 1312 Stonemill Court, Cincinnati OH 45215. (513)821-6670. Editor: Wm. E. Allendorf. Electronic Bulletin Board. "This is an attempt to revolutionize publishing—no paper, no rejection slips, no deadlines. For any person with access to a home computer and a modem." Estab. 1989. Circ. 2,400+.

Needs: "Any or all fiction and nonfiction categories are acceptable. Any size, topic, or inherent bias is acceptable. The only limitation is that the writer will not mind having his piece read, and an honest critique given directly by his readership." Plans future hardcopy anthology. Publishes ms 1-2 days after acceptance. Length: 2,000-10,000 words. Publishes short shorts, poetry, essays. "Critique given if not by editor, then by readers through Email."

How to Contact: Upload as EMAIL to the editor. Cover letter should include "titles, description (abstract), copyright notice." Reports in 1-2 days. Simultaneous submissions OK.

Payment: Pays in royalties, but charges fee for initial inputting (see below).

Terms: Charges $5 minimum subscription. Submissions cost $.50+ (deducted from subscription). Royalties are accrued each time the piece is read. Contact editor for details. Buys one-time rights.

Advice: "If the concept of the electronic magazine goes over with the public, then the market for fiction is limitless. Any piece that an author has taken the trouble to set to print is worth publishing. However, *The Hole* is looking for writers that want to be read—not ones that just want to write. The electronic magazine is an interactive medium, and pieces are judged on their ability to inspire a person to read them." Writers interested in submitting should: "Do it. You would be the first to be rejected by *The Hole*, if we did not use your piece; to make matters easier for all concerned, submit your piece as a ASCII text file via the modem. If you do not have access to a home computer with a modem, buy one, borrow one, steal one. This is the wave of the future for writers."

‡BLACK ICE (IV), Campus Box 494, Boulder CO 80306. (303)492-8947. Editor: Mark Amerika. Magazine: 5½ × 8½; 100 pages; glossy cover; photography on cover. "Publishes the most experimental innovative writing being written today for writers, critics, sophisticated readers." Published 3 times/year. Estab. 1984. Circ. 700.

Needs: Experimental, literary, translations. Does not want to see "anything that's not ground-breaking." Receives 50-75 unsolicited mss/month. Accepts approx. 12-15 mss/issue; approx. 40 mss/year. Publishes ms 2-4 months after acceptance. Recently published work by Raymond Federman, Eurudice, Ricardo Cruz, Diane Glancy. Sometimes critiques rejected mss and recommends other markets.

How to Contact: Send complete manuscript with cover letter. Reports in 1-3 months on queries; 3-4 months on mss. SASE. Simultaneous submissions OK. Sample copy $7. Fiction guidelines for #10 SAE and 1 first class stamp.

Payment: Pays in contributor's copies.

Terms: Acquires first rights.

Advice: "Expand your 'institutionalized' sense of what a story should be so that you include (open yourself up to) language play, innovative spatial composition, plots that die trying, de-characterizations whipped up in the food processor, themes barely capable of maintaining equilibrium in the midst of end-of-the-century energy crisis/chaos, etc."

BLACK JACK, (I), Seven Buffaloes Press, Box 249, Big Timber MT 59011. Editor: Art Cuelho. "Main theme: Rural. Publishes material on the American Indian, farm and ranch, American hobo, the common working man, folklore, the Southwest, Okies, Montana, humor, Central California, etc. for people who make their living off the land. The writers write about their roots, experiences and values they receive from the American soil." Annually. Estab. 1973. Circ. 750.

• *Black Jack* is published by Art Cuelho of Seven Buffaloes Press. He also publishes *Valley Grapevine* and *Azorean Express* also listed in this book. See also his listing for the press.

Needs: Literary, contemporary, western, adventure, humor, American Indian, American hobo, and parts of novels and long short stories. "Anything that strikes me as being amateurish, without depth, without craft, I refuse. Actually, I'm not opposed to any kind of writing if the author is genuine and has spent his lifetime dedicated to the written word." Receives approximately 10-15 unsolicited fiction mss/month. Acquires 5-10 mss/year. Length: 3,500-5,000 words (there can be exceptions).

How to Contact: Query for current theme with SASE. Reports in 1 week on queries; 2 weeks on mss. Sample copy for $5.75.

Payment: Pays 1-2 contributor's copies.

Terms: Acquires first North American serial rights and reserves the right to reprint material in an anthology or future *Black Jack* publications. Rights revert to author after publication.

Advice: "Enthusiasm should be matched with skill as a craftsman. That's not saying that we don't continue to learn, but every writer must have enough command of the language to compete with other proven writers. Save postage by writing first to the editor to find out his needs. A small press magazine always has specific needs at any given time. I sometimes accept material from country writers that aren't all that good at punctuation and grammar but make up for it with life's experience. This is not a highbrow publication; it belongs to the salt-of-the-earth people."

BLACK MOUNTAIN REVIEW, (IV), Lorien House, P.O. Box 1112, Black Mountain NC 28711-1112. (704)669-6211. Editor: David A. Wilson. Magazine: 5½×8½; 48 pages; 60 lb. offset paper; 65 lb. cover stock; occasionally illustrations and photographs. "Each issue covers an American writer and all material must fit the theme." Annually. Estab. 1987. Circ. 100-150.

Needs: Literary. "The category of fiction is not as important as meeting the requirements of the theme. Guidelines for SASE." Receives 10 unsolicited mss/month. Buys 1-2 mss/issue. Publishes ms 6 months to 1 year after acceptance. Published work by Maureen Williams. Length: 1,000 words preferred; 2,000 words maximum. Publishes short shorts.

How to Contact: Query first. Reports in 1 week. SASE. Sample copy for $6. Fiction guidelines for #10 SAE and 1 first class stamp.

Payment: Pays $15 maximum.

Terms: Pays on publication for one-time rights.

Advice: "Wait! Hold it! Don't send that ms ... until you have written for the guidelines. General material is not wanted. We are covering Tennessee Williams and Carl Sandburg in the near future. Submitted material is read carefully for content and (aagh!) spelling, but not the name/fame of the writers. There must be evidence of research within the story, and details must be accurate. There is still room for creativity. Do a good story, and you are welcome here."

BLACK RIVER REVIEW, (II), 855 Mildred Ave., Lorain OH 44052. (216)244-9654. Editor: Deborah Glaefke Gilbert. Fiction Editor: Jack Smith. Magazine: 8½×11; 60 pages; recycled paper; mat card cover stock; b&w drawings. "Contemporary writing and contemporary American culture; poetry, book reviews, essays on contemporary literature, short stories." Annually. Estab. 1985. Circ. 400.

Needs: Contemporary, experimental, humor/satire and literary. No "erotica for its own sake, stories directed toward a juvenile audience." Accepts up to 5 mss/year. Does not read mss May 1-Dec. 31. Publishes ms no later than July of current year. Published work by David Shields, Jeanne M. Leiby, Louis Gallo. Length: up to 3,500 words but will consider up to 4,000 maximum. Publishes short shorts. Also publishes literary essays, literary criticism, poetry. Sometimes critiques rejected mss and recommends other markets.

How to Contact: Reports on mss no later than July. SASE. No simultaneous submissions. Sample copy for $3 back issue; $3.50 current. Fiction guidelines for #10 SAE and 1 first class stamp. Reviews novels and short story collections.

Payment: Pays in contributor's copies.

Terms: Acquires one-time rights.

Advice: "Since it is so difficult to break in, much of the new writer's creative effort is spent trying to match trends in popular fiction, in the case of the slicks, or adapting to narrow themes ('Gay and Lesbian,' 'Vietnam War,' 'Women's Issues,' etc.) of little and literary journals. An unfortunate result, from the reader's standpoint, is that each story within a given category comes out sounding like all the rest. Among positive developments of the proliferation of small presses is the opportunity for writers to decide what to write and how to write it. My advice is support a little magazine that is both open to new writers and prints fiction you like. 'Support' doesn't necessarily mean 'buy all the back issues,' but, rather, direct involvement between contributor, magazine and reader needed to rebuild the sort of audience that was there for writers like Fitzgerald and Hemingway."

THE BLACK SCHOLAR, (II, IV), The Black World Foundation, Box 2869, Oakland CA 94609. (415)547-6633. Editor: Robert Chrisman. Magazine: 7×10; 56+ pages; newsprint paper; glossy, 24 lb. cover; illustrations; b&w photos. Magazine on black culture, research and black studies for Afro-Americans, college graduates and students. "We are also widely read by teachers, professionals and intellectuals, and are required reading for many black and Third World Studies courses." Quarterly. Estab. 1969. Circ. 10,000.
Needs: Literary, contemporary, juvenile, young adult and ethnic. No religious/inspirational, psychic, etc. Receives approximately 75 unsolicited fiction mss/month. Published new writers within the last year. Length: 2,000-5,000 words. Also publishes poetry.
How to Contact: Query with clips of published work and SASE. Reports in 2 months on queries, 1 month on mss.
Payment: Pays 10 contributor's copies and 1 year's subscription.
Terms: Acquires all rights.
Advice: "Poetry and fiction appear almost exclusively in our annual culture issue (generally, Sept./Oct. of given year)."

BLACK WARRIOR REVIEW, (II), Box 2936, Tuscaloosa AL 35487. (205)348-4518. Editor-in-Chief: James H.N. Martin. Fiction Editor: Leigh Ann Sackrider. Magazine: 6×9; approx. 144 pages; illustrations and photos sometimes. "We publish contemporary fiction, poetry, reviews, essays and interviews for a literary audience." Semiannually. Estab. 1974. Circ. 1,300-2,000.
• Work that appeared in the *Black Warrior Review* has been included in the *Pushcart Prize* anthology for 1991 and in *New Short Stories from the South. Esquire* (July 1992) noted *BWR* as a good place for budding writers.
Needs: Contemporary, literary, mainstream and prose poem. No types that are clearly "types." Receives 200 unsolicited fiction mss/month. Buys 5 mss/issue, 10 mss/year. Approximately 25% of fiction is agented. Recently published work by Dennis Johnson, Reneé Manfredi, Joy Williams; published new writers within the last year. Length: 7,500 words maximum; 3,000-5,000 words average. Also publishes literary criticism, poetry. Occasionally critiques rejected mss.
How to Contact: Send complete ms with SASE. Simultaneous submissions OK. Reports in 2-3 months. Publishes ms 2-5 months after acceptance. Sample copy $6. Fiction guidelines for SASE. Reviews novels and short story collections.
Payment: Pays $5-10/page and 2 contributor's copies.
Terms: Pays on publication.
Advice: "Become familiar with the magazine(s) being submitted to; learn the editorial biases; accept rejection slips as part of the business; keep trying. We are not a good bet for 'commercial' fiction. Each year the *Black Warrior Review* will award $500 to a fiction writer whose work has been published in either the fall or spring issue, to be announced in the fall issue. Regular submission deadlines are August 1 for fall issue, January 1 for spring issue."

BLACK WRITER MAGAZINE, (II), Terrell Associates, Box 1030, Chicago IL 60690. (312)924-3818. Editor: Mable Terrell. Fiction Editor: Herman Gilbert. Magazine: 8½×11; 40 pages; glossy paper; glossy cover; illustrations. "To assist writers in publishing their work." For "all audiences, with a special emphasis on black writers." Quarterly. Estab. 1972.

Needs: Ethnic, historical, literary, religious/inspirational, prose poem. Plans annual anthology. Receives 20 unsolicited mss/month. Acquires 15 mss/issue. Publishes ms on average of 6 months after acceptance. Length: 3,000 words preferred; 2,500 words average; 1,500 words minimum. Also publishes literary essays. Sometimes critiques rejected mss and recommends other markets.
How to Contact: Send complete ms with cover letter, which should include "writer's opinion of the work, and rights offered." Reports in 3 weeks. SASE. Simultaneous submissions OK. Sample copy for 8½ × 11 SAE and 70¢ postage. Fiction guidelines for SASE. Reviews novels and short story collections. Send books to the editor.
Payment: Pays subscription to magazine.
Terms: Acquires one-time rights.
Advice: "Write the organization and ask for assistance." Sponsors awards for fiction writers. Contest deadline May 30.

‡THE BLIZZARD RAMBLER (I), World's Most Unique Magazine, Box 54, Weiser ID 83672. Editor: Ron Blizzard. Fiction Editor: Dale Blizzard. Magazine: 7x8½; 80-120 pages; 20 lb. paper; 60 lb. cover; no art. Publishes "humor/satire and adventure (SF, fantasy, western), for those who don't take themselves too seriously." Publishes 3-4 issues/yr. Plans special fiction issue. Estab. 1983. Circ. 400.
Needs: Adventure, fantasy, humor/satire, mystery/suspense, prose poem, science fiction (hard science, soft/sociological), western (traditional, frontier). "We also like fictional 'news' stories." No erotica. Receives 35-50 unsolicited mss/month. Buys 70-90 mss/issue; 220-280 mss/year. Publishes ms 6-12 months after acceptance. Recently published work by Kenneth Wisman, Jess Wilbanks, Celeste Paul. Length: 3,000 words preferred; 2,500 words average; 50 words minimum; 8,000 words maximum. Sometimes critiques rejected mss and recommends other markets.
How to Contact: Send complete ms with cover letter. "Cover letter optional." Reports in 4-6 weeks on queries; 1-3 months on mss. No simultaneous submissions. Sample copy for $4 with writer's guidelines. Fiction guidelines for #10 SAE and 1 first class stamp.
Payment: Pays ¼¢/word and 1 contributor's copy.
Terms: Pays on acceptance for first rights. Sends galleys to author if requested.
Advice: "Is it entertaining? Is it a story, or just part of one? Is it clear what's happening? We would like to see old style westerns submitted. Send for a sample copy or writer's guidelines. Aim to entertain and send in the stories."

‡BLOOD & APHORISMS, A Journal of Literary Fiction, (II), Suite 711, 456 College St., Toronto, Ontario M6G 4A3 Canada. (416)972-0637. Publisher: Timothy Paleczny. Fiction Editor: Hilary G. Clark. Magazine: 8½ × 11; 72 pages; bond paper; illustrations on cover. "We publish new and emerging writers whose work is fresh and revealing, and impacts on a literary readership." Quarterly. Estab. 1990. Circ. 650.
Needs: Ethnic/multicultural, experimental, feminist (and men's issues), humor/satire, literary. No erotica, gratuitous violence or exploitive fiction. Publishes annual special fiction issue or anthology. Receives 50 unsolicited mss/month. Acquires 12-15 mss/issue; 45-55 mss/year. Publishes ms 3-6 months after acceptance. Recently published work by Lawrence Hill, Oakland Ross, Michelle Alfano. Length: 2,500-4,000 words average; 150 words minimum; 4,500 words maximum. Publishes short shorts. Often critiques rejected mss.
How to Contact: Send complete ms with a cover letter. Should include estimated word count, short bio, list of publications (optional) with submission. Reports in 2 weeks on queries; 6 weeks on mss. SASE or IRC for a reply to a query or return of ms. Simultaneous (please advise), electronic (disk with hard copy) submissions OK. Sample copy for $5 (Canadian). Fiction guidelines for SAE and 1 IRC. Reviews novels and short story collections. Send books to Craig Proctor, 9 Haslett Ave., Toronto, Ontario M4L 3R1.
Payment: Pays subscription to the magazine and 1 contributor's copy. Additional copies $4.
Terms: Acquires first North American serial rights.
Advice: "Be honest; take chances; find the strength in your own voice; show us your best—we're ready for anything and keep an open mind. Know the magazine you're sending to."

BLOODREAMS, A Magazine of Vampires & Werewolves, (II, IV), 1312 W. 43rd St., North Little Rock AR 72118. (501)771-2047. Editor: Kelly Gunter Atlas. Magazine: 8½ × 11; 40-50 pages; 20 lb. paper; 60 lb. stock cover; b&w drawings. "*Bloodreams* is dedicated exclusively to the preservation, continuance, and enhancement of the vampire and the werewolf legends for adult fans of the genre." Quarterly. Estab. 1991. Circ. 100.

Needs: Vampires and werewolves. "We do not want to see gore, unnecessary violence, or pornography." Receives 10-12 unsolicited mss/month. Acquires 4-6 mss/issue; 16-24 mss/year. Does not read mss in April, July, October, January. Publishes ms 2 months after acceptance. Recently published work by Gregory L. Norris and Deidra Cox. Length: 1,500 words average; 250 words minimum; 2,500 words maximum. Publishes short shorts. Length: 250-500 words. Also publishes poetry. Sometimes critiques rejected mss and recommends other markets.

How to Contact: Send complete ms with cover letter. Include a brief introduction and past credits if any. Reports in 1 week on queries; 4-6 weeks on mss. SASE. Simultaneous and reprint submissions OK. Sample copy for $4. Fiction guidelines for #10 SAE and 1 first class stamp.

Payment: Pays in contributor's copies. Charges for extras.

Terms: Acquires one-time rights.

Advice: "We look for well-written, concise short stories which are complete within themselves. We like writers who have their own sense of style and imagination who write with their own 'voice' and do not try to copy others' work. We are open to a variety of interpretations of the vampire and werewolf legends. For example, we like anything ranging from Stephen King to Anne Rice to Robert R. McCammon to Brian Lumley."

‡**THE BLUE WATER REVIEW (II)**, 8045 S.W. 100 St., Miami FL 33156. (305)596-7113. Editor/Publisher: Dennis M. Ross. Magazine: 5½×7; 45 pages; 60 lb. paper; standard cover stock; illustrations and photos. "No theme. We want quality writing: fiction, interviews with well known writers and critics, poetry, and photos." Semiannually. Estab. 1989. Circ. 5,000.

Needs: Adventure, contemporary, ethnic, experimental, humor/satire, literary, mainstream, mystery/suspense (private eye, police procedurals, amateur sleuth), regional, science fiction (soft/sociological), sports. "No pornography, no handwritten or single-spaced submissions, no manuscripts without SASE." Receives 15 unsolicited mss/month. Accepts 3-4 mss/issue; 10 mss/year. Publishes ms 1-3 months after acceptance. Agented fiction 10%. Length: 3,000 words maximum. Publishes short shorts. Sometimes critiques rejected mss.

How to Contact: Send complete manuscript with cover letter. Reports in 4-5 months. SASE. Simultaneous submissions OK. Fiction guidelines for #10 SAE and 1 first class stamp.

Payment: Pays 1 contributor's copy; charge for extras.

Terms: Acquires one-time rights.

Advice: "Manuscripts should have classic elements of short story, such as meaningful character change. Submit your best work no matter the publication. We want quality. Use standard form as illustrated in *Writer's Digest* (short stories)."

BLUELINE, (II, IV), English Dept., SUNY, Potsdam NY 13676. (315)267-2000. Editor-in-Chief: Alan Steinberg. Magazine: 6×9; 112 pages; 70 lb. white stock paper; 65 lb. smooth cover stock; illustrations; photos. "*Blueline* is interested in quality writing about the Adirondacks or other places similar in geography and spirit. We publish fiction, poetry, personal essays, book reviews and oral history for those interested in the Adirondacks, nature in general, and well-crafted writing." Annually. Estab. 1979. Circ. 700.

Needs: Adventure, contemporary, humor/satire, literary, prose poem, regional, reminiscences, oral history and nature/outdoors. Receives 8-10 unsolicited fiction mss/month. Accepts 6-8 mss/issue. Does not read January-August. Publishes ms 3-6 months after acceptance. Published fiction by Jeffrey Clapp. Published new writers within the last year. Length: 500 words minimum; 3,000 words maximum; 2,500 words average. Also publishes literary essays, poetry. Occasionally critiques rejected mss. Sometimes recommends other markets.

How to Contact: Send complete ms with SASE and brief bio. Submit mss Aug. 1-Nov. 30. Reports in 2-10 weeks. Reports in 2-10 weeks. Sample copy for $5.75. Fiction guidelines for 5×10 SAE with 1 first class stamp.

Payment: Pays 1 contributor's copy. Charges $3 each for 3 or more extra copies.

Terms: Acquires first rights.

Advice: "We look for concise, clear, concrete prose that tells a story and touches upon a universal theme or situation. We prefer realism to romanticism but will consider nostalgia if well done. Pay attention to grammar and syntax. Avoid murky language, sentimentality, cuteness or folksiness. We would like to see more good fiction related to the Adirondacks. Please include short biography and word count. If manuscript has potential, we work with author to improve and reconsider for publication. Our readers prefer fiction to poetry (in general) or reviews. Write from your own experience, be specific and factual (within the bounds of your story) and if you write about universal features such as love, death, change, etc., write about them in a fresh way. Triteness and mediocracy are the hallmarks of the majority of stories seen today."

BLUFF CITY, A Magazine of Poetry and Fiction, (II), Bluff City Press, P.O. Box 7697, Elgin IL 60121. Editor: Carol A. Morrison. Magazine: 5½ × 8½; 86 pages; 70 lb. paper; glossy heavy cover; occasionally illustrations. "Finely crafted poetry and short stories for a small press literary audience." Semiannually. Estab. 1990. Circ. 350.
Needs: Experimental, literary, prose poem. "No didactic, religious, special interest or unrevised drafts." Receives 30 unsolicited mss/month. Accepts 5-8 mss/issue; 10-16 mss/year. Publishes ms 6 months after acceptance. Recently published work by Thomas E. Kennedy, Patty Somlo, Rebecca Rule. Length: 2,500 words maximum. Publishes short shorts. Comments on or critiques rejected mss and recommends other markets.
How to Contact: Send complete ms with cover letter which should include previous publication credits, affiliations, a brief bio. Reports in 6-10 weeks on mss. SASE for ms. Simultaneous submissions OK. Sample copy for $4.50. Fiction guidelines for #10 SAE and 1 first class stamp.
Payment: Pays in contributor's copies.
Terms: Acquires first North American serial rights.
Advice: "Quite simply, we choose the best fiction we receive, from reactionary to dangerously experimental. We look for tension, surprise, and careful command of language. We like tightly constructed stories with fully developed characters, written by contributors with an ear for language, rhythms, and sound. This is not a market for hastily written first drafts. Revise and polish your work and read previous issues of *Bluff City* to form an eye for our market."

BLUR, Boston Literary Review, (II), Box 357, W. Somerville MA 02144. (617)625-6087. Editor: Gloria Mindock. Magazine: 5¼ × 13; 24 pages; 70 lb. offset paper; 80 lb. cover. Contemporary poetry and fiction. Semiannually. Estab. 1985. Circ. 500.
Needs: Contemporary, literary, experimental. "Non-mainstream work that has a strong and unique voice and that takes risks with form or content." Receives 50 unsolicited mss/month. Accepts 1-2 mss/issue; 2-4 mss/year. Publishes ms 6 months-1 year after acceptance. Length: 2,500 words maximum. Publishes short shorts. Sometimes critiques rejected mss.
How to Contact: Send complete ms with cover letter. Include estimated word count and list of publications. No simultaneous submissions. Reports in 2-4 weeks on queries. SASE. Sample copy for $4 and #10 SASE.
Payment: Pays 2 contributor's copies.
Terms: Acquires first North American serial rights. Sends galleys to author.

BOGG, A Magazine of British & North American Writing, (II), Bogg Publications, 422 N. Cleveland St., Arlington VA 22201. (703)243-6019. U.S. Editor: John Elsberg. Magazine: 6 × 9; 64-68 pages; 60 lb. white paper; 60 lb. cover stock; line illustrations. "American and British poetry, prose poems and other experimental short 'fictions,' reviews, and essays on small press." Published triannually. Estab. 1968. Circ. 750.
Needs: Very short experimental and prose poem. "We are always looking for work with British/Commonwealth themes and/or references." Receives 25 unsolicited fiction mss/month. Accepts 1-2 mss/issue; 3-6 mss/year. Publishes ms 3-12 months after acceptance. Published 50% new writers within the last year. Length: 500 words maximum. Also publishes literary essays, literary criticism, poetry. Occasionally critiques rejected mss.
How to Contact: Query first or send ms (2-6 pieces) with SASE. Reports in 1 week on queries; 2 weeks on mss. Sample copy for $3.50 or $4.50 (current issue). Reviews novels and short story collections.
Payment: Pays 2 contributor's copies. Reduced charge for extras.
Terms: Acquires one-time rights.
Advice: "Read magazine first. We are most interested in prose work of experimental or wry nature to supplement poetry."

BOTH SIDES NOW, An Alternative Journal of New Age/Aquarian Transformations, (II), Free People Press, 10547 State Highway 110 N., Tyler TX 75704-9537. (903)592-4263. Editor-in-Chief: Elihu Edelson. Magazine: 8½ × 11; 8-10 pages; bond paper and cover; b&w line illustrations; photos (screened for newsprint). Estab. 1969.

Needs: Material with new-age slant, including fantasy, feminist, humor/satire ("including political"), psychic/supernatural, spiritual, religious/inspirational, ecological fables, parables. "No violence (including S/M), prurience (pornography), or fascistic views." Length: "about 3 magazine pages at most." Also publishes some poetry. Occasionally critiques rejected mss with "brief note."
How to Contact: Send complete ms with SASE. Simultaneous submissions and previously published work OK. Reports in 3 months on mss. Sample copy for $1. Reviews "New Age and counterculture fiction."
Payment: Pays 6 contributor's copies. Charges $1 each for extra copies.
Terms: "Authors retain rights."
Advice: "Heed our editorial interests."

‡**BOTTOMFISH MAGAZINE, (II),** Bottomfish Press, Language Arts Division, De Anza College, 21250 Steven Creek Blvd., Cupertino CA 95014. (408)864-8538. Editor-in-Chief: Robert Scott. Magazine: 7×8½; 80-100 pages; White Bristol vellum cover; b&w high contrast illustrations and photos. "Contemporary poetry, fiction, b&w graphics and photos for literary and writing community." Annually. Estab. 1976. Circ. 500.
Needs: Experimental, literary and prose poem. "Literary excellence is our only criteria. We will consider all subjects except pornography." Receives 50-100 unsolicited fiction mss/month. Accepts 5-6 mss/issue. Length: 500 words minimum; 5,000 words maximum; 2,500 words average.
How to Contact: Send complete ms with cover letter, brief bio and SASE. No simultaneous submissions or reprints. Prefers letter-quality. Reports in 3-4 months. Publishes ms an average of 6 months-1 year after acceptance. Sample copy $4.
Payment: Pays 2 contributor's copies.
Terms: Acquires one-time rights.
Advice: "Strive for orginality and high level of craft; avoid clichéd or stereotyped characters and plots. We don't print slick, commercial fiction, regardless of quality."

BOULEVARD, (III), Opojaz Inc., P.O. Box 30386, Philadelphia PA 19103-8386. (215)561-1723. Editor: Richard Burgin. Magazine: 5½×8½; 150-225 pages; excellent paper; high-quality cover stock; illustrations; photos. "*Boulevard* aspires to publish the best contemporary fiction, poetry and essays we can print." Published 3 times/year. Estab. 1986. Circ. about 2,800.
Needs: Contemporary, experimental, literary, prose poem. Does not want to see "anything whose first purpose is not literary." Receives over 400 mss/month. Buys about 8 mss/issue. Publishes ms less than 1 year after acceptance. Agented fiction ⅓-¼. Length: 5,000 words average; 10,000 words maximum. Publishes short shorts. Published work by Lee K. Abbott, Francine Prose, Alice Adams. Also publishes literary essays, literary criticism, poetry. Sometimes critiques rejected mss and recommends other markets.
How to Contact: Send complete ms with cover letter. Reports in 2 weeks on queries; 2 months or less on mss. SASE. Simultaneous submissions OK. Sample copy for $6 and SAE with 5 first class stamps.
Payment: Pays $50-250; contributor's copies; charges for extras.
Terms: Pays on publication for first North American serial rights. Does not send galleys to author unless requested.
Advice: "Master your own piece of emotional real estate. Be patient and persistent."

MARION ZIMMER BRADLEY'S FANTASY MAGAZINE, (II, IV), Box 249, Berkeley CA 94701. (510)601-9000. Editor and Publisher: Marion Zimmer Bradley. Magazine: 8½×11; 64 pages; 60 lb. text paper; 10 lb. cover stock; b&w interior and 4 color cover illustrations. "Fantasy only; strictly family oriented." Quarterly.
 • This magazine is named for and published by one of the pioneers of fantasy fiction. Bradley is perhaps best known for the multi-volume Darkover series.
Needs: Fantasy. May include adventure, contemporary, humor/satire, mystery/suspense and young adult/teen (10-18) (all with fantasy elements). "No avant garde or romantic fantasy. No computer games!" Receives 50-60 unsolicited mss/week. Buys 8-10 mss/issue; 36-40 mss/year. Publishes 3-12 months after acceptance. Agented fiction 5%. Length: 3,000-4,000 words average; 7,000 words maximum. Publishes short shorts.

How to Contact: Send complete ms. SASE. Reports in 10 days. No simultaneous submissions. Sample copy $3.50. Fiction guidelines for #10 SASE.
Payment: Pays 3-10¢/word; contributor's copies.
Terms: Pays on acceptance. $25 kill fee "if held 12 months or more." Buys first North American serial rights.
Advice: "If I want to finish reading it—I figure other people will too. A manuscript stands out if I care whether the characters do well, if it has a rhythm. Make sure it has characters I will know *you* care about. If you don't care about them, how do you expect me to?"

BRAVO MUNDO NUEVO, Alternative Literature for a Brave New World, (I, II), La Sombra Publishing, P.O. Box 285, Hondo TX 78861. (512)426-5453. Editor: E.D. Santos. Newsletter: 8½ × 11; 8 pages; 70 lb. paper; illustrations. "Lesser known fiction writers are encouraged to submit to *BMN*. Fantasy, science fiction, social awareness type material are most welcome." Quarterly. Estab. 1990.
Needs: Fantasy, science fiction (soft/sociological), "social awareness" material. No "how-to; editorials; racist material; socially or environmentally flammable material." Publishes annual special fiction issue. Receives 5 unsolicited mss/month. Accepts 5 mss/issue; 20 mss/year. Publishes ms 6-9 months after acceptance. Recently published work by Angela deHoyos. Length: 600 words preferred; 20 words minimum; 1,200 words maximum. Publishes short shorts. Sometimes critiques rejected mss and recommends other markets.
How to Contact: Send complete ms with cover letter. Cover letter should include previous publications, if any, length of experience in writing, preferred genre of writing, current address and phone number. Reports in 2 months on mss. SASE. Simultaneous and reprint submissions OK. Sample copy free. Fiction guidelines for #10 SAE and 1 first class stamp.
Payment: Pays subscription to magazine.
Terms: Acquires one-time rights.
Advice: Looks for "originality and a gift for spontaneous storytelling as the principal criteria in choosing fiction for this publication. A manuscript need not be 'polished' to stand out; in point of fact, the more unrefined, the more authentic and genuinely appealing it is."

BREAKTHROUGH!, Showcase for Prose & Poetry (II), Aardvark Enterprises, (a division of Speers Investments Ltd.), 204 Millbank Dr. S.W., Calgary, Alberta T2Y 2H9 Canada. (403)256-4639. Editor: J. Alvin Speers. Magazine: 5½ × 8½; 52 pages; bond paper; color cardstock cover; illustrations. "Upbeat, informative and entertaining reading for general audience—articles, short stories, poetry, fillers and cartoons. General interest—popular with writers and readers for information and entertainment." Quarterly. Estab. 1982. Circ. 200+.
Needs: Adventure, historical (general), humor/satire, literary, mystery/suspense (amateur sleuth, young adult), regional, religious/inspirational, romance (contemporary, historical, romantic suspense, young adult), western. "No pornography, uncouth language, crudely suggestive, gay or lesbian." Receives 25 mss/month. Accepts 8-10 mss/issue; 30-40 mss/year. "Publication time varies with available space, held for season, etc." Length: 1,500 words; 500 words minimum; 2,500 words maximum. Publishes short shorts. Also publishes literary essays, literary criticism, poetry. Sometimes critiques rejected mss.
How to Contact: Subscribe, or buy sample and submit ms. Include brief bio. Reports in 1 week on queries. SASE. Simultaneous and reprint submissions OK. Sample copy $5. Fiction guidelines for #10 SAE, IRC, Canadian 48¢ stamp, or $1 U.S. quite acceptable. Reviews novels or short story collections by subscribers only.
Payment: By readers' vote small cash honorarium for best 3 items each issue, plus 4th place Honorable Mention Certificate.
Terms: Acquires one-time rights.
Advice: "We look for quality in line with editorial guidelines, clarity of presentation of story or information message. Be familiar with our style and theme—do not submit inappropriate material. We treat submittors with respect and courtesy."

THE BRIDGE, A Journal of Fiction & Poetry, (II), The Bridge, 14050 Vernon St., Oak Park MI 48237. Editor: Jack Zucker. Fiction Editor: Helen Zucker. Magazine: 5½ × 8½; 160 pages; 60 lb. paper; heavy cover. "Fiction and poetry for a literary audience." Semiannually. Estab. 1990.
Needs: Ethnic, mainstream, regional. Receives 80 unsolicited mss/month. Acquires 5-7 mss/issue; 10-14 mss/year. Publishes ms within one year of acceptance. Length: 3,000 words average; 7,500 words maximum. Publishes short shorts. Length: 1,000 words. Also publishes some short essays, some criticism, poetry.

How to Contact: Send complete manuscript with cover letter. Reports in 1 week on queries; 2-4 months on mss. SASE. Simultaneous submissions OK. Sample copy for $5 ($8 for 2). Reviews novels and short story collections.
Payment: Pays in contributor's copies.
Terms: Acquires first North American serial rights.
Advice: "Don't give us fiction intended for a popular/commercial market—we'd like to get 'real literature.'"

‡BRILLIANT STAR (II), National Spiritual Assembly of the Baha'is of the U.S., 915 Washington St., Evanston IL 60091. General Editor: Candace Moore Hill. Magazine: 8½×11; 33 pages; matte paper; glossy cover; illustrations; photos. "A magazine for Baha'i children about the history, teachings and beliefs of the Baha'i Faith." For children approx. 5-12 years old. Bimonthly. Estab. 1969. Circ. 2,300.
Needs: Adventure, children's/juvenile, ethnic, historical (general), humor/satire, mystery/suspense, spiritual, young adult/teen (10-18 years). "Accepts inspirational fiction if not overtly preachy or moralistic and if not directly Christian and related directly to Christian holidays." Upcoming themes: "From Racism to Unity" (March 1993); "The Purpose of Life" (May 1993); "Role of Women" (July 1993); "Leadership" (September 1993); "Courage" (November 1993); "Marriage & Family" (January 1994). Receives 30 unsolicited mss/month. Accepts 3-4 mss/issue; 18-24 mss/year. Publishes ms no sooner than 6 months after acceptance. Recently published work by Susan Pethick and John Paulits; published new writers within the last year. Length: 750 words preferred; 250 words minimum; 1,000 words maximum. Publishes short shorts. Also publishes poetry.
How to Contact: No queries. Send complete ms. Cover letter not essential. Reports in 6-10 weeks on mss. SASE. Simultaneous submissions OK "but please make a notation that it is a simultaneous sub." Sample copy for 9×12 SAE and 5 oz. postage. Fiction guidelines for #10 SAE with 1 first class stamp.
Payment: Pays in contributor's copies (two); charges for extras.
Terms: "Writer can retain own copyright or grant to the National Spiritual Assembly of the Baha'is of the U.S."
Advice: "We enjoy working with beginning writers and try to develop a constructive collaborative relationship with those who show promise and sensitivity to our aims and focus. We feel that the children's market is open to a wide variety of writers: fiction, nonfiction, science, photo-essays. Our needs for appealing fiction especially for pre-schoolers and young readers make us a good market for new writers. *Please*, have a story to tell! The single main reason for rejection of manuscripts we review is lack of plot to infuse the story with energy and make the reader want to come along. Seeking writers from Afro-American, Hispanic, Asian and Native American backgrounds to increase multi-ethnic focus of our magazine."

BROOMSTICK, A National, Feminist Periodical by, for, and About Women Over Forty, (II, IV), 3543 18th St. #3, San Francisco CA 94110. (415)552-7460. Editors: Mickey Spencer and Polly Taylor. Magazine: 8½×11; 40 pages; line drawings. "Our first priority in selecting and editing material is that it convey clear images of women over 40 that are positive, that it show the author's commitment against the denigration of midlife and long-living women which pervades our culture, and that it offer us alternatives which will make our lives better." For "women over 40 interested in being part of a network which will help us all develop understanding of our life situations and acquire the skills to improve them." Quarterly. Estab. 1978. Circ. 3,000.
Needs: Feminist experience in political context, old women, age and agism, humor, ethnic. No mss of "romantic love, nostalgic, saccharine acceptance, by or about men or young women." Receives 10 unsolicited fiction mss/month. Accepts 2-3 mss/issue; 20 mss/year. Published work by Astra, Wilma Elizabeth McDaniel, Ruth Harriet Jacobs; published new writers within the last year. Recommends magazine subscription before sending ms. Critiques rejected mss.
How to Contact: Send complete mss with 2 SASEs. Simultaneous and previously published submissions OK. Reports in 3 months on queries and mss. Sample copy for $5. Writer's guidelines for 50¢ or SASE.
Payment: Pays 2 contributor's copies; $5 charge for extras.
Advice: "Don't use stereotypes to establish character. Give protagonists names, not just roles (e.g. 'mother'). Avoid using "you," which sounds preachy. Read our editorials."

BROWNBAG PRESS, (II), Hyacinth House Publications, P.O. Box 120, Fayetteville AR 72702-0120. Editors: Shannon Frach, Randal Seyler. Magazine: Digest-sized; 30-55 pages; 20 lb. paper; cardstock cover; black & white illustrations. "*Brownbag Press* is a digest of poetry, fiction, and experimental writing that is seeking avant-garde, forceful, and often bizarre literature for a literate, adult audience that is bored to death with the standard offerings of modern mainstream fiction." Semiannually. Estab. 1989. Circ. 300.

• Hyacinth House Publications also publishes *Psychotrain* listed in this book. No need to send to both publications, says the editor, as submissions will be considered for both.

Needs: Condensed/excerpted novels, contemporary, erotica, ethnic, experimental, feminist, gay, horror, humor/satire, lesbian, literary, prose poem, psychic/supernatural/occult, translations, "Punk, psychedelia, fringe culture, Dada, surrealism. A sense of dark humor is definitely a plus. No religious, romance, or criminally boring mainstream. No tedious formula fiction. No yuppie angst. Nothing saccharine." Receives 150 unsolicited ms/month. Acquires 4-6 ms/issue. Publishes ms 1 year after acceptance. Recently published work by Brooks Caruthers, Bob Black, and Richard Behrens. Length: 100-5,000 words. Publishes short shorts. Length: 100 words or longer. Sometimes critiques rejected mss and recommends other markets.

How to Contact: Send complete ms with or without cover letter. "Don't use a cover letter to brag about how great you are; if you're that good, I guarantee we'll have heard of you." Reports in 1-5 months on ms. SASE. Simultaneous and reprint submissions OK. Sample copy for $3. Make checks out to "Hyacinth House Publications". Cash is also OK. Fiction guidelines for #10 SAE and 1 first class stamp.

Payment: Pays 1 contributor's copy; charges for extras.

Terms: Acquires one-time rights.

Advice: "Since our listing in these pages last year, competition for space in *Brownbag* has become quite fierce. Many of the pieces we're rejecting are being sent in by people who obviously failed to read our listing carefully. Despite all that we've said, we still receive blind submissions of inspirational pieces and romance stories, although those genres are completely inappropriate in relation to what we actually print. Also, we get a great deal of writing from people who seemingly cannot punctuate a paragraph of English, much less correctly spell the words contained therein. On the whole, we'd like to see more forceful, hard-hitting writing. Writers must capture our attention from line 1. Send bold, dynamic, unrepentant fiction that reveals an innate mastery of the language."

BYLINE, (I, II), Box 130596, Edmond OK 73013. (405)348-5591. Editor-in-Chief: Marcia Preston. Managing Editor: Kathryn Fanning. Monthly magazine "aimed at encouraging and motivating all writers toward success, with special information to help new writers." Estab. 1981.

• *Byline* is fast becoming known as an excellent starting place for new writers. For more information check out our close-up interview with the editor in the 1991 edition of this book. The magazine is ranked #40 in the 1992 *Writer's Digest* Fiction 50 list. The magazine also sponsors the *Byline* Literary Awards listed in this book.

Needs: Literary, genre and general fiction. Receives 75-100 unsolicited fiction mss/month. Buys 1 ms/issue, 12 mss/year. Recently published work by Brenda Burnham and Michael Bugeja; published many new writers within the last year. Length: 4,000 words maximum; 1,000 words minimum. Also publishes poetry.

How to Contact: Send complete ms with SASE. Simultaneous submissions OK, "if notified." "For us, no cover letter is needed." Reports in 3-6 weeks. Publishes ms an average of 3 months after acceptance. Sample copy, guidelines and contest list for $3.

Payment: Pays $50 and 2 contributor's copies.

Terms: Pays on acceptance for first North American rights.

Advice: "We're very open to new writers. Submit a well-written, professionally prepared ms with SASE. No erotica or senseless violence; otherwise, we'll consider most any theme. We also sponsor short story and poetry contests."

CALLALOO, A Journal of Afro-American and African Arts and Letters, (II, IV), Dept. of English, University of Virginia, Charlottesville VA 22903. (804)924-6637. Editor: Charles H. Rowell. Magazine: 7×10; 200 pages. Scholarly magazine. Quarterly. Plans special fiction issue in future. Estab. 1976. Circ. 1,000.

Needs: Contemporary, ethnic (black culture), feminist, historical (general), humor/satire, literary, prose poem, regional, science fiction, serialized/excerpted novel, translations. Acquires 3-5 mss/issue; 10-20 mss/year. Length: no restrictions.

How to Contact: Submit complete ms and cover letter with name and address. Reports on queries in 2 weeks; 2-3 months on mss. Simultaneous submissions OK. Previously published work accepted "occasionally." Sample copy $5.

Payment: Pays in contributor's copies.
Terms: Acquires all rights. Sends galleys to author.

CALLIOPE, (II, IV), Creative Writing Program, Roger Williams College, Bristol RI 02809. (401)254-3217. Co-ordinating Editor: Martha Christina. Magazine: 5½×8½; 40-56 pages; 50 lb. offset paper; vellum or 60 lb. cover stock; occasional illustrations and photos. "We are an eclectic little magazine publishing contemporary poetry, fiction, and occasionally interviews." Semiannually. Estab. 1977. Circ. 300.
Needs: Literary, contemporary, experimental/innovative. "We try to include at least 2 pieces of fiction in each issue." Receives approximately 10-20 unsolicited fiction mss each month. Does not read mss mid-March to mid-August. Published new writers within the last year. Length: 3,750 words. Publishes short shorts under 20 pages. Critiques rejected mss when there is time.
How to Contact: Send complete ms with SASE. Reports immediately or up to 3 months on mss. Sample copy $1.
Payment: Pays 2 contributor's copies and one year's subscription beginning with following issue.
Terms: Rights revert to author on publication.
Advice: "We are not interested in reading anyone's very first story. If the piece is good, it will be given careful consideration. Reading a sample copy of *Calliope* is recommended. Let the characters of the story tell their own story; we're very often (painfully) aware of the writer's presence. Episodic is fine; story need not (for our publication) have traditional beginning, middle and end."

CALYX, A Journal of Art & Literature by Women, (II), Calyx, Inc., P.O. Box B, Corvallis OR 97339. (503)753-9384. Managing Editor: Margarita Donnelly. Editors: Rebecca Gordon, Cheryl McLean, Catherine Holdorf, Linda Varsell Smith, Beverly McFarland. Magazine: 7×8; 128 pages per single issue, 250 per double; 60 lb. coated matte stock paper; 10 pt. chrome coat cover; original art. Publishes prose, poetry, art, essays, interviews and critical and review articles. "*Calyx* editors are seeking innovative and literary works of exceptional quality." Biannually. Estab. 1976. Circ. 3,000.
 • *Calyx* won the Bumbershoot Small Press Best Literary Journal Award in 1985 and 1991, the CCLM Literary Magazine Editors Award for Excellence in 1990 and other awards for literary excellence.
Needs: Accepts 3-5 fiction mss/issue, 9-15 mss/year. Receives approximately 300 unsolicited fiction mss each month. Reads mss only from March 1-April 15 and October 1-November 15 each year. Submit only during these periods. Published works by Ruthann Robson, Shirley Sikes, S.C. Wisenberg; published new writers within the last year. Length: 5,000 words maximum. Also publishes literary essays, literary criticism, poetry.
How to Contact: Send ms with SASE and biographical notes. Simultaneous submissions OK. Reports in up to 6 months on mss. Publishes ms an average of 6 months after acceptance. Sample copy $8 plus $1.25 postage. Reviews novels and short story collections.
Payment: Pays in copies and subscriptions.
Advice: Most mss are rejected because "the writers are not familiar with *Calyx*—writers should read *Calyx* and be familiar with the publication."

THE CAPILANO REVIEW, (II), 2055 Purcell Way, North Vancouver, British Columbia V7J 3H5 Canada. (604)984-1712. Editor: Robert Sherrin. Magazine: 6×9; 80-100 pages. Magazine of "fresh, innovative art and literature for literary/artistic audience." Quarterly. Estab. 1972. Circ. 1,000.
Needs: Contemporary, experimental, literary and prose poem. Receives 30 unsolicited mss/month. Buys 1-2 mss/issue; 4 mss/year. Published works by Bill Gaston, Sharon Thesen and Myrna Kostash. Published "lots" of new writers within the last three years. Length: 2,000-6,000 words. Publishes short shorts. Also publishes literary essays. Occasionally recommends other markets.
How to Contact: Send complete ms with cover letter. Sample copy for $8 (Canadian).
Payment: Pays $160 maximum ($40/page), 2 contributor's copies and one year subscription.
Terms: Pays on publication.

THE CARIBBEAN WRITER, (IV), The University of the Virgin Islands, RR 02, Box 10,000—Kingshill, St. Croix, Virgin Islands 00850. (809)778-0246. Editor: Erika Smilowitz-Waters. Magazine: 6×9; 130 pages; 60 lb. paper; glossy cover stock; illustrations and photos. "*The Caribbean Writer* is an international magazine with a Caribbean focus. The Caribbean should be central to the work, or the work should reflect a Caribbean heritage, experience or perspective." Annually. Estab. 1987. Circ. 1,500.

Needs: Contemporary, historical (general), humor/satire, literary, mainstream and prose poem. Receives 300 unsolicited mss/year. Acquires 10 mss/issue. Length: 300 words minimum; 3,750 words maximum. Also accepts poetry.
How to Contact: Send complete ms with cover letter. "Blind submissions only. Send name, address and title of ms on separate sheet. Title only on ms. Mss will not be considered unless this procedure is followed." Reports "once a year." SASE. Simultaneous submissions OK. Sample copy for $7 and $2 postage. Fiction guidelines for SASE.
Payment: Pays 1 contributor's copy. Annual prizes for best story ($400); for best poem ($250).
Terms: Acquires one-time rights.

CAROLINA QUARTERLY, (II), Greenlaw Hall CB #3520, University of North Carolina, Chapel Hill NC 27599-3520. (919)962-0244. Editor-in-Chief: Amber Vogel. Fiction Editor: Marielle Blais. Literary journal: 90-100 pages; cover illustrations and photos. "Fiction, poetry, graphics and some reviews, for an audience interested in good poetry and short fiction." Triannually. Estab. 1948. Circ. 1,000.
Needs: Receives 150-200 unsolicited fiction mss/month. Buys 5-7 mss/issue; 15-20 mss/year. Publishes ms an average of 10 weeks after acceptance. Recently published work by Barry Hannah, Nanci Kincaid, Rick Bass. Published new writers within the last year. Length: 7,000 words maximum; no minimum. Also publishes short shorts, literary essays, poetry. Occasionally critiques rejected mss.
How to Contact: Send complete ms with cover letter and SASE to fiction editor. No simultaneous submissions. Reports in 2-4 months. Sample copy for $5; Writer's guidelines for SASE and $1 postage. Reviews novels and short story collections.
Payment: Pays $15/contributor/issue and 2 contributor's copies.
Terms: Pays on publication for first North American serial rights.
Advice: "We publish many unsolicited stories and love publishing a new writer for the first time. Read what gets published in the journal/magazine that interests you. Our space is limited so the average length of mss we publish is 20 for short stories.

CAROUSEL LITERARY ARTS MAGAZINE, (I, II), Room 217, University Centre, University of Guelph, Guelph, Ontario N1G 2W1 Canada. Editors: Michael Carbert, Shirley Senoff. Magazine: 5½ × 8½; 80 pages; illustrations and photographs. Annually. Estab. 1985. Circ. 500.
Needs: Adventure, contemporary, ethnic, experimental, fantasy, feminist, gay, horror, humor/satire, lesbian, literary, mystery/suspense, prose poem, religious/inspirational, romance, science fiction, sports, and western. Receives 5 unsolicited mss each month. Accepts 3-4 mss per issue. Publishes ms 1-2 months after acceptance. Published work by Leon Rooke and J.J. Steinfield. Length: 3,000 words maximum. Also publishes literary essays, interviews, poetry.
How to Contact: Send complete ms. Include bio with manuscript. No simultaneous submissions. Reports in 1 month on queries; 4 months on mss. SASE. Sample copy $5 (Canadian).
Payment: Pays in contributor's copies.
Terms: Acquires one-time rights.
Advice: "We want work which takes chances in style, point of view, characterization. We are open to new writers."

CATALYST, A Magazine of Heart & Mind, (II, IV), Catalyst, Inc. 34 Forsyth St. SW, #400, Atlanta GA 30303-3700. (404)730-5785. Editor: Pearl Cleage. Magazine: 8 × 11; 130 pages; newsprint; photographs. "Seeks to stimulate the worldwide flow of ideas. Publishes fiction, drama, short stories, poetry and criticism for a general audience." Semiannually. Estab. 1986. Circ. 5,000.
  • Catalyst was voted "Best Literary Boost" by *Atlanta Magazine* in 1991.
Needs: Open. Publishes annual special fiction issue. Receives 100-200 unsolicited mss/month. Buys 75-100 mss/issue. Publishes ms 6 months after acceptance. Recently published work by Lois Lyles, Zaron Burnett, Jr. Length: 3,000 words maximum. Publishes short shorts. Recommends other markets.
How to Contact: Query first. Simultaneous submissions OK. Reports in 1 week on queries; 6 months on mss. SASE. Sample copy for $2.50 and 9 × 12 SAE. Fiction guidelines for #10 SAE.
Payment: Pays $10-200, contributor's copies. Charges for extras.
Terms: Pays on publication. Rights remain with author.
Advice: "Attend workshops; join a writing organization; read a variety of different writers' works; learn good writing skills; and seek advice from established writers."

CHALK TALK, (IV), 1550 Mills Road, RR2, Sidney, British Columbia V8L 3S1 Canada. (604)656-1858. Editor: Virginia Lee. Magazine: Pony tabloid-sized; 24 pages; recycled newsprint paper. "Writing by children only for children, ages 5-14." Monthly. Estab. 1988. Circ. 3,600.

Needs: *Children writers only.* Juvenile, young adult. "No war or violence." Publishes mss 1-4 months after acceptance. Length: 200 words preferred. Publishes short shorts. Critiques or comments on rejected mss and recommends other markets.
How to Contact: Send complete ms with cover letter. Reports in 3 months. SASE. (IRCs) Sample copy and fiction guidelines free.
Payment: Pays in contributor's copies.
Terms: Acquires one-time rights. Sponsors occasional contests for children only.

CHAMINADE LITERARY REVIEW, (II), Chaminade Press, 3140 Waialae Ave., Honolulu HI 96816. (808)735-4723. Editor: Loretta Petrie. Magazine: 6×9; 175 pages; 50 lb. white paper; 10 pt. C1S cover; photographs. "Multicultural, particularly Hawaii—poetry, fiction, artwork, criticism, photos, translations for all English-speaking internationals, but primarily Hawaii." Semiannually. Estab. 1987. Circ. 350.
Needs: Excerpted novel, ethnic, experimental, humor/satire, literary, religious/inspirational, translations. "We have published a variety including translations of Japanese writers, a fishing story set in Hawaii, fantasy set along the Amazon, but the major point is they are all 'literary.' No erotica, horror, children's or young adult, confession, lesbian, gay." Receives 8 unsolicited mss/month. Acquires 5-8 mss/issue. Publishes ms 3-6 months after acceptance. "We haven't published short shorts yet, but would depending on quality." Sometimes critiques rejected ms.
How to Contact: Send complete ms with cover letter. Include short contributor's note. Reporting time depends on how long before deadlines of May 15 and December 15. SASE. Reprint submissions OK. Sample copy for $3.50.
Payment: Pays subscription to magazine.
Terms: Acquires one-time rights.
Advice: "We look for good writing; appeal for Hawaii audience and writers everywhere. *CLR* was founded to give added exposure to Hawaii's writers, both here and on the mainland, and to juxtapose Hawaii writing with mainland and international work."

CHANGING MEN, Issues in Gender, Sex, & Politics, (II), Feminist Men's Publications, Inc., 306 N. Brooks, Madison WI 53715. (608)256-2565. Editor: Michael Biernbaum. Fiction Editor: Paul Matalucci. Magazine: 8½×11; 64 pages; bond paper; glossy card stock cover; illustrations and photographs. "Issues in gender, sex and politics for pro-feminist men (largely)." Biannual. Estab. 1979. Circ. 6,000.
● Focusing on the changing roles of men in our society, this publication was nominated for the *Utne Reader* Alternative Press Award in both 1991 and 1992.
Needs: Contemporary, erotica, experimental, feminist, gay, humor/satire, lesbian, literary, sports. "Fiction should be pro-feminist or pro-gay/lesbian or deal with issues in leftist/radical politics." Upcoming themes: "Changing Men of All Colors"; "New Perspectives on Gender." Receives 5-10 unsolicited mss/month. Acquires 1-2 mss/issue. Publishes ms 6 months-1 year after acceptance. Published work by Bob Shelby, S. Kolankiewicz, Keith Kelly. Length: 1,500-2,000 words average; 1,000 words minimum; 4,000 words maximum. Sometimes critiques rejected mss.
How to Contact: Send complete ms with cover letter. Include brief description of work enclosed. Reports in 6 months on mss. SASE. "May consider" simultaneous submissions. Sample copy for $6. Fiction guidelines for SASE.
Payment: Pays contributor's copies.
Terms: Acquires first North American serial rights. Sends galleys to author.
Advice: "Fresh perspectives on feminist, gay/lesbian and political issues. Writer should ideally be familiar with our magazine, know our spheres of interest and know what we have recently published to avoid excessive similarity/duplication."

CHAPTER ONE, For the Unpublished Writer in All of Us, (I), 12018 State Route 45, Lisbon OH 44432. Editor: Belinda J. Puchajda. Magazine: 5¼×8; 100-200 pages. "For short stories and poems." Quarterly. Estab. 1989.
● *Chapter One* ranked #26 on the 1992 *Writer's Digest* Fiction 50 list. After an unexpected move and a deluge of submissions Editor Puchajda decided to hire additional staff. To help defray costs she now charges a small reading fee (see terms). Also note the $1 sample copy is a "sampling" of work from the magazine—not a complete copy. Copies of *Chapter One* cost $4.95.
Needs: Adventure, confession, contemporary, erotica, ethnic, experimental, fantasy, feminist, historical (general), horror, humor/satire, juvenile (5-9 years), literary, mainstream, preschool (1-4 years), prose poem, psychic/supernatural/occult, regional, religious/inspirational, romance (contemporary, historical, young adult), mystery/suspense (private eye, amateur sleuth, young adult, romantic sus-

pense), science fiction, senior citizen/retirement, sports, western (traditional, frontier stories), young adult/teen (10-18 years). "No pornography." Receives 400-450 unsolicited mss/week. Buys 25-35 mss/ issue. Publishes ms 12-18 months after acceptance. Length: 4,500 words average; 100 words minimum; 10,000 maximum. Publishes short shorts. Length: 100 words. Sometimes critiques rejected mss and recommends other markets.

How to Contact: Send complete ms with cover letter. Include biographical information. Reports in 1-2 months on queries; 4-5 months on ms. Simultaneous submissions OK. Accepts 5¼ disk. IBM-compatible submissions. Sample copy for $1 and 2 first class stamps and SAE. Fiction guidelines for #10 SAE and 1 first class stamp.

Payment: Pays $50 maximum; contributor's copies.

Terms: *Charges $2.50 reading fee for less than 1,500 words; $5 for 1,500 words or more.* Pays on publication for one-time rights.

Advice: "We feel that there is a lot of talent out there, and we want to see it. Whether it be a story from a housewife who never wrote anything before, or a writer who has been writing for years and has never got published. We want to get you in print."

THE CHARITON REVIEW, (II), Northeast Missouri State University, Kirksville MO 63501. (816)785-4499. Editor: Jim Barnes. Magazine: 6×9; 100+ pages; 60 lb. paper; 65 lb. cover stock; photographs on cover. "We demand only excellence in fiction and fiction translation for a general and college readership." Semiannually. Estab. 1975. Circ. 700+.

Needs: Literary, contemporary and translations. Buys 3-5 mss/issue; 6-10 mss/year. Published work by Steve Heller, John Deming, Eve Shelnutt; published new writers within the last year. Length: 3,000-6,000 words. Also publishes literary essays, poetry. Critiques rejected mss when there is time. Sometimes recommends other markets.

How to Contact: Send complete ms with SASE. No book-length mss. No simultaneous submissions. Reports in less than 1 month on mss. Publishes ms an average of 6 months after acceptance. Sample copy for $3 with SASE. Reviews novels and short story collections.

Payment: Pays $5/page up to $50 maximum; contributor's copy; $3.50 for extras.

Terms: Pays on publication for first North American serial rights; rights returned on request.

Advice: "Do not ask us for guidelines: the only guidelines are excellence in all matters. Write well and study the publication you are submitting to. We are interested only in the very best fiction and fiction translation. We are not interested in slick material. We do not read photocopies or carbon copies. Know the simple mechanics of submission – SASE, no paper clips, no odd-sized SASE, etc. Know the genre (short story, novella, etc.). Know the unwritten laws."

THE CHATTAHOOCHEE REVIEW, (II), DeKalb College, 2101 Womack Rd., Dunwoody GA 30338. (404)551-3166. Editor: Lamar York. Magazine: 6×9; 150 pages; 70 lb. paper; 80 lb. cover stock; illustrations; photographs. Quarterly. Estab. 1980. Circ. 1,250.

Needs: Literary, mainstream. No juvenile, romance, sci-fi. Receives 500 unsolicited mss/month. Accepts 5 mss/issue. Published work by Leon Rooke, R.T. Smith; published new writers within the last year. Length: 2,500 words average. Also publishes literary essays, literary criticism, poetry. Sometimes critiques rejected mss and recommends other markets.

How to Contact: Send complete ms with cover letter, which should include sufficient bio for notes on contributors' page. Reports in 2 months. SASE. May consider simultaneous submission "reluctantly." Sample copy for $4. Fiction guidelines available on request. Reviews novels and short story collections.

Payment: Pays in contributor's copies.

Terms: Acquires first rights.

Advice: "Arrange to read magazine before you submit to it."

‡CHELSEA (II), Chelsea Associates, Inc., Box 5880, Grand Central Station, New York NY 10163. Editor: Sonia Raiziss. Magazine: 6×9; 185-235 pages; 60 lb. white paper; glossy cover stock; artwork; occasional photos. "We have no consistent theme except for single special issues. Otherwise, we use general material of an eclectic nature: poetry, prose, artwork, etc., for a sophisticated, literate audience interested in avant-garde literature and current writing, both national and international." Annually. Estab. 1958. Circ. 1,300.

● *Chelsea* sponsors the Chelsea Awards also listed in this book. Entries to that contest will also be considered for the magazine, but writers may submit directly to the magazine as well. The magazine was the recipient of an NEA grant in 1992.

Needs: Literary, contemporary, poetry and translations. No humorous, scatological, purely confessional or child/young-adult experiences. Receives approximately 100 unsolicited fiction mss each month. Approximately 1% of fiction is agented. Recently published work by Susan Sonde, Josip Novakovich, Roberta Allen. Length: not over 25 printed pages. Publishes short shorts of 4-6 pages. Critiques rejected mss when there is time.
How to Contact: Send complete ms with with SASE and succint cover letter with previous credits. No simultaneous submissions. Reports in 3 months on mss. Publishes ms within a year after acceptance. Sample copy $5 plus postage.
Payment: Pays contributor's copies, $5 per printed page; annual Chelsea Award, $500 (send SASE for guidelines).
Terms: Buys first North American serial rights plus one-time non-exclusive reprint rights.
Advice: "Familiarize yourself with issues of the magazine for character of contributions. Manuscripts should be legible, clearly typed, with minimal number of typographical errors and cross-outs, sufficient return postage. Most mss are rejected because they are conventional in theme and/or style, uninspired, contrived, etc."

"We generally publish about five stories in each issue," says David Nicholls, editor of the **Chicago Review,** *where special issues are a specialty. "This cover, commissioned for our special issue on Indian literatures, includes (in calligraphic form) fragments of the poems, stories and essays found in the issue in English translation. We chose the cover to highlight the process of translation and the 13 languages translated inside." Nicholls says they read all unsolicited manuscripts and "cultivate writers of promise." The cover was designed by G.R. Santosh, a painter and calligrapher in the Tantric tradition who lives and works in the Bharti Artists' Colony in New Delhi, India. (Cover, © 1992 by* **Chicago Review.***)*

CONTEMPORARY INDIAN LITERATURES

CHICAGO REVIEW, 5801 S. Kenwood Ave., Chicago IL 60637. Fiction Editor: Andy Winston. Magazine for a highly literate general audience: 6½×9; 96 pages; offset white 60 lb. paper; illustrations; photos. Quarterly. Estab. 1946. Circ. 2,000.
• *Chicago Review* was labeled a "literary root" by *Esquire* (July 1992).
Needs: Literary, contemporary, and especially experimental. Accepts up to 5 mss/issue; 20 mss/year. Receives 80-100 unsolicited fiction mss each month. No preferred length, except will not accept book-length mss. Also publishes literary essays, literary criticism, poetry. Sometimes critiques rejected mss "upon request." Sometimes recommends other markets.
How to Contact: Send complete ms with cover letter. SASE. Simultaneous submissions OK. Reports in 4-5 months on mss. Sample copy for $5. Guidelines with SASE. Reviews novels and short story collections. Send books to Book Review Editor.
Payment: Pays 3 contributor's copies and subscription.
Advice: "We look with interest at fiction that addresses subjects inventively, work that steers clear of clichéd treatments of themes. We're always eager to read writing that experiments with language, whether it be with characters' viewpoints, tone or style."

CHIPS OFF THE WRITER'S BLOCK, (I), Box 83371, Los Angeles CA 90083. Editor: Wanda Windham. Newsletter. "Freelancer's forum, the beginner's chance to be published." Bimonthly.
• Wanda Windham, editor of *Chips Off the Writer's Block* has been very helpful and quick to respond when I've contacted her on behalf of writers. A good sign in a magazine devoted to working with new writers.

Needs: "We will consider all categories of fiction, as our publication gives writers a chance to be 'critiqued' by fellow writers." No pornographic or offensive material. Upcoming theme: Christmas Issue (December 1993). Published new writers within the last year. "Always" critiques rejected mss.
How to Contact: Submit complete ms. "Cover letters are not necessary. Please note the word count on the first page of the story." Reports in 6 weeks to 2 months. SASE. Simultaneous submissions OK. Sample copy for $3. Fiction guidelines for #10 SAE and 1 first class stamp.
Payment: Pays in contributor's copies.
Advice: "The editor works directly with the author if editing is necessary or if the story needs to be reworked. The writer's peer group also sends in comments, suggestions, etc., once the story is in print. The comments are discussed in later issues."

CHIRICÚ, (II, IV), Ballantine Hall 849, Indiana University, Bloomington IN 47405. Editor: Sean T. Dwyer. "We publish essays, translations, poetry, fiction, reviews, interviews and artwork (illustrations and photos) that are either by or about Hispanics. We have no barriers on style, content or ideology, but would like to see well-written material." Annually. Estab. 1976. Circ. 500.
Needs: Contemporary, ethnic, experimental, fantasy, feminist, humor/satire, literary, mainstream, prose poem, science fiction, serialized/excerpted novel, translations. No fiction that has nothing to do with Hispanics (when not written by one). Recently published work by Ricardo Lindo, Eduardo Galeano; published new writers within the last year. Length: 7,000 words maximum; 3,000 words average. Occasionally critiques rejected mss. Sometimes recommends other markets.
How to Contact: Send complete ms with cover letter. "Include some personal information along with information about your story." SASE. No simultaneous submissions. Reports in 5 weeks. Publishes ms 6-12 months after acceptance. Sample copy for $5. Guidelines for #10 SAE.
Advice: "Realize that we are an Hispanic literary review so that if you are not Hispanic, then your work must reflect an interest in Hispanic issues or have an Hispanic bent to it in literature." Mss rejected "because beginning writers force their language instead of writing from genuine sentiment, because of multiple grammatical errors and because writers think that naming a character José gives their story a Hispanic slant."

CHIRON REVIEW, (I), Rt. 2, Box 111, St. John KS 67576-2212. (316)792-5025. Editor: Michael Hathaway. Tabloid: 10×13; 24+ pages; newsprint; illustrations; photos. Publishes "all types of material, no particular theme; traditional and off-beat, no taboos." Estab. 1982. Circ. 1,200.
Needs: Contemporary, experimental, humor/satire, literary. Receives 6 mss/month. Accepts 1 ms/issue; 4 mss/year. Publishes ms within 6-18 months of acceptance. Length: 3,500 words preferred. Publishes short shorts. Sometimes recommends other markets to writers of rejected mss.
How to Contact: Query. Reports in 6-8 weeks. SASE. No simultaneous submissions. Sample copy $2 ($4 overseas). Fiction guidelines for #10 SAE and 1 first class stamp.
Payment: Pays 1 contributor's copy. Charge for extra copies, 50% discount.
Terms: Acquires first rights.

CHRYSALIS, Journal of the Swedenborg Foundation, (II), The Swedenborg Foundation, 139 E. 23rd St., New York NY 10010. (212)673-7310. Send mss to: Rt. 1, Box 184, Dillwyn VA 23936. (804)983-3021. Editor-in-Chief: Carol S. Lawson. Fiction Editor: Phoebe Loughrey. Magazine: 7½×10; 80 pages; archival paper; coated cover stock; illustrations; photos. "A literary magazine centered around one theme per issue. Publishes fiction, articles, poetry, book and film reviews for intellectually curious readers interested in spiritual topics." Triannually. Estab. 1985. Circ. 3,000.
Needs: Adventure (leading to insight), contemporary, experimental, historical (general), literary, mainstream, mystery/suspense, science fiction, spiritual, sports. No religious, juvenile, preschool. Upcoming themes: "Time" (Spring 1993); "Work" (Summer 1993); "Family" (Autumn 1993); "The Future of Religion" (Spring 1994); "Music" (Summer 1994). Receives 40 mss/month. Buys 4-5 mss/issue; 12-18 mss/year. Publishes ms within 12 months of acceptance. Recently published work by Larry Dossey, Frances Vaughan, John Hitchcock, Perry Martin; published new writers within the last year. Length: 1,500 words minimum; 2,500 words maximum. Publishes short shorts. Also publishes literary essays, literary criticism, poetry. Sometimes critiques rejected mss and recommends other markets.
How to Contact: Query first and send SASE for guidelines. Reports in 2 months. SASE. No simultaneous, reprinted or inpress material. Sample copy for $5. Fiction guidelines for #10 SAE and 1 first class stamp.

Payment: Pays $75-250, subscription to magazine and 5 contributor's copies.
Terms: Pays on publication for one-time rights. Sends galleys to author.
Advice: Looking for "1. *Quality*; 2. appeal for our audience; 3. relevance to/illumination of an aspect of issue's theme."

CICADA, (II, IV), 329 "E" St., Bakersfield CA 93304. (805)323-4064. Editor: Frederick A. Raborg, Jr. Magazine: 5½ × 8¼; 24 pages; Matte cover stock; illustrations and photos. "Oriental poetry and fiction related to the Orient for general readership and haiku enthusiasts." Quarterly. Estab. 1985. Circ. 600.
● *Cicada* is edited by Frederick A. Raborg, Jr., who is also editor of *Amelia* and *SPSM&H* listed in this book. See also the listing for the *Amelia* Magazine Awards.
Needs: *All with Oriental slant*: Adventure, contemporary, erotica, ethnic, experimental, fantasy, feminist, historical (general), horror, humor/satire, lesbian, literary, mainstream, mystery/suspense, psychic/supernatural/occult, regional, contemporary romance, historical romance, young adult romance, science fiction, senior citizen/retirement and translations. "We look for strong fiction with Oriental (especially Japanese) content or flavor. Stories need not have 'happy' endings, and we are open to the experimental and/or avant-garde. Erotica is fine (the Japanese love their erotica); pornography, no." Receives 30+ unsolicited mss/month. Buys 1 ms/issue; 4 mss/year. Publishes ms 6 months-1 year after acceptance. Agented fiction 5%. Published work by Gilbert Garand and Jim Mastro. Length: 2,000 words average; 500 words minimum; 3,000 words maximum. Critiques rejected ms when appropriate. Always recommends other markets. Also publishes poetry.
How to Contact: Send complete ms with cover letter. Include Social Security number and appropriate information about the writer in relationship to the Orient. Reports in 2 weeks on queries; 3 months on mss (if seriously considered). SASE. Sample copy $4.50. Fiction guidelines for #10 SAE and 1 first class stamp.
Payment: Pays $10-25 plus contributor's copies; charge for extras.
Terms: Pays on publication for first North American serial rights. $5 kill fee.
Advice: Looks for "excellence and appropriate storyline. Strong characterization and knowledge of the Orient are musts. Neatness counts high on my list for first impressions. A writer should demonstrate a high degree of professionalism."

CIMARRON REVIEW, (II), Oklahoma State University, 205 Morrill, Stillwater OK 74078-0135. (405)744-9476. Editor: Gordon Weaver. Managing Editor: Deborah Bransford. Magazine: 6 × 9; 100 pages; illustrations on cover. "Poetry and fiction on contemporary themes; personal essay on contemporary issues that cope with life in the 20th century, for educated literary readers. We work hard to reflect quality." Quarterly. Estab. 1967. Circ. 700.
● *Esquire* dubbed the *Cimarron Review* a "literary root" in the July 1992 issue.
Needs: Literary and contemporary. No collegiate reminiscences or juvenilia. Buys 6-7 mss/issue; 24-28 mss/year. Published works by Peter Makuck, Mary Lee Settle, W. D. Wetherell, John Timmerman; published new writers within the last year. Also publishes literary essays, literary criticism, poetry. Sometimes recommends other markets.
How to Contact: Send complete ms with SASE. "Short cover letters are appropriate but not essential, except for providing *CR* with the most recent mailing address available." No simultaneous submissions. Reports in 6-8 weeks on mss. Publishes ms within 12 months after acceptance. Sample copy with SASE and $3. Reviews novels, short story collections, and poetry collections.
Payment: Pays one-year subscription to author, plus $50 for each prose piece and $15 for each poem.
Terms: Buys all rights on publication. "Permission to reprint granted freely."
Advice: "Short fiction is a genre uniquely suited to the modern world. *CR* seeks an individual, innovative style that focuses on contemporary themes."

CLIFTON MAGAZINE , (II), University of Cincinnati Communications Board, 204 Tangeman University Center, ML 136, Cincinnati OH 45221. (513)556-6379. Editor: Steve Libbey (1992-93). Editors change each year. "Send future correspondence to 'Editor.' " Magazine: 8 × 11; 48 pages; 70 lb. enamel coated paper; illustrations; photos. "*Clifton* is the magazine of the University of Cincinnati, presenting fiction, poetry and feature articles of interest to the University community. It is read by a highly literate

---

● *A bullet introduces comments by the editor of* Novel & Short Story Writer's Market *indicating special information about the listing.*

audience of students, academics and professionals looking for original and exciting ideas presented in our award-winning format." Quarterly. Estab. 1972. Circ. 30,000.
  • This student-run college magazine has won numerous awards over the years including the Columbia Scholastic Gold Crown Award in 1992 and the Silver Crown in 1991.
Needs: Literary, contemporary, science fiction (soft/sociological), fantasy, feminist, erotica, horror, prose poem, regional and ethnic. "Will consider anything we haven't read a thousand times before. We try to have no preconceptions when approaching fiction." Accepts 1-2 mss/issue, 5 mss/year. Length: 5,000 words maximum. Publishes short shorts. Also publishes poetry. Receives approximately 30 unsolicited fiction mss each month.
How to Contact: Send complete ms with SASE. Simultaneous submissions OK. Reports in 6-8 weeks on mss. Sample copy $2.75. Guidelines with #10 SASE. Reviews novels. Send books to Fiction Editor.
Payment: Pays 3 contributor's copies.
Terms: Acquires first rights.
Advice: "There is a trend in literature to overglorify the mundane, resulting in bland stories with lukewarm themes. Too often we find ourselves rejecting well-written stories that have no punch to them. Literary does not necessitate navel gazing. Literature is a mirror (usually the funhouse variety) to the world, and is just as dirty, ugly and sweaty, if not more so. Good writing feels right, like an expensive steak, and takes as long to eat. Don't be afraid to be different. Don't be different for the sake of being different. We read manuscripts first as readers, then as editors. If we as readers are bored, we as editors don't waste our time. A story should be mechanically sound, intricate, concise and lyrical. New and young writers are encouraged to submit. Work by UC students, grads and faculty is especially welcome."

CLOCKWATCH REVIEW, A Journal of the Arts, (II), Dept. of English, Illinois Wesleyan University, Bloomington IL 61702. (309)556-3352. Editor: James Plath. Magazine: 5½×8½; 64-80 pages; coated stock paper; glossy cover stock; illustrations; photos. "We publish stories which are *literary* as well as alive, colorful, enjoyable—stories which linger like shadows," for a general audience. Semiannually. Estab. 1983. Circ. 1,500.
Needs: Contemporary, experimental, humor/satire, literary, mainstream, prose poem and regional. Receives 50-60 unsolicited mss/month. Accepts 2 mss/issue; 4 mss/year. Recently published work by Ellen Hunnicutt, Beth Brandt, Charlotte Mandel; published new writers within the last year. Length: 2,500 words average; 1,200 words minimum; 4,000 words maximum. Occasionally critiques rejected mss if requested.
How to Contact: Send complete ms. Reports in 2 months. SASE. Publishes ms 3-12 months after acceptance. Sample copy for $4.
Payment: Pays 3 contributor's copies and small cash stipend. (Currently $50, but may vary).
Terms: Buys first serial rights.
Advice: "*Clockwatch* has always tried to expand the audience for quality contemporary poetry and fiction by publishing a highly visual magazine that is thin enough to invite reading. We've included interviews with popular musicians and artists in order to further interest a general, as well as academic, public and show the interrelationship of the arts. Give us characters with meat on their bones, colorful but not clichéd; give us natural plots, not contrived or melodramatic. Above all, give us your *best* work."

COCHRAN'S CORNER, (I), Box 2036, Waldorf MD 20601. (301)843-0485. Editor: Debra G. Tompkins. Magazine: 5½×8; 52 pages. "We publish fiction, nonfiction and poetry. Our only requirement is no strong language." For a "family" audience. Quarterly. Estab. 1986. Circ. 500.
Needs: Adventure, historical (general), horror, humor/satire, children's/juvenile, mystery/suspense, religious/inspirational, romance, science fiction and young adult/teen (10-18 years). "Mss must be free from language you wouldn't want your/our children to read." Plans a special fiction issue. Receives 50 mss/month. Accepts 4 mss/issue; 8 mss/year. Publishes ms by the next issue after acceptance. Published work by Juni Dunkin, Ruth Cox Anderson, Becky Knight. Length: 500 words preferred; 300 words minimum; 1,000 words maximum. Also publishes literary essays, literary criticism, poetry. Sometimes critiques unsolicited mss and recommends other markets.
How to Contact: "Right now we are forced to limit acceptance to *subscribers only*." Send complete ms with cover letter. Reports in 3 weeks on queries; 3 months on mss. SASE for manuscript. Simultaneous and reprint submissions OK. Sample copy for $5, 9×12 SAE and 90¢ postage. Fiction guidelines for #10 SAE and 1 first class stamp. Reviews novels and short stories. Send books to Ada Cochran, President.

Payment: Pays in contributor's copies.

Terms: Acquires one-time rights.

Advice: "I feel the quality of fiction is getting better. The public is demanding a good read, instead of having sex or violence carry the story. I predict that fiction has a good future. We like to print the story as the writer submits it if possible. This way writers can compare their work with their peers and take the necessary steps to improve and go on to sell to bigger magazines. Stories from the heart desire a place to be published. We try to fill that need."

THE COE REVIEW, (II), Student Senate of Coe College, 1220 1st St., Cedar Rapids IA 52402. (319)399-8660. Contact: Marcy Nissan. Magazine: 8½ × 5½; 100-150 pages; illustrations; photos. Annual anthology of "quality experimental writing in both poetry and fiction. Especially directed to an academic or experimental literary audience that is concerned with current literature." Annually. Estab. 1972. Circ. 500.

Needs: Literary, contemporary, psychic/supernatural, science fiction, fantasy, feminist, gay/lesbian, erotica, quality ethnic, regional, serialized and condensed novels, translations. "We publish students, unsolicited professional and solicited professional mss. *The Coe Review* is growing and it is our goal to become nationally acknowledged in literary circles as a forerunner in the publication of experimental writing. We support writing workshops and invite both writing professors and student writers to submit." No "religious propaganda, gothic, romance, western, mystery or adventure." Length: 500-4,000 words.

How to Contact: Send complete ms with SASE. "Mss sent in summer will possibly not be returned until fall depending on availability of a fiction editor in summer." Sample copy $4.

Payment: Pays $25-100 for solicitations and 1 contributor's copy; $4 charge for extras.

Terms: Pays on publication "but possibly sooner with solicited mss. Upon request we will reassign rights to the author." Buys all rights.

Advice: "We desire material that seeks to explore the vast imaginative landscape and expand the boundaries thereof. Study experimental writers such as Borges, Vonnegut, Brautigan, J. Baumbach and Manual Puig. Avoid sentimentalism. Do not be afraid to experiment or to write intelligent fiction."

COLLAGES AND BRICOLAGES, The Journal of International Writing, (II), P.O. Box 86, Clarion PA 16214. (814)226-2340. Editor: Marie-José Fortis. Magazine: 8 × 11; 100-150 pages; illustrations. "The theme, if there is any, is international post-modern/avant-gardist culture. The magazine may include essays, short stories, short plays, poems that show innovative promise." Annually. Estab. 1987. Plans special fiction issue.

Needs: Contemporary, ethnic, experimental, feminist, humor/satire, literary, philosophical works. "Also post-modern, surrealist b&w designs/illustrations are welcome." Upcoming themes: "China," "Academia" (1993). Receives about 10 unsolicited fiction mss/month. Publishes ms 6-9 months after acceptance. Recently published work by Marilou Awiakta, Boris Vian, Diane Hamill Metzgerr, Eric Basso; published new writers within the last year. Publishes short shorts. Also publishes literary essays, literary criticism, poetry. Sometimes critiques rejected ms; recommends other markets when there is time.

How to Contact: Send complete ms with cover letter that includes a short bio. Reports in 2-3 months. SASE. Simultaneous submissions OK. Sample copy $6. Reviews novels and short story collections. "How often and how many per issue depends on reviewers available."

Payment: Pays 2 contributor's copies.

Terms: Acquires first rights. Rights revert to author after publication.

Advice: "As far as fiction is concerned, it seems that everything has been said before. Hence, the writer's despair. This literary despair should be an asset to today's young writer. It should be his motif. The only innovation that can still be done is language innovation, playfulness, humor (with a sense of doom). We are now living in a neo-dada age, in a 'post-modern aura.' Hence, the writer's input should concentrate on these premises. Writing about the decadence of inspiration can bring us to a new age in literature. (The Dadaist despair was, after all, answered with surrealism.)We encourage experimental and literary writers who do not shy away from reading the classics."

‡COLLECTIONS, A Quarterly Literary and Arts Magazine, Artisan Lehigh Valley, P. O. Box 3452, Easton PA 18043-3452. (215)559-1040. Editor: Jeff Adler. Fiction Editors: Dave Rex and Eric Henthorn. Magazine: 8½ × 11; approx 75 pages; b&w illustrations and photos. Quarterly. Estab. 1992. Circ. 500.

Needs: Adventure, experimental, fantasy, horror, humor/satire, literary, science fiction. Receives 50-100 unsolicited mss/month. Buys 2-10 mss/issue; 8-50 mss/year. Publishes 1 month-1 year after acceptance. Length: 1,000 words average; 200 words minimum; 2,000 words maximum. Publishes short shorts. Length: 100-500 words. Also publishes literary essays.
How to Contact: Send complete ms with a cover letter. Should include short bio. Reports in 2 months on queries; 3 months on mss. Disposable copy of the ms. Simultaneous and reprint submissions OK. Sample copy $3. Fiction guidelines for #10 SAE and 1 first class stamp.
Payment: Pays in contributor's copies.
Terms: Acquires one-time rights; all work submitted is considered to have author's consent to be published for one year after receipt.
Advice: "Send us your stories, poems, black and white art. Lehigh Valley is a non-profit organization dedicated to providing publishing opportunities for aspiring writers, poets, and artists. We're still young, small and improving . . . "

COLORADO-NORTH REVIEW, (I, II), University of Northern Colorado, Greeley CO 80639. (303)351-1350. Editor: Jamey Birts. Magazine: 5½ × 8½; 64 pages; 70 lb. paper; 80 lb. cover stock; illustrations; photos. "Magazine of poetry, short fiction, translations, photography, interviews and graphic arts for writers or those interested in contemporary creativity." Published in winter and spring. Estab. 1968. Circ. 2,500.
Needs: Contemporary, literary and prose poem. Receives 100 unsolicited fiction mss/month. Acquires 70 mss/issue (including poetry), 140 mss/year. Published work by James Lentestey and Dennis Vannatta. Length: 1,000 words maximum. Critiques rejected mss by request. Also publishes poetry.
How to Contact: Send complete ms with SASE and brief biographical info for contributor's section. Reports in 3 months. Publishes ms 2-3 months after acceptance. Sample copy $3.50; free guidelines with SASE.
Payment: Pays in contributor's copies.
Advice: "We print poetry, art, and short fiction, so space is limited for short fiction, averaging three to four stories an issue. Obviously we must be very selective so send your best work. We are looking for stories whose form is dictated by its content. Innovative work is welcome as long as the innovation meets its own standards for quality. Work with insight is always appreciated. Please do not send simultaneous submissions."

COLUMBIA: A MAGAZINE OF POETRY & PROSE, (II), 404 Dodge Hall, Columbia University, New York NY 10027. (212)854-4391. Editors-in-Chief: Darlene Gold, Joshua Sinel. Editors change each year. Magazine: 5¼ × 8¼; approximately 200 pages; coated cover stock; illustrations, photos. "We accept short stories, novel excerpts, translations, interviews, nonfiction and poetry." Biannually.
Needs: Literary and translations. Accepts 3-10 mss/issue. Receives approximately 125 unsolicited fiction mss each month. Does not read mss May 1 to August 31. Published work by Philip Lopate, Amy Hempel, Madison Smartt Bell, John McNally; published 5-8 unpublished writers within the year. Length: 25 pages maximum. Publishes short shorts.
How to Contact: Send complete ms with SASE. Simultaneous submissions OK. Reports in 1-2 months. Sample copy $5.
Payment: Pays $100 for prose.
Advice: "Don't overwhelm editors. Send work that's not longer than 20 pages."

COMMUNITIES: JOURNAL OF COOPERATION, (II), Rt. 1, Box 155, Rutledge MO 63563. (816)883-5543. Business Manager: Laird Schaub. Editors change each issue. "Features articles on intentional communities, urban collectives, rural communes, politics, health, alternative culture and workplace democracy for people involved in cooperative ventures." Quarterly. Estab. 1973. Circ. 4,000.
Needs: Feminist, science fiction (soft/sociological), utopian and cooperative. Accepts "maybe 1 manuscript in 2 years (would do more if we got them)." Length: 1,000 words minimum; 5,000 words maximum. Occasionally critiques rejected ms.
How to Contact: Query first or send complete ms. Reports in 1 month on queries; 6 weeks on mss. Simultaneous and previously published submissions OK. Sample copy for $4.
Payment: Pays 1 year subscription and 3 contributor's copies.
Terms: Acquires one-time rights.

A COMPANION IN ZEOR, (I, II, IV), 307 Ashland Ave., McKee City NJ 08232. Editor: Karen Litman. Fanzine: 8½ × 11; 60 pages; "letter" paper; heavy blue cover; b&w line illustrations; occasional b&w photographs. Publishes science fiction based on the various Universe creations of Jacqueline Lichtenberg. Occasional features on Star Trek, and other interests, convention reports, reviews of movies and books, recordings, etc. Published irregularly. Estab. 1978. Circ. 300.

● *Companion in Zeor* is one of three fanzines devoted to the work and characters of Jacqueline Lichtenberg. Lichtenberg's work includes several future world, alien and group culture novels and series including the Sime/Gen Series and The Dushau trilogy. She's also penned two books on her own vampire character and she co-authored *Star Trek Lives*.

Needs: Fantasy, humor/satire, prose poem, science fiction. "No vicious satire. Nothing X-rated. Homosexuality prohibited unless *essential* in story. We run a clean publication that anyone should be able to read without fear." Occasionally receives one manuscript a month. Accepts "as much as can afford to print." Publication of an accepted ms "can take years, due to limit of finances available for publication." Occasionally critiques rejected mss and recommends other markets.

How to Contact: Query first or send complete ms with cover letter. "Prefer cover letters about any writing experience prior, or related interests toward writing aims." Reports in 1 month. SASE. Simultaneous submissions OK. Sample copy price depends on individual circumstances. Fiction guidelines for #10 SAE and 1 first class stamp. "I write individual letters to all queries. No form letter at present." SASE for guidelines required. Reviews sf/fantasy collections or titles.

Payment: Pays in contributor's copies.

Terms: Acquires first rights.

Advice: "We take fiction based on any and all of Jacqueline Lichtenberg's published novels. The contributor should be familiar with these works before contributing material to my fanzine. Also accepts manuscripts on cassette from visually handicapped if submitted. 'Zines also on tape for those individuals."

COMPOST NEWSLETTER, (IV), Compost Coven, 729 Fifth Ave., San Francisco CA 94118. (415)751-9466. Editor: Valerie Walker. Newsletter: 7×8½; 28 pages; bond paper; illustrations and scanned photographs. Publishes "humor/satire from a pagan/punk perspective." Quarterly. Estab. 1981. Circ. under 100.

Needs: Experimental, fantasy, feminist, gay, humor/satire, lesbian, psychic/supernatural/occult, science fiction, serialized novel, pagan. No Christian. Publishes ms within 3 or 4 issues after acceptance. Length: 500 words minimum; 2,000 words maximum.

How to Contact: Query with clips of published work. Reports in 3 months. SASE. Simultaneous and reprint submissions OK. Accepts electronic submissions via Macintosh disk. Sample copy $2.50. (Make checks/MO's out to Valerie Walker; mark "for CNL".)

Payment: Pays in contributor's copies.

Terms: Acquires one-time rights. Publication not copyrighted.

Advice: "If you don't like the magazine market, go out and make one of your own. Type single space on white paper, or send a Macintosh disk in MacWrite or Microsoft Word. Don't bother to format unless it's essential for the feel of the piece. Entertain us, even if you're serious. Get strange." Publishes ms "if it is funny, bizarre, or we agree with its politics."

CONCHO RIVER REVIEW, (I, II, IV), Fort Concho Museum Press, 213 East Avenue D, San Angelo TX 76903. (915)657-4441. Editor: Terence A. Dalrymple. Magazine: 6½×9; 100-125 pages; 60 lb. Ardor offset paper; Classic Laid Color cover stock; b&w drawings. "We publish any fiction of high quality—no thematic specialties—contributors must be residents of Texas or the Southwest generally." Semiannually. Estab. 1987. Circ. 300.

● The magazine is considering featuring "guest editors" with each issue, but mss should still be sent to the editor, Terence A. Dalrymple.

Needs: Contemporary, ethnic, historical (general), humor/satire, literary, regional and western. No erotica; no science fiction. Receives 10-15 unsolicited mss/month. Accepts 3-6 mss/issue; 8-10 mss/year. Publishes ms 4 months after acceptance. Published work by Robert Flynn, Clay Reynolds, Roland Sodowsky. Length: 3,500 words average; 1,500 words minimum; 5,000 words maximum. Also publishes literary essays, poetry. Sometimes critiques rejected mss and recommends other markets.

How to Contact: Send complete ms with SASE; cover letter optional. Reports in 3 weeks on queries; 3-8 weeks on mss. Simultaneous submissions OK (if noted). Sample copy $4. Fiction guidelines for #10 SAE and 1 first class stamp. Reviews novels and short story collections. Send books to Terence A. Dalrymple, % English Dept., Angelo State University, San Angelo TX 76909.

Payment: Pays in contributor's copies; $4 charge for extras.

Terms: Acquires first rights.

Advice: "We prefer a clear sense of conflict, strong characterization and effective dialogue."

CONFRONTATION, (II), English Dept., C.W. Post of Long Island University, Greenvale NY 11548. (516)299-2391. Editor: Martin Tucker. Magazine: 6×9; 190-250 pages; 70 lb. paper; 80 lb. cover; illustrations; photos. "We like to have a 'range' of subjects, form and style in each issue and are open to all forms. Quality is our major concern. Our audience is literate, thinking people; formally or self-educated." Semiannually. Estab. 1968. Circ. 2,000.
  • *Confrontation* has garnered a long list of awards and honors including the Editor's Award for Distinguished Achievement from CCLM (now the Council of Literary Magazines and Presses) and NEA. Work from the magazine has appeared in numerous anthologies including the *Pushcart Prize, Best Short Stories* and *O. Henry Prize Stories*.
Needs: Literary, contemporary, prose poem, regional and translations. No "proseletyzing" literature. Plans special fiction issue on new South African literature. Upcoming theme: "Self-Censorship." Buys 30 mss/issue; 60 mss/year. Receives 400 unsolicited fiction mss each month. Does not read June-Sept. Approximately 10-15% of fiction is agented. Recently published work by Jerzy Kosinski, Irvin Faust, Jayne Cortez; published many new writers within the last year. Length: 500-4,000 words. Publishes short shorts. Also publishes literary essays, poetry. Critiques rejected mss when there is time. Sometimes recommends other markets.
How to Contact: Send complete ms with SASE. "Cover letters acceptable, not necessary. We accept simultaneous submissions but do not like it." Accepts diskettes if accompanied by computer printout submissions. Reports in 6-8 weeks on mss. Publishes ms 6-12 months after acceptance. Sample copy for $3. Reviews novels and short story collections.
Payment: Pays $10-$100; 1 contributor's copy; half price for extras.
Terms: Pays on publication for all rights "with transfer on request to author."
Advice: "Keep trying."

CONJUNCTIONS (II), 33 W. 9th St., New York NY 10011. (212)477-1136. Editor: Bradford Morrow. Magazine: 6×9; 294 pages; 55 lb. woven paper; heavy cream laid paper cover stock; illustrations; photos. "*Conjunctions*: a conjoining of texts by many diverse writers; a forum of work-in-progress by both well-known and new writers. We represent no clique but are concerned solely with publishing works of high artistic and technical calibre." Semiannually. Estab. 1981. Circ. 5,500.
Needs: Experimental, literary and translations. Receives 200 unsolicited fiction mss/month. Accepts 65 mss/year. "Recent issues have included new work by John Hawkes, William T. Vollman and Mary Caponegro." Published new writers within the last year. No preferred length.
How to Contact: Send complete ms with SASE. Reports in 8-12 weeks on mss.
Payment: Pays 3 contributor's copies; extra copies available at 40% discount to contributors.
Terms: Acquires one-time rights. Sends galleys to author.
Advice: "Gain a far wider personal experience than that which is possible in writing schools. A broader reading base than is evident in most of the unsolicited work we receive would be useful. So much has already been accomplished, and it seems to us the literacy rate among writers is only barely higher than any other community or profession."

‡CORNFIELD REVIEW, (IV), The Ohio State University-Marion, 1465 Mt. Vernon Ave., Marion OH 43302. (614)389-2361. Editor: Stuart Lishan. Editors change each year. Send future mss to "Academic Advisor." Magazine: 8½×11; 48-52 pages. "Work centered in the Midwest or by writers from the Midwest." Annually. Estab. 1975. Circ. 300.
  • *Cornfield Review* has received grants from the Ohio Arts Council for the last four years.
Needs: Literary. Receives 50 unsolicited mss/month. Acquires 2-3 mss/year. Reads mss November-February only. Publishes ms 6 months after acceptance. Agented fiction 1%. Length: 2,000 words average; 500 words minimum; 3,000 words maximum. Publishes short shorts. Also publishes literary essays and poems.
How to Contact: Send complete ms with cover letter. Should include bio (50 words). SASE (or IRC) for return of the ms. No simultaneous submissions.
Payment: Pays contributor's copies.
Terms: Acquires one-time rights.

CORONA, Marking the Edges of Many Circles, (II), Department of History and Philosophy, Montana State University, Bozeman MT 59717. (406)994-5200. Co-Editors: Lynda Sexson, Michael Sexson. Managing Editor: Sarah Marrillo. Magazine: 7×10; 130 pages; 60 lb. "mountre matte" paper; 65 lb. Hammermill cover stock; illustrations; photos. "Interdisciplinary magazine—essays, poetry, fiction, imagery, science, history, recipes, humor, etc., for those educated, curious, with a profound interest in the arts and contemporary thought." Annually. Estab. 1980. Circ. 2,000.

Needs: Comics, contemporary, experimental, fantasy, feminist, gay, lesbian, humor/satire, literary, preschool, prose poem, psychic/supernatural/occult, regional, romance and senior citizen/retirement. "Our fiction ranges from the traditional Talmudic tale to fiction engendered by speculative science, from the extended joke to regional reflection—if it isn't accessible and original, please don't send it." Receives varying number of unsolicited fiction mss/month. Accepts 6 mss/issue. Published work by Rhoda Lerman and Stephen Dixon; published new writers within the last year. Publishes short shorts. Also publishes literary essays, poetry. Occasionally critiques rejected mss. Sometimes recommends other markets.
How to Contact: Query. Reports in 6 months on mss. Sample copy $7.
Payment: Pays minimal honorarium; 2 free contributor's copies; discounted charge for extras.
Terms: Acquires first rights. Sends galleys to author upon request.
Advice: "Be knowledgeable of contents other than fiction in *Corona*; one must know the journal."

COSMIC LANDSCAPES, An Alternative Science Fiction Magazine, (I, IV), % Dan Petitpas, 19 Carroll Ave., Westwood MA 02090. Editor: Dan Petitpas. Magazine: 7×8½; 32-56 pages; white bond paper and cover stock; illustrations; photos occasionally. "A magazine which publishes science fiction for science-fiction readers; also articles and news of interest to writers and SF fans. Occasionally prints works of horror and fantasy." Annually. Estab. 1983. Circ. 100.
Needs: Science fiction (hard science, soft/sociological). Receives 10-15 unsolicited mss/month. Accepts 8 mss/issue. Published new writers in the last year. Length: 2,500 words average; 25 words minimum. Will consider all lengths. "Every manuscript receives a personal evaluation by the editor." Sometimes recommends other markets.
How to Contact: Send complete ms with info about the author. Reports usually in 1 week-3 months. SASE. Simultaneous submissions OK. Sample copy for $3.50. Fiction guidelines with SASE.
Payment: Pays 2 contributor's copies; $2 for extras.
Terms: Acquires one-time rights.
Advice: "Writers should send a cover letter; include SASE and a return address. I like to know a little about them. Please give some background, and how the story pertains to their experience. Learn manuscript formats. Get E. B. White's *Elements of Style*. Don't get all your ideas from TV shows or movies. Try to know the basics."

‡COTTONWOOD, Magazine and Press, (II), 400 Kansas Union, Box 20, University of Kansas, Lawrence KS 66045. (913)864-3777. Editor: George F. Wedge. Magazine: 6×9; 112 pages; illustrations; photos. "Publish most types of 'literary' fiction. Intended audience: educated, sophisticated reader." Triannually. Estab. 1965. Circ. 500.
Needs: Ethnic/multicultural, experimental, literary, mainstream/contemporary, regional, science fiction. Publishes annual special fiction issue or anthology. Receives 20 unsolicited mss/month. Acquires 5 mss/issue; 15 mss/year. Publishes ms 12-18 months after acceptance. Agented fiction less than 5%. Length: 2,500-4,000 words average; 500 words minimum; 8,000 words maximum. Also publishes poetry. Sometimes critiques or comments on rejected mss.
How to Contact: Send complete ms with cover letter. Should include bio (25 words), list of publications. Reports in 2 weeks on queries; 1-2 months on mss. SASE (or IRC) for return of ms. No simultaneous submissions. Sample copy for $3. Fiction guidelines for #10 SAE and 1 first class stamp.
Payment: Pays 1 contributor's copy.
Terms: Acquires first rights. Fiction published in the magazine is eligible for annual Alice Carter Awards for the best fiction and poetry published in *Cottonwood*.

‡CRAB CREEK REVIEW, (II), 4462 Whitman Ave. N., Seattle WA 98103. (206)633-1090. Editor: Linda Clifton. Fiction Editor: Carol Orlock. Magazine: 6×10 minitab; 32 pages; ultrabright newsprint paper; self cover; line drawings. "Magazine publishing poetry, short stories, art and essays for adult, college-educated audience interested in literary, visual and dramatic arts and in politics." Triquarterly. Estab. 1983. Circ. 350.
● Note *Crab Creek Review* is backlogged with submissions until the end of 1993.
Needs: Contemporary, humor/satire, literary and translations. No confession, erotica, horror, juvenile, preschool, religious/inspirational, romance or young adult. Receives 20-30 unsolicited mss/month. Accepts 2 mss/issue; 6 mss/year. Recently published work by Rebecca Wells, Ben Groff; published new writers within the last year. Length: 3,000 words average; 1,200 words minimum; 4,000 words maximum. Publishes short shorts. Occasionally critiques rejected mss.

How to Contact: *Not reading unsolicited mss until December, 1993.* Send complete ms with short list of credits. Reports in 3 months. SASE. No simultaneous submissions. Sample copy $3.

Payment: Pays 2 contributor's copies; $2 charge for extras.

Terms: Acquires first rights. Rarely buys reprints.

Advice: "We appreciate 'sudden fictions.' Type name and address on each piece. Enclose SASE. Send no more than one story in a packet (except for short shorts—no more than 3, 10 pages total)."

CRAZYHORSE, (III), Dept. of English, Univ. of Arkansas, Little Rock, AR 72204. (501)569-3160. Managing Editor: Zabelle Stodola. Fiction Editor: Judy Troy. Magazine: 6×9; 140 pages; cover and front page illustrations only. "Publishes original, quality literary fiction." Biannually. Estab. 1960. Circ. 1,000.

● Stories appearing in *Crazyhorse* regularly appear in the *Pushcart Prize* and *Best American Short Stories* anthologies.

Needs: Literary. No formula (science-fiction, gothic, detective, etc.) fiction. Receives 100-150 unsolicited mss/month. Buys 3-5 mss/issue; 8-10 mss/year. Does not read mss in summer. Past contributors include Lee K. Abbott, Frederick Busch, Andre Dubus, Pam Durban, H.E. Francis, James Hannah, Gordon Lish, Bobbie Ann Mason and Maura Stanton; published new writers within the last year. Publishes short shorts. Also publishes literary essays, literary criticism, poetry. "Rarely" critiques rejected mss.

How to Contact: Send complete ms with cover letter. Reports in 1-3 months. SASE. No simultaneous submissions. Sample copy $5. Reviews novels and short story collections. Send books to fiction editor.

Payment: Pays $10/page and contributor's copies.

Terms: Pays on publication for first North American serial rights. *Crazyhorse* awards $500 to the author of the best work of fiction published in a given year.

Advice: "Read a sample issue and submit work that you believe is as good as or better than the fiction we've published."

CRAZYQUILT, (II), P.O. Box 632729, San Diego CA 92163-2729. (619)688-1023. Editor: Jim Kitchen. Magazine: 5½×8½; 92 pages; illustrations and photos. "We publish short fiction, poems, nonfiction about writing and writers, one-act plays and b&w illustrations and photos." Quarterly. Estab. 1986. Circ. 175.

Needs: Contemporary, ethnic, fantasy, gay, historical, humor/satire, literary, mainstream, mystery/suspense, science fiction, excerpted novel. "Shorter pieces are preferred." Receives 85-100 unsolicited mss/quarter. Accepts 1-3 mss/issue; 4-12 mss/year. Publishes 1 year after acceptance. Published work by Louis Phillips, Geraldine Little, David Mouat; published new writers within the last year. Length: 1,500 words minimum; 4,000 words maximum. Also publishes literary essays, literary criticism, poetry. Occasionally critiques rejected mss.

How to Contact: Send complete ms with cover letter. Reports in 3 weeks on mss. Simultaneous submissions OK. Sample copy $4.50 ($2.50 for back issue). Fiction guidelines for SAE and 1 first class stamp.

Payment: Pays 2 contributor's copies.

Terms: Acquires first North American serial rights or one-time rights.

Advice: "Write a story that is well constructed, develops characters and maintains interest."

THE CREAM CITY REVIEW, (II), University of Wisconsin-Milwaukee, Box 413, Milwaukee WI 53201. (414)229-9708. Editor: Sandra Nelson. Fiction Editor: Patricia Montalbano. Editors rotate. Magazine: 5½×8½; 200-300 pages; 70 lb. offset/perfect-bound paper; 80 lb. cover stock; illustrations; photos. "General literary publication—an electric selection of the best we receive." Semiannually. Estab. 1975. Circ. 2,000.

● *Esquire* named *Cream City Review* a "literary root" in a July 1992 article.

Needs: Ethnic, experimental, humor/satire, literary, prose poem, regional and translations. Receives approximately 200 unsolicited fiction mss each month. Accepts 6-10 mss/issue. Published work by Eve Shelnutt, Stuart Dybek, Robley Wilson, William Kittredge and Marge Piercy; published new writers within the last year. Length: 1,000-10,000 words. Publishes short shorts. Also publishes literary essays, literary criticism, poetry. Critiques rejected mss when there is time. Recommends other markets "when we have time."

How to Contact: Send complete ms with SASE. Simultaneous submissions OK. Reports in 2 months. Sample copy $4.50. Reviews novels and short story collections.
Payment: Pays 2 contributor's copies.
Terms: Acquires first rights. Sends galleys to author. Rights revert to author after publication.
Advice: "Read as much as you write so that you can examine your own work in relation to where fiction has been and where fiction is going."

THE CRESCENT REVIEW, (II), The Crescent Review, Inc., 1445 Old Town Rd., Winston-Salem NC 27106-3143. (919)924-1851. Editor: Guy Nancekeville. Magazine: 6×9; 160 pages. Estab. 1983.
• Work appearing in *The Crescent Review* has been included in past editions of the *Best American Short Stories, Pushcart Prize* and *Black Southern Writers* anthologies. A story from the journal was selected for the 1990 *Year's Best Horror Stories* and, more recently, in the 1992 *New Stories from the South.*
Needs: "All kinds of stories." Does not read submissions May-June; Nov.-Dec.
How to Contact: Reports in 2 weeks-4 months. SASE. No simultaneous submissions. Sample issue for $5.
Payment: Pays 2 contributor's copies; discount for contributors.
Terms: Acquires first North American serial rights.

CRIME CLUB, (I), Suite 171, 6172 Bollinger Rd., San Jose CA 95129. (408)257-0442. Editors: Rob Oxoby and Marc Oxoby. Magazine. "Journal of poetry, prose and visual arts." Quarterly. Estab. 1991. Circ. 400.
Needs: Any genre. Adventure, experimental, fantasy, historical, humor/satire, literary, mainstream, mystery/suspense, psychic/supernatural/occult, regional, religious, science fiction, serialized novel, prose poem. Length: 5,000 words maximum. Publishes short shorts. Length: 200-500 words. Also accepts poetry.
How to Contact: Query first or send complete ms with cover letter. Simultaneous submissions OK. Accepts electronic submissions (query first). Reports in 2 months.
Payment: Pays 1 contributor's copy.
Terms: Acquires first North American serial rights.
Advice: "Be honest, be smart and have fun with it. We are serious but do this because we enjoy it. We'll publish anything of quality."

CRUCIBLE, (I, II), English Dept., Barton College, College Station, Wilson NC 27893. (919)399-6456. Editor: Terrence L. Grimes. Magazine of fiction and poetry for a general, literary audience. Annually. Estab. 1964. Circ. 500.
Needs: Contemporary, ethnic, experimental, feminist, gay, lesbian, literary, regional. Receives 5 unsolicited mss/month. Accepts 5-6 mss/year. Publishes ms 4-5 months after acceptance. Does not read mss from April 30 to December 1. Recently published work by William Hutchins, Guy Nancekeville. Length: 8,000 words maximum. Publishes short shorts.
How to Contact: Send complete ms with cover letter which should include a brief biography, "in case we publish." Reports in 2 weeks on queries; by June 15 on mss. SASE. Sample copy for $4. Fiction guidelines free.
Payment: Pays contributor's copies.
Terms: Pays on publication for first rights.
Advice: "Write about what you know. Experimentation is fine as long as the experiences portrayed come across as authentic, that is to say, plausible."

CUTBANK, (II), English Department, University of Montana, Missoula MT 59812. Editors-in-Chief: Judy Blunt, Bob Hackett. Fiction Editor: Mary Vanek. Editors change each year. Terms run from June-June. After June 1993, address to "Fiction Editor." Magazine: 5½×8½; 115-130 pages. "Publishes highest quality fiction, poetry, artwork, for a general, literary audience." Semiannually. Estab. 1973. Circ. 600.
Needs: Receives 200 unsolicited mss/month. Accepts 6-12 mss/year. Does not read mss from February 28-August 15. Publishes ms up to 6 months after acceptance. Published new writers within the last year. Length: 40 pages maximum. Also publishes literary essays, literary criticism, poetry. Occasionally critiques rejected mss.

How to Contact: Send complete ms with cover letter, which should include "name, address, publications." Reports in 1-4 months on mss. SASE. Simultaneous submissions OK. Sample copy $4 (current issue $6.95). Fiction guidelines for SASE. Reviews novels and short story collections. Send books to fiction editor.
Payment: Pays 2 contributor's copies.
Terms: Rights revert to author upon publication, with provision that *Cutbank* receives publication credit.
Advice: "Strongly suggest contributors read an issue. We have published stories by David Long, William Kittredge, Rick DeMarinis, Patricia Henley, Melanie Rae Thon and Michael Dorris in recent issues, and like to feature new writers alongside more well-known names. Send only your best work."

CWM, (II, III, IV), 1300 Kicker Rd., Tuscaloosa AL 35404. (205)553-2284. Editor: David C. Kopaska-Merkel. Co-editor: Geof Huth, 317 Princeton Rd., Apt. 451, Schenectady NY 12306. (518)374-7143. Magazine: Variable size; pages, paper quality, cover variable; ink drawings or others possible. "Each issue has a theme; that of the 2nd issue is: 'What Lies Beneath the Surface' (to be published in late 1993). We publish fiction, art and poetry for anyone interested in something a little bit different." Estab. 1990.
Needs: "Any submission fitting the theme." Receives 5-10 mss/month. Accepts 1-5 mss/issue; 2-10 mss/year. Publishes ms within 2 years of acceptance. Length: 10,000 words maximum. Publishes short shorts; any length is acceptable. Also publishes poetry. Sometimes comments on rejected mss and recommends other markets.
How to Contact: Query first or send complete manuscript with cover letter. Reports in 1-4 weeks on queries; 1-8 weeks on mss. SASE. No simultaneous submissions. Accepts computer printout submissions. Accepts electronic submissions via disk. Fiction guidelines for #10 SAE and 1 first class stamp.
Payment: Pays contributor's copies.
Terms: Acquires one-time rights.
Advice: "A manuscript must meet our theme for the issue in question. It stands out if it begins well and is neatly and clearly prepared. Given a good beginning, the story must hold the reader's interest all the way to the end and not let go. It helps if a story haunts the reader even after it is put aside."

D.C., (I), K3, 18 Taylor Ave., Earlville NY 13332. (315)691-9431. Editor: Katrina Kelly. Newsletter: 8½ × 11; 12-14 pages; illustrations. "*D.C.* is interested in funny and/or interesting materials, sick humor is good, too. Our audience is people of the punk genre and the sarcastically morbid." Monthly. Estab. 1988. Circ. 150.
Needs: Horror, humor/satire, psychic/supernatural/occult. Receives 10-15 unsolicited mss/month. Acquires 3 (depending on length) mss/issue. Publishes ms soon after acceptance. Published work by Katrina Kelly, Kevin Miller, James Shepard, Frank Hart. Length: 2,000 words average. Publishes short shorts.
How to Contact: Query first. Reports in 2 weeks. Simultaneous submissions OK. Sample copy for $1.50. Fiction guidelines for SAE and 2 first class stamps.
Payment: Pays subscription to magazine. Must write often to stay on mailing list.
Advice: "I like submissions that are well written, are *somewhat* logical and interest or amuse." Magazine known for fiction "of the disgusting, revolting kind."

DAGGER OF THE MIND, Beyond The Realms Of Imagination, (II), K'yi-Lih Productions (a division of Breach Enterprises), 1317 Hookridge Dr., El Paso TX 79925. (915)591-0541. Editor: Arthur William Lloyd Breach. Magazine. 8½ × 11; 62-86 pages; hibright paper; high glossy cover; from 5-12 illustrations. Quarterly. Estab. 1990. Circ. 5,000.
Needs: Lovecraftian. Adventure, experimental, fantasy, horror, mystery/suspense (private eye, police procedural), science fiction (hard science, soft/sociological). Nothing sick and blasphemous, vulgar, obscene, racist, sexist, profane, humorous, weak, exploited women stories and those with idiotic puns. Plans special paperback anthologies. Receives 250 unsolicited mss/month. Buys 8-15 mss/issue; 90-100 mss/year depending upon length. Publishes ms 1 year after acceptance. Agented fiction 30%. Published work by Sidney Williams, Jessica Amanda Salmonson, Donald R. Burleson. Length: 4,500 words average; 5,000 minimum; 10,000 words maximum. Publishes short shorts. Length: Under 1,000 words. Also publishes literary essays, literary criticism, poetry. Sometimes comments on rejected mss.
How to Contact: Send complete manuscript with cover letter. "Include a bio and list of previously published credits with tearsheets. I also expect a brief synopsis of the story." Reports in 3-3½ months on mss. SASE. Simultaneous submissions OK. Accepts electronic submissions. Sample copy for $3.50, 9 × 12 SAE and 5 first class stamps. Fiction guidelines for #10 SAE and 1 first class stamp.

Payment: Pays ½-1¢/word plus 1 contributor's copy.
Terms: Pays on publication for first rights (possibly anthology rights as well).
Advice: "I'm a big fan of the late H.P. Lovecraft. I love reading through Dunsanian and Cthulhu Mythus tales. I'm constantly on the lookout for this special brand of fiction. If you want to grab my attention immediately, write on the outside of the envelope 'Lovecraftian submission enclosed.' There are a number of things which make submissions stand out for me. Is there any sensitivity to the tale? I like sensitive material, so long as it doesn't become mushy. Another thing that grabs my attention is characters which leap out of the pages and grab you. Then there are those old standards for accepting a manuscript: good imagery, story plot and originality. Move me, bring a tear to my eye; make me stop and think about the world and people around me. Frighten me with little spoken of truths about the human condition. In short, bring out all my emotions (except humor, I detest humor) and show me that you can move me in such a way as I have never been moved before."

THE DALHOUSIE REVIEW, (II), Room 314, Dunn Building, Dalhousie University, Halifax, Nova Scotia B3H 3J5 Canada. Editor: Dr. Alan Andrews. Magazine: 15cm × 23cm; approximately 140 pages; photographs sometimes. Publishes articles, book reviews, short stories and poetry. Quarterly. Circ. 800.
Needs: Literary. Length: 5,000 words maximum. Also publishes literary essays, literary criticism, poetry.
How to Contact: Send complete ms with cover letter. SASE (Canadian stamps). Sample copy $6.50 (Canadian) plus postage. Occasionally reviews novels and short story collections.

DANCE CONNECTION, A Canadian Dance Journal, (II, IV), 603, 815 1st St. SW, Calgary, Alberta, T2P 1N3 Canada. (403)237-7327. Editor: Heather Elton. Magazine: 8½ × 11; 56 pages; recycled bond paper; illustrations and b&w photographs. "Dance: Interview, essay, commentary, reviews for dance lovers, academics, educators, professionals, artists." Published 5 times per year. Estab. 1983. Circ. 5,000.
Needs: Dance. "Do not send anything not related to dance. No poems about ballet." Plans special fiction issue. Upcoming theme: Dance and Sport. Receives 10 unsolicited mss/month. Buys 1 mss/issue; 3 mss/year. Publishes ms 3 months after acceptance. Length: 1,100 words average; 400 words minimum; 2,500 words maximum. Publishes short shorts. Length: 800 words.
How to Contact: Query with clips of published work or send complete manuscript with cover letter. Reports in 2 months. SASE. Simultaneous and reprint submissions OK. Accepts electronic submissions; prefers Macintosh disk (Microsoft Word). Sample copy for 9 × 12 SAE. Fiction guidelines for #10 SAE.
Payment: Pays $25-250 (Canadian), subscription to magazine and contributor's copies.
Terms: Pays on publication for first rights or one-time rights.

DANDELION MAGAZINE, (II), Dandelion Magazine Society, 922 9th Ave., Calgary, Alberta T2C 0S4 Canada. (403)265-0524. Fiction Editor: Flora Malteure. Magazine: 100 pages. Semiannually. Estab. 1972. Circ. 700.
Needs: Literary. Receives 50 unsolicited mss/month. Accepts 5 mss/issue; 10 mss/year. Publishes ms 6 months after acceptance. Pubilshes short shorts. Sometimes critiques rejected mss.
How to Contact: Send complete ms with cover letter. Reports in 6 months on mss. SASE. Reviews novels and short story collections by Alberta authors. Sample copy for $6. Fiction guidelines for SAE.
Payment: No payment.
Terms: Acquires one-time rights.
Advice: "The best way to understand what we publish is by reading *Dandelion*. We invite you to subscribe. We publish reviews of books by Alberta authors, poetry, visual arts, short fiction and the occasional article. We try to be eclectic in what we publish. Please remember that since we only publish twice a year this sometimes gives rise to a delay in returning manuscripts. For our June issue we consider manuscripts during January through to the end of March. For our December issue we consider manuscripts during July through to the end of September. Manuscripts without SASE, or without sufficient postage will not be returned."

DARK TOME, (I, IV), P.O. Box 705, Salem OR 97308. Editor: Michelle Marr. Magazine: 5½ × 8½; 30-80 pages; 20 lb. paper; 60 lb. cover; illustrations. "We publish horror fiction for mature readers who are not easily offended." Bimonthly. Estab. 1990. Circ. 150.

Needs: Horror, psychic/supernatural/occult. "I want original nightmares, not classic ghost stories." Receives 50 unsolicited mss/month. Acquires 6-10 mss/issue; 30-60 mss/year. Publishes manuscript 2-4 months after acceptance. Length: 1,500 words average; 4,000 words maximum. Especially looking for short shorts (to 1,000 words).
How to Contact: Send complete manuscript with cover letter. Reports in 2-5 weeks. SASE. Sample copy for $2.75 payable to Michelle Marr. Fiction guidelines for #10 SASE.
Payment: Pays in contributor's copies and small cash payment.
Terms: Buys first North American serial rights.
Advice: "I am looking for stories with vivid images that will remain in the mind of the reader, and horrors that affect only a small number of people."

DAUGHTERS OF SARAH, (II, IV), 3801 N. Keeler, Box 411179, Chicago IL 60618. (312)736-3399. Editor: Reta Finger. Magazine: 5½ × 8½; 64 pages; illustrations and photos. "Christian feminist publication dealing with Christian theology, history, women and social issues from a feminist point of view." Quarterly. Estab. 1974. Circ. 5,000.
Needs: Historical, religious/inspirational, feminist and spiritual (Christian feminist). "No subjects unrelated to feminism from Christian viewpoint." Upcoming themes: "Women and War," "Feminism on Prophecy," "Birth, Adoption, Abortion," "Prostitution," "Women in Ministry." Receives 6-8 unsolicited fiction mss/month. Buys 4-6 mss/year. Published work by Mary Cartledge-Hayes. Length: 1,800 words maximum. Publishes short shorts. Also publishes poetry. Occasionally critiques rejected mss "if related and close to acceptance."
How to Contact: Query first with description of ms and SASE. Include cover letter stating why ms was written; biography of author. Simultaneous and previously published submissions OK "but won't pay." Reports in 2 weeks on queries. Publishes "most" ms 3 months to 1 year after acceptance. Sample copy for $2.50. Reviews novels and short story collections. Send books to Dulcie Gannett.
Payment: Pays $15/printed page; 3 free contributor's copies. Offers kill fee of one-half stated fee.
Terms: Pays upon publication for first North American serial or one-time rights.
Advice: "Make sure topic of story fits with publication. We get many stories that are either Christian stories, women's stories, Christian women's stories, but not necessarily feminist. We believe that the Christian gospel was meant to be radically egalitarian and we try to integrate it with the feminist insights and analysis available today."

DEATHREALM, (II), 3223-F Regents Park, Greensboro NC 27455. (919)288-9138. Editor: Mark Rainey. Magazine: 8½ × 11; 50-60 pages; 20 lb. bond paper; 8 pt. glossy coated cover stock; pen & ink, screened illustrations; b&w photos. Publishes "fantasy/horror," for a "mature" audience. Quarterly. Estab. 1987. Circ. 1,200.
● This horror and dark fantasy magazine won the Small Press Writers and Artists Organization's "Best Magazine" award and the editor won the "Best Editor" award in the same year (1990). Right now the editor is looking for more fiction with supernatural-based plots.
Needs: Experimental, fantasy, horror, psychic/supernatural/occult and science fiction. "Sci-fi tales should have a horror slant. *Strongly* recommend contributor buy a sample copy of *Deathrealm* before submitting." Receives 200-300 mss/month. Buys 6-8 mss/issue; 30 mss/year. Publishes ms within 1 year of acceptance. Published work by Joe R. Lansdale, Fred Chappell, Kevin J. Anderson, Jessica Amanda Salmonson. Length: 5,000 words average; 10,000 words maximum. Publishes short shorts. Also publishes literary criticism, poetry. Sometimes critiques rejected mss and recommends other markets.
How to Contact: Send complete ms with cover letter, which should include "publishing credits, some bio info, where they heard about *Deathrealm*. Never reveal plot in cover letter." May accept simultaneous submissions, but "not recommended." Reports in 2 weeks on queries; 6-8 weeks on ms. SASE. Sample copy for $4 and $1 postage. Fiction guidelines for #10 SAE and 1 first class stamp. Reviews novels and short story collections. Send books to Randy Johnston, 3114 NW 41, Oklahoma City OK 73112.
Payment: Pays $5 minimum; higher rates for established professionals; contributor's copies.
Advice: "Concentrate on characterization; development of ideas; strong atmosphere, with an important setting. I frown on gratuitous sex and violence unless it is a mere side effect of a more sophisticated story line. Stay away from overdone themes—foreboding dreams come true; being a frustrated writer; using lots of profanity and having a main character so detestable you don't care what happens to him."

DENVER QUARTERLY, (II, III), University of Denver, Denver CO 80208. (303)871-2892. Editor: Donald Revell. Magazine: 6 × 9; 144-160 pages; occasional illustrations. "We publish fiction, articles and poetry for a generally well-educated audience, primarily interested in literature and the literary experience. They read *DQ* to find something a little different from a strictly academic quarterly or a creative writing outlet." Quarterly. Estab. 1966. Circ. 1,200.

Needs: "We are now interested in experimental fiction (minimalism, magic realism, etc.) as well as in realistic fiction." Also publishes poetry.

How to Contact: Send complete ms with SASE. Does not read mss May-September 15. Do not query. Reports in 1-2 months on mss. Publishes ms within a year after acceptance. Published work by Joyce Carol Oates, Jay Clayton, Charles Baxter; published new writers within the last year. No simultaneous submissions. Sample copy $5 with SASE.

Payment: Pays $5/page for fiction and poetry, 2 free author's copies plus 3 tear sheets.

Terms: Buys first North American serial rights.

Advice: "We'll be looking for serious, realistic and experimental fiction. Nothing so quickly disqualifies a manuscript as sloppy proofreading and mechanics. Read the magazine before submitting to it. Send clean copy and a *brief* cover letter. We try to remain eclectic and I think we do, but the odds for beginners are bound to be long considering the fact that we receive nearly 8,000 mss per year and publish only about 16 short stories."

DESCANT, (II), Box 314, Station P, Toronto, Ontario M5S 2S8 Canada. (416)927-7059. Editor: Karen Mulhallen. Magazine: 5¾ × 8¾; 100-300 pages; heavy paper; good cover stock; illustrations and photos. "High quality poetry and prose for an intelligent audience who wants to see a broad range of literature." Quarterly. Estab. 1970. Circ. 1,000.

● In past years *Descant* has won Canada's National Magazine Award for both poetry and fiction.

Needs: Literary, contemporary, translations. "Although most themes are acceptable, all works must have literary merit." Upcoming theme: "First Nations" (Summer 1993). Receives 100-200 unsolicited mss/month. Published work by Tim Lilburn, Douglas Glover, George Bowering. Publishes short shorts. Also publishes literary essays, poetry. Critiques rejected mss when there is time.

How to Contact: Send complete ms with cover letter. SAE, IRC. Simultaneous submissions OK ("but we only print unpublished material"). Reports in 4 months on mss. Sample copy for $7.50 plus $2 for postage to U.S.

Payment: Pays a modest honorarium and 1 year subscription. Extra contributor's copies at discount.

Advice: "*Descant* has plans for several special issues in the next two years. Unsolicited work is less likely to be accepted in the coming months, and will be kept on file for longer before it appears."

DESCANT, (II), Department of English, Texas Christian University, Fort Worth TX 76129. (817)921-7240. Editors: Betsy Colquitt, Stanley Trachtenberg, Harry Opperman, Steve Sherwood. "*Descant* uses fiction and poetry. No restriction on style, content or theme. *Descant* is a 'little' literary magazine, and its readers are those who have interest in such publications." Semiannually. Estab. 1955. Circ. 500.

Needs: Literary, contemporary and regional. No genre or category fiction. Receives approximately 50 unsolicited fiction mss each month. Does not read mss in summer. Published new writers within the last year. Length: 1,500-5,000 words. Publishes short shorts. Sometimes recommends other markets. Also publishes poetry.

How to Contact: Send complete ms with SASE. Reports usually within 6 weeks on ms. Sample copy $8 (old copy).

Payment: Pays 2 free author's copies. (Pays $8 charge/extra copy.)

Advice: "Submit good material. Even though a small publication, *Descant* receives many submissions, and acceptances are few compared to the total number of mss received." Mss are rejected because they "are badly written, careless in style and development, shallow in characterization, trite in handling and in conception. We offer a $500 annual prize for fiction—the Frank O'Connor Prize. Award is made to the story considered (by a judge not connected to the magazine) to be the best published in a given volume of the journal."

DEUTERIUM, A Digest of Poems, Prose, and Art, (I), P.O. Box 20013, Dayton OH 45420-0013. (513)252-5784. Editor: Randy Watts. Magazine: 5½ × 8½; 16 pages; some illustrations. "For beginning, thought provoking writers." Semiannually. Estab. 1991. Circ. 100.

Needs: Confession, contemporary, experimental, fantasy, gay, historical (general), mainstream, mystery/suspense, prose poem, regional, romance (contemporary, historical), science fiction. Length: Open. Publishes short shorts. Also accepts poetry. Recommends other markets.

How to Contact: Query first. Simultaneous and reprint submissions OK. Sample copy free.

Payment: Pays contributor's copies.

Terms: Acquires one-time rights.

Advice: "I personally like down-to-earth writers. Don't write over the average American head."

‡DIFFUSIONS, (I), P. O. Box 50084, Washington DC 20091. Editors: K. Sawhill, S. Payne, B.D. Reisberg. Magazine: 7×8; 30 pages; illustrations and photos. "To provide a forum for artists of all languages and cultures." Quarterly. Estab. 1991. Circ. 500.
Needs: Adventure, condensed novel, erotica, ethnic/multicultural, experimental, fantasy, feminist, gay, horror, humor/satire, lesbian, literary, mainstream/contemporary, mystery/suspense, psychic/supernatural/occult, regional, religious/inspirational, romance, science fiction, senior citizen/retirement, serialized novel, sports, translations, westerns. Also, "pieces written in language other than English, Spanish or French must be briefly translated." Publishes special fiction issue or anthology. Receives 50 mss/month. Acquires 3 mss/issue; 10 mss/year. Recently published work by Danielle Hell, Eva Disgust, Geoffrey Peard. Length: 100-500 words average; 500 words maximum. Publishes short shorts. Length: under 500 words. Also publishes poetry.
How to Contact: Send complete manuscript with a cover letter. Should include 20 word bio with submission. Reports in 1 year on queries; 6 months on mss. Send SASE (IRC) for reply, return of ms, or send a disposable copy of the ms. Simultaneous submissions OK. Sample copy $3, fiction guidelines $1.
Payment: Pays 2 contributor's copies; additional copies half price.
Terms: Rights revert back to author after publication.
Advice: Looks for "originality in subject/theme, excellence (i.e., writing skill), political awareness of issues."

‡DOOR COUNTY ALMANAK, (IV), The Dragonsbreath Press, 10905 Bay Shore Dr., Sister Bay WI 54234. (414)854-2742. Editor: Fred Johnson. Magazine: 6×9; 200-300 pages; good uncoated paper; antique vellum cover stock; illustrations; photos. "The major focus is Door County WI and its surrounding areas. Covering the history, recent and distant, of the area and its people, including contemporary profiles of people and businesses. Each issue has a major theme. Also uses poetry and fiction for general audience, mainly aimed at people familiar with the area." No set publication schedule. Estab. 1982.
Needs: Adventure, contemporary, fantasy, historical (general), humor/satire, literary, mystery/suspense, regional. "Prefer to have the fiction in some way related to the area, at least to the issue's theme." No romance. Receives 10-20 unsolicited fiction mss/month. Buys 1-2 mss/issue. Does not read mss April-September. Published new writers within the last year. Length: 4,000 words average; 500 words minimum; 6,000 words maximum.
How to Contact: Query first. Reports in 3-4 weeks on queries; 2-3 months on mss. SASE for query and ms. Simultaneous submissions and reprints OK. Sample copy: $9.95 with 7×10 SAE and $1.50 postage. Fiction guidelines for #10 SAE and 1 first class stamp.
Payment: Pays $10-$35 plus contributor's copies.
Terms: Pays on publication for first North American serial rights and other rights.
Advice: "Query first to find out what coming issue's theme is and what the needs are. We're always looking for nonfiction articles also. Keep in mind this is definitely a regional magazine."

DREAM INTERNATIONAL/QUARTERLY, (I, IV), U.S. Address: Charles I. Jones, 121 N. Ramona St. #27, Ramona CA 92065. Australia address: Dr. Les Jones, 256 Berserker St., No. Rockhampton, Queensland 4701, Australia. Editors: Les and Chuck Jones. Magazine: 5×7; 60-80 pages; Xerox paper; parchment cover stock; some illustrations and photos. "Publishes fiction and nonfiction that is dream-related or clearly inspired by a dream. Also dream-related fantasy." Quarterly. Estab. 1981. Circ. 600.
Needs: Adventure, confession, contemporary, erotica, ethnic, experimental, fantasy, historical (general), horror, humor/satire, literary, mainstream, mystery/suspense, prose poem, psychic/supernatural/occult, romance, science fiction, translations, young adult/teen (10-18). Upcoming themes: "We are planning to solicit and encourage subjects related to the paranormal . . . possibly a contest associated with such subject sometime early in 1993." Receives 20-30 unsolicited mss/month. Publishes ms 6-8 months after acceptance. Length: 1,000 words minimum; 1,500 words maximum. Published new writers within the last year. Publishes short shorts. Length: 500-800 words. Also publishes literary essays,

The double dagger before a listing indicates that the listing is new in this edition. New Markets are often the most receptive to submissions by new writers.

poetry. Occasionally critiques rejected mss. Sometimes recommends other markets.
How to Contact: Reports in 6 weeks on queries; 3 months on mss. SASE. Simultaneous and reprint submissions OK. Sample copy for $5 (add $1.50 to single copy purchases to cover postage and handling), SAE and 2 first class stamps. Guidelines for $1.50 SAE and 1 first class stamp. "Accepted mss will not be returned unless requested at time of submission."
Payment: Pays in contributor's copies (contributors must pay $1.50 for postage and handling); sometimes offers magazine subscription.
Terms: Acquires one-time rights.
Advice: "Use your nightly dreams to inspire you to literary flights. Avoid stereotypes and clichés. Avoid Twilight Zone type stories. When contacting U.S. editor, make all checks, money orders, and overseas drafts payable to *Charles Jones.*"

DREAMS & NIGHTMARES, The Magazine of Fantastic Poetry, (IV), 1300 Kicker Rd., Tuscaloosa AL 35404. (205)553-2284. Editor: David C. Kopaska-Merkel. Magazine: 5½ × 8½; 20 pages; ink drawing illustrations. "*DN* is mainly a poetry magazine, but I *am* looking for short-short stories. They should be either fantasy, science fiction, or horror." Estab. 1986. Circ. 200.
  • Two poems first appearing in *Dreams & Nightmares* were selected for inclusion as Honorable Mentions in the 1991 *Year's Best Fantasy and Horror*, edited by Ellen Datlow and Terry Windling.
Needs: Experimental, fantasy, horror, humor/satire, science fiction. "Try me with anything *except*: senseless violence, misogyny or hatred (unreasoning) of any kind of people, sappiness." Receives 4-8 unsolicited fiction mss/month. Buys 0-1 ms/issue; 0-2 mss/year. Publishes ms 1-9 months after acceptance. Published work by Ron McDowell, D.F. Lewis. Length: 500 words average; 1,000 words maximum. Publishes short shorts. Length: 500 or fewer words. Sometimes critiques rejected mss and recommends other markets. Also publishes poetry.
How to Contact: Send complete manuscript. Reports in 1-3 weeks on queries; 1-6 weeks on mss. SASE. No simultaneous submissions. Accepts electronic submissions. Sample copy for $1.25 in stamps. Fiction guidelines for #10 SAE and 1 first class stamp.
Payment: Pays $3 and 2 contributor's copies.
Terms: Pays on acceptance for one-time rights.
Advice: "A story must grab the reader and hold on to the end. I want to be *involved*. Start with a good first line, lead the reader where you want him/her to go and end with something that causes a reaction or provokes thought."

DREAMS & VISIONS, New Frontiers in Christian Fiction, (II), Skysong Press, RR1, Washago, Ontario L0K 2B0 Canada. Editor: Steve Stanton. Fiction Editor: Wendy Stanton. Magazine: 5½ × 8½; 48 pages; 20 lb. bond paper; Mayfair Fancy cover; illustrations on cover. "Contemporary Christian fiction in a variety of styles for adult Christians." Triannually. Estab. 1989. Circ. 300.
Needs: Contemporary, experimental, fantasy, humor/satire, literary, religious/inspirational, science fiction (soft/sociological). "All stories should portray a Christian world view or expand upon Biblical themes or ethics in an entertaining or enlightening manner." Receives 20 unsolicited mss/month. Accepts 7 mss/issue; 21 mss/year. Publishes ms 2-6 months after acceptance. Length: 2,500 words; 1,500 words minimum; 7,500 words maximum. Sometimes critiques rejected mss.
How to Contact: Send complete ms with cover letter. "Bio is optional: degrees held and in what specialties, publishing credits, service in the church, etc." Reports in 1 month on queries; 8-10 weeks on mss. SASE. Simultaneous submissions OK. Sample copy for $3.95. Fiction guidelines for SAE and 1 IRC.
Payment: Pays in contributor's copies; extras at ⅓ discount.
Terms: Acquires first North American serial rights and one-time, non-exclusive reprint rights.
Advice: "In general we look for work that has some literary value, that is in some way unique and relevant to Christian readers today. Our first priority is technical adequacy, though we will occasionally work with a beginning writer to polish a manuscript. Ultimately, we look for stories that glorify the Lord Jesus Christ, stories that build up rather than tear down, that exalt the sanctity of life, the holiness of God, and the value of the family."

EAGLE'S FLIGHT, A Literary Magazine, (I), 2501 Hunters Hill Dr., #822, Enid OK 73703. Editor: Shyamkant Kulkarni. Fiction Editor: Rekha Kulkarni. Tabloid: 8½ × 11; 4-8 pages; bond paper; broad sheet cover. Publication includes "fiction and poetry for a general audience." Quarterly.

Needs: Literary, mainstream, mystery/suspense, romance. Plans to publish special fiction issue in future. Accepts 2-4 mss/year. Does not read mss June-December. Recently published work by Dr. Leroy Thomas, Laura Dawson, Chad Born, Branley Branson. Length: 1,500 words preferred; 1,000 words minimum; 2,000 maximum. Publishes short shorts. Also publishes literary criticism, poetry.
How to Contact: Query first. Reports in 6 weeks on queries; 3 months on mss. SASE. Sample copy or fiction guidelines for $1 and #10 SAE and 1 first class stamp. Reviews novels and short story collections.
Payment: Pays $5-20 or subscription to magazine, contributor's copies; charge for extras.
Terms: Pays on publication for first North American serial rights or one-time rights.
Advice: "We look for form, substance and quality. Read and study what one wants to write and work at."

EARTH'S DAUGHTERS, (II), A Feminist Arts Periodical, Box 41, Central Park Station, Buffalo NY 14215. (716)835-8719. Collective editorship. Business Manager: Bonnie Johnson. Magazine: usually 5½×8½; 50 pages; 60 lb. paper; coated cover; 2-4 illustrations; 2-4 photos. "We publish poetry and short fiction; also graphics, art work and photos; our focus is the experience and creative expression of women." For a general/women/feminist audience. Quarterly. Published special topical issues last year; plans more this year. Estab. 1971. Circ. 1,000.
Needs: Contemporary, erotica, ethnic, experimental, fantasy, feminist, humor/satire, literary, prose poem. "Keep the fiction short." Receives 25-50 unsolicited fiction mss/month. Accepts 2-4 mss/issue; 8-12 mss/year. Published work by Gabrielle Burton, Mary Jane Markell, Meredith Sue Willis and Julia Alvarez; published several new writers within the last year. Length: 400 words minimum; 1,000 words maximum; 800 words average. Occasionally critiques rejected mss and recommends other markets.
How to Contact: Send complete ms. SASE. Simultaneous submissions OK. Reports in 3 weeks on queries; 3 weeks to 3 months on mss. Publishes ms an average of 1 year after acceptance. Sample copy for $4.
Payment: Pays 2 contributor's copies, additional copies half price.
Terms: Acquires first rights. Copyright reverts to author upon publication.
Advice: "We require work of technical skill and artistic intensity; we welcome submissions from unknown writers. Send SASE in April of each year for themes of upcoming issues. Please do not inquire as to the status of your work too soon or too often—the US Mail is dependable, and we have yet to lose a manuscript."

ECHOES, (II), The Hudson Valley Writers Association, Box 7, LaGrangeville NY 12540. (914)223-5489. Editor: Marcia Grant. Fiction Editor: Don Monaco. Magazine: 5½×8½; 44 pages; illustrations. Quarterly. Estab. 1985. Circ. 300.
Needs: "We do not categorize material—we consider material of *all* types." Receives 15-30 unsolicited mss/month. Acquires 2-5 mss/issue; 8-20 mss/year. Publishes ms 8-12 weeks after acceptance. Published work by Arnold Lipkind, C.C. Doucette; "often encourages promising authors." Length: 1,500 words preferred; 750 words minimum; 3,000 words maximum. Publishes short shorts. Sometimes critiques rejected mss and recommends other markets.
How to Contact: Send complete ms with cover letter. Reports in 6-8 weeks. SASE. Simultaneous submissions and reprints OK, if author owns rights. Sample copy for $4.50. Back issues $3. Fiction guidelines for SAE.
Payment: Pays 1 contributor's copy.
Terms: Acquires one-time rights.
Advice: "Suggest reading a sample copy. We look for quality writing, engaging ideas and writing that we can get excited about."

EIDOS: Sexual Freedom and Erotic Entertainment for Women, Men & Couples, (IV), Box 96, Boston MA 02137-0096. (617)262-0096. Editor: Brenda Loew Tatelbaum. Tabloid: 10×14; 60 pages; web offset printing; illustrations; photos. Magazine of erotica for women, men and couples of all sexual orientations, preferences and lifestyles. "Explicit material regarding language and behavior formed in relationships, intimacy, moment of satisfaction—sensual, sexy, honest. For an energetic, well informed, international erotica readership." Quarterly. Estab. 1984. Circ. 7,000.
Needs: Erotica. Humorous or tongue-in-cheek erotic fiction is especially wanted. Publishes at least 4 pieces of fiction/year. Published new writers within the last year. Length: 1,000 words average; 500 words minimum; 2,000 words maximum. Also publishes literary criticism, poetry. Occasionally critiques rejected mss and recommends other markets.

How to Contact: Send complete ms with SASE. "Cover letter with history of publication or short bio is welcome." Reports in 1 month on queries; 2 months on mss. Simultaneous submissions OK. Sample copy $10. Fiction guidelines for #10 envelope with 1 first class stamp. Reviews novels and short story collections, "if related to subject of erotica (sex, politics, religion, etc.)."
Payment: Pays in contributor's copies.
Terms: Acquires first North American serial rights.
Advice: "We receive more erotic fiction manuscripts now than in the past. Most likely because both men and women are more comfortable with the notion of submitting these manuscripts for publication as well as the desire to see alternative sexually explicit fiction in print. Therefore we can publish more erotic fiction because we have more material to choose from. There is still a lot of debate as to what erotic fiction consists of. This is a tough market to break into. Manuscripts must fit our editorial needs and it is best to order a sample issue prior to writing or submitting material. Honest, explicitly pro-sex, mutually consensual erotica is void of unwanted power, control and degradation—no rape or coercion of any kind."

ELDRITCH SCIENCE, (I,IV), Greater Medford Science Fiction Society, 87-6 Park, Worcester MA 01605. Editor: George Phillies. Magazine: 8½×11; 30 pages; 20 lb. paper; 60 lb. cover; illustrations. Science fiction and fantasy for adults. Annually. Estab. 1988.
Needs: Adventure, fantasy, literary, science fiction (hard science, soft/sociological). "No horror, contemporary, erotica." Receives 5-10 unsolicited mss/month. Accepts 4 mss/issue; 8 mss/year. Publishes mss 4-6 months after acceptance. Published work by Cabot, Moxley, Reedman. Length: 8,000 words; 5,000 words minimum; 15,000 words maximum. Also publishes literary essays. Sometimes critiques rejected mss and recommends other markets.
How to Contact: Send complete ms with cover letter. Reports in 2 weeks on queries; 6-8 weeks on mss. SASE. No simultaneous submissions. Prefers electronic submissions via disk (MS-DOS, low density). Sample copy for 9×12 SAE and 5 first class stamps. Free fiction guidelines.
Payment: Pays in contributor's copies.
Terms: Acquires one-time rights. Publication not copyrighted.
Advice: "Clear plots, heroes who think and solve their problems, and sparkling, literary prose. Make a manuscript stand out. Read the guidelines!"

‡ELDRITCH TALES (II, IV), Yith Press, 1051 Wellington Rd., Lawrence KS 66044. (913)843-4341. Editor-in-Chief: Crispin Burnham. Magazine: 5½×8; 120 pages (average); glossy cover; illustrations; "very few" photos. "The magazine concerns horror fiction in the tradition of the old *Weird Tales* magazine. We publish fiction in the tradition of H.P. Lovecraft, Robert Bloch and Stephen King, among others, for fans of this particular genre." Semiannually. Estab. 1975. Circ. 1,000.
Needs: Horror and psychic/supernatural/occult. "No mad slasher stories or similar nonsupernatural horror stories." Receives about 8 unsolicited fiction mss/month. Buys 12 mss/issue, 24 mss/year. Published work by J.N. Williamson, William F. Wu and Charles Grant. Published new writers within the last year. Length: 50-100 words minimum; 20,000 words maximum; 10,000 words average. Occasionally critiques rejected mss. Sometimes recommends other markets.
How to Contact: Send complete ms with SASE and cover letter stating past sales. Previously published submissions OK. Prefers letter-quality submissions. Reports in 4 months. Publication could take up to 5 years after acceptance. Sample copy $6 and $1 for postage and handling.
Payment: ¼¢/word; 1 contributor's copy. $1 minimum payment.
Terms: Pays in royalties on publication for first rights.
Advice: "Buy a sample copy and read it thoroughly. Most rejects with my magazine are because people have not checked out what an issue is like or what type of stories I accept. Most rejected stories fall into one of two categories: non-horror fantasy (sword & sorcery, high fantasy) or non-supernatural horror (mad slasher stories, 'Halloween' clones, I call them). When I say that they should read my publication, I'm not whistling Dixie. We hope to up the magazine's frequency to a quarterly. We also plan to be putting out one or two books a year, mostly novels, but short story collections will be considered as well."

11TH STREET RUSE, (II), 322 E. 11th St., #23, New York NY 10003. Editor: Violet Snow. Newsletter: 8½×11; 4 pages; bond paper. "Mythical travel; goddess religion; the homeless; for young intellectuals with poor spelling." Bimonthly. Estab. 1988. Circ. 150.
Needs: "We need sublime writers, who can *hear* what they write—preferably have studied poetry." Receives 5 unsolicited mss/month. Accepts 1 ms/year. Publishes ms 2 months after acceptance. Published work by RLS, Violet Snow and Lucid. Length: 500 words average; 6 words minimum; 1,000

words maximum. Publishes short shorts. Length: 300 words. Also publishes literary essays, poetry. Sometimes comments on rejected mss.

How to Contact: Send complete manuscript with cover letter. Include "bio, hatsize." Reports in 3 months. SASE. Simultaneous submissions OK. Sample copy for $1, #10 SAE and 1 first class stamp. Fiction guidelines for #10 SAE and 1 first class stamp. Make checks payable to Ellen Carter.

Payment: Pays contributor's copies.

Terms: Acquires one-time rights. Publication not copyrighted.

ELF: ECLECTIC LITERARY FORUM, (II), P.O. Box 392, Tonawanda NY 14150. (716)693-7006. Editor: C.K. Erbes. Magazine: 8½ × 11; 56 pages; 60 lb. white offset paper; coated cover; 2-3 illustrations; 2-3 photographs. "Well-crafted short stories, poetry, essays on literary themes for a sophisticated audience." Quarterly. Estab. 1991. Circ. 5,000.
  • For more on *ELF*, see the Close-up interview with advisor, editor, Gloria Bane in the 1992 *Poet's Market*.

Needs: Adventure, contemporary, ethnic, fantasy, feminism, historical (general), humor/satire, literary, mainstream, mystery/suspense (private eye), prose poem, regional, science fiction (hard science, soft/sociological), sports, western. No violence and obscenity (horror/erotica). Accepts 4-6 mss/issue; 16-24 mss/year. Publishes ms up to 1 year after acceptance. Recently published work by Jess W. Henryes, Sandra Gouldford, Alyce Ingram, David Comfort. Length: 3,500 words average. Publishes short shorts. Length: 500 words. Sometimes critiques rejected mss and recommends other markets.

How to Contact: Send complete ms with optional cover letter. Reports in 4-6 weeks on mss. SASE. Simultaneous submissions OK (if so indicated). Sample copy for $4.50 ($6 foreign). Fiction guidelines for #10 SAE and 1 first class stamp.

Payment: Pays contributor's copies.

Terms: Acquires first North American serial rights.

Advice: "Short stories stand out when dialogue, plot, character, point of view and language usage work together to create a unified whole on a significant theme, one relevant to most of our readers. We also look for writers whose works demonstrate a knowledge of grammar and how to manipulate it effectively in a story. Each story is read by an Editorial Board comprised of English professors who teach creative writing and are published authors."

EPIPHANY, A Journal of Literature, (II), P.O. Box 2699, University of Arkansas, Fayetteville AR 72701. (501)524-3326. Editors: Charles Freeland, Gordon Grice, Bob Zordani. Magazine: Digest-sized; 80-120 pages; saddle-stapled; laser-printed; matte card cover. "Mainstream literature for a general and academic audience." Quarterly. Estab. 1990. Circ. 300.
  • Note the change in editors and the change in *Epiphany*'s needs. The magazine is now primarily interested in traditional literary fiction.

Needs: Mainstream literary fiction. Receives 30-50 unsolicited mss/month. Buys 5-10 mss/issue; 20-40 mss/year. Publishes ms 3-5 months after acceptance. Length: Up to 10,000 words. Publishes short shorts. Also publishes poetry and literary essays. Often makes brief comment on rejected mss, occasionally recommends other markets.

How to Contact: Send complete ms with SASE. "Cover letter OK but unnecessary." Reports in 1 month. "Considers simultaneous submissions, but writer should notify us promptly of acceptance elsewhere. No previously published material." Sample copy for $4.

Payment: Pays in contributor's copies, plus small honorarium when funds are available.

Terms: Acquires first rights.

Advice: "The flaws we see most often are sloppy proofreading, inadequate development, point-of-view problems, and insufficient attention to language. We aren't interested in anything nonsensical, trite, dogmatic or 'inspirational'."

EPOCH MAGAZINE, (II), 251 Goldwin Smith Hall, Cornell University, Ithaca NY 14853. (607)255-3385. Editor: Michael Koch. Fiction and poetry editors rotate each issue. Submissions should be sent to Michael Koch. Magazine: 6 × 9; 80-100 pages; good quality paper; good cover stock. "Top level fiction and poetry for people who are interested in and capable of being entertained by good literature." Published 3 times a year. Estab. 1947. Circ. 1,000.
  • Work originally appearing in this quality literary journal has appeared in numerous anthologies including *Best American Short Stories, Best American Poetry, Pushcart Prize, The O. Henry Prize Stories, Best of the West* and *New Stories from the South*.

Needs: Literary, contemporary and ethnic. Buys 4-5 mss/issue. Receives approximately 100 unsolicited fiction mss each month. Does not read in summer. Recently published work by Denis Johnson, Harriet Doerr, Lee K. Abbott; published new writers in the last year. Length: 10-30 typed, double-spaced pages. Also publishes literary essays (usually solicited), poetry. Critiques rejected mss when there is time. Sometimes recommends other markets.
How to Contact: Send complete ms with SASE. May accept simultaneous submissions if indicated in cover letter ("but prefer not to"). Reports in 2-8 weeks on mss. Publishes ms an average of 3 months after acceptance. Sample copy for $5.
Terms: Pays on publication for first North American serial rights.
Advice: "Read and be interested in the journals you're sending work to."

EROTIC FICTION QUARTERLY, (I, II, IV), EFQ Publications, Box 424958, San Francisco CA 94142. Editor: Richard Hiller. Magazine: 5×8; 186 pages; perfect-bound; 50 lb. offset paper; 65 lb. cover stock. "Small literary magazine for thoughtful people interested in a variety of sexual themes. Irregularly published."
Needs: Any style heartfelt, intelligent erotica. Also, stories not necessarily erotic whose subject is some aspect of authentic sexual experience. No standard pornography; no "men's magazine" stories; no contrived plots or gimmicks; no broad satire, parody or obscure "literary" writing. Length: 500 words minimum; 5,000 words maximum; 1,500 words average. Occasionally critiques rejected ms.
How to Contact: Send complete ms only. Send mss with SASE for reply, return or send a disposable copy of the ms. Fiction guidelines for SASE.
Payment: Pays $50.
Terms: Pays on acceptance for first rights.
Advice: "Wanted: unpublished as well as published writers who have something to say regarding sexual attitudes, emotions, roles, etc. Story ideas should come from real life, not media; characters should be real people. There are essentially no restrictions regarding content, style, explicitness, etc."

EVENT, (II), Douglas College, Box 2503, New Westminster, British Columbia V3L 5B2 Canada. Editor: Dale Zieroth. Fiction Editor: Maurice Hodgson. Managing Editor: Bonnie Bauder. Magazine: 6×9; 136 pages; quality paper and cover stock; illustrations; photos. "Primarily a literary magazine, publishing poetry, fiction, reviews, occasionally plays and graphics; for creative writers, artists, anyone interested in contemporary literature." Triannually. Estab. 1970. Circ. 1,000.
Needs: Literary, contemporary, feminist, adventure, humor, regional. No technically poor or unoriginal pieces. Buys 6-8 mss/issue. Receives approximately 50 + unsolicited fiction mss/month. Recently published work by Tom Wayman, Edith Pearlman, Richard Lemm; published new writers within the last year. Length: 5,000 words maximum. Also publishes poetry. Critiques rejected mss "when there is time."
How to Contact: Send complete ms with SASE and bio (*must* be Canadian postage or IRC). Reports in 4 months on mss. Publishes ms an average of 6-12 months after acceptance. Sample copy $5.
Payment: Pays $20/page and 2 contributor's copies.
Terms: Pays on publication for first North American serial rights.
Advice: "A good narrative arc is hard to find."

THE EVERGREEN CHRONICLES, A Journal of Gay & Lesbian Literature, (II), Box 8939, Minneapolis MN 55408. Managing Editor: Jim Berg. Magazine: 5½×8½; 90-100 pages; linen bond paper; b&w line drawings and photos. "No one theme, other than works must have a lesbian or gay appeal. Works sensual and erotic are considered. We look for poetry and prose, but are open to well-crafted pieces of nearly any genre." Semiannually. Estab. 1985. Circ. 400.
Needs: Gay or lesbian: adventure, confession, contemporary, ethnic, experimental, fantasy, feminist, humor/satire, literary, romance (contemporary), science fiction, serialized/excerpted novel, suspense/mystery. "We are interested in works by gay/lesbian artists in a wide variety of genres. The subject matter need not be specifically lesbian or gay-themed, but we do look for a deep sensitivity to that experience. Accepts 1-2 mss/issue; 12-15 mss/year. Publishes ms approx. 2 months after acceptance. Published work by Terri Jewel, Lev Raphael and Ruthann Robson; published new writers in the last year. Length: 3,500-4,500 words average; no minimum; 5,200 words maximum. 25 pages double-spaced

---

Read the Business of Fiction Writing section to learn the correct way to prepare and submit a manuscript.

maximum on prose. Publishes short shorts. Sometimes comments on rejected mss.
How to Contact: Send 4 copies of complete ms with cover letter. "It helps to have some biographical info included." Reports on queries in 3 weeks; on mss in 3-4 months. SASE. Sample copy for $8, 6×9 SAE and $1 postage. Fiction guidelines for #10 SAE and 1 first class stamp.
Payment: Pays in contributor's copies.
Terms: Acquires one-time rights.
Advice: "Perseverance is on a par with skill at the craft."

‡**EXIT, A Journal of the Arts,** Rochester Routes/Creative Arts Projects, 232 Post Ave., Rochester NY 14619-1313. (716)328-2144. Editor/Publisher: Frank Judge. "Our magazine has no theme and no particular bias but *quality*. We assume our readership is the 'little magazine' audience; we've had nothing to disprove this assumption so far." Published irregularly. Estab. 1976. Circ. 1,000.
Needs: Literary, contemporary, science fiction, fantasy, mystery and translations. "Science fiction, fantasy and mystery submissions should have a 'literary' slant giving a broader appeal than that of the respective forms; query preferred for these categories." No religious/inspirational, psychic/supernatural, feminist, gay/lesbian, confession, gothic, romance, western, adventure, juvenile, young adult, ethnic, or serialized or condensed novels. Accepts 1-2 mss/issue. Receives 20-30 unsolicited fiction mss each month. Length: 2,000 words maximum. Also publishes literary essays, literary criticism, poetry.
How to Contact: Send query or complete ms with SASE. Accepts disk submissions compatible with PC XT/AT, Mac, Apple II=, IIc, IIe. Reports in 3 weeks on queries, 3p6 months on mss. Publishes ms 6-12 months after acceptance. Sample copy $5. Reviews novels and short story collections.
Payment: 3 free author's copies; $5 charge for extras.
Terms: Pays on publication for first North American serial rights and second serial rights.
Advice: Mss are rejected because they are "loaded with adolescent clichés and trite concepts, revel in 'experimental' obscurantising, and/or have no sense of plot, liveliness."

‡**EXPERIMENTAL (BASEMENT), (I),** eXpErImENtAL (bAsEemEnT) pReSs, # A-191, 3740 N. Romero Rd., Tucson AZ 85705. (602)293-3287. Editor: Charles L. Champion. Magazine or newsletter; 25-75 pages; black and white illustrations and photographs. "Much of our philosophy is a branch off of the classic DaDaist thoughts." Published: spontaneously (3-5 issues, depending on funds). Estab. 1990. Circ. 250.
• Note that this magazine spells its name eXpErImENtAL (bAsEmEnT).
Needs: Experimental. "Constructivist fiction, visualature, conceptual fiction." Publishes special fiction issue or anthology. Receives 2-5 mss/month. Acquires 1-2 mss/issue; 7 mss/year. Publishes ms 1 month after acceptance. Recently published work by Karl Kempton, Jeff Skeates, Richard Kostelanetz. Length: "no longer than 12 legal size pieces of paper." Publishes short shorts. Also publishes literary essays, literary criticism and poetry. Often critiques rejected mss.
How to Contact: Send complete manuscript with a cover letter. "If writer is not familiar with the term 'vizlation' it would be wise to send SASE or $1 for info." Reports in 1 month. SASE. Simultaneous submissions OK. Sample copy $3. Reviews novels and short story collections.
Payment: Pays 1 contributor copy.
Terms: Not copyrighted.
Advice: Looks for "an author who extends the beauty of a language by experiment."

EXPLORATIONS '93, University of Alaska Southeast, 11120 Glacier Highway, Juneau AK 99801. (907)789-4418. Editor: Art Petersen. Magazine: 5½×8¼; 44 pages; heavy cover stock; illustrations and photographs. "Poetry, prose and art—we strive for artistic excellence." Annually. Estab. 1980. Circ. 250.
Needs: Experimental, humor/satire. Receives 1,700 mss/year.
How to Contact: Send complete ms with cover letter, which should include bio. Name and address on *back* of first page of each submission. All submissions entered in contest. Reading/entry fee $4/ story required. Submission deadline is March 21, postmarked by. Reports in 2-3 months. SASE. Simultaneous and reprint submissions OK. Accepts computer printout submissions. Sample copy $4 ($3 for back issues).
Payment: Pays 2 contributor's copies. *Charges $4 reading fee for non-UAS fiction contributors.* Also awards 4 annual prizes of $100 and $150 each: 2 for poetry, 2 for fiction. Judges: '91, Bill Hotchkiss; '92, Charles Bukowski; '93, James B. Hall. Write for guidelines.
Terms: Acquires one-time rights (rights remain with the author).

EXPLORER MAGAZINE, (I), Flory Publishing Co., Box 210, Notre Dame IN 46556. (219)277-3465. Editor: Ray Flory. Magazine: 5½ × 8½; 20-32 pages; 20 lb. paper; 60 lb. or stock cover; illustrations. Magazine with "basically an inspirational theme including love stories in good taste." Christian writing audience. Semiannually. Estab. 1960. Circ. 200 +.

Needs: Literary, mainstream, prose poem, religious/inspirational, romance (contemporary, historical, young adult) and science fiction. No pornography. Buys 2-3 mss/issue; 5 mss/year. Length: 600 words average; 300 words minimum; 900 words maximum. Also publishes literary essays. Occasionally critiques rejected mss.

How to Contact: Send complete ms with SASE. Reports in 1 week. Publishes ms up to 3 years after acceptance. Simultaneous submissions OK. Sample copy $3. Fiction guidelines for SAE and 1 first class stamp.

Payment: Pays up to $25.

Terms: Cash prizes of $25, $20, $15 and $10 based on subscribers' votes. A plaque is also awarded to first place winner.

Advice: "See a copy of magazine first; have a good story to tell—in *good* taste! Most fiction sent in is too *long*! Be yourself! Be honest and sincere in your style. Write what you know about. Our philosophy is to reach the world with Christian literature, drawing others closer to God and nature."

EYES, (I), Apt. 301, 2715 S. Jefferson Ave., Saginaw MI 48601. (517)752-5202. Editor: Frank J. Mueller, III. Magazine: 8½ × 11; 28-32 pages; 20 lb. paper; Gilbert Laid 65 lb. cover. "No specific theme yet. Hopefully, horror-related surreal; surrealism most welcome. For a general, educated, not necessarily literary audience." Estab. 1991. Circ. 30-40.

Needs: Contemporary, experimental, fantasy (dark), horror, mainstream, prose poem, romance (gothic). Nothing pornographic; no preachiness; children's fiction discouraged. As of now receives average of 8-9 unsolicited mss/month. Accepts 3-6 mss/issue. Publishes ms up to 1 year after acceptance. Length: 3,500 words preferred; 6,000 words maximum. Sometimes critiques rejected mss.

How to Contact: Query first or send complete ms. Reports in 1 month (or less) on queries; 4-6 weeks on mss. SASE. No simultaneous submissions. Sample copy for $3. Fiction guidelines for #10 SAE and 1 first class stamp.

Payment: No payment.

Terms: Acquires one-time rights.

Advice: "Write and write again. If rejected, try again. If you have a manuscript you like and would like to see it in *Eyes*, send it to me. I may agree with you. Try to have your manuscript say something."

FAG RAG, Box 15331, Kenmore Station, Boston MA 02215. (617)661-7534. Editor: E. Carlotta. Magazine of gay male liberation. Annually. Estab. 1970. Circ. 5,000.

Needs: Gay male material only: adventure, comics, confession, erotica, fantasy, historical, men's, prose poem. Receives 5 unsolicited fiction mss/month. Acquires 5 mss/issue. Length: 1-10,000 words.

How to Contact: Query first. Reports in 2 months on queries; 9 months on mss. SASE for query. Accepts disk submissions compatible with IBM-PC/Macintosh. Sample copy $5.

Payment: Pays in 2 contributor's copies.

Terms: Acquires first North American serial rights.

THE FARMER'S MARKET, (II), Midwestern Farmer's Market, Inc., Box 1272, Galesburg IL 61402. Editor: Jean C. Lee. Magazine: 5½ × 8½; 100-140 pages; 60 lb. offset paper; 65 lb. cover; b&w illustrations and photos. Magazine publishing "quality fiction, poetry, nonfiction, author interviews, etc., in the Midwestern tradition for an adult, literate audience." Semiannually. Estab. 1982. Circ. 500.

 • *The Farmer's Market* has received numerous grants and awards including Illinois Arts Council Literary Awards for 1985-1991 and Illinois Arts Council grants for 1983-1992. Work published in the magazine has been selected for the *O. Henry Prize* anthology.

Needs: Contemporary, feminist, humor/satire, literary, regional and excerpted novel. "We prefer material of clarity, depth and strength; strong plots, good character development." No "romance, juvenile, teen." Accepts 10-20 mss/year. Published work by Mary Maddox, David Williams; published new writers within the last year. Also publishes literary essays, poetry. Occasionally critiques rejected mss or recommends other markets.

How to Contact: Send complete ms with SASE. Reports in 1-3 months. No simultaneous submissions. Publishes ms 4-8 months after acceptance. Sample copy for $4.50 and $1 postage and handling.
Payment: Pays 1 contributor's copy. (Other payment dependent upon grants).
Terms: Authors retain rights.
Advice: "We're always interested in regional fiction but that doesn't mean cows and chickens and home-baked apple pie, please. We are publishing more fiction and we are looking for exceptional manuscripts. Read the magazines before submitting. If you don't want to buy it, ask your library. We receive numerous mss that are clearly unsuitable. We're not sweet and we're not cute."

FAT TUESDAY, (II), RD2, Box 4220, Manada Gap Rd., Grantville PA 17028. Editor-in-Chief: F.M. Cotolo. Editors: B. Lyle Tabor and Thom Savion. Associate Editors: Lionel Stevroid and Kristen vonOehrke. Journal: 8½×11 or 5×8; 27-36 pages; good to excellent paper; heavy cover stock; b&w illustrations; photos. "Generally, we are an eclectic journal of fiction, poetry and visual treats. Our issues to date have featured artists like Patrick Kelly, Charles Bukowski, Joi Cook, Chuck Taylor and many more who have focused on an individualistic nature with fiery elements. We are a literary mardi gras—as the title indicates—and irreverancy is as acceptable to us as profundity as long as there is fire! Our audience is anyone who can praise literature and condemn it at the same time. Anyone too serious about it on either level will not like *Fat Tuesday*." Annually. Estab. 1981. Circ. 700.
Needs: Comics, erotica, experimental, humor/satire, literary, prose poem, psychic/supernatural/occult, serialized/excerpted novel and dada. "Although we list categories, we are open to feeling out various fields if they are delivered with the mark of an individual and not just in the format of the particular field." Receives 20 unsolicited fiction mss/month. Accepts 4-5 mss/issue. Published new writers within the last year. Length: 1,000 words maximum. Publishes short shorts. Occasionally critiques rejected mss.
How to Contact: Send complete ms with SASE. "No previously published material considered." No simultaneous submissions. Reports in 1 month. Publishes ms 3-10 months after acceptance. Sample copy for $5.
Payment: Pays 1 contributor's copy.
Terms: Acquires one-time rights.
Advice: "As *Fat Tuesday* enters its second decade, we find that publishing small press editions is more difficult than ever. Money remains a problem, mostly because small press seems to play to the very people who wish to be published in it. In other words, the cast is the audience, and more people want to be in *Fat Tuesday* than want to buy it. It is through sales that our magazine supports itself. This is why we emphasize buying a sample issue ($5) before submitting. We have calculated that if only 25% of the submissions we received in the last year had bought sample issues, we could have published four or five issues in 1991 as opposed to the one we struggled to release. As far as what we want to publish—send us shorter works. 'Crystals of thought and emotion which reflect your individual experiences. As long as you dig into your guts and pull out pieces of yourself. Your work is your signature . . . Like time itself, it should emerge from the penetralia of your being and recede into the infinite region of the cosmos,' to coin a phrase, and remember *Fat Tuesday* is mardi gras—so fill up before you fast. Bon soir."

FELICITY, (I), Weems Concepts, HCR-13, Box 21AA, Artemas PA 17211. (814)458-3102. Editor: Kay Weems-Winter. Newsletter: 8½×11; 20 lb. bond paper; illustrations. "Publishes articles, poetry and short stories. Poetry has different theme each month. No theme for stories." Bimonthly. Estab. 1988. Circ. 200.
Needs: Open. Short stories, any genre in good taste. No erotica, translations. All submissions treated as contest entries. Entry fee is $5 and the deadline is the 30th of each month. Length: 800-2,500 words. Publishes short shorts. Length up to 800 words; entry fee $2. Editor will consider stories that do not win for *My Legacy* or recommends other markets. Publishes 3-4 months after acceptance.
How to Contact: Send complete ms with cover letter or enter monthly contests. "Send SASE for return of ms or tell me to destroy it if not accepted." Reports in 3-4 months. SASE. Simultaneous and reprint submissions OK as long as author still retains rights. Sample copy for $2, #10 SAE and 65¢ postage. Fiction guidelines for #10 SAE and 1 first class stamp or check *The Bottom Line*, market listing for contests.
Payment: Pays in contributor's copies and ½ of entry fee collected for Short Story Contest. All entries receive copy of the issue.
Terms: Acquires one-time rights. "We will be" copyrighted. "We sponsor monthly contests. Winner receives half of entry fees collected for the short story contest. Submit ms along with entry fee and you will be entered in the contest. Deadline is the 30th of each month. Read both of our publications—

Felicity and *The Bottom Line Publications*. Our contests are listed there."
Advice: Looks for "good opening sentence, realistic characters, nice descriptions, strong plot with believable ending. Use natural conversations. Let me *feel* your story. Keep me interested until the end. Keep trying. A lot of mss I read are from new writers. Personally I enjoy stories and articles which will create a particular emotion, build suspense, or offer excitement or entertainment. Don't spell out everything in detail—keep me guessing."

‡**FEMINIST BASEBALL (I)**, Box Dog Press, Box 9609, Seattle WA 98109. Editor: Jeff Smith. Magazine: 5½ × 8½; 60 pages; 80 lb. cover stock; illustrations and photos. "Film reviews, fiction, music, etc. for a diverse to general audience." Semiannually. Estab. 1985. Circ. 500.
Needs: Experimental, fantasy, gay, horror, humor/satire, lesbian, literary, science fiction, young adult/teen (10-18 years). "Nothing racist, bad, long (over 5 pages)." Receives 10 unsolicited mss/month. Accepts 1 ms/issue; 2 mss/year. Recently published work by Peter Wick, Nancy Ostrander, Joanna Bond. Length: 1,000 words average; 250 words minimum; 4,000 words maximum. Publishes short shorts (275-825 words). Sometimes critiques rejected mss and recommends other markets.
How to Contact: Send complete manuscript with cover letter. Reports in 6 weeks on queries. No simultaneous submissions. Sample copy for $3 (make checks payable to Jeff Smith).
Payment: Pays with subscription to magazine.

‡**FEMINIST STUDIES, (II)**, Women's Studies Program, University of Maryland, College Park MD 20742. (301)405-7413, 7415. Editor: Claire G. Moses. Fiction Editor: Alicia Ostriker. Magazine: Journal-sized; about 200 pages; photographs. "Scholarly manuscripts, fiction, book review essays for professors, graduate/doctorial students; scholarly interdisciplinary feminist journal." Triannually. Estab. 1974. Circ. 7,500.
Needs: Contemporary, ethnic, feminist, gay, lesbian. Receives about 15 poetry and stories/month. Acquires 2-3 mss/issue. "We review fiction twice a year. Deadline dates are May 1 and December 1. Authors will receive notice of the board's decision by June 30 and January 30, respectively." Publishes short shorts. Sometimes comments on or critiques a rejected ms and recommends other markets.
How to Contact: Send complete ms with cover letter. SASE. No simultaneous submissions. Sample copy for $10. Fiction guidelines free.
Payment: Pays 2 contributor's copies and 10 tearsheets.
Terms: Send galleys to authors.

FICTION, (II), % Dept. of English, City College, 138th St. & Convent Ave., New York NY 10031. (212)650-6319/650-6317. Editor: Mark Jay Mirsky. Managing Editor: Allan Aycock. Magazine: 6 × 9; 150-250 pages; illustrations and occasionally photos. "As the name implies, we publish *only* fiction; we are looking for the best new writing available, leaning toward the unconventional. *Fiction* has traditionally attempted to make accessible the unaccessible, to bring the experimental to a broader audience." Biannually. Estab. 1972. Circ. 2,000.
Needs: Contemporary, experimental, feminist, humor/satire, literary and translations. No romance, science-fiction, etc. Receives 50-100 unsolicited mss/month. Acquires 12-20 mss/issue; 24-40 mss/year. Does not read mss May-October. Publishes ms 1-6 months after acceptance. Agented fiction 10-20%. Recently published work by Harold Brodkey, Joyce Carol Oates, Peter Handke, Max Frisch and Adolfo Bioy-Casares. Length: Open. Publishes short shorts. Sometimes critiques rejected mss and recommends other markets.
How to Contact: Send complete ms with cover letter. Reports in 1-3 months on mss. SASE. Simultaneous submissions OK, but please advise. Photocopied submissions OK. Accepts computer printout submissions. Sample copy $5. Fiction guidelines free.
Payment: Pays in contributor's copies.
Terms: Acquires first rights.
Advice: Submit "something different, off-the-wall—we would favor a less-polished but stylistically adventurous piece over a more-polished formulaic piece."

FICTION INTERNATIONAL, (II), English Dept., San Diego State University, San Diego CA 92182. (619)594-6220. Editors: Harold Jaffe and Larry McCaffery. "Serious literary magazine of fiction, extended reviews, essays." Magazine: 200 pages; illustrations; photos. "Our twin biases are progressive politics and post-modernism." Biannually. Estab. 1973. Circ. 2,500.
Needs: Literary, political and innovative forms. Receives approximately 300 unsolicited fiction mss each month. Unsolicited mss will be considered only from September 1 through December 15 of each year. Published new writers within the last year. No length limitations but rarely use manuscripts over

25 pages. Portions of novels acceptable if self-contained enough for independent publication.
How to Contact: Send complete ms with SASE. Reports in 1-3 months on mss. Sample copy for $9:
query Harry Polkin-Horn, managing editor.
Payment: Pays in contributor's copies.
Advice: "Study the magazine. We're highly selective. A difficult market for unsophisticated writers."

THE FIDDLEHEAD, (II), University of New Brunswick, Campus House, Box 4400 Fredericton, New
Brunswick E3B 5A3 Canada. (506)453-3501. Editor: Don McKay. Fiction Editors: Bill Bauer, Diana
Austin, Banny Belyea, Ted Colson and Linda McNutt. Magazine: 6×9; 104-128 pages; ink illustrations; photos. "No criteria for publication except quality. For a general audience, including many poets
and writers." Quarterly. Estab. 1945. Circ. 1,000.
Needs: Literary. No non-literary fiction. Receives 100-150 unsolicited mss/month. Buys 4-5 mss/issue;
20-40 mss/year. Publishes ms up to 1 year after acceptance. Small percent agented fiction. Recently
published work by Aryeh Stollman; published new writers within the last year. Length: 50-3,000 words
average. Publishes short shorts. Occasionally critiques rejected mss.
How to Contact: Send complete ms with cover letter. SASE. "Canadian stamps or international
reply coupons!" for mss. Reprint submissions OK. No simultaneous submissions. Reports in 2-6
months. Sample copy for $5.50 (Canadian). Reviews novels and short story collections—*Canadian
only*.
Payment: Pays $10-12 (Canadian)/published page and 1 contributor's copy.
Terms: Pays on publication for first or one-time rights.
Advice: "Less than 5% of the material received is published."

FIGHTING WOMAN NEWS, (IV), 6741 Tung Ave. West, Theodore AL 36582. Editor: Debra Pettis.
Magazine: 8½×11; 16-32 pages; 60 lb. offset bond paper; slick cover; illustrations; photos. "Women's
martial arts, self defense, combative sports. Articles, reviews, etc., related to these subjects. Well-
educated adult women who are actually involved with martial arts read us because we're there and
we're good." Quarterly. Estab. 1975. Circ. 3,500.
Needs: Science fiction, fantasy, feminist, adventure, mystery/suspense (police procedural, private
eye) and translations. "No material that shows women as victims, incompetents, stereotypes; no 'fight
scenes' written by people who don't know anything about fighting skills." Receives very few unsolicited
fiction mss. Published work by Phyllis Ann Karr, Lauren Wright Douglas and Janrae Frank. Length:
2,500 words.
How to Contact: Query with clips of published work with SASE. Enclose cover letter with ms.
Simultaneous submissions OK, but "we must know if it is a simultaneous submission." Reports as
soon as possible on queries and mss. Sample copy $3.50. Specify "fiction" when asking for samples.
Guidelines for #10 SASE.
Payment: Pays contributor's copies and subscription.
Terms: Acquires one-time rights. Will print author's copyright if desired.
Advice: "We are now getting unsolicited mss from published writers who have what we want; i.e., a
good, competent story that's just a bit too martial-arts oriented for their regular markets. Our readers
have expressed a strong preference for more technique and theory with a few specific complaints
about too much fiction or poetry. So even with a more regular publication schedule and corresponding
increase in total pages, we are not likely to use more fiction. Read the magazine before submitting. I
also think the theme of death in combat can do with a rest."

FIGMENT MAGAZINE, Tales from the Imagination, (I, II, IV), P.O. Box 3128, Moscow ID 83843-
0477. Editors: Barb & J.C. Hendee. Magazine: 5½×8½; 60 pages; slick stock cover; illustrations.
"Poetry/stories/vignettes/novelettes in genres of sf, fantasy, and sf/f related horror, for adults." Quarterly. Estab. 1989.
 ● *Figment Magazine* was rated #35 on the 1992 *Writer's Digest* Fiction 50 list. See editor, J.C.
 Hendee's article in the front section of this book, Eating Your Eggshells. Hendee also edits
 the new *Fugue* listed in this book.
Needs: Fantasy, science fiction (hard science, soft/sociological). "We're open to standard plotting
through slightly experimental, as long as the story is interesting, comprehensible and always *entertaining.*" Receives 400+ mss/month. Buys 8-12 mss/issue; 32-48 mss/year. Publishes ms within 6 months
after acceptance. Recently published work by Nina Kiriki Hoffman, Ardath Mayhar, T. Jackson King,
Kiel Stuart. Length: 100-10,000 words; 3,000 words preferred. Also publishes poetry. Sometimes critiques rejected manuscripts and recommends other markets.

How to Contact: "Send for guidelines first." Send complete ms with cover letter; include Social Security number, bio, SASE and listing of publishing credits (year to date only) including where and when. Reports in 2 weeks on queries; 1 month average on mss. No simultaneous submissions. Encourages disk submissions. Sample copy for $4. Fiction guidelines for #10 SASE. Reviews novels and short story collections. Send to J.P. McLaughlin, reviewer.
Payment: Pays ½-1¢/word (for fiction).
Terms: Pays within 30 days of acceptance for first North American serial rights only. Sends galleys to author.
Advice: "Looks for original ideas or original methods used with old ideas. Cutting edge material that is fantastical and far-reaching but always entertaining! Don't tell us what your story is about in your cover letter; if we can't figure it out from the manuscript, then some more work needs to be done before you submit. We expect professional submissions in the proper format."

FINE MADNESS, (II), Box 31138, Seattle WA 98103-1138. Magazine: 5×8; 64 pages; 65 lb. paper; 60 lb. cover stock. Estab. 1981. Circ. 800.
Needs: Contemporary, experimental, literary, prose poem and translations. Receives 10 unsolicited mss/month. Accepts 1-2 mss/issue; 2-4 mss/year. Publishes ms no more than 1 year after acceptance. Published work by Naomi Nye, David Downing, Hillel Schwarz and Michael Novak. Length: "approx. 12 pages max." Publishes short shorts. Also "would like to see" literary essays.
How to Contact: Query first or send complete ms with cover letter. No simultaneous submissions. Reports in 1 month on queries; 3 months on mss. Sample copy $4. Guidelines free.
Payment: Pays subscription to magazine and contributor's copies.
Terms: Acquires first North American serial rights. Copyright reverts to author upon publication.

‡FIREWEED, A Feminist Quarterly, Box 279, Station B, Toronto, Ontario M5T 2W2 Canada. (416)323-9512. Editors: The Fireweed Collective. Women's literary and cultural journal, with an emphasis on race, class and sexuality. Quarterly. Estab. 1978. Circ. 2,000.
Needs: Fiction, poetry, nonfiction, articles, book reviews, lesbian, working class, and women of color content. No "women's formula style." Receives 60 unsolicited fiction mss/month. Buys 30 mss/issue; 120 mss/year. Length: 1,200 words minimum; 18,000 words maximum; 6,000 words average. Occasionally critiques rejected ms.
How to Contact: Query first with SASE. Photocopied submissions OK. Reports in 6 months on queries. Sample copy $5 in Canada, $6 in U.S.
Payment: $20 and 2 free contributor's copies.
Terms: Author retains copyright.

FISH DRUM MAGAZINE, (II), % 626 Kathryn Ave., Santa Fe NM 87501. Editor: Robert Winson. Magazine: 5½×8½; 40-odd pages; glossy cover; illustrations and photographs. "Lively, emotional vernacular modern fiction, art and poetry." Published 2-4 times/year. Estab. 1988. Circ. 500.
Needs: Contemporary, erotica, ethnic, experimental, fantasy, gay, lesbian, literary, prose poem, regional, science fiction. "We're interested in material by New Mexican writers; also on the practice of Zen. Most of the fiction we've published is in the form of short, heightened prose-pieces." Receives 6-10 unsolicited mss/month. Accepts 1-2 mss/issue; 2-8 mss/year. Publishes ms 6 months-1 year after acceptance. Also publishes literary essays, literary criticism, poetry. Recommends other markets.
How to Contact: Send complete manuscript. No simultaneous submissions. Reports on mss in 1-3 months. SASE. Sample copy for $3. Reviews novels and short story collections.
Payment: Pays in contributor's copies. Charges for extras.
Terms: Acquires first North American serial rights. Sends galleys to author.

FIVE FINGERS REVIEW, (II), Box 15426, San Francisco CA 94115. (415)255-2159. Editors: John High, Thovean Lovell. Magazine: 6×9; 125-150 pages; photographs on cover. "*Five Fingers* is dedicated to publishing well wrought poetry and prose from various aesthetic viewpoints. The magazine provides a forum from which talented writers (new and known, traditional and experimental) act as conscientious objectors, as creative witnesses to the passions and possibilities of our time." Semiannually. Estab. 1984. Circ. 1,000.
● Work from the *Five Fingers Review* appeared in the *Pushcart Prize* anthology in 1992.
Needs: Ethnic, experimental, feminist, gay, humor/satire, lesbian, literary, regional, prose poems, prose vignettes and works that move between the genres. Receives 15-20 unsolicited mss/month. Accepts 2-5 mss/issue. Published work by Molly Giles, W.A. Smith and Peter Johnson; published new writers in the last year. Publishes short shorts. Also publishes poetry.

How to Contact: Query with clips of published work. SASE. Simultaneous and reprint submissions OK. Reports in 3 months. Sample copy for $6.
Payment: Pays in contributor's copies.
Advice: "We are particularly looking for short-short stories, prose poems, prose vignettes and works of translations."

FLIPSIDE, (II), Professional Writing Program, Dixon 110, California University, California PA 15419. (412)938-4082. Editors: Jim Black, Jonathan Bagamery. Tabloid: 11½×17; 45-60 pages; illustrations; photos. "Emphasis on 'new journalism.' Fiction, nonfiction, poetry, humor." Semiannually. Estab. 1987. Circ. 2,000.
Needs: Contemporary, experimental, literary. No genre fiction. Receives 5-6 unsolicited mss/month. Accepts 2-3 mss/issue; 6-8 mss/year. Does not read June-August. Publishes ms 1-6 months after acceptance. Length: 1,000-5,000 words average; 10,000 words maximum. Also publishes literary essays, literary criticism, some poetry.
How to Contact: Send complete manuscript with or without cover letter. Reports in 2-4 weeks on queries; 1-2 months on mss. SASE. Simultaneous submissions OK. Sample copy and fiction guidelines for 9×12 SAE and $1.24 postage.
Payment: Pays 3 contributor's copies.
Terms: Acquires first North American serial rights.
Advice: "Experimental and alternative fiction are always welcome here. Traditional fiction, darkly executed, is also encouraged. Read all you can, buy lots of envelopes."

THE FLORIDA REVIEW, (II), Dept. of English, University of Central Florida, Orlando FL 32816. (407)823-2038. Contact: Russell Kesler. Magazine: 5½×8½; 128 pages. Semiannually. Estab. 1972. Circ. 1,000.
• Work from this quality literary journal was selected for the *Editor's Choice III: Fiction, Poetry & Art From the US Small Presses* (1984-1990), published by the Spirit That Moves Us Press.
Needs: Contemporary, experimental and literary. "We welcome experimental fiction, so long as it doesn't make us feel lost or stupid. We aren't especially interested in genre fiction (science fiction, romance, adventure, etc.), though a good story can transcend any genre." Receives 120 mss/month. Acquires 8-10 mss/issue; 16-20 mss/year. Publishes ms within 3-6 months of acceptance. Published work by Stephen Dixon, Richard Grayson and Liz Rosenberg. Publishes short shorts. Also publishes literary criticism, poetry.
How to Contact: Send complete ms with cover letter. Reports in 2-4 months. SASE. Simultaneous submissions OK. Sample copy for $4.50; free fiction guidelines. Reviews novels and short story collections.
Payment: Pays in contributor's copies. Small honorarium occasionally available.
Terms: "Copyright held by U.C.F.; reverts to author after publication. (In cases of reprints, we ask that a credit line indicate that the work first appeared in the *F.R.*)"
Advice: "We publish fiction of high 'literary' quality—stories that delight, instruct, and aren't afraid to take risks."

FOLIO: A LITERARY JOURNAL, (II), Literature Department, American University, Washington DC 20016. (202)885-2971. Editor changes yearly. Until May 1993, send mss to Elizabeth Poliner, editor. Magazine: 6×9; 64 pages. "Fiction is published if it is well written. We look for language control, skilled plot and character development." For a scholarly audience. Semiannually. Estab. 1984. Circ. 400.
Needs: Contemporary, literary, mainstream, prose poem, translations, essay, b&w art or photography. No pornography. Occasional theme-based issues. See guidelines for info. Receives 150 unsolicited mss/month. Accepts 3-5 mss/issue; 6-10 mss/year. Does not read mss during May-August or December-January. Published work by Henry Taylor, Kermit Moyer, Linda Pastan; publishes new writers. Length: 2,500 words average; 4,500 words maximum. Publishes short shorts. Occasionally critiques rejected mss.
How to Contact: Send complete ms with cover letter, which should include a brief bio. Reports in 1-2 weeks on queries; 1-2 months on mss. SASE. Simultaneous and reprint submissions OK (if noted). Sample copy for $5. Guidelines for #10 SAE and 1 first class stamp.
Payment: Pays in contributor's copies.
Terms: Acquires first North American rights. "$75 award for best fiction and poetry. Query for guidelines."

FOOTWORK, The Paterson Literary Review, (I, II), Passaic County Community College, College Blvd., Paterson NJ 07509. (201)684-6555. Editor: Maria Mazziotti Gillan. Magazine: 8×11; 120 pages; 60 lb. paper; 70 lb. cover; illustrations; photos. Plans fiction issue in future.

• *Footwork* was chosen by *Library Journal* as one of the 10 best magazines in the US.

Needs: Contemporary, ethnic, experimental. "We are interested in quality short stories, with no taboos on subject matter." Receives about 60 unsolicited mss/month. Accepts 4 mss/issue. Publishes ms about 6 months-1 year after acceptance. Published new writers within the last year. Length: 2,500-3,000 words. Also publishes literary essays, literary criticism, poetry.

How to Contact: Reports in 1 year or less on mss. SASE. Simultaneous submissions OK. Sample copy $5. Reviews novels and short story collections.

Payment: Pays in contributor's copies.

Terms: Acquires first North American rights.

Advice: "We look for original, vital, powerful work. The short story is—when successful—a major achievement. Because we publish relatively little work, we cannot consider stories which are slight, however charming."

FORBIDDEN LINES, (I, IV), The Science Fiction Writers' Group, P.O. Box 23, Chapel Hill NC 27514. (919)942-3194. Managing Editor: Charles Overbeck. Magazine: 8×11; 64 pages; newsprint; 50 lb. white cover; illustrations and photographs. "We publish the strange, the awful, the wonderful (science fiction, horror, fantasy). Our readers are mostly college-aged to mid 30s, well educated, equal numbers m/f." Bimonthly. (May go quarterly in 1993; increase to 80+ pages.) Estab. 1990. Circ. 800.

Needs: Condensed/excerpted novel, experimental, fantasy, horror, humor/satire, psychic/supernatural/occult, science fiction (hard science, soft/sociological)."No juvenile, no romance, no religious." Receives 10-30 mss/month (varies widely). Accepts 6/7 mss/issue; 30-40 mss/year. Publishes ms 2-4 weeks after acceptance. Recently published work by Del Stone, Jr., Michael Burris, Monica Eiland. Length: open. Publishes short shorts. Sometimes critiques rejected mss and recommends other markets.

How to Contact: Send complete ms with cover letter. "Please don't bore us with previous credits. We'll consider every story equally." Reports in 1 week on queries; 2 weeks-1 month on mss. SASE for queries "We do not return mss!!" Reprint submissions OK. Simultaneous submissions OK (but "we require exclusivity upon purchase"). Accepts electronic submissions via disk or modem (on Apple MacIntosh *only*). Sample copy for $2.50. Fiction guidelines for #10 SAE and 1 first class stamp.

Payment: Pays 2 contributor's copies. Charges for extras at cost, $1 each.

Terms: Acquires one-time rights.

Advice: "We ask is it original? Is it strange? How does reading it make us (the staff) *feel*? Stories are chosen by majority vote of the staff. The editor has veto power, but rarely disagrees with the majority. Send us a professionally prepared ms, too weird or wild for the pro zines. Be fresh. Be *real*, while being *unreal*. We get a lot of horror submissions (too many in fact). We would like to get more science fiction, more fantasy."

‡THE FOUR DIRECTIONS, American Indian Literary Quarterly, (II, IV), Snowbird Publishing Company, P. O. Box 729, Tellico Plains TN 37385. (615)982-7261. Senior Editor: Joanna Meyer. Assistant Editor: William Meyer. Magazine: 8×10½; 68 pages; 70 lb. paper; 100+ lb. cover; 10-20 illustrations; 2-6 photographs. "All writing must be by American Indian authors. We prefer writing that furthers the positive aspects of the American Indian spirit. We publish poetry, fiction, essays and reviews." Quarterly. Estab. 1992. Circ 600.

Needs: American Indian only: adventure, children's/juvenile; erotica; ethnic/multicultural; experimental; fantasy; feminist; historical (general); horror; humor/satire; literary; mystery/suspense; psychic/supernatural/occult; regional; science fiction; sports; translations; westerns; young adult/teen (10-18 years). "Writing should reflect Indian issues and views in all categories." Upcoming themes: "All-Women's Issue" (Vol. I, No. 4); "Indian Prisoners' Issue" (Vol. II, No. 2); "Children's Issue" (Vol. II, No. 4). Will publish special fiction issue or anthology. Receives 10 mss/month. Buys 8-12 mss/issue; 32-48 mss/year. Publishes ms 2-9 months after acceptance. Recently published Lise McCloud, Mary Lockwood, Joe Bruchac. Length: 2,000 words; 300 words minimum; 6,000 words maximum. Publishes short shorts. Length: 350 words. Also publishes literary essays, criticism, poetry. Often critiques rejected mss.

How to Contact: Query with clips of published work or send complete manuscript with a cover letter. Should include estimated word count, 1-page or less bio, list of publications, tribal affiliation. Reports on queries in 2-6 weeks on queries; 2-10 weeks on ms. Send SASE (IRC) for reply, return of ms, or send a disposable copy of the ms. Simultaneous, reprint or electronic submissions OK. Sample copy

for 8½×11 SAE and 4 first class stamps or IRCs. Fiction guidelines for #10 SAE and 1 first class stamp.
Payment: Pays 2¢/word plus 4 contributor's copies.
Terms: Pays on publication for one-time rights. Sends galleys to author, when schedule allows.
Advice: "Writing we'll consider must be relevant, creative, original and of interest to a wide readership, both Indian and non-Indian. We seek professional quality writing, and work, if *about* Indians, that is accurate and authentic. We want work that shows positive spiritual strengths. We've not seen enough theater scripts/drama. We'd like to see more. And we *know* there's more humorous writing than has been submitted."

FRICTION, Wampus Multimedia 6130 Calico Pool Lane, Burke VA 22015. (703)250-6010. Editor: Mark W. Doyon. Newsletter: 8½×11; 12-16 pages; 70 lb. diamond ultrafelt cover; line art only. "Thematically linked fiction . . . ." Quarterly. Estab. 1989.
Needs: Contemporary, humor/satire, literary. "*No genre fiction.*" Upcoming themes: send for editorial calendar. Receives 10-15 unsolicited mss/month. Accepts 3-5 mss/issue; 12-20 mss/year. Publishes ms 2-6 months after acceptance. Recently published work by Stephen Gerard, C.R. Torrey, John Shaw and Kevin Kerr. Length: 1,500-2,000 words average; 500 words minimum; 2,500 words maximum. Publishes short shorts. Sometimes critiques rejected mss and recommends other markets.
How to Contact: Send complete ms with cover letter. Reports in 2 weeks on queries; 6 weeks on mss. SASE. Simultaneous submissions OK. Accepts electronic submissions via disk (PC-formatted). Sample copy for $2, 9×12 SAE and 3 first class stamps. Fiction guidelines free.
Payment: Pays subscription to magazine.
Terms: Acquires one-time rights.
Advice: "We look for mss with strong thematic and editorial content. The writing should be concise and linear, but ultimately it's a strong point-of-view that makes or breaks a piece. If a submission reflects a strong vision, we'll often edit the language as necessary. Ultimately a ms must complement the issue's stated THEME (e.g. 1992 themes were: Politically Correct; Maximum Utility; Smoke-Filled Room; Goodwill Toward Men). Make sure that you have *something to say*. And then say it as concisely and elegantly as possible. Stay away from 'cute' or 'wacky' characterizations. Avoid 'clever' language. Present complex themes in a simple way."

FRITZ, (II), P.O. Box 170694, San Francisco CA 94117-0694. Editor: Lisa McElroy. Magazine: 8½×11; 24 pages; 60 lb. paper; vellum cover; illustrations and photographs. "A format for short stories, prose, poetry, photos, comics, nonfiction articles and some reviews for artists and writers who are absorbed by and/or objectify pop culture. Also, classic forms of writing as well as experimental." Annually. Estab. 1991. Circ. 500.
Needs: Erotica, ethnic, experimental, feminist, gay, historical (general), humor/satire, lesbian, literary, prose poem. No gore, sexist/racist for the sake of being sexist/racist. No formula genres. Receives 10-20 unsolicited mss/month. Accepts 5-10 mss/issue. Publishes ms 6 months (possibly more) after acceptance. Length: 2,500 words maximum. Publishes short shorts. Also accepts poetry.
How to Contact: Send complete ms with cover letter. Reports in 2 weeks on queries; 2-4 months on mss. SASE. Simultaneous submissions (if noted) and reprint submissions OK. Sample copy for $3. Fiction guidelines for #10 SAE and 1 first class stamp.
Payment: Pays contributor's copies.
Terms: Acquires one-time rights.
Advice: Looks for "intelligent observation of human behavior. A new way of expressing an opinion. An ability to create a rhythmic flow of words. A heart-felt opinion. A sense of humor. A sense of pathos."

‡FUGUE, Literary Digest of the University of Idaho, (II), Brink Hall, Rm. 200, University of Idaho, Moscow ID 83843. Executive Editor: J.C. Hendee. Editors change each year. Send to Executive Editor. Magazine: 5½×8½; 40-60 pages; 20 lb. stock paper. "We are interested in all classifications of fiction—we are not interested in pretentious 'literary' stylizations. We expect stories to be written in a manner engaging for anyone, not just academics and the pro-literatae crowd." Semiannually. Estab. 1990. Circ. 200+.
    ● J.C. Hendee is also editor of *Figment* listed in this book and author of Eating Your Eggshells included at the front of this edition.
Needs: Adventure, ethnic/multicultural, experimental, fantasy, historical (general), horror, humor/satire, literary, mainstream/contemporary, mystery/suspense, regional, romance, science fiction, sports, westerns. Receives 50+ unsolicited mss/month. Buys 4-8 mss/issue; 8-16 mss/year. Does not

read May-July. Publishes ms 3-5 months after acceptance. Length: 3,000 words average; 50 words minimum; 7,000 words maximum. Publishes short shorts. Also publishes literary essays and poetry. Sometimes critiques or comments on rejected mss.

How to Contact: Send complete ms with cover letter. "Obtain guidelines first." Should include estimated word count, Social Security number and list of publications. Report in 2 weeks on queries; 2 months on mss. SASE (or IRC) for a reply to a query or return of ms. No simultaneous submissions. Sample copy for $3. Fiction guidelines for #10 SAE and 1 first class stamp or IRC.

Payment: Pays ½¢/word plus 1 contributor's copy. Additional copies $2.

Terms: Pays on publication for first North American serial rights.

Advice: Looks for "competent writing, clarity and consideration for the reader above stylism. Do not send us the traditional themes considered to be 'literary'."

THE G.W. REVIEW, (II), The George Washington University, Box 20, The Marvin Center, 800 21st St., N.W., Washington DC 20052. (202)994-7288. Editor: Sarah Aitken. Magazine: 6×9; 64 pages; 60 lb. white offset paper; 65 lb. Patina cover; cover photo. "*The G.W. Review* is a literary magazine that publishes poetry, short fiction and essays for the university community, the Washington DC metropolitan area and an increasing number of national subscribers." Semiannually. Estab. 1980. Circ. 4,000 (annually).

Needs: Condensed/excerpted novel, contemporary, experimental, humor/satire, literary, mainstream, prose poem, translations. "*The G.W. Review* does not accept previously published material. No pornography or proselytizing religious manuscripts." Does not read mss May 15-August 15. Publishes ms up to 6 months after acceptance. Recently published work by Julia Alvarez and Richard McCann. Length: 2,500 words average; 6,000 words maximum. Publishes short shorts. Also publishes literary essays, poetry. Sometimes critiques rejected mss.

How to Contact: Send complete ms with cover letter. Include biographical information, places previously published, previous books, etc. Reports in 3-6 weeks on queries; 4-10 weeks on mss. SASE. Simultaneous submissions OK. Sample copy for $3. Fiction guidelines for 9×12 SASE.

Payment: Pays in contributor's copies.

Terms: Acquires one-time rights.

Advice: "*The G.W. Review* seeks to publish the best contemporary writing from outside the University community as well as the best from within. Initially intended for distribution to university students and the surrounding Washington DC metropolitan area, *The G.W. Review* has since begun to attain a more widespread national distribution and readership."

‡GASLIGHT, Tales of the Unsane, (II), Strait-Jacket Publications, P.O. Box 21, Cleveland MN 56017-0021. (507)931-6712. Editor: Melissa Gish. Magazine: 5½×8½; 44-52 pages; 60 lb. white paper; 100 lb. color cover; illustrations. "Highly imaginative sci-fi, fantasy, macabre fiction borne out of the darkest recesses of the creator's mind. Eager to work with new and/or unpublished writers." Quarterly. Estab. 1992. Circ. 150.

Needs: Experimental, fantasy (science, horror), horror, mystery/suspense (macabre), science fiction (hard science, soft/sociological, horror). Upcoming themes: "Grave Perspectives," undead issue (March 1993); "Parallel Lines," time travel issue (September 1993); "Darwin Tribute," strange creatures issue (December 1993). List of upcoming themes available for SASE. Publishes annual special fiction issue or anthology. Receives 50-60 unsolicited mss/month. Buys 10-12 mss/issue; 40-50 mss/year. Publishes ms 2-3 months or less after acceptance. Recently published work by D.F. Lewis, Lenora K. Rogers, Joshua Waterman. Length: 2,500 words average; 150 words minimum; 3,000 words maximum. Publishes short shorts. Length: 300 words. Also publishes poetry. Often critiques or comments on rejected mss.

How to Contact: Send complete ms with cover letter. Should include estimated word count, brief bio, list of recent publications, request for workshopping of ms. Reports in 2 weeks on queries; 3-4 weeks on mss. Send SASE for reply, return of mss or send a disposable copy of the ms. Simultaneous and reprint submissions OK. Sample copy for $4.25; $5 Canada; $6 overseas. Fiction guidelines for #10 SAE and 1 first class stamp or IRC. Reviews novels and short story collections.

Payment: Pays 2¢/word maximum, subscription to the magazine (featured author only), 1 contributor's copy plus 15% discount on additional copies.

Terms: Pays on acceptance for first North American serial rights or reprint rights, if ms is a reprint. Sponsors Annual Fiction Chapbook Contest, send #10 SASE (29¢) for application and guidelines.

Advice: "Ideas must be fresh. Prose must be clean and tight with a good command of grammar. Original plots, well-developed characters. Individual style must be apparent—no rehash or copycat material." Looks for "visits from other beings—fresh ideas for alien cultures. New slants on dragon themes. Militaristic sci-fi. Good blends of horror/sci-fi or of fantasy/horror. Please, no serial killers, no stripper-hooker murders, no sexism, no racism, no specism, no heavy profanity, blood and slime is only acceptable if it is relevant to the plot. No monster movie rip-offs, no cliché or ambiguous endings."

‡GAY CHICAGO MAGAZINE (II), Ultra Ink, Inc. 3121 N. Broadway, Chicago IL 60657-4522. (312)327-7271. Publisher: Ralph Gernhardt. Associate Publisher: Jerry Williams. Magazine: 8½×11; 80-144 pages; newsprint paper and cover stock; illustrations; photos. Entertainment guide, information for the gay community.
Needs: Erotica (but no explicit hard core), lesbian, gay and romance. Receives "a few" unsolicited mss/month. Acquires 10-15 mss/year. Published new writers within the last year. Length: 1,000-3,000 words.
How to Contact: Send complete ms with SASE. Accepts disk submissions compatible with Merganthaler Crtronic 200. Must have hard copy with disk submissions. Reports in 4-6 weeks on mss. Free sample copy for 9×12 SAE and $1.45 postage.
Payment: Minimal. 5-10 free contributor's copies; no charge for extras "if within reason."
Terms: Acquires one-time rights.
Advice: "I use fiction on a space-available basis, but plan to use more because we have doubled our format size to 8½×11."

‡GEORGETOWN REVIEW, (II), G & R Publications, Box 227, 400 E. College St., Georgetown KY 40324. (502)863-8308. Editor: Steven Carter. Magazine: 6×9; 85-100 pages; 60 lb. offset paper; 65 lb. cover; illustrations. "We want to publish quality fiction and poetry. Our audience is people who are interested in reading quality fiction and poetry." Annually. Estab. 1993. Circ. 500.
Needs: Literary. No romance, juvenile, fantasy. Receives 7-10 mss/year. Does not read mss June-August. Publishes 3-6 months after acceptance. Length: open. Publishes short shorts. Length: 400-500 words. Also publishes poetry.
How to Contact: Send complete ms with a cover letter. Reports in 3-4 months on mss. SASE (IRC). Simultaneous submissions OK. Sample copy $5, 9×12 SAE and 5 first class stamps.
Payment: Pays 2 contributor's copies.
Terms: Acquires first North American serial rights. Sends galleys to author.
Advice: "We simply look for quality work, no matter what the subject or style."

THE GEORGIA REVIEW, (II, III), The University of Georgia, Athens GA 30602-9009. (706)542-3481. Editor-in-Chief: Stanley W. Lindberg. Associate Editor: Stephen Corey. Journal: 7×10; 208 pages (average); 50 lb. woven old style paper; 80 lb. cover stock; illustrations; photos. *"The Georgia Review*, winner of the 1986 National Magazine Award in Fiction, is a journal of arts and letters, featuring a blend of the best in contemporary thought and literature—essays, fiction, poetry, graphics and book reviews—for the intelligent nonspecialist as well as the specialist reader. We seek material that appeals across disciplinary lines by drawing from a wide range of interests." Quarterly. Estab. 1947. Circ. 5,700.
 • This magazine has an excellent reputation for publishing high-quality fiction. It won the National Magazine Award for fiction in 1988.
Needs: Experimental and literary. "We're looking for the highest quality fiction—work that is capable of sustaining subsequent readings, not throw-away pulp magazine entertainment. Nothing that fits too easily into a 'category.' " Receives about 400 unsolicited fiction mss/month. Buys 3-4 mss/issue; 12-15 mss/year. Does not read unsolicited mss in June, July or August. Would prefer *not* to see novel excerpts. Published work by Lee K. Abbott, Marjorie Sandor, John Edgar Wideman; published new writers within the last year. Length: Open. Also publishes literary essays, literary criticism, poetry. Occasionally critiques rejected mss.
How to Contact: Send complete ms with SASE. No multiple submissions. Reports in 2-3 months. Sample copy $6; guidelines for #10 SAE with 1 first class stamp. Reviews short story collections.
Payment: Pays minimum: $35/printed page; 1 year complimentary subscription; 1 contributor's copy, reduced charge for extra.
Terms: Pays on publication for first North American serial rights. Sends galleys to author.

THE GETTYSBURG REVIEW, (II), Gettysburg College, Gettysburg PA 17325. (717)337-6770. Editor: Peter Stitt. Assistant Editor: Jeff Mock. Magazine: 6¾×10; approx. 170 pages; acid free paper; full color illustrations and photos. "Quality of writing is our only criterion; we publish fiction, poetry and essays." Quarterly. Estab. 1988. Circ. 2,500.
 • *The Gettysburg Review* won CELJ awards for Best New Journal and Best Design in 1988. Since that time the journal has published work that has appeared in several prize anthologies includ-

ing *Best American Poetry*, *Pushcart Prize* and *The O. Henry Awards*.

Needs: Contemporary, experimental, historical(general), humor/satire, literary, mainstream, regional and serialized novel. "We require that fiction be intelligent, and aesthetically written." Receives approx. 125 mss/month. Buys approx. 4-6 mss/issue; 16-24 mss/year. Publishes ms within 3-6 months of acceptance. Recently published work by Jill McCorkle, Rita Dove. Length: 3,000 words average; 1,000 words minimum; 20,000 words maximum. Occasionally publishes short shorts. Also publishes literary essays, some literary criticism, poetry. Sometimes critiques rejected mss.

How to Contact: Send complete mss with cover letter, which should include "education, credits." Reports in 3-6 months. SASE. No simultaneous submissions. Sample copy for $6 (postage paid). Does not review books per se. "We do essay-reviews, treating several books around a central theme." Send review copies to editor.

Payment: Pays $25/printed page plus subscription to magazine, contributor's copy. Charge for extra copies.

Terms: Pays on publication for first North American serial rights.

Advice: "Reporting time can take three months. It is helpful to look at a sample copy of *The Gettysburg Review* to see what kinds of fiction we publish before submitting."

THE GINGERBREAD DIARY, Alternative Lifestyles in Interracial Love, (I, IV), Box 3333, New York NY 10185. (212)904-0512. Editor: Gary David. Fiction Editors: Gary David, Julie David. Magazine: 8½×11; 40-50 pages; bond paper; color Xerox paper cover; illustrations; photos. "We feature essays, stories, poems on the theme of interracial love and relating, as well as material embracing other 'human interest' topics, basically for those who are involved in, or who have thought about, interracial relationships; also those who are the products of interracial unions." Published 5 times/year. Plans special fiction issue. Estab. 1986. Circ. 50.

Needs: Erotica, ethnic, experimental, fantasy, gay, historical (general), humor/satire, lesbian, literary, mainstream, prose poem, spiritual, regional, romance (contemporary, historical, young adult). "As noted above, we accept for consideration material dealing with a broad range of subjects; bear in mind that we do not restrict ourselves to black/white issues, but include all other 'races' as well, the object being, of course, to illuminate the emotional and intellectual interplay between people of different racial and cultural backgrounds within the context of their relationship." Acquires 1-2 mss/issue; 8-9 mss/year. Publishes ms "2 issues hence" after acceptance. Length: 4,000 words average; 550 words minimum; 5,000 words maximum. Publishes short shorts. Also publishes literary essays, poetry. Sometimes critiques rejected mss and recommends other markets.

How to Contact: Send complete ms with cover letter, which should include "some personal information about the author, a brief genesis of his/her work and why the author chose us." Reports in 1-2 months on queries; 3-4 months on mss. No SASE. Simultaneous submissions OK. Sample copy for $1. Fiction guidelines for #10 SAE and 1 first class stamp.

Payment: Pays in contributor's copies, charges for extras, voluntary donations.

Terms: Acquires all rights.

Advice: "Anyone interested in being published in the *Diary* would have to keep in mind that we are a new enterprise and, as such, are testing the waters of 'special-interest' literature in the hopes of building a readership of open-minded and intelligent people. Translation: You won't get rich and famous with us, if that is your aim. But ... if you have a good imagination and are willing to tackle subject matter 'beyond your ken' (as interracial loving will most likely be) then we will be more than happy to consider your work. We like to think of ourselves as one of the few publications willing to take a chance on raw, undiscovered talent."

GOLDEN ISIS MAGAZINE, (I, IV), Suite 137, 23233 Saticoy St., Bldg. 105, West Hills CA 91304. Editor: Gerina Dunwich. Magazine: Digest-sized; approx. 8 pages; 20 lb. stock; paper cover; illustrations. "*Golden Isis* is a mystical New Age literary magazine of occult fiction, Goddess-inspired poetry, Pagan artwork, Wiccan news, letters, occasional book reviews and classified ads." Quarterly. Estab. 1980. Circ. 4,000 (including 2 libraries).

Needs: Psychic/supernatural/occult, bizarre humor, fantasy and mystical Egyptian themes. "Please do not send us pornographic, religious, racist or sexist material. We will not consider stories written in present tense." Receives 100+ mss/month. Acquires 1-2 mss/issue; 4-8 mss/year. Published fiction by Rod R. Vick, Cary G. Osborne and Gypsy Electra; published many new writers within the last year. Length: 1,500 words maximum. Publishes short shorts. Also publishes poetry. Occasionally critiques rejected mss and often recommends other markets.

How to Contact: Send complete ms. SASE. Simultaneous submissions OK. Reports in up to 1 month. Sample copy $2. Fiction guidelines for #10 SAE and 1 first class stamp.
Payment: Payment varies from 1 contributor's copy to $5.
Terms: Pays on publication for first North American serial rights.
Advice: "Submit short fiction that is well-written, atmospheric and equipped with a good surprise ending. Originality is important. Quality writing is a must. Avoid clichés, poor grammar, predictable endings, unnecessary obscenity and run-on sentences, for these things will only bring you a fast rejection slip. Also publishes chapbooks: $5 reading fee; length up to 50 pages; query first or send complete ms. Sample chapbook $5."

GOTTA WRITE NETWORK LITMAG, (I), Maren Publications, 612 Cobblestone Circle, Glenview IL 60025. Editor: Denise Fleischer. Magazine: 8½×11; 36-48 pages; saddle-stapled ordinary paper; matte card or lighter weight cover stock; illustrations. Magazine "serves as an open forum to discuss new markets, successes and difficulties. Gives beginning writers their first break into print." Distributed through the US, Canada and England. Semiannually. Estab. 1988. Circ. 200.
Needs: Adventure, contemporary, fantasy, historical, humor/satire, literary, mainstream, prose poem, romance (gothic), science fiction (hard science, soft/sociological), young adult/teen, western (traditional). Receives 75-150 unsolicited ms per month. Accepts 1-3 mss per issue; up to 20 mss a year. Publishes mss 6-12 months after acceptance. Published work by Don Stockard, Chuck Howland, Carol Vinci and Jeff VanderMeer. Length: 8 pages maximum for short stories. Also publishes poetry. Recommends other markets.
How to Contact: Send complete ms with cover letter and query letter. Include "who the writer is, type of work submitted, previous publications and the writer's focused area of writing." Reports in 1-2 months. SASE. May consider simultaneous submissions. Reprints considered "at times." Sample copy for $5. Fiction guidelines for SASE.
Payment: Pays in contributor's copies; charge for extras.
Terms: Acquires first North American serial rights.
Advice: "If I still think about the direction of the story after I've read it, I know it's good. Organize your thoughts on the plot and character development (qualities, emotions) before enduring 10 drafts. Make your characters come alive by giving them a personality and a background and then give them a little freedom. Let them take you through the story."

‡GRAFFITI OFF THE ASYLUM WALLS, An Illiterary Journal, (I, IV), P.O. Box 515, Fayetteville AR 72702-0515. Curator: Bryan Westbrook. Magazine: Digest-sized; number of pages varies; glossy cover; illustrations. "The stuff you would be afraid to show your mother, priest and/or psychiatrist. Humor preferred." Publishes "whenever enough material is available." Estab. 1992. Circ. 200.
Needs: Erotica, experimental, feminist, horror, humor/satire, psychic/supernatural/occult, political (anti-Republican). "Nothing pro-religious, pro-animal rights, anything high fallutin'." Recently published work by Robert W. Howington, Allen Renfro, Marc Swan. Length: open, "but nothing Homeric." Also publishes literary essays and poetry. Often critiques or comments on rejected mss.
How to Contact: Send complete ms with cover letter. Should include bio (personal bio not publication list). Reports in 2 or 3 weeks on mss. Send SASE for reply, return of ms or send a disposable copy of ms. Simultaneous and reprint submissions OK. Sample copy for $2.50. Reviews novels and short story collections.
Payment: Pays 1 contributor's copy.
Terms: Acquires one-time rights.
Advice: "If it can make me laugh (not an easy task) or shock me (also a challenge) it will make it. Non-narrative stories have a harder time here. Forget everything you've ever read in school or been told in writing classes. I want to hear from the real you."

GRAIN, (I, II), Saskatchewan Writers' Guild, Box 1154, Regina, Saskatchewan S4P 3B4 Canada. Editor: Geoffrey Ursell. Fiction Editor: Edna Alford. Literary magazine: 5½×8½; 144 pages; Chinook offset printing; chrome-coated stock; illustrations; some photos. "Fiction and poetry for people who enjoy high quality writing." Quarterly. Estab. 1973. Circ. 1,800-2,000.
 • *Grain*, known as one of the most prestigious Canadian journals, won the Western Magazine Award for Fiction (in Canada) for both 1991 and 1992.
Needs: Contemporary, experimental, literary, mainstream and prose poem. "No propaganda—only artistic/literary writing." No mss "that stay *within* the limits of conventions such as women's magazine type stories, science fiction; none that push a message." Receives 80 unsolicited fiction mss/month. Buys 8-12 mss/issue; 32-48 mss/year. Agented fiction approximately 1%. Recently published 2 short

stories by emerging writers selected for the third *Journey Prize Anthology.* Length: "No more than 50 pages." Also publishes poetry. Occasionally critiques rejected mss.

How to Contact: Send complete ms with SAE, IRC and brief letter of 1-2 sentences. "Let us know if you're just beginning to send out." No simultaneous submissions. Reports within 6 months on ms. Publishes ms an average of 4 months after acceptance. Sample copy $5.

Payment: Pays $30-100; 2 contributor's copies.

Terms: Pays on publication for one-time North American rights. "We expect acknowledgment if the piece is republished elsewhere."

Advice: "Submit a story to us that will deepen the imaginative experience of our readers. *Grain* has established itself as a first-class magazine of serious fiction. We receive submissions from around the world. If Canada is a foreign country to you, we ask that you *do not* enclose US postage stamps on your return envelope. If you live outside Canada and neglect the International Reply Coupons, we *will not* read or reply to your submission."

‡GRAND STREET, 131 Varick St., #906, New York NY 10013. (212)807-6548. Fax (212)807-6544. Editor: Jean Stein. Magazine: 7×9; 220-240 pages; illustrations; photographs. "We seek new fiction and nonfiction of all types. We welcome experimental work. The only real criterion for acceptance is quality." Quarterly. Estab. 1981. Circ. 5,000.

• *Grand Street* is ranked #46 on the 1992 *Writer's Digest* Fiction 50 list.

Needs: Fiction, poetry, essays, translations. Receives 400 unsolicited mss/month. Buys 4 mss/issue; 16 mss/year. Time between acceptance of the ms and publication varies. Agented fiction 90%. Recently published work by David Foster Wallace, David Holper, Beth Nugent, Yehudit Katzir, Sandra Cisneros, William T. Vollman. Length: 6,000 words average; 1,000 words minimum; 9,000 words maximum. Sometimes critiques or comments on rejected mss.

How to Contact: Send complete ms with a cover letter. Reports in 6 weeks on mss. Send SASE (or IRC) for return of the ms or a disposable copy of the ms. Simultaneous and electronic submissions OK. Sample copy for $10.40.

Payment: Pays $250-1,200 and 2 contributor's copies. Additional copies at a reduced rate, $4.25.

Terms: Pays on publication for first North American serial rights. Sends galleys to author.

Advice: What magazine looks for is "hard to say, other than first-rate writing. We are fairly eclectic in our publishing policies. Look at a copy of the magazine first. That will give you a good idea of what we're looking for."

GRASSLANDS REVIEW, (I), Mini-Course—University of North Texas, N.T. Box 13706, Denton TX 76203. Editor: Laura B. Kennelly. Magazine: 6×9; 80 pages. *Grasslands Review* prints creative writing of all types; poetry, fiction, essays for a general audience. Semiannually. Estab. 1989. Circ. 200.

Needs: Adventure, contemporary, ethnic, experimental, fantasy, horror, humor/satire, literary, mystery/suspense, prose poem, regional, science fiction and western. Nothing pornographic or overtly political or religious. Accepts 5-8 mss/issue. Reads only in October and March. Publishes ms 6 months after acceptance. Recently published work by Carol Vopat, John Engell, Robert Weaver, Paul Bolognese, Laura Sofeh. Length: 1,500 words average; 100-3,500 words. Publishes short shorts (100-150 words). Also publishes poetry. Sometimes critiques rejected mss and recommends other markets.

How to Contact: Send complete ms in October or March *only* with cover letter. No simultaneous submissions. Reports on mss in 2 months. SASE. Sample copy for $2. May review novels or short story collections.

Payment: Pays in contributor's copies.

Terms: Acquires one-time rights. Publication not copyrighted.

Advice: "We are looking for fiction which leaves the reader with a strong feeling or impression—or a new perspective on life. The *Review* began as an in-class exercise to allow experienced creative writing students to learn how a little magazine is produced. We now wish to open it up to outside submissions so that our students can gain an understanding of how large the writing community is in the United States and so that they may have experience in working with other writers."

‡GREEN EGG/HOW ABOUT MAGIC?, (IV), Church of All Worlds, Box 1542, Ukiah CA 95482. (707)485-7787. Editor: Diane Darling. Magazine: 8½×11; 56 pages; recycled paper; 4 color glossy cover; b&w illustrations; and photographs. "Magical fantasy, ecological, historical having to do with pagan civilizations." Quarterly. Estab. 1988. Circ. 6,000.

• *Green Egg* won Silver Awards in 1990 and 1991 from the Wiccan Pagan Press Alliance.

Needs: Magical, Pagan and ecological themes: adventure, children's/juvenile (5-9 and 10-12 years), erotica, ethnic/multicultural, experimental, fantasy (science fantasy, sword and sorcery, children's fantasy), historical (general), humor/satire, psychic/supernatural/occult, religious/inspirational (Pagan). "No porn, mystery, sports, western, modern life, Christian, evil and painful." Upcoming themes: "Gender Polarity in Magic" (Spring 1993). Receives 2-3 unsolicited mss/month. Acquires 4 mss/year. Recently published work by Stephen Pearl, Fiona Firefall, Ivo Dominguez. Length: 600 words minimum; 2,000 words maximum. Publishes short shorts. Length: 500 words. Also publishes poetry. Sometimes critiques or comments on rejected mss.
How to Contact: Send complete ms with cover letter. Should include estimated word count and bio (1 paragraph—50 words). Reports in 2 months. Send SASE for reply, return of ms or send disposable copy of the ms. Simultaneous, reprint and electronic submissions OK. Sample copy $6.25. Fiction guidelines for SAE and 1 first class stamp or IRC. Reviews novels and short story collections.
Payment: Pays subscription to the magazine or contributor's copies.
Terms: Acquires one-time rights.
Advice: "Looks for economy of prose, artistic use of language, but most important is that the subject matter be germaine to our Pagan readership. Magical stories teaching ethics for survival as healthy biosphere heroines, human/animal/otherworld interface; transformative experiences; tidy plots; good grammar, spelling, punctuation; humor; classical deities and ethnic stuff."

GREEN MOUNTAINS REVIEW, (II), Johnson State College, Box A-58, Johnson VT 05656. (802)635-2356, ext. 339. Editor: Neil Shepard. Editor: Tony Whedon. Magazine: Digest-sized; 125-150 pages. Semiannually. Estab. 1975 (new series, 1987). Circ. 1,000.
Needs: Adventure, contemporary, experimental, humor/satire, literary, mainstream, serialized/excerpted novel, translations. Receives 30 unsolicited mss/month. Accepts 5 mss/issue; 10 mss/year. Publishes ms 4-6 months after acceptance. Length: 25 pages maximum. Publishes short shorts. Also publishes literary criticism, poetry. Sometimes critiques rejected mss.
How to Contact: Send complete ms with cover letter. Reports in 1 month on queries; 3-4 months on mss. SASE. Simultaneous submissions OK. Sample copy for $7.50.
Payment: Pays in contributor's copies.
Terms: Acquires first North American serial rights. Sends galleys to author upon request.

GREEN'S MAGAZINE, Fiction for the Family, (II), Green's Educational Publications, Box 3236, Regina, Saskatchewan S4P 3H1 Canada. Editor: David Green. Magazine: 5¼×8; 100 pages; 20 lb. bond paper; matte cover stock; line illustrations. Publishes "solid short fiction suitable for family reading." Quarterly. Estab. 1972.
Needs: Adventure, fantasy, humor/satire, literary, mainstream, mystery/suspense and science fiction. No erotic or sexually explicit fiction. Receives 20-30 mss/month. Accepts 10-12 mss/issue; 40-50 mss/year. Publishes ms within 3-6 months of acceptance. Agented fiction 2%. Published work by Solomon Pogarsky, Ann Beacham, Hélène Scheffler-Mason. Length: 2,500 words preferred; 1,500 words minimum; 4,000 words maximum. Also publishes poetry. Sometimes critiques rejected mss and recommends other markets.
How to Contact: Send complete ms. "Cover letters welcome but not necessary." Reports in 2 months. SASE. "Must include international reply coupons." No simultaneous submissions. Sample copy for $4. Fiction guidelines for #10 SAE and international reply coupon. Reviews novels and short story collections.
Payment: Pays in contributor's copies.
Terms: Acquires first North American serial rights.

GREENSBORO REVIEW, (II), University of North Carolina at Greensboro, Dept. of English, Greensboro NC 27412. (919)334-5459. Editor: Jim Clark. Fiction Editor: Blake Maher. Fiction editor changes each year. Send future mss to the editor. Magazine: 6×9; approximately 136 pages; 60 lb. paper; 65 lb. cover. Literary magazine featuring fiction and poetry for readers interested in contemporary literature. Semiannually. Circ. 500.
Needs: Contemporary and experimental. Accepts 6-8 mss/issue, 12-16 mss/year. Recently published work by Jill McCorkle, Robert Morgan and Peter Taylor. Published new writers within the last year. Length: 7,500 words maximum.
How to Contact: Send complete ms with SASE. No simultaneous submissions. Unsolicited manuscripts must arrive by September 15 to be considered for the winter issue and by February 15 to be considered for the summer issue. Manuscripts arriving after those dates may be held for the next consideration. Reports in 2 months. Sample copy for $2.50.

Payment: Pays in contributor's copies.
Terms: Acquires first North American serial rights.
Advice: "We want to see the best being written regardless of theme, subject or style. Recent stories from *The Greensboro Review* have been included in *The Best American Short Stories*, *Prize Stories: The O. Henry Awards*, *New Stories from the South* and *Best of the West*, anthologies recognizing the finest short stories being published."

‡**GRUE MAGAZINE, (II, IV)**, Hell's Kitchen Productions, Box 370, New York NY 10108. Editor: Peggy Nadramia. Magazine: 5½ × 8½; 96 pages; 60 lb. paper; 10 pt. CIS film laminate cover; illustrations; photos. "Quality short fiction centered on horror and dark fantasy—new traditions in the realms of the gothic and the macabre for horror fans well read in the genre, looking for something new and different, as well as horror novices looking for a good scare." Triannually. Estab. 1985.
Needs: Horror, psychic/supernatural/occult. Receives 250 unsolicited fiction mss/month. Buys 10 mss/issue; 25-30 mss/year. Publishes ms 1-2 years after acceptance. Published work by Thomas Ligotti, Joe R. Lansdale, Don Webb; published new writers within the last year. Length: 4,000 words average; 6,500 words maximum. Sometimes critiques rejected ms and recommends other markets.
How to Contact: Send complete ms with cover letter. "I like to hear where the writer heard about *Grue*, his most recent or prestigious sales, and maybe a word or two about himself." Reports in 3 weeks on queries; 4 months on mss. SASE for ms. Sample copy $4.50. Fiction guidelines for #10 SAE and 1 first class stamp.
Payment: Pays 2 contributor's copies plus ½¢ per word.
Terms: Pays on publication for first North American serial rights.
Advice: "Editors actually vie for the work of the better writers, and if your work is good, you will sell it—you just have to keep sending it out. But out of the 250 mss I read in September, maybe three of them will be by writers who cared enough to make their plots as interesting as possible, their characterizations believable, their settings unique, and who took the time to do the rewrites and polish their prose. Remember that readers of *Grue* are mainly seasoned horror fans, and *not* interested or excited by a straight vampire, werewolf or ghost story—they'll see all the signs, and guess where you're going long before you get there. Throw a new angle on what you're doing; put it in a new light. How? Well, what scares *you*? What's *your* personal phobia or anxiety? When the writer is genuinely, emotionally involved with his subject matter, and is totally honest with himself and his reader, then we can't help being involved, too, and that's where good writing begins and ends."

GULF COAST, A Journal of Literature & Art, (II), Dept. of English, University of Houston, 4800 Calhoun Rd., Houston TX 77204-5641. (713)749-3431. Contact: Fiction Editors. Editors change each year. Magazine: 6 × 9; 108 pages; stock paper, gloss cover; illustrations and photographs. "Fiction on the cusp for the literary-minded." Estab. 1984. Circ. 1,500.
Needs: Condensed/excerpted novel, contemporary, ethnic, experimental, humor/satire, literary, regional, translations, special interest: *translations* from emerging literatures, South America, Africa, China, etc. No children's, religious/inspirational. Plans special fiction issue. Receives 40 unsolicited mss/month. Accepts 3-4 mss/issue; 6-8 mss/year. Publishes ms 6 months-1 year after acceptance. Agented fiction 5%. Published work by Larry Woiwode, John Hawkes and Oscar Hijuelos. Length: No limit. Publishes short shorts. Sometimes critiques rejected mss.
How to Contact: Send complete manuscript with cover letter. "As few words as possible; please notify us if the submission is being considered elsewhere." Reports in 1-3 months. Simultaneous submissions OK ("but prefer not to"). Sample copy for $5, 9 × 12 SAE and 4 first class stamps. Fiction guidelines for #10 SAE and 1 first class stamp.
Payment: Pays contributor's copies.
Terms: Acquires one-time rights. "Write for guidelines."
Advice: "We are most intrigued by those who take risks, experiment with language."

GULF STREAM MAGAZINE, (II), Florida International University, English Dept., North Miami Campus, N. Miami FL 33181. (305)940-5599. Editor: Lynne Barrett. Associate Editor: Chris Gleason. Editors change every 1-2 years. Magazine: 5½ × 8½; 96 pages; bond paper; laminate (1 color, b&w) cover; cover illustrations only; cover photographs only. "We publish all *good quality*—fiction, nonfiction and poetry for a predominately literary market." Semiannually. Estab. 1989. Circ. 500.
Needs: Contemporary, humor/satire, literary, mainstream, mystery/suspense, regional. Nothing "radically experimental." Plans special issues. Receives 80 unsolicited mss/month. Acquires 5 mss/issue; 10 mss/year. Does not read mss during the summer. Publishes ms 6 weeks-3 months after acceptance. Published work by Alan Cheuse, Ann Hood. Length: 5,000 words average; 7,500 words maximum.

Publishes short shorts. Also publishes poetry. Sometimes critiques rejected mss.

How to Contact: Send complete manuscript with cover letter including "previous publications/short bio." Reports in 3 months. SASE. Simultaneous submissions OK "if noted." Sample copy $4. Free fiction guidelines.

Payment: Pays subscription and 2 contributor's copies.

Terms: Acquires first North American serial rights.

Advice: "Looks for good concise writing—well plotted; interesting characters."

GYPSY, Die Sympathische Alternative, (II), Vergin Press, 10708 Gay Brewer, El Paso TX 79935. (915)592-3701. Editors: Belinda Subraman and S. Ramnath. Magazine: 8½ × 11; 84 pages; 20-60 lb. offset paper; 60 lb. card cover; drawings; sometimes photographs. "Quality writing, occasionally limited to theme, for the literary and artistic community." Semiannually. Estab. 1984. Circ. 1,000.

• See the Close-up interview with *Gypsy* Editor Belinda Subraman in this book.

Needs: Experimental, feminist, literary, serialized novel, translations. Upcoming theme: The Positive Book: Growing Through Hard Times (Deadline: July 15).Receives 100 unsolicited fiction mss/month. Accepts 2-4 mss/issue; 6-10 mss/year. Publishes ms 1-8 months after acceptance. Length: "open, but short is better—perhaps 500-2,500 words." Publishes short shorts. Also publishes literary essays, literary criticism, poetry. Sometimes critiques or comments on rejected mss. Sometimes recommends other markets.

How to Contact: Query first or send complete ms with cover letter. Reports in 2-4 months. SASE. Reprint submissions sometimes OK. May accept simultaneous submissions if noted, but "prefer not to." Sample copies for $7. Fiction guidelines for #10 SAE and 1 first-class stamp.

Payment: Pays in contributor's copies.

Terms: Acquires one-time rights.

HABERSHAM REVIEW, (I, II), Piedmont College, P.O. Box 10, Demorest GA 30535. (404)778-2215. Editors: David L. Greene, Lisa Hodgens Lumpkin. Magazine. "General literary magazine with a regional (Southeastern U.S.) focus for a literate audience." Semiannually. Estab. 1991.

Needs: Contemporary, experimental, literary, mainstream, regional. Receives 100 unsolicited mss/month. Acquires 6-10 mss/issue. Publishes ms 6 month-1 year after acceptance. Publishes short shorts. Sometimes critiques rejected mss.

How to Contact: Send complete ms with cover letter. Reports in 6 months on mss. SASE. No simultaneous submissions. Accepts electronic submissions via disk or modem. Sample copy for $6.

Payment: Pays in contributor's copies.

Terms: Acquires first rights.

HALF TONES TO JUBILEE, (II), English Dept. Pensacola Junior College, 1000 College Blvd., Pensacola FL 32504. (904)484-1416. Editors: Allan Peterson and Walter Spara. Magazine: 6 × 9; approx. 100 pages; 70 lb. laid stock; 80 lb. cover. "No theme, all types published." Annually. Estab. 1985. Circ. 500.

Needs: Open. Receives 4-6 unsolicited mss/month. Accepts approx. 6 mss/issue. "We publish in September." Recently published work by Rachel Cann, Dusty Sklar, Johnathan Gillman, Mark Spencer. Length: 1,500 words average. Publishes short shorts. Also publishes poetry. Sometimes critiques rejected mss and recommends other markets.

How to Contact: Send complete manuscript with cover letter. SASE. Sample copy $4. Free fiction guidelines.

Payment: Pays 2 contributor's copies.

Terms: Acquires one-time rights.

‡HAPPINESS HOLDING TANK, (II), 9727 S.E. Reedway, Portland OR 97266. Editor: Albert Drake. Magazine: 8½ × 11; 30-50 pages; 20 lb. bond paper; Bristol cover stock; illustrations, photos sometimes. Primarily a magazine of poetry, articles, reviews, and literary information for poets, students, teachers, other editors and laypeople. "I think a good many people read it for the literary information, much of which isn't available elsewhere." Published irregularly. Estab. 1970. Circ. 300-500.

Needs: Literary. "We publish a limited amount of fiction: very short stories, parables, prose poems, fragments and episodes. Not a good market for traditional fiction." Accepts 4-5 mss/year. Receives very few unsolicited fiction mss each month. Does not read mss in summer. Critiques rejected mss "when there is time."

Close-up

Belinda Subraman
Co-Editor
Gypsy, Die Sympatische Alternative

© S. Ramnath

Belinda Subraman, co-editor of *Gypsy*, defines her magazine as "an alternative magazine in the sense that it doesn't follow established lines, not even the unspoken established lines of the small press." This nonconformist streak motivates many aspects of this magazine's philosophy, from the offbeat submissions she welcomes to experiments in paper color and stock. Subraman strives to make the magazine "express [her] individuality." She and co-editor S. Ramnath cringe at the thought of being a typical small literary magazine, says Subraman.

A more complete explanation of this magazine's name is found in Subraman's lifestyle in the early 1980s. She was living in Germany at the time, working for the United States government. The magazine's title evokes the "colorful" life of traveling in which she was engaged. The second part of the title reflects her desire to create a "congenial alternative" to literary magazines which give cold and abrupt rejections to submissions. She has vivid memories of her days as an aspiring author, and the unfriendly responses she received. As a result, her attitude in *Gypsy* is to avoid being cruel to anybody, she says.

The magazine is a semiannual. One issue each year is published in standard format and is open to "a wide variety of topics . . . tending more toward serious subjects." The other issue has evolved into a themed trade paperback edition. The first came out in 1992 and included many different perspectives on the Gulf War. The second (due out in April 1993) focuses on the ecological problems facing the earth. The next will be titled *The Positive Book: Growing Through Hard Times* and will showcase short selections on the subject of positive growth after violence and devastation. Under the aegis of the closely related Vergin Press, Subraman will accept submissions for this issue until July 15, 1993.

Subraman's ultimate criteria for publication are that a piece must have "a reason for being there and it must change me in some little way." Her goal, she says, is to create a dynamic fusion of art, poetry and prose. In recent years, however, Subraman has tried to shift her focus away from poetry, claiming that she sees too much "shallow work" in this genre and gets simply too many submissions. Though the ratio of prose to poetry is about 50/50, she would like to receive and include more well-written prose.

Through her own experiences in getting published, Subraman has discovered that writing fiction is not an easy process. In fact, she says "Writing, like any other art, takes years to develop. You learn through the doing of it."

—David G. Tompkins

How to Contact: Query. SASE. Simultaneous submissions OK. Reports in 1 week on queries, 3 weeks on mss. Publishes ms 3-5 months after acceptance. Sample copy $1 plus 68¢ postage.
Payment: Pays 2 contributor's copies.
Terms: Acquires one-time rights with automatic return of all rights to author.
Advice: "Be more careful about what you send out. Rewrite. Tighten. Compress. Read it aloud."

‡**HARD ROW TO HOE DIVISION, (II)**, Misty Hill Press, P.O. Box 541-I, Healdsburg CA 95448. (707)433-9786. Editor: Joe Armstrong. Newspaper: 8½×11; 12 pages; 60 lb. white paper; illustrations and photos. "Book reviews, short story and poetry of rural USA including environmental and nature subjects." Triannually. Estab. 1982. Circ. 150.
  • See the listing for Misty Hill Press in the Small Press section of this book.
Needs: Rural America. Receives 8-10 unsolicited mss/month. Acquires 1 ms/issue; 3-4 mss/year. Publishes ms 6-9 months after acceptance. Length: 1,500 words average; 2,000-2,200 words maximum. Publishes short shorts. Sometimes critiques rejected mss and tries to recommend other markets.
How to Contact: Send complete ms with cover letter. Reports in 2-3 weeks on mss. SASE. Simultaneous submissions OK. Sample copy for $2. Fiction guidelines for legal-size SAE and 1 first class stamp.
Payment: Pays 5 contributor's copies.
Terms: Acquires one-time rights.
Advice: "Be certain the subject fits the special need."

HARDBOILED, (I,II), Gryphon Publications, Box 209, Brooklyn NY 11228-0209. Editor: Gary Lovisi. Magazine: Digest-sized; 100 pages; offset paper; card stock cover; illustrations. Publishes "cutting edge, hard, noir fiction with impact! Query on nonfiction and reviews." Quarterly. Estab. 1988.
Needs: Mystery/suspense (private eye, police procedural, young adult). Receives 20-30 mss/month. Buys 20-30 mss/year. Publishes ms within 6 months-2 years of acceptance. Recently published work by Andrew Vachss, Richard Lupoff, Frank Grubber, Eugene Jzzi; published new writers within the last year. Length: 2,000 words minimum; 4,000 words maximum. Sometimes critiques rejected mss and recommends other markets.
How to Contact: Query first or send complete ms with cover letter. Reports in 2 weeks on queries; 2-6 weeks on mss. SASE. Simultaneous submissions OK, but query first. Sample copy $6.
Payment: Pays $5-50 and 2 contributor's copies.
Terms: Pays on publication for first North American serial rights. Copyright reverts to author.

HAUNTS, Tales of Unexpected Horror and the Supernatural, (II, IV), Nightshade Publications, Box 3342, Providence RI 02906. (401)781-9438. Editor: Joseph K. Cherkes. Magazine: 6×9 digest; 80-100 pages; 50 lb. offset paper; perfect-bound; pen and ink illustrations. "We are committed to publishing only the finest fiction in the genres of horror, fantasy and the supernatural from both semi-pro and established writers. We are targeted towards the 18-35 age bracket interested in tales of horror and the unknown." Quarterly. Plans special fiction issue. Estab. 1984. Circ. 1,200.
Needs: Fantasy, horror, psychic/supernatural/occult. No pure adventure, explicit sex, or blow-by-blow dismemberment. Receives 700-750 unsolicited fiction mss/month. Buys 10-12 mss/issue; 50-75 mss/year. Publishes ms 6-9 months after acceptance. Published work by Mike Hurley, Kevin J. Anderson, Frank Ward; published new writers within the last year. Length: 3,500 words average; 1,000 words minimum; 8,500 words maximum. Critiques rejected mss and recommends other markets.
How to Contact: Query first. "Cover letters are a nice way to introduce oneself to a new editor." Open to submissions January 1 to June 1, inclusive. Reports in 2-3 weeks on queries; 2-3 months on mss. SASE for query. Accepts magnetic media (IBM PC-MS/DOS Ver 2.0 or higher), and most major word processing formats. Sample copy $3.95 plus $1 postage and handling. Fiction guidelines for #10 SASE.
Payment: Pays $5-50 (subject to change), contributor's copies, charge for extras.
Terms: Pays on publication for first North American serial rights.
Advice: "Follow writers' guidelines closely. They are a good outline of what your publisher looks for in fiction. If you think you've got the 'perfect' manuscript, go over it again—carefully. Check to make sure you've left no loose ends before sending it out. Keep your writing concise. If your story is rejected, don't give up. Try to see where the story failed. This way you can learn from your mistakes. Remember, success comes to those who persist. We plan to open to advertising on a limited basis, also plan a media campaign to increase subscriptions and distributed sales."

HAWAII PACIFIC REVIEW, (II), Hawaii Pacific University, 1060 Bishop St., Honolulu HI 96813. (808)544-0214. Editor: Elizabeth Fischel. Magazine: 6×9; 100-150 pages; quality paper; glossy cover; illustrations and original artwork. "The *Review* seeks to reflect the cultural diversity that is the hallmark of Hawaii Pacific University. Consequently, we welcome material on a wide variety of themes and we encourage experimental styles and narrative techniques. Categories: fiction, poetry, essays and scholarly writing." Annually. Estab. "nationwide in 1988."
Needs: Adventure, contemporary, ethnic, experimental, fantasy, humor/satire, literary, mainstream, regional, science fiction, suspense/mystery, translations. No romance, confessions, religious or juvenile. Receives approx. 50 unsolicited fiction mss/month. Accepts 4-8 mss/issue. Deadline for the Spring annual issue is January 1. Does not read in summer. Publishes ms 3-12 months after acceptance. Published new writers within the last year. Length: 5,000 words maximum. Publishes short shorts. Also publishes literary essays, literary criticism, poetry. Sometimes critiques rejected mss or recommends other markets.
How to Contact: Send complete manuscript with cover letter, which should include a brief bio. Reports in 3 months. SASE. Simultaneous submissions OK. Fiction guidelines for #10 SAE and 1 first class stamp.
Payment: Pays in contributor's copies.
Terms: Acquires first North American serial rights. Rights revert to author upon publication.
Advice: "As more publication opportunities arise and more writers become visible, a new writer must find fresh, innovative ways of storytelling to truly stand out and move the genre forward."

HAWAII REVIEW, (II), University of Hawaii English Dept., 1733 Donaghho Rd., Honolulu HI 96822. (808)956-3030. Editor: Jeanne Tsutsui. Magazine: 6½×9½; 150-170 pages; illustrations; photos. "We publish short stories as well as poetry and reviews by new and experienced writers. As an international literary journal, we hope to reflect the idea that cultural diversity is of universal interest." For residents of Hawaii and non-residents from the continental US and abroad. Triannually. Plans special fiction issue on environmental concerns. Estab. 1972. Circ. 5,000.
Needs: Contemporary, ethnic, experimental, humor/satire, literary, prose poem, regional and translations. Receives 40-50 mss/month. Buys no more than 40 mss/issue; 130 mss/year. Published work by William Pitt Root, Ursule Molinaro and Ian Macmillan; published new writers within the last year. Length: 4,000 words average; no minimum; 8,000 words maximum. Occasionally critiques mss. Also publishes poetry. Recommends other markets.
How to Contact: Send complete manuscript with SASE. Reports in 3-4 months on mss. Sample copy for $5. Fiction guidelines free.
Payment: Payment "varies depending upon funds budgeted. Last year, we paid $35-70 per story;" 2 contributor's copies.
Terms: Pays on publication for all rights. Sends galleys to author upon request. After publication, copyright reverts to author upon request.

HAYDEN'S FERRY REVIEW, (II), Arizona State University, Matthews Center ASU, Tempe AZ 85287-1502. (602)965-1243. Managing Editor: Salima Keegan. Editors change every 1-2 years. Magazine: 6×9; 128 pages; fine paper; illustrations and photographs. "Contemporary material by new and established writers for a varied audience." Semiannually. Estab. 1986. Circ. 600.
• Work from *Hayden's Ferry Review* was selected for inclusion in the *Pushcart Prize* anthology in 1992.
Needs: Contemporary, ethnic, experimental, fantasy, feminist, gay, historical (general), humor/satire, literary, mainstream, prose poem, psychic/supernatural/occult, regional, romance (contemporary), science fiction, senior citizen/retirement. Possible special fiction issue. Receives 150 unsolicited mss/month. Accepts 5 mss/issue; 10 mss/year. Does not read mss in the summer. Publishes mss 3-4 months after acceptance. Published work by Raymond Carver, Ken Kesey, Rita Dove, Chuck Rosenthal and Rick Bass. Length: No preference. Publishes short shorts. Also publishes literary essays.
How to Contact: Send complete manuscript with cover letter. No simultaneous submissions. Reports in 2-3 months from deadline on mss. SASE. Sample copy for $6. Fiction guidelines for SAE.
Payment: Pays 2 contributor's copies.
Terms: Buys first North American serial rights. Sends galleys to author.

‡**HEART ATTACK MAGAZINE, Myocardial Infarction Horror, (I, IV)**, Coronary Press, 518 Lowell St., Methuen MA 01844. (508)685-2342. Editor: David Gordon. Magazine: 8½×11; 60-80 pages; 20 lb. bond paper; 80 lb. gloss cover; illustrations; photographs. "Horror, sci-fi, dark fantasy. Mostly

publish horror. Humor is good too (especially black). Audience ranges from 16 years-70 years." Bi-monthly. Estab. 1991. Circ. 1,000.

• *Heart Attack* was nominated by the Small Press Writers and Artists Organization as "Best New Magazine/Editor" in 1991.

Needs: Erotica, fantasy (science fantasy), horror, humor/satire, mystery/suspense (horror slant), psychic/supernatural/occult, romance (gothic), science fiction (hard science, soft/sociological). "All stories should have a horror slant. No pornography or racism but sex and profanity is okay." Upcoming themes: Halloween (October) "All stories must have to do with Halloween. Ghost and witch stories are the best kinds." Receives 125-150 unsolicited mss/month. Acquires 7-8 mss/issue; 48 mss/year. Publishes ms 4-6 months after acceptance. Agented fiction 5%. Recently published work by John B. Rosenman, Brad J. Boucher, Marthayn Pelegrimas, Gregory L. Norris. Length: 2,000 words preferred; 150 words minimum; 3,000 words maximum. Publishes short shorts. Length: 400 words. Also publishes literary criticism, poetry. Always critiques or comments on rejected mss.

How to Contact: Send complete ms with cover letter or send for guidelines. Include estimated word count, bio (2 paragraphs), list of publications (if any). Reports in 1 week on queries; 4-6 weeks on mss. Send SASE for reply, return of mss or disposable copy of the ms. No simultaneous submissions. Reprint submission OK. Sample copy for $4. Fiction guidelines for #10 SAE and 1 first class stamp or IRC. Reviews novels and short story collections. Send published book (horror and sf only) review copies to Brad Boucher, P.O. Box 750, E. Hampstead NH 03826.

Payment: Pays 1 contributor's copy; additional copies at a reduced rate, $3.10.

Terms: Acquires first North American serial rights.

Advice: Looks for "good plot, constant suspense, detail, enjoyable characters. Traditional horror (monsters, aliens, etc.) are okay as long as it is written well. Personally, friendliness is important, but also professionalism. Know that the editor is the boss even if you don't agree. Remember that an editor's policy is mainly built on his opinion. Take an editor's critique into consideration, but don't accept it as *law*, unless it is grammatical errors. Just be kind and professional and able to accept constructive criticism. Most manuscripts lately have seemed to be lacking in great suspense. I like to be captivated almost immediately, but also to be held there throughout the story. Also, I don't see enough sci-fi, dark fantasy or dark humor. All I get mostly is horror."

THE HEARTLANDS TODAY, (II), The Firelands Writing Center, Firelands College of BGSU, Huron OH 44839. (419)433-5560. Editors: Larry Smith and Nancy Dunham. Magazine: 6×9; 160 pages; b&w illustrations; 25-30 photographs. Material must be set in the Midwest . . . prefer material that reveals life in the Midwest today for a general, literate audience. Annually. Estab. 1991.

Needs: Ethnic, humor, literary, mainstream, regional (Midwest). Upcoming theme: Socially Engaged Writing (Midwest location). Receives 10 unsolicited mss/month. Buys 6 mss/issue. Does not read mss August-December. Publishes ms 6 months after acceptance. Recently published work of Wendell Mayo, Tony Tomassi, Gloria Bowman. Length: 4,500 words maximum. Also publishes literary essays, poetry. Sometimes critiques rejected mss and recommends other markets.

How to Contact: Send complete ms with cover letter. Reports in 1 month on mss. SASE for ms, not needed for query. Simultaneous submissions OK, if noted. Sample copy for $5.

Payment: Pays $20-25 and 2 contributor's copies.

Terms: Pays on publication for first rights.

Advice: "We look for writing that connects on a human level, one that moves us with its truth and opens our vision of the world. If writing is a great escape for you, don't bother with us. We're in it for the joy, beauty or truth of the art. We look for a straight, honest voice dealing with human experiences. We do not define the Midwest, we hope to be a document of the Midwest. If you feel you are writing from the Midwest, send. We look first at the quality of the writing."

HEAVEN BONE, (IV), Heaven Bone Press, Box 486, Chester NY 10918. (914)469-9018. Editors: Steven Hirsch, Kirpal Gordon. Magazine: 8½×11; 49-78 pages; 60 lb. recycled offset paper; recycled C1S cover; computer clip art, graphics, line art, cartoons, halftones and photos scanned in tiff format. "New consciousness, expansive, fine literary, earth and nature, spiritual path. We use current reviews, essays on spiritual and esoteric topics, creative stories and fantasy. Also: reviews of current poetry releases and expansive literature." Readers are "spiritual seekers, healers, poets, artists, musicians, students." Semiannually. Estab. 1987. Circ. 1,200.

Needs: Experimental, fantasy, psychic/supernatural/occult, esoteric/scholarly, regional, religious/inspirational, spiritual. "No violent, thoughtless or exploitive fiction." Receives 45-110 unsolicited mss/month. Accepts 5-15 mss/issue; 12-30 mss/year. Publishes ms 2 weeks-6 months after acceptance. Recently published work by Fielding Dawson, Janine Pommy-Vega, Charles Bukowski, Marge Piercy;

published new writers within the last year. Length: 3,500 words average; 1,200 words minimum; 6,000 words maximum. Publishes short shorts. Also publishes literary essays, literary criticism, poetry. Sometimes critiques rejected mss and may recommend other markets.

How to Contact: Send complete ms with cover letter, which should include short bio of recent activities. Reports in 2 weeks on queries; 2 weeks-6 months on mss. SASE. Reprint submissions OK. Accepts electronic submissions via "Apple Mac SE/30 versions of Macwrite, Microsoft Word v. 4.0 or Writenow v. 3.0." Sample copy $5. Fiction guidelines free. Reviews novels and short story collections.

Payment: Pays in contributor's copies; charges for extras.

Terms: Acquires first North American serial rights. Sends galleys to author, if requested.

Advice: "Our fiction needs are temperamental, so please query first before submitting. We prefer shorter fiction. Do not send first drafts to test them on us. Please refine and polish your work before sending. Always include SASE. We are looking for the unique, unusual and excellent."

HERESIES: A Feminist Publication on Art & Politics, (IV), Box 1306, Canal St. Station, New York NY 10013. Magazine: 8½ × 11; 96 pages; non-coated paper; b&w illustrations and photos. "We believe that what is commonly called art can have a political impact and that in the making of art and all cultural artifacts our identities as women play a distinct role . . . A place where diversity can be articulated. International and North American readership; carried by many college libraries, alternative bookshops, and art schools." Published 1-2 times/year. Estab. 1977. Circ. 8,000.

Needs: Feminist and lesbian. Upcoming themes: "Women on Men;" "Viva Latina;" "Biography/ Autobiography;" "Hair." "Due to reliance on volunteer editors and the extensive cuts in arts funding, notification for acceptance or rejection may take up to 1 year, particularly for nonthematic submissions." Published new writers within the last year. Publishes stories up to 25 typed pages maximum. Also publishes poetry.

How to Contact: Query. Guidelines with SASE.

Payment: Small payment post publication and several contributor's copies.

Advice: "Try not to imitate what you think is a successful, saleable style. Try to stick to concrete stuff you've experienced yourself so as to sharpen your narrative/dialogue skills on a foundation of familiarity."

HERSPECTIVES, The Dialogue of the Common Woman for Wise Women, Strong Women, Healers, & Peacemakers, (II, IV), Box 2047, Squamish, British Columbia V0N, 3G0 Canada. (604)892-5723. Editor: Mary E. Billy. Magazine: 8½ × 11; 30-40 pages; bond paper; b&w illustrations and photographs. "Feminist; ecology; spirituality; poetry; articles; cartoons; graphics; letters; short short fiction for women. Quarterly. Estab. 1989. Circ. 300.

Needs: Condensed/excerpted novel, confession, contemporary, erotica, ethnic, experimental, fantasy, feminist, humor/satire, juvenile, lesbian, mainstream, prose poem, senior citizen/retirement, young adult/teen (10-18 years) (for women). "No sexist, racist, homophobic; prefer positive perspective." Receives 3 unsolicited mss/month. Accepts 2-4 mss/issue; 6 mss/year. Publishes ms 3-24 months after acceptance. Recently published work by Louise Allin, Gina Bergamino. Length: 1,000-2,000 words average; 200 words minimum; 3,000 words maximum. Publishes short shorts. Sometimes critiques rejected mss.

How to Contact: Send complete ms with cover letter. Include "where you heard about or read *Herspectives*, international coupons for ms return if outside of Canada. Reports in 2-6 weeks. SASE. Simultaneous and reprint submissions OK. Sample copy for $5. Fiction guidelines for #10 SAE and 1 first class Canadian stamp or IRC.

Payment: Pays 1 contributor's copy.

Terms: Acquires first rights. Not copyrighted.

Advice: Looks for "clean tight writing, ring of honesty and guts, humor, a positive attitude without sounding Pollyanaish. Absolutely no violence."

Market conditions are constantly changing! If you're still using this book and it is 1994 or later, buy the newest edition of Novel & Short Story Writer's Market *at your favorite bookstore or order directly from Writer's Digest Books.*

HIGH PLAINS LITERARY REVIEW, (II), Suite 250, 180 Adams Street, Denver CO 80206. (303)320-6828. Editor-in-Chief: Robert O. Greer, Jr. Magazine: 6 × 9; 135 pages; 70 lb. paper; heavy cover stock. "The *High Plains Literary Review* publishes poetry, fiction, essays, book reviews and interviews. The publication is designed to bridge the gap between high-caliber academic quarterlies and successful commercial reviews." Triannually. Estab. 1986. Circ. 950.

● *High Plains Literary Review* was named a "literary root" by *Esquire* (July 1992).

Needs: Most pressing need: outstanding essays, serious fiction, contemporary, humor/satire, literary, mainstream, regional. No true confessions, romance, pornographic, excessive violence. Receives approximately 200 unsolicited mss/month. Buys 4-6 mss/issue; 12-18 mss/year. Publishes ms usually 6 months after acceptance. Published work by Richard Currey, Joyce Carol Oates, Nancy Lord and Rita Dove; published new writers within the last year. Length: 4,200 words average; 1,500 words minimum; 8,000 words maximum; prefers 3,000-6,000 words. Also publishes literary essays, literary criticism, poetry. Occasionally critiques rejected mss. Sometimes recommends other markets.

How to Contact: Send complete ms with cover letter, which should include brief publishing history. Reports in 6 weeks. SASE. Simultaneous submissions OK. Sample copy for $4.

Payment: Pays $5/page for prose and 2 contributor's copies.

Terms: Pays on publication for first North American serial rights. "Copyright reverts to author upon publication." Sends copy-edited proofs to the author.

Advice: "*HPLR* publishes *quality* writing. Send us your very best material. We will read it carefully and either accept it promptly, recommend changes or return it promptly. Do not start submitting your work until you learn the basic tenets of the game including some general knowledge about how to develop characters and plot and how to submit a manuscript. I think the most important thing for any new writer interested in the short story form is to have a voracious appetite for short fiction, to see who and what is being published, and to develop a personal style."

HILL AND HOLLER: Southern Appalachian Mountains, (II), Seven Buffaloes Press, Box 249, Big Timber MT 59011. Editor: Art Cuelho. Magazine: 5½ × 8½; 80 pages; 70 lb. offset paper; 80 lb. cover stock; illustrations; photos rarely. "I use mostly rural Appalachian material: poems and stories. Some folklore and humor. I am interested in heritage, especially in connection with the farm." Annually. Published special fiction issue. Estab. 1983. Circ. 750.

● Art Cuelho of Seven Buffaloes Press also edits *Azorean Express*, *Black Jack* and *Valley Grape-vine* listed in this book. See also the listing for the publishing company for more information.

Needs: Contemporary, ethnic, humor/satire, literary, regional, rural America farm. "I don't have any prejudices in style, but I don't like sentimental slant. Deep feelings in literature are fine, but they should be portrayed with tact and skill." Receives 10 unsolicited mss/month. Accepts 4-6 mss/issue. Publishes ms 6 months-1 year after acceptance. Length: 2,000-3,000 words average. Also publishes short shorts of 500-1,000 words.

How to Contact: Query first. Reports in 2 weeks on queries. SASE. Sample copy $6.75.

Payment: Pays in contributor's copies; charge for extras.

Terms: Acquires first North American serial rights "and permission to reprint if my press publishes a special anthology." Sometimes sends galleys to author.

Advice: "In this Southern Appalachian rural series I can be optimistic about fiction. Appalachians are very responsive to their region's literature. I have taken work by beginners that had not been previously published. Be sure to send a double-spaced clean manuscript and SASE. I have the only rural press in North America; maybe even in the world. So perhaps we have a bond in common if your roots are rural."

‡HIS GARDEN MAGAZINE, (II, IV), 216 N. Vine St., Kewanee IL 61443. (309)852-0332. Editor: Margi L.Washburn. Magazine: 8½ × 11; 32 pages; 20 lb. white paper; 20 lb. color cover; illustrations. "*His Garden* is an inspirational publication. I like to print a good variety of uplifting material. If I can bring a smile or make someone aware of the good things in life, that will be my goal." Triannually. Estab. 1992. Circ. 150.

Needs: Fantasy (spiritual warfare). No erotica, horror, science fiction, mystery. Receives 35 + unsolicited mss/month. Buys 3-5 mss/issue; 10-15 mss/year. Publishes ms 4-6 months after acceptance. Recently published work by Lois Hayn, Nathaniel Johnson, Jr. Length: 250 words minimum; 2,500 words maximum. Publishes short shorts. Also publishes poetry. Always critiques or comments on rejected mss.

How to Contact: Send complete ms with cover letter. Should include estimated word count, bio and list of publications. Reports in 3 weeks on queries; 2 months on mss. Send SASE for reply, return of ms or send a disposable copy of the ms. Simultaneous and reprint submissions OK. Sample copy for

$3.50. Fiction guidelines for SASE. Reviews novels and short story collections.

Payment: Pays $5 and 1 contributor's copy. Additional copies $2.

Terms: Buys one-time rights. Not copyrighted.

Advice: "I need to feel emotion of some kind. If a writer can make me care what happens to the character(s) in a story, I'll consider acceptance. I love subtle messages that really touch my heart. I'd like to see more written about how our changing world has affected our values, our children, the family and the elderly."

‡**HOB-NOB (I)**, 994 Nissley Rd., Lancaster PA 17601. Editor/Publisher: Mildred K. Henderson. Magazine: 8½ × 11; 76+ pages; 20 lb. bond paper; 20 lb. (or heavier) cover stock; b&w illustrations; few photos. "*Hob-Nob* is a small (one-person), amateur publication currently with a literary emphasis on original prose and poetry. This publication is directed toward amateur writers and poets, but many of them would like to be professional. For some, appearance in *Hob-Nob* is simply an opportunity to be published somewhere, while others possibly see it as a springboard to bigger and better things." Semiannually. Estab. 1969. Circ. 450.

Needs: Literary, adventure, contemporary, humor, fantasy, psychic/supernatural/occult, prose poem, regional, romance (gothic), religious/inspirational, science fiction, spiritual, sports, mystery (amateur sleuth, English cozy), juvenile, young adult, senior citizen/retirement, western (frontier, young adult), very brief condensed novels, excerpts from novels. "Upbeat" subjects are preferred. Family emphasis. "Clean only. No erotica, works with excessive swearing or blatantly sexual words, gross violence, suicide, etc." Accepts 25-35 mss/issue. Does not read new contributor's submissions March 1-December 31, to prevent a backlog; any received before January will be returned. Receives 8-10 fiction mss each month. Recently published work by Keith Slater, Bernard Hewitt, Diana Kwiatkowski Rubin, Bonnie Newton; published many new writers within the last year. Length: preferably 500-2,000 words. Sometimes serializes a longer story (2 installments). Critiques rejected mss when there is time. Sometimes recommends other markets.

How to Contact: Send complete ms with SASE. No simultaneous submissions. Reports in several months on acceptance, "less for rejections." Publishes ms at least 1½-2 years after acceptance. Sample copy for $3.50 or $3 for a back issue.

Payment: Pays 1 contributor's copy for first appearance only. $3.50 for one extra, $3 each for additional. Readers' choice contest every issue – votes taken on favorite stories and poems. Small prizes up to $10.

Terms: Acquires first rights.

Advice: "Include name and address on at least the first page, and name on others. State 'original and unpublished.' I especially appreciate the 'light' touch in both fiction and nonfiction – family stories and light romance (*no* erotica); offbeat, whimsical, humorous, maybe even cornball at times." Includes "some recurring humorous characters from certain established contributors. Occasional two-part stories (*under* 5,000 words total)."

HOBSON'S CHOICE (I), Starwind Press, Box 98, Ripley OH 45167. (513)392-4549. Editor: Susannah West. Magazine: 8½ × 11; 16 pages; 60 lb. offset paper and cover; b&w illustrations; line shot photos. "Science fiction and fantasy for young adults and adults with interest in science, technology, science fiction and fantasy." Monthly. Estab. 1974. Circ. 2,000.

Needs: Fantasy, science fiction (hard science, soft/sociological). "We like SF that shows hope for the future and protagonists who interact with their environment rather than let themselves be manipulated by it." No horror, pastiches of other authors, stories featuring characters created by others (i.e. Captain Kirk and crew, Dr. Who, etc.). Receives 50+ unsolicited mss/month. Buys 4-6 mss/issue; 16-24 mss/year. Publishes ms between 4 months-2 years after acceptance. Published work by Barbara Myers, Allen Byerle, Kurt Hyatt; published new writers within the last year. Length: 3,000-8,000 words average; 1,000 words minimum; 8,000 words maximum. Also publishes literary criticism and "occasionally" literary essays. Occasionally critiques rejected mss.

How to Contact: Send complete ms. Reports in 2-3 months. "If an author hasn't heard from us by 4 months, he/she should feel free to withdraw." SASE for ms. No simultaneous submissions. Accepts electronic submissions via disk for the IBM PC or PC compatible and Macintosh. Sample copy $1.75; issue #2-5 $2.50. Fiction guidelines for #10 SAE and 1 first class stamp. Tipsheet packet (all guidelines plus tips on writing science fiction) for $1 and SASE.

Payment: Pays 1-4¢/word and contributor's copies.
Terms: Pays 25% on acceptance; 75% on publication. "25% payment is kill fee if we decide not to publish story." Rights negotiable. Sends galleys to the author.
Advice: "I certainly think a beginning writer can be successful if he/she studies the publication *before* submitting, and matches the submission with the magazine's needs. Get our guidelines and study them *before* submitting. Don't submit something *way over* or *way under* our word length requirements. Be understanding of editors; they can get swamped very easily, *especially* if there's only one editor handling all submissions. You don't need to write a synopsis of your story in your cover letter – the story should be able to stand on its own."

‡HOME PLANET NEWS, (II), Home Planet Publications, P. O. Box 415, New York NY 10009. (718)769-2854. Tabloid: 11½ × 16; 24 pages; newsprint; illustrations; photos. "*Home Planet News* publishes mainly poetry along with some fiction, as well as reviews (books, theater and art), and articles of literary interest. We see *HPN* as a quality literary journal in an eminently readable format – and in content urban, urbane and politically aware." Triannually. Estab. 1979. Circ. 1,000.
• Poetry by Daniel Berrigan and Frank Murphy appearing in *HPN* has been included in the *Pushcart Prize* and *Editor's Choice* anthologies.
Needs: Ethnic/multicultural, experimental, feminist, gay, historical (general), lesbian, literary, mainstream/contemporary, science fiction (soft/sociological). No "children's or genre stories (except rarely for some SF")." Upcoming themes: "AIDS" (9/93). Publishes special fiction issue or anthology. Receives 12 mss/month. Buys 1 ms/issue; 3 mss/year. Publishes 1 year after acceptance. Recently published Maureen McNeil, B.A. Niditch, Enid Dame. Length: 2,500 words average; 500 words minimum; 3,000 words maximum. Publishes short shorts. Also publishes literary criticism, poetry.
How to Contact: Send complete ms with a cover letter. Reports in 3-6 months on mss. Send SASE (IRC) for reply, return of ms or send a disposable copy of the ms. Sample copy $3. Fiction guidelines for SAE.
Payment: Pays 4 contributor's copies; additional copies $1.
Terms: Acquires one-time rights.
Advice: "We use very little. It just has to grab us. We need short pieces of some complexity." Looking for "well-written, well-plotted stories with well-developed, believable characters."

THE HOPEWELL REVIEW, (III, IV), (formerly *Arts Indiana Literary Supplement*), Arts Indiana, Inc., #701, 47 S. Pennsylvania St., Indianapolis IN 46204. (317)632-7894. Editor: Alison Jester. Magazine: 9 × 12; 32 pages; 80 lb. signature gloss paper; self-cover; illustrations. "The *Hopewell Review* is an annual anthology of fiction and poetry published in a magazine format. The primary criterion for selection is high literary quality for well-educated, active patrons of the arts." Annually. Estab. 1989.
• *The Hopewell Review* recently changed its name from the *Arts Indiana Literary Supplement*. It's still distributed with the Indiana-based arts publication and features the work of Indiana writers, but the editors decided to change the name to better reflect the "indigenous quality" of the work. The Hopewells, a "pre-literate" group of mound-building people native to Indiana, southwest Ohio and Illinois, were the inspiration for the title change.
Needs: Condensed/excerpted novel, contemporary, experimental, humor/satire, literary, prose poem, regional, translations. "Writers must currently live in Indiana or have an extraordinary tie." Receives 600 unsolicited mss/year. Buys 4-6 mss/issue. Publishes annually (September). Recently published work by Scott Russell Sanders, Maura Stanton and James Walton. Length: 4,000 words maximum. Sometimes critiques rejected mss.
How to Contact: Send complete ms with cover letter which should include brief biography. Annual deadline: February. Notification: June. SASE. Simultaneous submissions OK with notification. Sample copy for $2.95 and $2 postage. Fiction guidelines for SAE and 1 first class stamp.
Payment: Pays $125-625 ($500 award of excellence); and 2 contributor's copies. Charges for extras.
Terms: Pays on publication for first rights, one-time rights.
Advice: "Fresh perspectives and use of the English language make a ms stand out."

‡HOPSCOTCH: THE MAGAZINE FOR GIRLS, (II), The Bluffton News Publishing & Printing Co., P.O. Box 164, Bluffton OH 45817. (419)358-4610. Fax: (419)358-5027. Editor: Marilyn Edwards. Magazine: 7 × 9; 50 pages; enamel paper; pen & ink illustrations; photographs. Bimonthly. Estab. 1989. Circ. 8,000.
• *Hopscotch* is indexed in the *Children's Magazine Guide* and *Ed Press*. For more, see the close-up with a *Hopscotch* editor in the 1991 *Children's Writer's & Illustrator's Market*.

Needs: Children's/juvenile (5-9, 10-12 years): adventure, ethnic/multicultural, fantasy, historical (general), sports. Upcoming themes: "Dogs" (Feb./March 1993); "Gardening" (April/May 1993); "The Sky-Airplanes & Astronomy" (June/July 1993); "Grandmothers & Granddaughters" (Oct./Nov. 1993). List of upcoming themes available for SASE. Receives 300-400 unsolicited mss/month. Buys 20-40 mss/year. Agented fiction 2%. Recently published work by Lois Grambling, Wayne Hogan, VaDonna Jean Leaf. Length: 700-1,000 words preferred; 300 words minimum; 1,000 maximum. Publishes short shorts. Length: 250-400 words. Also publishes poetry, puzzles, hidden pictures and crafts. Always comments on rejected mss.
How to Contact: Send complete ms with cover letter. Should include estimated word count, 1-page bio, Social Security number, list of publications. Reports in 2-4 weeks on queries; 6-10 weeks on mss. Send SASE for reply, return of ms or send disposable copy of the ms. Simultaneous and reprint submissions OK. Sample copy for $3. Fiction guidelines for #10 SASE. Reviews novels and short story collections.
Payment: Pays 5-10¢/word (extra for usable photos or illustrations) and 1-2 contributor's copies. Additional copies $3; $2 for 10 or more.
Terms: Pays 6 months before publication for first North American serial rights.
Advice: Looks for "age of girl involved (6-12 years), length under 1,000 words, typewritten—having been proofread."

HOR-TASY, (II, IV), Ansuda Publications, Box 158-J, Harris IA 51345. Editor/Publisher: Daniel R. Betz. Magazine: 5½ × 8½; 72 pages; mimeo paper; index stock cover; illustrations on cover. "*Hor-Tasy* is bringing back actual *horror* to horror lovers tired of seeing so much science fiction and SF passed off as horror. We're also very much interested in true, poetic, pure fantasy."
Needs: Fantasy and horror. "Pure fantasy: Examples are trolls, fairies and mythology. The horror we're looking for comes from the human mind—the ultimate form of horror. It must sound real—so real that in fact it could very possibly happen at any time and place. We must be able to feel the diseased mind behind the personality. No science fiction in any way, shape or form. We don't want stories in which the main character spends half his time talking to a shrink. We don't want stories that start out with: 'You're crazy,' said so and so." Accepts 6 mss/issue. Receives 15-20 unsolicited fiction mss each month. Published work by Charmaine Parsons, M. C. Salemme, Jude Howell; published new writers within the last year. Critiques rejected mss "unless it's way off from what we're looking for." Sometimes recommends other markets.
How to Contact: Query or send complete ms with SASE. Simultaneous submissions OK ("if we know about it.") Reports in 1 day on queries. "If not interested (in ms), we return immediately. If interested, we may keep it as long as 6 months." Publishes ms an average of 1 year after acceptance. Sample copy for $2.95. Guidelines for #10 SASE.
Payment: Pays 2 contributor's copies. Extras at cover price less special discount rates.
Terms: Acquires first North American serial rights.
Advice: "Most stories rejected are about spooks, monsters, haunted houses, spacemen, etc. Because *Hor-Tasy* is a unique publication, I suggest the potential writer get a sample copy. Only unpublished work will be considered."

HOUSEWIFE-WRITER'S FORUM, (I), P.O. Box 780, Lyman WY 82937. (307)786-4513. Editor: Diane Wolverton. Fiction Editor: Bob Haynie. Magazine: 6½ × 10; 32-40 pages; glossy cover; illustrations. "Support for the woman who juggles writing with family life. We publish short fiction, poetry, essays, nonfiction, line drawings, humor and hints. For women of all ages; house husbands who write." Bimonthly. Estab. 1988. Circ. over 1,200.
● This magazine also includes fiction marketing tips and information. It is ranked #48 on the 1992 *Writer's Digest* Fiction 50 list and also won first place in the Wyoming Media Professionals annual contest for regularly published magazines. See also our listing for the contest sponsored by the magazine, Best Short Story Rejected by *Redbook* (or other large market).
Needs: Contemporary, experimental, historical (general), humor/satire, literary, mainstream, mystery/suspense, romance (contemporary, historical). No pornographic material. Receives 100-200 mss/month. Buys 1-2 mss/issue; 6-12 mss/year. Publishes ms within 6 months-1 year after acceptance. Recently published work by Elaine McCormick, Carol Shenold and Carole Bellacera. Length: 1,500 words preferred; 500 words minimum; 2,000 words maximum. Publishes short shorts. Publishes critiques of accepted mss.
How to Contact: Send complete ms with cover letter. Reports in 3 months on mss. SASE "with *adequate* postage." Simultaneous and reprint submissions OK. Sample copy for $4. Fiction guidelines for #10 SAE and 1 first class stamp.

Payment: Pays 1¢/word, plus 1 contributor's copy. Half price for extra copies.
Terms: Pays on acceptance for first North American rights. Sponsors awards for fiction writers. "We sponsor occasional contests geared to the interests of housewife-writers. First place winners are published in the magazine. Entry fees: $4. Prize: $30. Send #10 SAE with 1 first class stamp for guidelines and further information."
Advice: "Fiction Editor Bob Haynie reads all mss and sometimes offers suggestions on the rejections. All published materials are printed with Mr. Haynie's critiques. Here are a few samples to show you what he's looking for: 'Life is made up of small details. Writing often consists of finding the right ones out of the thousands that make up even the briefest moment and using them to convey information to the reader. There's more to this than just a bunch of required items and small details, though. There is also believable dialogue, controlled pacing, and a fine ending that fits the tone and the action and the narrator just right. I look for the overall effect of the story—the product of its theme, its narrative skill, its handling of detail and pace and dialogue, its felicity of beginning, transition and ending. The degree to which all these things mesh and contribute to a whole meaning that surpasses the mere sum of the constituents is the degree to which a story succeeds.' "

HOWLING DOG, (II), 8419 Rhode, Utica MI 48317. Magazine: 6×9; 64 pages; 65 lb. paper; some illustrations; some photographs. "A wild and crazy literary magazine for a diverse audience." Estab. 1985. Circ. 500.
Needs: Contemporary, experimental, humor/satire, literary and mainstream. Upcoming theme: "Music issue," stories and interviews of musicians. Receives 40 unsolicited mss/month. Accepts 2 mss/issue. Publishes ms 6 months after acceptance. Recently published work by M.L. Liebler and Gregory Burnham. Length: 800 words average; 300 words minimum; 1,000 words maximum. Publishes short shorts. Also publishes literary essays, literary criticism, poetry. Sometimes critiques rejected mss and recommends other markets.
How to Contact: Send complete ms. No cover letter. Reports in 1 year. Sample copy for $4. Reviews novels and short story collections.
Payment: Pays in contributor copies; discount charge for extras.
Terms: Acquires one-time rights.
Advice: "We look for crazy, *provocative*, quick, detailed, memorable, smooth reading, emotional or otherwise interesting. Keep it *less than* 1,000 words."

‡THE HUNTED NEWS, (II), The Subourban Press, P.O. Box 9101, Warwick RI 02889. (401)739-2279. Editor: Mike Wood. Magazine: 8½×11; 25-30 pages; photocopied paper. "I am looking for good writers, in the hope that I can help their voices be heard. Like most in the small press scene, I just wanted to create another option for writers who otherwise might not be heard." Triannually. Estab. 1991. Circ. 200.
Needs: Children's/juvenile (1-4 and 10-12 years), erotica, experimental, gay, humor/satire, lesbian, literary, mainstream/contemporary, serialized novel, translations. No SF; politically-biased; romance. Publishes annual special fiction issue or anthologies. Receives 5-10 unsolicited mss/month. Acquires 1-2 mss/issue; 6 mss/year. Publishes ms within 3 months after acceptance. Recently published work by Darryl Smyers, Robert Howington. Length: 500 words minimum; 900 words maximum. Publishes short shorts. Length: 300+ words. Also publishes literary essays, literary criticism and poetry. Always critiques or comments on rejected mss.
How to Contact: Send complete ms with cover letter. Should include bio. Reports in 1 month. Send SASE for reply, return of ms or send disposable copy of the ms. Simultaneous and reprint submissions OK. Sample copy for 8½×11 SAE and 3 first class stamps. Fiction guidelines free. Reviews novels or short story collections.
Payment: Pays up to 5 contributor's copies.
Terms: Acquires one-time rights.
Advice: "I look for an obvious love of language and a sense that there is something at stake in the story, a story that somehow needs to be told. Write what you need to write, say what you think you need to say, no matter the subject, and take a chance and send it to me; a writer will always find an audience if the work is true."

HURRICANE ALICE, A Feminist Quarterly, (II), Hurricane Alice Fn., Inc., 207 Church St. SE, Minneapolis MN 55455. Executive Editors: Martha Roth, Patricia Cumbie. Fiction is collectively edited. Tabloid: 11×17; 12-16 pages; newsprint stock; illustrations and photos. "We look for feminist fictions with a certain analytic snap, for serious readers, seriously interested in emerging forms of feminist art/artists." Quarterly. Estab. 1983. Circ. 600-700.

Needs: Erotica, experimental, feminist, gay, humor/satire, lesbian, science fiction, translations. No coming-out stories, defloration stories, abortion stories. Upcoming themes: "Women and Travel" (Spring 1993); "Native American Women Writers" (Summer 1993); "Women and Politics" (Fall 1993). Receives 80 unsolicited mss/month. Publishes 8-10 stories annually. Publishes mss up to 1 year after acceptance. Recently published work by Beth Brant, Nona Caspers, Joanna Kadin, Toni McNaron; published new writers within the last year. Length: up to 3,000 words maximum. Publishes short shorts. Occasionally critiques rejected mss.

How to Contact: Send complete ms with cover letter. "A brief biographical statement is never amiss. Writers should be sure to tell us if a piece was commissioned by one of the editors." Reports in 3-4 months. SASE for ms. Simultaneous submissions OK. Sample copy for $2.50, 11 × 14 SAE and 2 first class stamps.

Payment: Pays 5 contributor's copies.

Terms: Acquires one-time rights.

Advice: "Fiction is a craft. Just because something happened, it isn't a story; it becomes a story when you transform it through your art, your craft."

HYPERBOLE STUDIOS, The Art of Digital Storytelling, (I, II), 1412 W. Alabama, Houston TX 77006. (713)529-9696. Editor: Greg Roach. Fiction Editor: Paul Wayne Hiaumet. Computer disk magazine: illustrations and photographs. "Published on computer disks—no general theme—fiction, poetry, graphics." Bimonthly. Estab. 1990. Circ. 350.

Needs: Adventure, condensed/excerpted novel, contemporary, erotica, experimental, fantasy, historical (general), horror, humor/satire, literary, mainstream, mystery/suspense, prose poem, science fiction, serialized novel, translations. Plans special fiction issue. Receives 4 unsolicited mss/month. Buys 1-3 mss/issue; 10-20 mss/year. Publishes ms 2-4 months after acceptance. Recently published work by Michael Banks, Christopher Woods, Hanz Doppler. Length: Open. Publishes short shorts. Also publishes poetry. Sometimes critiques rejected mss and recommends other markets.

How to Contact: Send complete ms with cover letter. Include Social Security number. Reports in 2 weeks on queries; 1 month on mss. SASE. Reprint submissions OK. Sample copy for $3. Fiction guidelines for #10 SAE and 1 first class stamp.

Payment: Pays $5 flat or $1/page and contributor's copies.

Terms: Pays on publication for first rights.

Advice: "Hypermedia opens up new doors for fiction writers—it's a whole new genre. *Hyperbole* is a disk based publication—no printed paper is involved. While *Hyperbole* runs on computers (Apple Macintosh & IIGS) it is not about computers. We are dedicated to exploring hypermedia (the integration of text, graphics, music, animation and sound on a computer) as a legitimate mode of communication and a viable opportunity for artists and writers."

‡HYPHEN MAGAZINE, Chicago's Magazine of the Arts, (I), Shoestring Publications, Suite 6, 3458 W. Devon, Lincolnwood IL 60659. (312)478-3609. Editor: Eduardo Cruz Eusebio. Fiction Editors: Margaret Lewis, Dave Mead. Magazine: 8½ × 11; 72 pages; white bond paper; glossy cover; illustrations and photos. Purpose is "to bring the arts together, and to bring the arts to the people in a format that is inviting, intriguing and attractive. We publish interviews, fiction and nonfiction about the arts, artists, and anything that might interest artists and art supporters." Quarterly. Estab. 1991. Circ. 1,000.

Needs: Erotica, ethnic/multicultural, experimental, feminist, gay, historical (general), humor/satire, lesbian, literary, mainstream/contemporary, psychic/supernatural/occult, regional, science fiction, serialized novel, translations. No romance. Publishes special fiction issue or anthology. Receives 15 unsolicited mss/month. Acquires 4 mss/issue; 16 mss/year. Publishes ms 2-4 months after acceptance. Recently published work by Phillip Brooks, Jennifer Sheridan, Zoe Keithley. Length: 2,500 words average; 5,000 words maximum. Publishes short shorts. Length: 400 words. Also publishes literary essays and poetry. Often critiques or comments on rejected mss.

How to Contact: Send complete ms with cover letter. Should include a one paragraph bio with submission. Reports in 1 month on queries; 5 months on mss. Send SASE (IRC) for reply, return of ms or send disposable copy of ms. Simultaneous, reprint submissions OK. Sample copy for $4. Fiction guidelines for #10 SAE and 1 first class stamp. Reviews novels and short story collections.

Payment: Pays 2 contributor's copies, subscription. Additional copies for $3.

Terms: Pays on publication for first North American serial rights or one-time rights.

Advice: Looks for "committed and vigorous writing. Never send a first draft, but never forget your first impulse. If the story doesn't move you, it will not move anyone else."

‡THE ICONOCLAST, (II), Wagner Labs & Enterprises, 1675 Amazon Rd., Mohegan Lake NY 10547. Editor: Phil Wagner. Newsletter: 8½×11; 8 pages; 20 lb. white paper; 20 lb. cover stock; illustrations; photographs. *"The Iconoclast* is a self-supporting, independent, unaffiliated general interest magazine with an appreciation of the profound, absurd and joyful in life. Material is limited only by *its* quality and *our* space. We want readers who are open-minded, unafraid to think, and actively engaged with the world." Published 8/year. Estab. 1992. Circ. 150.
Needs: Adventure, ethnic/multicultural, humor/satire, literary, mainstream/contemporary, science fiction, sports. "Nothing militant, solipsistic, or silly." Receives 10 unsolicited mss/month. Accepts 1-2 mss/issue; 10-15 mss/year. Publishes ms 1 week-6 months after acceptance. Length: 1,500 words preferred; 100 words minimum; 2,000 words maximum. Publishes short shorts. Also publishes literary essays, literary criticism and poetry. Often critiques or comments on rejected mss.
How to Contact: Send complete ms. Reports in 1 month. Send SASE for reply, return of mss or send a disposable copy of the ms. Simultaneous and reprint submissions OK. Sample copy for $1.25. Reviews novels and short story collections.
Payment: Pays 1 contributor's copy; additional copies 75¢ (40% discount).
Terms: Acquires one-time rights.
Advice: "We like fiction that has something to say (and not about its author). We hope for work that is observant, intense and multi-leveled. Follow Pound's advice – 'make it new.' Write what you want in whatever style you want – then pray there's someone who can appreciate your sensibility."

IMMANENT FACE MAGAZINE, (I), P.O. Box 492, New Town Branch, Boston MA 02258. Editor: Carl Quesnel. Magazine: 8½×11; 20-25 pages; 25 lb. paper; 60 lb. cover; illustrations and photographs. "Theme: The expression of personal and global concerns of individuals. Types: From writing for the common people, to the esoteric, for anyone age 12-100 who really cares about our reality." Quarterly. Estab. 1987. Circ. 250.
Needs: Condensed/excerpted novel, contemporary, experimental, fantasy, literary, prose poem, science fiction (hard science, soft/sociological), serialized novel, translations. "We do *not* want to see material that is not final-draft quality, nor do we want to see material that is impossible to comprehend unless it has a stated, worthy purpose." Receives 10 unsolicited mss/month. Accepts 2 mss/issue; 10 mss/year. Publishes ms 2-5 months after acceptance. Recently published work by D. Castleman, Lyn Lifshin. Length: 1,750 words preferred; 3,000 words maximum. Publishes short shorts. Sometimes comments on rejected mss and recommends other markets.
How to Contact: Send complete ms with cover letter. Include "name, address, greeting, how the writer heard of our magazine, biographical tidbit maybe, *not* a list of previous publications." Reports in 1 month on queries; 2 months on mss. SASE. Simultaneous and reprint submissions OK. Accepts electronic submissions via disk. Sample copy for $1.50. Fiction guidelines for #10 SAE and 1 first class stamp.
Payment: Pays contributor's copies.
Terms: Not copyrighted.
Advice: "Manuscripts that stand out make me feel strongly – either positive or negative – or else they capture an atmosphere really well. Description is very important."

INDIAN YOUTH OF AMERICA NEWSLETTER, (II, IV), Indian Youth of America, Inc., P.O. Box 2786, Sioux City IA 51106. (712)252-3230. Contact: Paige Gordon. Newsletter: 8½×11; 12 or more pages; 100 lb. lustre paper; illustrations and photographs. "We are looking for Native American authors who write on a variety of themes for a broad audience, from children (former campers and others) through adults; nationwide, international." Quarterly. Estab. 1987.
Needs: Adventure, condensed/excerpted novel, contemporary, historical, literary, western, Native American. "Unsolicited manuscripts are welcome, and should be about 5-6 pages typed, double-spaced. Author should include biographical information and a photo (returnable) of himself/herself. Illustrations for the story can also be used, provided space is available. The author should also include tribal affiliation. All authors should be of Native American descent." Does not want to see "extremely abstract themes; extreme violence; sexual situations." Unsolicited mss received each month "varies greatly." Acquires one ms/issue; 4 mss/year. Publishes ms usually within a year after acceptance. Agented fiction 50%. Published work by Joseph Bruchac, Mary Tall Mountain, Louis Littlecoon Oliver, Virginia Driving Hawk Sneve. Length: 800 words average; 650-700 words minimum; 1,200 words maximum. Recommends other markets.

How to Contact: Send complete manuscript with cover letter that includes information about the author, tribal affiliation, other published works and awards, if applicable. Reports in 2-4 weeks on queries; 4-6 weeks on mss. Simultaneous and reprint submissions OK. Sample copy and fiction guidelines free.
Payment: Pays free subscription to magazine and contributor's copies.

INDIANA REVIEW, (II), 316 N. Jordan Ave., Indiana University, Bloomington IN 47405. (812)855-3439. Editor: Dorian Gossey. Associate Editor: Gretchen Knapp. Editors change every 2 years. Send future submissions to "Fiction Editor." Magazine: 6×9; 224 pages; 60 lb. paper; Glatfelter cover stock. "Magazine of contemporary fiction and poetry in which there is a zest for language, some relationship between form and content, and awareness of the world. For fiction writers/readers, followers of lively contemporary poetry." Biannually. Estab. 1976. Circ. 650.
• A close-up interview with Editor Dorian Gossey appears in the 1992 *Writer's Market* (at the time she was associate editor).
Needs: Literary, contemporary, experimental, mainstream. "We are interested in innovation, logic, unity, a social context, a sense of humanity. All genres that meet some of these criteria are welcome. We would also consider novellas, novel excerpts and 'suites' of 3 related stories." Buys 3-4 mss/issue. Recently published work by Ursula LeGuin, David Michael Kaplan, Ann Packer; published new writers within the last year. Length: 1-35 magazine pages. Also publishes literary essays, poetry.
How to Contact: Send complete ms with cover letter. "Don't describe or summarize the story." SASE. No simultaneous submissions. Reports in 3 months. Publishes ms an average of 2-10 months after acceptance. Sample copy $7.
Payment: Pays $5/page.
Terms: Buys North American serial rights.
Advice: "Refrain from the chatty cover letter. Send one story at a time (unless they're really short), and no simultaneous submissions."

‡INFINITY LIMITED, A Journal for the Somewhat Eccentric, (II), The Infinity Group, P.O. Box 2713, Castro Valley CA 94546-0546. (510)581-8172. Editor: Genie Lester. Magazine: 8½×11; 40 pages; bond paper; parchment cover; illustrations and photos. "Stories with plots for professional people, readers, writers. No vulgar language, senseless violence, or graphic sex please." Quarterly. Estab. 1988. Circ. 1,000.
Needs: Adventure, contemporary, ethnic, experimental, fantasy, historical (general), humor/satire, literary, mystery/suspense, prose poem, psychic/supernatural/occult, regional, romance (contemporary, historical), science fiction, translations. "No pretentious prose, erotica, horror (unless *very* well done); stories without a plot or point, war recollections." Plans to publish annual special fiction issue or anthology. Receives 10-12 unsolicited mss/month. Acquires 5-7 mss/issue; 20-28 mss/year. Does not read mss June-August, December 15-January 15. Publishes ms 2 months-1 year after acceptance. Recently published work by Charles Rampp, Thomas Chase, Ken Johnson. Length: 10,000 words maximum. Publishes short shorts. Sometimes critiques rejected mss and recommends other markets.
How to Contact: Send complete ms with cover letter. Include brief bio. Reports in 1-6 months on mss. SASE. Simultaneous and reprint submissions OK. Accepts electronic submissions. Sample copy for $3.95 and 9×12 SAE. Fiction guidelines for #10 SAE and 1 first class stamp.
Payment: Pays in contributor's copies.
Terms: Acquires one-time and reprint rights. Sends galleys to author.
Advice: "Our editorial board is a group of volunteers of widely-varying ages, political and religious persuasions, ethnic groups, races and professions. If they agree on a manuscript, we are fairly sure that our readers will find it acceptable. If one of us gets excited about a work, the rest usually agree to its publication. Make sure your manuscript is readable, accompanied by an SASE, identified with your name on every page, and *not* stapled. Please have patience with us. We try to respond promptly, but we are volunteers spending our own money and time."

INNISFREE, (I, II), Box 277, Manhattan Beach CA 90266. (310)545-2607. FAX (310)546-5862. Editor: Rex Winn. Magazine: 8½×11; 50+ pages; 90 lb. cover stock; illustrations and photos. Publishes "fiction, poetry, essays—open forum." Bimonthly. Estab. 1981. Circ. 350.
Needs: Adventure, contemporary, ethnic, fantasy, literary, mainstream, mystery/suspense (private eye, police procedural), regional and science fiction. "No political or religious sensationalism." Accepts 12-15 mss/issue; approx. 80 mss/year. Publishes ms within 12 months of acceptance. Published work by Fran C. Goodman, Arlene J. Pollack and A. David Sydney. Length: 3,000 words average. Publishes short shorts. Sometimes critiques rejected mss.

How to Contact: Send complete mss with cover letter. Reports in 6-8 weeks. SASE. May accept simultaneous submissions, but "reluctantly." Accepts electronic submissions via IBM disk. Sample copy for $4. Free fiction guidelines.
Payment: No payment. Prizes offered.
Terms: Acquires one-time rights.
Advice: "Fiction market is on the decline. This is an attempt to publish new writers who take pride in their work and have some talent."

"Innisfree attempts to create a tranquil environment in which artists and writers may express themselves. This drawing of a dog and rabbit represents that, but it also represents a curiosity about life," says Editor Rex Winn. "In their craft, writers share their vision of how they fight difficulties. Hopefully, readers will experience a power and a beauty from these stories that will enrich their lives and help them be more happy and free. Innisfree strives for the rediscovery of the age-old art of storytelling. Fiction should be emotionally involving, humorous or thought-provoking." This drawing was originally submitted by Jim Martin along with his short story, "Horse and Rabbit." Winn decided to use it on the magazine's 10th anniversary cover instead.

INTERIM, (II), Dept. of English, University of Nevada, Las Vegas NV 89154. (702)739-3172. Editor and Founder: A. Wilber Stevens. Magazine: 6×9; 48-64 pages; heavy paper; glossy cover; cover illustrations. Publishes "poetry and short fiction for a serious, sophisticated, educated audience." Semiannually. Estab. 1944; revived 1986. Circ. 600-800.
Needs: Contemporary and experimental, literary. Accepts 2-3 mss/issue. Publishes ms within 6 months-1 year of acceptance. Recently published work by Gladys Swan and James B. Hall. Length: 4,000 words preferred; 7,500 words maximum. Also publishes poetry.
How to Contact: Send complete ms with cover letter. Reports on mss in 2 months. SASE. Sample copy $5.
Payment: Pays in contributor's copies and two-year subscription to magazine.

THE IOWA REVIEW, (II), University of Iowa, 308 EPB, Iowa City IA 52242. (319)335-0462. Editor: David Hamilton. Magazine: 6×9; 200 pages; first grade offset paper; Carolina C1S-10 pt. cover stock. "Stories, essays, poems for a general readership interested in contemporary literature." Triannually. Estab. 1970. Circ. 1,200.
• Work published in *Iowa Review* regularly has been selected for inclusion in the *Pushcart Prize* and *Best American Short Stories* anthologies.
Needs: Receives 150-200 unsolicited fiction mss/month. Agented fiction less than 10%. Buys 4-5 mss/issue, 12-16 mss/year. Does not read mss May-August. Published work by Mary Swander, Charles Baxter and Donald Hall; published new writers within the last year. Also publishes literary essays, literary criticism, poetry.
How to Contact: Send complete ms with SASE. "Don't bother with queries." Simultaneous submissions OK. Reports in 4 months on mss. Publishes ms an average of 4-12 months after acceptance. Sample copy $5. Reviews novels and short story collections (3-6 books/year).
Payment: Pays $10/page; 2 contributor's copies; charge for extras: 30% off cover price.
Terms: Pays on publication for first North American serial rights. Hardly ever buys reprints.
Advice: In cover letters, "be moderate. Be decent. Be brief."

IOWA WOMAN, P.O. Box 680, Iowa City IA 52244. Editor: Marianne Abel. Nonprofit magazine "dedicated to encouraging and publishing women writers and artists internationally." Quarterly. Estab. 1979. Circ. 2,500.

• *Iowa Woman* has received numerous awards and honors including most recently an Honorable Mention, Non-Academic Periodical, Chicago Women in Publishing (1992) and Finalist, Iowa Arts Council Outstanding Achievement Award (1992) and Iowa Community Cultural Grant Awards (1991 and 1992). The magazine has also had essays included in the *Best American Essays* and *Notable American Essays*. See the *Iowa Woman* Writing Contest listed also in this book.

Needs: Historical, literary, regional, women's. Upcoming theme: "Crafts," broad concept of crafts for 1993 Year of American Craft, especially the book arts. Receives 30 unsolicited mss/month. Buys 3 mss/issue; 12 mss/year. Length: 6,500 words maximum. Also publishes literary essays, literary criticism, and sponsors contest.

How to Contact: Send complete ms. Reports in 3 months. SASE. Sample copy for $6. Fiction or contest guidelines for SAE with 1 first class stamp. Reviews novels and short story collections. Send books to Coleen Maddy, Books Editor.

Payment: Pays 2 contributor's copies; $4 charge for extras, $5 per published page. During 1992-93, will pay $20 bonus to Iowa resident (current or former) and $100 bonus on contest prize if an Iowa writer wins.

Terms: Buys first serial rights.

Advice: "Our editorial collective often responds critically with rejections. Our guidelines are clear, but we still get stories without women or women's experience as the center. New writers have a better chance with regular submissions than with our annual writing contest which is quite competitive."

ipsissima verba/the very words, (I), Haypenny Press, 211 New St., West Paterson NJ 07424-3329. Editor: P.D. Jordan. Magazine: 5½×8½; b&w illustrations. "Short fiction, poetry, essays *written in the first person singular* for an adult/literary/general audience." Semiannually (soon to be triannually). Estab. 1989.

Needs: First person writing *only.* Adventure, contemporary, ethnic, experimental, fantasy, feminist, historical (general), humor/satire, literary, mainstream, mystery/suspense, prose poem, psychic/supernatural/occult, regional, romance (contemporary), science fiction, senior citizen/retirement, serialized novel, sports, translations, western. "Will consider any type or genre of story, as long as the 'first person' rule is met . . . . Prefer suspense over true horror. No pornography." Publishes annual special fiction issue. Receives 50-75 unsolicited mss/month. Accepts up to 10 mss/issue. Publishes ms within 6 months after acceptance. Recently published work by Jim Adams, Thomas Wilson, Tommy Lee Curtis. Length: varies. Publishes short shorts. Length: 1-4 pages. Sometimes critiques rejected mss and recommends other markets.

How to Contact: Send complete ms with cover letter. Reports in 2 weeks on queries; up to 2 months on mss. SASE. Simultaneous and reprint submissions OK. Sample copy for 4 first class stamps. Fiction guidelines for #10 SAE.

Payment: Pays contributor's copies.

Terms: Acquires one-time rights.

Advice: "Remember the 'first person' rule. The single factor is the *ease* with which the writer 'speaks.' The more natural the 'voice,' the more likely it will be accepted. Read Barry Yourgrau, Tom DeHaven, P.D. Jordan . . . get a sample copy of the magazine. Write from your own self. First-person writing isn't for everyone, but if you can write as if you are talking you are on the right track."

IRIS: A Journal About Women, (II, IV), Box 323 HSC, University of Virginia, Charlottesville VA 22908. (804)924-4500. Editor: Rebecca Hyman. Fiction Editor: Kristen Staby Rembold. Magazine: 8½×11; 72 pages; glossy paper; heavy cover; illustrations and photographs. "Material of particular interest to women. For a feminist audience, college educated and above." Semiannually. Estab. 1980. Circ. 2,500.

• *Iris* received the Best in Virginia Award for a black-and-white magazine in 1992.

Needs: Experimental, feminist, lesbian, literary, mainstream. "I don't think what we're looking for particularly falls into the 'mainstream' category—we're just looking for well-written stories of interest to women (particularly feminist women)." Receives 300 unsolicited mss/year. Accepts 5 mss/year. Publishes ms within 1 year after acceptance. Length: 4,000 words average. Sometimes critiques rejected mss.

How to Contact: Send complete ms with cover letter. Include "previous publications, vocation, other points that pertain. Make it brief!" Reports in 3 months on mss. SASE. Simultaneous submissions OK. Accepts electronic submissions via disk or modem. Sample copy for $5. Fiction guidelines for #10 SAE and 1 first class stamp.
Payment: Pays in contributor's copies and 1 year subscription.
Terms: Acquires one-time rights.
Advice: "I select mss which are lively imagistically as well as in the here-and-now; I select for writing which challenges the reader. My major complaint is with stories that don't elevate the language above the bland sameness we hear on the television and everyday. Read the work of the outstanding women writers, such as Alice Munroe and Louise Erdrich."

‡ITALIAN AMERICANA, (II, IV), VRI/CCE 199 Promenade St., Providence RI 02908-5090. (401)277-6180. Editor: Carol Bonomo Albright. Magazine: 7×9; 150 pages; varnished cover; photographs. "Italian experience in America; historical articles; fiction; memoirs all concerning Italian experience in the Americas." Semiannually. Estab. 1974. Circ. 1,000.
Needs: Italian American: literary. Publishes special fiction issue or anthology. Receives 10 mss/month. Buys 3 mss/issue; 6-7 mss/year. Publishes up to 1 year after acceptance. Agented fiction 5%. Recently published Salvatore LaPuma; Rita Ciresi, Maria Bruno. Length: 20 double spaced pages. Publishes short shorts. Also publishes literary essays, literary criticism, poetry. Often critiques rejected mss.
How to Contact: Send complete manuscript (in triplicate) with a cover letter. Should include 3-5 line bio, list of publications. Reports in 4-8 weeks on queries; 2-6 months on manuscripts. Send SASE (IRC) for reply, return of ms or send a disposable copy of ms. No simultaneous submissions. Sample copy $5. Fiction guidelines for SAE and 1 first class stamp. Reviews novels and short story collections. Send books to Professor John Paul Russo, English Dept., Univ. of Miami, Coral Gables, FL 33124.
Payment: Pays $50, plus 1 contributor copy and free subscription to magazine; additional copies $7.
Terms: Pays on publication for first North American serial rights.
Advice: "Please individualize characters, instead of presenting types (i.e., lovable uncle, aunt, etc.)."

JAPANOPHILE, (II, IV), Box 223, Okemos MI 48864. (517)349-1795. Editor-in-Chief: Earl Snodgrass. Magazine: 5¼×8½; 50 pages; illustrations; photos. Magazine of "articles, photos, poetry, humor, short stories about Japanese culture, not necessarily set in Japan, for an adult audience, most with college background; travelers." Quarterly. Estab. 1974. Circ. 600.
  • Note that because of the mandatory entry fee for the contest, published stories not winning the contest net $10 of the $20 payment. However, the winning story receives $100. See the *Japanophile* Short Story Contest listed in this book.
Needs: Adventure, historical (general), humor/satire, literary, mainstream, and mystery/suspense. Published special fiction issue last year; plans another. Receives 40-100 unsolicited fiction mss/month. Buys 6 ms/issue, 20-30 mss/year. Recently published work by Mimi Hinman, Bobbi Crudup, Gerald Y. Kinro; published new writers within the last year. Length: 2,000 words minimum; 9,000 words maximum; 4,000 words average. Also publishes literary essays, literary criticism, poetry. Sometimes recommends other markets.
How to Contact: Send complete ms with SASE and cover letter with brief author bio and information about story. Simultaneous and reprint submissions OK. Reports in 2 months on mss. Sample copy for $4; guidelines for #10 SAE and 1 first class stamp.
Payment: Pays $20 on publication, for short stories. All stories submitted to the magazine are entered in the annual contest. *A $10 entry fee must accompany each submission.* Prizes include $100 plus publication for the best short story. Deadline December 31.
Terms: Pays on publication for all rights, first North American serial rights or one-time rights (depends on situation).
Advice: "Short stories usually involve Japanese and 'foreign' (non-Japanese) characters in a way that contributes to understanding of Japanese culture and the Japanese people. However, a *good* story dealing with Japan or Japanese cultural aspects anywhere in the world will be considered, even if it does not involve this encounter or meeting of Japanese and foreign characters. Some stories may also be published in an anthology."

JEOPARDY, Literary Arts Magazine, (II), CH 132, Western Washington University, Bellingham WA 98225. (206)676-3118. Contact: Editors. Editors change every year. Magazine: 6×9; 108 pages; 70 lb. paper; Springhill 215 cover stock; illustrations and photographs. Material published: fiction, nonfiction, poetry, photographed artwork (slide form) for "all inclusive" audience. Annually. Estab. 1965. Circ. 3,000-4,000.

Needs: Adventure, contemporary, ethnic, experimental, fantasy, feminist, humor/satire, literary, mainstream, prose poem, regional, contemporary romance, science fiction and translations. No long stories. Accepts 7-10 mss/year. Length: 4 pages (average 800-1,000 words). Also publishes literary essays, literary criticism, poetry.
How to Contact: Submissions accepted between September and February. Mss sent during summer months may not be read immediately. Send complete ms. SASE. No simultaneous submissions. Previously published submissions OK. Reports in 4 months. Sample copy $4.
Payment: Pays 2 contributor's copies.
Advice: "We are a student-run university literary publication. We are happy to look at any fiction. Sometimes, if staff is large enough, at writer's request we will comment on the work."

JEWISH CURRENTS MAGAZINE, (IV), 22 E. 17th St., New York NY 10003. (212)924-5740. Editor-in-Chief: Morris U. Schappes. Magazine: 5½ × 8½; 48 pages. "We are a progressive monthly, broad in our interests, printing feature articles on political and cultural aspects of Jewish life in the US and elsewhere, reviews of books and film, poetry and fiction, Yiddish translations; regular columns on Israel, US Jewish community, current events, Jewish women today, secular Jewish life. Monthly themes include Holocaust and Resistance, Black-Jewish relations, Jewish Book Month, Jewish Music Month, etc. National audience, literate and politically left, well educated." Monthly. Estab. 1946. Circ. 3,000.
● This magazine may be slow to respond. They are backlogged through 1993.
Needs: Contemporary, ethnic, feminist, historical (general), humor/satire, literary, senior citizen/retirement, translations. "We are interested in *authentic* experience and readable prose; Jewish themes; humanistic orientation. No religious, political sectarian; no porn or hard sex, no escapist stuff. Go easy on experimentation, but we're interested." Receives 6-10 unsolicited fiction mss/month. Accepts 0-1 ms/issue; 8-10 mss/year. Recently published work by Morton Stavis, Julius Lester; published new writers within the last year. Length: 1,000 words minimum; 3,000 words maximum; 1,800 words average. Also publishes literary essays, literary criticism, poetry.
How to Contact: Send complete ms with cover letter. "Writers should include brief biographical information, especially their publishing histories." SASE. No simultaneous submissions. Reports in 2 months on mss. Publishes ms 2 months-2 years after acceptance. Sample copy for $2 with SASE and 3 first class stamps. Reviews novels and short story collections.
Payment: Pays complimentary one-year subscription; 6 contributor's copies.
Terms: "We readily give reprint permission at no charge." Sends galleys to author.
Advice: Noted for "stories about Jewish family life, especially intergenerational relations, and personal Jewish experience—e.g., immigrant or holocaust memories, assimilation dilemmas, etc. Matters of character and moral dilemma, maturing into pain and joy, dealing with Jewish conflicts OK. Space is increasingly a problem. Tell the truth, as sparely as possible."

THE JOURNAL, (II), Dept of English, Ohio State University, 164 W. 17th St., Columbus OH 43210. (614)292-4076. Editors: Kathy Fagan (poetry); Michelle Herman (fiction). Magazine: 6 × 9; 80 pages. "We are open to all forms of quality fiction." For an educated, general adult audience. Semiannually. Estab. 1973. Circ. 1,300.
Needs: "Interested in all literary forms." No romance or religious/devotional. Accepts 2 mss/issue. Receives approximately 100 unsolicited fiction mss each month. "Usually" publishes ms within 1 year of acceptance. Agented fiction 10%. Published work by Liza Wieland, M.V. Clayton; published new writers within the last year. Length: Open. Also accepts poetry. Critiques rejected mss when there is time.
How to Contact: Send complete ms with cover letter. Reports "as soon as possible," usually 3 months. SASE. Sample copy $5.50; fiction guidelines for SASE.
Payment: Pays $25 stipend when funds are available; contributor's copies; $5.50 charge for extras.
Terms: Acquires First North American serial rights. Sends galleys to author.
Advice: Mss are rejected because of "lack of understanding of the short story form, shallow plots, undeveloped characters. Cure: read as much well-written fiction as possible. Our readers prefer 'psychological' fiction rather than stories with intricate plots. Take care to present a clean, well-typed submission."

THE JOURNAL, (II), Poetry Forum, 5713 Larchmont Dr., Erie PA 16509. (814)866-2543. Fax: (814)866-2543 (Faxing hours: 8-10 a.m. and 5-8 p.m.) Editor: Gunvor Skogsholm. Newspaper: 7 × 8½; 18-20 pages; card cover; photographs. "Good writing—material on writing for late teens to full adulthood." Quarterly. Estab. 1989. Circ. 200.
● *The Journal* is edited by Gunvor Skogsholm, the editor of *Poetry Forum Short Stories.* Although

this magazine is not strictly a pay-for-publication, she really means it when she says "subscribers come first." See the listing for *Poetry Forum Short Stories*.

Needs: Mainstream. Plans annual special fiction issue. Receives 25-30 unsolicited mss/month. Accepts 1 ms/issue; 7-10 mss/year. Publishes mss 2 weeks-7 months after acceptance. Agented .1% . Length: 500 words preferred; 300 words average; 150 words minimum. Publishes short shorts. Length: 400 words.

How to Contact: Send complete ms. Reports in 2 weeks to 7 months on mss. SASE. Simultaneous submissions OK. Accepts electronic submission via disk. Sample copy for $3. Fiction guidelines for SASE.

Payment: No payment.

Terms: Acquires one-time rights. Not copyrighted.

Advice: "Subscribers come first!" Looks for "a good lead stating a theme, support of the theme throughout and an ending that rounds out the story or article. 1.) Let it be believable; 2.) Please don't preach; 3.) Avoid propaganda; 4.) Don't say: 'This is a story about a retarded person.' Instead prove it by your writing."

JOURNAL OF POLYMORPHOUS PERVERSITY, (II), Wry-Bred Press, Inc., 10 Waterside Plaza, Suite 20-B, New York NY 10010. (212)689-5473. Editor: Glenn Ellenbogen. Magazine: 6¾×10; 24 pages; 60 lb. paper; antique india cover stock; illustrations with some articles. "*JPP* is a humorous and satirical journal of psychology, psychiatry, and the closely allied mental health disciplines." For "psychologists, psychiatrists, social workers, psychiatric nurses, *and* the psychologically sophisticated layman." Semi-annually. Estab. 1984.

Needs: Humor/satire. "We only consider materials that are 1) funny, 2) relate to psychology *or* behavior." Receives 10 unsolicited mss/month. Acquires 8 mss/issue; 16 mss/year. Published work by Kathleen Donald, Ph.D. Most writers published last year were previously unpublished writers. Length: 1,500 words average; 4,000 words maximum. Comments on rejected ms.

How to Contact: Send complete ms *in triplicate*. Reports in 1-3 months on mss. SASE. Sample copy for $5. Fiction guidelines for #10 SAE and 1 first class stamp.

Payment: Pays 2 contributor's copies; charge for extras: $5.

Advice: "We will *not* look at poetry or short stories. We only want to see intelligent spoofs of scholarly psychology and psychiatry articles written in scholarly scientific languages. Take a look at *real* journals of psychology and try to lampoon their *style* as much as their content. There are few places to showcase satire of the social sciences, thus we provide one vehicle for injecting a dose of humor into this often too serious area. Occasionally, we will accept a piece of creative writing written in the first person, e.g. 'A Subjective Assessment of the Oral Doctoral Defense Process: I Don't Want to Talk About It, If You Want to Know the Truth' (the latter being a piece in which Holden Caulfield shares his experiences relating to obtaining his Ph.D. in Psychology). Other creative pieces have involved a psychodiagnostic evaluation of The Little Prince (as a psychiatric patient) and God being refused tenure (after having created the world) because of insufficient publications and teaching experience."

JOURNAL OF REGIONAL CRITICISM, (II), Arjuna Library Press, 1025 Garner St. D, Space 18, Colorado Springs CO 80905. Editor: Joseph A. Uphoff, Jr. Pamphlet: size variable; number of pages variable; Xerox paper; Bristol cover stock; b&w illustrations and photos. "Surrealist and dreamlike prose poetry and very short surrealist stories to illustrate accompanying mathematical, theoretical material in the fine arts for a wide ranging audience interested in philosophical sophistication and erudite language." Variable frequency. Estab. 1979.

Needs: Adventure, contemporary, ethnic, experimental, fantasy, historical (general), horror, humor/satire, literary, mainstream, prose poem, psychic/supernatural/occult, regional, religious/inspirational, contemporary romance, science fiction. Upcoming theme: "English as a Second Language (for those confused by irony)." Receives 0-1 unsolicited fiction ms/month. Accepts 1-5 mss/issue. Recently published work by Robert W. Howington, Walter Kuchinsky, Rich Murphy. Short short stories preferred. Also publishes literary criticism, poetry. Sometimes critiques rejected mss and recommends other markets.

How to Contact: Send complete ms with cover letter. Manuscript will *not* be returned. Cover letter should include goals, behind-the-scenes explanation, and biographical material or résumé, date of birth, degrees, awards, offices and publications. SASE for query. Simultaneous and reprint submissions OK. Sample copy, if and when available, for $1 postage. Reviews novels and short story collections.

Payment: Pays by contract after profit; contributor's copies.
Terms: Acquires "prototype presentation rights." Publication copyrighted—limited edition procedure copyrights.
Advice: "Piles of manuscripts contain undifferentiated nonentities. A story is like any work of art. It is a picture. These are ambitiously composed and buried by writers who are afraid to reread them, or they are courageously studied through readings separated by days, weeks or months. When the artist can stand the repeated sight of a polished image it is ready to be read aloud in public. It helps if the editor has some biographical knowledge of the author, a picture or a philosophical statement."

‡JUST A MOMENT, (I, II), Pine Grove Press, P.O. Box 40, Jamesville NY 13078. (315)423-9268. Editor: Gertrude S. Eiler. Magazine: 5½×8½; 75+ pages; 60 lb. offset paper; 65 lb. cover stock. "Our aim from the beginning has been to publish work of quality by authors with talent and ability whether previously published or not." Estab. 1990. Circ. 300.
 ● In the past few years *Just a Moment* has held a contest for college students, deadline each February. If interested, contact them to find out if there will be one planned for 1994.
Needs: Adventure, ethnic/multicultural, experimental, fantasy, historical, horror, humor/satire, literary, mainstream/contemporary, mystery/suspense, psychic/supernatural/occult, regional, romance, science fiction, senior citizen/retirement, sports, westerns (traditional, adult western, frontier). Receives 40 unsolicited mss/month. Acquires 9-10 mss/issue; 40 mss/year. Publishes ms up to 1 year after acceptance. Length: 3,500 words maximum. Publishes short shorts. Also publishes poetry. Often critiques or comments on rejected mss.
How to Contact: Send complete ms with cover letter. Should include estimated word count, bio, Social Security number (optional), list of publications (nice but optional). Reports in 2 weeks on queries; up to 6 months on mss. Send SASE for reply, return of ms, or disposable copy of the ms. No simultaneous submissions. Sample copy for $2.50. Fiction guidelines for any size SAE and 1 first class stamp.
Payment: Pays subscription to the magazine.
Terms: Acquires one-time rights.
Advice: Looks for "quality writing, unusual subject matter, fresh and imaginative slant. Don't over-write! Don't be afraid to cut! Would like to see more "Action! Adventure! Humor!

KALEIDOSCOPE: International Magazine of Literature, Fine Arts, and Disability, (II, IV), 326 Locust St., Akron OH 44302. (216)762-9755. Editor-in-Chief: Darshan Perusek, Ph.D. Senior Editor: Gail Willmott. Magazine: 8½×11; 56-64 pages; non-coated paper; coated cover stock; illustrations (all media); photos. "*Kaleidoscope* is a literary arts magazine with a disability focus; writers and artists both with and without disabilities are featured, with the understanding that those without a disability limit themselves to our focus in order to solidify a connection with the magazine's purpose of creatively expressing the way disability does, or does not, affect how society reacts to disability." Semiannually. Estab. 1979. Circ. 1,500.
 ● Editor Darshan Perusek was featured in a Close-up interview in the 1990 edition of *Novel & Short Story Writer's Market*. She received the Ohioanna Award for Editorial Excellence in 1988.
Needs: Personal experience, drama, fiction, essay, artwork. Upcoming themes: "Disability and Chronic Illness" (March 1993); "Disability and Body Image" (August 1993). Receives 20-25 unsolicited fiction mss/month. Buys 10 mss/year. Approximately 1% of fiction is agented. Recently published work by Kemp Pheley, Nancy Mairs, Oliver Sacks, Lisa Novick. Published new writers within the last year. Length: 5,000 words maximum. Also publishes poetry.
How to Contact: Query first or send complete ms and cover letter, which should include SASE, author's educational and writing background, if author has a disability, how the disability has influenced the writing. Simultaneous submissions OK. Reports in 1 month on queries; 6 months on mss. Sample copy for $3. Guidelines for #10 SAE and 1 first class stamp.
Payment: Pays cash ranging from $10-125; 2 contributor's copies; charge for extras: $4.50.
Terms: Pays on publication for first rights. Reprints are permitted with credit given to original publication.
Advice: "Read the magazine and get submission guidelines. Writers with disabilities may write on any topic; non-disabled writers must limit themselves to the theme of disability. *Kaleidoscope* seeks work that challenges stereotypical images of people with disabilities by presenting balanced, realistic portrayals of those who have disabilities."

KALLIOPE, A Journal of Women's Art, (II), Florida Community College at Jacksonville, 3939 Roosevelt Blvd., Jacksonville FL 32205. (904)381-3511. Editor: Mary Sue Koeppel. Magazine: 7¼ × 8¼; 76-88 pages; 70 lb. coated matte paper; Bristol cover; 16-18 halftones per issue. "A literary and visual arts journal for women, *Kalliope* celebrates women in the arts by publishing their work and by providing a forum for their ideas and opinions." Short stories, poems, plays, essays, reviews and visual art. Triannually. Estab. 1978. Circ. 1,250.
Needs: "Quality short fiction by women writers." Upcoming themes: "Women of the Future" (deadline April 1993). Accepts 2-4 mss/issue. Receives approximately 100 unsolicited fiction mss each month. Published work by Layle Silbert, Robin Merle, Claudia Brinson Smith, Colette; published new writers within the last year. Preferred length: 750-3,000 words, but occasionally publishes longer (and shorter) pieces. Also publishes poetry. Critiques rejected mss "when there is time and if requested."
How to Contact: Send complete ms with SASE and short contributor's note. No simultaneous submissions. Reports in 2-3 months on ms. Publishes ms an average of 1-6 months after acceptance. Sample copy: $7 for current issue; $4 for issues from '78-'88. Reviews novels and short story collections.
Payment: Pays 3 contributor's copies or year's subscription. $7 charge for extras, discount for 4 or more.
Terms: Acquires first rights. "We accept only unpublished work. Copyright returned to author upon request."
Advice: "Read our magazine. The work we consider for publication will be well written and the characters and dialogue will be convincing and have strength and movement. We like a fresh approach and are interested in new or unusual forms. Make us believe your characters; give readers an insight which they might not have had if they had not read you. We would like to publish more work by minority writers." Manuscripts are rejected because "1) nothing *happens!*, 2) it is thinly disguised autobiography (richly disguised autobiography is OK), and 3) ending is either too pat or else just trails off."

KANSAS QUARTERLY, (I, II), Kansas Quarterly Association, 122 Denison Hall, English Dept., Kansas State University, Manhattan KS 66506-0703. (913)532-6716. Editors: Harold Schneider (emeritus), Ben Nyberg, John Rees, G.W. Clift and Jonathan Holden. Magazine: 6 × 9; 104-356 pages; 70 lb. offset paper; Frankcote 8 pt. coated cover stock; illustrations occasionally; unsolicited photos rarely. "A literary and cultural arts magazine publishing fiction and poetry. Special material on selected, announced topics in literary criticism, art history, folklore and regional history. For well-read, general and academic audiences." Quarterly. Published double and single fiction issues last year; plans repeat. Estab. 1968. Circ. 1,300.
Needs: "We consider most categories as long as the fiction is of sufficient literary quality to merit inclusion, though we have no interest in children's literature. We resist translations and parts of novels, but do not absolutely refuse them." Accepts 30-50 mss/year. Limited reading done in summer. Agented fiction approximately 1%. Recently published work by Stephen Dixon, D.E. Steward and Jerry Bumpus; published new writers within the last year. Length: 350-12,000 words. Sometimes recommends other markets.
How to Contact: Send complete ms with SASE. Reports in 3 months + on mss. Publishes ms an average of 18-24 months after acceptance. Sample copy $6.
Payment: Pays 2 contributor's copies and annual awards to the best of the stories published.
Terms: Acquires all rights. Sends galleys to author. "We reassign rights on request at time of republication." Sponsors awards: *KQ*/KAC (national); Seaton awards (for Kansas natives or residents). Each offers 6-10 awards from $25-$250.
Advice: "Always check a sample copy of the magazine to which you send your stories — note its editors' likes and interests."

KARAMU, (II), English Dept., Eastern Illinois University, Charleston IL 61920. (217)581-5614. Editor: Peggy L. Brayfield. Magazine: 5 × 8; 60 pages; cover illustrations. "We like fiction that builds around real experiences, real images and real characters, that shows an awareness of current fiction and the types of experiments that are going on in it, and that avoids abstraction, sentimentality, over-philosophizing and fuzzy pontifications. For a literate, college-educated audience." Annually. Estab. 1967. Circ. 500.
    • *Karamu* received two Illinois Arts Council Awards in 1990.
Needs: Literary, contemporary. Receives approximately 20-30 unsolicited fiction mss/month. Accepts 5-8 mss/issue. Recently published work by Emilio DeGrazia, Jefferson Humphries, Jere Hoar, Ellen Winter. Published new writers within the last year. Length: 2,000-7,000 words. Also publishes literary essays, poetry. Critiques rejected mss when time permits.

How to Contact: Send complete ms with SASE. "Initial screening within 1 week, surviving mss may be held until May or June." Publishes ms an average of 1 year after acceptance. Sample copy $3; 2 issues for $5.

Payment: Pays 1 contributor's copy; half price charge for extras.

Advice: "Send for a sample copy, read it, and send a complete ms if your stories seem to match our taste. Please be patient—we sometimes get behind in our reading, especially between May and September. Mss submitted between January and June have the shortest waiting time, if they survive initial screening. We feel that much of the best writing today is being done in short fiction."

‡**KELSEY REVIEW, (II, IV),** Mercer County College, P.O. Box B, Trenton NJ 08690. (609)586-4800. Editor: Robin Shore. Magazine: 8 × 14; 64 pages; glossy paper; soft cover. "Must live or work in Mercer County, NJ." Annually. Estab. 1988. Circ. 1,000.

Needs: Open. Regional (Mercer County only). Receives 70 unsolicited mss/year. Acquires 18 mss/issue. Reads mss only in May. Publishes ms 2-3 months after acceptance. Length: 2,000 words maximum. Publishes short shorts. Also publishes literary essays, literary criticism and poetry. Always critiques or comments on rejected mss.

How to Contact: Send complete ms with cover letter. SASE or IRC for return of ms. No simultaneous submissions. Sample copy free. Reviews novels and short story collections.

Payment: Pays 5 contributor's copies.

Terms: Acquires rights, revert to author on publication.

Advice: Looks for "quality: intellect and grace and guts."

"We publish between 20 and 24 short stories and/or novel excerpts each year, and at least 25 percent of the fiction we publish comes from writers whose work we have solicited," says Marilyn Hacker, editor of The Kenyon Review, *an international journal of literature, culture and the arts. "We strongly discourage writers from submitting work simply because they've gotten our address from a market book. Buy or at least borrow and read an issue first!" she says. This cover illustration, titled "The Blue Fox Rolls Away the Stone," is mixed media on paper by Gina Gilmour. "We've used her work for all four 1992 issues and we may showcase other artists' work similarly in subsequent volumes," Hacker says. The cover design is by Nanette Black.*

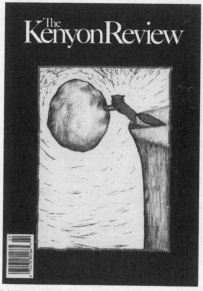

KENNESAW REVIEW, (II), Kennesaw State College, English Dept., P.O. Box 444, Marietta GA 30061. (404)423-6297. Editor: Dr. Robert W. Hill. Fiction Editor: Dr. Paula Yow. Magazine. "Just good fiction, all themes, for a general audience." Semiannually. Estab. 1987.

Needs: Condensed/excerpted novel, contemporary, ethnic, experimental, fantasy, feminist, gay, horror, humor/satire, literary, mainstream, psychic/supernatural/occult, regional. No romance. Receives 25-60 mss/month. Accepts 2-4 mss/issue. Publishes ms 6-12 months after acceptance. Recently published work by Julie Brown, Stephen Dixon, Robert Morgan, Carolyn Thorman. Length: 9-30 pages. Publishes short shorts. Length: 500 words. Often comments on or critiques rejected mss.

How to Contact: Send complete ms with cover letter. Include previous publications. Reports in 3 weeks on queries; 2 months on mss. SASE. Simultaneous submissions OK. Sample copy and fiction guidelines free.

Payment: Pays in contributor's copies.

Terms: Acquires first publication rights only. Acknowledgment required for subsequent publication.

Advice: "Use the language well and tell an interesting story. Send it on. Be open to suggestions."

‡KENTUCKY WRITING, (II), Somerset Community College, 808 Monticello St., Somerset KY 42501. (606)679-8501. Editors: Betty Peterson, Wanda Fries. Magazine: 5½×9½; 80 pages; illustrations; photographs. "We publish poetry, short fiction, literary essays, cartoons, drawings, black-and-white photos. We also publish one anthology of Kentucky student work, K-12, once a year." Annually. Estab. 1985. Circ. 1,500.
Needs: Mainstream/contemporary. Publishes annual special fiction issue or anthology. Receives 25 unsolicited mss/month. Acquires 8 mss/issue; 16 mss/year. Does not read mss in summer. Publishes ms 6 months-1 year after acceptance. Recently published work by Gurney Norman, Meredith Sue Willis. Length: 7,000 words maximum. Publishes short shorts. Also publishes literary essays and poetry. Sometimes critiques or comments on rejected mss.
How to Contact: Send complete ms with cover letter. Should include bio. Reports in 3-12 months on mss. SASE for return of ms. No simultaneous submissions. Sample copy for $5. Fiction guidelines for #10 SAE and 1 first class stamp.
Payment: Pays 1 contributor's copy.
Terms: Acquires first North American serial rights.
Advice: "We look for strong characterization, vivid detail, a strong sense of place, conflict and resolution." Would like to see more "authentic voice; a genuine exploration of place, rather than reliance on clichés and stereotypes." Avoid sending "sentimental treatment of Appalachian themes."

THE KENYON REVIEW, (II), Kenyon College, Gambier OH 43022. (614)427-3339. Editor: Marilyn Hacker. "Fiction, poetry, essays, book reviews." Quarterly. Estab. 1939. Circ. 4,500.
• Work published in the *Kenyon Review* has been selected for inclusion in the *Pushcart Prize* anthology for the past three years and the prestigious Iowa Short Fiction Award went to a collection of stories by a writer whose title story from the book was first published in *Kenyon Review*. The editor is well-known poet Marilyn Hacker.
Needs: Condensed/excerpted novel, contemporary, ethnic, experimental, feminist, gay, historical, humor/satire, lesbian, literary, mainstream, translations. Upcoming theme: "Contemporary Theater" (Spring 1993, deadline Oct. 1, 1992). Receives 300 unsolicited fiction mss/month. Buys up to 3 mss/issue; up to 12 mss/year. Does not read mss April-August. Publishes ms 12-18 months after acceptance. 50% of fiction is agented. Length: 3-15 (typeset) pages preferred. Rarely publishes short shorts. Sometimes comments on rejected ms.
How to Contact: Send complete ms with cover letter. Reports on mss in 2-3 months. SASE. No simultaneous submissions. Sample copy for $7.
Payment: Pays $10/page for fiction.
Terms: Pays on publication for one-time rights and option on anthology rights. Sends copy-edited version to author for approval.
Advice: "Read several issues of our publication. We remain invested in encouraging/reading/publishing work by (in particular) writers of color, writers expanding the boundaries of their genre, unpredictable voices and points of view."

‡KESTREL, A Journal of Literature and Art in the New World, (II), Division of Language and Literature, Fairmont State College, 1201 Locust Ave., Fairmont WV 26554. (304)367-4717. Editors: Martin Lammon, Valerie N. Colander, John King. Magazine: 6×9; illustrations and photographs. "An eclectic journal publishing the best fiction, poetry, creative nonfiction and artwork for a literate audience. We strive to present contributors' work in depth." Semiannually. Estab. 1993. Circ. 500.
Needs: Ethnic/multicultural, experimental, feminist, literary, mainstream/contemporary, regional, translations. "No pornography, children's literature, romance fiction, pulp science fiction—formula fiction in general." Receives 30 unsolicited mss/month. Accepts 3-5 mss/issue; 6-10 mss/year. Publishes ms 6-12 months after acceptance. Length: 5,000 words maximum. Publishes short shorts. Also publishes literary essays and poetry. Sometimes critiques or comments on rejected mss.

Rocky Point visitors lose their way, find rocky road of Mexican justice

By Jerry Kammer
The Arizona Republic

Two wrong turns in the northern Mexico desert took separate groups of young Arizona men down a desolate desert road and into nightmarish encounters with Mexican police who accused them of attacking a bus and robbing its driver.

It is a story of life in borderland Mexico, where proximity to home makes some Americans careless. Add impetuosity, cross-cultural suspicions and a language barrier to the mix, and it can become combustible.

The trouble began Saturday evening, when the first group was heading home after a quick trip to Puerto Penasco, or Rocky Point, the popular Mexican resort town about 65 miles south of the Arizona border at Lukeville.

They are Josh Poles, 18; Brent Taubman, 18; Kevin Scott, 20; and Eddie Hernandez, 22.

They should have turned north at the junction just below Lukeville and crossed the border into the United States. But they headed west, into the chilly Sonoran Desert.

— See ROCKY POINT, page A18

"Do you see any mention of a knit cap on that page?" Bailey asked.

"No," Fuhrman said.

Bailey, in his second day of cross-examination, led Fuhrman through his account of his discovery and his description of the glove's condition.

"It appeared it had somewhat of a gleam or glisten to it," Fuhrman said.

Bailey dropped the subject, then returned to it later, asking Fuhrman whether he knows how long it takes for blood to dry at 60 degrees Fahrenheit, the overnight temperature June 13. The witness said he didn't know.

The attorney then observed that the detective has connected the glove to a noise that Simpson's house guest Brian "Kato" Kaelin said he heard the night before. This exchange followed:

How to Contact: Send complete ms with cover letter. Should include estimated word count, brief bio and list of publications with submission. Reports in 3 weeks on queries; 3 months on mss. SASE (or IRC) for return of ms or disposable copy of ms. No simultaneous submissions. Sample copy $5. Fiction guidelines for #10 SAE and 1 first class stamp or IRC.
Payment: Pays 2 contributor's copies.
Terms: Rights revert to contributor on publication.

KIOSK, (II), English Department, S.U.N.Y. at Buffalo, 302 Clemens Hall, Buffalo NY 14260. (716)636-2570. Editor: N. Gillespie. Magazine: 5½ × 8½; 100 pages; card stock cover. "We seek innovative, non-formula fiction and poetry." Plans special fiction issue. Annually (may soon be Biannually). Estab. 1986. Circ. 750.
Needs: Excerpted novel, short story, prose poem and translations. "No genre or formula fiction; we seek fiction that defies categorization — lush, quirky, flippant, challenging, etc. Stretch the boundaries." Receives 35 mss/month. Accepts 10-20 mss/issue. Publishes ms within 6 months of acceptance. Published work by Ray Federman, Carol Berge, James Sallis. Length: 3,000 words preferred; 7,500 words maximum. Publishes short shorts "the shorter the better." Also publishes poetry. Sometimes critiques rejected mss; rarely recommends other markets.
How to Contact: Send complete mss with cover letter. Does not read from May to September. Reports in 2-3 months on mss. "Most sooner; if we keep it longer, we're considering it seriously." SASE. Simultaneous and reprint submissions OK. Sample copy for 9×6 or larger SAE and 2 first class stamps.
Payment: Pays in contributor's copies.
Terms: Acquires one-time rights.
Advice: "First and foremost *Kiosk* is interested in sharp writing. There's no need to be dogmatic in terms of pushing a particular style or form, and we aren't. At the same time, we get tired of reading the same old story, the same old poem. Make it new, but also make it worth the reader's effort. Style without substance is a bugaboo. No gratuitous obscurity, but don't be afraid to take real chances. Though we consider all types, we definitely lean towards the experimental. Literary magazine writing is exciting when editors take chances and offer a place for writers who find other avenues closed."

‡KOLA, A Black Literary Magazine, (IV), Box 1602, Place Bonaventure, Montreal Quebec H5A 1H6 Canada. Editor: Dr. Horace I. Goddard. Magazine: 6×9; 40 pages; black and white illustrations. "Manuscripts that focus on the black experience in Africa and the African diaspora for a general audience." Estab. 1987. Circ. 300.
Needs: Contemporary, ethnic, feminist, literary, black. Accepts 3 mss/issue. Publishes ms 4 months after acceptance. Published work by Dr. Nigel Thomas, Randolph Homer and Yvonne Anderson. Length: 3,000-5,000 words; 2,000 words minimum; 6,000 words maximum. Sometimes critiques rejected mss.
How to Contact: Send complete manuscript with cover letter. Include bio-vita, previous publications. Reports in 3 months on mss. SASE for ms, not needed for query. No simultaneous submissions. Sample copy for $4 and 6×9 SAE.
Payment: Pays 2 contributor's copies.
Terms: Acquires first rights.
Advice: "The fiction must relate to the black experience. It must be of a high standard in structure: theme, plot, characterization, etc. Make sure you can follow grammar rules, use a dictionary, accept criticism, and keep on writing even though the rejection slips get you down."

‡KUMQUAT MERINGUE, "Dedicated to the Memory of Richard Brautigan", (I, II, IV), P.O. Box 5144, Rockford IL 61125. (815)968-0713. Editor: Christian Nelson. Magazine: Digest-sized; 32 pages; some illustrations and photographs. "Mostly poetry but always needing short, quirky, maybe sexy prose, preferably under 400 words. Unusual facets of love and sex. Like writing that puts us in the mood of Richard Brautigan." Published irregularly, approx. every 6-7 months. Estab. 1991. Circ. 500.
● Richard Brautigan's works include *Trout Fishing in America, The Hawkline Monster* and *In Watermelon Sugar.*
Needs: Adventure, erotica, ethnic/multicultural, experimental, feminist, gay, humor/satire, lesbian, literary, mainstream/contemporary, regional. No inspirational or regular science fiction. Receives 20 unsolicited mss/month. Acquires 2-4 mss/issue; 4-10 mss/year. Publishes ms 6-9 months after acceptance. Recently published work by Robert W. Howington, Paul R. Haenel, Howard Fine, Terry J. Fox. Length: 600 words maximum. Publishes short shorts. Also publishes literary essays and poetry. Often critiques or comments on rejected mss.

How to Contact: Send complete ms with cover letter. Reports in 1-2 months on mss. SASE for ms or send disposable copy of ms. Simultaneous submissions or reprints OK. Sample copy for $4. Fiction guidelines for #10 SAE.

Payment: Pays 1 contributor's copy.

Terms: Acquires first rights.

Advice: *"Kumquat Meringue* publishes literary works of uncommon and unusual virtue. We're very open to beginning or unpublished writers, but our editorial policy is an anomalous one. We never presume to judge whether a submitted piece is 'good' or 'bad.' The only judgment is whether or not we like it, and how it fits in with the feel of the magazine. And admittedly, we're hard to please. We do like concentration on the smaller details of everyday life, especially about love . . . and sex. We like to read about love gone wrong and love gone right. But we want the quirky side. So please, no hearts and flowers and none of that old worn out stuff about how much you love that certain someone. And no June moons or sleeping like spoons. We also like reading things 'to' or 'for' Richard Brautigan."

LACTUCA, (II), Box 621, Suffern NY 10901. Editor: Mike Selender. Magazine: Folded 8½×14; 72 pages; 24 lb. bond; soft cover; saddle-stapled; illustrations. Publishes "poetry, short fiction and b&w art, for a general literary audience." Published 2-3 times/year. Estab. 1986. Circ. 700.

Needs: Adventure, condensed/excerpted novel, confession, contemporary, erotica, literary, mainstream, prose poem and regional. No "self-indulgent writing or fiction about writing fiction." Receives 30 or more mss/month. Accepts 3-4 mss/issue; 10-12 mss/year. Publishes ms within 3-12 months of acceptance. Published work by Douglas Mendini, Tom Gidwitz, Ruthann Robson; published new writers within the last year. Length: around 12-14 typewritten double-spaced pages. Publishes short shorts. Often critiques rejected mss and recommends other markets.

How to Contact: Query first or send complete ms with cover letter. Cover letter should include "just a few brief notes about yourself. Please no long 'literary' résumés or bios. The work will speak for itself." Reports usually within 6 weeks. No longer than 3 months. SASE. No simultaneous or previously published work. Accepts electronic submissions via "MS DOS formatted disk. We can convert most word-processing formats." Sample copy for $4. Fiction guidelines for #10 SAE and 1 first class stamp.

Payment: Pays 2-5 contributor's copies, depending on the length of the work published.

Terms: Acquires first North American serial rights. Sends galleys to author if requested. Copyrights revert to authors.

Advice: "Too much of the poetry and fiction I have been reading over the past two years has been obsessed with the act of writing or life as a writer. We're not interested in this kind of writing. I place a strong emphasis on the readability of fiction. The dialogue should be clear, and the characters speaking readily discernible. It is worth making the extra revisions necessary to obtain this level of quality. We strongly suggest that writers send a SASE for our guidelines before submitting any fiction."

‡THE LAMPLIGHT, (II), The Society of Wretched Writers, Poets and Artists, 8110 N. 38 St., Omaha NE 68112. (402)453-4634. Editor: Richard R. Carey. Fiction Editor: Bruce Riley. Magazine: 8½×11; 40 pages; 20 lb. bond paper; 65 lb. stock cover; some illustrations; a few photographs. "Our purpose is to establish a new literature drawn from the past. We relish foreign settings in the 19th century when human passions transcended computers and fax machines. We are literary but appeal to the common intellect and the mass soul of humanity." Semiannually.

• The Society of Wretched Writers, Poets and Artists publishes *Raskolnikov's Cellar*, which alternates with *The Lamplight* and also publishes *Beggar's Folios* and *The Beggar's Review*. Write them for information on these other publications.

Needs: Historical (general), humor/satire, literary, mystery/suspense (literary), romance (gothic, historical). "Settings in the past. Psychological stories." Plans special fiction issue or anthology in the future. Receives 10-15 unsolicited mss/month. Accepts 2 mss/issue; 4 mss/year. Publishes ms 4 months-1 year after acceptance. Recently published work by Fredrick Zydek, John J. McKernan. Length: 2,000 words preferred; 500 words minimum; 3,500 words maximum. Publishes short shorts. Length: 300 words. Also publishes literary criticism and poetry. Sometimes critiques or comments on rejected mss.

How to Contact: Send complete ms with cover letter. Should include estimated word count, bio (a paragraph or two) and list of publications. Reports in 1 month on queries; 2½ months on mss. SASE. Simultaneous and reprint submission OK. Sample copy for $7, 9×12 SAE and 2 first class stamps. Fiction guidelines for $1, #10 SAE and 1 first class stamp. Reviews novels and short story collections.

Payment: Pays 2 contributor's copies. Additional copies at a reduced rate of 40% discount up to 5 additional copies.
Terms: Acquires first North American serial rights.
Advice: "We look first for writing style: syntax and diction, and literary restraint. The plot should beat in rhythm to this style. We are attracted to stories that go beyond conventional feelings, those that dig up the insanity of the normal intellect and the sanity of the madman. If the author lights the fuse in the first paragraph, we will read on for the explosion. We scan every manuscript for the fuse. Make your characters a unified mess—conflicting traits, unexplained compulsions, untied ends, revealing weaknesses. Learn at least 3 foreign languages, but be the master of your own. When you have read Dostoyevsky, Proust, Kafka and their like, then submit to us. Remember: the strongest way to say a thing is to never quite say it. We are a bit different from most publications; thus think differently. Don't be afraid to think and write above your own experiences."

LANGUAGE BRIDGES QUARTERLY, Polish-English Literary Magazine, (II, IV), Box 850792, Richardson TX 75085-0792. (214)530-2782. Editor: Eva Ziem. Fiction Editor: Zofia Przebindowska-Tousty. Magazine: 8½×11; 20+ pages; 60 lb. paper; 65 lb. cover; illustrations. "Today's Poland and Polish spirit are the main subject; a picture of life in Poland, with emphasis on the recent Polish emigration wave problems, however topics of general nature are being accepted. For both English and Polish speaking readers." Quarterly. Estab. 1989. Circ. 300.
Needs: Condensed/excerpted novel, fantasy, historical (general), humor/satire, literary, prose poem, religious/inspirational, translations, young adult/teen (10-18 years). "No horror, no vulgar language." Receives 1 unsolicited ms/month. Accepts one fiction ms every second issue. Publishes ms 3-6 months after acceptance. "Length does not matter. The longer works are broken into parts." Publishes short shorts. Sometimes critiques rejected mss and recommends other markets.
How to Contact: Send complete ms with cover letter. Reports in 2-3 months on mss. Simultaneous and reprint submissions OK. Accepts electronic submissions via disk. Free sample copy and fiction guidelines.
Payment: Pays contributor's copies.
Terms: Pays for one-time rights. Sends galleys to author.
Advice: "*LBQ* is the only fully bilingual Polish-English literary magazine in the U.S. It obviously helps Polish newcomers to learn English and Polish Americans to brush up on their Polish. Consequently, through translated Polish literary works, *LBQ* introduces the English-speaking reader to Polish culture and problems of Poles in Poland and abroad. *LBQ* creates a bridge between Polish and American writers as well as the readers. As the bilingual population of Polish Americans has recently grown in the U.S.A., *LBQ* also fulfills the increasing demand for crosscultural dialogue in seeking common roots and discovering differences."

THE LAUREL REVIEW, (II), Northwest Missouri State University, Dept. of English, Maryville MO 64468. (816)562-1265. Co-editors: Craig Goad, David Slater and William Trowbridge. Associate Editor: Randy Freisinger. Magazine: 6×9; 124-128 pages; good quality paper. "We publish poetry and fiction of high quality, from the traditional to the avant-garde. We are eclectic, open and flexible. Good writing is all we seek." Biannually. Estab. 1960. Circ. 800.
Needs: Literary and contemporary. Accepts 3-5 mss/issue, 6-10 mss/year. Receives approximately 60 unsolicited fiction mss each month. Approximately 1% of fiction is agented. Length: 2,000-10,000 words. Sometimes publishes literary essays; also publishes poetry. Critiques rejected mss "when there is time." Reads September to May.
How to Contact: Send complete ms with SASE. No simultaneous submissions. Reports in 1-4 months on mss. Publishes ms an average of 1-12 months after acceptance. Sample copy for $3.50.
Payment: Pays 2 contributor's copies, 1 year subscription.
Terms: Acquires first rights. Copyright reverts to author upon request.
Advice: Send $3.50 for a back copy of the magazine.

THE LEADING EDGE, Magazine of Science Fiction and Fantasy, (II, IV), 3163 JKHB, Provo UT 84604. Editor: Michael Carr. Fiction Editor: Tracy Kline. Magazine: 5×8; 120-144 pages; 20 lb. bond paper; 40 lb. card stock; 15-20 illustrations. "We are a magazine dedicated to the new and upcoming author, poet, and artist involved in the field of science fiction and fantasy. We are for the upcoming professional." Triannually. Circ. 500.
Needs: Adventure, experimental, fantasy, humor/satire, prose poem, science fiction (hard science, soft/sociological). "We are very interested in experimental sf and humorous stories, but all pieces should fall within the category of sf and fantasy. No graphic sex, violence, dismemberment, etc. No

outrageous religious commentary. No fannish/media stories; i.e., no Star Wars, Star Trek, Dr. Who, etc." Receives 40 unsolicited mss/month. Buys 6-8 mss/issue; 20-30 mss/year. Publishes ms 1-4 months after acceptance. Recently published work by Jane Yolen, Michael R. Collings, Thomas Easton, David Brin. Length: 5,000 words; 500 words minimum; 17,000 words maximum. Publishes short shorts. Also publishes literary essays, literary criticism, poetry. Critiques rejected mss.

How to Contact: Send complete ms with cover letter. Include name and address, phone number, title of story and classification of story (leave name off manuscript—put it on cover letter only). Reports in 3-4 months on mss. SASE. Simultaneous submissions OK. Sample copy for $2.50. Fiction guidelines for #10 SAE and 1 first class stamp. Sometimes reviews novels and short story collections.

Payment: Pays $5-100 plus contributor's copies.

Terms: Pays on publication for first North American serial rights. Sends galleys to author.

Advice: "All fiction must be original, innovative and interesting. We are very familiar with the body of sf and fantasy work, and look for new stories. Too many writers of sf and fantasy rely on existing cliché and convention. Humor, hard science, and experimental fantasy have the best chance for publication. Accurate science, vivid imagery, and strong characterization will impress the editors. We want stories about people with problems; the setting is there to illustrate the problem, not vice versa. Proofread!!! Please send clean, proofread copy. Just because we're small doesn't mean we're sloppy. Research! Be accurate. Our readers are *very* aware of science and history. We do not publish graphic violence or sex. Violence is okay if it is necessary to the story."

THE LEDGE POETRY AND FICTION MAGAZINE, (II), 64-65 Copper Ave., Glendale NY 11385. Editor: Timothy Monaghan. Magazine: 5½×8½; 80+ pages; typeset and perfect-bound; gloss cover; cover art. "Our only criteria is material of high literary merit." Semiannually. Estab. 1988. Circ. 450.

Needs: "Stories which possess a gritty, arresting and/or provocative quality that makes us sit up and take notice; stories grounded in contemporary and/or urban experience." Receives approx. 24 unsolicited fiction mss/month. Accepts 3 mss/issue; 6 mss/year. Publishes mss 1-4 months after acceptance. Recently published work by George Held, Mitch Levenberg, Diana Chang, Joyce Stewart. Length: "up to 12 pages, double-spaced." Publishes short shorts. Also publishes poetry. Comments on or critiques rejected mss occasionally, if warranted. Recommends other markets.

How to Contact: Send complete ms with cover letter (optional). Reports in 2-3 weeks on queries; 3 months or less on mss. SASE. Reprint submissions OK. Sample copy for $5. Fiction guidelines for #10 SASE.

Payment: Pays 1 contributor's copy.

Terms: Acquires one-time rights.

Advice: "We are open to all schools and slants, but especially value a story written in prose that demonstrates some mastery of the English language, an original slant on its theme, and an ending, whether loud or muted, naive or ironical, of some consequence."

‡LEFT BANK, (II, IV), Blue Heron Publishing, 24450 NW Hansen Rd., Hillsboro OR 97124. (503)621-3911. Editor: Linny Stovall. Book Form: 6×9; 160 pages; book paper; illustrations; photographs. "We only publish NW writers (OR, MT, ID, WA, AK, British Columbia and Alberta) and take only a few short stories—mostly essay format." Semiannually. Estab. 1991. Circ. 7,000.

● The publishers of *Left Bank* also publish the *Writer's Northwest Handbook* (by Media Weavers). It's chock full of market and writing information for the northwestern US.

Needs: Ethnic/multicultural, feminist, gay, humor/satire, lesbian, literary, mainstream/contemporary, regional. "Each issue is themed. Guidelines must be sent for since each issue is thematic. We also take excerpts from books in progress or recently in print (latter particularly if well-known author). Upcoming theme: "Gotta Earn a Living" (June 1993). List of upcoming themes available for SASE. Buys 2-6 fiction mss/issue. Publishes ms 4 months after acceptance. Agented fiction 50%. Recently published work by David Duncan, Ken Kesey. Length: 2,500 words preferred; 3,000 words maximum. Publishes short shorts. Length: 400-500 words. Also publishes literary essays and poetry.

How to Contact: Query first and get guidelines for SASE. Should include bio (1 page maximum), list of publications. Reports in 2-3 weeks on queries; 2 months on mss. SASE for a reply to a query or send a disposable copy of the ms. Simultaneous, reprint and electronic submissions OK. Sample copy for $7.95 plus $2 (postage and handling). Fiction guidelines for SASE.

Payment: Pays $50-150 and 1 contributor's copy.

Terms: Buys first North American serial rights or one-time rights.

LEFT CURVE, (II), Box 472, Oakland CA 94604. (510)763-7193. Editor: Csaba Polony. Magazine: 8½ × 11; 112 pages; 60 lb. paper; 100 pt. C1S Durosheen cover; illustrations; photos. "*Left Curve* is an artist-produced journal addressing the problem(s) of cultural forms emerging from the crises of modernity that strive to be independent from the control of dominant institutions, based on the recognition of the destructiveness of commodity (capitalist) systems to all life." Published irregularly. Estab. 1974. Circ. 1,200.

Needs: Contemporary, ethnic, experimental, historical, literary, prose poem, regional, science fiction, translations, political. Upcoming themes: "Computers and the Creative Process" (hypertext, virtual reality, etc.); "Post-Communist Culture". Receives approx. 6 unsolicited fiction mss/month. Accepts approx. 1 ms/issue. Publishes ms a maximum of 6 months after acceptance. Length: 1,200 words average; 500 words minimum; 2,500 words maximum. Publishes short shorts. Sometimes comments on rejected mss or recommends other markets.

How to Contact: Send complete ms with cover letter, which should include "statement on writer's intent, brief bio, why submitting to *Left Curve*." No simultaneous submissions. Reports in 3-6 months. SASE. Sample copy for $7, 9 × 12 SAE and 90¢ postage. Fiction guidelines for 2 first class stamps.

Payment: Pays in contributor's copies.

Terms: Acquires first rights.

Advice: "Be honest, realistic and gorge out the truth you wish to say. Understand yourself and the world. Have writing be a means to achieve or realize what is real."

LEGEND, A "Robin of Sherwood" Fanzine, (I, II, IV), 1036 Hampshire Rd., Victoria, British Columbia V8S 4S9 Canada. Editor: Janet P. Reedman. Magazine: Size varies; 170+ pages; bond paper; color print cover; illustrations. "Fantasy: Based on TV series 'Robin of Sherwood.' Annually. Estab. 1989. Circ. 200+.

Needs: Adventure, fantasy, historical, retold myths/legends. "All material must be based on 'Robin of Sherwood' in these genres. Nothing excessively violent/sexual, though adult themes are fine. Nothing sticky-sweet and saccharine, either!" Receives 2-3 unsolicited mss/month. Accepts 15-20 mss/issue; 15-20 mss/year. Publishes ms 4-18 months after acceptance. Length: 3,000 words preferred; 150 words minimum; 20,000 words maximum. Also publishes poetry. Sometimes critiques rejected mss and recommends other markets.

How to Contact: Query first. (I'll accept mss without queries, but it might be wise to write and ask if we're still open, overstocked, etc.). Reports in 1 month on queries; 2 months on mss. SASE. "Will accept loose stamps or IRCs, as I can use stamps from other countries." No simultaneous submissions. Fiction guidelines for #10 SAE and 1 loose first class stamp.

Payment: Pays in contributor's copies for material over 3 pages long.

Terms: Acquires first North American serial rights.

Advice: "Please support small publications, so they can *survive* to publish your work! *Read* a sample copy, so you don't waste postage and the editor's time! We have had handwritten mss, juveniles, no SASE, satires, experimental fiction, 5 stories crammed in one envelope . . . *despite explicit* guidelines! Also, *please, no* phone calls unless you are invited to phone via the mail first!! *Legend* may undergo a change of publisher, although I will remain as editor."

‡THE LETTER PARADE, (I), Bonnie Jo Enterprises, P.O. Box 52, Comstock MI 49041. Editor: Bonnie Jo. Newsletter: legal/letter-sized; 6 pages. Monthly. Estab. 1985. Circ. 113.

Needs: "Anything short." Receives 5-6 unsolicited mss/month. Acquires 1-2 mss/issue. Publishes ms up to a year after acceptance. Recently published work by Mimi Lipson, Ann Keniston, Chuck Jones. Length: 250-750 words preferred; 1,000 words maximum. Publishes short shorts. Also publishes literary essays.

How to Contact: Send complete ms with a cover letter. Send disposable copy of ms. Simultaneous and reprint submissions OK. Sample copy for $1. Reviews novels or short story collections. Send review copies to Christopher Magson.

Payment: Pays subscription to magazine.

Terms: Not copyrighted.

Advice: "My publication is small, so stories have got to be short. Good writing makes a manuscript stand out."

LIBIDO, The Journal of Sex and Sensibility, (II, IV), Libido, Inc., P.O. Box 146721, Chicago IL 60614. (312)281-5839. Editors: Jack Hafferkamp and Marianna Beck. Magazine: 5½ × 8½; 80 pages; 70 lb. non-coated; b&w illustrations and photographs. "Erotica is the focus. Fiction, poetry, essays, reviews for literate adults." Quarterly. Estab. 1988. Circ. 7,500.

● Specializing in "literary" erotica, this journal has attracted a number of top-name writers.

Needs: Condensed/excerpted novel, confession, erotica, gay, lesbian. No "dirty words for their own sake, violence, sexual exploitation." Receives 25-50 unsolicited mss/month. Buys about 5/issue; about 20 per year. Publishes ms up to 1 year after acceptance. Published work by Marco Vassi, Anne Rampling (Ann Rice), Larry Tritten. Length: 1,000-3,000 words; 300 words minimum; 3,000 words maximum. Also publishes literary essays, literary criticism. Sometimes critiques rejected ms and recommends other markets.

How to Contact: Send complete manuscript with cover letter including Social Security number and brief bio for contributor's page. Reports in 3 months on mss. SASE. No simultaneous submissions. Reprint submissions OK. Accepts electronic submissions via disk. Sample copy for $7. Free fiction guidelines. Reviews novels and short story collections.

Payment: Pays $15-50 and 2 contributor's copies.

Terms: Pays on publication for one-time or anthology rights.

Advice: "Humor is a strong plus. There must be a strong erotic element, and it should celebrate the joy of sex."

LIGHTHOUSE, (II), Box 1377, Auburn WA 98071-1377. Editor: Tim Clinton. Magazine: 5½ × 8½; 56 pages. "Timeless stories and poems for family reading—G rated." Bimonthly. Estab. 1986. Circ. 300.

Needs: Adventure, contemporary, historical, humor/satire, juvenile (5-9 years), mainstream, mystery/suspense, prose poem, regional, romance (contemporary, historical and young adult), senior citizen/retirement, sports, western, young adult/teen (10-18 years). Receives 300 mss/month. Accepts 15 mss/issue; 90 mss/year. Publishes ms within 2 years of acceptance. Recently published work by Will Ackerman, Nancy R. Herndon, Laura Battyanyi-Petose; published new writers within the last year. Length: 5,000 words maximum. Publishes short shorts.

How to Contact: Send complete mss, include Social Security number. No queries, please. Reports in 3 months or more on mss. SASE. No simultaneous submissions. Sample copy for $3 (includes guidelines). Fiction guidelines for #10 SAE and 1 first class stamp.

Payment: Pays up to $50 for stories; up to $5 for poetry.

Terms: Author copies discounted at $1.50 each. Payment on publication for first rights and first North American serial rights.

Advice: "If there is a message in the story, we prefer it to be subtly hidden in the action. We feel there is a market for quality fiction stories that are entertaining and have standards of decency as well."

THE LIMBERLOST REVIEW, (II), HC 33, Box 1113, Boise ID 83706-9702. (208)344-2120. Editor: Richard Ardinger. A magazine of poetry, fiction, interviews, memoirs. Publishes several issues a year. Estab. 1976. Circ. varies 500-1,500.

Needs: Contemporary and experimental. Issues of the magazine often devoted to chapbooks. Receives 10-15 unsolicited mss/month. Acquires 1-2 mss/issue. Occasionally comments on rejected ms. Also publishes literary essays, poetry. Special interest in writers from the Northwest.

How to Contact: Send complete ms with cover letter and short bio. Reports in 2 months. SASE. Photocopied submissions OK. Accepts computer printout submissions. Sample copy for $10 with SASE.

Payment: Contributor's copies; charge for extras: author's discount 20%.

Terms: Pays on publication for first rights. Sends galleys to author to check.

Advice: "Most recent issues have been devoted to single authors in the form of books and chapbooks. Issue No. 21, for example, appeared as a collection of short stories by John Rember, entitled *Coyote in the Mountains.*"

LIMESTONE: A LITERARY JOURNAL, (II), University of Kentucky, Dept. of English, 1215 Patterson Office Tower, Lexington KY 40506-0027. (606)257-7008. Contact: Editorial Committee. Magazine: 6 × 9; 50-75 pages; standard text paper and cover; illustrations; photos. "We publish a variety of styles and attitudes, and we're looking to expand our offering." Annually. Estab. 1981. Circ. 1,000.

Needs: Experimental, humor/satire, literary, mainstream, prose poem. Receives 200 mss/year. Acquires 15 mss/issue. Does not read mss May-Sept. Publishes ms an average of 6 months after acceptance. Publishes new writers every year. Length: 3,000-5,000 words preferred; 5,000 words maximum. Publishes short shorts. Sometimes critiques rejected mss.

How to Contact: Send complete ms with cover letter, which should include "publishing record and brief bio." Reports in 1 month on queries; 7 months or longer on mss. SASE. Simultaneous submissions OK. Sample copy $3.

Payment: Pays 2 contributor's copies.
Terms: Rights revert to author.
Advice: "We encourage all writers to send their most exacting, thought-filled writing. Send us writing where every word tells."

‡**LINDEN LANE MAGAZINE, (IV),** Linden Lane Magazine and Press, 103 Cuyler Rd., P.O. Box 2384, Princeton NJ 08543-2384. (609)921-7943. Fax (609)921-7943. Editor: Belkis Cuza-Malé. Tabloid: 28 pages; newsprint; illustrations and photographs. "Latin-American and American writers, in Spanish or English." Quarterly. Estab. 1982. Circ. 3,000.
Needs: Ethnic/multicultural, experimental, literary, mainstream/contemporary. Special interest: Latin American authors in US. Publishes special fiction issue or anthology. Receives 30 unsolicited mss/ month. Acquires 20 mss/year. Publishes ms 6 months after acceptance. Recently published work by Severo Sarduy, Mayra Montero, Guillermo Cabrera Imyante. Length: 800 words average. Also publishes literary essays, literary criticism and poetry. Sometimes critiques or comments on rejected mss.
How to Contact: Send complete ms with cover letter. Should include list of publications with submission. Reports on mss in 3 months. Send SASE (or IRC) for return of ms or a disposable copy of the ms. Will consider simultaneous submissions. Sample copy $2 with 8 × 11 SAE. Reviews novels and short story collections.
Payment: Pays 10 contributor's copies. Additional copies for $1.

‡**LINES IN THE SAND, (I, II),** LeSand Publications, 890 Southgate Ave., Daly City CA 94015. (415)992-4770. Editor: Nina Z. Sanders. Fiction Editors: Nina Z. Sanders and Barbara J. Less. Magazine: 5½ × 8½; 32 pages; 20 lb. bond; King James cost-coated cover; illustrations. "Stories should be well-written, entertaining and suitable for all ages. Our readers range in age from 7 to 90. No particular slant or philosophy." Bimonthly. Estab. 1992. Circ. 100.
Needs: Adventure, children's/juvenile (10-12 years), experimental, fantasy (science fantasy, children's fantasy), horror, humor/satire, literary, mainstream/contemporary, mystery/suspense (private eye/ hard-boiled, amateur sleuth, cozy, romantic suspense), science fiction (soft/sociological), senior citizen/retirement, westerns (traditional, frontier, young adult western), young adult/teen (10-18 years). "No erotica, pornography." Receives 20-30 unsolicited mss/month. Buys 8-10 mss/issue; 50-60 mss/ year. Publishes ms 2-4 months after acceptance. Recently published work by Jane Dachtelberg, John Moir, Beatrice Eckstein. Length: 1,200 words preferred; 250 words minimum; 2,500 words maximum. Publishes short shorts. Length: 250 words. Also publishes poetry. Often critiques or comments on rejected mss.
How to Contact: Send complete ms with cover letter. Should include estimated word count, bio (3-4 sentences). Reports in 2-6 months on mss. Send SASE for reply, return of ms or disposable copy of themes. Simultaneous and reprint submissions OK. Sample copy for $3.50. Fiction guidelines for #10 SAE and 1 first class stamp.
Payment: Pays $3-10 and 2 contributor's copies.
Terms: Pays on publication. Buys first North American serial rights. Sends galleys to author. Sponsors contests. To enter contest submit 2 copies of story, 2,000 words maximum, double-spaced typed and $5 reading fee for each story submitted.
Advice: "Use fresh, original approach, show, don't tell,' conform to guidelines, use dialogue when appropriate, be grammatically correct. Stories should have some type of conflict. Read a sample copy (or two). Study the guidelines. Use plain language; avoid flowery, 'big' words unless appropriate in dialogue."

LININGTON LINEUP, (IV), Elizabeth Linington Society, 1223 Glen Terrace, Glassboro NJ 08028-1315. Editor: Rinehart S. Potts. Newsletter: 8½ × 11; 16 pages; bond paper and cover stock; illustrations and photographs. "For those interested in the publications of Elizabeth Linington (a/k/a Lesley Egan, Egan O'Neill, Anne Blaisdell, Dell Shannon) — historical fiction and detective mysteries — therefore material must relate in some way thereto." Bimonthly. Plans special fiction issue. Estab. 1984. Circ. 400.

 ● Elizabeth Linington wrote several books under her many pen names. Among the mysteries she wrote as Del Shannon are *The Dispossessed*, *Destiny of Death* and *Chaos of Crime*. As Lesley Egan she wrote several books including *Little Boy Lost* and *The Miser*.
Needs: *Charges reading fee of $1. Requires magazine subscription of $12 before reading.* Historical (general), literary, mystcry/suspense. Upcoming themes: LAPD in Fiction, Deliz Riordan, RIP. Receives 3-4 fiction mss/month. Accepts 1 ms/issue; 6 mss/year. Publishes ms 3 months after acceptance. Pub-

lishes short shorts. Also publishes literary essays, literary criticism, poetry. Sometimes comments on rejected mss.
How to Contact: Query first. Reports in 1 month. SASE. No simultaneous submissions. Reprint submissions OK. Sample copy for $3. Reviews novels, short story collections and reference books/criticism in mystery field.
Payment: Pays subscription to magazine.
Terms: Acquires first rights.
Advice: "Become familiar with Miss Linington's books and continuing characters. We have been receiving material which completely disregards the information cited above."

LITE MAGAZINE, The Journal of Satire and Creativity, (I, II), #13, 8057 Winding Wood Rd., Glen Burnie MD 21061-5029. (410)247-8804. Editor: David W. Kriebel. Magazine: 8½ × 11; 52 pages; 30 lb. newprint paper; glossy cover; 12-24 illustrations; some photographs. "Satire, poetry, short fiction, occasional nonfiction pieces. Our audience is intelligent, literate, and imaginative. They have the ability to step back and look at the world from a different perspective." Quarterly. Estab. 1989. Circ. 10,000.
Needs: Experimental, fantasy, historical (general), horror, humor/satire, literary, mystery/suspense (private eye), psychic/supernatural/occult, science fiction (hard science, soft/sociological). "No erotica, gay, lesbian. Nothing demeaning to any ethnic or religious group. No stories with an obvious or trite 'message.' No violence for its own sake." Receives 10-20 unsolicited mss/month. Accepts 4-8 mss/issue; 16-32 ms/year. Publishes mss 1-3 months after acceptance. Recently published work by Richard Gardner, Bill Jones. Length: 2,500 words preferred; 6,000 words maximum. Publishes short shorts. Also publishes poetry. Sometimes comments on or critiques rejected mss.
How to Contact: Request guidelines, then send ms and cover letter. Include "information on the writer, focusing on what led him to write or create visual art. We want to know the person, both for our contributors guide 'Names in Lite' and to help build a network of creative people." Reports in 1 month. SASE. Simultaneous submissions OK, but prefer them not to be sent to other Baltimore publications. Sample copy for $1.25, 9 × 12 SAE and 3 first class stamps. Fiction guidelines for #10 SAE and 1 first class stamp.
Payment: Pays contributor's copies; extras for 25% discount.
Terms: Acquires one-time rights.
Advice: "We first look for quality writing, then we look at content and theme. It's not hard to tell a dedicated writer from someone who only works for money or recognition. Fiction that resonates in the heart makes us take notice. It's a joy to read such a story."

THE LITERARY REVIEW, An International Journal of Contemporary Writing, Fairleigh Dickinson University, 285 Madison Ave., Madison NJ 07940. (201)593-8564. Editor-in-Chief: Walter Cummins. Magazine: 6 × 9; 128-152 pages; illustrations; photos. "Literary magazine specializing in fiction, poetry, and essays with an international focus." Quarterly. Estab. 1957. Circ. 2,000.
Needs: Works of high literary quality only. Upcoming theme: "New Myths - 500 Years After Columbus" (Fall 1992). Receives 30-40 unsolicited fiction mss/month. Approximately 1-2% of fiction is agented. Published Anne Brashler, Thomas E. Kennedy, Henry H. Roth; published new writers within the last year. Acquires 10-12 mss/year. Also publishes literary essays, literary criticism, poetry. Occasionally critiques rejected mss. Sometimes recommends other markets.
How to Contact: Send complete ms with SASE. "Cover letter should include publication credits." Reports in 3 months on mss. Publishes ms an average of 1-1½ years after acceptance. Sample copy for $5; guidelines for SASE. Reviews novels and short story collections.
Payment: Pays 2 contributor's copies; 25% discount for extras.
Terms: Acquires first rights.
Advice: "Too much of what we are seeing today is openly derivative in subject, plot and prose style. We pride ourselves on spotting new writers with fresh insight and approach."

THE LITTLE MAGAZINE, (II), State University of New York at Albany, English Department, Albany NY 12222. Editors: Ron MacLean, Katie Yates. Magazine: 5½ × 8½; 300 pages; 70 lb. Nikusa paper; 10 pt. high gloss cover; cover illustrations. "Fiction and poetry for a literary audience." Annually. Estab. 1965.
Needs: Ethnic, experimental, feminist, gay, humor/satire, lesbian, literary, prose poem. No romance. Receives "roughly" 600 mss/issue over a 3-month reading period. Accepts 10 mss/issue. Reads only from September 15 to December 15. Publishes ms 6 months after acceptance. Published work by Edward Kleinschmidt, Lydia Davis, Ralph Lombreglia. Length: 3,000 words preferred; 5,000 words

maximum. Publishes short shorts. Critiques or comments on rejected mss.
How to Contact: Send complete ms with SASE, but only send between September 15 and December 15. Reports in 1 month on queries; in 2 months on mss. Simultaneous and reprint submissions OK. Sample copy for $6.
Payment: Pays 2 contributor's copies.
Terms: Acquires first North American serial rights.
Advice: "We like a wide variety of work from traditional to experimental."

‡**LIVING WATER MAGAZINE, A Magazine by, for, and about Christians, (I, II, IV),** Sonshine Ministries, P.O. Box 750996, Houston TX 77275-0996. (713)944-6441. Editor: Lew Engle. Magazine: 8½ × 11; 20 pages; 20 lb. bond paper; pulp cover; 1-3 illustrations. "The philosophy is that all Christians have something to share—*Living Water* is that place where they can share it. We use fiction, nonfiction and poetry. Audience is Christians world-wide. Bimonthly. Estab. 1990. Circ. 75.
Needs: "Almost any fiction with a strong Christian slant." Adventure, children's/juvenile (10-12 years), historical (general), mainstream/contemporary, mystery/suspense (amateur sleuth, young adult), religious/inspirational, romance (contemporary, historical, young adult), young adult/teen (10-18 years). "Nothing humanistic, New Age, anti-Judeo-Christian." Receives 0-1 unsolicited mss/month. Buys 2-3 mss/issue; 12-18 mss/year. Publishes ms 2-6 months after acceptance. Length: 1,000 words preferred; 25 words minimum; 2,100 words maximum. Publishes short shorts. Length: 100 words. Also publishes poetry. Often critiques or comments on rejected mss.
How to Contact: Query first or send complete ms with cover letter. Should include estimated word count, bio (100 words), Social Security number. Reports in 1 month on queries; 2 months on mss. Send SASE for reply, return of ms or send disposable copy of the ms. Simultaneous submissions OK. Sample copy for 9 × 12 SAE and 3 first class stamps. Fiction guidelines for #10 SAE and 1 first class stamp. Reviews novels and short story collections.
Payment: Pays ½¢/word or $1-10, subscription and 3 contributor's copies. Obtain up to 10 additional copies for any donation.
Terms: Pays on publication for first North American serial rights. Not copyrighted.
Advice: Looks for work that is "sound in its use of the Scriptures, and has *real* people dealing with *real* life. Get a sample copy—write from your heart—let your honesty show in your work. Write what you feel God has given you—not what you think someone might expect—but still follow all basic writing rules (good grammar, punctuation, etc.)."

‡**LIZARD'S EYELID MAGAZINE, (I),** MDF Productions, P.O. Box 8561, Jupiter FL 33468-8561. (407)622-6696. Fax: (407)746-1055. Editor: Sterling Sandow. Newsletter: 8 ½ × 11; 28-32 pages; illustrations and photos. "Political, underground music magazine aimed at 16-30 year olds." Quarterly. Estab. 1989. Circ. 2,500.
Needs: Ethnic/multicultural, experimental, feminist, horror, humor/satire, psychic/supernatural/occult. Receives 20 unsolicited mss/month. Acquires 1-2 mss/issue; 4-6 mss/year. Publishes 2-3 months after acceptance. Recently published work by Charles Bukowski, Brooke Beetler, Asiamus Nonamet. Length: 500 words average; 50 words minimum; 1,500 words maximum. Publishes short shorts. Length: 250 words. Also publishes literary essays, literary criticism and poetry. Often critiques or comments on rejected mss.
How to Contact: Send complete ms with cover letter. Should include word count and bio (½ page or less). Reports on mss in 3 weeks. Send SASE (or IRC) for ms. Will consider simultaneous submissions. Sample copy $2. Fiction guidelines for #10 SAE and 1 first class stamp or IRC. Reviews novels and short story collections.
Payment: Pays 1-3 contributor's copies. Additional copies for $1.
Terms: Acquires one-time rights. Sends galleys to author.
Advice: "We are always looking for the type of manuscript that is entirely uncensored and uninhibited. The type of story that makes you stop and think. Write what you feel, use the words and expressions that you mean."

LLAMAS MAGAZINE, The International Camelid Journal, (IV), Clay Press Inc., Box 100, Herald CA 95638. (916)448-1668. Editor: Cheryl Dal Porto. Magazine: 8½ × 11; 128+ pages; glossy paper; 80 lb. glossy cover stock; illustrations and pictures. For llama owners and lovers. 8 issues/year. Estab. 1979. Circ. 5,500.
Needs: Adventure, historical, humor. Receives 15-25 unsolicited fiction mss/month. Accepts 1-6 mss/issue; 12-24 mss/year. Publishes ms usually 3-4 months after acceptance. 15% of fiction is agented. Length: 2,000-3,000 words average. Publishes short shorts 300-1,000 words in length.

How to Contact: Send query to: Susan Ley, *Llamas* Asst. Editor. Reports in 1 month. Reprint submissions OK. Accepts electronic submissions via Apple 2 disk. Fiction guidelines free.
Payment: Pays $25-500, subscription to magazine and contributor's copies.
Terms: Pays on publication for first rights, first North American serial rights and one-time rights.

LONG SHOT, Box 6238, Hoboken NJ 07030. Editors: Jack Wiler, Jessica Chosid, Tom Pulhamus, Danny Shot. Magazine: 5½ × 8½; 128 pages; 60 lb. paper; 10 pt. C1S cover; illustrations; photos. Estab. 1982. Circ. 1,500.
Needs: Adventure, confession, contemporary, erotica, ethnic, experimental, fantasy, feminist, gay, horror, humor/satire, lesbian, political, prose poem, psychic/supernatural/occult, science fiction, suspense/mystery, western. Receives 100 unsolicited mss/month. Accepts 4-5 mss/issue. Does not read mss in August. Publishes ms within 6 months after acceptance. Published work by Allen Ginsberg, Charles Bukowski, Amiri Baraka, June Jordan; published new writers within the last year. Publishes short shorts. Also publishes poetry. Sometimes recommends other markets.
How to Contact: Send complete ms. Reports in 2-3 months. SASE. Simultaneous submissions OK. Sample copy for $5 plus $1 postage.
Payment: Pays in contributor's copies.
Terms: Acquires one-time rights.

THE LONG STORY, (II), 11 Kingston St., North Andover MA 01845. *May be change of address in coming year. Please watch writing periodicals for notice.* (508)686-7638. Editor: R.P. Burnham. Magazine: 5½ × 8½; 150-200 pages; 60 lb. paper; 65 lb. cover stock; illustrations (b&w graphics). For serious, educated, literary people. No science fiction, adventure, romance, etc. "We publish high literary quality of any kind, but especially look for stories that have difficulty getting published elsewhere— committed fiction, working class settings, left-wing themes, etc." Annually. Estab. 1983. Circ. 700.
Needs: Contemporary, ethnic, feminist and literary. Receives 30-40 unsolicited mss/month. Accepts 6-7 mss/issue. Length: 8,000 words minimum; 20,000 words maximum. Sometimes recommends other markets.
How to Contact: Send complete ms with a brief cover letter. Reports in 2+ months. Publishes ms an average of 3 months to 1 year after acceptance. SASE. May accept simultaneous submissions ("but not wild about it"). Sample copy for $5.
Payment: Pays 2 contributor's copies; $4 charge for extras.
Terms: Acquires first rights.
Advice: "Read us first and make sure submitted material is the kind we're interested in. Send clear, legible manuscripts. We're not interested in commercial success; rather we want to provide a place for long stories, the most difficult literary form to publish in our country."

‡LOONFEATHER (II), Bemidji Arts Center, 426 Bemidji Ave., Bemidji MN 56601. (218)751-4869. Editors: Betty Rossi and Jeane Sliney. Magazine: 6 × 9; 48 pages; 60 lb Hammermill Cream woven paper; 65 lb vellum cover stock; illustrations; occasional photos. A literary journal of short prose, poetry and graphics. Mostly a market for Northern Minnesota, Minnesota and Midwest writers. Semi-annually. Estab. 1979. Circ. 300.
Needs: Literary, contemporary, prose poem and regional. Accepts 2-3 mss/issue, 4-6 mss/year. Published work by Richard Jewell, Gary Erickson, James C. Manolis. Published new writers within the last year. Length: 600-1,500 words (prefers 1,500).
How to Contact: Send complete ms with SASE, and short autobiographical sketch. Reports in 3 months. Sample copy $2 back issue; $4.95 current issue.
Payment: Free author's copies.
Terms: Acquires one-time rights.
Advice: "Send carefully crafted and literary fiction. Because of increase in size of magazine, we can include more, slightly longer fiction.The writer should familiarize himself/herself with the type of fiction published in literary magazines as opposed to family magazines, religious magazines, etc."

LOST, A Magazine of Horror and Dark Humor, (II), Lupus Publishing, 67 Seyler St., New Hamburg, Ontario N0B 2G0 Canada. (519)662-2725. Editor: Adam Thornton. Magazine: 5¾ × 8½; 40 pages; illustrations and photographs. "Horrific or black comedy in both stories and artwork. Graphic or quiet poems accepted as well." Estab. 1990.
Needs: Experimental, horror, prose poem, psychic/supernatural/occult. "Must be morbid or horrific." No "fantasy or science." Receives 20-25 unsolicited mss/month. Acquires 10 mss/issue. Publishes ms 1 or 2 months after acceptance. Length: 1,000 words average; 500 words minimum; 3,000 words maxi-

mum. Publishes short shorts. Length: 400 words. Always comments on rejected mss and recommends other markets.
How to Contact: Send complete manuscript with cover letter that includes some biographical info. Reports in 1 week. Accepts electronic submissions. Fiction guidelines for SASE.
Payment: Pays in contributor's copies. Publication is not copyrighted.
Advice: "Read popular horror stories, then send us something unlike the stuff you read. We are looking for fiction along the lines of Steve Rasnic Tem, Charles L. Grant, Douglas E. Winter, Richard Christian Matheson."

LOST AND FOUND TIMES, (II), Luna Bisonte Prods, 137 Leland Ave., Columbus OH 43214. (614)846-4126. Editor: John M. Bennett. Magazine: 5½×8½; 40 pages; good quality paper; good cover stock; illustrations; photos. Theme: experimental, avant-garde and folk literature, art. Published irregularly. Estab. 1975. Circ. 300.
Needs: Literary, contemporary, experimental, prose poem. Prefers short pieces. Also publishes poetry. Accepts approximately 2 mss/issue. Published work by Spryszak, Steve McComas, Willie Smith, Rupert Wondolowski, Al Ackerman; published new writers within the last year. Sometimes recommends other markets.
How to Contact: Query with clips of published work. SASE. No simultaneous submissions. Reports in 1 week on queries, 2 weeks on mss. Sample copy for $4.
Payment: Pays 1 contributor's copy.
Terms: Rights revert to authors.

LOST WORLDS, The Science Fiction and Fantasy Forum, (I, IV), HBD Publishing, P.O. Box 605, Concord NC 28025. (704)933-7998. Editor: Holley B. Drye. Newsletter: 8½×11; 24 pages; 24 lb. bond paper; b&w illustrations. "General interest science fiction and fantasy, as well as some specialized genre writing. For a broad-spectrum age groups, anyone interested in newcomers." Monthly. Estab. 1988. Circ. 150.
Needs: Experimental, fantasy, horror, psychic/supernatural/occult, science fiction (hard science, soft/sociological), serialized novel. Publishes annual special fiction issue. Receives 7-15 unsolicited mss/month. Accepts 7-10 mss/issue; 100 and up mss/year. Publishes ms 3 months after acceptance (unless otherwise notified). Length: 3,000 words preferred; 2,000 words minimum; 5,500 words maximum. Publishes short shorts. Sometimes critiques rejected mss and recommends other markets. "Although we do not publish every type of genre fiction, I will, if asked, critique anyone who wishes to send me their work. There is no fee for reading or critiquing stories."
How to Contact: Query first. "Cover letters should include where and when to contact the author, a pen name if one is preferred as well as their real name, and whether or not they wish their real names to be kept confidential." Reports in 1 month on queries; 2 months on mss. SASE (only if they wish return of their manuscript.) Simultaneous and reprint submissions OK. Accepts electronic submissions via disk or modem. Sample copy for $2. Fiction guidelines free.
Payment: Pays contributor's copies.
Terms: Acquires one-time rights.
Advice: "I look for originality of story, good characterization and dialogue, well-written descriptive passages, and over-all story quality. The presentation of the work also makes a big impression, whether it be good or bad. Neat, typed manuscripts will always have a better chance than hand-written or badly typed ones. All manuscripts are read by either three or four different people, with an eye towards development of plot and comparison to other material within the writer's field of experience. Plagiarism is not tolerated, and we do look for it while reading a manuscript under consideration. Never be afraid to send us anything, we really are kind people."

LOUISIANA LITERATURE, A Review of Literature and Humanities, (II), Southeastern Louisiana University, Box 792, Hammond LA 70402. (504)549-5022. Editor: David Hanson. Magazine: 6¾×9¾; 100 pages; 70 lb. paper; card cover; illustrations; photos. "We publish literary quality fiction and essays by anyone. Essays should be about Louisiana material, but creative work can be set anywhere." Semiannually. Estab. 1984. Circ. 400 paid; 700 printed.
Needs: Literary, mainstream, regional. No sloppy ungrammatical manuscripts. Receives 60 unsolicited mss/month. Buys 3 mss/issue; 6 mss/year. Does not read mss June-July. Publishes ms 6 months maximum after acceptance. Published work by Kelly Cherry and Louis Gallo; published new writers within the last year. Length: 3,500 words preferred; 1,000 words minimum; 6,000 words maximum. Also publishes literary essay (Louisiana themes), literary criticism, poetry. Sometimes comments on rejected mss.

How to Contact: Send complete ms. Reports in 1-2 months on mss. SASE. Sample copy for $4. Reviews novels and short story collections by Louisiana authors only.
Payment: Pays up to $25 and contributor's copies.
Terms: Pays on publication for one-time rights.
Advice: "Cut out everything that is not a functioning part of the story. Make sure everything is spelled correctly. Use relevant specific detail in every scene."

THE LOUISVILLE REVIEW, (II), Department of English, University of Louisville, Louisville KY 40292. (502)588-6801. Editor: Sena Naslund. General Editor: Karen S. Mann. Magazine: 6 × 8¾; 100 pages; Warren's Old Style paper; cover photographs. Semiannually. Estab. 1976. Circ. 750.
Needs: Contemporary, experimental, literary, prose poem. Receives 30-40 unsolicited mss/month. Acquires 6-10 mss/issue; 12-20 mss/year. Publishes ms 2-3 months after acceptance. Published work by Maura Stanton, Patricia Goedicke, Michael Cadnum. Length: 50 pages maximum. Publishes short shorts.
How to Contact: Send complete ms with cover letter. Reports on queries in 2-3 weeks; 2-3 months on mss. SASE. Sample copy for $4. Fiction guidelines for #10 SAE and 1 first class stamp.
Payment: Pays in contributor's copies.
Terms: Acquires first North American serial rights.
Advice: Looks for "original concepts, fresh ideas, good storyline, engaging characters, a story that works."

LYNX, Journal of Renga, (II, IV), Spirit Lake Press, P.O. Box 169, Toutle WA 98649. (206)274-6661 or 274-6352. Editor: Terri Lee Grell. Magazine: 24-36 pages; newsprint paper; b&w illustrations and photographs. "Poetry commentary, stories and renga. Renga is linked verse; two or more poets cooperate to make a renga. The form dates back to 12th century Japan. For an adventurous audience." Quarterly. Estab. 1989. Circ. 500.
Needs: Experimental, literary, prose poem, translations. "No slick fiction. If it squeaks, send it to NYC." Receives 3-4 unsolicited mss/month. Acquires 1 ms/issue; 4 mss/year. Publishes ms within 4 months after acceptance. Recently published work by Hiroaki Sato, Gerald Burns, Miyazawa Kenji. Length: 2,000 words maximum. Publishes short shorts. Length: 250-500 words. Also accepts poetry. Sometimes critiques rejected mss and recommends other markets.
How to Contact: Send complete ms with cover letter. Reports in 1-2 months. SASE. Sample copy for $2.
Payment: Pays contributor's copies and some payment by arrangement.
Terms: Pays on publication. Acquires first North American serial rights. Not copyrighted.
Advice: "If it can't easily slip into one genre or another, we love it. If a manuscript is perfect to a fault, we hate it. We despise factory fiction. We love fiction writers who finally give up on factory fiction, let go of the reins and tell us something dry and outrageous, fast and holy, truly. Make my day."

THE MACGUFFIN, (II), Schoolcraft College, Department of English, 18600 Haggerty Rd., Livonia MI 48152. (313)591-6400, ext. 449. Editor: Arthur J. Lindenberg. Fiction Editor: Elizabeth Hebron. Magazine: 5½ × 8½; 128 pages; 60 lb. paper; 110 lb. cover; b&w illustrations and photos. "*The MacGuffin* is a literary magazine which publishes a range of material including poetry, nonfiction and fiction. Material ranges from traditional to experimental. We hope our periodical attracts a variety of people with many different interests." Triannually. Quality fiction a special need. Estab. 1984. Circ. 500.
Needs: Adventure, contemporary, ethnic, experimental, fantasy, historical (general), humor/satire, literary, mainstream, prose poem, psychic/supernatural/occult, science fiction, translations. No religious, inspirational, confession, romance, horror, pornography. Upcoming theme: 10th Anniversary Issue (June 1993). Receives 25-40 unsolicited mss/month. Accepts 5-10 mss/issue; 10-30 mss/year. Does not read mss between July 1 and August 15. Publishes 6 months to 2 years after acceptance. Agented fiction: 10-15%. Recently published work by Arlene McKanic, Joe Schall, Joseph Benevento; published new writers within the last year. Length: 2,000-2,500 words average; 400 words minimum; 4,000 words maximum. Publishes short shorts. Length: 400 words. Also publishes literary essays. Occasionally critiques rejected mss and recommends other markets.
How to Contact: Send complete ms with cover letter, which should include: "1. *Brief* biographical information; 2. Note that this *is not* a simultaneous submission." Reports in 2+ months. SASE. Reprint submissions OK. Sample copy for $3. Fiction guidelines free.

Payment: Pays 2 contributor's copies.
Terms: Acquires one-time rights.
Advice: "Be persistent. If a story is rejected, try to send it somewhere else. When we reject a story, we may accept the next one you send us. When we make suggestions for a rewrite, we may accept the revision. There seems to be a great number of good authors of fiction, but there are far too few places for publication. However, I think this is changing. Make your characters come to life. Even the most ordinary people become fascinating if they live for your readers."

THE MADISON REVIEW, (II), Department of English, Helen C. White Hall, 600 N. Park St., University of Wisconsin, Madison WI 53706. (608)263-3800. Rotating Editors. Magazine: 6 × 9; 180 pages. "Magazine of fiction and poetry with special emphasis on literary stories and some emphasis on midwestern writers." Published semiannually. Estab. 1978. Circ. 500.
Needs: Experimental and literary stories, prose poems and excerpts from novels. Receives 50 unsolicited fiction mss/month. Acquires 7-12 mss/issue. Published work by Richard Cohen, Fred Chappell and Janet Shaw. Published new writers within the last year. Length: no preference. Also publishes poetry.
How to Contact: Send complete ms with cover letter and SASE. "The letters should give one or two sentences of relevant information about the writer—just enough to provide a context for the work." Reports in 2 months on mss. Publishes ms an average of 4 months after acceptance. "We often do not report on mss during the summer." Sample copy $4.
Payment: Pays 2 contributor's copies; $2.50 charge for extras.
Terms: Acquires first North American serial rights.
Advice: "We are now willing to accept chapters of novels in progress and short short fiction. Write with surgical precision—then revise. Often the label 'experimental' is used to avoid reworking a piece. If anything, the more adventurous a piece of fiction is, the more it needs to undergo revision."

MAGIC CHANGES, (II), Celestial Otter Press, P.O. Box 658, Warrenville IL 60555. (708)416-3111. Editor: John Sennett. Magazine: 8½ × 11; 110 pages; 60 lb. paper; construction paper cover; illustrations; photos. "Theme: transformation by art. Material: poetry, songs, fiction, stories, reviews, art, essays, etc. For the entertainment and enlightenment of all ages." Biannually. Estab. 1979. Circ. 500.
Needs: Literary, prose poem, science fiction (soft/sociological), sports fiction, fantasy and erotica. "Fiction should have a magical slant." Upcoming themes: "Last Gasp of a Lost Grasp, "Music, Time, Magic." Accepts 8-12 mss/year. Receives approximately 15 unsolicited fiction mss each month. Published work by J. Weintraub, David Goodrum, Anne F. Robertson; published new writers within the last year. Length: 3,500 words maximum. Also publishes literary essays, literary criticism, poetry.
How to Contact: Send complete ms with SASE. Simultaneous submissions OK. Accepts disk submissions compatible with IBM or Macintosh; prefers hard copy with disk submissions. Reports in 3 months. Publishes ms an average of 8 months after acceptance. Sample copy $5. Make check payable to John Sennett. Reviews novels and short story collections.
Payment: Pays 1-2 contributor's copies; $5 charge for extras.
Terms: Acquires first North American serial rights.
Advice: "Write about something fantastic in a natural way, or something natural in a fantastic way. We need good stories—like epic Greek poems translated into prose."

MAGIC REALISM, (II, IV), Pyx Press, P.O. Box 620, Orem UT 84059-0620. Editors: C. Darren Butler and Julie Thomas. Magazine: 5½ × 8½; 60 pages; 20 lb. paper; card stock or bond cover; b&w illustrations. "Magic realism, exaggerated realism, some genre fantasy/dark fantasy, literary fantasy, occasionally glib fantasy of the sort found in the folk and fairy tales; myths for a general, literate audience." Triannually. Estab. 1990. Circ. 400.
Needs: Experimental, fantasy, literary, magic realism. "No sorcery/wizardry, sleight-of-hand magicians, occult, or the Edward Eager *Half-Magic* sort of story that begins "The magic started when . . ." Receives 80-100 unsolicited mss/month. Accepts 5-12 mss/issue; 20-30 mss/year. Publishes ms 4-24 months after acceptance. Recently published work by Bruce Taylor, Steve Rasnic Tem, Janice Eidus. Length: 4,000 words preferred; 100 words minimum; 8,000 words maximum; query for more than 8,000 words. Publishes short shorts. Length: 500-1,500 words. Sometimes critiques rejected mss and recommends other markets.
How to Contact: Send complete ms with cover letter. Include bio, list of credits. "Response time is generally within 3 months, but acceptance can take up to 6 months. SASE. Simultaneous and reprint submissions (if noted) OK. Sample copy for $4.95 (checks to C. Darren Butler). Fiction guidelines for SAE and 1 first class stamp.

Payment: Pays contributor's copies. Charges for extras.
Terms: Acquires first North American serial rights or one-time rights and nonexclusive reprint rights in case we want to use the work in an anthology.
Advice: "I like finely controlled feats of association; works wherein the human imagination defines reality. Magic realism subverts reality by shaping it into a human mold; bringing it closer to the imagination and to the subconscious. For example, people used to believe that swans migrated to the moon in Autumn or that high-speed vehicles would be useless because human bodies would break apart at high speeds. We have accepted borderline literary stories wherein the exaggerated elements are extremely subtle or part of the author's style—evident in metaphor or plotting or characterization—rather than the story's reality."

MANOA , A Pacific Journal of International Writing, (II), English Dept., University of Hawaii Press, Honolulu HI 96822. (808)948-8833. Editors: Robert Shapard, Frank Stewart. Fiction Editor: Ian MacMillan. Magazine: 7×10; 240 pages. "An American literary magazine, emphasis on top US fiction and poetry, but each issue has a major guest-edited translated feature of recent writings from an Asian/Pacific country." Semiannually. Estab. 1989.
● See the Close-up interview with Editor Robert Shapard in the 1992 *Novel & Short Story Writer's Market*.
Needs: Excerpted novel, contemporary, literary, mainstream and translation (from nations in or bordering on the Pacific). "Part of our purpose is to present top US fiction from throughout the US, not only to US readers, but to readers in Asian and Pacific countries. Thus we are not limited to stories related to or set in the Pacific—in fact, we do not want exotic or adventure stories set in the Pacific, but good US literary fiction of any locale." Accepts 10-12 mss/issue; 20-24/year. Publishes ms 6 months-1 year after acceptance. Agented fiction 10%. Published work by Anne Beattie, Ron Carlson and W.S. Merwin. Publishes short shorts. Also publishes literary essays, literary criticism, poetry.
How to Contact: Send complete ms with cover letter or through agent. Reports in 6 weeks. SASE. Simultaneous submissions OK. Sample copy $7. Reviews novels and short story collections. Send books to Reviews Editor.
Payment: "Highly competitive rates paid so far." Pays contributor copies.
Terms: Pays for first North American serial, plus one-time reprint rights. Sends galleys to author.
Advice: "Hawaii has come of age literarily and wants to contribute to the best of US mainstream. It's readership is (and is intended to be) mostly national, not local. It also wants to represent top US writing to a new international market, in Asia and the Pacific. Altogether we hope our view is a fresh one; that is, not facing east toward Europe but west toward 'the other half of the world.' We mostly run short stories."

MARK, A Journal of Scholarship, Opinion, and Literature, (II), University of Toledo, 2801 W. Bancroft SU2514, Toledo OH 43606. (419)537-4407. Editors: Danielle Demuche, Julie Bevins. Magazine: 6×9; 72 pages; acid-free paper; some illustrations; photographs. "General theme is exploration of humanity and man's effort to understand the world around him." Annually. Estab. 1967. Circ. 3,500.
Needs: Contemporary, ethnic, humor/satire, literary, regional and science fiction. "We do not have the staff to do rewrites or heavy copyediting—send clean, legible mss only." No "typical MFA first-person narrative—we like stories, not reportage." Receives 20-25 unsolicited fiction mss/month. Acquires 7-10 mss/year. Does not read June to September. Publishes ms 6 months after acceptance. Publishes short shorts.
How to Contact: Send complete ms with cover letter, name, address and phone. Reports in January each year. Sample copy $3 plus 7×10 SAE with 72¢ postage.
Payment: Pays 2 contributor's copies.
Terms: Acquires one-time rights.
Advice: "Beginning fiction writers should write in a style that is natural, not taught to them by others. More importantly, they should write about subjects they are familiar with. Be prepared for rejection, but good writing will always find a home."

THE MARYLAND REVIEW, Department of English and Modern Languages, University of Maryland Eastern Shore, Princess Anne MD 21853. (301)651-2200, ext. 262. Editor: Chester M Hedgepeth. Magazine: 6×9; 100-150 pages; quality paper stock; heavy cover; illustrations; "possibly" photos. "We have a special interest in black literature, but we welcome all sorts of submissions. Our audience is literary, educated, well-read." Annually. Estab. 1986. Circ. 500.

Needs: Contemporary, humor/satire, literary, mainstream, black literature. No genre stories; no religious, political or juvenile material. Accepts approx. 12-15 mss/issue. Publishes ms "within 1 year" after acceptance. Published work by John K. Crane, David Jauss; published new writers within the last year. Publishes short shorts. "Length is open, but we do like to include some pieces 1,500 words and under." Also publishes poetry.
How to Contact: Send complete ms with cover letter, which should include a brief autobiography. Reports "as soon as possible." SASE, *but does not return mss*. No simultaneous submissions. "No fax copies, please." Sample copy for $6.
Payment: Pays in contributor's copies.
Terms: Acquires all rights.
Advice: "Think primarily about your *characters* in fiction, about their beliefs and how they may change. Create characters and situations that are utterly new. We will give your material a careful and considerate reading. Any fiction that is flawed by grammatical errors, misspellings, etc. will not have a chance. We're seeing a lot of fine fiction these days, and we approach each story with fresh and eager eyes. Ezra Pound's battle-cry about poetry refers to fiction as well: 'Make it New!' "

THE MASSACHUSETTS REVIEW, (II), Memorial Hall, University of Massachusetts, Amherst MA 01002. (413)545-2689. Editors: Mary Heath, Jules Chametzky, Paul Jenkins. Magazine: 6×9; 172 pages; 52 lb. paper; 65 lb. vellum cover; illustrations and photos. Quarterly.
Needs: Short stories. Does not read mss June 1-October 1. Published new writers within the last year. Approximately 5% of fiction is agented. Critiques rejected mss when time permits.
How to Contact: Send complete ms. No ms returned without SASE. Simultaneous submissions OK, if noted. Reports in 2 months. Publishes ms an average of 9-12 months after acceptance. Sample copy $5.50. Guidelines available for SASE.
Payment: Pays $50 maximum.
Terms: Pays on publication for first North American serial rights.
Advice: "Shorter rather than longer stories preferred (up to 28 pages). There are too many stories about 'relationships,' domestic breakups, etc."

MATI, Ommation Press, 5548 N. Sawyer, Chicago IL 60625. Editor: Effie Mihopoulos. "Primarily a poetry magazine, but we do occasional special fiction and science fiction issues." Quarterly. Estab. 1975. Circ. 1,000.
   ● Ommation Press publishes this and *Salome,* a publication dedicated to performing arts, also listed in this book.
Needs: Literary, contemporary, science fiction, feminist, translations. No mystery, gothic, western, religious. Receives approximately 20 unsolicited fiction ms each month. Length: 1-2 pages. Also publishes poetry. Occasionally sends ms on to editors of other publications. Sometimes recommends other markets.
How to Contact: Send complete ms with SASE. Reports in 1 week-2 months. Sample copy $1.50 with 9×12 SAE (preferred) plus 90¢ postage.
Payment: Pays 1 contributor's copy; special contributor's rates available for extras.
Terms: Acquires first North American serial rights. "Rights revert to authors but *Mati* retains reprint rights."
Advice: "We want to see good quality writing and a neat ms with sufficient return postage; same size return as outside envelope and intelligent cover letter. Editor to be addressed as 'Dear Sir/Ms' instead of 'Dear Sir' when it's a woman editor."

MERLYN'S PEN, The National Magazine of Student Writing, Grades 7-10, (IV), Box 1058, East Greenwich RI 02818. (401)885-5175. Editor: R. Jim Stahl. Magazine: 8⅛×10⅞; 36 pages; 50 lb. paper; 70 lb. gloss cover stock; illustrations; photos. Student writing only—grades 7 through 10, for libraries, homes and English classrooms. Bimonthly (September-April). Estab. 1985. Circ. 22,000.
Needs: Adventure, experimental, fantasy, historical (general), horror, humor/satire, literary, mainstream, mystery/suspense, regional, romance, science fiction, western, young adult/teen, editorial reviews, puzzles, word games, poetry. Must be written by students in grades 7-10. Receives 500 unsolicited fiction mss/month. Accepts 25 mss/issue; 100 mss/year. Publishes ms 3 months to 1 year after acceptance. Length: 1,500 words average; 25 words minimum; 4,000 words maximum. Publishes short shorts. Responds to rejected mss.
How to Contact: Send complete ms and cover letter with name, grade, age, home and school address, home and school telephone number, supervising teacher's name and principal's name. Reports in 10-12 weeks. SASE for ms. Sample copy for $3.

Payment: Pays 3 contributor's copies, charge for extras. Each author published receives a free copy of *The Elements of Style*.
Terms: Published works become the property of Merlyn's Pen, Inc.
Advice: "Write what you *know*; write where you are."

‡MESHUGGAH, A Journal of Oddball Fiction and Subversive Thoughts, (II), Feh! Press, #603, 147 Second Ave., New York NY 10003. Editor: Simeon Stylites. Fiction Editor: Morgana Malatesta. Magazine: 16 pages; bond paper; illustrations. "We publish what interests us, which tends to be unusual and offbeat in subject matter, though not experimental in style. Eclectic. Our audience: a mixed bunch." Quarterly. Estab. 1991. Circ. 100.
Needs: Erotica, fantasy (science fantasy), humor/satire, mainstream/contemporary, psychic/supernatural/occult, science fiction (hard science, soft/sociological). Special interests: surreal fiction, political fiction, very short fiction. Receives 2 unsolicited mss/month. Acquires 6-7 mss/issue; 25 mss/year. Publishes ms 6 months after acceptance. Recently published work by Crad Kilodney, David Huberman, Al Ackerman. Length: 1,000 words average; 50 words minimum; 4,000 words maximum. Publishes short shorts. Also publishes literary essays and literary criticism. Sometimes critiques or comments on rejected mss.
How to Contact: Send complete ms with cover letter. Should include bio with submission. Reports in 2-4 weeks. Send SASE (IRC) for reply, return of ms or send disposable copy of ms. Will consider simultaneous submissions, reprints and electronic submissions. Sample copy $1. Fiction guidelines for #10 SAE and 1 first class stamp or IRC.
Payment: Pays 1 contributor's copy. Additional copies for 50¢.
Terms: Acquires one-time rights.
Advice: Looks for "interesting, short, thought-provoking, unconventional subject matter, intelligent offbeat fiction, intelligent fiction on unusual subjects."

METROPOLITAIN, (II), City of Light Publications, 6307 N. 31st St., Arlington VA 22207. Editor: J.L. Bergsohn. Magazine: 5½ × 8½; 50 pages; 24 lb. Hammermill paper; illustrated cover; b&w illustrations. "*Metropolitain* is primarily geared toward showcasing the talents of Washington area writers." Quarterly. Estab. 1991. Circ. 250.
• Note *Metropolitain* has cut down on the number of subject categories acceptable.
Needs: Contemporary, ethnic, literary, mainstream, regional, translations. Receives 75 unsolicited mss/month. Accepts 4 mss/issue; 16 mss/year. Publishes ms up to 1 year after acceptance. Length: 5,000 words maximum. Publishes short shorts. Also publishes poetry. Sometimes comments on or critiques rejected mss.
How to Contact: Send complete ms with cover letter. Include brief bio with list of publication credits. Reports in 2 weeks on queries; 1 month on mss. SASE. Simultaneous and reprint submissions OK. Accepts computer printout submissions. Sample copy for $3.
Payment: Pays 1 contributor's copy; charges for extras.
Terms: Acquires one-time rights. Sends galleys to author.
Advice: "We look for clean, polished prose and dialogue that rings true. A firm command of both the English language and the craft of fiction writing is imperative."

MICHIGAN QUARTERLY REVIEW, University of Michigan, 3032 Rackham, Ann Arbor MI 48109-1070. (313)764-9265. Editor: Laurence Goldstein. "An interdisciplinary journal which publishes mainly essays and reviews, with some high-quality fiction and poetry, for an intellectual, widely read audience." Quarterly. Estab. 1962. Circ. 1,800.
• *Esquire* (July 1992) named *Michigan Quarterly Review* a "literary root."
Needs: Literary. No "genre" fiction written for a "market." Upcoming themes: "Male Body" issue (Fall 1993); "Cuban theme" (Winter 1994). Receives 200 unsolicited fiction mss/month. Buys 2 mss/issue; 8 mss/year. Published work by Charles Baxter, Bell Gale Chevigny and Jay Neugeboren; published new writers within the last year. Length: 1,500 words minimum; 7,000 words maximum; 5,000 words average. Also publishes poetry, literary essays.
How to Contact: Send complete ms with cover letter. "I like to know if a writer is at the beginning, or further along, in his or her career. Don't offer plot summaries of the enclosed story, though a background comment is welcome." SASE. No simultaneous submissions. Sample copy for $2 and 2 first class stamps.

Payment: Pays $8-10/printed page.
Terms: Pays on publication for first rights. Awards the Lawrence Foundation Prize of $500 for best story in *MQR* previous year.
Advice: "Read back issues to get a sense of tone; level of writing. *MQR* is very selective; only send the very finest, best-plotted, most-revised fiction."

MID-AMERICAN REVIEW, (II), Department of English, Bowling Green State University, Bowling Green OH 43403. (419)372-2725. Fiction Editor: Ellen Behrens. Magazine: 5½ × 8½; 200 pages; 60 lb. bond paper; coated cover stock. "We publish serious fiction and poetry, as well as critical studies in contemporary literature, translations and book reviews." Biannually. Estab. 1981.
• *Mid-American Review* sponsors the Sherwood Anderson Short Fiction Prize listed in this book.
Needs: Experimental, traditional, literary, prose poem, excerpted novel and translations. Upcoming theme: "Fall 1993 issue is expected to be devoted to work by Asian-Americans." Receives about 80 unsolicited fiction mss/month. Buys 5-6 mss/issue. Does not read June-August. Approximately 5% of fiction is agented. Recently published work by Steven Schwartz, Eve Shelnut, Philip Graham, Dan O'Brien; published new writers within the last year. Also publishes literary essays, literary criticism, poetry. Occasionally critiques rejected mss. Sometimes recommends other markets.
How to Contact: Send complete ms with SASE. No simultaneous submissions. Reports in about 3 months. Publishes ms an average of 3-6 months after acceptance. Sample copy for $4. Reviews novels and short story collections. Send books to reviews editor.
Payment: Pays $7/page up to $50; 2 contributor's copies; $2 charge for extras.
Terms: Pays on publication for one-time rights.
Advice: "We just want *quality* work of whatever vision and/or style. We are now looking for more translated fiction."

MIDDLE EASTERN DANCER, The International Monthly Magazine of Middle Eastern Dance & Culture, (II), Box 181572, Casselberry FL 32718-1572. (407)831-3402. Editor: Karen Kuzsel. Fiction Editor: Jeanette Spencer. Magazine: 8½ × 11; 36 pages; 60 lb. stock; enamel cover; illustrations; photos. "Our theme is Middle Eastern dance and culture. We run seminar listings, professional directory, astrology geared to dancers, history, interviews, poetry, recipes, reviews of movies, clubs, shows, records, video, costuming, personal beauty care, exercise and dance choreography." Monthly. Estab. 1979. Circ. 2,500.
Needs: No fiction that does not relate to Middle-Eastern dance or culture. Receives 5 unsolicited ms/month. Publishes ms within 4 months after acceptance. Published work by Alan Fisher, Jeanette Larson and Sid Hoskins; published new writers within the last year. *Charges $10 if comments are desired.* Occasionally critiques rejected mss. Recommends other markets.
How to Contact: Send complete ms with cover letter, which should include "background in Middle Eastern dance or culture, why they came to write this story and how they know of the magazine." Reports in 1 month on queries. SASE. Reprint submissions OK "if not to other Middle Eastern dance and culture publication." Sample copy $1 or send 9x12 SAE and 75¢ postage.
Payment: Pays $10-25 and 2 contributor's copies.
Terms: Pays on acceptance for one-time rights.
Advice: "Stick strictly to Middle Eastern dance/culture."

MIDLAND REVIEW, An Annual Journal of Contemporary Lit, Lit. Crit. & Art, (II), Oklahoma State University, English Dept., Morrill Hall, Stillwater OK 74078. Editors change every year. Send to "Editor." Magazine: 6½ × 9½; 128 pages; 80 lb. paper; perfect bond cover stock; illustrations; photos. "A mixed bag of quality work." For "anyone who likes to read and for those that want news that folks in Oklahoma are alive. Publishes 30-40% OSU student material." Annually. Estab. 1985. Circ. 500.
Needs: Ethnic, experimental, feminist, historical (general), literary, prose poem, regional, translations. Receives 15 unsolicited fiction mss/month. Accepts 4 mss/issue. Publishes ms 2-6 months after acceptance. Published work by Jene Friedemann, Steffie Corcoran, Bruce Michael Gans; published new writers within the last year. Length: 4-10 pages double-spaced, typed. Publishes short shorts of 2-4 pages. Also publishes literary essays, literary criticism, poetry.
How to Contact: Send complete ms with cover letter. Reports in 6-8 weeks on queries. SASE for ms. Simultaneous submissions OK. Sample copy for $5, 90¢ postage and 9 × 12 SAE. Fiction guidelines for #10 SAE and 1 first class stamp.

Payment: Pays 1 contributor's copy.

Terms: Copyright reverts to author.

Advice: "We want to encourage good student stories by giving them an audience with more established writers."

MIDNIGHT ZOO, (II), Experiences Unlimited, P.O. Box 8040, Walnut Creek CA 94596. (510)825-4434. Editor: Jon L. Herron. Fiction Editors: Elizabeth Martin-Burk and Debbie Baker. Fiction editors change every year. Magazine: 11 × 17; 64+ pages; 20 lb. bond paper; 100 lb. glossy cover; b&w illustrations and photographs. "Horror, science fiction and fantasy stories and poems plus science fact, interviews, reviews, writer's information, profiles, strange happenings for all ages interested in this genre." Monthly. Estab. 1990. Circ. 3,000+.

  • Stories from *Midnight Zoo* were included in the Nebula Award Nominations (1991), and the Small Press Writers and Artists Organization nominated "Best Poet," "Best New Writer" and "Best Editor" from the magazine in 1992. Jon L. Herron also edits *Aberations* listed in this book.

Needs: Fantasy, horror, prose poem, psychic/supernatural/occult, science fiction (hard science, soft/sociological). We will accept stories up to 10,000 words. Receives 120 unsolicited mss/month. Buys 15 mss/issue. 180+ mss/year. Publishes ms within 2 issues after acceptance. Recently pubished work by Ardath Mayhar, Kevin O'Donnell, Jr., Kevin J. Anderson. Length: 3,000 words preferred; 500 words minimum; 10,000 words maximum (except for anthology—15,000). Publishes short shorts. Sometimes critiques rejected mss and recommends other markets.

How to Contact: Send complete ms with cover letter. Include Social Security number, telephone number and a short bio. Reports in 2 months on queries; 2 weeks-4 months on mss. SASE. Simultaneous and reprint (very few) submissions OK. Accepts electronic submissions via disk or modem (Micro-Soft Word 5, Word Perfect or ASCII). Sample copy for $6. Fiction guidelines for SAE and 1 first class stamp.

Payment: Pays ½¢/word; $12 maximum; subscription to magazine; contributor's copies; reduced charge for extras.

Terms: Pays on publication for first North American serial rights. Sometimes sends galleys to author.

Advice: "First a ms must be well written and have an original idea or an original twist on an established idea. Good spelling and grammar are important. However, we work with writers who we feel show potential and in many cases have gone through 5 or 6 re-writes in order to get the best possible story from the writer. We remain dedicated to assisting new and under-published writers attain publication through our magazine and have even assisted writers in getting published in other magazines." Sponsors contest: $5 entry fee for stories. Prizes each year—$100 best fiction, 2nd and 3rd prizes and honorable mentions.

‡THE MILWAUKEE UNDERGRADUATE REVIEW, (I), P.O. Box 71079, Milwaukee WI 53211. Editor: Dean Andrade. Fiction Editor: Jennifer Dunajski. Magazine: 5½ × 8; 50 pages; 70 lb. glossy paper; 67 lb. card stock cover; b&w illustrations. Semiannually. Estab. 1989. Circ. 1,000.

Needs: Adventure, ethnic/multicultural, experimental, fantasy (science fantasy, sword and sorcery), feminist, gay, historical, horror, humor/satire, lesbian, literary, mainstream/contemporary, mystery/suspense (private eye/hard-boiled, amateur sleuth, cozy, police procedural, romantic suspense), psychic/supernatural/occult, regional, religious/inspirational, romance (contemporary, gothic, historical), science fiction (hard science, soft/sociological), sports, westerns (traditional, adult, frontier). Receives 10-20 unsolicited mss/month. Acquires 6-8 mss/issue; 12-16 mss/year. Publishes 10-12 weeks after acceptance. Recently published work by Christopher Grimes, Ottillia Willis, Peter J. Theis. Length: 2,000 words average; 200 words minimum; 5,000 words maximum. Publishes short shorts. Length: 400 words. Also publishes literary essays, literary criticism and poetry. Often critiques or comments on rejected mss.

How to Contact: Send complete ms with cover letter. Should include 200 word bio, electronic copy (if available) with submission. Reports on queries in 2 weeks; 8-10 weeks on mss. Send SASE (IRC) for reply, return of ms or send disposable copy of the ms. Will consider simultaneous, electronic submissions. Sample copy $2.50. Fiction guidelines for #10 SAE and 1 first class stamp or IRC.

Payment: Pays 2 contributor's copies.

Terms: Acquires first North American serial rights.

Advice: Looks for "detail, resonance, compression, originality, ambiguity. Work that is well-informed yet subtle."

‡MIMSY MUSING, A Review of Ideas on Nursing and the Care of Children, (I, IV), Box 161613, Sacramento CA 95816. Editor: David Hutchinson, RN. Newsletter: 8½×11; 16-20 pages; 20 lb. bond paper; 20 lb. bond cover; pen & ink illustrations. "For health care professionals, parents, anyone with an interest in kids, nursing *or* literature/ideas." Bimonthly. Estab. 1991. Circ. 400.
Needs: Humor/satire, juvenile (1-4 years, 5-9 years), mainstream, young adult/teen (10-18 years). "Nursing, pediatrics, medicine, hospital life, life and death, pain. No erotic; horror; lit-school experimental." Publishes ms less than 2 months after acceptance. Length: 1,000 words average; 5,000 words maximum. Publishes short shorts. Sometimes critiques or comments on rejected mss. Sometimes recommends other markets.
How to Contact: Send complete ms with cover letter. Include "author's interest or background relative to kids/nursing/medicine. Something personal perhaps, or at least complementary to the story." Reports in 1 week on queries; 1 month on mss. SASE. Simultaneous and reprint submissions OK. Sample copy for $2, #10 SAE and 2 first class stamps. Fiction guidelines for #10 SAE and 1 first class stamp.
Payment: $20 maximum and contributor's copies.
Terms: Pays on acceptance for one-time rights. Sometimes sends galleys to author.
Advice: "Work should be on a topic close to the author's heart (or mind). Every manuscript stands out in its own way; and each author has to find his/her own path to the rare land of polished writing. Honest effort is the minimum requirement; improvement generally follows."

MINAS TIRITH EVENING-STAR, (IV), W.W. Publications, Box 373, Highland MI 48357-0373. (813)585-0985. Editor: Philip Helms. Magazine: 8½×11; 40+ pages; typewriter paper; black ink illustrations; photos. Magazine of J.R.R. Tolkien and fantasy—fiction, poetry, reviews, etc. for general audience. Quarterly. Published special fiction issue; plans another. Estab. 1967. Circ. 500.
● *Minas Tirith Evening-Star* is the official publication of the American Tolkein Society. Contact the magazine for information on joining. The publisher, W.W. Publications also appears in this book in the small press section.
Needs: "Fantasy and Tolkien." Upcoming theme: "J.R.R. Tolkien's 100th Birthday!" Receives 5 unsolicited mss/month. Accepts 1 ms/issue; 5 mss/year. Published new writers within the last year. Length: 1,000-1,200 words preferred; 5,000 words maximum. Publishes short shorts. Also publishes literary essays, literary criticism, poetry. Occasionally critiques rejected ms.
How to Contact: Send complete ms and bio. Reports in 1-2 months. SASE. No simultaneous submissions. Reprint submissions OK. Sample copy for $1. Reviews novels and short story collections.
Terms: Acquires first rights.
Advice: Goal is "to expand knowledge and enjoyment of J.R.R. Tolkien's and his son Christopher Tolkien's works and their worlds."

MIND IN MOTION, A Magazine of Poetry and Short Prose, (II), Box 1118, Apple Valley CA 92307. (619)248-6512. Editor: Céleste Goyer. Magazine: 5½×8½; 60 pages; 20 lb. paper; 50 lb. cover. "We prefer to publish works of substantial brilliance that engage and encourage the readers' mind." Quarterly. Estab. 1985. Circ. 350.
Needs: Experimental, fantasy, humor/satire, literary, prose poem, science fiction. No "mainstream, romance, nostalgia, un-poetic prose; anything with a slow pace or that won't stand up to re-reading." Receives 50 unsolicited mss/month. Acquires 10 mss/issue; 40 mss/year. Publishes ms 2 weeks to 3 months after acceptance. Recently published work by Robert E. Brimhall, Don Stockard, Maria L. Escola. Length: 2,000 words preferred; 250 words minimum; 3,500 words maximum. Also publishes poetry. Sometimes critiques rejected mss and occasionally recommends other markets.
How to Contact: Send complete ms. "Cover letter or bio not necessary." SASE. Simultaneous (if notified) submissions OK. Sample copy for $3.50. Fiction guidelines for #10 SAE and 1 first class stamp.
Payment: One contributor's copy when financially possible; charge for extras.
Terms: Acquires first North American serial rights.
Advice: "We are now able to take more stories per issue, and they may be a bit longer than previously, due to a format modification. *Mind in Motion* is noted for introspective, philosophical fiction with a great deal of energy and originality."

MIND MATTERS REVIEW, (I,II), Box 234, 2040 Polk St., San Francisco CA 94109. (415)775-4545. Editor: Carrie Drake. Magazine: 8 1/2×11; 30-64 pages; illustrations and photos. "*MMR* is basically a philosophical publication. We have published two short stories that were written in the form of parables." Audience is "conservative intellectually, but liberal fiscally." Quarterly. Estab. 1988. Circ. 1,000.

Needs: Historical (general), literary, prose poem. Accepts 4 mss/year. Publishes ms 6-12 months after acceptance. Recently published Ralph Tyler, Barbara Jarvik. Length: 800 words preferred; 400 words minimum; 1,000 words maximum.

How to Contact: Query first. Reports in 3 weeks. SASE. Simultaneous and reprint submissions OK. Sample copy for $3.50. Fiction guidelines for SASE.

Payment: Pays contributor's copies.

Terms: Acquires one-time rights. Sends galleys to author.

Advice: "A beginning fiction writer for *MMR* should first be familiar with the overall frame of reference of *MMR* and its range of flexibility and limitations. We seek writers who are able to tap moral principles as a source of imagination and inspiration. The moral principle can be atheistic or Christian or Buddhist—whatever—as long as there is a logical structure. Characters and plots do not have to be complex or have strong emotional appeal as long as they draw attention to life experiences that give the reader something to think about."

MINDSCAPES, A Literary Magazine of Short Fiction, (II), Juno Press, 2252 Beverly Glen Place, Los Angeles CA 90077. (213)474-0959. Editor: Beverly Bernstein. Magazine: 8½×11; 60 pages; 60 lb. paper; illustrations. *Mindscapes* prints "literary and mainstream short story fiction for an educated adult audience." Semiannually. Estab. 1991. Circ. 350.

Needs: Adventure, contemporary, experimental, humor/satire, literary, mainstream. No pornography, no fragments. Receives 60 unsolicited mss/month. Accepts 12 mss/issue; 20-24 mss/year. Publishes ms within 6 months after acceptance. Recently published work by Donald Rawley, Terry Wolverton, Marlene Buono, Mel Green. Length: 1,500 words preferred; 500 words minimum; 4,000 words maximum. Publishes short shorts. Sometimes critiques rejected mss and recommends other markets.

How to Contact: Send complete ms with cover letter. Include previous publications and one-sentence summary of the story. Simultaneous submissions OK. Reports in 1 month. SASE. Sample copy $7.50.

Payment: Pays 1 contributor's copy.

Terms: Acquires one-time rights.

Advice: "Send us clean, correct manuscripts. We are interested in dynamic, unique stories. If you can hold an audience reading it aloud, it stands a good chance for being right for us. Strong characterrs, dramatic plots and tales that touch the heart are what we're looking for. Dense material with obscure symbolism and no point should go to somebody else."

THE MINNESOTA REVIEW, A Journal of Committed Writing, (II), Dept. of English, East Carolina University, Greenville NC 27858. (919)757-6388. Editor: Jeffrey Williams. Fiction Editor: Fred Pfeil. Magazine: 5¼×8; approximately 200 pages; some illustrations; occasional photos. "We emphasize socially and politically engaged work." Semiannually. Estab. 1960. Circ. 1,000.

Needs: Experimental, feminist, gay, historical (general), lesbian, literary, science fiction. Receives 20 mss/month. Accepts 3-4 mss/issue; 6-8 mss/year. Publishes ms within 6 months to 1 year after acceptance. Recently published work by Harold Jaffe, Linda Schor, John Berger. Length: 5,000-6,000 words preferred. Publishes short shorts. Also publishes literary essays, literary criticism, poetry. Sometimes critiques rejected mss and recommends other markets.

How to Contact: Send complete ms with optional cover letter. Reports in 2-3 weeks on queries; 2-3 months on mss. SASE. Simultaneous submissions OK. Reviews novels and short story collections. Send books to book review editor.

Payment: Pays in contributor's copies. Charge for extra copies.

Terms: Acquires first rights.

Advice: "We look for socially and politically engaged work, particularly work that stretches boundaries."

MIORITA, A JOURNAL OF ROMANIAN STUDIES, (IV), The Dept. FLLL, Dewey 482, University of Rochester, Rochester NY 14627. (716)275-4258 or (716)275-4251. Co-Editors: Charles Carlton and Norman Simms. Magazine: 5½×8½; Xerox paper; occasional illustrations. Magazine of "essays, reviews, notes and translations on all aspects of Romanian history, culture, language and so on," for academic audience. Annually. Estab. 1973. Circ. 200.

Needs: Ethnic, historical, literary, regional and translations. "All categories contingent upon relationship to Romania." Receives "handful of mss per year." Accepts "no more than one per issue." Length: 2,000 words maximum. Occasionally critiques rejected mss.

How to Contact: Send complete ms. SASE preferred. Previously published work OK (depending on quality). Accepts computer printout submissions.
Payment: "We do not pay."

MISSISSIPPI REVIEW, (I, II), University of Southern Mississippi, Box 5144, Hattiesburg MS 39406. (601)266-4321. Editor: Frederick Barthelme. "Literary publication for those interested in contemporary literature—writers, editors who read to be in touch with current modes." Semiannually. Estab. 1972. Circ. 1,500.
Needs: Literary, contemporary, fantasy, humor, translations, experimental, avant-garde and "art" fiction. No juvenile. Buys varied amount of mss/issue. Does not read mss in summer. Length: 100 pages maximum.
How to Contact: Send complete ms with SASE including a short cover letter. Sample copy for $5.50.
Payment: Pays in contributor's copies.
Terms: Acquires first North American serial rights.

MISSISSIPPI VALLEY REVIEW, (III), Western Illinois University, Dept. of English, Simpkins Hall, Macomb IL 61455. Editors: John Mann and Tama Baldwin. Magazine: 64 pages; original art on cover. "A small magazine, *MVR* has won 16 Illinois Arts Council awards in poetry and fiction. We publish stories, poems and reviews." Biannually. Estab. 1971. Circ. 800.
Needs: Literary, contemporary. Upcoming theme: "The Writer as Witness" (Spring, 1992). Does not read mss in summer. Published work by Ray Bradbury, Gwendolyn Brooks, Louise Erdrich, Al Hirschfeld. Also publishes poetry.
How to Contact: Send complete ms with SASE. Reports in 3 months. Sample copy for $5.
Payment: Pays 2 contributor's copies.
Terms: Individual author retains rights.
Advice: "Persistence."

THE MISSOURI REVIEW, (II), 1507 Hillcrest Hall, University of Missouri, Columbia MO 65211. (314)882-4474. Editors: Speer Morgan, Greg Michalson. Magazine: 6×9; 256 pages. Theme: fiction, poetry, essays, reviews, interviews, cartoons. "All with a distinctly contemporary orientation. For writers, and the general reader with broad literary interests. We present non-established as well as established writers of excellence. The *Review* frequently runs feature sections or special issues dedicated to particular topics frequently related to fiction." Published 3 times/academic year. Estab. 1977. Circ. 4,500.
  • A Close-up interview with Managing Editor Speer Morgan appeared in the 1992 *Novel & Short Story Writer's Market.*
Needs: Literary, contemporary; open to all categories except juvenile, young adult. Receives approximately 300 unsolicited fiction mss each month. Buys 6-8 mss/issue; 18-25 mss/year. Published new writers within the last year. No preferred length. Also publishes literary essays, poetry. Critiques rejected mss "when there is time."
How to Contact: Send complete ms with SASE. Reports in 10 weeks. Sample copy for $6.
Payment: Pays $20/page minimum.
Terms: Pays on signed contract for all rights.
Advice: Awards William Peden Prize in fiction; $1,000 to best story published in *Missouri Review* in a given year. Also sponsors Editors' Prize Contest with a prize of $1,000.

MOBIUS, The Journal of Social Change, (II), 1149 E. Mifflin, Madison WI 53703. (608)255-4224. Editor: Fred Schepartz. Magazine: 8½×11; 16-32 pages; 60 lb. paper; 60 lb. cover. "Looking for fiction which uses social change as either a primary secondary theme. This is broader than most people think. Need social relevance in one way or another. For an artistically and politically aware and curious audience." Quarterly. Estab. 1989. Circ. 150.
Needs: Contemporary, ethnic, experimental, fantasy, feminist, gay, historical (general) horror, humor/ satire, lesbian, literary, mainstream, prose poem, science fiction. "No porn, no racist, sexist or any other kind of ist. No Christian or spiritually proselytizing fiction." Receives 15 unsolicited ms/month. Accepts 2-3 mss/issue. Publishes ms 3-9 months after acceptance. Recently published work by Larry Edgerton, Andrea Musher, Dennis Trudell. Length: 3,500 words preferred; 500 words minimum; 5,000 words maximum. Publishes short shorts. Length: 300 words. Sometimes critiques rejected mss.
How to Contact: Send complete ms with cover letter. Reports in 1-2 months. SASE. Simultaneous and reprint submissions OK. Sample copy for $2, 9×12 SAE and 3 first class stamps. Fiction guidelines for 9×12 SAE and 4-5 first class stamps.

Payment: Pays contributor's copies.
Terms: Acquires one-time rights.
Advice: Looks for "first and foremost, good writing. Prose must be crisp, polished, story must pique my interest and make me care due to a certain intellectual, emotional aspect. Second, *Mobius* is about social change. We want stories that make some statement about the society we live in, either on a macro or micro level. Not that your story needs to preach from a soapbox (actually, we prefer that it doesn't) but your story needs to have *something* to say."

THE MONOCACY VALLEY REVIEW, (II), Mt. St. Mary's College, Emmitsburg MD 21727. (301)447-6122. Editor: William Heath. Fiction Editor: Roser Camiacals-Heath. Magazine: 8½×11; 72 pages; high-quality paper; illustrations and photographs. For readers in the "Mid-Atlantic region; all persons interested in literature." Annually. Estab. 1986. Circ. 500.
Needs: Adventure, contemporary, experimental, historical, humor/satire, literary, mainstream, prose poem reviews. "We would not exclude any categories of fiction, save pornographic or obscene. Our preference is for realistic fiction that dramatizes things that matter." Receives 20-25 unsolicited mss/ month. Buys 3-5 mss/issue. Does not read mss March, October. Publishes ms 6 weeks after acceptance. Published work by Ann Knox; Maxine Combs; Doris Selinsky. Length: 3,000-4,000 words preferred; no minimum; 10,000 words maximum. Also publishes poetry. Sometimes critiques rejected mss.
How to Contact: Query first or ask for submission guidelines. Send 50-word bio. Reports in 4 weeks on queries; 1-4 months on mss. SASE. Simultaneous submissions OK. Sample copy for $5. Fiction guidelines for #10 SAE and 1 first class stamp. Reviews novels and short story collections.
Payment: Pays $10-25 and contributor's copies.
Terms: Pays on publication.
Advice: "Be patient in receiving a response. Manuscript readings take place about eight weeks before the publication date (April 15). Submit in Fall and early Winter. I would not advise submitting in November and December. Deadline for submissions: January 15th."

THE MONTHLY INDEPENDENT TRIBUNE TIMES JOURNAL POST GAZETTE NEWS CHRONICLE BULLETIN, The Magazine to Which No Superlatives Apply, (II), 1630 Allston Way, Berkeley CA 94703. Editor: T.S. Child. Fiction Editor: Denver Tucson. Magazine: 5½×8; 8 pages; 60 lb. paper; 60 lb. cover; illustrations and photographs. "Our theme is the theme of utter themelessness. We publish anything. In the past, we have published short stories, short short stories, the world's shortest story, plays, game show transcriptions, pictures made of words, teeny-weeny novelinis." Published irregularly. Estab. 1983. Circ. 500.
Needs: Adventure, experimental, humor/satire, mystery/suspense (private eye, amateur sleuth), psychic/supernatural/occult. "If it's serious, literary, perfect, well-done or elegant, we don't want it. If it's wacky, bizarre, unclassifiable, funny, cryptic or original, we might." Nothing "pretentious; serious; important; meaningful; honest." Receives 10 unsolicited mss/month. Accepts 1-2 mss/issue. Accept manuscripts published in next issue. Length: 400 words preferred. 1,200 words maximum. Publishes short shorts. Length: 400 words. Sometimes critiques rejected mss.
How to Contact: Send complete ms with cover letter. Reports in 2 months. SASE. "May" accept simultaneous submissions. Sample copy $.50, any size SAE and 1 first class stamp.
Payment: Pays subscription (2 issues); 3 contributor's copies.
Terms: Not copyrighted.
Advice: "First of all, work must be *short*—1,200 words maximum, but the shorter the better. It must make me either laugh or scratch my head, or both. Things that are slightly humorous, or written with any kind of audience in mind are returned. We want writing that is spontaneous, unconscious, boundary-free. If you can think of another magazine that might publish your story, send it to them, not us. Send us your worst, weirdest stories, the ones you're too embarrassed to send anywhere else."

THE MOODY STREET REVIEW, (II), Edge Press, Apt. 2, 205 E. 78th St., New York NY 10021. (212)772-2332. Editor: David Gibson. Magazine: 8½×11; 65-75 lb. cover; illustrations and photographs. "Beat sensitivity, not style—fiction, poetry, nonfiction. For literary, artistic, down to earth bare bones types." Annually. Estab. 1988. Circ. 300.
Needs: Condensed/excerpted novel, contemporary, ethnic, humor/satire, literary, mainstream, regional, translations (from French). Receives 50-75 unsolicited mss/month. Publishes 2 mss/issue. Does not read mss August-April. Recently published work by Rod Kessler, Catherine Gammon. Length: 10,000 words preferred; 5,000 words minimum; 20,000 words maximum. Sometimes critiques rejected mss and recommends other markets.

How to Contact: Reports in 1-3 months on mss. SASE. Sample copy $5 (payable to David Gibson). Fiction guidelines for $1, 5½ × 8½ SAE and $1-1.50 postage.
Payment: *Charges $1 reading fee.* Pays 2 contributor's copies.
Terms: Not copyrighted.
Advice: "Of course, use of vivid imagery and sentence rhythm are important. But most of all, a proportionate sense of distance between the narrator—whether, it be an omniscient or limited one—and the subjects of a given story is the hardest to achieve. Stories should have all of these aspects as well as emotionally involving the reader in the very first few sentences. This does not, of course, mean it should imitate the pseudo-pathos and melodrama of television programs. As long as a character's feelings stand out, as a real person's world—that is what will draw a reader into the story. Know what a beat sensitivity is. Read Blake Whitman, the symbolist poets, Thomas Wolfe, the surrealist poets; and so on. Don't imitate, emulate, and know the difference between these two words."

mOOn, (II), Qamar Illustrated, 363 W. 18th St., New York NY 10011. (212)255-4362. Co-Editors: Kevin Gray, Nelson Kim, Cameron McWhirter and Margaret Mittelbach. Magazine: 8 1/2 × 11; 40 pages; card cover; illustrations and photographs. "*mOOn* prints quality writing, all styles—fiction, poetry, nonfiction—for a cryptic, squamous audience." Triannually. Estab. 1991. Circ. 300.
Needs: Contemporary, ethnic, experimental, feminist, gay, horror, humor/satire, lesbian, literary, prose poem, psychic/supernatural/occult, translations. Receives 15 unsolicited mss/month. Accepts 5-8 mss/issue; 15-24 mss/year. Publishes ms 2-4 months after acceptance. Recently published work by Peter Meinke, Percy Magus and Hakim Bey. Length: 300 words minimum; 3,000 words maximum. Publishes short shorts. Sometimes critiques rejected mss.
How to Contact: Send complete ms with cover letter. Reports in 6 weeks. SASE. Simultaneous and reprint submissions OK. Sample copy for $4.
Payment: Pays contributor's copies.
Terms: Acquires one-time rights. Sends galleys to author.
Advice: "We're trying to encourage good, new American writing that helps define the times we live (or don't live) in and the times to come. We are interested in any theme and any style of writing that is of good quality, that will fit into our lit-zine format."

THE MOUNTAIN LAUREL, Monthly Journal of Mountain Life, Foundation Inc., P.O. Box 562, Wytheville VA 24382. (703)228-7282. Editor: Susan M. Thigpen. Tabloid: 28 pages; newsprint; illustrations and photographs. "Everyday details about life in the Blue Ridge Mountains of yesterday, for people of all ages interested in folk history." Monthly. Estab. 1983. Circ. 20,000.
Needs: Historical, humor, regional. "Stories must fit our format—we accept seasonal stories. There is always a shortage of good Christmas stories. A copy of our publication will be your best guidelines as to what we want. We will not even consider stories containing bad language, sex, gore, horror." Receives approximately 40 unsolicited fiction mss/month. Accepts up to 5 mss/issue; 60 mss/year. Publishes ms 2-6 months after acceptance. Length: 500-600 words average; no minimum; 1,000 words maximum. Publishes short shorts. Length: 300 words. Sometimes critiques rejected mss. Recommends other markets.
How to Contact: Send complete ms with cover letter, which should include "an introduction to the writer as though he/she were meeting us in person." Reports in 1 month. SASE. Simultaneous submissions OK. Sample copy for 9 × 12 SAE and 5 first class stamps. Fiction guidelines for #10 SAE and 1 first class stamp.
Payment: Pays in contributor's copies.
Terms: Acquires one-time rights.
Advice: "Tell a good story. Everything else is secondary. A tightly written story is much better than one that rambles. Short stories have no room to take off on tangents. *The Mountain Laurel* has published the work of many first-time writers as well as works by James Still and John Parris. First publication ever awarded the Blue Ridge Heritage Award."

‡MUSE PORTFOLIO, (I, II), 25 Tannery Rd., Box 8, Westfield MA 01085. Editor: Haemi Balgassi. Magazine: 5½ × 8½; 29 pages; 20 lb. paper; color cover; illustrations. "*M.P.* welcomes submissions from sincere, eloquent freelancers who crave the opportunity to share and support one another's writing through a casual forum." Semiannually (may increase to quarterly in 1993). Estab. 1992. Circ. 180.
Needs: Ethnic/multicultural, feminist, historical (general), literary, mainstream/contemporary, mystery/suspense (amateur sleuth, cozy, romantic suspense, general), regional, romance (contemporary, young adult, anything tasteful), senior citizen/retirement, young adult/teen (10-18 years). No pornogra-

phy, vulgarity, excessive violence, profanity. Receives 10-15 unsolicited mss/month. Acquires 2-5 mss/issue; 4-10 mss/year. Publishes ms 6-12 months after acceptance. Recently published work by Lois Hayn, Bobbi Sinha, Joseph Balgassi. Length: 1,000 words preferred; 300 words minimum; 3,000 words maximum. Publishes short shorts. Length: 300-500 words. Also publishes literary essays and poetry. Sometimes critiques or comments on rejected mss.
How to Contact: Send complete ms with cover letter. "No phone queries, please." Should include estimated word count, bio (short paragraph), list of publications (optional). Reports in 2 weeks on queries; 3-8 weeks on mss. SASE for a reply to query or return of ms. Simultaneous and reprint submissions OK. Sample copy for $1.25, 6×9 or larger SAE and 3 first class stamps. Fiction guidelines for #10 SAE and 1 first class stamp.
Payment: Pays 1 contributor's copy.
Terms: Acquires one-time rights. Not copyrighted, but author copyright notices included in issues.
Advice: "We are eager to review the 'personal best' efforts of sincere, earnest writers of all levels. We especially encourage the beginning freelancer, and also appreciate submissions from more experienced writers who are willing to share their work with newer colleagues. Be sincere, and treat yourself, your writing and the freelance process with respect. Remember the 'three P's': Be *patient, persistent* and *professional.* Develop as *polished* a voice as possible. We are excited and appreciative when we discover the rare creative gem that has obviously been polished through *necessary revisions.*"

MYSTERY NOTEBOOK (Ashenden), (II, IV), Box 1341, F.D.R. Station, New York NY 10150. Editor: Stephen Wright. Journal and Newsletter: 8½×11; 10-16 pages and occasional double issues; photocopied; self cover; illustrations and photos sometimes. "Mystery books, news, information; reviews and essays. Ashenden section is devoted to Somerset Maugham and his works." For mystery readers and writers and for Maugham readers and scholars. Quarterly. Estab. 1984. Circ. (approx.) 1,000.
Needs: Excerpted novel (suspense/mystery). Receives few unsolicited mss. Length: brief. Short shorts considered. Also publishes articles and essays (brief) on Maugham and his works. Occasionally comments on rejected ms.
How to Contact: Query. Reports in 3 weeks on queries; 1 month on mss. SASE for ms. Simultaneous and previously published submissions OK (if query first). Sample copies or back issues $7.50, double issues $15.
Payment: None. "If author is a regular contributor, he or she will receive complimentary subscription. Usually contributor receives copies of the issue in which contribution appears."
Advice: "Mystery magazines use all kinds of stories in various settings. This is also true of mystery books except that no matter what kind of detective is the protagonist (private eye, amateur, police, female operative) the novel must be the best of its kind—even for consideration. Mystery fiction books have increased in demand—*but* the competition is more keen than ever. So only those with real talent *and* a superb knowledge of mystery-writing craft have *any* chance for publication. Do try to get the reader interested in the first few pages. It also helps if you know and understand the current market."

‡MYSTERY STREET, The new wave of crime fiction, (II, IV), P.O. Box 1378, Eugene OR 97440. (503)344-6742. Fax: (503)683-3412. Editor: O'Neil De Noux. Magazine: 8½×11; 64 pages; electra-bright paper; slick cover; illustrations on cover. "For a general mystery audience. Will publish short stories: mystery, police procedural, private-eye, espionage, suspense and thrillers—in all forms—hard-boiled, softboiled and traditional British cozy." Bimonthly. Estab. 1992. Circ. 6,000+
● This is a new magazine from the publishers of *Pulphouse* and *Tomorrow* listed in this book.
Note: At press time we learned Pulphouse *plans to put* Mystery Street *on hiatus indefinitely.*
Needs: Mystery/suspense (private eye/hard-boiled, amateur sleuth, cozy, police procedural, espionage). Receives 100+ unsolicited mss/month. Buys 10 mss/issue; 60 mss/year. Publishes ms 2-6 months after acceptance. Agented fiction 20%. Recently published work by John Lutz, Bill Pronzini, Kate Wilhelm. Length: 5,000 words preferred; 250 words minimum; 10,000 words maximum. Publishes short shorts. Length: 350 words. Often critiques or comments on rejected mss.
How to Contact: Send complete ms with cover letter. Should include estimated word count, 50-word bio, Social Security number, list of publications, list of organizations (M.W.A.) Reports in 1 week on queries; 1 month on mss. Send SASE for reply, return of ms or send a disposable copy of the ms. Simultaneous submissions OK (if noted). Sample copy for $3.95, 9×12 SAE and 4 first class stamps. Fiction guidelines for #10 SAE and 1 first class stamp. Reviews novel and short story collections.
Payment: Pays 4-7¢/word, subscription and 3 contributor's copies.
Terms: Pays on publication for first rights. Sends galleys to author.
Advice: "We are very interested in seeing stories with private-eye or police officer heroes/heroines."

MYSTERY TIME, An Anthology of Short Stories, (I), Box 2907, Decatur IL 62526. Editor: Linda Hutton. Booklet: 5½×8½; 44 pages; bond paper; illustrations. "Annual collection of short stories with a suspense or mystery theme for mystery buffs." Estab. 1983.

● Hutton Publications, publisher of *Mystery Time* and several other small journals has informed us of a number of changes. *Mystery Time* has a new address (see above) and *Christian Outlook*, *Rhyme Time*, *Story Time* and *Writer's Info* will no longer be published.

Needs: Suspense/mystery only. Receives 10-15 unsolicited fiction mss/month. Buys 10-12 mss/year. Recently published work by Elizabeth Lucknell, Helen Mitchell, Billie Marsh. Published new writers within the last year. Length: 1,500 words maximum. Occasionally critiques rejected mss and recommends other markets.

How to Contact: Send complete ms with SASE. "No cover letters." Simultaneous and previously published submissions OK. Reports in 1 month on mss. Publishes ms an average of 6-8 months after acceptance. Sample copy for $3.50. Fiction guidelines for #10 SAE and 1 first class stamp.

Payment: Pays ¼¢/word minimum; 1¢/word maximum; 1 contributor's copy; $2.50 charge for extras

Terms: Buys one-time rights. Buys reprints.

Advice: "Study a sample copy and the guidelines. Too many amateurs mark themselves as amateurs by submitting blind."

THE MYTHIC CIRCLE, (I), The Mythopoeic Society, Box 6707, Altadena CA 91001. Co-Editors: Tina Cooper and Christine Lowentrout. Magazine: 8½×11; 50 pages; high quality photocopy paper; illustrations. "A tri-quarterly fantasy-fiction magazine. We function as a 'writer's forum,' depending heavily on letters of comment from readers. We have a very occasional section called 'Mythopoeic Youth' in which we publish stories written by writers still in high school/junior high school, but we are not primarily oriented to young writers. We have several 'theme' issues (poetry, American fantasy) and plan more of these in the future." Triquarterly. Estab. 1987. Circ. 150.

Needs: Short fantasy. "No erotica, no graphic horror, no 'hard' science fiction." Receives 25 + unsolicited ms/month. Accepts 19-20 mss/issue. Publishes ms 1-2 years after acceptance. Published work by Charles de Lint, Gwyneth Hood, Angelee Sailer Anderson; published new writers within the last year. Length: 3,000 words average. Publishes short shorts. Length: 8,000 words maximum. Always critiques rejected mss; may recommend other markets."

How to Contact: Send complete ms with cover letter. "We give each ms a personal response. We get many letters that try to impress us with other places they've appeared in print—that doesn't matter much to us." Reports in 6-12 weeks. SASE. No simultaneous submissions. Accepts electronic submissions, IBM or MAC floppies. Sample copy for $6.50; fiction guidelines for #10 SASE.

Payment: Pays in contributor's copies; charges for extras.

Terms: Acquires one-time rights.

Advice: "There are very few places a fantasy writer can send to these days. *Mythic Circle* was started up because of this; also, the writers were not getting any kind of feedback when (after nine or ten months) their mss were rejected. We give the writers personalized attention—critiques, suggestions—and we rely on our readers to send us letters of comment on the stories we publish, so that the writers can see a response. Don't be discouraged by rejections, especially if personal comments/suggestions are offered."

NAHANT BAY, (II), What Cheer Press, 45 Puritan Rd., Swampscott MA 01907. (617)595-3722. Editors: Kim A. Pederson and Kalo Clarke. Magazine: 5¼×8½; 60-65 pages; 20 lb. bond paper; illustrations and photographs. "Short stories, essays and poetry for those interested in quality fiction." Annually. Estab. 1990.

Needs: Adventure, condensed/excerpted novel, contemporary, erotica, ethnic, experimental, fantasy, feminist, gay, historical, horror, humor/satire, lesbian, literary, mainstream, mystery/suspense, prose poem, psychic/supernatural/occult, regional, science fiction, translations. No romance, juvenile, teen, religious, confession. Receives 5-10 unsolicited mss/month. Accepts 2-3 mss/issue. Recently published work by Sara Spurgeon, Leonard Goodman and Jaimee Wristow Colbert. Length: 1,250 words minimum; 2,500 words maximum. Publishes short shorts. Sometimes critiques rejected mss and recommends other markets.

How to Contact: Send complete ms with cover letter. Include brief biographical information. Reports in 2 months on mss. SASE. Simultaneous submissions OK. Accepts electronic submissions via disk or modem. Sample copy for $6, SAE and 5 first class stamps. Fiction guidelines for #10 SAE and 1 first class stamp.

Payment: Pays contributor's copies. Charge for extras.
Terms: Acquires first North American serial rights.
Advice: Looks for striking use of language; compelling characters and story; sense of humor; sense of irony.

NASSAU REVIEW, (I, II), Nassau Community College, State University of New York, Stewart Ave., Garden City NY 11596. (516)222-7186. Editor: Paul A. Doyle. Fiction Editor: Virginia A. Moran. Magazine: 5½ × 8½; 80-120 pages; heavy stock paper; b&w illustrations and photographs. For "college teachers, libraries, educated college-level readers." Annually. Estab. 1964.
Needs: Contemporary, fantasy, historical (general), literary, mainstream, serialized novel. Receives 200 unsolicited mss/year. Accepts 5 mss/issue. Does not read mss January-August. Publishes ms 6 months after acceptance. Published work by Dick Wimmer, Louis Phillips, Norbert Petsch. Length: 800-1,500 words preferred; 1,000 words minimum; 1,500 words maximum. Publishes short shorts.
How to Contact: Send complete ms with cover letter. Include basic publication data. Reports in 1 month on queries; 8 months on mss. SASE. No simultaneous submissions. Sample copy for 9 × 12 SAE.
Payment: No payment.
Terms: Acquires first rights or one-time rights.
Advice: Looks for "imaginative, concrete writing on interesting characters and scenes." Send story ms before Oct. 15, $150 prize to best story published each year.

NCASA JOURNAL, A Publication of the National Coalition Against Sexual Assault, (I, IV), Suite 500, 123 S. 7th St., Springfield IL 62701. (217)753-4117. Editor: Becky Bradway. Newsletter: 8½ × 11; 12-16 pages; illustrations and photographs. "*NCASA Journal* is a forum for commentary, information and creative work concerning sexual assault and the anti-sexual assault movement." Quarterly. Estab. 1985. Circ. 1,500.
Needs: Condensed/excerpted novel, contemporary, ethnic, experimental, feminist, gay, humor/satire, literary, prose poem, regional, serialized novel, translations. Fiction and poetry are included in a special section, "Voices of Survivors." Work should be written by survivors of rape or incest. "All fiction must be grounded in a feminist perspective." Accepts 1-2 mss/issue; 4-6 mss/year. Publishes ms up to 1 year after acceptance. Length: 2,000 words average; 500 words minimum; 3,000 words maximum. Publishes short shorts. Sometimes critiques rejected mss and recommends other markets.
How to Contact: Send complete manuscript with cover letter. Reports in 2 weeks on mss. SASE. Simultaneous and reprint submissions OK. Sample copy $4. Fiction guidelines for SASE and 1 first class stamp.
Payment: Pays 3 contributor's copies.
Terms: Acquires first rights.
Advice: "*NCASA Journal* is looking for well-written, thoughtful fiction and poetry from survivors of rape and incest. Fiction may be based upon personal experience, but should utilize the mechanics of the story form: plot, characterization, dialogue, etc. Stories should have fully realized characters who ring true as fiction. Personal exploration should be done within the context of the story. Please do not be discouraged by rejection; this magazine has very limited space for creative work."

NEBO, A Literary Journal, (II), Arkansas Tech University, Dept. of English, Russellville AR 72801. (501)968-0256. Editors change each year. Contact Editor or Advisor: Dr. Michael Karl Ritchie. Literary, fiction and poetry magazine: 5 × 8; 50-60 pages. For a general, academic audience. Annually. Estab. 1983. Circ. 500.
Needs: Literary, mainstream, reviews. Receives 20-30 unsolicited fiction mss/month. Accepts 2 mss/issue; 6-10 mss/year. Does not read mss May 1-Sept. 1. Published new writers within the last year. Length: 3,000 words maximum. Also publishes literary essays, literary criticism, poetry. Occasionally critiques rejected mss.
How to Contact: Send complete ms with SASE and cover letter with bio. Simultaneous submissions OK. Reports in 3 months on mss. Publishes ms an average of 6 months after acceptance. Sample copy $5. "Submission deadlines for all work are Nov. 15 and Jan. 15 of each year." Reviews novels and short story collections.

Payment: Pays 1 contributor's copy.
Terms: Acquires one-time rights.
Advice: "A writer should carefully edit his short story before submitting it. Write from the heart and put everything on the line. Don't write from a phony or fake perspective. Frankly, many of the manuscripts we receive should be publishable with a little polishing. Manuscripts should *never* be submitted with misspelled words or on 'onion skin' or colored paper."

THE NEBRASKA REVIEW, (II), University of Nebraska at Omaha, ASH 212, Omaha NE 68182-0324. (402)554-2771. Fiction Editor: James Reed. Magazine: 5½×8½; 72 pages; 60 lb. text paper; chrome coat cover stock. "*TNR* attempts to publish the finest available contemporary fiction and poetry for college and literary audiences." Publishes 2 issues/year. Estab. 1973. Circ. 500.
Needs: Contemporary, humor/satire, literary and mainstream. Receives 40 unsolicited fiction mss/month. Acquires 4-5 mss/issue, 8-10 mss/year. Does not read April 1-September 1. Published work by Elizabeth Evans, Stephen Dixon and Peter Leach; published new writers within the last year. Length: 5,000-6,000 words average. Also publishes poetry.
How to Contact: Send complete ms with SASE. Reports in 1-2 months. Publishes ms an average of 6-9 months after acceptance. Sample copy $2.50.
Payment: 2 free contributor's copies plus 1 year subscription; $2 charge for extras.
Terms: Acquires first North American serial rights.
Advice: "Write 'honest' stories in which the lives of your characters are the primary reason for writing and techniques of craft serve to illuminate, not overshadow, the textures of those lives. Sponsors a $300 award/year—write for rules."

NEOPHYTE, (I, IV), Jemar Publishing, 11220 Hooper Rd., Baton Rouge LA 70818-3803. (504)261-4251. Editor: Jeffery W. Behrnes. Magazine: Digest-sized; 40 pages; bond paper; illustrations. "Science fiction/science fiction short stories." Bimonthly. Estab. 1991. Circ. 100.
Needs: Science fiction (hard science, soft/sociological) and articles on writing science fiction. Plans special fiction issue in the future. Receives 20-40 unsolicited mss/month. Accepts 2-4 mss/issue; 12-20 mss/year. Publishes ms 2-3 months after acceptance. Recently published work by J. Walker Bell, David J. Adams, H.L. Levine, Pam Chillemi-Yeager. Length: 3,000 words preferred; 2,000 words minimum; 10,000 words maximum. Sometimes critiques rejected mss and recommends other markets.
How to Contact: Send complete ms with cover letter. Include "short description of story and brief background on author (introduce yourself)." Reports in 2-4 weeks. SASE. May accept simultaneous submissions, if notified. Reprint submissions OK. Accepts electronic submissions via disk (IBM, ASCII or WordPerfect). Sample copy for $2. Fiction guidelines for #10 SAE and 1 first class stamp.
Payment: Pays in contributor's copies. Charge for extras.
Terms: Acquires one-time rights.
Advice: "The criteria used are that the story *is* a story in the science fiction genre and that it contains all components that make it a story. Read lots of science fiction, both the classics and the experimental. We work with new or previously unpublished authors."

‡NEW ANGLICAN REVIEW, A Monthly Forum for Anglican Fiction & Opinion, (I, IV), Dayspring Press, 18600 W. 58th Ave., Golden CO 80403-1070. (303)279-2462. Editor: C. Brainerd. Magazine: 5½×8½; 60 pages; 20 lb. bond paper; 40 lb. bond cover; line drawings. "NAR is open to all genres of general or technical interest to Anglicans—traditional or liberal." Monthly. Estab. 1986. Circ. 627.
● Dayspring Press, which is listed in the Small Press Section of this book, also publishes the *New Catholic Review* and *Fiction Forum*.
Needs: Anglican. Open to all categories "as long as there is some Anglican connection." Plans a "best of" annual. Receives 16 unsolicited mss/month. Buys 4 mss/issue; 58 mss/year. Publishes ms 1-3 months after acceptance. Agented fiction 10%. Recently published work by Alvin C. Davis, Jules A.T. Messner, Ford Pilkingham. Length: 500-2,500 words preferred. Publishes short shorts. Length: 50-500 words. Also publishes literary essays, literary criticism and poetry. Always critiques or comments on rejected mss.
How to Contact: Send complete ms with cover letter. Should include estimated word count, bio (500 words), Social Security number, list of publications. Reports in 1-4 weeks on queries; 1-3 months on mss. SASE for return of ms. Simultaneous and reprint submissions OK. Sample copy for $2.57 and 6×9 SAE. Fiction guidelines for $2.57 and 6×9 SAE. Reviews novels and short story collections.

Payment: Pays 50% of net sales.
Advice: *"NAR* is a forum publication, which means that it attempts to publish almost everything it receives. Therefore, the criteria of acceptability are purely mechanical rather than aesthetic in any sense."

‡NEW CATHOLIC REVIEW, A Monthly Forum for Catholic Fiction & Opinion, (I, IV), Dayspring Press, 18600 W. 58th Ave., Golden CO 80403-1070. (303)279-2462. Editor: John C. Brainerd. Magazine: 5½ × 8½; 60 pages; 20 lb. printer's bond paper; 40 lb. gloss cover; line drawings. *"NCR* is open to all genres of general and technical interest to Catholics – traditional and liberal." Monthly. Estab. 1987. Circ. 568.
Needs: Catholic. Open to any genre as long as there is a Catholic connection. Plans a "best of" annual. Receives 25 unsolicited mss/month. Buys 6 mss/issue; 70 mss/year. Publishes ms 1-3 months after acceptance. Agented fiction 10%. Recently published work by Harley Cracker, Thelma Johnson, Jason Orllard. Length: 500-2,500 words preferred. Publishes short shorts. Length: 500-1,500 words. Also publishes literary essays, literary criticism and poetry. Always critiques or comments on rejected mss.
How to Contact: Send complete ms with cover letter. Should include estimated word count, bio (500 words), Social Security number, list of publications. Reports in 1-4 weeks on queries; 1-3 months on mss. SASE for return of ms. Simultaneous and reprint submissions OK. Sample copy for $2.57 and 6×9 SAE. Fiction guidelines for $2.57 and 6×9 SAE. Reviews novels and short story collections.
Payment: Pays 50% of net sales.
Advice: *"NCR* is a forum publication, which means that it attempts to publish almost everything it receives. Therefore, the criteria of acceptability are purely mechanical rather than aesthetic in any sense."

THE NEW CRUCIBLE, A Magazine About Man and His Environment, (I), RRI, Box 76, Stark KS 66775-9802. Editor: Garry De Young. Magazine: 8½ × 11; variable number of pages; 20 lb. paper; soft cover; illustrations and photographs. Publishes "environmental material – includes the total human environment." Monthly. Plans special fiction issue. Estab. 1964.
Needs: Atheist. "Keep material concise, use clear line drawings. Environmentalists must be Materialists because the environment deals with matter. Thus also evolutionists. Keep this in mind. Manuscripts not returned. Will not accept religious or other racist or sexist material." Upcoming theme: "Why churches, synagogues and mosques must be taxed. We are looking for input on this theme!" Length: concise preferred. Publishes short shorts. Also publishes literary criticism, poetry. Sometimes critiques rejected mss. Publishes original cartoons.
How to Contact: Send complete ms with cover letter. Cover letter should include "biographical sketch of author." SASE. Simultaneous and reprint submissions OK. Sample copy for $2, 9×12 SAE and 4 first class stamps.
Payment: Pays in contributor's copies.
Terms: *Charges $1/page reading fee.* "Will discuss rights with author."
Advice: "Be gutsy! Don't be afraid to attack superstitionists. Attack those good people who remain so silent – people such as newspaper editors, so-called scientists who embrace superstition such as the Jesus myth or the Virgin Mary nonsense. We publish the works of Elbert Hubbard and also the Haldeman-Julius Little Blue Books which were the forerunners of the present paperbacks. Many are considered taboo by local libraries. We also solicit material critical of Zionist expansionism."

NEW DELTA REVIEW, (II), English Dept./Louisiana State University, Baton Rouge LA 70803. (504)388-5922. Editor: Janet Wondra. Fiction Editor: Joshua Russell. Magazine: 6×9; 75-125 pages; high quality paper; glossy card cover; illustrations; photographs. "No theme or style biases. Poetry, fiction primarily; also creative essays, literary interviews and reviews." Semi-annually. Estab. 1984.
● *New Delta Review* also sponsors the Eyster Prizes for fiction and poetry. See the listing in the Contest and Awards Section of this book. Work from the magazine has been included in the *Pushcart Prize* anthology.
Needs: Contemporary, experimental, humor/satire, literary, mainstream, prose poem, translations. Receives 120 unsolicited mss/ month. Accepts 4-8 mss/issue. Recently published work by Wayne Wilson, Charlotte Forbes, Mitchell Levenberg, Jacques Servin; published new writers within the last year. Length: 20 ms pages average; 250 words minimum. Publishes short shorts. Also publishes poetry. Sometimes critiques rejected mss.

How to Contact: Send complete ms with cover letter. Cover letter should include "credits, if any; no synopses, please." No simultaneous submissions. Reports on mss in 2-3 months. SASE. Mss deadlines September 1 for fall; February 15 for spring. Sample copy $4. Reviews novels and short story collections.

Payment: Pays in contributor's copies. Charge for extras.

Terms: Acquires first North American serial rights. Sponsors award for fiction writers in each issue. Eyster Prize-$50 plus notice in magazine. Mss selected for publication are automatically considered.

Advice: "The question we are asked most is still what *kind* of fiction we like. We answer: The good kind. Be brave. Explore your voice. Make sparks fly off your typewriter. Send your best work, even if others have rejected it. Don't send a story simply because it mentions the Mississippi. We seek top quality fiction, not local color. And don't forget the SASE if you want a response."

‡NEW ENGLAND REVIEW, (III), Middlebury College, Middlebury VT 05753. (802)388-3711, ext. 5075. Editors: T.R. Hummer, Devon Jersild. Magazine: 6×9; 140 pages; 70 lb paper; coated cover stock; illustrations; photos. A literary quarterly publishing fiction, poetry and essays on life and the craft of writing. For general readers and professional writers. Quarterly. Estab. 1977. Circ. 2,000.

 • *New England Review* has long been associated with Breadloaf Writer's Conference, held at Middlebury College.

Needs: Literary. Receives 250 unsolicited fiction mss/month. Accepts 5 mss/issue; 20 mss/year. Does not read ms June-August. Recently published work by W.D. Wetherell, Susan Minot, Gore Vidal; published new writers within the last year. Publishes ms 3-9 months after acceptance. Agented fiction: less than 5%. Publishes short shorts. Sometimes critiques rejected mss.

How to Contact: Send complete ms with cover letter. "Cover letters that demonstrate that the writer knows the magazine are the ones we want to read. We don't want hype, or hard-sell, or summaries of the author's intentions. Will consider simultaneous submissions, but must be stated as such." Reports in 8-10 weeks on mss. SASE.

Payment: Pays $10/page; subscription to magazine; contributor's copies; charge for extras.

Terms: Pays on publication. Acquires first rights and reprint rights. Sends galleys to author.

Advice: "It's best to send one story at a time, and wait until you hear back from us to try again."

NEW FRONTIER, (IV), 46 North Front, Philadelphia PA 19106. (215)627-5683. Editor: Sw. Virato. Magazine: 8×10; 48-60 pages; pulp paper stock; illustrations and photos. "We seek new age writers who have imagination yet authenticity." Monthly. Estab. 1981. Circ. 60,000.

Needs: New age. "A new style of writing is needed with a transformation theme." Receives 10-20 unsolicited mss/month. Accepts 1-2 mss/issue. Publishes ms 3 months after acceptance. Agented fiction "less than 5%." Published work by John White, Laura Anderson; published work by new writers within the last year. Length: 1,000 words average; 750 words minimum; 2,000 words maximum. Publishes short shorts. Length: 150-500 words. Occasionally critiques rejected mss and recommends other markets.

How to Contact: Send complete ms with cover letter, which should include author's bio and credits. Reports in 2 months on mss. SASE for ms. Simultaneous and reprint submissions OK. Sample copy for $2. Fiction guidelines for #10 SAE and 1 first class stamp.

Terms: Acquires first North American serial rights and one-time rights.

Advice: "The new age market is ready for a special kind of fiction and we are here to serve it. Don't try to get an A on your term paper. Be sincere, aware and experimental. Old ideas that are senile don't work for us. Be fully alive and aware—tune in to our new age audience/readership."

NEW LAUREL REVIEW, (II), 828 Lesseps St., New Orleans LA 70117. (504)947-6001. Editor: Lee Meitzen Grue. Magazine: 6×9; 120 pages; 60 lb. book paper; Sun Felt cover; illustrations; photo essays. Journal of poetry, fiction, critical articles and reviews. "We have published such internationally known writers as James Nolan, Tomris Uyar and Yevgeny Yevtushenko." Readership: "Literate, adult audiences as well as anyone interested in writing with significance, human interest, vitality, subtlety, etc." Annually. Estab. 1970. Circ. 500.

Needs: Literary, contemporary, fantasy and translations. No "dogmatic, excessively inspirational or political" material. Acquires 1-2 fiction mss/issue. Receives approximately 50 unsolicited fiction mss each month. Length: about 10 printed pages. Also publishes literary essays, literary criticism, poetry. Critiques rejected mss when there is time.

How to Contact: Send complete ms with SASE. Reports in 3 months. Sample copy $6. Reviews novels and short story collections.
Payment: Pays 1 contributor's copy.
Terms: Acquires first rights.
Advice: "We are interested in international issues pointing to libraries around the world. Write fresh, alive 'moving' work. Not interested in egocentric work without any importance to others. Be sure to watch simple details such as putting one's name and address on ms and clipping all pages together. Caution: Don't use overfancy or trite language."

NEW LETTERS MAGAZINE, (I, II), University of Missouri-Kansas City, 5100 Rockhill Rd., Kansas City MO 64110. (816)235-1168. Fax: (816)235-5191. Editor: James McKinley. Magazine: 14 lb. cream paper; illustrations. Quarterly. Estab. 1971 (continuation of *University Review*, founded 1935). Circ. 2,500.
    ● This magazine is another "literary root" according to *Esquire* (July 1992).
Needs: Contemporary, ethnic, experimental, humor/satire, literary, mainstream, translations. No "bad fiction in any genre." Upcoming theme: New Letters Literary Awards Issue (Winter 1993). Published work by Richard Rhodes, Jascha Kessler, Josephine Jacobsen; published work by new writers within the last year. Agented fiction: 10%. Also publishes short shorts. Occasionally critiques rejected mss.
How to Contact: Send complete ms with cover letter. Does not read mss May 15-October 15. Reports in 3 weeks on queries; 6-8 weeks on mss. SASE for ms. No simultaneous or multiple submissions. Sample copy: $8.50 for issues older than 5 years; $5.50 for 5 years or less.
Payment: Pays honorarium—depends on grant/award money; 2 contributor's copies. Sends galleys to author.
Advice: "Seek publication of representative chapters in high-quality magazines as a way to the book contract. Try literary magazines first."

NEW MEXICO HUMANITIES REVIEW, (II), Humanities Dept., New Mexico Tech, Box A, Socorro NM 87801. (505)835-5445. Editors: John Rothfork and Jerry Bradley. Magazine: 5½ × 9½; 150 pages; 60 lb. Lakewood paper; 482 ppi cover stock; illustrations; photos. Review of poetry, essays and prose of Southwest. Readership: academic but not specialized. Published 2 times/year. Estab. 1978. Circ. 650.
Needs: Literary and regional. "No formula." Accepts 40-50 mss/year. Receives approximately 50 unsolicited fiction mss/month. Length: 6,000 words maximum. Publishes short shorts. Critiques rejected mss "when there is time." Sometimes recommends other markets.
How to Contact: Send complete ms with SASE. Reports in 2 months. Publishes ms an average of 6 months after acceptance. Sample copy $5.
Payment: Pays 1 year subscription.
Terms: Sends galleys to author.
Advice: Mss are rejected because they are "unimaginative, predictable and technically flawed. Don't be afraid to take literary chances—be daring, experiment."

NEW ORLEANS REVIEW, (II), Box 195, Loyola University, New Orleans LA 70118. (504)865-2294. Editor: John Biguenet. Magazine: 8½ × 11; 100 pages; 60 lb. Scott offset paper; 12 + King James C1S cover stock; photos. "Publishes poetry, fiction, translations, photographs, nonfiction on literature and film. Readership: those interested in current culture, literature." Quarterly. Estab. 1968. Circ. 1,000.
Needs: Literary, contemporary, translations. Buys 9-12 mss/year. Length: under 40 pages.
How to Contact: Send complete ms with SASE. Does not accept simultaneous submissions. Accepts computer printout submissions. Accepts disk submissions; inquire about system compatibility. Prefers hard copy with disk submission. Reports in 3 months. Sample copy $9.
Payment: "Inquire."
Terms: Pays on publication for first North American serial rights. Sends galleys to author.

THE NEW PRESS LITERARY QUARTERLY, (II), 53-35 Hollis Court Blvd., Flushing NY 11365. (718)229-6782. Publisher: Bob Abramson. Magazine: 8½ × 11; 32 pages; medium bond paper and glossy cover stock; illustrations and photographs. "Poems, short stories, commentary, personal journalism. Original, informative and entertaining." Quarterly. Estab. 1984.
Needs: Adventure, confession, ethnic, experimental, fantasy, humor/satire, literary, mainstream, prose poem, serialized/excerpted novel, spiritual, sports, translations. No gratuitous violence. Upcoming theme: Summer/Beach. Receives 20 unsolicited mss/month. Accepts 4 mss/issue; 16 mss/year. Publishes ms 12 months after acceptance. Published new writers within the last year. Length: 4,000

words maximum; 100 words minimum. Also publishes literary essays, literary criticism, poetry. Sometimes critiques rejected mss and recommends other markets.

How to Contact: Send complete ms with cover letter. Reports in 2 months. SASE. "Fiction over 10 pages only reviewed through June." Simultaneous and reprint submissions OK. Sample copy $4; fiction guidelines free. $15 for one-year (4 issues) subscription.

Payment: Pays 3 contributor's copies, $25 for each prose piece and $75 for the best essay in each issue.

Terms: Buys one-time rights.

THE NEW QUARTERLY, New Directions in Canadian Writing, (II, IV), ELPP, University of Waterloo, Waterloo, Ontario N2L 3G1 Canada. (519)885-1212, ext. 2837. Managing Editor: Mary Merikle. Fiction Editors: Peter Hinchcliffe, Kim Jernigan. Magazine: 6×9; 80-120 pages; perfect-bound cover, b&w cover photograph; photos with special issues. "We publish poetry, short fiction, excerpts from novels, interviews. We are particularly interested in writing which stretches the bounds of realism. Our audience includes those interested in Canadian literature." Quarterly.

Needs: "I suppose we could be described as a 'literary' magazine. We look for writing which is fresh, innovative, well crafted. We promote beginning writers alongside more established ones. Ours is a humanist magazine—no gratuitous violence, though we are not afraid of material which is irreverent or unconventional. Our interest is more in the quality than the content of the fiction we see." Published recent special issues on magic, realism in Canadian writing, family fiction and Canadian Mennonite writing. Receives approx. 50 unsolicited mss/month. Buys 5-6 mss/issue; 20-24 mss/year. Publishes ms usually within 6 months after acceptance. Recently published work by Diane Schoemperlen, Patrick Roscoe and Steven Heighton; published new writers within the last year. Length: up to 20 pages. Publishes short shorts. Also publishes poetry. Sometimes recommends other markets.

How to Contact: Send complete ms with cover letter, which should include a short biographical note. Reports in 1-2 weeks on queries; approx. 3 months on mss. SASE for ms. Sample copy for $4.

Payment: Pays $100 and contributor's copies.

Terms: Pays on publication for first North American serial rights.

Advice: "Send only one well polished manuscript at a time. Persevere. Find your own voice. The primary purpose of little literary magazines like ours is to introduce new writers to the reading public. However, because we want them to appear at their best, we apply the same standards when judging novice work as when judging that of more established writers."

the new renaissance, (II), 9 Heath Rd., Arlington MA 02174. Fiction Editors: Louise T. Reynolds, Harry Jackel and Patricia Michaud. Magazine: 6×9; 144-208 pages; 70 lb. paper; laminated cover stock; artwork; photos. "An international magazine of ideas and opinions, emphasizing literature and the arts, *tnr* takes a classicist position in literature and the arts. Publishes a variety of very diverse, quality fiction, always well crafted, sometimes experimental. *tnr* is unique among literary magazines for its marriage of the literary and visual arts with political/sociological articles and essays. We publish the beginning as well as the emerging and established writer." Biannually. Estab. 1968. Circ. 1,500.

● Few magazines can make this boast: October 1991 was declared "*the new renaissance* Month in Greater Boston," by Boston's Mayor Flynn. Work published in *the new renaissance* has been chosen for inclusion in *Editor's Choice III*.

Needs: Literary, humor, prose poem, translations, off-beat, quality fiction and, occasionally, experimental fiction. "We don't want to see heavily plotted stories with one-dimensional characters or heavily academic or 'poetic' writing, or fiction that is self-indulgent." Buys 5-6 mss/issue, 8-13 mss/year. Receives approximately 75-130 unsolicited fiction mss each month. Reads only from Jan. 2 thru June 30. Agented fiction approx. 8-12%. Recently published work by Philip Greene, Kurt Kusenbert, Lauren Hahn (translation). Published new writers within the last year. Length of fiction: 3-36 pages. Also publishes literary essays, literary criticism, poetry. Comments on rejected mss "when there is time and when we want to encourage the writer or believe we can be helpful."

How to Contact: Send complete ms with SASE (IRCs) of sufficient size for return. "Inform us if multiple submission." Reluctantly accepts simultaneous submissions. Reports in 5-8 months. Publishes ms an average of 18-24 months after acceptance. Sample copy $6.75 for 2 back issues, $7.50 or $9 for recent issue. Reviews novels and short story collections.

Payment: Pays $40-80 after publication; 1 contributor's copy. Query for additional copies.

Terms: Buys all rights in case of a later *tnr* book collection; otherwise, rights return to the writer.

Advice: "We represent one of the best markets for writers because we publish a greater variety (of styles, statements, tones) than most magazines, small or large. Study *tnr* and then send your best work; we will read 2 manuscripts only if they are 4 pages or less; for mss 6 pages or more, send only one ms.

Manuscripts are rejected because writers do not study their markets and send out indiscriminately. Fully one-quarter of our rejected manuscripts fall into this category; others are from tyro writers who haven't yet mastered their craft or writers who are not honest or who haven't fully thought their story through or from writers who are careless about language. Also, many writers feel compelled to 'explain' their stories to the reader instead of letting the story speak for itself."

NEW VIRGINIA REVIEW, An anthology of literary work by and important to Virginians, (II), 1306 East Cary St., 2A, Richmond VA 23219. (804)782-1043. Editor: Mary Flinn. Magazine: 6½×10; 180 pages; high quality paper; coated, color cover stock. "Approximately one half of the contributors have Virginia connections; the other authors are serious writers of contemporary fiction. Occasionally guest editors set a specific theme for an issue, e.g. 1986 Young Southern Writers." Published January, May and October. Estab. 1978. Circ. 2,000.
Needs: Contemporary, experimental, literary, mainstream, serialized/excerpted novel. No blue, sci-fi, romance, children's. Receives 50-100 unsolcited fiction mss/month. Accepts an average of 15 mss/issue. Does not read from April 1 to September 1. Publishes ms an average of 6-9 months after acceptance. Length: 5,000-6,500 words average; no minimum; 8,000 words maximum. Also publishes poetry. Sometimes critiques rejected mss.
How to Contact: Send complete ms with cover letter, name, address, telephone number, brief biographical comment. Reports in 6 weeks on queries; up to 6 months on mss. "Will answer questions on status of ms." SASE. Sample copy $13.50 and 9x12 SAE with 5 first-class stamps.
Payment: Pays $10/printed page; contributor's copies; charge for extras, ½ cover price.
Terms: Pays on publication for first North American serial rights. Sponsors contests and awards for Virginia writers only.
Advice: "Since we publish a wide range of styles of writing depending on the tastes of our guest editors, all we can say is—try to write good strong fiction, stick to it, and try again with another editor."

‡NEW VOICES IN POETRY AND PROSE, (I), New Voices Publishing, P.O. Box 52196, Shreveport LA 71135. (318)797-8243. Editor: Cheryl White. Magazine: 8½×11; 16-24 pages; linen paper; illustrations. " Dedicated to publishing new writers; appreciate many types of fiction." Semiannually. Estab. 1991. Circ. 400.
 • *New Voices* also sponsors a contest listed in this book.
Needs: Adventure, fantasy, historical (general), horror, humor/satire, literary, mainstream/contemporary, mystery/suspense, psychic/supernatural/occult, regional, religious/inspirational, romance, science fiction (soft/sociological). No "controversial themes; political; racist." Receives 20 unsolicited mss/month. Buys 3 mss/issue; 6-8 mss/year. Publishes ms 6 months after acceptance. Recently published work by Dan Schwala, Joan Shaw. Length: 4,000 words maximum. Publishes short shorts. Also publishes poetry. Often critiques or comments on rejected mss.
How to Contact: Send complete ms with cover letter. Should also send estimated word count, very brief bio and list of publications with submission. Reports in 2 months on mss. Send SASE (IRC) for return of ms. Will consider simultaneous submissions and reprints. Sample copy $5. Fiction guidelines free. Reviews novels and short story collections.
Payment: Pays 1 contributor's copy.
Terms: Acquires one-time rights.
Advice: "A short story appeals to us when it *really tells a story* about human nature, or offers up a basic lesson about life. Develop characters well, so they are fleshed-out and real to life. Complicated plots can be a hindrance; stick to the simple."

‡NeWEST REVIEW (II, IV), Box 394, Sub P.O. 6, Saskatoon, Saskatchewan S7N 0W0 Canada. Editor: Gail Youngberg. Magazine: 48 pages; book stock; illustrations; photos. Magazine devoted to western Canada regional issues; "fiction, reviews, poetry for middle- to high-brow audience." Bimonthly (6 issues per year). Estab. 1975. Circ. 1,000.
Needs: "We want fiction of high literary quality, whatever its form and content. But we do have a heavy regional emphasis." Receives 15-20 unsolicited mss/month. Buys 1 ms/issue; 10 mss/year. Length: 2,500 words average; 1,500 words minimum; 5,000 words maximum. Sometimes recommends other markets.
How to Contact: "We like *brief* cover letters. Reports very promptly in a short letter. SAE, IRCs or Canadian postage. No multiple submissions. Sample copy $3.50.
Payment: Pays $100 maximum.
Terms: Pays on publication for one-time rights.
Advice: "Polish your writing. Develop your story line. Give your characters presence. If we, the readers, are to care about the people you create, you too must take them seriously."

Close-up

Francine Ringold
Editor-in-Chief
Nimrod

© Steve Jennings

"Our mission is to serve both the writer and the reader," says *Nimrod* Editor-in-Chief, Francine Ringold. "We do this through discovery of the language and the literature which, in its different shapes and possibilities, moves us toward delight and understanding."

Nimrod is a semiannual, devoting one of its issues to a theme determined by its editorial board. World events and current issues play a major role in determining these themes, and the editors have displayed a knack for focusing on nations and issues at the center of world attention. For instance, the spring issue in 1990 presented literature from the republics of the former Soviet Union. The 1992 edition offered work by Eastern European authors, including writers from war-torn Yugoslavia. The 1993 edition will feature fiction and poetry of Australian authors, whose country is struggling to redefine its relationship to its original inhabitants and the rest of the region.

The second of the two issues each year features fiction and poetry from two sources. The "Awards" issue contains the finalists and honorable mentions from the annual Ruth G. Hardman Literary Awards competition as well as the best of unsolicited submissions during the year. *Nimrod* accepts unsolicited submissions, receiving about 100 per month of both poetry and prose. However, if a particular unsolicited work is good and time remains, the fiction editor often recommends the writer enter it in the fiction contest.

What is good fiction for *Nimrod*? Ringold says it is writing "in which neither content nor aesthetic is irrelevant. 'Voice' is important—something that is a combination of style and content." A good beginning will also spark attention. "That first paragraph must be arresting," she says. "Energy, vigor and vitality are important."

Ringold uses words like surprising and arresting when describing the work she prefers. She agrees unusual approaches to fiction, handled well, are often the difference between getting and not getting a reading. "The element of surprise, what we used to call the 'hook,' and a complete text in which each moment is fresh and an enlightenment—both are important," says Ringold. "It is that resonance that will draw the reader on."

However, Ringold advises against defining "arresting" fiction as prose using style or story line that is different simply for the sake of being different. "I don't like overwriting or writing that is precious or calls attention to itself—in other words, writing that takes more delight in technique and craft than in character and the story itself."

Nimrod's editor also advises both caution and risk-taking to aspiring writers. "Don't be eager to publish," she says. "Be eager to write well. On the other hand, don't be afraid to submit; you may get good advice. And be willing to listen to that advice, especially on an unsolicited submission. Remember, it's from someone who has taken the time, someone who cares and is tantalized enough by your work to comment."

—Michael Oxley

NEXT PHASE, (I, II), Phantom Press, 33 Court St., New Haven CT 06511. (203)772-1697. Editor: Kim Means. 8½×11; 16 pages. "Features the best of fiction, poetry and illustration by up-and-coming writers and artists. We publish quality work as long as it is environmentally and humanely oriented." Quarterly. Estab. 1989. Circ. 1,000.

Needs: Experimental, fantasy. Receives 10-15 unsolicited mss/month. Accepts 3 mss/issue; 15 mss/year. Publishes short shorts. Also publishes poetry. Critiques rejected mss and recommends other markets.

How to Contact: Send complete manuscript with cover letter. SASE. Simultaneous and reprint submissions OK. Reports in 3 weeks. Sample copy for $3 per issue includes postage.

Payment: Pays contributor's copies.

Terms: Acquires one-time rights.

Advice: "We are now accepting a broader range of fiction at longer lengths—up to 2,000 words. Environmentally-oriented fiction or fantasy, experimental pieces encouraged."

NIGHT OWL'S NEWSLETTER, (II, IV), Julian Associates, 6831 Spencer Hwy., #203, Pasadena TX 77505. (404)889-2597. Editor: Robin Parker. Newsletter: 8½×11; 16 pages; 20 lb. copy paper; cartoons. A newsletter for "night owls—people who can't sleep through much of the hours between midnight and 6 a.m. and often want to sleep late in the morning." Quarterly. Estab. 1990.

Needs: Excerpted novel, experimental, fantasy, humor/satire, literary. "All variations must relate to the subject of night and/or night owls. No erotica." Accepts 1-2 mss/issue; 4-10 mss/year. Publishes ms 3-9 months after acceptance. Recently published work by Catharine Mason. Length: 500-700 words preferred; 250 words minimum; 1,000 words maximum. Publishes short shorts. Critiques or comments on rejected mss. Recommends other markets.

How to Contact: Send complete ms with cover letter. Include short bio and credits. Reports in 2-3 months. SASE. Simultaneous and reprint submissions OK. Accepts electronic submissions. Sample copy for $3.50. Fiction guidelines for #10 SAE and 1 first-class stamp.

Payment: Pays $1 minimum plus 1 contributor's copy; charges for extras.

Terms: Buys one-time rights.

Advice: "We are most interested in a humorous and intelligent approach to the problem of people not being able to get to sleep or stay asleep at night and/or unable to wake up in the morning. This means the writer must understand the problem and have information to help others (besides suggesting drugs, alcohol or sex) or offer humorous support."

NIGHTSUN, Department of English, Frostburg State University, Frostburg MD 21532. Co-Editors: Doug DeMars and Barbara Wilson. Magazine: 5½×8½; 64 pages; recycled paper. "Although *Nightsun* is now primarily a journal of poetry and interviews, we are still looking for excellent short-short fiction (3 pgs. maximum)." Annually. Estab. 1981. Circ. 300-500.

How to Contact: Send inquiry with SASE. No simultaneous submissions. Reports within 3 months. Sample copy $6.50.

Payment: Pays 2 contributor's copies.

Terms: Acquires one-time rights (rights revert to author after publication).

NIMROD, International Journal of Prose and Poetry, (II), Arts & Humanities Council of Tulsa, 2210 S. Main, Tulsa OK 74114. Editor-in-Chief: Francine Ringold. Magazine: 6×9; 160 pages; 60 lb. white paper; illustrations; photos. "We publish one thematic issue and one awards issue each year. "A recent theme was 'Making Language: 35th Anniversary Issue,' a compilation of poetry, prose and fiction by authors from countries such as Austria, Bulgaria, Finland, Germany, Greece, Romania, Hungary. We seek vigorous, imaginative, quality writing." Published semiannually. Estab. 1956. Circ. 3,000+.

• Look for the Close-up interview with *Nimrod's* Editor-in-Chief Francine Ringold in this book.

Needs: "We accept contemporary poetry and/or prose. May submit adventure, ethnic, experimental, prose poem, science fiction or translations." Upcoming themes: "Australian Issue" (Spring, 1993); "Canadian Issue" (1994). Receives 120 unsolicited fiction mss/month. Published work by Josephine Jacobson, Alice Walker, Francois Camoin, Gish Jen; published new writers within the last year. Length: 7,500 words maximum. Also publishes poetry.

How to Contact: Reports in 3 weeks-3 months. Sample copy: "to see what *Nimrod* is all about, send $4.50 for a back issue. To receive a recent awards issue, send $6.90 (postage incl.)
Payment: Pays 2 contributor's copies, plus $5/page up to $25 total per author per issue.
Terms: Buys one-time rights.
Advice: "Read the magazine. Write well. Be courageous. No superfluous words. No clichés. Keep it tight but let your imagination flow. Read the magazine. Strongly encourage writers to send #10 SASE for brochure for annual literary contest with prizes of $1,000 and $500.

NO IDEA MAGAZINE, (I), P.O. Box 14636, Gainesville FL 32604-4636. Editor: Var Thëlin. Magazine: 8½×11; 64 pages, 16 four-color pages; 37 lb. newsprint; illustrations and photographs. Each issue comes with a hard-vinyl 7-inch record. "Mostly underground/punk/hardcore music and interviews, but we like delving into other art forms as well. We publish what we feel is good—be it silly or moving." Sporadically. Estab. 1985.
Needs: Adventure, contemporary, experimental, fantasy, horror, humor/satire, mystery/suspense (amateur sleuth, private eye), science fiction. "Humor of a strange, odd manner is nice. We're very open." Receives 5-10 mss/month. Publishes ms up to 6 months after acceptance. Publishes mostly short shorts. Length: 1-6 pages typed.
How to Contact: Send complete manuscript with cover letter. Simultaneous submissions OK. Sample copy $3. Checks to Var Thëlin. Reviews novels and short story collections.
Payment: Pays in contributor's copies.
Terms: Acquires one-time rights.
Advice: "A query with $3 will get you a sample of our latest issue and answers to any questions asked. Just because we haven't included a writer's style of work before doesn't mean we won't print their work. Perhaps we've never been exposed to their style before."

THE NOCTURNAL LYRIC, (I), Box 77171, San Francisco CA 94107-7171. (415)621-8920. Editor: Susan Moon. Digest: 5½×8½; 26 pages; illustrations. "We are a non-profit literary journal, dedicated to printing fiction by new writers for the sole purpose of getting read by people who otherwise might have never seen their work." Bimonthly. Estab. 1987. Circ. 150.
Needs: Experimental, fantasy, horror, humor/satire, psychic/supernatural/occult, science fiction, poetry. "We will give priority to unusual, creative pieces." Receives approx. 50 unsolicited mss/month. Publishes ms 6-10 months after acceptance. Publishes short shorts. Length: 2,000 words maximum. Also publishes poetry.
How to Contact: Send complete ms with cover letter. Cover letter should include "something about the author, what areas of fiction he/she is interested in." Reports in 1 week on queries; 2-3 months on mss. SASE. Simultaneous and reprint submissions OK. Sample copy $1.50 (checks made out to Susan Moon, editor). Fiction guidelines for #10 SAE and 1 first class stamp.
Payment: No payment. Pays neither in cash nor contributor's copies.
Terms: Publication not copyrighted.
Advice: "Please stop wasting your postage sending us things that are in no way bizarre. We're getting more into strange, surrealistic horror and fantasy, or silly, satirical horror. If you're avant-garde, we want you! We're mainly accepting things that are bizarre all the way through, as opposed to ones that only have a surprise bizarre ending."

‡NOISY CONCEPT, The Journal of Voluntary Insanity, (I), #3, 960 Morris Rd., Kent OH 44240. (216)678-1576. Editor: "Insane" Mike Thain. Magazine: Digest-sized; bond paper; bond cover; illustrations. "Generally we intend to promote voluntary insanity, currently through such topics as hemp legalization, animal rights, anti-authoritarianism, vegetarianism and music. all viewpoints are considered, yet stupidity is ridiculed." Bimonthly. Estab. 1989. Circ. 200-500.
Needs: Adventure, erotica, experimental, fantasy (science fantasy), feminist, horror, humor/satire, literary, mainstream/contemporary, mystery/suspense, psychic/supernatural/occult, science fiction (hard science, soft/sociological), young adult/teen (10-18 years). Does not want to see "anything that promotes fascism, oppression or the capitalist machine." Buys 1 ms/issue; 6 ms/year. Publishes ms up to 1 year after acceptance. Length: 400 words average; 500 words maximum. Publishes short shorts. Also publishes poetry.
How to Contact: Send complete ms. Reports in 2 months on ms. Send SASE (IRC) for reply, return of ms or send disposable copy of ms. Will consider simultaneous submissions, reprints, electronic submissions (IBM WordPerfect 5.0, 3.5 in. disk *only*). Sample copy 50¢. Reviews novels and short story collections.

Payment: Pays 1 contributor's copy. Additional copies 25¢ each/10 or more.
Terms: Acquires one-time rights. Not copyrighted.
Advice: "Insanity is a label attached to a person who is different. It is synonymous with 'originality,' 'creativity,' and 'individuality.' I make no rules and I expect writers not to follow them. Don't read a sample copy first. Just write from the heart. Too many writers want to fit into a mold because too many publications have too many rules."

NOMOS, Studies in Spontaneous Order, (II, IV), Nomos Press, Inc., 257 Chesterfield, Glen Ellyn IL 60137. (708)858-7184. Editor: Carol B. Low. 8½×11; 32 pages; original illustrations. "Essays, poems, fiction, letters relating to Libertarian concepts and culture for a Libertarian audience." Quarterly. Estab. 1982. Circ. 450 paid; 1,000 total.
Needs: Historical (general), humor/satire, mystery/suspense (police procedurals), science fiction (hard science). Upcoming theme: Environmental Issues. "We are a strictly hard-core Libertarian magazine and only consider relevant fiction. Reviews of novels also accepted." Receives 1 unsolicited ms/month. Accepts 1 ms/issue; 4 mss/year. Publishes ms 4-8 months after acceptance. Length: 500-2,000 words average; 2,000 words maximum. Publishes short shorts. Occasionally critiques rejected mss.
How to Contact: Send complete manuscript with cover letter. Reports in 5-6 months on mss. SASE. No simultaneous submissions. Accepts electronic submissions. Sample copy $4.50. Fiction guidelines for #10 SAE. Reviews novels.
Payment: Pays choice of subscription to magazine or contributor's copies.
Terms: Acquires one-time rights. Sends galleys or letter detailing edits or desired corrections to author.

THE NORTH AMERICAN REVIEW, University of Northern Iowa, Cedar Falls IA 50614. (319)273-6455. Editor: Robley Wilson. Publishes quality fiction. Quarterly. Estab. 1815. Circ. 4,500.
Needs: "We will not be reading any new material until January, 1994, due to backlog."
How to Contact: Send complete ms with SASE. Sample copy $3.50.
Payment: Pays approximately $10/printed page; 2 contributor's copies. $3.50 charge for extras.
Terms: Pays on acceptance for first North American serial rights.
Advice: "We stress literary excellence and read 3,000 manuscripts a year to find an average of 35 stories that we publish. Please *read* the magazine first."

NORTH ATLANTIC REVIEW, (II), North Eagle Corp. of NY, 15 Arbutus Ln., Stony Brook NY 11790. (516)751-7886. Editor: John Gill. Magazine: 7×9; 200 pages; glossy cover. "General interest." Estab. 1989. Circ. 1,000.
Needs: "General fiction and fiction about the sixties." Has published special fiction issue. Accepts 12 mss/issue; 25 mss/year. Publishes ms 6-10 months after acceptance. Length: 3,000-7,000 words average. Publishes short shorts. Sometimes critiques rejected mss and recommends other markets.
How to Contact: Send complete ms with cover letter. Reports in 4-6 months on queries. SASE. Simultaneous submissions OK. Sample copy for $10.

NORTH DAKOTA QUARTERLY, (II), University of North Dakota, Box 8237, University Station, Grand Forks ND 58202. (701)777-3321. Editor: Robert W. Lewis. Fiction Editor: William Borden. Poetry Editor: Jay Meek. Magazine: 6×9; 200 pages; bond paper; illustrations; photos. Magazine publishing "essays in humanities; some short stories; some poetry." University audience. Quarterly. Estab. 1910. Circ. 800.
Needs: Contemporary, ethnic, experimental, feminist, historical (general), humor/satire and literary. Upcoming theme: "Contemporary Yugoslav literature in English translation" (Fall 1992). Plans an annual anthology or special edition. Receives 15-20 unsolicited mss/month. Acquires 4 mss/issue; 16 mss/year. Recently published work by Jerry Bumpus, Dusty Sklar, Daniel Curley; published new writers within the last year. Length: 3,000-4,000 words average. Also publishes literary essays, literary criticism, poetry. Sometimes critiques rejected mss.
How to Contact: Send complete ms with cover letter. "But they need not be much more than hello; please read this story; I've published (if so, best examples) . . ." SASE. Reports in 3 months. Publishes ms an average of 6-8 months after acceptance. Sample copy $5. Reviews novels and short story collections.

Payment: Pays 5 contributor's copies; 20% discount for extras; year's subscription.
Terms: Acquires one-time rights.
Advice: "We may publish a higher average number of stories in the future — 4 rather than 2. Read widely. Write, write; revise, revise."

NORTH EAST ARTS MAGAZINE, (II), Boston Arts Organization, Inc., J.F.K. Station, P.O. Box 6061, Boston MA 02114. Editor: Mr. Leigh Donaldson. Magazine: 6½ × 9½; 32-40 pages; matte finish paper; card stock cover; illustrations and photographs. Bimonthly. Estab. 1990. Circ. 750.
  • For more on North East ARTS see the Close-up interview with Editor Leigh Donaldson in the 1992 *Poet's Market*.
Needs: Ethnic, gay, historical (general), literary, mystery/suspense (private eye), prose poem. No obscenity, racism, sexism, etc. Upcoming themes: "the culinary arts, window-dressing, unique boat building, jazz history . . ." Receives 50 unsolicited mss/month. Accepts 1-2 mss/issue; 5-7 mss/year. Publishes ms 2-4 months after acceptance. Agented fiction 20%. Length: 750 words preferred. Publishes short shorts. Sometimes critiques rejected mss.
How to Contact: Send complete ms with cover letter. Include short bio. Reports in 3 weeks on queries; 2-4 months on mss. SASE. Simultaneous submissions OK. Sample copy for $4.50, SAE and 75¢ postage. Fiction guidelines free.
Payment: Pays 2 contributor's copies.
Terms: Acquires first North American serial rights. Sometimes sends galleys to author.
Advice: Looks for "creative/innovative use of language and style. Unusual themes and topics."

THE NORTHWEST GAY & LESBIAN READER, Art, Opinion and Literature, (I, IV), Beyond the Closet Bookstore, 1501 Belmont Ave., Seattle WA 98122. (206)322-4609. Editor: Ron Whiteaker. Tabloid: 11 × 17; 16 pages; newsprint paper, illustrations, photographs. "A wide range of formats reflecting the gay/lesbian/bisexual experience." Bimonthly. Estab. 1989. Circ. 4,000.
Needs: Gay, lesbian, bisexual. "Light erotica OK. No hard-core erotica, or 'abusive attitude' fiction." Receives 2 unsolicited mss/month. Accepts 1 ms/issue. Publishes ms 2 months after acceptance. Published work by William Freeberg, Aubrey Hart Sparks, Jill Sunde. Length: 2,000 words preferred; 1,000 words minimum; 3,500 words maximum. Publishes short shorts.
How to Contact: Send complete ms with cover letter. Include "a bit about the story and its author." Reports in 2 weeks on queries; 2 months on mss. SASE. Accepts electronic submissions — IBM compatible disk in generic (ASCII) word processing format. Sample copy for 75¢, 9 × 12 SAE and 3 first class stamps. Fiction guidelines for #10 SAE and 1 first class stamp.
Payment: Pays in contributor's copies and free subscription.
Terms: Acquires one-time rights.
Advice: "A story that is clever and well-written and contains original ideas is considered first, rather than the hackneyed, over-done story lines containing redundant dogma and irritating buzzwords. Reflect the gay/lesbian/bisexual experience."

NORTHWEST REVIEW, (II), 369 PLC, University of Oregon, Eugene OR 97403. (503)346-3957. Editor: John Witte. Fiction Editor: Hannah Wilson. Magazine: 6 × 9; 140-160 pages; high quality cover stock; illustrations; photos. "A general literary review featuring poems, stories, essays and reviews, circulated nationally and internationally. For a literate audience in avant-garde as well as traditional literary forms; interested in the important younger writers who have not yet achieved their readership." Triannually. Estab. 1957. Circ. 1,200.
Needs: Literary, contemporary, feminist, translations and experimental. Accepts 4-5 mss/issue, 12-15 mss/year. Receives approximately 100 unsolicited fiction mss each month. Published work by Susan Stark, Madison Smartt Bell, Maria Flook, Charles Marvin; published new writers within the last year. Length: "Mss longer than 40 pages are at a disadvantage." Also publishes literary essays, literary criticism, poetry. Critiques rejected mss when there is time. Sometimes recommends other markets.

Stay informed! Keep up with changes in the market by using the latest edition of Novel & Short Story Writer's Market. *If this is 1994 or later, buy a new edition at your favorite bookstore or order directly from Writer's Digest Books.*

How to Contact: Send complete ms with SASE. "No simultaneous submissions are considered." Reports in 3-4 months. Sample copy $3.50. Reviews novels and short story collections. Send books to John Witte.
Payment: Pays 3 contributor's copies and a one-year subscription; 40% discount on extras.
Terms: Acquires first rights.
Advice: "Persist. Copy should be clean, double-spaced, with generous margins. Careful proofing for spelling and grammar errors will reduce slowing of editorial process." Mss are rejected because of "unconvincing characters, overblown language, melodramatic plot, poor execution."

‡NOSTOC MAGAZINE (II), Arts End Books, Box 162, Newton MA 02168. Editor: Marshall Brooks. Magazine: size varies; 60 lb. book paper; illustrations; photos. Biannually. Estab. 1973. Circ. 300.
Needs: "We are open-minded." Receives approximately 15 unsolicited fiction mss each month. Published new writers within the last year. Publishes short shorts. Prefers brief word length. Frequently critiques rejected mss and recommends other markets.
How to Contact: Query. SASE for ms. No simultaneous submissions. Reports in 1 week on queries, 2-3 weeks on mss, ideally. Sample copy $3.50. Send SASE for catalog.
Payment: Modest payment.
Terms: Sends galleys to author. Rights revert to author.
Advice: "We tend to publish *short* short stories that are precise and lyrical. Recently, we have been publishing *short* short story collections by one author, which are issued as a separate number of the magazine. We are always on the outlook for new material for these small collections. We publish fiction because of the high quality; quite simply, we believe that good writing deserves publication."

NOW & THEN, (IV), Center for Appalachian Studies and Services, East Tennessee State University, Box 70556, Johnson City TN 37614-0556. (615)929-5348. Editor: Pat Arnow. Magazine: 8½×11; 36-52 pages; coated paper and cover stock; illustrations; photographs. Publication focuses on Appalachian culture, present and past. Readers are mostly people in the region involved with Appalachian issues, literature, education." Triannually. Estab. 1984. Circ. 1,000.
Needs: Ethnic, literary, regional, serialized/excerpted novel, prose poem, spiritual and sports. "Absolutely has to relate to Appalachian theme. Can be about adjustment to new environment, themes of leaving and returning, for instance. Nothing unrelated to region." Upcoming themes: "Civil War in Appalachia" (Summer '93, deadline March '93). Appalachian Storytellers (Fall '93, deadline July '93). Buys 2-3 mss/issue. Publishes ms 3-4 months after acceptance. Recently published work by Lee Smith, Pinckney Benedict, Gurney Norman, George Ella Lyon; published new writers within the last year. Length: 3,000 words maximum. Publishes short shorts. Also publishes literary essays, poetry.
How to Contact: Send complete ms with cover letter. Reports in 3 months. Include "information we can use for contributor's note." SASE. Simultaneous submissions OK, "but let us know when it has been accepted elsewhere right away." Sample copy $3.50. Reviews novels and short story collections.
Payment: Pays up to $50 per story, contributor's copies, one year subscription.
Terms: Buys first-time rights.
Advice: "We're emphasizing Appalachian culture, which is not often appreciated because analysts are so busy looking at the trouble of the region. We're doing theme issues. Beware of stereotypes. In a regional publication like this one we get lots of them, both good guys and bad guys: salt of the earth to poor white trash. Sometimes we get letters that offer to let us polish up the story. We prefer the author does that him/herself." Send for list of upcoming themes.

NUCLEAR FICTION, (II,V), P.O. Box 49019, Austin TX 78765. (512)478-7262. Editor: Brian Martin. Magazine. "A bimonthly magazine of sci-fi, fantasy and horror. Includes film and book reviews, art, poetry." Estab. 1988.
Needs: Horror, fantasy and science fiction. Length: Open. Also publishes literary criticism, poetry.
How to Contact: Send complete ms; cover letter optional. Reports in 4-6 weeks on average. Sample copy for $3. Reviews novels and short story collections. Send books to Brian Martin, Editor, 2518 Leon St. #107, Austin TX 78705.
Payment: Pays ½¢/word for fiction. (Minimum payment $7.50.)
Terms: Pays on acceptance; for first North American serial rights.
Advice: "Be mindful of the fundamentals of story telling. Otherwise, no strict requirements here; good work is to be found in all types of imaginative fiction."

LA NUEZ, (II, IV), P.O. Box 023617, Brooklyn NY 11202. (718)624-8936. Editor: Rafael Bordao. Magazine: 8½×11; 32 pages; 60 lb. offset paper; glossy cover; illustrations and photographs. "*Spanish language* literary magazine (poetry, short fiction, criticism, reviews) for anyone who reads Spanish and loves poetry and literature. Many of our readers are professors, writers, critics and artists. Triannually. Estab. 1988. Circ. 1,000.
Needs: Spanish only. Literary. "Nothing more than 6 pages. No political or religious themes." Publishes "very few" mss/issue, "because of space limitations." Publishes ms 3-6 months after acceptance. Length: 6 pages or less. Publishes short shorts. Also publishes literary essays, literary criticism, poetry.
How to Contact: Send complete ms with cover letter and short bio, SASE. Only unpublished work. No simultaneous submissions. Reports in 6-8 weeks. Sample copy for $3.50. Fiction guidelines for #10 SAE and 1 first class stamp. Reviews novels and short story collections.
Payment: Pays 2 contributor's copies.
Advice: Publication's philosophy is "to publish the high quality poetry and literature in Spanish of writers from the rich diversity of cultures, communities and countries in the Spanish-speaking world."

THE OAK, (I), 1530 7th St., Rock Island IL 61201. (309)788-3980. Editor: Betty Mowery. 8½×11; 8-14 pages. "Anything of help to writers." Bimonthly. Estab. 1991. Circ. 385.
Needs: Adventure, contemporary, experimental, historical (general), humor/satire, mainstream, mystery/suspense, prose poem, regional, romance (gothic). No erotica. Receives about 12 mss/month. Accepts up to 6 mss/issue. Publishes ms within 3 months of acceptance. Published new writers within the last year. Length: 500 words maximum. Publishes short shorts. Length: 200 words.
How to Contact: Send complete ms. Reports in 1 week. SASE. Simultaneous and reprint submissions OK. Sample copy $2. Subscription $10 for 6 issues.
Payment: Pays in contributor's copies.
Terms: Acquires first rights.
Advice: "Just send a manuscript, but first read a copy of our publication to get an idea of what type of material we take. Please send SASE. If not, manuscripts *will not* be returned. Be sure name and address is on the manuscript."

‡OFFICE NUMBER ONE, (I), 2111 Quarry Rd., Austin TX 28703. (512)320-8243. Editor: Charles Edwards. Magazine: 8½×11; 12 pages; 60 lb. standard paper; b&w illustrations and photos. "I look for short stories or essays (500-800 words) that can put a reader on edge – but *not* because of profanity or obscenity, rather because the story serves to jolt the reader away from a consensus view of the world." Quarterly. Estab. 1989. Circ. 1,000.
Needs: Experimental, fantasy, horror, humor/satire, literary, psychic/supernatural/occult, fictional news articles. Upcoming themes: "I have a generic bad news page, and generic good news. Need articles about escaping from somewhere or something. Limericks about fishing and fish, lawyers, insanity, dogs and space ships." Receives 1 unsolicited ms/month. Buys 1 ms/issue; 4 mss/year. Does not read mss during December. Publishes ms 4-6 months after acceptance. Recently published work by Joe Sumral. Length: 500 word minimum; 1,000 words maximum. Also publishes literary essays, literary criticism and poetry. Sometimes critiques or comments on rejected mss.
How to Contact: Send complete ms with cover letter. Should include estimated word count and summary of article and intent ("How does this reach who?") with submission. Reports in 2-4 weeks on mss. Send SASE (IRC) for reply, return of ms or send disposable copy of ms. Will consider simultaneous submissions, reprints. Sample copy for $2 with SAE and 3 first class stamps or 3 IRCs. Fiction guidelines for SAE and 1 first class stamp or 1 IRC. Reviews novels and short story collections.
Payment: Pays ¼ cent/word and 1 contributor's copy. Additional copies for $1 plus postage.
Terms: Payment on publication. Purchases one-time rights.
Advice: "Clean writing, no unnecessary words, perfect word choice, clear presentation of an idea. Make the piece perfect. Express one good idea. Write for an audience that you can identify. Be able to say why you write what you write."

THE OHIO REVIEW, (II), 209C Ellis Hall, Ohio University, Athens OH 45701-2979. (614)593-1900. Editor: Wayne Dodd. Assistant Editor: Robert Kinsley. Magazine: 6×9; 144 pages; illustrations on cover. "We attempt to publish the best poetry and fiction written today. For a mainly literary audience." Triannually. Estab. 1971. Circ. 2,000.
Needs: Contemporary, experimental, literary. "We lean toward contemporary on all subjects." Receives 150-200 unsolicited fiction mss/month. Buys 3 mss/issue. Does not read mss June 1-August 31. Publishes ms 6 months after acceptance. Agented fiction: 1%. Also publishes poetry. Sometimes critiques rejected mss and/or recommends other markets.

How to Contact: Query first or send complete ms with cover letter. Reports in 6 weeks. SASE. Sample copy $4.25. Fiction guidelines for #10 SASE.
Payment: Pays $5/page, free subscription to magazine, 2 contributor's copies.
Terms: Pays on publication for first North American serial rights. Sends galleys to author.
Advice: "We feel the short story is an important part of the contemporary writing field and value it highly. Read a copy of our publication to see if your fiction is of the same quality. So often people send us work that simply doesn't fit our needs."

OLD HICKORY REVIEW, (II), Jackson Writers Group, Box 1178, Jackson TN 38302. (901)668-3717 or (901)664-5959. President: William Nance, Jr.. Editor: Edna Lackie. Fiction Editors: Dorothy Stanfill and Donald Phillips. Magazine: 8½×11; approx. 90 pages. "Usually two short stories and 75-80 poems—nothing obscene or in poor taste. For a family audience." Semiannually. Plans special fiction issue. Estab. 1969. Circ. 300.
Needs: Contemporary, experimental, fantasy, literary, mainstream. Receives 4-5 unsolicited fiction mss/month. Acquires 2 mss/issue; 4 mss/year. Publishes ms no more than 3-4 months after acceptance. Length: 2,500-3,000 words. Publishes short shorts. Also publishes poetry. Sometimes critiques rejected mss and recommends other markets.
How to Contact: Send complete ms with cover letter, which should include "credits." Reports on queries in 2-3 weeks; on mss in 1-2 months. SASE. Sample copy available. Fiction guidelines for SAE.
Payment: Pays in contributor's copies; charge for extras. Sponsors contests for fiction writers, "advertised in literary magazine and with flyers."
Advice: "We are tired of war, nursing homes, abused children, etc. We are looking for things which are more entertaining. No pornographic fiction, no vile language. Our publication goes into schools, libraries, etc."

THE OLD RED KIMONO, (II), Box 1864, Rome GA 30162. (706)295-6312. Editors: Ken Anderson and Jonathan Hershey. Magazine: 8×11; 65-70 pages; white offset paper; 10 pt. board cover stock. Annually. Estab. 1972. Circ. 1,200.
Needs: Literary. "We will consider good fiction regardless of category." Receives 20-30 mss/month. Accepts 6-8 mss/issue. Does not read mss March 15-September 1. "Issue out in May every year." Published work by Thomas Feeny, David Huddle, Peter Huggins. Length: 2,000-3,000 words preferred; 5,000 words maximum. Publishes short shorts. "We prefer short fiction." Also publishes poetry.
How to Contact: Send complete ms with cover letter. Reports in 2 weeks on queries; 2-3 months on mss. SASE. Simultaneous submissions OK, but "we would like to be told." Fiction guidelines for #10 SAE and 1 first class stamp.
Payment: Pays in contributor's copies.
Terms: Acquires first rights.

ONCE UPON A WORLD, (II), Route 1, Box 110A, Nineveh IN 46164. Editor: Emily Alward. Magazine: 8½×11; 80-100 pages; standard white paper; colored card stock cover; pen & ink illustrations. "A science fiction and fantasy magazine with emphasis on alternate-world cultures and stories of idea, character and interaction. Also publishes book reviews and a few poems for an adult audience, primarily readers of science fiction and fantasy." Annually. Estab. 1988. Circ. 100.
Needs: Fantasy, science fiction. No realistic "stories in contemporary settings"; horror; stories using Star Trek or other media characters; stories with completely negative endings." Receives 20 unsolicited mss/month. Accepts 8-12 mss/issue; per year "varies, depending on backlog." Publishes ms from 2 months to 1½ years after acceptance. Published work by Janet Reedman and Mark Andrew Garland. Length: 3,000 words average; 400 words minimum; 10,000 words maximum. Publishes short shorts. Also publishes poetry. Sometimes critiques rejected mss and recommends other markets.
How to Contact: Send complete manuscript. Reports in 2-4 weeks on queries; 2-16 weeks on mss. SASE. "Reluctantly" accepts simultaneous submissions, if noted. Sample copy $8.50; checks to Emily Alward. Fiction guidelines for #10 SAE and 1 first class stamp. Reviews novels and short story collections.
Payment: Pays contributor's copies.
Terms: Acquires first rights. "Stories copyrighted in author's name; copyrights not registered."
Advice: "Besides a grasp of basic fiction technique, you'll need some familiarity with the science fiction and fantasy genres. We suggest reading some of the following authors whose work is similar to what we're looking for: Isaac Asimov, Poul Anderson, Norman Spinrad, David Brin, Anne McCaffrey, Marion Zimmer Bradley, Mercedes Lackey, Katharine Kimbriel."

ONIONHEAD, Literary Quarterly, (II), Arts on the Park, Inc., 115 N. Kentucky Ave., Lakeland FL 33801. (813)680-2787. Editors: Charles Kersey, Dennis Nesheim, Dudley Uphoff. Editorial Assistant: Anna Wiseman. Magazine: Digest-sized; 40 pages; 20 lb. bond; glossy card cover. "Provocative political, social and cultural observations and hypotheses for a literary audience—an open-minded audience." Estab. 1989. Circ. 250.

Needs: Contemporary, ethnic, experimental, feminist, gay, humor/satire, lesbian, literary, prose poem, regional. "Must have a universal point (International)." Publishes short fiction in each issue. Receives 100-150 unsolicited titles/month. Acquires approximately 28 mss/issue; 100 titles (these numbers include: poetry, short prose and essays)/year. Publishes ms within 18 months of acceptance. Published work by Lyn Lifshin, A.D. Winans, Jessica Freeman, Laurel Speer. Length: 3,000 words average; 4,000 words maximum. Publishes short shorts. Also publishes poetry.

How to Contact: Send complete manuscript with cover letter that includes brief bio and SASE. Reports in 2 weeks on queries; 2 months on mss. No simultaneous submissions. Sample copy $3 postpaid. Fiction guidelines for #10 SAE and 1 first class stamp.

Payment: Pays in contributor's copy. Charge for extras.

Terms: Acquires first North American serial rights.

Advice: "Review a sample copy of *Onionhead* and remember *literary quality* is the prime criterion. Avoid heavy-handed approaches to social commentary—be subtle, not didactic."

‡OREGON EAST (II, IV), Hoke College Center, EOSC, La Grande OR 97850. (503)962-3787. Editor: Christian Reiten. Magazine: 6×9; 80 pages; illustrations and photographs. "*Oregon East* prefers fiction about the Northwest. The majority of our issues go to the students of Eastern Oregon State College; staff, faculty and community members receive them also, and numerous high school and college libraries." Annually. Estab. 1950. Circ. 900.

Needs: Humor/satire, literary, prose poem, regional, translations. No juvenile/children's fiction. Receives 20 unsolicited mss/month. Accepts 3-6 mss/issue. Does not read April to August. Publishes ms an average of 5 months after acceptance. Published work by Ursula LeGuin, Madeline de Trees and George Venn. Published new writers within the last year. Length: 2,000 words average; 3,000 words maximum. Publishes short shorts. Sometimes critiques rejected mss.

How to Contact: Send complete ms with cover letter which should include name, address, brief bio. Reports in 1 week on queries; 3 months on mss. SASE. Sample copy $5; fiction guidelines for #10 SASE.

Payment: 2 contributor's copies.

Terms: Rights revert to author.

Advice: "Follow our guidelines, please! Keep trying: we have limited space because we must publish 50% on-campus material. *Oregon East* has been around for almost 40 years, and it has always strived to represent the Northwest's great writers and artists, as well as several from around the world."

OTHER VOICES, (II), The University of Illinois at Chicago, Dept of English (M/C 162), Box 4348, Chicago IL 60680. (312)413-2209. Editors: Sharon Fiffer and Lois Hauselman. Magazine: 5⅞×9; 168-205 pages; 60 lb. paper; coated cover stock; occasional photos. "Original, fresh, diverse stories and novel excerpts" for literate adults. Semiannually. Estab. 1985. Circ. 1,500.

Needs: Contemporary, experimental, humor/satire, literary, excerpted novel. No taboos, except ineptitude and murkiness. No fantasy, horror, juvenile, psychic/occult. Receives 100 unsolicited fiction mss/month. Accepts 20-23 mss/issue. Published work by Barbara Lefcowitz, Susan B. Weston; published new writers within the last year. Length: 4,000 words average; 5,000 words maximum. Also publishes short shorts "if paired together" of 1,000 words. Only occasionally critiques rejected mss or recommends other markets.

How to Contact: Send mss with SASE or submit through agent. Cover letters "should be brief and list previous publications. Also, list title of submission. Most beginners' letters try to 'explain' the story—a big mistake." Simultaneous submissions OK. Reports in 10-12 weeks on mss. SASE. Sample copy $5.90 (includes postage). Fiction guidelines for #10 SAE and 1 first class stamp.

Payment: Pays in contributor's copies and modest cash gratuity (when possible).

Terms: Acquires one-time rights.

Advice: "There are so *few* markets for *quality* fiction! We—by publishing 40-45 stories a year—provide new and established writers a forum for their work. Send us your best voice, your best work, your best best."

OTHER WORLDS, Science Fiction-Science Fantasy, (II), Gryphon Publications, Box 209, Brooklyn NY 11228. Editor: Gary Lovisi. Magazine: 5 × 8; 60+ pages; offset paper; card cover; illustrations and photographs. "Adventure—or action-oriented SF—stories that are fun to read." Annually. Estab. 1988. Circ. 300.
Needs: Science fiction (hard science, soft/sociological). No high fantasy, sword and sorcery. Receives 12 unsolicited mss/month. Accepts 2-4 mss/issue. Publishes ms 1-2 years (usually) after acceptance. Length: 3,000 words maximum. Publishes short shorts. Length: 500-1,000 words. Sometimes critiques rejected mss and recommends other markets.
How to Contact: Send complete ms with cover letter. Simultaneous submissions OK. Reports in 2 weeks on queries; 1 month on mss. SASE. Sample copy $5.
Payment: Pays 2 contributor's copies.
Terms: Acquires first North American serial rights. Copyright reverts to author.
Advice: Looks for "harder sf stories, with *impact!*"

‡OTTERWISE, For Kids into Saving Animals and the Environment, (II, IV), P.O. Box 1374, Portland ME 04104. (207)283-2964. Editor: Cheryl Miller. Fiction Editor: Marianne Matte. Newsletter: 8½ × 11; 16 pages; recycled paper; illustrations; photographs. "For kids 8-13, short stories about animal welfare and saving the environment." Quarterly. Estab. 1988. Circ. 3,000.
Needs: Children's/Juvenile (5-9 years, 10-12 years): fantasy (children's fantasy), mystery/suspense (young adult mystery), young adult/teen (10-18 years), animal welfare, environmental. Receives 10 unsolicited mss/month. Acquires 1 ms/issue; 4 mss/year. Publishes ms up to 3 months after acceptance. Length: 800 words preferred; 100 words minimum; 1,000 words maximum. Publishes short shorts.
How to Contact: Send complete ms with cover letter. Reports in 1 month. Send SASE for reply, return of ms or send disposable copy of the ms. Simultaneous, reprint and electronic submissions OK. Sample copy for $2. Fiction guidelines free.
Payment: No payment.
Terms: Acquires one-time rights.
Advice: Looks for "story written from animal's point of view that shows action on part of kids—well written. Don't write 'down' to kids, check spelling and grammar. Don't be too obvious and corny."

OUROBOROS, (II), 3912 24th St., Rock Island IL 61201-6223. Editor and Publisher: Erskine Carter. Magazine: 6 × 9; 76 pages; 60 lb. offset paper; 80 lb. cover; b&w illustrations. "We publish fiction (short stories), poetry and art for thoughtful readers." Published irregularly. Estab. 1985. Circ. 400.
Needs: Adventure, contemporary, experimental, fantasy, historical (general), horror, humor/satire, literary, mainstream, mystery/suspense, psychic/supernatural/occult, science fiction. "We are mainly interested in stories about people, in situations of conflict or struggle. We want to see *real* characters at odds with others, themselves, their universe. No racist/right-wing/anti-minority material." Receives 40-50 unsolicited mss/month. Accepts 8-10 mss/issue; 32-40 mss/year. Publishes ms 3 months to 1 year after acceptance. Published work by W. Rose, C. Stevenson, D. Starkey; published new writers within the last year. Length: 2,500 words average; 3,500 words maximum. Publishes short shorts. Length: 500 words. Also publishes poetry. Sometimes critiques rejected mss and recommends other markets.
How to Contact: Request guidelines and a sample copy. Reports in 2 weeks. SASE. Reprint submissions OK. Sample copy of current issue $4.50. Back issues available.
Payment: Pays in contributor's copies.
Terms: Rights revert to author. Sends galleys to author.
Advice: "The beginning writer *can* break in here and learn valuable lessons about writing and publishing. Obtain a sample copy, write something you think will grab us, then submit. Get to know the markets. Don't waste time, energy and postage without researching."

OUTERBRIDGE, (II), English A-323, The College of Staten Island (CUNY), 715 Ocean Terr., Staten Island NY 10301. (718)390-7779. Editor: Charlotte Alexander. Magazine: 5½ × 8½; approx. 110 pages; 60 lb. white offset paper; 65 lb. cover stock. "We are a national literary magazine publishing mostly fiction and poetry. To date, we have had three special focus issues (the 'urban' and the 'rural' experience, 'Southern'). For anyone with enough interest in literature to look for writing of quality and writers on the contemporary scene who deserve attention. There probably is a growing circuit of writers, some academics, reading us by recommendations." Annually. Estab. 1975. Circ. 500-700.
Needs: Literary. "No *Reader's Digest* style; that is, very popularly oriented. We like to do interdisciplinary features, e.g., literature and music, literature and science and literature and the natural world." Upcoming themes: "Animal World;" "Farms and Farming;" "Send-ups of PC," (politically correct language). Accepts 8-10 mss/year. Does not read in July or August. Published work by William Davey,

Ron Berube, Patricia Ver Ellen; published new writers within the last year. Length: 10-25 pages. Also publishes poetry. Sometimes recommends other markets.
How to Contact: Query. Send complete ms with cover letter. "Don't talk too much, 'explain' the work, or act apologetic or arrogant. If published, tell where, with a brief bio." SASE. Reports in 2 weeks on queries, 2 months on mss. Sample copy $5 for annual issue.
Payment: Pays 2 contributor's copies. Charges ½ price of current issue for extras to its authors.
Terms: Acquires one-time rights. Requests credits for further publication of material used by *OB*.
Advice: "Read our publication first. Don't send out blindly; get some idea of what the magazine might want. A *short* personal note with biography is appreciated. Competition is keen. Read an eclectic mix of classic and contemporary. Beware of untransformed autobiography, but *everything* in one's experience contributes."

‡OWEN WISTER REVIEW, (II), ASUW Student Publications Board, P.O. Box 4238, University of Wyoming, Laramie WY 82071. (307)766-3819. Fax: (307)766-4027. Editor: Spence Keralis. Fiction Editors: "Fiction Selection Committee." Editors change each year. After 1993, contact selection committee. Magazine: 6×9; 92 pages; 60 lb. matte paper; 80 lb. glossy cover; illustrations; photographs. "Though we are a university publication, our audience is wider than just an academic community." Semiannually. Estab. 1978. Circ. 500.
• *Owen Wister Review* has won numerous awards and honors far surpassing many student-run publications. Nine poems from *OWR* were nominated for inclusion in the *Pushcart Prize* anthology (1992-1993). The magazine received Best of Show award from the Associated Collegiate Press/College Media Advisors Inc. and six individual Gold Circle Awards from the Columbia Scholastic Press Association.
Needs: Ethnic/multicultural, experimental, feminist, gay, humor/satire, lesbian, literary, translations. No science fiction or fantasy. Plans special fiction issue or anthology.
Receives 12-15 unsolicited mss. Acquires 3 mss/issue; 6-8 mss/year. "Summer months are generally down time for *OWR*." Publishes 2-3 months after acceptance. Recently published work by Mark Jenkins, John Bennet, the Kunstwaffen art collaborative, Sue Thornton. Length: 1,300 words average; 3,500 words maximum. Publishes short shorts. Also publishes literary essays, literary criticism and poetry. Often critiques or comments on rejected mss.
How to Contact: Send complete ms with cover letter. Should include estimated word count, bio, list of publications. Reports in 2-3 weeks on queries; 2-3 months on mss. Send SASE for reply, return of ms or send disposable copy of the ms. Simultaneous submissions OK. Sample copy for $5. Free fiction guidelines. Reviews poetry and short story collections. Send books to fiction committee — review.
Payment: Pays 1 contributor's copy. 10% off additional copies.
Terms: Acquires one-time rights. Sends galleys to author.
Advice: "In the last few issues we have geared the material toward what we think of as 'underpublished' groups — minorities, veterans, the gay community — survivor groups. This has broadened our audience to include just about anyone who wishes to be challenged by their reading material. Our committee likes to hear a fresh voice. Experimental fiction is encouraged. Consistency is very important. We look for and encourage young writers but insist on quality. Metafiction and short humor stand out among the longer works. We want to be hooked and not let go; regardless of subject matter, the approach should be compelling and relentless."

OXALIS, A Literary Magazine, (II), Stone Ridge Poetry Society, P.O. Box 3993, Kingston NY 12401. (914)687-7942. Editor: Shirley Powell. Fiction Editor: Mildred Barker. Magazine: 8½×11; 48-60 pages; 60 lb. recycled paper; 65 lb. recycled cover. "A selection of the best in poetry and fiction presented in an attractive package. For people interested in good writing." Quarterly. Estab. 1988. Circ. 350.
Needs: Adventure, contemporary, erotica, ethnic, experimental, fantasy, feminist, gay, historical, horror, humor/satire, lesbian, literary, mainstream, mystery/suspense, prose poem, regional, romance (contemporary, historical), science fiction, senior citizen/retirement, sports, western (frontier stories), contemporary issues: environment, human rights. "Nothing sentimental or preachy." No children's literature. Upcoming theme: Contest Issue (fiction and poetry) (spring/summer). Receives 10 unsolicited mss/month. Accepts 2-7 mss/issue; 12 mss/year. (Magazine is about half poetry, half fiction.) Publishes ms 6-15 months after acceptance. Recently published work by Emilie Glen, Stephen Dunn, Lucy Honig. Length: 4,000 words maximum. Publishes short shorts. Also publishes poetry.
How to Contact: Include "2 or 3 sentence bio suitable for Contributors' Page." Reports in up to 3 months. SASE. May accept simultaneous submissions, but "prefer not to." Sample copy for $4. Fiction guidelines for #10 SAE and 1 first class stamp.

Payment: Pays 2 contributor's copies.
Terms: Acquires first rights or one-time rights.
Advice: Looks for "something different from anything I've read before. Something that changes my mind or shakes me up. Fiction I can't forget. Read *Oxalis* and acquaint yourself with contemporary writing. Then write something better."

OXFORD MAGAZINE, (II), Bachelor Hall, Miami University, Oxford OH 45056. (513)529-5256. Fiction Editor: Keith Banner. Editors change every year. Send future submissions to "Fiction Editor." Magazine: 6×9; 85-100 pages; illustrations. Biannually. Estab. 1985. Circ. 500-1,000.
● This college literary has published work selected for the *Pushcart Prize* anthology in 1991.
Needs: Ethnic, experimental, feminist, gay, humor/satire, lesbian, literary, translations. Receives 50-60 unsolicited mss/month. Does not read mss May through August. Published new writers within the last year. Length: 2,000-3,000 words average; 4,000 words maximum. Publishes short shorts. Also publishes literary essays, literary criticism, poetry.
How to Contact: Send complete ms with cover letter, which should include a short bio or interesting information. No simultaneous submissions. Reports in 3-4 months on mss. SASE. Sample copy for $4, 10×12 SAE and 4 first class stamps. Reviews novels and short story collections. Send books to managing editor.
Payment: Pays a small honorarium and 1 year subscription.
Terms: Acquires one-time rights.
Advice: "We look for writing that makes sense: fiction that makes you put down your spoon and reread the page until your soup goes cold. *Oxford Magazine* is looking for fiction that moves the mind. Unfortunately, this is a quality which eludes definition. We are interested in fresh voices, not educated imitations of other authors. Call us optimistic, but we believe that literature has a place in modern (post-modern?) culture, and we like our magazine to reflect that. That doesn't mean stories which end happily; it means stories which are significant. We are interested in providing a forum for voices which don't normally receive one, and in subject matters which reflect the potential of those voices."

P.I. MAGAZINE, Fact and Fiction about the World of Private Investigators, (II), 755 Bronx, Toledo OH 43609. (419)382-0967. Editor: Bob Mackowiak. Magazine: 8½×11; about 50 pages; coated white paper and cover; illustrations and photographs. "All about private eyes: personality profiles and stories about professional investigators; original fiction; books, movie, video, games, etc. Audience includes private eye and mystery fans." Quarterly. Estab. 1988. Circ. 1,300
Needs: Adventure, humor/satire, suspense/mystery. "Principal character must be a private detective – not a police detective, spy or school teacher who solves murders on the side. No explicit sex." Buys 4-6 mss/issue. Publishes ms 2-3 months after acceptance. Published work by Curtis Fischer; column by Bill Palmer. Length: 3,000-5,000 words preferred. Publishes short shorts. Sometimes critiques rejected ms and recommends other markets if possible.
How to Contact: Send complete ms with cover letter. Reports in 4 months. SASE. Simultaneous submissions OK. Single copy for $4.75."
Payment: Pays $15 minimum; $25 for fiction; contributor's copies; charge for extras.
Terms: Pays on publication for one-time rights.
Advice: "Private eye stories do not need to be murder mysteries, and they do not need to start with a client walking into the detective's run-down office. How about a successful private investigator making good money. Most of the real P.I.s run profitable businesses."

THE P.U.N. (PLAY ON WORDS), (II), The Silly Club and Michael Rayner, Box 536-583, Orlando FL 32853. (407)898-0463. Editor: Danno Sullivan. Newsletter: 8 pages; cartoons. "All polite humor. Polite, meaning no foul language, sex, etc. As a joke, something like 'Child Abuse with Dr. Seuss' is OK. We have an intelligent readership. They don't mind puzzling a bit to get the joke, but they also enjoy plain silliness." Published bimonthly. Estab. 1982. Circ. 400.
Needs: Humor/satire. Receives 20 unsolicited fiction mss/month. Buys 1-3 mss/issue; 10-20 mss/year. Publishes ms "usually next issue" after acceptance. Length: short shorts, 1 page or less. Sometimes critiques rejected mss.

How to Contact: Send complete ms with cover letter. Reports in 2-3 weeks. SASE. Simultaneous and reprint submissions OK. Sample copy for #10 SASE and $1.
Payment: Pays $1 minimum, $15 maximum; contributor's copies.
Terms: Pays on acceptance for one-time rights.
Advice: "Keep it short. Keep it obviously (even if it's subtle) funny. Above all, don't write like Erma Bombeck. We get a lot of 'cute' material—*Readers Digest*-style, which is not for us. We like short *articles*, as opposed to stories. Fiction presented as fact."

PABLO LENNIS, The Magazine of Science Fiction, Fantasy and Fact, (I, IV), Deneb Press, Fandom House, 30 North 19th St., Lafayette IN 47904. Editor: John Thiel. Magazine: 8½×11; 22 pages; standard stock; illustrations and "occasional" photos. "Science fiction, fantasy, science, research and mystic for scientists and science fiction and fantasy appreciators." Monthly.
Needs: Fantasy, psychic/supernatural/occult, science fiction, spiritual. Receives 25 unsolicited mss/year. Accepts 3 mss/issue; 35 mss/year. Publishes ms 6 months after acceptance. Recently published work by P.M. Fergusson, Michael Kube-McDowell, Darrin Kidd; published new writers within the last year. Length: 1,500 words average; 3,000 words maximum. Also publishes literary criticism, poetry. Occasionally critiques rejected mss and recommends other markets.
How to Contact: "Method of submission is author's choice but he might prefer to query. No self-statement is necessary." No simultaneous submissions. Reports in 2 weeks. Does not accept computer printouts.
Payment: Pays 1 contributor's copy.
Terms: Publication not copyrighted.
Advice: "I have taboos against unpleasant and offensive language and want material which is morally or otherwise elevating to the reader. I prefer an optimistic approach, and favor fine writing. With a good structure dealt with intelligently underlying this, you have the kind of story I like. I prefer stories that have something to say to those which have something to report."

‡PACIFIC REVIEW (II), Dept. of English and Comparative Lit., San Diego State University, San Diego CA 92182-0295. (619)594-5200. Contact: Editor. Magazine: 6×9; 100-150 pages; book stock paper; paper back, extra heavy cover stock; illustrations, photos. "There is no designated theme. We publish high-quality fiction, poetry, and familiar essays: academic work meant for, but not restricted to, an academic audience." Biannually. Estab. 1973. Circ. 1,000.
Needs: "We do not restrict or limit our fiction in any way other than quality. We are interested in all fiction, from the very traditional to the highly experimental. Accceptance is determined by the quality of submissions." Does not read June-August. Published new writers within the last year. Publishes short shorts. Length: 4,000 words max.
How to Contact: Send original ms with SASE. No unsolicited submissions. Reports in 3-5 months on mss. Sample copy $6.
Payment: 1 author's copy.
Terms: "First serial rights are *Pacific Review*'s. All other rights revert to author."

PAINTED BRIDE QUARTERLY, (II), Painted Bride Art Center, 230 Vine St., Philadelphia PA 19106. (215)925-9914. Editor: Teresa Leo. Literary magazine: 6×9; 96-100 pages; illustrations; photos. Quarterly. Estab. 1975. Circ. 1,000.
Needs: Contemporary, ethnic, experimental, feminist, gay, lesbian, literary, prose poem and translations. Receives 10 unsolicited mss/week. Acquires 2 mss/issue; 8 mss/year. Published new writers within the last year. Length: 3,000 words average; 5,000 words maximum. Publishes short shorts. Also publishes literary essays, literary criticism, poetry. Occasionally critiques rejected mss.
How to Contact: Send complete ms. Reports in 3 weeks-3 months. SASE. Sample copy $5. Reviews novels and short story collections. Send books to Lou McKee.
Payment: Pays 1 contributor's copy, 1 year free subscription, 50% off additional copies.
Terms: Acquires first North American serial rights.
Advice: "We want quality in whatever—we hold experimental work to as strict standards as anything else. Many of our readers write fiction; most of them enjoy a good reading. We hope to be an outlet for quality. A good story gives, first, enjoyment to the reader. We've seen a good many of them lately, and we've published the best of them."

PAINTED HILLS REVIEW, (II), P.O. Box 494, Davis CA 95617. Editors: Michael Ishii, Kara Kosmatka. Magazine: 5½×8½; 48 pages. "Our only criterion for the work we publish is it be solid, well-written work. We publish poems, fiction (short stories and novel excerpts), plus b&w art for those interested in the literary arts, in the *craft* of writing." Triannually. Estab. 1990. Circ. 300.

Needs: Excerpted novel, confession, contemporary, ethnic, experimental, historical (general), humor/satire, literary, prose poem, regional, religious/inspirational, translations. No "gay/lesbian, pornography, occult/New Age, horror/shock fiction." Plans special fiction issue. Receives 10-30 unsolicited mss/month. Accepts 8-10 mss/year. Publishes ms 2 months to 1 year after acceptance. Recently published work by Omar Castañeda, Mark Wisniewski, James Sallis, Lia Smith. Length: 2,500 words preferred; 4,000 words maximum. Publishes short shorts. Sometimes critiques rejected mss.

How to Contact: Send complete ms with cover letter. Include a short bio of author (a paragraph). Reports in 2 weeks on queries; 1-2 months on mss. SASE. Sample copy for $3. Fiction guidelines for #10 SAE and 1 first class stamp.

Payment: Pays 1 or more contributor's copies.

Terms: Acquires first North American serial rights. All rights revert to author upon publication.

Advice: Ask: "Does it look as if it was written in one sitting and never looked at again? Or has it been worked on? Does the narration flow smoothly? Is the language awkward? Is there an interesting-enough conflict and resolution in the story? Basically, is it well-written?" Sponsors annual fiction contest; send SASE for details.

PALACE CORBIE, (II), Merrimack Books, P.O. Box 158, Lynn IN 47355. (317)935-0232. Editor: Wayne Edwards. Magazine: 6×9, perfect-bound trade paperback; card stock cover; b&w illustrations. "Perseverance in the face of adversity, doom and despair for a horror/dark fantasy audience." Semiannually. Estab. 1992.

Needs: Adventure, contemporary, erotica, ethnic, experimental, fantasy, feminist, gay, historical (general), horror, lesbian, literary, psychic/supernatural/occult, religious/inspirational, science fiction, translations. Receives about 100 unsolicited mss/month. Accepts 10-12 mss/issue; 20-24 mss/year. Publishes ms 6 months after acceptance. Length: 2,000-8,000 words preferred. Sometimes critiques rejected mss and recommends other markets.

How to Contact: Send complete ms, cover letter (optional). No simultaneous submissions. Reprint submissions OK. Accepts electronic submissions via disk (ASCII, Word for Windows). Reports in 2 weeks on queries; 3 weeks on mss. SASE. Fiction guidelines for #10 SAE and 1 first class stamp.

Payment: Pays contributor's copies. Charges for extras.

Terms: Acquires one-time rights. Sends galleys to author.

Advice: Looks for "quality of writing only. What aggravates me the most, however, is a story with *no* plot. I see a lot of those."

PANDORA, (I), 2844 Grayson, Ferndale MI 48220. Editor: Meg Mac Donald. Anthology: 5½×8½; 72 pages; offset paper; perfect-bound, 2-color laminated cover; b&w illustrations. Magazine for science fiction and fantasy readers. Published 2 times/year. Estab. 1978. Circ. 700.

Needs: Fantasy, science fiction (soft/sociological). "Nothing X-rated; no horror; no gratuitous violence or sex. Unless the author created the universe, she/he should not send us stories in that universe." Upcoming themes: "#29 (March/April) will feature fairytales, myths, legends, etc. with SF/F twists." Receives 200 unsolicited fiction mss/month. Buys 6-10 mss/issue, 20 mss/year. Publishes ms 6 months-1 year after acceptance on average, sometimes as long as 2 years. Published many new writers within the last year. Length: 6,000 words average; 10,000 words maximum. Always critiques rejected mss if accompanied by a SASE. Also publishes poetry. Sometimes recommends other markets.

How to Contact: Send complete ms with cover letter, which should include relevant publication history. Previously published submissions OK. No electronic submissions of any kind. "Grudgingly" accepts simultaneous submissions. Reports in 2 weeks on queries; 2-3 months on mss. Sample copy $5 (US); $7 (Canada/Mexico); $10 overseas. Fiction guidelines for SASE.

Payment: Pays 1-2¢/word and 1 contributor's copy.

Terms: Pays on publication for first North American serial rights, second rights or one-time rights on previously published mss.

Advice: "Like most magazines, *Pandora* makes guidelines available to writers for a SASE and we hope you'll take advantage of this service. In the meantime, here are a few bits of advice. If you are writing horror, New Age-inspired fantasy, occultic material, or stories heavy on sex, violence, and profanity, you can assume *Pandora* is not the right market for you. If you are writing character-oriented fantasy and science fiction, stories about other worlds and fascinating characters with believable problems, *Pandora* might be for you. If your characters are active not passive, if you use Christian elements in your fiction, if you have a wacky sense of humor that isn't dependant on insults or cheap puns, *Pandora* might be for you. Above all, we hope that you are writing what your heart leads you to write. Write to enlighten and lift and challenge the hearts and minds of your readers. Good luck!"

THE PANHANDLER, A Magazine of Poetry and Fiction, (II), The University of West Florida, English Dept., Pensacola FL 32514. (904)474-2923. Editors: Michael Yots, Stanton Millet and Laurie O'Brien. Magazine: 6×9; 64 pages; 40 lb. paper; 70 lb. cover stock. Semiannually. Estab. 1976. Circ. 500.
  ● Although all work on *The Panhandler* is under the direction of the editors, they inform me the magazine is used as a teaching tool for the University of West Florida's "Magazine Editing and Publishing" class and as a Directed Study instrument for exceptional students.
Needs: Contemporary, ethnic, experimental, humor/satire, literary and mainstream. No sci fi, horror, erotica. Plans to publish special fiction or anthology issue in the future. Receives 15+ unsolicited mss/month. Accepts 2-4 mss/issue; 8-10 mss/year. Publishes ms 3-8 months after acceptance. Length: 1,500-3,000 words; 2,500 average. Sometimes critiques rejected mss and recommends other markets.
How to Contact: Send complete ms with cover letter. Should include writing experience, publications. Reports in 1-4 months. SASE. Simultaneous submissions OK. Sample copy $4. Fiction guidelines for #10 SAE and 1 first class stamp.
Payment: Pays in contributor's copies.
Terms: Acquires first rights.
Advice: "We look for engaging narrative voice. Characters whose concerns are of interest to readers. Real, everyday problems, dilemmas. Clear, efficient narrative style. Manuscript must lead the reader through the story and make him feel on completion that it was worth the trip."

THE PAPER BAG, (I, II), Box 268805, Chicago IL 60626-8805. (312)285-7972. Editor: Michael H. Brownstein. Magazine: 5½×8½; 25-40 pages; cardboard cover stock; illustrations. Quarterly. Estab. 1988. Circ. 300.
Needs: Adventure, contemporary, erotica, ethnic, experimental, fantasy, feminist, horror, literary, mainstream, mystery/suspense, prose poem and western. Plans to publish special fiction or anthology issue in the future. Receives 10 unsolicited mss/month. Accepts 2-4 mss/issue; 36-60 mss/year. Publishes mss 3 months to 1 year after acceptance. Under 500 words preferred; 500 words maximum. "Has to be under 500 words." Sometimes critiques rejected mss and recommends other markets.
How to Contact: Send complete ms with cover letter. "Include brief bio for our contributor's page." Reports in 1 week on queries; 1 week to 3 months on mss. SASE. Sample copy $2.50. Fiction guidelines for SAE and 1 first class stamp.
Payment: Pays in contributor's copies.
Terms: Acquires first rights. Sometimes sends pre-publication galleys to the author.

PAPER RADIO, (I,II), P.O. Box 4646, Seattle WA 98104-0646. Editor: N.S. Kvern. Magazine: 8½×11; 48-64 pages; photocopied and/or offset paper and cover; illustrations; b&w photographs. "We're open to anything, but it has to be short—usually less than 2,500 words." Readers are "mostly people who are interested in avant garde, political, bizarre, surrealism, cyberpunk, literary/experimental writing and computers." Published 2-3 times/year. Estab. 1986. Circ. 2,000.
Needs: Erotica, experimental, fantasy, literary, prose poem, science fiction. Receives 50 unsolicited fiction mss/month. Accepts 4-5 mss/issue; 12-15 mss/year. Publishes ms an average of 2-3 months after acceptance. Length: 2,000 words average; 3,500 words maximum. Publishes short shorts. Sometimes critiques rejected mss.
How to Contact: Send complete ms with cover letter. "some autobiographical information is helpful—one or two paragraphs—and I like to know where they hear about our magazine." Reports in 2 months. SASE. Simultaneous submissions OK. Sample copy $4.
Payment: Pays contributor's copies.
Terms: Acquires first rights, "artist can publish material elsewhere simultaneously."
Advice: "We are devoted to the cause of experimentation and literature and we like a wide variety of fiction. Best to see a sample copy. Our publication is orderly in its chaos, wild and untameable in its order."

PARAGRAPH, A Magazine of Paragraphs, (II), 92 E. Manning St., Providence RI 02906. (401)331-7748. Co-Editors: Walker Rumble and Karen Donovan. Magazine: 4¼×5½; 38 pages. "No particular theme—we publish collections of paragraphs for a general audience." Published 3 times/year. Estab. 1985. Circ. 700.
Needs: "Any topic is welcome, including experimental writing. Our only requirement is that paragraphs must be 200 words or less." Receives 30-40 unsolicited mss/month. Accepts 30-33 mss/issue; 90 mss/year. Publishes ms 2-3 months after acceptance. Published work by Lisa Shea, Laurel Speer, Conger Beasley Jr., Jennifer Lodde, Gary Fincke. Length: 200 words. Also publishes literary essays, but 200 words maximum, of coursc. Sometimes critiques rejected mss.

How to Contact: Send complete manuscript with cover letter. Reports in 1 week on queries; 2 months on mss. SASE. Simultaneous submissions OK. Sample copy $3. Fiction guidelines for SAE and 1 first class stamp.
Payment: Pays contributor's copies and charges for extras.
Terms: Acquires first rights. Sends galleys to author.

THE PARIS REVIEW (II), 45-39 171 St. Pl., Flushing NY 11358 (*business office only, send mss to address below in How to Contact subhead*). Editor: George A. Plimpton. Managing Editor: James Linville. Magazine: 5¼×8½; about 240 pages; illustrations and photographs (unsolicited artwork not accepted). "Fiction and poetry of superlative quality, whatever the genre, style or mode. Our contributors include prominent, as well as less well-known and previously unpublished writers. 'The Art of Fiction' interview series includes important contemporary writers discussing their own work and the craft of writing." Quarterly.
• George Plimpton, editor of the well-respected *Paris Review*, also edits a popular series of interviews with well-known writers whose work has appeared in the magazine.
Needs: Literary. Receives about 1,000 unsolicited fiction mss each month. Published work by Raymond Carver, Elizabeth Tallent, Rick Bass, John Koethe, Sharon Olds, Derek Walcott, Carolyn Kizer, Tess Gallagher, Peter Handke, Denis Johnson, Bobbie Ann Mason, Harold Brodkey, Joseph Brodsky, John Updike, Andre Dubus, Galway Kinnell, E.L. Doctorow and Philip Levine. Published new writers within the last year. No preferred length. Also publishes literary essays, poetry.
How to Contact: *Send complete ms with SASE to Fiction Editor, 541 E. 72nd St., New York NY 10021.* Simultaneous submissions OK. Sample copy $8.
Payment: Pays for material.
Terms: Pays on publication for first North American serial rights. Sends galleys to author.

PARTING GIFTS, (II), 3413 Wilshire, Greensboro NC 27408. Editor: Robert Bixby. Magazine: 5×8; 40 pages. "High quality insightful fiction, very brief and on any theme." Semiannually. Estab. 1988.
Needs: "Brevity is the second most important criterion behind literary quality." Publishes ms within one year of acceptance. Length: 250 words minimum; 1,000 words maximum. Also publishes literary criticism, poetry. Sometimes critiques rejected mss.
How to Contact: Send complete ms with cover letter. Simultaneous submissions OK. Reports in 1 day on queries; 1-7 days on mss. SASE.
Payment: Pays in contributor's copies.
Terms: Acquires one-time rights.
Advice: "Read the works of Amy Hempel, Jim Harrison, Kelly Cherry, C.K. Williams and Janet Kauffman, all excellent writers who epitomize the writing *Parting Gifts* strives to promote. I need more than ever for my authors to be better read. I need for my authors to have read all kinds of fiction and nonfiction, and I sense that many unaccepted writers have not put in the hours reading."

PARTISAN REVIEW, (II), 236 Bay State Rd., Boston MA 02215. (617)353-4260. Editor: William Phillips. Executive Editor: Edith Kurzweil. Magazine: 6×9; 160 pages; 40 lb. paper; 60 lb. cover stock. "Theme is of world literature and contemporary culture: fiction, essays and poetry with emphasis on the arts and political and social commentary, for the general intellectual public; scholars." Quarterly. Estab. 1934. Circ. 8,000.
Needs: Contemporary, experimental, literary, prose poem, regional and translations. Receives 100 unsolicited fiction mss/month. Buys 2 mss/issue; 8 mss/year. Published work by José Donoso, Isaac Bashevis Singer, Doris Lessing; published new writers within the last year. Length: open. Publishes short shorts.
How to Contact: Send complete ms with SASE and cover letter listing past credits. No simultaneous submissions. Accepts computer printout submissions. Reports in 4 months on mss. Sample copy for $5 and $1.50 postage.
Payment: Pays $25-200; 1 contributor's copy.
Terms: Pays on publication for first rights.
Advice: "Please, research the type of fiction we publish. Often we receive manuscripts which are entirely inappropriate for our journal. Sample copies are available for sale and this is a good way to determine audience."

PASSAGER, A Journal of Remembrance and Discovery, (II, IV), University of Baltimore, 1420 N. Charles, Baltimore MD 21201-5779. Editor: Kendra Kopelke. Fiction Editor: Sally Darnowsky. Magazine: 8¼ square; 32-36 pages; 70 lb. paper; 80 lb. cover; photographs. "We publish stories and novel excerpts to 3,000 words, poems to 50 lines. Query for interviews." Quarterly. Estab. 1990. Circ. 750.

Needs: "Publishes personal voices that speak about the strangeness and wonder of the passage of time. Special interest in older writers, but publishes all ages." Receives 300 unsolicited mss/month. Accepts 3-4 prose mss/issue; 12-15/year. Publishes ms up to 1 year after acceptance. Recently published work by Elisavietta Ritchie, Lawrence Durrell, Edmund Keeley, Ronnie Gilbert. Length: 250 words minimum; 3,000 words maximum. Publishes short shorts. Also publishes literary essays, poetry. Length: 250 words. Often critiques rejected mss.

How to Contact: Send complete ms with cover letter. Reports in 2-3 months on mss. SASE. Simultaneous submissions OK, if noted. Sample copy for $3.50. Fiction guidelines for #10 SAE and 1 first class stamp.

Payment: Pays subscription to magazine and contributor's copies.

Terms: Acquires first North American serial rights. Sometimes sends galleys to author.

Advice: "*Get a copy* so you can see the quality of the work we use. We often reject beautifully written work that is bland in favor of rougher work that has the spark we're looking for. In those cases, we try to work with the author to bring the work to a publishable condition—if possible."

PASSAGES NORTH, (II), Kalamazoo College, 1200 Academy St., Kalamazoo MI 49007. Editor: Michael Barrett. Associate Editors: Cullen Bailey Burns, Peter Ingalls. Magazine: 5¼ × 8½; 100 pages; original art and photography. "*Passages North* publishes quality fiction, poetry and creative nonfiction by emerging and established writers." Readership: General and literary. Semiannual. Estab. 1979. Circ. 1,500.

Needs: "Excellence is our only criteria. We seek outstanding fiction regardless of subject, form or style." Accepts 5-10 mss/year. Does not read June-August. Published works by Susan Straight, Gary Gildner, Rennie Sparks; published new writers within the last year. Length: Open. Critiques returned mss when there is time.

How to Contact: Send complete mss with SASE and brief letter of previous publication, awards. Simultaneous submissions OK, if writer's phone number is included. Reports in 3 weeks to 2 months. Publishes an average of 3-6 months after acceptance. Sample copy $3.

Payment: Pays 3 contributor's copies. Frequent honoraria.

Terms: Rights revert to author on publication. No reprints.

PEARL, A Literary Magazine, (II, IV), Pearl, 3030 E. Second St., Long Beach CA 90803. (310)434-4523. Editors: Joan Jobe Smith, Marilyn Johnson and Barbara Hauk. Magazine: 5½ × 8½; 72 pages; 60 lb. bond paper; 80 lb. gloss cover; b&w drawings and graphics. "We are primarily a poetry magazine, but we do publish some *very short* fiction and nonfiction. We are interested in lively, readable prose that speaks to *real* people in direct, living language; for a general literary audience." Triannually. Estab. 1974 ("folded" after 3 issues but began publishing again in 1987). Circ. 500.

● *Pearl* editors plan to publish an annual fiction issue beginning in 1993. This has increased their fiction needs greatly.

Needs: Contemporary, humor/satire, literary, mainstream, prose poem. "We will only consider short-short stories up to 1,200 words. Longer stories (up to 4,000 words) may only be submitted to our short story contest. All contest entries are considered for publication. Although we have no taboos stylistically or subject-wise, obscure, predictable, sentimental, or cliché-ridden stories are a turn-off." Publishes a special fiction issue each year. Receives 4-5 unsolicited mss/month. Accepts 1-10 mss/issue; 2-12 mss/year. Publishes ms 6 months to 1 year after acceptance. Recently published work by MacDonald Harris, Sara Backer, C. Marcus Parr, Margaret Kaufmann, Donna Hilbert. Length: 1,000 words average; 500 words minimum; 1,200 words maximum. Also publishes poetry.

How to Contact: Send complete ms with cover letter including publishing credits and brief biographical information. No simultaneous submissions. Reports in 6-8 weeks on mss. SASE. Sample copy $5 (postpaid). Fiction guidelines for #10 SAE and 1 first class stamp.

Payment: Pays 2 contributor's copies.

Terms: Acquires first North American serial rights. Sends galleys to author. "*Pearl* holds an annual short story contest. Submission period: December 1-March 1. Award: $50, publication in *Pearl*, 10 copies. $5 entry fee. Maximum length: 4,000 words. Send SASE for complete guidelines."

Advice: "We look for vivid, *dramatized* situations and characters, stories written in an original 'voice,' that make sense and follow a clear narrative line. What makes a manuscript stand out is more elusive, though—more to do with feeling and imagination than anything else . . ."

‡PECKERWOOD, (II), 1503-1465 Lawrence W, Toronto, Ontario M6L 1B2 Canada. (416)248-2675. Editor: Ernie Ourique. Magazine: 7 × 8½; 45 pages; 20 lb. bond paper; illustrations. "The alternative to a lively bout of oral sex." Triannually. Estab. 1987. Circ. 300.
Needs: Literary, regional, translations. Receives 17 unsolicited mss/month. Acquires 1 ms/issue; 2 mss/year. Publishes ms 1 month after acceptance. Length: 500 words minimum; 3,000 words maximum. Publishes short shorts. Length: 250 words. Also publishes literary essays, literary criticism and poetry. Often critiques or comments on rejected mss.
How to Contact: Send complete ms with cover letter. Should include 50-word bio. Reports in 1 month. Send SASE for reply, return of ms or send disposable copy of the ms. No simultaneous submissions. Sample copy for $2 (Canadian), 7 × 8½ SAE and 2 IRCs. Fiction guidelines for #10 SAE and 1 IRC.
Payment: Pays 3 contributor's copies.
Terms: Acquires first rights.
Advice: Looks for "fiction that is unafraid to be crossed over into poetry. The sad beautiful reality of living in a world where you're born, suffer and work, love. Don't listen to anybody, read everything, stop writing, start listening to yourself. Never explain yourself."

THE PEGASUS REVIEW, (I, IV), Box 134, Flanders NJ 07836. (201)927-0749. Editor: Art Bounds. Magazine: 5½ × 8½; 6-8 pages; illustrations. "Our magazine is a bimonthly, entirely in calligraphy, illustrated. Each issue is based on specific themes. More pages in 1993." Estab. 1980. Circ. 250.
Needs: Humor/satire, literary, prose poem and religious/inspirational. Upcoming themes: "Challenges" (January/February); "Education" (March/April); "Childhood" (May/June); "Civilization" (July/August); "Heroes" (September/October); "Beliefs" (November/December). "Themes may be approached by humor, satire, inspirational, autobiographical, prose. Try to avoid the obvious." Receives 50 unsolicited mss/month. Accepts 65-75 mss/year. Published work by new writers within the last year. Publishes short shorts 3 pages; 500 words. Themes are subject to change, so query if in doubt. "Occasional brief critiques."
How to Contact: Send complete ms. SASE "a must." Brief cover letter with author's background and full name—no initials. Simultaneous submissions acceptable, if so advised. Sample copy $2. Fiction guidelines for SAE.
Payment: Pays 2 contributor's copies. Occasional book awards.
Terms: Acquires one-time rights.
Advice: "Read what is being written today but also read the classics. Pay as much attention to your markets as to your writing. Persevere. Because of calligraphy format brevity is the key."

PEMBROKE MAGAZINE, (I, II), Box 60, Pembroke State University, Pembroke NC 28372. (919)521-4214, ext. 433. Editor: Shelby Stephenson. Fiction Editor: Stephen Smith. Magazine: 9 × 10; 225 pages; illustrations; photos. Magazine of poems and stories plus literary essays. Annually. Estab. 1969. Circ. 500.
Needs: Open. Receives 120 unsolicited mss/month. Publishes short shorts. Published work by Fred Chappell, Robert Morgan; published new writers within the last year. Length: open. Occasionally critiques rejected mss and recommends other markets.
How to Contact: Send complete ms. No simultaneous submissions. Reports in up to 3 months. SASE. Accepts computer printout submissions. Sample copy $3 and 9 × 10 SAE.
Payment: Pays 1 contributor's copy.
Advice: "Write with an end for *writing*, not publication."

PENNSYLVANIA ENGLISH, (II), English Department, Penn State University—Erie, Humanities Division, Erie PA 16563. Editor: Dean Baldwin. Fiction Editor: Chris Dubbs. Magazine: 7 × 8½; 100 pages; 20 lb. bond paper; 65 lb. matte cover. For "teachers of English in Pennsylvania at the high school and college level." Semiannually. Estab. 1985. Circ. 300.
Needs: Literary, contemporary mainstream. Does not read mss from May to August. Publishes ms an average of 6 months after acceptance. Length: 5,000 words maximum. Publishes short shorts. Also publishes literary essays, literary criticism, poetry. Sometimes critiques rejected mss.

Check the Category Indexes, located at the back of the book, for publishers interested in specific fiction subjects.

How to Contact: Send complete ms with cover letter. Reports in 2 months. SASE. Simultaneous submissions OK.
Payment: Pays in contributor's copies.
Terms: Acquires first North American serial rights.

‡**PENNSYLVANIA REVIEW,** University of Pittsburgh, 526 C.L./English Dept., Pittsburgh PA 15260. (412)624-0026. Managing Editor: Julie Parson-Nesbitt. Magazine: 7×10; 70-100 pages. Magazine of fiction, poetry, nonfiction, interviews, reviews, novel excerpts, long poems for literate audience. Semi-annually. Estab. 1985. Circ. 1,000.
Needs: Ethnic, experimental, feminist, gay, humor/satire, lesbian, literary, prose poem, regional, translations. "High quality!" Receives 75 unsolicited fiction mss/month. Accepts 3-5 mss/issue; 6-10 mss/year. Deadlines: Dec. 1 and March 1. Mss not read in summer months. Recently published work by Sharon Doubiago and Maggie Anderson; published new writers within the last year. Length: 5,000 maximum words for prose. Comments on rejected mss "rarely and only if we've had some interest."
How to Contact: Send complete ms. Reports in 2 weeks on queries; 2-3 months on ms. SASE for ms. Simultaneous submissions OK, if informed when ms is accepted elsewhere. Sample copy $5. Fiction guidelines for #10 SAE and 1 first class stamp.
Payment: Pays 1 contributor's copy.
Advice: "Don't be discouraged when your work is returned to you. Returns are not necessarily a comment on the quality of the writing. Keep trying."

PEOPLENET, "Where People Meet People," (IV), Box 897, Levittown NY 11756. (516)579-4043. Editor: Robert Mauro. Newsletter: 8½×11; 12 pages; 20 lb. paper; 20 lb. cover stock. "Romance stories featuring disabled characters." Quarterly. Estab. 1987. Circ. 200.
Needs: Romance, contemporary and disabled. Main character must be disabled. Upcoming theme: "Marriage between disabled and non-disabled." Accepts 1 ms/issue; 3 mss/year. Publishes ms up to 2 years after acceptance. Length: 500-1,000 words; 800-1,000 average. Publishes short shorts. Also publishes literary criticism, poetry.
How to Contact: Send complete ms and SASE. Reports in 1 month *"only* if SASE there." No simultaneous submissions. Sample copy $3. Fiction guidelines for #10 SAE and 1 first class stamp.
Payment: Pays 1¢/word on acceptance.
Terms: Acquires first rights.
Advice: "We are looking for stories of under 1,000 words on romance with a disabled man or woman as the main character. No sob stories or 'super crip' stories. Just realistic romance. No porn. Love, respect, trust, understanding and acceptance are what I want."

PERCEPTIONS, (I), 1530 Phillips, Missoula MT 59802. (406)543-5875. Editor: Temi Rose. Magazine: 4×5; 20 pages. Publishes "primarily women's perceptions," for readers of "all ages, both sexes." Triannually. Estab. 1982. Circ. 100.
• Work published in *Perceptions* has been selected regularly to appear in the *Pushcart Prize* anthology. The magazine is also included in *Ms* magazine's list of feminist publications.
Needs: Adventure, condensed/excerpted novel, confession, contemporary, experimental, fantasy, feminist, mystery/suspense, prose poem, psychic/supernatural/occult, religious/inspirational, science fiction. Publishes short shorts. Collected by University of Wisconsin, Madison Serials Library; produces poetry videos with permission of writers. Critiques rejected mss "only if requested."
How to Contact: Query first. Reports in 1 month. SASE. Simultaneous and reprint submissions OK. Accepts electronic submissions via disk or modem. Sample copy $5. Fiction guidelines for SAE and 1 first class stamp.
Payment: Pays in contributor's copies.

‡**PERCEPTIONS, The Journal of Imaginative Sensuality, (II, IV),** Sensuous SIG, Inc., P.O. Box 2867, Toledo OH 43606-0867. Fax: (419)474-1009. Editor: Victoria. Magazine: 5½×8½; 44 pages; 20 lb. bond paper; 60 lb. cover; illustrations; photographs. *"Perceptions* is a journal celebrating the nature of sensuality. We celebrate a realization that virtually everything sexual is sensual, but that sensuality's diversity far exceeds only a sexual purview." Quarterly. Estab. 1988. Circ. 250.
Needs: Erotica, experimental, gay, humor/satire, lesbian, psychic/supernatural/occult, science fiction (soft/sociological). "Any fiction with a sensual slant. We do not accept pornography or graphically obscene fiction." Receives 10 unsolicited mss/month. Acquires 4-5 mss/issue; 20 mss/year. Publishes ms 2-6 months after acceptance. Recently published work by Vlasa Glen, Bud Martin, Bart Geraci, Alan Schwartz.. Length: 800 words preferred; 400 words minimum; 1,600 words maximum (unless

serialized). Publishes short shorts. Length: 400-800 words. Also publishes literary essays, literary criticism and poetry. Always critiques or comments on rejected mss.

How to Contact: Send $3 for 44-page sample issue and submission guidelines. Should include 3-4 sentence bio. Reports in 2 weeks on queries; 2 months on mss. Send SASE for reply, return of ms or send disposable copy of ms. Simultaneous and reprint submissions OK. Electronic submission preferred. Sample copy for $3 (fiction guidelines included).

Payment: Pays 1 contributor's copy. Additional copies $2.

Terms: Acquires one-time rights.

Advice: "We prefer fiction that has an original or unusual story or angle. We attempt to publish fiction from a variety of viewpoints. Steer away from the temptation to depict sexuality or erotic issues in a graphic or obscene way. We prefer more sensual or 'intellectual' stories."

PEREGRINE, The Journal of Amherst Writers and Artists, (II), Amherst Writers and Artists Press, Box 1076, Amherst MA 01004. (413)253-3307. Fiction Editor: Kathy Dunn. Fiction editors change every year. Send future submissions to Pat Schneider, editor. Magazine: 5 × 7; 90 pages; sturdy matte white paper; heavier cover stock. "Poetry and prose—short stories, short short stories, and occasionally prose fantasies or reflections that are fiction yet are not stories." Annually.

• *Peregrine* has been awarded grants from the Massachusetts Cultural Council for the past six years.

Needs: "No specific 'category' requirements; we publish what we love." Accepts 2-4 mss/issue. Publishes ms an average of 6 months after acceptance. Recently published work by Anna Kirwan Vogel, Jane Yolen, Barbara VanNoord; published new writers within the last year. Length: 1,000-2,500 words preferred. Publishes short shorts. "Short pieces have a better chance of publication."

How to Contact: Send complete ms with cover letter, which should include brief biographical note. Reports in 3-6 months. SASE. Simultaneous submissions OK. Sample copy $3 plus $2 postage.

Payment: Pays contributor's copies.

Terms: All rights return to writer upon publication.

Advice: "Every manuscript is read by 3 or more readers. We publish what we love most—and it has varied widely."

‡PHOEBE, An Interdisciplinary Journal of Feminist Scholarship, (II, IV), Theory and Aesthetics, Women's Studies Program, State University of New York, College at Oneonta, Oneonta NY 13820. (607)431-2014. Editor: Kathleen O'Mara. Fiction Editor: Charlotte Walker. Journal: 8½ × 11; 115 pages; 80 lb. paper; illustrations and photos. "Feminist material for feminist scholars and readers." Semiannually. Estab. 1989. Circ. 400.

Needs: Feminist: ethnic, experimental, gay, humor/satire, lesbian, literary, translations. Receives 6 unsolicited mss/month. "One-third to one-half of each issue is short fiction and poetry." Does not read mss in summer. Publishes ms 3-4 months after acceptance. Length: 1,500-2,500 words preferred. Publishes short shorts. Sometimes critiques rejected mss and recommends other markets.

How to Contact: Send complete ms with cover letter. Reports in 1 month on queries; 15 weeks on mss. Sample copy for $7.50. Fiction guidelines free.

Payment: Pays in contributor's copies.

Terms: Acquires one-time rights.

Advice: "We look for writing with a feminist perspective. *Phoebe* was founded to provide a forum for cross-cultural feminist analysis, debate and exchange. The editors are committed to providing space for all disciplines and new areas of research, criticism and theory in feminist scholarship and aesthetics. *Phoebe* is not committed to any one conception of feminism. All work that is not sexist, racist, homophobic, or otherwise discriminatory, will be welcome. *Phoebe* is particularly committed to publishing work informed by a theoretical perspective which will enrich critical thinking."

PHOEBE, A Journal of Literary Arts, (II), George Mason University, 4400 University Dr., Fairfax VA 22030. (703)993-2915. Editor: Jeff McDaniel. Fiction Editors: Scott Garson, Piers Marchant, Adrian Lurssen. Editors change each year. Magazine: 6 × 9; 116 pages; 80 lb. quality paper; 0-5 illustrations per issue; 0-10 photographs per issue. "We publish fiction, poetry, photographs, illustrations and some reviews." Published 2 times/year. Estab. 1972. Circ. 2,500.

Needs: "Looking for a broad range of poetry, fiction and essays. Encourage writers and poets to experiment, to stretch the boundaries of genre." No romance, western, juvenile, erotica. Receives 20 mss/month. Accepts 5-7 mss/issue; 20-28 mss/year. Does not read mss in summer. Deadlines for mss are: September 25th for Fall issue; February 10th for Spring issue. Publishes ms 3-6 months after acceptance. Length: "no more than 35 pages. Also publishes literary essays, literary criticism, poetry.

How to Contact: Send complete ms with cover letter. Include "name, address, phone. Brief bio." SASE. Simultaneous submissions OK. Sample copy $3.25.

Payment: Pays 4 contributor's copies.

Terms: Acquires one-time rights. All rights revert to author.

Advice: "We are interested in a variety of fiction, poetry and nonfiction. We suggest potential contributors study previous issues."

PIG IRON, (II), Box 237, Youngstown OH 44501. (216)783-1269. Editor: Jim Villani. Magazine. 8½ × 11; 128 pages; 60 lb. offset paper; 85 pt. coated cover stock; b&w illustrations; b&w 120 line photographs. "Contemporary literature by new and experimental writers." Annually. Estab. 1975. Circ. 1,000.

Needs: Literary and thematic. No mainstream. Upcoming theme: "The American Dream" (deadline: September 1992). Buys 10-20 mss/issue. Receives approximately 75-100 unsolicited fiction mss each month. Recently published work by Laural Speer, Eve Shelnutt, Reg Saner, Rhona McAdam. Length: 8,000 words maximum. Also publishes literary essays, poetry.

How to Contact: Send complete ms with SASE. No simultaneous submissions. Reports in 3 months. Sample copy $3.

Payment: Pays $5/printed page; 2 contributor's copies; $5 charge for extras.

Terms: Pays on publication for first North American serial rights.

Advice: "Looking for works that do not ignore psychological development in character and plot/ action." Mss are rejected because of "lack of new ideas and approaches. Writers need to work out interesting plot/action and setting/set. Read a lot; read for stylistic innovation. Send SASE for current theme list."

THE PIKESTAFF FORUM, (II), Box 127, Normal IL 61761. (309)452-4831. Editors: Robert D. Sutherland, James Scrimgeour, James McGowan and Curtis White. Tabloid: 11½ × 17½; 40 pages; newsprint paper; illustrations; photos. "*The Pikestaff Forum* is a general literary magazine publishing poetry, prose fiction, drama." Readership: "General literary with a wide circulation in the small press world. Readers are educated (but not academic) and have a taste for excellent serious fiction." Published irregularly—"whenever we have sufficient quality material to warrant an issue." Estab. 1977. Circ. 1,000.

Needs: Literary and contemporary with a continuing need for good short stories or novel excerpts. "We welcome traditional and experimental works from established and non-established writers. We look for writing that is clear, concise and to the point; contains vivid imagery and sufficient concrete detail; is grounded in lived human experience; contains memorable characters and situations. No confessional self-pity or puffery; self-indulgent first or second drafts; sterile intellectual word games or five-finger exercises or slick formula writing, genre-pieces that do not go beyond their form (westerns, mysteries, gothic, horror, science fiction, swords-and-sorcery fantasy), commercially oriented mass-market stuff, violence for its own sake, racist or sexist material or pornography (sexploitation)." Accepts 1-4 mss/issue. Receives approximately 15-20 unsolicited fiction mss each month. Published work by Constance Pierce, Linnea Johnson; published new writers within the last year. Length: from 1 paragraph to 4,000 or 5,000 words. Also publishes poetry. Critiques rejected mss when there is time.

How to Contact: Query. Send complete ms. SASE. "Reluctantly" accepts simultaneous submissions. Reports in 3 weeks on queries, 3 months on mss. Publishes ms up to 1 year after acceptance. Sample copy $2.

Payment: Pays 3 contributor's copies. Cover price less 50% discount for extras.

Terms: Acquires first rights. Copyright remains with author.

Advice: "We are highly selective, publishing only 3% of the stories that are submitted for consideration. Read other authors with an appreciative and critical eye; don't send out work prematurely; develop keen powers of observation and a good visual memory; get to know your characters thoroughly; don't let others (editors, friends, etc.) define or 'determine' your sense of self-worth; be willing to learn; outgrow self-indulgence. Develop discipline. Show, don't tell; and leave some work for the reader to do. Write for the fun of it (that way there's a sure return for the investment of time and effort). Always write to achieve the best quality you can; be honest with yourself, your potential readers, and your story. Learn to become your own best editor: know when you've done well, and when you haven't done as well as you can. Remember: there's a lot of competition for the available publication slots, and editorial bias is always a factor in what gets accepted for publication. Develop a sense of humor about the enterprise."

THE PINEHURST JOURNAL, Pinehurst Press, P.O. Box 360747, Milpitas CA 95036. (408)945-0986. Editor: Michael K. McNamara. Contributing Editor: Kathleen M. McNamara. Magazine: 8½×11; 48 pages; recycled 24 lb. paper; 60 lb. cover; illustrations. "Fiction, nonfiction and poetry for an educated audience appreciative of polished, thought-provoking work." Quarterly. Estab. 1990. Circ. 300.
Needs: Contemporary, experimental, feminist, gay, historical (general), horror, humor/satire, lesbian, literary, mainstream, mystery/suspense, prose poem. "No hard sci-fi, fantasy, occult, swords and sorcery, slasher or porn, travel or religious. No formula western or romance." Receives 80 mss/month. Accepts 17 mss/issue; 65-70 mss/year. Publishes ms 1-4 months after acceptance. Length: 2,000 words average; 750 words minimum; 4,000 words maximum. Publishes literary essays, some literary and poetry criticism. Critiques mss and recommends other markets.
How to Contact: Send complete manuscript with cover letter and short bio which includes publishing successes, if any. Indicate whether piece is a simultaneous submittal. Reports in 1 month or less on queries; 2 months or less on mss. SASE. Simultaneous submissions OK. Sample copy for $5. Guidelines for #10 SAE and 1 first class stamp.
Payment: Pays $5 and 1 contributor's copy for fiction. Charge for extras.
Terms: Buys one-time rights.
Advice: "Try to make each word pull its own weight and polish, polish, polish then punctuate, punctuate, punctuate."

‡PIRATE WRITINGS, A Literary and Poetry Collective, (II), 53 Whitman Ave., Islip NY 11751. Poetry Editor: Mark Cudak. Fiction Editor: Edward J. McFadden. Magazine. "We are looking for poetry and short stories that entertain." Semiannually. Estab. 1992. Circ. 1,000.
Needs: Adventure, fantasy (science fantasy, sword and sorcery), literary, mystery/suspense, science fiction. Plans to publish special fiction issue or anthology in the future. Receives 10-20 unsolicited mss/month. Buys 4 mss/issue; 8-10 mss/year. Publishes ms 6 months-1 year after acceptance. Length: 1,750 words average; 750 words minimum; 3,000 words maximum. Also publishes poetry. Sometimes critiques or comments on rejected mss.
How to Contact: Send complete ms with cover letter. Should include estimated word count, 1 paragraph bio, social security number, list of publications with submission. Reports in 1 week on queries; 2 months on mss. Send SASE (or IRC) for reply or return of ms or disposable copy of ms. Will consider simultaneous submissions. Sample copy $3. Fiction guidelines for #10 SAE.
Payment: Pays 2 contributor's copies.
Terms: Acquires first North American serial rights.
Advice: "We want the best fiction by new and under-published writers. Think about what you write. Send your best!"

‡PLÉIADES MAGAZINE/PHILAE (I), Box 357, Suite D, 6677 W. Colfax, Lakewood CO 80215. John Moravec, Pléiades Productions. Magazine: 8½×11; 30-50 pages; 30 lb. paper; illustrations. "We want well thought out material; no sex stories, and good rhymed poetry and carefully written prose. We want articles about national issues." Both magazines will, in the future, be published twice a year; *Philae* more often depending on material. *Philae* estab. 1947, *Pléiades*, estab. 1984. Circ. 10,000.
Needs: Literary, fantasy, horror, mystery/suspense, senior citizen/retirement, serialized/excerpted novel, western. Receives 50-100 unsolicited mss/month. Publishes ms 3 months or less after acceptance. Length: 1,200-1,800 words average; 500-800 words minimum.
How to Contact: Send complete ms with short cover letter. SASE. Reports in 2-3 weeks. Simultaneous submissions OK. Sample copy $3.75. (Checks made out to John L. Moravec). Fiction guidelines for #10 SAE and 1 first class stamp.
Payment: Pays in contributor's copies, awards, trophies.
Advice: "Learn to write, and take lessons on punctuation. Shorter fiction and articles considered first."

PLOUGHSHARES, (II), Emerson College, 100 Beacon St., Boston MA 02116. (617)578-8753. Executive Director: DeWitt Henry. "Our theme is new writing (poetry, fiction, personal essays) that addresses contemporary adult readers who look to fiction and poetry for help in making sense of themselves and of each other." Triquarterly. Estab. 1971. Circ. 3,800.
 • *Ploughshares* also sponsors a writing seminar in Holland. See the 1991 *Novel & Short Story Writer's Market* for a Close-up on the conference and the listing in the Conference section of this edition.

Needs: Literary, prose poem. "No genre (science fiction, detective, gothic, adventure, etc.), popular formula or commercial fiction whose purpose is to entertain rather than to illuminate." Buys 20+ mss/year. Receives approximately 400-600 unsolicited fiction mss each month. Published work by Rick Bass, Joy Williams, Andre Dubus; published new writers within the last year. Length: 300-6,000 words.
How to Contact: "Query with #10 SASE for guidelines and examine a sample issue. Reading periods and needs vary." Cover letter should include "previous pubs." SASE. Reports in 3-5 months on mss. Sample copy $8.95. (Please specify fiction issue sample.)
Payment: Pays $10/page to $50 maximum, plus copies. Offers 50% kill fee for assigned ms not published.
Terms: Pays on publication for first North American serial rights.
Advice: "Be familiar with our fiction issues, fiction by our writers and by our various editors (e.g., Rosellen Brown, Tim O'Brien, Jay Neugeboren, Jayne Anne Phillips, James Alan McPherson) and more generally acquaint yourself with the best short fiction currently appearing in the literary quarterlies, and the annual prize anthologies (*Pushcart Prize, O. Henry Awards, Best American Short Stories*). Also realistically consider whether the work you are submitting is as good as or better than—in your own opinion—the work appearing in the magazine you're sending to. What is the level of competition? And what is its volume? (In our case, we accept about 1 ms in 200.) Never send 'blindly' to a magazine, or without carefully weighing your prospect there against those elsewhere. Always keep a copy of work you submit."

THE PLOWMAN, (II), Box 414, Whitby Ontario L1N 5S4 Canada. Editor: Tony Scavetta. Tabloid: 112 pages; illustrations and photos. Monthly. Estab. 1988. Circ. 15,000.
● The publisher of *The Plowman* also produces several hundred chapbooks each year.
Needs: "An international journal publishing all holocaust, relition, didactic, ethnic, eclectic, love and other stories."
How to Contact: Send complete ms with cover letter. Reports in 1 week. Enclose IRCs. Simultaneous and reprint submissions OK. Sample copy and fiction guidelines for SAE.
Payment: Pays in contributor's copies; charges for extras.
Terms: Acquires one-time rights. Sends galleys to author.

POETIC SPACE, Poetry & Fiction, (I, II), P.O. Box 11157, Eugene OR 97440. Editor: Don Hildenbrand. Fiction Editor: Thomas Strand. Magazine: 8×11; 16 pages; light paper; medium cover; b&w art. "Social, political, avant-garde, erotic, environmental material for a literary audience." Biannually (Sept. and March). Estab. 1983. Circ. 600.
● *Poetic Space* received a grant from the Lane Arts Council (Eugene, Oregon) for 1992. This is the magazine's fourth year receiving a Council grant.
Needs: Contemporary, erotica, ethnic, experimental, fantasy, feminist, gay, humor/satire, lesbian, literary, prose poem, regional, serialized novel, translations. No sentimental, romance, mainstream. Plans special anthology issue Spring '92. Receives 10-12 unsolicited mss/month. Accepts 2 mss/issue; 4-6 mss/year. Publishes ms 3-4 months after acceptance. Recently published work by Nathan Versace and Louise A. Blum. Length: 1,500-2,000 words average. Publishes short shorts. Also publishes literary essays, literary criticism, poetry. Sometimes critiques rejected mss and recommends other markets.
How to Contact: Send complete ms with cover letter that includes basic info/credits. Reports in 1-2 weeks on queries; 1-2 months on mss. SASE. No simultaneous submissions. Sample copy for $3, 4×9 SAE and 45¢ postage. Fiction guidelines for #10 SAE and 1 first class stamp. Reviews novels and short story collections. Send books to Don Hildenbrand.
Payment: Pays contributor's copies.
Terms: Acquires one-time rights or "reserves anthology rights."

POETRY FORUM SHORT STORIES, (I, II), Poetry Forum, 5713 Larchmont Dr., Erie PA 16509. (814)866-2543. Fax: (814)866-2543 (fax hours 8-10 a.m., 5-8 p.m.). Editor: Gunver Skogsholm. Newspaper: 7×8½; 34 pages; card cover; illustrations. "Human interest themes (no sexually explicit or racially biased or blasphemous material) for the general public—from the grassroot to the intellectual." Quarterly. Estab. 1989. Circ. 400.
● The editor of this publication also edits *The Journal* (see the listing in this section). Note the publication policy charging for membership to the magazine for publication.
Needs: Confession, contemporary, ethnic, experimental, fantasy, feminist, historical, literary, mainstream, mystery/suspense, prose poem, religious/inspirational, romance, science fiction, senior citizen/retirement, young adult/teen. "No blasphemous, sexually explicit material." Publishes annual special fiction issue. Receives 50 unsolicited mss/month. Accepts 12 mss/issue; 40 mss/year. Publishes ms 6

months after acceptance. Agented fiction less than 1%. Recently published work by Bernard Hewitt, Don Peyer, Jess Wilbanks. Length: 2,000 words average; 500 words minimum; 5,000 words maximum. Also publishes literary essays, literary criticism, poetry.

How to Contact: *This magazine charges a "professional members" fee of $36.* The fee entitles you to publication of a maximum of 3,000 words. Send complete ms with cover letter. Reports in 3 weeks to 2 months on mss. SASE. Simultaneous and reprint submissions OK. "Accepts electronic submissions via disk gladly." Sample copy $3. Fiction guidelines for SAE and 1 first class stamp. Reviews novels and short story collections.

Terms: Charges for publication (see above). Acquires one-time rights.

Advice: Also sponsors contest.

POETRY MAGIC PUBLICATIONS, (I), 1630 Lake Dr., Haslett MI 48840. (517)339-0583. Editor: Lisa Roose-Church. Magazine: 8½×11; b&w illustrations. "Publishes poetry and articles relating to writing. Have used other themes. We will consider just about anything of high quality." Quarterly. Estab. 1988.

Needs: Contemporary, humor, prose poem. No pornography, science fiction, horror, fantasy. "We publish anthologies that writers can submit work for. Receives over 100 mss/month. Accepts 2 mss/issue. Publishes ms within 6 months of acceptance. Published work by Scott Sonders. Length: 50-500 words preferred; 50 words minimum; 1,000 words sometimes. Also publishes poetry. Sometimes critiques rejected mss and recommends other markets.

How to Contact: Query first, query with clips of published work or send complete ms with cover letter. Reports in 2-6 weeks. SASE. Simultaneous (if stated) and reprint submissions OK. Sample copy of newsletter for $4.50. Anthology sample available for $5 plus $2 postage. Fiction guidelines for #10 SAE and 1 first class stamp.

Payment: Pays in contributor's copies (minimum) to $100 (maximum) for newsletter only.

Terms: Acquires first rights or one-time rights.

Advice: "Correct usage of grammar, punctuation, etc. is important. We prefer fiction that is quality reading, which entices the reader for more from that author. Because we get less fiction than poetry, we are selective because our readers want to be enticed, enthralled and overwhelmed with a story. If it doesn't do this for the editor she will not accept it. Experiment and create your own style."

POETRY MOTEL, (II), Suburban Wilderness Press, 1619 Jefferson, Duluth MN 55812. Editor: Pat McKinnon. Fiction Editor: Bud Bracken. Magazine: 7×8½; 50-80 pages; 20 lb. paper; various cover; various amount of illustrations and photographs. "We're wide open though we lean toward wry satire and hilarity." 1-2 times annually. Estab. 1984. Circ. 500.

Needs: Condensed/excerpted novel, contemporary, erotica, ethnic, fantasy, feminist, gay, humor/satire, lesbian, literary, prose poem, science fiction. "Nothing along the popular/genre lines." Receives 2-5 unsolicited mss/month. Accepts 2-5 mss/issue; 2-10 mss/year. Publishes ms 1 month to 2 years after acceptance. Recently published work by Willie Smith, Gregory Burnham, Hugh Knox. Length: 300 words average; 25 words minimum; 1,500 words maximum. Publishes short shorts. Length: 300-500 words. Also publishes literary essays, literary criticism, poetry. Sometimes critiques rejected mss.

How to Contact: Send complete ms with cover letter. Reports in 1 week on queries; 1 week to 1 month on mss. SASE. Simultaneous and reprint submissions OK. Sample copy $5.95. Fiction guidelines for #10 SAE and 1 first class stamp. Reviews novels and short story collections.

Payment: Pays contributor's copies. Charge for extras.

Terms: Acquires one-time rights.

Advice: "Read what we print first since it is beyond description and never what you might imagine."

THE POINTED CIRCLE, (II), Portland Community College-Cascade, 705 N. Killingsworth St., Portland OR 97217. (503)244-6111 ext. 5405. Editors: Student Editorial Staff. Magazine: 7×8½; approx. 80 pages; b&w illustrations and photographs. "Anything of interest to educationally/culturally mixed audience." Annually. Estab. 1980.

Needs: Contemporary, ethnic, literary, prose poem, regional. "We will read whatever is sent, but encourage writers to remember we are a quality literary/arts magazine intended to promote the arts in the community." Acquires 3-7 mss/year. We accept submissions only December 1-March 1, for October 1 issue. Length: 3,500 words average; 500 words minimum; 5,000 words maximum. Publishes short shorts. Length: 100 words. Rarely critiques rejected mss and sometimes recommends other markets.

How to Contact: Send complete ms with cover letter and brief bio. SASE. Simultaneous submissions OK. Sample copy for $3.50. Fiction guidelines for #10 SAE and 1 first class stamp.
Payment: Pays in contributor's copies.
Terms: Acquires one-time rights.
Advice: "Looks for quality—topicality—nothing trite. The author cares about language and acts responsibly toward the reader, honors the reader's investment of time and piques the reader's interest."

‡**PORTABLE LOWER EAST SIDE, (IV),** P.O. Box 30323, New York NY 10011. Editor: Arthur Nersesian. Magazine: 5x11; 170 pages; 10 pt. cover stock; photos. "New York work, different themes." Semiannually. Estab. 1983. Circ. 2,000.
Needs: Erotica, ethnic/multicultural, gay, lesbian, literary, mainstream/contemporary, mystery/suspense, regional (New York). Upcoming themes: "Afro-American" (7/93). Publishes anthologies. Receives 30 unsolicited mss/month. Buys 2 mss/issue; 4 mss/year. Does not read mss during summer. Publishes ms 3-6 months after acceptance. Agented fiction 50%. Recently published work by Ginsberg, Benders. Length: 2,000 words minimum; 5,000 words maximum. Also publishes literary essays, poetry.
How to Contact: Send complete ms with cover letter. Reports in 2-3 months. Send SASE (IRC) for reply, return of ms or send disposable copy of ms. No simultaneous submissions. Sample copy $5.
Payment: Pays 2-3 contributor's copies. Additional copies $4.
Terms: Acquires one-time rights.

THE PORTABLE WALL, (II), Basement Press, 215 Burlington, Billings MT 59101. (406)256-3588. Editor: Daniel Struckman. Magazine: 6×9¼; 40 pages; cotton rag paper; best quality cover; line engravings; illustrations. "We consider all kinds of material. Bias toward humor." Semiannually. Estab. 1977. Circ. 400.
Needs: Adventure, contemporary, ethnic, experimental, feminist, historical, humor/satire, literary, mainstream, prose poem, regional, science fiction, senior citizen, sports, translations. "We favor short pieces and poetry." Receives 5-10 unsolicited mss/month. Accepts 3-4 mss/issue; 6-8 mss/year. Publishes ms 6 months to a year after acceptance. Published works by Gray Harris, Wilbur Wood. Length: 2,000 words preferred. Publishes short shorts. Also publishes literary essays, literary criticism, poetry. Sometimes critiques rejected mss.
How to Contact: Send complete ms with cover letter. No simultaneous submissions. Reports in 2-4 weeks on mss. SASE. Sample copy $6.50.
Payment: Pays subscription to magazine.
Terms: Acquires one-time rights.
Advice: "We like language that evokes believable pictures in our minds and that tells news."

BERN PORTER INTERNATIONAL, Bern Porter Books, 22 Salmond St., Belfast ME 04915. (207)338-6798. Editor: Bern Porter. Magazine: 8½×11; 98-132 pages; illustrations and photographs. "High literary quality with international flavor." Bimonthly. Estab. 1991.
Needs: Experimental, literary, prose poem, translations, international. Publishes special fiction issue. Receives 30-50 unsolicited mss/month. Buys 10-15 mss/issue. Publishes ms immediately after acceptance. Length: Open. Publishes short shorts. Comments on or critiques rejected mss and recommends other markets.
How to Contact: Query first. Reports in 1 week. SASE. Simultaneous and reprint submissions OK. Accepts electronic submissions via disk or modem. Sample copy and fiction guidelines free.
Payment: Pays 6¢/word.
Terms: Pays on publication. Buys world rights. Sends galleys to author.

POSKISNOLT PRESS, Yesterday's Press, (I, II, IV), Yesterday's Press, JAF Station, Box 7415, New York NY 10116-4630. (718)680-3899. Editor: Patricia D. Coscia. Magazine: 7×8½; 20 pages; regular typing paper. Estab. 1989. Circ. 100.
Needs: Contemporary, erotica, ethnic, experimental, fantasy, feminist, gay, humor/satire, lesbian, literary, mainstream, prose poem, psychic/supernatural/occult, romance, young adult, senior citizen/ retirement, western, young adult/teen (10-18 years). "X-rated material is not accepted!" Plans to publish a special fiction issue or anthology in the future. Receives 50 unsolicited mss/month. Accepts 30 mss/issue; 100+ mss/year. Publishes ms 6 months after acceptance. Length: 200 words average; 100 words minimum; 500 words maximum. Publishes short shorts. Length: 100-500 words. Sometimes critiques rejected mss and recommends other markets.

How to Contact: Query first with clips of published work or send complete manuscript with cover letter. Reports in 1 week on queries; 6 months on mss. SASE. Accepts simultaneous submissions. Sample copy for $4 with #10 SASE and $2 postage. Fiction guidelines for #10 SASE and $2 postage.
Payment: Pays with subscription to magazine or contributor's copies; charges for extras.
Terms: Acquires all rights, first rights or one-time rights.

THE POST, (II), Publishers Syndication International, Suite 856, 1377 K St., Washington DC 20005. Editor: A.P. Samuels. Newspaper: 8½×11; 32 pages. Monthly. Estab. 1988.
Needs: Adventure, mystery/suspense (private eye), romance (romantic suspense), western (traditional). "No explicit sex, gore, extreme violence or bad language." Receives 75 unsolicited mss/month. Buys 1 ms/issue; 12 mss/year. Time between acceptance and publication varies. Agented fiction 10%. Length: 10,000 words average.
How to Contact: Send complete manuscript with cover letter. Reports on mss in 5 weeks. No simultaneous submissions. Fiction guidelines for #10 SAE and 1 first class stamp.
Payment: Pays ½¢ to 4¢/word.
Terms: Pays on acceptance for all rights.

POTATO EYES, (II), Nightshade, Box 76, Troy ME 04987. (207)948-3427. Editors: Carolyn Page and Roy Zarucchi. Fiction Editor: Dr. Ted Holmes. Magazine: 5½×8½; 108 pages; 60 lb. text paper; 80 lb. Curtis flannel cover. "We tend to showcase Appalachian talent from Alabama to Quebec, and in doing so, we hope to dispel hackneyed stereotypes and political borders. However, we don't limit ourselves to this area, publishing always the best that we receive. Our subscribers have included: boat builder, teacher, dairy farmer, college prof, doctor, lawyer, world traveler, lumberman . . . and that was just in last week's batch." Estab. 1988. Circ. 800.
  • The publishers of *Potato Eyes* were featured in a Close-up interview in the 1991 *Novel & Short Story Writer's Market*. They also operate Nightshade Press listed in the Small Press section of this book.
Needs: Contemporary, humor/satire, literary, mainstream, regional, and rural themes. Published a *1992 Nightshade Short Story Reader*. Receives 50 unsolicited mss/month. Accepts 5-6 mss/issue; 10-12 mss/year. Publishes ms 2 months-2 years after acceptance. Recently published work by Ann Williams, Pat Carr, Rebecca Rule, Robert Chute and Alice Sink. Length: 3,000 words maximum; 2,000 average. Publishes short shorts. Length: 450 words. Also publishes poetry (looking for English/French translations of Franco poems). Sometimes critiques rejected mss and recommends other markets.
How to Contact: Send complete ms with cover letter. Reports in 3 weeks-4 months on mss. SASE. Sample copy $5, including postage. Fiction guidelines with #10 SAE.
Payment: Pays in contributor's copies.
Terms: Acquires first North American serial rights.
Advice: "We care about the larger issues, including pollution, ecology, bio-regionalism, uncontrolled progress and 'condominia,' as well as the rights of the individual, particularly the elderly. We care about television, the great sewer pipe of America, and what it is doing to America's youth. We are exploring these issues with writers who have originality, a reordered perspective, and who submit to us generous sprinklings of humor and satire. Although we do occasionally comment on valid fiction, we have walked away unscathed from the world of academia and refuse to correct manuscripts. We respect our contributors and treat them as professionals, however, and write personal responses to every submission if given an SASE. We expect the same treatment—clean copy without multi folds or corrections. We like brief non-Narcissistic cover letters containing the straight scoop. We suggest that beginning fiction writers spend the money they have set aside for creative writing courses or conferences and spend it instead on subscriptions to good little literary magazines."

POTPOURRI, (II), P.O. Box 8278, Prairie Village KS 66208. (913)642-1503. Editor: Polly W. Swafford. Fiction Editor: Candy Schock. Newspaper: 12×14; 24 pages. "Literary journal: short stories, verse, essays, travel, prose-poetry for a general adult audience." Offers annual awards in fiction and poetry. Monthly. Estab. 1989. Circ. 6,000.
Needs: Adventure, contemporary, ethnic, experimental, fantasy, historical (general), humor/satire, literary, mainstream, mystery/suspense (private eye), prose poem, romance (contemporary, historical, romantic suspense), science fiction (soft/sociological), western (frontier stories). "*Potpourri* accepts a broad genre; hence its name. Guidelines specify no religious, confessional, racial, political, erotic, abusive or sexual preference materials unless fictional and necessary to plot." Plans special fiction issue. Receives 75 unsolicited mss/month. Accepts 8-10 mss/issue; 100-120 mss/year. Publishes ms 3-6 months after acceptance. Agented fiction 1%. Recently published work by William Wu, David Ray,

Layle Silbert, Wilma Yeo, C. Marcus Parr. Length: 2,500 words maximum. Also publishes poetry. Sometimes critiques on rejected mss and recommends other markets.

How to Contact: Send complete ms with cover letter. Include "complete name, address, phone number, brief summary statement about submission, short bio on author." Reports in 3-6 weeks on queries; 2-4 months on mss. SASE. Simultaneous submissions OK. Sample copy for 9×12 SAE and 3 first class stamps. Fiction guidelines for #10 SAE and 1 first class stamp.

Payment: Pays contributor's copies.

Terms: Acquires first rights.

Advice: Looks for "first: Reader appeal and mastery of craft. Does the manuscript spark immediate interest and the introduction create the effect that will dominate? Second: Action in dialogue or narration that tells the story. Third: Escalation of conflicts and resolution. Conclusion needs to leave something with the reader to be long remembered. We look for the unusual twist. Ask yourself: Is the story idea different? Does the story hold the reader's interest from the very beginning to the end? Try reading your story aloud to yourself and to others. Does your mind wander? Watch the body language of your listeners for positive or negative reactions."

THE POTTERSFIELD PORTFOLIO, (II), Wild East Publishing Co-operative Ltd., 151 Ryan Court, Fredericton, New Brunswick E3A 2Y9 Canada. Editors: Joe Blades, Margaret McLeod. Magazine: 6×9; 96 pages; book paper; perfect-bound; coated cover stock; artwork. "Quality fiction, poetry, essays, drama, etc. in English, French and Spanish from a diversity of visions and voices." Semiannually. Estab. 1979.

Needs: Receives 15-30 fiction mss/month. Buys 5-6 fiction mss/issue. Recently published work by William Bauer, Claudia Gahlinger, Don Acker, Sylvia Mortce; published new writers within the last year. Publishes short shorts. Sometimes comments on rejected mss.

How to Contact: Send complete ms with cover letter and enough information for short bio in journal. No simultaneous submissions. Reports in 2 months. SASE. Sample copy $6 (US).

Payment: Pays $10/printed page and contributor's copies.

Terms: Pays on publication for first Canadian serial rights.

Advice: "We have opened up our mandate to encompass more than Atlantic Canadian. And we are particularly interested in feminist writing/fiction including nontraditional fiction forms and feminist fantasy."

PRAIRIE FIRE, (II), Prairie Fire Press Inc., Room 423, 100 Arthur St., Winnipeg, Manitoba R3B 1H3 Canada. (204)943-9066. Managing Editor: Andris Taskans. Magazine: 6×9; 128 pages; offset bond paper; sturdy cover stock; illustrations; photos. "Essays, critical reviews, short fiction and poetry. For writers and readers interested in Canadian literature." Published 4 times/year. Estab. 1978. Circ. 1,200.

Needs: Literary, contemporary, experimental, prose poem, reviews. "We will consider work on any topic of artistic merit, including short chapters from novels-in-progress. We wish to avoid gothic, confession, religious, romance and pornography." Buys 3-6 mss/issue, 12-24 mss/year. Does not read mss in summer. Recently published work by David Arnason, Holley Rubinsky, Diane Schoemperlen; published new writers within the last year. Receives 24-30 unsolicited fiction mss each month. Publishes short shorts. Length: 8,000 maximum; 3,000 words average. Also publishes literary essays, literary criticism, poetry. Critiques rejected mss "if requested and when there is time." Sometimes recommends other markets.

How to Contact: Send complete ms with IRC w/envelope and short bio. No simultaneous submissions. Reports in 3-4 months. Sample copy for $7 (Canadian). Reviews novels and short story collections. Send books to Andris Taskans.

Payment: Pays $60 for the first page, $30 for each additional page; 2 contributor's copies; 60% of cover price for extras.

Terms: Pays on publication for first North American serial rights. Rights revert to author on publication.

Advice: "We are publishing more fiction, and we are commissioning illustrations. Read our publication before submitting. We prefer Canadian material. Most mss are not ready for publication. Be neat, double space, and put your name and address on everything! Be the best writer you can be."

PRAIRIE SCHOONER, (II), University of Nebraska, English Department, 201 Andrews Hall, Lincoln NE 68588-0334. (402)472-3191. Editor: Hilda Raz. Magazine: 6×9; 144 pages; good stock paper; heavy cover stock. "A fine literary quarterly of stories, poems, essays and reviews for a general audience that reads for pleasure." Quarterly. Estab. 1927. Circ. 3,000.

• *Prairie Schooner*, one of the oldest publications in this book, has garnered several awards and honors over the years. Work appearing in the magazine has been selected for various anthologies and this year *Esquire* identified the magazine as one of the "root" publications for new writers. See the Close-up interview with the editor in the 1993 *Writer's Market*.

Needs: Good fiction. Upcoming theme: "Fall 1993 will be 'Canadian Women Writers' — a special issue of *Prairie Schooner*." Accepts 4-5 mss/issue. Receives approximately 150 unsolicited fiction mss each month. Recently published work by Leo Litwak, Ursula Hegi, Wayne Karlin, Kyoko Mori; published new writers within the last year. Length: varies. Also publishes poetry.

How to Contact: Send complete ms with SASE and cover letter listing previous publications — where, when. Reports in 3 months. Sample copy $3.50. Reviews novels and short story collections.

Payment: Pays in contributor's copies and prize money awarded.

Terms: Acquires all rights. Will reassign rights upon request after publication.

Advice: "*Prairie Schooner* is eager to see fiction from beginning and established writers. Be tenacious. Accept rejection as a temporary setback and send out rejected stories to other magazines. *Prairie Schooner* is not a magazine with a program. We look for good fiction in traditional narrative modes as well as post modernist, meta-fiction or any other form or fashion a writer might try." Annual prize of $500 for best fiction, $500 for best new writer (poetry or fiction), $500 for best poetry; additional prizes, $250-1,000.

PRIMAL VOICES, (I), Lambert/McIntosh Enterprises, P.O. Box 3179, Poughkeepsie NY 12603. Fiction Editors: Carol Lambert, Susan McIntosh, Lee Schryver. Magazine: 8½ × 11; 52 pages; 20 lb. paper; glossy cover; illustrations and photographs. "Endangered species, homeless, seniors, handicapped, retarded, incarcerated (the voiceless) for humanitarians." Quarterly. Estab. 1990. Circ. 100.

Needs: Condensed/excerpted novel, ethnic, experimental, fantasy, feminist, gay, historical (general), horror, humor/satire, literary, prose poem, regional, senior citizen/retirement, sports (exceptional), translations, western (frontier stories). No "hunting, human or animal abuse, violence or sexist writing." Upcoming theme: "We would like to focus on Native Americans. Black and white photos to accompany article would be helpful (illustrations also)." Receives 20 unsolicited mss/month. Accepts no more than 2 mss/issue; 8 mss/year. Does not read mss in August. Publishes ms 2 months after acceptance. Recently published work by Patty Somlo. Length: 1,200 words preferred; 500 words minimum; 1,500 words maximum. Sometimes critiques rejected mss and recommends other markets.

How to Contact: Send complete ms with cover letter. Include "a short bio for our Contributor's Notes." Reports in 8-10 weeks. SASE. Simultaneous and reprint submissions OK. Sample copy for $3.75, SAE and 4 first class stamps. Fiction guidelines for #10 SAE and 1 first class stamp.

Payment: Pays contributor's copies.

Terms: Acquires one-time rights.

Advice: Looks for "characters and story that are both real and believable. The story is well written and proofread by the author with attention paid to grammar and spelling in the text. Think about your own concerns and about the things in our society that need to be addressed and/or changed."

PRIMAVERA, (II, IV), Box 37-7547, Chicago IL 60637. (312)324-5920. Editorial Board. Magazine: 5½ × 8½; 100 pages; 60 lb. paper; glossy cover; illustrations; photos. Literature and graphics reflecting the experiences of women: poetry, short stories, photos, drawings. Readership: "an audience interested in women's ideas and experiences." Annually. Estab. 1975. Circ. 1,000.

• *Primavera* has won grants from the Illinois Arts Council and from Chicago Women in Publishing.

Needs: Literary, contemporary, science fiction, fantasy, feminist, gay/lesbian and humor. "We dislike slick stories packaged for more traditional women's magazines. We publish only work reflecting the experiences of women, but also publish mss by men." Accepts 6-10 mss/issue. Receives approximately 40 unsolicited fiction mss each month. Recently published work by Kathryn Christman, Dawn Newton, C.D. Collins; published new writers within the last year. Length: 25 pages maximum. Also publishes poetry. Critiques rejected mss when there is time. Often gives suggestions for revisions and invites resubmission of revised ms. Occasionally recommends other markets.

How to Contact: Send complete ms with SASE. Cover letter not necessary. No simultaneous submissions. Reports in 1 week – 5 months on mss. Publishes ms up to 1 year after acceptance. Sample copy $5; $7 for recent issues. Guidelines for SASE.

Payment: Pays 2 contributor's copies.

Terms: Acquires first rights.

PRISM INTERNATIONAL, (II), E462-1866 Main Mall, University of British Columbia, Vancouver, British Columbia V6T 1Z1 Canada. (604)822-2514. Executive Editor: Patricia Gabin. Editor: Murray Logan. Magazine: 6×9; 72-80 pages; Zephyr book paper; Cornwall, coated one side cover; photos on cover. "A journal of contemporary writing—fiction, poetry, drama, creative non-fiction and translation. *Prism*'s audience is world-wide, as are our contributors." Readership: "Public and university libraries, individual subscriptions, bookstores—an audience concerned with the contemporary in literature." Quarterly. Estab. 1959. Circ. 1,200.
Needs: Literary, contemporary, prose poem or translations. "Most any category as long as it is *fresh*. No overtly religious, overtly theme-heavy material or anything more message- or category-oriented than self-contained." Buys approximately 70 mss/year. Receives 50-100 unsolicited fiction mss each month. Published new writers within the last year. Length: 5,000 words maximum "though flexible for outstanding work." Publishes short shorts. Also publishes poetry. Critiques rejected mss when there is time.
How to Contact: Send complete ms with SASE or SAE, IRC and cover letter with bio, information and publications list. "Keep it simple. US contributors take note: US stamps are not valid in Canada and your ms will not likely be returned if it contains US stamps. Send International Reply Coupons instead." Reports in 3 months. Sample copy $5 (U.S./Canadian).
Payment: Pays $20 (Canadian)/printed page, 1 year's subscription.
Terms: Pays on publication for first North American serial rights.
Advice: "Too many derivative, self-indulgent pieces; sloppy construction and imprecise word usage. There's not enough attention to voice and not enough invention. We are committed to publishing outstanding literary work in all genres." Sponsors annual short fiction contest. Contest issue comes out in April. Grand prize is $2,000 (Canadian). Send SASE (IRC) for details.

PRISONERS OF THE NIGHT, An Adult Anthology of Erotica, Fright, Allure and . . . Vampirism, (II, IV), MKASHEF Enterprises, Box 368, Poway CA 92074-0368. Editor: Alayne Gelfand. Fiction and Poetry Editor for issue #7: Wendy Rathbone. Future submissions should go to Editor. Magazine: 8½×11; 50-80 pages; 20 lb. paper; slick cover; perfect-bound; illustrations. "An adult, erotic vampire anthology of original character stories and poetry. Heterosexual and homosexual situations included." Annually. Estab. 1987. Circ. approx. 5,000.
Needs: "All stories must be vampire stories, with unique characters, unusual situations." Adventure, contemporary, erotica, experimental, fantasy, feminist, gay, lesbian, literary, mystery/suspense, prose poem, psychic/supernatural/occult, romance (gothic, romantic suspense), science fiction (soft/sociological), western (adult). No fiction that deals with anyone else's creations, i.e., no "Dracula" stories. Receives 30-50 unsolicited fiction mss/month. Buys 5-12 mss/issue. Publishes ms 1-11 months after acceptance. Recently published work by Taerie Bryant, Charles Gramlich, Charlee Jacob, F.A. McMahan; published new writers within the last year. Length: under 10,000 words. Publishes short shorts. Sometimes critiques rejected mss. Recommends other markets.
How to Contact: Send complete ms with short cover letter. "A brief introduction of author to the editor; name, address, *some* past credits if available." Reports in 1-3 weeks on queries; 2-4 months on mss. Reads *only* September-March. SASE. No simultaneous submissions. Accepts electronic submissions via IBM Word Perfect (4.2 or 5.1) disk. Sample copy #1-4, $15; #5, $12; #6, $9.95. Fiction guidelines for #10 SAE and 1 first class stamp.
Payment: Pays 1¢/word for fiction.
Terms: Pays on publication for first North American serial rights.
Advice: "Unusual, unique *types* of vampires in surprising and unexpected situations will appeal to me most readily. The staid, cliched, ordinary character or setting will lose my attention immediately. Full-fleshed, detailed characterization is required. I do not want pornography: sex for shock value is an absolute negative. No 'singles' bars' or prostitution themes. No 'counts' or 'countesses.' No gore or gratuitous blood and guts. Graphic erotica *is* very welcome. Be original, be bold and fresh in your approach."

PROCESSED WORLD, (II), #1829, 41 Sutter St., San Francisco CA 94104. (415)626-2160. Editor: Chris Carlsson. Magazine: 8½×11; 64 pages; 20 lb. bond paper; glossy cover stock; illustrations; photos. "Magazine about work, office work, computers and hi-tech (satire)." Biannually. May publish special fiction issue. Estab. 1981. Circ. 5,000.
Needs: Comics, confession, "tales of toil," contemporary, fantasy, humor/satire, literary, science fiction. Acquires 1-2 mss/issue; 3-6 mss/year. Recently published work by James Pollack. Published new writers within the last year. Length: 1,250 words average; 100 words minimum; 1,500 words maximum. Occasionally critiques rejected ms.

How to Contact: Send complete ms. Reports in 4 months. SASE. Simultaneous submissions OK. Sample copy $5.
Payment: Pays subscription to magazine.
Terms: Acquires one-time rights.
Advice: "Make it real. Make it critical of the status quo. Read the magazine before you send us a story."

PROPHETIC VOICES, An International Literary Journal, (II), Heritage Trails Press, 94 Santa Maria Dr., Novato CA 94947. (415)897-5679. Editor: Goldie L. Morales. Fiction Editors: Ruth Wildes Schuler and Jeanne Leigh Schuler. Magazine: 6¾ × 8¼; 100-144 pages; bond paper; textured cover; illustrations and photographs. "Material with a social awareness/ecology slant for an adult audience. Interested in material from other countries." Semiannually.
Needs: Historical (general) and prose poem. "We want gripping material that is also educational." No religious, sexual, juvenile, sports, young adult. Receives 10 unsolicited mss/month. Acquires 1 or 2 mss/issue; 3 or 4 mss/year. Publishes ms 1-3 years after acceptance. Recently published work by P. Raja, Denver Stull and Kirpal Gordon. Publishes short shorts. Recommends other markets.
How to Contact: Send complete manuscript. Reports in 5 weeks on queries; 3 months on mss. SASE. Simultaneous and reprint submissions OK. Sample copy $6.
Payment: Pays contributor's copy.
Terms: Acquires one-time rights.
Advice: "A story should be different, educational—one that a reader is not likely to forget. Material must have universal and timeless appeal. We are not interested in trendy stories or those appealing only to a limited region or geographical locale."

PROVINCETOWN ARTS, (II), Provincetown Arts, Inc., 650 Commercial St., P.O. Box 35, Provincetown MA 02657. (508)487-3167. Editor: Christopher Busa. Magazine: 9 × 12; 184 pages; 60 lb. uncoated paper; 12 pcs. cover; illustrations and photographs. "*PA* focuses broadly on the artists, writers and theater of America's oldest continuous art colony." Annually. Estab. 1985. Circ. 8,000.
● This large-format arts publication has had work included in *Best American Poetry* and *Best American Essays*.
Needs: Plans special fiction issue. Receives 300 unsolicited mss/year. Buys 5 mss/issue. Publishes ms 3 months after acceptance. Recently published work by Carole Maso and Hilary Masters. Length: 3,000 words average; 1,500 words minimum; 8,000 words maximum. Publishes short shorts. Length: 1,500-8,000 words. Also publishes literary essays, literary criticism, poetry. Sometimes critiques rejected mss and recommends other markets.
How to Contact: Send complete ms with cover letter including previous publications. No simultaneous submissions. Reports in 2 weeks on queries; 3 months on mss. SASE. Sample copy $7.50. Reviews novels and short story collections.
Payment: Pays $75-300.
Terms: Pays on publication for first rights. Sends galleys to author.

PSI, (II), Suite 856, 1377 K Street NW, Washington DC 20005. Editor: A.P. Samuels. Magazine: 8½ × 11; 32 pages; bond paper; self cover. "Mystery and romance." Bimonthly. Estab. 1987.
Needs: Romance (contemporary, historical, young adult), mystery/suspense (private eye), western (traditional). Receives 35 unsolicited mss/month. Buys 1-2 mss/issue. Length: 10,000 words average. Critiques rejected mss "only on a rare occasion."
How to Contact: Send complete ms with cover letter. Reports in 2 weeks on queries; 1 month on mss. SASE. No simultaneous submissions. Accepts electronic submissions via disk.
Payment: Pays 1-4¢/word plus royalty.
Terms: Pays on acceptance for first North American serial rights.
Advice: "Manuscripts must be for a general audience. Just good plain story telling (make it compelling). No explicit sex or ghoulish violence."

PSYCHOTRAIN, (II), Hyacinth House Publications, P.O. Box 120, Fayetteville AR 72702-0120. Editor: Shannon Frach. Magazine: 8½ × 11; 25-35 pages; 20 lb. paper; cardstock; illustrations. "*PsychoTrain* is a journal of poetry, fiction, and art that welcomes intense, earthy, decadent, and often risqué work from a wide array of authors, including both beginners and more established. I publish for a generally left-of-center audience that appreciates humor noir, radical writing, and tough, edgy fiction." Estab. 1991. Circ. 200.
● Hyacinth House Publications also publishes *Brownbag Press*. There is no need to submit to

both, says the editor, because manuscripts will be considered for all.

Needs: Condensed/excerpted novel, erotica, ethnic, experimental, feminist, gay, horror, humor/satire, lesbian, literary, prose poem, psychic/supernatural/occult, translations, "Pagan, Dada/surrealism, counterculture, subcultural writing of any and all persuasions." "No candy-coated, dandyfied fiction here. Just pure, old-fashioned decadence. Nothing didactic. No hand-wringing sentimentalism. No whining unless it's really damned funny." Plans special fiction issue. Receives 40 unsolicited mss/month. Accepts 5-7 mss/issue. Publishes ms 1 year after acceptance. Recently published work by Gomez Robespierre, Janice Hedin, Joseph Benzola, Rafael Carvajal. Length: 50 words minimum; 4,500 words maximum. Publishes short shorts. Sometimes critiques rejected mss and recommends other markets.

How to Contact: Send complete ms with cover letter. "A cover letter is not necessary. If you send one, don't give me a mere list of credits or whine about how nobody understands you because you're a sensitive artist. And no plot synopses, please. Reports in 2-5 months on mss. SASE. Simultaneous and reprint submissions OK. Sample copy for $3 and 4 first class stamps. Fiction guidelines for #10 SAE and 1 first class stamp.

Payment: Pays 1 contributor's copy; charges for extras.

Terms: Acquires one-time rights.

Advice: "Send the most twisted, bizarre, abrasive material you've got, but beware—being crass is not all it takes to get published here. It's also going to take fast-paced, dynamic, energetic, well-crafted writing. For some reason, a lot of people seem to think we'd be fascinated by stories about clinical psychotherapy, or asylum narratives. Out of vast mountains of manuscripts, we've taken one story about a psychiatrist, one story about Reichian therapy, and one asylum narrative—and we're not exactly looking for any more. Also, we're getting too much really bad genre fiction—horror and detective mysteries are the supreme offenders here. Avoid Cro-magnon 'frat-boy' humor that relies upon beer or breasts the size of medicine balls to get the story rolling. Every week, we get stories in which a male narrator labels a woman a 'bitch' for not sleeping with him and then the rest of the story focuses on how he cleverly, intellectually expresses his dissatisfaction by murdering her. Send us one of these, and win your own free rejection slip."

‡PUCK!, The Unofficial Journal of the Irrepressible, (II), Permeable Press, Studio 15, 900 Tennessee, San Francisco CA 94107-3014. (415)648-2175. Editor: Brian Clark. Fiction Editor: Kurt Putnam. Magazine: 8½×11; 60 pages; recycled uncoated paper; coated cover; illustrations and photos. "Our audience does not accept mainstream media as presenting anything even vaguely resembling reality. We publish poetry, prose and dozens of review in our humble attempt to counteract the hogwash of *Time, Paris Review,* et al." Triannually. Estab. 1984. Circ. 500.

Needs: Condensed novel, erotica, ethnic/multicultural, experimental, fantasy (science fantasy), feminist, gay, historical (general) horror, humor/satire, lesbian, literary, psychic/supernatural/occult, regional, religious/inspirational, science fiction (hard science, soft/sociological, cyber punk), translations. Upcoming themes: Plans a 10th Anniversary Issue (October 1994). List of upcoming themes available for SASE. Receives 25 unsolicited mss/month. Buys 3-10 mss/issue; 25 mss/year. Publishes ms within 6 months after acceptance. Agented fiction 10%. Recently published work by Stan Henry, Hugh Fox, Belinda Subraman. Publishes short shorts. Also publishes literary essays, literary criticism, poetry. Sometimes critiques or comments on rejected mss.

How to Contact: Send complete ms with cover letter. Should include bio (under 50 words), list of publications. Reports in 2 months. Send SASE (IRC) for reply or return of ms. No simultaneous submissions. Accepts reprints and electronic (disk or modem) submissions. Sample copy $6.50. Fiction guidelines for #10 SAE and 2 first class stamps or IRCs. Reviews novels and short story collections. Send review copies to Attn: Reviews Editor at above address.

Payment: Pays 2 or more contributor's copies plus honorarium (40%)

Terms: Payment on publication. Purchases first North American serial rights.

Advice: Looks for "a certain 'je ne sais quois'—as if the work has been channeled or written in a fit of brilliant rage. Keep trying to pull your head out of this ocean of bogus media we're being drowned in. Subscribe."

PUCKERBRUSH REVIEW, (I, II), Puckerbrush Press, 76 Main St., Okono ME 04473. (207)866-4868/581-3832. Editor: Constance Hunting. Magazine: 9×12; 80-100 pages; illustrations. "We publish mostly new Maine writers; interviews, fiction, reviews, poetry for a literary audience." Semiannually. Estab. 1979. Circ. approx. 500.

Needs: Experimental, gay (occasionally), literary, belles-lettres. "Nothing cliché." Receives 30 unsolicited mss/month. Accepts 6 mss/issue; 12 mss/year. Publishes ms 1 year after acceptance. Recently published work by Dwight Cathcart, Tema Nason. Sometimes publishes short shorts. Also publishes literary essays, literary criticism, poetry. Sometimes critiques rejected mss and recommends other markets.
How to Contact: Send complete ms with cover letter. Reports in 2 months. SASE. Simultaneous submissions OK. Sample copy $2. Fiction guidelines for SASE. Sometimes reviews novels and short story collections.
Payment: Pays in contributor's copies.
Advice: "Just write the story as it would like you to do."

PUERTO DEL SOL, (I), New Mexico State University, Box 3E, Las Cruces NM 88003. (505)646-3931. Editor-in-Chief: Antonya Nelson. Magazine: 6×9; 200 pages; 60 lb. paper; 70 lb. cover stock; photos sometimes. "We publish quality material from anyone. Poetry, fiction, art, photos, interviews, reviews, parts-of-novels, long poems." Semiannually. Estab. 1961. Circ. 1,500.
Needs: Contemporary, ethnic, experimental, literary, mainstream, prose poem, excerpted novel and translations. Receives varied number of unsolicited fiction mss/month. Acquires 8-10 mss/issue; 12-15 mss/year. Does not read mss May-August. Published work by Ken Kuhlken, Susan Thornton; published new writers within the last year. Also publishes poetry. Occasionally critiques rejected mss.
How to Contact: Send complete ms with SASE. Simultaneous and photocopied submissions OK. Accepts computer printout submissions. Reports in 2 months. Sample copy $7.
Payment: Pays 2 contributor's copies.
Terms: Acquires one-time rights (rights revert to author).
Advice: "We are open to all forms of fiction, from the conventional to the wildly experimental, as long as they have integrity and are well written. Too often we receive very impressively 'polished' mss that will dazzle readers with their sheen but offer no character/reader experience of lasting value."

PULPHOUSE, A Fiction Magazine, (II), Box 1227, Eugene OR 97440. Editor: Dean Wesley Smith. Magazine: 8½×11; 48 pages; saddle-stitched; web-printed. Estab. 1988. Has 10,000 copies in print.
   • Pulphouse Publishing has several lines of books, mostly featuring short stories or novellas by single authors. Submissions are by invitation *only*. They also publish the new *Mystery Street* listed in this book. *Pulphouse* magazine ranked #3 on the *Writer's Digest* Fiction 50 list.
Needs: Fantasy, horror, science fiction, speculative fiction. Published work by Harlan Ellison, Kate Wilhelm, Michael Bishop, Charles de Line, George Alec Effinger; published new writers within the last year. Length: 7,500 words maximum.
How to Contact: Send complete ms with cover letter "that gives publication history, work history, or any other information relevant to the magazine. Don't tell us about the story. The story will tell us about the story." SASE. Sample copy for $2.50. Fiction guidelines for #10 SAE and 1 first class stamp.
Payment: Pays 3-6¢/word.
Terms: Pays on acceptance for first serial rights.
Advice: "*Pulphouse* needs fiction that takes risks, that presents viewpoints not commonly held in the field. Although such fiction can include experimental writing, it is usually best served by clean, clear prose. We are looking for strong characterization, fast-moving plot, and intriguing settings."

PULSAR, Science Fiction and Fantasy, (II), Anthony Ubelhor, P.O. Box 886, Evansville IN 47706. (812)421-8361. Editor: Anthony Ubelhor. Magazine: 8×11; 60 pages; 20 lb. paper; glossy cover; b&w illustrations and photographs. "Science fiction and fantasy stories, articles, interviews for an adult audience. Prefer science fiction with psychological, or metaphysical themes." Semiannually. Estab. 1986. Circ. 400.
Needs: Fantasy, science fiction (soft/sociological). "Always looking for articles and retrospectives on the science fiction field, as well as interviews with writers." No horror. Publishes annual special fiction issue. Receives 20 unsolicited mss/month. Accepts 5-10 mss/issue; 10-20 mss/year. Publishes ms 1-12 months after acceptance. Recently published work by Mike Resnick, Arlan Andrews, C.S. Williams. Length: 6,000 words average; 1,500 words minimum; 10,000 words maximum. Publishes short shorts. Length: about 6,000-10,000 words. Also publishes literary essays, literary criticism, poetry. Sometimes critiques rejected mss.
How to Contact: Send complete manuscript with cover letter. No simultaneous submissions. Reprint submissions OK. Reports in 4-6 weeks on queries; 1-3 months on mss. SASE. Sample copy $4. Fiction guidelines for SAE and 1 first class stamp. Reviews novels and short story collections (science fiction/fantasy works only).

Payment: Pays in contributor's copies. Charge for extras.
Terms: Acquires first North American serial rights.
Advice: "We encourage beginning writers. A rejection from us is always an invitation to submit again."

‡**QUANTA, (I),** # 203, 5437 Ellsworth Ave., Pittsburgh PA 15232. (412)621-8793. Fax: (412)268-8192. Editor: Daniel K. Applequist. Magazine: 8½×11; 35-40 pages; illustrations; photos. "*Quanta* is primarily an electronic publication, distributed across computer networks to an international audience. It is dedicated to bringing the works of new and amateur authors to a wide readership." Bimonthly. Estab. 1989. Circ. 2,000.
Needs: Fantasy (science fantasy), psychic/supernatural/occult. science fiction (hard science, soft/sociological). Plans special fiction issue or anthology. Receives 20 mss/month. Buys 5 mss/issue; 20 mss/year. Publishes 1-2 months after acceptance. Recently published J. Palmer Hall, Michael C. Berch, Jason Suell, Phillip Nolte. Publishes short shorts. Also publishes literary essays, literary criticism, poetry. Always critiques rejected manuscripts.
How to Contact: Send complete ms with a cover letter; send ms in electronic form (disk or e-mail). Should include estimated word count, short bio and list of publications. Reports in 3 weeks on queries; 2 months on manuscripts. Send SASE (IRC) for reply, return of ms or send disposable copy of ms. Simultaneous, reprint and electronic submissions OK. Sample copy for SAE and 5 first class stamps. Fiction guidelines for 8½×11 SAE.
Payment: Pays 1 contributor copy.
Terms: Acquires one-time rights.
Advice: Looks for "interesting or novel narratorial style or good content. I shy away from 'formula' pieces (e.g., hook 'n' slash fantasy)."

QUARRY, (II), Quarry Press, Box 1061, Kingston, Ontario K7L 4Y5 Canada. (613)548-8429. Editor: Steven Heighton. Magazine: 5½×8½; 120 pages; #1 book 120 paper; 160 lb. Curtis Tweed cover stock; illustrations; photos. "Quarterly anthology of new Canadian poetry, prose. Also includes graphics, photographs and book reviews. We seek readers interested in vigorous, disciplined, new Canadian writing." Published special fiction issue; plans another. Estab. 1952. Circ. 1,100.
Needs: Experimental, fantasy, literary, serialized/excerpted novel and translations. "We do not want highly derivative or clichéd style." Receives 80-100 unsolicited fiction mss/month. Buys 4-5 mss/issue; 20 mss/year. Does not read in July. Less than 5% of fiction is agented. Published work by Diane Schoemperlen, David Helwig, Joan Fern Shaw; published new writers within the last year. Length: 3,000 words average. Publishes short shorts. Usually critiques rejected mss and recommends other markets.
How to Contact: Send complete ms with SAE, IRC and brief bio. Publishes ms an average of 3-6 months after acceptance. Sample copy $5 with 4×7 SAE and 35¢ Canadian postage or IRC.
Payment: Pays $10/page; 1 year subscription to magazine and 1 contributor's copy.
Terms: Pays on publication for first North American serial rights.
Advice: "Read previous *Quarry* to see standard we seek. Read Canadian fiction to see Canadian trends. We seek aggressive experimentation which is coupled with competence (form, style) and stimulating subject matter. We also like traditional forms. Our annual prose issue (spring) is always a sellout. Many of our selections have been anthologized. Don't send US stamps or SASE (if outside Canada). Use IRC. Submit with brief bio."

‡**QUARRY WEST (II),** Porter College, UCSC, Santa Cruz CA 95064. (408)459-2155. Editor: Kenneth Weisner. Fiction Editors: Kathy Chetkovich and Thad Nodine. Magazine: 6¾×8¼; 120 pages; 60 lb stock opaque paper; cover stock varies with cover art; illustrations sometimes; photos. Magazine of fiction, poetry, general nonfiction, art, graphics for a general audience. Semiannually. Estab. 1971. Circ. 750.
Needs: Traditional, experimental. Acquires 2-5 mss/issue; 4-10 mss/year. Length: 6,000 words maximum. Occasionally critiques rejected ms.
How to Contact: Send complete ms with SASE. Photocopied submissions OK. Reports in 6 weeks on mss. Publishes ms an average of 1-3 months after acceptance. Does not read mss July and August. Sample copy $3.50.

Payment: 2 free contributor's copies.
Terms: Acquires first North American serial rights. Sponsors fiction contest.
Advice: "We're interested in good writing—we've published first-time writers and experienced professionals. Don't submit material you are unsure of or perhaps don't like just for the sake of publication—only show your *best* work—read the magazine for a feeling of the kind of fiction we've published. Type double-spaced and legibly."

QUARTERLY WEST, (II), University of Utah, 317 Olpin Union, Salt Lake City UT 84112. (801)581-3938. Editors: Jeffrey Vasseur, Marty Williams. Fiction Editor: Lee Mortensen. Editors change every 2 years. Magazine: 6×9; 150+ pages; 60 lb. paper; 5-color cover stock; illustrations and photographs rarely. "We try to publish a variety of fiction and poetry from all over the country based not so much on the submitting author's reputation but on the merit of each piece. Our publication is aimed primarily at an educated audience which is interested in contemporary literature and criticism." Semiannually. "We sponsor biennial novella competition." Estab. 1976. Circ. 1,000.
Needs: Literary, contemporary, translations. Buys 4-6 mss/issue, 10-12 mss/year. Receives approximately 100 unsolicited fiction mss each month. Published work by Andre Dubus and Chuck Rosenthal; published new writers within the last year. No preferred length; interested in longer, "fuller" short stories. Critiques rejected mss when there is time. Sometimes recommends other markets.
How to Contact: Send complete ms. Cover letters welcome. SASE. Simultaneous submissions OK. Reports in 2 months; "sooner, if possible." Sample copy for $4.50.
Payment: Pays $15-300.
Terms: Pays on publication for first North American serial rights.
Advice: "Write a clear and unified story which does not rely on tricks or gimmicks for its effects." Mss are rejected because of "poor style, formula writing, clichés, weak characterization. We solicit quite frequently, but tend more toward the surprises—unsolicited. Don't send more than one story per submission, but submit as often as you like."

QUEEN OF ALL HEARTS, (II), Queen Magazine, Montfort Missionaries, 26 S. Saxon Ave., Bay Shore NY 11706. (516)665-0726. Managing Editor: Roger M. Charest, S.M.M. Magazine: 7¾×10¾; 48 pages; self cover stock; illustrations; photos. Magazine of "stories, articles and features on the Mother of God by explaining the Scriptural basis and traditional teaching of the Catholic Church concerning the Mother of Jesus, her influence in fields of history, literature, art, music, poetry, etc." Bimonthly. Estab. 1950. Circ. 5,000.
Needs: Religious/inspirational. "No mss not about Our Lady, the Mother of God, the Mother of Jesus." Length: 1,500-2,000 words. Sometimes recommends other markets.
How to Contact: Send complete ms with SASE. No simultaneous submissions. Reports in 1 month on mss. Publishes ms 6 months to one year after acceptance. Sample copy $2.50 with 9×12 SAE.
Payment: Varies. Pays 6 contributor's copies.
Advice: "We are publishing stories with a Marian theme."

QUEEN'S QUARTERLY, A Canadian Review, (II, IV), Queen's University, Kingston, Ontario K7L 3N6 Canada. (613)545-2667. Editor: Boris Castel. Magazine: 6×9; 800 pages/year; illustrations. "A general interest intellectual review, featuring articles on science, politics, humanities, arts and letters. Book reviews, poetry and fiction." Published quarterly. Estab. 1893. Circ. 3,000.
Needs: Adventure, contemporary, experimental, fantasy, historical (general), humor/satire, literary, mainstream, science fiction and women's. "*Special emphasis on work by Canadian writers.*" Buys 2 mss/issue; 8 mss/year. Published work by Janette Turner Hospital; published new writers within the last year. Length: 5,000 words maximum. Also publishes literary essays, literary criticism, poetry.
How to Contact: "Send complete ms and a copy on disk in Wordperfect—only one at a time—with SASE." No simultaneous or multiple submissions. Reports within 3 months. Sample copy $6.50. Reviews novels and short story collections.
Payment: Pays $100-300 for fiction, 2 contributor's copies and 1-year subscription; $5 charge for extras.
Terms: Pays on publication for first North American serial rights. Sends galleys to author.

RADIO VOID, (II), P.O. Box 5983, Providence RI 02903. Publisher: Brian T. Gallagher. Fiction Editor: Christopher Pierson. Magazine: 8½×11; 112 pages; newsprint paper; illustrations and photographs (varies). "Conflicting, themeless variety...an eclectic blend in which, when sifted, can be found a common literary thread." Biannually. Estab. 1986. Circ. 1,000.

Needs: Open to all types of fiction. Receives approx. 20 unsolicited fiction mss/month. Accepts 15-20 mss/issue; 80-100 mss/year. Publishes ms 3-4 months after acceptance. Recently published work by Cynthia Wachtell, Jonathan Thomas. Length: Open. Publishes short shorts. Also publishes literary essays, literary criticism, poetry. Critiques or comments on rejected mss.
How to Contact: Send complete ms with cover letter. Include name, address, biographical paragraph. No simultaneous submissions. Reports in 2 months on queries; in 3-5 months on mss. SASE. Sample copy for $3. Fiction guidelines for #15 SAE and 1 first class stamp. Reviews novels and short story collections. Send books to Zoë Pierson.
Payment: Pays in contributor's copies and free business card-size ad.
Terms: "We do not purchase rights--author offers us a loan."

‡**RAFALE, Supplement Littéraire, (II)**, Franco-American Research Organization Group, University of Maine, Franco American Center, Orono ME 04469. (207)581-3775. Fax: (207)581-3764. Editor: Rhea Côté. Tabloid insert: 4 pages; newsprint; illustrations and photos. Publication was founded to stimulate and recognize creative expression among Franco-Americans, all types of readers, including literary and working class." Monthly except July and August. Estab. 1986. Circ. 5,000.
Needs: "We will consider any type of short fiction, poetry and critical essays of good quality, in French as well as English." Receives about 10 unsolicited mss/month. Accepts 2-4 mss/issue. Recently published work by Robert Cormier; published new writers within the last year. Length: 1,000 words average; 750 words minimum; 2,500 words maximum. Occasionally critiques rejected mss.
How to Contact: Send complete ms with cover letter, which should include a short bio and list of previous publications. Reports in 3 weeks on queries; 1 month on mss. SASE. Simultaneous and reprint submissions OK.
Payment: Pays $10 and 3 copies.
Terms: Buys one-time rights.
Advice: "Write honestly. Start with a strongly felt personal experience and develop it with a beginning, middle and end. If you make us feel what you have felt, we will publish it."

RAG MAG, (II), Box 12, Goodhue MN 55027. (612)923-4590. Publisher/Editor: Beverly Voldseth. Magazine: 6 × 9; 60 pages; varied paper quality; illustrations; photos. "We are eager to print poetry, prose and art work. We are open to all styles." Semiannually. Estab. 1982. Circ. 200.
Needs: Adventure, comics, contemporary, erotica, ethnic, experimental, fantasy, feminist, literary, mainstream, prose poem, regional. "Anything well written is a possibility. No extremely violent or pornographic writing." Receives 100 unsolicited mss each month. Accepts 1-2 mss/issue. Published work by Egon Ludowese, Rusty McKenzie, Spencer Reece, Tracy Nordstrom; published new writers within the last year. Length: 1,000 words average; 2,200 words maximum. Occasionally critiques rejected mss. Sometimes recommends other markets.
How to Contact: Send complete ms. Reports in 2 months. SASE. Simultaneous and previously published submissions OK. Single copy $6.
Payment: Pays 1 contributor's copy; $4.50 charge for extras.
Terms: Acquires one-time rights.
Advice: "Submit clean copy on regular typing paper (no tissue-thin stuff). We want fresh images, sparse language, words that will lift us out of our chairs. I like the short story form. I think it's powerful and has a definite place in the literary magazine."

RAINBOW CITY EXPRESS, (I,II,IV), Box 8447, Berkeley CA 94707-8447. Editor: Helen B. Harvey. Magazine: 8½ × 11; 60-80 pages; 20 lb. bond paper; illustrations. "We are only interested in topics pertaining to spiritual awakening and evolution of consciousness. For highly educated, well-read, psychologically sophisticated, spiritually evolving and ecologically conscious free-thinkers." Quarterly. Estab. 1988. Circ. 1,000.
Needs: Feminist, literary, prose poem, religious/inspirational and spirituality. "We only accept *short fiction* and absolutely no novels or long fiction. No immature, romantic, violent, sexist material." Receives 60-90 unsolicited mss/month. Buys 4-10 mss/issue; 20-40 mss/year. Publishes ms 3-6 months after acceptance. Length: 200-1,000 words; 500-800 average. Almost always critiques rejected mss and sometimes recommends other markets.
How to Contact: "Order a sample copy and *read it first!* Then send a complete manuscript with SASE." Reports on queries in 2-4 weeks; 3-6 months on mss. All submissions *must* contain SASE! Sample copy $7 postpaid. Writer's guidelines for #10 SASE and 2 first class stamps.

Payment: "Payment is arranged on individual basis. Some cash 'honorariums' and every contributor always receives a copy of issue containing her or his work." Pays $5-50.

Terms: Pays on publication for one-time rights.

Advice: Looks for "intelligent, lively, well-written material, with a substantial and plausible plot and characters. Topics must be related to our Spirituality/Consciousness slant. *Read* 1-2 copies of *RCE* first! *Rainbow City Express* is very unique and it is impossible to write for our publication without first becoming familiar with it. Please study a recent issue before submitting. We prefer *true* (nonfiction) stories related to spiritual awakening."

"This cover reflects the speculative, otherworldly vision of the fiction, poetry and artwork that we publish," says Jeff Dennis, editor and publisher of the recently founded magazine Random Realities. *"We felt that the image of a fortune-teller working with a skull rather than a crystal ball would give our premiere publication more of a supernatural feel and indicate our leanings toward dark fantasy, horror and science fiction. Seventy percent of Random* Realities *consists of short fiction. The balance is poetry, artwork, video and book reviews, and occasional interviews with writers and artists." The cover illustrator for this issue was Cathy Shanks, who also wrote and illustrated one of the stories inside.*

‡**RANDOM REALITIES, (II),** 5043 Audubon Place, Norcross GA 30093. Editor: Jeff Dennis. Magazine: 5½ × 8½; 50-70 pages; 60 lb. cream offset paper; semi-gloss 65 lb. cover; b&w illustrations and photographs. "Science fiction, horror, and fantasy for a literate audience of 25 and up. These readers are interested in commercial fiction that is unique, often blending styles from several genres. Our aim is a wide variety of speculative fiction in every issue." Semiannually. Estab. 1992. Circ. 300.

• *Random Realities* plans to go quarterly in 1994, so watch for an increase in needs.

Needs: Fantasy (science fantasy, horror, sword and sorcery, children's fantasy), psychic/supernatural/occult, science fiction (hard science, soft/sociological). No "Star Trek, possessed children, or blatant slasher stories. No mindless violence or unnecessary gore." Plans special fiction issue or anthology in the future. Receives 15-25 unsolicited mss/month. Acquires 8-10 mss/issue; 16-20 mss/year. Publishes ms 3-9 months after acceptance. Length: 5,000 words preferred; 1,000 words minimum; 7,000 words maximum. Also publishes poetry. Often critiques or comments on rejected mss.

How to Contact: Send complete ms with cover letter. Should include estimated word count, bio (50-100 words), Social Security number, list of publications. Reports in 6-10 weeks on mss. Send a disposable copy of ms "with #10 SASE for reply." No simultaneous submissions. Accepts reprints. Sample copy for $4.50 plus $1.50 postage and handling. (Checks/money orders payable to Jeff Dennis only.) Fiction guidlines for #10 SASE. Reviews novels and short story collections. Send books to Michael S. Watkins.

Payment: Pays 5¢/word and 1 contributor's copy on publication. Additional copies 30% off cover.

Terms: Buys first North American serial rights. Sends galleys to author.

Advice: "Our readers and staff are well-read in the sci-fi, horror, and fantasy genres. Therefore, we've seen most of the standard plots and are looking for unique twists on the old tried-and-true, or, preferably, new and imaginative plots that center around the human condition. Stories should contain some type of human interaction so that our readers can identify with what happens to the characters. Pull us into your world on that first page, keep the story moving, give us some human interaction and a twist here and there, and you've probably got a sale."

‡THE RAVEN CHRONICLES, a magazine of multicultural art, literature and the spoken word, (II), The Raven Chronicles, P. O. Box 95918, Seattle WA 98145. (206)543-0249. Editors: Phoebe Bosché, Phil Red-Eagle. Fiction Editor: Kathleen Alcalá. Magazine: 8½×11; 48-64 pages; 50 lb. book paper; glossy cover; b&w illustrations; photos. *"The Raven Chronicles* is designed to promote multicultural art, literature and the spoken word." Triannually. Estab. 1991. Circ. 1,000.

• This magazine is a frequent winner of Bumbershoot awards.

Needs: Ethnic/multicultural, literary, regional. Receives 5-10 mss/month. Buys 2-3 mss/issue; 8 mss/year. Publishes 3-6 months after acceptance. Recently published Jewell Rhodes, Leonard Goodman, Kathleen de Azevedo, Daniel F. Aga. Length: 2,000 words average; 2,500 words maximum. Publishes short shorts. Length: 300-500 words. Also publishes literary essays, literary criticism, poetry. Sometimes critiques rejected mss.

How to Contact: Send complete ms with cover letter. Should include estimated word count. Reports in 3-6 months on manuscripts. Send SASE (IRC) for return of ms. Simultaneous submissions OK. Sample copy $2. Fiction guidelines for #10 SAE and 1 first class stamp.

Payment: Pays $10-25 plus 2 contributor's copies; additional copies at half cover cost.

Terms: Pays on publication for first North American serial rights. Sends galleys to author.

Advice: Looks for "clean, direct language, written from the heart. Read sample copy, or look at *Before Columbus* anthologies, *Greywolf Annual* anthologies."

RE ARTS & LETTERS [REAL], (II), "A Liberal Arts Forum," Stephen F. Austin State University, P.O. Box 13007, Nacogdoches TX 75962. (409)568-2101. Editor: Lee Schultz. Academic Journal: 6×10; perfect-bound; 120-150 pages; "top" stock. "65-75% of pages composed of fiction (2-4 stories per issue), poetry (20-60 per issue), an occasional play, book reviews (assigned after query), and interviews. Other 25-35% comprised of articles in scholarly format. Work is reviewed based on the intrinsic merit of the scholarship and creative work and its appeal to a sophisticated international readership (U.S., Canada, Great Britain, Ireland, Brazil, Puerto Rico, Italy)." Semiannual. Estab. 1968. Circ. 400+.

Needs: Adventure, contemporary, genre, feminist, science fiction, historical, experimental, regional. No beginners. Receives 35-70 unsolicited mss per month. Accepts 2-5 fiction mss/issue. Publishes 1-6 months after acceptance; one year for special issues. Published work by Joe R. Lansdale, Lewis Shiner, Walter McDonald, Peter Mattheisson. Length 1,000-7,000 words. Occasionally critiques rejected mss and conditionally accepts on basis of critiques and changes. Recommends other markets.

How to Contact: Send complete ms with cover letter. No simultaneous submissions. Reports in 2 weeks on queries; 3-4 weeks on mss. SASE. Sample copy and writer's guidelines $5. Guidelines for SASE.

Payment: Pays 1 contributor's copy; charges for extras.

Terms: Rights revert to author.

Advice: "Please study an issue. Have your work checked by a well-published writer—who is not a good friend."

RECONSTRUCTIONIST, (II), Federation of Reconstructionist Congregations & Havurot, Church Rd. and Greenwood Ave., Wyncote PA 19095. (215)887-1988. Editor: Joy Levitt. Magazine: 8½×11; 32 pages; illustrations; photos. "Review of Jewish culture—essays, fiction, poetry of Jewish interest for American Jews." Published 6 times/year. Estab. 1935. Circ. 9,000.

Needs: Ethnic. Receives 10 unsolicited mss/month; buys 15 mss/year. Publishes ms 1-2 years after acceptance. Published work by Myron Taube, Lev Raphael; published new writers within the last year. Length: 2,500 words average; 3,000 words maximum. Publishes short shorts. Recommends other markets.

How to Contact: *Send mss only to Joy Levitt, Box 1336, Roslyn Heights NY 11577.* All other material should be sent to the Pennsylvania address. Send complete ms with cover letter. Reports in 6-8 weeks. SASE for mss. Sample copy free.

Payment: Pays $25-36 and contributor's copies.

Terms: Pays on publication for first rights.

RED CEDAR REVIEW, (II), Dept. of English, 17C Morrill Hall, Michigan State University, East Lansing MI 48825. (517)355-7570. Editors change. Editor until June 1993 is Jacqueline A. Justice. After that, contact Fiction Editor. Magazine: 5½×8½; 60-80 pages; quality b&w illustrations and b&w photos. Theme: "literary—poetry, fiction, book reviews, one-act plays, interviews, graphics, artwork." Biannually. Estab. 1963. Circ. 400+.

Needs: Literary, feminist, regional and humorous. Accepts 3-4 mss/issue, 6-10 mss/year. Published new writers within the last year. Length: 500-7,000 words. Also publishes poetry.
How to Contact: Send complete ms with SASE. Simultaneous submissions OK. Reports in 2-3 months on mss. Publishes ms up to 4 months after acceptance. Sample copy $2.
Payment: Pays 2 contributor's copies. $5 charge for extras.
Terms: Acquires first rights.
Advice: "Read the magazine and good literary fiction. There are many good writers out there who need a place to publish, and we try to provide them with that chance for publication. We prefer short stories that are experimental and take risks. Make your style unique—don't get lost in the mainstream work of the genre."

‡**REDCAT MAGAZINE, (I)**, 6309 Wiley St., Hollywood FL 33023. (305)983-5684. Editor: Jim Pettit. Magazine: 5½×8½; 40-80 pages; 20 lb. bond paper; 60 lb. laminated cover. "Easy reading, fright-provoking, non-pretentious horror for the masses. Consider us a training ground." Bimonthly. Estab. 1991. Circ. 150.
Needs: Fantasy (dark), horror. No "gothic horror; no sword and sorcery; no science fiction; no movie rip-offs." Receives 25 unsolicited submissions/month. Buys 3-6 mss/issue; 18-36 mss/year. Publishes ms 2 months maximum after acceptance. Recently published work by Eugene James, Donald Goodwin, D.L. Green. Length: 3,500 words preferred; 1,000 words minimum; 12,000 words maximum. Always critiques or comments on rejected mss.
How to Contact: Send complete ms with cover letter. Should include estimated word count, Social Security number. "Not absolutely *necessary* but we'd like to know a *little* about you." Reports in 1 month on mss. SASE or send disposable copy of ms. No simultaneous submissions. Sample copy for $3.50. Fiction guidelines for #10 SAE and 1 first class stamp.
Payment: Pays $5-10 and 1 contributor's copy. Additional copies $2.
Terms: Pays on publication for one-time rights. Not copyrighted.
Advice: "Write to please yourself. You can't produce good work if you're not having fun trying. Good horror—at least as defined by us—comes when everyday people find themselves neck deep in some negative situation that's totally beyond their control. And remember—we're not the ultimate arbiters of taste. A rejection by us may be due more to our lack of taste than your lack of talent. Keep trying. And please—read us before submitting."

THE REDNECK REVIEW OF LITERATURE, (I, II), 2919 N. Donner Ave., Milwaukee WI 53211. (414)332-6881. Editor: Penelope Reedy. Magazine: 8½×11; 80 pages; offset paper; cover varies from semi-glossy to felt illustrations; photos. "I consider *Redneck* to be one of the few—perhaps the only—magazines in the West seeking to bridge the gap between literate divisions. My aim is to provide literature from and to the diverse people in the western region. Readership is extremely eclectic including ranchers, farmers, university professors, writers, poets, activists, civil engineers, BLM conservation officers, farm wives, attorneys, judges, truck drivers." Semiannually. Estab. 1975. Circ. 500.
Needs: "Publishes poetry, fiction, plays, essays, book reviews and folk pieces." Upcoming themes: "Language" (Spring 1993), "The West on Wheels" (Fall 1993). Receives 10 "or so" unsolicited mss/month. Receives 4-5 mss/issue. Recently published work by Rafael Zepeda, Clay Reynolds and Gerald Haslam; published new writers within the last year. Length: 1,500 words minimum; 2,500 words maximum. Also publishes literary essays, literary criticism, poetry.
How to Contact: Send complete ms. SASE. May accept simultaneous submissions. Reprint submissions from established writers OK. Reports in 2 weeks to 2 months. Sample copy for $6 with $1 postage.
Payment: Pays in contributor's copies.
Terms: Rights returned to author on publication.
Advice: "Give characters action, voices. Tell the truth rather than sentimentalize. *Redneck* deals strictly with a contemporary viewpoint/perspective, though the past can be evoked to show the reader how we got here. Nothing too academic or sentimental reminiscences. I am not interested in old-time wild west gunfighter stories."

REFLECT, (II, IV), 3306 Argonne Ave., Norfolk VA 23509. (804)857-1097). Editor: W.S. Kennedy. Magazine: 5½×8½; 48 pages; pen & ink illustrations. "Spiral Mode fiction and poetry for writers and poets—professional and amateur." Quarterly. Estab. 1979.
Needs: Spiral fiction. "The four rules to the Spiral Mode fiction form are: (1) The story a situation or condition. (2) The outlining of the situation in the opening paragraphs. The story being told at once, the author is not overly-involved with dialogue and plot development, may concentrate on *sound*, *style*, *color*—the superior elements in art. (3) The use of a concise style with euphonic wording. Good

poets may have the advantage here. (4) The involvement of Spiral Fiction themes—as opposed to Spiral Poetry themes—with love, and presented with the mystical overtones of the Mode." No "smut, bad taste, anarchist . . ." Accepts 2-6 mss/issue; 8-24 mss/year. Publishes ms 3 months after acceptance. Recently published work by Ruth Wildes Schuler, B.Z. Niditch, Patricia Anne Treat. Length: 1,500 words average; 2,500 words maximum. Publishes short shorts. Sometimes critiques rejected mss and recommends other markets.

How to Contact: Send complete ms with cover letter. Reports in 2 months on mss. SASE. No simultaneous submissions. Sample copy $2. Free fiction guidelines.

Payment: Pays contributor's copies.

Terms: Acquires one-time rights. Publication not copyrighted.

Advice: "Subject matter usually is not relevant to the successful writing of Spiral Fiction, as long as there is some element or type of *love* in the story, and provided that there are mystical references. (Though a dream-like style may qualify as 'mystical.')"

‡REJECTS, The Magazine for Rejected Dark Fantasy, (I), 3496 Turner Rd., SE, Salem OR 97302. (503)588-5444. Editor: Kenneth Brady. Magazine: digest-sized; 30-40 pages; 20 lb. white paper; card cover; illustrations. "Fiction and poetry with a dark slant." Bimonthly. Estab. 1992. Circ. 150.

Needs: Rejected mss. "Must be accompanied by 5 rejection slips from other publications. Fantasy (dark), horror, psychic/supernatural/occult, science fiction. Buys 6-8 mss/issue; 36-48/year. Publishes 2-6 months after acceptance. Length: 3,000 words maximum (possibly more). Publishes short shorts. Also publishes poetry. Always comments on rejected mss.

How to Contact: Send complete ms with a cover letter ("must have some deep wisdom of life"). Should include estimated word count, brief bio, list of publications (if any) and 5 rejection slips from other publications. Reports in 1 month. SASE. No simultaneous submissions. Accepts electronic submissions (MS DOS ASCII format). Sample copy $2.50 (payable to Ken Brady). Fiction guidelines for #10 SAE and 1 first class stamp.

Payment: Pays 2 contributor's copies.

Terms: Acquires first North American serial rights.

Advice: "*Rejects* is a publication for stories and poetry on the dark side that have met with no success so far, but that doesn't mean they're not good stories—maybe the right editor has yet to see them."

RENEGADE, (II), Box 314, Bloomfield MI 48303. (313)972-5580. Editor: Michael E. Nowicki. Co-Editors: Larry Snell, Miriam Jones. Magazine: 5½×8½; 32 pages; 4-5 illustrations. "We are open to all reviews except erotica and we publish whatever we find good." Estab. 1988. Circ. 100.

Needs: Adventure, condensed/excerpted novel, contemporary, experimental, fantasy, feminist, historical (general), horror, humor/satire, literary, mainstream, mystery/suspense, prose poem, psychic/supernatural/occult, religious/inspirational, romance, science fiction, translations and western. Receives 40-50 unsolicited mss/month. Accepts 2 mss/issue; 4 mss/year. Publishes ms 6 months after acceptance. Published work by Sam Astrachan. Length: 400-4,000 words; 3,000 average. Publishes short shorts. Length: 400 words. Also publishes literary essays, literary criticism, poetry. Sometimes critiques rejected mss and recommends other markets.

How to Contact: Send complete ms with cover letter. Simultaneous submissions OK. Reports in 2 weeks to 1 month on queries; 3 weeks to 4 months on mss. SASE. Sample copy $3. Fiction guidelines for #10 SAE and 1 first class stamp. Reviews novels and short story collections.

Payment: Pays in contributor's copies.

Terms: All rights revert to author. Publication not copyrighted.

Advice: "We look for characters which appear to be real and deal with life in a real way, as well as the use of plot to forefront the clash of personalities and the theme of the work. Take advice cautiously and apply what works. Then submit it. We are always happy to critique work we read."

RENOVATED LIGHTHOUSE PUBLICATIONS, (II), P.O. Box 644, Reynoldsburg OH 43068. Editor: R. Allen Dodson. 5½×8½; 48 pages; card cover; illustrations and photographs. "Mostly poetry-related, but will consider all literary and artistic mediums and subjects for freelancers and general audiences with literary interest." Estab. 1986. Circ. 200.

Needs: Adventure, experimental, fantasy, historical (general), literary, mainstream, prose poem, regional, science fiction (soft/sociological), New Age. Receives 30 unsolicited mss/month. Buys 12 mss/year. Publishes ms 1 year average after acceptance. Also publishes literary essays, literary criticism, poetry. Sometimes critiques rejected mss and sometimes recommends other markets.

How to Contact: Query with cover letter and credits; *we're overstocked for 1993.* "Personal information and comments about the story—I like to get to know my writers." Reports in 1 month. SASE. No simultaneous submissions. Sample copy $3.25. Guidelines available.
Payment: Pays $1.25 and 1 contributor's copy per printed page.
Terms: Buys first rights.

RESPONSE, A Contemporary Jewish Review, (II, IV), 27 W. 20th St., 9th Floor, New York NY 10011. (212)675-1168. Editors: Adam Margolis, Bennett Lovett-Graff. Magazine: 6×9; 64 pages; 70 lb. paper; 10 pt. C1S cover; illustrations; photos. "Fiction, poetry and essays with a Jewish theme, for Jewish students and young adults." Quarterly. Estab. 1967. Circ. 1,500.
Needs: Contemporary, ethnic, experimental, feminist, historical (general), humor/satire, literary, prose poem, regional, religious, spirituals, translations. "Stories in which the Holocaust plays a major role must be exceptional in quality. The shrill and the morbid will not be accepted." Receives 5-10 unsolicited mss/month. Accepts 5-10 mss/issue; 10-15 mss/year. Publishes ms 2-4 months after acceptance. Length: 15-20 pages (double spaced). Publishes short shorts. Sometimes recommends other markets.
How to Contact: Send complete ms with cover letter; include brief biography of author. "Do not summarize story in cover letter." Reports in 2-3 months on mss. SASE. No simultaneous submissions. Sample copy $6; free guidelines.
Payment: Pays in contributor's copies.
Terms: Acquires all rights.
Advice: "In the best pieces, every word will show the author's conscious attention to the craft. Subtle ambiguities, quiet ironies and other such carefully handled tropes are not lost on *Response*'s readers. Pieces that also show passion that is not marred by either shrillness or pathos are respected and often welcomed. Writers who write from the gut or the muse are few in number. *Response* personally prefers the writer who thinks about what he or she is doing, rather than the writer who intuits his or her stories."

REVIEW, LATIN AMERICAN LITERATURE AND ARTS, 680 Park Ave., New York NY 10021. (212)249-8950. Editor: Alfred Mac Adam. "Magazine of Latin American fiction, poetry and essays in translation for academic, corporate and general audience." Biannually.
Needs: Literary. No political or sociological mss. Upcoming themes: "Latin American Travelers" (Spring 1993); "Latin American Women's Writing" (Fall 1993); "Cuban Literature and Arts" (Spring 1994). Receives 5 unsolicited mss/month. Buys 8 mss/issue; 16 mss/year. Length: 1,500-2,000 words average. Occasionally critiques rejected mss.
How to Contact: Query first or send complete ms. Reports in several months. Previously published submissions OK if original was published in Spanish. Simultaneous submissions OK, if notified of acceptance elsewhere. Sample copy free. Reviews novels and short story collections. Send books to Daniel Shapiro, Managing Editor.
Payment: Pays $50-200, and 2-3 contributor's copies.
Terms: Pays on publication.
Advice: "We are always looking for good translators."

‡RFD, A Country Journal for Gay Men Everywhere, (I, II, IV), Short Mountain Collective, P.O. Box 68, Liberty TN 37095. (615)536-5176. Contact: The Collective. Magazine: 8½×11; 64-80 pages. "Focus on radical faeries, gay men's spirituality—country living." Quarterly. Estab. 1974. Circ. 1,100.
Needs: Gay: Erotica, ethnic/multicultural, experimental, fantasy, feminist, humor/satire, literary, mainstream/contemporary, mystery/suspense, psychic/supernatural/occult, regional, romance. Receives 10 unsolicited mss/month. Acquires 3 mss/issue; 12 mss/year. Length: open. Publishes short shorts. Also publishes literary essays, literary criticism and poetry.
How to Contact: Send complete ms with cover letter. Should include estimated word count. Usually reports in 6-9 months. Send SASE for reply, return of ms or send disposable copy of ms. Simultaneous, reprint and electronic submissions OK. Sample copy for $5.50. Free fiction guidelines.
Payment: Pays 1 or 2 contributor's copies.
Terms: Not copyrighted.

RHINO, (II), 8403 W. Normal Ave., Niles IL 60714. Fiction Editor: Kay Meier. Magazine: 5½×8; 80 pages, "best" quality paper; 65 lb. Tuscani cover stock; cover illustrations only. "Exists for writers of short prose and poetry—for new writers whose eyes and ears for language are becoming practiced, and whose approaches to it are individualistic. Aimed toward the poetically inclined." Annually. Estab. 1976. Circ. 500.

Needs: "Short prose (up to 10 pages). We aim for artistic writing; we also accept the well-written piece of wide or general appeal." Receives approximately 100 unsolicited fiction mss each month. Published work by Gary Fincke and Lois Hauselmann; published new writers within the last year. Also publishes poetry. Critiques rejected mss "when there is time." Sometimes recommends other markets.

How to Contact: *Charges $3 reading fee.* Send complete ms with cover letter with credits and SASE. No simultaneous submissions. Sample copy $6 plus $1.05 postage.

Payment: Pays 1 contributor's copy.

Terms: Acquires one-time rights.

Advice: "We recommend you know how to construct a variety of idiomatic English sentences; take as fresh an approach as possible toward the chosen subject; and take time to polish the ms for its keenest effect. Don't be afraid to experiment with form. We like strong writing—human warmth, humor, originality, beauty!"

RIVER STYX, (II), Big River Association, 14 S. Euclid, St. Louis MO 63108. (314)361-0043. Editor: Lee Fournier. Magazine: 6×8; 90 pages; visual art (b&w). "No theme restrictions, high quality, intelligent work." Triannual. Estab. 1975.

Needs: Excerpted novel chapter, contemporary, ethnic, experimental, feminist, gay, satire, lesbian, literary, mainstream, prose poem, translations. "Avoid 'and then I woke up' stories." Receives 15 unsolicited mss/month. Buys 1-3 mss/issue; 3-8 mss/year. Reads only in September and October. Published work by Bonita Friedman, Leslie Becker, Fred Viebahn. Length: no more than 20-30 manuscript pages. Publishes short shorts. Also publishes poetry. Sometimes critiques rejected mss and recommends other markets.

How to Contact: Send complete manuscript with name and address on every page. Reports in 4 months on mss. Reprint submissions OK. Simultaneous submissions OK. Sample copy $7. Fiction guidelines for #10 SAE and 1 first class stamp.

Payment: Pays $8/page maximum, free subscription to magazine and contributor's copies.

Terms: Pays on publication for first North American serial rights.

Advice: Looks for "writer's attention to the language and the sentence; responsible, controlled narrative."

RIVERSIDE QUARTERLY, (II,IV), Box 5507 Drew Station, Lake Charles LA 70606. (318)433-2227. Editor: Leland Sapiro. Fiction Editor: Redd Boggs. Magazine: 5½×8½; 64 pages; illustrations. Quarterly. Estab. 1964. Circ. 1,100.

Needs: Fantasy and science fiction (hard science, soft/sociological). Accepts 1 ms/issue; 4 mss/year. Publishes ms 6 months after acceptance. Length: 3,500 words maximum; 3,000 words average. Publishes short shorts. Also publishes literary essays, literary criticism, poetry. Critiques rejected mss.

How to Contact: *Send directly to fiction editor, Redd Boggs, Box 1111, Berkeley CA 94701.* Send complete ms with cover letter. Reports in 2 weeks. SASE. Simultaneous submissions OK. Accepts electronic submissions. Sample copy $2.50. Reviews novels and short story collections.

Payment: Pays in contributor's copies.

Terms: Acquires one-time rights. Sends galleys to author.

Advice: "Would-be contributors are urged to first inspect a copy or two of the magazine (available at any major college or public library) to see the *kind* of story we print."

RIVERWIND, (II,IV), General Studies/Hocking College, Nelsonville OH 45764. (614)753-3591 (ext. 2375). Editors: Audrey Naffziger, C.A. Dubielak. Fiction Editor: Robert Clark Young. Magazine: 6×9; 60 lb. paper; cover illustrations. "College press, small literary magazine." Annually. Estab. 1975.
 ● In addition to receiving funding from the Ohio Arts Council since 1985, *Riverwind* won the Septa Award in 1992.

Needs: Adventure, contemporary, erotica, ethnic, feminist, historical (general), horror, humor/satire, literary, mainstream, prose poem, spiritual, sports, regional, translations, western. No juvenile/teen fiction. Receives 30 mss/month. Does not read during the summer. Recently published work by Roy Bentley, Greg Anderson; published new writers within the last year. Sometimes critiques rejected mss.

How to Contact: Send complete ms with cover letter. No simultaneous submissions. Reports on mss in 1-4 months. SASE.
Payment: Pays in contributor's copies.
Advice: "Your work must be strong, entertaining. It helps if you are an Ohio/West Virginia writer. We hope to print more fiction. We now publish mainly regional writers (Ohio, West Virginia, Kentucky)."

ROANOKE REVIEW, (II), Roanoke College, English Department, Salem VA 24153. (703)375-2500. Editor: Robert R. Walter. Magazine: 6×9; 40-60 pages. Semiannually. Estab. 1967. Circ. 300.
Needs: Receives 30-40 unsolicited mss/month. Accepts 2-3 mss/issue; 4-6 mss/year. Publishes ms 6 months after acceptance. Length: 2,500 words minimum; 7,500 words maximum. Publishes short shorts. Occasionally critiques rejected mss.
How to Contact: Send complete ms with cover letter. Reports in 1-2 weeks on queries; 8-10 weeks on mss. SASE for query. Sample copy $2.
Payment: Pays in contributor's copies.

THE ROCKFORD REVIEW, (II), The Rockford Writers Guild, Box 858, Rockford IL 61105. Editor-in-Chief: David Ross. Magazine: 5⅜×8½; 96 pages; b&w illustrations; b&w photos. "We look for prose and poetry with a fresh approach to old themes or new insights into the human condition." Annually. Estab. 1971. Circ. 500.
  ● The Rockford Writers Guild publishes this and *Tributary*, also listed in this book.
Needs: Ethnic, experimental, fantasy, humor/satire, literary, regional, science fiction (hard science, soft/sociological). Upcoming theme: "The Next Decade"—How the human condition is apt to change in the future. Recently published work by David Olsen, Judith Beth Cohen, Thomas E. Kennedy, Michael Driver. Length: Up to 2,500 words. Also publishes one-acts and essays.
How to Contact: Send complete ms. "Include a short biographical note—no more than four sentences." Simultaneous submissions OK. Reports in 4-6 weeks on mss. SASE. Sample copy $6. Fiction guidelines for SASE.
Payment: Pays contributor's copies. "Two $50 editor's choice cash prizes per issue."
Terms: Acquires first North American serial rights.
Advice: "Any subject or theme goes as long as it enhances our understanding of our humanity."

ROHWEDDER, International Journal of Literature & Art, (II, IV), Rough Weather Press, Box 29490, Los Angeles CA 90029. Editor: Hans-Jurgen Schacht. Fiction Editors: Robert Dassanowsky-Harris and Nancy Antell. Magazine: 8½×11; 50+ pages; 20 lb. paper; 90 lb. cover; illustrations; photos. "Multilingual/cultural poetry and short stories. Graphic art and photography." Annually. Estab. 1986.
Needs: Contemporary, ethnic, experimental, feminist, literary, regional, translations (with rights). No fillers. Upcoming themes: Contemporary Media (Fall 1993). Receives 20-50 unsolicited mss/month. Accepts 6 mss/year. Publishes ms 6-9 months after acceptance. Length: 1,500-2,500 words average; 200 words minimum; 2,500 words maximum. Publishes short shorts. Also publishes literary essays, poetry. Sometimes critiques rejected mss and recommends other markets.
How to Contact: Include bio with submission. Reports in 1 month on queries; 3 months on mss. SASE. Sample copy $5.
Payment: Pays in contributor's copies, charges for extras.
Terms: Acquires one-time rights.
Advice: "Go out as far as you have to but remember the basics: clear, concise style and form."

RUBY'S PEARLS, (I, II), A.C. Aarbus Publishing Inc., 3803 Cypress Ave., Sanford FL 32773. Editor: Del Freeman. Fiction Editor: Patsy Sauls. Magazine: Electronic; page number varies. "All fiction, no porn, no poetry, general interest." Monthly. Estab. 1991. "Uploaded electronically to BBSs nationwide."
  ● *Ruby's Pearls* won a Digital Quill Award (sponsored by the Disktop Publishing Association) this year. The editor plans an annual year-end anthology called *Ruby's Pearl's: One Perfect Strand*. By using other bulletin boards and "echoing" across the country the magazine is accessible to 35 of the 50 states, on Genie and Compuserve and in boards in London, Hong Kong, Japan and Singapore.
Needs: Condensed/excerpted novel, contemporary, experimental, humor/satire, mainstream, mystery/suspense. "Stories can be submitted on either size disk, ASCII, IBM format only. Will return if mailer (pre-paid) is enclosed." No porn, erotica. Buys 1-2 mss/issue; 24-30 mss/year. Publishes ms 1-2 months after acceptance. Recently published work by Patsy Sauls, Betty Duckworth, Mary Ellen Wofford. Publishes short shorts. Length: 250 up (unless it's really killer). Sometimes comments on rejected ms.

How to Contact: Submissions are by 5.25 disk; stories in IBM-ASCII format only or they can be made by modem by calling "Treasures BBS" 1-407-831-9130 and uploading to the RP Conf., 157-Files. Contact by mail, by disk, complete story. Reports in 1-2 months. "Prepaid disk mailer is required." Simultaneous submissions OK. Accepts electronic submissions via disk or modem. For sample copy: "Write me and I'll respond with name and number of nearest BBS where it can be found."
Payment: No payment.
Terms: Only the privilege to reproduce electronically once. All rights remain with author.
Advice: "We're looking for something different. March to a different drummer."

SALAD, A Reader, (I, II), Moonface Press, Box 64980-306, Dallas TX 75206. (214)696-8990. Editor: Elaine Liner. Magazine: 5×6½; 74 pages; 20 lb. bond; handmade paper, Strathmore Beau Brilliant cover. "New fiction and poetry. Not too serious. Not ultra-lit. Open to oddities such as lists, eulogies, letters, short-short plays or scenes from plays. For people who are as sick as we are of water-image poems and long, wordy stories about New York writers and models and what they eat and drink." Annually. Estab. 1990.
Needs: Contemporary, experimental, humor/satire, literary, regional. "No violent fiction, please. No stories expressing violence toward women, children or animals." Receives 30-50 unsolicited mss/month. Buys 10-15 mss/issue. Publishes ms up to 9 months after acceptance. Recently published work by Sheryl Nelms, John Shore, John Eaton, Clay McNear. Length: 1,000 words preferred. Publishes short shorts. Sometimes critiques rejected mss ("if I think I want to see more work by that author").
How to Contact: Send complete ms with cover letter. Include "a little bio info, mention previously published work, some background perhaps on why submitting this mss to *Salad*." Reports in 3 months. SASE. Simultaneous submissions OK. Sample copy for $5.
Payment: Pays 2 contributor's copies. Charges for extras.
Terms: Acquires first North American serial rights or one-time rights.
Advice: "If the writer has a sense of humor, that's an immediate grabber. I like to be surprised, get a little shove, see a little experimentation in how the words are used. A new, fresh voice—not the humdrum type of super-serious literary, I'll-see-you-at-the-next-poetry-reading stuff—interests us. Neatness counts a lot. Read an issue first. Then, take your best story and edit out at least a third of it. We like tight, bright writing. Read your story aloud to yourself or to a friend and when it sounds great, send that version."

SALMON MAGAZINE, (I, II), P.O. Box 440313, Somerville MA 02144. Editor: Andrew Tang. Fiction Editor: Anna Watson. Magazine: 5½×8; 150-200 pages; glossy cardstock cover; illustrations and photographs. For "a literary audience." Quarterly. Estab. 1991.
Needs: Excerpted novel, contemporary, erotica, ethnic, experimental, fantasy (as long as there's no unicorn), feminist, gay, horror, lesbian, literary, mystery/suspense, prose poem, regional, science fiction, senior citizen/retirement, translation. No "pornography, religious fiction, men's adventure, political propaganda." Receives 50-100 unsolicited mss/month. Accepts 12-14 mss/issue; 24-28 mss/year. Does not read mss July and August. Accepted manuscripts published in next issue. Recently published work by Edwidge Danticat, Katherine Min, Val Gerstle. Length: 3,000 words. Submit "one story at a time." Publishes short shorts. Sometimes critiques rejected ms and recommends other markets.
How to Contact: Send complete ms with or without cover letter. Reports in 1-2 weeks on queries; 1-4 months on mss. SASE. Simultaneous (if noted) and reprint submissions OK.
Payment: Pays 1 contributor's copy. Charges for extras; 40% discount.
Terms: Acquires one-time rights. Sends pre-publication galleys to the author "on occasion—we check before changing anything big."
Advice: "The most important quality is emotional honesty. If a manuscript lacks integrity, if it is manipulative, I become uninterested. I like writing that makes me see words and phrases in a new light; I'm interested in stories incorporating questions of gender, race . . . identity. I like to be surprised, shocked, moved . . . ."

SALOME: A JOURNAL FOR THE PERFORMING ARTS, (I, II, IV), Ommation Press, 5548 N. Sawyer, Chicago IL 60625. Editor: Effie Mihopoulos. "*Salome* seeks to cover the performing arts in a thoughtful and incisive way." Quarterly. Estab. 1976. Circ. 1,000.
  ● Ommation Press publishes this and *Mati*, also listed in this book.
Needs: Literary, contemporary, science fiction, fantasy, women's, feminist, gothic, romance, mystery, adventure, humor, serialized novels, prose poems, translations. "We seek good quality mss that relate to the performing arts or fiction with strong characters that somehow move the reader." Receives approximately 25 unsolicited fiction mss each month; accepts 40 mss/year. No preferred length. Some-

times sends mss on to editors of other publications and recommends other markets.
How to Contact: Send complete ms with SASE. Reports in 1 month. Sample copy $4, 9×12 SASE with $1.05 (book-rate) postage preferred.
Payment: Pays 1 contributor's copy. Contributor's rates for extras upon request.
Terms: Acquires first North American serial rights. "Rights revert to author, but we retain reprint rights."
Advice: "Write a well-written story or prose poem." Rejected mss are "usually badly written—improve style, grammar, etc.—too often writers send out mss before they're ready. See a sample copy. Specify fiction interest."

SALT LICK PRESS, (II), Salt Lick Foundation, P.O. Box 15471, Austin TX 78761-5471. Editor: James Haining. Magazine: 8½×11; 64 pages; 60 lb. offset stock; 80 lb. text cover; illustrations and photos. Irregularly. Estab. 1969.
Needs: Contemporary, erotica, ethnic, experimental, feminist, gay, lesbian, literary. Receives 25 unsolicited mss each month. Accepts 2 mss/issue. Length: open. Occasionally critiques rejected mss.
How to Contact: Send complete ms with cover letter. Reports in 2 weeks on queries; 1 month on mss. SASE. Simultaneous and reprint submissions OK. Sample copy $5, 9×12 SAE and 3 first class stamps.
Payment: Pays in contributor's copies.
Terms: Acquires first North American serial rights. Sends galleys to author.

SAN GABRIEL VALLEY MAGAZINE, (IV), Miller Books, 2908 W. Valley Blvd., Alhambra CA 91803. (213)284-7607. Editor: Joseph Miller. Magazine: 5¼×7¼; 48 pages; 60 lb. book paper; vellum bristol cover stock; illustrations; photos. "Regional magazine for the Valley featuring local entertainment, dining, sports and events. We also carry articles about successful people from the area. For upper-middle-class people who enjoy going out a lot." Bimonthly. Published special fiction issue last year; plans another. Estab. 1976. Circ. 3,000.
Needs: Contemporary, inspirational, psychic/supernatural/occult, western, adventure and humor. No articles on sex or ERA. Receives approximately 10 unsolicited fiction mss/month. Buys 2 mss/issue; 20 mss/year. Length: 500-2,500 words. Also publishes short shorts. Recommends other markets.
How to Contact: Send complete ms with SASE. Reports in 2 weeks on mss. Sample copy $1 with 9×12 SASE.
Payment: Pays 5¢/word; 2 contributor's copies.
Terms: Payment on acceptance for one-time rights.

SAN JOSE STUDIES, (II), San Jose State University, One Washington Square, San Jose CA 95192. Editor: Fauneil J. Rinn. Magazine: Digest-sized; 112-144 pages; good paper and cover; occasional illustrations and photos. "A journal for the general, educated reader. Covers a wide variety of materials: fiction, poetry, interviews, interdisciplinary essays. Aimed toward the college-educated common reader with an interest in the broad scope of materials." Triannually. Estab. 1975. Circ. 500.
Needs: Social and political, literary, humor, ethnic and regional. Receives approximately 20 unsolicited fiction mss each month. Published work by Molly Giles, Richard Flanagan. Length: 2,500-5,000+ words. Also publishes literary essays, literary criticism, poetry. Critiques rejected mss when there is time. Sometimes recommends other markets.
How to Contact: Send complete ms with SASE. No simultaneous submissions. Reports in 2 months. Publishes ms an average of 6 months to 1 year after acceptance. Sample copy $4.
Payment: Pays 2 contributor's copies. Annual $100 award for best story, essay or poem.
Terms: Acquires first rights. Sends galleys to author.
Advice: "Name should appear *only* on cover sheet. We seldom print beginning writers of fiction or poetry."

‡SAN MIGUEL WRITER, (II), Tenerias #9, San Miguel de Allende, GTO Mexico 37700. (011)52-465-22225. Editor: Carl Selph. Magazine: 5½×8½; 80 pages; illustrations. "We accept fiction, nonfiction, poetry, etc., based on 'literary' quality definable only as it is perceived by a group of approximately 5 well-read editors sensitive to a community of artists of all kinds and professionals—many retired—from all fields." Semiannually. Estab. 1989. Circ. 3,000.
● Even though this magazine is published in Mexico, work is primarily in English and since it is based in North America we included it here rather than in the foreign section.

Needs: Adventure, ethnic/multicultural, experimental, fantasy (science fantasy, sword and sorcery), feminist, gay, historical (general), humor/satire, lesbian, literary, mystery/suspense (police procedural, romantic suspense), psychic/supernatural/occult, regional, romance (contemporary, historical), science fiction (soft/sociological), senior citizen/retirement, serialized novel, translations. "Our special interest is manuscripts in Spanish from Latino writers." Nothing pornographic unless with redeeming literary quality; no simplistic action. Receives 30 unsolicited mss/month. Acquires 3-6 mss/issue. Publishes ms 3-5 months after acceptance. Recently published work by Ann Ireland, Alice K. Barten, Madelene Carr. Length: 6,000 words maximum. Publishes short shorts. Also publishes literary essays, literary criticism and poetry.
How to Contact: Send complete ms with cover letter. Should include estimated word count, one-paragraph bio, list of publications. Reports in 3 months on mss. SASE for return of ms or send disposable copy of ms. No simultaneous submissions. Electronic submissions OK. Reviews novels and short story collections.
Payment: Pays 1 contributor's copy.
Terms: Rights remain with author. Writers can participate in contest "simply by submitting their work for acceptance. $100 prize each for the best selection in poetry and prose, English or Spanish, chosen annually."
Advice: "Though principally an English-language publication, we relish our presence in San Miguel and eagerly solicit work in Spanish. The editors impose no restrictions on subject and style but stipulate that, in their judgment, manuscripts be of literary merit and of interest to our readers. San Miguel, a town with an unrelenting flow of painters, writers, musicians — artists of all kinds and people representing careers of all kinds — provides a challenging readership for contributors to the *San Miguel Writer*. Our editors, attuned to such an environment, are not only discriminating but, yes, elitist — in the most serious sense of that word — about the calibre of the magazine they are producing."

SANSKRIT, Literary Arts Publication of UNC Charlotte, (II), University of North Carolina at Charlotte, Highway 49, Charlotte NC 28223. (704)547-2326. Editor: Jeff Byers. Fiction Editor: Scott Buchanan. Magazine: 9 × 15, 60-90 pages. "We are a general lit/art mag open to all genres, if well written, for college students, alumni, writers and artists across the country." Annually. Estab. 1968.
Needs: Contemporary, erotica, ethnic, experimental, feminist, gay, humor/satire, lesbian, literary, mainstream, prose poem, regional, translations. No formula, western, romance. Upcoming theme: How literature reflects/affects/influences REAL LIFE. Receives 2-4 unsolicited mss/month. Acquires 3-6 mss/issue. Does not read mss in summer. Publishes in late March. Recently published work by Nann Budd, P.L. Thomas, Jerry Saviano. Length: 250 words minimum; 5,000 words maximum. Publishes short shorts. Also publishes poetry. Sometimes critiques rejected mss.
How to Contact: Send complete manuscript with cover letter. SASE. Simultaneous submissions OK. Sample copy $6. Fiction guidelines for #10 SAE.
Payment: Pays contributor's copies.
Terms: Acquires one-time rights. Publication not copyrighted.
Advice: "A tight cohesive story, in an often shattered world, wins my heart. I like quirkiness just to the point of self indulgence. There is a fine line . . . there are many fine lines . . . walk as many as you can."

SANTA MONICA REVIEW, (III), Santa Monica College, 1900 Pico Blvd., Santa Monica CA 90405. (213)450-5150. Editor: James Krusoe. Magazine: 5½ × 8; 140 pages, rag paper. Semiannually. Estab. 1988. Circ. 1,000.
Needs: Contemporary, literary. Accepts 5 mss/issue; 10 mss/year. Publishes mss varying amount of time after publication. Published work by Ann Beattie, Arturo Vivante, Guy Davenport and Barry Hannah.
How to Contact: Send complete ms with cover letter. Reports in 3 months on mss. SASE. Simultaneous submissions OK. Sample copy $7.
Payment: Pays subscription to magazine, contributor's copies.
Terms: Acquires one-time rights.
Advice: "We are *not* actively soliciting beginning work. We want to combine high quality West Coast, especially Los Angeles, writing with that from the rest of the country."

‡SCREAM OF THE BUDDHA, (III), Buddha Rose Publications, P.O. Box 548, Hermosa Beach CA 90254. (310)543-3809. Fax: (310)543-9673. Editor: Scott Shaw, Ph.D. Fiction Editor: Elliot Sebastian. Magazine: 8½ × 11; 30 pages; card cover; illustrations; photos. "To publish the abstract, the literally

obscene, the mystical, the powerful. We here are literary anarchists." Bimonthly. Estab. 1988. Circ. 1,000.
Needs: Adventure, erotica, experimental, literary, psychic/supernatural/occult, science fiction. "Not boring, traditional junk." Receives 800 mss/month. Buys 3 mss/issue; 12-15 mss/year. Publishes 3 months after acceptance. Agented fiction 80%. Recently published Charles Bukowski, Scott Shaw, Hae Won Shin, James F. Spezze III. Length: 1,000 words. Publishes short shorts. Also publishes literary essays, literary criticism, poetry. Sometimes critiques rejected mss.
How to Contact: Send complete ms with a cover letter or submit through an agent. Should include minimal bio. Reports 1 day-1 month. Send SASE (IRC) for reply, return of ms or send disposable copy of ms. Simultaneous reprint submissions OK. Sample copy $5. Reviews novels and short story collections.
Payment: Pays 1-3 contributor's copies.
Terms: Acquires first rights.
Advice: Looks for "a ms that screams a form of passion that we have never read before. So often, we see the same old ego-filled material; telling someone else where it is at, from one individual's point of view. Junk. Some people love us—most hate us—WE DON'T CARE! Forget structure. Forget all that you have been taught. Forget what the 'masters' have written, because that is all nonsense. Scream your own vision and an audience will come to you."

THE SEATTLE REVIEW, (II), Padelford Hall GN-30, University of Washington, Seattle WA 98195. (206)543-9865. Editor: Donna Gerstenberger. Fiction Editor: Charles Johnson. Magazine: 6×9. "Includes general fiction, poetry, craft essays on writing, and one interview per issue with a Northwest writer." Semiannually. Published special fiction issue. Estab. 1978. Circ. 1,000.
Needs: Contemporary, ethnic, experimental, fantasy, feminist, gay, historical, horror, humor/satire, lesbian, literary, mainstream, mystery/suspense, prose poem, psychic/supernatural/occult, regional, science fiction, excerpted novel, translations, western. "We also publish a series called Writers and their Craft, which deals with aspects of writing fiction (also poetry)—point of view, characterization, etc., rather than literary criticism, each issue." Does not want to see "anything in bad taste (porn, racist, etc.)." Receives about 50 unsolicited mss/month. Buys about 3-6 mss/issue; about 4-10 mss/year. Reads mss all year but "slow to respond in summer." Agented fiction 25%. Published work by David Milofsky, Lawson Fusao Inada and Liz Rosenberg; published new writers within the last year. Length: 3,500 words average; 500 words minimum; 10,000 words maximum. Publishes short shorts. Sometimes critiques rejected mss. Occasionally recommends other markets.
How to Contact: Send complete ms. "If included, cover letter should list recent publications or mss we'd seen and liked, but been unable to publish." Reports in 3 months. SASE. Sample copy "half-price if older than one year." Current issue $4.50; some special issues $5.50-6.50.
Payment: Pays 0-$100, free subscription to magazine, 2 contributor's copies; charge for extras.
Terms: Pays on publication for first North American serial rights. Copyright reverts to writer on publication; "please request release of rights and cite *SR* in reprint publications." Sends galleys to author.
Advice: "Beginners do well in our magazine if they send clean, well-written manuscripts. We've published a lot of 'first stories' from all over the country and take pleasure in discovery."

THE SECRET ALAMEDA, A Dent in the Pacific Rim, (II), P.O. Box 527, Alameda CA 94501. (510)521-5597. Editor: Richard Whittaker. Magazine: 8½×11; 48-60 pages; 70 lb. coated paper; illustrations and photographs. "We're a magazine put together by artists. We publish art portfolios, interviews, articles, and fiction." Audience is "hard to define. We think we have an educated audience, probably over 30 years old for the most part. People who appreciate the visual arts as well as the literary arts." Quarterly. Estab. 1991. Circ. 1,500-2,500.
Needs: "Literary work—sometimes serious, sometimes humorous—but always work of substance and depth. We prefer honest, personal work based on lived experience. Will consider nonfiction along these lines also. Not interested in most 'genres' of writing." Recently published work by George Lakoff, Barbara Minton, Wm. Dudley, Ronald Hobbs. Length: 500-2,500 words. Sometime critiques rejected mss.
How to Contact: Send complete ms with cover letter. Reports in 4-6 weeks. SASE. Simultaneous and reprint submissions OK. Sample copy for $4.
Payment: Pays subscription and up to 10 contributor's copies.
Terms: Acquires one-time rights.
Advice: "Read a copy of the magazine."

SEEMS, (II), Lakeland College, Sheboygan WI 53081. (414)565-3871. Editor: Karl Elder. Magazine: 7×8½; 40 pages. "We publish fiction and poetry for an audience which tends to be highly literate. People read the publication, I suspect, for the sake of reading it." Published irregularly. Estab. 1971. Circ. 300.
Needs: Literary. Accepts 4 mss/issue. Receives approximately 12 unsolicited fiction mss each month. Published work by John Birchler; published new writers within the last year. Length: 5,000 words maximum. Publishes short shorts. Also publishes poetry. Critiques rejected mss when there is time.
How to Contact: Send complete ms with SASE. Reports in 2 months on mss. Publishes ms an average of 1-2 years after acceptance. Sample copy $3.
Payment: Pays 1 contributor's copy; $3 charge for extras.
Terms: Rights revert to author.
Advice: "Send clear, clean copies. Read the magazine in order to help determine the taste of the editor." Mss are rejected because of "lack of economical expression, or saying with many words what could be said in only a few. Good fiction contains all of the essential elements of poetry; study poetry and apply those elements to fiction. Our interest is shifting to story poems, the grey area between genres."

‡SEMIOTEXT(E), (II), Autonomedia, P.O. Box 568, Brooklyn NY 11211. (718)387-6471. Editor: Jim Fleming. Fiction Editor: Sylviere Lotringer. Magazine: 7×10; 160 pages; 50 lb. paper; 10 pf cover; illustrations and photos. "Radical/marginal for an arts/academic audience." Annually. Estab. 1974. Circ. 8,000.
Needs: Erotica, ethnic, experimental, fantasy, feminist, gay, literary, psychic/supernatural/occult, science fiction, translations. Recently published work by Kathy Acker, William Burroughs. Publishes short shorts. Sometimes recommends other markets.
How to Contact: Query first. Reporting time varies. SASE for ms. Simultaneous submissions OK. Accepts electronic submissions. Sample copy for $10.
Payment: Pays in contributor's copies.
Terms: Acquires first North American serial rights. Sends galleys to author.

SENSATIONS MAGAZINE, (I,II), 2 Radio Ave., A5, Secaucus NJ 07094. Founder: David Messineo. Magazine: 8½×11; 50-70 pages; 20 lb. inside paper, 67 lb. cover paper; vellum cover; black ink line illustrations. "We publish short stories and poetry, no specific theme, for a liberal, worldly audience who reads for pleasure." Magazine also includes the Rediscovering America in Poetry research series. Semiannually. Estab. 1987. Circ. 250.
Needs: Adventure, contemporary, fantasy, gay, historical, horror, humor/satire, lesbian, literary, mainstream, mystery/suspense (private eye), prose poem, regional, romance (historical), science fiction, western (traditional). "We're not into gratuitous profanity, pornography, or violence. Sometimes these are needed to properly tell the tale. We'll read anything unusual, providing it is submitted in accordance with our submission policies. No abstract works only the writer can understand." Upcoming theme: " A theme issue on Coney Island's amusement parks is anticipated for either the summer of 1993 or the summer of 1994." Accepts 2-4 mss/issue. Publishes ms 2 months after acceptance. Recently published work by Jay Jacobs and Robert Dumont.
How to Contact: "Send name, address, a paragraph of background information about yourself, a paragraph about what inspired the story. We'll send submission guidelines when we are ready to judge material." Reports in 1-2 weeks on queries; 4-6 weeks on mss. SASE for brochure. Simultaneous submissions OK. Accepts electronic submissions (Macintosh only). *Must first purchase* sample copy $8. Check payable to David Messineo. *"Do not submit material before reading submission guidelines."* Next deadline: late 1994. Only accepting Fiction Contest entries during 1993.
Payment: No payment.
Terms: Acquires one-time rights.
Advice: "Each story must have a strong beginning that grabs the reader's attention in the first two sentences. Characters have to be realistic and well-described. Readers must like, hate, or have some emotional response to your characters. Setting, plot, construction, attention to detail—all are important. We work with writers to help them improve in these areas, but the better the stories are written before they come to us, the greater the chance for publication. Purchase sample copy first and read the stories, then determine which of your stories is most appropriate to submit. Our research project offers the first collection of poetry written in and about America in the 1500s and 1600s, which may also be of interest to you. Send SASE for information on our Fiction Contest (Top Prize $250) before July 1, 1993."

THE SEWANEE REVIEW, (III), University of the South, Sewanee TN 37375. (615)598-1245. Editor: George Core. Magazine: 6×9; 192 pages. "A literary quarterly, publishing original fiction, poetry, essays on literary and related subjects, book reviews and book notices for well-educated readers who appreciate good American and English literature." Quarterly. Estab. 1892. Circ. 3,000.

Needs: Literary, contemporary. No translations, juvenile, gay/lesbian, erotica. Buys 10-15 mss/year. Receives approximately 100 unsolicited fiction mss each month. Does not read mss June 1-August 31. Published new writers within the last year. Length: 6,000-7,500 words. Critiques rejected mss "when there is time." Sometimes recommends other markets.

How to Contact: Send complete ms with SASE and cover letter stating previous publications, if any. Reports in 1 month on mss. Sample copy $6 plus 50¢ postage.

Payment: Pays $10-12/printed page; 2 contributor's copies; $3.50 charge for extras. Writer's guidelines for SASE.

Terms: Pays on publication for first North American serial rights and second serial rights by agreement.

Advice: "Send only one story at a time, with a serious and sensible cover letter. We think fiction is of greater general interest than any other literary mode."

short fiction • essays • book reviews
&
conversations with

DANIEL RICHLER • DOUGLAS COOPER

"This cover was chosen to reflect the two sides of Canada and Canadian youth," says Evan Solomon, editor-in-chief of Shift, a literary magazine created to provide a forum for Canadian writers ages 35 and under. "The diner shot under our logo is so typical of the kind of place young writers inhabit, while the beautiful shot of the man on the water suggests how connected Canadians are to their land and nature," he says. "We are moving toward publishing a wider range of writing, such as essays and travelogues, but Shift is primarily a magazine for short fiction." The cover photographs were taken by Steven Angel, an animator and freelance artist. The layout was designed by Mark Hyland, a researcher for CBC television.

SHATTERED WIG REVIEW, (I, II), Shattered Wig Productions, 523 E. 38th St., Baltimore MD 21218-1930. (301)243-6888. Editor: Collective. Magazine: 70 pages; "average" paper; cardstock cover; illustrations and photos. "Open forum for the discussion of the absurdo-miserablist aspects of everyday life. Fiction, poetry, graphics, essays, photos." Semiannually. Estab. 1988. Circ. 500.

Needs: Confession, contemporary, erotica, ethnic, experimental, feminist, gay, humor/satire, juvenile (5-9 years), lesbian, literary, preschool (1-4 years), prose poem, psychic/supernatural/occult, regional, senior citizen/retirement, serialized/excerpted novel, translations, young adult/teen (10-18), meat, music, film, art, pickles, revolutionary practice." Does not want "anything by Ann Beattie or John Irving." Receives 15-20 unsolicited mss/month. Publishes ms 2-4 months after acceptance. Published work by Al Ackerman, Jake Berry, Bella Donna; published new writers within the last year. Publishes short shorts. Also publishes literary criticism, poetry. Sometimes critiques rejected mss and recommends other markets.

How to Contact: Send complete ms with cover letter or "visit us in Baltimore." Reports in 1 month. SASE for ms. Simultaneous and reprint submissions OK. Sample copy for $4.

Payment: Pays in contributor's copies.

Terms: Acquires one-time rights.

Advice: "The arts have been reduced to imploding pus with the only material rewards reserved for vapid stylists and collegiate pod suckers. The only writing that counts has no barriers between imagination and reality, thought and action. Send us at least 3 pieces so we have a choice."

‡SHIFT MAGAZINE, Short Fiction by Young Canadian Writers, (II), Solomon-Heintzman, 88 Roxborough St. East, Toronto, Ontario M4W 1V8 Canada. (416)482-9955. Fax: (416)920-1933. Editors: Evan Solomon, Andrew Heintzman. Magazine: 8½ × 11; 32-48 pages; 20 lb. glossy paper; 80 lb. glossy cover; illustrations; photographs. "Writers under the age of 35 are encouraged to submit all genres of fiction, including travelogs, memoirs and essays on culture and literature." Quarterly. Estab. 1992. Circ. 1,100.

Needs: Adventure, condensed novel, erotica, ethnic/multicultural, experimental, feminist, gay, historical, humor/satire, lesbian, literary, mainstream/contemporary, regional, serialized novel, translations. No pornography. Plans special fiction issue or anthology in the future. Receives 50-80 unsolicited mss/month. Acquires 5-9 mss/issue; 20-35 mss/year. Publishes ms 1-5 months after acceptance. Recently published work by Rinaldo Columbi, Evan Solomon, John Sullivan. Length: 4,000 words maximum. Publishes short shorts. Also publishes literary essays and literary criticism. Often critiques or comments on rejects mss.

How to Contact: Send complete ms with cover letter. Should include estimated word count, bio (2 lines), list of publications. Reports in 2 weeks on queries; 6 weeks on mss. SASE (IRC). Simultaneous submissions, reprint (if noted) and electronic submissions (3.5 disks with hard copy) OK. Sample copy for $4 (Canadian) and 8½ × 11 SAE. Fiction guidelines for 8½ × 11 SAE. Reviews novel and short story collections.

Payment: Pays 1 contributor's copy.

Terms: Acquires one-time rights.

Advice: Looks for "new, exciting fiction which seeks to say something relevant and informative to our readers. It should be clearly written. *But* all styles are examined. Story must be good on its own terms."

SHOCKBOX, The Literary/Art Magazine with Teeth, (II), P.O. Box 7226, Nashua NH 03060. (603)888-8549. Editor: C.F. Roberts. Magazine: Digest-sized; 44 pages. "We publish raw, jarring experimental literary fiction. For generally alternative art/lit., underground audience." Quarterly. Estab. 1991.

Needs: Experimental, humor/satire, literary. "No slick, watered-down prose. No contrived TV-Movie-of-the-Week fodder." Receives 10 unsolicited mss/month. Accepts 3 mss/issue; 20 mss/year. Time varies between acceptance and publication. Recently published work by Robert W. Howington, Christopher Woods, Skip Rhudy, Joseph Benzola. Length: 1,000 words or less preferred. Publishes short shorts. Sometimes comments on rejected mss and recommends other markets.

How to Contact: Query first. Include name, address, short bio. Reports in 2 weeks on queries; 2-3 months on mss. SASE. Simultaneous and reprint submissions OK. Sample copy for $2.50. Fiction guidelines for #10 SAE. Make check payable to C.F. Roberts.

Payment: Pays in contributor's copies.

Terms: Acquires first rights or one-time rights.

Advice: "More and more nowadays, I find that I am bored and annoyed by mainstream 'literature' and all the preconceived ideas associated with it. Please do step out of these bounds and give me something startling and unusual to read. I want to hedge away from the status quo and all it entails. SURPRISE ME."

SHOOTING STAR REVIEW, (II, IV), 7123 Race St., Pittsburgh PA 15208. (412)731-7464. Editor: Sandra Gould Ford. Magazine: 8½ × 11; 32 pages; 60 lb. white paper; 80 lb. enamel glossy cover; generously-illustrated; photos. "Dedicated to the Black African-American experience." Quarterly. Estab. 1987. Circ. 1,500.

Needs: Contemporary, experimental, literary, regional, young adult, translations. Each issue has a different theme: "Behind Bars" (deadline March 1); "Marching to a Different Beat" (deadline June 1); "A Salute to African-American Male Writers" (deadline September 1); "Mothers and Daughters" (deadline November 15). Writers should send SASE for guidelines. No juvenile, preschool. Receives 30-40 unsolicited mss/month. Publishes 5-8 mss/issue. Publishes ms 4-12 months after acceptance. Length: 1,800 words preferred; 3,500 words maximum. Publishes short shorts. Length: 1,000 words or less. Sometimes critiques rejected mss and recommends other markets.

How to Contact: Send complete ms with cover letter. "We like to promote the writer as well as their work and would appreciate understanding who the writer is and why they write." Reports within 1 month on queries; 10-12 weeks on mss. SASE. Simultaneous, photocopied and reprint submissions OK. Accepts electronic submissions via "IBM compatible, 5¼" double sided/double density disk, ASCII non-formated." Sample copy for $3. Fiction guidelines for #10 SAE and 1 first class stamp.

Payment: Pays $15-50 maximum and 2 contributor's copies; charge for extras.

Terms: Pays on publication for first North American serial rights. Sends galleys to author upon request, if time permits.

Advice: "*Shooting Star Review* was started specifically to provide a forum for short fiction that explores the Black experience. We are committed to this art form and will make space for work that satisfies our guidelines. Upcoming themes—"Home & Community"—exploring the worlds that make us; "Star Child"—fanciful studies of the zodiac; "The Heritage"—thoughts about what growing old can mean; "Juneteenth"—the celebration of emancipation.

‡SHORT FICTION BY WOMEN, (IJ, IV), Box 1276, Stuyvesant Station, New York NY 10009. Editor: Rachel Whalen. Magazine: Journal-sized; illustrations and photographs on cover only. "*Short Fiction By Women* publishes very readable fiction which meets standards of literary excellence. For everyone who enjoys fine fiction." Triannually. Estab. 1991.

Needs: Condensed/excerpted novel, contemporary, ethnic, experimental, feminist, gay, lesbian, literary, translations. "We are interested in all good stories by women writers. No romance, horror, mystery, erotica, Christian/inspirational." Receives 150-200 unsolicited mss/month. Buys 5-15 mss/issue; 15-45 mss/year. Publishes ms 6 months after acceptance. Recently published work by Roberta Allen, Jennifer Lodde, Kat Meads, Tricia Tunstall. Length: 20,000 words maximum. Publishes short shorts. Sometimes critiques rejected mss and recommends other markets.

How to Contact: Send complete ms with cover letter. If unsure, send for writers's guidelines. Reports in 6 weeks on mss. Simultaneous submissions OK. Sample copy for $6. Fiction guidelines for #10 SAE and 1 first class stamp.

Payment: "Payment is based on length of story and funds available. Our long-term goal is to pay writers a 'living wage.' "

Terms: Pays on publication for first serial rights.

Advice: "Proofread, rewrite, clarify. Read and analyze literature. Study the many excellent books available on fiction writing."

THE SHORT STORY DIGEST, (I, II), Caldwell Publishing, Box 1183, Richardson TX 75083. Editor: Jack T. Hess. Magazine: 5⅛ × 8½; 40-50 pages; 20 lb. paper; 70 Warren Flo cover; illustrations and photographs. "We want to open a new market for short fiction." Quarterly. Estab. 1991. Circ. 1,000.

Needs: Adventure, contemporary, fantasy, horror, humor/satire, mainstream, mystery/suspense (private eye, amateur sleuth, romantic suspense), psychic/supernatural/occult, science fiction (hard science), western (traditional). "Please no excessive blood and guts, porno." No sword and sorcery. Receives 50-100 unsolicited mss/month. Buys 8-12 mss/issue; 32-50 mss/year. Recently published work by Douglas Bryce, Maggie Cooper, H.W. Christopher. Length: 1,500-2,000 words preferred; 500 words minimum; 3,000 words maximum. Publishes short shorts (but not often).

How to Contact: Send complete ms with cover letter. Reports in 8-10 weeks on mss. SASE. No simultaneous submissions. Accepts electronic submissions via disk. Sample copy for $3. Fiction guidelines for #10 SAE and 1 first class stamp.

Payment: Pays 1¢/word (more if ms is exceptional).

Terms: Pays on publication for first North American serial rights and 1 reprint in case we publish a "Best Of."

Advice: "Have a friend read it. If he likes it, then the flow of the story is good. A new author can sometimes edit their own story to death, thinking it is not good enough to submit. Take a chance, the worst that can happen is a rejection notice in the mail. Don't get mad at rejection. Sometimes a ms is rejected because of lack of space or the idea does not fit what the editor is looking for at that time."

SHORT STUFF MAGAZINE FOR GROWN-UPS, (II), Bowman Publications, P.O. Box 7057, Loveland CO 80537. (303)669-9139. Editor: Donna Bowman. Magazine: 8½ × 11; 40 pages; bond paper; enamel cover; b&w illustrations and photographs. "Nonfiction is regional—Colorado and adjacent states. Fiction and humor must be tasteful, but can be any genre, any subject. We are designed to be a 'Reader's Digest' of fiction. We are found in professional waiting rooms, etc." Monthly.

Needs: Adventure, contemporary, historical (general), humor/satire, mainstream, mystery/suspense (private eye, police procedural, amateur sleuth, romantic suspense, English cozy), regional, romance (contemporary, gothic, historical), western (frontier). No erotica. Plans special fiction issue. Receives 100 unsolicited mss/month. Buys 9-12 mss/issue; 76 mss/year. Publishes ms 3 months after acceptance. Recently published work by Dean Ballenger and Dorothy Roberts. Length: 1,000 words average; 1,500 words maximum. Also publishes some poetry.

How to Contact: Send complete ms with cover letter. SASE. Reports in 3 months. Simultaneous and reprint submissions OK. Sample copies with SAE and 98¢ postage. Fiction guidelines for SAE. Reviews novels and short story collections.
Payment: Pays $10-50 and subscription to magazine.
Terms: Pays on publication for first North American serial rights.
Advice: "We seek a potpourri of subjects each issue. A new slant, a different approach, fresh viewpoints—all of these excite us. We don't like gore, salacious humor or perverted tales. Prefer third person. Be sure it is a story with a beginning, middle and end. It must have dialogue. Many beginners do not know an essay from a short story."

SIDE SHOW, Short Story Annual, (II), Somersault Press, P.O. Box 1428, El Cerrito CA 94530-1428. (510)215-2207. Editor: Shelley Anderson, Kathe Stoltz and Marjorie K. Jacobs. Book (paperback): 5½ × 8½; 300 pages; 50 lb. paper. "Quality short stories for a general, literary audience." Annually. Estab. 1991. Circ. 250.
Needs: Contemporary, ethnic, feminist, gay, humor/satire, lesbian, literary, mainstream. Nothing genre, religious, pornographic. Receives 50-60 unsolicited mss/month. Buys 25-30 mss/issue. Does not read mss in August. Publishes ms up to 9 months after acceptance. Recently published work by Dorothy Bryant, Molly Giles and Jeff A. McQueen. Length: Open. Publishes short shorts. Critiques rejected mss and recommends other markets.
How to Contact: All submissions entered in contest. *$10 entry fee* (includes subscription to 1993-94 *Side Show*). Deadline: June 30, 1993. No guidelines. Send complete ms with cover letter and entry fee. Reports in 2-3 weeks on mss. SASE. Simultaneous submissions OK. Sample copy for $12.50 and $2.50 postage and handling ($1.03 sales tax CA residents).
Payment: Pays $5/printed page.
Terms: Pays on publication for first North American serial rights. Sends galleys to author. All submissions entered in our contest for cash prizes $30 (1st); $25 (2nd); $20 (3rd).
Advice: Looks for "readability, vividness of characterization, coherence, inspiration, interesting subject matter, point of view, originality, plausibility."

SIDETREKKED, (I, IV), Science Fiction London, 304-25 Grand Ave., London, Ontario N6C 1L3 Canada. (519)660-8883. Editor: Timothy Blahout. Editors change by election. Timothy Blahout will remain editor at least until next election (June 1993). Newspaper: 7 × 8½; 36-40 pages; bond paper; b&w drawings, halftone photographs. "Science fiction for science fiction readers, mostly adults." Quarterly. Estab. 1980. Circ. 200.
Needs: Fantasy, science fiction (hard science, soft/sociological). "We will consider any story with a science fictional slant. Because sf tends to be all-embracing, that could include horror, humor/satire, romance, suspense, feminist, gay, ethnic, etc.—yes, even western—but the science fiction classification must be met, usually by setting the story in a plausible, futuristic universe." Receives 3-5 unsolicited fiction mss/month. Accepts 3-8 mss/issue. Time between acceptance and publication varies. Published work by Joe Beliveau, Dave Seburn. Length: 1,000-5,000 words preferred. "No hard-and-fast rules, but we can't accommodate novelettes or novellas." Publishes short shorts. Critiques or comments on rejected mss, if requested by the author. Recommends other markets on occasion.
How to Contact: Send complete ms with cover letter. No simultaneous submissions. Reports in 3 weeks on queries; in 1 month on mss. SASE. Sample copy for $2 (Canadian) and 9 × 10 SAE.
Payment: Pays in contributor's copies.
Terms: Acquires first North American serial rights.
Advice: "We are more forgiving than most fiction markets and we try to work with new writers. What makes us want to work with a writer is some suggestion that he or she understands what makes a good story. What makes a manuscript stand out? Tell a good story. The secondary things are fixable if the story is there, but if it is not, no amount of tinkering can fix it."

‡SIDEWALKS, (II), P.O. Box 321, Champlin MN 55316. (612)421-3512. Editor: Tom Heie. Magazine: 5½ × 8½; 60-75 pages; 60 lb. paper; textured recycled cover. "*Sidewalks* . . . place of discovery, of myth, power, incantation . . . places we continue to meet people, preoccupied, on our way somewhere . . . tense, dark, empty places . . . place we meet friends & strangers, neighborhood sidewalks, place full of memory, paths that bring us home." Semiannually. Estab. 1991. Circ. 500.
Needs: Experimental, humor/satire, literary, mainstream/contemporary, regional. No violent, pornographic kinky material. Acquires 6-8 mss/issue; 12-16 mss/year. Publishes ms 1-3 months after acceptance. Recently published work by Lin Enger, Paul Hintz. Length: 2,500 words preferred; 3,000 words maximum. Publishes short shorts. Also publishes poetry.

How to Contact: Send complete ms with cover letter. Should include estimated word count, very brief bio, list of publications. Reports in 1 week on queries; 2-3 months on mss. Send SASE for reply, return of ms or send a disposable copy of the ms. No simultaneous submissions. Accepts electronic submissions. Sample copy for $5.
Payment: Pays 1 contributor's copy. Additional copies $4.
Terms: Acquires one-time rights.
Advice: "We look for a story with broad appeal, one that is well-crafted and has strong narrative voice, a story that leaves the reader thinking after the reading is over."

SIGN OF THE TIMES, A Chronicle of Decadence in the Atomic Age, (II), 221 Boylston Ave. E., Seattle WA 98102. (206)323-6764. Editor: Mark Souder. Tabloid: 8×10; 32 pages; book paper; 120 lb. cover stock; illustrations; photos. "Decadence in all forms for those seeking literary amusement." Semiannually. Published special fiction issue last year; plans another. Estab. 1980. Circ. 750.
Needs: Comics, erotica, experimental, gay, lesbian. No religious or western manuscripts. Receives 6 unsolicited mss/month. Buys 10 mss/issue; 20 mss/year. Published work by Gary Smith, Willie Smith, Ben Satterfield. Length: 3,000 words average; 500 words minimum, 5,000 words maximum. Publishes short shorts. Sometimes comments on rejected mss and recommends other markets.
How to Contact: Send complete ms with cover letter and bio. Reports in 6 weeks on mss. SASE. Sample copy $3.50. Fiction guidelines for #10 SASE.
Payment: Pays up to $20, subscription to magazine, 2 contributor's copies; 1 time cover price charge for extras.
Terms: Pays on publication for first rights plus anthology in the future.

THE SIGNAL, (II), Network International, Box 67, Emmett ID 83617. Editors: Joan Silva and David Chorlton. Magazine: 8½×11; 68 pages; good paper; some art; photos. "Wide open. Not restricted to 'literature.' Poetry, essays, reviews, comment, interviews, speculative thought." Semiannually. Estab. 1987.
Needs: Literary, translations. No "religious dogma, journeys of self-discovery in a '57 Chevrolet, catalogues of family members." Receives few unsolicited mss/month. Accepts "perhaps 1" ms/issue. Publishes ms 6 months to 1 year after acceptance. Length: 3,000 words maximum. Publishes short shorts. Also publishes literary essays, literary criticism, poetry.
How to Contact: "Just send us the story. Cover letter optional." Reports in 10 weeks on mss. SASE. Simultaneous submissions OK. Sample copy $4. Fiction guidelines for #10 SAE and 1 first class stamp. Reviews novels and short story collections.
Payment: Pays in contributor's copies.
Terms: Acquires first rights.
Advice: "We want to remain open to all writing. Although unable to publish very much fiction, we do look for ideas expressed in any form."

SILVERFISH REVIEW, (II), Silverfish Press, Box 3541, Eugene OR 97403. (503)344-5060. Editor: Rodger Moody. High quality literary material for a general audience. Published irregularly. Estab. 1979. Circ. 750.
Needs: Literary. Accepts 1-2 mss/issue. Also publishes literary essays, poetry, interview, translations.
How to Contact: Send complete ms with SASE. No simultaneous submissions. Reports in 2-3 months on mss. Sample copy $3 and $1 for postage.
Payment: Pays 5 contributor's copies; $5/page when funding permits.
Terms: Rights revert to author.
Advice: "We publish primarily poetry; we will, however, publish good quality fiction. *SR* is mainly interested in the short short story (one-minute and three-minute)."

SING HEAVENLY MUSE!, (II), Box 13320, Minneapolis MN 55414. Editor: Sue Ann Martinson. Magazine: 6×9; 125 pages; 55 lb. acid-free paper; 10 pt. glossy cover stock; illustrations; photos. Women's poetry, prose and artwork. Annually. Estab. 1977.
Needs: Literary, feminist, prose poem and ethnic/minority. Receives approximately 30 unsolicited fiction mss each month. Published work by Helene Cappuccio, Erika Duncan, Martha Roth. Publishes short shorts. Also publishes literary essays, poetry. Sometimes recommends other markets.
How to Contact: Query for information on theme issues, reading periods or variations in schedule. Include cover letter with "brief writing background and publications." No simultaneous submissions. Reports in 1-6 months on queries and mss. Publishes ms an average of 1 year after acceptance. Sample copy $3.50.

Payment: Pays 2 contributor's copies.
Terms: Acquires first rights.
Advice: "Try to avoid preaching. Look for friends also interested in writing and form a mutual support-and-criticism group."

THE SINGLE SCENE (II, IV), Box 30856, Gahanna OH 43230. (614)476-8802. Editor: Jeanne Marlowe. Magazine: 8 × 11; 24 pages; illustrations; photos. Single living, male-female relationship topics covered for single adults. Bimonthly. Estab. 1985. Circ. 7,000.
Needs: Confession, contemporary, experimental, fantasy, humor/satire, mainstream, mystery/suspense. Buys 6-12 mss/year. Publication time varies "now that I have a backlog." Recently published work by Paul Wolf, J.C. Reagan; published new writers within the last year. Length: 3,000 words maximum; "shorter mss more likely to be accepted." Publishes short shorts. Occasionally critiques rejected mss.
How to Contact: Send complete ms with a statement granting one-time rights in exchange for copies. Reports in 2 weeks on queries; 1 month on mss. SASE for ms, "unless you don't want ms returned." Simultaneous and reprint submissions OK, "if not from regional publications (OH)." Sample copy for $2. Reviews novels and short story collections.
Payment: Contributor's copies and advertising trade for most; $25 plus advertising trade maximum.
Terms: Pays on publication for one-time rights.
Advice: "My readers are primarily interested in meeting people, dating/relating to the other sex. I like to include a biographical note about my contributors' relation to singles. Although I have little space, I like to tackle tough problems and integrate fiction with editorial and personal experience. I don't shy away from the controversial, but reject the superficial."

SINISTER WISDOM, (IV), Box 3252, Berkeley CA 94703. Editor: Elana Dykewomon. Magazine: 5½ × 8½; 128-144 pages; 55 lb. stock; 10 pt C1S cover; illustrations; photos. Lesbian-feminist journal, providing fiction, poetry, drama, essays, journals and artwork. Quarterly. 1992 issues included "Lesbians of Color," and "Resistance." Estab. 1976. Circ. 3,000.
Needs: Lesbian: adventure, contemporary, erotica, ethnic, experimental, fantasy, feminist, historical, humor/satire, literary, prose poem, psychic, regional, science fiction, sports, translations. No heterosexual or male-oriented fiction; nothing that stereotypes or degrades women. Receives 50 unsolicited mss/month. Accepts 25 mss/issue; 75-100 mss/year. Publishes ms 1 month to 1 year after acceptance. Published work by Sapphire, Melanie Kaye/Kantrowitz, Adrienne Rich, Terri L. Jewell and Gloria Anzaldúa; published new writers within the last year. Length: 2,000 words average; 500 words minimum; 4,000 words maximum. Publishes short shorts. Also publishes literary essays, literary criticism, poetry. Occasionally critiques rejected mss. Sometimes recommends other markets.
How to Contact: Send 2 copies of complete ms with cover letter, which should include a brief author's bio to be published when the work is published. Simultaneous submissions OK, if noted. Reports in 2 months on queries; 9 months on mss. SASE. Sample copy $6.25. Reviews novels and short story collections. Send books to "Attn: Book review."
Payment: Pays in contributor's copies.
Terms: Rights retained by author.
Advice: The philosophy behind *Sinister Wisdom* is "to reflect and encourage the lesbian movements for social change, especially change in the ways we use language."

SKYLARK, (I), Purdue University, 2200 169th St., Hammond IN 46323. (219)989-2262. Editor: Pamela Hunter. Magazine: 8½ × 11; 100 pages; illustrations; photos. Fine arts magazine — short stories, poems and graphics for adults. Annually. Estab. 1971. Circ. 500-1,000.
• This college magazine has received three Columbia Scholastic Press Association awards for its essays and poetry.
Needs: Contemporary, ethnic, experimental, fantasy, feminist, humor/satire, literary, mainstream, mystery/suspense (English cozy), prose poem, regional, romance (gothic), science fiction, serialized/excerpted novel, spiritual, sports and western (frontier stories). Upcoming theme: Humor (submit December 1992-May 1993). Receives 20 mss/month. Accepts 12-15 mss/issue. Recently published work by Michael Beres, Eunice Madison, Susan Erler, Margaret Davis; published new writers within the last year. Length: 4,000 words maximum. Also publishes literary essays, poetry.

How to Contact: Send complete ms. SASE for ms. Simultaneous submissions OK, but notify if accepted elsewhere. Reports in 10 weeks. Sample copy $5; back issue $3.
Payment: Pays 1 contributor's copy.
Terms: Acquires first rights. Copyright reverts to author.
Advice: "The goal of *Skylark* is to encourage *creativity* and give beginning and published authors showcase for their work. Manuscripts *must* be carefully prepared and proofread."

SLATE AND STYLE, Magazine of the National Federation of the Blind Writers Division, (IV), NFB Writer's Division, 2704 Beach Drive, Merrick NY 11566. (516)868-8718. Editor: Loraine E. Stayer. Fiction Editor: Loraine Stayer. Newsletter: 8 × 10; 32 print/Braille pages; cassette and large print. "Articles of interest to writers, and resources for blind writers." Quarterly. Estab. 1982. Circ. 200.
Needs: Adventure, contemporary, fantasy, humor/satire, blindness. No erotica. "Avoid theme of death and handicapped." Does not read June, July. Length: 1,000 words average. Publishes short shorts. Also publishes literary criticism, poetry. Critiques rejected mss only if requested. Sometimes recommends other markets.
How to Contact: Query first. Reports on queries in 2 weeks; 1 month on mss. Photocopied submissions OK. Sample copy $2.50 and cassette mailer if tape requested. Large print copies also available. "Sent Free Matter For The Blind. If not blind, send 2 stamps."
Payment: Pays in contributor's copies.
Terms: Acquires one-time rights. Publication not copyrighted. Sponsors contests for fiction writers.
Advice: "Keep a copy. Editors can lose your work. Consider each first draft as just that and review your work before you send it. SASE a must."

SLIPSTREAM, (II, IV), Box 2071, New Market Station, Niagara Falls NY 14301. (716)282-2616. Editor: Dan Sicoli. Fiction Editors: R. Borgatti, D. Sicoli and Livio Farallo. Magazine: 7 × 8½; 80-120 pages; high quality paper and cover; illustrations; photos. "We use poetry and short fiction with a contemporary urban feel." Estab. 1981. Circ. 300.
Needs: Contemporary, erotica, ethnic, experimental, humor/satire, literary, mainstream and prose poem. No religious, juvenile, young adult or romance. Receives over 75 unsolicited mss/month. Accepts 2-8 mss/issue; 6-12 mss/year. Length: under 15 pages. Publishes short shorts. Published work by Gregory Burnham, Nan D. Hayes and Kurt Nimmo. Rarely critiques rejected mss. Sometimes recommends other markets.
How to Contact: "We are currently backlogged with fiction. Query before submitting." Reports within 2 months. SASE. Sample copy $5. Fiction guidelines for #10 SASE.
Payment: Pays 2 contributor's copies.
Terms: Acquires one-time rights on publication.
Advice: "Writing should be honest, fresh; develop your own style. Check out a sample issue first. Don't write for the sake of writing, write from the gut as if it were a biological need. Write from experience and mean what you say, but say it in the fewest number of words."

THE SMALL POND MAGAZINE, (II), Box 664, Stratford CT 06497. (203)378-4066. Editor: Napoleon St. Cyr. Magazine: 5½ × 8½; 42 pages; 60 lb. offset paper; 65 lb. cover stock; illustrations (art). "Features contemporary poetry, the salt of the earth, peppered with short prose pieces of various kinds. The college educated and erudite read it for good poetry, prose and pleasure." Triannually. Estab. 1964. Circ. 300.
Needs: "Rarely use science fiction or formula stories you'd find in *Cosmo*, *Redbook*, *Ladies Home Journal*, etc." Buys 10-12 mss/year. Longer response time in July and August. Receives approximately 50 unsolicited fiction mss each month. Length: 200-2,500 words. Critiques rejected mss when there is time. Sometimes recommends other markets.
How to Contact: Send complete ms with SASE and short vita. Reports in 2 weeks-3 months. Publishes ms an average of 2 months to 1 year after acceptance. Sample copy $3; $2.50 for back issues.
Payment: Pays 2 contributor's copies; $2.50/copy charge for extras.
Terms: Acquires all rights.
Advice: "Send for a sample copy first. All mss must be typed. Name and address and story title on front page, name of story on succeeding pages and paginated." Mss are rejected because of "tired plots and poor grammar; also over-long—2,500 words maximum. Don't send any writing conference ms unless it got an A or better."

SNAKE NATION REVIEW, (II), Snake Nation Press, Inc., 110, #2 West Force St., Valdosta GA 31601. (912)249-8334. Editor: Roberta George. Fiction Editor: Janice Daugharty. Newspaper: 6×9; 110 pages; acid free 70 lb. paper; 90 lb. cover; illustrations and photographs. "We are interested in all types of stories for an educated, discerning, sophisticated audience." Semiannually. Estab. 1989. Circ. 700.

Needs: "Short stories of 5,000 words or less, poems (any length), art work that will be returned after use." Condensed/excerpted novel, contemporary, erotica, ethnic, experimental, fantasy, feminist, gay, horror, humor/satire, lesbian, literary, mainstream, mystery/suspense, prose poem, psychic/supernatural/occult, regional, science fiction, senior citizen/retirement. "We want our writers to have a voice, a story to tell, not a flat rendition of a slice of life." Plans annual anthology. Receives 50 unsolicited mss/month. Buys 8-10 mss/issue; 20 mss/year. Publishes ms 3-6 months after acceptance. Agented fiction 1%. Recently published work by Judith Oitiz Cofer, Victor Miller. Length: 3,500 words average; 300 words minimum; 5,500 words maximum. Publishes short shorts. Length: 500 words. Also publishes literary essays, poetry. Sometimes critiques rejected mss and recommends other markets.

How to Contact: Send complete ms with cover letter. Reports on queries in 3 months. SASE. Sample copy for $5, 8×10 SAE and 90¢ postage. Fiction guidelines for SAE and 1 first class stamp.

Payment: Pays $100 maximum and contributor's copies.

Terms: Buys first rights. Sends galleys to author.

Advice: "Looks for clean, legible copy and an interesting, unique voice that pulls the reader into the work." Spring contest: short stories (5,000 words); $300 first prize, $200 second prize, $100 third prize; entry fee: $5 for stories, $1 for poems.

SNAKE RIVER REFLECTIONS, (I), 1863 Bitterroot Dr., Twin Falls ID 83301. (208)734-0746 (evenings). Editor: Bill White. Newsletter: 5½×8½; 8 pages; illustrations. "General interest newsletter with social commentary." Published 10 times/year. Estab. 1990. Circ. approximately 300.

Needs: Literary, mystery/suspense, regional, humor/satire, science fiction (soft/sociological) and western. No erotica, gay, lesbian, religious or occult fiction. Accepts 1 ms/issue; 10 mss/year. Publishes ms within 1-2 months of acceptance. Length: 500 words maximum. Also publishes literary essays, literary criticism, poetry. Sometimes critiques rejected mss and recommends other markets.

How to Contact: Include SASE. No simultaneous submissions. Sample copy 55¢. Fiction guidelines for #10 SASE.

Payment: Pays 2 contributor's copies.

Terms: Acquires first rights.

Advice: "Be persistent. Study a sample of our publication. Make your story exciting."

‡SNOWY EGRET (II), The Fair Press, P.O. Box 9, Bowling Green IN 47833. (812)829-1910. Editors: Karl Barnebey, Mike Aycock; Magazine: 8½×11; 50 pages; text paper; heavier cover; illustrations. "Literary exploration of the abundance and beauty of nature and the ways human beings interact with it." Semiannually. Estab. 1922. Circ. 500.

Needs: Nature writing, including 'true' stories, eye-witness accounts, descriptive sketches and traditional fiction. "We are particularly interested in fiction that celebrates abundance and beauty of nature, encourages a love and respect for the natural world, and affirms the human connection to the environment. No works written for popular genres: horror, sci fi, romance, detective, western, etc." Receives 25 unsolicited ms/month. Buys up to 6 mss/issue; up to 12 mss/year. Publishes ms 6 months-1 year after acceptance. Recently published works by Jane Candia Coleman, Stephen Lewandowski and Margarita Mondrus Engle. Length: 1,000-3,000 words preferred; 500 words minimum; 10,000 words maximum. Publishes short shorts. Length: 400-500 words. Sometimes critiques rejected mss and recommends other markets.

How to Contact: Send complete ms with cover letter. "Cover letter optional: do not query." Reports in 2 months. SASE. Simultaneous submissions OK if noted. Sample copy for $8, 9×12 SAE. Send #10 SASE for writer's guidelines.

Payment: Pays $2/page, 2 contributor's copies; charge for extras.

Terms: Pays on publication. Purchases first North American serial rights. Sends galleys to author. Publication copyrighted.

Advice: Looks for "honest, freshly detailed pieces with plenty of description and/or dialogue which will allow the reader to identify with the characters and step into the setting. Characters who relate strongly to nature, either positively or negatively, and who, during the course of the story, grow in their understanding of themselves and the world around them."

SONOMA MANDALA, (II), Dept. of English, Sonoma State University, 1801 E. Cotati Ave., Rohnert Park CA 94928. (707)664-3902. Faculty Advisor: Elizabeth Herron. Magazine: 7 × 8½; approx. 100 pages; bond paper; card cover stock; some illustrations; some photos. "We have no static thematic preference. We publish several short pieces (up to 2,500 words) of fiction in each issue." For campus community of a small liberal arts college and the surrounding rural/residential area. Annually. Estab. 1972. Circ. 500-1,000.
Needs: Contemporary, ethnic, experimental, feminist, gay, humor/satire, lesbian, literary, mainstream, prose poem, translations, western, regional. Receives 10-15 unsolicited fiction mss/month. Accepts 3-5 mss/issue. Does not read ms August 15 to November 15. Publishes 9-12 months after acceptance. Published new writers within the last year. Length: 1,000 words average; 2,500 words maximum. Publishes short shorts.
How to Contact: Send complete ms with cover letter. "Include info on simultaneous submissions, which we allow, if so indicated in cover letter. Always include address and telephone number, if needed." Reports in 1-5 months. SASE for ms. Photocopied submissions OK. Sample copy $6 postpaid.
Payment: Pays 2 contributor's copies.
Terms: Acquires one-time rights; rights revert to author upon publication.
Advice: "Read the literary magazines, and, if you believe in your work, keep submitting it to other publications. Especially interested in SSU and SF Bay area writers, but consider all quality submissions."

SONORA REVIEW, (II), University of Arizona, Department of English, Tucson AZ 85721. (602)621-1836 or (602)626-8383. Contact: Fiction Editor. Editors change each year. Magazine: 6 × 9; 150 pages; 16 lb. paper; 20 lb. cover stock; photos seldom. *Sonora Review* publishes short fiction and poetry of high literary quality. Semiannually. (In 1992-93, will do a double issue). Estab. 1980. Circ. 650.
● For more on this magazine, see the Close-up with the 1992 editor in last year's *Novel & Short Story Writer's Market*. Work published in *Sonora Review* has been selected for inclusion in the *Pushcart Prize, O. Henry Awards, Best of the West* and *Best American Poetry* anthologies.
Needs: Literary. "We are open to a wide range of stories with accessibility and vitality being important in any case. We're not interested in genre fiction, formula work." Acquires 4-6 mss/issue. Agented fiction 10%. Published work by Nancy Lord, Robyn Oughton, Ron Hansen. Length: open, though prefers work under 25 pages. Also publishes literary essays, literary criticism, poetry. Sometimes recommends other markets.
How to Contact: Send complete ms with SASE and cover letter with previous publications. Simultaneous submissions OK. Reports in 2 months on mss, longer for work received during summer (May-August). Publishes ms an average of 2-6 months after acceptance. Sample copy $5.
Payment: Pays 2 contributor's copies; $4 charge for extras. Annual cash prizes.
Terms: Acquires first North American serial rights. Fiction contest: 1st prize, $150; 2nd prize $50. Please write for submission guidelines. Send #10 SASE.
Advice: "Let the story sit for several months, then review it to see if you still like it. If you're unsure, keep working on it *before* sending it out. All mss are read carefully, and we try to make brief comments if time permits. Our hope is that an author will keep us interested in his or her treatment of a subject by using fresh details and writing with an authority that is absorbing." Mss are rejected because "1) we only have space for 6-8 manuscripts out of several hundred submissions annually, and 2) most of the manuscripts we receive have some merit but are not of publishable quality. It would be helpful to receive a cover letter with all manuscripts."

SOUNDINGS EAST, (II), English Dept., Salem State College, Salem MA 01970. (508)741-6270. Advisory Editor: Rod Kessler. Magazine: 5½ × 8½; 64 pages; illustrations; photos. "Mainly a college audience, but we also distribute to libraries throughout the country." Biannually. Estab. 1973. Circ. 3,000.
Needs: Literary, contemporary, prose poem. No juvenile. Publishes 4-5 stories/issue. Receives 30 unsolicited fiction mss each month. Does not read April-August. Published work by James Brady, Terry Farish and Christina Shea; published new writers within the last year. Length: 250-5,000 words. "We are open to short pieces as well as to long works."
How to Contact: Send complete ms with SASE between September and March. Accepts partial novels and multiple submissions if notified. Reports in 1-3 months on mss. Sample copy $3.
Payment: Pays 2 contributor's copies.
Terms: All publication rights revert to authors.
Advice: "We're impressed by an excitement—coupled with craft—in the use of the language. It also helps to reach in and grab the reader by the heart."

SOUTH DAKOTA REVIEW, (II), University of South Dakota, Box 111, University Exchange, Vermillion SD 57069. (605)677-5966. Editor: John R. Milton. Associate Editor: Brian Bedard. Magazine: 6×9; 150+ pages; book paper; glossy cover stock; illustrations sometimes; photos on cover. "Literary magazine for university and college audiences and their equivalent. Emphasis is often on the West and its writers, but will accept mss from anywhere. Issues are generally fiction and poetry with some literary essays." Quarterly. Estab. 1963. Circ. 500.
Needs: Literary, contemporary, ethnic, experimental, excerpted novel, regional and translations. "We like very well-written stories. Contemporary western American setting appeals, but not necessary. No formula stories, sports or adolescent 'I' narrator." Receives 30 unsolicited fiction mss/month. Accepts about 10-20 mss/year, more or less. Assistant editor accepts mss in June-July, sometimes August. Agented fiction 5%. Publishes short shorts of 5 pages double-spaced typescript. Published work by Ed Loomis, Max Evans, Dennis Lynds; published new writers within the last year. Length: 1,300 words minimum; 6,000 words maximum. (Has made exceptions, up to novella length.) Sometimes recommends other markets.
How to Contact: Send complete ms with SASE. "We like cover letters that are not boastful and do not attempt to sell the stories but rather provide some personal information about the writer." No multiple submissions. Reports in 1 month. Publishes ms an average of 1-6 months after acceptance. Sample copy $5.
Payment: Pays 2-4 contributor's copies, depending on length of ms; $3 charge for extras.
Terms: Acquires first rights and second serial rights.
Advice: Rejects mss because of "careless writing; often careless typing; stories too personal ('I' confessional), adolescent; working manuscript, not polished; subject matter that editor finds trivial. We are trying to use more fiction and more variety. We would like to see more sophisticated stories. Do not try to outguess editors and give them what you think they want. Write honestly. Be yourself."

SOUTHEASTERN FRONT, (I, II), Southeastern Front Organization, 565 17th St. NW, Cleveland TN 37311. Editor: Robin Merritt. Magazine: 8½×11; 40-60 pages; glossy cover; illustrations and photos. "*Southeastern Front* is an artists and writers representation service, a gallery in a magazine. Our aim is to provide exposure for artists and writers from all over the country. We hope to create an excellent medium of presentation for artists from isolated geographic areas." Estab. 1986. Circ. 1,500.
Needs: "There are no stylistic limitations on submissions or subject matter. We are interested in finding high quality new work by new and/or emerging artists and writers and helping them to obtain exposure. No pieces which are devoid of intellectual or aesthetic merit, nor commercially designed work." Receives 12-15 unsolicited mss/month. Accepts 6-8 mss/issue; 18-20 mss/year. Published new writers within the last year. Length: no restrictions. Publishes short shorts. Critiques rejected mss. Recommends other markets.
How to Contact: Send complete ms with cover letter. Reports on ms at time of publication. SASE for ms. Simultaneous and reprint submissions OK *occasionally*. For sample copy send SASE. Fiction guidelines for SAE and 1 first class postage.
Payment: Pays contributor's copies; charge for extras at wholesale rates for more than 5 copies.
Terms: Writers retain all rights.
Advice: "Allow yourself total creative and intellectual freedom, but never forget to be an artist, a craftsman who is conscious of aesthetic values. Be sure to include substantial human experience in your plots."

‡SOUTHERN CALIFORNIA ANTHOLOGY (II), Master of Professional Writing Program–USC, MPW-WPH 404 USC, Los Angeles CA 90089-4034. (213)740-3252. Contact: Richard Aloia. Magazine: 5½×8½; 142 pages; semi-glossy cover stock. "The *Southern California Anthology* is a literary review that is an eclectic collection of previously unpublished quality contemporary fiction, poetry and interviews with established literary people, published for adults of all professions; of particular interest to those interested in serious contemporary literature." Annually. Estab. 1983. Circ. 1,500.
Needs: Contemporary, ethnic, experimental, feminist, historical (general), humor/satire, literary, mainstream, regional, serialized/excerpted novel. No juvenile, religious, confession, romance, science fiction. Receives 30 unsolicited fiction mss each month. Accepts 10-12 mss/issue. Does not read February-September. Publishes ms 4 months after acceptance. Length: 10-15 pages average; 2 pages minimum; 25 pages maximum. Publishes short shorts.
How to Contact: Send complete ms with cover letter or submit through agent. Cover letter should include list of previous publications. Reports on queries in 1 month; on mss in 4 months. SASE. Sample copy $2.95. Fiction guidelines for #10 SAE and 1 first class stamp.

Payment: Pays in contributor's copies.
Terms: Acquires first rights.
Advice: "The *Anthology* pays particular attention to craft and style in its selection of narrative writing."

SOUTHERN EXPOSURE, (II, IV), Institute for Southern Studies, P.O. Box 531, Durham NC 27702. (919)419-8311. Editor: Eric Bates. Magazine: 8½×11; 64 pages. "Southern politics and culture — investigative reporting, oral history, fiction for an audience of Southern changemakers — scholars, journalists, activists." Quarterly. Estab. 1972. Circ. 5,000.
  • *Southern Exposure* has won numerous awards for its reporting including the Sidney Hillman Award for reporting on racial justice issues.
Needs: Contemporary, ethnic, feminist, gay, humor/satire, lesbian, literary, regional. Upcoming theme: 20th Anniversary Issue (Spring/Summer 1993). Receives 50 unsolicited mss/month. Buys 1 mss/issue; 4 mss/year. Publishes ms 3-6 months after acceptance. Agented fiction 25%. Published work by Clyde Egerton, Jill McCorkle and Larry Brown. Length: 3,500 words preferred.
How to Contact: Send complete ms with cover letter. No simultaneous submissions. Reports in 4-6 weeks on mss. SASE for ms. Sample copy for $4, 8½×11 and $1.85 postage. Fiction guidelines for #10 SAE and 1 first class stamp.
Payment: Pays $100, subscription to magazine and contributor's copies.
Terms: Pays on publication for first rights.

SOUTHERN HUMANITIES REVIEW, (II, IV), Auburn University, 9088 Haley Center, Auburn University AL 36849. Co-Editors: Dan R. Latimer and R.T. Smith. Magazine: 6×9; 96 pages; 60 lb. neutral pH, natural paper, 65 lb. neutral pH med. coated cover stock; occasional illustrations and photos. "We publish essays, poetry, fiction and reviews. Our fiction has ranged from very traditional in form and content to very experimental. Literate, college-educated audience. We hope they read our journal for both enlightenment and pleasure." Quarterly. Estab. 1967. Circ. 800.
  • *Poet's Market* 1993 features a Close-up in interview with R.T. Smith, poet and co-editor of *SHR.*
Needs: Serious fiction, fantasy, feminist, humor and regional. Receives approximately 25 unsolicited fiction mss each month. Accepts 1-2 mss/issue, 4-6 mss/year. Slower reading time in summer. Published work by Anne Brashler, Heimito von Doderer and Ivo Andric; published new writers within the last year. Length: 3,500-5,000 words. Also publishes literary essays, literary criticism, poetry. Critiques rejected mss when there is time. Sometimes recommends other markets.
How to Contact: Send complete ms with SASE and cover letter with an explanation of topic chosen — special, certain book, etc., a little about author if they have never submitted. Reports in 90 days. Sample copy $5. Reviews novel and short story collections.
Payment: Pays 2 contributor's copies; $5 charge for extras.
Terms: Acquires all rights. Sends galleys to author.
Advice: "Send us the ms with SASE. If we like it, we'll take it or we'll recommend changes. If we don't like it, we'll send it back as promptly as possible. Read the journal. Send a typewritten, clean copy carefully proofread. We also award annually the Hoepfner Prize of $100 for the best published essay or short story of the year. Let someone whose opinion you respect read your story and give you an honest appraisal. Rewrite, if necessary, to get the most from your story."

THE SOUTHERN REVIEW, (II), Louisiana State University, 43 Allen Hall, Baton Rouge LA 70803. (504)388-5108. Editors: James Olney and Dave Smith. Magazine: 6¾×10; 240 pages; 50 lb. Glatfelter paper; 65 lb. #1 grade cover stock; occasional photos. "A literary quarterly publishing critical essays, poetry and fiction for a highly intellectual audience." Quarterly. Published special fiction issue. Estab. 1935. Circ. 3,000.
  • This quality literary journal was ranked #50 on the 1992 *Writer's Digest* Fiction 50 list.
Needs: Literary and contemporary. "We emphasize style and substantial content. No mystery, fantasy or religious mss." Buys 7-8 mss/issue. Receives approximately 100 unsolicited fiction mss each month. Agented fiction 5%. Recently published work by Gloria Naylor, Wendell Berry, Jill McCorkle; published new writers within the last year. Length: 2,000-10,000 words. Also publishes literary essays, literary criticism, poetry. Sometimes recommends other markets.
How to Contact: Send complete ms with cover letter and SASE. "Prefer brief letters giving information on author concerning where he/she has been published before, biographical info and what he/she is doing now." Reports in 2 months on mss. Publishes ms an average of 1-2 years after acceptance. Sample copy $5. Reviews novels and short story collections.

Payment: Pays $12/printed page; 2 contributor's copies.
Terms: Pays on publication for first North American serial rights. "We transfer copyright to author on request." Sends galleys to author.
Advice: "Develop a careful style with characters in depth." Sponsors annual contest for best first collection of short stories published during the calendar year.

SOUTHWEST REVIEW, (II), 307 Fondren Library West, Box 4374, Southern Methodist University, Dallas TX 75275. (214)373-7440. Editor: Willard Spiegelman. Magazine: 6×9; 160 pages. "The majority of our readers are college-educated adults who wish to stay abreast of the latest and best in contemporary fiction, poetry, literary criticism and books in all but the most specialized disciplines." Quarterly. Estab. 1915. Circ. 1,600.
Needs: "High literary quality; no specific requirements as to subject matter, but cannot use sentimental, religious, western, poor science fiction, pornographic, true confession, mystery, juvenile or serialized or condensed novels." Receives approximately 200 unsolicited fiction mss each month. Published work by Brad Conard, Ellen Akins, Rick Bass and Millicent Dillon. Length: prefers 3,000-5,000 words. Also publishes literary essays, poetry. Occasionally critiques rejected mss. Sometimes recommends other markets.
How to Contact: Send complete ms with SASE. Reports in 3 months on mss. Publishes ms 6 months to 1 year after acceptance. Sample copy $5. Free guidelines for SASE.
Payment: Payment varies; writers receive 3 contributor's copies.
Terms: Pays on publication for first North American serial rights. Sends galleys to author.
Advice: "We have become less regional. A lot of time would be saved for us and for the writer if he or she looked at a copy of the *Southwest Review* before submitting. We like to receive a cover letter because it is some reassurance that the author has taken the time to check a current directory for the editor's name. When there isn't a cover letter, we wonder whether the same story is on 20 other desks around the country."

SOU'WESTER, (II), Southern Illinois University-Edwardsville, Edwardsville IL 62026-1438. (618)692-3190. Managing Editor: Fred W. Robbins. Magazine: 6×9; 88 pages; Warren's Olde Style paper; 60 lb. cover. General magazine of poetry and fiction. Triannually. Estab. 1960. Circ. 300.
Needs: Receives 40-50 unsolicited fiction mss/month. Accepts 3 mss/issue, 9 mss/year. Published work by Robert Wexelblatt, Robert Solomon; published new writers within the last year. Length: 10,000 words maximum. Also publishes poetry. Occasionally critiques rejected mss.
How to Contact: Send complete ms with SASE. Simultaneous submissions OK. Reports in 4 months. Publishes ms an average of 6 months after acceptance. Sample copy $5.
Payment: Pays 2 contributor's copies; $5 charge for extras.
Terms: Acquires first serial rights.

SOZORYOKU, Quarterly Journal of the Imagination, (II), Running Dinosaur Press, 265 Fifth Ave., Chula Vista CA 91910. Editor: Ralph E. Vaughan. Magazine: 5½×8½; 36-44+ pages; bond paper; pen & ink illustrations. "Myth, fantasy and science fiction of cosmic import for a highly eclectic and literate audience." Quarterly. Estab. 1990. Circ. 100.
Needs: Adventure, ethnic, experimental, fantasy, feminist, historical, horror, literary, mainstream, mystery/suspense, prose poem, psychic/supernatural/occult, regional, science fiction, weird western. "No romance, erotica, mundane fiction." Receives 50 unsolicited mss/month. Buys 8-12 mss/issue; 30-50 mss/year. Publishes ms 1-3 months after acceptance. Recently published work by David Barker, Eric Holmes, t. Winter-Damon. Length: 200 words minimum; 2,500 words maximum. Publishes short shorts. Sometimes critiques rejected mss.
How to Contact: Send complete ms with cover letter; ask for guidelines. No simultaneous submissions. Reports in 2-4 weeks on mss. SASE. Sample copy for $2. Fiction guidelines for #10 SAE and 1 first class stamp.
Payment: Pays ¼-½¢/word.
Terms: Pays on acceptance for one-time rights.
Advice: "I look for a story with sharply drawn characters and plausible settings and conflicts, with a style that draws me into the story and makes me care. I look for stories that stay with me long after the reading, stories with vision and a sense of the cosmic."

SPECTRUM, (II), Anna Maria College, Box 72-C, Sunset Lane, Paxton MA 01612. (617)849-3450. Editor: Robert H. Goepfert. Magazine: 6×9; 64 pages; illustrations and photos. "An interdisciplinary publication publishing fiction as well as poetry, scholarly articles, reviews, art and photography. Sub-

missions are especially encouraged from those affiliated with liberal arts colleges." Semiannually. Estab. 1985. Circ. 1,000.
Needs: Contemporary, experimental, historical, literary, mainstream. No western, mystery, erotica, science fiction. Receives an average of 15 unsolicited fiction ms/month. Accepts 4-6 mss/issue. Publishes ms approx. 6 months after acceptance. Length: 2,000-5,0000 words preferred; 3,000 words average; 10,000 words maximum. Publishes short shorts. Also publishes literary essays, literary criticism, poetry. Sometimes critiques rejected mss and recommends other markets.
How to Contact: Send complete ms with cover letter. Reports in 6 weeks. SASE for ms. No simultaneous submissions. Sample copy for $3. Fiction guidelines free with SASE.
Payment: Pays $20 and 2 contributor's copies.
Terms: Pays on publication for first North American serial rights. Sends pre-publication galleys to author. Publication not copyrighted.
Advice: "Our chief aim is diversity."

SPINDRIFT, (II), Shoreline Community College, 16101 Greenwood Ave. North, Seattle WA 98133. (206)546-4785. Editor: Carol Orlock, adviser. Magazine: 140 pages; quality paper; photographs; b&w artwork. "We look for fresh, original work that is not forced or 'straining' to be literary." Annually. Estab. around 1967. Circ. 500.
Needs: Contemporary, ethnic, experimental, historical (general), prose poem, regional, science fiction, serialized/excerpted novel, translations. No romance, religious/inspirational. Receives up to 150 mss/year. Accepts up to 20 mss/issue. Does not read during spring/summer. Publishes ms 3-4 months after acceptance. Published work by David Halpern, Jana Harris; published new writers within the last year. Length: 250 words minimum; 3,500-4,500 words maximum. Publishes short shorts.
How to Contact: Send complete ms, and "bio, name, address, phone and list of titles submitted." Reports in 2 weeks on queries; 6 months on mss with SASE. Sample copy for $6, 8×10 SAE and $1 postage.
Payment: Pays in contributor's copies; charge for extras.
Terms: Acquires first rights. Publication not copyrighted.
Advice: "The tighter the story the better. The more lyric values in the narrative the better. Read the magazine, keep working on craft. Submit several pieces by February 1."

THE SPIRIT THAT MOVES US, (II), Box 820-N, Jackson Heights NY 11372-0820. (718)426-8788. Editor: Morty Sklar. Publishes fiction, essays, poetry and artwork. "We want feeling and imagination, work coming from the human experience." Semiannually. Estab. 1975. Circ. 1,500-2,000.
● The Spirit That Moves Us Press (also listed in this book) publishes the *Editor's Choice* anthologies, featuring the best of the small press.
Needs: "SASE first to find out what our needs are." Literary and contemporary—"anything goes, if it is fiction, poetry or art." Upcoming theme: "Phoenix: Stories, Essays & Poetry from Former Drug Addicts." Buys 5-6 mss/issue and about 15 mss for special fiction issues. Receives approximately 90 unsolicited fiction mss each month. Recently published work by W.P. Kinsella, Julia Alvarez, Bhararti Mukherjee, Jaime Manriqué; published new writers within the last year. Length: 10,000 words maximum. Also publishes literary essays, poetry. Critiques rejected mss when there is time.
How to Contact: Send SASE first for theme and plans. "A cover letter sort of makes the exchange more personal." Simultaneous submissions OK, if noted. Reports in 1 week-1 month on mss. Publishes ms an average of 6 months after acceptance. Sample copy $5 for *Free Parking*, our 15th Anniversay collection.
Payment: Pays cash and free cloth copy, 40% discount for paperbacks; 25% on all other publications.
Terms: Acquires first rights. Buys reprints for anthology issue.
Advice: "Query first for theme with SASE. We're small but good and well-reviewed. Send the work you love best. Write from yourself and not from what you feel is the fashion or what the editor wants. This editor wants what you want if it has heart, imagination and skill. Aside from the obvious reason for rejection, poor writing, the main reason for rejection is lack of human concerns—that is, the writer seems to be concerned with style more than content. Read a copy of the magazine you'll be submitting work to. Don't rely on your writing for money unless you're in it for the money. Have time to write, as much time as you can get (be anti-social if necessary)."

SPIT: A JOURNAL OF THE ARTS, (I), East River SPIT, 240 E. 9th St., #7, New York NY 10003. (212)505-9590; 673-3546. Magazine: 8½×11; 50-75 pages; illustrations and photographs. "We are a magazine for emerging (new) artists of all kinds, as well as for more established artists who support the work we do. We consider fiction/prose of any style. Audience is varied, though at the moment, mostly youngish; avant-garde." Published every 6-9 months. Estab. 1990. Circ. 400.

Needs: Contemporary, erotica, ethnic, experimental, fantasy, feminist, gay, historical (general), horror, humor/satire, lesbian, literary, mystery/suspense, prose poem, regional, science fiction, senior citizen/retirement, translations. Receives 10 unsolicited mss/month. Accepts 4-5 mss/issue. Publishes ms up to 6 months after acceptance. Recently published work by Jennifer Blowdryer, Steven Schrader, Jeremy Stoljar. Length: 2,500 words average; 6,000 words maximum. Publishes short shorts. Sometimes critiques rejected mss.

How to Contact: Send complete ms with cover letter. Include a brief biographical statement. Reports in 2 weeks on queries; up to 6 months on mss. SASE. Simultaneous, photocopied and reprint submissions OK. Sample copy for $3. Fiction guidelines for any size SAE and 1 first class stamp.

Payment: Pays in contributor's copies.

Terms: Acquires one-time rights.

Advice: "We are interested in discovering and supporting new writers of all styles, experiences, backgrounds and orientations. It is not necessary that our writers be thoroughly developed or polished; a unique voice, vision or use of language is what will draw our editors to a work of fiction or prose."

‡SPITBALL (I), 6224 Collegevue Pl., Cincinnati OH 45224. (513)541-4296. Editor: Mike Shannon. Magazine: 5½ × 8½; 52 pages; 20 lb white paper; 65-67 lb cover stock; illustrations; photos. Magazine publishing "fiction and poetry about *baseball* exclusively for an educated, literary segment of the baseball fan population." Quarterly. Estab. 1981. Circ. 1,000.

Needs: Confession, contemporary, experimental, historical, literary, mainstream and suspense. "Our only requirement concerning the type of fiction written is that the story be *primarily* about baseball." Receives "100 or so" unsolicited fiction mss/year. Accepts 7-8 mss/year. Published work by Dallas Wiebe, Michael Gilmartin, Rick Wilber. Published new writers within the last year. Length: no limit. The longer it is, the better it has to be. Will critique rejected mss if asked.

How to Contact: Send complete ms with SASE, and cover letter with brief bio about author. Previously published submissions OK. Reporting time varies. Publishes ms an average of 3 months after acceptance. Sample copy $5.

Payment: "No monetary payment at present. We may offer nominal payment in the near future." 2 free contributor's copies per issue in which work appears.

Terms: Acquires first North American serial rights. Buys reprints "if the work is good enough and it hasn't had major exposure already."

Advice: "Our audience is mostly college educated and knowledgeable about baseball. The stories we have published so far have been very well written and displayed a firm grasp of the baseball world and its people. In short, audience response has been great because the stories are simply good as stories. Thus, mere use of baseball as subject is no guarantee of acceptance. We are always seeking submissions. Unlike many literary magazines, we have no backlog of accepted material. Consult *The Best of Spitball* (1988) by Pocket Books, Div. of Simon & Schuster. Still in print even if not in local bookstore. Fiction is a natural genre for our exclusive subject, baseball. There are great opportunities for writing in certain areas of fiction, baseball being one of them. Baseball has become the 'in' spectator sport among intellectuals, the general media and the 'yuppie' crowd. Consequently, as subject matter for adult fiction it has gained a much wider acceptance than it once enjoyed."

SPOOFING!, Yarns and Such, (I, IV), Creative With Words Publications, Box 223226, Carmel CA 93922. (408)649-5627. Editor: Brigitta Geltrich. Editors rotate. Booklet: 5½ × 8½; approx. 60 pages; bond paper; illustrations. Folklore. Annually. Estab. 1975. Circ. varies.

Needs: Ethnic, humor/satire, juvenile (5-9 years), mystery/suspense (private eye, amateur sleuth), preschool (1-4 years), regional, young adult/teen (10-18 years), folklore. "Once a year we publish an anthology of the writings of young writers, titled: *We are Writers Too!*" No violence or erotica, religious fiction. Upcoming themes: "Fairy Tales from a Different Perspective;" "Tall Tales (for the family);" "Impossible Loves (clean family reading)." Receives 100 unsolicited fiction mss/month. Does not read mss July-August. Publishes ms 2-6 months after acceptance. Publishes after set deadlines: after July 31 or December 31 of any given year. Published new writers within the last year. Length: 1,000 words average. Critiques rejected mss "when requested, *then we charge $20/prose, up to 1,000 words.*"

How to Contact: Query first or send complete ms with cover letter. "Reference has to be made to which project the manuscript is being submitted. Unsolicited mss without SASE will be destroyed after holding them 1 month." Reports in 1 week on queries; 2 months on mss; longer on specific seasonal anthologies. SASE. No simultaneous submissions. Accepts electronic submissions via Radio Shack Model 4/6 disk and Macintosh. Sample copy price $5 for children's issues, $6 for adult issues. Fiction guidelines for #10 SASE.

Payment: No payment. 20% reduction on each copy ordered.
Terms: Acquires one-time rights.

SPSM&H, (II, IV), *Amelia* Magazine, 329 "E" St., Bakersfield CA 93304. (805)323-4064. Editor: Frederick A. Raborg, Jr. Magazine: 5½ × 8¼; 24 pages; Matte cover stock; illustrations and photos. "*SPSM&H* publishes sonnets, sonnet sequences and fiction, articles and reviews related to the form (fiction may be romantic or Gothic) for a general readership and sonnet enthusiasts." Quarterly. Estab. 1985. Circ. 600.
  • This magazine is edited by Frederick A. Raborg, Jr., who is also editor of *Amelia* and *Cicada*.
  See also the listing for the *Amelia* Magazine Awards.
Needs: Adventure, confession, contemporary, erotica, ethnic, experimental, fantasy, feminist, gay, historical (general), horror, humor/satire, lesbian, literary, mainstream, mystery/suspense, regional, contemporary and historical romance, science fiction, senior citizen/retirement, translations and western. All should have romantic element. "We look for strong fiction with romantic or Gothic content, or both. Stories need not have 'happy' endings, and we are open to the experimental and/or avant-garde. Erotica is fine; pornography, no." Receives 30+ unsolicited mss/month. Buys 1 ms/issue; 4 mss/year. Publishes ms 6 months-1 year after acceptance. Agented fiction 5%. Published work by Mary Louise R. O'Hara and Clara Castelar Bjorlie. Length: 2,000 words average; 500 words minimum; 3,000 words maximum. When appropriate critiques rejected ms; recommends other markets.
How to Contact: Send complete ms with cover letter. Should include Social Security number. Reports in 2 weeks. SASE. Sample copy $4.50. Fiction guidelines for #10 SAE and 1 first class stamp.
Payment: Pays $10-25; contributor's copies; charge for extras.
Terms: Pays on publication for first North American serial rights.
Advice: "A good story line (plot) and strong characterization are vital. I want to know the writer has done his homework and is striving to become professional."

SQUARE ONE, A Magazine of Fiction, (I, II), Tarkus Press, Box 11921, Milwaukee WI 53211-0921. Editor: William D. Gagliani. Magazine: 7 × 8½; 75-90 pages; 20 lb. white bond paper; 80 lb. colored linen cover; illustrations; pen and ink drawings or any black on white. "There is no specific theme at *Square One*, but we publish only fiction and illustrations. Aimed at a general literate audience—people who *enjoy* reading fiction." Annually. Estab. 1984. Circ. 250.
Needs: Open to all categories including mainstream, mystery, science fiction, horror (all subgenres), fantasy, suspense, etc. "We like exciting stories in which things happen and characters *exist*." Receives 40-50 unsolicited fiction mss/month. Does not read mss between May and September. Accepts 6-12 mss/issue, depending on lengths; 6-12 mss/year. Publishes ms generally 1-14 months after acceptance. Published new writers within the last year. Length: 3,000 words average; 7,500 words maximum. Occasionally publishes short shorts but not vignettes. "It is editorial policy to comment on at least 75% of submissions rejected, but *please* be patient—we have a very small staff."
How to Contact: Send complete ms with cover letter. "Too many letters explain or describe the story. Let the fiction stand on its own. If it doesn't, the letter won't help. We like a brief bio and a few credits, but some writers get carried away. Use restraint and plain language—don't try to impress (it usually backfires)." Reports in 1-14 months on mss. SASE for ms. Simultaneous (if so labeled) and reprint submissions OK. Can accept electronic submissions via disk, "DS/DD, 3.5" Atari Mega ST Disks (using WordPerfect 4.1 for Atari) and HD or DS/DD 3.5" disks (using Microsoft Word 4.0, Works, or WordPerfect 2.0+ for Macintosh). Hard copy should accompany any electronic submissions." Sample copy $3.50, 9 × 12 SAE, and 6 first class stamps (recent issue). Fiction guidelines for #10 SAE and 1 first class stamp. Please make checks payable to William D. Gagliani.
Payment: Pays 2 contributor's copies.
Terms: Acquires one-time rights.
Advice: "*Square One* is not a journal for beginners, despite what the name may imply. Rather, the name refers to the back-to-basics approach that we take—fiction must first and foremost be compelling. We want to see stories that elicit a response from the reader. We are currently seeking more horror/dark fantasy (all subgenres welcome), but still like to see variety—strong fiction in any genre remains an overall theme. We must stress that, since we are an irregular publication, contributors should expect long response lags. Our staff is small and *Square One* is a part-time endeavor. Patience is the best advice we can offer. Also, we oppose the absurdity of asking that writers subscribe to every magazine they would like to write for, especially given most writers' financial state. Check local public and college libraries and bookstores to see what's going on in the small press and literary markets, and—as a matter of dignity—consider carefully before submitting to magazines that routinely charge reading fees."

STARLIGHT, Star Books, Inc., 408 Pearson St., Wilson NC 27893. (919)237-1591. Editor: Irene Burk Harrell. Magazine: Digest-sized 5½ × 7½; 64 pages; 20 lb. paper; b&w illustrations and photographs. "Christian inspirational material for men and women of all ages, some children." Quarterly. Estab. 1987.
Needs: Religious/inspirational. Wants "any genre, for any age, as long as it is exciting, God-honoring, in conformity with biblical truth." Publishes ms less than 3 months after acceptance. Published work by Anthony Chiarilli and John R. Price. Length: "10-12 double-spaced pages but open to longer or shorter." Also publishes poetry. Sometimes critiques rejected mss and suggests rewrite.
How to Contact: Send complete ms with cover letter. No simultaneous submissions. Reports in 1 month. SASE. Sample copy $4. Fiction guidelines for #10 SAE and 2 first class stamps.
Payment: Pays 3 contributor's copies.
Terms: Acquires first rights.
Advice: "We want to see the surprises the Lord assigns to His people. First-person, personal, pro-life."

STARRY NIGHTS, (I, II, IV), Merry Men Press, 274 Roanoke Road, El Cajon CA 92020. Editor: Robin Hood. Magazine: 8½ × 11; 200 pages; 20 lb. paper; 90 lb. cover stock. Erotic science fiction/fantasy, poetry, art "for a mature audience." Estab. 1990.
Needs: Erotica: mystery (romantic suspense), romance (gothic), science fiction (hard science). "See guidelines for definition of erotica. There's a big difference between *E* and *pornography*." Has published special fiction issue in the past. Receives 7 unsolicited mss per month; buys up to 15 mss per issue. Publishes ms 1-11 months after acceptance. "Will accept multiple stories from same author." Also publishes poetry. Comments on rejected mss and recommends other markets.
How to Contact: Reports in 1 week on queries; 1 month on mss. SASE. No simultaneous submissions. Accepts electronic submissions, "hard copy must be included." Fiction guidelines for SAE and 1 first class stamp.
Payment: Pays .01/word and 1 contributor's copy.
Terms: Pays on publication for first North American serial rights.

STONE SOUP, The Magazine By Children, (I, IV), Children's Art Foundation, Box 83, Santa Cruz CA 95063. (408)426-5557. Editor: Gerry Mandel. Magazine: 6 × 8¾; 48 pages; high quality paper; Sequoia matte cover stock; illustrations; photos. Stories, poems, book reviews and art by children through age 13. Readership: children, librarians, educators. Published 5 times/year. Estab. 1973. Circ. 13,000.
 • This is known as "the literary journal for children." *Stone Soup* has won the Edpress Golden Lamp Honor Award in 1992 and the Parent's Choice Award in 1991.
Needs: Fiction by children on themes based on their own experiences, observations or special interests. No clichés, no formulas, no writing exercises; original work only. Receives approximately 1,000 unsolicited fiction mss each month. Accepts approx. 15 mss/issue. Published new writers within the last year. Length: 150-2,500 words. Also publishes literary essays, poetry. Critiques rejected mss upon request.
How to Contact: Send complete ms with cover letter. "We like to learn a little about our young writers, why they like to write, and how they came to write the story they are submitting." SASE. No simultaneous submissions. Reports in 1 month on mss. Publishes ms an average of 1-6 months after acceptance. Sample copy $4. Guidelines for SASE. Reviews children's books.
Payment: Pays $10 plus 2 contributor's copies; $2 charge for extras.
Terms: Buys all rights.
Advice: Mss are rejected because they are "derivatives of movies, TV, comic books; or classroom assignments or other formulas."

Market categories: (I) Open to new writers; (II) Open to both new and established writers; (III) Interested mostly in established writers; (IV) Open to writers whose work is specialized.

STORY, (II), F&W Publications, 1507 Dana Ave., Cincinnati OH 45207. (513)531-2222. Editor: Lois Rosenthal. Magazine: 6¼×9½; 128 pages; uncoated, recycled paper; uncoated index stock. "We publish finest quality short stories. Will consider unpublished novel excerpts if they are self-inclusive." Quarterly. Estab. 1931.
• *Story* won the National Magazine Award for Fiction in 1992.
Needs: Literary, experimental, humor, mainstream, translations. No genre fiction—science fiction, detective, young adult, confession, romance, etc. Buys approximately 12 mss/issue. Agented fiction 50-60%. Published work by Joyce Carol Oates, Bobbie Ann Mason, Tobias Wolff, Madison Smartt Bell, Rick DeMarinis, Antonya Nelson, Rick Bass, Charles Baxter, Hortense Calisher, Robert Olmstead, Melissa Pritchard; published new writers within the last year. Length: 1,000 words minimum; 8,000 words maximum.
How to Contact: Send complete ms with or without cover letter, or submit through agent. SASE necessary for return of ms and response. May accept simultaneous submissions (reluctantly). Sample copy for $5.95, 9×12 SAE and $2.40 postage. Fiction guidelines for #10 SAE and 1 first class stamp.
Payment: Pays $250 plus 5 contributor's copies.
Terms: Pays on acceptance for first North American serial rights. Sends galleys to author.
Advice: "We accept fiction of the highest quality, whether by established or new writers. Since we receive over 300 submissions each week, the competition for space is fierce. We look for original subject matter told through fresh voices. Read issues of *Story* before trying us."

‡STORYQUARTERLY, (II), Box 1416, Northbrook IL 60065. (312)433-0741. Co-Editors: Anne Brashler and Diane Williams. Magazine: approximately 6×9; 130 pages; good quality paper; illustrations; photos. A magazine devoted to the short story and committed to a full range of styles and forms. Semiannually. Estab. 1975. Circ. 3,000.
• *Esquire* (July 1992) named *Storyquarterly* one of America's "literary roots."
Needs: Accepts 12-15 mss/issue, 20-30 mss/year. Receives 200 unsolicited fiction mss/month. Published new writers within the last year.
How to Contact: Send complete ms with SASE. Simultaneous submissions OK. Reports in 3 months on mss. Sample copy $4.
Payment: Pays 3 contributor's copies.
Terms: Acquires one-time rights. Copyright reverts to author after publication.
Advice: "Send one manuscript at a time, subscribe to the magazine, send SASE."

STROKER MAGAZINE, (II), 124 N. Main St., #3, Shavertown PA 18708. Editor: Irving Stettner. Magazine: 5½×8½; average 48 pages; medium paper; 80 lb. good cover stock; illustrations; photos. "*An un-literary* literary review interested in sincerity, verve, anger, humor and beauty. For an intelligent audience—non-academic, non-media dazed in the US and throughout the world." Published 3-4 times/year. Estab. 1974, 50 issues to date. Circ. 600.
Needs: Literary, contemporary. Published new writers within the last year. Also publishes poetry. No academic material. Length: "3-8 pages preferred but not essential."
How to Contact: Send complete ms with SASE. Simultaneous submissions OK. Reports in 6 weeks. Sample copy $4.50.
Payment: Pays 2 contributor's copies. $1 charge for extras.
Terms: Acquires one-time rights.
Advice: "We are interested in fiction. Be sure your name and address are on the manuscript."

STRUGGLE, A Magazine of Proletarian Revolutionary Literature, (IV), Marxist-Leninist Party USA, Detroit Branch, Box 13261, Harper Station, Detroit MI 48213-0261. Editor: Tim Hall. Magazine: 5½×8½; 24-48 pages; 20 lb. white bond paper; colored cover; illustrations; occasional photographs. Publishes material related to "the struggle of the working class and all progressive people against the rule of the rich—including their war policies, racism, exploitation of the workers, oppression of women, etc." Quarterly. Estab. 1985.
Needs: Contemporary, ethnic, experimental, feminist, historical (general), humor/satire, literary, mystery/suspense, prose poem, regional, science fiction, senior citizen/retirement, translations, young adult/teen (10-18). "The theme can be approached in many ways, including plenty of categories not listed here." No romance, psychic, western, erotica, religious. Receives 5-6 unsolicited fiction mss/month. Publishes ms 3 months or less after acceptance. Recently published work by Willie Abraham Howard, Jr., Judy Fitzgerald, R.G. Wilfong; published new writers within the last year. Length: 1,000-3,000 words average; 5,000 words maximum. Publishes short shorts. Normally critiques rejected mss.

How to Contact: Send complete ms; cover letter optional but helpful. "Tries to" report in 3 months. SASE. Simultaneous and reprint submissions OK. Sample copy for $1.50. Checks to Tim Hall-Special Account.
Payment: Pays 2 contributor's copies.
Terms: No rights acquired. Publication not copyrighted.
Advice: "Write about the oppression of the working people, the poor, the minorities, women, and if possible, their rebellion against it—we are not interested in anything which accepts the status quo. We are not too worried about plot and advanced technique (fine if we get them!)—we would probably accept things others would call sketches, provided they have life and struggle. Just describe for us a situation in which some real people confront some problem of oppression, however seemingly minor. Observe and put down the real facts. We have increased our fiction portion of our content in the last 2 years. We get poetry and songs all the time. We want 1-2 stories per issue."

STUDIO ONE, (II, IV), College of St. Benedict, St. Joseph MN 56374. Editor: Jennifer Coe. Magazine: 7 × 10; 76-100 pages; illustrations (7-10/issue); photographs (10-15/issue). "Studio One is a regional magazine for literary and visual art. We publish photographs, drawings, paintings, poetry and short fiction for the academic community in the Midwest, particularly for the College of St. Benedict and St. John's University." Annually. Estab. 1976. Circ. 900.
Needs: Contemporary, ethnic, feminist, humor/satire, literary, mainstream, prose poem, regional. "We will consider all work submitted and we welcome submissions. The categories above reflect what we tend to publish annually." No "violent erotica, smut." Receives "maybe 1" unsolicited fiction ms/month. Acquires "5 out of 20" mss/year. Does not read mss in summer. Publishes ms 1-2 months after acceptance. Length: 500-1,000 words preferred; 5,000 words maximum. Publishes short shorts.
How to Contact: Send complete ms with cover letter. Include "return address, phone number and brief history of the work submitted (whether it has be published before)." Reports in 2-3 weeks on queries; 1-6 months on mss. SASE. Simultaneous and reprint submissions OK.
Payment: Pays in contributor's copies.
Terms: Acquires all rights (or reprint rights).
Advice: "If the story strikes us as interesting, we consider it. But manuscripts that arrest us with their color, word choice, form or message are the manuscripts we publish. It is so difficult to define what we look for in a work other than quality. Usually the work simply tells us that it intends to be published...Please be patient with acceptance letters. If you submitted, we will respond before publication. Our deadline is always in February, so please submit by then."

SUB-TERRAIN (I,II), Anvil Press, Box 1575, Stn. A, Vancouver BC V6C 2P7 Canada. (604)876-8710. Editor: D.E. Bolen, J.L. McCarthy and P. Pitre. Magazine: 7 × 10; 28-32 pages; offset printed paper; illustrations; photos. "Sub-Terrain functions as a literary magazine with a social conscience. *Sub-Terrain* provides a forum for work that pushes the boundaries in form or content." Estab. 1988.
Needs: "We are looking for work that expresses the experience of urban existence as we approach the closing of the century." Erotica, experimental, humor/satire and literary. Upcoming themes: "Tatooed Women & Tattooed Men," anything on the subject of stigma, branding, being marked; "A Full Frontal," the theme of exposure; "Asleep at the Watchtower," material concerned with the corruption of institutionalized religion. Receives 20-30 unsolicited mss/month. Accepts 3-4 mss/issue. Publishes ms 1-4 months after acceptance. Length: 200-3,000 words; 400-500 average. Publishes short shorts. Length: 200 words. Also publishes literary essays, literary criticism, poetry. Sometimes critiques rejected mss and "at times" recommends other markets.
How to Contact: Send complete ms with cover letter. Simultaneous submissions OK, if notify when ms is accepted elsewhere. Reports in 3-4 weeks on queries; 2-3 months on mss. SASE. Sample copy $3. Occasionally reviews novels and short story collections. Send books marked "Review Copy, Managing Editor."
Payment: Pays in contributor's copies.
Terms: Acquires one-time rights.
Advice: "We look for something special in the voice or style. Not simply something that is a well-written story. A new twist, a unique sense or vision of the world. The stuff that every mag is hoping to find. Write about things that are important to you: issues that *must* be talked about; issues that frighten, anger you. The world has all the cute, well-made stories it needs."

THE SUN, (II), The Sun Publishing Company, Inc., 107 N. Roberson St., Chapel Hill NC 27516. (919)942-5282. Editor: Sy Safransky. Magazine: 8½ × 11; 40 pages; offset paper; glossy cover stock; illustrations; photos. "*The Sun* is a magazine of ideas. We publish all kinds of writing—fiction, articles, poetry. Our only criteria are that the writing make sense and enrich our common space. We direct *The Sun* toward interests which move us, and we trust our readers will respond." Monthly. Estab. 1974. Circ. 15,000.

Needs: Open to all fiction. Accepts 3 ms/issue. Receives approximately 400 unsolicited fiction mss each month. Published work by Eleanore Devine, Earl C. Pike, Deborah Shouse; published new writers within the last year. Length: 10,000 words maximum. Also publishes poetry.

How to Contact: Send complete ms with SASE. Reports in 3 months. Publishes ms an average of 6-12 months after acceptance. Sample copy $3.

Payment: Pays up to $100 on publication, plus 2 contributor's copies and a complimentary subscription.

Terms: Acquires one-time rights. Publishes reprints.

SUN DOG: THE SOUTHEAST REVIEW, (II), English Department, 406 Williams, Florida State University, Tallahassee FL 32306. (904)644-4230. Editor: Pat MacEnulty. Magazine: 6 × 9; 60-100 pages; 70 lb. paper; 10 pt. Krome Kote cover; illustrations; photos. Biannually. Estab. 1979. Circ. 2,000.

Needs: "We want stories which are well written, beautifully written, with striking images, incidents and characters. We are interested more in quality than in style or genre." Accepts 20 mss/year. Receives approximately 60 unsolicited fiction mss each month. Reads less frequently during summer. Critiques rejected mss when there is time. Occasionally recommends other markets (up to 5 poems or 1 story.)

How to Contact: Send complete ms with SASE. "Short bio or cover letter would be appreciated." Publishes ms an average of 2-6 months after acceptance. Sample copy $4.

Payment: Pays 2 contributor's copies. $2 charge for extras.

Terms: Acquires first North American serial rights which then revert to author.

Advice: "Avoid trendy experimentation for its own sake (present-tense narration, observation that isn't also revelation). Fresh stories, moving, interesting characters and a sensitivity to language are still fiction mainstays. Also publishes winner and runners-up of the World's Best Short Short Story Contest sponsored by the Florida State University English Department."

SWIFT KICK, (II), 1711 Amherst St., Buffalo NY 14214. (716)837-7778. Editor: Robin Kay Willoughby. Magazine: size, number of pages, paper quality, cover stock vary; illustrations; photos, b&w line art, xerographs. "Specializes in unusual formats, hard-to-classify works, visual poetry, found art, etc. for pataphysical, rarified audience." Published special fiction issue; plans another. Estab. 1981. Circ. 100.

Needs: Open. "If it doesn't seem to fit a regular category, it's probably what we'd like! No boring, slipshod, everyday stuff like in mass-market magazines." Receives 5 unsolicited fiction mss/month. Accepts 1-2 mss/issue. Does not read just before Christmas. Publishes ms depending on finances (6 months-1 year) after acceptance. Publishes short shorts of 1,000 words (or 1 picture). Sometimes recommends other markets.

How to Contact: Query first for longer works or send complete ms with cover letter for short work. Reports in 2 months to 1 year. SASE ("or include reply card with OK to toss enclosed work"). Simultaneous submissions OK. Will consider reprints of astoundingly good work (out of print). Sample copy for $7; "sample purchase recommended to best understand magazine's needs."

Payment: Pays in contributor's copies; half price for extras.

Terms: Acquires one-time rights. Rights revert to artists/authors. Sends galleys to author if requested.

Advice: "We always get less fiction than poetry – if a story is good, it has a good chance of publication in little mags. Editorially, I'm a snob, so don't write like anyone else; be *so* literate your writing transcends literature and (almost) literacy. Don't submit over 10 pages first time. Submit a 'grabber' that makes an editor ask for more. Don't neglect the stories in your own life for someone else's castles-in-the-air."

SYCAMORE REVIEW, (II), Department of English, Purdue University, West Lafayette IN 47907. (317)494-3783. Editor: Linda E. Haynes. Fiction Editor: Troy Hickman. Editors change every two years. Send future submissions to "Fiction Editor." Magazine: 5½ × 8½; 130 pages; heavy, textured, uncoated paper; heavy matte cover. "Journal devoted to contemporary literature. We publish both traditional and experimental fiction, personal essay and poetry." Semiannually. Estab. 1989. Circ. 1,000.

Needs: Contemporary, experimental, historical (general), humor/satire, literary, mainstream, regional, sports, translations. "We generally avoid genre literature, but maintain no formal restrictions on style or subject matter. No science fiction, romance, children's." Publishes ms 3 months-1 year after acceptance. Length: 3,750 words preferred; 250 words minimum. Also publishes poetry. Sometimes critiques rejected mss and recommends other markets.

How to Contact: Send complete ms with cover letter. Cover letter should include previous publications, address changes. Reports in 4 months. SASE. Simultaneous submissions OK. Sample copy $5. Fiction guidelines for #10 SAE and 1 first class stamp.
Payment: Pays in contributor's copies; charge for extras.
Terms: Acquires one-time rights.
Advice: "We publish both new and experienced authors but we're always looking for stories with strong emotional appeal, vivid characterization and a distinctive narrative voice; stories that appeal to the heart more than the head. Avoid gimmicks and trite, predictable outcomes. Write stories that have a ring of truth, the impact of felt emotion. Don't be afraid to submit, send your best."

TAL, A Torch Magazine of the Arts, (II, IV), (formerly *Mosaic*), 318 Ave. F, Brooklyn NY 11218. Editor: Y. David Shulman. Magazine: 5½ × 7½; 10-20 pages; 20 lb. paper; illustrations. "Forum for writers and artists involved with Torah stories, translations, poetry, interviews, artwork. For those interested in literature and the arts and the Judaic tradition." Published irregularly. Estab. 1990. Circ. 200.
Needs: Ethnic. Accepts 1-2 mss/issue. Length: 2,000 words preferred. Publishes short shorts. Sometimes critiques rejected mss.
How to Contact: Send complete ms with cover letter. Include estimated word count. Reports in 1 month. Send SASE (IRC) for reply, return of ms or send a disposable copy of ms. Simultaneous and reprint submissions OK. Sample copy for $1.
Payment: Pays 2 contributor's copies.
Terms: Acquires one-time rights.
Advice: "Provides a forum for Torah-involved writers and artists."

‡TAMAQUA, (II), C120, Humanities Dept., Parkland College, Champaign IL 61821. (217)351-2217. Editor-in-Chief: James McGovern. Fiction Editor: Marci Dodds. Magazine: 5½ × 8½; 160-256 pages; 80 lb. paper; 12 point cover; some illustrations; 12-40 photos every issue. "No theme; top quality fiction, poetry, nonfiction (reviews, thoughtful essays, autobiography, biography, insightful travel, etc.) for a literate audience." Semiannually. Estab. 1990. Circ. 1,500.
Needs: Literary, condensed/excerpted novel, contemporary, ethnic, experimental, feminist, gay, humor/satire, prose poem, regional. "No stupid writing, no polemics, no demagogues, no zipperheads— that is, we want good, solid, intelligent, *professional* writing." Publishes special fiction issues (Native American issue, Pan American issue). Buys 4-10 mss/issue; 8-20 mss/year. Publishes ms 6 months after acceptance. Recently published work by Gerald Vizenor, Ralph Salisbury, Lisa McCloud. Length: 10,000 words maximum. Publishes short shorts. Length: under 1,000 words. Sometimes critiques rejected mss.
How to Contact: Send complete ms with cover letter. Reports in 3-4 weeks on queries; 6-8 weeks on mss. SASE. Simultaneous submissions OK. Prefers electronic submissions. Sample copy for $6, 8½ × 11 SAE and 72¢ postage. Fiction guidelines for #10 SAE and 1 first class stamp.
Payment: Pays $10-50, subscription to magazine, contributor's copies; charge for extras.
Terms: Pays on publication for first North American serial rights.
Advice: "The most influential ingredient for the growing market in fiction (as well as all other writing) is the reduced costs of production because of desk-top publishing. Purchase a copy and *study* the magazine, or others of similar quality, to distinguish between good, solid professional writing and that which is not."

TAMPA REVIEW, (III), 401 W. Kennedy Blvd., Box 19F, University of Tampa, Tampa FL 33606-1490. (813)253-3333, ext. 3621. Editor: Richard Mathews. Fiction Editor: Andy Solomon. Magazine: 7½ × 10½; approximately 70 pages; acid-free paper; visual art; photos. "Interested in fiction of distinctive literary quality." Semiannually. Estab. 1988.
Needs: Contemporary, ethnic, experimental, fantasy, historical, humor/satire, literary, mainstream, prose poem, translations. "We are far more interested in quality than in genre. No sentimental as opposed to genuinely moving, nor self-conscious style at the expense of human truth." Buys 4-5 mss/issue. Publishes ms within 7 months-1 year of acceptance. Agented fiction 60%. Published work by Lee K. Abbott, Lorrie Moore, Tim O'Connor, Scott Bradfield. Length: 1,000 words minimum; 6,000 words maximum. Publishes short shorts "if the story is good enough." Also publishes literary essays (must be labeled nonfiction), poetry. Sometimes critiques rejected mss and recommends other markets.

How to Contact: Send complete mss with cover letter. Should include brief bio and publishing record. Include Social Security number. No simultaneous submissions. SASE. Reads September-December; reports January-March. Sample copy for $5 (includes postage) and 9 × 12 SAE. Fiction guidelines for #10 SAE and 1 first class stamp.
Payment: Pays $10 per printed page.
Terms: Pays on publication for first North American serial rights. Sends galleys to author—upon request.
Advice: "There are more good writers publishing in magazines today than there have been in many decades. Unfortunately, there are even more bad ones. In T. Gertler's *Elbowing the Seducer*, an editor advises a young writer that he wants to hear her voice completely, to tell (he means 'show') him in a story the truest thing she knows. We concur. Rather than a trendy workshop story or a minimalism that actually stems from not having much to say, we would like to see stories that make us believe they mattered to the writer and, more importantly, will matter to a reader. Trim until only the essential is left, and don't give up belief in yourself. And it might help to attend a good writers conference, e.g. Wesleyan or Bennington."

‡**TEMPORARY CULTURE, (II),** P.O. Box 43072, Upper Montclair NJ 07043. Editor: H. Wessells. 4½ × 11; 24-32 pages; b&w illustrations. "Creating new mythologies from the bankrupt post-industrial landscapes. Pushing language to new terrain." Semiannually. Estab. 1988. Circ. 250.
Needs: Experimental, prose poem, science fiction, ecological. "No workshop confessionals and narrow-minded egocentric visions of the world. No self indulgence." Publishes special fiction issue or anthology. Receives 0-2 unsolicited mss/month. Acquires 4 mss/year. Publishes short shorts. Sometimes critiques or comments on rejected mss.
How to Contact: Send complete ms with cover letter. Reports in 1-1½ months. SASE. Simultaneous submissions OK. Sample copy for $5.
Payment: Pays in contributor's copies.
Terms: Acquires one-time rights. Sometimes sends galleys to author.

THE TEXAS REVIEW, (II), Sam Houston State University Press, Huntsville TX 77341. (713)294-1423. Editor: Paul Ruffin. Magazine: 6 × 9; 148-190 pages; best quality paper; 70 lb. cover stock; illustrations; photos. "We publish top quality poetry, fiction, articles, interviews and reviews for a general audience." Semiannually. Estab. 1976. Circ. 700.
Needs: Literary and contemporary fiction. "We are eager enough to consider fiction of quality, no matter what its theme or subject matter. No juvenile fiction." Accepts 4 mss/issue. Receives approximately 40-60 unsolicited fiction mss each month. Published work by George Garrett, Ellen Gilchrist, Fred Chappell; published new writers within the last year. Length: 500-10,000 words. Critiques rejected mss "when there is time." Recommends other markets.
How to Contact: Send complete ms with cover letter. SASE. Reports in 3 months on mss. Sample copy $3.
Payment: Pays contributor's copies plus one year subscription.
Terms: Acquires all rights. Sends galleys to author.

‡**THEATRE OF THE NIGHT, Scripture Ov Die Apokalypse, (I),** Nuclear Trenchcoated Subway Prophets Ministries, 118 E. Goodheart Ave., Lake Mary FL 32746. Editor: Ms. Lake Vajra. Fiction Editor: Asomati. Magazine: 40-50 pages; glossy paper; heavy glossy cover; pen & ink and collage illustrations; half-tone photographs. "Writings and art celebrating the beauty of darkness. Includes in-depth interviews with the darkest creative minds of the underworld: bands, editors, writers, artists, magicians, witches, vampyres, masters and slaves ... goth, industrial, ambient, ritual ... DARK SURREAL SENSUALITY." Quarterly. Estab. 1992. Circ. 5,000.
Needs: Children's/juvenile (scary fairytales), erotica, experimental, fantasy (dark fantasy/horror), feminist, gay, horror, lesbian, literary, occult, religious, romance (contemporary, gothic), "sm/bd, mythology, fairytale nightmares, decadent." No sports, western, sf. Plans special fiction issue or anthology in the future. Receives 12 unsolicited mss/month. Acquires 5 mss/issue. Publishes ms 3 months or less after acceptance. Recently published work by Shannon Frach, Todd Mecklem, Beij Beltrisi, Cayte Dallas. Length: open. Publishes short shorts. Also publishes literary essays, literary criticism and poetry. Often critiques or comments on rejected mss.
How to Contact: Send complete ms with cover letter. Should include bio and list of publications. Reports in 1-2 months. SASE for a reply to a query or send a disposable copy of the ms. Simultaneous submissions, reprints and electronic submissions OK. Sample copy for $5, $1 for catalog of magazines we publish. Fiction guidelines (bimonthly newsletter) for $1. Reviews novel and short story collections.

Payment: Pays contributor's copies. Additional copies $4.
Terms: All rights belong to the writers.
Advice: Looks for "surreally flowing stream ov (sub)consciousness, dream-like, nightmarish imagery, heavily descripted . . . employing any of the following words: vampire, witch, angel, rain, water, dark, night, dawn, pale, strange, and/or kiss . . . heh heh. Get the catalog and newsletter to see which of our publications your writings would best suit, then sample copy of the magazine. We publish 7 magazines at the moment. I would like to see more "dark surreal sensuality—vampirerotica, gotherotica, dark fantasy, introversion, fetish, decadence, morbid trancewritings, melancholy, ecstatic visions . . . ."

THEMA, (II,IV), Box 74109, Metairie LA 70033-4109. Editor: Virginia Howard. Magazine: 5½×8½; 200 pages; Grandee Strathmore cover stock; b&w illustrations. "Different specified theme for each issue—short stories, poems, b&w artwork must relate to that theme." Quarterly. Estab. 1988.
 • *Thema* editor, Virginia Howard, was featured in a Close-up interview in the 1991 *Novel & Short Story Writer's Market*. The magazine ranks #32 on the 1992 *Writer's Digest* Fiction 50 list.
Needs: Adventure, contemporary, experimental, humor/satire, literary, mainstream, mystery/suspense, prose poem, psychic/supernatural/occult, regional, science fiction, sports, western. "Each issue is based on a specified premise—a different unique theme for each issue. Many types of fiction acceptable, but must fit the premise. No pornographic, scatologic, erotic fiction." Upcoming themes: "Dust" (deadline February 1); "The Dreamland Café" (deadline May 1); "Talking to a Stranger" (deadline August 1); "Mirror image" (deadline November 1). Publishes ms within 3-4 months of acceptance. Published work by Edith Pearlman, A.L. Sirois, William Luvas. Length: fewer than 6,000 words preferred. Publishes short shorts "if very clever." Length: 300-900 words. Also publishes poetry. Sometimes critiques rejected mss and recommends other markets.
How to Contact: Send complete ms with cover letter, which should include "name and address, brief introduction, specifying the intended target issue for the mss." Simultaneous submissions OK. Reports on queries in 1 week; on mss in 8-10 weeks after deadline for specified issue. SASE. Sample copy $5. Free fiction guidelines.
Payment: Pays $25.
Terms: Pays on acceptance for one-time rights.
Advice: "Do not submit a manuscript unless you have written it for a specified premise. If you don't know the upcoming themes, send for guidelines first, before sending a story. We need more stories told in the Mark Twain/O. Henry tradition in magazine fiction."

THIN ICE, (II), 379 Lincoln Ave., Council Bluffs IA 51503. (712)322-9125. Editor/Publisher: Kathleen Jurgens. Magazine: Digest-sized; 95-104 pages; 16-20 lb. paper; enamel cover; b&w, pen and ink illustrations. "Horror and dark fantasy—short stories, poetry, interviews, art." Triannually. Estab. 1987. Circ. 250.
 • Editor Kathleen Jurgens was voted "Best Editor" by the Small Press Writers and Artists Organization in 1991.
Needs: Experimental, fantasy (dark), horror, black humor/satire, poetry, psychic/supernatural/occult. No "racist, preachy, straight porn for shock value." Receives 50-100 unsolicited mss/month. Accepts approx. 10 mss/issue; approx. 40 mss/year. Publishes ms 1-2 years after acceptance. Published work by Bentley Little, J. N. Williamson, Colleen Drippe, Jeannette Hopper. Length: 1,000-4,000 words preferred. Also publishes poetry. Critiques rejected mss.
How to Contact: Send complete ms with cover letter. Cover letter should include "a personal introduction, mention a few prior 'sales' if desired (though not necessary), where the writers heard of *Thin Ice*." No simultaneous submissions. Reports in 1 week on queries; 1-2 months on mss. SASE. Sample copy for $4.50 to Kathleen Jurgens ($6 outside of the U.S.). Fiction guidelines with #10 SASE.
Payment: Pays in contributor's copies.
Terms: Acquires first North American serial rights.
Advice: "Invest in a copy of the magazine and read it from cover to cover. Get a 'feel' for the overall mood, tone, and subject matter. Don't apologize for misspellings or coffee stains on the manuscript—retype it. While I prefer informal query letters, I become quite irate when potential contributors treat me unprofessionally. I respond to all submissions personally, frequently offering editorial commentary. Always include a SASE with the correct amount of postage. Give me the full 2 months to respond. Absolutely no simultaneous or multiple submissions considered. Please, do not summarize the story in your cover letter."

13TH MOON, A Feminist Magazine, (IV), SUNY-Albany, Dept. of English, Albany NY 12222. (518)442-4181. Editor: Judith Johnson. Magazine: 6×9; 200 pages; 50 lb. paper; heavy cover; photographs. "Feminist literary magazine for feminist women and men." Annually. Estab. 1973. Circ. 1,500.
Needs: Excerpted novel, experimental, feminist, lesbian, literary, prose poem, science fiction, translations. No fiction by men. Accepts 1-3 mss/issue. Does not read mss May-Sept. Time varies between acceptance and publication. Recently published work by F.R. Lewis, Jan Ramjerdi, Wilma Kahn. Length: Open. Publishes short shorts. Also publishes poetry. Sometimes critiques rejected mss.
How to Contact: Send complete ms with cover letter and SASE. Reports in 1 month on queries; 4 months on mss. SASE. Accepts electronic submissions via disk (WordPerfect 5.1 only). Sample copy for $8.
Payment: Pays 2 contributor's copies.
Terms: Acquires first North American serial rights.
Advice: Looks for *"unusual* fiction with feminist appeal."

THIS MAGAZINE, (II), Red Maple Foundation, 16 Skey Lane, Toronto, Ontario M6J 3S4 Canada. (416)588-6580. Editor: Judy MacDonald. Fiction Editor: Phil Hall. Magazine: 8½×11; 42 pages; bond paper; coated cover; illustrations and photographs. "Alternative general interest magazine." Estab. 1973. Circ. 12,000.
Needs: Ethnic, contemporary, experimental, fantasy, feminist, gay, lesbian, literary, mainstream, prose poem, regional. No "commercial/pulp fiction." Receives 15-20 unsolicited mss/month. Buys 1 mss/issue; 8 mss/year. Published work by Margaret Atwood and Peter McGehee. Length: 1,500 words average; 2,500 words maximum. Sometimes critiques rejected mss.
How to Contact: Query with clips of published work. Reports in 6 weeks on queries; 3-6 months on mss. SASE. No simultaneous submissions. Sample copy $4 (includes postage and GST). Fiction guidelines for #9 SAE and 48¢ U.S., 43¢ Canadian.
Payment: Pays $100 (Canadian) fiction; $25/poem published.
Terms: Buys one-time rights.
Advice: "It's best if you're familiar with the magazine when submitting work; a large number of mss that come into my office are inappropriate. Style guides are available. Manuscripts and queries that are clean and personalized really make a difference. Let your work speak for itself—don't try to convince us."

‡THE THREEPENNY REVIEW, (II), P.O. Box 9131, Berkeley CA 94709. (510)849-4545. Editor: Wendy Lesser. Tabloid: 10×17; 40 pages; Electrobrite paper; white book cover; illustrations. "Serious fiction." Quarterly. Estab. 1980. Circ. 8,000.
  • *The Threepenny Review* has received GE Writers Awards, CLMP Editor's Awards, NEA grants, Lila Wallace grants and inclusion of work in the Pushcart Prize Anthology. It was ranked # 36 on the 1992 *Writer's Digest* Fiction 50 List.
Needs: Literary. "Nothing 'experimental' (ungrammatical)." Receives 300-400 mss/month. Buys 3 mss/issue; 12 mss/year. Publishes 6-12 months after acceptance. Agented fiction 5%. Recently published Sigrid Nunez, Dagobato Gilb, Ann Packer, Leonard Michaels. Length: 5,000 words maximum. Publishes short shorts. Also publishes literary essays, literary criticism, poetry.
How to Contact: Send complete ms with cover letter. Reports in 2-4 weeks on queries;1-2 months on mss. Send SASE for reply, return of ms or send disposable copy of ms. No simultaneous submissions. Sample copy $5. Fiction guidelines for #10 SAE and 1 first class stamp. Reviews novels and short story collections.
Payment: Pays $200 plus free subscription to the magazine; additional copies at half price.
Terms: Pays on acceptance. Acquires first North American serial rights. Sends galleys to author.

‡THRUST, Experimental and Underground Prose, (II), Experimental Chapbook Press, P.O. Box 1602, Austin TX 78767. Editor: Skip Rhudy. Magazine: Digest-sized; 50-70 pages; 60 lb. offset paper; 65 lb. card cover; illustrations on cover. "*Thrust* is a magazine for writers and readers bored with the standard offerings of university-affiliated magazines, which pump out mainstream stories by the dumpster-full." Semiannually. Estab. 1992. Circ. 100.
Needs: Experimental, translations (prose only). "Absolutely no mainstream." Plans anthology in the future. Receives 5-10 unsolicited mss/month. Acquires 5-10 mss/issue; 15-30 mss/year. Publishes ms 6 weeks-6 months after acceptance. Recently published work by Daniel Quinn, Wolfgang Hilbig, Robert Howington. Length: open. Publishes short shorts. Often critiques or comments on rejected mss.

How to Contact: Send complete ms with cover letter. Should include one-paragraph bio. Reports in 2 weeks on queries; 6 weeks on mss. Send SASE for reply, return of ms or send a disposable copy of the ms. Simultaneous submissions OK. Sample copy for $3.50 (check made out to Skip Rhudy; cash; stamps). Reviews novels and short story collections.
Payment: Pays 1 contributor's copy.
Terms: Acquires one-time rights.
Advice: "Material should be experimental in nature; we will consider anything that is not clearly mainstream. That means we will not consider genre work of any kind, *unless* the writer incorporates experimental elements in the language or perspective. Short, tightly-written prose stands the best chance of acceptance at *Thrust*. No strict guidelines regarding subject matter exist, but we are most interested in controversial themes generally disregarded or avoided by establishment literary magazines. We want powerful voices from the underbelly, the fringe, the ghetto, voices telling stories about the random ugliness of modern, urban life. Translation of work that is experimental or underground in nature will also be considered."

TICKLED BY THUNDER, A Newsmagazine for Writers, (II), Tickled by Thunder Pub. Co., 7385 129th St., Surrey, British Columbia V3W 7B8 Canada. (604)591-6095 (phone, voice or fax). Editor: Larry Lindner. Magazine: Digest-sized; bond paper; bond cover; illustrations and photographs. "Totally open. For writers." Quarterly. Estab. 1990. Circ. 100.
Needs: Adventure, contemporary, fantasy, humor/satire, literary, mainstream, mystery/suspense, prose poem, psychic/supernatural, religious/inspirational, science fiction, western. "No pornography." Receives 40 unsolicited mss/month. Buys 1-4 mss/issue; 4-16 mss/year. Publishes ms next issue after acceptance. Length: 1,500 words average; 2,000 words maximum. Publishes short shorts. Length: No preference. Also publishes poetry. Sometimes critiques rejected mss and recommends other markets.
How to Contact: Query with clips of published work if any including "Brief resume/history of writing experience, photo, credits, etc." Reports in 3-4 months. SASE. Simultaneous submissions OK. Sample copy $2.50 (Canadian) or 3 IRCs. Fiction guidelines for legal SAE and 1 first class stamp.
Payment: Pays $1 maximum.
Terms: Buys first rights.
Advice: "Send for guidelines, read a sample copy and ask questions. Send SASE for info on contest for fiction and poetry."

‡TIMBERLINES, (II), Lake City Writers Forum, P.O. Box 38, Lake City CO 81235. Contact: Editorial Panel. Magazine: 6½ × 9½; 55-75 pages; line drawings. "Contemporary, general fiction, poetry. While all themes and styles will be considered, *Timberlines'* orientation is toward quality work reflecting western, mountain or outdoor ambience or theme."Annually. Estab. 1991. Circ. 1,000.
Needs: Adventure, ethnic/multicultural, historical (general), humor/satire, literary, mainstream/contemporary, regional, senior citizen/retirement, young adult/teen. Receives 200 unsolicited mss/year. Reads mss only from August-December. Publishes short shorts. Also publishes literary essays.
How to Contact: Send complete ms with cover letter. Should include one-paragraph bio and list of publications. SASE for return of ms or send a disposable copy of the ms. Simultaneous and reprint submissions OK. Sample copy for $4, 7 × 10 or larger SAE and 5 first class stamps.
Payment: Pays 3 contributor's copies. Additional copies at our cost (it varies).
Terms: Acquires one-time rights. Not copyrighted.
Advice: Looks for "good writing—interesting story line, general appeal. Original approach. Learn what makes a good story and how to put it together."

‡TOMORROW, Speculative Fiction, (II), Pulphouse, Inc., P.O. Box 6038, Evanston IL 60204. (708)864-3668. Editor: Algis Budrys. Magazine: 8¼ × 10¾; 64 pages; newsprint; slick cover; illustrations. "Any good science fiction, fantasy and horror, for an audience of fiction readers." Bimonthly. Estab. 1993.
  ● This magazine is published by noted science fiction and mystery publisher, Pulphouse. See the listing for the press and their other magazine, *Pulphouse* in this book.
Needs: Fantasy, horror, science fiction. Receives 100 mss/month. Buys 8-12 mss/issue; 48-82 mss/year. Publishes 2-3 issues after acceptance. Agented fiction 5%. Recently published Gene Wolak, M. Shayne Bell, Rob Chilson. Length: 4,000 words average. Publishes short shorts. Always critiques rejected mss.
How to Contact: Send complete ms with cover letter. Should include estimated word count, 25-word bio, social security number. Reports in 2 weeks. Send SASE (IRC) for reply, return of ms or send a disposable copy of the ms. No simultaneous submissions. Sample copy $3.95 plus postage, to Tomorrow Single Copy Sales, Pulphouse, Inc., Box 1227, Eugene, OR 97440.

Payment: $50 minimum; 7¢/word maximum plus 2 contributor's copies.
Terms: Pays halfway betwen acceptance and publication. Acquires first North American serial rights. Sends galleys to author.
Advice: "Read my ongoing series on writing in the magazine."

TRADESWOMEN, A Quarterly Magazine for Women in Blue-Collar Work, (I, IV), Tradeswomen, Inc., P.O. Box 40664, San Francisco CA 94140. (415) 821-7334. Magazine: 8½×11; 40 pages; b&w photographs. Quarterly. Estab. 1981. Circ. 1,500.
Needs: "Looking for fiction about women in blue-collar employment; on-the-job stories, 'what it's like' stories by women and men." Upcoming themes: "Nontraditional Training Centers for Women"; "Women of Color and Their Needs." Receives 2 unsolicited mss/month; accepts 1-2 mss/issue. Publishes ms 3-6 months after acceptance. Length: 2,000 words average; 3,000 words maximum. Publishes short shorts. Recommends other markets for rejected mss.
How to Contact: Send complete ms with cover letter. Reports on queries in 1 month; on ms in 2 months. SASE. Simultaneous and reprint submissions OK. Sample copy $3.50 plus $1.20 postage. Fiction guidelines free.

TRANSLATION, (II), The Translation Center, Columbia University, 412 Dodge, New York NY 10027. (212)854-2305. Director: Frank MacShane. Editors change each year. (One guest each issue). Magazine: 6×9; 200-300 pages; coated cover stock; photos. Semiannually. Estab. 1972. Circ. 1,500.
Needs: Literary translations only. Upcoming themes: Czech, Israeli, African issues. Accepts varying number of mss/year. Receives approximately 10-15 unsolicited fiction mss each month. Length: very short or excerpts; not in excess of 15 mss pages. Critiques rejected mss "rarely, because of time involved."
How to Contact: "Please query the magazine's current needs—will respond within 2 weeks to queries." Simultaneous submissions OK. Reports in 3-6 months on mss. Sample copy $9.
Payment: Payment varies.
Terms: Acquires first North American serial rights for that volume publication only.
Advice: "We are particularly interested in translations of previously untranslated work. Annual awards of $1,000 for outstanding translation of a substantial part of a book-length literary work. Translator must have letter of intent to publish from a publisher. Write for description and application for awards program."

TRIBUTARY, (II), The Rockford Writers Guild, Box 858, Rockford IL 61105. Editor: David Ross. Magazine: 5⅜×8½; b&w illustrations and photographs. "Devices with a fresh approach to old themes or new insights into the human condition whether prose or poetry." Quarterly supplement to annual *Rockford Review*. Estab. 1990. Circ. 200.
● The Rockford Writers Guild publishes this and *The Rockford Review*, also listed in this book.
Needs: Ethnic, experimental, fantasy, humor/satire, science fiction (hard science, soft/sociological). Publishes short shorts up to 500 words.
How to Contact: Send complete ms. Simultaneous submissions OK, if noted. Reports in 4-6 weeks. SASE. Sample copy for $2.50. Fiction guidelines for #10 SAE and 1 first class stamp.
Payment: Pays in contributor's copies. Submissions considered for $25 Readers' Poll prize.
Terms: Acquires first North American serial rights.

TRIQUARTERLY, (II), Northwestern University, 2020 Ridge Ave., Evanston IL 60208. (708)491-7614. Fiction Editors: Reginald Gibbons and Susan Hahn. Magazine: 6×9¼; 240+ pages; 60 lb. paper; heavy cover stock; illustration; photos. "A general literary quarterly especially devoted to fiction. We publish short stories, novellas or excerpts from novels, by American and foreign writers. Genre or style is not a primary consideration. We aim for the general but serious and sophisticated reader. Many of our readers are also writers." Triannually. Estab. 1964. Circ. 5,000.
● In 1991 the publishers of *Triquarterly* published *Fiction of the '80s*, a collection of the best fiction published in the magazine during the 1980s. The magazine ranks #49 on the 1992 *Writer's Digest* Fiction 50 list.

● *A bullet introduces comments by the editor of* Novel & Short Story Writer's Market *indicating special information about the listing.*

Needs: Literary, contemporary and translations. "No prejudices or preconceptions against anything *except* genre fiction (sci fi, romances, etc.)." Buys 10 mss/issue, 30 mss/year. Receives approximately 500 unsolicited fiction mss each month. Does not read May 1-Sept. 30. Approximately 10% of fiction is agented. Published work by Stanley Elkin, Chaim Potsk, Alice Fulton; published new writers within the last year. Length: no requirement. Publishes short shorts.
How to Contact: Send complete ms with SASE. No simultaneous submissions. Reports in 3-4 months on mss. Publishes ms an average of 6 months to 1 year after acceptance. Sample copy $4.
Payment: Pays $100-500, 2 contributor's copies. Cover price less 40% discount for extras.
Terms: Pays on publication for first North American serial rights. Sends galleys to author.

TUCUMCARI LITERARY REVIEW, (I, II), 3108 W. Bellevue Ave., Los Angeles CA 90026. Editor: Troxey Kemper. Magazine: 5½×8½; 32 pages; 20 lb. bond paper; 110 lb. cover; few illustrations; Xerox photographs. "Old-fashioned fiction that can be read and reread for pleasure; no weird, strange pipe dreams." Bimonthly. Estab. 1988. Circ. small.
Needs: Adventure, contemporary, ethnic, historical (general), humor/satire, literary, mainstream, mystery/suspense, regional (southwest USA), senior citizen/retirement, western (frontier stories). No science fiction, drugs/acid rock, pornography, horror, martial arts. "No talking animals or plants. No talking with God or telling what He told you." Accepts 6 or 8 mss/issue; 35-40 mss/year. Publishes ms 2 to 6 months after acceptance. Length: 400-1,200 words preferred. Also publishes rhyming poetry.
How to Contact: Send complete ms with or without cover letter. Reports in 2 weeks. SASE. Simultaneous and reprint submissions OK. Sample copy $1.50 plus 50¢ postage. Fiction guidelines for #10 SAE and 1 first class stamp.
Payment: Pays in contributor's copies.
Terms: Acquires one-time rights. Publication not copyrighted.
Advice: "Does the work 'say something' or is it a hodgepodge of sentence fragments and paragraphs, not tied together into a story? No 'it was all a dream' endings."

TURNSTILE, (II), Suite 2348, 175 Fifth Ave., New York NY 10010. Editor: Mitchell Nauffts. Magazine: 6×9; 128 pages; 55 lb. paper; 10 pt. cover; illustrations; photos. "Publishing work by new writers." Biannually. Estab. 1988. Circ. 1,000.
• *Turnstile* was a CCLM (now CLMP) seed grant recipint in 1989 and has received grants from the New York State Council of the Arts for the last three years.
Needs: Contemporary, experimental, humor/satire, literary, regional. No genre fiction. Upcoming theme: 2nd Annual Fiction Contest in Fall 1993. Receives approx. 80 unsolicited fiction mss/month. Publishes approx. 5 short story mss/issue. Recently published work by James Applewhite, Richard Russo; published new writers within the last year. Length: 2,000 words average; 4,000 words maximum. Publishes some short shorts. Also publishes poetry. Sometimes comments on rejected mss.
How to Contact: Query first or send complete ms with cover letter. Reports on queries in 3-4 weeks; on mss in 6-10 weeks. SASE. Simultaneous submissions OK. Sample copy $6.50 and 7×10 SAE; fiction guidelines for #10 SAE and 1 first class stamp.
Payment: Pays in contributor's copies; charge for extras.
Terms: Acquires one-time rights.
Advice: "Also publishes interviews with writers, essays and subjective nonfiction. More than ever we're looking for *well-crafted* stories that address the sometimes unpleasant realities of the world we live in. We're known for publishing a range of new voices, and favor stories that rely on traditional narrative techniques (e.g. characterization, plot, effective endings)."

‡TWISTED, P.O. Box 1249, Palmetto GA 30268-1249. (404)463-1458. Editor: Christine Hoard. Magazine: 8½×11; 152 pages; 60 lb. paper; 67 lb. cover; illustrations; photos. "Emphasis on contemporary horror and fantasy, anything on the dark side of reality." For readers of horror, "weird," fantasy, etc. Published irregularly. Estab. 1985. Circ. 300.
Needs: "We are mostly interested in adult-oriented horror." Fantasy, horror, prose poem, psychic/supernatural/occult. "No hard science fiction, no sword and sorcery. Graphic horror or sex scenes OK if tastefully done. Sexist-racist writing turns me off." Receives approx. 30 unsolicited fiction mss/month. Accepts 10 mss/issue. Publishes ms 2 months to 2 years after acceptance. Published work by David Bruce, Joe Faust, Bentley Little, Kathleen Jurgens; published new writers within the last year. Length: 2,000 words average; 200 words minimum; 5,000 words maximum. Sometimes critiques rejected mss and recommends other markets.

How to Contact: Reporting time varies. Cover letters not necessary but appreciated. No simultaneous or multiple submissions. Sample copy $6. Fiction guidelines for #10 SAE and 1 first class stamp.
Payment: Pays in contributor's copies.
Terms: Acquires first rights.
Advice: "Sometimes we are overstocked so probably best to inquire first."

2 AM MAGAZINE, (I, II, IV), Box 6754, Rockford IL 61125-1754. Editor: Gretta M. Anderson. Magazine: 8½×11; 60 or more pages; 60 lb. offset paper; 70 lb. offset cover; illustrations; photos occasionally. "Horror, science fiction, fantasy stories, poetry, articles and art for a sophisticated adult audience." Quarterly. Summer fiction issue planned. Estab. 1986. Circ. 1,500.
• This horror, science fiction and fantasy magazine ranks #16 on the 1992 *Writer's Digest* Fiction 50 list.
Needs: Experimental, fantasy, horror, humor/satire, mystery/suspense (police procedurals, romantic suspense), prose poem, psychic/supernatural/occult, romance (gothic), science fiction (hard science, soft/sociological). No juvenile. Receives 400 unsolicited mss/month. Buys 12-14 mss/issue; 50 mss/year. Publishes ms an average of 6-9 months after acceptance. Published work by J. N. Williamson, Elizabeth Engstrom, Leonard Carpenter; published new writers within the last year. Length: 1,800 words average; 500 words minimum; 5,000 words maximum. Publishes short shorts. Sometimes critiques rejected mss and recommends other markets.
How to Contact: Send complete ms with cover letter (cover letter optional). Simultaneous submissions OK. Reports in 1 month on queries; 10-12 weeks on mss. SASE. Sample copy $4.95 and $1 postage. Fiction guidelines for #10 SASE.
Payment: Pays ½¢/word minimum, negotiable maximum; 1 contributor's copy; 40% discount on additional copies.
Terms: Pays on acceptance for one-time rights with non-exclusive anthology option. Sends prepublication galleys to author.
Advice: "Publishing more pages of fiction, more sf, and mystery, as well as horror. Put name and address on manuscript, double-space, use standard ms format. Pseudonym should appear under title on first manuscript page. True name and address should appear on upper left on first ms page."

THE TWOPENNY PORRINGER, (I, II), P.O. Box 1456, Tacoma WA 98401. Editor: Adrian Taylor. Magazine: Digest-sized; 70-80 pages; b&w illustrations and photographs. "General literary and arts (poetry, short stories, photos, artwork)." Quarterly. Estab. 1992. Circ. 2,000.
Needs: Contemporary, experimental, literary, prose poem, science fiction (soft/sociological), translations. Receives 2+ unsolicited mss/month. Buys a minimum of 4 mss/year. Length: Open. Publishes short shorts. Also accepts poetry.
How to Contact: Send complete ms with cover letter. Reports in 2 months on mss. SASE. Simultaneous submissions OK. Sample copy for $2.
Payment: Pays 2 contributor's copies and 3 subsequent issues.
Terms: Acquires one-time rights. Sends galleys to author.
Advice: "I am very open to all styles. The work should be original and have a captivating quality about it that will keep the interest of the reader. Reality expressed in a creative manner is always best."

THE ULTIMATE WRITER, (I), Perry Terrell Publishing, 1617 Newport Place #24, Kenner LA 70065. (504)465-9412. Editor: Perry Terrell. Magazine: 8½×11; bond paper. "Poetry, fiction, essays, articles for an audience of all ages, geared toward creativity in writing and expression." Monthly. Estab. 1990. Circ. 632.
Needs: Adventure, confession, ethnic, experimental, fantasy, historical, humor/satire, juvenile, mainstream, mystery/suspense, religious/inspirational, romance, science fiction, western; also plays, fillers. No pornographic material. Plans special fiction issue. Accepts 48 mss/year. Publishes ms 4-8 months after acceptance, depending on length of ms. Length: 99 words minimum, no maximum, "but more than 5,000 words will be printed in 2 or 3 issues." Also publishes literary essays, literary criticism, poetry.
How to Contact: Query first or send complete ms with cover letter. Simultaneous submissions OK. Reports in 1 week on queries; 4-6 months on mss. SASE. Sample copy for $3.75. Fiction guidelines for #10 SAE and 1 first-class stamp. Reviews novels and short story collections.
Payment: Pays 2 contributor's copies or three-month subscription.
Advice: Sponsors fiction, essay, poetry, article contest. Write for details.

UNDERPASS, (II), Underpass Press, #574-21, 10405 Jasper Ave., Edmonton, Alberta T5J 3S2 Canada. Editor: Barry Hammond. Magazine: 5¼×8¼; pages vary; 60 lb. bond paper; Mayfair cover; some illustrations. "Mainly a poetry annual for an adult audience." Annually. Estab. 1987. Circ. 200-300.

Needs: Contemporary, experimental, literary, prose poem. "We have only published a few short stories. We are mainly a poetry annual. No religious or nature poetry." Receives 6 mss/month. Buys 1 or 2 mss/issue. Does not read mss Nov.-Jan. Publishes ms within 6 months after acceptance. Recently published work by Wade Bell. Length: 2,000 words average; 500 words minimum; 6,000 words maximum. Publishes short shorts. Length: No preference. Sometimes critiques rejected mss.

How to Contact: Send complete mss with cover letter including "brief bio and publishing history (if any)." Reports in 6 weeks. "Our deadline is August 31st each year." SASE. Simultaneous submissions OK. Sample copy for $6.95, 6×9 SAE and 2 first class stamps. Fiction guidelines for #10 SAE and 1 first class stamp.

Payment: Pays $10 minimum and contributor's copies.

Terms: Buys one-time rights. Sends galleys to author.

Advice: "Try poetry before submitting prose."

UNIVERSITY OF PORTLAND REVIEW, (II), University of Portland, 5000 N. Willamette Blvd., Portland OR 97203. (503)283-7144. Editor-in-Chief: Thompson M. Faller. Magazine: 5×8; 40-55 pages. "Magazine for the college-educated layman of liberal arts background. Its purpose is to comment on the human condition and to present information in different fields with relevance to the contemporary scene." Published semiannually. Established 1948. Circ. 1,000.

Needs: "Only fiction that makes a significant statement about the contemporary scene will be employed." Receives 4 unsolicited mss/month. Acquires 2-3 mss/issue, 4-6 mss/year. Published new writers within the last year. Length: 1,500 words minimum; 3,500 words maximum; 2,000 words average. Sometimes recommends other markets.

How to Contact: Send complete ms with SASE. Reports in 3 weeks on queries; 6 months on mss. Publishes ms up to 1 year after acceptance. Sample copy 50¢.

Payment: Pays 5 contributor's copies; 50¢ charge for extras.

Terms: Acquires all rights.

UNMUZZLED OX, (III), Unmuzzled Ox Foundation Ltd., 105 Hudson St., New York NY 10013. Editor: Michael Andre. Tabloid. "Magazine about life for an intelligent audience." Quarterly. Estab. 1971. Circ. 20,000.

• At press time the editor said the next few issues of this magazine would include poetry, essays and art only. You may want to check before sending submissions or expect a long response time.

Needs: Contemporary, literary, prose poem and translations. No commercial material. Receives 20-25 unsolicited mss/month. Also publishes poetry. Occasionally critiques rejected mss.

How to Contact: "Cover letter is significant." Reports in 1 month. SASE. Sample copy $7.50.

Payment: Contributor's copies.

‡UNREALITY, A Magazine of Fantastic Fiction, (II), P.O. Box 1155, Columbia SC 29202-1155. (803)783-9156. Editor: David Schindler. Magazine: 7×8½; 40-60 pages; 20 lb. paper; b&w illustrations. "The theme of the magazine is the overlapping of reality and the unreal. The philosophy is to allow writers the freedom to explore dark or fantastic themes without having to pander to the requirements of any particular genre." Quarterly. Estab. 1992. Circ. 100.

Needs: Fantasy, horror, psychic/supernatural/occult. "I'm open to anything so long as it has a dark or unreal theme." Receives 50 unsolicited mss/month. Acquires 6-10 mss/issue; 30-40 mss/year. Publishes ms 3-6 months after acceptance. Recently published work by D.F. Lewis, Lenora K. Rogers, Bobby G. Warner. Length: 4,000 words maximum. Also publishes poetry. Often critiques or comments on rejected mss.

How to Contact: Send complete ms with cover letter. Should include brief bio. Reports in 4-6 weeks on mss. Send SASE for reply, return of ms or send a disposable copy of the ms. Simultaneous submissions OK, if identified as such. Sample copy for $3. Fiction guidelines for #10 SAE and 1 first class stamp.

Payment: Pays 2 contributor's copies for stories. Additional copies for cost; query for prices.
Terms: Acquires first North American serial rights.
Advice: Looks for "a well-written, intelligent story that deals with dark or fantastic themes. I'm looking for quality fiction, not just a good scare. Beginning writers who have never read anything but horror fiction will probably have a hard time placing a story here. Expose yourself to great fiction, then write the stories you want to write. Would like to see more subtle horror."

THE UNSILENCED VOICE, An Anything but Toast Publication, (I), #29, 9333 N. Lombard, Portland OR 97203. (503)240-0120. Editor: Clint C. Wilkinson. Magazine: 4×5; 19 pages; illustrations. "Leftist, politically and socially oriented also weird, fringe fiction, poetry, reporting and cartoons for an open minded, politically aware audience." Bimonthly. Estab. 1990. Circ. 25.
Needs: Experimental, horror, humor/satire, mystery/suspense (private eye, police procedural, amateur sleuth), psychic/supernatural/occult, western (traditional, frontier). No erotic, religious, racist material. Plans future special fiction issue. Accepts 2 mss/issue; 20 mss/year. Publishes ms 2 months after acceptance. Recently published work by James Burchill, Mike Brann, Mark Howell. Length: 300 words preferred; 600 words maximum. Publishes short shorts. Sometimes critiques rejected mss and recommends other markets.
How to Contact: Send complete ms. Reports in 1 month. SASE. Simultaneous and reprint submissions OK. Sample copy for $1. Fiction guidelines for #10 SAE and 1 first class stamp.
Payment: Pays in contributor's copies.
Terms: Acquires one-time rights. Publication not copyrighted.
Advice: "I look for well-told stories in which well-developed, real characters participate. If it's really weird, that's good too. Send stuff to underground publications to build up credits and confidence for attacking the big leagues. Use your writing to wake people up and as a force for change. We live in scary times, and artists need to be at the forefront of the battle to make the world better."

‡URBANUS/RAIZIRR, (II), Urbanus Press, P.O. Box 192561, San Francisco CA 94119-2561. Editors: Peter Drizhal, Cameron Bamberger. Magazine: 5½×8½; 48 pages; 60 lb. offset paper; 10 pt. coated cover; illustrations; a few photographs. "We seek writing for an audience that is generally impatient with mainstream writing and poetry; social slants, shock value, dark undercurrents, normal people in strange but semi-plausible circumstances . . ." Semiannually. Estab. 1988. Circ. 400.
Needs: Erotica, ethnic/multicultural, experimental, feminist, gay, horror, humor/satire, lesbian, "social" contemporary, science fiction (soft/sociological). Does not accept "anything that would be better suited for a mainstream audience/publication." Receives 10-20 unsolicited mss/month. Buys 3-5 mss/year. Publishes ms 6-18 months after acceptance. Length: 5,000 words maximum. Publishes short shorts. Also publishes poetry. Sometimes comments on or critiques rejected mss.
How to Contact: Send complete ms with a brief (1 paragraph) cover letter. Should include estimated word count, 50-word bio, Social Security number, list of publications (3-5). Reports in 1-2 weeks on queries; 2-8 weeks on mss. Send SASE for reply, return of ms or send a disposable copy of the ms. No multiple or simultaneous submissions. Sample copy for $5 for most recent or $7 for 2 most recent issues. (Payable to Urbanus Press).
Payment: Pays ¼¢/word and 1 contributor's copy.
Terms: Pays on publication for first North American serial rights.
Advice: "Don't flood us with a succession of stories, if rejected. Either read a copy to see what's up — or wait a number of months, and try with a new approach." Looks for "an understanding of the market to which you are submitting. Pot-shot submissions will get reciprocal treatment."

US1 WORKSHEETS, (II), Postings Box 1, Ringoes NJ 08551. (609)448-5096. Editor: Rotating board. Magazine: 11½×17; 20-25 pages. Publishes poetry and fiction. Annually. Estab. 1973.
Needs: "No restrictions on subject matter or style. Good story telling or character deliniation appreciated. Audience does not include children." Publishes ms within 3 months of acceptance. Published work by Alicia Ostriker, Toi Derricotte, J.A. Perkins, Cynthia Goodling, Judith McNally. Publishes short shorts.
How to Contact: Query first. Reports on queries "as soon possible." SASE. Sample copy $4.
Payment: Pays in contributor's copies.
Terms: Acquires one-time rights. Copyright "reverts to author."

VALLEY GRAPEVINE, (I, IV), Seven Buffaloes Press, Box 249, Big Timber MT 59011. Editor/Publisher: Art Cuelho. Theme: "poems, stories, history, folklore, photographs, ink drawings or anything native to the Great Central Valley of California, which includes the San Joaquin and Sacramento valleys.

Focus is on land and people and the oil fields, farms, orchards, Okies, small town life, hobos." Readership: "Rural and small town audience, the common man with a rural background, salt-of-the-earth. The working man reads *Valley Grapevine* because it's his personal history recorded." Annually. Estab. 1978. Circ. 500.

• *Valley Grapevine* is published by Art Cuelho of Seven Buffaloes Press. He also publishes *Azorean Express, Black Jack, Hill and Holler,* listed in this book. See also his listing for the press.

Needs: Literary, contemporary, western and ethnic (Okie, Arkie). No academic, religious (unless natural to theme), gay/lesbian or supernatural material. Receives approximately 4-5 unsolicited fiction mss each month. Length: 2,500-10,000 (prefers 5,000) words.

How to Contact: Query. SASE for query, ms. Reports in 1 week. Sample copy available to writers for $5.75.

Payment: Pays 1-2 contributor's copies.

Terms: Acquires first North American serial rights. Returns rights to author after publication, but reserves the right to reprint in an anthology or any future special collection of Seven Buffaloes Press.

Advice: "Buy a copy to get a feel of the professional quality of the writing. Know the theme of a particular issue. Some contributors have 30 years experience as writers; most 15 years. Age does not matter; quality does."

VALLEY WOMEN'S VOICE, Feminist Newsjournal, (II, IV), 321 Student Union, University of Massachusetts, Amherst MA 01002. (413)545-2436. Contact: Carol McMaster.Newspaper: 16 pages. "Feminist analysis, feminist poetry, stories, health articles, revolution-visionary-action oriented, interviews, book reviews, music/art reviews, profiles and ideas for ongoing columns." For women readers. Monthly. Estab. 1979. Circ. 5,000.

Needs: Ethnic, feminist, lesbian, prose poem, spiritual, women's sports. Any subject "as long as it is feminist—especially news and feature articles. Photos with ms a plus." Plans special summer fiction issue (possible). Receives 3-10 mss/month. Publishes new writers regularly. New women writers encouraged to send their best work. Length: no more than five pages. "Fiction accepted up to 20 pages, but the longer it is, the harder it is for us to print it. Please, double spaced." Also publishes literary essays, literary criticism, poetry.

How to Contact: Send complete ms with cover letter. "Cover letter should include short biographical statement which provides a context for work submitted." SASE. Simultaneous and reprint submissions OK. Sample copy $1. Reviews novels and short story collections.

Payment: Pays 1 contributor's copy.

‡VANDELOECHT'S FICTION MAGAZINE, (I), P.O. Box 515, Montross VA 22520. Editor: Mike Vandeloecht. Magazine: 8½ × 11; 40 pages; 20 lb. bond paper; 67 lb. color cover; b&w illustrations. "Eclectic in nature." Quarterly. Estab. 1991.

Needs: Adventure, experimental, fantasy (science fantasy), horror, humor/satire, literary, mainstream/contemporary, mystery/suspense (cozy), psychic/supernatural/occult, regional, romance (contemporary), science fiction (hard science, soft/sociological), sports, westerns (traditional). Publishes annual special fiction issue or anthology. Receives 20 unsolicited mss/month. Acquires 60 mss/issue; 240 mss/year. Publishes ms 3 months after acceptance. Recently published work by Logan McNeil, Hampton Creed, D.F. Lewis, Anke Kriske. Length: 1,000 words preferred; 5 words minimum; 2,500 words maximum. Publishes short shorts. Also publishes poetry. Always critiques or comments on rejected mss.

How to Contact: Send complete ms with cover letter. Should include estimated word count, bio (1 paragraph), Social Security number, list of publications. Reports in 1 week. Send SASE for reply, return of ms or send a disposable copy of the ms. No simultaneous submissions. Sample copy for $2. Fiction guidelines for SASE.

Payment: Pays 1 contributor's copy.

Terms: Acquires first North American serial rights. Send SASE for information.

Advice: Looks for "the uniqueness of the writer's voice. Be honest and don't quit."

‡VeriTales®, Short Stories with a Ring of Truth, (II), Fall Creek Press, P.O. Box 1127, Fall Creek OR 97438. (503)744-0938. Editor: Helen Wirth. Trade Paperback Anthologies: 5½ × 8½; 192 pages; recycled, uncoated 50-70 lb. paper; 10 pt C1S recycled cover; illustrations. "Description of a veri-tale: Through a well-developed and forward-moving short story, the reader is sensitized to an opportunity for spiritual growth. Fiction with substance, for 'thinking' adults." Publishes 2 titles/year with varying publication dates. Estab. 1993.

Needs: Adventure, condensed novel, ethnic/multicultural, experimental, fantasy (science fantasy, sword and sorcery), feminist, gay, historical, humor/satire, lesbian, literary, mainstream/contemporary, mystery/suspense (private eye/hard-boiled, amateur sleuth, cozy, romantic suspense), psychic/supernatural/occult, regional, religious/inspirational, romance (contemporary, gothic, historical), science fiction (hard science, soft/sociological), senior citizen/retirement, sports, translations, westerns (traditional, adult western, frontier)."We publish exclusively anthologies of short stories which meet the criteria of VeriTales." Receives 40-60 unsolicited mss/month. Buys 8-15 mss/issue; 16-30 mss/year. Publishes ms a maximum of 3 years after acceptance. Recently published work by William Luvaas, Ron Suppa, John Vorhaus, Terry Wolverton. Length: 9,000 words maximum. Publishes short shorts. Sometimes critiques or comments on rejected mss.
How to Contact: Query first; request author guide; enclose #10 SASE; identify where you learned of Fall Creek Press. "After reviewing author guide, submit disposable copy of entire ms with estimated word count and SASE for reply. Reports in 1 month. Simultaneous submissions OK. Samples of our trade paperbacks will be available at list price + shipping."
Payment: Pays royalties and 1 contributor's copy. Additional copies 40% discount from list.
Terms: Buys all rights. Sends galleys to author.
Advice: Looks for "short stories that 'go somewhere.' The protagonists are not the same people at the end that they were at the beginning. They may not be acting differently, but they are thinking differently, because of the experience contained within the story. We look for stories that address a new subject or that apply a new treatment to an old subject, frequently ending with an unexpected 'twist.' All stories must affirm or imply an element of hope."

VERVE, (II), P.O. Box 3205, Simi Valley CA 93093. Editor: Ron Reichick. Fiction Editor: Marilyn Hochheiser. Magazine: Digest-sized, 40 pages, 70 lb. paper, 80 lb. cover, cover illustrations or photographs. "Each issue has a theme." Quarterly. Estab. 1989. Circ. 700.
Needs: Contemporary, experimental, fantasy, humor/satire, literary, mainstream, prose poem. No pornographic material. Upcoming themes: "Letters From Home" (deadline: Feb. 15, 1993); "Counterclockwise" (deadline: May 15, 1993); "Close Encounters" (deadline: August 15, 1993); "Growing Pains" (deadline: November 15, 1993). Receives 100 unsolicited fiction mss/month. Accepts 4-6 mss/issue; 16-24 mss/year. Publishes ms 2 months after acceptance. Length: 1,000 words maximum. Publishes short shorts. Also publishes literary criticism, poetry.
How to Contact: "Request guidelines before submitting manuscript." Reports 4-6 weeks after deadline. SASE. Simultaneous submissions OK. Sample copy for $3.50. Fiction guidelines for #10 SAE and 1 first-class stamp. Reviews short story collections.
Payment: Pays in contributor's copies.
Terms: Acquires one-time rights.

VIDEOMANIA, The Video Collectors Newspaper, (I, II), LegsOfStone Publishing Co., Box 47, Princeton WI 54968. (414)295-4377. Editor: Bob Katerzynske. Tabloid; 10½×16; 32+ pages; newsprint paper; ground wood cover; b&w/color illustrations and photographs. "Slanted towards the home entertainment buff, individuals with a *real* interest in home video and entertainment. Publishes *anything* we feel is of interest to our readers—fiction and non-fiction. Audience is mostly male (90%), but female readership is always increasing." Bimonthly. Estab. 1982. Circ. 5-6,000.
• Tagged to the bottom of *Videomania*'s listing this year was an emphatic note, which reads in part, "We have enough poems. We don't need any more poems. Poems are laying all over the floor . . . No more poetry, please . . . " Poets take note.
Needs: Movie-related themes. Experimental, fantasy, feminist, horror, humor/satire, lesbian, mainstream, science fiction (soft/sociological), video/film. Receives 3-4 unsolicited mss/month. Buys 1-2 mss/issue; 6-9 mss/year. Publishes ms 2-6 months after acceptance. Length: 800 words maximum; 500 words minimum. Publishes short shorts. Length: 500 words. Sometimes critiques rejected mss and recommends other markets.
How to Contact: Send complete ms with cover letter. No simultaneous submissions. Reports in 1-2 months. SASE. Sample copy for $2.50, 9×12 SAE and $1 postage. Fiction guidelines for #10 SAE and 1 first class stamp.
Payment: Pays $2.50 token payment in certain cases; contributor's copies.
Terms: Pays on publication for all rights or as writer prefers.
Advice: "If the editor likes it, it's in. A good manuscript should not be too heavy; a *touch* of humor goes a long way with us. Don't expect to get rich off of us. On the other hand, we're more willing than other publications to look at the first-time, non-published writer. We've published established writers in the past that wanted to use our publication as sort of a sounding board for something experimental."

Close-up

Kimberly Willardson
Editor
The Vincent Brothers Review

A bit of mystery surrounds *The Vincent Brothers Review*. When asked about the name, editor Kimberly Willardson replies: "We want to keep it a secret ... as long as the Vincent Brothers remain secret, the magazine will be a success." Since its founding in Ohio in 1988 this has been true, as the magazine has achieved worldwide circulation and a place on *Writer's Digest* magazine's list of 50 top fiction markets.

There is, however, little mystery in the editorial philosophy of the magazine. Willardson's goal is: "to encourage, support, and promote creative writers." As part of this mission, she tries to comment on and critique every work she receives. She solicits submissions from "writers dedicated to practicing the craft of fiction [writing]." This does not mean only those who have long lists of publishing credits, Willardson says. "We work with new writers, but new writers have to meet our standards, which are pretty high."

The inspiration for publishing the magazine came in 1987 when Willardson attended a conference on small literary magazines. She met several editors of other magazines and "was struck by the energy and dedication of these crazy people." She has never regretted her role as editor and calls it "the perfect job—it makes me aware of what people are writing currently and helps me with my own writing."

The Vincent Brothers Review publishes poetry, prose, essays and book reviews three times yearly. Two of these issues have themes brainstormed by Willardson and her two co-editors. Most recently, the fall '92 issue focused on superstition and the supernatural. The spring '93 issue "will be dedicated to Ohio—submissions that center around Ohio legends—rumors, gossip and history," says Willardson. The deadline is April 15, 1993.

Willardson has a loose set of guidelines which govern her choice of materials to publish. "The main thing we look for is knowing that the writer has control of the story—that they're aware of all aspects of the story: Every word is chosen carefully; point of view is maintained; characters are believable enough so that we would know them if we met them," she says. But the fundamental requirements are that the piece "reveals some aspect of life we've taken for granted or never considered before" and that "we are haunted by a story. We are thinking about it long after it is put down."

As final advice, she says: "Study the market—it will help focus your writing as well as support the work of your peers."

—David G. Tompkins

‡VIET NAM GENERATION, A Journal of Recent History & Contemporary Issues, (II, IV), 2921 Terrace Dr., Chevy Chase MD 20815. (301)608-0622. Fax: (301)608-0761. Editor: Kalí Tal. Magazine: 8½×11; 120-140 pages; 60 lb. white offset paper; 65 lb. Vellum Bristol cover; line art illustrations; half-tone photographs. "Full coverage of the tumultuous events of the 1960s and 1970s requires an interdisciplinary approach. Since our first issue we have offered our readers a rich and diverse mixture of academic writing, new fiction and poetry, political analyses, personal narrative and review essays." Quarterly. Estab. 1989. Circ. 400.
Needs: "Must be related to 1960s or Viet Nam War or veterans issues." Ethnic/multicultural, experimental, feminist, gay, lesbian, literary, translations. No children's, sports, psychic. "We are always interested in the subjects of race, class and gender as they relate to the Viet Nam War, the 1960s and veterans issues." Publishes annual special fiction issue or anthology. Receives 10-15 mss/month. Acquires 5-10 mss/issue; 30-35 mss/year. Usually publishes ms 4-6 months after acceptance. Recently published work by W.D. Ehrhart, Wayne Karlin, David A. Willson, Nguyen Huy Thiep. Length: open. Publishes short shorts. Also publishes literary essays, literary criticism and poetry. Always critiques or comments on rejected mss.
How to Contact: Send complete ms with cover letter. Should include one-paragraph bio and list of publications. Reports in 2 weeks on queries; 2 months on mss. Send SASE for reply, return of ms or send a disposable copy of the ms. Simultaneous, reprint (sometimes) and electronic submissions OK. Sample copy for $8. Reviews novels and short story collections.
Payment: Pays 2 contributor's copies. Additional copies at cost.
Terms: Acquires certain reprint rights.
Advice: "We look first for strong prose style, then for interesting treatments of the Viet Nam War or the 1960s. An unusual perspective helps. Sample topics include: counterculture, antiwar movement, women's movement, black liberation movement, veterans readjustment, American Indian movement, Viet Nam War narratives."

THE VILLAGE IDIOT, (II), Mother of Ashes Press, Box 66, Harrison ID 83833-0066. Editor: Joe M. Singer. Magazine: 48 pages; illustrations; photos.
Needs: "A good read—stories, essays, articles, some poetry."
How to Contact: Send complete ms with SASE. No simultaneous submissions. Reports within 1 month. Sample copy $3. Reviews novels and short story collections. Send books to Art Droll.
Payment: Pays 2 contributor's copies.
Terms: Acquires one-time rights (copyright for author).

THE VILLAGER, (I,II), 135 Midland Ave., Bronxville NY 10707. (914)337-3252. Editor: Amy Murphy. Fiction Editor: Mrs. Anton Tedesko. Magazine: 28-40 pages. "Magazine for a family audience." Publishes monthly, but for 9-months only—October-June. Estab. 1928. Circ. 1,000.
Needs: Adventure, historical, humor/satire, literary, prose poem, romance (historical), mystery/suspense. Length: Open. Publishes short shorts. Also publishes poetry.
How to Contact: Send complete ms with cover letter. SASE. Sample copy for $1.25.
Payment: Pays 2 contributor's copies.

THE VINCENT BROTHERS REVIEW, (II), Vincent Brothers Publishing, 4566 Northern Circle, Mad River Twp., Dayton OH 45424. Editor: Kimberly Willardson. Magazine: 5½×8½; 64-84 pages; 60 lb. white coated paper; 60 lb. Oxford (matte) cover; b&w illustrations and photographs. "We publish two theme issues per year. Writers must send SASE for information about upcoming theme issues. Each issue of *TVBR* contains poetry, b&w art, at least 3 short stories and usually 1 book review. For a mainstream audience looking for an alternative to the slicks." Triannually. Estab. 1988. Circ. 400.
● Ranked #37 on the 1992 *Writer's Digest* Fiction 50 list, *Vincent Brothers Review* has also received grants from the Ohio Arts Council for the last four years. An interview with the editor appears in this book.
Needs: Adventure, condensed/excerpted novel, contemporary, ethnic, experimental, feminist, historical (general), humor/satire, literary, mainstream, mystery/suspense (private eye, amateur sleuth, cozy), prose poem, regional, science fiction (soft/sociological), senior citizen/retirement, serialized novel, translations, western (traditional, adult, frontier). "We don't like to exclude any category—we might very much enjoy a fantasy (or western) story if it is well crafted. We focus on the way the story is presented rather than the genre of the story. No racist, sexist, fascist, etc. work." Upcoming theme: Issue #15 theme is "Ohio Legends, Folklore, History" (deadline: April 15, 1993). Send SASE for themes. Receives 120-150 unsolicited mss/month. Buys 3-5 mss/issue; 9-15 mss/year. Publishes ms 2-4 months after acceptance. Recently published work by Janice Levy, James S. Dorr and Constance

Garcia-Barrio. Length: 2,500 words average; 300 words minimum; 3,500 words maximum. Publishes short shorts. Length: 300-1,000 words. Also publishes literary essays, literary criticism, poetry. Often critiques rejected mss and sometimes recommends other markets.

How to Contact: Send complete ms with cover letter. Include Social Security number. "Include previous publications; if the manuscript should be returned (SASE must be included) or if the manuscript is photocopied." Simultaneous submissions OK, but not preferred. Reports in 3-4 weeks on queries; 4-8 months on mss. SASE. Sample copy $4.50. Fiction guidelines for #10 SAE and 1 first class stamp. Reviews novels and short story collections.

Payment: Pays $10 minimum and 2 contributor's copies. Charge (discounted) for extras.

Terms: Buys one-time rights.

Advice: "We are average readers—we want to be hooked immediately and rendered unable to put the story down until we've read the last word of it. I strongly recommend that writers read a sample copy *before* submitting stories to us. Blindly submitting stories to *any* magazine address is a foolish habit for a writer to have. It is part of the writer's job to study the market."

VINTAGE NORTHWEST, (I, IV), Northshore Senior Center (Sponsor), Box 193, Bothell WA 98041. (206)487-1201. Editor: Margie Brons. Magazine: 7×8½; 64 pages; illustrations. "We are a senior literary magazine, published by and for seniors. All work done by volunteers except printing." For "all ages who are interested in our seniors' experiences." Published winter and summer. Estab. 1980. Circ. 500.

● *Vintage Northwest* received the Sage Walker Merit Award for helping senior writers in 1992.

Needs: Adventure, comedy, condensed novel (1,000 words maximum), fantasy, historical, humor/satire, inspirational, mystery/suspense, poetry, senior citizen/retirement, western (frontier). No religious or political mss. Upcoming themes: "Travel and Adventure" (Summer 1993); "Recording Only the Sunny Hours" (Winter 1993). Receives 2-3 unsolicited mss/month. Accepts 2 mss/issue. Published work by Dave Kneeshaw, Sylvia Tacker; published new writers within the last year. Length: 1,000 words maximum. Also publishes literary essays. Occasionally critiques rejected mss.

How to Contact: Send complete ms. SASE. Simultaneous and previously published submissions OK. Reports in 3-6 months. Sample copy $2.50. Fiction guidelines with SASE.

Payment: Pays 1 contributor's copy.

Advice: "Our only requirement is that the author be over 50 or physically handicapped when submission is written."

VIRGIN MEAT, (I), 2325 W.K 15, Lancaster CA 93536. (805)722-1758. Editor: Steve Blum. Digest: 5×8½; 26 pages. Published "about once every 3 months." Estab. 1987. Circ. 350.

Needs: Horror. Receives 3-4 mss/day. Length: 2,000 words maximum. Also publishes poetry.

How to Contact: Send complete ms with cover letter. Reports in 1 week. Simultaneous and reprint submissions OK. Sample copy $2. Reviews novels and short story collections.

Payment: Pays in contributor's copies.

Terms: Acquires one-time rights. Publication not copyrighted.

Advice: "Horror fiction should be horrific all the way through, not just at the end. Avoid common settings, senseless violence and humor."

VIRGINIA QUARTERLY REVIEW, (III), One West Range, Charlottesville VA 22903. (804)924-3124. Editor: Staige Blackford. "A national magazine of literature and discussion. A lay, intellectual audience, people who are not out-and-out scholars but who are interested in ideas and literature." Quarterly. Estab. 1925. Circ. 4,500.

Needs: Literary, contemporary, feminist, romance, adventure, humor, ethnic, serialized novels (excerpts) and translations. "No pornography." Buys 3 mss/issue, 20 mss/year. Length: 3,000-7,000 words.

How to Contact: Query or send complete ms. SASE. No simultaneous submissions. Reports in 2 weeks on queries, 2 months on mss. Sample copy $5.

Payment: Pays $10/printed page. Offers Emily Clark Balch Award for best published short story of the year.

Terms: Pays on publication for all rights. "Will transfer upon request."

Advice: "Because of the competition, it's difficult for a nonpublished writer to break in."

VISION, Science Fiction Magazine, (II), 561 Dalton Way, Goleta CA 93117. Editor: Steven B. Joy. Fiction Editor: Roy Smith. Magazine: 5¼×8½; 38 pages; bond paper; ledger cover; b&w illustrations. "Sci-Fi in 2,000 words or less." Bimonthly. Estab. 1989.

Needs: Adventure, experimental, fantasy, prose poem, science fiction. No sex, violence, war, horror. Receives 30 unsolicited mss/month. Buys 10-13 mss/issue; 72 mss/year. Publishes ms 2-4 months after acceptance. Agented fiction 1%. Recently published work by Herb Kauderer. Length: 2,000 words preferred; 100 words minimum; 3,000 words maximum. Publishes short shorts. Also publishes poetry. Sometimes critiques rejected mss and recommends other markets.
How to Contact: Send complete ms with cover letter. Include "age, some credits, name of story, word count, where you learned of *VISION*." Reports in 2-3 weeks on queries; 3-4 weeks on ms. SASE. Simultaneous and reprint submissions OK. Sample copy for $1.75 and 6×9 SAE with 53¢ postage. Fiction guidelines for #10 SAE and 1 first class stamp.
Payment: Pays $15 maximum, contributor's copies, charges $1 for extras.
Terms: Pays on publication for one-time rights. Sends galleys to author.
Advice: Looks for "1. A good ending; 2. Cause an emotion; 3. Was thought provoking. Our magazine is primarily dedicated to the short, short science fiction story. We are looking for mss from new authors who are especially interested in stories about robots, technology, the future, aliens, bioengineering, computers, cyber-punk, space travel, tear-jerkers, time travel, and science fiction art."

‡WAGONS OF STEEL MAGAZINE, (II, IV), P.O. Box 1435, Vason WA 98070. Editor: Gaffo Jones. Fiction Editor: Natalie Kosovac. Newsletter: 6×4. "A magazine of humor and satire with an emphasis on the station wagon. Anecdotes, essays, fiction, photos, comics for mostly Seattle-area collegians and young urbanites. Quarterly. Estab. 1990. Circ. 500.
Needs: Adventure, erotica, experimental, fantasy (automotive), horror, humor/satire, psychic/supernatural/occult. Receives 50 mss/month. Buys 3 mss/issue; 12 mss/year. Recently published B.B. Cunningham, Doug Ingle. Length: open. Publishes short shorts. Also publishes poetry. Sometimes critiques rejected mss.
How to Contact: Send complete ms with a cover letter. Should include very short bio. Reports in 4-6 weeks on manuscripts. Send SASE (IRC) for reply, return of ms or send a disposable copy of the ms. Simultaneous submissions OK. Sample copy $3 and postage. Fiction guidelines for #10 SAE.
Payment: Pays 1 contributor's copy; additional copies $2.
Terms: Acquires first rights.
Advice: Looks for "originality, humor, irreverance, a basic understanding of what we're trying to do here."

WASHINGTON REVIEW, (II, IV), Friends of the Washington Review of the Arts, Box 50132, Washington DC 20091. (202)638-0515. Fiction Editor: Jeff Richards. "We publish fiction, poetry, articles and reviews on all areas of the arts. We have a particular interest in the interrelationships of the arts and emphasize the cultural life of the DC area." Readership: "Artists, writers and those interested in cultural life in this area." Bimonthly. Estab. 1975. Circ. 10,000.
Needs: Literary. Accepts 1-2 mss/issue. Receives approximately 50-100 unsolicited fiction mss each month. Length: Prefers 3,000 words or less. Critiques rejected mss when there is time.
How to Contact: Send complete ms with SASE. Reports in 2 months. Publishes ms an average of 6 months after acceptance. Copy for tabloid-sized SASE and $2.50.
Payment: Pays contributor's copies plus small payment whenever possible.
Terms: Pays on publication for first North American serial rights.
Advice: "Edit your writing for redundant adjectives. Make sure everything makes sense: the plot, character, motivation. Try to avoid clichés."

WEBSTER REVIEW, (II), Webster Review, Inc., Webster University, 470 E. Lockwood, Webster Groves MO 63119. (314)432-2657. Editor: Nancy Schapiro. Magazine: 5×8; 120 pages; 60 lb. white paper; 10pt. C1S; cover illustrations and photographs. "Literary magazine, international, contemporary. We publish many English translations of foreign fiction writers for academics, writers, discriminating readers." Annually. Estab. 1974.
Needs: Contemporary, literary, translations. No erotica, juvenile. Receives 100 unsolicited mss/month. Accepts 3-5 mss/issue; 6-10 mss/year. Publishes ms one year or more after acceptance. Agented fiction less than 1%. Published work by David Williams and Anjana Appachana. Publishes short shorts. Sometimes critiques rejected mss.
How to Contact: Send complete manuscript with cover letter. Reports in 2-4 months on mss. SASE. Simultaneous submissions OK. Sample copy for 6×9 SAE and 2 first class stamps.
Payment: Pays contributor's copies.
Terms: Acquires first rights.

WEIRDBOOK, (II), Box 149, Amherst Branch, Buffalo NY 14226. (716)839-2415. Editor: W. Paul Ganley. Magazine: 8½×11; 64 pages; self cover; illustrations. "Latter day 'pulp magazine' along the lines of the old pulp magazine *Weird Tales*. We tend to use established writers. We look for an audience of fairly literate people who like good writing and good characterization in their fantasy and horror fiction, but are tired of the clichés in the field." Semiannually. Estab. 1968. Circ. 1,000.
Needs: *Presently overstocked. Inquire first.* Psychic/supernatural, fantasy, horror and gothic (not modern). No psychological horror; mystery fiction; physical horror (blood); traditional ghost stories (unless original theme); science fiction; swords and sorcery without a supernatural element; or reincarnation stories that conclude with 'And the doctor patted him on ... THE END!' " Buys 8-12 mss/issue. Length: 15,000 words maximum. Also publishes poetry. Sometimes recommends other markets.
How to Contact: Send complete ms with SASE. Reports in 3 months on mss. Sample copy $6.80. Guidelines for #10 SASE.
Payment: Pays 1¢/word minimum and 1 contributor's copy.
Terms: Pays on publication ("part on acceptance only for solicited mss") for first North American serial rights plus right to reprint the entire issue.
Advice: "Read a copy and then some of the best anthologies in the field (such as DAW's 'Best Horror of the Year,' Arkham House anthologies, etc.) Occasionally we keep mss longer than planned. When sending a SASE marked 'book rate' (or anything not first class) the writer should add 'Forwarding Postage Guaranteed.' "

‡WEST, (II), Bluestone Press, P.O. Box 1186 Hampshire College, Amherst MA 01002. Editors: J. Horoschak, J.Beckman. Magazine: 5½×8½; 150 pages; laid or equivalent paper; 80 lb. matte cover; illustrations; photographs. "We consider traditional as well as 'avant-garde' material, including pictorial essays, artist's books, letters, artwork, etc. Audience is mostly writers, but also a substantial number of institutions plus libraries." Quarterly. Estab. 1990. Circ. 200.
Needs: Condensed novel, erotica, ethnic/multicultural, experimental, feminist, gay, historical, humor/ satire, lesbian, literary, mainstream/contemporary, regional, translations. "We accept submissions of any style, but do not frequently publish genre fiction." List of upcoming themes available for SASE. Publishes special fiction issue or anthology. Receives 60 unsolicited mss/month. Acquires 5 mss/issue; 20 mss/year. Publishes ms usually 1 month after acceptance. Agented fiction 5%. Recently published work by Alice Mattison, Louise Blum, Paul Beckman. Length: 2,000-3,000 words preferred. Publishes short shorts. Also publishes literary essays, literary criticism and poetry. Sometimes critiques or comments on rejected mss.
How to Contact: Send complete ms with cover letter. Should include one-paragraph bio, list of publications. Reports in 1 month on queries; 3 months on mss. Send SASE for reply, return of ms or send a disposable copy of ms. Simultaneous and electronic submissions OK. Sample copy for $6. Fiction guidelines for #10 SASE.
Payment: Pays 2 contributor's copies.
Terms: Acquires first North American serial rights. Sponsors annual fiction contest. Write for entry guidelines, include SASE.
Advice: "In general, we look for fiction that combines a compelling theme with control of language. Manuscripts that challenge traditional formats or uses of language stand out. However, we do always respect a well-written piece in a more traditional vein."

WEST BRANCH, (II), Bucknell Hall, Bucknell University, Lewisburg PA 17837. Editors: K. Patten and R. Taylor. Magazine: 5½×8½; 96-120 pages; quality paper; illustrations; photos. Fiction and poetry for readers of contemporary literature. Biannually. Estab. 1977. Circ. 500.
Needs: Literary, contemporary, prose poems and translations. No science fiction. Accepts 3-6 mss/ issue. Recently published work by Chuck Martin, David Milofsky, Sharon Sheehe Stark; published new writers within the last year. No preferred length.
How to Contact: Send complete ms with cover letter, "with information about writer's background, previous publications, etc." SASE. No simultaneous submissions. Reports in 6-8 weeks on mss. Sample copy $3.
Payment: Pays 2 contributor's copies and one-year subscription; cover price less 25% discount charge for extras.
Terms: Acquires first rights.
Advice: "Narrative art fulfills a basic human need—our dreams attest to this—and storytelling is therefore a high calling in any age. Find your own voice and vision. Make a story that speaks to your own mysteries. Cultivate simplicity in form, complexity in theme. Look and listen through your characters."

WEST
ISSUE #6 SPRING 1992

"The idea of West is to publish work that is seeking new ground and working to create and uncover," says Editor Joshua Saul Beckman. "We felt that this image of Harry Houdini as a child was interesting and intriguing. All his life Houdini embraced and created mystery. This search and creation of mystery is what made him grow and expand. The same is often true for writers," he says. "We publish fiction from one sentence long to one hundred pages long, that is, we publish one novella or group of short stories each year through our annual fiction contest." Beckman says the cover image was "appropriated and redrawn by us from an uncopyrighted image by Louis Glanzman."

WESTVIEW, A Journal of Western Oklahoma, (I, II), Southwestern Oklahoma State University, 100 Campus Dr., Weatherford OK 73096-3098. (405)774-3077. Editor: Dr. Leroy Thomas. Magazine: 8½ × 11; up to 44 pages; 24 lb. paper; slick cover; illustrations and photographs. "Various themes for people who like nostalgia." Quarterly. Estab. 1981. Circ. 800.

● The editor was recently inducted into the Western Oklahoma Historical Society Hall of Fame for his work on *Westview*.

Needs: Experimental, historical (general), literary, mainstream, western. "The subject must be Western Oklahoma—west of Interstate 35." Upcoming themes: All Western Oklahoma—"Lawmen and Outlaws" (Spring 1993); "Feast" (Summer 1993); "Farmhouses" (Winter 1993); "Youth" (Spring 1994); "Flora and Fauna" (Summer 1994). Receives 2-5 unsolicited mss/month. Accepts 10 ms/issue; 40 mss/year. Publishes ms 1 month-2 years after acceptance. Published work by Orv Owens, Leroy Thomas and Margie Snowden North. Length: 2,000 words average; 1,000 words minimum; 3,000 words maximum. Publishes short shorts. Length: 400 words. Also publishes literary essays, literary criticism, poetry. Always critiques rejected mss and sometimes recommends other markets.

How to Contact: Query first. Reports in 3 weeks on queries. SASE. Simultaneous submissions OK. Sample copy for $4 and 9 × 12 SAE. Fiction guidelines for #10 SAE and 1 first class stamp. Reviews novels and short story collections.

Payment: Pays contributor's copies.

Terms: Acquires first rights.

Advice: "Write for a copy of our stylesheet and for our list of themes for future issues. Don't neglect the SASE."

WHETSTONE, (II), English Dept., University of Lethbridge, Lethbridge, Alberta T1K 3M4 Canada. (403)329-2367. Contact: Professor Martin Oordt. Magazine: approximately 6 × 9; 48-64 pages; superb-ond paper; photos. Magazine publishing "poetry, prose, drama, prints, photographs and occasional music compositions for a university audience." Twice yearly. Estab. 1971. Circ. 500.

Needs: Experimental, literary and mainstream. "Interested in works by native writers/artists. Interested in multi-media works by individuals or collaborators. Yearly writing contest with cash prizes." Upcoming theme: "Typically marginalized writers will be our focus for upcoming season." Receives 1 unsolicited fiction ms/month. Accepts 1-2 ms/issue, 3-4 mss/year. Does not read May through August. Published new writers within the last year. Length: 12 double-spaced pages maximum. Also publishes literary essays, literary criticism, poetry.

How to Contact: Send complete ms with SASE, or SAE with IRC and cover letter with author's background and experience. Simultaneous submissions OK. Reports in 5 months on mss. Publishes ms an average of 3-4 months after acceptance. Sample copy $5 (Canadian) and 7½ × 10½ or larger SAE and 2 Canadian first class stamps or IRCs.

Payment: Pays 2 contributor's copies.
Terms: Acquires no rights.
Advice: "We seek most styles of quality writing. Avoid moralizing."

WHISKEY ISLAND MAGAZINE, University Center 7, Cleveland State University, Cleveland OH 44115. (216)687-2056. Contact: Editor. Editors change each year. Magazine of fiction, poetry, photography with no specific theme. Published 1-2 times/year. Estab. 1978. Circ. 2,500.
Needs: Receives 20-30 unsolicited fiction mss/month. Acquires 3-4 mss/issue. Length: 5,000 words maximum; 2,000-3,000 words average. Also publishes poetry.
How to Contact: Send complete ms with SASE. No simultaneous or previously published submissions. Reports in 2 months on mss. Sample copy $3.
Payment: Pays 2 contributor's copies.
Terms: Acquires one-time rights.
Advice: "Please include brief bio."

WHISPER, (II), (formerly *Helter Skelter*), Scream Press, 509 Enterprise Dr., Rohnert Park CA 94928. Editor: Anthony Boyd. Magazine: 8½×11; 20 pages; 20 lb. paper; 60 lb. cover; illustrations and photographs. "Horror is *not* a theme. *Whisper* is general interest. Audience: youngest reader 11, oldest reader 77—all ages, all professions." Semiannually. Estab. 1987. Circ. 250.
Needs: Adventure, contemporary, fantasy, humor/satire, mystery/suspense, science fiction. "No gore, no porn." Receives 2 unsolicited mss/month. Accepts 1 ms/issue; 2 mss/year. Publishes ms up to 11 months after acceptance. Length: 1,000 words average; 1,200 words maximum.
How to Contact: Send complete ms with cover letter. Include "a short bio, a few publication credits, and anything else I may find interesting. Tell me a joke so I'm in a good mood to read your story." Reports in 1 week on queries; 1 month on mss. SASE. Reprint submissions OK, if stated. No simultaneous submissions. Sample copy for $2.50.
Payment: Pays in contributor's copies.
Terms: Acquires one-time rights.
Advice: "I like a lot of what *Pandora* publishes, good plot, and some strong twists. Looks for neatness, a good cover letter, and appropriateness—I'm not interested in crude, violent drivel, and if the first 2 paragraphs don't get my attention, I send it back."

THE JAMES WHITE REVIEW, A Gay Men's Literary Quarterly, (II, IV), The James White Review Association, 3356 Butler Quarter Station, Minneapolis MN 55403. (612)291-2913. Editor: Collective of 3. Tabloid: 17×26; 16 pages; illustrations; photos. "We publish work by *male* gay writers—any subject for primarily gay and/or gay sensitive audience." Quarterly. Estab. 1983. Circ. 3,500.
 • *The James White Review* won an award for Publisher Service from the Lambda Literary Awards in 1990.
Needs: Contemporary, adventure, experimental, gay, humor/satire, literary, prose poem, translations. No pornography. Upcoming theme: "African American" (June 1993). Receives 50 unsolicited fiction mss/month. Buys 3 mss/issue; 12 mss/year. Publishes ms 3 months or sooner after acceptance. Recently published work by Felice Picano, George Stambolian; published new writers within the last year. Length: 22 pages, double-spaced. Sometimes critiques rejected mss. Recommends other markets "when we can."
How to Contact: Send complete ms with cover letter with short bio. SASE. No simultaneous submissions. Reports in 2-3 months. Sample copy $3. Fiction guidelines $1.
Payment: Pays 3 contributor's copies and $25.
Terms: Buys one-time rights; returns rights to author.
Advice: "We are publishing longer stories and serializing."

WHITE WALL REVIEW, 63 Gould St., Toronto, Ontario M5B 1E9 Canada. Editors change annually. Send mss to "Editors." Magazine: 5¾×8¾; 160 pages; Zephyr Antique paper; soft cover, glossy; two-tone illustrations; b&w photographs. "Book of poetry, prose, art, plays, music and photography. Publishes unknown, international and professional writers. For international audience." Annually. Estab. 1976. Circ. 600.
Needs: "No content 'requirements.' " Must be reasonably short. Nothing "spawning hate, prejudice or obscenity." Accepts 100+ mss/book. Accepts mss from September to 1st week in December of a given year. Published work by Steven Heighton, Robert Hough, Ruth Olsen Latta; published new writers within the last year. Also publishes poetry.

How to Contact: Send complete ms with cover letter. "The cover letter should contain important information about why the writer is submitting to our publication, where he/she saw our information and some biographical information." Reports on mss "when accepted." SASE or SAE and IRC for ms. No simultaneous submissions. Sample copy $8.
Payment: Pays 1 contributor's copy.
Terms: Acquires first or one-time rights.
Advice: "Keep it *short*. We look for creativity but not to the point of obscurity."

‡WICKED MYSTIC, (I, II, IV), P.O. Box 3087, Astoria NY 11103. (718)545-6713. Editor: Andre Scheluchin. Magazine: Digest-sized; 80 pages; 20 lb. paper; 28 lb. cover. "Horror, gothic, gore, vampires, violence, blood, death." Bimonthly. Estab. 1990. Circ. 1,000.
Needs: Erotica, horror, psychic/supernatural/occult, vampires. No romance. Receives 30 unsolicited mss/month. Acquires 10 mss/issue; 60 mss/year. Time between acceptance of the ms and publication varies. Recently published work by Kin Elizabeth, Michael Arnzen, Gregory Nyman, Mark Fewell. Length: 2,000 words preferred; 500 words minimum; 3,000 words maximum. Also publishes literary essays, literary criticism and poetry.
How to Contact: Send complete ms with cover letter. Should include estimated word count, short and basic bio, list of publications. Reports in 2-4 weeks. Send SASE for reply, return of mss or send a disposable copy of the ms. Simultaneous and electronic submissions OK. Sample copy for $4. Free fiction guidelines.
Payment: Pays 1 contributor's copy.
Terms: Acquires first rights.
Advice: Looks for "more originality. Take a topic that either has not been done before or take one that has been done before and give it a new and bizarre twist. I don't like stories that are too predictable."

THE WIDENER REVIEW, (II), Widener University, One University Place, Chester PA 19013. (215)499-4341. Fiction Editor: Michael Clark. Magazine: 5¼ × 8½; 80 pages. Fiction, poetry, essays, book reviews for general audience. Annually. Estab. 1984. Circ. 250.
Needs: Contemporary, experimental, literary, mainstream, regional, serialized/excerpted novel. Receives 15 unsolicited mss/month. Publishes 3-4 mss/issue. Does not read mss in summer. Publishes ms 3-9 months after acceptance. Length: 1,000 words minimum; 5,000 words maximum. Occasionally critiques rejected mss.
How to Contact: Send complete ms with cover letter. Reports in 3 months on mss. Deadline for submission: March 15, notification by June 15. SASE for ms. No simultaneous submissions or reprints. Sample copy $4. Fiction guidelines for #10 SAE and first class stamp.
Payment: Pays 1 contributor's copy; charge for extras.
Terms: Acquires first serial rights.

THE WILLIAM AND MARY REVIEW, (II), P.O. Box 8795, Campus Center, The College of William and Mary, Williamsburg VA 23187-8795. Editor: Stacy Payne. Magazine: 100 pages; graphics; photography. "We publish high quality fiction, poetry, essays, interviews with writers and art. Our audience is primarily academic." Annually. Estab. 1962. Circ. 3,500.
• In 1992 *The William and Mary Review* received second place for literary magazines and an honorable mention for overall excellence from the Society for Collegiate Journalists.
Needs: Literary, contemporary and humor. Receives approximately 90 unsolicited fiction mss each month. Accepts 9 mss/issue. Published work by Paul Wood, W.S. Penn and Dana Gioia; published new writers within the last year. Length: 7,000 words maximum. Also publishes poetry. Usually critiques rejected mss.
How to Contact: Send complete ms with SASE and cover letter with name, address and phone number. "Cover letter should be as brief as possible." Simultaneous submissions OK. Reports in 2 months. Fiction department closed in June, July and August. Sample copy $5. May review novels and short story collections.
Payment: Pays 5 contributor's copies.
Terms: Acquires first rights.
Advice: "We want original, well written stories. Staff requests names be attached separately to individual works. Page allotment to fiction will rise in relation to quality fiction received. The most important aspect of submitting ms is to be familiar with the publication and the types of material it accepts. For this reason, back copies are available."

WILLOW REVIEW, (II), College of Lake County, 19351 West Washington St., Grayslake IL 60030. (708)223-6601 ext. 550 or 555. Editor: Paulette Roeske. Magazine: 6×9; 68-76 pages; 70 lb. paper; 80 lb. cover; b&w illustrations and photographs. "*Willow Review* is nonthematic and publishes short fiction, memoir, poetry, photographs and b&w artwork. For a general andliterary adult audience." Annually. Estab. 1969. Circ. 1,000.
Needs: Contemporary, ethnic, experimental, feminist, historical, humor/satire, literary, prose poem, regional. "There is no bias against an particular subject matter, although there is a clear editorial preference for literary fiction." No "popular genre fiction; children/young adult." Plans special fiction issue. Receives 50 unsolicited mss/month. Buys 7-8 mss/issue. Does not read mss June-August. Accepted mss published in April of each year. Recently published work by Gregory Orr, Lisel Mueller, Joe Breckenridge. Length: 1,500 words minimum; 3,500 words maximum. Publishes short shorts. Length: 500 words. Sometimes comments on rejected mss and recommends other markets.
How to Contact: Send complete ms with cover letter. Include Social Security number, complete mailing address, telephone number, list of several previous publications, other recognition (awards, etc. if applicable). Reports in 1-2 months on mss. SASE (if writer would like it returned). Sample copy for $3. Fiction guidelines for #10 SAE and 1 first class stamp.
Payment: Pays contributor's copies to $100 maximum. All manuscripts are automatically considered for the annual *Willow Review* awards: $100 for first place, $50 for second and $25 for third.
Terms: Pays on publication for first North American serial rights. Not copyrighted.
Advice: "*Willow Review*, because of its 68-76 page length, is forced to make word count a factor although we would publish an exceptional story which exceeds our recommended length. Beyond that, literary excellence is our sole criteria. Perhaps voice, more than any other factor, causes a manuscript to stand out. Study the craft—read the best little magazines, subscribe to them, maintain contact with other writers through writer's groups or informally, attend fiction readings and ask the writers questions in the discussion periods which typically follow, read Eudora Welty's *One Writer's Beginnings* or John Gardner's *On Becoming a Novelist* or Flannery O'Connor on writing fiction or the articles in *Poets & Writers*. Consider writing a discipline, a field of study—it won't kill 'inspiration' or 'creativity' but will augment it to help you write the best story you can write."

WILLOW SPRINGS, (II, III), MS-1, Eastern Washington University, Cheney WA 99004. (509)458-6424. Editor: Nance Van Winckel. Semiannually. Estab. 1977. Circ. 1,000.
Needs: Parts of novels, short stories, literary, prose poems, poems and translations. Receives 70 unsolicited mss/month. Accepts 3-4 mss/issue; 6-8 mss/year. Does not read mss June 1-August 31. Recently published work by Alberto Rios, Alison Baker; published new writers within the last year. Length: 5,000 words maximum. Rarely critiques rejected mss.
How to Contact: Send complete ms with SASE. No simultaneous submissions. Reports in 2-3 months on mss. Publishes ms an average of 1-6 months after acceptance. Sample copy for $4.
Payment: Pays 2 contributor's copies; plus small honorarium.
Terms: Acquires first North American rights.
Advice: "We hope to attract good fiction writers to our magazine, and we've made a commitment to publish four stories per issue. We like fiction that exhibits a fresh approach to language. Our most recent issues, we feel, indicate the quality and level of our commitment."

WISCONSIN ACADEMY REVIEW, (II, IV), Wisconsin Academy of Sciences, Arts & Letters, 1922 University Ave., Madison WI 53705. (608)263-1692. Editor-in-Chief: Faith B. Miracle. Magazine: 8½×11; 48-52 pages; 75 lb. coated paper; coated cover stock; illustrations; photos. "The *Review* reflects the focus of the sponsoring institution with its editorial emphasis on Wisconsin's intellectual, cultural, social and physical environment. It features short fiction, poetry, essays and Wisconsin-related book reviews for well-educated, well-traveled people interested in furthering regional arts and literature and disseminating information about sciences." Quarterly. Estab. 1954. Circ. 2,000.
Needs: Experimental, historical (general), humor/satire, literary, mainstream, prose poem. "Author must have lived or be living in Wisconsin or fiction must be set in Wisconsin." Receives 5-6 unsolicited fiction mss/month. Accepts 1-2 mss/issue; 6-8 mss/year. Published new writers within the last year. Length: 1,000 words minimum; 4,000 words maximum; 3,000 words average. Also publishes poetry; "will consider" literary essays, literary criticism.
How to Contact: Send complete ms with SAE and state author's connection to Wisconsin, the prerequisite. Publishes ms an average of 6-9 months after acceptance. Sample copy $2. Fiction guidelines for SAE and 1 first class stamp. Reviews books on Wisconsin themes.
Payment: Pays 5 contributor's copies.
Terms: Pays on publication for first rights.

THE WISCONSIN RESTAURATEUR, (I, II), Wisconsin Restaurant Association, 125 W. Doty, Madison WI 53703. (608)251-3663. Editor: Jan LaRue. Magazine: 8½×11; 80 pages; 80 lb. enamel cover stock; illustrations; photos. "Published for foodservice operators in the state of Wisconsin and for suppliers of those operations. Theme is the promotion, protection and improvement of the foodservice industry for foodservice workers, students, operators and suppliers." Monthly except December/January combined. Estab. 1933. Circ. 4,200.
Needs: Literary, contemporary, feminist, science fiction (soft/sociological), regional, western, mystery (private eye, amateur sleuth, young adult), adventure, humor, juvenile and young adult. "Only exceptional fiction material used. No stories accepted that put down persons in the foodservice business or poke fun at any group of people. No off-color material. No religious, no political." Buys 1-2 mss/issue, 12-24 mss/year. Receives 15-20 unsolicited fiction mss/month. Length: 500-2,500 words. Critiques rejected mss "when there is time."
How to Contact: Send complete ms with SASE. Simultaneous submissions OK. Reports in 1-2 months. Sample copy for 9×12 SASE. Guidelines for SASE.
Payment: Pays $2.50-$20; contributor's copy; 50¢ charge for extra copy.
Terms: Pays on acceptance for first rights and first North American serial rights.
Advice: "Make sure there is some kind of lesson to be learned, a humorous aspect, or some kind of moral to your story." Mss are rejected because they are not written for the restaurateur/reader.

‡WISCONSIN REVIEW, (II), Box 158, Radford Hall, University of Wisconsin, Oshkosh WI 45901. (414)424-2267. Editor: Valerie Jahns. Editors change every year. Send future submissions to "Fiction Editor." Magazine: 6×9; 60-100 pages; illustrations. Literary prose and poetry. Triquarterly. Estab. 1966. Circ. 2,000.
Needs: Literary and experimental. Receives 30 unsolicited fiction mss each month. Published new writers within the last year. Length: up to 5,000 words. Publishes short shorts. Critiques rejected mss when there is time. Occasionally recommends other markets.
How to Contact: Send complete ms with SASE and cover letter with bio notes. Simultaneous submissions OK. Reports in 2-4 months. Publishes ms an average of 1-2 months after acceptance. Sample copy $2.
Payment: Pays in contributor's copies.
Terms: Acquires first rights.
Advice: "We look for well-crafted work with carefully developed characters, plots and meaningful situations. The editors highly appreciate work of original and fresh thought when considering a piece of experimental fiction."

WITNESS, (II), Oakland Community College, Orchard Ridge Campus, 27055 Orchard Lake Road, Farmington Hills MI 48334. (313)996-5732. Editor: Peter Stine. Magazine: 6×9; 160 pages; 60 lb. white paper; perfect-bound; often illustrations and photos. "Fiction, poetry, essays that highlight the role of the modern writer as witness to the times." Biannually. Estab. 1987. Circ. 3,000.
• *Witness* received an NEA grant in 1992.
Needs: Condensed/excerpted novel, contemporary, experimental, fantasy, feminist, literary and sports. "Alternate special or thematic issues: consult back issues or write for themes." Upcoming theme: "American Humor." Plans to publish a special fiction issue or an anthology in the future. Receives 150 unsolicited mss/month. Buys 10 mss/issue; 40 mss/year. Publishes ms 3 months-1 year after acceptance. Agented fiction 20%. Published work by Joyce Carol Oates, Amy Hempel and Richard Currey. Length: 3,500 words average. Publishes short shorts—500 words. Sometimes critiques rejected mss.
How to Contact: Send complete ms with cover letter. Reports in 3 months on mss. SASE. Simultaneous submissions OK. Accepts electronic submissions. Sample copy $5. Fiction guidelines for #10 SAE and 1 first class stamp.
Payment: Pays $6/page minimum and contributor's copies.
Terms: Pays on publication for first North American serial rights.
Advice: Looks for "intelligence, compassion, lucidity, original voice. *Witness* blends features of literary and issue-oriented magazine and highlights the writer as witness. Alternate special issues (*Holocaust, Writings from Prison, Sixties,* etc.)"

‡THE WITTENBERG REVIEW, An Undergraduate Journal of the Liberal Arts, (I), Wittenberg University, P.O. Box 720, Springfield OH 45501. (513)327-6231. Fax: (513)327-6340. Editor: Professor Richard Veler. Magazine: 6×9; 125 pages; 60 lb. paper; 80 lb. cover; illustrations; photographs. "A national publication of scholarly and creative work by undergraduates for undergraduates and those interested in undergraduate education." Semiannually. Estab. 1990. Circ. 6,000.

Needs: Open. "Each manuscript is considered on its own merits." Receives 3 unsolicited mss/month. Acquires 2 mss/issue; 4 mss/year. Publishes ms 2 months after acceptance. Length: 2,500-3,000 words preferred. Also publishes literary essays, literary criticism and poetry. Often critiques or comments on rejected mss.

How to Contact: Send complete ms with cover letter. Should include estimated word count, one-page bio, Social Security number, list of publications. Reports in 2 weeks. Send SASE for reply, return of ms or send a disposable copy of the ms. Simultaneous, reprint and electronic submissions OK. Sample copy free. Fiction guidelines free.

Payment: Pays in contributor's copies.

Terms: Acquires all rights.

Advice: Work "should exceed a mere synthesis of resources, emphasize author's own insights and demonstrate imagination and creativity." Sponsors contest: "All writers that are published are eligible and anyone who submits a piece is eligible."

‡THE WOLSKE'S BAY STAR, The International Public Newspaper, (II), The Corporation for Public Newspapers, Rt. 1 Box 186-A, Caledonia MN 55921-9801. (507)724-5532. Editor: Francis Nied. Newsletter: 8½×11; 24+ pages; 20 lb. bond paper; illustrations; photographs. "The philosophy is to speak in the positive. Good work is desired. Circulation begins at 1,000 issues and continues to all beings capable of reading printed English." Published irregularly. Estab. 1983. Circ. 1,000.

Needs: Open to all fiction categories. Publishes special fiction issues or anthologies. Recently published work by Johnny Tachyon, Timo III. Publishes short shorts. Also publishes literary essays, literary criticism and poetry. Always critiques or comments on rejected mss.

How to Contact: Query with clips of published work or send complete ms with cover letter. Should include a short bio. Reports in 13 weeks. Send SASE for reply or return of ms or send a disposable copy of ms. Simultaneous submissions OK. Sample copy for $2, 8×10 SAE and 6 first class stamps. Reviews novels and short story collections.

Payment: Pays $15 minimum, subscription to magazine and 5 contributor's copies. Additional copies 50¢ each.

Terms: Pays on acceptance for one-time rights.

Advice: "Truth . . . seek it out . . . tell a story . . . tell truth through/in fiction. Set example for reader."

THE WORCESTER REVIEW, Worcester Country Poetry Association, Inc., 6 Chatham St., Worcester MA 01609. (508)797-4770. Editor: Rodger Martin. Magazine: 6×9; 60-100 pages; 60 lb. white offset paper; 10 pt. C1S cover stock; illustrations and photos. "We like high quality, creative poetry, artwork and fiction. Critical articles should be connected to New England." Semiannually. Estab. 1972. Circ. 1,000.

Needs: Literary, prose poem. "We encourage New England writers in the hopes we will publish at least 30% New England but want the other 70% to show the best of writing from across the US." Receives 10-20 unsolicited fiction mss/month. Accepts 2-4 mss/issue. Publishes ms an average of 6 months to 1 year after acceptance. Agented fiction less than 10%. Published work by Debra Friedman, Carol Glickfeld. Length: 2,000 words average; 1,000 words minimum; 4,000 words maximum. Publishes short shorts. Also publishes literary essays, literary criticism, poetry. Sometimes critiques rejected mss and recommends other markets.

How to Contact: Send complete ms with cover letter. Reports in 2 weeks on queries; 4-5 months on mss. SASE. Simultaneous submissions OK if other markets are clearly identified. Sample copy $4; fiction guidelines free.

Payment: Pays 2 contributor's copies and honorarium if possible.

Terms: Acquires one-time rights.

Advice: "Send only one short story—reading editors do not like to read two by the same author at the same time. We will use only one. We generally look for creative work with a blend of craftsmanship, insight and empathy. This does not exclude humor. We won't print work that is shoddy in any of these areas."

WORDS OF WISDOM, (II), 612 Front St., Glendora NJ 08029-1133. (609)863-0610. Editor: J.M. Freiermuth. Newsletter: 5½×8½; 36-44 pages; copy paper; some illustrations and photographs. "Fiction, satire, humerous poetry and travel for a general audience —90% of readers have B.A." Monthly. Estab. 1981. Circ. 180.

Needs: Adventure, contemporary, ethnic, feminist, historical (general), humor/satire, mainstream, mystery/suspense (private eye, cozy), regional, western (traditional, adult, frontier). No religion, children's, gay, romance. Plans special "All Woman Author" issue (August 1993). Receives 20-30 unsolicited mss/month. Accepts 6-10 mss/issue; 75-100 mss/year. Publishes ms 2-4 months after acceptance. Recently published work by Tim Strong, Don Stockard, Carole Vopat, Linda Raymond. Length: 2,000-3,000 words average; 1,200 words minimum; 7,000 words maximum. Publishes short shorts. Length: "Long enough to develop a good bite." Sometimes critiques rejected mss and recommends other markets.

How to Contact: Send complete manuscript copy and/or DOS floppy with cover letter including "name, address, SASE." Reports in 2-3 weeks on mss. SASE. Simultaneous and reprint submissions OK. Accepts electronic submissions. Sample copy for $1, 6×9 SAE and 75¢ postage. Reviews novels and short story collections.

Payment: Pays subscription to magazine for first publication and contributor's copies for subsequent publications.

Terms: Acquires one-time rights. Publication not copyrighted.

WORDSMITH, (II), Box 891, Ft. Collins CO 80522-0891. Editor: Judith Kaufman. Magazine: Digest-sized; 60-80 pages; 60 lb. paper; glossy cover. Annually. Estab. 1992. Circ. 400.

Needs: Adventure, condensed/excerpted novel, contemporary, ethnic, experimental, fantasy, historical (general), horror, humor/satire, literary, mainstream, mystery/suspense, prose poem, psychic/supernatural/occult, religious/inspirational, romance, science fiction, senior citizen/retirement, serialized novel, sports, western, young adult/teen. "We'll look at almost anything. Please, no gay/lesbian, erotica or porno. There are plenty of publications earmarked for those forms." Buys 4-5 mss/issue. Length: up to 4,000 words. Sometimes critiques rejected mss and recommends other markets.

How to Contact: Send complete ms with cover letter. Include "short bio, credits, (if any)." SASE. No simultaneous submissions. Reports in 1 month. Sample copy for $3. Fiction guidelines for SASE.

Payment: Pays $10 minimum. Cash prize for best story of the issue.

Terms: Pays on publication for one-time rights.

Advice: "Truth strikes us like a hammer. Manuscripts that are poorly prepared, lack spelling skills and punctuation are disqualified to make our editorial task easier. When we read a piece, we want to be amazed. Be it the characters, or the plot, or the rhythm of the words, let us see quality in your work."

‡WORKING CLASSICS (I,II,IV), Red Wheelbarrow Press, 298 Ninth Ave., San Francisco CA 94118. (415)332-0305. Editor: David Joseph. Magazine: 8½×11; 24 pages; 70 lb cover stock; illustrations; photos. Magazine of "creative work, fiction, nonfiction, poetry, interviews, reviews, comics, by and for working people — especially the organized, trade unionists (both rank and file and leadership), artists, leftists, progressives." Semiannually. Plans special fiction issue. Estab. 1982. Circ. 1,000.

Needs: Comics, contemporary, ethnic, experimental, feminist, gay, historical, humor/satire, lesbian, literary, prose poem and regional. No psychic/supernatural/occult, religious/inspirational. Receives 12 unsolicited mss/month. Accepts 2 mss/issue; 4 mss/year. Published the works of Paul Casey and Carrie Jenkins; published new writers within the past year. Length: 2,400 words average; 250 words minimum; 18,000 words maximum. Occasionally critiques rejected mss. Recommends other markets.

How to Contact: Send complete ms. "We're interested in the concrete process involved in your actual conditions. We like to know why you believe your story is for our audience of working people and working writers." Reports in 3 months. SASE. Simultaneous and previously published submissions OK. Accepts disk submissions for IBM or compatible; prefers hard copy with disk submission. Sample copy $3.

Payment: Pays 1 contributor's copy; reduced charge for extras.

Terms: Acquires one-time rights.

Advice: "The recent expansion in the short fiction market seems to have come to a halt. I think it will remain open with room for new developments in fiction. Dirty realism is not the last word in fiction. Yet realism often may be necessary for focusing details taken from observation. The combination of imagination and observation creates the dynamics of short fiction."

WORM, (I), Macronex, 115 Grand St., Brooklyn NY 11211-4123. Fax: (718)782-0747. Editor: Kit Blake. Newsletter: 8½×11; 20 pages; 20 lb. paper; colored paper cover; computer graphics, illustrations and photographs. "Cultural media magazine for a modern audience." Monthly. Estab. 1991.

Needs: Contemporary, erotica, ethnic, experimental, gay, historical, lesbian, literary, science fiction (hard science, soft/sociological, techno). No fantasy, romance, sports. Publishes special fiction issue. Upcoming themes: Exploring the present and potential political power of minor media (i.e. camcorders, indie labels, small press, etc; evolution, both physical and social, in an age of biotechnology and instant communication. Receives 2 unsolicited mss/month. Accepts 1 mss/issue; 12 mss/year. Recently published work by Ian Keldoulis, David Brody. Length: 2,000 words preferred; 300 words minimum; 3,000 words maximum. Publishes short shorts. Length: 300-500 words. Recommends other markets.
How to Contact: Send complete ms with cover letter. Reports in 3 weeks on queries; 1 month on mss. SASE. Simultaneous and reprint submissions OK. Recommends electronic submissions via disk or modem (Mac format preferred). Sample copy for $2.
Payment: Pays contributor's copies.
Terms: Acquires one-time rights. Not copyrighted.
Advice: Looks for "otherworldliness. Make a micro model for a macro world."

THE WORMWOOD REVIEW, (II, IV), P.O. Box 4698, Stockton CA 95204. (209)466-8231. Editor: Marvin Malone. Magazine: 5½×8½; 48 pages; 60 lb. matte paper; 80 lb. matte cover; illustrations. "Concentrated on the prose-poem specifically for literate audience." Quarterly. Estab. 1959. Circ. 700.
Needs: Prose poem. No religious or inspirational. Receives 500-600 unsolicited mss/month. Buys 30-40 mss/issue; 120-160 mss/year. Publishes ms 6-18 months after acceptance. Published work by Charles Bukowski, Dan Lenihan. Length: 300 words preferred; 1,000 words maximum. Critiques or comments on rejected mss.
How to Contact: Send complete ms with cover letter. Reports in 1-2 months. SASE. No simultaneous submissions. Sample copy for $4. Fiction guidelines for #10 SAE and 1 first-class stamp.
Payment: Pays $12-140 or equivalent in contributor's copies.
Terms: Pays on publication for all rights.
Advice: A manuscript that stands out has "economical verbal style coupled with perception and human values. Have something to say—then say it in the most economical way. Do *not* avoid wit and humor."

WRIT MAGAZINE, (II), 2 Sussex Ave., Toronto, Ontario M5S 1J5 Canada. (416)978-4871. Editor: Roger Greenwald. Assoc. Editor: Richard Lush. Magazine: 6×9; 96 pages; Zephyr laid paper; cover stock varies; cover illustrations. "Literary magazine for literate readers interested in the work of new writers." Annually. Publishes occasional special fiction issues. Estab. 1970. Circ. 700.
Needs: Literary, short stories, short shorts, parts of novels, translations. Accepts 10-15 mss/year. Does not read mss May-August. Published fiction by Leon Rooke, Nawal El Saadawi, Michael Stephens; published new writers in the last year. Length: 300-20,000 words. Critiques rejected mss "when there is time. Sometimes recommends other markets."
How to Contact: Send complete ms with SASE (Canadian stamps or IRCs) and brief biographical note on author and/or translator, and a phone number. Translators must send copy of original text. No simultaneous submissions. Reports in 2-3 months. Sample copy $7.50.
Payment: Pays 2 contributor's copies. Negotiates charge for extras.
Terms: Acquires first North American serial rights. Copyright reverts to author.
Advice: "Look at your target magazine before submitting."

WRITERS' FORUM, (II), University of Colorado at Colorado Springs, Colorado Springs CO 80933-7150. Editor: Dr. Alex Blackburn. "Ten to fifteen short stories or self-contained novel excerpts published once a year along with 25-35 poems. Funded by grants from National Endowment for the Arts, Council for Literary Magazines, University of Colorado and others. Highest literary quality only: mainstream, avant-garde, with preference to western themes. For small press enthusiasts, teachers and students of creative writing, commercial agents/publishers, university libraries and departments interested in contemporary American literature." Estab. 1974.
• Work published in *Writer's Forum* appears regularly in *Best of the West, Pushcart Prize* and *Best American Short Stories* anthologies. Ohio University Press and Swallow Press will publish an anthology in late 1993 titled *Higher Elevations: Stories From Writer's Forum.*
Needs: Literary, contemporary, ethnic (Native American, Chicano, not excluding others) and regional (West). No "sentimental, fantasy (sexual, extra-terrestrial), passionless, placeless, undramatized, etc. material." Accepts 10-12 mss/issue. Receives approximately 40 unsolicited fiction mss each month and will publish new as well as experienced authors. Recently published fiction by Robert Olen Butler, Charles Baxter, Gladys Swan; published many new writers within the last year. Length: 1,500-10,000

words. Also publishes literary essays, literary criticism, poetry. Critiques rejected mss "when there is time and perceived merit."

How to Contact: Send complete ms and letter with relevant career information with SASE. Simultaneous submissions OK. Reports in 3-5 weeks on mss. Publishes ms an average of 6 months after acceptance. Sample back copy $7 to *NSSWM* readers. Current copy $10. Check payable to "University Press of Colorado/Writers' Forum."

Payment: Pays 1 contributor's copy. Cover price less 60% discount for extras.

Terms: Acquires one-time rights. Rights revert to author.

Advice: "Read our publication. Be prepared for constructive criticism. We especially seek submissions that show immersion in place (trans-Mississippi West) and development of credible characters. Turned off by slick content. Probably the TV-influenced fiction with trivial dialogue and set-up plot is the most quickly rejected. Our format—a 5½×8½ professionally edited and printed paperback book—lends credibility to authors published in our imprint."

‡**WRITERS' OPEN FORUM, (I),** Bristol Publishing, P.O. Box 516, Tracyton WA 98393. Editor: Sandra E. Haven. Magazine: 5½×8½; 32 pages; slick cover; illustrations. *"Writers' Open Forum* is designed to help writers improve their skills and marketability. We offer information on writing, market listings and print several stories and articles per issue for the expressed purpose of letting other writers critique those pieces. Critiques are both published and mailed on to the originating author." Bimonthly. Estab. 1990.

Needs: Adventure, childrens/juvenile (5-9 years, 10-12 years), fantasy, historical (general), humor/satire, mainstream/contemporary, mystery/suspense, psychic/supernatural/occult, regional, romance (contemporary, young adult), science fiction, senior citizen/retirement, sports, westerns, young adult/teen. "No graphic sex, violence, slice-of-life or wildly experimental formats." Plans special fiction issue or anthology. Buys 4-7 mss/issue; 30-42mss/year. Publishes 4 months after acceptance. Length: 100 words minimum; 2,000 words maximum. Publishes short shorts. Always comments on rejected mss.

How to Contact: Send complete ms with a cover letter. Should include brief bio. Reports in 2 months on mss. Send SASE (IRC) for reply, return of ms or send a disposable copy of the ms. Sample copy #3. Fiction guidelines for #10 SAE and 1 first class stamp.

Payment: Pays $5 minimum plus 2 contributor's copies; additional copies $2.50 each for 1-5, $2 each for 6 or more.

Terms: Pays on acceptance. Acquires first rights.

Advice: "We will not consider any manuscript with graphic sex, violence, or slice-of-life or experimental formats. We prefer stories with a protagonist the reader can care about, a problem to resolve, complications along the way, and a resolution resulting from the protagonist's decision or action. It may be a chapter from a book or journal, but must be so stated in the cover letter and still suit our requirements."

WRITERS' RENDEZVOUS, (I), P.O. Box 105, Sacramento CA 95812. Editor: Karen Campbell. Newsletter: 8½×11; approx. 24 pages; bond paper; no cover; line drawings. "Writer-oriented, publish only work relating to freelance writing and penpalling." Quarterly. Estab. 1986. Circ. 100.

Needs: No fiction "not related to writing/penpalling. No erotica!!" Receives approx. 10 unsolicited fiction mss/month. Publishes approx. 2 mss/issue; approx. 10 mss/year. Publishes ms 6 weeks-1 year after acceptance. Published work by Bettye Griffin, Jan McDaniel, Linda Hutton; published new writers within the last year. Length: 750 words average; 1,500 words maximum. Publishes short shorts. Sometimes comments on rejected mss and recommends other markets. Also publishes literary criticism, poetry.

How to Contact: Send complete ms with cover letter. Reports in 2-3 months. SASE. Simultaneous and reprint submissions OK. Sample copy for $3.50, #10 SAE and 3 first class stamps; fiction guidelines for #10 SAE and 1 first class stamp. Reviews novels and short story collections.

Payment: Pays in contributor's copies.

Terms: Acquires one-time rights. Publication not copyrighted. Sponsors contests for fiction writers. "SASE for guidelines; $2 entry fee. Cash prize."

Advice: "Proofread. Then proofread again. Then ask a friend or teacher to proofread. Use your dictionary—both for spelling and meaning. Read the guidelines carefully. And, if you want cash for your work, be sure you aren't submitting to markets which pay copies. (I've had several acceptances fall through when I advised the author of our non-payment policy)."

XAVIER REVIEW, (I, II), Xavier University, Box 110C, New Orleans LA 70125. (504)486-7411, ext. 7481. Editor: Thomas Bonner, Jr. Magazine of "poetry/fiction/nonfiction/reviews (contemporary literature) for professional writers/libraries/colleges/universities." Semiannually. Estab. 1980. Circ. 500.
Needs: Contemporary, ethnic, experimental, historical (general), literary, Latin-American, prose poem, Southern, religious, serialized/excerpted novel, translations. Receives 30 unsolicited fiction mss/month. Accepts 2 mss/issue; 4 mss/year. Length: 10-15 pages. Occasionally critiques rejected mss.
How to Contact: Send complete ms. SASE. Sample copy $5.
Payment: Pays 2 contributor's copies.

YELLOW SILK: Journal of Erotic Arts, (II), Verygraphics, Box 6374, Albany CA 94706. Editor/Publisher: Lily Pond. Magazine: 8½ × 11; 60 pages; matte coated stock; glossy cover stock; 4-color illustrations; photos. "We are interested in nonpornographic erotic literature: joyous, mad, musical, elegant, passionate. 'All persuasions; no brutality' is our editorial policy. Literary excellence is a priority; innovative forms are welcomed, as well as traditional ones." Quarterly. Estab. 1981. Circ. 16,000.
Needs: Comics, erotica, ethnic, experimental, fantasy, feminist/lesbian, gay, humor/satire, literary, prose poem, science fiction and translations. No "blow-by-blow" descriptions; no hackneyed writing except when used for satirical purposes. Nothing containing brutality. Buys 4-5 mss/issue; 16-20 mss/year. Published work by William Kotzwinkle, Gary Soto, published new writers within the last year. Length: no preference. Occasionally critiques rejected ms.
How to Contact: Send complete ms with SASE and include short, *personal* bio notes. No queries. No pre-published material. No simultaneous submissions. Name, address and phone number on each page. Submissions on disk OK *with* hard copy only. Reports in 3 months on mss. Publishes ms up to 3 years after acceptance. Sample copy $7.50.
Payment: Pays 3 contributor's copies plus minimum of $10 per prose item.
Terms: Pays on publication for all periodical and anthology rights for one year following publication, at which time rights revert back to author; and non-exclusive reprint and anthology rights for the duration of the copyright.
Advice: "Read, read, read! Including our magazine—plus Nabokov, Ntozake Shange, Rimbaud, Virginia Woolf, William Kotzwinkle, James Joyce. Then send in your story! Trust that the magazine/editor will not rip you off—they don't. As they say, 'find your own voice,' then trust it. Most manuscripts I reject appear to be written by people without great amounts of writing experience. It takes years (frequently) to develop your work to publishable quality; it can take many re-writes on each individual piece. I also see many approaches to sexuality (for my magazine) that are trite and not fresh. The use of language is not original, and the people do not seem real. However, the gems come too, and what a wonderful moment that is. Please don't send me anything with blue eye shadow."
submissions OK. Sample copy for $2. Fiction guidelines for #10 SAE and 1 first-class stamp.

YOUNG VOICES MAGAZINE, The Magazine of Young People's Creative Work, (I, II, IV), Box 2321, Olympia WA 98507. (206)357-4863. Editor: Steve Charak. Magazine: "All materials are by elementary through high school students for children and adults interested in children's work." Bimonthly. Estab. 1988. Circ. 1,000.
Needs: Adventure, experimental, historical (general), humor/satire, juvenile (5-18), literary, mainstream, mystery/suspense (young adult), prose poem, and science fiction. "Everything must be written by elementary, middle or high school students. (12th grade is the limit.)" No excessive violence or sexual content. Plans a special fiction issue or an anthology in the future. Receives 100 unsolicited mss/month. Buys 30 mss/issue; 160-200 mss/year. Publishes ms 4-6 months after acceptance. Recently published work by Steven Shetterly and Maren Connolly. Length: 500 words average. Publishes short shorts. Also publishes poetry. Always critiques rejected mss and recommends other markets.
How to Contact: Send complete ms with cover letter. Make sure age, grade and school are in the letter. Simultaneous and reprint submissions OK. Sample copy $3. Fiction guidelines for SASE.
Payment: Pays $3-5 and contributor's copies.
Terms: Pays on acceptance for one-time rights.

ZERO HOUR, "Where Culture Meets Crime," (I, II, IV), Box 766, Seattle WA 98111. (206)621-8829. Editor: Jim Jones. Tabloid: 11 × 16; 36 pages; newsprint paper; illustrations and photos. "We are interested in fringe culture. We publish fiction, poetry, essays, confessions, photos, illustrations, interviews, for young, politically left audience interested in current affairs, non-mainstream music, art, culture." Semiannually. Estab. 1988. Circ. 3,000.

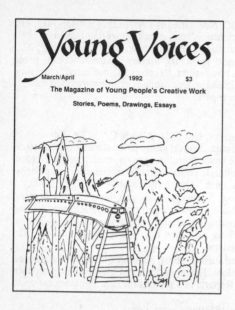

Young Voices

March/April 1992 $3

The Magazine of Young People's Creative Work

Stories, Poems, Drawings, Essays

"I first saw this drawing when I looked at a collection of young people's artwork that was being assembled by a local hospital as a coloring book for the children admitted as patients," Steve Charak, publisher of Young Voices, says of this cover. "I was immediately struck by its perspective." Young Voices provides an outlet for the work of elementary through high school-age youth, he says. This drawing was created by Jeff Spohn, as a fourth grader at L.P. Brown Elementary in Olympia, Washington. "Until now, Young Voices has been about 75 percent fiction, the rest being poetry and reviews. This will change as we look for more young people who wish to write essays and features. Still, fiction will be featured in every issue," Charak says.

Needs: Confessions, erotica, ethnic, experimental, feminist, gay, humor/satire, psychic/supernatural/occult and translations. "Each issue revolves around an issue in contemporary culture: cults and fanaticism, addiction, pornography, etc." No romance, inspirational, juvenile/young, sports. Receives 5 unsolicited mss/month. Accepts 3 mss/issue; 9 mss/year. Publishes ms 2-3 months after acceptance. Published work by Jesse Bernstein and Mike Allmayer. Length: 1,200 words average; 400 words minimum; 1,500 words maximum. Publishes short shorts. Length: 400 words. Also publishes literary essays, literary criticism, poetry. Sometimes critiques rejected mss.

How to Contact: Query first. Reports in 2 weeks on queries; 1 month on mss. SASE. Simultaneous submissions OK. Sample copy $3, 9 × 12 SAE and 5 first class stamps. Fiction guidelines free. Reviews novels and short story collections.

Payment: Pays in contributor's copies.

Terms: Acquires one-time rights. Sends galleys to author.

Advice: "Does it fit our theme? Is it well written, from an unusual point of view or on an unexplored/underexplored topic?"

ZOIKS!, Curdling the Cream of the Mind, (I, II, IV), P.O. Box 33561, Raleigh NC 27636. Editor: Skip Elsheimer. Fiction Editor: David Jordan. Magazine: illustrations and photos. "*Zoiks!* is interested in new ideas and new ways of thinking. Or at least using old ideas in a new way. Exploring the world through innocent absurdism." Plans special fiction issue. Estab. 1986.

Needs: Experimental, humor/satire, psychic/supernatural/occult, translations, underground literature, conspiracy-oriented fiction. "I'm interested in anything that will make you question your surroundings. No fiction that is pretentious, lacking humor." Upcoming themes: "Food—Freud's Other Obsession," "Cartoon's—Morality Plays of Our Time." Receives 2-3 unsolicited mss/month. Accepts 1-2 mss/issue; 6-12 mss/year. Published work by Harrison Nutkins, B.Z. Niditch; published new writers within the last year. Publishes short shorts. Sometimes critiques rejected mss or recommends other markets.

How to Contact: Query first with clips of published work or send complete ms with cover letter, which should include address. Should tell something about the author. Reports in 2 months. Simultaneous and reprint submissions OK. Accepts electronic submissions via Macintosh 800K. Sample copy $1.50. Make checks payable to Skip Elsheimer.

Payment: Pays in contributor's copies; charges for extras at cost plus postage.

Terms: Publication not copyrighted. Work belongs to the author.

Advice: "I feel that magazine fiction is too industry oriented. Everyone should have a shot at getting published. Express *yourself*!"

ZYZZYVA, The Last Word: West Coast Writers and Artists, (II, IV), Suite 1400, 41 Sutter St., San Francisco CA 94104. (415)255-1282. Editor: Howard Junker. Magazine: 6×9; 144 pages; Starwhite Vicksburg smooth paper; graphics; photos. "Literate" magazine. Quarterly. Estab. 1985. Circ. 3,500.
Needs: Contemporary, experimental, literary, prose poem. West Coast writers only. Receives 300 unsolicited mss/month. Buys 5 fiction mss/issue; 20 mss/year. Agented fiction: 10%. Recently published work by Isabel Allende, Dennis Cooper, Elizabeth Tallent; published new writers within the last year. Length: varies. Also publishes literary essays.
How to Contact: Send complete ms. "Cover letters are of minimal importance." Reports in 2 weeks on mss. SASE. No simultaneous submissions or reprints. Sample copy $8. Fiction guidelines on masthead page.
Payment: Pays $50-250.
Terms: Pays on acceptance for first North American serial rights.
Advice: "Keep the faith."

International literary and small circulation magazines

The following is a list of literary and small circulation publications from countries outside the U.S. and Canada that accept or buy short fiction in English (or in the universal languages of Esperanto or Ido).

Before sending a manuscript to a publication in another country, it's a good idea to query first for information on the magazine's needs and methods of submission. Send for sample copies, or try visiting the main branch of your local library, a nearby college library or bookstore to find a copy.

All correspondence to markets outside your own country must include International Reply Coupons, if you want a reply or material returned. You may find it less expensive to send copies of your manuscript for the publisher to keep and just enclose a return postcard with one IRC for a reply. Keep in mind response time is slow for many overseas publishers, but don't hesitate to send a reply postcard with IRC to check the status of your submission. You can obtain IRCs from the main branch of your local post office. The charge for one in U.S. funds is 95¢.

THE ABIKO LITERARY QUARTERLY RAG, 8-1-8 Namiki, Abiko-Shi, Chiba-Ken 270-11 Japan. Tel./Fax: (0471)84-7904. Editor: Anna Livia Plurabelle. Fiction Editor: D.C. Palter. Quarterly. Circ. 500. Publishes 4 stories/issue. "We are a semi-bilingual (Japanese/English) magazine for Japanese and foreigners living in Japan." Needs: contemporary, erotica, experimental, historical, humor, literary, mainstream, regional. Length: 3,000 average; 5,000 maximum. Send entire manuscript with SAE and IRCs. Pays in 5 contributor's copies. "A story submitted in both English and Japanese receives special consideration. I look for strong character development as well as a good plot. Most stories I receive are exclusively character development or plot, but both are necessary to stand a good chance of being published." Follow proper format and submission procedures. Sponsors contest. Write for details. Sample copy for 700 yen plus 300 yen postage.

ACUMEN, 6, The Mount, Furzeham, Brixham, Devon TQ5 8QY England. Fiction Editor: Patricia Oxley. Circ. 700. Semiannual. "Literary magazine with an emphasis on poetry. I use 1-2 short stories/year (2 issues) which are around 1,500 words, have a clear statement and are written in a literary style. Writers paid in extra copies of *Acumen*. Writers receive copies of the issue containing their work. Send sufficient IRCs to cover return postage. Make sure name and address are on manuscript (not just covering letter or, worse still, on outside of envelope.)"

AQUARIUS, Flat 10, Room-A, 116 Sutherland Ave., Maida-Vale, London W9 England. Fiction Editor: Sean Glackin. Editor: Eddie Linden. Circ. 5,000. Publishes five stories/issue. Interested in humor/satire, literary, prose poem and serialized/excerpted novels. "We publish prose and poetry and reviews." Payment is by agreement. "We only suggest changes. Most stories are taken on merit." Price in UK £5 plus postage and packing; in US $18 plus $3 postage. Next issue devoted to women writers.

‡AUGURIES, 48 Anglesey Road, Alverstoke, Gosport, Hampshire P012 2EQ England. Editor: Nik Morton. Circ. 300. Averages 30-40 stories/year. "Science fiction and fantasy, maximum length 4,000 words." Pays £2 per 1,000 words plus complimentary copy. "Buy back issues, then try me!" Sample copy $5. Subscription $20 (4 issues). Member of the New SF Alliance.

CAMBRENSIS, 41 Heol Fach, Cornelly, Bridgend, Mid-Glamorga, CF33 4LN Wales. Editor: Arthur Smith. Quarterly. Circ. 500. "Devoted solely to the short story form, featuring short stories by writers born or resident in Wales/or with some Welsh connection; receives grants from the Welsh Arts' Council and the Welsh Writers' Trust; uses art-work—cartoons, line-drawings, sketches etc." Length: 2,500 words maximum. Writers receive 3 copies of magazine. Writer has to have some connection with Wales. SAE and International Reply Coupon or similar should be enclosed "Air mail" postage to avoid long delay. Send international reply coupon for a sample copy. Subscriptions via Blackwell's Periodicals, P.O. Box 40, Hythe Bridge Street, Oxford, OX1 2EU, UK or Faxon Europe, P.O. Box 297, 10000A D Amsterdam, Holland.

CHAPMAN, 4 Broughton Place, Edinburgh EH1 3RX Scotland. Fiction Editor: Joy Hendry. Quarterly. Circ. 2,000. Publishes 4-6 stories/issue. "Founded in 1970 *Chapman*, Scotland's quality literary magazine, is a dynamic force in Scotland, publishing poetry, fiction, criticism, reviews; articles on theatre, politics. language and the arts." Length: 1,000 words minimum; 6,000 words maximum. Include SAE and return postage (IRCs) with submissions. Pays £8.50/page.Sample copy available for £3.50 (includes postage).

‡CONTRAST, Box 3841, Cape Town 8000 South Africa. Editor: Douglas Reid Skinner. Circ. 750. Averages 6-8 short stories/year. "A literary journal of Southern Africa; emphasis on publishing short stories (max 6,500 words), poetry and literary articles." No payment—contributor's copies sent. "Include self-addressed envelope."

CREATIVE FORUM, Bahri Publications, 997A Gobindpuri Kalkaj, P.O. Box 4453, New Delhi 110019 India. Telephones: 011-6445710, 011-6448606. Fax: 91.11-6460796. Fiction Editor: U.S. Bahri. Circ. 1,800. Publishes 8-12 stories annually. "We accept short stories only for our journal, *Creative Forum*. Novels/novellas accepted if suitable subsidy is forthcoming from the author." Length: 2,000-3,000 words. Pays in copies. Manuscripts should be "neatly typed and not beyond 200 sheets." Subscriptions $40 US. "Short stories accompanied with $25 US towards annual subscription of the journal are given preferential treatment and priority."

‡DILIMAN REVIEW, Rm. 208 Palma Hall Annex (Phan), University of the Phillippines, Diliman, Quezon City 3004 Philippines. Editor: Lilia Quindoza Santiago.

EOD (The Esoteric Order of Dagon) MAGAZINE, P.O. Box 7545, St., Kilda Rd., Melbourne, Victoria 3004 Australia. Fiction Editor: Chris A. Masters. Quarterly. Circ. 500. "*EOD* is an amateur, small press magazine, the aim of which is to encourage up-and-coming horror writers, artists and poets in Australia to develop their talents and to promote their work. Due to the limited outlets for horror fiction in Australia, *EOD* is interested mainly in publishing Australian writers, but I will try to print one or two stories per issue from outside Australia." Length: 10,000 words maximum. Writers receive a copy of the issue in which their story appears. "Unfortunately, I cannot afford to pay for contributions but I do sponsor a short story competition (prizes: $80, $40, $20 Australian) in which the writer's 3 most popular stories receive a small sum for their effort. All contributions to *EOD* should in some way relate to the horror genre and be entertaining. All work should be typed, word processed or on 5¼" disk (360K IBM in ASCII file format). (Guidelines sheet available for SASE or 2 IRCs if outside Australia.) Contributions should also include SASE for reply or appropriate envelope and postage if work is to be returned. For overseas writers, your best bet would be to seek publication in the much larger British and U.S. market." Sample copy available for $5 (US) or $12 (US) for subscription.

FOOLSCAP, 78 Friars Road, East Ham, London E6 1LL England. Fiction and Poetry Editor: Judi Benson. Quarterly. Publishes 2-3 stories/issue. "We are primarily poetry though can handle short fiction of up to 5 pages. This could include a scene from a novel. We are looking for strong quality work but will give careful consideration to all submissions. Any subject considered, also nonfiction." Length: 420-2,000 words. Pays 1 contributor's copy. "Do not send work exceeding 10 typed pages as the magazine does not have the space. Send manuscript in typed form with SAE and enough IRCs for return." Sample copy available for $5.

FORESIGHT (IV), 44 Brockhurst Rd., Hodge Hill, Birmingham B36 8JB England. Editor: John Barklam. Fiction Editor: Judy Barklam. Quarterly. Magazine including "new age material, world peace, psychic phenomena, research, occultism, spiritualism, mysticism, UFOs, philosophy, etc. Shorter articles required on a specific theme related to the subject matter of *Foresight* magazine." Length: 300-1,000 words. Pays in contributor's copies. Send SAE with IRC for return of ms. Sample copy for 30p and 25p postage.

FRANK, An International Journal of Contemporary Writing and Art, B.P. 29 94301 Vincennes Cedex, France. US Office: A-L Books, Suite 305, 45 Newbury St., Boston, MA 02116. Editor: David Applefield. Semiannual. "Eclectic, serious fiction, favors innovative works that convey social, political, environmental concern — all styles, voices — and translations, novel extracts" for literary international audience. "Send your best work, consult a copy of the journal before submitting." Published work by Frederick Barthelme, Robert Coover, Rita Dove, Italo Calvino, Vaclav Havel, and Sony Labou Tansi. Special foreign dossiers of work little known to American readers. Including: The Congo, Pakistan, Phillippines. Length: 3,000 words maximum. Pays 2 copies and $5 (US)/printed page. "Send work that conveys a sense of necessity and soulfulness." Sample copy $10 (US).

GLOBAL TAPESTRY JOURNAL, (II), BB Books, 1 Spring Bank, Longsight Rd., Copster Green, Blackburn, Lancashire BB1 9EU England. Editor: Dave Cunliffe. "Post-underground with avant-garde, experimental, alternative, counterculture, psychedelic, mystical, anarchist etc. fiction for a bohemian and counterculture audience." Recently published fiction by Gregory Stephenson, Arthur Moyse and David Tipton; published work by new writers within the last year. Sample copy $4 (Sterling Cheque, British Money Order or dollar currency).

GOING DOWN SWINGING, Box 64, Coburg Victoria 3058 Australia. Fiction Editors: Kevin Brophy and Myron Lysenko. Circ. 1,000. Annual. Publishes approx. 80 pages of fiction/year. "We publish short stories, prose poetry, poetry, interviews and reviews. We try to encourage young or new writers as well as established writers. Interested in experimental writing." Payment: $20 (Australian) per contribution. Writers receive 1 contributor's copy. Send ms, 2 International Reply Coupons and a short biographical note. Include 2-3 stories. Deadline: December 15. "We are interested in innovative, contemporary writing with the aim of publishing an equal balance of female and male writers of considerable talent." Sample copies $8 (Australian). Writer's guidelines available. Send SAE and IRC.

GRANTA, 2/3 Hanover Yard, Noel Road, Islington, London N1 8BE England. U.S. Associate Publisher: Anne Kinard. Editor: Bill Buford. U.S. office: 250 W. 57th St., New York NY 10107. Quarterly. "Paperback magazine (256 pages) publishing fiction (including novellas and works-in progress), essays, political analysis, journalism, etc." Potential contributors *must* be familiar with the magazine.

‡**THE HARDCORE**, P.O. Box 1899, London N9 8JT England. Fiction Editor: J. Nuit. Quarterly. Circ. 500. Publishes 3 stories/issue. "The magazine at the edge of contemporary culture. We print high speed, hard edged, glitteringly intellegent stories set from the absolute present to the near future." Length: 1,500 words minimum; 10,000 words maximum. "Complimentary copy always sent to writer/artist. Payment by share of profits in English pounds." Write to enquire. Send $4 US (cash or money order) to editorial address.

‡**HECATE**, Box 99, St. Lucia Q4067 Australia. Fiction Editor: Carole Ferrier. Circ. 2,000. Publishes 5-8 stories annually. "Socialist feminist; we like political stories (broadly defined)." Writers receive $50 (Australian) and 5 copies. "We only rarely publish non-Australian writers of fiction."

‡**THE HONEST ULSTERMAN**, 102 Elm Park Mansions, Park Walk, London SW10 OAP U.K. Fiction Editor: Robert Johnstone. Circ. 1,000. Publishes 3-4 stories/year. "Mainly poetry, book review, socio-political comment, short stories, novel extracts, etc. Main interest is Ireland/Northern Ireland." Writers receive small payment and two contributor's copies. For 4 issues send UK £14 airmail or sample issue US $7. "Contributors are strongly advised to read the magazine before submitting anything."

HRAFNHOH, 32 Strŷd Ebeneser, Pontypridd Mid Glamorgan CF37 5PB Wales. Fiction Editor: Joseph Biddulph. Circ. 300-500. Published irregularly. "Now worldwide and universal in scope. Suitable: fictionalized history, local history, family history. Explicitly Christian approach. Well-written stories or general prose opposed to abortion and human embryo experimentation particularly welcome. No payment made, but free copies provided. Be brief, use a lot of local colour and nature description, in a controlled, resonant prose or in dialect. Suitable work accepted in Esperanto and other languages, including Creole. Stamps and U.S. currency are no use to me. IRC (International Reply Coupon) will cover a brief response. But mss however small are expensive to return, so please send copy." Sample copy free, but 3 International Reply Coupons would cover real cost of sending it overseas.

‡ILLUMINATIONS, Ryde School, Queens Rd., Ryde, Isle of Wight P033 3BE England. Annual. Circ. 500. Publishes 1-2 short pieces (c. 2,000 words/issue). "*Illuminations* is an international magazine of contemporary writing, concentrating on poetry, very open to translation, taking only a limited amount of fiction. All material is read on its own merits; we have no genre or formula expectations." Length: 3,000 words maximum. Pays 2 contributor's copies plus 1 subsequent issue. Sample copies ($5) available from address given.

IMAGO, (formerly *Imago Literary Magazine*), School of Communication, QUT, GPO Box 2434, Brisbane 4001 Australia. Contact: Dr. Philip Neilsen or Helen Horton. Published 3 times/year. Circ. 750. 30-50% fiction. *Imago* is a literary magazine publishing short stories, poetry articles, interviews and book reviews. "While content of articles and interviews should have some relevance either to Queensland or to writing, stories and poems may be on any subject. The main requirement is good writing." Length: 1,000 words minimum; 3,000 words maximum; approximately 2,000 words preferred. Pays on publication in accordance with Australia Council rates: short stories, $A80 minimum; articles, $A80 minimum; reviews, $A50. Also provides contributor's copy. "Contributions should be typed double-spaced on one side of the paper, each page bearing the title, page number and author's name. Name and address of the writer should appear on a cover page of longer mss, or on the back, or bottom, of single page submissions. A SASE (or SAE and IRCs) with sufficient postage to cover the contents, should be sent for the return of ms or for notification of acceptance or rejection. No responsibility is assumed for the loss of or damage to unsolicited manuscripts." Sample copy available for $A7. Guidelines, as above, available on request.

‡INDIAN LITERATURE, Sahitya Akademi, National Academy of Letters, Rabindra Bhavan, 35 Ferozeshah Rd., New Delhi 110 001 India. Editor: Professor K. Sachidanandan. Circ. 3,100. Publishes 6 issues/year; 144-240 pages/issue. "Presents creative work from 22 Indian languages including Indian English." Sample copy $7.

IRON MAGAZINE, (II), Iron Press, 5 Marden Ter., Cullercoats, North Shields, Tyne & Wear NE30 4PD England. Editor: Peter Mortimer. Circ. 800. Published 3 times/year. Publishes 14 stories/year. "Literary magazine of contemporary fiction, poetry, articles and graphics." Length: 6,000 words maximum. Pays approx. £10/page. No simultaneous submissions. Five poems, two stories per submission the limit. Sample copy for $8 (US) (no bills-no checks). "Please see magazine before submitting and don't submit to it before you're ready! Many stories submitted are obviously only of interest to the domestic market of the writer. Always try there first! And do try to find something out about the publication, or better, see a sample copy, before submitting."

ISLAND, P.O. Box 207, Sandy Bay 7005 Australia. Fiction Editor: Dr. Cassandra Pybus. Quarterly. Circ. 2,000. Publishes 4 stories/issue. "*Island* is a quarterly of ideas, criticism, fiction and poetry. It features essays on a range of issues (environmental, political, literary, personal) plus short fiction and poetry." Length: 2,000-5,000 words. Pays $80 (Australian) minimum. Send "double-spaced laser print *not* dot matrix. A *small* amount of relevant biographical detail. Only *one* piece at a time. If you are unpublished at home you are unlikely to be published abroad." Sample copy: $10 (Australian).

LA KANCERKLINIKO, (IV), 162 rue Paradis, 13006 Marseille France. Phone: 91-3752-15. Fiction Editor: Laurent Septier. Circ. 300. Quarterly. Publishes 40 pages of fiction annually. "An esperanto magazine which appears 4 times annually. Each issue contains 32 pages. *La Kancerkliniko* is a political and cultural magazine. General fiction, science fiction, etc. Short stories or very short novels. The short story (or the very short novel) must be written only in esperanto, either original or translation from any other language." Length: 15,000 words maximum. Pays in contributor's copies. Sample copy on request with 3 IRCs from Universal Postal Union.

KRAX MAGAZINE, 63 Dixon Ln., Leeds LS12 4RR, Yorkshire Britain, U.K. Publishes 9 monthly issues. "*Krax* is a poetry magazine which contains one short story per edition. Usually preferred length is 800-1,500 words." Pays one contributor's copy. "Lighted-hearted material only—no politics not even spoofs." Send IRC's for reply postage (*not* stamps), enquire or send synopsis before sending large manuscripts. Sample copies $1 each, no guidelines.

‡LANDFALL/CAXTON PRESS, P.O. Box 25-088, Christchurch, New Zealand. Fiction Editor: Anne Kennedy. Publishes 20 stories/year. "We are willing to consider any type of serious fiction, whether the style is regarded as conservative or avant-garde." Length: maximum 15,000 words. Pays NZ $30-80, depending on length of story. "In New Zealand we follow English spelling conventions. Without wishing to be unduly nationalist, we would normally give first preference to stories which contain some kind of North American-New Zealand connection."

LONDON MAGAZINE, 30 Thurloe Place, London SW7 England. Editor: Alan Ross. Bimonthly. Circ. 5,000. Publishes 3-4 stories/issue. "Quality is the only criteria." Length: 1,500-5,000 words. Pays £50-100, depending on length, and contributor's copy. "Send only original and literary, rather than commercial, work."

‡MANUSHI, A Journal About Women and Society, C/202 Lajpat Nagar 1, New Delhi 110024 India. Editor: Madhu Kishwar. Bimonthly. Circ. up to 8,000. Publishes one fiction story/issue. "*Manushi* is a magazine devoted to human rights and women's rights issues with a focus on the Indian subcontinent and the situation of Indian communities settled overseas. It includes poetry, fiction, historical and sociological studies, analysis of contemporary politics, review of mass media and literature, biographies, profiles and histories of various movements for social change." Length: 12,000 words maximum. Duplicate mss preferred.

‡MASSACRE, BCM 1698, London WC1N 3XX United Kingdom. Editor: Roberta McKeown. Annual. Circ. 300. Published 19 stories in 1992 (from 1,000 to 5,000 words each). *Massacre* is "an annual anthology (paperback, perfect-bound) dedicated to anti-naturalistic and marginal writings. Looking for the subjective—satire, parodies, surrealism, the 'absurd' are particularly welcome. No slice-of-life stories, sci-fi or poetry, please." Length: 2,000 words maximum. "SAE a must (or IRCs). No simultaneous submissions, please." Pays 1 contributor's copy plus 50% discount on further copies (plus postage). "*Massacre* is quirky and many mss submitted are not suitable. Try to read a sample copy before submitting. This magazine is not for everybody." Sample copy from Indelible Inc., BCM 1698, London WC1N 3XX UK. Price: £6.50 (in sterling, checks payable to Indelible Inc.) or $13 (in dollars, checks payable to R. McKeown).

‡MEANJIN, University of Melbourne, Parkville, Victoria 3052 Australia. Fiction Editor: Jenny Lee. Circ. 3,500. "*Meanjin*'s emphasis is on publishing a wide range of writing by new and established writers. Our primary orientation is toward Australian writers, but material from overseas sources is also published." Writer receives approx. $60 (Australian) per 1,000 words and 2 copies. "Please submit typed manuscript and enclose return addressed envelope with IRCs."

NEW HOPE INTERNATIONAL, 20 Werneth Ave., Hyde, SK14 5NL England. Fiction Editor: Gerald England. Circ. 750. Publishes 2-6 stories annually. Publishes "mainly poetry. Fiction used must be essentially literary but not pretentious. Only short fiction used (max 2,000 words). Would use more fiction but the standard submitted (in comparison to the poetry) has been rather poor." Payment: 1 complimentary copy. Guidelines available for IRC. Sample copy: $5 (cash, if cheque, send $10, due to bank charges).

NEW OUTLOOK, MIDDLE EAST MAGAZINE, (IV), 9 Gordon Street, 63458 Israel. Editor: Chaim Shur. "Middle East peace issues, for a progressive audience." Monthly. Estab. 1957. Circ. 4,500. Needs: ethnic, historical (general), translations, Palestinian literature. Pays in contributor's copies. "We publish Palestinian fiction and controversial Israeli works in English in order to broaden potential audience for these works."

‡THE NEW WELSH REVIEW, 49 Park Place, Cardiff Wales CF1 3AT UK. Editor: Robin Reeves. "*NWR*, a quarterly, publishes stories, poems and critical essays." Accepts 16-20 mss/year. Pays "cheque on publication and one free copy." Length: 2,000-3,000 words.

NORTHERN PERSPECTIVE, Box 41246, Casuarina 0811 Australia. Editor: Dr. Lyn Riddett. Circ. 1,000. Semiannual. Publishes about 200 pages of fiction annually. "Publishes short stories, poems, book reviews, articles. *Northern Perspective* is a liberal arts/literary magazine." Length: 1,500-4,000 words.

Writers are paid $10 (Australian)/1,000 words and receive contributor's copies. "Strive for 'form' and style in short story; image in poetry."

NUTSHELL QUARTERLY, 8 George Marston Rd, Binley, Coventry CV3 2HH England. Fiction Editor: Tom Roberts. Circ. 1,000. Accepts 30-40 mss/year. "*Nutshell* is a small press (64-80 pages) magazine featuring short stories, poetry, interviews, articles and reviews. Pleased to receive fiction of any length and of high quality." Pays 1 contributor's copy and choice of payment (nominal) or reduces subscription price. Length: 1,000-3,000 words preferred; 7,000 words maximum. Send SAE with IRCs and a short biography. "We are also interested in hearing about the surroundings in which people work and in receiving correspondence."

‡OUTRIDER, Journal of Multicultural Literare, P.O. Box 210, Indooroopilly, Queensland 4068, Australia. Fiction Editor: Manfred Jurgensen. Circ. 1,000. Publishes approx. 20 short stories plus other prose features annually. "*Outrider* aims to extend the concept of Australian literature. It publishes literary prose, poetry and articles dealing wth literature in Australia. Translated works are welcome." Pays $10/1,000 words. "We expect a professional presentation of manuscripts (enclose self-addressed stamped envelope!). There are no restrictions on what we publish, provided it is good writing."

PANURGE, (I), 15 Westwood Ave., Heaton, Newcastle Upon Tyne, NE6 5QT, U.K. Tel: 091-265-5910. Fiction Editor: David Almond. Circ. 1,000. Published twice/year. Perfect-bound, 120 pages. "Dedicated to short fiction by new and up-and-coming names. Each issue features several previously unpublished names. Several *Panurge* writers have been included in major anthologies, approached by agents, offered contracts by publishers. We seek work that shows vitality of language, command of form, an individual approach." Pays 1 month after publication, 1 contributor's copy. Pays £10/3 printed pages. Overseas subscription $22; Airmail $27. Sample copy $12.

PARIS TRANSCONTINENTAL, A Magazine of Short Stories, Institut des Pays Anglophones, Sorbonne Nouvelle, 5, rue de l'Ecole de Medecine, 75006 Paris, France. Fiction Editors: Claire Larrière, Albert Russo and Dee Goldberg. Semiannually. Circ. 1,000. Publishes short stories exclusively; no poetry, nonfiction or artwork. "*Paris Transcontinental,* purports to be a forum for writers of excellent stories whose link is the English language, wherever it is spoken. It purports thus to be global in scope and to introduce the best among today's authors, whether they hail from Europe or the Americas, from Oceania, Africa or Asia, for new literatures are evolving that reflect our post-colonial and computerized societies in ways that do not necessarily converge but certainly enrich our common space, hopefully also spurring our mutual understanding." Length: 2,000 words minimum; 4,000 words maximum. "Submitters should send us no more than 3 stories at a time, along with a few lines about themselves and their work (approx. 100 words), one IRC to let them know of our decision, and *extra* IRCs (at least 3) for the return of their manuscripts. (No stamps please!)" Pays 2 contributor's copies. "Have an authentic voice and be professional. Write with your gut and read from all quarters. Author's featured include Al Brooks, Stephen Dixon, Jayanta Mahapatra, Joyce Carol Oates, Albert Russo, Alan Sillitoe and Michael Wielding." Send IRC for guidelines. For a sample copy, send a check for FF70 (or 70 French Francs) drawn on your own local bank.

‡PASSPORT MAGAZINE, 5 Parsonage St., Wistow, Huntingdon, Cambridgeshire PE17 2QD England. Fiction Editor: Thomas McCarthy. Semiannual. Circ. 500. Publishes 8-9 pieces of fiction/issue. "A magazine of new international writing. We aim to publish writers new to British readers, i.e., unknown writers, or well-known foreign writers in newly translated work." Length: 500 words minimum; 10,000 words maximum. Pays 2 contributor's copies and a minimum of £10/thousand words on publication. Guidelines for SAE or IRC. Sample copy £5.95 in the UK; £6.92 outside UK.

PHLOGISTON, (II,IV), Burning Tiger Press, Box 11-708 Manners St., Wellington, Aotearoa, New Zealand. Fiction Editor: Alex Heatley. Circ. 100. Quarterly. Publishes 8 stories/year. "Specializes in 'science fiction, fantasy, humor/satire,' but also considers general material." Length: 2,000-10,000 words. Pays in contributor's copies. "Try a copy to get our flavor, take an Alka Seltzer, then send us your best and most unusual work."

PLANET-THE WELSH INTERNATIONALIST, P.O. Box 44, Aberystwyth, Dyfed, Cymru/ Wales UK. Fiction Editor: John Barnie. Bimonthly. Circ. 1,300. Publishes 1-2 stories/issue. "A literary/cultural/ political journal centered on Welsh affairs but with a strong interest in minority cultures in Europe and elsewhere." Length: 1,500-4,000 words maximum. No submissions returned unless accompanied by an SAE. Writers submitting from abroad should send at least 3 IRCs. Writers receive 1 contributor's copy. Payment is at the rate of £40 per 1,000 words (in the currency of the relevant country if the author lives outside the UK). "We do not look for fiction which necessarily has a 'Welsh' connection, which some writers assume from our title. We try to publish a broad range of fiction and our main criterion is quality. Try to read copies of any magazine you submit to. Don't write out of the blue to a magazine which might be completely inappropriate to your work. Recognize that you are likely to have a high rejection rate, as magazines tend to favor writers from their own countries." Sample copy: cost (to USA & Canada) £2.87. Writers' guidelines for SAE.

THE PLAZA, A Space for Global Human Relations, U-Kan Inc., Yoyogi 2-32-1, Shibuya-Ku, Tokyo Japan 151. Tel: (81)3-3379-3881. Fax: (81)3-3379-3882. Editor: Joel Baral. Fiction Editor: Taylor Mignon. Quarterly. Circ. 8,000. Publishes about 3 stories/issue. *"The Plaza* is an intercultural and bilingual magazine (English and Japanese). Our focus is the 'essence of being human.' All works are published in both Japanese and English (translations by our staff if necessary). The most important criteria is artistic level. We look for works that reflect simply 'being human.' Stories on intercultural (not international) relations are desired. *The Plaza* is devoted to offering a spiritual *Plaza* where people around the world can share their creative work. We introduce contemporary writers and artists as our generation's contribution to the continuing human heritage." Length: 200-1,200 words, minimalist short stories are welcomed. Send complete ms with cover letter. Sample copy and guidelines free.

"The cover of The Plaza *is designed to show that this magazine is a cultural publication with a high artistic level. It is not an international or educational magazine, but an intercultural and creative one. It is not an information magazine, but an opinion one," says Editor Joel Baral. "Our intent is to dig up talented writers from around the world and introduce them globally. Also, through the theme of the cover, our intent is to show a plaza that exists in the mind of the artist, where no national boundaries are found and human feelings and sensibilities are most highly considered. Every cover of* The Plaza *has adopted the work of Kazuo Omori, an artist born in the 19th century."*

PRINTED MATTER, Hikari Biru 303, 3-7-10 Takadanobaba, Shinjuku-ku, Tokyo 169 Japan. Editor: Stephen Forster. Quarterly. Circ. 600. About 1/3 of each issue is fiction. *"Printed Matter* is an English-language literary journal that features fiction, poetry, reviews, interviews, essays and artwork, now in its sixteenth year of publication. Though based in Japan, the magazine has an international outlook: we are not especially looking for a backdrop of cherry blossoms and Mt. Fuji. Any type of fiction is acceptable; the sole criterion is quality." Length: up to 5,000 words. Pays 2 contributor's copies. "As with submissions anywhere, study the magazine first. Submit clearly typed manuscripts together with the usual enclosures (SASE or IRCs)." Sample copy: 600 yen; £3; US $5; Australian $6.

‡QUADRANT, Box 1495, Collingwood, Victoria 3066 Australia. Fiction Editor: Mr. Les Murray. Monthly. Circ. 5,000. Publishes 1-2 stories/issue. "Magazine of current affairs, culture, politics, economics, the arts, literature, ideas; stories: general and varied." Length: 4,000 words maximum. Pays contributor's copies and a minimum of $80 (Australian). For sample copy "write to us, enclosing cheque (or equivalent) for $10 (Australian)."

ROMANIAN REVIEW, Redactia Publicatiilor Pentru Strainatate, Piata Presei Libere NR1, 71341 Bucuresti Romania. Fiction Editor: Mrs. Andreea Ionescu. Monthly. Fiction 40%. "Our review is scanning the Romanian history and cultural realities, the cooperation with other countries in the cultural field and it is also a mean of acquaintance with Romanian and overseas writers. We publish the *Romanian Review* in six languages (English, German, French, Spanish, Russian, Chinese). Any kind of well-written fiction may enter the pages of the review, on the sole condition that it would be decent." Length: 2,000 words minimum; 5,000 words maximum. "As we do not have the possibility of payment in foreign currency, we can only offer "lei" 800-2,000/story, depending on its length and qualities. The exchange may be done on the writer's account." Sample copies available; write for information.

‡SCARP, (II), % School of Creative Arts, University of Wollongong, Locked Mailbag 8844, South Coast Mail Centre 2521, Australia. Editor: Ron Pretty. Circ. 1,000. Publishes 15,000-20,000 words of fiction annually. Published twice a year. "We look for fiction in a contemporary idiom, even if it uses a traditional form. Preferred length: 1,000-3,000 words. We're looking for energy, impact, quality." Payment: $20 (Australian) per 1,000 words; contributor's copies supplied. "Submit to reach us in April and/or August. Include SASE. In Australia the beginning writer faces stiff competition – the number of paying outlets is not increasing, but the number of capable writers is."

SEPIA, Poetry & Prose Magazine, (I), Kawabata Press, Knill Cross House, Higher Anderton Rd., Millbrook, Nr Torpoint, Cornwall England. Editor-in-Chief: Collin David Webb. Published 3 times/year. "Magazine for those interested in modern un-clichéd work." Contains 32 pages/issue. Length: 200-4,000 words (for short stories). Pays 1 contributor's copy. Always include SAE with IRCs. Send $1 for sample copy and guidelines.

‡SF NEXUS, P.O. Box 1123 Brighton BN1 6EX England. Fiction Editor: P. Brazier. Quarterly. Circ. 2,000. Publishes 3 stories/issue. "Science fiction and related genre. Light or humorous work is favoured." Length: 2,000 words minimum; 4,000 words maximum. Pays 2 contributor's copies and £50, per 1,000 words. "Subscribe to the magazine and read several issues first. We always read subscribers manuscripts ahead of unknown submissions."

‡SMOKE, (II), Windows Project, 40 Canning St., Liverpool L8 7NP England. Contact: Dave Ward. Magazine of poetry, fiction, art, long poems, collages, concrete art, photos, cartoons. "N.B. Fiction up to 2,000 words."

SOCIAL ALTERNATIVES, % Dept. of Government, University of Queensland, St. Lucia, Queensland 4072 Australia. Fiction Editor: John Knight. Circ. 3,000. Quarterly. Publishes 2-3 stories in each quarterly issue. "The journal is socio-political, but stories of any theme or style will be considered. The criterion is excellence." Length: 1,000-3,000 words. Pays writers "if we have money – we usually don't." Writers receive one contributor's copy. Send "3 copies of story, immaculately presented so no sub-editing is necessary. SASE for return."

STAND MAGAZINE, 179 Wingrove Rd., Newcastle Upon Tyne, NE4 9DA England. Fiction Editor: Lorna Tracy. Circ. 4,500. Quarterly. Averages 16-20 stories/year. "*Stand* is an international quarterly publishing poetry, short stories, reviews, criticism and translations." Length: 5,000 words maximum. Payment: £30 per 1,000 words of prose on publication (or in US dollars); contributor's copies. "Read copies of the magazine before submitting. Enclose sufficient IRCs for return of mss/reply. No more than 6 poems or 2 short stories at any one time. Avoid specific genre writing – e.g. science fiction, travel etc. Should not be under consideration elsewhere." Sponsors biennial short competition: First prize, $1,500. Send 2 IRCs for information. Sample copy: $6.50. Guidelines on receipt of 2 IRCs/SASE (U.K. stamps).

STAPLE, Tor Cottage 81, Cavendish Rd., Matlock DE4 3MD U.K.. Fiction Editor: Don Measham. Published 3 times/year. Circ. up to 500. Publishes up to 50% fiction. Staple is "70-80 pages, perfect-bound; beautifully designed and produced. Stories used by *Staple* have ranged from social realism (through autobiography, parody, prequel, parable) to visions and hallucinations. We don't use unmodified genre fiction, i.e. adventure, crime or westerns. We are interested in extracts from larger works – provided author does the extraction." Length: 200 words minimum; 5,000 words maximum. Adequate IRCs and large envelope for return, if return is required. Otherwise IRC for decision only. Pays complimentary copy plus subscription for US contributors. Get a specimen copy of one of the issues with strong prose representation. Send 10 IRCs for airmail dispatch, 5 IRCs for surface mail. The monograph series *Staple First Editions* is being re-launched. IRC for details March 1993. For guidelines: editorial of *Staple 22* is designed to guide prose writers. Send appropriate cash or draft.

STUDIO: A JOURNAL OF CHRISTIANS WRITING, (II), 727 Peel St., Albury 2640 Australia. Fiction Editor: Paul Grover. Circ. 300. Quarterly. Averages 20-30 stories/year. "*Studio* publishes prose and poetry of literary merit, offers a venue for new and aspiring writers, and seeks to create a sense of community among Christians writing." Length: 500-5,000 words. Pays in copies. Sample copy $8 (Australian). Subscription $40 (Australian) for four issues (one year). International draft in Australian dollars.

SUNK ISLAND REVIEW, P.O. Box 74, Lincoln LN1 1QG England. Fiction Editor: Michael Blackburn. Biannual. "A biannual magazine of new fiction, poetry, translations. Articles and graphics. Short stories, SF and excerpts from novels, novellas are all welcome not romance, historical fiction etc." Length: Open. Send cover letter and no more than 2 short stories at a time. Pays on publication. "Read the magazine first. We prefer disposable mss. All mss must be accompanied by adequate number of IRCs for reply or return."

TAK TAK TAK, P.O. Box 7, Bulwell, Nottingham NG6 OHW England. Fiction Editors: Andrew and Tim Brown. Circ. 500. "An occasional anthology on a set theme containing several pieces of fiction. Also several books each year. *Tak Tak Tak* is in paperback book form with cassette for music and the spoken word. We use all sorts of fiction relevant to the theme, but for reasons of space it can't be too long. (2,500 words maximum)." Pays one contributor's copy. "Write for more details, sample copies and guidelines."

‡TAKAHE, QUARTERLY LITERARY MAGAZINE, P.O. Box 13-335, Christchurch New Zealand. Fiction Editors: Sandra Arnold and James Norcliffe. "We publish short fiction and poetry. We have no preconceived specifications as to form, subject-matter, style or purpose. We believe that literature, among other things, is an art of significant silence. It demands an active reader whose trust in language matches that of the writer." Payment is by issues of the magazine, with a small money order at the editors' discretion.

TEARS IN THE FENCE, (II), 38 Hod View, Stourpaine, Nr. Blandford Forum, Dorset DT11 8TN England. Editor: David Caddy. Semiannual. A magazine of poetry, fiction and graphics, "blended with a conservation section to develop the concepts of ecology and conservation beyond their present narrow usage." Publishes 3-4 stories/issue. Pays £7.50 per story plus complimentary copy of the magazine. Sample copy $4 (US).

THE THIRD HALF MAGAZINE, "Amikeco," 16, Fane Close, Stamford, Lincolnshire PE9 1H9 England. Fiction Editor: Kevin Troop. Quarterly. "*The Third Half* literary magazine publishes mostly poetry, but editorial policy is to publish as much *short* short story writing as possible in each issue. Short stories especially for children, for use in the classroom, with 'questions' and 'work to do' are occasionally produced, along with poetry books, as separate editions. I wish to expand on this." Length: 1,800 words maximum. Pays in contributor's copies.

‡TOGETHER, For All Concerned with Christian Education, The National Society, Church House, Great Smith St., London SW1P 3NZ England. Editor-in-Chief: Mrs. P. Egan. Magazine of forward-looking Christian education for children under 12. Short stories, plays, services, projects, etc. Also songs, carols, occasional poems. Readers are primary school and Sunday school teachers, clergy.

‡WASAFIRI, P.O. Box 195, Canterbury, Kent CT2 7BX England. Fiction Editor: Ms. Susheila Nasta. Semi-annual. Circ. 700. Publishes 2-3 short stories/issue. "Publishes critical articles, interviews, fiction and poetry by and about African, Asian, Carribbean, Pacific and Black British writers." Length: 500 words miminum; 2,000 words maximum. Pays contributor's copies. "We welcome any writing for consideration which falls into our areas of interest. Work from writers outside Britain is a major part of our interest. Articles should be double-spaced and follow MLA guidelines."

WEBBER'S, 15 McKillop St., Melbourne, Victoria 3000 Australia. Contact: The Editor. Biannual. "*Webber's* is a relatively new literary magazine specializing in short fiction, poetry, reviews, essays and interviews. It attempts to encourage new writers as well as established ones." Length: 2,000 words maximum. Material submitted must be previously unpublished and include SAE with IRCs. Pays approximately $60-75 (Australian) and 1 contributor's copy. "We are always interested in receiving new manuscripts and consider each contribution carefully. In writing about what *they* know, writers from other countries will be providing Australian readers with material about which they do not know. This is always very positive."

WESTERLY, English Dept., University of Western Australia, Nedlands, 6009 Australia. Caroline Horobin, Administrator. Quarterly. Circ. 1,000. "A quarterly of poetry, prose and articles of a literary and cultural kind, giving special attention to Australia and Southeast Asia." Pays $50 (AUS) minimum and 1 contributor's copy. Sample copy for $6 (AUS).

‡THE WRITERS' ROSTRUM, (I), 14 Ardbeg Rd., Rothesay, Bute PA20 0NJ Scotland. Fiction Editor: Jenny Chaplin. Circ. 1,000. Publishes approx. 15 short stories annually. "My magazine, *The Writers' Rostrum*, has been described as 'cozy' and being like 'tea and cream buns on a Sunday afternoon.' From this, you will gather that I refuse to publish anything that is in any way controversial, political or obscene. Short stories are on such topics as family life, friendship, telepathy and other aspects of the supernatural. Also seasonal topics: beauties of nature, etc. Writers in Britain receive cheque (£1-£5) on publication, together with a copy of the particular issue in which their work appears. Writers abroad receive complimentary copy. Keep to the required wordage, 900 words maximum. If at all possible, study the magazine. Always send SASE and/or IRC. Where possible, I will suggest other UK markets, since my main aim is to help handicapped/beginners/retired people get started on the craft of writing and see their work published. All profits from The Writers' Rostrum are sent to a variety of medical charities, with main recipient being Parkinson's disease research funds."

Literary and small circulation magazines/'92-'93 changes

The following literary magazines appeared in the 1992 edition of *Novel & Short Story Writer's Market* but are not in the 1993 edition. Those publications whose editors did not respond to our request for an update of their listings may not have done so for a variety of reasons — they may be out of business, for example, or they may be overstocked with submissions. These "no responses" are listed with no additional explanation below. Some responded too late for inclusion and this is indicated. If an explanation was given, it appears in parentheses next to the listing name.

American Fiction (asked to be left out this year)
The Armchair Detective (asked to be left out this year)
Belles Lettres (contest only)
The Bellingham Review
Berkeley Fiction Review
Blatant Artifice (out of business)
Blind Iguana Press (out of business)
Blue Light Red Light (asked to be left out this year)
Blue Ryder
Bone Saw (asked to be left out this year)
BVI-Pacifica Newsletter (out of business)
Canadian Author & Bookman (Okanagan Short Fiction Award only)
Canadian Fiction Magazine
Cathedral Of Insanity
Ceilidh (out of business)
Center Magazine (asked to be deleted)
Central Park
Chakra (asked to be deleted)

Champagne Horror (asked to be left out this year)
Cimmerian Journal (discontinued indefinitely)
Cipher (asked to be deleted)
City Scriptum (no longer using outside work)
Cold-Drill Magazine
Colorado Review
Common Lives/Lesbian Lives
Crosscurrents (asked to be left out this year)
Culture Concrete
Dan River Anthology
Dead Tree Product
The Ecphorizer
Emrys Journal
Encounters Magazine (ceased publication)
Eotu
Ergo! (contest only)
The Escapist
The Gamut (suspended publication)
Great Stream Review
Groundswell (ceased publication)
Hippo (out of business)

Hobo Jungle (out of business)
Humerus
Imagine (ceased publication)
Inlet (out of business)
Jacaranda Review (no unsolicited fiction)
Joyeux Erotique (out of business)
Kings Review
Lake Effect (out of business)
Latin American Literary Review (inappropriate submissions)
Left-Footed Wombat (ceased publication)
Lost Creek Letters
The Mage (ceased publication)
The Malahat Review (asked to be deleted)
The Midcoaster
Minnesota Ink (asked to be deleted)
The Miss Lucy Westenra Society Of The Undead
Moving Out
Negative Capability
New Kent Quarterly
New Methods

Nexus
No Newz
Northern Arizona Mandala
Notebook/Cuaderno: A Literary Journal
Notes From The Southwest
NRG (out of business)
Our Write Mind (suspended publication)
Oyez Review
Pikeville Review
The Pipe Smoker's Ephemeris
Plots Magazine (ceased publication)
Poetry Halifax Dartmouth
Portland Review
Potent Aphrodisiac
The Prairie Journal of Canadian Literature
Probe Post (ceased publication)
Reflections (out of business)
Review La Booche

River City
Samisdat (out of business)
Sand Hills Review
Scrivener
Sequoia
Shawnee Silhouette (out of business)
The Silver Web
Sisyphus
Smile
The Sneak Preview (local material only)
South Carolina Review
The South Hill Gazette (ceased publication)
The Standing Stone (out of business)
Starsong (out of business)
Syzygy (at their request)
Tandava (ceased publication)
Terror Time Again
Third Woman (ceased publication)

Toad Hiway (no longer published)
Two-Ton Santa
Uncle (out of business)
Underground Forest/La Selve Subterranea (inappropriate submissions)
A Very Small Magazine (asked to be left out this year)
Visibilities
Wascana Review (asked to be left out this year)
Welter (asked to be left out this year)
Wind Magazine (out of business)
Woman Of Power
The Writers' Bar-B-Q (out of business)
Writer's Guidelines
Yesterday's Magazette (asked to be deleted)
Young Judaean

Commercial Periodicals

We noted last year that the country's economic woes had taken a toll on the magazine industry. Experts promised a recovery, but it has been very slow and publishers are continuing their belt-tightening measures of the last few years. While often fiction is one of the first things added when a magazine attempts a redesign, it is also one of the first things sacrificed when pages are lost for lack of advertising dollars. This year, we saw fiction cut from some well-known markets including *McCall's* and *Mademoiselle*.

Despite these losses, all is not gloom and doom. More magazines chose to keep their listings this year than last and we added 23 magazines this edition (a modest increase over last year). Many of the new listings are not from newly established magazines. More so in this section than in any other, editors tend to drop their listings for a year or two when they become overstocked with submissions, only to return later when they are ready for more.

Types of magazines

The commercial magazine market for short fiction is highly competitive. By our definition, commercial means magazines with circulations of 10,000 or more and which have a commercial focus. The number of these markets is shrinking, and the fact is most commercial publications accept only one or two stories per issue. Quite a few only take fiction once or twice a year or only, occasionally, if the fiction involves a very narrow topic such as trout fishing or juggling.

Magazines that have a reputation for publishing top-flight fiction are excellent opportunities but the competition is even more keen. This is not to say new writers are not encouraged. *The Atlantic* and *Harper's*, for example, are open to submissions from new and established writers. Keep in mind, however, these editors are looking for work of exceptional quality.

This section also includes the top markets for genre fiction such as mystery and science fiction. *Omni* encourages new writers but accepts about 20 stories each year, while *Ellery Queen's Mystery Magazine* is all fiction and publishes several stories each issue. These magazines are known to book publishers as fertile ground for budding novelists.

Choosing where to submit

Unlike small journals and publications, most of the magazines listed in this section are available at newsstands and bookstores. The best way to start your search, therefore, is to take a look at recent issues of those that interest you. You may also want to browse through this section. If your writing concerns a particular subject or type of fiction, check the Category Index for a list of magazines under the appropriate heading. The index starts on page 616. For more on narrowing your search, see How to Get the Most Out of This Book starting on page 3.

You also may want to use our ranking codes as a guide, especially if you are a new writer. As with the literary and small circulation publications, the magazines listed in this section are ranked by Roman numerals according to their level of openness to submissions. For details on these codes see the end of this introduction.

Reading the listings

In addition to looking at several recent issues, reading a magazine's listing will give you clues to its focus. For information common to all listings in this book, see How to Get the Most Out of This Book. Under the "Needs" subhead you will find a list of the types of fiction the magazine is most interested in. We've added to this a number of subcategories this year describing more about some of the different categories. Under mystery, for example, we've included information on the type of mystery, such as private eye, police procedural, amateur sleuth, cozy or romantic suspense. A statement about what the magazine does *not* want to receive may follow the list of needs.

Other information in the Needs subhead will give you an idea how stiff your competition may be. We've included how many manuscripts the magazine receives and how many it actually publishes. The greater the difference between the two figures, of course, the higher your odds for being published. You may also recognize some of the writers the magazine has recently published. Reading their work will help you see exactly what material interests the editor.

After the Needs subhead, you'll find How to Contact. Most magazines want to see the whole manuscript. While it is rare, some magazines in this section will ask for a query first. For these, send a brief letter describing the topic of your story in one or two sentences and, if you like, one or two short writing samples. Some commercial magazines also take novel excerpts. If you don't see any specifics on submitting an excerpt, write to inquire.

New to this edition

This year we've added a new feature to the listings that enables us to tell you additional information not covered by the listing format. Our own editorial comments appear in some listings set off by a bullet (•). This is where we can tell you about awards or honors the magazine has received, whether we list other magazines by the same publisher, about any special interests or requirements and any information from our readers that will help you learn even more about the publication. We've checked several sources, including the magazines themselves for information. Since this is a new feature, we do not claim to include every award or every publication honored and we hope to increase the amount of this information in the future. Your input is welcome.

You may want to take a look at the *Writer's Digest* Fiction 50 list frequently mentioned in the editorial comments. Each year the editors of *Writer's Digest* magazine put together a list of top magazines for fiction writers (based on a set of established criteria) and publish it in the June issue.

Also this year we've clarified whether a magazine accepts simultaneous submissions. More and more publications are accepting submissions they know have been sent to other publications for consideration. Reporting time (the time it takes an editor to get back to you regarding your submission) is increasing, and editors realize writers just don't have the time to give them an exclusive review of a manuscript.

Keep in mind, however, it is common courtesy to inform editors if a submission is being sent to more than one editor at a time. If your story is accepted by one of them, it is also courteous to let everyone involved know the story has been sold. Establish your own criteria beforehand on what you will do if you receive more than one acceptance. Many writers feel it is fairest to take the first response.

Submitting your work

For particulars on submitting work to commercial magazines, see the Business of Fiction Writing. Unless otherwise informed, send a brief cover letter with your manuscript. If you want your manuscript returned, include a large self-addressed, stamped envelope. If you'd rather just send a disposable copy and save the postage, you may want to include a business-size SASE or postcard for a reply.

Both U.S. and Canadian magazines are listed in this section, followed by a section of International Commercial Periodicals. When sending work to a country other than your own, include International Reply Coupons (IRCs) rather than stamps for return mail. These are available at the main branch of your local post office.

For more on trends in commercial fiction, take a look at our Commercial Fiction Trends Report starting on page 68. For more on commercial magazines in general, see issues of *Writer's Digest* and industry trade publications such as *MagazineWeek* and *Folio*.

The ranking system for listings in this section is as follows:

I **Periodical encourages beginning or unpublished writers to submit work for consideration and publishes new writers regularly.**

II **Periodical publishes work by established writers and by new writers of exceptional talent.**

III **Magazine does not encourage beginning writers; prints mostly writers with previous publication credits and very few new writers.**

IV **Special-interest or regional magazine, open only to writers on certain topics or from certain geographical areas.**

ABORIGINAL SCIENCE FICTION, (II, IV), Box 2449, Woburn MA 01888-0849. Editor: Charles C. Ryan. Magazine: 8½×11; 68 pages; 40 lb. paper; 60 lb. cover; 4-color illustrations; photos. "*Aboriginal Science Fiction* is looking for good science fiction stories. While 'hard' science fiction will get the most favorable attention, *Aboriginal Science Fiction* also wants good action-adventure stories, *good* space opera, humor and science fantasy for adult science fiction readers." Quarterly. Estab. 1986. Circ. 31,000+.
● This leading science fiction magazine ranked #43 on the 1992 *Writer's Digest* Fiction 50 list.
Needs: Science fiction. Original, previously unpublished work only. "No fantasy, sword and sorcery, horror, or Twilight-Zone type stories." Receives 120-140 unsolicited mss/week. Buys 12 mss/issue; 30-42 mss/year. Publishes ms 6 months to 1 year after acceptance. Agented fiction 5%. Published work by Larry Niven, David Brin and Walter Jon Williams; published new writers within the last year. Length: 2,500 words minimum; 6,000 words maximum. Some shorter material accepted, but "no shorter than 1,500-2,000 words for fiction. Jokes may be 50-150 words." Sometimes comments on rejected mss.
How to Contact: Send complete ms. Reports in 2-3 months. SASE. Sample copy for $4.95 (double issue) plus $1.05 postage and handling. Fiction guidelines for #10 SAE and 1 first class stamp. Reviews novels and short story collections. Send books to Janice M. Eisen, Apt. 454, 225 State St., Schenectady NY 12305 or Darrell Schweitzer, 113 Deepdale Rd., Strafford PA 19087.
Payment: Pays "$250 flat" and 2 contributor's copies.
Terms: Pays on publication for first North American serial rights and non-exclusive reprint and foreign options.
Advice: "Stories with the best chance of acceptance will make unique use of science ideas; have lively, convincing characters; an ingenious plot; a powerful and well integrated theme, and use an imaginative setting. Read all the science fiction classics and current magazines to understand the field and to avoid clichés."

AIM MAGAZINE, (I, II), 7308 S. Eberhart Ave., Chicago IL 60619. (312)874-6184. Editor: Ruth Apilado. Fiction Editor: Mark Boone. Newspaper: 8½×11; 48 pages; slick paper; photos and illustrations. "Material of social significance: down-to-earth gut. Personal experience, inspirational." For "high

school, college and general public." Quarterly. Estab. 1973. Circ. 10,000.
* *Aim* sponsors an annual short story contest listed in this book.
Needs: Open. No "religious" mss. Published special fiction issue last year; plans another. Receives 25 unsolicited mss/month. Buys 15 mss/issue; 60 mss/year. Published work by Thomas J. Cottle, Karl Damgaard, Richie Zeiler; published new writers within the last year. Length: 800-1,000 words average. Publishes short shorts. Sometimes comments on rejected mss.
How to Contact: Send complete ms. SASE with cover letter and author's photograph. Simultaneous submissions OK. Sample copy for $3.50 with SAE (9 × 12) and $1 postage. Fiction guidelines for #10 envelope and 1 first class stamp. Reviews novels and short story collections occasionally. Send books to fiction editor.
Payment: Pays $15-25.
Terms: Pays on publication for first rights.
Advice: "Search for those who are making unselfish contributions to their community and write about them. Our objective is to purge racism from the human bloodstream. Write about your own experiences."

ALIVE NOW!, (I, II), The Upper Room, Box 189, Nashville TN 37202-0189. (615)340-7218. Magazine of devotional writing and visuals for young adults. Bimonthly. Estab. 1971. Circ. 75,000.
Needs: Religious/inspirational. Buys 4 mss/issue; 12 mss/year. Length: 10 words minimum; 300 words maximum.
How to Contact: Send complete mss with SASE. Previously published submissions OK. Reports in 3 months on mss. Sample copy free. Fiction guidelines free. Enclose SASE.
Payment: Pays $25; 12 contributor's copies.
Terms: Pays on publication for first rights, one-time rights, newspaper and periodical rights. Occasionally buys reprints.

ALOHA, The Magazine of Hawaii and the Pacific, (IV), Davick Publishing Co., Suite 309, 49 South Hotel St., Honolulu HI 96813. (808)523-9871. Fax: (808)533-2055. Associate Publisher/Editor: Cheryl Tsutsumi. Magazine about the 50th state. Upscale demographics. Bimonthly. Estab. 1979. Circ. 65,000.
* The publisher of *Aloha* has published a coffee-table book, *The Best of Aloha*, which won the Grand Award of Excellence from the Hawaii Visitors Bureau Travel Writing Competition.
Needs: "Only fiction that illuminates the true Hawaiian experience. No stories about tourists in Waikiki or contrived pidgin dialogue." Receives 6 unsolicited mss/month. Publishes ms up to 1 year after acceptance. Length: 1,000-2,500 words average.
How to Contact: Send complete ms. No simultaneous submissions. Reports in 2 months. SASE. Sample copy for $2.95.
Payment: Pays between $200-500.
Terms: Pays on publication for first-time rights.
Advice: "Submit only fiction that is truly local in character. Do not try to write anything about Hawaii if you have not experienced this culturally different part of America."

AMAZING® STORIES, (II), TSR, Inc., Box 111, Lake Geneva WI 53147. (414)248-3625. Editor: Mr. Kim Mohan. Magazine: 8⅜ × 10¾; 96 (or more) pages; 80 lb. enamel; 100 lb. Northcote cover stock; perfect-bound; color illustrations; rarely b&w illustrations; rarely photos. Magazine of science fiction, fantasy and horror fiction stories for adults and young adults. Monthly. Estab. 1926. Circ. 20,000.
* *Amazing Stories* ranked #5 on the 1992 *Writer's Digest* Fiction 50 list. See our listing for TSR's *Dragon* and for the press listing in this book.
Needs: Science fiction (hard science, soft sociological), fantasy, horror. "We prefer science fiction to dominate our content, but will not turn away a well-written story regardless of genre. Low priority to heroic, pseudo-Medieval fantasy; no hack-'n'-slash or teen exploitation horror." Receives 700-1,000 unsolicited fiction mss/month. Buys 8-10 mss/issue; 100-120 mss/year. Publishes ms 4-8 months after acceptance. Agented fiction approximately 5%. Recently published work by Robert Silverberg, Roger Zelazny, Ursula K. Le Guin, Harry Turtledove; published new writers within the last year. Length: 1,000 words minimum; 25,000 words maximum; will consider serialization of or excerpts from longer works. Usually critiques rejected mss.
How to Contact: Send complete ms with cover letter (list other professional credits in SF, fantasy or horror). Reports in 10-12 weeks. SASE. No simultaneous submissions. Sample copy for $5. Fiction guidelines for #10 SASE.

Payment: Pays 6-10¢/word.
Terms: Pays on acceptance for first worldwide rights in the English language. Sends prepublication galleys to author.
Advice: "*AMAZING® Stories* is interested in all forms of science fiction, with an emphasis on strong plot lines and believable characterization. Avoid rehashes of old ideas and stereotypical story lines or characters. We encourage writers to experiment with innovative styles and approaches, but not at the expense of comprehensibility. All of that advice holds true for fantasy and horror as well. Read the magazine and others of its type, to get an idea of the competition you're up against before trying to write for it. Send us a story that deserves to be called Amazing, and we'll find a place for it."

AMERICAN ATHEIST, A Journal of Atheist News and Thought, (II, IV), American Atheist Press, P.O. Box 2117, Austin TX 78768-2117. Editor: R. Murray-O'Hair. Magazine: 8½×11; 56 pages; 40 lb. offset paper; 80 lb. glossy cover; illustrations and photographs. "The *American Atheist* is devoted to the history and lifestyle of atheism, as well as critiques of religion. It attempts to promote an understanding of atheism, while staying aware of religious intrusions into modern life. Most of its articles are aimed at a general—but atheistic—readership. Most readers are college or self-educated." Monthly. Estab. 1958. Circ. 30,000.
Needs: Contemporary, feminist, historical (general), humor/satire, atheist, anti-religious. "All material should have something of particular interest to atheists." No religious fiction. Receives 0-6 mss/month. "We would like to publish 1 story per issue; we do *not* receive enough quality mss to do so." Publishes ms "1-3 months" after acceptance. Length: 2,000-3,000 words preferred; 800 words minimum; 5,000 words maximum. Sometimes critiques rejected mss.
How to Contact: Send complete ms with cover letter and biographical material. Reports in 3 months. SASE. Accepts electronic submissions, "WordPerfect compatible or in ASCII. Should be accompanied by printout." Sample copy for 9×12 SAE or label. Fiction guidelines for #10 SASE. Reviews novels and short story collections. Send books to book review editor.
Payment: Pays $15/1,000 words, free subscription to the magazine and contributor's copies.
Terms: Pays on acceptance for one-time rights.
Advice: "Submit material carefully, after reviewing the publication in question. We receive a lot of submissions that are entirely inappropriate, and this slows down our ability to respond."

THE AMERICAN CITIZEN ITALIAN PRESS, 13681 "V" St., Omaha NE 68137. Editor: Diana C. Failla. Magazine. Quarterly.
Needs: Ethnic, historical (general), sports, celebrity, human interest, mainstream and translations. Receives 4-5 unsolicited mss/month. Buys 1-2 mss/issue. Length: 80 words minimum; 1,200 words maximum. Publishes short shorts.
How to Contact: Send complete ms with cover letter. Reports in 1 month on queries. Simultaneous submissions OK. Sample copy and fiction guidelines for 9×12 SAE.
Payment: Pays $20-25.
Terms: Pays on publication for one-time rights.

ANALOG SCIENCE FICTION & FACT, (II), Dell Magazines Fiction Group, 380 Lexington Ave., New York NY 10168-0035. (212)557-9100. Editor: Stanley Schmidt. Magazine: 5³/₁₆×7⅜; 178 pages; illustrations (drawings); photos. "Well-written science fiction based on speculative ideas and fact articles on topics on the present and future frontiers of research. Our readership includes intelligent laymen and/or those professionally active in science and technology." Thirteen times yearly. Estab. 1930. Circ. 85,000.
   ● *Analog* is considered one of the leading science fiction pubilcations. The magazine has won a number of Hugos and Nebula Awards. It ranked #6 on the 1992 *Writer's Digest* Fiction 50 list. *Asimov's* (also listed in this book) is the Dell Magazine's other science fiction publication.
Needs: Science fiction (hard science, soft/sociological) and serialized novels. "No stories which are not truly science fiction in the sense of having a plausible speculative idea *integral to the story*." We do two double-size issues per year (January and July). Receives 300-500 unsolicited fiction mss/month. Buys 4-8 mss/issue. Agented fiction 30%. Published work by Lois McMaster Bujold, Anne McCaffrey, Jerry Oltion, Timothy Zahn and Charles Sheffield; published new writers within the last year. Length: 2,000-80,000 words. Publishes short shorts. Critiques rejected mss "when there is time." Sometimes recommends other markets.
How to Contact: Send complete ms with SASE. Cover letter with "anything that I need to know before reading the story, e.g. that it's a rewrite I suggested or that it incorporates copyrighted material. Otherwise, no cover letter is needed." Query with SASE only on serials. Reports in 1 month on both

query and ms. No simultaneous submissions. Fiction guidelines for SASE. Sample copy for $2.50. Reviews novels and short story collections. Send books to Tom Easton.
Payment: Pays 5-8¢/word.
Terms: Pays on acceptance for first North American serial rights and nonexclusive foreign rights. Sends galleys to author.
Advice: Mss are rejected because of "inaccurate science; poor plotting, characterization or writing in general. We literally only have room for 1-2% of what we get. Many stories are rejected not because of anything conspicuously *wrong*, but because they lack anything sufficiently *special*. What we buy must stand out from the crowd. Fresh, thought-provoking ideas are important. Familiarize yourself with the magazine—but don't try to imitate what we've already published."

APPALACHIA JOURNAL, (II, IV), Appalachian Mountain Club, 5 Joy St., Boston MA 02108. (617)523-0636. Editor: Sandy Stott. Magazine: 6×9; 160 pages; 50 lb. recycled paper; 10 pt. C1S cover; 5-10 illustrations; 20-30 photographs. "*Appalachia* is the oldest mountaineering and conservation journal in the country. It specializes in backcountry recreation topics (hiking, canoeing, cross-country skiing, etc.) for outdoor (including armchair) enthusiasts." Semiannually. Estab. 1876. Circ. 10,000.
Needs: Prose, poem, sports. Receives 5-10 unsolicited mss/month. Buys 1-4 mss/issue; 2-8 mss/year. Publishes ms 6-12 months after acceptance. Length: 500-4,000 words average. Publishes short shorts.
How to Contact: Send complete ms with cover letter. No simultaneous submissions. Reports in 1 month on queries; 6 weeks on mss. SASE for query. Sample copy for $5. Fiction guidelines for #10 SAE.
Payment: Pays contributor's copies. Occasionally pays $100-300 for a feature—usually assigned.
Advice: "All submissions should be related to conservation, mountaineering, and/or backcountry recreation both in the Northeast and throughout the world."

ARIZONA COAST, (II), Hale Communications, Inc., 912 Joshua, Parker AZ 85344. (602)669-6464. Editor: Jerry Hale. Magazine: 5½×8½; 40 pages; 70 lb. gloss; illustrations; photos. Publication prints stories about tourism, old West, lifestyle for young travel-oriented family audiences, snowbirds and senior citizens. Bimonthly. Estab. 1988. Circ. 15,000.
Needs: Condensed/excerpted novel, historical (general), senior citizen/retirement, serialized novel, western. Receives 1 unsolicited ms/month. Accepts 1 ms/issue; 6 mss/year. Publishes ms within 6 months after acceptance. Publishes short shorts. Sometimes critiques rejected mss and recommends other markets.
How to Contact: Send complete ms with cover letter. Reports in 2 months. Simultaneous submissions OK. Accepts electronic submissions. Sample copy free. Reviews novels and short story collections.
Payment: Pays free subscription to magazine.
Terms: Acquires one-time rights.
Advice: "Don't give up!"

ART TIMES, A Cultural and Creative Journal, (II), CSS Publications, Inc., 16 Fite Rd., Saugerties NY 12477. (914)246-6944. Fax: Same. Editor: Raymond J. Steiner. Magazine: 12×15; 20 pages; Jet paper and cover; illustrations; photos. "Arts magazine covering the disciplines for an over 40, affluent, arts-conscious and literate audience." Monthly. Estab. 1984. Circ. 15,000.
Needs: Adventure, contemporary, ethnic, fantasy, feminist, gay, historical, humor/satire, lesbian, literary, mainstream and science fiction. "We seek quality literary pieces. Nothing violent, sexist, erotic, juvenile, racist, romantic, political, etc." Receives 30-50 mss/month. Buys 1 ms/issue; 11 mss/year. Publishes ms within 18-24 months of acceptance. Length: 1,500 words maximum. Publishes short shorts.
How to Contact: Send complete ms with cover letter. Simultaneous submissions OK. Reports in 6 months. SASE. Sample copy for $1.75, 9×12 SAE and 3 first class stamps. Fiction guidelines for #10 SAE and 1 first class stamp.
Payment: Pays $15, free subscription to magazine (one year); 6 contributor's copies.
Terms: Pays on publication for first North American serial rights.
Advice: "Competition is greater (more submissions received), but keep trying. We print new as well as published writers."

ASIMOV'S SCIENCE FICTION, (II), (formerly *Isaac Asimov's Science Fiction Magazine*), Dell Magazines, 380 Lexington Ave., New York NY 10168-0035. Editor: Gardner Dozois. Magazine: 5³/₁₆×7⅜ (trim size); 192 pages; 29 lb. newspaper; 70 lb. to 8 pt. C1S cover stock; illustrations; rarely photos.

Magazine consists of science fiction and fantasy stories for adults and young adults. Published 13 issues/year. Estab. 1977. Circ. 120,000.
● Named for a science fiction "legend," *Asimov's* ranked #2 on the 1992 *Writer's Digest* Fiction 50 list and regularly receives Hugo and Nebula Awards. Editor Gardner Dozois has received several awards for editing including Hugos and those from *Locus* and *Science Fiction Chronicle* magazines. *Locus* also named *Asimov's* "Best Magazine" in 1992. Dell Magazine's other science fiction magazine is *Analog* also listed in this book.
Needs: Science fiction (hard science, soft/sociological) and fantasy. No horror or psychic/supernatural. "We have two double-issues per year (April and November)." Receives approximately 800 unsolicited fiction mss each month. Buys 10 mss/issue. Publishes ms 6-12 months after acceptance. Agented fiction 30%. Published work by George Alec Effinger, Connie Willis, Walter Jon Williams, Gregory Benford and Judith Moffett; published new writers in the last year. Length: up to 20,000 words. Publishes short shorts. Critiques rejected mss "when there is time." Sometimes recommends other markets.
How to Contact: Send complete ms with SASE. No simultaneous submissions. Reports in 1-2 months. Fiction guidelines for #10 SASE. Sample copy for $3.50 and 9×12 SASE. Reviews novels and short story collections. Send books to book reviewer.
Payment: Pays 6-8¢/word for stories up to 7,500 words; 5¢/word for stories over 12,500; $450 for stories between those limits.
Terms: Pays on acceptance for first North American serial rights plus specified foreign rights, as explained in contract. Very rarely buys reprints. Sends galleys to author.
Advice: "We are looking for character stories rather than those emphasizing technology or science. New writers will do best with a story under 10,000 words. Every new science fiction or fantasy film seems to 'inspire' writers—and this is not a desirable trend. Be sure to be familiar with our magazine and the type of story we like; workshops and lots of practice help. Try to stay away from trite, cliched themes. Start in the middle of the action, starting as close to the end of the story as you possibly can."

THE ASSOCIATE REFORMED PRESBYTERIAN, (II), The Associate Reformed Presbyterian, Inc.; 1 Cleveland St., Greenville SC 29601. (803)232-8297. Editor: Ben Johnston. Magazine: 8½×11; 32-48 pages; 50 lb. offset paper; illustrations; photos. "We are the official magazine of our denomination. Articles generally relate to activities within the denomination—conferences, department work, etc., with a few special articles that would be of general interest to readers." Monthly. Estab. 1976. Circ. 6,300.
Needs: Contemporary, juvenile, religious/inspirational, spiritual and young adult/teen. "Stories should portray Christian values. No retelling of Bible stories or 'talking animal' stories. Stories for youth should deal with resolving real issues for young people." Receives 30-40 unsolicited fiction mss/month. Buys 1 ms/some months; 10-12 mss/year. Publishes ms within 1 year after acceptance. Recently published work by Kevin Robinson, Jan Johnson and Marilyn Phemister. Length: 300-750 words (children); 1,250 words maximum (youth). Sometimes critiques rejected mss. Occasionally recommends other markets.
How to Contact: Query and cover letter preferred. Reports in 6 weeks on queries and mss. Simultaneous submissions OK. Sample copy for $1.50; fiction guidelines for #10 SAE and 1 first class stamp.
Payment: Pays $20-50 and contributor's copies.
Terms: Buys first rights.

THE ATLANTIC, (II), (formerly *Atlantic Monthly*), 745 Boylston St., Boston MA 02116. (617)536-9500. Fax: (617)536-3975. Editor: William Whitworth. Senior Editors: Michael Curtis, Jack Beatty. Managing Editor: Cullen Murphy. General magazine for the college educated with broad cultural interests. Monthly. Estab. 1857. Circ. 500,000.
● *The Atlantic* ranks #1 on the 1992 *Writer's Digest* Fiction 50 list.
Needs: Literary and contemporary. "Seeks fiction that is clear, tightly written with strong sense of 'story' and well-defined characters." Buys 15-18 stories/year. Receives approximately 1,000 unsolicited fiction mss each month. Published work by Alice Munro, E.S. Goldman, Charles Baxter and T.C.

The double dagger before a listing indicates that the listing is new in this edition. New Markets are often the most receptive to submissions by new writers.

"Our publication doesn't have a 'philosophy,' other than a desire to be truthful and fair and alert to issues of great public importance as well as to writers of convincing talent and sophistication," says C. Michael Curtis, senior editor of The Atlantic. Although they generally publish only one story in each issue, Curtis says, "We have published fiction for 135 years and don't think we'd be the same magazine without it." The artwork featured on this cover was created by Karen Barbour, who is the illustrator for a variety of publications as well as four children's books she has also written. Her work "evoked, we thought, an apt and understandable take on the article inside," Curtis says.

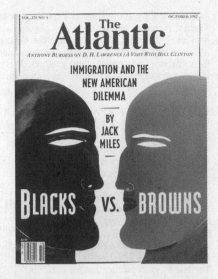

Boyle; published new writers within the last year. Preferred length: 2,000-6,000 words.
How to Contact: Send cover letter and complete ms with SASE. Reports in 2 months on mss.
Payment: Pays $2,500/story.
Terms: Pays on acceptance for first North American serial rights.
Advice: When making first contact, "cover letters are sometimes helpful, particularly if they cite prior publications or involvement in writing programs. Common mistakes: melodrama, inconclusiveness, lack of development, unpersuasive characters and/or dialogue."

‡ATLANTIC SALMON JOURNAL, (IV), The Atlantic Salmon Federation, 1435 St. Alexandre #1030, Montreal, Quebec H3A 2G4 Canada. (514)842-8059. Editor: Harry Bruce. Magazine: 8½×11; 48-56 pages; illustrations; photographs. Conservation of Atlantic salmon: History, research, angling, science and management articles for conservationists, biologists, anglers and politicians. Quarterly. Estab. 1952. Circ. 20,000.
Needs: Historical (general), humor/satire. Receives 2-3 unsolicited mss/month. Buys 2 mss/issue. Publishes ms 2-6 months after acceptance. Length: 2,000-3,000 words average; 1,500 words minimum; 3,000 words maximum. Publishes short shorts.
How to Contact: Query with clips of published work or send complete manuscript with cover letter. Reports in 4-6 weeks on queries; 6-8 weeks on mss. SASE. Simultaneous submissions OK. Accepts electronic submissions via IBM floppy diskette, Wordstar or Word-Perfect. Sample copy for 9×12 SAE and 51¢ postage. Fiction guidelines for #8 or #10 SAE and 39¢ postage.
Payment: Pays $50-350 and contributor's copies.
Terms: Pays on publication for first rights or first North American serial rights.

THE BABY CONNECTION NEWS JOURNAL, (IV), Parent Education for Infant Development, P.O. Drawer 13320, San Antonio TX 78213. Editor: G. Morris-Boyd. Newspaper: 35″ web press; 10¾×16; 16 pages; newsprint paper; newsprint cover; illustrations and photographs. "Material on pregnancy, infant sensory development, birthing and breastfeeding for new and expectant parents, midwives, nurses, ob/gyn's." Quarterly. Estab. 1986. Circ. 36,000.
Needs: Humor/satire, mainstream, romance (contemporary), pregnancy, parenting. Receives 40-60 unsolicited mss/month. Accepts 6-7 mss/quarter; 24 mss/year. Publishes ms 2-3 months after acceptance. Published work by Susan Ludington, Vicki Lansky. Length: 800 words average; 800 words minimum; 1,100 words maximum. Publishes short shorts.
How to Contact: Query with clips of published work. Send complete manuscript with cover letter. "Always include a brief personal bio—not all about works published but info on the writer personally. Married? Children? Hobbies? Our readers like to feel they know the writers personally." Simultaneous sukbmissions OK. Reports in 6-9 months. Sample copy for 10×13 SAE with 2 first class stamps and $3. Fiction guidelines for #10 SAE and 1 first class stamp and $1.50.

Payment: Pays in contributor's copies. Charges for extras.
Terms: Acquires all rights.
Advice: "We especially encourage the male perspective. Everyone knows about kids and babies—so a fiction base should be a breeze for our selected themes of birthing, pregnancy, raising kids, finding time for self and spouse, family values. Write real! Fiction can be life-experienced based and often makes for a workable formula. Take time to read what you have written! Proof your manuscript before sending it in."

‡BALLOON LIFE, The Magazine for Hot Air Ballooning, (II,IV), 2145 Dale Ave., Sacramento CA 95815. (916)922-9648. Editor: Glen Moyer. Magazine: 8½×11; 48+ pages; 80 lb. Tahoe Gloss; color, b&w photos. "Sport of hot air ballooning. Readers participate in hot air ballooning as pilots, crew, official observers at events and spectators."
Needs: Humor/satire, sports and hot air ballooning. "Manuscripts should involve the sport of hot air ballooning in any aspect." Buys 4-6 mss/year. Publishes ms within 3-4 months after acceptance. Published work by Carl Kohler and Lorna Powers; published new writers within the last year. Length: 800 words minimum; 1,500 words maximum; 1,200 words average. Publishes 400-500 word shorts. Sometimes critiques rejected mss and recommends other markets.
How to Contact: Send complete ms with cover letter that includes Social Security number. Reports in 3 weeks on queries; 2 weeks on mss. SASE. Simultaneous and reprint submissions OK. Sample copy for 9×12 SAE and $1.90 postage. Fiction guidelines for #10 SAE and 1 first class stamp.
Payment: Pays $25-75 and contributor's copies.
Terms: Pays on publication for first North American serial, one-time or other rights. 50-100% kill fee.
Advice: "Generally the magazine looks for humor pieces that can provide a light-hearted change of pace from the technical and current event articles. An example of a work we used was titled 'Balloon Astrology' and dealt with the character of a hot air balloon based on what sign it was born (made) under."

BALTIMORE JEWISH TIMES, (II, IV), 2104 N. Charles St., Baltimore MD 21218. (301)752-3504. Local News Editor: Barbara Pash. Magazine: 160 pages a week, average; illustrations; photos. Magazine with subjects of interest to Jewish readers. Weekly. Estab. 1918. Circ. 20,000.
Needs: Contemporary Jewish themes only. Receives 7-10 unsolicited fiction mss/month. Buys 10-15 mss/year. Length: 3,500 words maximum (or 6-15 typed pages). Occasionally critiques rejected mss.
How to Contact: Send complete ms. Simultaneous and previously published submissions OK "on occasion." Reports in 2 months on mss. Sample copy $2 and #10 envelope.
Payment: Pays $35-150.
Terms: Pays on publication.

‡BEAR, Masculinity . . . without the trappings, (IV), COA, 2215 R Market St. #148, San Francisco CA 94114. (415)552-1506. Fax: (415)552-3244. Editor: Richard H. Bulger. Magazine: 60-120 pages; Vista paper; 70 lb. gloss cover stock; illustrations and photos. "Bear is about the average American working man—who happens to be gay. For gay men 25-55." Bimonthly. Estab. 1987. Circ. 40,000.
Needs: Confession, erotica, humor/satire and serialized novel. "Must be sex-positive. Don't make a big deal about an individual's sexual preference. Use masculine American archetypes. No youth-oriented fiction; sex-negative or self-hating pieces; leather sex." Plans to publish special fiction issue or anthology in the future. Receives 10-15 unsolicited mss/month. Buys 1-2 mss/issue. Publishes ms 3-6 months after acceptance. Published work by Jay Shaffer, Furr and C.C. Ryder. Length: 500 words minimum; 3,000 words average. Publishes short stories. Sometimes critiques rejected mss and recommends other markets.
How to Contact: Send complete ms with cover letter that includes Social Security number. Reports in 2-3 weeks on queries; 1-2 months on mss. SASE. Simultaneous, photocopied and reprint submissions OK. Accepts computer printout submissions. Prefers electronic submissions via disk or modem. Sample copy $6. Fiction guidelines for #10 SAE and 1 first class stamp.
Payment: Pays $25-150 and 1 contributor's copy for first North American serial and first rights.
Terms: Pays half on acceptance, half on publication. 50% kill fee.

BECKETT BASEBALL CARD MONTHLY, (IV), Statabase, Suite 200, Statabase, 4887 Alpha Rd., Dallas TX 75244. (214)991-6657. Editor: Dr. James Beckett. Fiction Editor: Mike Payne. Magazine: 8½×11; 96 pages; coated glossy paper; 8 pt. Sterling cover; 12 illustrations; 100+ photographs. "Collecting baseball cards is a leisure-time avocation. It's wholesome and something the entire family can do together. We emphasize its positive aspects. For card collectors and sports enthusiasts, 6-60." Monthly. Estab. 1984. Circ. 800,000+ paid.

Needs: Humor/satire, sports, young adult/teen (10-18 years). "Sports hero worship; historical fiction involving real baseball figures; fictionalizing specific franchises of national interest such as the Yankees, Dodgers or Mets." No fiction that is "unrealistic sportswise." Publishes ms 4-6 months after acceptance. Length: 1,500 words average; 2,500 words maximum. Publishes short shorts. Sometimes comments on rejected mss or recommends other markets "if we feel we can help the reader close the gap between rejection and acceptance."

How to Contact: Send complete ms with cover letter. Include Social Security number. Reports in 6 weeks. SASE. Will consider reprints "if prior publication is in a very obscure or very prestigious publication." Sample copy for $3. Fiction guidelines free.

Payment: Pays $80-400.

Terms: Pays on acceptance for first rights.

Advice: "Fiction must be baseball oriented and accessible to both pre-teenagers and adults; fiction must stress redeeming social values; fictionalization must involve the heroes of the game (past or present) or a major-league baseball franchise with significant national following. The writer must have a healthy regard for standard English usage. A prospective writer must examine several issues of our publication prior to submission. Our publication is extremely successful in our genre, and our writers must respect the sensitivities of our readers. We are different from other sports publications, and a prospective writer must understand our distinctiveness to make a sale here."

BEPUZZLED, (II, IV), Lombard Marketing, Inc., 45 Wintonbury Ave., Bloomfield CT 06002. (203)286-4222. Editor: Luci Seccareccia. "Mystery jigsaw puzzles . . . includes short mystery story with clues contained in puzzle picture to solve the mystery for preschool, 8-12 year olds, adults." Estab. 1987.

• Most of the large bookstore chains and specialty shops carry *bePuzzled* and other mystery puzzles. See "Off the Beaten Path" in the 1991 *Novel & Short Story Writer's Market* for more on *bePuzzled*.

Needs: Mystery: Adventure, juvenile, mainstream, preschool, young adult, suspense--all with mystery theme. Receives 3 unsolicited fiction mss/month. Buys 20 mss/year. Publishes ms 6-18 months after acceptance. Recently published work by John Lutz, Matt Christopher, Alan Robbins, Henry Slesar. Length: 4,000 words preferred; 4,000 words minimum; 5,000 words maximum. Sometimes recommends other markets.

How to Contact: Query for submission guidelines. Reports in 2 months. SASE. Simultaneous submissions OK. Fiction guidelines free.

Payment: Pays $200 minimum.

Terms: Payment is made on delivery of final ms. Buys all rights.

Advice: "Thoughtful, challenging mysteries that can be concluded with the visual element of a puzzle. Many times we select certain subject matter and then send out these specifics to our pool of writers . . . Think out the mystery. Work backwards. List clues and red herrings. Then write the story containing supporting information. Play one of our mystery thrillers so you understand the relationship between the story and the picture."

BIKE REPORT, (I, IV), Bikecentennial, Box 8308, Missoula MT 59807. (406)721-1776. Editor: Daniel D'Ambrosio. Magazine on bicycle touring: 8½×11; 24 pages; coated paper; self cover; illustrations and b&w photos. Published 9 times annually. Estab. 1974. Circ. 18,000.

Needs: Adventure, fantasy, historical (general), humor/satire, regional and senior citizen/retirement with a bicycling theme. Buys variable number of mss/year. Published new writers within the last year. Length: 2,000 words average; 1,000 words minimum; 2,500 words maximum. Publishes short shorts. Occasionally comments on a rejected ms.

Market categories: (I) Open to new writers; (II) Open to both new and established writers; (III) Interested mostly in established writers; (IV) Open to writers whose work is specialized.

How to Contact: Send complete ms with SASE. Reports in 6 weeks. Simultaneous and previously published submissions OK. Accepts electronic submissions; prefers hard copy with disk submission. Sample copy for $1, 9×12 SAE and 60¢ postage. Fiction guidelines for #10 SAE and 1 first class stamp.
Payment: Pays $25-65/published page.
Terms: Pays on publication for first North American serial rights.

BLACK BELT, (II), Rainbow Publications, Inc., 24715 Ave. Rockefeller, Valencia CA 91355. (805)257-4066. Executive Editor: Jim Coleman. Magazine: 112 pages. Emphasizes "martial arts for both practitioner and layman." Monthly. Circ. 100,000.
Needs: Martial arts-related, historical and modern-day. Buys 1-2 fiction mss/year. Publishes ms 3 months to 1 year after acceptance. Published work by Glenn Yancey.
How to Contact: Query first. Reports in 2-3 weeks.
Payment: Pays $100-200.
Terms: Pays on publication for first North American serial rights; retains right to republish.

BOMB MAGAZINE, New Art Publications, Suite 1002A, 594 Broadway, New York NY 10012. (212)431-3943. Editor: Betsy Sussler. Magazine: 11×14; 100 pages; 70 lb. gloss cover; illustrations and photographs. "Artist-and-writer-edited magazine." Quarterly. Estab. 1981.
● *Bomb* ranked #47 on *Writer's Digest* Fiction 50 list.
Needs: Contemporary, ethnic, experimental, serialized novel. Publishes "Summer Reading" issue. Receives 40 unsolicited mss/month. Buys 6 mss/issue; 24 mss/year. Publishes ms 3-6 months after acceptance. Agented fiction 20%. Recently published work by Dennis Cooper, Ed Vega, Sandra Cisneros, Hilton Als. Length: 10-12 pages average. Publishes short interviews.
How to Contact: Send complete manuscript with cover letter. Simultaneous submissions OK. Reports in 4 months on mss. SASE. Sample copy $4 with $2.50 postage.
Payment: Pays $100 and contributor's copies.
Terms: Pays on publication for first or one-time rights. Sends galleys to author.

BOSTON REVIEW, (II), Boston Critic Inc., 33 Harrison Ave., Boston MA 02111. Publisher/Editor: Joshua Cohen. "A bimonthly magazine of politics, arts and culture." Tabloid: 11×17; 24-32 pages; jet paper. Estab. 1975. Circ. 20,000.
● While *Boston Review* is still accepting fiction submissions, their "New Voices" program has been discontinued. For more on the magazine, see our close-up in the 1991 *Novel & Short Story Writer's Market* (note editors have since changed).
Needs: Contemporary, ethnic, experimental, literary, prose poem, regional, and translations. Receives 100+ unsolicited fiction mss/month. Buys 4-6 mss/year. Publishes ms an average of 4 months after acceptance. Published work by Joyce Carol Oates, Yasunari Kawabata, Stephen Dixon. Length: 4,000 words maximum; 2,000 words average. Publishes short shorts. Occasionally critiques rejected ms.
How to Contact: Send complete ms with cover letter and SASE. "You can almost always tell professional writers by the very thought-out way they present themselves in cover letters. But even a beginning writer should find some link between the work (its style, subject, etc.) and the publication—some reason why the editor should consider publishing it." Reports in 2-3 months. Simultaneous submissions OK (if noted). Sample copy for $4. Reviews novels and short story collections. Send books to Deborah Noyes, managing editor.
Payment: Pays $50-200 and 1 contributor's copy.
Terms: Pays after publication for first rights.
Advice: "We believe that original fiction is an important part of our culture—and that this should be represented by the *Boston Review*."

BOSTONIA MAGAZINE, (IV), The magazine of culture and ideas, Boston University, 10 Lenox St., Brookline MA 02146. (617)353-3081/2917. Editor-in-Chief: Keith Botsford. Senior Editor: Tom D'Evelyn. Magazine: 8½×11; 88 pages; 60 lb. paper; 80 lb. cover stock. "Thoughtful provocative prose for national audience." Quarterly. Estab. 1900. Circ. 140,000.
Needs: "Especially strong in these areas: literature, music, politics; sophisticated international focus throughout including fiction." Length: 3,000 words average; 1,500 words minimum; 4,000-5,000 words maximum.

How to Contact: Send complete ms with cover letter. Reporting time varies. SASE. Sample copy $4. Free fiction guidelines.
Payment: Payment (cash) varies; pays contributor's copies, charges for extras.
Terms: Pays on acceptance for first North American serial rights.

BOWBENDER, Canada's Archery Magazine, (II, IV), Suite 200, 807 Manning Rd. N.E., Calgary, Alberta T2E 7M8 Canada. (403)569-9520. Fax: (403)569-9590. Editor: Pat Parker. Contact: John Bataiuk. Magazine: 8¼ × 10⅞; 48 pages; 60 lb. gloss stock; 100 lb. gloss cover; illustrations; photos. "We publish material dealing with hunting, wildlife, conservation, equipment, nature and Olympic team coverage etc., for outdoorsmen, especially hunters and competitive archers." Published 6 times/ year. Estab. 1984. Circ. 45,000.
Needs: Adventure, sports and western. "*Might* publish fiction if it concerns (bow) hunting, archery or traveling in the Canadian outdoors." Does not want to see anything veering off the topic of archery in Canada. Publishes ms within 1 year after acceptance. Length: 1,200 words average; 500 words minimum; 2,000 words maximum.
How to Contact: Query first or send complete manuscript with cover letter, which should include a brief autobiography (archery) to be included in the magazine. Reports in 1 week on queries; 3 weeks on mss. SASE for ms. Sample copy for $2.95 (Canadian), 9 × 12 SAE and $1.12 (Canadian postage). Editorial/Photography guidelines for #10 SAE and 42¢ (Canadian), 30¢ (U.S.) postage.
Payment: Pays $300 maximum. (Roughly 10¢/word depending on regularity of submission, quality photo complement, etc.) Free contributor's copies; charge for extras.
Terms: Pays on publication for first North American serial rights, or first Canadian if requested and acceptable.
Advice: "Fiction remains a 'big' maybe. Write for guidelines and review a sample copy first."

BOWHUNTER MAGAZINE, The Magazine for the Hunting Archer, (IV), Cowles Magazines, Inc., Box 8200, Harrisburg PA 17105. (717)657-9555. Fax: (717)657-9526. Editor: M.R. James. Editorial Director: Dave Canfield. Magazine: 8¼ × 10¾; 150 pages; 75 lb. glossy paper; 150 lb. glossy cover stock; illustrations and photographs. "We are a special interest publication for people who hunt with the bow and arrow. We publish hunting adventure and how-to stories. Our audience is predominantly male, 30-50, middle income." Bimonthly. Circ. 230,000.
Needs: Bowhunting, outdoor adventure. "Writers must expect a very limited market. We buy only one or two fiction pieces a year. Writers must know the market—bowhunting—and let that be the theme of their work. No 'me and my dog' types of stories; no stories by people who have obviously never held a bow in their hands." Receives 1-2 unsolicited fiction mss/month. Buys 1-2 mss/year. Publishes ms 3 months to 2 years after acceptance. Length: 1,500 words average; 500 words minimum; 2,000 words maximum. Publishes short shorts. Length: 500 words. Sometimes critiques rejected mss and recommends other markets.
How to Contact: Query first or send complete ms with cover letter. Reports in 2 weeks on queries; 6 weeks on mss. Sample copy for $2 and 8½ × 11 SAE with appropriate postage. Fiction guidelines for #10 SAE and 1 first class stamp.
Payment: Pays $50-300.
Terms: Pays on acceptance for first North American serial rights.
Advice: "We have a resident humorist who supplies us with most of the 'fiction' we need. But if a story comes through the door which captures the essence of bowhunting and we feel it will reach out to our readers, we will buy it. Despite our macho outdoor magazine status, we are a bunch of English majors who love to read. You can't bull your way around real outdoor people—they can spot a phony at 20 paces. If you've never camped out under the stars and listened to an elk bugle and try to relate that experience without really experiencing it, someone's going to know. We are very specialized; we don't want stories about shooting apples off people's heads or of Cupid's arrow finding its mark. James Dickey's *Deliverance* used bowhunting metaphorically, very effectively . . . while we don't expect that type of writing from everyone, that's the kind of feeling that characterizes a good piece of outdoor fiction."

BOYS' LIFE, For All Boys, (III), Boy Scouts of America, Magazine Division, Box 152079, 1325 Walnut Hill Lane, Irving TX 75015-2079. (214)580-2000. Fiction Editor: Kathleen V. DaGroomes. Magazine: 8 × 11; 68 pages; slick cover stock; illustrations; photos. "*Boys' Life* covers Boy Scout activities and general interest subjects for ages 8 to 18, Boy Scouts, Cub Scouts and others of that age group." Monthly. Estab. 1911. Circ. 1,300,000.

• Ranked #20 on the 1992 *Writer's Digest* Fiction 50 list, *Boy's Life* has received numerous awards.

Needs: Adventure, humor/satire, mystery/suspense (young adult), science fiction, western (young adult) and sports. "We publish short stories aimed at a young adult audience and frequently written from the viewpoint of a 10- to 16-year-old boy protagonist." Receives approximately 150 unsolicited mss/month. Buys 12-18 mss/year. Published work by William Forstchen, Maureen Crane Wartski, Gary Paulsen, E.M. Hunnicutt; published new writers within the last year. Length: 500 words minimum; 1,500 words maximum; 1,200 words average. "Very rarely" critiques rejected ms.

How to Contact: Send complete ms with SASE. "We'd much rather see manuscripts than queries." Reports in 6 weeks. Simultaneous submissions OK. For sample copy "check your local library." Writer's guidelines available; send SASE.

Payment: Pays $500 and up, "depending on length and writer's experience with us."

Terms: Pays on acceptance for one-time rights.

Advice: "*Boys' Life* writers understand the readers. They treat them as intelligent human beings with a thirst for knowledge and entertainment. We tend to use many of the same authors repeatedly because their characters, themes, etc., develop a following among our readers."

BUFFALO SPREE MAGAZINE, (II, IV), Spree Publishing Co., Inc., 4511 Harlem Rd., Buffalo NY 14226. (716)839-3405. Editor: Johanna V. Shotell. "City magazine for professional, educated and above-average income people." Quarterly. Estab. 1967. Circ. 21,000.

Needs: Literary, contemporary, feminist, mystery, adventure, humor and ethnic. No pornographic or religious. Buys about 15 mss/issue; 60 mss/year. Length: 2,500 words maximum.

How to Contact: Send complete ms with SASE. Reports within 3-6 months. Sample copy for $2 with 9×12 SASE and $2.40 postage.

Payment: Pays $80-150; 1 contributor's copy.

Terms: Pays on publication for first rights.

‡BUZZ, The Talk of Los Angeles, (II, IV), Buzz Inc., 11835 W. Olympic #450, Los Angeles CA 90064. (310)473-2721. Fax: (310)473-2876. Editor: Allan Mayer. Fiction Editor: Renée Vogel. Magazine: 9×10⅞; 96-120 pages; coated paper. Published 10 times/year. Estab. 1990. Circ. 70,000.

Needs: Literary, mainstream/contemporary, regional. Receives 75-100 unsolicited mss/month. Buys 1 ms/issue; 10 mss/year. Recently published work by Frederick Raphael, Charles Bukowski, Barry Gifford, Amy Gerstler. Length: 2,000 words minimum; 5,000 words maximum. Also publishes literary essays. Sometimes critiques or comments on rejected mss.

How to Contact: Send complete ms with a cover letter. Reports on mss in 2 months. SASE for return of ms. Simultaneous and electronic submissions OK. Sample copy for $2.50, 11×14 SAE and $2.90 postage. Fiction guidelines for SASE. Send books to Renée Vogel.

Payment: Pays $500-3,000 and contributor's copies.

Terms: Buys first North American serial rights. Sends galleys to author.

Advice: Looks for "A distinct, individual voice."

CAMPUS LIFE MAGAZINE, (II), Christianity Today, Inc., 465 Gundersen Drive, Carol Stream IL 60188. (312)260-6200. Fax: (708)260-0114. Editor: James Long. Senior Editor: Christopher Lutes. Magazine: 8¼×11¼; 100 pages; 4-color and b&w illustrations; 4-color and b&w photos. "General interest magazine with a religious twist. Not limited strictly to Christian content." Articles "vary from serious to humorous to current trends and issues, for high school and college age readers." Monthly except combined May-June and July-August issues. Estab. 1942. Circ. 130,000.

• *Campus Life* regularly receives awards from the Evangelical Press Association.

Needs: Condensed novel, humor/satire, prose poem, serialized/excerpted novel. "All submissions must be contemporary, reflecting the teen experience in the 90s. We are a Christian magazine but are *not* interested in sappy, formulaic, sentimentally religious stories. We *are* interested in well crafted stories that portray life realistically, stories high school and college youth relate to. Nothing contradictory of Christian values. If you don't understand our market and style, don't submit." Buys 5 mss/year. Reading and response time slower in summer. Published work by Barbara Durkin, Christopher Conn; published new writers within the last year. Length: 1,000-3,000 words average, "possibly longer." Publishes short shorts.

How to Contact: Query with short synopsis of work, published samples and SASE. Does not accept unsolicited manuscripts. Reports in 4-6 weeks on queries. Sample copy $2 and 9½×11 envelope.
Payment: Pays "generally" $250-400; 2 contributor's copies.
Terms: Pays on acceptance for one-time rights.
Advice: "We print finely crafted fiction that carries a contemporary teen (older teen) theme. First person fiction often works best. Ask us for sample copy with fiction story. Fiction communicates to our reader. We want experienced fiction writers who have something to say to or about young people without getting propagandistic."

CANADIAN MESSENGER, (IV), Apostleship of Prayer, 661 Greenwood Ave., Toronto, Ontario M4J 4B3 Canada. (416)466-1195. Editors: Rev. F.J. Power, S.J.; Alfred De Manche. Magazine: 7×10; 32 pages; glossy paper; self cover; illustrations; photos. Publishes material with a "religious theme or a moral about people, adventure, heroism and humor, for Roman Catholic adults." Monthly. Estab. 1891. Circ. 17,000.
• The Apostleship of Prayer also publishes *Messenger of the Sacred Heart* listed in this book.
Needs: Religious/inspirational. Receives 10 mss/month. Buys 1 ms/issue. Publishes ms within 1-1½ years of acceptance. Length: 500 words minimum; 1,500 words maximum.
How to Contact: Send complete ms with cover letter. No simultaneous submissions. Reports on mss in "a few" weeks. SASE. Sample copy for $1. Fiction guidelines for $1 and 7½×10½ SAE.
Payment: Pays 4¢/word.
Terms: Pays on acceptance for first North American rights.

CAPPER'S, (II), Stauffer Communications, Inc., 1503 S.W. 42nd St., Topeka KS 66609-1214. (913)295-1108. Editor: Nancy Peavler. Magazine: 24-48 pages; newsprint paper and cover stock; photos. A "clean, uplifting and nonsensational newspaper for families from children to grandparents." Biweekly. Estab. 1879. Circ. 375,000.
• Stauffer Communications also publishes *Grit* listed in this book.
Needs: Serialized novels. "We accept only novel-length stories for serialization. No fiction containing violence, sexual references or obscenity." Receives 2-3 unsolicited fiction mss each month. Buys 2-3 stories/year. Published work by Juanita Urbach, Colleen L. Reece, John E. Stolberg; published new writers within the last year.
How to Contact: Send complete ms with SASE. Cover letter and/or synopsis helpful. Reports in 5-6 months on ms. Sample copy for 85¢.
Payment: Pays $75-250 for one-time serialization and contributor's copies (1-2 copies as needed for copyright).
Terms: Pays on acceptance for second serial (reprint) rights and one-time rights.
Advice: "Please proofread and edit carefully. We've seen major characters change names partway through the manuscript."

CAREER FOCUS, COLLEGE PREVIEW, DIRECT AIM, JOURNEY, VISIONS, (IV), Communications Publishing Group, Inc., 3100 Broadway, 225 PennTower, Kansas City MO 64111. Editor: Georgia Clark. Magazines: 70 pages; 50 lb. paper; gloss enamel cover; 8×10 or 5×7 (preferred) illustrations; camera ready photographs. *Career Focus*, "For Today's Professionals" includes career preparation, continuing education and upward mobility skills for advanced Black and Hispanic college students and college graduates. Annually. *College Preview*, "For College-Bound Students" is designed to inform and motivate Black and Hispanic high school students on college preparation and career planning. *Direct Aim*, "A Resource for Career Strategies," is designed for Black and Hispanic college students. Discusses career preparation advancement and management strategies as well as life-enhancement skills. Quarterly. Circ. 600,000. *Journey*, "A Success Guide for College and Career-Bound Students" is for Asian American high school and college students who have indicated a desire to pursue higher education through college, vocational/technical or proprietary schools. Semiannually. *Visions*, "A Success Guide for Career-Bound Students" is designed for Native American students who want to pursue a higher education through college, vocational/technical or proprietary schools. Semiannually. Specialized publication limited to certain subjects or themes.
Needs: Adventure, condensed/excerpted novel, contemporary, ethnic, experimental, historical (general), humor/satire, prose poem, romance (contemporary, historical, young adult), science fiction, sports, suspense/mystery. Receives 2-3 unsolicited mss/month. Buys 2-4 mss/year. After acceptance of ms, time varies before it is published. Length: 1,000 words minimum; 4,000 words maximum. Publishes short shorts. Does not usually comment on rejected ms.

How to Contact: Query with clips of published work (include Social Security number) or send copy of resume and when available to perform. Reports in 4-6 weeks. SASE. Simultaneous and reprint submissions OK. Sample copy and fiction guidelines for 9 × 10 SASE.
Payment: Pays 10¢ per word.
Terms: Pays on acceptance for first rights and second serial (reprint) rights.
Advice: "Today's fiction market is geared toward stories that are generated from real-life events because readers are more sophisticated and aware of current affairs. But because everyday life is quite stressful nowadays, even young adults want to escape into science fiction and fairytales. Fiction should be entertaining and easy to read. Be aware of reader audience. Material should be designed for status-conscious young adults searching for quality and excellence. Do not assume readers are totally unsophisticated and avoid casual mention of drug use, alcohol abuse or sex. Avoid overly ponderous, overly cute writing styles. Query describing the topic and length of proposed article. Include samples of published work if possible. Must be typed, double spaced on white bond paper (clean copy only)."

CAT FANCY, (IV), Fancy Publications, P.O. Box 6050, Mission Viejo CA 92690. (714)855-8822. Editor-in-Chief: Debbie Phillips-Donaldson. General cat and kitten magazine, for "people interested in the responsible care of their pets." Monthly. Circ. 278,000.
Needs: Cat-related themes only. "Stories should focus on a cat or cats, not just be about people who happen to have a cat." Receives approximately 40 unsolicited fiction mss/month. Accepts 3-4 mss/year. Publishes ms 2-10 months after acceptance. Agented fiction 10%. Published work by Barbara L. Diamond, Edward W. Clarke and Sandi Fisher; published new writers within the last year. Length: 3,000 words maximum. Sometimes recommends other markets.
How to Contact: "Please query first, and enclose copies of published clips, if available." No simultaneous submissions. Reports in 2-3 months. SASE. Sample copy for $4.50. Fiction guidelines for SASE.
Payment: Pays 5-10¢/word and 2 contributor's copies.
Terms: Rarely buys reprints.
Advice: "Don't let rejections discourage you. We reject many well-written stories because we simply don't have space for them all. At the same time, don't assume your story is beyond reproach. Seek out the opinions of teachers and of writers you respect—and not just those who will be kind to you. Do the best you can to 'develop backbone' and to look hard at your work. Then consider the market of the magazine in which you want to be published. Send out your story and if rejected, revise or choose another market and try, try again. Remember: You never really fail until you stop trying."

‡CHANGES, The Magazine for Personal Growth, (II), U.S. Journal Inc., 3201 SW 15th St., Deerfield Beach FL 33442. (305)360-0909. Associate Editor: Andrew Meacham. Managing Editor: Jeffrey Laign. Magazine: 8½ × 11; 80 pages; slick paper; glossy cover; illustrations; photos. "Fiction often deals with growth and recovery from undesirable or painful pasts; or character change through realization." Bimonthly. Estab. 1986. Circ. 60,000.
Needs: "Quality, professional fiction, typed, double-spaced." Receives 30 mss/month. Buys 3-4 mss/year. Publishes mss within several months of acceptance. Agented fiction 5%. Recently published work by Carol Konek, Elizabeth Benedict. Length: 2,000 words maximum. Publishes short shorts.
How to Contact: Query with clips of published work or send complete ms with cover letter which should include Social Security number and "a short professional bio." Reports in 6 weeks. SASE. Simultaneous submissions OK. Sample copy for SAE. Fiction guidelines for #10 SAE and 1 first class stamp.
Payment: Pays 15¢/word.
Terms: Pays on publication for first North American serial rights. Publication copyrighted.
Advice: "Too much of the fiction we read is superficial and imitative. We're looking for bold new writers who have something to say. A too-subtle message is better than a predictable one."

CHESS LIFE, (IV), U.S. Chess Federation, 186 Route 9W, New Windsor NY 12553. (914)562-8350. Editor: Glenn Petersen. Magazine: 8¼ × 10¾; 68 pages; slick paper; illustrations and photos. "Chess: news, theory, human interest, for chess players (mostly male)." Monthly. Circ. 58,000.
Needs: "Chess must be central to story." Receives 3 unsolicited mss/month. Accepts 2 mss/year. Publishes short shorts. Occasionally critiques rejected mss.
How to Contact: Query first. Free sample copy and fiction guidelines.

CHIC, (II), Larry Flynt Publications, Suite 300, 9171 Wilshire Blvd., Beverly Hills CA 90210. Executive Editor: Doug Oliver. Magazine: 100 pages; illustrations; photos. "Men's magazine, for men and women." Published 13 times/year. Estab. 1976. Circ. 100,000.

Needs: Erotica. Receives 20-30 unsolicited mss/month. Buys 1 ms/issue; 13 mss/year. Publishes ms 1-6 months after acceptance. Published new writers within the last year. Length: 3,000 words average; 2,500 words minimum; 3,500 words maximum. Seldom critiques rejected mss.

How to Contact: Send complete ms with cover letter, which should include "writer's name, address, telephone number and whether the manuscript has been or is being offered elsewhere." No simultaneous submissions. Reports in 4-6 weeks. SASE for ms. Fiction guidelines for SASE.

Payment: Pays $500.

Terms: Pays on acceptance for all rights.

Advice: "Readers have indicated a desire to read well-written erotic fiction, which we classify as a good story with a sexual undercurrent. The writer should read several published short stories to see the general tone and style that we're looking for. The writer should keep in mind that the first requirement is that the story be a well-written piece of fiction, preferably third person, and that it include at least one clinically descriptive sex account of one-and-a-half pages in length. We are not interested in 3,000-word sex scenes."

CHICKADEE, The Magazine for Young Children from OWL, (II), Young Naturalist Foundation, Suite 306, 56 The Esplanade, Toronto, Ontario M5E 1A7 Canada. (416)868-6001. Fax: (416)868-6009. Editor: Lizann Flatt. Magazine: 8½ × 11¾; 32 pages; glossy paper and cover stock; illustrations and photographs. "*Chickadee* is created to give children under nine a lively, fun-filled look at the world around them. Each issue has a mix of activities, puzzles, games and read-to-me stories." Monthly except July and August. Estab. 1979. Circ. 130,000.

● *Chickadee* has won several awards including the 1991 Ed Press Golden Lamp Honor award and the Parents' Choice Golden Seal Award.

Needs: Juvenile. No religious or anthropomorphic material. Buys 1 ms/issue; 10 mss/year. Publishes ms an average of 1 year after acceptance. Published work by Jo Ellen Bogart, Patti Farmer and Marilyn Pond; published new writers within the last year. Length: 300 words minimum; 800 words maximum; 500 words average.

How to Contact: Send complete ms and cover letter with $1 to cover postage and handling. Simultaneous submissions OK. Reports in 2 months. Sample copy for $4.50. Free fiction guidelines for SAE.

Payment: Pays $25-250 (Canadian); 2 contributor's copies.

Terms: Pays on acceptance for all rights. Occasionally buys reprints.

Advice: "Read back issues to see what types of fiction we publish. Common mistakes include: loose, rambling and boring prose; stories that lack a clear beginning, middle and end; unbelievable characters; and overwriting."

CHILD LIFE, (IV), Children's Better Health Institute, Box 567, 1100 Waterway Blvd., Indianapolis IN 46206. (317)636-8881. Editor: Stan Zukowski. Juvenile magazine for youngsters ages 9-11. Looking for adventure, humor, contemporary situations, folk and fairy tales and especially stories that deal with an aspect of health, nutrition, exercise (sports) or safety.

● The Children's Better Health Institute also publishes *Children's Digest, Children's Playmate, Humpty Dumpty, Jack and Jill* and *Turtle* magazines listed in this book.

Needs: Juvenile. No adult or adolescent fiction. Recently published work by Nancy Sweetland, Ben Westfried, Joseph Sherman, Eileen Spirelli. Published new writers within the last year. Length: 1,000 words maximum.

How to Contact: Send complete ms with SASE. Reports in 8-10 weeks. Sample copy $1.25. Writer's guidelines for SASE.

Payment: Approximately 10¢/word for all rights.

Terms: Pays on publication.

Advice: "Always keep in mind your audience's attention span and interests: grab their attention quickly, be imaginative, and try to make your dialogue free and as natural as possible. We are staying away from heavy narrative. Writers who make liberal use of dialogue to expound situations are more likely to be taken seriously."

CHILDREN'S DIGEST, (II, IV), Children's Better Health Institute, P.O. Box 567, 1100 Waterway Blvd., Indianapolis IN 46206. Editor: Elizabeth A. Rinck. Magazine: 6½ × 9; 48 pages; reflective and preseparated illustrations; color and b&w photos. Magazine with special emphasis on health, nutrition, exercise and safety for preteens.

● Other magazines published by Children's Better Health Institute and listed in this book are *Child Life, Children's Playmate, Humpty Dumpty, Jack and Jill* and *Turtle.*

Needs: "Realistic stories, short plays, adventure and mysteries. We would like to see more stories that reflect today's society: concern for the environment, single-parent families and children from diverse backgrounds. Humorous stories are highly desirable. We especially need stories that *subtly* encourage readers to develop better health or safety habits. Stories should not exceed 1,500 words." Receives 40-50 unsolicited fiction mss each month. Published work by Charles Ghigna, Frances Gorman Risser and Julia Lieser; published new writers within the last year.
How to Contact: Send complete ms with SASE. "A cover letter isn't necessary unless an author wishes to include publishing credits and special knowledge of the subject matter." Reports in 10 weeks. Sample copy for $1.25. Guidelines with SASE.
Payment: Pays 10¢/word minimum with up to 10 contributor's copies.
Terms: Pays on publication for all rights.
Advice: "We try to present our health-related material in a positive—not a negative—light, and we try to incorporate humor and a light approach wherever possible without minimizing the seriousness of what we are saying. Fiction stories that deal with a health theme need not have health as the primary subject but should include it in some way in the course of events. Most rejected health-related manuscripts are too preachy or they lack substance. Children's magazines are not training grounds where authors learn to write 'real' material for 'real' readers. Because our readers frequently have limited attention spans, it is very important that we offer them well-written stories."

CHILDREN'S PLAYMATE, (IV), Children's Better Health Institute, P.O. Box 567, 1100 Waterway Blvd., Indianapolis IN 46206. (317)636-8881. Editor: Elizabeth A. Rinck. Magazine: 6½×9; 48 pages; preseparated and reflective art; b&w and color illustrations. Juvenile magazine for children ages 6-8 years.
• *Child Life, Children's Digest, Humpty Dumpty, Jack and Jill* and *Turtle* magazines are also published by Children's Better Health Institute and listed in this book.
Needs: Juvenile with special emphasis on health, nutrition, safety and exercise. "Our present needs are for short, entertaining stories with a subtle health angle. Seasonal material is also always welcome." No adult or adolescent fiction. Receives approximately 150 unsolicited fiction mss each month. Published work by Nancy Gotter Gates, Kathleen Nekich, Jean Leedale Hobson and Marge O'Harra; published new writers within the last year. Length: 700 words or less.
How to Contact: Send complete ms with SASE. Indicate word count on material. Reports in 8-10 weeks. Sample copy for $1.25.
Payment: Pays up to 15¢/word and up to 10 contributor's copies.
Terms: Pays on publication for all rights.
Advice: "Stories should be kept simple and entertaining. Study past issues of the magazine—be aware of vocabulary limitations of the readers."

‡CHRISTIAN SINGLE, (II), Baptist Sunday School Board, 127 Ninth Ave, North, MSN 140, Nashville TN 37234. (615)251-2228. Magazine: 8½×11; 50 pages; illustrations; photographs. "We reflect the doctrine and beliefs of Southern Baptist single adults. We prefer positive, uplifiting, encouraging fiction written from the single perspective." Monthly. Estab. 1979. Circ. 90,000.
• The Baptist Sunday School Board also publishes *Home Life, Living with Teenagers* and *The Student* listed in this book.
Needs: Religious/inspirational. Receives 1 unsolicited ms/month. Buys 1 ms/issue; 4-5 mss/year. Publishes ms 14 months to 2 years after acceptance. Length: 600-1,200 words average. Publishes short shorts. Also publishes poetry.
How to Contact: Send complete ms with a cover letter. Should include estimated word count and Social Security number. Reports in 1-2 weeks on queries; 3-6 weeks on mss. Send SASE (or IRC) for reply, return of ms or send a disposable copy of the ms. No simultaneous submissions. Accepts reprint and electronic submissions. Sample copy for 9×12 SAE and 4 first class stamps.
Payment: Pays 5½¢/word and 3 contributor's copies.
Terms: Pays on acceptance. Buys all rights, first rights, first North American serial rights or one-time rights.
Advice: Looks for mss that are "intended for a single audience, are not preachy, but are entertaining with an inspirational message."

CLUBHOUSE, Your Story Hour, (II), Box 15, Berrien Springs MI 49103. (616)471-3701. Editor-in-Chief: Elaine Trumbo. Magazine: 6×9; 32 pages; 60 lb. offset paper; self cover stock; illustrations and some photos. "A Christian magazine designed to help young people feel good about themselves. Our primary goal is to let them know there is a God and that He loves kids. Stories are non-moralistic in

tone and full of adventure." Readers are "children 9-14 years old. Stories are selected for the upper end of the age range. Primary audience—kids without church affiliation." Published 6 times/year. Estab. 1951 under former name *The Good Deeder*. Circ. 10,000.
Needs: Adventure, contemporary, historical (general), religious, young adult/teen. No Christmas stories that refer to Santa, elves, reindeer, etc. No Halloween/occult stories. Receives 250+ unsolicited fiction mss/month. Buys 6 mss/issue, 40 mss/year. Reads mss in March-April only. Publishes ms 6-18 months after acceptance. Published new writers within the last year. Length: 1,000-1,200 words. Occasionally critiques rejected mss and recommends other markets.
How to Contact: Send complete ms, in April. Reports in 2 months. SASE always. Simultaneous submissions and previously published work OK. Sample copy with 6×9 SAE and 3 first class stamps. Fiction guidelines for #10 SAE and 1 first class stamp.
Payment: Pays $25-35 and contributor's copies.
Terms: Pays within about 6 months for any rights offered. Buys reprints.
Advice: "Especially interested in stories in which children are responsible, heroic, kind, etc., not stories in which children are pushed into admitting that a parent, sibling, friend, etc., was right all along. I want upbeat, fun, exciting stories. Do not mention church, Sunday School, etc., just because this is a Christian magazine. General tone of the magazine is warmth, not criticism. Remember that a story should follow a plot sequence and be properly wrapped up at the end. Most stories I reject involve kids who have regrettable turns of behavior which they finally change, appeal to a too-young age group, are preachy, are the wrong length or lack sparkle. Fiction can be more exact than truths, because details can be fashioned to complete the plot which might by necessity be omitted if the account were strictly factual."

‡COMMON TOUCH MAGAZINE, (II), Straub Association, 132 Grandview Rd., St. Marys PA 15857. (814)834-2445. Editor: Catherine Straub. Fiction Editor: Gen Conroy. Magazine: 8½×11; 48-60 pages; gloss #70 paper; gloss #120 cover; illustrations; photographs. "Success and enjoyment centered items for few men, women, age 25 to 70. The short-short stories we look for have a conversational down-to-earth, concise delivery. The pattern; not the rule." Quarterly. Estab. 1991. Circ. 20,000.
Needs: Adventure, condensed novel, experimental, fantasy, feminist, historical (general), mainstream/contemporary, mystery/suspense (amateur sleuth, cozy, romantic suspense), religious/inspirational, romance (amateur sleuth, cozy, romantic suspense), serialized novel, sports, comics or short quips. List of upcoming themes available for SASE. Buys 3-6 mss/issue; 18-24 mss/year. Publishes ms 1-1½ years after acceptance. Recently published work by Mike Morgan, Dorothy Brooks, Ross Bunch. Length: 1,000 words average; 300 words minimum; 1,500 words maximum. Publishes short shorts. Also publishes poetry. Sometimes critiques or comments on rejected mss.
How to Contact: Send complete ms with a cover letter. Should include estimated word count, Social Security number, rights available. Reports in 1-3 months on queries; 1-6 months on mss. Send SASE (or IRC) for reply, return of ms or send a disposable copy of the ms. Simultaneous, reprint and electronic submissions OK. Sample copy for $2.49 plus $1.21 postage. Fiction guidelines for #10 SAE and 1 first class stamp. Reviews novels and short story collections.
Payment: Pays $15-50 and 3 contributor's copies. Additional copies $1.95 plus $1.21 postage.
Terms: Pays on publication. Buys first rights, first North American serial rights, one-time rights or second rights.
Advice: "Remember you stand a better chance being published if you keep your work short-short and the subject interesting to the public."

THE COMPANION OF ST. FRANCIS AND ST. ANTHONY, (II), Conventual Franciscan Friars, Box 535, Postal Station F, Toronto, Ontario M4Y 2L8 Canada. (416)463-5442. Editor-in-Chief: Betty McCrimmon. Associate Editor: Fr. Rick Riccoli CFM Conv. Magazine. Publishes material "emphasizing religious and human values and stressing Franciscan virtues—peace, simplicity, joy." Monthly. Estab. 1936. Circ. 10,000.
Needs: Adventure, humor, mainstream, religious. Canadian settings preferred. Receives 50 unsolicited fiction mss/month. Buys 2/issue. Time varies between acceptance and publication. Length: 800 words minimum; 1,500 words maximum. Publishes short shorts, 200 words preferred.
How to Contact: Send complete mss. Reports in 3 weeks to 1 month on mss. SASE with "cash to buy stamps" or IRC. Sample copy and fiction guidelines free.
Payment: Pays 6¢/word (Canadian funds).
Terms: Pays on publication for first North American serial rights.

COMPUTOREDGE, San Diego's Free Weekly Computer Magazine, (IV), The Byte Buyer, Inc., Box 83086, San Diego CA 92138. (619)573-0315. Fax: (619)573-0205. Editor: Leah Steward-Shidan. Magazine: 8½×11; 75-100 pages; newsprint paper; 50 lb. bookwrap cover; illustrations. Publishes material relating to "personal computers from a human point of view. For new users/shoppers." Weekly. Estab. 1983. Circ. 90,000.
Needs: Fiction that includes computers. "Keep it short! Can be science fiction including computers or 'future' stories." Receives up to 3 unsolicited fiction mss/month. Buys 10 fiction mss/year. Publishes ms 1-4 months after acceptance. Length: 800 words minimum; 1,200 words maximum.
How to Contact: Send complete ms with cover letter. Include Social Security number and phone number. Reports in 1 month. SASE. Reprint submissions OK. Electronic submission of *accepted* mss *only*. Sample copy for 9×12 SAE and $1.50 postage; writer's guidelines for #10 SAE and 1 first class stamp.
Payment: Pays 8-10¢/word.
Terms: Pays on publication for first rights or first North American serial rights. Offers $15 kill fee.
Advice: Magazine fiction today is "too trendy. Reader should be able to come away from article moved, enlightened, edified."

CONTACT ADVERTISING, (IV), Box 3431, Ft. Pierce FL 34948. (407)464-5447. Editor: Herman Nietzche. Magazines and newspapers. Publications vary in size, 40-56 pages. "Group of 14 erotica, soft core publications for swingers, single males, married males." Bimonthly, quarterly and monthly. Estab. 1975. Circ. combined is 60,000.
● This a group of regional publications with *very* explicit sexual content, graphic personal ads, etc. Not for the easily offended.
Needs: Erotica, fetish, fantasy, feminist, gay and lesbian. Receives 8-10 unsolicited mss/month. Buys 1-2 mss/issue; 40-50 mss/year. Publishes ms 1-3 months after acceptance. Length: 2,000 words minimum; 3,500 words maximum; 2,500-3,500 words average. Sometimes critiques rejected mss and recommends other markets.
How to Contact: Query first, query with clips of published work or send complete ms with cover letter. Reports in 1-2 weeks on queries; 3-4 weeks on mss. SASE. Simultaneous and reprint submissions OK. Sample copy for $6. Fiction guidelines free.
Payment: 1st submission, free subscription to magazine; subsequent submissions $25-75; all receive three contributor's copies.
Terms: Pays on publication for all rights or first rights. Sends galleys to author if requested.
Advice: "Know your grammar! Content must be of an adult nature but well within guidelines of the law. Fantasy, unusual sexual encounters, swinging stories or editorials of a sexual bend are acceptable."

‡CORNERSTONE MAGAZINE, (II), Cornerstone Communications, Inc., 939 W. Wilson Ave., Chicago IL 60640. (312)989-2080. Fax (312)989-2076. Editor: Dawn Herrin. Fiction Editor: Jennifer Ingerson. Magazine: 11×15; 40 pages; 35 lb. coated matte paper; self cover; illustrations and photos. "For young adults, 18-35. We publish nonfiction (essays, personal experience, religious), music interviews, current events, film and book reviews, fiction, poetry. *Cornerstone* challenges readers to look through the window of biblical reality. Known as avante-garde, yet attempts to express orthodox belief in the language of the nineties." Approx. bimonthly. Estab. 1972. Circ. 60,000.
● *Cornerstone Magazine* has won numerous awards from the Evangelical Press Association. It has also received a number of design awards, including one from *Print* magazine."
Needs: Ethnic/multicultural, fantasy (science fantasy, sword and sorcery), humor/satire, literary, mainstream/contemporary, religous/inspirational, young adult/teen (10-18 years). Special interest in "issues pertinent to contemporary society, seen with a biblical worldview." No "pornography, cheap shots at non-Christians, unrealistic or syrupy articles." Upcoming theme: "Racism." Plans to publish special fiction issue or anthology. Receives 25 unsolicited mss/month. Buys 1 mss/issue; 3-4 mss/year. Does not read mss during Christmas/New Year's week and the first week of July. Recently published work by Dave Cheadle, C.S. Lewis, J.B. Simmonds. Length: 1,200 words average; 250 words minimum; 2,500 words maximum. Publishes short shorts. Length: 250-450 words. Also publishes literary essays, literary criticism, poetry.
How to Contact: Send complete ms (photocopy only). Should include estimated word count, bio (50-100 words), list of publications, and name, address, phone and fax number on every item submitted. Send disposable copy of the ms. Will consider simultaneous submissions, reprints and electronic (disk or modem) submissions. Sample copy for 11x15 SAE and 6 first class stamps or IRCs. Reviews novels and short story collections.

Payment: Pays 8¢/word minimum; 10¢/word maximum; also 6 contributor's copies. Additional copies for $1.
Terms: Payment on publication. Purchases first serial rights.
Advice: "Articles may express Christianworld view but shouldn't be unrealistic or syrupy. We're looking for high-quality fiction with skillful characterization and plot development and imaginative symbolism." Looks for "mature Christian short stories, as opposed to those more fit for church bulletins or Christian women's magazines. We want fiction with bite and an edge but with a Christian worldview."

COSMOPOLITAN MAGAZINE, (III), The Hearst Corp., 224 W. 57th St., New York NY 10019. (212)649-2000. Editor: Helen Gurley Brown. Fiction Editor: Betty Kelly. Associate Fiction Editor: Suzanne Bober. Most stories include male-female relationships, traditional plots, characterizations. Single career women (ages 18-34). Monthly. Circ. just under 3 million.
 • *Cosmopolitan* ranks #22 on the *Writer's Digest* Fiction 50 list.
Needs: Contemporary, romance, mystery and adventure. "Stories should include a romantic relationship and usually a female protagonist. The characters should be in their 20s or 30s (i.e., same ages as our readers). No highly experimental pieces. Upbeat endings." Buys 1 short story plus a novel or book excerpt/issue. Agented fiction 98%. Recently published excerpts by Danielle Steel, Pat Booth and Belva Plain; published new writers within the last year. Length: short shorts (1,500 words); longer (2,000-4,000 words). Occasionally recommends other markets.
How to Contact: Send complete ms with SASE. Guidelines for #10 SASE. Publishes ms 6-18 months after acceptance.
Payment: Pays $750-2,000.
Terms: Pays on acceptance for first North American serial rights. Buys reprints.
Advice: "It is rare that unsolicited mss are accepted. We tend to use agented, professional writers. The majority of unsolicited short stories we receive are inappropriate for *Cosmo* in terms of characters used and situations presented, or they just are not well written."

COUNTRY AMERICA, (IV), 1716 Locust St., Des Moines IA 50336. (515)284-3790. Editor: Danita Allen. Magazine: 8¼ × 10½; 100 pages. "*Country America* celebrates and serves the country way of life including country music for an audience who loves rural values and traditions." Monthly. Estab. 1989. Circ. 750,000.
Needs: Receives "very few" unsolicited mss/month. Buys 2 or 3 mss/year. Publishes ms approximately 6 months after acceptance. Published fiction by Charlie Daniels.
How to Contact: Query first. Reports in 1 month. SASE for mss. Sample copy for $3.30.
Payment: Pays 35-75¢/word.
Terms: Pays on acceptance. Buys all rights.

COUNTRY WOMAN, (IV), Reiman Publications, Box 643, Milwaukee WI 53201. (414)423-0100. Editor: Ann Kaiser. Managing Editor: Kathleen Pohl. Magazine: 8½ × 11; 68 pages; excellent quality paper; excellent cover stock; illustrations and photographs. "Articles should have a rural theme and be of specific interest to women who live on a farm or ranch, or in a small town or country home, and/or are simply interested in country-oriented topics." Bimonthly. Estab. 1971. Circ. 1,000,000.
Needs: Fiction must be upbeat, heartwarming and focus on a country woman as central character. "Many of our stories and articles are written by our readers!" Published work by Lori Ness, Wanda Luttrell and Dixie Laslett Thompson; published new writers within last year. Publishes 1 fiction story per issue. Length: 750-1,000 words.
How to Contact: All manuscripts should be sent to Kathy Pohl, Managing Editor. Reports in 2-3 months. Include cover letter and SASE. Simultaneous reprint submissions OK. Sample copy and writer's guidelines for $2 and SASE. Guidelines for #10 SASE.
Payment: Pays $90-125.
Terms: Pays on acceptance for one-time rights.
Advice: "Read the magazine to get to know our audience. Send us country-to-the-core fiction, not yuppie-country stories—our readers know the difference!"

CREATIVE KIDS, (I, IV), GCT, Inc., Box 6448, Mobile AL 36660. (205)478-4700. Editor: Fay L. Gold. Magazine: 8½ × 11; 32 pages; illustrations; photos. Material by children for children. Published 8 times/year. Estab. 1980. Circ. 13,000.
 • *Creative Kids* featuring work by children has won Ed Press and Parents' Choice Gold Awards.

Needs: "We publish work by children ages 5-18." Juvenile (5-9 years); young adult/teen (10-18 years). Non sexist, racist or violent. Upcoming themes: Environment (March); Spring/Flowers (April); Summer/Sports (May); Fall/Halloween/School (October); International Issue (potpourri) (November); Winter/Sports (December); Animals (January); People/Feelings/Friends (February). Accepts 8-10 mss/issue; 60-80 mss/year. Publishes ms up to one year after acceptance. Published new writers within the last year. Publishes short shorts.
How to Contact: Send complete ms with cover letter, which should include name, age, home address, school name and address, statement of originality signed by teacher or parent. Reports in 2 weeks on queries; 1 month on mss. SASE. No simultaneous submissions. Sample copy for $3.
Payment: Pays contributor's copy only.
Terms: Acquires all rights.
Advice: "Ours is a magazine to encourage young creative writers to use their imaginations, talent and writing skills. Type the manuscript—double space. Include all vital information about author. Send to one magazine at a time."

CRICKET MAGAZINE, (II), Carus Corporation, P.O. Box 300, Peru IL 61354. (815)224-6656. Editor-in-Chief: Marianne Carus. Magazine: 7 × 9; 64 pages; illustrations; photos. Magazine for children, ages 7-14. Monthly. Estab. 1973. Circ. 100,000.
 • *Cricket* ranked #34 on the 1992 *Writer's Digest* Fiction 50 List. Carus Corp. also publishes *Ladybug* listed in this book.
Needs: Juvenile, including literary, contemporary, science fiction, historic fiction, folk and fairytales, fantasy, mystery, adventure, humorous, ethnic and translations. No adult articles. All issues have different "mini-themes." Receives approximately 1,100 unsolicited fiction mss each month. Publishes ms 6-24 months or longer after acceptance. Buys 180 mss/year. Agented fiction 1-2%. Published work by Peter Dickinson, Mary Stolz, Jane Yolen; published new writers within the last year. Length: 500-1,500 words.
How to Contact: Do not query first. Send complete ms with SASE. List previous publications. Reports in 3 months on mss. Sample copy for $2; Guidelines for SASE.
Payment: Pays up to 25¢/word; 2 contributor's copies; $2 charge for extras.
Terms: Pays on publication for first rights. Sends edited mss for approval. Buys reprints.
Advice: "Do not write *down* to children. Write about well-researched subjects you are familiar with and interested in, or about something that concerns you deeply. Children *need* fiction and fantasy. Carefully study several issues of *Cricket* before you submit your manuscript." Sponsors contests for children, ages 5-14.

CRUSADER MAGAZINE, (II), Calvinist Cadet Corps, Box 7259, Grand Rapids MI 49510. (616)241-5616. Fax: (616)241-5558. Editor: G. Richard Broene. Magazine: 8½ × 11; 24 pages; 50 lb. white paper and cover stock; illustrations; photos. Magazine to help boys ages 9-14 discover how God is at work in their lives and in the world around them. 7 issues/year. Estab. 1958. Circ. 12,000.
Needs: Adventure, comics, juvenile, religious/inspirational, spiritual and sports. Receives 60 unsolicited fiction mss/month. Buys 3 mss/issue; 18 mss/year. Publishes ms 4-11 months after acceptance. Published work by Sigmund Brouwer, Alan Cliburn and Betty Lou Mell. Length: 800 words minimum; 1,500 words maximum; 1,200 words average. Publishes short shorts.
How to Contact: Send complete ms and SASE with cover letter including theme of story. Reports in 3-5 weeks. Simultaneous and previously published submissions OK. Sample copy with a 9 × 12 SAE and 3 first class stamps. Fiction guidelines for #10 SAE and 1 first class stamp.
Payment: Pays 2-5¢/word; 1 contributor's copy.
Terms: Pays on acceptance for one-time rights. Buys reprints.
Advice: "On a cover sheet list the point your story is trying to make. Our magazine has a theme for each issue, and we try to fit the fiction to the theme."

DETROIT JEWISH NEWS, 27676 Franklin Rd., Southfield MI 48034. (313)354-6060. Associate Editor: Alan Hitsky. Newspaper: 120+ pages; illustrations and photos. Jewish news. Weekly. Estab. 1942. Circ. 20,000.
 • *Detroit Jewish News* has received the Rockower Award for Jewish Journalism an average of four times each year for the last four years.
Needs: "For fiction, we prefer articles on any subject with a Jewish flavor." Receives 3-4 unsolicited mss/month. Buys 6 mss/year. Publishes ms 2-3 months after acceptance. Length: 1,000-2,000 words averge. Publishes short shorts. Sometimes critiques rejected mss.

How to Contact: Send complete ms with cover letter that includes Social Security number. Reports in 2 weeks on queries; 1 month on mss. SASE. Simultaneous and reprint submissions OK. Sample copy for $1.

Payment: Pays $40-100 and contributor's copies; charge for extras.

Terms: Pays on publication for one-time rights. Offers kill fee.

‡**DIALOGUE, The Magazine for the Visually Impaired, (I, II),** Blindskills Inc., P.O. Box 5181, Salem OR 97304. (503)581-4224. Editor/Publisher: Carol McCarl. Magazine: 9×11; 115 pages; matte stock. Publishes information on blind-related technology and human interest articles for blind, deaf-blind and visually impaired adults. Quarterly. Estab. 1961. Circ. 50,000.

Needs: Adventure, contemporary, humor/satire, literary, mainstream, regional, senior citizen/retirement and suspense/mystery. No erotica, religion, confessional or experimental. Receives approximately 10 unsolicited fiction mss/month. Buys 3 mss/issue, 12 mss/year. Publishes ms an average of 6 months after acceptance. Recently published work by Patrick Quinn, Marieanna Pape and John Dasney; published new writers within the last year. Length: 1,500 words average; 500 words minimum; 2,000 words maximum. Publishes short shorts. Occasionally critiques rejected mss. Sometimes recommends other markets. "We give top priority to blind or visually impaired (legally blind) authors."

How to Contact: Query first or send complete ms with SASE. Also send statement of visual handicap. Reports in 2 weeks on queries; 6 weeks on mss. Reprint submissions OK. Accepts electronic submissions on disk; IBM and compatible; Word Perfect preferred. Sample copy for $5 and #10 SAE with 1 first class stamp; free to visually impaired. Fiction guidelines free.

Payment: Pays $5-50 and contributor's copy.

Terms: Pays on acceptance for first rights. "All fiction published in *Dialogue* automatically enters the Victorin Memorial Award Contest held annually. One winner per year.

Advice: "Study the magazine. This is a very specialized field. Remember the SASE!"

DISCOVERIES, (II), Nazarene Publishing House, 6401 The Paseo, Kansas City MO 64131. Editor: Latta Jo Knapp. Story paper: 8½×11; 4 pages; illustrations. "Committed to reinforce the Bible concept taught in Sunday School curriculum, for ages 8-10 (grades 3-4)." Weekly.

• Other Nazarene-affiliated publications include *Kindergarten Listen*, *Standard* and *Teens Today* listed in this book.

Needs: Religious, puzzles. Buys 1-2 stories and 1-2 puzzles/issue. Publishes ms 1-2 years after acceptance. Length: 500-700 words.

How to Contact: Send complete ms with cover letter and SASE. Send SASE for sample copy and guidelines.

Payment: Pays 5¢/word for multiple rights.

Terms: Pays on acceptance or on publication.

Advice: "Stories should vividly portray definite Christian emphasis or character building values, without being preachy."

DRAGON MAGAZINE, The Monthly Adventure Role-Playing Aid, (IV), TSR, Inc., P.O. Box 111, Lake Geneva WI 53147. (414)248-3625. Editor: Roger E. Moore. Fiction Editor: Barbara G. Young. Magazine: 8½×11; 120 pages; 50 penn. plus paper; 80 lb. northcote cover stock; illustrations; rarely photos. "*Dragon* contains primarily nonfiction—articles and essays on various aspects of the hobby of fantasy and science fiction role-playing games. One short fantasy story is published per issue. Readers are mature teens and young adults; over half our readers are under 18 years of age. The majority are male." Monthly. Estab. 1976. Circ. 85,000.

• TSR also has a listing in the Commercial Publishers section of this book. See also TSR's other publication, *Amazing Stories* in this book.

Needs: "We are looking for all types of fantasy (not horror) stories. We are *not* interested in fictionalized accounts of actual role-playing sessions." Upcoming themes: "fantasy humor" (April 1993); "Dark Sun™ game world" (September 1993); "gothic horror" (October 1993). Receives 50-60 unsolicited fiction mss/month. Buys 10-12 mss/year. Publishes ms 6-12 months after acceptance. Recently published work by Lois Tilton, Heather Lynn Sarik, Jean Lorrah; published new writers within the last year. Length: 1,500 words minimum; 8,000 words maximum; 3,000-4,000 words average. Occasionally critiques rejected mss.
How to Contact: Send complete ms, estimated word length, SASE. List only credits of professionally published materials within genre. No simultaneous submissions. Reports in 4-6 weeks. Sample copy for $4.50. Fiction guidelines for #10 SAE and 1 first class stamp. Reviews fantasy and science fiction novels for their application to role-playing games.
Payment: Pays 5-8¢/word; 2 free contributor's copies; $2 charge for extras.
Terms: Pays on acceptance for fiction only for first worldwide English language rights.
Advice: "It is *essential* that you actually see a copy (better, several copies) of the magazine to which you are submitting your work. Do not rely solely on market reports, as stories submitted to the wrong publication waste both your time and the editor's. We see *lots* of stories about dragons—try a less conventional fantasy creature: ogre, pixie, dwarf."

DRUMMER, (II, IV), Desmodus, Inc., Box 410390, San Francisco CA 94141. (415)252-1195. Editor: Joseph W. Bean. Magazine: 8½ × 11; 84 pages; glossy full-color cover; illustrations and photos. "Gay male erotica, fantasy and mystery with a leather, SM or other fetish twist." Monthly. Estab. 1975. Circ. 20,000.
Needs: Adventure, erotica, fantasy, gay, horror, humor/satire, mystery/suspense, science fiction and western. "Fiction must have an appeal to gay men." Receives 20-30 unsolicited fiction mss/month. Accepts 3 mss/issue. Publishes ms 6-8 months after acceptance.
How to Contact: Send complete ms with cover letter. SASE. Simultaneous submissions OK. Reprints OK "only if previously in foreign or very local publications." Accepts electronic submissions compatible with IBM PC. Reports in approximately 3 months. Sample copy for $5. Fiction guidelines for #10 SASE. Reviews novels and short story collections.
Payment: Pays $100 and contributor's copies.
Terms: Pays on publication for first North American serial rights.

EMERGE MAGAZINE, (III), Our Voice In Today's World, Emerge Communications, 170 Varick St., New York NY 10013. (212)627-4151. Editor: Mr. Wilmer C. Ames, Jr. Fiction Editor: Gerald Gladney. Magazine: 8⅛ × 10⅞; 84 pages; 40 lb. paper; 70 lb. cover stock; 5-6 illustrations; 45 photographs. "*Emerge* is an African American news monthly that covers politics, arts and lifestyles for the college educated, middle class African American audience." Estab. 1989.
Needs: Ethnic, fantasy, humor/satire, literary, psychic/supernatural/occult, science fiction, sports, suspense/mystery. "*Emerge* is looking for humorous, tightly written fiction no longer than 3,000 words about African Americans."
How to Contact: Submit ms through agent only. Reviews novels and short story collections. Send to Susan McHenry, executive editor.
Payment: Pays $1,000-3,000 and contributor's copies.
Terms: Pays 25% kill fee. Buys first North American serial rights.
Advice: "*Emerge* stories must accomplish with a fine economy of style what all good fiction must do: make the unusual familiar. The ability to script a compelling story is what has been missing from most of our submissions."

ESQUIRE, 1790 Broadway, New York NY 10019. Prefers not to share information.

EVANGEL, (IV), Light & Life Press, P.O. Box 535002, Indianapolis IN 46253-5002. (317)244-3660. Editor: Vera Bethel. Sunday school take-home paper for distribution to young adults who attend church. Fiction involves young couples and singles coping with everyday crises, making decisions that show growth; for readers ages 25-35. Magazine: 5½ × 8½; 8 pages; 2-color illustrations; b&w photos. Weekly. Estab. 1896. Circ. 35,000.
Needs: Religious/inspirational. "No fiction without any semblance of Christian message or where the message clobbers the reader." Receives approximately 75 unsolicited fiction mss each month. Buys 1 ms/issue, 52 mss/year. Published work by C. Ellen Watts, Jeanne Zornes and Betty Steele Everett. Length: 1,000-1,200 words.

How to Contact: Send complete ms with SASE. Reports in 1 month. Sample copy and fiction guidelines with 6×9 SASE.

Payment: Pays $45; 2 contributor's copies; charge for extras.

Terms: Pays on publication for simultaneous, first, second serial (reprint), first North American serial or one-time rights.

Advice: "Choose a contemporary situation or conflict and create a good mix for the characters (not all-good or all-bad heroes and villains). Don't spell out everything in detail; let the reader fill in some blanks in the story. Keep him guessing." Rejects mss because of "unbelievable characters and predictable events in the story."

THE FAMILY, (II, IV), Daughters of St. Paul, 50 St. Paul's Ave., Boston MA 02130. (617)522-8911. Editor: Sr. Donna William Giaimo FSP. Magazine: 8½×11; 40 pages; glossy paper; self-cover; illustrations and photos. Family life—themes include parenting issues, human and spiritual development, marital situations for teen-adult, popular audience predominantly Catholic. Monthly, except July-Aug. Estab. 1953. Circ. 10,000.

• Another magazine published by the Daughters of St. Paul is *My Friend* listed in this book.

Needs: Religious/inspirational. "We favor upbeat stories with some sort of practical or moral message." No sex, romance, science fiction, horror, western. Receives about 100 unsolicited mss/month. Buys 3-4 mss/issue; 30-40 mss/year. Publishes ms 4-6 months after acceptance. Length: 800 words minimum; 1,500 words maximum; 1,200 words average.

How to Contact: Send complete ms with cover letter that includes Social Security number and list of previously published works. Reports in 2 months on mss. SASE. Reprint submissions OK. Sample copy for $1.75, 9×12 SAE and 5 first class stamps. Guidelines for #10 SAE and 1 first class stamp.

Payment: Pays $50-150.

Terms: Pays on publication for first North American serial or one-time rights (reprints). Sends galleys to author "only if substantive editing was required."

Advice: "We look for 1) message; 2) clarity of writing; 3) realism of plot and character development. If seasonal material, send at least 7 months in advance. We're eager to receive submissions on family topics. And we love stories that include humor."

"We publish stories that are short and entertaining and, although they are not all a reality, our readers can relate to them," says Linda L. Lindeman, publisher and editor of Fifty Something, a magazine for adults age 50 and over that likes to present nostalgia to its readers. The cover of this edition for northeastern Ohio shows Bob Hope with Lucille Ball. "Bob Hope is originally from Cleveland and we like the idea of using an old picture that our readers might recognize and enjoy," Lindeman says. A two-page photo spread of Hope, recalling his days in Cleveland, is included inside the issue. The photos were provided by Bob Hope's publicity staff.

‡**FIFTY SOMETHING MAGAZINE,** "For the Fifty-and-Better," Media Trends Publications, 8250 Tyler Blvd., Mentor OH 44060. (216)974-9594. Editor: Linda L. Lindeman. Magazine: 8×11; 32-48 pages; #50 gloss paper; illustrations and photos. "Light-hearted issues on aging. 50+ is the best time of your life. Positive approach to getting older. Tradition—how things used to be." Bimonthly. Estab. 1990. Circ. 25,000.

Needs: Adventure, historical (general), humor/satire, romance (historical), senior citizen/retirement, westerns. Nothing "high tech." Receives 60 unsolicited mss/month. Buys 4 mss/issue; 24 mss/year. Recently published work by Patricia Mote, Ron DeCarlo, Caryl Jost. Length: 1,000 words average; 400 words minimum; 1,500 words maximum. Publishes short shorts. Also publishes literary essays and poetry. Always critiques or comments on rejected mss.
How to Contact: Send complete ms with cover letter. Should include estimated word count with submission. Reports in 2 weeks on queries; 5 weeks on mss. Send SASE (IRC) for reply, return of ms or send disposable copy of ms. Will consider simultaneous submissions, reprints and electronic (disk or modem) submissions. Sample copy for 9 × 12 SAE and $1.21 postage. Fiction guidelines for #10 SAE and 1 stamp or IRC. Reviews novels and short story collections.
Payment: Pays 10 contributor's copies. Additional copies for postage.
Terms: Acquires one-time rights.
Advice: "Photos always help make the story more interesting. Just go for it!"

FIRST, (II), For Women, Heinrich Bauer North America Inc., 270 Sylvan Ave., Englewood Cliffs NJ 07632. (201)569-6699. Editor: Dennis Neeld. Magazine: 150 pages; slick paper; illustrations and photos. "Women's service magazine for women age 18 up — no upper limit — middle American audience." Monthly. Estab. 1989. Circ. 2 million.
 • Fiction Editor Elinor Nauen was profiled in a close-up interview for the 1992 *Novel & Short Story Writer's Market*. The magazine ranks #11 on the *Writer's Digest* Fiction 50 list.
Needs: Contemporary, literary, mainstream and regional. "No experimental, romance, formula fiction, fantasy, sci-fi, or stories with foreign settings." Receives 200 unsolicited mss/month. Buys 1 ms/issue; 16 mss/year. Time between acceptance and publication varies. Agented fiction 33⅓%. Published work by Chuck Wachtel, Tima Smith and P.J. Platz. Length: 2,000 words minimum; 2,200 words maximum. "No short shorts." Sometimes critiques rejected mss.
How to Contact: Send complete ms with cover letter. "Cover letter should be brief, mention previous publications and agent if any, and tell us if material is seasonal. No queries please." Reports in 8-10 weeks on mss. SASE for ms or reply. Reprint submissions OK. Fiction guidelines for #10 SAE and 1 first class stamp. Send seasonal material 6 months in advance.
Payment: Pays $1,500 (less for reprinted material).
Terms: Pays on acceptance for first North American serial rights.
Advice: "We especially like a fresh sensibility and a sensitive handling of themes of interest to contemporary women. Read at least 3 issues of the magazine. Send us the story you had to write for yourself, not one you concocted 'especially for *First*.' "

FIRST HAND, Experiences for Loving Men, (II, IV), First Hand Ltd., Box 1314, Teaneck NJ 07666. (201)836-9177. Fax: (201)836-5055. Editor: Bob Harris. Magazine: digest size; 130 pages; illustrations. "Half of the magazine is made up of our readers' own gay sexual experiences. Rest is fiction and columns devoted to health, travel, books, etc." Monthly. Estab. 1980. Circ. 60,000.
Needs: Erotica, gay. "Should be written in first person." No science fiction or fantasy. Erotica should detail experiences based in reality. Receives 75-100 unsolicited mss/month. Buys 6 mss/issue; 72 mss/year. Publishes ms 9-18 months after acceptance. Recently published work by John Hoff, Rick Jackson, Jack Sofelot; published new writers within the last year. Length: 3,000 words preferred; 2,000 words minimum; 3,750 words maximum. Sometimes critiques rejected mss.
How to Contact: Send complete ms with cover letter which should include writer's name, address, telephone and Social Security number and "should advise on use of pseudonym if any. Also whether selling all rights or first North American rights." No simultaneous submissions. Reports in 3-4 months. SASE. Sample copy for $5. Fiction guidelines for #10 SAE and 1 first class stamp.
Payment: Pays $100-150.
Terms: Pays on publication for all rights or first North American serial rights.
Advice: "Avoid the hackneyed situations. Be original. We like strong plots."

FLORIDA WILDLIFE, (IV), Florida Game & Fresh Water Fish Commission, 620 South Meridian St., Tallahassee FL 32399-1600. (904)488-5563. Editor: Andrea H. Blount. Assistant Editor: Scott Ball. Magazine: 8½ × 11; 52 pages. "Conservation-oriented material for an 'outdoor' audience." Bimonthly. Estab. 1947. Circ. 30,000.

Needs: Adventure, sports. "Florida-related adventure or natural history only." Buys 3-4 mss/year. Length: 1,200 words average; 500 words minimum; 1,500 words maximum.
How to Contact: Send complete ms with cover letter including Social Security number. "We prefer to review article. Response varies with amount of material on hand." Sample copy for $1.25.
Payment: Pays $50 per published page.
Terms: Pays on publication for one-time rights.
Advice: "Send your best work."

FREEWAY, (II), Box 632, Glen Ellyn IL 60138. (708)668-6000 (ext. 310). Editor: Amy J. Cox. Magazine: 8½ × 11; 4 pages; newsprint paper; illustrations; photos. Weekly Sunday school paper "specializing in first-person true stories about how God has worked in teens' lives," for Christian teens ages 15-21.
• Another magazine for teens by this publisher, *Teen Power,* is listed in this book.
Needs: Comics, humor/satire, spiritual, allegories and parables. Length: 1,000 words average; 1,200 words maximum. Occasionally critiques rejected mss.
How to Contact: Send complete ms with SASE. Reports in 2-3 months. Simultaneous submissions OK. Sample copy or fiction guidelines available for SASE.
Payment: Pays 6-10¢/word.
Terms: Pays on acceptance for one-time rights.
Advice: "Send us humorous fiction (parables, allegories, etc.) with a clever twist and new insight on Christian principles. Do *not* send us typical teenage short stories. Watch out for cliché topics and approaches."

THE FRIEND MAGAZINE, (II), The Church of Jesus Christ of Latter-day Saints, 23rd Floor, 50 E. North Temple, Salt Lake City UT 84150. (801)240-2210. Editor: Vivian Paulsen. Magazine: 8½ × 10½; 50 pages; 40 lb. coated paper; 70 lb. coated cover stock; illustrations; photos. Publishes for 3-11 year-olds. Monthly. Estab. 1971. Circ. 220,000.
• The Church of Jesus Christ of Latter-Day Saints also publishes *New Era* listed in this book.
Needs: Adventure, ethnic, some historical, humor, mainstream, religious/inspirational, nature. Length: 1,000 words maximum. Publishes short shorts. Length: 250 words.
How to Contact: Send complete ms. "No query letters please." Reports in 6-8 weeks. SASE. Sample copy for 9½ × 11 SAE and 98¢ postage.
Payment: Pays 9-10¢/word.
Terms: Pays on acceptance for all rights.
Advice: "The *Friend* is particularly interested in stories with substance for tiny tots. Stories should focus on character-building qualities and should be wholesome without moralizing or preaching. Boys and girls resolving conflicts is a theme of particular merit. Since the magazine is circulated worldwide, the *Friend* is interested in stories and articles with universal settings, conflicts, and character. Other suggestions include rebus, picture, holiday, sports, and photo stories, or manuscripts that portray various cultures. Very short pieces (up to 250 words) are desired for younger readers and preschool children. Appropriate humor is a constant need."

GALLERY MAGAZINE, (IV), Montcalm Publishing Corporation, 401 Park Avenue South, New York NY 10016. (212)779-8900. Editor: Barry Janoff. Fiction Editor: John Bowers. Magazine: 130 pages; illustrations and photographs. Magazine for men, 18-34. Monthly. Estab. 1972. Circ. 425,000.
Needs: Adventure, erotica, humor/satire, literary, mainstream, suspense/mystery. Receives 100 unsolicited fiction mss/month. Accepts 6 mss/year. Publishes ms 5 months after acceptance. Less than 10% of fiction is agented. Length: 1,500-3,000 words average; 1,000 words minimum; 3,500 words maximum. Sometimes critiques rejected mss and recommends other markets.
How to Contact: Send complete ms. Reports in 2 months. SASE. No photocopied submissions. Accepts electronic submissions if Mac or compatible disk available. Sample copy $6.25. Fiction guidelines for #10 SAE and 1 first class stamp.
Payment: Pays $500, contributor's copies.
Terms: Pays 50% on acceptance/50% on publication. Buys first North American serial rights.

THE GEM, (II), Churches of God, General Conference, Box 926, Findlay OH 45839. (419)424-1961. Editor: Marilyn Rayle Kern. Magazine: 6 × 9; 8 pages; 50 lb. uncoated paper; illustrations (clip art). "True-to-life stories of healed relationships and growing maturity in the Christian faith for senior high students through senior citizens who attend Churches of God, General Conference Sunday Schools." Weekly. Estab. 1865. Circ. 8,000.

Needs: Adventure, feminist, humor, mainstream, religious/inspirational, senior citizen/retirement. Nothing that denies or ridicules standard Christian values. Receives 30 unsolicited fiction mss/month. Buys 1 ms every 2-3 issues; 20-25 mss/year. Publishes ms 4-12 months after submission. Published work by Betty Steele Everett, Todd Lee and Betty Lou Mell. Length: 1,500 words average; 1,000 words minimum; 1,700 words maximum.

How to Contact: Send complete ms with cover letter ("letter not essential, unless there is information about author's background which enhances story's credibility or verifies details as being authentic"). Reports in 6 months. SASE for ms. Simultaneous and reprint submissions OK. Sample copy and fiction guidelines for #10 SAE and 1 first class stamp. "If more than one sample copy is desired along with the guidelines, will need 2 oz. postage."

Payment: Pays $10-15 and contributor's copies. Charge for extras (postage for mailing more than one).

Terms: Pays on publication for one-time rights.

Advice: "Competition at the mediocre level is fierce. There is a dearth of well-written, relevant fiction which wrestles with real problems involving Christian values applied to the crisis times and 'passages' of life. Humor which puts the daily grind into a fresh perspective and which promises hope for survival is also in short supply. Write from your own experience. Avoid religious jargon and stereotypes. Conclusion must be believable in terms of the story—don't force a 'Christian' ending. Avoid simplistic solutions to complex problems. Listen to the storytelling art of Garrison Keillor. Feel how very particular experiences of small town life in Minnesota become universal."

GENT, (II), Dugent Publishing Corp., Suite 600, 2600 Douglas Rd., Coral Gables FL 33134. (305)443-2378. Editor: Bruce Arthur. "Men's magazine designed to have erotic appeal for the reader. Our publications are directed to a male audience, but we do have a certain percentage of female readers. For the most part, our audience is interested in erotically stimulating material, but not exclusively." Monthly. Estab. 1959. Circ. 175,000.

• Another magazine in this publisher's sexually explicit line, *Cavalier*, has been discontinued.

Needs: Contemporary, science fiction, horror, erotica, mystery, adventure and humor. *Gent* specializes in "D-Cup cheesecake," and fiction should be slanted accordingly. "Most of the fiction published includes several sex scenes. No fiction that concerns children, religious subjects or anything that might be libelous." Receives approximately 30-50 unsolicited fiction mss/month. Buys 2 mss/issue; 24 mss/year. Publishes ms an average of 6 weeks after acceptance. Agented fiction 10%. Published new writers within the last year. Length: 2,000-3,500 words. Critiques rejected mss "when there is time."

How to Contact: Send complete ms with SASE. Reports in 1 month. Sample copy for $5. Fiction guidelines for legal-sized SASE.

Payment: Pay starts at $200; 1 contributor's copy.

Terms: Pays on publication for first North American serial rights.

Advice: "Since *Gent* magazine is the 'Home of the D-Cups,' stories and articles containing either characters or themes with a major emphasis on large breasts will have the best chance for consideration. Study a sample copy first." Mss are rejected because "there are not enough or ineffective erotic sequences, plot is not plausible, wrong length, or not slanted specifically for us."

GEORGIA SPORTSMAN, (II, IV), Game & Fish Publications, P.O. Box 741, Marietta GA 30061. (404)953-9222. Editor: Jimmy Jacobs. Magazine: 8 × 10¾; 80 pages; slick paper; slick cover; illustrations and photographs. "Adventure, humor and nostalgia dealing with hunting and fishing in Georgia for hunters and fishermen." Monthly. Estab. 1976. Circ. 48,000.

• Game & Fish Publications publishes a series of regional and state-based outdoor sport publications.

Needs: Adventure, humor/satire. "Fiction must take place in or pertain to Georgia and center on hunting and fishing. Such activities as hiking, camping, canoeing or boating are OK as long as they have a hunting or fishing connection. No strictly camping, hiking, boating or canoeing stories or pieces ascribing human characteristics to animals and fish." Receives 6-8 unsolicited mss/month. Buys 1 ms/issue; 6-12 mss/year. Publishes ms 6 months to 1 year after acceptance. Recently published work by Bob Kornegay, LeRoy Powell, William Parlasca. Length: 1,500 words average, 1,400 words minimum; 1,600 words maximum.

How to Contact: Send complete ms with cover letter including "who the writer is, and how to contact him/her." SASE. Simultaneous submissions OK. Reports in 6-8 weeks. Sample copy for $2.50. Free fiction guidelines.

Payment: Pays $125.

Terms: Pays 2½ months prior to publication for first North American serial rights.

THE GIFTED CHILD TODAY, (IV), GCT Inc., P.O. Box 6448, Mobile AL 36660. (205)478-4700. Editor: Marvin Gold. Magazine: 8½ × 11; 64 pages; coated paper; self-cover; illustrations and photographs. "Focuses on materials about gifted, creative, and talented children and youth. For parents and professionals." Bimonthly. Estab. 1978. Circ. 10,000.

● *The Gifted Child Today* has won serveral Ed Press awards, the most recent in 1992.

Needs: "As long as the subject matter deals with gifted, creative, and/or talented individuals in some way, material will be considered." Does not want to see "protagonist(s) and/or antagonist(s) that are not gifted, creative and/or talented individuals." Receives 3-4 unsolicited mss each month. Accepts 1 ms/issue. Publishes ms 1-2 years after acceptance. Length: 1,800 words average; 1,000 words minimum; 5,000 words maximum. Publishes short shorts. Length: 500 words.

How to Contact: Send complete ms with cover letter. No simultaneous submissions. Reports in 1 month on queries; 2 months on mss. SASE. Sample copy for $5. Reviews novels and short story collections "only if material deals with gifted individuals as subject."

Payment: Pays in contributor's copies. Charges for extras.

Terms: Acquires first rights.

GOLF JOURNAL, (II), United States Golf Assoc., Golf House, Far Hills NJ 07931. (908)234-2300. Managing Editor: David Earl. Magazine: 40-48 pages; self cover stock; illustrations and photos. "The magazine's subject is golf—its history, lore, rules, equipment and general information. The focus is on amateur golf and those things applying to the millions of American golfers. Our audience is generally professional, highly literate and knowledgeable; presumably they read *Golf Journal* because of an interest in the game, its traditions, and its noncommercial aspects." Published 8 times/year. Estab. 1949. Circ. 285,000.

Needs: Humor. "Fiction is very limited. *Golf Journal* has had an occasional humorous story, topical in nature. Generally speaking, short stories are not used. Golf jokes will not be used." Buys 10-12 mss/year. Published new writers within the last year. Length: 1,000-2,000 words. Recommends other markets. Critiques rejected mss "when there is time."

How to Contact: Send complete ms with SASE. Reports in 2 months on mss. Sample copy for SASE.

Payment: Pays $500-1,000; 1-10 contributor's copies.

Terms: Pays on acceptance.

Advice: "Know your subject (golf); familiarize yourself first with the publication." Rejects mss because "fiction usually does not serve the function of *Golf Journal*, which, as the official magazine of the United States Golf Association, deals chiefly with nonfiction subjects."

GOOD HOUSEKEEPING, (II), 959 Eighth Ave., New York NY 10019. Editor: John Mack Carter. Fiction Editor: Lee Quarfoot. Magazine: 8 × 10; approximately 250 pages; slick paper; thick, high-gloss cover; 4-color illustrations, b&w and color photos. Homemaking magazine of informational articles, how-to's for homemakers of all ages. Monthly. Circ. 20 million.

● *Good Housekeeping* ranked #10 on the 1992 *Writer's Digest* Fiction 50 list.

Needs: "*Good Housekeeping* looks for stories of emotional interest to women—courtship, romance, marriage, family, friendship, personal growth, coming-of-age. The best way to know if your story is appropriate for us is to read several of our recent issues. (We are sorry but we do not furnish free sample copies of the magazine.)" Buys 1 short story/issue. Agented fiction 90%. Length: 1,000-3,000 words.

How to Contact: Send complete disposable ms with cover letter. *Unsolicited manuscripts will not be returned* (see Advice). Simultaneous submissions OK. Reports in 4-6 weeks. Publishes ms an average of 6 months after acceptance.

Payment: Pays standard magazine rates.

Terms: Pays on acceptance for first North American serial rights.

Advice: "It is now our policy that all submissions of unsolicited fiction received in our offices will be read and, if found to be unsuitable for us, destroyed by recycling. If you wish to introduce your work to us, you will be submitting material that will not be critiqued or returned. The odds are long that we will contact you to inquire about publishing your submission or to invite you to correspond with us directly, so please be sure before you take the time and expense to submit it that it is our type of material."

GOREZONE, (II, IV), Starlog Communications, Inc., 475 Park Ave. S., New York NY 10016. (212)689-2830. Editor: Tony Timpone. Fiction Editor: Michael Gingold. Magazine: 8 × 11; 66 pages; glossy paper; 4-color cover; illustrations; photographs for nonfiction. "We are a horror magazine looking for

quality, original and scary short horror stories for teens, mostly male, age 16-22." Quarterly. Estab. 1988. Circ. 180,000.
Needs: Horror only. No "obscenity, 'it was only a dream,' movie-inspired ripoffs, etc." Receives 20 unsolicited mss/month. Buys 1 ms/issue; 4 mss/year ("so it's very competitive."). Publishes ms 4-8 months after acceptance. Agented fiction 10%. Recently published work by Steve Rasnic Tem, Wayne Allen Sallee and Jeffrey Thomas. Length: 2,400 words preferred; 2,000 words minimum; 3,100 words maximum.
How to Contact: Query first with SASE for guidelines or submit through agent. No simultaneous submissions. Reports in 3 weeks on queries; 2 months on mss. SASE. Sample copy for $4.50, 8½ × 11 SAE and $1.05 postage. Fiction guidelines for #10 SAE and 1 first class stamp.
Payment: Pays $150-200 and 2 contributor's copies.
Terms: Pays on publication. Buys all rights.
Advice: "Fiction has to be good, presented professionally. Writer must have a strong knowledge of the horror market and our magazine. Read our magazine and back issues to determine what kinds of stories have already been published. Don't call offices ever."

‡**GRIT, America's Family Magazine, (II),** Stauffer Communications, Inc., 616 Jefferson, Topeka KS 66607. (913)295-1147. Executive Editor: Roberta J. Peterson. Tabloid: 50 pages; 30 lb. newsprint; illustrations and photos. "*Grit* is a 'good news' publication and has been since 1881. Fiction should be approx. 2,500 words and interesting, inspiring, perhaps compelling in nature. Audience is *conservative*; readers tend to be 40+ from smaller towns, rural areas." Biweekly. Estab. 1881. Circ. 400,000.
● *Grit* is considered one of the leading family-oriented publications. Stauffer Communications also publishes *Cappers*, listed in this book.
Needs: Adventure, condensed novelette, mainstream/contemporary (conservative), mystery/suspense, light religious/inspirational, romance (contemporary, historical), science fiction, westerns (traditional, frontier). Buys 1 mss/issue; 26 mss/year. Length: 2,500 words average; 2,300 words minimum; 2,700 words maximum. Also publishes poetry.
How to Contact: Send complete ms with cover letter. Should include estimated word count, brief bio, social security number, list of publications with submission. Reports in 2 months. Send SASE (IRC) for reply, return of ms or send disposable copy of ms. No simultaneous submissions. Will consider electronic (disk or modem) submissions (Macintosh). Sample copy $1.50.
Payment: $150 minimum; $225 maximum.
Terms: Purchases first North American serial rights.
Advice: Looks for "well-written, simple and readable; fresh approach; strong start."

THE GUIDE: Gay Travel, Entertainment, Politics, and Sex, (II, IV), Box 593, Boston MA 02199. (617)266-8557. Fax: (617)266-1125. Editor: French Wall. Magazine: 8 × 10; 124-156; newsprint; 70 lb. cover stock; photos. "Gay liberation and sex positive information, articles and columns; radical political and radical religious philosophies welcome. Audience is primarily gay men, some lesbians, bar crowd and grassroots politicos." Monthly. Estab. 1981. Circ. 30,000.
Needs: Adventure, erotica, ethnic, experimental, fantasy, feminist, gay, historical (general), humor/satire, lesbian, regional, religious/inspirational romance (contemporary, historical and young adult), science fiction, senior citizen, spiritual, sports, suspense/mystery. "Focus on empowerment—avoidance of 'victim' philosophy appreciated." Receives 4 mss/month. Publishes ms within 3 months to 1 year after acceptance. Length: 1,800 words average; 500 words minimum; 5,000 words maximum. Recently published work by Lars Eighner, John Champagne and A.J. Johnson; published new writers within the last year. Publishes short shorts. Sometimes critiques rejected mss.
How to Contact: Query first. Reports in 2-4 weeks. SASE; include cover letter and phone number. Simultaneous submissions OK. Sample copy for 9 × 13 SAE and 8 first class stamps.
Payment: Pays $50-180.
Terms: Pays on acceptance for all rights or first rights.
Advice: "*The Guide*'s format and extensive distribution in this area makes it an excellent vehicle for writers anxious to be read. *The Guide* has multiplied its press run fourfold in the past years and is committed to continued growth."

‡**GUIDE MAGAZINE, (I, II, IV),** Review & Herald Publishing Association, 55 W. Oak Ridge Dr., Hagerstown MD 21740. (301)791-7000. Fax: (301)791-7012. Editor: Jeannette Johnson. Magazine: 6 × 9; 32 pages; glossy (coated) paper; illustrations; photographs. "*Guide* is a weekly Christian journal geared toward 10- to 14-year-olds. Stories and other features presented are relevant to the needs of

today's young person, and emphasize positive aspects of Christian living." Weekly. Estab. 1953. Circ. 40,000.

● Affiliated with the Seventh-day Adventist Church, *Guide* has won awards from the Protestant Church Publishing Association, Associated Church Press and Evangelical Church Press.

Needs: Religious/inspirational: adventure (10-14 years), humor, sports, young adult/teen (10-18 years); mainstream/contemporary. No romance, sci fi, horror, etc. "We use four general categories in each issue: spiritual/devotional; personal growth; adventure/nature; humor." Receives 80-100 unsolicited mss/month. Buys 2-3 mss/issue; 150 mss/year. Publishes ms 3-12 months after acceptance. Length: 1,000-1,200 words average. Publishes short shorts. Often critiques or comments on rejected mss.

How to Contact: Send complete ms. Should include estimated word count, Social Security number. Reports in 2 weeks. SASE for return of ms or a send disposable copy. Simultaneous and reprint submissions OK. Sample copy for #10 SAE and 2 first class stamps. Fiction guidelines for #10 SAE and 1 first class stamp.

Payment: Pays 3-5¢/word and 3 contributor's copies. Additional copies 50¢ each.

Terms: Pays on acceptance. Buys first, first North American serial, one-time, reprint or simultaneous rights.

Advice: "The aim of *Guide* magazine is to reflect in creative yet concrete ways the unconditional love of God to young people 10 to 14 years of age. Believing that an accurate picture of God is a prerequisite for wholeness, our efforts editorially and in design will be focused on accurately portraying His attributes and expectations."

GULFSHORE LIFE, The Lifestyle Magazine of Southwest Florida, (II, IV), 2975 S. Horseshoe Dr., Naples FL 33942. (813)643-3933. Editor: Tim Whitaker. Magazine: 100 pages; 50 lb. Sommerset paper; 100 lb. Warren Flow cover; photographs. "Lifestyle magazine for older, upscale audience-visitors and residents to southwest Florida." Estab. 1970. Circ. 20,000.

Needs: Literary, mainstream, regional (southwest Florida). No "erotica, gay, preschool." Receives 2-3 unsolicited mss/month. Buys 1 mss/year. Publishes ms 3-6 months after acceptance. Length: 1,800 words preferred; 1,200 words minimum; 3,000 words maximum. Publishes short shorts. Length: 500 words. Sometimes comments on rejected ms.

How to Contact: Send complete ms with cover letter. Reports in 1-2 months. SASE. Simultaneous submissions OK. Accepts electronic submission via disk or modem. Sample copy for $2.95, 8½×11 SAE and $2.50 postage. Fiction guidelines for #10 SAE and 1 first class stamp.

Payment: Pays 14¢/word.

Terms: Payment is on publication. Offers 30% kill fee. Buys first North American serial rights. Sends galleys to author.

Advice: Looks for writing that "keeps me riveted to the page from word #1! Seldom see enough development of main character(s) or details. Writers try to cover too much with too little detail. Focus everything more!"

HADASSAH MAGAZINE, (IV), 50 W. 58th St., New York NY 10019. Executive Editor: Alan M. Tigay. Senior Editor: Zelda Shluker. General interest magazine: 8½×11; 48-70 pages; coated and uncoated paper; slick, medium weight coated cover; drawings and cartoons; photos. Primarily concerned with Israel, the American Jewish community, Jewish communities around the world and American current affairs. Monthly except combined June/July and August/September issues. Circ. 375,000.

Needs: Ethnic (Jewish). Receives 20-25 unsolicited fiction mss each month. Recently published fiction by Anita Desai and Lori Ubell; published new writers within the last year. Length: 1,500-2,500 words.

How to Contact: Query first with writing samples. Reports in 3 months or less on mss. "Not interested in multiple submissions or previously published articles."

Payment: Pays $300 minimum.

Terms: Pays on publication for U.S. publication rights.

Advice: "Stories on a Jewish theme should be neither self-hating nor schmaltzy."

HARPER'S MAGAZINE, (II, III), 11th Floor, 666 Broadway, New York NY 10012. (212)614-6500. Editor: Lewis H. Lapham. Magazine: 8×10¾; 80 pages; illustrations. Magazine for well educated, widely read and socially concerned readers, college-aged and older, those active in political and community affairs. Monthly. Circ. 200,000.

● This is considered a top but tough market for contemporary fiction. The magazine was a National Magazine Award Finalist for fiction in 1991. For more information see the close-up interview with Lewis Lapham in the 1992 *Writer's Market*.

Needs: Contemporary and humor. Stories on contemporary life and its problems. Does a summer reading issue usually in August. Receives approximately 300 unsolicited fiction mss/month. Published new writers within the last year. Length: 1,000-5,000 words.

How to Contact: Query to managing editor, or through agent. Reports in 6 weeks on queries.

Payment: Pays $500-1,000.

Terms: Pays on acceptance for rights, which vary on each author and material. Negotiable kill fee. Sends galleys to author.

Advice: Buys very little fiction but *Harper's* has published short stories traditionally.

HI-CALL, (II), Gospel Publishing House, 1445 Boonville Ave., Springfield MO 65802-1894. (417)862-2781. Editor: Deanna S. Harris. Take-home Sunday school paper for teenagers (ages 12-17). Weekly. Estab. 1936. Circ. 80,000.

Needs: Religious/inspirational, mystery/suspense, adventure, humor, spiritual and young adult, "with a strong but not preachy Biblical emphasis." Receives approximately 100 unsolicited fiction mss/month. Published work by Betty Steele Everett, Alan Cliburn and Michelle Starr. Published new writers within the last year. Length: up to 1,500 words.

How to Contact: Send complete ms with SASE. Reports in 1-3 months. Simultaneous and reprint submissions OK. Free sample copy and guidelines.

Payment: Pays 2-3¢/word.

Terms: Pays on acceptance for one-time rights.

Advice: "Most manuscripts are rejected because of shallow characters, shallow or predictable plots, and/or a lack of spiritual emphasis. Send seasonal material approximately 18 months in advance."

HIGH ADVENTURE, (II), General Council Assemblies of God (Gospel Publishing Co.), 1445 Boonville, Springfield MO 65802. (417)862-2781, ext. 4178. Editor: Marshall Bruner. Magazine: 8⁵⁄₁₆ × 11⅛; 16 pages; lancer paper; self cover; illustrations; photos. Magazine for adolescent boys. "Designed to provide boys with worthwhile, enjoyable, leisure reading; to challenge them in narrative form to higher ideals and greater spiritual dedication; and to perpetuate the spirit of the Royal Rangers program through stories, ideas and illustrations." Quarterly. Estab. 1971. Circ. 86,000.

Needs: Adventure, historical (general), mystery/suspense, religious/inspirational and western. Published new writers within the last year. Length: 1,200 words minimum. Publishes short shorts to 1,000 words. Occasionally critiques rejected mss.

How to Contact: Send ms with SASE. Include Social Security number. Reports in 2 months. Simultaneous and reprint submissions OK. Free sample copy and fiction guidelines for 9 × 12 SASE.

Payment: Pays 2-3¢/word (base) and 3 contributor's copies.

Terms: Pays on acceptance for first rights and one-time rights.

Advice: "Ask for list of upcoming themes."

HIGHLIGHTS FOR CHILDREN, 803 Church St., Honesdale PA 18431. (717)253-1080. Editor: Kent L. Brown, Jr. Address fiction to: Beth Troop, Manuscript Coordinator. Magazine: 8½ × 11; 42 pages; uncoated paper; coated cover stock; illustrations; photos. Published 11 times/year. Circ. 2.8 million.

● *Highlights* is very supportive of writers. The magazine sponsors a contest and a workshop each year at Chatauqua (New York). See the listings for these and for their press, Boyds Mills Press in other sections of this book. The magazine ranked #24 on the 1992 *Writer's Digest* Fiction 50 list.

Needs: Juvenile (ages 2-12). Unusual stories appealing to both girls and boys; stories with good characterization, strong emotional appeal, vivid, full of action. "Begin with action rather than description, have strong plot, believable setting, suspense from start to finish." Length: 400-900 words. "We also need easy stories for very young readers (100-400 words)." No war, crime or violence. Receives 600-800 unsolicited fiction mss/month. Buys 6-7 mss/issue. Also publishes rebus (picture) stories of 125 words or under for the 3-to 7-year-old child. Recently published work by Dianne MacMillan, Judith Logan Lehne and Don Reed; published new writers within the last year. Critiques rejected mss occasionally, "especially when editors see possibilities in story."

How to Contact: Send complete ms with SASE and include a rough word count and cover letter "with any previous acceptances by our magazine; any other published work anywhere." No simultaneous submissions. Reports in 6 weeks. Free guidelines on request.

Payment: Pays 14¢ and up per word.

Terms: Pays on acceptance for all rights. Sends galleys to author.

Advice: "We accept a story on its merit whether written by an unpublished or an experienced writer. Mss are rejected because of poor writing, lack of plot, trite or worn-out plot, or poor characterization. Children *like* stories and learn about life from stories. Children learn to become lifelong fiction readers by enjoying stories."

ALFRED HITCHCOCK MYSTERY MAGAZINE, (I, II), Dell Magazines Fiction Group, 380 Lexington Ave., New York NY 10168-0035. (212)856-6300. Editor: Cathleen Jordan. Mystery fiction magazine: 5¹⁄₁₆ × 7⅜; 160 pages; 28 lb. newsprint paper; 60 lb. machine-/coated cover stock; illustrations; photos. Published 13 times/year. Estab. 1956. Circ. 225,000.

●   Stories published in *Alfred Hitchcock Mystery Magazine* have won several Edgar Awards for "Best Mystery Story of the Year," Shamus Awards for "Best Private Eye Story of the Year" and Robert L. Fish Awards for "Best First Mystery Short Story of the Year." It ranks #14 on the 1992 *Writer's Digest* Fiction 50 list. See *Ellery Queen's Mystery Magazine* also listed in this book.

Needs: Mystery (private eye, police procedural, amateur sleuth, cozy) and detection. No sensationalism. Number of mss/issue varies with length of mss. Length: up to 14,000 words. Also publishes short shorts.

How to Contact: Send complete ms and SASE. Simultaneous submissions OK, if indicated. Reports in 2 months. Guideline sheet for SASE.

Payment: Pays 6½¢/word on acceptance.

THE HOME ALTAR, Meditations for Families with Children, (I), P.O. Box 590179, San Francisco CA 94159-0179. Editor: M. Elaine Dunham. Magazine: 5¼ × 7¼; 64 pages; newsprint paper; coated 4-color cover; 2-color illustrations. "*The Home Altar* is a magazine of daily devotions. For each day, there is a designated Bible reading, a short story (fiction or nonfiction) which reflects the central message of the biblical passage, and a concluding prayer." Readers are "primarily Lutheran (ELCA) families—with children between 6 and 14 years of age." Quarterly. Estab. 1940. Circ. 75,000.

Needs: Juvenile (5-9 years) and religious/inspirational. "No unsolicited manuscripts are accepted for publication in *The Home Altar*. All writing is done on assignment, to reflect specific Bible readings and themes." Accepts up to 90 mss/issue; approximately 365 mss/year. Publishes ms an average of 6-12 months after acceptance. Published work by Barbra Minar, Normajean Matzke and Jerome Koch. Length: 150 words average; 125 words minimum; 170 words maximum. Sometimes critiques rejected mss.

How to Contact: Query with clips of published or unpublished work. Reports on queries in 3 months; on assigned mss in 2 weeks. Sample copy and fiction guidelines free.

Payment: Pays $10/"story"; contributor's copies.

Terms: Pays on acceptance for all rights.

Advice: "We're trying to serve a diverse group of readers—children of all ages as well as adults. A well-written story often has several levels of meaning and will touch people of different ages and experiences in different ways. Write stories in which children are the protagonists. Keep your sentences short. Use inclusive language when referring to human beings or to God."

HOME LIFE, (II), The Sunday School Board of the Southern Baptist Convention, 127 9th Ave. N., Nashville TN 37234. (615)251-2271. Editor: Charlie Warren. A Christian family magazine: 8⅛ × 11; 66 pages; coated paper; separate cover stock; illustrations; photos. "Top priorities are strengthening and enriching marriage; parenthood; family concerns and problems; and spiritual and personal growth. Most of our readers are married couples and parents between the ages of 25-50. They read it out of a desire for Christian growth and discipleship." Monthly. Estab. 1947. Circ. 650,000.

●   Other family and relationship magazines published by The Sunday School Board include *Christian Singles*, *Living with Teenagers* and *The Student*.

Needs: Contemporary, prose poem, religious/inspirational, spiritual, humor and young adult. "We do not want distasteful, risqué or raunchy fiction. Nor should it be too fanciful or far-fetched." Receives approximately 100-200 unsolicited fiction mss/month. Buys 1-2 mss/issue; 12-24 mss/year. Publishes ms 12-20 months after acceptance. Published work by Irene J. Kutz, Mary C. Perham, Ann Beacham; published new writers within the last year. Length: 750-1,800 words. Publishes short shorts of 500+ words. Recommends other markets.

How to Contact: Query or send complete ms. Reports in 1 month on queries; 2 months on mss. SASE always. Simultaneous submissions OK. Sample copy for $1.
Payment: Pays up to 5½¢/word for unsolicited mss; 3 contributor's copies.
Terms: Pays on acceptance for all rights, first rights or first North American serial rights. Rarely buys reprints.
Advice: "Work must be believable."

‡HOME TIMES, (I, II, IV), Neighbor News, Inc., P.O. Box 16096, West Palm Beach FL 33416. (407)439-3509. Editor: Dennis Lombard. Newspaper: tabloid; 12-24 pages; newsprint; illustrations and photographs. "Interdenominational Christian news, views, fiction, poetry, sold to general public, *not* through churches." Monthly. ("May go weekly in late 1990-early 1991"). Estab. 1980. Circ. 13,000.
Needs: Adventure, historical (general), humor/satire, literary, mainstream, religious/inspirational, romance, sports. "All fiction needs to be related to the publication's religious content—we feel you must examine a sample issue because *Home Times* is *different*." Nothing "preachy or doctrinal." Plans special fiction issue and other topical specials. Receives unsolicited mss/month. Buys 75 mss/issue. Publishes ms 1-6 months after acceptance. Published work by Michelle Starr. Length: 900 words average; 500 words minimum; 1,000 words maximum. "Will consider any length under 1,000."
How to Contact: Send complete manuscript with cover letter including Social Security number. "Absolutely no queries." "1-2 sentences on what the piece is and on who you are." Reports on mss in 1 week. SASE. Simultaneous and reprint submissions OK. Sample copy for $1, 9×12 SAE and 2 first class stamps. Guidelines for #10 SAE and 1 first class stamp.
Payment: Pays $5-35.
Terms: Buys one-time rights.
Advice: "Read our newspapers—get the drift of our rather unusual interdenominational non-doctrinal content. Send $5 for a writer's 1-year subscription (12 issues, reg. $9)."

HORSE ILLUSTRATED, (IV), Fancy Publications, Box 6050, Mission Viejo CA 92690. (714)855-8822. Fax: (714)855-3045. Editor: Susan Wills. Associate Editor: Kathryn Shayman. "General all-breed horse magazine for horse lovers of all ages but mainly women riding for show and pleasure. All material is centered around horses; both English and western riding styles are profiled." Monthly. Estab. 1982. Circ. 120,000.
Needs: Adventure, humor and suspense/mystery. "Must concern horses. Liberal—nothing unsuitable to a younger audience, although we do not want mss aimed directly at young readers." Receives 3-5 unsolicited mss/month. Buys 5-6 mss/year. Publishes ms 4-10 months after acceptance. Published work by Cooky McClung, Elizabeth Vaugh; published new writers within the last year. Length: 1,500-2,000 words average; 1,000 words minimum; 2,500 words maximum. Occasionally critiques rejected mss if asked to do so.
How to Contact: Query first or send complete ms. Reports in 2 months on queries; 3 months on mss. SASE. Sample copy for $3.25. Fiction guidelines for SASE.
Payment: Pays $50-150; 2 contributor's copies; $2 charge for extras ("free if request is for a reasonable number of copies").
Terms: Pays on publication for one-time rights.
Advice: "Write about adult women—*no* little girl, wild stallion or cowboy and Indian stories, please."

‡HOT 'N' NASTY, (II, IV), AJA Publishing Corp., P.O. Box 470, Port Chester NY 10573. Editor: Julie Silver. Magazine: digest-sized; 106 pages; newsprint paper; board 10 pt. cover; illustrations; photographs. "Sexually explicit material." Publishes 8 issues/year.
• AJA Publishing also publishes *Options* magazine listed in this book.
Needs: Erotica. Buys 13 mss/year; 104 mss/year. Length: 750-1,000 ("Letters") or 2,000-3,000 ("Stories"). "Rejects go out with checklist showing some reasons for rejection."
How to Contact: Send complete ms with or without a cover letter. Should include estimated word count and disk in Mac format if available. Reports in about 3 weeks. Send SASE for reply, return of ms or send disposable copy of ms (with SASE for response). No simultaneous submissions. Accepts electronic (disk only) submissions. Sample copy for $3.50, 6×9 SAE and 4 first class stamps. Fiction guidelines for SAE and 1 first class stamp.
Payment: Pays $15 (letter), $100 (story).
Terms: Pays on publication. Buys all rights.
Advice: "Stories must 'read real,' be hot, be interesting, have *some* storyline, and get to the hot part by the bottom of page 3 at the latest. Letters must get to the hot part by top of page 2. Strongly urge writers to send for guidelines for further info, as there is too much to print here. We don't care what

you've had published before, only that you write well, follow our guidelines and, if possible, strive for some originality. You do not have to be a 'name' writer with a track record. You *do* have to write well and *hot*."

‡**HOT SHOTS, (IV),** Sunshine Publishing Company, Inc., 7060 Convoy Court, San Diego CA 92111. (619)278-9080. Editor: Ralph Cobar. Magazine; digest sized; 100 pages; Dombrite paper; 4-color cover; color centerfold and photographs. "Adult erotica, real life fantasies, and true reader experience. Explicit fiction about 18-50 year old males only. For gay males." Monthly. Plans special fiction issue. Estab. 1986. Circ. 35,000.
Needs: Confession, erotica, gay. No subjugation, rape, heavy s&m, beastiality, incest, unless characters are of consenting age. Accepts 100-150 mss/year. Length: 2,500 words average; 2,000 words minimum; 3,000 words maximum. Sometimes critiques rejected mss.
How to Contact: Send complete ms with cover letter. Reports in 1-2 months. Accepts electronic submissions via disk convertable to ASCII format or WP5.1. Requires hard copy when sending disk submissions. Sample copy $5. Fiction guidelines free.
Payment: Pays $100, contributor's copies.
Terms: Pays on publication for all rights.
Advice: "Keep all sexual activity between fictional characters within the realm of possibility. Do not overexaggerate physical characteristics. We want stimulating fiction, not comedy. The overall tone of *Hot Shots* is always exciting, up beat, compassionate."

HUMPTY DUMPTY'S MAGAZINE, (II), Children's Better Health Institute, Box 567, 1100 Waterway Blvd., Indianapolis IN 46206. Editor: Christine French Clark. Magazine: 6½ × 9⅛; 48 pages; 35 lb. paper; coated cover; illustrations; rarely photos. Children's magazine stressing health, nutrition, hygiene, exercise and safety for children ages 4-6. Publishes 8 issues/year.
• Children's Better Health Institute also publishes *Child Life, Children's Digest, Children's Playmate, Jack and Jill* and *Turtle* listed in this book.
Needs: Juvenile health-related material and material of a more general nature. No inanimate talking objects. Rhyming stories should flow easily with no contrived rhymes. Receives 250-300 unsolicited fiction mss/month. Buys 3-5 mss/issue. Length: 600 words maximum.
How to Contact: Send complete ms with SASE. No queries. Reports in 8-10 weeks. Sample copy for $1.25. Editorial guidelines for SASE.
Payment: Pays minimum 10-20¢/word for stories plus 2 contributor's copies (more upon request).
Terms: Pays on publication for all rights. (One-time book rights returned when requested for specific publication.)
Advice: "In contemporary stories, characters should be up-to-date, with realistic dialogue. We're looking for health-related stories with unusual twists or surprise endings. We want to avoid stories and poems that 'preach.' We try to present the health material in a positive way, utilizing a light humorous approach wherever possible." Most rejected mss "are too wordy. Cover letters should be included only if they give pertinent information—list of credits, bibliography, or mention of any special training or qualifications that make author an authority."

HUSTLER, Larry Flynt Publications, Suite 300, 9171 Wilshire Blvd., Beverly Hills CA 90210. Does not accept outside fiction; all fiction is staff written.

HUSTLER BUSTY BEAUTIES, (I, IV), HG Publications, Inc., Suite 300, 9171 Wilshire Blvd., Beverly Hills CA 90210. (310)858-7100. Editor: N. Morgen Hagen. Magazine: 8 × 11; 100 pages; 60 lb. paper; 80 lb. cover; illustrations and photographs. "Adult entertainment and reading centered around large-breasted women for an over-18 audience, mostly male." Monthly. Estab. 1988. Circ. 150,000.
Needs: Adventure, erotica, fantasy, mystery/suspense. All must have erotic theme. Receives 25 unsolicited fiction mss/month. Buys 1 ms/issue; 6-12 mss/year. Publishes mss 3-6 months after acceptance. Published work by Mike Dillon, H.H. Morris. Length: 1,600 words preferred; 1,000 words minimum; 2,000 words maximum.
How to Contact: Query first. Then send complete ms with cover letter. Reports in 2 weeks on queries; in 2-4 weeks on mss. SASE. Sample copy for $5. Fiction guidelines free.
Payment: Pays $80-500.
Terms: Pays on publication for all rights.
Advice: Looks for "1. Plausible plot, well-defined characters, literary ingenuity. 2. Hot sex scenes. 3. Readable, coherent, grammatically sound prose."

I.D., (IV), David C. Cook Publishing Co., 850 N. Grove, Elgin IL 60120. (708)741-2400. Editors: Douglas Schmidt; Lorraine Triggs. A take-home Sunday school paper: 5½×8½; 8 pages; Penegra paper and cover; full color illustrations and photos. For senior high classes. Weekly.

• *I.D.* won First Place for a humorous article awarded by Evangelical Press Association.

Needs: Christian spiritual. Writers work mostly on assignment. "Each piece must present some aspect of the Christian life without being preachy. No closing sermons and no pat answers. Any topic appropriate to senior high is acceptable." Buys 5-10 mss/year. Length: 900-1,200 words.

How to Contact: Send complete ms with SASE. No queries please. Cover letter with brief bio, religious credentials and experience with senior highs. Simultaneous submissions OK. Reports in 2 months on mss. Guidelines for SASE.

Payment: Pays $100-125.

Terms: Pays on acceptance for all rights.

Advice: "You've got to know kids and be aware of the struggles Christian kids are facing today. Don't write about how things were when you were a teenager—kids don't want to hear it."

IDEALS MAGAZINE, (II), Ideals Publishing Corp., Suite 890, 565 Marriott Dr., Nashville TN 37210. (615)885-8270. Associate Editor: Tim Hamling. Vice President of Publishing: Patricia Pingry. Magazine: 8⁷⁄₁₆×10⅞; 80 pages; 60 lb Cougarpaper; 12 pt C1S cover; illustrations; photos. "*Ideals* is a family-oriented magazine with issues corresponding to seasons and based on traditional values." Published 8 times a year. Estab. 1944.

Needs: Seasonal, inspirational, spiritual, or humorous short, short fiction or prose poem. Length: 700 words maximum.

How to Contact: Send complete ms with SASE. Reports in 3-4 months on mss.

Payment: Varies.

Terms: Pays on publication for one-time rights.

Advice: "We publish fiction that is appropriate to the theme of the issue and to our audience."

INDIA CURRENTS, (II,IV), The Complete Indian American Magazine, Box 21285, San Jose CA 95151. (408)274-6966. Fax: (408)274-2733. Editor: Arvind Kumar. Magazine: 8½×11; 104 pages; newsprint paper; illustrations and photographs. "The arts and culture of India as seen in America for Indians and non-Indians with a common interest in India." Monthly. Estab. 1987. Circ. 30,000.

• *India Currents* recently won an award for "Cultural Awareness Through Journalism" from the Federation of Indian American Associations.

Needs: All Indian content: contemporary, ethnic, feminist, historical (general), humor/satire, literary, mainstream, prose poem, psychic/supernatural/occult, regional, religious/inspirational, romance, translations (from Indian languages). "We seek material with insight into Indian culture, American culture and the crossing from one to another." Receives 12 unsolicited mss/month. Buys 1 ms/issue; 12 mss/year. Publishes ms 2-6 months after acceptance. Published work by Chitra Divakaruni, Jyotsna Sreenivasan, Mathew Chacko; published new writers within the last year. Length: 1,500 words average; 1,000 words minimum; 3,000 words maximum. Publishes short shorts. Length: 500 words.

How to Contact: Send complete ms with cover letter and clips of published work. Reports in 2-3 months on mss. SASE. Simultaneous and reprint submissions OK. Accepts electronic submissions. Sample copy $3.

Payment: Pays $25/1,000 words.

Terms: Pays on publication for one-time rights.

Advice: "Story must be related to India and subcontinent in some meaningful way. The best stories are those which document some deep transformation as a result of an Indian experience, or those which show the humanity of Indians as the world's most ancient citizens."

INDIAN LIFE MAGAZINE, (II, IV), Intertribal Christian Communications, Box 3765, Station B, Winnipeg, Manitoba R2W 3R6 Canada. (204)661-9333 or (800)665-9275 in Canada only. Fax: (204)661-3982. Contact: Editor. Magazine: 8½×11; 24 pages; newsprint paper and cover stock; illustrations; photos. A nondenominational Christian magazine written and read mostly by North American Indians. Bimonthly. Estab. 1979. Circ. 65,000.

• *Indian Life Magazine* has won several awards for "Higher Goals in Christian Journalism" and "Excellence" from the Evangelical Press Association. The magazine also won awards from the Native American Press Association.

Needs: Adventure, confession, ethnic (Indian), historical (general), juvenile, religious/inspirational and young adult/teen. Receives 10 unsolicited mss/month. Buys 1 ms/issue; 4-5 mss/year. Published new writers within the last year. Length: 1,000-1,200 words average. Publishes short shorts of 600-900 words. Occasionally comments on rejected mss.

How to Contact: Query first, send complete ms (with cover letter, bio and published clips), or query with clips of published work. Simultaneous submissions OK. Reports in 1 month on queries; in 2 months on mss. IRC or SASE ("US stamps no good up here"). Sample copy $1 and 8½×11 SAE. Fiction guidelines for $1 and #10 SAE.

Payment: Write for details on payment.

Terms: Pays on publication for first rights.

Advice: "Keep it simple with an Indian viewpoint at about a 7th grade reading level. Read story out loud. Have someone else read it to you. If it doesn't come across smoothly and naturally, it needs work."

INIQUITIES, The Magazine of Great Wickedness & Wonder, (I, II), Suite 1346, 235 E. Colorado Blvd., Pasadena CA 91101. Editors: J.F. Gonzalez and Buddy Martinez. Magazine: 8½×11; 96 pages; slick glossy paper; illustrations and photographs. "Horror fiction, nonfiction in relation to horror and relating subjects (see guidelines) for anybody who has an interest in horror (books, film, etc.)." Quarterly. Estab. 1990. Circ. 10,000.

Needs: Horror, mystery, (police procedural) psychic/supernatural/occult; suspense and (soft/sociological) science fiction. No sword and sorcery, romance, confessional, pornography. Receives 250 unsolicited mss/month. Buys 6-8 mss/issue; 30-35 mss/year. Publishes ms 6 months-1½ years after acceptance. Published work by Peter Straub, Clive Barker, Ray Bradbury. Length: 4,000-6,000 words preferred; 10,000 words maximum. Publishes short shorts. Sometimes critiques rejected mss and recommends other markets.

How to Contact: Send complete ms with cover letter. Include "credits, if any, name, address and phone number. I don't want the writer to tell me about the story in the cover letter." Reports in 1-3 weeks on queries; 3 months on mss. SASE. Simultaneous and reprint submissions OK. Sample copy for $4.95. Fiction guidelines for #10 SAE and 1 first class stamp.

Payment: Pays 3¢-5¢/word.

Terms: Offers kill fee of half the amount. Buys first North American serial rights. Sends galleys to author.

Advice: Looks for "believable characters and original ideas. Good writing. Fantastic writing. Make the words flow and count for the story. If the story keeps us turning the pages with bated breath. It has a great chance. If we get through the first two pages and it's sloppy, displays weak, or uninteresting characters or a contrived plot, we won't even finish it. Chances are the reader won't either. Know the genre and what's been done. *Invest in a sample copy*. While we are open to different styles of horror. We have high expectations for the fiction we publish. The only way a beginner will know what we expect is to buy the magazine and read what we've published."

INSIDE, The Magazine of the Jewish Exponent, (II), Jewish Federation, 226 S. 16th St., Philadelphia PA 19102. (215)893-5700. Editor-in-Chief: Jane Biberman. Magazine: 175-225 pages; glossy paper; illustrations; photos. Aimed at middle- and upper-middle-class audience, Jewish-oriented articles and fiction. Quarterly. Estab. 1980. Circ. 80,000.

Needs: Contemporary, ethnic, humor/satire, literary and translations. No erotica. Receives approximately 10 unsolicited fiction mss/month. Buys 1-2 mss/issue; 4-8 mss/year. Published new writers within the last year. Length: 1,500 words minimum; 3,000 words maximum; 2,000 words average. Occasionally critiques rejected mss.

How to Contact: Query first with clips of published work. Reports on queries in 3 weeks. SASE. Simultaneous submissions OK. Sample copy for $3. Fiction guidelines for SASE.

Payment: Pays $100-600.

Terms: Pays on acceptance for first rights. Sometimes buys reprints. Sends galleys to author.

Advice: "We're looking for original, avant-garde, stylish writing."

INSIGHTS, NRA News for Young Shooters, (II, IV), National Rifle Association of America, 1600 Rhode Island Ave. NW, Washington DC 20036. (202)828-6075. Editor: John Robbins. Magazine: 8⅛×10⅞; 24 pages; 60 lb. Midset paper and cover; illustrations and photos."*InSights* publishes educational yet entertaining articles, teaching young hunters and shooters ways to improve their performance. For boys and girls ages eight to 20." Monthly. Estab. 1981. Circ. 50,000.

Needs: Hunting or competition shooting. No "anti-hunting, anti-firearms." Receives 5-10 unsolicited mss/month. Accepts 1 ms/issue; 12 mss/year. Publishes ms an average of 1 month to 1 year after acceptance. Published work by Dan Anderson, Michael Manley and John Robbins; published new writers within the last year. Length: 1,000 words minimum; 1,500 words maximum. Publishes short shorts. Sometimes critiques rejected ms; occasionally recommends other markets.
How to Contact: Query with clips of published work and cover letter. Reports in 1 month on query; 6-8 weeks on mss. SASE. Free sample copy and fiction guidelines.
Payment: Pays up to $250.
Terms: Pays on acceptance.
Advice: "Writing is an art but publishing is a business — a big business. Any writer who understands his market place has an edge over a writer who isn't familiar with the publications that want his kind of writing. We have become more discriminating in the fiction that we buy. Story has to have a strong plot and must present a lesson, whether it is gun safety, ethics or hunting knowledge."

INTERNATIONAL BOWHUNTER, (I, II, IV), P.O. Box 67, Pillager MN 56473-0067. (218)746-3333. Editor: Johnny Boatner. Magazine: 8¼ × 10¾; 68 pages; enamel paper; illustrations and photographs. "Bowhunting articles only for bowhunters." Published 6 times/year. Estab. 1990. Circ. 50,000+.
Needs: Adventure and sports. "We want articles by people who are actually bowhunters writing about their experience." Receives 30 unsolicited mss/month. Buys 7-12 mss/issue; 49-84/year. Publishes ms 1-6 months after acceptance. Length: 1,200 words preferred; 600 words minimum; 4,000 words maximum. Publishes short shorts. Length: 500 words. Sometimes critiques rejected mss and recommends other markets.
How to Contact: Send complete ms with cover letter. Include Social Security number and bio. Reports on queries in 2 weeks. SASE. Sample copy for $2, #10 SAE and 1 first class stamp. Fiction guidelines for #10 SAE and 1 first class stamp.
Payment: Pays $25-150 and contributor's copies; charge for extras.
Terms: Buys first rights.
Advice: "Read your guidelines."

JACK AND JILL, (IV), The Children's Better Health Institute, Box 567, 1100 Waterway Blvd., Indianapolis IN 46206. (317)636-8881. Editor: Steve Charles. Children's magazine of articles, stories and activities many with a health, safety, exercise or nutritional-oriented theme, ages 6-8 years. Monthly except January/February, March/April, May/June, July/August. Estab. 1938.
• Other publications by this publisher listed in this book include *Child Life, Children's Digest, Children's Playmate, Humpty Dumpty* and *Turtle.*
Needs: Science fiction, mystery, sports, adventure, historical fiction and humor. Health-related stories with a subtle lesson. Published work by Peter Fernandez, Adriana Devoy and Myra Schomberg; published new writers within the last year. Length: 500-1,500 words.
How to Contact: Send complete ms with SASE. Reports in 10 weeks on mss. Sample copy 75¢. Fiction guidelines for SASE.
Payment: Pays 8¢/word.
Terms: Pays on publication for all rights.
Advice: "Try to present health material in a positive — not a negative — light. Use humor and a light approach wherever possible without minimizing the seriousness of the subject. We need more humor and adventure stories."

JIVE, BLACK CONFESSIONS, BLACK ROMANCE, BRONZE THRILLS, BLACK SECRETS, (I, II), Sterling's Magazines/Lexington Library, 355 Lexington Ave., New York NY 10017. (212)949-6850. Editor: Tonia L. Shakespeare. Magazine: 8½ × 11; 72 pages; newsprint paper; glossy cover; 8 × 10 photographs. "We publish stories that are ultra romantic and have romantic lovemaking scenes in them. Our audience is basically young and in high school and college. However, we have a significant audience base of divorcees and housewives. The age range is from 18-49." Bimonthly (*Jive* and *Black Romance* in odd-numbered months; *Black Confessions* and *Bronze Thrills* in even-numbered months). 6 issues per year. Estab. 1962. Circ. 100,000.

● *A bullet introduces comments by the editor of* Novel & Short Story Writer's Market *indicating special information about the listing.*

Needs: Confession, romance (contemporary, young adult). No "stories that are stereotypical to black people, ones that do not follow the basic rules of writing, or ones that are too graphic in content and lack a romantic element." Receives 200 or more unsolicited fiction mss/month. Buys 6 mss/issue (2 issues/month); 144 mss/year. Publishes ms an average of 3-6 months after acceptance. Recently published work by Linda Smith; published new writers within the last year. Length: 18-23 pages. Always critiques rejected mss; recommends other markets.

How to Contact: Query with clips of published work or send complete ms with cover letter. "A cover letter should include an author's bio and what he or she proposes to do. Of course, address and phone number." Reports in 3-6 months. SASE. Simultaneous submissions OK. "Please contact me if simultaneously submitted work has been accepted elsewhere." Sample copy for 9 × 12 SAE and 5 first class stamps; fiction guidelines for #10 SAE and 2 first class stamps.

Payment: Pays $75-100.

Terms: Pays on publication for first rights or one-time rights.

Advice: "Our five magazines are a great starting point for new writers. We accept work from beginners as well as established writers. Please study and research black culture and lifestyles if you are not a black writer. Stereotypical stories are not acceptable. Set the stories all over the world and all over the USA—not just down south. We are not looking for 'the runaway who gets turned out by a sweet-talking pimp' stories. We are looking for stories about all types of female characters. Any writer should not be afraid to communicate with us if he or she is having some difficulty with writing a story. We are available to help at any stage of the submission process. Also, writers should practice patience. If we do not contact the writer, that means that the story is being read or is being held on file for future publication. If we get in touch with the writer, it usually means a request for revision and resubmission. Do the best work possible and don't let rejection slips send you off 'the deep end.' Don't take everything that is said about your work so personally. We are buying all of our work from freelance writers."

JUGGLER'S WORLD, (IV), International Juggler's Association, Box 443, Davidson NC 28036. (704)892-1296. Editor: Bill Giduz. Fiction Editor: Ken Letko. Magazine: 8½ × 11; 40 pages; 70 lb. paper and cover stock; illustrations and photos. For and about jugglers and juggling. Quarterly.

Needs: Historical (general), humor/satire, science fiction. No stories "that don't include juggling as a central theme." Receives "very few" unsolicited mss/month. Accepts 2 mss/year. Publishes ms an average of 6-12 months to 1 year after acceptance. Length: 1,000 words average; 500 words minimum; 2,000 words maximum. Sometimes critiques rejected mss.

How to Contact: Query first. Reports in 1 week. Simultaneous submissions OK. Prefers electronic submissions via IBM or Macintosh compatible disk. Sample copy for $2.50.

Payment: Pays $25-50, free subscription to magazine and 3 contributor's copies.

Terms: Pays on acceptance for first rights.

JUNIOR TRAILS, (I, II), Gospel Publishing House, 1445 Boonville Ave., Springfield MO 65802. (417)862-2781. Elementary Editor: Sinda S. Zinn. Magazine: 5½ × 8½; 8 pages; 36 lb. coated offset paper; art illustrations; photos. "A Sunday school take-home paper of nature articles and fictional stories that apply Christian principles to everyday living for 9-to 12-year-old children." Weekly. Estab. 1954. Circ. 70,000.

Needs: Contemporary, religious/inspirational, spiritual, sports and juvenile. Adventure stories are welcome. No Biblical fiction or science fiction. Buys 2 mss/issue. Published work by Betty Lou Mell, Mason M. Smith, Nanette L. Dunford; published new writers within the last year. Length: 1,200-1,500 words. Publishes short shorts.

How to Contact: Send complete ms with SASE. Reports in 6-8 weeks. Free sample copy and guidelines.

Payment: Pays 3¢/word. 3 free author's copies.

Terms: Pays on acceptance.

Advice: "Know the age level and direct stories relevant to that age group. Since junior-age children (grades 5 and 6) enjoy action, fiction provides a vehicle for communicating moral/spiritual principles in a dramatic framework. Fiction, if well done, can be a powerful tool for relating Christian principles. It must, however, be realistic and believable in its development. Make your children be children, not overly mature for their age. We would like more stories with a *city* setting."

KID CITY, (II), Children's Television Workshop, 1 Lincoln Plaza, New York NY 10023. (212)595-3456. Editor-in-Chief: Maureen Hunter-Bone. Magazine: 8½ × 11; 32 pages; glossy cover; illustrations; photos. General interest for children 6-10 "devoted to sparking kids' interest in reading and writing about the world around them." Published 10 times/year. Estab. 1974. Circ. 350,000.

Needs: Adventure, mystery, juvenile (6-10 years), science fiction. Publishes ms "at least" 6 months after acceptance. Length: 600-750 words average; 1,000 words maximum.
How to Contact: Send complete ms with cover letter. Reports in 1-2 months on mss. SASE. Sample copy for $1.50 and 9 × 12 SAE with 75¢ postage. Writers' guidelines for 9 × 12 SAE with 75¢ postage.
Payment: Pays $200-400 and contributor's copies.
Terms: Pays on acceptance for all rights (some negotiable).
Advice: "We look for bright and sparkling prose. Don't talk down. Don't stereotype. Don't use cutesy names, animals or plots. No heavy moralizing or pat dilemmas."

KINDERGARTEN LISTEN, (IV), WordAction Publishing Company, 6401 The Paseo, Kansas City MO 64109. (816)931-1900 or (816)333-7000 (editorial). Editor: Janet R. Reeves. Fiction Editor: Amy Lofton. Tabloid: 4-page story paper; 8½ × 11; newsprint; newsprint cover; b&w and 4-color illustrations; 4-color photos. Stories follow a 2-year topic cycle. Readers are kindergarten 5s and early 6s. Weekly. Estab. 1981. Circ. 45,000.
● Other magazines associated with the Nazarene in this book are *Discoveries, Standard* and *Teens Today*.
Needs: Contemporary, prose poem, religious/inspirational, spiritual, Christian topic themes. Published work by Katharine Ruth Adams, Helen Ott, Minnie Wells. Length: 300 words minimum; 400 words maximum. Sometimes critiques rejected mss and recommends other markets.
How to Contact: Request guidelines and theme list first "if unfamiliar with 2-year topic cycle" or send complete mss. Writers must include SASE for each submission. Simultaneous submissions OK. Reports in 1 month on mss. SASE. Accepts electronic submissions via disk or modem in ASCII text only. Sample copy and fiction guidelines for 8½ × 11 SAE and 1 first class stamp.
Payment: Pays 5¢/word or $25 for stories (whichever is greater) and 4 contributor's copies. Charges for extra copies.
Terms: Pays on acceptance for multiple use rights. No remuneration for reprinting stories when issues are recycled. Authors are free to submit to other publications whose audiences do not overlap that of *Listen*.
Advice: "A majority of submissions we've received lately are of poor quality. Dialogue and actions of main child characters are unrealistic to the young age group our magazine ministers to. Actions and dialogue of parent characters is often too unrealistic as well. They're either too good to be true or very stilted in actions and speech. Because today's children are growing up in a rough world, we seek to help them deal with a variety of situations from divorce to the simple worries of a young child, like being left with a new babysitter. We seek to portray fictional children finding real solutions in the love and guidance of Christ, assisted by parent and other adult figures. Too many submissions appear to come from writers who don't take the children's market seriously or view it as an easy area to write prose for. In fact, children's stories require research and realism, and much effort in writing and rewriting. Writers have to know the audience well, not just guess or try to recall what it was like to be a pre-K child. Few writers can relate well enough to produce good manuscripts without these efforts." Criteria used in choosing fiction: "(1) Does it relate to our theme titles for the 2-year cycle? (2) Is the story interesting to children? (3) Does it assist them in understanding some vital area of the Christian life, God's love, etc.? (4) Is it realistic in portrayal of all characters? (5) Does it flow naturally and make for good reading? (6) Does the story line progress logically? (7) Does it include any references to inappropriate parent behavior, or unacceptable practices, or doctrines, of the Church of the Nazarene. Ex: We've had a hair-raising number of writers portraying scenes where children are left unattended in shopping malls or some other public place — which is highly inappropriate parental behavior considering the abduction situation that has terrorized our country's parents and families. The portrayal shows little insight on the writer's part."

LADIES' HOME JOURNAL, (III), Published by Meredith Corporation, 100 Park Ave., New York NY 10017. Editor-in-Chief: Myrna Blyth. Fiction/Articles Editor: Jane Farrell. Magazine: 190 pages; 34-38 lb. coated paper; 65 lb. coated cover; illustrations and photos.
● *Ladies' Home Journal* has won several awards for journalism. It ranks #21 on the 1992 *Writer's Digest* Fiction 50 list.
Needs: Book mss and short stories, *accepted only through an agent*. Return of unsolicited material cannot be guaranteed. Recently published work by Fay Weldon, Anita Shreve, Jane Shapiro, Anne Rivers Siddons. Length: approximately 3,500 words.

Close-up

Lisa Rao
Senior Editor
Kid City

Writers hoping to sell fiction in today's children's magazine market take heart. The market is "absolutely" healthy, says Lisa Rao, senior editor of *Kid City* magazine. "I would say in my three years with *Kid City* almost every major publishing house has come out with a children's magazine."

Published by Children's Television Workshop, *Kid City* has a fairly well-established niche in this increasingly diverse market. Launched in 1971 as *Electric Company* magazine, the publication changed titles to *Kid City* in 1988, when the television program was discontinued. Aside from dropping references to the television program characters, the magazine's format has remained the same.

Kid City is an "easy-to-read literacy magazine," according to Rao, which makes it accessible to children with a broad range of reading skills. "Whereas a magazine like *Cricket* has wonderful stories, it's aimed at very good readers," she says.

For children aged six through 10, *Kid City* to "instills an interest in reading in low-level readers," Rao says. "We try to keep things as simple as possible to generate interest in a six-year-old and to hold the interest of an eight- or nine-year-old as they continue to be excited about reading." To do this, each issue includes regular features such as puzzles, games, news, reader-submitted jokes and cartoons, and fiction.

According to Rao, the magazine receives 100 freelance fiction submissions per month, of which four or five are accepted. Recently, *Kid City* has been seeking more heavy-hitting subject matter in its short stories. By heavy-hitting, Rao suggests "anything that in the life of a ten-year-old would be a difficult topic," such as death, divorce, peer pressure and ethical issues. The trick is achieving simplicity without sermonizing. "Keep the language simple but don't talk down," Rao says. "We really don't like to use preachy stories. Discuss it from the kid's point of view."

Other *Kid City* fiction needs include mysteries and "create your own adventure" stories, in which several plot options branch out from one story premise. Readers choose a plot path and, in some cases, write their own endings.

Good humorous fiction pieces are also in short supply, Rao says. "Kids at that age range love anything with puns and plays on words," she says. "And if it's a funny story, don't be afraid to make it silly, because that's what appeals to our age range. The best test a freelancer can give any story is to give it to a seven-year-old for a critique," Rao adds. "On borderline stories here, we give them to children of people in the office and ask them what they think. They're real honest—that's the best part."

Each issue of *Kid City* is thematic (the Olympics, baseball, and bugs, for example) and while it's not imperative that fiction be tailored to the theme, it helps. "We're always looking for new submissions," Rao says, "and everything gets read. The only thing that matters is that we like it."

—Anne M. Bowling

How to Contact: Send complete ms with cover letter (credits). Simultaneous submissions OK. Publishes ms 4-12 months after acceptance.
Terms: Buys First North American rights.
Advice: "Our readers like stories, especially those that have emotional impact. We are using fiction every month, whether it's an excerpt from a novel or a short story. Stories about relationships between people — husband/wife — mother/son — seem to be subjects that can be explored effectively in short stories. Our reader's mail and surveys attest to this fact: Readers enjoy our fiction, and are most keenly tuned to stories dealing with children. Fiction today is stronger than ever. Beginners can be optimistic; if they have talent, I do believe that talent will be discovered."

"One of our goals is to foster in children a love of reading, so fiction plays a central role in each issue," says Paula Morrow, editor of Ladybug, a magazine for the two to seven age-group. "We look for rich, evocative language to stimulate a child's imagination and developing taste. The main character should be someone children can identify with. The story should be age-appropriate but not condescending, and must hold enjoyment for both parent and child through repeated read-aloud sharings. If we like a story, we will develop a theme around it." This cover illustration, by Lynn Munsinger, accompanies the issue's excerpt of Hedgehog Bakes a Cake, a picture book by Maryann Macdonald that Munsinger illustrated. (Artwork, © 1992 Lynn Munsinger.)

LADYBUG, (II, IV), Carus Corporation, P.O. Box 300, Peru IL 61354. (815)224-6643. Editor-in-Chief: Marianne Carus. Contact: Submissions Editor. Magazine: 8 × 9¼; 36 pages plus 4-page pullout section; illustrations. "*Ladybug* publishes original stories and poems and reprints written by the world's best children's authors. For young children, ages 2-6." Monthly. Estab. 1990. Circ. 130,000.
 • Carus Corporation's magazine for older children, *Cricket* is also listed in this book.
Needs: Juvenile, fantasy (children's), preschool, read-out-loud stories, picture stories, folk tales, fairy tales. Length: 300-750 words preferred. Publishes short shorts.
How to Contact: Send complete ms with cover letter. Include word count on ms (do not count title). Reports in 3 months. SASE. Reprints are OK. Fiction guidelines for SAE and 1 first class stamp. Sample copy: $2.
Payment: Pays up to 25¢/word (less for reprints).
Terms: Pays on publication for first publication rights or second serial (reprint) rights. For recurring features, pays flat fee and copyright becomes property of Carus Publishing.

LADY'S CIRCLE, (II), Lopez Publications, Suite 906, 152 Madison Ave., New York NY 10016. (212)689-3933. Editor: Mary Bemis. Magazine. "A lot of our readers are in Midwestern states." Bimonthly. Estab. 1963. Circ. 100,000.
Needs: Historical, humor/satire, mainstream, religious/inspirational, senior citizen/retirement. Receives 100 unsolicited fiction mss/month. Buys about 6-7 fiction mss/year. Time between acceptance and publication "varies, usually works 6 months ahead." Length: 1,000 words minimum; 1,200 words maximum. Accepts short shorts "for fillers." Sometimes critiques rejected ms.
How to Contact: Query first. Reports in 3 months on queries. SASE. Simultaneous and reprint submissions OK. Accepts electronic submissions via disk or modem. Sample copy for $3.95; fiction guidelines for SAE.
Payment: Pay varies, depending on ms.
Terms: Pays on publication for first North American serial rights.

‡**LAF!, (I),** Scher Maihem Publishing, Ltd., Box 313, Avilla IN 46710. (219)897-2674. Editor: Julie Scher. Magazine: 11¼ × 11½; 8 pages; newsprint paper; cartoon illustrations. "Ridiculous reality and personal experience humor aimed at middle-America, general circulation. Publishes short (600 wd.) humor pieces and cartoons." Monthly. Estab. 1991. Circ. 10,000.
Needs: Humor/satire. "No religious, political, offensive material." Plans special fiction issue or anthology in the future. Receives 100 unsolicited submissions/year. Buys 10 mss/issue; 120 mss/year. Publishes ms 3-4 issues after acceptance. Recently published work by Vivian Sade, Lizzie Sinn, Lee Sauer. Length: 600 words maximum. Publishes short shorts. Length: 250-500 words.
How to Contact: Query with clips of published work or send complete ms with a cover letter. Should include estimated word count. Reports in 1 month on queries; 6 weeks on mss. Send SASE (or IRC) for reply, return of ms or send a disposable copy of the ms. Simultaneous and reprint submissions OK. Sample copy for 9 × 12 SAE and 56¢ postage. Fiction guidelines for #10 SAE and 1 first class stamp.
Payment: Pays $5-20 and 1 contributor's copy. Additional copies 50¢.
Terms: Pays on publication. Buys one-time rights.
Advice: Looks for work that is "Surprising, has great command of language, is imaginative and easily understood by a wide audience."

LETHBRIDGE MAGAZINE, (I, II), 248684 Alberta Ltd., P.O. Box 1203, Lethbridge, Alberta T1J 4A4 Canada. (403)327-3200. Editor: Richard Burke. Magazine: 8 ½ × 11; 48 pages; glossy paper; illustrations and photos. "*Lethbridge Magazine* prints general interest topics relating to Lethbridge and Southern Alberta for an audience of all ages. Bimonthly. Estab. 1981. Circ. 17,218.
Needs: Adventure, historical (general), humor/satire, literary, regional. Receives 10 unsolicited mss/month. Buys 1 ms/year. Publishes ms 2 months after acceptance. Length: 1,500 words preferred; 1,000 words minimum; 2,000 words maximum. Publishes short shorts.
How to Contact: Query first with clips of published work or send complete ms with cover letter. Reports in 2 months. SASE. Simultaneous and reprint submissions OK. Accepts electronic submissions. Sample copy for $2. Fiction guidelines for SASE.
Payment: Pays 5-12¢/word. Provides contributor's copies.
Terms: Pays on publication for first North American serial rights.
Advice: "Space requirements usually dictate if we can use a submission. Originality and quality of writing make a manuscript stand out. Keep the length short (800 words)."

LIGUORIAN, (I, IV), "A Leading Catholic Magazine," Liguori Publications, 1 Liguori Dr., Liguori MO 63057. (314)464-2500. Editor-in-Chief: Allan Weinert, CSS.R. Managing Editor: Francine M. O'Connor. Magazine: 5 × 8½; 64 pages; b&w illustrations and photographs. "*Liguorian* is a Catholic magazine aimed at helping our readers to live a full Christian life. We publish articles for families, young people, children, religious and singles—all with the same aim." Monthly. Estab. 1913. Circ. 430,000.
Needs: Religious/inspirational, young adult and senior citizen/retirement (with moral Christian thrust), spiritual. "Stories submitted to *Liguorian* must have as their goal the lifting up of the reader to a higher Christian view of values and goals. We are not interested in contemporary works that lack purpose or are of questionable moral value." Receives approximately 25 unsolicited fiction mss/month. Buys 12 mss/year. Recently published work by Tom Dowling, Sharon Helgens, Jim Auer, Ann Urrein and Jon A. Ripslinger; published new writers within the last year. Length: 1,500-2,000 words preferred. Also publishes short shorts. Occasionally critiques rejected mss "if we feel the author is capable of giving us something we need even though this story did not suit us." Occasionally recommends other markets.
How to Contact: Send complete ms with SASE. Accepts disk submissions compatible with TRS-80 Model III; prefers hard copy with disk submission. Reports in 6 weeks on mss. Sample copy and free fiction guidelines for 6 × 9 SASE."
Payment: Pays 10-12¢/word and 6 contributor's copies. Offers 50% kill fee for assigned mss not published.
Terms: Pays on acceptance for all rights.
Advice: "First read several issues containing short stories. We look for originality and creative input in each story we read. Since most editors must wade through mounds of manuscripts each month, consideration for the editor requires that the market be studied, the manuscript be carefully presented and polished before submitting. Our publication uses only one story a month. Compare this with the 25 or more we receive over the transom each month. Also, many fiction mss are written without a specific goal or thrust, i.e., an interesting incident that goes nowhere is *not a story*. We believe fiction

is a highly effective mode for transmitting the Christian message and also provides a good balance in an unusually heavy issue."

LILITH MAGAZINE, The Jewish Women's Magazine, (I, II, IV), Suite 2432, 250 W. 57th St., New York NY 10107. (212)757-0818. Editor: Susan Weidman Schneider. Fiction Editor: Julia Wolf Mazow. Magazine: 8½ × 11; 32 pages; 80 lb. cover; b&w illustrations; b&w and color photos. Publishes work relating to Jewish feminism, for Jewish feminists, feminists and Jewish households. Quarterly. Estab. 1975. Circ. 10,000.
Needs: Ethnic, feminist, lesbian, literary, prose poem, psychic/supernatural/occult, religious/inspirational, senior citizen/retirement, spiritual, translation, young adult. "Nothing that does not in any way relate to Jews, women or Jewish women." Receives 15 unsolicited mss/month. Accepts 1 ms/issue; 3 mss/year. Publishes ms 2-6 months after acceptance. Published work by Leslea Newman and Fredelle Maynard. Publishes short shorts.
How to Contact: Send complete ms with cover letter, which should include a 2-line bio. Reports in 2 months on queries; 2-6 months on mss. SASE. Simultaneous and reprint submissions OK. Sample copy for $5. Fiction guidelines for #10 SAE and 1 first class stamp. Reviews novels and short story collections. Send books to Rachel Dobkin.
Payment: Varies.
Terms: Acquires first rights.

LIVE, (IV), Assemblies of God, 1445 Boonville, Springfield MO 65802. (417)862-2781. Editor: Lorraine Mastrorio. "A take-home story paper distributed weekly in young adult/adult Sunday school classes. *Live* is a fictional story paper primarily. True stories in narrative style are welcome. Articles are acceptable. Poems, first-person anecdotes and humor are used as fillers. The purpose of *Live* is to present in short story form realistic characters who utilize biblical principles. We hope to challenge readers to take risks for God and to resolve their problems scripturally." Weekly. Circ. 180,000.
Needs: Religious/inspirational, prose poem and spiritual. "Inner city, ethnic, racial settings." No controversial stories about such subjects as feminism, war or capital punishment. Buys 2 mss/issue. Published work by Maxine F. Dennis, E. Ruth Glover and Larry Clark; published new writers within the last year. Length: 500-2,000 words.
How to Contact: Send complete ms. Social Security number and word count must be included. Simultaneous submissions OK. Reports in up to 1 year. Sample copy and guidelines for SASE.
Payment: Pays 3¢/word (first rights); 2¢/word (second rights).
Terms: Pays on acceptance.
Advice: "Stories should go somewhere! Action, not just thought-life; interaction, not just insights. Heroes and heroines, suspense and conflict. Avoid simplistic, pietistic conclusions, preachy, critical or moralizing." Reserves the right to change titles, abbreviate length and clarify flashbacks in stories for publication.

LIVING WITH TEENAGERS, (II), Baptist Sunday School Board, MSN 140, 127 9th Ave. North, Nashville TN 37234. (615)251-2273. Editor: Jimmy Hester. Magazine: 10⅜ × 8⅛; 50 pages; illustrations; photos. Magazine especially designed "to enrich the parent-teen relationship, with reading material from a Christian perspective" for parents of teenagers. Quarterly. Estab. 1978. Circ. 50,000.
• *Home Life, Christian Singles* and *The Student*, also published by The Sunday School Board, are listed in this section.
Needs: Religious/inspirational, spiritual and parent-teen relationships. Nothing not related to parent-teen relationships or not from a Christian perspective. Receives approximately 50 unsolicited fiction mss/month. Buys 2-5 mss/issue. Length: 600-1,200 words (short shorts).
How to Contact: Query with clips of published work or send complete ms. Cover letter with reason for writing article; credentials for writing. Reports in 2 months on both queries and mss. SASE always. Sample copy for 9 × 12 SAE and proper postage.
Payment: Pays 5½¢/published word and 3 contributor's copies for all rights.
Terms: Pays on acceptance for all and first rights.
Advice: "Sometimes a fictitious story can communicate a principle in the parent-youth relationship quite well."

LOLLIPOPS MAGAZINE, (II), Good Apple, Inc., Box 299, Carthage IL 62321. (217)357-3981. Editor: Mary Lindeen. Magazine: 8½ × 11; 64 pages; illustrations. "Preschool-2nd grade publication for teachers and their students. All educational material. Short stories, poems, activities, math, gameboards." Published 5 times/year. Circ. 18,000.

Needs: Preschool-grade 2. Submissions cover all areas of the curriculum. Seasonal materials considered. Receives 40-50 unsolicited mss/month. Number of fiction mss bought varies per issue. Published new writers within the last year. Occasionally accepts short stories (500-750 words).
How to Contact: Query first or write for guidelines and a free sample copy. Reports in 1 week on queries. SASE for ms.
Payment: Payment varies; depends on story.
Terms: Pays on publication for all rights.

THE LOOKOUT, (II), Standard Publishing, 8121 Hamilton Ave., Cincinnati OH 45231. (513)931-4050. Fax: (513)931-0904. Editor: Simon J. Dahlman. Magazine: 8½ × 11; 16 pages; newsprint paper; newsprint cover stock; illustrations; photos. "Conservative Christian magazine for adults." Weekly. Estab. 1894. Circ. 120,000.
• *The Lookout* has won awards from the Evangelical Press Association and placed #29 on the 1992 *Writer's Digest* Fiction 50 list. Standard Publishing also publishes *Radar* and *Seek* listed in this book.
Needs: Religious/inspirational. No predictable, preachy material. Taboos are blatant sex and swear words. Receives 50 unsolicited mss/month. Buys 1 fiction ms/issue; 45-50 mss/year. Publishes ms 2-12 months after acceptance. Published work by Bob Hartman, Myrna J. Stone, Dave Cheadle and Daniel Schantz; published new writers within the last year. Length: 1,200-2,000 words.
How to Contact: Send complete ms with SASE. Reports in 2-3 months on ms. Simultaneous and reprint submissions OK. Sample copy for 50¢. Guidelines for #10 SASE.
Payment: Pays 5-7¢/word for first rights; 4-5¢/word for other rights and contributor's copies.
Terms: Pays on acceptance for one-time rights. Buys reprints.
Advice: "We would like to see a better balance between stories that focus on external struggles (our usual fare in the past) and those that focus on internal (spiritual, emotional, psychological) struggles. Send us good stories—not good sermons dressed up as stories. Keep stories in a contemporary setting with an adult's point of view. A Christian perspective is necessary, but you don't need to preach or make explicit references to religion in the story. Be true to life."

THE LUTHERAN JOURNAL, (II), Outlook Publications, Inc., 7317 Cahill Rd., Minneapolis MN 55435. (612)941-6830. Editor: Rev. A.U. Deye. "A family magazine providing wholesome and inspirational reading material for the enjoyment and enrichment of Lutherans." Quarterly. Estab. 1936. Circ. 136,000.
Needs: Literary, contemporary, religious/inspirational, romance (historical), senior citizen/retirement and young adult. Must be appropriate for distribution in the churches. Buys 2-4 mss/issue. Length: 1,000-1,500 words.
How to Contact: Send complete ms with SASE. Sample copy for SASE with 59¢ postage.
Payment: Pays $10-25 and 6 contributor's copies.
Terms: Pays on publication for all and first rights.

McCALL'S, 110 5th Ave., New York NY 10011-5603. No longer publishes fiction.

MADEMOISELLE MAGAZINE, Condé Nast Publications, Inc., 350 Madison Ave., New York NY 10017. No longer publishes fiction.

THE MAGAZINE FOR CHRISTIAN YOUTH!, (II, IV), The United Methodist Publishing House, 201 8th Avenue S., Nashville TN 37202. (615)749-6463. Contact: Editor. Magazine: 8½ × 11; 48 pages; slick, matte finish paper. *"The Magazine for Christian Youth!* tries to help teenagers develop Christian identity and live their faith in contemporary culture. Fiction and nonfiction which contributes to this purpose are welcome." Monthly. Estab. 1985. Circ. 30,000.
• *The Magazine for Christian Youth* has won awards from the Evangelical Press Association and The Associated Church Press. The United Methodist Publishing House also publishes *Mature Years* listed in this book.
Needs: Adventure, contemporary, ethnic, fantasy, humor/satire, mystery/suspense, prose poem, religious/inspirational, science fiction, spiritual, translations, young adult/teen (10-18 years). Upcoming theme: "100% All Teen Issue," all fiction, articles, photos and illustrations done by teens. (November 1993). Receives 25-50 unsolicited mss/month. Buys 1-2 mss/issue; 12-24 mss/year. Publishes ms 9-12 months after acceptance. Length: 700-1,500 words.

How to Contact: Send complete ms with cover letter. Reports in 3-6 months. SASE. Simultaneous and reprint submissions OK. Sample copy and fiction guidelines for 9½×12½ SAE and 5 first class stamps. Fiction limited to teenaged writers.
Payment: Pays 5¢/word.
Terms: Pays on acceptance for first North American serial rights or one-time rights.
Advice: "Get a feel for our magazine first. Don't send in the types of fiction that would appear in Sunday school curriculum just because it's a Christian publication. Reflect the real world of teens in contemporary fiction. Don't preach; but story should have a message to help teenagers in some way or to make them think more deeply about an issue." Writing contest announced in March issue. Deadline is early April.

‡MAGAZINE OF FANTASY AND SCIENCE FICTION, (II), P.O. Box 11526, Eugene OR 97440. Editor: Kathryn Rusch. Magazine: illustrations on cover only. Publishes "science fiction and fantasy. Our readers are age 13 and up who are interested in science fiction and fantasy." Monthly. Estab. 1949.
 • *Magazine of Fantasy and Science Fiction* has won numerous awards including two Nebulas in 1991. The magazine ranks 15 on the *Writer's Digest* Fiction 50 list.
Needs: Fantasy and science fiction. Receives "hundreds" of unsolicited fiction submissions/month. Buys 8 fiction mss/issue ("on average"). Time between acceptance and publication varies. Length: 20,000 words maximum. Publishes short shorts. Critiques rejected ms, "if quality warrants it." Sometimes recommends other markets.
How to Contact: Send complete ms with cover letter. Reports in 6-8 weeks. SASE. No simultaneous submissions. Reprint submissions OK. Sample copy for $3 or $5 for 2. Fiction guidelines for SAE.
Payment: Pays 5-7¢/word.
Terms: Pays on acceptance for first North American serial rights; foreign, option on anthology if requested.

MATURE LIVING, (II), Sunday School Board of the Southern Baptist Convention, MSN 140, 127 Ninth Ave. N., Nashville TN 37234. (615)251-2191. Acting Editor: Judy Pregel. Magazine: 8½×11; 48 pages; non-glare paper; slick cover stock; illustrations; photos. "Our magazine is Christian in content and the material required is what would appeal to 60+ age group: inspirational, informational, nostalgic, humorous. Our magazine is distributed mainly through churches (especially Southern Baptist churches) that buy the magazine in bulk and distribute it to members in this age group." Monthly. Estab. 1977. Circ. 360,000.
Needs: Contemporary, religious/inspirational, humor, prose poem, spiritual and senior citizen/retirement. Avoid all types of pornography, drugs, liquor, horror, science fiction and stories demeaning to the elderly. Buys 1 ms/issue. Publishes ms an average of 1 year after acceptance. Published work by Burndean N. Sheffy, Pearl E. Trigg, Joyce M. Sixberry; published new writers within the last year. Length: 425-900 words (prefers 900). "Also, please use 42 characters per line."
How to Contact: Send complete ms with SASE. Reports in 2 months. Sample copy for $1. Guidelines for SASE.
Payment: Pays $21-73; 3 contributor's copies. 85¢ charge for extras.
Terms: Pays on acceptance. First rights 15% less than all rights, reprint rights 25% less. Rarely buys reprints.
Advice: Mss are rejected because they are too long or subject matter unsuitable. "Our readers seem to enjoy an occasional short piece of fiction. It must be believable, however, and present senior adults in a favorable light."

MATURE YEARS, (II), United Methodist Publishing House, 201 Eighth Ave. S., Nashville TN 37202. (615)749-6468. Editor: Marvin W. Cropsey. Magazine: 8½×11; 112 pages; illustrations and photos. Magazine "helps persons in and nearing retirement to appropriate the resources of the Christian faith as they seek to face the problems and opportunities related to aging." Quarterly. Estab. 1953.
 • United Methodist Publishing House also publishes a magazine for teens, the *Magazine for Christian Youth*, listed in this book.
Needs: Religious/inspirational, nostalgia, humor, intergenerational relationships, prose poem, spiritual (for older adults). "We don't want anything poking fun at old age, saccharine stories or anything not for older adults." Buys 3-4 mss/issue, 12-16 mss/year. Usually publishes ms 12-18 months after acceptance. Published new writers within the last year. Length: 1,000-1,800 words.

How to Contact: Send complete ms with SASE and Social Security number. No simultaneous submissions. Reports in 2 months. Sample copy for 10½ × 11 SAE and $3.50 postage.
Payment: Pays 4¢/word.
Terms: Pays on acceptance for all and first rights.
Advice: "Practice writing dialogue! Listen to people talk; take notes; master dialogue writing! Not easy, but well worth it! Most inquiry letters are far too long. If you can't sell me an idea in a brief paragraph, you're not going to sell the reader on reading your finished article or story."

MESSENGER OF THE SACRED HEART, (II), Apostleship of Prayer, 661 Greenwood Ave., Toronto, Ontario M4J 4B3 Canada. (416)466-1195. Editors: Rev. F.J. Power, S.J. and Alfred DeManche. Magazine: 7 × 10; 32 pages; coated paper; self-cover; illustrations; photos. Magazine for "Canadian and U.S. Catholics interested in developing a life of prayer and spirituality; stresses the great value of our ordinary actions and lives." Monthly. Estab. 1891. Circ. 18,000.
• *Canadian Messenger*, also published by the Apostleship of Prayer, is listed in this book.
Needs: Religious/inspirational. Stories about people, adventure, heroism, humor, drama. No poetry. Buys 1 ms/issue. Recently published work by Ken Thoren, Rev. Charles Dickson, Ph.D., and Rev. John M. Scott, S.J.; published new writers within the last year. Length: 750-1,500 words. Recommends other markets.
How to Contact: Send complete ms with SAE or IRC. No simultaneous submissions. Reports in 1 month. Sample copy for $1.50 (Canadian).
Payment: Pays 4¢/word, 3 free author's copies.
Terms: Pays on acceptance for first North American serial rights. Rarely buys reprints.
Advice: "Develop a story that sustains interest to the end. Do not preach, but use plot and characters to convey the message or theme. Aim to move the heart as well as the mind. If you can, add a light touch or a sense of humor to the story. Your ending should have impact, leaving a moral or faith message for the reader."

METRO SINGLES LIFESTYLES, (II), Metro Publications, Box 28203, Kansas City MO 64118. (816)436-8424. Editor: Robert L. Huffstutter. Fiction Editor: Earl R. Stonebridge. Tabloid: 36 pages; 30. lb newspaper stock; 30 lb. cover; illustrations; photos. "Positive, uplifting, original, semi-literary material for all singles: widowed, divorced, never-married, of all ages 18 and over." Bimonthly. Estab. 1984. Circ. 25,000.
Needs: Humor/satire, literary, prose poem, religious/inspirational, romance (contemporary), special interest, spiritual, single parents. No erotic, political, moralistic fiction. Receives 2-3 unsolicited mss/month. Buys 1-2 mss/issue; 12-18 mss/year. Publishes ms 2 months after acceptance. Length: 1,500 words average; 1,200 words minimum; 4,000 words maximum. Publishes short shorts. Published work by Patricia Castle, Libby Floyd, Donald G. Smith; published new writers within the last year. Length: 1,200. Occasionally critiques rejected mss. Recommends other markets.
How to Contact: Send complete ms with cover letter. Include short paragraph/bio listing credits (if any), current profession or job. Reports in 3 weeks on queries. SASE. Sample copy $3.
Payment: Pays $25-50, free subscription to magazine and contributor's copies.
Terms: Payment on publication.
Advice: "A question I ask myself about my own writing is: will the reader feel the time spent reading the story or article was worth the effort? Personally, I enjoy stories and articles which will create a particular emotion, build suspense, or offer excitement or entertainment. Features accompanied by photos receive special attention."

MIDSTREAM, A Monthly Jewish Review, (II, IV), Theodor Herzl Foundation, 110 E. 59th St., New York NY 10022. (212)339-6021. Editor: Joel Carmichael. Magazine: 8½ × 11; 48 pages; 50 lb. paper; 65 lb. white smooth cover stock. "We are a Zionist journal; we publish material with Jewish themes or that would appeal to a Jewish readership." Monthly. Estab. 1955. Circ. 10,000.
Needs: Historical (general), humor/satire, literary, mainstream, translations. Receives 15-20 unsolicited mss/month. Accepts 1 mss/issue; 10 mss/year. Publishes ms 6-18 months after acceptance. Agented fiction 10%. Published work by I. B. Singer, Anita Jackson, Enid Shomer. Length: 2,500 words average; 1,500 words minimum; 3,000 words maximum. Sometimes critiques rejected mss.
How to Contact: Send complete ms with cover letter, which should include "address, telephone, identification or affiliation of author; state that the ms is fiction." Reports in 1-2 weeks. SASE. Sample copy for 9 × 12 SAE. Fiction guidelines for #10 SASE.

Payment: Pays 5¢/word and contributor's copies.
Terms: Pays on publication for first rights.
Advice: "Always include a cover letter and double space."

MILITARY LIFESTYLE, (II), Downey Communications, Inc., Suite 710, 4800 Montgomery Lane, Bethesda MD 20814-5341. Editor: Hope M. Daniels. Magazine: 8½ × 11; avg. 72 pages; coated paper; illustrations and photos. Monthly magazine for military families worldwide. Publishes 10 issues per year. Estab. 1969. Circ. 530,000.

• See the listing for the *Military Lifestyle* Short Story Contest listed in the Contests and Awards Section.

Needs: Contemporary. "Fiction must deal with lifestyle or issues of particular concern to our specific military families audience." Receives 50 unsolicited mss/month. Buys 1-2 mss/issue; 10-15 mss/year. Publishes ms 2-6 months after acceptance. Published new writers within the last year. Length: 1,500 words average. Generally critiques rejected mss. Recommends other markets if applicable.
How to Contact: Send complete ms with cover letter, which should include info on writer and writing credits and history. No simultaneous submissions. Reports in 6-8 weeks on mss. SASE. Sample copy for $1.50, 9 × 12 SAE and 4 first class stamps. Fiction guidelines for #10 SASE and 1 first class stamp. Reviews novels and short story collections.
Payment: Pays $400 minimum and 2 contributor's copies.
Terms: Pays generally on publication unless held more than 6 months; then on acceptance for first North American serial rights.
Advice: "Fiction is slice-of-life reading for our audience. Primarily written by military wives or military members themselves, the stories deal with subjects very close to our readers: prolonged absences by spouses, the necessity of handling child-raising alone, the fear of accidents while spouses are on maneuvers or in dangerous situations, etc. The important point: Target the material to our audience— military families—and make the characters real, empathetic and believable. Read your copy over as an objective reader rather than as its author before submission. Better yet, read it aloud!"

MODERN GOLD MINER AND TREASURE HUNTER, (II), P.O. Box 47, Happy Camp CA 96039. (916)493-2029. Editor: Dave McCracken. Fiction Editor: Gary Brooks. Magazine: 8 × 10⅞; 48 pages; 50 lb. coated #5 paper; 80 lb. Sterling Web cover; pen-and-ink illustrations; photographs. "Recreational and small-scale gold mining, treasure and relic hunting. All stories must be related to these topics. For recreational hobbyists, adventure loving, outdoor people." Bimonthly. Estab. 1988. Circ. 50,000.
Needs: Adventure, experimental, historical, humor, mystery/suspense, senior citizen/retirement. "Futuristic stories OK, but not sci-fi. No erotica, gay, lesbian--absolutely no 'cussing!' " Buys 1-2 mss/ issue; 6-16 mss/year. Publishes ms 4-6 months after acceptance. Published work by Ken Hodgson and Michael Clark. Length: 2,000 words preferred; 900 words minimum; 2,700 words maximum. Publishes short shorts. Length: 400-500 words. Sometimes critiques or comments on rejected mss.
How to Contact: Send complete ms with cover letter. Include Social Security number, "brief outline of the story and something about the author." Reports in 2 weeks on queries; 4-6 weeks on mss. SASE for mss. Accepts electronic submissions. Sample copy for $2.95 (U.S.), $3.50 (Canada). Free fiction guidelines.
Payment: Pays 3¢/word minimum and contributor's copies.
Terms: Pays on publication for all rights.
Advice: Looks for "as always, quality writing. We can edit small changes but the story has to grab us. Our readers love 'real life' fiction. They love exploring the 'that could happen' realm of a good fiction story. Keep your story geared to gold mining or treasure hunting. Know something about your subject so the story doesn't appear ridiculous. Don't try to dazzle readers with outlandish adjectives and keep slang to a minimum." Sponsors fiction contest—look for rules in upcoming issues.

MOMENT MAGAZINE, (II, IV), Suite 300, 3000 Connecticut Ave. NW, Washington DC 20008. (202)387-8888. Publisher/Editor: Hershel Shanks. Managing Editor: Suzanne F. Singer. Magazine: 8½ × 11; 64 pages; 60 lb. coated paper; 80 lb. cover stock; illustrations and photos. Modern, historical magazine publishing material on intellectual, cultural and political issues of interest to the Jewish community. Audience is college-educated, liberal, concerned with Jewish affairs. Bimonthly. Estab. 1975. Circ. 30,000.
Needs: Contemporary, ethnic, historical, religious, excerpted novel and translations. "All fiction should have Jewish content. No sentimental stories about 'Grandma' etc. Do not encourage Holocaust themes." Receives 60-80 unsolicited fiction mss/month. Buys 2-3 mss/year. Publishes ms 1-24 months

after acceptance. Length: 2,000 words minimum; 4,000 words maximum; 3,000 words average. Publishes short shorts.

How to Contact: Query first or send complete ms. Cover letter with bio. Reports in 1 month on queries; 2 months on mss. SASE always. No multiple submissions. Sample copy for $4. Fiction guidelines for #10 SAE and 1 first class stamp.

Payment: Varies.

Terms: Pays on publication for first rights.

Advice: "We caution against over-sentimentalized writing which we get way too much of all the time. Query first is helpful; reading stories we've published a must."

MONTANA SENIOR CITIZENS NEWS, (II,IV), Barrett-Whitman Co., Box 3363, Great Falls MT 59403. (406)761-0305. Editor: Jack Love. Tabloid: 11×17; 50-60 pages; newsprint paper and cover; illustrations; photos. Publishes "everything of interest to seniors, except most day-to-day political items like Social Security and topics covered in the daily news. Personal profiles of seniors, their lives, times and reminiscences." Bimonthly. Estab. 1984. Circ. 23,000.

Needs: Historical, senior citizen/retirement, western (historical or contemporary). No fiction "unrelated to experiences to which seniors can relate." Buys 1 or fewer mss/issue; 4-5 mss/year. Publishes ms within 6 months of acceptance. Published work by Anne Norris, Helen Clark, Juni Dunklin. Length: 500-800 words preferred. Publishes short shorts. Length: under 500 words.

How to Contact: Send complete ms with cover letter and phone number. Only responds to selected mss. SASE. Simultaneous and reprint submissions OK. Accepts electronic submission via WordPerfect disk. Sample copy for 9×12 SAE and $2 postage and handling.

Payment: Pays $2/column inch.

Terms: Pays on publication for first rights or one-time rights.

MY FRIEND, The Catholic Magazine for Kids, (II), Daughters of St. Paul, 50 St. Paul's Ave., Boston MA 02130. (617)522-8911. Editor: Sister Anne Joan. Magazine: 8½×11; 32 pages; smooth, glossy paper and cover stock; illustrations; photos. Magazine of "religious truths and positive values for children in a format which is enjoyable and attractive. Each issue contains Bible stories, lives of saints and famous people, short stories, science corner, contests, projects, etc." Monthly during school year (September-June). Estab. 1979. Circ. 10,000.

• Daughters of St. Paul also publish *The Family* listed in this book.

Needs: Juvenile, religious/inspirational, spiritual (children), sports (children). Receives 30 unsolicited fiction mss/month. Accepts 3-4 mss/issue; 30-40 mss/year. Recently published work by Eileen Spinelli, Bob Hartman and M. Donaleen Howitt; published new writers within the past year. Length: 200 words minimum; 900 words maximum; 600 words average.

How to Contact: Send complete ms with SASE. Reports in 1-2 months on mss. Publishes ms an average of 1 year after acceptance. Sample copy for 9×12 SAE and 90¢ postage.

Payment: Pays $20-150 (stories, articles).

Advice: "We prefer child-centered stories in a real-world setting. Children enjoy fiction. They can relate to the characters and learn lessons that they might not derive from a more 'preachy' article. We accept only stories that teach wholesome, positive values. We are particularly interested in science articles and in material for boys aged 8-10."

NA'AMAT WOMAN, Magazine of NA'AMAT USA, The Women's Labor Zionist Organization of America, (IV), 200 Madison Ave., New York NY 10016. (212)725-8010. Editor: Judith A. Sokoloff. "Magazine covering a wide variety of subjects of interest to the Jewish community—including political and social issues, arts, profiles; many articles about Israel; and women's issues. Fiction must have a Jewish theme. Readers are the American Jewish community." Published 5 times/year. Estab. 1926. Circ. 30,000.

Read the Business of Fiction Writing section to learn the correct way to prepare and submit a manuscript.

Needs: Contemporary, literary. Receives 10 unsolicited fiction mss/month. Buys 3-5 fiction mss/year. Length: 1,500 words minimum; 3,000 words maximum. Also buys nonfiction.
How to Contact: Query first or send complete ms with SASE. Reports in 3 months on mss. Free sample copy for 9×11½ SAE and 98¢ postage.
Payment: Pays 8¢/word; 2 contributor's copies.
Terms: Pays on publication for first North American serial rights; assignments on work-for-hire basis.
Advice: "No maudlin nostalgia or romance; no hackneyed Jewish humor and no poetry."

NEW ERA MAGAZINE, (II, IV), The Church of Jesus Christ of Latter-day Saints, 50 E. North Temple St., Salt Lake City UT 84150. (801)532-2951. Editor: Richard M. Romney. Magazine: 8×10½; 51 pages; 40 lb. coated paper; illustrations and photos. "We will publish fiction on any theme that strengthens and builds the standards and convictions of teenage Latter-day Saints ('Mormons')." Monthly. Estab. 1971. Circ. 200,000.
● This publisher also publishes *The Friend* listed in this book.
Needs: Stories on family relationships, self-esteem, dealing with loneliness, resisting peer pressure and all aspects of maintaining Christian values in the modern world. "All material must be written from a Latter-day Saint ('Mormon') point of view—or at least from a generally Christian point of view, reflecting LDS life and values." Receives 30-35 unsolicited mss/month. Accepts 1 ms/issue; 12 mss/year. Publishes ms 3 months to 5 years after acceptance. Length: 1,500 words average; 250 words minimum; 2,000 words maximum.
How to Contact: Query letter preferred; send complete ms. Reports in 6-8 weeks. SASE. Sample copy for $1 and 9×12 SAE with 2 first class stamps. Fiction guidelines for #10 SASE.
Payment: Pays $50-375 and contributor's copies.
Terms: Pays on acceptance for all rights (reassign to author on request).
Advice: "Each magazine has its own personality—you wouldn't write the same style of fiction for *Seventeen* that you would write for *Omni*. Very few writers who are not of our faith have been able to write for us successfully, and the reason usually is that they don't know what it's like to be a member of our church. You must study and research and know those you are writing about. We love to work with beginning authors, and we're a great place to break in if you can understand us." Sponsors contests and awards for LDS fiction writers. "We have an annual contest; entry forms are in each September issue. Deadline is January; winners published in August."

NEW MYSTERY, (III), The Best New Mystery Stories, #2001, 175 Fifth Ave., New York NY 10010. (212)353-1582. Editor: Charles Raisch. Magazine: 8½×11; 96 pages; illustrations and photographs. "Mystery, suspense and crime." Quarterly. Estab. 1990. Circ. 50,000.
● For more on *New Mystery* see the close-up interview with Editor Charles Raisch in the 1991 *Novel & Short Story Writer's Market*.
Needs: Mystery/suspense. Plans special annual anthology. Receives 150+ unsolicited mss/month. Buys 6-10 mss/issue. Agented fiction 50%. Published work by Lawrence Block, Herb Resnicow, Michael Avallone, Stu Kaminsky. Length: 3,000-5,000 words preferred. Sometimes critiques rejected mss and recommends other markets.
How to Contact: Send complete ms with cover letter. Reports on ms in 1 month. SASE. Accepts electronic submissions. Sample copy for $5, 9×12 SAE and 4 first class stamps.
Payment: Pays $25-250.
Terms: Pays on publication for all rights.
Advice: Stories should have "believable characters in trouble; sympathetic lead; visual language." Sponsors "Annual First Story Contest."

THE NEW YORKER, (III), The New Yorker, Inc., 20 W. 43rd St., New York NY 10036. (212)840-3800. Fiction Department. A quality magazine of interesting, well written stories, articles, essays and poems for a literate audience. Weekly. Estab. 1925. Circ. 622,000.
How to Contact: Send complete ms with SASE. Reports in 8-10 weeks on mss. Publishes 1-2 mss/ issue.
Payment: Varies.
Terms: Pays on acceptance.
Advice: "Be lively, original, not overly literary. Write what you want to write, not what you think the editor would like. Send poetry to Poetry Department."

‡**NOAH'S ARK, A Newspaper for Jewish Children, (II, IV),** Suite 250, 8323 Southwest Freeway, Houston TX 77074. (713)771-7143. Editors: Debbie Israel Dubin and Linda Freedman Block. Tabloid: 4 pages; newsprint paper; illustrations; photos. "All material must be on some Jewish theme. Seasonal material relating to Jewish holidays is used as well as articles and stories relating to Jewish culture (charity, Soviet Jewry, ecology), etc." for Jewish children, ages 6-12. Monthly Sept.-June. Estab. 1979. Circ. 450,000.
Needs: Juvenile (6-12 years); religious/inspirational; ages 6-12 Jewish children. "Newspaper is not only included as a supplement to numerous Jewish newspapers and sent to individual subscribers but is also distributed in bulk quantities to religious schools; therefore all stories and articles should have educational value as well as being entertaining and interesting to children." Receives 10 unsolicited mss/month. Buys "few mss but we'd probably use more if more appropriate mss were submitted." Published new writers within the last year. Length: 600 words maximum.
How to Contact: Send complete ms with SASE. "The cover letter is not necessary; the submission will be accepted or rejected on its own merits." Simultaneous submissions and reprints OK. Sample copy for #10 envelope and 1 first class stamp. "The best guideline is a copy of our publication."
Payment: Varies; contributor's copies.
Terms: Pays on acceptance for one-time rights.
Advice: "Our newspaper was created by two writers looking for a place to have our work published. It has grown in only 10 years to nearly 1 million readers throughout the world. Beginners with determination can accomplish the impossible."

NORTHEAST, the Sunday Magazine of the Hartford Courant, (IV), 285 Broad St., Hartford CT 06115. (203)241-3700. Editor: Lary Bloom. Magazine: 10 × 11½; 32-100 pages; illustrations; photos. "A regional (New England, specifically Connecticut) magazine, we publish stories of varied subjects of interest to our Connecticut audience" for a general audience. Weekly. Published special fiction issue and a special college writing issue for fiction and poetry. Estab. 1981. Circ. 300,000.
● *Northeast* ranked #38 on the 1992 *Writer's Digest* Fiction 50 list.
Needs: Contemporary and regional. No children's stories or stories with distinct setting outside Connecticut. Receives 100 unsolicited mss/month. Buys 1 ms/issue. Publishes short shorts. Length: 750 words minimum; 3,500 words maximum.
How to Contact: Send complete ms with SASE. Reports in 6-8 weeks. Simultaneous submissions OK. No reprints or previously published work. Sample copy and fiction guidelines for 10 × 12 or larger SASE.
Payment: Pays $250-1,000.
Terms: Pays on acceptance for one-time rights.

OMNI, (II), General Media, 1965 Broadway, New York NY 10023. Fiction Editor: Ellen Datlow. Magazine: 8½ × 11; 114-182 pages; 40-50 lb. stock paper; 100 lb. Mead off cover stock; illustrations; photos. "Magazine of science and science fiction with an interest in near future; stories of what science holds, what life and lifestyles will be like in areas affected by science for a young, bright and well-educated audience between ages 18-45." Monthly. Estab. 1978. Circ. 1,000,000.
● *Omni* has won numerous awards (see "Advice" below). They rank #25 on the 1992 *Writer's Digest* Fiction 50 list and Editor Ellen Datlow was featured in the 1990 *Novel & Short Story Writer's Market*. Datlow also edits *The Year's Best Horror* and other anthologies.
Needs: Science fiction, contemporary fantasy and technological horror. No sword and sorcery or space opera. Buys 20 mss/year. Receives approximately 400 unsolicited fiction mss/month. Agented fiction 5%. Recently published work by Joyce Carol Oates, William Gibson, Lucius Shepard and Pat Cadigan. Length: 2,000 words minimum, 10,000 words maximum. Critiques rejected mss that interest me "when there is time." Sometimes recommends other markets.
How to Contact: Send complete ms with SASE. No simultaneous submissions. Reports within 3 weeks. Publishes ms 3 months to 2 years after acceptance.
Payment: Pays $1,250-2,250; 3 free author's copies.
Terms: Pays on acceptance for first North American serial rights with exclusive worldwide English language periodical rights and nonexclusive anthology rights.
Advice: "Beginning writers should read a lot of the best science fiction short stories today to get a feeling for what is being done. Also, they should read outside the field and nonfiction for inspiration. We are looking for strong, well written stories dealing with the next 100 years. Don't give up on a market just because you've been rejected several times. If you're good, you'll get published eventually. Don't ever call an editor on the phone and ask why he/she rejected a story. You'll either find out in a personal rejection letter (which means the editor liked it or thought enough of your writing to

comment) or you won't find out at all (most likely the editor won't remember a form-rejected story)."
Recent award winners and nominees: "Tower of Babylon," by Ted Chiang won the Nebula award for
novelette and has been nominated for a Hugo. "They're Made out of Meat," by Terry Bisson, was
nominated for the Nebula Award. Ellen Datlow has been nominated in Best Professional editor
category of the Hugos 3 years running.

GROWING LIFE ON MARS

STUNNING
FICTION:
HARLAN ELLISON
RETURNS!
OLYMPIC SCIENCE
SPAIN
CREATES
THE
FUTURE

Dwayne Flinchum, senior art director at Omni, selected artwork by Rafal Olbinski for this cover of the magazine because "it reflected the ideals and editorial niche that Omni is known for," he says. "Although it is not directly related to the content of the issue, it reflects the identity of the magazine well. It represents the poetic coexistence of 'science and art' as well as the more surreal, futuristic aspects of our editorial. Also, as a painting, it is less illustrative and falls more within the bounds of fine art which Omni has always showcased." As for fiction, Flinchum says, "it's an integral part of the magazine and always has been." This issue, in fact, includes work by Harlan Ellison. (Artwork, © 1992 Rafal Olbinski.)

ON OUR BACKS, Entertainment for the Adventurous Lesbian, (II, IV), Blush Productions, 526
Castro St., San Francisco CA 94114. (415)861-4723. Editor: Marcy Sheiner. Magazine: 8½×11; 50
pages; slick paper; illustrations; photos. "Lesbian erotica, short stories, nonfiction, commentary, news
clips, photos." Bimonthly. Estab. 1984. Circ. 30,000.
 • *On Our Backs* recently won a design award from the Gay and Lesbian Press Association.
Needs: Erotica, fantasy, humor/satire, nonfiction of interest to lesbians. No "non-erotic, heterosexual" fiction. Receives 20 mss/month. Buys 2-3 mss/issue. Publishes ms within 1 year of acceptance.
Published new writers within the last year. Length: 2,500 words minimum; 5,000 words maximum.
How to Contact: Send complete ms. Simultaneous submissions OK. Reports in 6 weeks. Accepts
electronic submissions via (Mac) disk. Sample copy for $6. Fiction guidelines for #10 SAE and 1 first
class stamp.
Payment: Pays $20-100 and contributor's copies.
Terms: Pays on publication for first North American serial rights.
Advice: "Ask yourself—does it turn me on? Ask a friend to read it—does it turn her on as well? Is it
as well-written as any well-crafted non-erotic story? We love to read things that we don't see all the
time—originality is definitely a plus! We're looking for lesbian erotica that deals with relationship
issues—as well as sex, stories that have high literary merit."

ON THE LINE, (II), Mennonite Publishing House, 616 Walnut Ave., Scottdale PA 15683-1999.
(412)887-8500. Editor: Mary Meyer. Magazine: 7×10; 8 pages; illustrations; b&w photos. "A religious
take-home paper with the goal of helping children grow in their understanding and appreciation of
God, the created world, themselves and other people." For children ages 10-14. Weekly. Estab. 1970.
Circ. 10,000.
 • *Purpose, Story Friends* and *With*, listed in this book, are also published by the Mennonite
 Publishing House.
Needs: Adventure and religious/inspirational for older children and young teens (10-14 years). Receives 50-100 unsolicited mss/month. Buys 1 ms/issue; 52 mss/year. Recently published work by Michael LaCross, Betty Lou Mell, Virginia Kroll; published new writers within the last year. Length:
750-1,000 words.

How to Contact: Send complete ms noting whether author is offering first-time or reprint rights. Reports in 1 month. SASE. Simultaneous and previously published work OK. Free sample copy and fiction guidelines.

Payment: Pays on acceptance for one-time rights.

Advice: "We believe in the power of story to entertain, inspire and challenge the reader to new growth. Know children and their thoughts, feelings and interests. Be realistic with characters and events in the fiction. Stories do not need to be true, but need to *feel* true."

OPTIONS, The *Bi*-**Monthly, (I, II, IV)**, AJA Publishing, Box 470, Port Chester NY 10573. Associate Editor: Diana Sheridan. Magazine: Digest-sized; 114 pages; newsprint paper; glossy cover stock; illustrations and photos. Sexually explicit magazine for and about bisexuals. 10 issues/year. Estab. 1982. Circ. 100,000.

● AJA Publishing has discontinued their other magazine, *Turn On Letters* but has started a new one, *Hot 'N' Nasty* listed in this book.

Needs: Erotica, gay, lesbian. "First person as-if-true experiences." Accepts 6 unsolicited fiction mss/issue. "Very little" of fiction is agented. Published new writers within the last year. Length: 2,000-3,000 words average; 2,000 words minimum. Sometimes critiques rejected mss.

How to Contact: Send complete ms with or without cover letter. No simultaneous submissions. Reports in approximately 3 weeks. SASE. "Submissions on Macintosh disk welcome, but please include hard copy too." Sample copy for $2.95 and 6 × 9 SAE with 5 first class stamps. Fiction guidelines for SASE.

Payment: Pays $100.

Terms: Pays on publication for all rights.

Advice: "Read a copy of *Options* carefully and look at our spec sheet before writing anything for us. That's not new advice, but to judge from some of what we get in the mail, it's necessary to repeat. We only buy 2 bi/lesbian pieces per issue; need is greater for bi/gay male mss. Though we're a bi rather than gay magazine, the emphasis is on same-sex relationships. If the readers want to read about a male/female couple, they'll buy another magazine. Gay male stories sent to *Options* will also be considered for publication in *Beau*, our gay male magazine. *Most important:* We *only* publish male/male stories that feature 'safe sex' practices unless the story is clearly something that took place pre-AIDS."

ORANGE COAST MAGAZINE, The Magazine of Orange County, (II), Suite 8, 245-D Fischer Ave., Costa Mesa CA 92626. (714)545-1900. Editor: Palmer Thomason Jones. Managing Editor: Erik Himmelsbach. Associate Editor: Lynn Allison. Magazine: 8½ × 11; 200 pages; 50 lb. Sonoma gloss paper; 10. Warrenflo cover; illustrations and photographs. *Orange Coast* publishes articles offering insight into its affluent, well-educated Orange County readers. Monthly. Estab. 1974. Circ. 35,000.

● *Orange Coast* won First Place for Fiction from the Maggie Awards in 1990 and 1991.

Needs: All genres. Receives 10 unsolicited mss/month. Buys 2 mss/year. Publishes ms 4-6 months after acceptance. Published work by Robert Ray. Length: 2,500 words average; 1,500 words minimum; 4,000 words maximum.

How to Contact: Send complete ms with cover letter that includes Social Security number. Reports in 3 months. SASE. Simultaneous submissions OK. Sample copy for 9 × 12 SASE.

Payment: Pays $250.

Terms: Pays on acceptance for first North American serial rights.

ORGANICA QUARTERLY, (II), Organica Press, 4419 N. Manhattan Ave., Tampa FL 33614. (813)876-4879. Editor: Susan Hussey. Fiction Editor: Silvia Curbelo. Tabloid: 28 pages. "Intelligent, literary." Quarterly. Circ. 200,000.

Needs: Contemporary, ethnic, experimental, humor/satire, literary. "Have strong aversion to 'New Age' genre; to self-indulgent writing of all kinds." Buys 3-4 mss/year. Time from acceptance to publishing varies. Recently published work by Ann Darby, Joele Renée Ashley, Mark Wisniewsky, Garry Mealor. Length: 2,500-3,000 words average; 5,000 words maximum. Publishes short shorts.

How to contact: Send complete ms with cover letter. "Not necessary; previous publications might be listed if cover letter is enclosed." No simultaneous submissions. Reports in 2-3 months on mss. Sample copy $1.

Payment: "Varies, but competitive."

Terms: Pays on publication for first North American serial rights. Sends galleys to author.

Advice: "Our only criteria is quality. We are looking for intelligent fiction and a fresh approach to language."

THE OTHER SIDE, (III), 300 W. Apsley St., Philadelphia PA 19144-4221. (215)849-2178. Editor: Mark Olson. Fiction Editor: Jennifer Wilkins. Magazine: 8½×11; 64 pages; illustrations and photographs. Magazine of justice rooted in discipleship for Christians with a strong interest in peace, social and economic justice. Bimonthly. Estab. 1965. Circ. 14,000.
Needs: Contemporary, ethnic, experimental, feminist, humor/satire, literary, mainstream, mystery/ suspense, spiritual. Receives 30 unsolicited fiction mss/month. Buys 6 mss/year. Publishes ms 3-9 months after acceptance. Published work by Laurie Skiba, James Schaap and Shirley Pendlebury. Length: 500 words minimum; 5,000 words maximum; 2,500 words average.
How to Contact: Send complete ms with SASE. Reports in 6-8 weeks. No simultaneous submissions or pre-published material. Sample copy for $4.50.
Payment: Pays $50-250; free subscription to magazine; 6 contributor's copies.
Terms: Pays on acceptance for all or first rights.

OUI MAGAZINE, (II), 15th Floor, 519 8th Ave., New York NY 10018. (212)967-6262. Editor: Richard Kidd. Magazine: 8×11; 112 pages; illustrations; photos. Magazine for college-age males and older. Monthly. Estab. 1972. Circ. 1 million.
Needs: Contemporary, fantasy, lesbian, men's, mystery and humor. Buys 1 ms/issue; 12 mss/year. Receives 200-300 unsolicited fiction mss/month. Published new writers within the last year. Length: 1,500-3,000 words.
How to Contact: Send complete ms with SASE. Include cover letter with author background, previous publications, etc. Reports in 6-8 weeks on mss.
Payment: Pays $250 and up.
Terms: Pays on publication for first rights.
Advice: "Many mss are rejected because writers have not studied the market or the magazine. We want writers to take chances and offer us something out of the ordinary. Look at several recent issues to see what direction our fiction is headed."

OUT MAGAZINE, (II, IV), YOU the Publications, Box 5, 359 Davenport Rd., Toronto, Ontario M5R 1K5 Canada. Editor: Shawn Venasse. Prose Editor: Robert Pinet. Tabloid: 11×17; 24 pages; news-print; illustrations and photographs. "*By* and *for gay men* – short fiction, essays, poetry, interviews, photos, illustrations for gay men, age 18-54." Monthly. Estab. 1986. Circ. 25,000 +.
Needs: Gay: Adventure, condensed/excerpted novel, erotica, ethnic, experimental, fantasy, historical (general), humor/satire, literary, mystery/suspense, prose poem, suspense/mystery, translations. "We are looking for 'original' bold, innovative, distinctive writing that both explores and celebrates the *gay male* spirit. We are not particularly interested in clichéd work, i.e. 70's porn, 'coming out' stories (unless they are really good) nor AIDS stories (again, not unless they are exceptional)." Nothing homophobic, sexist, racist nor *porn* written in a clichéd manner. Plans special fiction issue. Receives 10 unsolicited mss/month. Accepts 2 mss/issue; 12 mss/year. Publishes ms up to 2 months after acceptance. Agented fiction 10%. Published work by Peter Crossley, Jim Nason. Length: 1,500 words average; 1,000 words minimum; 2,000 words maximum. Publishes short shorts. Length: 400-500 words. Some-times critiques rejected mss and recommends other markets.
How to Contact: Send complete manuscript with cover letter. Include bio material, intent of story, why writer chose *Out!* Reports in 2 weeks on queries; 4-6 weeks on mss. SASE. Accepts electronic submissions via disk (Word Perfect 5.1 preferred). Sample copy $2.
Payment: Pays free subscription and contributor's copies.
Terms: Acquires one-time rights.
Advice: "We look for bold, innovative words coupled with a strong voice. A writer who is not afraid to challenge his readers. A strong visual/descriptive sense. 'Passionate, honest, thoughtful' – key words."

OUTLAW BIKER, (II, IV), Outlaw Biker Enterprises, Suite #2305, 450 7th Ave., New York NY 10123-2305. (212)564-0112. Fax: (212)465-8350. Publisher/Editor: Casey Exton. Magazine: 8½×11; 96 pages; 50 lb. color paper; 80 lb. cover stock; illustrations; photos. Publication for hard-core bikers, their partners and for tattoo enthusiasts. Monthly. Special issue 6 times/year, *Tattoo Review*. Estab. 1984. Circ. 225,000.

Needs: Biker fiction and humor. Receives 20 unsolicited mss/month. Accepts 3 fiction mss/issue. Publishes ms 4 months after acceptance. Length: 1,000 words minimum; 2,500 words maximum.
How to Contact: Send complete ms with cover letter. SASE very important. Reports on queries in 1 month. Sample copy $3.50.
Payment: Pays $50-150.
Terms: Pays on publication for all rights.
Advice: "Timely biker events with photos used constantly. Photos do not have to be professionally taken. Clear snapshots of events with the short story usually accepted. Send to: Casey Exton, Attention."

PILLOW TALK, (II), 801 2nd Ave., New York NY 10017. Editor: Asia Fraser. Magazine: digest-sized; 98 pages; photos. Bimonthly erotic letters magazine.
• This is also the publisher of *Private Letters* listed in this book.
Needs: "We use approximately 20 short letters of no more than five manuscript pages per issue, and five long letters of between seven and nine manuscript pages." Published new writers within the last year. Recommends other markets.
How to Contact: "We encourage unsolicited manuscripts. Writers who have proven reliable will receive assignments."
Payment: Pays $5 per page for short letters and a $75 flat rate for long letters and articles.
Terms: Pays on acceptance.
Advice: "Keep it short and sensual. We buy many more short letters than long ones. This is a 'couples-oriented' book; the sex should be a natural outgrowth of a relationship, the characters should be believable, and both male and female characters should be treated with respect. No S&M, bondage, male homosexuality, incest, underage characters or anal sex—not even in dialogue, not even in implication. No language that even implies sexual violence—not even in metaphor. No ejaculation on any part of a person's body. Romance is a big plus."

PLAYBOY MAGAZINE, 680 N. Lake Shore Dr., Chicago IL 60611. Did not respond.

POCKETS, Devotional Magazine for Children, (II), The Upper Room, Box 189, 1908 Grand Ave., Nashville TN 37202. (615)340-7333. Editor-in-Chief: Janet R. McNish. Magazine: 7×9; 32 pages; 50 lb. white econowrite paper; 80 lb. white coated, heavy cover stock; color and 2-color illustrations; some photos. Magazine for children ages 6-12, with articles specifically geared for ages 8 to 11. "The magazine offers stories, activities, prayers, poems—all geared to giving children a better understanding of themselves as children of God." Published monthly except for January. Estab. 1981. Estimated circ. 68,000.
• *Pockets* was nominated by *MagazineWeek* for an Excellence Award in 1991. The magazine has also received honors from the Educational Press Association of America. *Pockets* ranks #44 on the 1992 *Writer's Digest* Fiction 50 list.
Needs: Adventure, contemporary, ethnic, fantasy, historical (general), juvenile, religious/inspirational and suspense/mystery. "All submissions should address the broad theme of the magazine. Each issue will be built around several themes with material which can be used by children in a variety of ways. Scripture stories, fiction, poetry, prayers, art, graphics, puzzles and activities will all be included. Submissions do not need to be overtly religious. They should help children experience a Christian lifestyle that is not always a neatly wrapped moral package, but is open to the continuing revelation of God's will. Seasonal material, both secular and liturgical, is desired. No violence, horror, sexual and racial stereotyping or fiction containing heavy moralizing." Receives approximately 120 unsolicited fiction mss/month. Buys 2-3 mss/issue; 22-33 mss/year. Publishes short shorts. A peace-with-justice theme will run throughout the magazine. Published work by Peggy King Anderson, Angela Gibson and John Steptoe; published new writers last year. Length: 600 words minimum; 1,500 words maximum; 1,200 words average.
How to Contact: Send complete ms with SASE. Previously published submissions OK, but no simultaneous submissions. Reports in 2 months on mss. Publishes ms 1 year to 18 months after acceptance. Sample copy for $1.95. Fiction guidelines and themes with SASE. "Strongly advise sending for themes before submitting."

Payment: Pays 12¢/word and up and 2-5 contributor's copies. $1.95 charge for extras; $1 each for 10 or more.
Terms: Pays on acceptance for newspaper and periodical rights. Buys reprints.
Advice: "Do not write *down* to children." Rejects mss because "we receive far more submissions than we can use. If all were of high quality, we still would purchase only a few. The most common problems are overworked story lines and flat, unrealistic characters. Most stories simply do not 'ring true', and children know that. Each issue is theme-related. Please send for list of themes. Include SASE." Sponsors annual fiction writing contest. Deadline: Oct. (1,000-1,600 words.)

PORTLAND MAGAZINE, Maine's City Magazine, (II), 578 Congress St., Portland ME 04101. (207)775-4339. Editor: Colin Sargent. Magazine: 68 pages; 60 lb. paper; 80 lb. cover stock; illustrations and photographs. "City lifestyle magazine—style, business, real estate, controversy, fashion, cuisine, interviews, art." Monthly. Estab. 1986. Circ. 22,000.
Needs: Contemporary, historical, literary. Receives 20 unsolicited fiction mss/month. Buys 1 mss/issue; 12 mss/year. Publishes short shorts. Recently published work by Janwillem Van de Wetering, Sanford Phippen, Mamene Medwood. Length: 3 double-spaced typed pages. Query first.
How to Contact: "Fiction below 700 words, please." Send complete ms with cover letter. Reports in 3 months. SASE. Accepts electronic submissions.
Terms: Pays on publication for first North American serial rights.
Advice: "We publish ambitious short fiction featuring everyone from Frederick Barthelme to newly discovered fiction by Edna St. Vincent Millay."

‡POWERPLAY MAGAZINE, (II, IV), Brush Creek Media, Inc., #148, 2215R Market St., San Francisco CA 94114. (415)552-1506. Fax (415)552-3274. Editor: Stephen Staffora. Magazine: 8 ½ × 11; 64-72 pages; white husky paper; gloss cover; b&w photos. "Geared toward gay men. *Powerplay* is kink-oriented." Quarterly. Estab. 1992. Circ. 38,000.
● This publisher also publishes *Bear* listed in this book.
Needs: Gay: erotica, humor/satire. Receives 5-10 unsolicited mss/month. Buys 2-3 mss/issue; 15-20 mss/year. Length: Open. Sometimes critiques or comments on reject mss.
How to Contact: Send complete ms with cover letter. Should include bio and social security number with submission. Send SASE (IRC) for return or send disposable copy of ms. Will consider simultaneous submissions and electronic (disk or modem) submissions. Sample copy $6.50. Fiction guidelines free.
Payment: $75-125. Also pays 2-3 contributor's copies.
Terms: May pay on acceptance or publication. Purchases first North American serial rights.

‡PRIME TIME SPORTS AND FITNESS, (IV), Prime Time Publishing, P.O. Box 6097, Evanston IL 60204. (708)864-8113. Editor: Dennis Dorner. Fiction Editor: Linda Jefferson. Magazine; 8½ × 11; 40-80 pages; coated enamel paper and cover stock; 10 illustrations; 42 photographs. "For active sports participants." Estab. 1975. Circ. 67,000.
● *Prime Time Sports and Fitness* has won several awards for "recreational reporting."
Needs: Adventure, contemporary, erotica, fantasy, historical, humor/satire, mainstream, mystery/suspense (romantic suspense), sports, young adult/teen (10-18 years). No gay, lesbian. Receives 30-40 unsolicited mss/month. Buys 1-2 mss/issue; 20/year. Publishes ms 3-8 months after acceptance. Agented fiction 10%. Recently published work by Dennis Dorner, Sally Hammill. Length: 2,000 words preferred; 250 words minimum; 3,000 words maximum. Publishes short shorts. Length: 250-500 words. Sometimes critiques rejected ms and recommends other markets.
How to Contact: Send complete ms with cover letter, include Social Security number. "Do *not* include credits and history. We buy articles, not people." Reports in 1 to 3 months on queries; 1 week to 3 months on mss. SASE. Simultaneous and reprint submissions OK. Sample copy for 10 × 12 SAE and $1.40 postage. Fiction guidelines free for SAE.
Payment: Pays $25-500.
Terms: Pays on publication for all rights, first rights, first North American serial rights, one-time rights; "depends on manuscript."
Advice: "Be funny, ahead of particular sports season, and enjoy your story. Bring out some human touch that would relate to our readers."

PRIVATE LETTERS, (I, II), 801 2nd Ave., New York NY 10017. Editor: Asia Fraser. Magazine: digest-sized; 98 pages; illustrations; photographs. Bimonthly letters magazine.
● The publisher of *Private Letters* also publishes *Pillow Talk* listed in this book.

Needs: Erotica, written in letter form. No S&M, incest, homosexuality, anal sex or sex-crazed women and macho, women-conquering studs. "We use approximately 40 short letters per issue of no more than four double-spaced manuscript pages and five long letters of about 10 double-spaced manuscript pages." Published work by Diana Shamblin, Frank Lee and Shirley LeRoy; published new writers within the last year. Recommends other markets.

How to Contact: Send complete ms. "The majority of the material is assigned to people whose writing has proven consistently top-notch. They usually reach this level by sending us unsolicited material which impresses us. We invite them to send us some more on spec, and we're impressed again. Then a long and fruitful relationship is hopefully established. We greatly encourage unsolicited submissions. We are now printing two additional issues each year, so naturally the demand for stories is higher."

Payment: Pays $5 per page for short letters; $75 for long (7-10 page) letters.

Terms: Pays on acceptance.

Advice: "If you base your writing on erotic magazines other than our own, then we'll probably find your material too gross. We want good characterization, believable plots, a little romance, with sex being a natural outgrowth of a relationship. (Yes, it can be done. Read our magazine.) Portray sex as an emotionally-charged, romantic experience—not an animalistic ritual. *Never* give up, except if you die. In which case, if you haven't succeeded as a writer yet, you probably never will. (Though there have been exceptions.) Potential writers should be advised that each issue has certain themes and topics we try to adhere to. It would be greatly to one's benefit to write to ask for a copy of the writer's guidelines *and* a list of themes and topics for upcoming issues. Also, while the longer stories of more than seven pages pay more, there are only about five of them accepted for each issue. We buy far more four to six-page mss."

PURPOSE, (II), Mennonite Publishing House, 616 Walnut Ave., Scottdale PA 15683-1999. (412)887-8500. Editor: James E. Horsch. Magazine: 5⅜ × 8⅜; 8 pages; illustrations; photos. "Magazine focuses on Christian discipleship—how to be a faithful Christian in the midst of tough everyday life complexities. Use story form to present models and examples to encourage Christians in living a life of faithful discipleship." Weekly. Estab. 1969. Circ. 18,000.

● Mennonite Publishing House also publishes *On the Line*, *Story Friends* and *With* listed in this book.

Needs: Historical, religious/inspirational. No militaristic/narrow patriotism or racism. Receives 100 unsolicited mss/month. Buys 3 mss/issue; 40 mss/year. Recently published work by Melodie Davis, Lonni Collins Pratt and Sandy Sheppard. Length: 700 words average; 1,000 words maximum. Occasionally comments on rejected mss.

How to Contact: Send comlpete ms only. Reports in 2 months. Simultaneous and previously published work OK. Sample copy for 6 × 9 SAE and 2 first class stamps. Writer's guidelines free with sample copy only.

Payment: Pays up to 5¢/word for stories and 2 contributor's copies.

Terms: Pays on acceptance for one-time rights.

Advice: Many stories are "situational—how to respond to dilemmas. Write crisp, action moving, personal style, focused upon an individual, a group of people, or an organization. The story form is an excellent literary device to use in exploring discipleship issues. There are many issues to explore. Each writer brings a unique solution. Let's hear them. The first two paragraphs are crucial in establishing the mood/issue to be resolved in the story. Work hard on developing these."

ELLERY QUEEN'S MYSTERY MAGAZINE, (II), Dell Magazines Fiction Group, 380 Lexington Ave., New York NY 10017. (212)557-9100. Editor: Janet Hutchings. Magazine: Digest-sized; 160 pages with special 288-page issues in March and October. Magazine for lovers of mystery fiction. Published 13 times/year. Estab. 1941. Circ. 279,000.

● Dell Magazines other mystery publication is *Alfred Hitchcock Mystery Magazine* listed in this book. *Ellery Queen's* is ranked #18 on the 1992 *Writer's Digest* Fiction 50 list. The magazine has won numerous awards.

Needs: "We accept only mystery, crime suspense and detective fiction." Receives approximately 300 unsolicited fiction mss each month. Buys 10-15 mss/issue. Publishes ms 6-12 months after acceptance. Agented fiction 50%. Published work by Clark Howard, Robert Barnard and Ruth Rendell; published new writers within the last year. Length: up to 7,000 words, occasionally longer. Publishes 2-3 short novels of up to 17,000 words per year by established authors. Minute mysteries of 250 words, and short mystery verse. Critiques rejected mss "only when a story might be a possibility for us if revised." Sometimes recommends other markets.

How to Contact: Send complete ms with SASE. Cover letter should include publishing credits and brief biographical sketch. Simultaneous submissions OK. Reports in 3 months or sooner on mss. Fiction guidelines with SASE. Sample copy for $2.75.
Payment: Pays 3¢/word and up.
Terms: Pays on acceptance for first North American serial rights. Occasionally buys reprints.
Advice: "We have a Department of First Stories and usually publish at least one first story an issue— i.e., the author's first published fiction. We select stories that are fresh and of the kind our readers have expressed a liking for. In writing a detective story, you must play fair with the reader re clues and necessary information. Otherwise you have a better chance of publishing if you avoid writing to formula."

R-A-D-A-R, (II), Standard Publishing, 8121 Hamilton Ave., Cincinnati OH 45231. (513)931-4050. Editor: Margaret Williams. Magazine: 12 pages; newsprint; illustrations; a few photos. "*R-A-D-A-R* is a take-home paper, distributed in Sunday school classes for children in grades 3-6. The stories and other features reinforce the Bible lesson taught in class. Boys and girls who attend Sunday school make up the audience. The fiction stories, Bible picture stories and other special features appeal to their interests." Weekly. Estab. 1978.
• *Seek* and *The Lookout*, also published by Standard, are listed in this book.
Needs: Fiction—The hero of the story should be an 11- or 12-year-old in a situation involving one or more of the following: history, mystery, animals, prose poem, spiritual, sports, adventure, school, travel, relationships with parents, friends and others. Stories should have believable plots and be wholesome, Christian character-building, but not "preachy." No science fiction. Receives approximately 75-100 unsolicited mss/month. Published work by Betty Lou Mell, Betty Steele Everett and Alan Cliburn; published new writers within the last year. Length: 900-1,000 words average; 400 words minimum; 1,200 words maximum. Publishes short shorts.
How to Contact: Send complete ms. Reports in 2 weeks on queries; 6-8 weeks on mss. SASE for ms. No simultaneous submissions; reprint submissions OK. Free sample copy and guidelines.
Payment: Pays 3-7¢/word; contributor's copy.
Terms: Pays on acceptance for first rights, reprints, etc.
Advice: "Send for sample copy, guidesheet, and theme list. Follow the specifics of guidelines. Keep your writing current with the times and happenings of our world."

RADIANCE, The Magazine for Large Women, (II), Box 30246, Oakland CA 94604. (510)482-0680. Editor: Alice Ansfield. Fiction Editors: Alice Ansfield and Carol Squires. Magazine: 8½ × 11; 48-52 pages; glossy/coated paper; 70 lb. cover stock; illustrations; photos. "Theme is to encourage women to live fully now, whatever their body size. To stop waiting to live or feel good about themselves until they lose weight." Quarterly. Estab. 1984. Circ. 35,000.
• In 1991 *Radiance* was nominated for a "Best of the Alternative Press" award by the *Utne Reader* magazine.
Needs: Adventure, contemporary, erotica, ethnic, fantasy, feminist, historical, humor/satire, mainstream, mystery/suspense, prose poem, science fiction, spiritual, sports, young adult/teen. "Would prefer fiction to have in it a larger-bodied character; living in a positive, upbeat way. Our goal is to empower women." Receives 30+ mss/month. Buys 15 mss/year. Publishes ms within 1 year of acceptance. Published work by Marla Zarrow and Dan Davis. Length: 1,800 words preferred; 800 words minimum; 2,500 words maximum. Publishes short shorts. Sometimes critiques rejected mss and recommends other markets.
How to Contact: Query with clips of published work and send complete mss with cover letter. Reports in 2-3 months. SASE. Simultaneous and reprint submissions OK. Sample copy for $3.50. Fiction guidelines for #10 SASE. Reviews novels and short story collections ("with at least 1 large-size heroine.")
Payment: Pays $50-100 and contributor's copies.
Terms: Pays on publication for one-time rights. Sends galleys to the author if requested.
Advice: "Read our magazine before sending anything to us. Know what our philosophy and points of view are before sending a manuscript. Look around within your community for inspiring, successful and unique large women doing things worth writing about. At this time, prefer fiction having to do with a larger woman (man, child). *Radiance* is one of the leading resources in the size acceptance movement. Each issue profiles dynamic large women from all walks of life, along with articles on health, media, fashion and politics. Our audience is the 30 million American women who wear a size 16 or over. Feminist, emotionally-supportive, quarterly magazine."

Close-up

Dawn Raffel
Fiction Editor
Redbook

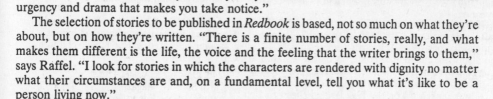

© Kathleen M. Heins

You'll increase your chances of making a sale to *Redbook* if you stretch your idea of what you think a woman's magazine should be. Instead of tailoring your stories to fit its market (young mothers between the ages of 25-45), Dawn Raffel, *Redbook*'s fiction editor, recommends writers submit stories they wouldn't expect to find in a woman's magazine.

"We're not a literary magazine but we do look for stories that have the emotional complexity, care and composition that you'd find in a literary magazine," says Raffel.

Stories that work for *Redbook* grab your attention as well as your heart. "Ultimately we want the reader to be moved by the story," says Raffel. "There should also be a sense of urgency and drama that makes you take notice."

The selection of stories to be published in *Redbook* is based, not so much on what they're about, but on how they're written. "There is a finite number of stories, really, and what makes them different is the life, the voice and the feeling that the writer brings to them," says Raffel. "I look for stories in which the characters are rendered with dignity no matter what their circumstances are and, on a fundamental level, tell you what it's like to be a person living now."

For ideas, Raffel suggests looking inward. "Look at your own experiences. I'm not saying that everybody has to write autobiographical stories. You should look at what's going on in the world around you, but you have to see where you connect with that."

Certain stories, however, don't work for the magazine. If you've just finished a story about a woman's glorious triumph over a shattering divorce, for example, think twice before sending it. "I've seen it a hundred times and unless you're really bringing something different to the story, there's no life in it," says Raffel, who is also not interested in stories that lecture. "If you want to make a political point, or teach a lesson, this is the wrong forum."

After seven years at *Redbook*, Raffel says she can usually tell by the first page of a story whether a writer has hit the mark. "There's a certain amount you can do in revision, but I'm a patient reader and if I can't stay with it I don't think our readers will either."

Whenever possible, Raffel tries to send written responses to those writers who show promise, even if their work is currently not suitable for publication. How long should you wait for a reply? Although turnover time for short-story submissions to *Redbook* is usually fairly quick, backlogs can result in six-week response times.

What does Raffel enjoy most about her work? "It's wonderful to find a new writer," says Raffel, "especially when that person brings something to our readership that's moving and effective and that they haven't seen before!"

—Kathleen M. Heins

RANGER RICK MAGAZINE, (II), National Wildlife Federation, 1400 16th St. NW, Washington DC 20036-2266. (703)790-4278. Editor: Gerald Bishop. Fiction Editor: Deborah Churchman. Magazine: 8 × 10; 48 pages; glossy paper; 60 lb. cover stock; illustrations; photos. "*Ranger Rick* emphasizes conservation and the enjoyment of nature through full-color photos and art, fiction and nonfiction articles, games and puzzles, and special columns. Our audience ranges in ages from 6-12, with the greatest number in the 7 to 10 group. We aim for a fourth grade reading level. They read for fun and information." Monthly. Estab. 1967. Circ. 900,000 + .
  • *Ranger Rick* has won several Ed Press awards and was a runner up for the National Magazine Award for single issue in 1991.
Needs: Fantasy, mystery (amateur sleuth), adventure, science fiction, sports, and humor. "Interesting stories for kids focusing directly on nature or related subjects. Fiction that carries a conservation message is always needed, as are adventure stories involving kids with nature or the outdoors. Moralistic 'lessons' taught children by parents or teachers are not accepted. Human qualities are attributed to animals only in our regular feature, 'Adventures of Ranger Rick.' " Receives about 150-200 unsolicited fiction mss each month. Buys about 6 mss/year. Published fiction by Leslie Dendy. Length: 900 words maximum. Critiques rejected mss "when there is time."
How to Contact: Query with sample lead and any clips of published work with SASE. May consider simultaneous submissions. Reports in 1-2 months on queries and mss. Publishes ms 8 months to 1 year after acceptance, but sometimes longer. Sample copy for $2. Guidelines for legal-sized SASE.
Payment: Pays $550 maximum/full-length ms.
Terms: Pays on acceptance for all rights. Very rarely buys reprints. Sends galleys to author.
Advice: "For our magazine, the writer needs to understand kids and that aspect of nature he or she is writing about—a difficult combination! Mss are rejected because they are contrived and/or condescending—often overwritten. Some mss are anthropomorphic, others are above our readers' level. We find that fiction stories help children understand the natural world and the environmental problems it faces. Beginning writers have a chance equal to that of established authors *provided* the quality is there. Would love to see more science fiction and fantasy, as well as mysteries."

REDBOOK, (II), The Hearst Corporation, 224 W. 57th St., New York NY 10019. Fiction Editor: Dawn Raffel. Magazine: 8 × 10¾; 150-250 pages; 34 lb. paper; 70 lb. cover; illustrations; photos. "*Redbook*'s readership consists of American women, ages 25-44. Most are well-educated, married, have children and also work outside the home." Monthly. Estab. 1903. Circ. 4,000,000.
  • See the close-up interview with *Redbook* Fiction Editor Dawn Raffel in this section. Work published in *Redbook* has been selected for the O. Henry Award anthology in 1992. The magazine is ranked #4 on the 1992 *Writer's Digest* Fiction 50 list.
Needs: "*Redbook* generally publishes one or two short stories per issue. Stories need not be about women exclusively; but must appeal to a female audience. We are interested in new voices and buy up to a quarter of our stories from unsolicited submissions. Standards are high: Stories must be fresh, felt and intelligent; no formula fiction. Receives up to 3,000 unsolicited fiction mss each month; published new writers within the last year. Length: up to 22 ms pages.
How to Contact: Send complete ms with SASE. No queries, please. Simultaneous submissions OK. Reports in 4-6 weeks.
Terms: Pays on acceptance for first North American serial rights.
Advice: "Superior craftsmanship is of paramount importance: We look for emotional complexity, dramatic tension, precision of language. Note that we almost never run stories that look back on the experiences of childhood or adolescence. Please read a few issues to get a sense of what we're looking for."

REFORM JUDAISM, (II), Union of American Hebrew Congregations, 838 5th Ave., New York NY 10021. (212)249-0100, ext. 400. Editor: Aron Hirt-Manheimer. Managing Editor: Joy Weinberg. Magazine: 8½ × 11; 48 or 64 pages; illustrations; photos. "We cover subjects of Jewish interest in general and Reform Jewish in particular, for members of Reform Jewish congregations in the United States and Canada." Quarterly. Estab. 1972. Circ. 295,000.
Needs: Humor/satire, religious/inspirational. Receives 30 unsolicited mss/month. Buys 3 mss/year. Publishes ms 6 months after acceptance. Length: 1,200 words average; 600 words minimum; 3,000 words maximum. Sometimes recommends other markets.
How to Contact: Send complete ms with cover letter. Reports in 3 weeks. SASE for ms. Simultaneous submissions OK. Sample copy for $2 and SAE.
Payment: Pays 10¢/word.
Terms: Pays on publication for first North American serial rights.

ROAD KING MAGAZINE, (I), William A. Coop, Inc., Box 250, Park Forest IL 60466. (708)481-9240. Magazine: 5¾ × 8; 48-88 pages; 60 lb. enamel paper; 60 lb. enamel cover stock; illustrations; photos. "Bimonthly leisure-reading magazine for long-haul, over-the-road professional truckers. Contains short articles, short fiction, some product news, games, puzzles and industry news. Truck drivers read it while eating, fueling, during layovers and at other similar times while they are en route."
Needs: Truck-related, western, mystery, adventure and humor. "Remember that our magazine gets into the home and that some truckers tend to be Bible Belt types. No erotica or violence." Receives 200 unsolicited fiction mss each year. Buys 1 ms/issue; 6 mss/year. Publishes ms 1-2 months after acceptance. Published work by Forrest Grove and Dan Anderson. Length: 1,200 words, maximum.
How to Contact: Send complete ms with SASE. No simultaneous submissions. Reports in 3-6 months. Sample copy with 6 × 9 SASE.
Payment: Pays $400 maximum.
Terms: Pays on acceptance for all rights.
Advice: "Don't phone. Don't send mss by registered or insured mail or they will be returned unopened by post office. Don't try to get us involved in lengthy correspondence. Be patient. We have a small staff and we are slow." Mss are rejected because "most don't fit our format . . . they are too long; they do not have enough knowledge of trucking; there is too much violence. Our readers like fiction. We are a leisure reading publication with a wide variety of themes and articles in each issue. Truckers can read a bit over coffee, in the washroom, etc., then save the rest of the magazine for the next stop. Know the trucker market. We are not interested in stereotypical image of truckers as macho, beer guzzling, women-chasing cowboys."

ST. ANTHONY MESSENGER, (II), 1615 Republic St., Cincinnati OH 45210-1298. Editor: Norman Perry, O.F.M. Magazine: 8 × 10¾; 56 pages; illustrations; photos. "*St. Anthony Messenger* is a Catholic family magazine which aims to help its readers lead more fully human and Christian lives. We publish articles which report on a changing church and world, opinion pieces written from the perspective of Christian faith and values, personality profiles, and fiction which entertains and informs." Monthly. Estab. 1893. Circ. 347,000.
● This is a leading Catholic magazine, but has won awards for both religious and secular journalism and writing. In 1992 the magazine received 7 awards from the Catholic Press Association and 9 awards from the Cincinnati Editors Association. *St. Anthony Messenger* ranks #39 on the 1992 *Writer's Digest* Fiction 50 list.
Needs: Contemporary, religious/inspirational, romance, senior citizen/retirement and spiritual. "We do not want mawkishly sentimental or preachy fiction. Stories are most often rejected for poor plotting and characterization; bad dialogue — listen to how people talk; inadequate motivation. Many stories say nothing, are 'happenings' rather than stories." No fetal journals, no rewritten Bible stories. Receives 70-80 unsolicited fiction mss/month. Buys 1 ms/issue; 12 mss/year. Publishes ms up to 1 year after acceptance. Published work by Marjorie Franco, Joseph Pici, Joan Savro and Philip Gambone. Length: 2,000-2,500 words. Critiques rejected mss "when there is time." Sometimes recommends other markets.
How to Contact: Send complete ms with SASE. No simultaneous submissions. Reports in 6-8 weeks. Sample copy and guidelines for #10 SASE. Reviews novels and short story collections. Send books to Barbara Beckwith, book review editor.
Payment: Pays 14¢/word maximum; 2 contributor's copies; $1 charge for extras.
Terms: Pays on acceptance for first North American serial rights.
Advice: "We publish one story a month and we get up to 1,000 a year. Too many offer simplistic 'solutions' or answers. Pay attention to endings. Easy, simplistic, deus ex machina endings don't work. People have to feel characters in the stories are real and have a reason to care about them and what happens to them. Fiction entertains but can also convey a point in a very telling way just as the Bible uses stories to teach."

ST. JOSEPH'S MESSENGER AND ADVOCATE OF THE BLIND, (II), Sisters of St. Joseph of Peace, 541 Pavonia Ave., Jersey City NJ 07306. (201)798-4141. Magazine: 8½ × 11; 16 pages; illustrations; photos. For Catholics generally but not exclusively. Theme is "religious — relevant — real." Quarterly. Estab. 1903. Circ. 20,000.
● *St. Joseph's Messenger and Advocate of the Blind* ranked #30 on the 1992 *Writer's Digest* Fiction 50 list.
Needs: Contemporary, humor/satire, mainstream, religious/inspirational, romance and senior citizen/retirement. Receives 30-40 unsolicited fiction mss/month. Buys 3 mss/issue; 20 mss/year. Publishes ms an average of 1 year after acceptance. Published work by Eileen W. Strauch; published new writers

within the last year. Length: 800 words minimum; 1,800 words maximum; 1,500 words average. Occasionally critiques rejected mss.

How to Contact: Send complete ms with SASE. Simultaneous and previously published submissions OK. Sample copy for #10 SAE and 1 first class stamp. Fiction guidelines for SASE.

Payment: Pays $15-40 and 2 contributor's copies.

Terms: Pays on acceptance for one-time rights.

Advice: Rejects mss because of "vague focus or theme. Write to be read—keep material current and of interest. *Do not preach*—the story will tell the message. Keep the ending from being too obvious. Fiction is the greatest area of interest to our particular reading public."

SASSY MAGAZINE, (II), Lang Communications, 230 Park Ave., New York NY 10169. (212)551-9500. Editor: Mary Kaye Schilling. Fiction Editor: Christina Kelly. Magazine; 9½×11; 100-130 pages; glossy 40 lb. stock paper and cover; illustrations and photographs. "Lifestyle magazine for girls, ages 14-19, covering entertainment, fashion as well as serious subjects." Monthly. Estab. 1988. Circ. 650,000.

• *Sassy*, known for its gutsy approach to writing for young women, has received a *MagazineWeek* Award for Editorial Excellence in 1992 and was nominated in 1991 for an ASME general excellence award. It ranked #9 on the 1992 *Writer's Digest* Fiction 50 list.

Needs: Contemporary, ethnic, experimental, feminist, gay, humor/satire, literary, mainstream, prose poem, regional, young adult/teen (10-18 years). "No typical teenage romance." Publishes annual special fiction issue. Receives 300 unsolicited mss/month. Buys 1 ms/issue; 12 mss/year. Publishes ms 3-6 months after publication. Published Christina Kelly, John Elder, Elizabeth Mosier. Length: 2,000 words; 1,000 words minimum; 3,500 words maximum. Sometimes critiques rejected mss and recommends other markets.

How to Contact: Send complete manuscript with cover letter. Include social security number and address, brief background, perhaps one sentence on what story is about or like. Reports in 3 months. SASE. Simultaneous submissions OK. Sample copy for $2. Fiction guidelines are free.

Payment: Pays $1,000 and contributor's copies.

Terms: Pays on acceptance. Offers 20% kill fee. Buys all rights or first North American serial righs. Send galleys to author (if requested).

Advice: "We look for unusual new ways to write for teenagers. It helps if the story has a quirky, vernacular style that we use throughout the magazine. Generally our stories have to have a teenage protagonist but they are not typical teen fiction. In the end, our only real criterion is that a story is original, intelligent, well-crafted and moves us."

SEEK, (II), Standard Publishing, 8121 Hamilton Ave., Cincinnati OH 45231. Editor: Eileen H. Wilmoth. Magazine: 5½×8½; 8 pages; newsprint paper; art and photos in each issue. "Inspirational stories of faith-in-action for Christian young adults; a Sunday School take-home paper." Weekly. Estab. 1970. Circ. 40,000.

• Standard Publishing also publishes *Radar* and *The Lookout* listed in this book.

Needs: Religious/inspirational. Buys 150 mss/year. Publishes ms an average of 1 year after acceptance. Published new writers within the last year. Length: 500-1,200 words.

How to Contact: Send complete ms with SASE. No simultaneous submissions. Reports in 4-6 weeks. Free sample copy and guidelines. Reviews "some" novels and short story collections.

Payment: Pays 5-7¢/word.

Terms: Pays on acceptance. Buys reprints.

Advice: "Write a credible story with Christian slant—no preachments; avoid overworked themes such as joy in suffering, generation gaps, etc. Most mss are rejected by us because of irrelevant topic or message, unrealistic story, or poor character and/or plot development. We use fiction stories that are believable."

SEVENTEEN, (II), Klll Magazine Corp., 850 3rd Ave., New York NY 10022. (212)759-8100. Fiction Editor: Joe Bargmann. Magazine: 8½×11; 125-400 pages; 40 lb. coated paper; 80 lb. coated cover stock; illustrations; photos. A general interest magazine with fashion, beauty care, pertinent topics such as current issues, attitudes, experiences and concerns during the teenage years. Monthly. Estab. 1944. Circ. 1.7 million.

Needs: High-quality literary fiction. Receives 300 unsolicited fiction mss/month. Buys 1 mss/issue. Agented fiction 50%. Published work by Margaret Atwood, Joyce Carol Oates; published new writers within the last year. Length: approximately 1,500-3,500 words. Also publishes short shorts.

"Seventeen welcomes stories that are relevant to adolescents and their experiences, fiction that somehow touches contemporary young adult life," says Associate Editor Christine Genna. "Submissions should be accessible and appealing to our readers, ages 13 to 21, as well as challenging and inspiring. In essence, we publish stories that possess the quality and integrity of today's best literary short fiction." This cover pictures Lillian Martinez, winner of the magazine's 1992 Cover Model Contest. "Lillian is a natural beauty—she is young, healthy and has the look that appeals to our readers, one which they can relate to," Genna says. The cover photographer was Antoine Verglas.

How to Contact: Send complete ms with SASE and cover letter with relevant credits. Reports in 2 months on mss. Guidelines for with SASE.

Payment: Pays $700-2,500.

Terms: Pays on acceptance for one-time rights.

Advice: "Respect the intelligence and sophistication of teenagers. *Seventeen* remains open to the surprise of new voices. Our commitment to publishing the work of new writers remains strong; we continue to read every submission we receive. We believe that good fiction can move the reader toward thoughtful examination of her own life as well as the lives of others—providing her ultimately with a fuller appreciation of what it means to be human. While stories which focus on female teenage experience continue to be of interest, the less obvious possibilities are equally welcome. We encourage writers to submit literary short stories concerning subjects that may not be immediately identifiable as 'teenage,' with narrative styles that are experimental and challenging. Too often, unsolicited submissions possess voices and themes condescending and unsophisticated. Also, writers hesitate to send stories to *Seventeen* which they think too violent or risqué. Good writing holds the imaginable and then some, and if it doesn't find its home here, we're always grateful for the introduction to a writer's work."

SHOFAR, For Jewish Kids On The Move, (I, II, IV), 43 Northcote Dr., Melville NY 11747. (516)643-4598. Editor: Gerald H. Grayson, Ph.D. Magazine: 8½×11; 32-48 pages; 60 lb. paper; 80 lb. cover; illustration; photos. Audience: Jewish children in fourth through eighth grades. Monthly (October-May). Estab. 1984. Circ. 10,000.

Needs: Adventure, contemporary, ethnic, fantasy, humor, juvenile (5-9 years), prose poem, religious/inspirational, spiritual, sports, suspense/mystery, translations, young adult/teen (10-18 years) and Jewish. Receives 12-24 unsolicited mss/month. Buys 3-5 mss/issue; 24-40 mss/year. Published work by Caryn Huberman, Diane Claerbout and Rabbi Sheldon Lewis. Length: 750-1,000 words. Occasionally critiques rejected mss. Recommends other markets.

How to Contact: Send complete ms with cover letter. Reports in 6-8 weeks. SASE. Simultaneous and reprint submissions OK. Sample copy for 9×12 SAE and 5 first class stamps. Fiction guidelines for 3½×6½ SAE and 1 first class stamp.

Payment: Pays 7¢/word.

Terms: Pays on publication for first North American serial rights.

Advice: "Know the magazine and the religious-education needs of Jewish elementary-school-age children. If you are a Jewish educator, what has worked for you in the classroom? Write it out; send it on to me; I'll help you develop the idea into a short piece of fiction. A beginning fiction writer eager to break into *Shofar* will find an eager editor willing to help."

THE SINGLE PARENT, Journal of Parents Without Partners, (IV), Parents Without Partners, Inc., 8807 Colesville Rd., Silver Spring MD 20910-4346. (301)588-9354. Fax: (301)588-9216. Editor: Rene McDonald. Magazine: 8×10¾; 48 pages; 38 lb. glossy paper; illustrations; photos. Publication for divorced, separated, widowed or never-married parents and their children. Published 6 times/year. Estab. 1957. Circ. 105,000.
  ● *The Single Parent* won the 1990 Award for Excellence in magazine writing on children of divorce from the National Council of Children's Rights. Parents Without Partners is a national organization for single parents.
Needs: Short stories for *children only*, not adults. Stories should deal with issues that children from one-parent families might face. Buys 2 mss/issue. Published new writers within the last year. Length: 1,500 words maximum.
How to Contact: Send complete ms with SASE. Simultaneous submissions OK. Reports within 2 months. Sample copy for $1.25 or 10×12 manila SAE with $1.25 postage. Reviews short story collections occasionally.
Payment: Pays up to $75; 2 contributor's copies.
Terms: Pays on publication.
Advice: "Write about real children facing (and coping with) the real problems that crop up in single parent households."

SINGLELIFE MAGAZINE (II), Single Life Enterprises, Inc., Suite 703, 606 W. Wisconsin Ave., Milwaukee WI 53203. (414)271-9700. Fax: (414)271-5263. Editor: Gail Levine. Magazine: 8×11; 64 pages; slick paper; illustrations; photos. "Material deals with concerns of single persons of 24-60 age group." Primarily a nonfiction magazine. Bimonthly. Estab. 1982. Circ. 25,000.
Needs: Humor/satire, literary, travel, relationships, self-help, seasonal food and entertaining. Receives 50 unsolicited mss/month. Publishes ms 2-4 months after acceptance. Length: 1,000 words minimum; 3,500 words maximum.
How to Contact: Send complete ms. Reports in 1 week, "depends on production schedule." SASE for ms. Simultaneous and reprint submissions OK. Sample copy $3.50. Writers' guidelines for SAE and 1 first class stamp.
Payment: Pays $50-150 and contributor's copies.
Terms: Pays on publication for one-time rights.

SOJOURNER, A Women's Forum, (II, IV), 42 Seaverns, Jamaica Plain MA 02130. (617)524-0415. Editor: Karen Kahn. Magazine: 11×17; 48 pages; newsprint paper; illustrations; photos. "Feminist journal publishing interviews, nonfiction features, news, viewpoints, poetry, reviews (music, cinema, books) and fiction for women." Published monthly. Estab. 1975. Circ. 33,000.
Needs: Contemporary, ethnic, experimental, fantasy, feminist, lesbian, humor/satire, literary, prose poem and women's. Upcoming themes: May publish "Fiction/Poetry" issue (February); "Annual Health Supplement" (March). Receives 20 unsolicited fiction mss/month. Accepts 10 mss/year. Agented fiction 10%. Published new writers within the last year. Length: 1,000 words minimum; 4,000 words maximum; 2,500 words average. Recommends other markets.
How to Contact: Send complete ms with SASE and cover letter with description of previous publications; current works. Simlultaneous submissions OK. Publishes ms an average of 6 months after acceptance. Sample copy $2 with 10×13 SASE and 86¢ postage. Fiction guidelines for SASE.
Payment: Pays subscription to magazine and 2 contributor's copies, $15. No extra charge up to 5; $1 charge each thereafter.
Terms: Buys first rights only.
Advice: "Pay attention to appearance of manuscript! Very difficult to wade through sloppily presented fiction, however good. Do write a cover letter. If not cute, it can't hurt and may help. Mention previous publication(s)."

SPORTS AFIELD, Hearst Magazine, 250 W. 55th St., New York NY 10019. Prefers not to share information.

STANDARD, (II, IV), Nazarene International Headquarters, 6401 The Paseo, Kansas City MO 64131. (816)333-7000. Editor: Beth A. Watkins. Magazine: 8½×11; 8 pages; illustrations; photos. Inspirational reading for adults. Weekly. Estab. 1936. Circ. 165,000.
  ● Other magazines listed in this book associated with the Nazarene are *Discoveries, Kindergarten Listen* and *Teens Today.*

Needs: Religious/inspirational, spiritual. Receives 350 unsolicited mss/month (both fiction and nonfiction). Accepts 240 mss/year. Publishes ms 14-18 months after acceptance. Published new writers within the last year. Length: 1,000 words average; 300 words minimum; 1,700 words maximum. Also publishes short shorts of 300-350 words.
How to Contact: Send complete ms with name, address and phone number. Reports in 1-2 months on mss. SASE. Simultaneous submissions OK but will pay only reprint rates. Sample copy and guidelines for SAE and 1 first class stamp.
Payment: Pays 3½¢/word; 2¢/word (reprint); contributor's copies.
Terms: Pays on acceptance for one-time rights.
Advice: "Too much is superficial; containing the same story lines. Give me something original, humorous, yet helpful. I'm also looking for more stories on current social issues. Make plot, characters realistic. Contrived articles are quick to spot and reject."

STORY FRIENDS, (II), Mennonite Publishing House, 616 Walnut Ave., Scottdale PA 15683. (412)887-8500. Editor: Marjorie Waybill. Sunday school publication which portrays Jesus as a friend and helper. Nonfiction and fiction for children 4-9 years of age. Weekly.
• *Story Friends* ranks #42 on the *Writer's Digest* Fiction 50 list. The Mennonite Publishing House listed in this book also include *On the Line, Purpose* and *With* magazines.
Needs: Juvenile. Stories of everyday experiences at home, in church, in school or at play, which provide models of Christian values. Length: 300-800 words.
How to Contact: Send complete ms with SASE. Seasonal or holiday material should be submitted 6 months in advance. Free sample copy.
Payment: Pays 3-5¢/word.
Terms: Pays on acceptance for one-time rights. Buys reprints. Not copyrighted.
Advice: "It is important to include relationships, patterns of forgiveness, respect, honesty, trust and caring. Prefer exciting yet plausible short stories which offer different settings, introduce children to wide ranges of friends and demonstrate joys, fears, temptations and successes of the readers."

STRAIGHT, (II), Standard Publishing Co., 8121 Hamilton Ave., Cincinnati OH 45231. (513)931-4050. Editor: Carla Crane. "Publication helping and encouraging teens to live a victorious, fulfilling Christian life. Distributed through churches and some private subscriptions." Magazine: 6½ × 7½; 12 pages; newsprint paper and cover; illustrations (color); photos. Quarterly in weekly parts. Estab. 1951. Circ. 75,000.
• *Straight* ranked #31 on the *Writer's Digest* Fiction 50 list.
Needs: Contemporary, religious/inspirational, romance, spiritual, mystery, adventure and humor—all with Christian emphasis. "Stories dealing with teens and teen life, with a positive message or theme. Topics that interest teenagers include school, family life, recreation, friends, church, part-time jobs, dating and music. Main character should be a 15- or 16-year-old boy or girl, a Christian and regular churchgoer, who faces situations using Bible principles." Receives approximately 100 unsolicited fiction mss/month. Buys 1-2 mss/issue; 75-100 mss/year. Publishes ms an average of 1 year after acceptance. Less than 1% of fiction is agented. Published work by Alan Cliburn, Marian Bray, Teresa Cleary; published new writers within the last year. Length: 800-1,200 words. Recommends other markets.
How to Contact: Send complete ms with SASE and cover letter (experience with teens especially preferred from new writers). Reports in 1 month. Sample copy and guidelines for SASE.
Payment: Pays 3-7¢/word.
Terms: Pays on acceptance for first and one-time rights. Buys reprints.
Advice: "Get to know us before submitting, through guidelines and sample issues (free with a SASE). And get to know teenagers. A writer must know what today's teens are like, and what kinds of conflicts they experience. In writing a short fiction piece for the teen reader, don't try to accomplish too much. If your character is dealing with the problem of prejudice, don't also deal with his/her fights with sister, desire for a bicycle, or anything else that is not absolutely essential to the reader's understanding of the major conflict."

‡STREET NEWS, (II), Suite 8040, 543 W. 43rd St., New York NY 10036. Editor: John Conolley. Tabloid: 12 × 15; 20 pages; newsprint; illustrations. "*Street News* is published to be sold by the homeless. Philosophy is objectivist or libertarian. We would publish short fiction, but we're not presently in a position to pay money for it. That may change later." Biweekly. Estab. 1989. Circ. 20,000.
Needs: Children's/juvenile (5-9 years, 10-12 years), ethnic/multicultural, humor/satire, literary, mainstream/contemporary, mystery/suspense (young adult), regional, senior citizen/retirement, serialized novel, sports, translations, young adult/teen (10-18 years). "No erotica, no hard genre stuff. Will

consider fantasy in here-and-now setting." Receives 1-2 unsolicited mss/month. Publishes ms 1-2 months after acceptance. Length: 400 words minimum; 2,000 words maximum. Also publishes poetry.
How to Contact: Send complete ms with cover letter. Should include estimated word count, bio (one or two sentences), and list of publications with submission. Reports in 1 month. Send SASE (IRC) for reply, return of ms or send disposable copy of ms. Sample $2 or $1 and 9×12 SAE and 3 oz. postage.
Payment: Pays 3 contributor's copies. Additional copies for SAE.
Terms: Acquires one-time rights.
Advice: Looks for "an interesting point; a new, or even oddball, way of looking at things. When you've finished the first draft (or maybe better, the second draft), go back and look for ways to prepare your reader better for understanding your point. Read 'The Power of Plot Irony' and 'The Sport of Fiction' in October '92 *Writer's Digest*."

THE STUDENT, A Christian Collegiate Magazine, (I, II), Student Ministry Department of the Baptist Sunday School Board, 127 Ninth Ave., North, Nashville TN 37234. (615)251-2788. Editor: Milt Hughes. Magazine: 8¼×11; 50 pages; uncoated paper; coated cover stock; illustrations; photos. Magazine for Christians and non-Christians about life and work with Christian students on campus and related articles on living in dorm setting, dating life, missions activities, Bible study, and church ministry to students. Monthly. Estab. 1922. Circ. 40,000.
• Other family and relationship magazines published by The Sunday School Board include *Christian Singles*, *Home Life* and *Living with Teenagers*.
Needs: Adventure, humor, comics, confession, contemporary, ethnic, and religious/inspirational. Does not want to see mss "without purpose or without moral tone." Receives approximately 25 unsolicited fiction mss/month. Buys 1-2 mss/issue; 12-24 mss/year. Length: 300 words minimum (or less, depending on treatment); 1,500 words maximum; 750 words average.
How to Contact: Query first with SASE. Cover letter with bio and description of published works. Simultaneous and previously published submissions OK. Reports in 3 weeks on queries; 6 weeks on mss. Sample copy 75¢. Fiction guidelines for SASE.
Payment: Pays 5¢/word and 3 contributor's copies.
Terms: Pays on publication for all rights, first rights, one-time rights, and assignments for work-for-hire basis.
Advice: "Fit writing to format and concept of the piece. View many issues of the magazine before you write. Our readers demand fiction which conveys our message in an interesting way."

STUDENT LEADERSHIP JOURNAL, (IV), InterVarsity Christian Fellowship, P.O. Box 7895, 6400 Schroeder Rd., Madison WI 53707-7895. (608)274-9001. Managing Editor: Jeff Yourison. "The journal is a networking and leadership development tool for audience described below. We publish articles on leadership, spiritual growth and evangelism. We publish occasional poetry, short stories and allegories. The audience is Christian student leaders on secular college campuses." Quarterly. Estab. 1988. Circ. 8,000.
Needs: Religious/inspirational, prose poem. "The form of fiction is not nearly as important as its quality and content. Fiction published by *Student Leadership* will always reflect a Christian worldview." No romance or children's fiction. Receives 10-15 unsolicited fiction mss/month. Buys up to 1 ms/issue; 4 mss/year. Publishes ms up to 2 years after acceptance. Length: 2,000 words preferred; 200 words minimum; 2,500 words maximum.
How to Contact: Query first with clips of published work. "A good cover letter will demonstrate familiarity with the magazine and its needs and will briefly describe the submission and any relevant information." Reports in up to 2 months on queries; up to 3 months on mss. SASE. Simultaneous and reprint submissions OK. Sample copy for $3, 9×12 SAE and $1 postage. Fiction guidelines for #10 SAE and 1 first class stamp. Reviews novels and short story collections "if they address our audience *and* contemporary cultures."
Payment: Pays $25-200.
Terms: Pays on acceptance for first or one-time rights. Sends pre-publication galleys to author.
Advice: "Read! Read! Read! The short story author must be an *artist* with words in so short a space. *Read* the best work of others. Observe it; get it into your bones. Just like a picture, a story must be vivid, colorful, well-balanced and eye-catching. Write! Write! Write! Don't be afraid to have at it! Picasso pitched many of his sketches. You'll pitch most of yours. But it's good practice, and it keeps your creative mind flowing."

SUNDAY JOURNAL MAGAZINE, (IV), *The Providence Journal-Bulletin*, 75 Fountain St., Providence RI 02902. (401)277-7349. Editor: Elliot Krieger. Magazine: 10×11½; 28 pages; coated newsprint paper; illustrations; photos. "Magazine which has appeared weekly for 40 years in the *Providence Sunday Journal*." Circ. 280,000.
Needs: Regional. "We will accept fiction centered around Rhode Island or Northeastern US only." Published fiction by Paul Watkins and Ann Hood; published new writers within the last year.
How to Contact: Submit with SASE.
Payment: Pays $175-400.
Terms: Buys one-time rights. Sponsors short-story contest for New England writers.

SUNSHINE MAGAZINE, (II), Henrichs Publications, Box 40, Sunshine Park, Litchfield IL 62056. Magazine: 5¼×7¼; 48 pages; matte paper and cover stock; illustrations. "To promote goodwill for the betterment of our society. We publish short, nondenominational, inspirational material." Monthly. Estab. 1924. Circ. 60,000.
● *Sunshine* ranks #7 on the 1992 *Writer's Digest* Fiction 50 list.
Needs: "Light" fiction, humor, juvenile (5-9 years), preschool (0-4 years), senior citizen/retirement. No fiction that is lengthy, fantasy, sexual, specifically religious, violent or dealing with death, drugs, divorce or alcohol. Receives 500 unsolicited fiction mss/month. Buys 12 mss/issue; 140 mss/year. Publishes ms within a year of acceptance. Published work by Robert Tefertillar, Gail Geddes, Joanna Captain; published new writers within the last year. Length: 750 words average; 100 words minimum; 1,250 words maximum. Publishes short shorts. Sometimes critiques rejected ms and recommends other markets.
How to Contact: Send complete ms with SASE and cover letter with name, address, rights offered. Simultaneous submissions OK. Reports in 2 months on mss. SASE. Sample copy for 50¢ or 6×8 SAE with 2 first class stamps. Fiction guidelines for #10 SASE.
Payment: Pays $10-100, contributor's copies; charge for extras.
Terms: Pays on acceptance for first North American serial rights.
Advice: "Always know the magazine you're submitting to. Read the guidelines *thoroughly* and examine one or two sample copies."

SURFING MAGAZINE (IV), Western Empire, Box 3010, San Clemente CA 92672. (714)492-7873. Editor: Nick Carroll. Editorial Director/Dept. Manager: David Gilovich. Magazine: 8×11; 140 pages; 45 lb. free sheet paper; 80 lb. cover stock; photos. Magazine covering "all aspects of the sport of surfing for young, active surfing enthusiasts." Monthly. Estab. 1964. Circ. 92,000.
Needs: Surfing-related fiction. Receives 2 unsolicited mss/month. Buys 3 mss/year. Length: 2,000-3,000 words average. Occasionally critiques rejected mss. Also publishes short shorts.
How to Contact: Cover letter with background on surfing. Query first. Reports in 2 weeks. SASE. Free sample copy and fiction guidelines.
Payment: Pays 15-20¢/word.
Terms: Pays on publication for one-time rights.
Advice: "Establish yourself as a *Surfing* general contributor before tackling fiction."

‡SWANK MAGAZINE, (II, IV), Broadway Publishing Company, 1700 Broadway, New York NY 10019. Editor: Brian J. English. Magazine: 8½×11; 116 pages; 20 lb. paper; 60 lb. coated stock; illustrations; photos. "Men's sophisticate format. Sexually-oriented material. Our readers are after erotic material." Published 13 times a year. Estab. 1952. Circ. 350,000.
Needs: High-caliber erotica. "Fiction always has an erotic or other male-oriented theme; also eligible would be mystery or suspense with a very erotic scene. Writers should try to avoid the clichés of the genre." Buys 1 ms/issue, 18 mss/year. Receives approximately 80 unsolicited fiction mss each month. Published new writers within the last year. Length: 1,500-2,750 words.
How to Contact: Send complete ms with SASE and cover letter, which should list previous publishing credits. No simultaneous submissions. Reports in 2 weeks on mss. Sample copy $5.95 with SASE.
Payment: Pays $250-400. Offers 25% kill fee for assigned ms not published.
Terms: Buys first North American serial rights.
Advice: "Research the men's magazine market." Mss are rejected because of "typical, overly simple storylines and poor execution. We're looking for interesting stories—whether erotic in theme or not—that break the mold of the usual men's magazine fiction. We're not only just considering strict erotica. Mystery, adventure, etc. with erotica passages will be considered."

SYNDICATED FICTION PROJECT, (I), (formerly PEN Syndicated Fiction Project), P.O. Box 15650, Washington DC 20003. (202)543-6322. Director: Caroline Marshall. "Fiction syndicate created to market quality short fiction to a broad, national audience via radio (The Sound of Writing, co-produced with NPR), newspaper Sunday magazines and regional magazines (a varying group) and literary publications, including *American Short Fiction* published by the University of Texas Press."
   • For more on this unique project see the close-up interview with Director Caroline Marshall in the 1992 *Writer's Market* and "Off the Beaten Path" in the 1991 *Novel & Short Story Writer's Market*.
Needs: Literary. Receives 2,500-5,000 submissions/year. Buys 50 unpublished mss/year. Only reads in January. Length: 2,500 words maximum. Publishes short shorts.
How to Contact: Please send for guidelines first. Send 2 copies of complete ms with cover letter and brief bio. Up to 2 stories may be submitted at one time, but no one story may exceed 2,500 words. Decisions made by late May. SASE. Fiction guidelines for #10 SASE.
Payment: Pays $500 plus $100 per print publication. "Realistic possible potential: $1,000."
Terms: Pays $500 on return of contract; syndication fees paid on semiannual basis. Buys worldwide serial rights, audio and anthology rights.
Advice: "Newspaper and radio audiences prefer short pieces of general, topical or family interest. Submitters are encouraged to imagine seeing their work in a Sunday magazine with accompanying illustration or hearing it on the air to judge a story's suitability."

'TEEN MAGAZINE, (II), Petersen Publishing Co., 8490 Sunset Blvd., Los Angeles CA 90069. Editor: Roxanne Camron. Magazine: 100-150 pages; 34 lb. paper; 60 lb. cover; illustrations and photos. "The magazine contains fashion, beauty and features for the young teenage girl. The median age of our readers is 16. Our success stems from our dealing with relevant issues teens face, printing recent entertainment news and showing the latest fashions and beauty looks." Monthly. Estab. 1957. Circ. 1.1 million.
   • Note this magazine has doubled its payment rate.
Needs: Romance, adventure, mystery, humor and young adult. Every story, whether romance, mystery, humor, etc., must be aimed for teenage girls. The protagonist should be a teenager, preferably female. No experimental, science fiction, fantasy or horror. Buys 1 ms/issue; 12 mss/year. Generally publishes ms 3-5 months after acceptance. Published work by Emily Ormand, Louise Carroll and Linda Bernson; published new writers within the last year. Length: 3,000 words. Publishes short shorts.
How to Contact: Send complete ms and short cover letter with SASE. Reports in 10 weeks on mss. Sample copy for $2.50. Guidelines for SASE.
Payment: Pays $200.
Terms: Pays on acceptance for all rights.
Advice: "Try to find themes that suit the modern teen. We need innovative ways of looking at the age-old problems of young love, parental pressures, making friends, being left out, etc. *'TEEN* would prefer to have romance balanced with a plot, re: a girl's inner development and search for self. Handwritten mss will not be read."

TEEN POWER, (IV), Scripture Press Publications, Inc., Box 632, Glen Ellyn IL 60138. (708)668-6000. Editor: Amy Cox. Magazine: 5⅜ × 8⅜; 8 pages; non-glossy paper and cover; illustrations and photographs. "*Teen Power* publishes true stories and fiction with a conservative Christian slant—must help readers see how principles for Christian living can be applied to everyday life; for young teens (11-16 years); many small town and rural; includes large readerships in Canada, England and other countries in addition to U.S." Estab. 1966.
   • Another magazine by this publisher, *Freeway*, is listed in this book. *Teen Power* won an Award of Merit in 1992 from the Evangelical Press Association.
Needs: Adventure, humor/satire, religious/inspirational, young adult/teen (11-16 years). "All must have spiritual emphasis of some sort." Receives approximately 50-75 unsolicited mss/month. Buys 1 ms/issue; about 50 mss/year. Publishes ms at least 1 year after acceptance. Published work by Alan Cliburn, Betty Steele Everett and Michael La Cross; published new writers within the last year. Length: 1,000 words preferred; 250 words minimum; 1,100 words maximum. Publishes short shorts. Length: 300-500 words. Sometimes critiques rejected mss and recommends other markets.

How to Contact: Send complete ms with cover letter. Reports in 6-8 weeks. SASE. Simultaneous and reprint submissions OK. Sample copy and fiction guidelines for #10 SAE and 1 first class stamp.
Payment: Pays $20 minimum; $120 maximum; contributor's copies.
Terms: Pays on acceptance. Buys first rights and one-time rights.
Advice: "We look for spiritual emphasis (strong but not preachy), writing style, age appropriateness, creativity in topic choice and presentation. A writer for *Teen Power* must know something about young teens and what is important to them, plus have a working knowledge of basic principles for Christian living, and be able to weave the two together."

TEENS TODAY, (II), Church of the Nazarene, 6401 The Paseo, Kansas City MO 64131. (816)333-7000. Editor: Karen DeSollar. Sunday school take-home paper: 8½×11; 8 pages; illustrations; photos. "For junior and senior high students involved with the Church of the Nazarene who find it interesting and helpful to their areas of life." Weekly. Circ. 60,000.
   • Other Nazarene-affiliated magazines listed in this book are *Discoveries, Kindergarten Listen* and *Standard*.
Needs: Contemporary, religious/inspirational, romance, humor, juvenile, mystery/suspense (romantic suspense), science fiction (soft sociological), young adult and ethnic. "Nothing that puts teens down or endorses lifestyles not in keeping with the denomination's beliefs and standards." Buys 1-2 mss/issue. Published new writers within the last year. Length: 1,000-1,500 words.
How to Contact: Send complete ms with SASE. Simultaneous submissions OK. Reports in 2 months on mss. Publishes ms 8-10 months after acceptance. Sample copy and guidelines for SASE.
Payment: Pays 4¢/word and 3½¢/word on second reprint.
Terms: Pays on acceptance for first and second serial rights. Buys reprints.
Advice: "Don't be too juvenile."

TEXAS CONNECTION MAGAZINE, (IV), Box 541805, Dallas TX 75220. (214)951-0316. Editor: Alan Miles. Magazine: 8½×11; 168 pages; book offset paper; 100 lb. enamel cover; illustrations and photographs. "Adult erotica, for adults only." Monthly. Estab. 1985. Circ. 50,000.
Needs: Erotica, erotic cartooning, sexual fantasy, feminist, gay, humor/satire and lesbian. "Publishes new quarterly digest—100% fiction." Receives 20-30 unsolicited mss/month. Buys 2-3 mss/issue. Publishes ms 2-3 months after acceptance. Length: 1,750 words preferred; 1,000 words minimum; 2,500 words maximum.
How to Contact: Send complete ms with cover letter. Cover letter must state writer/author's age (18 yrs. minimum). Reports in 4-6 weeks. SASE for ms, not needed for query. Simultaneous and reprint submissions OK. Sample copy for $8.50. Free fiction guidelines. Reviews erotic fiction only.
Payment: Pays $25-200. Free subscription to magazine and contributor's copies.
Terms: Pays on publication. Purchases all rights on some, first rights on most.
Advice: "We publish an adult, alternative lifestyle magazine that is (uniquely) distributed both in the adult store market and mass-market outlets (convenience stores) throughout 5 states: Texas (main), Oklahoma, Arkansas, Louisiana, New Mexico. We are, of course, interested in fresh, erotic fiction only."

‡THRASHER, Skateboard Magazine, (I, II), High Speed Productions, P.O. Box 884570, San Francisco CA 94188-4570. (415)822-3083. Fax: (415)822-8359. Editor: Kevin Thatcher. Fiction Editor: Brian Brannon. Magazine: 20.5 × 27.7 cm; 88-114 pages; coated paper; 4-color and b&w illustrations and photographs. "*Thrasher* is a blunt and honest hardcore publication for youth, skateboarding and sincere music." Monthly. Estab. 1981. Circ. 200,000.
Needs: Must deal with skateboarding in some manner. Receives 5-10 unsolicited mss/month. Buys 0-4 mss/issue; 8-15 mss/year. Publishes ms 3-36 months after acceptance. Recently published work by Mike Gumkowski, Don Redondo, Jake Phelps. Length: 500 words preferred; 25 words minimum; 1,500 words maximum. Publishes short shorts. Also publishes literary essays, criticism and poetry.

Successful marketing requires the proper tools. Make sure you have the latest edition of Novel & Short Story Writer's Market. *If you're still using this book and it's 1994 or later, buy the new edition at your favorite bookstore or order directly from Writer's Digest Books.*

How to Contact: Send complete ms with a cover letter. Should include estimated word count, Social Security number, list of publications. SASE for return of ms or send disposable copy of ms. No simultaneous submissions. Accepts electronic submissions. Sample copy for 9 × 12 SAE. Fiction guidelines for 9 × 12 SAE.
Payment: Pays 15¢/word and 5 contributor's copies, if requested.
Terms: Pays on publication. Buys first rights.
Advice: Looks for "creative thought involving skateboarding, music, snowboarding, fiction, youth culture. Keep submitting manuscripts whenever you have them. Our over-worked staff may not always reply, but we do read them."

TIKKUN, A Bimonthly Jewish Critique of Politics, Culture and Society, (III), Institute for Labor and Mental Health, 5100 Leona St., Oakland CA 94619. (510)482-0805. Editor: Michael Lerner. Magazine: 8 × 11; 96 pages; high quality paper. "*Tikkun* was created as the liberal alternative to *Commentary Magazine* and the voices of Jewish conservatism, but is not aimed just at a Jewish audience. Readers are intellectuals, political activists, Washington policy circles, writers, poets." Bimonthly.
Needs: Condensed/excerpted novel, contemporary, feminist, gay, historical (general), humor/satire, lesbian, literary, mainstream, translations, Jewish political. "No narrowly Jewish fiction. At least half of our readers are not Jewish. Or anything that is not of highest quality." Receives 150 unsolicited mss/month. Buys 1 ms/issue. Publishes ms 6-9 months after acceptance. Agented fiction 50%. Published work by Amos Oz, Lynne Sharon Schwartz, E.M. Broner. Length: 4,000 words preferred. Publishes short shorts. Almost always critiques rejected mss.
How to Contact: Send complete ms with cover letter. Reports in 2-3 months. SASE. Sample copy for $7.50.
Payment: Pays $100-250.
Terms: Pays on publication for first rights.
Advice: Looks for creativity, sensitivity, intelligence, originality, profundity of insight. "Read *Tikkun*, at least 3-4 issues worth, understand the kinds of issues that interest our readers, and then imagine yourself trying to write fiction that delights, surprises and intrigues this kind of an audience. Do not write what you think will feel sweet or appealing to this audience – but rather that which will provoke, bring to life and engage them."

TOUCH, (II), Calvinettes, Box 7259, Grand Rapids MI 49510. (616)241-5616. Editor: Joanne Ilbrink. Magazine: 8½ × 11; 24 pages; 50 lb. paper; 50 lb. cover stock; illustrations and photos. "Our purpose is to lead girls into a living relationship with Jesus Christ. Puzzles, poetry, crafts, stories, articles, and club input for girls ages 9-14." Monthly. Circ. 16,000.
● *Touch* won fourth place for fiction from the Evangelical Press Association awards in 1992.
Needs: Adventure, ethnic, juvenile and religious/inspirational. "Articles must help girls discover how God is at work in their world and the world around them." Each issue has a theme; write for biannual update. Receives 50 unsolicited fiction mss/month. Buys 3 mss/issue; 30 mss/year. Usually does not read during February, March, September and October. Published work by Ida Mae Petsock; published new writers within the last year. Length: 500 words minimum; 1,000 words maximum; 1,000 words average.
How to Contact: Send complete ms with 8 × 10 SASE. Prefers no cover letter. Reports in 4 months. Simultaneous and previously published submissions OK. Sample copy for 8 × 10 SASE. Free guidelines.
Payment: Pays 3-5¢/word.
Terms: Pays on acceptance for simultaneous, first or second serial rights.
Advice: "Try new and refreshing approaches. The one-parent, new girl at school is a bit overdone in our market. We have been dealing with issues like AIDS, abuse, drugs, and family relationships in our stories – more awareness-type articles."

TQ (TEENQUEST), (II), Good News Broadcasting Co., Box 82808, Lincoln NE 68501. (402)474-4567. Fax: (402)474-4519. Editor: Chris Lyon. Magazine: 8 × 10¾; 48 pages; illustrations; photos. "*TQ* is designed to aid the spiritual growth of young teen Christian readers by presenting Biblical principles." Publishes 11 issues/year. Estab. 1946. Circ. 60,000.
Needs: Religious/inspirational, regional, romance, adventure, fantasy, science fiction and mystery. "Stories must be grounded in Biblical Christianity and should feature teens in the 14-17 year range." Buys 3-4 mss/issue; 35-40 mss/year. Receives 50-60 unsolicited fiction mss/month. Published work by Nancy Rue, Stephen Bly, Marian Bray, Scott Pinzon; published new writers within the last year. Length: up to 2,000 words.

How to Contact: Managing editor reads all query letters. All other mss screened. Send SASE and cover letter. Reports in 2 months. Publishes ms 6 months to 2 years after acceptance. Sample copy and guidelines for 9×12 SASE.

Payment: Pays 7-10¢/word for unassigned fiction. More for assignments. Pays 3¢/word for reprints.

Terms: Pays on acceptance for first or reprint rights.

Advice: "The most common problem is that writers don't understand the limitations of stories under 2,500 words and try to cram a 6,000-word plot into 2,000 words at the expense of characterization, pacing and mood. We feel that fiction communicates well to our teenage readers. They consistently rank fiction as their favorite part of the magazine. We get hundreds of stories on 'big issues' (death, drugs, etc). Choose less dramatic subjects that are important to teenagers and give us a new storyline that has a Biblical emphasis, but isn't preachy. Although our magazine is based on Christian principles, we do not want fiction where the lesson learned is blatantly obvious. We're looking for subtlety. Before you try to write for teens, get to know some — talk to them, watch their TV shows, read their magazines. You'll get ideas for stories and you'll be able to write for our audience with accurate and up-to-date knowledge." Teen fiction writers under age 20 may enter annual contest.

TURTLE MAGAZINE FOR PRESCHOOL KIDS, (I, II), Children's Better Health Institute, Benjamin Franklin Literary & Medical Society, Inc., Box 567, 1100 Waterway Blvd., Indianapolis IN 46206. Editor: Christine French Clark. Magazine of picture stories and articles for preschool children 2-5 years old.

● Children's Better Health Institute also publishes magazines for older children including *Child Life, Children's Digest, Children's Playmate, Jack and Jill* and *Humpty Dumpty* listed in this book.

Needs: Juvenile (preschool). Special emphasis on health, nutrition, exercise and safety. Also has need for "action rhymes to foster creative movement and retold folktales for use in 'Pokey Toes Theatre.' " Receives approximately 100 unsolicited fiction mss/month. Published work by Ginny Winter, Robin Krautbauer and Ann Devendorf; published new writers within the last year. Length: 8-24 lines for picture stories; 500 words for bedtime or naptime stories.

How to Contact: Send complete ms with SASE. No queries. Reports in 8-10 weeks. Send SASE for Editorial Guidelines. Sample copy for $1.25.

Payment: Pays 10-20¢/word (approximate). Payment varies for poetry and activities.

Terms: Pays on acceptance for all rights. (One-time book rights may be returned when requested for specific publication.)

Advice: "Become familiar with past issues of the magazine and have a thorough understanding of the preschool child. You'll find we are catering more to our youngest readers, so think simply. Also, avoid being too heavy-handed with health-related material. First and foremost, health features should be fun! Because we have developed our own turtle character ('Pokey Toes'), we are not interested in fiction stories featuring other turtles."

THE VANCOUVER CHILD, (II), 757 Union St., Vancouver, British Columbia V6A 2C3 Canada. (604)251-1760. Editor: Wendy Wilkins. Tabloid: 10¼×15½; 12 or 16 pages; newsprint paper; newsprint cover; illustrations and b&w photographs. "*The Vancouver Child* celebrates children and families, and we primarily publish nonfiction articles on issues affecting children's daily lives for parents in the Lower Mainland (Vancouver and suburbs); children also read our kids' pages but most of our readers are parents." Monthly. Estab. 1988. Circ. 30,000.

Needs: Feminist, juvenile (5-9 years), literary, mainstream, preschool (1-4 years), regional. "Short stories should have something to do with family life or children. It is possible that we would print a short story for children on our kids' pages, if the story were very short and of good quality. No foul language, please." No confession, erotica, romance, religious. Receives 1 or 2 unsolicited mss/month. Buys 10 mss/year. Publishes ms 1-5 months after acceptance. Recently published work by Robert Stelnach, Dolores Wilkins, Tiffany Stone. Length: 750 words average; 1,000 words maximum. Publishes short shorts. Sometimes critiques rejected mss and recommends other markets.

How to Contact: Send complete ms with cover letter. "Complete manuscript more important than cover letter. We will read the story and judge it on its merits." Reports in 3-5 weeks. Send SAE with International Reply Coupon. Accepts electronic submissions via disk. Sample copy for 10×13 SAE and 2 first class stamps or IRC. Free fiction guidelines. Reviews only children's stories.

Payment: Pays 5¢/word.

Terms: Pays on publication for one-time rights.

Advice: "For our publication we favor writing that is 'tight' — i.e. every word counts. The language, however, should remain rich and evocative. We also prefer a good story to a specifically moralistic or socially relevant story. Thus if a writer has a point to make, we prefer the point of view to be embedded in the story and subtle rather than leaving nothing to the imagination and intelligence of the reader. Although we do not have a policy to print only Canadian authors, we prefer stories which make reference to Canadian locations rather than American locations. In some stories, it's not a problem, but a manuscript may be rejected on those grounds."

VIRTUE, The Christian Magazine for Women, (II), Virtue Ministries, Inc., Box 850, Sisters OR 97759. (503)549-8261. Editor: Marlee Alex. Magazine: 8⅛ × 10⅞; 80 pages; illustrations; photos. Christian women's magazine featuring food, fashion, family, etc.—"real women with everyday problems, etc." Published 6 times/year. Estab. 1978. Circ. 75,000.
Needs: Condensed novel, contemporary, humor, religious/inspirational and romance. "Must have Christian slant." Buys 1 ms/issue; 6 mss/year (maximum). Length: 1,200 words minimum; 2,000 words maximum; 1,200 words average. Publishes short shorts.
How to Contact: Reports in 6-8 weeks on ms. Sample copy for 9 × 13 SAE and $1.50 postage. Writer's guidelines for SASE. Reviews novels and short story collections.
Payment: Pays 15-25¢/published word.
Terms: Pays on publication for first rights or reprint rights.
Advice: "Send us descriptive, colorful writing with good style. *Please*—no simplistic, unrealistic pat endings or dialogue. We like the story's message to be implicit as opposed to explicit. Show us, inspire us—don't spell it out or preach it to us."

VISTA, (II), Wesley Press, Box 50434, Indianapolis IN 46953. (317)842-0444. Editor: Brenda Bratten. Magazine: 8½ × 11; 8 pages; offset paper and cover; illustrations and photos. "*Vista* is our adult take-home paper." Weekly. Estab. 1906. Circ. 50,000.
Needs: Humor/satire, religious/inspirational, senior citizen/retirement. Receives 100 unsolicited mss/month. Buys 4 mss/issue. Publishes ms 10 months after acceptance. Length: 500 words minimum; 1,300 words maximum.
How to Contact: Send complete ms with cover letter. Reports in 6-8 weeks. SASE. Simultaneous and reprint submissions OK. Sample copy for 9 × 12 SAE.
Payment: Pays 2-4¢/word.
Terms: Pays on acceptance for first or reprint.
Advice: "Manuscripts for all publications must be in keeping with early Methodist teachings that people have a free will to personally accept or reject Christ. Wesleyanism also stresses a transformed life, holiness of heart and social responsibility. Obtain a writers' guidelines before submitting ms."

THE WASHINGTONIAN, (IV), Suite 200, 1828 L St. NW, Washington DC 20036. (202)296-3600. Editor: John A. Limpert. Submit ms to Associate Editor: Diane Lazarus. General interest, regional magazine. Magazine: 8¼ × 10⅞; 200 pages; 40 lb. paper; 80 lb. cover; illustrations; photos. Monthly. Estab. 1965. Circ. 161,793.
  • *The Washingtonian* has won the National Magazine Award several times for reporting, feature writing and public service.
Needs: Short pieces set in Washington. Publishes a summer reading issue. Receives 8-10 unsolicited fiction mss/month. Buys 3 fiction mss/year. Length: 1,000 words minimum; 10,000 words maximum. Occasionally critiques rejected mss.
How to Contact: Send complete ms with SASE. Reports in 2 months. Simultaneous submissions OK. Sample copy for $4.
Payment: Pays 50¢/word.
Terms: Pays on publication for first North American rights. Negotiates kill fee for assigned mss not published.

WEIRD TALES, The Unique Magazine, (I, IV), Terminus Publishing Company, Inc., Box 13418, Philadelphia PA 19101. Editors: George Scithers and Darrell Schweitzer. Magazine: 8½ × 11; 80 pages; pen and ink illustrations. "This is a professional fantasy-fiction and horror-fiction magazine." Quarterly. Estab. 1923. Circ. 10,000.
  • *Weird Tales* ranked #19 on the 1992 *Writer's Digest* Fiction 50 list.
Needs: Fantasy, horror, supernatural/occult. "Writers should be familiar with the fantasy/horror genres; the editors are well read in the field and want fresh ideas rather than tired old retreads. To paraphrase Ursula K. LeGuin, 'If you want to write it, you gotta read it!' " Receives 400-500 unsolicited fiction mss/month. Buys 3-4 fiction mss/month; 48-80 mss/year. Publishes ms usually less than 2 years after acceptance. Published work by Gene Wolfe, Ramsey Campbell and Nancy Springer; published

new writers within the last year. Length: 20,000 words maximum. Publishes short shorts. Always comments on rejected mss.

How to Contact: Send complete ms, which should include return address. No simultaneous submissions. Reports within 1 month. SASE. Sample copy for $5. Fiction guidelines for #10 SAE and 1 first class stamp.

Payment: Pays 3-5¢/word, depending on length of story, plus 3 contributor's copies.

Terms: Pays on acceptance for first North American serial rights. Sends galleys to author.

Advice: *"Weird Tales* is a revival of a famous old 'pulp' magazine, but with new fiction by many top writers and talented newcomers to the field. Basically, we're trying to make this *Weird Tales* as it would be today had it continued uninterrupted to the present. Know the field. Know manuscript format. Be familiar with the magazine, its contents and its markets. Send only your best work."

WITH MAGAZINE, (I, IV), Faith & Life Press and Mennonite Publishing House, Box 347, Newton KS 67114. (316)283-5100. Magazine: 8½ × 11; 32 pages; 60 lb. coated paper and cover; illustrations and photos. "Our purpose is to help teenagers understand the issues that impact them and to help them make choices that reflect Mennonite-Anabaptist understandings of living by the Spirit of Christ. We publish all types of material—fiction, nonfiction, poetry, teen personal experience, etc." Published 8 times/year. Estab. 1968. Circ. 5,800.

● *With* won several awards from the Associated Church Press. Other Mennonite publications listed in this book include *On the Line, Purpose* and *Story Friends.*

Needs: Contemporary, ethnic, humor/satire, literary, mainstream, religious, translations, young adult/teen (13-18 years). "We accept issue-oriented pieces as well as religious pieces. No religious fiction that gives 'pat' answers to serious situations." Receives about 50 unsolicited mss/month. Buys 1-2 mss/issue; 8-10 mss/year. Publishes ms up to 1 year after acceptance. Published new writers within the last year. Length: 1,500 words preferred; 400 words minimum; 2,000 words maximum. Rarely critiques rejected mss.

How to Contact: Send complete ms with cover letter, which should include short summary of author's credits and what rights they are selling. Reports in 1-2 months on mss. SASE. Simultaneous and reprint submissions OK. Sample copy for 9 × 12 SAE and $1.21 postage. Fiction guidelines for #10 SAE and 1 first class stamp.

Payment: Pays 2¢/word for reprints; 4¢/word for simultaneous rights (one-time rights to an unpublished story). Supplies contributor's copies; charge for extras.

Terms: Pays on acceptance for one-time rights.

Advice: "Write with a teenage audience in mind, but don't talk down to them. Treat the audience with respect. Real life isn't always like that and teens will perceive the story as unbelievable. Do include ethnic minorities in your stories; our audience is both rural and urban. Except for humorous fiction (which can be just for laughs) each story should make a single point that our readers will find helpful through applying it in their own lives."

WOMAN'S DAY, 1633 Broadway, New York NY 10019. No longer accepts fiction.

WOMAN'S WORLD MAGAZINE, The Woman's Weekly, (II), Heinrich Bauer North America, 270 Sylvan Ave., Englewood Cliffs NJ 07632. (201)569-0006. Editor: Dena Vane. Fiction Editor: Jeanne Muchnick. Magazine; 9½ × 11; 54 pages; newspaper quality. "The magazine for 'Mrs. Middle America.' We publish short romances and mini-mysteries for all women, ages 18-68." Weekly. Estab. 1980. Circ. 1.5 million.

● *Woman's World* ranked #8 on the *Writer's Digest* Fiction 50 list. Heinrich Bauer NA also publishes *First* listed in this book.

Needs: Romance (contemporary), suspense/mystery. No humour, erotica. Receives 50 unsolicited mss/month. Buys 2 mss/issue; 104 mss/year. Publishes mss 6-10 weeks after acceptance. Agented fiction 2%. Published work by Tina Smith, P.J. Platz, Lisa Albert, Fay Thompson. Length: romances—1,900 words; mysteries—900 words. Publishes short shorts. Sometimes critiques rejected mss and recommends other markets.

How to Contact: Send complete manuscript with cover letter. *"No queries."* Reports in 6-8 weeks. SASE. Sample copy for $1. Fiction guidelines free.

Payment: Romances—$1,000, mysteries—$500.

Terms: Pays on acceptance. Buys first North American serial rights only.

‡**WOMEN'S AMERICAN ORT REPORTER, (II,IV),** Women's American ORT, 315 Park Ave. S., New York NY 10010. (212)505-7700. Editor: Eve Jacobson Kessler. 8⅛ × 10⅞; glossy; photographs. "Jewish women's issues; education, for membership." Quarterly. Estab. 1966. Circ. 110,000.
Needs: Condensed/excerpted novel, ethnic, feminist, humor/satire and literary. Receives 2 unsolicited mss/month. Buys 2 mss/year. Publishes ms 3 months after acceptance. Agented fiction 50%. Length: 2,500 words. Published work by A.B. Yehoshua. Possibly publishes short shorts. Sometimes critiques rejected ms and recommends other markets.
How to Contact: Send complete ms with cover letter. Include Social Security number. Reports in 3 weeks. SASE. Sample copy for SASE.
Payment: Varies.
Terms: Pays on publication for first North American serial rights.

WOMEN'S GLIB, A Collection of Women's Humor, (IV), Women's Glib™, P.O. Box 259, Bala Cynwyd, PA 19004. (215)668-4252. Editor: Rosalind Warren. Annual trade paperback book. 6 × 9; 200-300 pages; 60 lb. paper; (cartoons) and (photoessays). "Women's humor—humor written/drawn by women. Stories, essays, rhymed verse, cartoons, photoessays—short, hilarious feminist material." For "anybody who appreciates feminist humor." Annually. Estab. 1990. Circ. 30,000 in print (includes both *Women's Glib* and *Women's Glibber.*
• The first book in this series was a LAMBDA Literary Award finalist in 1992.
Needs: Women's humor: Contemporary, ethnic, feminist, gay, humor/satire, lesbian, literary, mainstream. "I need mostly short, hilariously (laugh-out-loud) funny material—don't be safe, be outrageous!—*by women only.* No domestic humor. No diet or weight loss humor or material about how svelte a girl should be. No stories in which aliens land on planet earth to share their intergalactic diet secrets with us. Nothing about how to catch or keep a man or about how men can't cook or do laundry. Nothing homophobic or racist or sexist. Female protagonists preferred." Receives 150 unsolicited mss/month. Buys 20 mss/issue. Publishes ms within a year after acceptance. Agented fiction 5%. Recently published work by Nora Ephron, Mollins Ivins, Judy Tenuta, Lynda Barry. Length: 1,000 words preferred; 3,000 words maximum. Publishes short shorts. Usually critiques rejected mss and recommends other markets.
How to Contact: Query with clips of published work or send complete ms with cover letter. Reports in 2 weeks. SASE. Simultaneous and reprint submissions OK. submissions. Sample copy for $11 (includes postage). Fiction guidelines for #10 SAE and 1 first class stamp.
Payment: Pays $5/page and 2 contributor's copies.
Terms: Pays on publication for one-time, nonexclusive rights.
Advice: "If it makes me laugh I publish it. I prefer short (2-10 pages) material. Some of the most popular material in the first two books (*Women's Glib*) and *Women's Glibber* was by previously unpublished writers. Read the first two books in the series. I need humor pieces—material written to amuse the reader. I get a lot of submissions that I can't use because rather than being humor pieces they're short fiction, told with some wit, but basically they're stories."

WONDER TIME, (II), World Action Publications, 6401 The Paseo, Kansas City MO 64131. (816)333-7000. Editor: Lois Perrigo. Magazine: 8¼ × 11; 4 pages; self cover; color illustrations; photos. Hand-out story paper published through World Action Publications; stories should follow outline of Sunday school lesson for 6-8 year-olds. Weekly. Circ. 45,000.
Needs: Religious/inspirational and juvenile. Stories must have first- to second-grade readability. No fairy tales or science fiction. Receives 50-75 unsolicited fiction mss/month. Buys 1 ms/issue. Publishes ms an average of 1 year after acceptance. Length: 300-550 words.
How to Contact: Send complete ms with SASE. Reports in 6 weeks. Guidelines for SASE.
Payment: Pays $25 minimum.
Terms: Pays on production (about 1 year after publication) for multi-use rights.

WY'EAST HISTORICAL JOURNAL, (II), Crumb Elbow Publishing, P.O. Box 294, Rhododendron OR 97049. (503)622-4798. Editor: Michael P. Jones. Journal: 5½ × 8½; 60 pages; top-notch paper; hardcover; illustrations and photographs. "Publishes historical or contemporary articles on the history of Oregon's Mt. Hood, the Columbia River, the Pacific NW, or the Old Oregon Country that includes Oregon, Washington, Idaho, Wyoming, Montana, Alaska, Northern California and British Columbia. For young adults to elderly." Quarterly. Estab. 1992. Circ. 10,000.
Needs: Open. Special interests include wildlife and fisheries, history of fur trade in Pacific Northwest, the Oregon Trail and Indians. "All materials should relate—somehow—to the region the publication is interested in." Plans to publish annual special fiction issue. Receives 10 unsolicited mss/month.

Buys 1-2 mss/issue; 22-24 mss/year. Publishes ms up to one year after acceptance. Recently published work by Joel Palmer. Publishes short shorts. Recommends other markets. "We have several other publications through Crumb Elbow Publishing where we can redirect the material."

How to Contact: Query with clips of published work or send complete ms with cover letter. Reports in 2 months "depending upon work load." SASE. Simultaneous and reprint submissions OK. Sample copy $5. Fiction guidelines for #10 SAE and 1 first class stamp.

Payment: Pays contributor's copies.

Terms: Pays on publication. Buys one-time rights.

Advice: "A ms has to have a historical or contemporary tie to the Old Oregon Country, which was the lands that lay west of the Rocky Mountains to the Pacific Ocean, south to and including Northern California, and north to and including Alaska. It has to be about such things as nature, fish and wildlife, the Oregon Trail, pioneer settlement and homesteading, the Indian wars, gold mining, wild horses—which are only a few ideas. It has to be written in a non-offensive style, meaning please remove all four-letter words or passages dealing with loose sex. Do not be afraid to try something a little different. No prima donnas, please! We wish to work with writers who are professionals, even if they haven't had any of their works published before. This is a great place to break into the publishing world as long as you are an adult who acts like an adult. Send copies only! And please note that we cannot be responsible for the U.S. Postal Service once you mail something to us, or we mail something to you. We are looking forward to working with those who love history and nature as much as we do."

XTRA MAGAZINE, Church-Wellesley Review (Literary Supplement) (IV, V), Pink Triangle Press, Box 7289, Stn. A, Toronto, Ontario M5W 1X9 Canada. (416)925-6665. Editor: Ken Popert. Fiction Editor: Dayne Ogilvie. Tabloid: 11½ × 17; 44-60 pages; newsprint paper; illustrations and photographs. "Gay/lesbian magazine, but fiction/poetry does not have to be about sexual orientation." Fiction supplement is annual. Estab. 1990 (supplement only). Circ. 20,000.

Needs: Gay, lesbian. Publishes annual special fiction issue. Receives 4-5 unsolicited mss/month. Buys up to 20 mss/year. Publishes mss spring after acceptance. Recently published work by Antler (American poet) Sky Gilbert (Canadian playwright). Length: 1,500 words maximum. Publishes short shorts. Sometimes critiques rejected mss and recommends other markets.

How to Contact: Send complete manuscript with cover letter. Reports in 1-2 months on mss. SASE. If notified, simultaneous and reprint submissions OK. Sample copy free.

Payment: Pays 70¢/word (slightly more for poetry) up to $150 maximum.

YANKEE MAGAZINE, (II, III), Yankee, Inc., Dublin NH 03444. Editor: Judson D. Hale. Fiction Editor: Edie Clark. Magazine: 6 × 9; 176 + pages; glossy paper; 4-color glossy cover stock; illustrations; color photos. "Entertaining and informative New England regional on current issues, people, history, antiques and crafts for general reading audience." Monthly. Estab. 1935. Circ. 1,000,000.

• *Yankee* ranked #12 on the 1992 *Writer's Digest* Fiction 50 list.

Needs: Literary. Fiction is to be set in New England or compatible with the area. No religious/inspirational, formula fiction or stereotypical dialect, novels or novellas. Buys 1 ms/issue; 12 mss/year. Published work by Andre Dubus, H. L. Mountzoures and Fred Bonnie; published new writers within the last year. Length: 2,000 words. Recommends other markets.

How to Contact: Send complete ms with SASE and previous publications. "Cover letters are important if they provide relevant information: previous publications or awards; special courses taken; special references (e.g. 'William Shakespeare suggested I send this to you . . . .')" Simultaneous submissions OK, "within reason." Reports in 4-6 weeks.

Payment: Pays $1,000.

Terms: Pays on acceptance; rights negotiable. Sends galleys to author.

Advice: "Read previous 10 stories in *Yankee* for style and content. Fiction must be realistic and reflect life as it is—complexities and ambiguities inherent. Our fiction adds to the 'complete menu'—the magazine includes many categories—humor, profiles, straight journalism, essays, etc. Listen to the advice of any editor who takes the time to write a personal letter. Go to workshops; get advice and other readings before sending story out cold."

THE YOUNG CRUSADER, (II, IV), National Woman's Christian Temperance Union, 1730 Chicago Ave., Evanston IL 60201. (708)864-1396. Editor-in-Chief: Mrs. Rachel Bubar Kelly. Managing Editor: Michael C. Vitucci. "Character building material showing high morals and sound values; inspirational, informational nature articles and stories for 6-12 year olds." Monthly. Estab. 1887. Circ. 10,000.

Needs: Juvenile. Stories should be naturally written pieces, not saccharine or preachy. Buys 3-4 mss/issue; 60 mss/year. Length: 600-650 words. Also prose and poetry. Published work by Nadine L. Mellott, Gloria L. Sollid and Veronica McClearin.
How to Contact: Send complete ms with SASE. Simultaneous submissions OK. Reports in 6 months or longer on mss. Sample copy for SASE.
Payment: Pays ½¢/word and contributor's copy. Pays ½¢/word for prose, 10¢/line for poetry.
Terms: "If I like the story and use it, I'm very lenient and allow the author to use it elsewhere. Don't write down to the child; the children of today are surprisingly bright and sophisticated." Mss/prose/poetry, if used, pays on publication. If not used mss/prose/poetry will be destroyed.

YOUNG SALVATIONIST/YOUNG SOLDIER, (II, IV), The Salvation Army, P.O. Box 269, 615 Slaters Lane, Alexandria VA 22313. (703)684-5500. Editor: Capt. M. Lesa Salyer. Magazine: 8×11; 16 pages (*Young Salvationist*); illustrations and photos. Christian emphasis articles for youth members of The Salvation Army. Monthly. Estab. 1984. Circ. 50,000.
• Note *Young Salvationist* no longer publishes children's stories. Their focus is on teens and college-age young adults.
Needs: Religious/inspirational, young adult/teen. Receives 150 unsolicited mss/month. Buys 9-10 ms/issue; 90-100 mss/year. Publishes ms 3-4 months after acceptance. Length: 1,000 words preferred; 750 words minimum; 1,200 words maximum. Publishes short shorts. Sometimes critiques rejected mss and recommends other markets.
How to Contact: Send complete ms. Reports in 1-2 weeks on queries; 2-4 weeks on mss. SASE. Simultaneous and reprint submissions OK. Sample copy for 9×12 SAE and 3 first class stamps. Fiction guidelines and theme list for #10 SAE with 1 first class stamp.
Payment: Pays 10¢/word.
Terms: Pays on acceptance for all rights, first rights, first North American serial rights and one-time rights.

International commercial periodicals

The following commercial magazines, all located outside the United States and Canada, also accept work from fiction writers. Countries represented here range from England, Ireland and Scotland to Czechoslovakia, Germany and Italy. Also included are South Africa, Australia and China.

As with other publications, try to read sample copies. While some of these may be available at large newsstands, most can be obtained directly from the publishers. Write for guidelines as well. Whereas one editor may want fiction with some connection to his or her own country, another may seek more universal settings and themes. Watch, too, for payment policies. Many publications pay only in their own currencies.

In all correspondence, use self-addressed envelopes (SAEs) with International Reply Coupons (IRCs) for magazines outside your own country. IRCs may be purchased at the main branch of your local post office. In general, send IRCs in amounts roughly equivalent to return postage. When submitting work to these international publications, you may find it easier to include a disposable copy of your manuscript and only one IRC with a self-addressed postcard for a reply. This is preferred by many editors, and it saves you the added cost of having your work returned.

‡EROTIC STORIES, Northern and Shell Bldg., Box 381, Mill Harbour, London E14 9TW England. Editor: Elizabeth Coldwell. Deputy Editor: Dominic Collier. Published 6 times/year. Buys 120 stories/year. "*Erotic Stories* is an international magazine of human relations, dealing with all aspects of relationships, sexuality and sexual health. We are looking for erotic stories in which plot and characterization are as important as erotic content." Length: 2,000-3,000 words. "Slightly longer stories are also acceptable. For guidelines send SAE with IRC." Pays 1 contributor's copy.

FAIR LADY, (III), P.O. Box 1802, Cape Town 2000 South Africa. Editor: Liz Butler. Bi-monthly. Circ. 180,000. Publishes 1/issue. "We are a magazine chiefly for women of all ages, working mothers or pensioners, teenagers or homemakers. We try to keep a high standard of writing in our short stories, since our readers are well-educated and discerning." Length: 1,000 words minimum; 3,000 words maximum. "We will try to provide tearsheets on request. Payment varies, but can be made in US dollars in some circumstances. Include a short, informative covering letter so that we know you have given the submission of your story to us some thought. Don't just send the ms to everybody."

FORUM, Northern and Shell Building, Box 381, Mill Harbour, London E14 9TW England. Fiction Editor: Elizabeth Coldwell. Circ. 30,000. Publishes 13 stories/year. "*Forum* is the international magazine of human relations, dealing with all aspects of relationships, sexuality and sexual health. We are looking for erotic stories in which the plot and characterisation are as important as the erotic content." Length: 2,000-3,000 words. Pays contributor's copy. "Try not to ask for the ms to be returned, just a letter of acceptance/rejection as this saves on your return postage. Anything which is very 'American' in language or content might not be as interesting to readers outside America. Writers can obtain a sample copy by saying they saw our listing."

GUIDE PATROL, 17-19 Buckingham Palace Rd., London SW1W OPT England. Editor: Mary Richardson. Circ. 25,000. Publishes 12 short stories annually. "Magazine aimed at girls aged 10-14. The official magazine for the Girl Guides Association. Stories need to be 1,000-1,500 words long with a Guiding background." Payment is £45 per 1,000 words plus contributor copy.

INTERZONE: Science Fiction and Fantasy, 217 Preston Drove, Brighton BN1 6FL England. Editor: David Pringle. Monthly. Circ. 10,000. Publishes 5-6 stories/issue. "We're looking for intelligent science fiction in the 2,000-7,000 word range. Send 2 IRCs with 'overseas' submissions and a *disposable* ms." Pays £30 per 1,000 words on publication and 2 contributor's copies. "Please *read the magazine* — available through specialist science-fiction dealers or direct by subscription." Sample copies to USA: $5. Write for guidelines.

IRELAND'S OWN, 1 North Main St., Wexford Ireland. Fiction Editor: Austin Channing. Weekly. Circ. 56,000. Publishes 3 stories/issue. "*Ireland's Own* is a homely family-oriented weekly magazine with a story emphasis on the traditional values of Irish society. Short stories must be written in a straightforward nonexperimental manner with an Irish orientation." Length: 2,000-3,000 words. Pays £20-25 on publication and contributor's copies. "Study and know the magazine's requirements, orientation and target market. Guidelines and copies sent out on request."

LOVING MAGAZINE, Room 2735, IPC, King's Reach Tower, Stamford St., London SE1 9LS England. Editor: Lorna Read. Monthly. Circ. 40,000. Publishes 17 stories/issue. Needs "romantic fiction in first or third person, from male or female point of view. No school stories, no heroes/heroines under 16. We also have a 'Something Different' section for historical, crime or even science fiction stories, provided they have a romance at the core. Stories must be typed and double-spaced, and a word count must be given. Please advise if story is available on disk." Length: 1,000 words minimum; 5,000 words maximum. Writers receive a contributor's copy. Payment is in authors' own currency and is on a sliding scale from £25-£50/1,000 words, according to how much editing work the story needs. Make plot universal enough to interest people in other countries and cultures. If a story is too parochial, it will alienate a foreign reader. We will sometimes send out a sample copy but cannot do it as a matter of course because we are only given a limited supply of each issue for distribution from our office." Write for guidelines.

‡MY WEEKLY, 80 Kingsway East, Dundee DD4 8SL Scotland. Editor: Sandy Monks. "*My Weekly* is a widely read magazine aimed at 'young' women of all ages. We are read by busy young mothers, active middle-aged wives and elderly retired ladies." Fiction (romance and humor) "should deal with real, down-to-earth themes that relate to the lives of our readers. Our rates compare favourably with other British magazines. Complete stories can be of any length from 1,500 to 4,000 words. Serials from 3 to 10 installments."

NEW WOMAN, Orange House, 20 Orange Street, London WC2 England. Fiction Editor: Samantha Harrison. Monthly. Circ. 250,000. Publishes 1 story/issue. "Mainstream quality women's magazine usually featuring established writers, but occasionally run outstanding submissions from unknown authors." Length: 1,500-3,500 words.

NOVA SF, Perseo Libri srl, Box 1240, I-40100 Bologna Italy. Fiction Editor: Ugo Malaguti. Bimonthly. Circ. 5,000. "Science fiction and fantasy short stories and short novels." Pays $100-600, depending on length, and 2 contributor's copies on publication. "No formalities required, we read all submissions and give an answer in about 20 weeks. Buys first Italian serial rights on stories."

PEOPLE'S FRIEND, 80 Kingsway East, Dundee Scotland. Fiction Editor: W. Balnave. Weekly. Circ. 566,000. Publishes 5 stories/issue. Length: 1,000-3,000 words. Pays $75-85 and contributor's copies. "British backgrounds preferred by our readership." Sample copy and guidelines available on application.

REALITY MAGAZINE, 75 Orwell Rd., Rathgar, Dublin 6 Ireland. Fiction Editor: Fr. Kevin H. Donlon. Monthly. Circ. 20,000. Publishes an average of 5 short stories annually. Length: 900-1,200 words. Pays £25-£35 (Ireland)/1,000 words and 2 contributor's copies. "Be clear, brief, to the point and practical. Write only about your own country. Sample copies supplied on request."

‡SCHOOL MAGAZINE, Private Bag 3, Ryde NSW 2112 Australia. Fiction Editor: Jonathan Shaw. Circ. 200,000. Publishes 40 stories/year. "Literary magazine for 8-11 year olds (much like *Cricket*). All types of stories—real life, fantasy, sci-fi, folk tales." Pays $137/1,000 words on acceptance—one use only. Two free copies.

THE SCOTS MAGAZINE, 2 Albert Square, Dundee DD1 9QJ Scotland. Editor: John Rundle. Monthly. Circ. 85,000. "World's oldest popular periodical. We use well-written fiction in a Scottish setting with a specific Scottish content." Length: 1,000-4,000 words. Payment made in pounds sterling, also contributor's copies. "No ghosts of Culloden or Glencoe, no haggis and no phoney Scotts dialogue." Guidelines available on request.

‡SUPERBIKE, Link House, Dingwall Ave., Croydon CR9 2TA England. Editor: John Cutts. Circ. 50,000. Publishes approximately 6-8 fiction pieces/year. "Monthly motorcycle magazine—high-performance motorcycles only—tests and features. Will consider any fiction relating to this genre, preferably not death-wish/ghost/horror stories. 3,000 words max." Writers paid on publication. Looks for "Double-spaced type—neat manuscripts! Good spelling. Outstandingly original humor."

WOMAN'S REALM, IPC Magazines, King's Reach Tower, Stamford St., London SE1 9LS England. Fiction Editor: Nick Vermuth. Weekly. Circ. 530,000. Publishes 2 stories/issue. Appeals to practical, intelligent, family-minded women, age 25 upwards. High standard of writing required. Originality important. "Nearest US equivalent to our kind of fiction is probably *Redbook*." Length: 1,000-1,200 words and 2,800-3,000 words. Payment starts from approximately £150. "We do not accept unsolicited fiction. However, if writers are interested, they can contact us with their idea. On the whole, we don't send out sample copies. However, if someone lives so far away that they cannot receive a copy, we'll send one. Guidelines are available for established writers. Publishes a wide range of stories including humorous, first- or third-person, single, divorcée, second marriage, perhaps with kids, career/home conflicts, 20s-30s. Stories narrated by men also welcome. Avoid doom and gloom."

THE WORLD OF ENGLISH, P.O. Box 1504, Beijing China. Chief Editor: Chen Yu-lun. Circ. 300,000+. "We welcome contributions of short articles that would cater to the interest of our reading public, new and knowledgeable writings on technological finds, especially interesting short stories and novels, etc. We can only pay in our currency which regrettably is inconvertible." Write for sample copy.

Commercial periodicals/'92-'93 changes

Most of the following commercial magazines appeared in the 1992 edition of *Novel & Short Story Writer's Market* but are not in the 1993 edition. Those publications whose editors did not respond this year to our request for an update are listed below without further explanation. They may have done so for a variety of reasons—they may be out of business, they are no longer taking fiction or they may be overstocked with submissions. They may have responded too late for inclusion in this edition.

If we received information about why a publication would not appear, we included the explanation next to its name below.

The American Newspaper Carrier
American Squaredance (out of business)
The Atlantic Advocate (ceased publication)
The B'Nai B'Rith International Jewish Monthly (asked to be deleted)
Bread
Buzzworm: The Environmental Journal (contest only)
Il Caffe
Catholic Forester (asked to be deleted)
Cavalier Magazine (out of business)
Chesapeake Bay Magazine (no fiction)
Christmas (asked to be deleted)
The Church Herald (asked to be deleted)

The Church Musician
Dog Fancy (asked to be deleted)
Family Magazine (no fiction)
The Flyfisher (sold magazine)
Flyfishing News, Views And Reviews (sold magazine)
Guide Magazine
Guys
In Touch For Men
Inside Texas Running (no fiction)
Lutheran Woman Today (asked to be deleted)
Mademoiselle (no fiction)
Manscape
The Modern Woodmen (asked to be left out this year)
National Lampoon
New Hampshire Life
New York Running News (asked to be deleted)

Nugget
Oh! Idaho (out of business)
Palouse Journal
The Plain Journal (asked to be deleted)
Screw Magazine
Shining Star
Sporting Times
Sports Afield (asked to be deleted)
Student Lawyer (no fiction)
Trailer Boats Magazine (asked to be deleted)
Turn-On Letters (ceased publication)
Vision (out of business)
Visions Magazine (ceased publication)
Western People (asked to be deleted)
Woman's Day (no fiction)

Small Press

With the current emphasis on "big books" and the tight economic climate, it's been increasingly difficult for new writers — especially those whose work is considered literary or experimental — to get published by the large commercial publishing houses. Introducing interesting, new writers to the reading public, therefore, has become the most important role played by the small press today.

Small presses have taken this role very seriously, introducing some of the world's finest writers. Many of the more successful small presses, such as Coffee House, Milkweed Editions and Graywolf, have built reputations for publishing award-winning fiction. In addition, better production, distribution and marketing have made many small presses competitive with their larger counterparts. More readers looking for new, talented writers are turning to the small press to find them.

Why publish with the small press?

Despite this success, most small presses are unable to pay six-figure advances or treat their authors to lavish parties and promotional tours. Still, small presses continue to offer opportunities to writers who would otherwise have only a slim chance at publication by larger houses.

Even though they cannot afford to pay big advances, small press publishing offers writers a number of benefits. For one thing, smaller houses tend to keep their books in print much longer than commercial publishers. More small presses are taking advantage of cooperative marketing and distribution networks, increasing their sales through group catalogs and advertising. This can actually mean more money for the writer in the long run.

Many writers say a good, stable editor/writer relationship is the main reason they've stayed with the small press. Editors at small presses tend to stay longer because they have more at stake in the business. In fact, many actually own the press and many are writers themselves.

Types of small presses

In this section we use the term "small press" in the broadest sense. Included in our definition are publishers not backed by large corporations. Most publish no more than 10-20 books each year. The section includes very small operations, nonprofit presses, university publishers and small- to mid-size independents.

The very small presses are sometimes called micropresses and are owned and operated by one to three people, usually friends or family members. Some are cooperatives of writers and most started out by publishing their own books or books by their friends. These presses can be easily swamped with submissions. Writers published by these very small presses, however, say they are treated as "one of the family."

Nonprofit presses depend on grants and donations to help meet operating costs. Because the economy has been slow to recover, many have lost some or all of their funding and have cut back on the number of books they publish. Keep in mind, too, some of these presses are funded by private organizations such as churches or clubs and books that reflect the backer's views or beliefs are most likely to be considered for publication.

Funding for university presses is often tied to government and private grants as well. Traditionally, universities tend to publish writers who are either affiliated with the university in some way or whose work is representative of the region in which the school is located.

Many publishers in this section are independent literary and regional presses. Several have become highly sophisticated about competing in the marketplace and in carving out their own niche.

Choosing a small press

It's a good idea to familiarize yourself with a press' focus and line. Visit independent and college bookstores and libraries to find books published by small presses. Write away for catalogs from the presses that interest you most.

To find a press specializing in a specific type of fiction or a particular genre, use the Category Index starting on page 616. Check under the category that best describes your work for a list of presses most interested in that type of work.

To focus your search even more, we provide a ranking system. Listings include a Roman numeral code placed after the press name. This code refers to the level of openness to new writers. For more on these codes, see the list at the end of this introduction.

In addition to the double dagger (‡) indicating whether a listing is new to this edition, book packagers are marked with a box (■) symbol. A packager creates books and then sells these to a publisher. Many produce fiction series written by one or several authors. Authors are generally paid a flat fee. Packagers are often very willing to work with new writers.

You may also see an asterisk (*) at the start of a listing. This lets you know the press sometimes funds the publication of its books through a subsidy arrangement. By our definition, a subsidy press is one that requires a writer to financially subsidize the production of his or her books. Although this enables small presses to publish more books, approach subsidy arrangements with caution. Find out exactly what type of production is involved and how many books will be produced. Check this figure with a local printer. If the press' figure is more, ask what type of marketing and distribution is planned and ask for proof.

Read the listings

The next step is to read the listings carefully. Each contains information on the needs, terms and submission procedures. In addition, listings also include a variety of information designed to tell you even more about the press. For a discussion of information common to all listings see How to Get the Most Out of This Book on page 3.

Within the "Needs" subcategory of a listing, you'll find the types of fiction needed by the press. Some listings also include information on what types of fiction the press does *not* want to see. Following this is a list of books published. If the listing says "recently published," the list of books was updated this edition. If it just says "published," the press has provided this list of books more than one year in a row. This may mean the press is very proud of these particular books or it may mean the press publishes only a few fiction titles. To find out more about the press, try to find one of their books in a store or library.

Other information included within the listing lets you know exactly how to approach a press, how long it will take for a response and how you will be paid. If a press asks for query first, make sure your letter is brief. If you are asked to send sample chapters, be sure to send the first three consecutive chapters. For more on submitting to publishers see the Business of Fiction Writing starting on page 76.

New to this edition

This year we've added a new feature that enables us to tell you additional information not covered within the listings. Our own editorial comments appear in some listings set off by a bullet (●). This is where we can tell you about awards or honors the press has received; whether we list other imprints, magazines or contests by the same publisher; about any special interests or requirements; and any information from our readers that will help you learn even more about the press. We've checked several sources, including the publishers themselves for information. One source we refer to in the editorial comments is *Esquire*, a magazine noted for its coverage of the literary scene. We note a few publishers who appeared in a list of good places for a writer to start from an article in the magazine's July 1992 issue. Since this is a new feature, we do not claim to include every award or every press honored, and we hope to increase the amount of this information in the future.

We've also added a number of subcategories to our Needs subhead. We've asked publishers to elaborate on the type of fiction they consider. For example, if a publisher publishes mysteries, we've asked what kind of mystery—police procedural, cozy, amateur sleuth, young adult or romantic suspense. With this additional information you can narrow your list of potential markets to those specifically interested in the type of fiction you write.

Submitting your work

For particulars on submitting work to small presses, see the Business of Fiction Writing. If the press accepts complete manuscripts, send it with a brief cover letter and any other information outlined in the listing. If you want your manuscript returned, include a large self-addressed, stamped envelope. If you'd rather just send a disposable copy and save the postage, you may want to include a business-size SASE or postcard for a reply.

For more small presses see the *International Directory of Little Magazines and Small Presses* published by Dustbooks (P.O. Box 100, Paradise CA 95967). To keep tabs of the small press industry check issues of the two major small press trade publications: *Small Press Review* (also published by Dustbooks) and *Small Press* (Colonial Hill/RFD 1, Mt. Kisco NY 10549).

Both U.S. and Canadian publishers are listed in this section, followed by a section of International Small Press. When sending work to a country other than your own, include International Reply Coupons (IRCs) rather than stamps for return mail. These are available at the main branch of your local post office.

The ranking system for listings in this section is as follows:

I **Publisher encourages beginning or unpublished writers to submit work for consideration and publishes new writers frequently.**

II **Publisher accepts work by established writers and by new writers of exceptional talent.**

III **Publisher does not encourage beginning writers; publishes mostly writers with extensive previous publication credits or agented writers and very few new writers.**

IV **Special-interest or regional publisher, open only to writers on certain topics or from certain geographical areas.**

ADVOCACY PRESS, (IV), Box 236, Santa Barbara CA 93102. Executive Director: Barbara Fierro-Lang. Estab. 1983. Small publisher with 3-5 titles/year. Hardcover and paperback originals. Books: perfect or Smythe-sewn binding; illustrations; average print order: 5,000-10,000 copies; first novel print order: 5,000-10,000. Averages 2 children's fiction (32-48 pg.) titles per year.
  ● Advocacy Press' books have won the Ben Franklin Award (*My Way Sally*) and the Friends of American Writers Award (*Tonia the Tree*).

Needs: Juvenile. Wants only feminist/nontraditional messages to boys or girls—picture books; self-esteem issues. Published *Father Gander Nursery Rhymes*, by Dr. Doug Larch (picture book); *Minou*, by Mindy Bingham (picture book); *Kylie's Song*, by Patty Sheehan (picture book).
How to Contact: Submit complete manuscript with SASE for return. Reports in 10 weeks on queries. Simultaneous submissions OK.
Terms: Pays in royalties of 5-10%. Book catalog for SASE.
Advice: "Only fictional stories for children 4-12 years old that give messages of self sufficiency for little girls; little boys can nurture and little girls can be anything they want to be, etc. Please review some of our publications *before* you submit to us. Because of our limited focus, most of our titles have been written in-house."

*AEGINA PRESS, INC., (I,II), 59 Oak Lane, Spring Valley, Huntington WV 25704. (304)429-7204. Imprint is University Editions, Inc. Managing Editor: Ira Herman. Estab. 1984. Independent small press. Publishes paperback and hardcover originals and reprints. Books: 50 lb. white text/10 point high gloss covers; photo-offset printing; perfect binding, illustrations; average print order: 500-1,000. Published new writers within the last year. Plans 5-10 first novels this year. Averages 30 total titles, 15 fiction titles each year. Sometimes comments on rejected ms.
Needs: Adventure, contemporary, experimental, faction, fantasy, historical, horror, literary, mainstream, regional, romance (gothic), science fiction (hard science, soft sociological), short story collections, mystery/suspense (young adult, romantic suspense), thriller/espionage. No racist, sexist, or obscene materials. Recently published *The Gentleman from Ocala*, by William Beatrice, Jr. (novel); *Death of a Shark*, by Lamberto Mancino (mystery novel); *Beneath the Snow*, by Irving Greenfield (novel).
How to Contact: Accepts unsolicited mss. Send outline/synopsis and 3 sample chapters or complete ms with cover letter. SASE. Agented fiction 5%. Reports in 3 weeks on queries; 1-2 months on mss. Simultaneous submissions OK.
Terms: Pays 15% royalties. *Subsidy publishes most new authors.* "If the manuscript meets our quality standards but is financially high risk, self-publishing through the University Editions imprint is offered. All sales proceeds go to the author until the subsidy is repaid. The author receives a 40% royalty thereafter. Remaining unsold copies belong to the author." Sends galleys to author. Publishes ms 6-9 months after acceptance. Writer's guidelines for #10 SASE. Book catalog for 9×12 SAE, 4 first class stamps and $2.

ALYSON PUBLICATIONS, INC., (II), 40 Plympton St., Boston MA 02118. (617)542-5679. Fiction Editor: Sasha Alyson. Estab. 1977. Medium-sized publisher specializing in lesbian- and gay-related material. Publishes paperback originals and reprints. Books: paper and printing varies; trade paper, perfect-bound; average print order: 8,000; first novel print order: 6,000. Published new writers within the last year; plans 4 first novels this year. Averages 15 total titles, 8 fiction titles each year.
Needs: "We are interested in all categories; *all* materials must be geared toward lesbian and/or gay readers." Recently published *Persistent Desire: A Femme-Butch Reader*, edited by Joan Nestle; *Arson!*, by Cap Iversen; *Short Rides*, by Wendy Borgstrom. Publishes anthologies. Authors may submit to them directly.
How to Contact: Query first with SASE. Reports in 3 weeks on queries; 2 months on mss.
Terms: "We prefer to discuss terms with the author." Sends galleys to author. Book catalog for SAE and 52¢ postage.

AMERICAN ATHEIST PRESS, (IV), Gustav Broukal Press, Box 140195, Austin TX 78714-0195. Editor: Robin Murray-O'Hair, Estab. 1960. Paperback originals and reprints. Books: bond and other paper; offset printing; perfect binding; illustrations "if pertinent." Averages 6 total titles/year. Occasionally critiques or comments on rejected mss.

 The asterisk indicates a publisher who sometimes offers subsidy arrangements. Authors are asked to subsidize part of the cost of book production. See the introduction for more information.

Needs: Contemporary, humor/satire, literary, science fiction. No "religious/spiritual/occult."
How to Contact: Query with sample chapters and outline. SASE. Reports in 2 months on queries; 3 months on mss. Simultaneous submissions OK. Accepts electronic submissions via IBM-PC/Word-Perfect on disk.
Terms: Pays 8-11% royalties. Writers guidelines for #9 SAE and 1 first class stamp. Book catalog free on request.
Advice: "We only publish fiction which relates to Atheism; we receive many queries for general interest fiction, which we do not publish."

ANNICK PRESS LTD., (IV), 15 Patricia Ave., Willowdale, Ontario M2M 1H9 Canada. (416)221-4802. Publisher of children's books. Publishes hardcover and paperback originals. Books: offset paper; full-color offset printing; perfect and library binding; full-color illustrations; average print order: 9,000; first novel print order: 7,000. Plans 18 first picture books this year. Averages approximately 20 titles each year, all fiction. Average first picture book print order 2,000 cloth, 12,000 paper copies. Occasionally critiques rejected ms.
Needs: Children's books only.
How to Contact: "Annick Press publishes only work by Canadian citizens or residents." Does not accept unsolicited mss. Query with SASE. Free book catalog.
Terms: Sends galleys to author.
Advice: "Publishing more fiction this year, because our company is growing. But our publishing program is currently full."

APPLEZABA PRESS, Box 4134, Long Beach CA 90804. Editorial Director: Shelley Hellen. Estab. 1977. "We are a family-operated publishing house, working on a part-time basis. We plan to expand over the years." Publishes paperback originals. Averages 1 fiction title each year.
Needs: Contemporary, literary, experimental, feminist, gay, lesbian, fantasy, humor/satire, translations, and short story collections. No gothic, romance, confession, inspirational, satirical, black humor or slapstick. Published *Horse Medicine and Other Stories*, by Raephael Zepecha; *Nude*, by Judson Jerome.
How to Contact: Accepts unsolicited mss. Submit complete ms with SASE. No simultaneous submissions. Reports in 2 months. Publishes ms 2-3 years after acceptance.
Terms: Pays in author's copies and 8-15% royalties; no advance. Free book catalog.
Advice: "Cover letter with previous publications, etc. is OK. Each book, first or twentieth, has to stand on its own. If a first-time novelist has had shorter works published in magazines, it makes it somewhat easier for us to market the book. We publish only book-length material."

ARIADNE PRESS, (I), 4817 Tallahassee Ave., Rockville MD 20853. (301)949-2514. President: Carol Hoover. Estab. 1976. Shoestring operation—corporation with 4 directors who also act as editors. Publishes hardcover and paperback originals. Books: 50 lb. alkaline paper; offset printing; Smyth-sewn binding. Average print order 1,000; average first novel print order 1,000. Plans 1 first novel this year. Averages 1 total title each year; only fiction. Sometimes critiques rejected mss. "We comment on selected mss of superior writing quality, even when rejected."
Needs: Adventure, contemporary, feminist, historical, humor/satire, literary, mainstream, mystery/suspense, psychological, family relations and marital, war. Looking for "literary-mainstream" fiction. No short stories, no science fiction, horror or mystery. Published *How to Write an Uncommonly Good Novel*, (nonfiction).
How to Contact: *Query first.* SASE. Agented fiction 5%. Reports in 1 month on queries; 2 months on mss. Simultaneous submissions OK.
Terms: Pays royalties of 10%. No advance. Sends pre-publication galleys to author. Writer's guidelines not available. List of books in stock for #10 SASE.
Advice: "We exist primarily for non-established writers. Try large, commercial presses first."

 The double dagger before a listing indicates that the listing is new in this edition. New Markets are often the most receptive to submissions by new writers.

‡ARJUNA LIBRARY PRESS, (II), Subsidiaries include: The Journal of Regional Criticism, 1025 Garner St., D, Space 18, Colorado Springs CO 80905-1774. Director: Joseph A. Uphoff, Jr.. Estab. 1979. "The Arjuna Library is an artist's prototype press." Publishes paperback originals. Books: 20 lb. paper; photocopied printing; perfect binding; b&w illustrations; average print order: 20. Averages 6 total titles, 3 fiction titles each year. Sometime comments on rejected ms.
• Arjuna Press has had exhibits at the Colorado Springs Fine Arts Center, KTSC Public Television (academic), University of Southern Colorado and The Poets House, New York, 1992.
Needs: Adventure, childrens/juvenile (fantasy), erotica, experimental, fantasy (surrealist), horror (supernatural), lesbian, romance (futuristic/time travel), science fiction (hard science/technological, soft/sociological), poetry, young adult/teen (fantasy/science fiction). Nothing obscene or profane. Recently published *Deep Ellum*, by Robert W. Howington (surrealist).
How to Contact: Accepts unsolicited mss. Submit complete ms with cover letter, resume. Include list of publishing credits, a disposable copy of the ms to be filed; will return samples in envelopes. Simultaneous and electronic submissions OK.
Terms: Pays 1 author's copy, plus potential for royalties. Writer's guidelines for SASE.
Advice: "A cynical attitude will lead the writer into habits of composition and delivery that are offensive to the audience and supportive individuals (who tend to be paranoid themselves). These unconscious mannerisms are very difficult to escape unless one practices a form of proper thought and behavior. Work that has been read aloud in public is more polished than works that the author wants to hide from!"

ARROWOOD BOOKS, (II), P.O. Box 2100, Corvallis OR 97339. (503)753-9539. Editor: Lex Runciman. Estab. 1985. Small, part-time, 2-person operation. Publishes hardcover and paperback originals. Books: acid free paper. Average print order 1,000; first novel print order varies. Averages 2 titles/year.
• Arrowood Books received a Bumpershoot (Seattle) publication prize in 1991. The press looks for work with a Northwest connection.
Needs: Contemporary, literary, mainstream. Published *Sorrowful Mysteries and Other Stories*, by Normandi Ellis.
How to Contact: Accepts unsolicited mss. Query first. Simultaneous submissions OK, if noted. Reports on queries in 3 weeks; 3 months on mss.
Terms: Advance is negotiable. Pays in royalties of 10-12%. Sends pre-publication galleys to author.

*‡ASYLUM ARTS, (II), P.O. Box 6203, Santa Maria CA 93456. (805)928-8774. Editor: Greg Boyd. Estab. 1985. Independent publisher. Publishes paperback originals. Books: acid-free paper; off-set printing; smythy-sewn/wrapper binding; some illustrations; average print order: 2,000; first novel print order: 2,000. Averages 6-8 total titles, 4 fiction titles each year. Sometimes comments on rejected ms.
Needs: Erotica, experimental, literary, short story collections, translations. Plans anthology French Romantic Reader; editors select stories. Recently published *The Gothic Twilight*, by Stephen-Paul Martin (stories); *Choose Your Own World*, by Edouard Roditi (stories); *Toothpaste with Chlorophyll*, by Elias Papadimitrakopoulos (stories). Publishes the Asylum Annual.
How to Contact: Accepts unsolicited mss. Query first. Include estimated word count, bio, list of publishing credits, Social Security number. Send SASE (or IRC) for a reply to a query. Reports in 1 month on queries; 4 months on mss. No simultaneous submissions.
Terms: Pays royalties of 10% and author's copies. Also "individual arrangement, book by book; some cooperative projects." Subsidy publishes 20%. Sends galleys to author. Publishes ms 1-2 years after acceptance. Book catalog free.
Advice: "We are publishing more paperback originals as they are easier to distribute."

‡THE ATLANTEAN PRESS, (II), 354 Tramway Dr., Milpitas CA 95035. (408)262-8478. Fax: (408)262-8478. Publisher: P. LeChevalier. Estab. 1990. "Very small (2-3 titles/year) independent; plans to expand in 1994." Publishes hardcover originals and reprints and paperback originals and reprints. Books: acid-free paper; Smythe-sewn case or sew and wrap; average print order: 2,000; first novel print order: 2,000. Averages 2-3 total titles, all fiction. Sometimes comments on rejected mss.
Needs: Adventure, childrens/juvenile, historical (general), literary, mainstream/contemporary, military/war, mystery/suspense (private eye/hardboiled, amateur sleuth, cozy, malice domestic, police procedural), short story collections, thriller/espionage, translations, western. Publishes annual anthology, "Atlantean Press Review." Send for guidelines, enclosing a description of your work. Recently published *Whisper the Guns*, by Edward Cline (suspense).

How to Contact: Accepts unsolicited mss. Query first. Include estimated word count, 1 page bio, writing experience, ambitions and philosophy. SASE. Reports in 2 months. Simultaneous and electronic submissions OK.

Terms: Pays royalties of 10% minimum; 25% maximum. Provides 5 or more author's copies. Pays honorarium ($15-100) or makes individual arrangement with author depending on the book. Sends galleys to author. Publishes ms 8-18 months after acceptance. Writer's guidelines for #10 SASE and 1 first class stamp. Book brochures are free.

Advice: "We are looking for good *romantic* fiction and drama. Not to be confused with "romance," this means serious fiction with a logical *plot*; strong, active motivated *characters* and a *theme*. Read Ayn Rand's *Romantic Manifesto*."

*AUTHORS UNLIMITED, (II), Imprints include Authors Unlimited and Military Literary Guild, 3324 Barham Blvd., Los Angeles CA 90068. (213)874-0902. Senior Editor: Renais J. Hill. Estab. 1983. Midsize independent publisher with plans to expand. Publishes hardcover and paperback originals. Books: 60 lb. paper; trade paper and hard cover binding; illustrations; average print order: 2,000. Published new writers within the last year. Plans 10 first novels this year. Averages 30 total titles, 15 fiction titles each year.

Needs: Adventure, contemporary, ethnic, faction, fantasy, feminist, gay, glitz, historical, horror, humor/satire, lesbian, literary, mainstream, military/war, mystery/suspense (amateur sleuth, private eye, police procedural), psychic/supernatural/occult, regional, religious/inspirational, romance, science fiction, short story collections, spiritual, thriller/espionage, western. No pornography. Recently published *Victors All*, by Monita I. Syll; *Labor of Love*, by Dr. LeRoy Weekes (Vol. I & II); *The Obstinate Embryo*, by Anita Lanrinean.

How to Contact: Accepts unsolicited mss. Submit complete ms with cover letter. SASE (IRC). Reports in 1 month. Simultaneous submissions OK.

Terms: *Subsidy publishes 10% of books* (cooperative terms, approx. 60/40%). No advance. Provides 50 author's copies. Sends galleys to author. Publishes ms 9 months after acceptance. Writer's guidelines for 9×12 SAE and $1.25 postage. Book catalog for 9×12 SAE and $1.25 postage.

BAMBOO RIDGE PRESS, (IV), P.O. Box 61781, Honolulu HI 96839-1781. (808)599-4823. Editors: Darrell Lum and Eric Chock. Estab. 1978. "Bamboo Ridge Press publishes *Bamboo Ridge: The Hawaii Writers' Quarterly*, a journal of fiction and poetry with special issues devoted to the work of one writer—fiction or poetry." Publishes paperback originals and reprints. Books: 60 lb. natural; perfect-bound; illustrations; average print order: 2,000. Published new writers within the last year. Averages 2-4 total titles.

Needs: Ethnic, literary and short story collections. "Interested in writing that reflects Hawaii's multicultural ethnic mix. No psuedo-Hawaiiana myths or Hawaii-Five-O type of mentality—stereotypical portrayals of Hawaii and its people." Published *Pass On, No Pass Back*, by Darrll Lum (short story collection).

How to Contact: Accepts unsolicited mss. Query first. SASE. Reports in 4-6 weeks on queries; 3-6 months on mss. Simultaneous submissions OK.

Terms: Payment depends on grant/award money. Sends galleys to author. Publishes ms 6 months-1 year after acceptance. Writer's guidelines for #10 SAE and 1 first class stamp. Book catalog for #10 SASE or IRC and 52¢ postage.

BARN OWL BOOKS, (I, IV), Box 226, Vallecitos NM 87581. (505)582-4226. Imprints include Amazon Press. Publisher: Gina Covina. Estab. 1983. Two-person small publisher; "author participation in publishing process encouraged." Publishes paperback originals. Books: quality paperback standard paper; offset litho printing; perfect binding; illustrations "if appropriate"; average print order: 2,000-5,000; first novel print order: 2,000. Averages 1 total title/year. Occasionally critiques or comments on rejected ms.

Needs: Contemporary, ethnic, feminist, gay, lesbian, literary, regional.

How to Contact: Accepts unsolicited mss. Query first. SASE. Reports in 1 month on queries; 2 months on mss.

Terms: Pays royalties of 7-12%. Sends galleys to authors.

FREDERIC C. BEIL, PUBLISHER, INC., (II), 414 Tattnall St., Savannah GA 31401. Imprints include The Sandstone Press. President: Frederic C. Beil III. Estab. 1983. General trade publisher. Publishes hardcover originals and reprints. Books: acid-free paper; letterpress and offset printing; Smythe-sewn,

hardcover binding; illustrations; average print order: 3,000; first novel print order: 3,000. Plans 2 first novels this year. Averages 10 total titles, 2 fiction titles each year.
Needs: Historical, literary, regional, short story collections, translations. Published *A Woman of Means*, by Peter Taylor.
How to Contact: Does not accept unsolicited mss. Query first. Reports in 1 week on queries.
Terms: Payment "all negotiable." Sends galleys to author. Book catalog free on request.

BETHEL PUBLISHING, (IV), 1819 S. Main, Elkhart IN 46516.(219)293-8585. Contact: Senior Editor. Estab. 1975. Mid-size Christian book publisher. Publishes paperback originals and reprints. Averages 3-5 total titles per year. Occasionally critiques or comments on rejected manuscripts.
Needs: Religious/inspirational, young adult/teen. No "workbooks, cookbooks, coloring books, theological studies, pre-school or elementary-age stories."
How to Contact: Accepts unsolicited manuscripts. Query first. Reports in 2 weeks on queries; 3 months on mss. Accepts simultaneous submissions. Publishes manuscripts 8-16 months after acceptance.
Terms: Pays royalties of 10% and 12 author's copies. Writer's guidelines and book catalog free on request.

BILINGUAL PRESS/EDITORIAL BILINGÜE, (II, IV), Hispanic Research Center, Arizona State University, Tempe AZ 85287-2702. (602)965-3867. Editor: Gary Keller. Estab. 1973. "University affiliated." Publishes hardcover and paperback originals, and reprints. Books: 60 lb. acid free paper; single sheet or web press printing; case-bound and perfect-bound; illustrations sometimes; average print order: 4,000 copies (1,000 case-bound, 3,000 soft cover). Published new writers within the last year. Plans 2 first novels this year. Averages 12 total titles, 6 fiction each year. Sometimes comments on rejected ms.
Needs: Ethnic, literary, short story collections and translations. "We are always on the lookout for Chicano, Puerto Rican, Cuban-American or other U.S. Hispanic themes with strong and serious literary qualities and distinctive and intellectually important themes. We have been receiving a lot of fiction set in Latin America (usually Mexico or Central America) where the main character is either an ingenue to the culture or spy, adventurer, or mercenary. We don't publish this sort of 'Look, I'm in an exotic land' type of thing. Also, novels about the Aztecs or other pre-Columbians are very iffy." Recently published *Distant Journeys*, by Rafael Castillo (short stories); *Peregrinos de Aztlán*, by Miguel Mèndez (novel); *Lenor Park*, by Nash Candelaria (novel).
How to Contact: Query first. SASE. Include Social Security number with submission. Reports in 3 weeks on queries, 2 months on mss. Simultaneous submissions OK.
Terms: Pays royalties of 10%. Average advance $300. Provides 10 author's copies. Sends galleys to author. Publishes ms 1 year after acceptance. Writer's guidelines not available. Book catalog free.
Advice: "Writers should take the utmost care in assuring that their manuscripts are clean, grammatically impeccable, and have perfect spelling. This is true not only of the English but the Spanish as well. All accent marks need to be in place as well as diacritical marks. When these are missing it's an immediate first indication that the author does not really know Hispanic culture and is not equipped to write about it. We are interested in publishing creative literature that treats the U.S. Hispanic experience in a distinctive, creative, revealing way. The kinds of books that we publish we keep in print for a very long time (certainly into the next century) irrespective of sales. We are busy establishing and preserving a U.S. Hispanic canon of creative literature."

BLACK HERON PRESS, (I, II), P.O. Box 95676, Seattle WA 98145. Publisher: Jerry Gold. Estab. 1984. One-person operation; no immediate plans to expand. Publishes paperback and hardback originals. Average print order: 1,000; first novel print order: 500-1,500. Averages 2 fiction titles each year.
Needs: Adventure, contemporary, experimental, humor/satire, literary, science fiction. Vietnam war novel—literary. "We don't want to see fiction written for the mass market. If it sells to the mass market, fine, but we don't see ourselves as a commercial press." Recently published *Newt*, by Ron Dakron; *The Census Taker*, by Marilyn Stablein (reprint); *The Remf Returns*, by David A. Willson.
How to Contact: Query and sample chapters only. Reports in 3 months on queries. Simultaneous submissions OK.
Terms: Pays standard royalty rates. No advance.
Advice: "A query letter should tell me: 1) number of words, 2) number of pages, 3) if ms is available on floppy disk, 4) if parts of novel been published? 5) where? If you're going to submit to *Black Heron*, make the work as good as you can. I'm a good editor but dI don't have the time to solve major problems with a manuscript."

BLACK MOSS PRESS, (II), Box 143 Station A, Windsor ON N9A-6L7 Canada. (519)252-2551. Editorial Contact Person: Kristina Russelo. Fiction Editor: Marty Gervais. Estab. 1969. "Small independent publisher assisted by government grants." Publishes paperback originals. Books: Zephyr paper; offset printing; perfect binding; 4-color cover, b&w interior illustrations; average print order: 500. Averages 10-14 total titles, 7 fiction titles each year. Sometimes comments on rejected mss.
Needs: Humor/satire, juvenile (5-9 years, including easy-to-read, contemporary), literary, preschool/picture book, short story collections. "Usually open to children's material. Nothing religious, moralistic, romance." Recently published *The Failure of Love*, by Paul Vasey; *Ethel on Fire*, by Helen Humphreys; *Priest's Boy*, by Clive Doucet.
How to Contact: Accepts unsolicited mss. Submit outline/synopsis and 2 sample chapters. SASE. Reports in 1-3 months. *Canadian authors only.*
Terms: Pays for children's in royalties; literary in author's copies. Sends galleys to author. Publishes ms 1-2 years after acceptance. Book catalog for SASE.
Advice: "Generally, originality, well developed plots, strong, multi-dimensional characters and some unusual element catch my interest. It's rare that we publish new authors' works, but when we do, that's what we want. (We do publish short story collections of authors who have had some stories in lit mags.) Because we are assisted by government grants which place certain restrictions on us, we are unable to publish any material by anyone other than a Canadian citizen or immigrant landed in Canada."

BLACK TIE PRESS, (I, II), Box 440004, 12655 Whittington Dr., Houston TX 77244. (713)789-5119. Publisher/Editor: Peter Gravis. Estab. 1986. "We are a tiny press interested in contemporary poetry and short fiction." Publishes hardcover and paperback originals. Books: Mohawk vellum, Glatfelter paper; combination offset and letter press printing; Smythe sewn; illustrations; average print order: varies.
Needs: Contemporary and experimental. "Our current aim is to publish an anthology of short fiction (4-6,000 words). No science fiction, romance, spiritual, religious, juvenile, historical."
How to Contact: Query or submit complete ms (with proper postage) with cover letter. SASE necessary for returns. Reporting time varies.
Terms: Usually pays in copies. "Payment will be determined on individual basis." Publishes ms one year after acceptance. Writer's guidelines free for SASE or IRC.

BLIND BEGGAR PRESS, Box 437, Bronx NY 10467. Imprint: LampLight Editions. Fiction Editors: Gary Johnston, C.D. Grant. Estab. 1975. Small press with plans to expand. Publishes paperback originals. Plans to publish first novels "dependent upon budget." Averages 2-3 total titles each year; "no fiction titles thus far." Average print order 2,000 copies. Occasionally critiques rejected ms.
Needs: Ethnic (Third World), experimental, juvenile (animal, easy-to-read, fantasy, historical), preschool/picture book, short story collections, translations and young adult/teen (historical).
How to Contact: Query first with SASE. Reports in 1 month on queries; 2 months on mss. Simultaneous submissions OK. Publishes ms 12-18 months after acceptance.
Terms: Pays in author's copies (10-15% of run). "If author wishes to pay all or part of production costs, we work out individual arrangements directly." Book catalog free on request.
Advice: Recent trends include ethnic historical (biographies, political history, etc.). In first novels interested in high quality, relevancy to Third World readers. "Within two years we plan to publish children's books, short stories and *maybe* a small novel."

BOOKS FOR ALL TIMES, INC., Box 2, Alexandria VA 22313. Publisher/Editor: Joe David. Estab. 1981. One-man operation. Publishes hardcover and paperback originals. Books: 60 lb. paper; offset printing; perfect binding; average print order: 1,000. "No plans for new writers at present." Has published 1 fiction title to date. Occasionally critiques rejected mss.
Needs: Contemporary, literary and short story collections. "No novels at the moment; hopeful, though, of someday soon publishing a collection of quality short stories. No popular fiction or material easily published by the major or minor houses specializing in mindless entertainment. Only interested in stories of the Victor Hugo or Sinclair Lewis quality."
How to Contact: Query first with SASE. Simultaneous submission OK. Reports in 1 month on queries.
Terms: Pays negotiable advance. "Publishing/payment arrangement will depend on plans for the book." Book catalog free on request.
Advice: Interested in "controversial, honest books which satisfy the reader's curiosity to know. Read Victor Hugo, Fyodor Dostoyevsky and Sinclair Lewis, for example. I am actively looking for short articles (up to 5,000 words) on contemporary education. I prefer material critical of the public schools when documented and convincing."

BOREALIS PRESS, (IV), 9 Ashburn Dr., Ottawa, Ontario K2E 6N4 Canada. Imprint includes *Journal of Canadian Poetry*. Editor: Frank Tierney. Fiction Editor: Glenn Clever. Estab. 1970. Publishes hardcover and paperback originals and reprints. Books: standard book-quality paper; offset printing; perfect and cloth binding; average print order: 1,000. Buys juvenile mss with b&w illustrations. Average number of titles: 4.

● Borealis Press has a series, "New Canadian Drama," with five books in print. They recently won an Ontario Arts Council grant.

Needs: Contemporary, literary, juvenile and young adult. "Must have a Canadian content or author; query first." Recently published *Margin of Error*, by Lelsey Choyce (young adult short stories of maritime Canada); *What Necessity Knows*, by Lily Dougall and Sister Woman, J.G. Sime (reprints of 19-century Canadian women novelists); *From My Vantage Point*, by Harold Gloade (stories of Canadian Micmac Indians).

How to Contact: Submit query with SASE (Canadian postage) or IRCs. No simultaneous submissions. Reports in 2 weeks on queries, 3-4 months on mss. Publishes ms 1-2 years after acceptance.

Terms: Pays 10% royalties and 3 free author's copies; no advance. Sends galleys to author. Free book catalog with SASE or IRC.

Advice: " Have your work professionally edited. We generally publish only material with a Canadian content or by a Canadian writer."

*BOTTOM DOG PRESS, (IV), Firelands College, Huron OH 44839. (419)433-5560. Editor/Publisher: Dr. Larry Smith. Estab. 1984. Four-person part-time operation assisted by grants from Ohio Arts Council. Publishes paperback originals. Books: fine paper; perfect binding; cover art illustrations; average print order: 1,500 fiction. Averages 3 total titles, 1-2 fiction titles each year. Always critiques or comments on rejected mss.

● Bottom Dog Press regularly receives grants from the Ohio Arts Council.

Needs: Literary, mainstream. Midwest life. Published *Best Ohio Fiction* collection (160 pages) with work by Jack Matthews, Robert Flanagan, Philip F. O'Connor, Robert Fox; *Loving Power: Stories*, by Robert Flanagan; *Human Anatomy: Three Fictions* (three books in one including *Martin's World*, by Philip O'Connor; *Well of Living Waters*, by Annabel Thomas and *Being a Poet*, by Jack Matthew).

How to Contact: Accepts unsolicited mss. Query first. Submit complete ms with cover letter. SASE. Reports on queries in 2 weeks; 2 months on mss.

Terms: Pays royalties of 10-15% minimum and 20 author's copies. Sends galleys to author. Has done 2 books co-operatively—50/50. Book catalog free on request.

Advice: "We do an 'Ohio Writers Series' specializing in chapbook collections of stories or novellas—emphasis on sense of place and strong human characters. All submissions must fall within the 40,000 word limit. We also do a 'Contemporary Midwest Fiction Series' of stories or novel (160 pgs.)."

BRITISH AMERICAN PUBLISHING, LTD., (III), Subsidiary of British American (distributed by Simon & Schuster), Imprints include Paris Review Editions, 19 British American Blvd., Latham NY 12110. (518)786-6000. Managing Editor: Kathleen A. Murphy. Estab. 1988. Midsize independent publisher with plans to expand. Publishes hardcover originals and reprints and paperback originals. Published new writers within the last year. Plans 2 first novels this year. Averages 10 total titles, 5 fiction, this year. Sometimes comments on rejected ms.

● This publisher was named as a "literary root" for American writers by *Esquire* (July 1992).

Needs: "General—all genres. Always interested in unusual, offbeat, humorous fiction and nonfiction." Recently published *Portable People*, by Paul West (biographical sketches); *Miracle Cure*, by Harlan Coben (suspense); *Boiling Rock*, by Remar Sutton (suspense mystery); *Frog*, by Stephen Dixon (1991 National Book Award finalist and PEN/Faulkner finalist).

How to Contact: Accepts unsolicited mss. Submit complete ms with cover letter. SASE (IRC). Agented fiction 90%. Reports in 4-6 weeks. Simultaneous submissions OK.

Terms: Pays royalties, negotiable advance. Sends pre-publication galleys to author. Publishes ms 1 year after a acceptance. Book catalog free.

Listings marked with a solid box are book packagers. See the introduction for more information.

■**BRYANS & BRYANS, (I) (Book Packager and Editorial Consultant)**, Box 121, Fairfield CT 06430. (203)454-2051. President: John B. Bryans. Fiction Editor: James A. Bryans. Arranges publication of paperback originals (packages). Books: paperback/mass market. *Critiques mss: $200 charge* "for 2-page evaluation only when this has been agreed upon in advance. Often I will offer comments and criticism at no charge where, based on a query, we have encouraged submission. Line-editing and ongoing consulting services to author and publishers."
Needs: Adventure, contemporary, historical, horror, humor/satire, literary, mainstream, romance (contemporary, historical). Recently produced *Baton Rouge* (historical with romance elements); *Portland* and *Omaha*, by Lee Davis Willoughby (packaged by us for Knightsbridge Publishing, Los Angeles).
How to Contact: Does not accept unsolicited mss. Query first. SASE. Agented fiction 50-90%. Reports in 2 weeks on queries; 1 month on mss. Electronic submissions OK via Microsoft Word on Macintosh disk.
Terms: Pays in royalties of 6-10%. Negotiable advance.
Advice: "Send us a letter, maximum 2 pages, describing the project and giving pertinent background info on yourself. Include an SASE and we will reply to let you know if we find the idea intriguing enough to see 3 sample chapters (the *first* three) and a detailed synopsis."

BURNING BOOKS, (IV), 690 Market St., Suite 1501, San Francisco CA 94104. (415)788-7480. Publishers: Kathleen Burch, Michael Sumner. Estab. 1979. Three-person part-time operation. Publishes paperback originals. Books: acid-free paper; offset and letterpress printing; spiral or signature sewn binding; illustrations; average print order: 1,000-3,000. Averages 1 title/year; 1 fiction title every 2 years. *Will provide detailed critique of ms for $100.*
Needs: Literary. No "commercially inspired" fiction. Published *Moment of Silence*, by Toma Longinovíc.
How to Contact: Does not accept unsolicited mss. Query first. Reports on queries in 6 weeks.
Terms: Pays in author's copies. Sends galleys to author. Book catalog free on request.

CACANADADADA, (I, II, IV), 3350 West 21 Ave., Vancouver BC V6S 1G7 Canada. (604)738-1195. President: Ronald B. Hatch. Fiction Editor: J. Michael Yates. Estab. 1988. Publishes paperback originals. Books: 60 lb. paper; photo offset printing; perfect binding; average print order: 1,000; first novel print order: 1,000. Plans 1 first novel this year. Averages 6 total titles, 3 fiction this year. Sometimes comments on rejected ms.
• A book published by Cacanadadada, Jancis M. Andrews' *Rapunzel...*, won the 1992 Women's Book of the Year award.
Needs: Experimental and literary. Recently published *Worlds in Small*, by John Robert Columbo; *Daymares*, by Robert Zend; *Rapunzel, Rapunzel, Let Down Down Your Hair*, by Jancis M. Andrews.
How to Contact: *Canadian authors only.* Accepts unsolicited mss. Submit outline/synopsis and 1 or 2 sample chapters. SASE. Short story collections must have some magazine publication. Reports in 1 week on queries; 1 month on mss.
Terms: Pays royalties of 10%. Provides author's copies. Sends galleys to author. Publishes ms 6 months after acceptance.
Advice: "We publish both fiction and poetry. We are a Canadian publishing house and depend on a partial government subsidy to publish books. Thus, authors *must* be Canadian."

CADMUS EDITIONS, (III), Box 126, Tiburon CA 94920. (707)431-8527. Editor: Jeffrey Miller. Estab. 1979. Emphasis on quality literature. Publishes hardcover and paperback originals. Books: Approximately 25% letterpress; 70% offset printing; perfect and case binding; average print order: 2,000; first novel print order: 2,000. Averages 3-5 total titles, 3 fiction titles each year.
Needs: Literary. Published *The Wandering Fool*, by Yunus Emre, translated by Edouard Roditi and Guzin Dino; *The Hungry Girls*, by Patricia Eakins; *Zig-Zag*, by Richard Thornley.
How to Contact: Does not accept or return unsolicited mss. Query first. SASE. Photocopied submissions OK.
Terms: Royalties negotiated per book. Sends galleys to author.

CALYX BOOKS, (II,IV), P.O. Box B, Corvallis OR 97339. (503)753-9384. Editor: M. Donnelly. Fiction Editor: Beverly McFarland. Estab. 1986. "We publish fine literature and art by women." Publishes hardcover and paperback originals. Books: offset printing; paper and cloth binding; average print order: 5,000-10,000 copies; first novel print order: 5,000. Published new writers within the last year. Averages 2-4 total titles each year.

Close-up

Steve Schrader
Publisher
Cane Hill Press

"I get several hundred manuscripts each year, but most of them are coming to the wrong place," says Steve Schrader, owner and publisher of Cane Hill Press. He says the biggest mistake a writer can make when submitting to a small press is not researching the press first. "The ideal person to submit to me is someone who can show me they really know the kind of books I publish. They've done the research and have an understanding of what I do—otherwise they're just wasting their time and mine."

Schrader describes his press as literary and says he spends most of his time reading manuscripts, although he publishes only two or three books each year. "Usually I ask that writers send me something short first (not a whole manuscript). I know quickly if the manuscript is right for me. What I'm interested in is original, lively, pure-spirited prose."

He says cover letters are useful in that they help him determine if the writer is familiar with the press. "But I'm not impressed with unsolicited praise from teachers or other advertisements for the work. The writer doesn't have to make a big case for the book—I'm not looking for bestsellers."

In fact, Schrader advises writers to try the big markets first, if they are looking for commercial success and large financial rewards. The rewards of working with a small press are real, but very different, he says. "I do receive manuscripts from writers who have had commercial success. They submit to me because they prefer to publish with a small press or because they have given up on the big presses. They know at big publishers a book can get lost, but I'm going to be behind it no matter what. I don't take on a book just because I think it will sell. It's more because I believe in it. This is a labor of love rather than a business."

Although the press is only four years old, Cane Hill authors and books have already won praise and some very good, well-placed reviews in *The New York Times* Book Review, *Publishers Weekly* and others. "I spend a lot of time sending books out for review. I may send 200 books to people. I go over each list carefully and do follow up letters." This individual, personal service is a main reason writers choose small presses, Schrader says.

"Small presses also try to keep books in print longer. I try to keep all mine in print. Sometimes I will call a college to persuade them to use a book in a course. This helps keep book orders up." Another boost to sales comes from authors who have gone on to bigger presses, he explains. "As these authors continue to turn out new work it generates interest in earlier works I've published."

To writers, Schrader says, "They say 'don't go to law school unless you really love law' and I think this is good advice for almost anything. You must really love to write and you must keep at it. And write as honestly as possible."

—Robin Gee

• *Calyx*, a literary journal by this publisher, is also listed in this book. Books published by Calyx have received the American Book Award, GLCA Fiction Award and Bumpershoot and other awards. They are not now working on an anthology but past anthologies include *Forbidden Stitch: An Asian American Women's Anthology* and *Women and Aging*.

Needs: Contemporary, ethnic, experimental, feminist, lesbian, literary, short story collections and translations. Recently published *Mrs. Vargas and the Dead Naturalist*, by Kathlean Alcalá (short stories); *Ginseng and Other Tales from Manila*, by Marianne Villanueva (short stories); *Killing Color*, by Charlotte Watson Sherman (short stories).

How to Contact: Query first or submit outline/synopsis and 3 sample chapters. Include SASE (IRC). Open for submissions Jan. 1993-March 1993. Reports in 1 month on queries; 6 months on mss.

Terms: Pays royalties of 10% minimum, author's copies, (depends on grant/award money). Sends galleys to author. Publishes ms 2 years after acceptance. Writer's guidelines for #10 SAE and 1 first class stamp or IRC. Book catalog free on request.

CANE HILL PRESS, 225 Varick St., 11th Floor, New York NY 10014. (212)316-5513. Publisher: Steve Schrader. Estab. 1988. "Literary press—contemporary fiction." Publishes paperback originals. Average print order: 2,000. Published new writers within the last year. Plans 1 first novel this year. Averages 2-3 total titles, all fiction, this year. Sometimes comments on rejected ms.

Needs: Literary, short story collections. No genre. Recently published *Getting Jesus in the Mood*, by Anne Brashler (story collection); *Phoenix*, by Melissa Pritchard (novel); and *All Backs Were Turned*, by Marek Hlasko (translation from a Polish novel).

How to Contact: Accepts unsolicited mss. Query first. Agented fiction 50%. Reports in 1 week on queries; 1 month on mss. Simultaneous submissions OK.

Terms: Pays in advance; $2,000-3,000. Also 50 author's copies. Sends galleys to author. Publishes ms 18 months after acceptance. Book catalog free on request.

‡CAPRA PRESS, (III), imprint of Joshua Odell Editions, P.O. Box 2068, Santa Barbara CA 93120. (805)966-4590. Fax: (805)965-8020. Publisher: Noel Young. Fiction Editor: Cynthia Cornett. Estab. 1969. Midsize independent publisher. Publishes paperback originals. Averages 12 total titles, 4 fiction titles each year.

Needs: Open. Recently published *Final Fate of the Alligators*, by Edward Hoagland (short stories); *Captain ZZYZX*, by Michael Petracca (contemporary); *Evening Redness*, by Lawrence Clark Powell (literary).

How to Contact: Accepts unsolicited mss. Submit outline/synopsis and 2 sample chapters. Include bio, list of publishing credits. SASE for reply to query or return of ms. Reports in 1 month. Simultaneous submissions OK.

Terms: Pays in royalties, advance and author's copies. Sends galleys to author. Time between acceptance of the ms and publishing varies. Writer's guidelines for #10 SAE and 1 first class stamp. Book catalog for #13 SAE and 2 first class stamps.

CARAVAN PRESS, (III), 15445 Ventura Bl. #279, Sherman Oaks CA 91403. (818)377-4301. Publisher: Jana Cain. Estab. 1979. "Small three-person publisher with expansion goals." Publishes hardcover and paperback originals, especially poetry collections. Plans 1-2 novels this year. Averages 6 total titles. Occasionally critiques or comments on rejected ms; fee varies.

Needs: Erotica, historical, humor/satire, literary, short story collections. *List for novels filled for next year or two.* Published *Litany*, by Scott Sonders (poems).

How to Contact: Query through agent only. SASE. Agented fiction 90%. Reports in 2 months on queries. Simultaneous submissions OK.

Terms: Payment rate is "very variable." Sends galleys to author.

Advice: "Be competent, be solvent. Know who you are. Target your market."

*CAROLINA WREN PRESS, (II,IV), 120 Morris St., Durham NC 27701. (919)560-2738. Imprints are Lollipop Power Books. Editor-in-Chief: Elaine Goolsby. Fiction Editor: Kathryn Lovatt. "Small non-profit independent publishing company which specializes in women's and minority work and non-sexist, multi-racial children's books." Publishes paperback originals. Books: off-set printing; perfect and saddle-stitching binding; illustrations mainly in children's; average print order: 1,000 adult, 3,000 children; first novel print order: 1,000. Published new writers within the last year. Plans 2 first novels this year. Averages 2-3 total titles each year. Sometimes comments on rejected mss.

Needs: Contemporary, ethnic, experimental, feminist, gay, juvenile (easy-to-read, fantasy, contemporary), lesbian, literary, preschool/picture book, regional, short story collections, translations. No standard clichéd stuff, romances, etc. No animals (children's books). "We are currently looking for short stories by women, in particular, Southern and minority writers are *especially* encouraged to apply." Published *Love, Or a Reasonable Facsimile*, by Gloree Rogers (ethnic); *Brother and Keeper, Sister's Child*, by Margaret Stephens (literary).
How to Contact: Accepts unsolicited mss. Submit outline/synopsis and 1 or 2 sample chapters. SASE. Reports in 6 months.
Terms: Pays in copies (10% of print run for adults, 5% for children's books). Pays cash advance and royalties if grants are available. Sends galleys to author. Publishes ms 2-3 years after acceptance. Writer's guidelines for #10 SAE and 2 first class stamps. Book catalog for #10 SAE and 2 first class stamps.
Advice: "We would like to see work from more black women writers."

CARPENTER PRESS, (I, II), Box 14387, Columbus OH 43214. Editorial Director: Robert Fox. Estab. 1973. One-man operation on part-time basis. Publishes paperback originals. Books: alkaline paper; offset printing; perfect or saddle stapled binding; illustrations sometimes; average print order: 500-2,500; first novel print order: 1,000.
Needs: Contemporary, literary, experimental, fantastical. "Literary rather than genre science fiction and fantasy." Published *Dawn of the Flying Pigs*, by Jerry Bumpus (short stories); and the 10th anniversary first novel contest winner, *The Three-Week Trance Diet*, by Jane Pirto. "Do not plan to publish more than one book/year including chapbooks, and this depends upon funding, which is erratic. Contemplating future competitions in the novel and short story."
How to Contact: Accepts unsolicited mss. Query. SASE. Simultaneous submissions OK. Reports promptly.
Terms: Pays in author's copies or 10% royalties. "Terms vary according to contract." No cash advance. Free book catalog with 52¢ postage.
Advice: "Know what we've published. Don't try to impress us with whom you've studied or where you've published. Read as much as you can so you're not unwittingly repeating what's already been done. I look for freshness and originality. I wouldn't say that I favor experimental over traditional writing. Rather, I'm interested in seeing how recent experimentation is tying tradition to the future and to the work of writers in other countries. We encourage first novelists."

CATBIRD PRESS, (II), 44 N. 6th Ave., Highland Park NJ 08904. Publisher: Robert Wechsler. Estab. 1987. Small independent trade publisher. Publishes hardcover and paperback originals and reprints. Books: acid-free paper; offset printing; cloth/paper binding; illustrations (where relevant). Average print order: 4,000; first novel print order: 3,000. Averages 5 total titles, 1-2 fiction titles each year.
Needs: Contemporary, humor (specialty); literary, translations (specialty Czech, French and German read in-house). No thriller, historical, science fiction, or other genre writing, only writing with a fresh style and approach. Recently published *Lifetime Employment*, by Floyd Kemske.
How to Contact: Accepts unsolicited mss but no queries. Submit outline/synopsis with sample chapters. SASE. Reports in 2-4 weeks on mss. Simultaneous submissions OK, but let us know if simultaneous.
Terms: Pays royalties of 7½-15%. Average advance: $2,000; offers negotiable advance. Sends prepublication galleys to author. Publishes ms approx. 1 year after acceptance. Terms depend on particular book. Writer's guidelines for #10 SAE with 1 first class stamp.
Advice: "We are interested in quality fiction particularly with a comic vision. We are definitely interested in unpublished novelists who combine a sense of humor with a true knowledge of and love for language, a lack of ideology, care for craft and self-criticism."

‡CAVE BOOKS, (IV), Subsidiary of Cave Research Foundation, 756 Harvard Ave., St. Louis MO 63130. (314)862-7646. Editor: Richard A. Watson. Estab. 1957. Small press. Publishes hardcover and paperback originals and reprints. Books: acid free paper; various methods printing; binding sewn in signatures; illustrations; average print order: 1,500; first novel print order: 1,500. Averages 4 total titles. Number of fiction titles varies each year. Critiques or comments on rejected ms.
• For years now Cave Books has been looking for realistic adventure novels involving caves. A writer with a *quality* novel along these lines would have an excellent chance for publication.
Needs: Adventure (cave exploration). Needs any realistic novel with caves as central theme. "No gothic, romance, fantasy or science fiction. Mystery and detective OK if the action in the cave is central and realistic. (What I mean by 'realistic' is that the author must know what he or she is talking about.)"

How to Contact: Accepts unsolicited mss. Submit complete ms with cover letter. Reports in 1 week on queries; 1 month on mss. Simultaneous submissions OK.
Terms: Pays in royalties of 10%. Sends galleys to author. Book catalog free on request.
Advice: Encourages first novelists. "We would like to publish more fiction, but we get very few submissions. Why doesn't someone write a historical novel about Mammoth Cave, Carlsbad Caverns, . . .?"

CHELSEA GREEN PUBLISHING CO., Route 113, P.O. Box 130, Post Mills VT 05058. (802)333-9073. Editor: Ian Baldwin. Estab. 1985. "Small independent trade publisher with plans to expand." Publishes hardcover and paperback originals. Averages 8-10 total titles, 1-2 fiction titles each year.
Needs: Serious fiction only . . . no genre fiction (ie. romance, spy, sci fi) or mainstream." Published *The Automotive History of Lucky Kellerman*, by Steve Heller (literary); *The Eight Corners of the World*, by Gordon Weaver (lit/comedy).
How to Contact: Query first. Prefers no unsolicited submissions. SASE.
Terms: Royalties to trade standards; small advances on royalties negotiable.
Advice: "Receptive to serious fiction that deepens the reader's understanding of the global environmental crisis."

‡CHEOPS BOOKS, (II, IV), Suite 179, 977 Seminole Trail, Charlottesville VA 22901. (804)973-7047. Fax: (804)973-1330. Vice President: Kay Bognar. Fiction Editors: Gary Bennet, Alice Bognar and Larry Bognar. Estab. 1990. "Four-person operation on part-time basis." Books: 50 lb. white paper; offset/litho printing; perfect binding; four color cover illustraitons; average print order: 2,000; first novel print order: 2,000. Averages 1 (fiction) title each year. Always comments on rejected ms; *charges $50/ms for proofread and edit plus comments sheet.*
Needs: Fantasy (mythological), historical (general, mythological), romance (historical), western (historical). "We want adult historical novels well-researched and with sense of voice and style." No historical costume dramas. Recently published *To Follow the Goddess*, by Linda Cargill (mythological historical).
How to Contact: Query first. Include estimated word count and list of publishing credits. SASE. Reports in 2 weeks on queries.
Terms: *Note: publisher charges $50 fee (see above).* Sends galleys to author. Book catalog for #10 SAE and 1 first class stamp.
Advice: "We are essentially a small 'mom and pop' operation. We don't acquire or publish many books due to time and budget constraints. Due to the recession we did not publish a title in 1992, but we plan to publish our next title in 1993. Sales are just starting to pick up again. Tip: Find a voice. Pretend the main character is telling the story to you as did the bards of old. You can hear it. We are very fond of the novels of Mary Renault and Robert Graves. We publish only historical fiction. No genre westerns, family sagas, romances or series books. We don't consider anything concerning the post 1914 world historical enough for our purposes. We even prefer unusual time periods and settings, the more exotic the better (but no pure fantasy or self-created worlds please)."

CLEAR LIGHT PUBLISHERS, (IV), 823 Don Diego, Santa Fe NM 87501. (505)989-9590. Publisher: Harmon Houghton. Estab. 1980. "Publish primarily on Southwest, traditional cultures." Publishes hardcover originals. Plans 3 first novels this year. Averages 10-12 total titles, 3 fiction titles each year. Sometimes comments on rejected ms.
Needs: Faction, historical, humor/satire, regional, spiritual, western. Looking for "Southwest, western, native American."
How to Contact: Query first or submit outline/synopsis and sample chapters or sample of writing. SASE. Reports in 6-9 weeks on queries. Simultaneous submissions OK.
Terms: Pays 10-12.5% royalties, negotiable advance. Sends galleys to author. Publishes ms 3-6 months after acceptance. Book catalog free.

CLEIS PRESS, P.O. Box 14684, San Francisco CA 94114-0684. Did not respond.

CLIFFHANGER PRESS, (II), Box 29527, Oakland CA 94604-9527. (415)763-3510. Editor: Nancy Chirich. Estab. 1986. Publishes trade paperback originals. Books: 60 lb. recycled paper; offset printing; perfect binding; average print order: 2,000; first novel print order: 2,000. Published all new writers within the last year; goal is 10 novels a year.

Needs: Suspense/mystery. "Need mystery/suspense (approximately 75,000 words); heavy on the American regional or foreign background. No grossly hardboiled detectives and no spies." (Send SASE for guidelines for specific needs.) Recently published *Beyond Saru*, by T.A. Roberts, and *Mayan Shadows*, Christopher Brennan; *The Small Rains*, by Lizbeth Piel.
How to Contact: Please first send for writer's guidelines, free on request for SASE. Query first with outline/synopsis and first three chapters as sample. SASE. If sample appears to be our style, we will request complete ms. Reports in 3 weeks on queries; approx. 12 weeks on requested mss. Unsolicited mss are returned unopened. Simultaneous submissions OK, but please let us know.
Terms: No advances. Pays royalties of 8-15%. Sends galleys to author.
Advice: "Cliffhanger Press publishes *original* first novels. Suspense is central to our books, but we are moving away from strictly mysteries to novels that transcend the genre." Looks for "themes that show American citizens of diverse ethnic or social backgrounds interacting in a realistic, ultimately mutually respectful way. This does not necessarily mean Goody Two-Shoes. It's *OK* to be entertaining! Say something to reflect American culture wherever in the world it is represented. Include rich, unusual locale, strong sense of place. Think regionally! Think globally!"

‡**CLOCKWATCH REVIEW PRESS, (I),** Dept. of English, Illinois Wesleyan University, Bloomington IL 61702-2900. (309)556-3352. Editor: James Plath. Estab. 1983. "Small independent publisher, not-for-profit corporation." Publishes hardcover and paperback originals. Books: recycled paper; offset printing; perfect binding; average print order: 1,600. Published new writers within the last year. Averages 1 title each year. Often comments on rejected ms.
● See also the listing for *Clockwatch Review* in the Literary/Small Circulation section of this book.
Needs: Literary, short story collections. "First books by authors who have served an apprenticeship in the little literary magazines." No genre material.
How to Contact: Accepts unsolicited mss. Submit outline/synopsis and 3 sample chapters or short stories. Include brief bio and list of publishing credits. Send SASE (or IRC) for reply, return of ms or send a disposable copy of the ms. Reports in 2 weeks on queries; 2-4 months on mss. No simultaneous submissions.
Terms: Pays 10% of print run, honorarium. Sends galleys to author. Publishes ms 1 year after acceptance. Writer's guidelines for SASE.

COFFEE HOUSE PRESS, (II), 27 N. 4th St., Minneapolis MN 55401. (612)338-0125. Editorial Assistant: Michael L. Wiegers. Fiction Editor: Allan Kornblum. Estab. 1984. "Nonprofit publisher with a small staff. We publish literary titles: fiction and poetry." Publishes paperback originals. Books: acid-free paper; offset and letterpress printing; Smythe sewn binding; cover illustrations; average print order: 2,500; first novel print order: 3,000-4,000. Published new writers within the last year. Plans one first novel this year. Averages 10 total titles, 5-6 fiction titles each year. Sometimes critiques rejected mss.
● This successful nonprofit small press has received numerous grants from various organizations including NEA, the Mellon Foundation and Lila Wallace/Readers Digest. Coffee House's award-winning author, Frank Chin, was featured in a close-up in the 1992 *Novel & Short Story Writer's Market*.
Needs: Contemporary, ethnic, experimental, humor/satire, literary, short story collections. Looking for "non-genre, contemporary, high quality, unique material." No westerns, romance, erotica, mainstream, sci-fi, mystery. Publishes anthologies, but they are closed to unsolicited submissions. Recently published *Brazil-Maru*, by Karen Tei Yamashita (our first hardcover edition); *How to Leave a Country*, by Cris Mazza; and *Price of Eggs*, by Anne Panning.
How to Contact: Accepts unsolicited mss. Submit samples or complete manuscript with cover letter. SASE. Agented fiction 10%. Reports in 3 months on queries; 9 months on mss.
Terms: Pays royalties of 8%. Average advance $500. Provides 15 author's copies. Writer's guidelines for #10 SASE or IRC.
Advice: "Be brilliant."

‡**COLONIAL PRESS, (I, II),** 1237 Stevens Rd. SE, Bessemer AL 35023. (205)428-2146. President: Bradley Twitty. Fiction Editors: Dr. Pat Grierson, Jo Barksdale. Estab. 1954. "Small independent publisher." Publishes hardcover and paperback originals. Books: 50-60 lb. offset paper; perfect binding; average print order: 1,000-50,000. Plans 2 first novels this year. Averages 20-50 total titles, very few fiction titles each year. Always comments on rejected mss.

Needs: Childrens/juvenile (historical, series), historical, new age/mystic/spiritual, psychic/supernatural/occult, regional (south), religious/inspirational (children's religious), short story collections, young adult/teen (historical).
How to Contact: Accepts unsolicited mss. Submit outline/synopsis and 1 sample chapter. Include bio. Send a disposable copy of the manuscript. Reports in 1 month on queries. Simultaneous submissions OK.
Terms: Pays royalties of 5-10%; 10 author's copies. Also makes individual arrangements with author. Publishes ms 6 months-2 years after acceptance. Book catalog free.

CONFLUENCE PRESS INC., (II), Spalding Hall, Lewis-Clark State College, Lewiston ID 83501. (208)799-2336. Imprints: James R. Hepworth Books and Blue Moon Press. Fiction Editor: James R. Hepworth. Estab. 1976. Small trade publisher. Publishes hardcover and paperback originals and reprints. Books: 60 lb. paper; photo offset printing; Smythe-sewn binding; average print order: 1,500-5,000 copies. Published new writers this year. Averages 5 total titles/year. *Critiques rejected mss for $25/ hour.*
• Books published by Confluence Press have received Western States Book Awards and awards from the Pacific Northwest Booksellers Association.
Needs: Contemporary, historical, literary, mainstream, short story collections, translations. "Our needs favor serious fiction, 1 novel and 1 short fiction collection a year, with preference going to work set in the contemporary western United States." Published *Angels and Others*, by Ken Smith; *Runaway*, by Mary Clearman Blew; *Passages West*, edited by Hugh Nichols.
How to Contact: Query first. SASE for query and ms. Agented fiction 50%. Reports in 6-8 weeks on queries and mss. Simultaneous submissions OK.
Terms: Pays in royalties of 10%; advance is negotiable; 10 author's copies; payment depends on grant/award money. Sends galleys to author. Book catalog for 6x9 SASE.
Advice: "We are very interested in seeing first novels from promising writers who wish to break into serious print. We are also particularly keen to publish the best short story writers we can find. We are also interested in finding volume editors for our American authors series. Prospective editors should send proposals."

COTEAU BOOKS, (IV), Thunder Creek Publishing Co-operative Ltd., 401-2206 Dewdney Ave., Regina, Saskatchewan S4R 1H3 Canada. (306)777-0170. Managing Editor: Shelley Sopher. Estab. 1975. Small, independent publisher; focus on first-time published works. Publishes hardcover and paperback originals. Books: #2 offset or 60 lb. hi-bulk paper; offset printing; perfect and Smythe-sewn binding; 4 color illustrations; average print order: 1,500-3,000; first novel print order: approx. 1,500. Published new writers within this year. Plans 1 first novel this year. Publishes 9-11 total titles, 5-6 fiction titles each year. Sometimes comments on rejected mss.
• Books published by Coteau Books have received Best First Book awards from the Commonwealth Writers Prize. The publisher does do anthologies and these will be announced when open to submissions.
Needs: No science fiction. Recently published *The Bonus Deal*, by Archie Crail; *Life Skills*, by Marlis Wesseler; *Sun Angel*, by Chirs Fisher.
How to Contact: *Canadian writers only.* Query first, then submit complete ms with cover letter. SASE. No simultaneous or multiple submissions. Agented fiction 10%. Reports on queries in 3 weeks; on mss in 4 months.
Terms: "We're a co-operative who receives subsidies from the Canadian, provincial and local governments. We do not accept payments from authors to publish their works." Sends galleys to author. Publishes ms 1-2 years after acceptance. Book catalog for 8½×11 SASE.
Advice: "We publish short-story collections, novels and poetry collections, as well as literary interviews and children's books. This is part of our mandate."

COUNCIL FOR INDIAN EDUCATION, (I,IV), 517 Rimrock Rd., Billings MT 59102. (406)252-7451. Editor: Hap Gilliland. Estab. 1963. Small, non-profit organization publishing Native American materials for schools. Publishes hardcover and paperback originals. Books: offset printing; perfect bound or saddle stitched binding; b&w illustrations; average print order: 1,000; first novel print order: 1,000. Published new writers within the last year; plans 3 first novels this year. Averages 5 total titles, 4 fiction titles each year. Usually critiques rejected ms.
Needs: All must be about Native Americans: Adventure, ethnic, family saga, historical, juvenile (historical, adventure and others), preschool/picture book, regional, western, young adult/teen (easy-to-read, mystery, western, historical), western (frontier). Especially needs "short novels, and short stories

accurately portraying American Indian life past or present—fast moving with high interest." No sex emphasis. Recently published *Old Lop Ear Wolf*, by Royce Holland (3 stories); *Mi'ca—Buffalo Hunter*, by Jane Bendix (novel); *Search for Identity*, by different authors (short stories).
How to Contact: Accepts unsolicited mss. Submit complete ms with SASE. Reports in 4 months. Simultaneous submissions OK.
Terms: Pays 10% of wholesale price or 1½¢/word. Sends galleys to author. Free writer's guidelines and book catalog.
Advice: Mostly publishes original fiction in paperback. "Be sure material is culturally authentic and good for the self-concept of the group about whom it is written. Send us only material on Native Americans, make sure it is true to the culture and way of life of a particular tribe at a particular time, and that you don't downgrade any group."

CREATIVE ARTS BOOK CO., (II), 833 Bancroft Way, Berkeley CA 94710. (415)848-4777. Imprints: Creative Arts Communications Books, Creative Arts Life and Health Books and Saturday Night Specials. Editorial Production Manager: Donald Ellis. Estab. 1975. Small independent trade publisher. Publishes hardcover originals and paperback originals and reprints. Average print order: 2,500-10,000; average first novel print order: 2,500-10,000. Published new writers within the last year. Plans 3 first novels this year. Averages 10-20 titles each year.
● Books published by Creative Arts have been finalists for the American Book Award and the press won *Bay Area Focus Magazine's Press of the Year* award in 1990. They've published fiction by William Saroyan, Allen Ginsberg and Aldous Huxley.
Needs: Contemporary, erotica (literary), feminist, historical, literary, mystery/suspense (Saturday night specials), regional, short story collections, translations, western. Publishes anthologies, *Black Lizard Crime Fiction* (Vols. I & II). Recently published *Journey to Paz* by Yoshi Ko Uchida; *Stolen Moments*, by Ed Michael Nagler; *Heaven*, by Al Young.
How to Contact: Accepts unsolicited ms. Submit outline/synopsis and 3 sample chapters (approx. 50 pages). SASE (IRC). Agented fiction 50%. Reports in 2 weeks on queries; 1 month on mss. Simultaneous submissions OK.
Terms: Pays royalties of 7½-15%; average advance of $1,000-10,000; 10 author's copies. Sends galleys to author. Writers guidelines and book catalog for SASE or IRC.

CREATIVE WITH WORDS PUBLICATIONS (II, III), Box 223226, Carmel CA 93922. Editor-in-Chief: Brigitta Geltrich. Estab. 1975. One-woman operation on part-time basis. Books: bond and stock paper; mimeographed printing; saddle stitch binding; illustrations; average print order varies. Publishes paperback anthologies of new and established writers. Averages 2 anthologies each year. *Critiques rejected mss; $10 for short stories; $20 for longer stories, folklore items, $5 for poetry.*
Needs: Humor/satire, juvenile (animal, easy-to-read, fantasy). "Editorial needs center on folkloristic items (according to themes): tall tales and such for annual anthologies." Needs seasonal short stories appealing to general public; "tales" of folklore nature, appealing to all ages, poetry and prose written by children. Recently published anthologies, "The Slavic People," "Christmas Stories" and "Seasons and Holidays." Prose not to exceed 1,000 words.
How to Contact: Accepts unsolicited mss. Query first; submit complete ms (prose no more than 1,000 words) with SASE and cover letter. Reports in 1 month on queries; 2 months on mss. Publishes ms 1-6 months after acceptance. Writer's guidelines (1 oz.) for SASE. No simultaneous submissions.
Terms: Pays in 20% reduced author copies.
Advice: "Our fiction appeals to general public: children-senior citizens. Follow guidelines and rules of *Creative With Words* publications and not those the writer feels CWW should have. We only consider fiction along the lines of folklore or seasonal genres. Be brief, sincere, well-informed and proficient!"

CREATIVITY UNLIMITED PRESS, (II), 30819 Casilina, Rancho Palos Verdes CA 90274. (310)377-7908. Contact: Rochelle Stockwell. Estab. 1980. One-person operation with plans to expand. Publishes paperback originals and self-hypnosis cassette tapes. Books: perfect binding; illustrations; average print order: 1,000; first novel print order 1,000 copies. Averages 1 title (fiction) each year.
Needs: Published *Insides Out*, by Shelley Stockwell (plain talk poetry); *Sex and Other Touchy Subjects*, (poetry and short stories): and *Timetravel: Do-It Yourself Past Life Regression Handbook*.
Advice: Write for more information.

CROSS-CULTURAL COMMUNICATIONS, (IV), 239 Wynsum Ave., Merrick NY 11566-4725.. (516)868-5635. Editorial Director: Stanley H. Barkan. Estab. 1971. "Small/alternative literary arts publisher focusing on the traditionally neglected languages and cultures in bilingual and multimedia format."

Publishes chapbooks, magazines, anthologies, novels, audio cassettes (talking books) and video cassettes (video books, video mags); hardcover and paperback originals. Publishes new women writers series, Holocaust series, Israeli writers series, Dutch writers series, Asian-American writers series.

Needs: Contemporary, literary, experimental, ethnic, humor/satire, juvenile and young adult folktales, and translations. "Main interests: bilingual short stories and children's folktales, parts of novels of authors of other cultures, translations; some American fiction. No fiction that is not directed toward other cultures. For an annual anthology of authors writing in other languages (primarily), we will be seeking very short stories with original-language copy (other than Latin script should be print quality 10/12) on good paper. Title: *Cross Cultural Review Anthology: International Fiction 1.* We expect to extend our *CCR* series to include 10 fiction issues: *Five Contemporary* (Dutch, Swedish, Yiddish, Norwegian, Danish, Yugoslav, Sicilian, Greek, Israeli, etc.) *Fiction Writers.*" Recently published *Sicilian Origin of the Odyssey*, by L.G. Pocock (bilingual English-Italian translations by Nat Scamacca); *Sikano Americano!* and *Bye Bye America*, by Nat Scammacca.

How to Contact: Accepts unsolicited mss. Query with SAE with $1 postage to include book catalog. "Note: Original language ms should accompany translations." Simultaneous submissions OK. Reports in 1 month.

Terms: Pays "sometimes" 10-25% in royalties and "occasionally" by outright purchase, in author's copies—"10% of run for chapbook series," and "by arrangement for other publications." No advance.

Advice: "Write because you want to or you must; satisfy yourself. If you've done the best you can, then you've succeeded. You will find a publisher and an audience eventually. Generally, we have a greater interest in nonfiction novels and translations. Short stories and excerpts from novels written in one of the traditional neglected languages are preferred—with the original version (i.e., bilingual). Our kinderbook series will soon be in production with a similar bilingual emphasis, especially for folktales, fairy tales, and fables."

‡CRYSTAL RIVER PRESS, P.O. Box 1382, Healdsburg CA 95448. Publisher/Editor-in-Chief: Thomas Watson. Midsize independent childrens and young adult publisher. Publishes hardcover and paperback originals and paperback reprints. Books: 80 lb. coated paper; offset printing; case and paper bound binding; average print order: 2,000-5,000. Averages 12-15 total titles, 9 fiction titles each year. Sometimes comments on rejected ms; *charges $15/short stories 3,000 words; $30 longer ms.*

Needs: Children's/juvenile, young adult/teen (10-18 years). Looking for environmental adventure—culture folklore. Publishes young adult shorts. Writers may submit to anthology editor. Publishes *Mr. Crowfeather* (Indian subject folklore based); *The Peach Street Kids* (adventures of friends various cultural backgrounds); *The Mountain* (environmental fantasy) series. All children's subjects covered.

How to Contact: Accepts unsolicited mss. Query first then submit outline/synopsis and 3 sample chapters. Include estimated word count and bio. SASE for reply to query or return of ms. Agented fiction 15-30%. Reports in 2 weeks on queries; 4-6 weeks on mss. Simultaneous submissions OK.

Terms: Pays royalties of 8-10% minimum; 15% maximum. Average advance $800. Provides 30 author's copies. Sends galleys to author. Publishes ms 8-10 months after acceptance. Writer's guidelines for #10 SAE and 1 first class stamp.

HARRY CUFF PUBLICATIONS LTD., (IV), 94 LeMarchant Rd., St. John's, Newfoundland A1C 2H2 Canada. (709)726-6590. Editor: Harry Cuff. Estab. 1981. "Small regional publisher specializing in Newfoundlandia." Publishes paperback originals. Books: offset printing; perfect binding; average print order: 1,000; first novel print order: 800. Averages 12 total titles, 1 fiction each year.

Needs: "Either about Newfoundland, or by a Newfoundlander, or both. No mainstream or erotica." Published *Collected Works of A.R. Scammell* (short story collection) and *Princes*, by Tom Finn (short story collection).

How to Contact: Accepts unsolicited mss. Submit outline/synopsis and 3 sample chapters. SASE (IRC) necessary for return of ms. Reports in 1 month on queries; 3-5 months on mss. Accepts electronic submissions via disk (query first).

Terms: Pays royalties of 10% minimum. Sends galleys to author. Publishes ms 6-18 months after acceptance. Writer's guidelines and book catalog free.

Advice: "I would like to see more good fiction, period, but it *has* to be about Newfoundland or by a Newfoundlander (note that these are entirely discrete categories) I don't want any more mss about the Vietnam War or running a radio station in Kansas City or the like! Our readers will not buy that from us."

*DAN RIVER PRESS, (I,II), Conservatory of American Letters, Box 88, Thomaston ME 04861. (207)354-0998. President: Robert Olmsted. Fiction Editor: R.S. Danbury III. Estab. 1976. Publishes hardcover and paperback originals. Books: 60 lb. offset paper; offset printing; perfect (paperback); hardcover binding; illustrations; average print order: 1,000; first novel print order: 1,000. Published new writers within the past year. Averages 4-5 total titles; 3 fiction titles last year.
Needs: Adventure, contemporary, experimental, fantasy, historical, horror, humor/satire, literary, mainstream, military/war, psychic/supernatural/occult, regional, science fiction, short story collections, western. "We want good fiction that can't find a home in the big press world. No mindless stuff written flawlessly." Recently published *Bound*, by William Hoffman, (novel); *Blue Collar and Other Stories*, by Tom Laird (short story collection); *The Dreams are Dying*, by Everett Whealdon.
How to Contact: Accepts unsolicited mss, but get guidelines. Large SASE please.
Terms: Pays $250 cash advance (minimum) on acceptance; 10% royalties on 1,000 copies, then 15%. Sends galleys to author. After acceptance, publication "depends on many things (funding, etc.). Probably in six months once funding is achieved." Writer's guidelines for #10 SAE and 2 first class stamps. Book catalog for 6x9 SAE and 2 first class stamps.
Advice: "Submit to us (and any other small press) when you have exhausted all hope for big press publication. Then, do not expect the small press to be a big press. We lack the resources to do things like 'promotion,' 'author's tours.' These things either go undone or are done by the author. When you give up on marketability of any novel submitted to small press, adopt a different attitude. Become humble, as you get to work on your second/next novel, grow, correct mistakes and create an audience. Remember . . . logic dictates that a small press can *not* market successfully. If they could, they'd be a large press, with no time for unknowns."

JOHN DANIEL AND COMPANY, PUBLISHERS, (I, II), Box 21922, Santa Barbara CA 93121. (805)962-1780. Fiction Editor: John Daniel. Estab. 1980/reestablished 1985. Small publisher with plans to expand. Publishes paperback originals. Books: 55-65 lb. book text paper; offset printing; perfect bound paperbacks; illustrations sometimes; average print order: 2,000; first novel print order: 2,000. Plans 2 first novels this year. Averages 5 total titles, 2-3 fiction titles each year. Sometimes critiques rejected ms.
Needs: "I'm open to all subjects (including nonfiction)." Literary, mainstream, short story collections. No pornographic, exploitive, illegal, or badly written fiction. Recently published *The Tall Uncut*, by Pete Fromm (stories); *Winter Return*, by John Espey (novel); and *The Year of the Buck*, by Susan Harper (stories), published new writers within the last year.
How to Contact: Accepts unsolicited mss. Query first. SASE. Submit outline/synopsis and 2 sample chapters. Reports in 3 weeks on queries; 2 months on mss. Simultaneous submissions OK.
Terms: Pays in royalties of 10% of net minimum. Sends galleys to author.
Advice: Encourages first novelists. "As an acquiring editor, I would never sign a book unless I were willing to publish it in its present state. Once the book is signed, though, I, as a developmental editor, would do hard labor to make the book everything it could become. Read a lot, write a lot, and stay in contact with other artists so you won't burn out from this, the loneliest profession in the world."

*MAY DAVENPORT PUBLISHERS, (I, II, IV), 26313 Purissima Rd., Los Altos Hills CA 94022. (415)948-6499. Editor/Publisher: May Davenport. Estab. 1975. One-person operation with independent subcontractors. Publishes hardcover and paperback originals. Books: 65-80 lb. paper; off-set printing; perfect binding/saddle stitch/plastic spirals; line drawing illustrations; average print order 500-3,000; average first novel print order: 3,000. Plans 1-3 first novels this year. Averages 3-5 total titles/year (including coloring books/reprints); 2-5 fiction titles/year. Sometimes critiques rejected mss.
Needs: "Overstocked with picture book mss. Prefer drama for junior and senior high students. Don't preach. Entertain!" Recently published *The Rebus Escape*, by Ray J. Lum; *Sumo, The Wrestling Elephant*, by Esther Y.P. Mok; *Leroy, the Lizard*, by Claudia Cherness (a coloring book).
How to Contact: Query first with SASE. Agented fiction 2%. Reports in 2-3 weeks.
Terms: Pays royalties of 10-15%; no advance. Sends galleys to author. "Partial subsidy whenever possible in advance sales of 3,000 copies, which usually covers the printing and binding costs only. The authors are usually teachers in school districts who have a special book of fiction or textbook relating to literature." Writer's guidelines free with your SASE.
Advice: "If you are print-oriented, remember the TV-oriented are not literate. They prefer visuals and verbalizing to writing. Personal tip: Combat illiteracy by creating material which will motivate children/young adults to enjoy words and actions. Write a play for this junior/senior high age. They will read anything which they think they can participate in dramatically for themselves. If you can't write a play, forget it. Try writing stories with social values for coloring books. It's how you use your

literary tools of expression that might impress future writers of literature."

DAWNWOOD PRESS, (III, IV), Fifth Floor, 387 Park Ave. South, New York NY 10016-8810. (212)532-7160. Fax: (212)213-2495. President: Kathryn Drayton. Fiction Editor: John Welch. Estab. 1984. Publishes hardcover originals. Books: 60 lb. Lakewood-white paper; offset litho printing; adhesive case binding; average print order: 5,000. Averages 1 fiction title each year.
Needs: Contemporary. "Our needs are taken care of for the next 2 years." No experimental. Published *History's Trickiest Questions*, by Paul Kuttner (history); *Killing Love*, by Paul Kuttner.
How to Contact: Does not accept unsolicited mss. Submit through agent only. Reports in 2 weeks on queries; 2 weeks on mss. Simultaneous submissions OK.
Terms: Advance negotiable. Sends galleys to author.
Advice: "Same advice since Dickens's days: Tell a story from the opening sentence in easily understood English, and if you must philosophize do so through action and colloquial dialogue."

*DAYSPRING PRESS, INC., (I,II), Box 135, Golden CO 80401. (303)279-2462. Editor: John C. Brainerd. Estab. 1984. "Fourteen-person 'little literary' and 'religious' operation on fulltime basis; 5 periodicals, tracts and paperbacks." Books: 20 lb. Cascade Bond Xerographic; photo offset printing; staple, spiral, perfect case-bound; b&w illustrations; average print order: 1,000; first novel print order: 500. Published new writers within the last year. Plans 12 first novels this year. Plans 16 fiction titles this year. Sometimes critiques rejected ms. "I would not reject any material categorically. Purposefully violent, scandalous and pejorative material would have to have very definite counter values."
  • Dayspring Press also publishes *New Anglican Review* and *New Catholic Review* listed in this book.
Needs: Sci-fi, period, and contemporary genre. Recently published *Gregory's Tide*, by Bobbie Daniels; *Housewives Around*, by Claire O'Malley; and *Pass a Billie*, by Dirk S. Cobb.
How to Contact: Accepts unsolicited mss. Submit complete ms with cover letter. Include SASE with submission. Reports in 1 month.
Terms: 50% net. Publishes ms 90 days after acceptance. Writer's guidelines for #10 SAE and 1 first class stamp. Catalog for $2.75.
Advice: "I would like to see more poignant trading in the hardcore human issues and less distraction in the trivial."

THE DRAGONSBREATH PRESS, (IV), 10905 Bay Shore Dr., Sister Bay WI 54234. Editor: Fred Johnson. Estab. 1973. One-man operation on part-time basis. Publishes paperback and hardback originals in small editions as handmade books. Books: varied paper; letterpress printing; hand binding; illustrations.
Needs: Contemporary, literary, experimental, erotica, science fiction, fantasy, and humor/satire. "NO NOVELS, but rather single short stories."
How to Contact: "We are not currently accepting any unsolicited mss." Query and when requested send complete ms with SASE. Simultaneous submissions OK. Reports in 1 month on queries, 2 months on mss. "Always include a cover letter and SASE."
Terms: Negotiates terms. No advance. "Since we are a small press, we prefer to work cooperatively, sharing the work and expenses between the author and the press. We are not a 'vanity press' ."
Advice: "This is a small press working with the book as an art form producing handmade limited-edition books combining original artwork with original writing. Since we work with hand-set type and have limited time and money, we prefer shorter writing suited to handwork and illustrating. We are not a typical publishing house; books would have limited distribution, mainly to art and book collectors. We are now also looking for regional (Wisconsin) writing for a regional magazine the press has begun publishing entitled *The Door County Alamanak*. Always include cover letter with brief description of story."

DUNDURN PRESS, (II), 2181 Queen St. E., #301, Toronto, Ontario M4L 1E5 Canada. (416)698-0454. Editorial Contact Person: Kirk Howard. Estab. 1972. Midsize independent publisher with plans to expand. Publishes hardcover and paperback originals. "We do not as yet publish fiction, but intend to start in 1992 or 1993."

Needs: Contemporary.
How to Contact: Accepts unsolicited mss. Submit outline/synopsis and sample chapters. SASE for ms. Simultaneous submissions OK. Accepts electronic submissions.
Terms: Pays royalties of 10-15%; $1,000 average advance; 10 author's copies. Sends galleys to author. Publishes ms 6-9 months after acceptance. Writer's guidelines not available. Book catalog free on request for SASE.

‡E.M. PRESS, INC., (I, II), P.O. Box 4057, Manassas VA 22110. (703)368-9828. Editor: Beth Miller. Estab. 1991. "Small, traditional publishing company." Publishes paperback originals. Books: 50 lb. text paper; offset printing; perfect binding; illustrations; average print order: 1,200-5,000. Averages 3 (all fiction) total titles. If requested comments on rejected ms.
Needs: Adventure, childrens/juvenile, family saga, fantasy, horror, humor/satire, literary, mainstream/contemporary, military/war, mystery/suspense, romance, thriller/espionage. Recently published *The Twisted Star*, by Don Lo Cicero (general); *Some Brief Cases of Inspector Alec Stuart of Scotland Yard*, by Archibald C. Wagner, MD (mystery).
How to Contact: Accepts unsolicited mss. Submit outline/synopsis and sample chapters or complete ms with cover letter. Include estimated word count. Send a SASE (or IRC) for reply, return of ms or send a disposable copy of the ms. Agented fiction 10%. Reports in 1 month on queries; 2 months on mss. Simultaneous submissions OK.
Terms: Amount of royalties and advances vary. Sends galleys to author. Publishes ms 4-9 months after acceptance. Writer's guidelines for SASE.

‡EARTH-LOVE PUBLISHING HOUSE, (IV), B4-111, 8031 Wadsworth Blvd., Arvada CO 80003. (303)420-1743. Fax: (303)431-2891. Director: Laodeciae Augustine. Estab. 1989. Small publisher. Publishes paperback originals and reprints. Books: 60 lb. paper; offset printing; sew and wrap binding; halftone illustrations; average print order: 5,000; first novel print order: 5,000. Averages 2 total titles, 1 fiction title each year. Often comments on rejected mss.
Needs: Adventure, mystery/suspense (amateur sleuth), new age/mystic/spiritual, metaphysical adventure.
How to Contact: Does not accept unsolicited mss. Query first. Include estimated word count and list of publishing credits with submission. SASE. Reports in 3 weeks on queries; 5 weeks on mss. Simultaneous submissions OK. Accepts electronic (disk) submissions.
Terms: Pays royalties of 8% minimum; 12% maximum or 10% of run for author's copies. Publishes ms 6-10 months after acceptance.

THE ECCO PRESS, (II), 100 West Broad St., Hopewell NJ 08525. (212)645-2214. Editor-in-Chief: Daniel Halpern. Estab. 1970. Small publisher. Publishes hardcover and paperback originals and reprints. Books: acid-free paper; offset printing; Smythe-sewn binding; occasional illustrations. Averages 25 total titles, 10 fiction titles each year. Average first novel print order 3,000 copies.
  ● Ecco Press publishes the prestigious literary, *Antaeus*, listed in this book.
Needs: Literary and short story collections. "We can publish possibly one or two original novels a year." No science fiction, romantic novels, western (cowboy). Recently published: *Where Is Here*, by Joyce Carol Oates; *Have You Seen Me*, by Elizabeth Graver; *Coming Up Down South*, by Cecil Brown.
How to Contact: Accepts unsolicited mss. Query first, especially on novels, with SASE. Reports in 2 to 3 months, depending on the season.
Terms: Pays in royalties. Advance is negotiable. Writer's guidelines for SASE. Book catalog free on request.
Advice: "We are always interested in first novels and feel it's important that they be brought to the attention of the reading public."

THE EIGHTH MT. PRESS, (II, IV), 624 SE 29th Ave., Portland OR 97214. (503)233-3936. Publisher: Ruth Gundle. Estab. 1984. One-person operation on full-time basis. Publishes paperback originals. Books: acid-free paper, perfect-bound; average print order: 5,000. Averages 2 total titles, 1 fiction title, each year.
Needs: Books written only by women. Ethnic, feminist, lesbian, literary, short story collections. Published *Cows and Horses*, by Barbara Wilson (feminist/literary).
How to Contact: Accepts unsolicited mss. Query first. SASE. Reports on queries in 2 weeks; on mss in 3 weeks.
Terms: Pays royalties of 8-10%. Sends galleys to author. Publishes ms within 1 year of acceptance.

‡EVERGREEN PUBLICATIONS, (II, IV), P.O. Box 220, Davison MI 48423. (313)658-1143. Publisher: Mary Beckwith. Estab. 1988. "Small independent book publisher." Publishes trade paperback originals. Books: 60 lb. offset paper; offset printing; perfect binding; average print order: 7,500. Published new writers within the last year. Plans 2 first novels this year. Averges 8 total titles, 2 fiction titles each year.
  • *Time Out!*, a book published by Evergreen Publications, won a Benjamin Franklin Award for Excellence in Independent Publishing in 1990.
Needs: Religious/inspirational (Christian), young adult/teen (10-18) (adventure, mystery/suspense). Plans poetry anthology. Recently published *Dear Suzanne*, by Sandra Bricker (adult); *Bloom Where You're Planted*, by Matilda Nordvedt (juvenile); *The First Day's the Hardest*, by Matilda Nordtvedt (juvenile). Publishes "Sarah" series.
How to Contact: Accepts unsolicited submissions. Submit outline/synopsis and 3 sample chapters. Include estimated word count, one page bio and list of publishing credits. SASE for a reply to query or return of ms. Reports in 6-8 weeks. Simultaneous submissions OK.
Terms: Pays royalties of 12%. Average advance $500. Sends galleys to author. Writer's guidelines for #10 SAE and 2 first class stamps. Book catalogs for #10 SAE and 2 first class stamps.
Advice: "Today Christian markets are more open to fiction. Please *read* and *observe* guidelines for proposing manuscripts to publishers."

FABER AND FABER, INC., (I, II), 50 Cross St., Winchester MA 01890. Small trade house which publishes literary fiction and collections. Averages 4-6 fiction titles each year.
Needs: Literary. No mystery/romances/thrillers/juvenile, please. Allow two months for response. Recently published *Higher Math*, by Jennifer Ball; *Flying Lessons*, by Susan Johnson; *Songs of the the Humpback Whale*, by Jodi Picoult; *The Loop*, by Joe Coomer.
How to Contact: "Prefer query and one or two sample chapters with SASE for reply. Require synopsis/description—cannot consider ms without this. Address to Editorial Assistant.
Advice: "Accepting very little original fiction at present."

FASA CORPORATION, (II, IV), 1026 West Van Buren, Chicago IL 60607. Editor: Donna Ippolito. "Company responsible for science fiction, adventure games, to include adventures, scenarios, game designs and novels, for an audience high school age and up." Published new writers within the last year.
Needs: Adventure, science fiction. Publishes ms an average of 9 months to 1 year after acceptance. Occasionally critiques or comments on rejected ms. Recommends other markets.
How to Contact: Query first. Reports in 2-6 weeks. Simultaneous submissions OK. Accepts electronic submissions via IBM ASCII or Macintosh disks.
Terms: Pays on publication for all rights. Sends galleys to author.
Advice: "Be familiar with our product and always ask about suitability before plunging into a big piece of work that I may not be able to use."

THE FEMINIST PRESS AT THE CITY UNIVERSITY OF NEW YORK, 311 East 94 St., New York NY 10128. (212)360-5790. Publisher: Florence Howe. Estab. 1970. "Nonprofit, tax-exempt, education organization interested in changing the curriculum, the classroom and consciousness." Publishes hardcover and paperback reprints. "We use a fine quality paper, perfect bind our books, four color covers; and some cloth for library sales if the book has been out of print for some time; we shoot from the original text when possible. We always include a scholarly and literary afterword, since we are introducing a text to a new audience; average print run: 4,000." Publishes no original fiction. Averages 12 total titles/year; 4-6 fiction titles/year (reprints of feminist classics only).

Market categories: (I) Open to new writers; (II) Open to both new and established writers; (III) Interested mostly in established writers; (IV) Open to writers whose work is specialized.

Needs: Contemporary, ethnic, feminist, gay, lesbian, literary, regional, science fiction, translations, women's.
How to Contact: Accepts unsolicited mss. Query first. Submit outline/synopsis and 1 sample chapter. SASE (IRC). Reports in 2 weeks on queries; 2 months on mss. Simultaneous submissions OK.
Terms: Pays royalties of 10% of net sales; $100 advance; 10 author's copies. Sends galleys to author. Book catalog free on request.

FICTION COLLECTIVE TWO, Publications Center Campus, Box 494, University of Colorado, Boulder CO 80309-0494. Did not respond.

‡FIFTH HOUSE PUBLISHERS, (I), 620 Duchess St., Saskatoon, Saskatchewan 57L 5V6 Canada. (306)242-4936. Fax: (306)242-7667. Managing Editor: Charlene Dobmeier. Estab. 1982. "Mid-size independent Canadian publisher." Publishes hardcover originals and reprints and paperback originals and reprints. Plans 1 first novel this year. Averages 14 total titles, 2-3 fiction titles each year.
Needs: Ethnic/multicultural (native), historical (general), literary, mainstream/contemporary. Recently published *Silent Words*, by Ruby Slipperjack (adult/young adult novel); *How Do You Spell Beautiful*, by Patrick Lane (short story); *Upstream*, by Sharon Butala (adult novel).
How to Contact: Accepts unsolicited mss. Submit outline/synopsis and 2-3 sample chapters. Include estimated word count and list of publishing credits. SASE for a reply to query or return of ms. Reports in 2 months.
Terms: Pays in royalties and advance depending on the book. Sends galleys to author. Publishes book 8-12 months after acceptance. Writer's guidelines for SASE. Books catalogs 8×10 SASE.
Advice: "We would like to continue expanding our fiction list with Canadian Native authors. We are more interested in novels than short fiction."

‡FIRE ISLAND PRESS, (II, IV), Liberation Inc., Room 203B, 89 Robin Lane, Fairfield CT 06430-3939. (203)330-9596. President: Joseph Letendre. Estab. 1991. "Three-person operation." Publishes paperback originals. Books: 50 lb. paper; perfect binding; average print order: 4,000. Plans 4 first novels this year. Averages 6 titles, all fiction. Sometimes comments on rejected mss.
 • Liberation Inc.'s other imprints include Lavender Press, Marie's Books, McKnight Books and J & P Books, also listed in this section.
Needs: Erotica (gay and lesbian). Especially "a need for lesbian erotica. No S & M." Recently published *Flesh Fable*, by Aaron Travis (gay erotica) and *Bitter Beauties*, by Tripp Vandertord (gay erotica).
How to Contact: Does not accept unsolicited mss. Submit outline/synopsis and 3 sample chapters. Include estimated word count. SASE. Reports in 2 months. Simultaneous submissions OK.
Terms: Pays royalties of 10% minimum; 25% maximum. Average advance: $250. Sends galleys to author. Book catalog free.
Advice: "The demand for erotica has increased, I believe, due to the crisis of AIDS."

FIREBRAND BOOKS, (II), 141 The Commons, Ithaca NY 14850. (607)272-0000. Contact: Nancy K. Bereano. Estab. 1985. Publishes quality trade paperback originals. Averages 8-10 total titles each year.
Needs: Feminist, lesbian. Recently published *Cecile*, by Ruthann Robson (short stories); *The Gilda Stories*, by Jewelle Gomez (novel).
How to Contact: Accepts unsolicited mss. Submit outline/synopsis and sample chapters or send complete ms with cover letter. SASE. Reports in 2 weeks on queries; 2 months on mss. Simultaneous submissions OK with notification.
Terms: Pays royalties.

1st AMENDMENT PUBLISHERS INC., (IV), P.O. Box 9222, Santa Fe NM 87504. (505)988-4838. Editor: Allen A. Nysse. Fiction Editor: Dawn-Marie Peterson. Estab. 1989. New mid-size independent publisher with plans to expand. Publishes hardcover and paperback originals and paperback reprints. Books: 50 lb. Lakewood, 444PPI paper; belt press printing; adhesive case binding; b&w illustrations; average print order: 3,000; first novel print order: 3,000. Published new writers within the last year. Plans 1 first novel this year. Averages 3 total titles, 2 fiction titles per year. Sometimes comments on rejected manuscripts.
Needs: Historical, literary, mainstream, military/war. Looking for novels that "encourage the reader to think about moral, social and philosophical problems; those that point out evils in society and challenge the reader to seek social and /or political reforms. Does not want to see "anything negative or with degenerating moral tendency, and all self-serving fiction." Published *America Within*, by Allen Nyssc (psychological novel).

How to Contact: Accepts unsolicited manuscripts. Query first, then send outline/synopsis and 3 sample chapters. SASE. Reports in 6 weeks on queries; 3 months on mss. Accepts simultaneous submissions.
Terms: Pays royalties of 2-10%; 100 contributor's copies. Publishes manuscripts 6-18 months after acceptance.

*FLORIDA LITERARY FOUNDATION PRESS, (II), distributed by Woldt Corp., 2516 Ridge Ave., Sarasota FL 34235. (813)957-1281. Chairman: Virginia G. McClintock. Fiction Editor: Patrick J. Powers. Estab. 1989. "Nonprofit literary foundation." Publishes paperback originals. Books: quality trade paper. Averages 4-5 total titles, 1 anthology fiction title each year. Sometimes comments on rejected ms.
● Woldt Corp. also distributes books by Starbooks listed in this book.
Needs: Literary. "Quality work on any subject—nothing clichéd." Recently published *Shells: Monuments to Life*, by M. John Childrey (anthology of short stories and poetry); *Moving Mother Out*, by Joanne Childers (poetry).
How to Contact: SASE. Submit outline/synopsis and sample chapters. SASE. Reports in 1 month on queries; 6 weeks on mss. Simultaneous submissions OK. Accepts electronic submissions.
Terms: Provides 10-50 author's copies, honorarium; payment depends on grant/award money. Individual arrangement with author depending on the book. Will consider subsidy publishing. Sends galleys to author. Publishes ms 6-8 months after acceptance. Writer's guidelines free.

FOUR WALLS EIGHT WINDOWS, Box 548, Village Station, New York NY 10014. (212)206-8965. Co-Publishers: John Oakes/Dan Simon. Estab. 1986. "We are a small independent publisher." Publishes hardcover and paperback originals and paperback reprints. Books: quality paper; paper or cloth binding; illustrations sometimes; average print order: 3,000-5,000; first novel print order: 3,000-5,000. Averages 20 total titles/year; approximately 7-8 fiction titles/year.
How to Contact: "Query letter accompanied by sample chapter and SASE is best. Useful to know if writer has published elsewhere, and if so, where." Accepts unsolicited mss. Submit outline/synopsis and 1 sample chapter. SASE (IRC). Agented fiction 70%. Reports in 2 months on mss. Simultaneous submissions OK.
Terms: Pays standard royalties; advance varies. Sends galleys to author. Book catalog free on request.

GAY SUNSHINE PRESS AND LEYLAND PUBLICATIONS, (IV), P.O. Box 410690, San Francisco CA 94141. (707)996-6082. Editor: Winston Leyland. Estab. 1970. Publishes hardcover and paperback originals. Books: natural paper; perfect-bound; illustrations; average print order: 5,000-10,000.
Needs: Literary, experimental and translations—all gay male material only. "We desire fiction on gay themes of *high* literary quality and prefer writers who have already had work published in literary magazines. We also publish erotica—short stories and novels." Published *Crystal Boys*, by Pai Hsienyung (novel).
How to Contact: "Do not send an unsolicited manuscript." Query with SASE. Reports in 3 weeks on queries, 2 months on mss. Send $1 for catalog.
Terms: Negotiates terms with author. Sends galleys to author. Royalties or outright purchase.
Advice: "We continue to be interested in receiving queries from authors who have book length manuscripts of high literary quality. We feel it is important that an author know exactly what to expect from our press (promotion, distribution etc.) before a contract is signed. Before submitting a query or manuscript to a particular press, obtain critical feedback from knowledgeable people on your manuscript, e.g. a friend who teaches college English. If you alienate a publisher by submitting a manuscript shoddily prepared/typed, or one needing very extensive re-writing, or one which is not in the area of the publisher's specialty, you will surely not get a second chance with that press."

GOOSE LANE EDITIONS, (I, II, IV), 361 Queen St., Fredericton, New Brunswick E3B 1B1 Canada. (506)450-4251. Acquisitions Editor: Laurel Boone. Estab. 1957. Publishes hardcover and paperback originals and occasional reprints. Books: some illustrations, average print run: 2,000; first novel print order: 1,500. Averages 12 total titles, 2-4 fiction, each year. Sometimes critiques rejected mss.
● For more on Goose Lane, see the close-up interview with managing editor Susanne Alexander in the 1992 *Writer's Market*.
Needs: Contemporary, historical, literary, short story collections. "Not suitable for mainstream or mass-market submissions." Recently published *Fadimatu*, by Jennifer Mitton (novel); *Mumsahib*, by Anne Montagnes (novel in stories); *The Last Tasmanian*, by Herb Curtis (novel).

How to Contact: Accepts unsolicited mss; complete work, or "samples." Query first. SASE "with Canadian stamps, International Reply Coupons, cash, check or money order. No US stamps please." Reports in 6 months. Simultaneous submissions OK.
Terms: *"Only mss from Canada."* Pays royalties of 8% minimum; 12% maximum. Average advance: $100-200, negotiable. Sends galleys to author. Writers guidelines for 9x12 SAE and IRCs.

GRAYWOLF PRESS, (III), 2402 University Ave., St. Paul MN 55114. (612)641-0077. Publisher: Scott Walker. Estab. 1974. Growing small press, nonprofit corporation. Publishes hardcover and paperback originals and paperback reprints. Books: acid-free quality paper; offset printing; hardcover and soft binding; illustrations occasionally; average print order: 3,000-10,000; first novel print order: 2,000-6,000. Averages 18-20 total titles, 6-8 fiction titles each year. Occasionally critiques rejected ms. No genre books (romance, western, suspense).
   • Graywolf Press books have won numerous awards. Most recently, *Cloud Street*, by Tim Winton received the Australian Miles Franklin Award; *Licorice*, by Abby Frucht received Quality Paperback Book's New Voices Award and *Skywater*, by Melinda Worth Popham received *Buzzworm*'s Edward Abbey Award. The press has recently started the Graywolf Discovery Series featuring reprint paperbacks of out-of-print "gems."
Needs: Literary, and short story collections. Published *The Last Studebaker*, by Robin Hemley (novel); *The Secret of Cartwheels*, by Patricia Henley (short stories); *Cloudstreet*, by Tim Winton (novel).
How to Contact: Query with SASE. Reports in 2 weeks. Simultaneous submissions OK.
Terms: Pays in royalties of 7½-10%; negotiates advance and number of author's copies. Sends galleys to author. Free book catalog.

GRIFFON HOUSE PUBLICATIONS, Box 81, Whitestone NY 11357. (212)767-8380. President: Frank D. Grande. Estab. 1976. Small press. Publishes paperback originals and reprints.
Needs: Contemporary, literary, experimental, ethnic (open), translations, reprints, and multinational theory.
How to Contact: Query with SASE. No simultaneous submissions. Reports in 1 month on queries, 6 weeks on mss.
Terms: Pays in 6 free author's copies. No advance.

‡GRYPHON PUBLICATIONS, (I, II), Imprints include Gryphon Books, Gryphon Doubles, P.O. Box 209, Brooklyn NY 11228. (718)646-6126 (after 6 pm EST). Owner/Editor: Gary Lovisi. Estab. 1983. "Small press." Publishes hardcover and paperback originals and paperback reprints. Books: bond paper; offset printing; perfect binding; average print order: 500-1,000. Published new writers within the last year. Plans 2 first novels this year. Averages 5-10 total titles, 4-8 fiction titles each year. Often comments on rejected ms.
Needs: Adventure, experimental, horror (psychological), mystery/suspense (private eye/hardboiled, crime and true crime), science fiction (hard science/technological, soft/sociological, short story collections, thriller/espionage. No romance, westerns. Plans anthology of hardboiled crime fiction. Authors may submit story. Recently published *The Dreaming Detective*, by Ralph Vaughn (mystery-fantasy-horror); *The Woman in the Dugout*, by Gary Lovisi and T. Arnone (baseball novel); *A Mate for Murder*, by Bruno Fischer (hardboiled pulp). Publishes Gryphon Double novel series.
How to Contact: Accepts unsolicited mss. Submit outline/synopsis and sample chapters or complete ms with cover letter. Include estimated word count, bio (50 words), short list of publishing credits, how they heard about us. Send SASE for reply, return of ms or send a disposable copy of the ms. Agented fiction 5-10%. Reports in 2-4 weeks on queries; 2-6 weeks on mss. Simultaneous and electronic submissions OK (with hard copy—disk in ASCII).
Terms: For magazines, $5-25 on publication plus 2 contributor's copies; for novels/collections payment varies and is much more. Usually sends galleys to author. Publishes ms 6 months-2 years after acceptance. Writers guidelines and book catalog for SASE.
Advice: "I am looking for better and better writing, more cutting-edge material with *impact*! Keep it lean and focused."

GUERNICA EDITIONS, (III, IV), 3160 Avenue de Carignan, Montréal, Québec H1N 2Y5 Canada. Editor: Antonio D'Alfonso. Fiction Editor: Umberto Claudio. Editor for women's books: Julia Gualtieri. Estab. 1978. Publishes paperback originals. Books: offset printing; perfect/sewn binding; average print order: 1,000; average first novel print order: 1,000. Plans to publish 1 first novel this year. Publishes 16-20 total titles each year.

Needs: Contemporary, ethnic, literary, translations of foreign novels. Looking for novels about women and ethnic subjects. No unsolicited works. Published *Bittersweet Pieces: Dutch Short Stories*, edited by Gerrie Bussink; *Infertility Rites*, by Mary Melfi; *The Tangible Word*, by France Thêoret.
How to Contact: Does not accept or return unsolicited mss. Query first. IRC. 100% of fiction is agented. Reports in 6 months. Electronic submissions via IBM WordPerfect disks.
Terms: Pays royalties of 7-10% and 10 author's copies. Book catalog for SAE and $2 postage. (Canadian stamps only).
Advice: Publishing "more pocket books."

*GUYASUTA PUBLISHER, (I,II), Subsidiary of Lee Shore Agency, Sterling Bldg., 440 Friday Rd., Pittsburgh PA 15209. (412)821-6211. Imprint is One Foot on the Mountain Press. Acquisitions Manager: Anna Aivaliotis. Fiction Editor: Trinette Kern. Estab. 1988. Publishes paperback originals. Books: offset printing; perfect-bound; illustrations; average print order: 750. Published new writers within the last year. Plans 4 first novels this year. Averages 30 total titles, 2 fiction titles each year. Sometimes comments on rejected ms.
Needs: Contemporary, erotica, short story collections. No "historical romances, experimental fiction, anything over 65,000 words." Recently published *Waltzing Through the Forbidden Forest*, by Tony Bowler (humor/satire).
How to Contact: Accepts unsolicited mss. Query first. SASE. Reports in 2 weeks on queries; 3 months on mss. Simultaneous submissions OK.
Terms: Pays royalties of 7% maximum. "We make individual arrangements with authors depending on the book. We do straight publishing and cooperative publishing. We send out press releases, include books in catalog, market mainly through mail and book conventions." Sends galleys to author. Publishes ms 6-9 months after acceptance. Writer's guidelines and book catalog for 4×9 SAE and 1 first class stamp.
Advice: "When submitting a manuscript do not send us your first draft. We will reject it. Work on your story, give it time to evolve. Read fiction and how-to books. Please type, double space and use healthy margins."

*HAYPENNY PRESS, (I), 211 New St., West Paterson NJ 07424. Estab. 1988. "Small independent publisher with plans to expand." Publishes paperback originals. Books: offset and/or mimeo printing; perfect binding. Published new writers within the last year. Plans 2-4 first novels this year. Averages 2-3 titles (all fiction). Sometimes comments on rejected ms. "No charge for comments . . . *for detailed (separate) critique: $25 (for ms under 200 pages.)*"
Needs: Contemporary, ethnic, experimental, fantasy, humor/satire, literary, mainstream, military/war, regional, science fiction, short story collections, young adult/teen (10-18 years) easy-to-read and problem novels. No horror, pornography or formula stories. Published *Cooper Street*, by P.D. Jordan (y/a).
How to Contact: Does not accept unsolicited mss. Query first (always!!). Include SASE. Reports in 2 weeks on queries; 1 month on ms.
Terms: Pays by "individual arrangement. Cooperative situations possible." Publishes ms up to 1 year after acceptance. Writer's guidelines for #10 SASE and 1 first class stamp.
Advice: "Prefer to work with authors who have a specific purpose/market/audience (ie: counselors at runaway shelters; teachers of literacy programs; etc.). The competition in 'general' markets is fierce and authors are expected to do all they can to help promote their work. We are open to suggestions/arrangements, if the work merits publication. Y/A writers: project something useful to your teen audience without being "preachy." Others: offbeat, unusual is fine . . . main criteria is to be good/original enough to stand out . . . Please no five-step plots or outlines."

*‡HEAVEN BONE PRESS, (II), 86 Whispering Hills Dr., Chester NY 10918. (914)469-9018. Editor: Steve Hirsch. Estab. 1986. "Literary publisher." Publishes paperback originals. Books: paper varies; saddle or perfect binding; average print order: 2,000. Averages 4 total titles, 1 fiction title each year. Sometimes comments on rejected ms.
• See the listing for *Heaven Bone* magazine in this book.
Needs: Experimental, literary, new age/mystic spiritual, psychic/supernatural, science fiction (hard science/technological, soft/sociological).
How to Contact: Accepts unsolicited mss. Query first. Include estimated word count, short bio, list of publishing credits. SASE. Agented fiction 10%. Reports in 1 month on queries; 6 months on mss. No simultaneous submissions. Accepts electronic submissions.

Terms: Pays author's copies (10% of press run); depends on grant/award money. "We also do cooperative arrangements or individual arrangement with author." Sends galleys to author. Publishes ms up to 18 months after acceptance. Writer's guidelines for #10 SAE and 2 first class stamps. Book catalog for #10 SAE and 2 first class stamps.

Advice: "Know our magazine. *Heaven Bone*, very well before attempting to be published by us. Looking for more experimental, surreal work—less workshop exercises."

HELICON NINE EDITIONS, (I,II), Subsidiary of Helicon Nine, Inc., 9000 W. 64th Terr., Merrian KS 66202. (913)722-2999. Publisher/Editor: Gloria Vando Hickok. Estab. 1990. Small press publishing poetry, fiction, creative nonfiction and anthologies. Publishes paperback originals. Books: 70 lb. Vellum paper; offset printing; perfect-bound; 4-color cover; average print order: 1,000-5,000. Published new writers within the last year. Plans 8 total titles, 2-4 fiction titles this year.

Needs: Contemporary, ethnic, experimental, literary, short story collections, translations. "We're only interested in fine literature." Nothing "commercial." Recently published *Sweet Angel Band*, by R.M. Kinder (short story collection).

How to Contact: Does not accept unsolicited mss. Query first or submit outline/synopsis and sample chapter. SASE. Reports in 1 week on queries; 3 months on mss.

Terms: Pays royalties, author's copies or honorarium. "Individual arrangement with author." Sends galleys to author. Publishes ms 1-6 months after acceptance. Writer's guidelines for SASE.

Advice: "Make it good. Check spelling and grammar before submitting. Be proud of your work. Submit a clean, readable copy in a folder or box—paginated with title and name on each page. Also, do not pre-design book, i.e. no illustrations—it's very amateurish. We'd like to see books that will be read 50-100 years from now. New classics."

‡HERALD PRESS, (II), Mennonite Publishing House, 616 Walnut Ave., Scottdale PA 15683. (412)887-8500. Book Editor: Michael A. King. Estab. early 1900s. "Midsize Christian denominational publisher." Publishes paperback originals. Books: full color press; squareback adhesive binding; average print order: 3,000; first novel print order: 3,500. Published new writers within the last year. Plans 2-4 first novels this year. Averages 30-35 total titles, 5-10 fiction titles each year. Sometimes comments on rejected mss.

Needs: Adventure, children's/juvenile (adventure, mystery, series), ethnic/multicultural (general), historical (general), mainstream/contemporary, religious/inspirational (general, children's religious), romance (contemporary), young adult/teen (adventure, easy-to-read, historical, mystery/suspense, problem novels, romance. Does not want to see "anything not suitable for a *Christian* publisher." Recently published *Hagar*, by James R. Shott (biblical fiction) and *Reuben*, by Mary Christner Borntrager (Amish fiction).

How to Contact: Accepts unsolicited mss. Submit outline/synopsis and 2 sample chapters. Should include estimated word count, one-page bio and list of publishing credits. Send SASE for reply, return of ms or send a disposable copy of the ms. Reports in 4-8 weeks on queries; 10 weeks on mss. Simultaneous submissions OK. Accepts electronic submissions.

Terms: Pays royalties of 10% minimum and 12 author's copies. Sends galleys to author. Publishes ms 14 months after acceptance. Writer's guidelines free; book catalog free for 9 × 12 SASE and 5 first class stamps.

Advice: "Keep in mind our Christian audience. We publish mostly biblical and Amish fiction or novels for our Mennonite/Christian readers. We're not interested in fantasy or end-of-the-world novels. We need more creative well-written novels with religious theme yet without preachy style."

*HERITAGE PRESS, (II, IV), Box 18625, Baltimore MD 21216. (301)383-9330. President: Wilbert L. Walker. Estab. 1979. One-man operation, full-time basis; uses contractual staff as needed. Publishes hardcover originals. Books: 60 lb. white offset paper; offset printing; sewn hardcover binding; average print order: 2,000; first novel print order: 1,000. Averages 2 total titles, 1-2 fiction titles each year.

Needs: Ethnic (black). Interested in "fiction that presents a balanced portrayal of the black experience in America, from the black perspective. No fiction not dealing with blacks, or which views blacks as inferior." Published *Stalemate at Panmunjon* (the Korean War), and *Servants of All*, by Wilbert L. Walker.

How to Contact: Does not accept unsolicited mss. Query first with SASE. Simultaneous submissions OK. Reports in 2 weeks on queries, 2 months on mss. Publishes ms an average of 9 months after acceptance.

Terms: Must return advance if book is not completed or is unacceptable. *"We plan to subsidy publish only those works that meet our standards for approval.* No more than 1 or 2 a year. Payment for publication is based on individual arrangement with author." Book catalog free on request.
Advice: "Write what you know about. No one else can know and feel what it is like to be black in America better than one who has experienced our dichotomy on race." Would like to see new ideas with broad appeal. "First novels must contain previously unexplored areas on the black experience in America. We regard the author/editor relationship as open, one of mutual respect. Editor has final decision, but listens to author's views."

‡HMS Press, (II), Spare Time Editions (Fredericion N.B.), Poetry Mute Swan Editions (Eufaula Alabama), P. O. Box 340, Stn. B, London, Ontario N6A 4WI Canada. (519)434-4740. President: Wayne Ray. "One-person operation on part-time basis." Publishes paperback originals. Books: saddle and perfect binding; average print order 300. Plans 1 first novel this year. Averages 6 total titles, 2 fiction titles each year. Often comments on rejected mss.
Needs: Erotica, historical (general), humor/satire, literary, regional (Ontario or Alabama). Recently published *Beatrice Dickerskin*, by W. Ray (humor). Plans series of Alabama "Tall Tales" from the 1940s.
How to Contact: Does not accept unsolicited mss. Query letter only first. Submit outline/synopsis and 1-2 sample chapters or contact through FidoNet BBS, RelayNet BBS, CircuitNet BBS (Writer's Conference post to Wayne Ray). Send SASE (IRC) for reply, return of ms or send a disposable copy of the ms. Reports in 1 month. Simultaneous submissions OK. Accepts electronic submissions (WP 5.1).
Terms: Pays royalties of 10% maximum and up to 100 books or individual arrangement with author. Sends galleys to author. Publishes ms 2 months after acceptance. Book catalog free.
Advice: "Prefer chapbook format—less than 48 pages."

*HOMESTEAD PUBLISHING, (I, II), Box 227, Moose WY 83012. (406)538-8960. Editor: Carl Schreier. Estab. 1980. Regional publishers for the Rocky Mountains, midsize firm. Publishes hardcover and paperback originals and reprints. Books: natural stock to enamel paper; web, sheet-feed printing; perfect or smythe-sewn binding; b&w or color illustrations; average print order: 10,000; first novel print order: 2,000-5,000. Plans 1-2 first novels this year. Averages 8-10 total titles; 1-2 fiction each year. Sometimes critiques rejected mss.
Needs: Historical, juvenile (wildlife, historical), literary, preschool/picture book, short story collection, western, young adult/teen (10-18 years, historical). Looking for "good quality, well written and contemporary" fiction. Recently published *The Great Plains: A Young Reader's Journal*, by Bullock (children's natural history-adventure); *Tales of the Grizzly*, by Dr. Tim Clark and Denise Casey.
How to Contact: Accepts unsolicited mss. Query first. SASE. Reports in 1 month. Sends galleys to author. Simultaneous submissions OK.
Terms: Pays royalties of 6-10%. Provides 6 author's copies. Subsidy publishes "occasionally, depending on project."

‡INDEPENDENCE PUBLISHERS OF GEORGIA INC., (I, II), 4771 East Conway Dr., Atlanta GA 30327. (404)843-8084. Editor: Stanley Beitler. Associate Editor: Walter Sturdivant. Estab. 1992. Small press. Publishes hardcover originals. Books: offset, sheetfed printing; case binding; halftone and line illustrations and drawings; first novel print order: 2,500. Rarely critiques rejected ms.
  ● This publisher underwent a reorganization recently. Under their old name, Independence *Publishers*, they published *Appalachian Patterns*, nominated for the American Academy and Institute of Arts and Letters prize for first fiction and the Townsend Prize for fiction.
Needs: Contemporary, experimental, historical, humor/satire, literary, mystery/suspense (cozy, private eye), regional, short story collections, thriller/espionage, translations, western (adult). Looks for "talented new and published writers of fiction and nonfiction." Published *Appalachian Patterns*, by Bo Ball (short-story collection).
How to Contact: Accepts unsolicited mss. Submit complete ms. SASE necessary for return of ms. Reports in 2 weeks on queries; 2 months on mss.
Terms: Pays royalties and advance.

INFINITE SAVANT PUBLISHING, (I, II), 5410 Wilshire Blvd. #601, Los Angeles CA 90036. (213)936-0483. Editor/Owner: James C. Jones II. Estab. 1990. "Two-person operation on part-time basis with plans to expand." Publishes paperback originals. Books: perfect binding; average print order: 500-

2,000; first novel print order: 1,000-3,000. Plans 5 first novels this year. Averages 6 total titles, all fiction this year. Sometimes comments on rejected ms.

Needs: Adventure, erotica, fantasy, feminist, gay, horror, lesbian, psychic/supernatural/occult, science fiction, suspense/mystery. Produces *UFPSS Friendship*, a special genre oriented magazine.

How to Contact: Accepts unsolicited mss. Query first. SASE (IRC). Reports in 2 weeks on queries; 2 months on mss. Simultaneous submissions OK. Accepts electronic submissions via (IBM PC-ASCII—5¼ or 3½; Commodore 128-ASCII—3½; Amiga-ASCII—3½) or BBS (*UFPSS Friendship*) (213)936-1432.

Terms: Pays royalties of 8-10%. Provides 10 author's copies. Publishes ms 1-2 years after acceptance. Writer's guidelines for SASE, #10 envelope and 1 first class stamp.

INVERTED-A, INC., (II), 401 Forrest Hill, Grand Prairie TX 75051. (214)264-0066. Editors: Amnon or Aya Katz. Estab. 1977. A small press which evolved from publishing technical manuals for other products. "Publishing is a small part of our business." Publishes paperback originals. Books: bond paper; offset printing; illustrations; average print order: 250; first novel print order: 250. Publishes 2 titles a year, in recent years mostly poetry, fiction is now about every other year. Also publishes a periodical *Inverted-A, Horn*, which appears irregularly and is open to very short fiction as well as excerpts from unpublished longer fiction. Comments on rejected mss.

Needs: "We are interested in justice and freedom approached from a positive and romantic perspective." Published *The Few Who Count*, by Aya Katz (novel); *Damned in Hell*, by A.A. Wilson (novella); *Inverted Blake* (collection); *Inverted Blake #2* (collection); *Undimmed by Tears* (collection).

How to Contact: Submit query with sample. SASE. Reports in 6 weeks on queries; 3 months on mss. Simultaneous submissions OK. Accepts electronic submissions via modem or ASCII file on a pc MSDOS diskette. Electronic submission mandatory for final ms of accepted work.

Terms: We do not pay except for author copies. Sends galleys to author. For current list send SAE and 1 first class stamp.

Advice: "Deal with more than personal problems. Project hope."

ISLAND HOUSE, (IV), 519½ Capp St., San Francisco CA 94110. (415)826-7113. Imprint: Cottage Books. Senior Editor: Susan Sullivan. Fiction Editor: Pat Healy. Estab. 1987. "Small Press, four person, full time." Publishes paperback originals. Books: acid-free paper; offset printing; perfect-bound; average print order: 2-3,000. Published new writers within the last year. Averages 3 total titles, 2 fiction titles each year. Sometimes comments on rejected ms; *$75 charge for critiques*.

Needs: Ethnic, experimental, faction, literary and short story collections. Looking for Irish-Celtic themes and quality. Published *The West*, by Ed Stack (short stories).

How to Contact: No unsolicited mss. Query first. Agented fiction 50%. Reports in 2 weeks on queries; 3 months on mss. Simultaneous submissions OK.

Terms: Pays royalties of 6-10%; offers negotiable advance. Sends galleys to author. Publishes ms 6-9 months after acceptance. Book catalog free.

ITALICA PRESS, (IV), 595 Main St., #605, New York NY 10044. (212)935-4230. Publishers: Eileen Gardiner and Ronald G. Musto. Estab. 1985. Small independent publisher. Publishes paperback originals. Books: 50-60 lb. natural paper; offset printing; Smythe-sewn binding; illustrations; average print order: 1,500. "First time translators published. We would like to see translations of well-known Italian writers in Italy who are not yet translated for an American audience." Publishes 6 total titles each year; 2 fiction titles. Sometimes critiques rejected mss.

Needs: Translations from Italian. Looking for "4 novels over next two years—exclusively translations of 20th Century Italian literature." Recently published *Dolcissimo*, by Giuseppe Bonaviri; *Man of Smoke*, by Aldo Palazzeschi; *Otronto*, by Maria Corti.

How to Contact: Accepts unsolicited mss. Query first. Reports in 3 weeks on queries; 2 months on mss. Simultaneous submissions OK. Electronic submissions via Macintosh disk.

Terms: Pays in royalties of 5-15% and 10 author's copies. Sends pre-publication galleys to author. Book catalog free on request.

Read the Business of Fiction Writing section to learn the correct way to prepare and submit a manuscript.

‡J & P Books, (I), Liberation Inc., Room J, 89 Robin Lane, Fairfield CT 06430-3939. Editor: Jay Peters. Estab. 1992. Publishes paperback originals.
• Other imprints of Liberation Inc. listed in this book are Fire Island Press, Marie's Books, McKnight Books and Lavender Press.
Needs: Humor/satire, mystery/suspense (private eye/hardboiled, amateur sleuth, cozy), western (traditional, adult western, frontier saga), young adult/teen (adventure, fantasy/science fiction, mystery/suspense, problem novels, romance).
How to Contact: Does not accept unsolicited mss. Query letter only first. Should include estimated word count. SASE (IRC). Reports in 1 month on queries.
Terms: Pays royalties of 10% minimum; 25% maximum. Sends galleys to author.

JESPERSON PRESS LTD., (I), 39 James Lane, St. John's, Newfoundland A1E 3H3 Canada. (709)753-0633. Trade Editor: Shelly Dawe. Midsize independent publisher. Publishes hardcover and paperback originals. Published new writers within the last year. Averages 7-10 total titles, 1-2 fiction titles each year. Sometimes comments on rejected ms.
Needs: Adventure, fantasy, humor/satire, juvenile (5-9 yrs.) including: animal easy-to-read, fantasy, historical, sports, spy/adventure and contemporary. Recently published *Daddy's Back*, by Barbara Ann Lane; *Fables, Fairies & Folklore of Newfoundland*, by Miké McCarthy and Alice Lannon; *Justice for Julie*, by Barbara Ann Lane.
How to Contact: Accepts unsolicited mss. Submit complete manuscript with cover letter. SASE. Reports in 3 months on mss.
Terms: Pays negotiable royalties. Sends galleys to author. Book catalog free.

*‡JORDAN ENTERPRIZES PUBLISHING COMPANY, (II), 6457 Wilcox Station, Box 38002, Los Angeles CA 90038. Imprint: The Lion. Managing Editor: Patrique Quintahlen. Estab. 1990. Publishes hardcover and paperback originals and reprints. Books: 50-60 lb weight paper; perfect bound; artists on staff for illustrations; average print order: 1,000-15,000. Averages 3 total titles/year; 2 fiction titles/year. *Offers editorial/publishing consultations services for new/unpublished writers for a fee.* Query for details.
Needs: Adventure, contemporary, ethnic, experimental, fantasy, historical, juvenile (animal, easy-to-read, fantasy, historical, contemporary), literary, mainstream, preschool/picture book, romance (contemporary, historical), science fiction, young adult/teen (easy-to-read, fantasy/science fiction, historical, problem novels, romance). "Looking for contemporary juvenile novels, interesting settings." No horror, gore, erotica, gay, occult, novels. No sexism, racism, or pornography. Recently published *The Strawberry Fox*, (middle reader), *The Strawberry Fox*, a play for children   all ages by Prentiss Van Daves Illustrations by Nancy Dominique James; *The Christmas* by Toy Welcome.
How to Contact: Accepts unsolicited mss. Query first. Submit outline/synopsis with 3 sample chapters. SASE (IRC). 50% of fiction is agented. Reports in 4 months on queries; in 6 months on mss. ·Accepts disk submissions from Macintosh Plus.
Terms: Pays royalties of 8-10%; average advance $500-5,000; advance is negotiable; advance is more for agented ms; 50 author's copies. Sends galleys to author. *Subsidy publishes 1% of books each year.* Subsidy publishes books of poetry only, 50-150 pages. Subjects: love, psychology, philosophy, new male/female relationships, family.
Advice: "Devote 90% of your time to finding an agent. To save time and expense, it is recommended that authors learn as much as possible about not simply their writing craft, but also the very art of publishing. I recommend studying self publishing at some point after the author has completed several works, learning the actual book making process, book design, marketing, sales, distribution, and publishing and the money saving typesetting advantages of today's word processing and computer options. This advice is to speed the 'submission-to-publication' process between author and small press operations. This is valuable in respect to new unpublished authors. The classical submissions methods of ms to major publishers still remains an important option to the author with a book with commercial value. For literary works of the highest quality small presses are the proven markets for success to the professional and the literary author."

KAR-BEN COPIES, INC., (II, IV), 6800 Tildenwood La., Rockville MD 20852. (301)984-8733. President: Judye Groner. Estab. 1974. Small publisher specializing in juvenile Judaica. Publishes hardcover and paperback originals. Books: 70-80 lb. patina paper; offset printing; perfect and case binding; 2-4 color illustrations; average print order: 5,000-10,000. Averages 8-10 total titles, 6-8 fiction titles each year. Published new writers within the last year.

Needs: Juvenile (3-10 years). Recently published *Two by Two, Favorite Bible Stories*, by Harry Arater; *Daddy's Chair*, by Sandy Lantor and four new board books for toddlers.
How to Contact: Accepts unsolicited mss. Submit outline/synopsis and sample chapters or complete ms with cover letter. SASE. Reports in 1 week on queries; 1 month on mss. Simultaneous submissions OK.
Terms: Pays in royalties of 5-10%; average advance: $1,000; 12 author's copies. Sends galleys to author. Writer's guidelines for SASE. Book catalog free on request.

‡KITCHEN TABLE: WOMEN OF COLOR PRESS, (II, IV), Box 908, Latham NY 12110. Publisher: Barbara Smith. Estab. 1981. "Independent press with several paid employees, very good distribution." Publishes paperback originals. Books: 50 lb stock paper; offset/web press printing; perfect binding; some b&w graphic elements/designs; average print order: 5,000; first novel print order: 3,000. "All of our books are trade paperbacks, a few of which are bound for libraries." Averages 2 total titles each year; 1 fiction title every two years. Occasionally critiques rejected ms.
Needs: Ethnic, feminist, lesbian, literary, short story collections. Needs for novels include novels by women of color—authors that reflect in some way the experiences of women of color. "We are looking for high quality, politically conscious writing and would particularly like to hear from American Indian women fiction writers." Has published *Cuentos: Stories by Latinas*, edited by Alma Gómez, Cherrie Moraga; Mariana Romo-Carmona (short story anthology with selections in both English and Spanish).
How to Contact: Accepts unsolicited mss. Query first. Submit outline/synopsis and 3 sample chapters. SASE. Reports in 1 month on queries; 6 months on mss. Simultaneous submissions OK.
Terms: Pays in royalties of 8-10% and 10 author's copies. Sends galleys to author. Book catalog for 2 first class stamps.
Advice: "One of the most common mistakes that our press tries to address is the notion that the first work a writer publishes should be a book as opposed to a submission to a periodical. Periodicals serve as a very valuable apprenticeship for a beginning writer. They should submit work to appropriate literary and other kinds of journals that publish fiction. By appropriate I mean appropriate for the kind of writing they do. Getting published in periodicals gives the writer experience and also creates a 'track record' that may interest the prospective book publisher."

KRUZA KALEIDOSCOPIX, INC., (IV), Box 389, Franklin MA 02038. (508)528-6211. Editor/President: J.A. Kruza. Fiction Editor: R. Burbank. Estab. 1976. Publishes hardcover and paperback originals. Books: 60-80 lb. coated paper; offset printing; saddle and perfect binding; illustrations; average print order: 10,000. Averages 12 total titles each year. Sometimes critiques rejected mss.
Needs: Historical (nautical); juvenile (5-9 yrs.) including: animal, lesson teachings about work ethic, historical. "Stories for children, ages 3-7, with problem and characters who work out solution to problem, i.e. work ethic."
How to Contact: Accepts and returns unsolicited mss. Submit complete ms with cover letter. SASE. Reports in 3 weeks on queries; 3 months on mss. Simultaneous submissions OK.
Terms: *Charges $3 reading fee.* Flat fee, depending on strength of story. Provides 10 author's copies. Writer's guidelines for #10 SAE with 1 first class stamp.

‡LAVENDER PRESS, (II), Liberation Inc., Room 203A, 89 Robin Lane, Fairfield CT 06430-3939. Editor: Peter Daniels. Estab. 1990. "Three-person operation." Publishes paperback originals. Books: 50 lb. paper; stitch or perfect binding; average print order: 4,000; first novel print order: 4,500. Plans 3 first novels this year. Averages 6 total titles, all fiction, this year. Sometimes comments on rejected mss.
  ● This press won the Lambda Gay Science Fiction Award for *Secret Matter*, by Toby Johnson in 1990. Other imprints of Liberation Inc. include Fire Island, Marie's Books, McKnight Books and J & P Books.
Needs: Gay, lesbian. Especially interested in "gay and lesbian science fiction, westerns. No gay romances." Recently published *Getting Life in Perspective*, by Toby Johnson (gay/spiritual/ghost).
How to Contact: Does not accept unsolicited mss. Submit outline/synopsis and 3 sample chapters. Should include estimated word count. SASE (IRC). Agented fiction 20%. Reports in 1 month on queries; 2 months on manuscripts.
Terms: Pays royalties of 10% minimum; 25% maximum. Average advance: $500. Sends galleys to author. Publishes up to 1 year after acceptance. Book catalog for #10 SASE and 1 first class stamp.

‡**LEE & LOW BOOKS, (I, II)**, 228 East 45th St., 14th Fl., New York NY 10017. (212)867-6155. Fax: (212)490-1846. Publisher: Philip Lee. Estab. 1991. "Independent multicultural children's book publisher." Publishes hardcover originals. Averages 6 total titles, 4-6 fiction titles each year. Sometimes comments on rejected ms.
Needs: Childrens/juvenile (preschool/picture book, historical, multicultural). Plans anthologies of poetry, short stories. Recently published *Abuela's Weave*, by Omar Castáneda (hardcover picture book); *Baseball Saved Us*, by Ken Mochizuki (hardcover picture book); *Joshua's Masai Mask*, by Dakari Hru (hardcover picture book).
How to Contact: Accepts unsolicited mss. Query first then submit outline/synopsis and 2 sample chapters, complete ms with cover letter or through an agent. Include estimated word count and bio (no more than one page). Send SASE for reply, return of ms or send a disposable of the ms. Agented fiction 30%. Reports in 3-5 weeks on queries; 4-6 weeks on mss. Simultaneous submissions OK.
Terms: Pays royalties. Offers advance. Sends galleys to author. Publishes ms 18 months after acceptance. Writer's guidelines for #10 SASE and 1 first class stamp. Book catalog for SASE.
Advice: "Writers should familiarize themselves with the styles and formats of recently published children's books. Lee & Low Books is a multicultural children's book publisher. We would like to see more contemporary stories set in the U.S. Animal stories are discouraged."

‡**LESTER PUBLISHING LIMITED, (II)**, 507A, 56 The Esplanade, Toronto, Ontario M53 1A7 Canada. (416)362-1032. Fax: (416)362-1647. Assistant Editor: Janice Weaver. Estab. 1991. Small independent publisher. Publishes hardcover and paperback originals. Published new writers within the last year. Plans 2 first novels this year. Averages 20 total titles, 3-5 fiction titles each year. Sometimes comments on rejected mss.
Needs: Children's/juvenile (preschool/picture book), historical (general), humor/satire, literary, mainstream/contemporary, short story collections, young adult/teen (adventure, historical, mystery/suspense, problem novels). No romance or science fiction. Recently published *The Rose Tree*, by Mary Walkin Keane (literary); *Hockey Night in the Dominion of Canada*, by Eric Zweig (historical); *Talking Power*, by David Lewis Stein (contemporary).
How to Contact: Accepts unsolicited mss. Submit outline/synopsis and 2-3 sample chapters. Should include estimated word count and cover letter. Send SASE (IRC) for reply, return of ms or send a disposable copy of the ms. Agented fiction 60-75%. Reports in 1 month on queries; 6 months on manuscripts.
Terms: Pays royalties, negotiable advance and 6-10 author's copies. Sends galleys to author. Publishes ms 6-18 months after acceptance. Writer's guidelines and catalog free.
Advice: "Fiction is a risky venture, especially in Canada. We publish very little and all in trade paperback (with the exception of young adult fiction, which we do as hardcover originals). I think we will, frankly, do less and less fiction and fewer first-time authors. Although we do not require them, an initial query letter is useful."

LOLLIPOP POWER BOOKS, (II), 120 Morris St., Durham NC 27701. (919)560-2738. Editor: Ruth A. Smullin. Estab. 1970. "Children's imprint of the Carolina Wren Press, a small, nonprofit press which publishes non-sexist, multi-racial picture books." Publishes paperback originals. Averages 1 title (fiction) each year. Average first book run 3,000 copies.
Needs: Juvenile. "Picture books only. Our current publishing priorities are: books with African American, Hispanic/Latino or Native American characters; bilingual (English/Spanish) books. Recently published *Maria Teresa*, by Mary Atkinson (bilingual); *In Christina's Toolbox*, by Diane Homan; *Grownups Cry Too*, by Nancy Hazen (bilingual).
How to Contact: Send complete manuscript with SASE. Do not send illustrations. Reports in 3 months on mss. Simultaneous submissions OK. Publishes ms from 1-2 years after acceptance. Guidelines for SASE.
Terms: Pays royalties of 10%.
Advice: "Lollipop Power Books must be well-written stories that will appeal to children. We are not interested in preachy tales where 'message' overpowers plot and character. We are looking for good stories told from a child's point of view. Our books present a child's perspective and feelings honestly and without condescension."

HENDRICK LONG PUBLISHING CO., (IV), Box 25123, Dallas TX 75225. (214)358-4677. Vice President: Joann Long. Estab. 1969. "Independent publisher focusing on Texas material geared primarily to a young audience. (K through high school). Cornerstone of company is a Texas history seventh grade textbook (state adopted)." Publishes hardcover and paperback originals and hardcover reprints.

Close-up

John Yow
Senior Editor
Longstreet Press

At Longstreet Press, Senior Editor John Yow has learned to function under what he describes as a harsh but undeniable reality: The market for quality fiction is "as broad as the world, but only an inch deep. People everywhere want literary fiction, but there's no concentration anywhere," he says.

For that reason, publishing fiction is both a labor of love and a risky business for this small press, which began four years ago. Of the approximately 25 books each year that Longstreet publishes, only two or three titles are fiction. The company's hope, Yow says, is to make enough profit selling nonfiction to support the fiction work it takes on.

A big advantage to working with a small press like Longstreet, Yow says, is the personalized attention authors receive. "All of our writers know us very well," he says. "There's no sense of intimidation in dealing with us."

The down side to a small press, he adds, is that "we can't pay six-figure advances, and we don't have million-dollar publicity budgets. We can't create a bestseller by running an ad in the *New York Times*."

Still, Longstreet does a pretty effective job of marketing its books. It employs two full-time publicity specialists, works with a network of 30 sales representatives, produces a slick sales catalog and strives to publish books that have "the high-quality look of the larger commercial houses," Yow says.

In addition, Longstreet was purchased in 1992 by Cox Newspapers, which owns numerous newspapers across the country. The acquisition provides an infusion of funds but no change in Longstreet's mode of operation and gives the small press more resources and opportunities to expand its markets, Yow says.

Yow describes the company's range of fiction as "pretty narrow," explaining that Longstreet concentrates on fairly traditional literary novels and has been known to turn away some excellent avant-garde work. It also has turned down "zillions" of romance novels, historical novels and thrillers—genres that the company's guidelines expressly rule out.

Longstreet receives an average of 20 manuscripts a day, mostly unsolicited, which puts a strain on the 14-member staff. But the publisher is reluctant to close the door on unsolicited submissions. "Every now and then we find something we like. And if everybody closes the door, it gets mighty tough for a first-time writer to find a home," he says.

For an author seeking a home at Longstreet, the best approach is to send a cover letter detailing his or her writing background and publication credits. The letter should be accompanied by a one-page description of the novel, and 50 to 75 sample pages.

"What I'm looking for is something that lets me know immediately I'm hearing a voice I've never heard before. I'm looking for fiction that moves me—to laughter or to tears—fiction that speaks to the heart," says Yow.

—Perri Weinberg-Schenker

Books: average print order: 2,000 (except textbooks which have a much longer run.) Published new writers within the last year. Averages 8 total titles, 4 fiction titles each year. Sometimes comments on rejected ms.

Needs: Texas themes: historical, regional, for juvenile, young adult, teen. "No material not suitable for junior high/high school audience." Recently published *Boomer's Kids*, by Ruby C. Tolliver; *Johnny Texas*, by Carol Hoff (reprint); *Shipwrecked on Padre Island*, by Isabel Marvin.

How to Contact: Query first or submit outline/synopsis and sample chapters (at least 2—no more than 3). SASE. Reports in 2 weeks on queries; 2 months on ms.

Terms: Offers negotiable advance. Sends galleys to author. Publishes ms 18 months after acceptance. Writer's guidelines for SASE. Book catalog for $1.

LONGSTREET PRESS, (II), Suite 118, 2140 Newmarket Parkway, Marietta GA 30067. (404)980-1488. Associate Editor: Suzanne Comer Bell. Estab. 1988. "Small independent publisher with plans to grow." Publishes hardcover and paperback originals. Published new writers within the last year. Averages 20-25 total titles, 2-3 fiction titles each year. Sometimes comments on rejected ms.

• See the close-up interview with Senior Editor John Yow in this book.

Needs: Literary, mainstream. "Quality fiction." No "genre fiction, highly experimental work, ya, juvenile." Recently published *The Kingdom of Brooklyn*, by Merrill Joan Gerber (literary); *Holy Orders*, by Carolyn Thorman; *Moonblind*, by Linda Chandler Munson.

How to Contact: Accepts unsolicited mss. Submit outline/synopsis and sample chapters. SASE. Agented fiction 50%. Reports on queries in 6 weeks; on mss in 3 months. Simultaneous (if told) submissions OK.

Terms: Pays in royalties; advance is negotiable; author's copies. Sends galleys to author. Publishes ms 6 months-1 year after acceptance. Writer's guidelines for #10 SASE and 1 first class stamp. Book catalog for 9×12 envelope with 4 first class stamps.

Advice: "Read good contemporary literary fiction—know the field."

LOS HOMBRES PRESS, (II,IV), Box 632729, San Diego CA 92163-2729. (619)234-6710. Publisher: James D. Kitchen. Estab. 1989. Small publisher with plans to do 5 books in 1992. Publishes paperback originals. Books: 60 lb. paper; offset printing; perfect-bound; average print order: 2,000; first novel print order: 2,000. Published new writers within the last year. Plans 2 first novels this year. Averages 4-5 total titles, 3 fiction titles each year. Sometimes comments on rejected mss.

Needs: Gay and lesbian. "Novels including mainstream, literary, science fiction (soft sociological), mystery, fantasy, futuristic, adventure, western (adult). Open to most categories with a gay theme; short story collections." No men's action, pornography. Recently published *Perverted Proverbs*, by Marsh Cassady; *Movie Hooky*, by Dan Foster; *Persephone's Song*, by Mary Schmidt.

How to Contact: Accepts unsolicited mss. Query first or submit 3 sample chapters. SASE. Include social security number with submission. Agented fiction 50%. Reports on queries in 2 weeks; mss in 2 months. Simultaneous submissions OK.

Terms: Pays 10-15% royalties and 10 author's copies. Sends galleys to author. Publishes ms 1 year after acceptance. Writer's guidelines for #10 SASE and 1 first class stamp.

LUCKY HEART BOOKS, (I), Subsidiary of Salt Lick Press, P.O. Box 15471, Austin TX 78761-5471. Editor/Publisher: James Haining. Estab. 1969. Small press with significant work reviews in several national publications. Publishes paperback originals and reprints. Books: offset/bond paper; offset printing; stitch, perfect bound; illustrations; average print order: 500; first novel print order: 500. Sometimes comments on rejected mss.

Needs: Open to all fiction categories.

How to Contact: Accepts unsolicited mss. SASE. Agented fiction 1%. Reports in 2 weeks to 4 months on mss.

Terms: Pays 10 author's copies. Sends pre-publication galleys to author.

McKNIGHT BOOKS, (I), Liberation Inc., Room 203M, 89 Robin Lane, Fairfield CT 06430-3939. (203)330-9596. President: Joseph Letendre. Fiction Editor: Peter R. McKnight. Estab. 1992. Four-person publisher. Publishes paperback originals. Plans 10 first novels this year. Averages 12 titles, all fiction.

• Other imprints of Liberation Inc. listed in this book include Lavender Press, Fire Island Press, Marie's Books, J & P Books.

Needs: Fantasy (space fantasy, sword and sorcery), science fiction (soft/sociological, space trilogy/series). Plans anthology (space fantasy). Writers may submit to editor.

How to Contact: Does not accept unsolicited mss. Submit outline/synopsis and 5 sample chapters. Should include estimated word count, one-page bio and list of publishing credits if available. SASE. Reports in 3 weeks on queries; 2 months on mss. Simultaneous submissions OK.

Terms: Pays royalties of 10% minimum; 25% maximum. Sends galleys to author.

MADWOMAN PRESS, (I, IV), P.O. Box 690, Northboro MA 01532. (508)393-3447. Editor/Publisher: Diane Benison. Estab. 1991. Independent small press publishing lesbian fiction. Publishes paperback originals. Books: perfect binding; average print order: 4,000-6,000; first novel print order: 5,000. Averages 2-4 total titles, 2 fiction titles each year. Sometimes comments on rejected ms.

Needs: "All must have lesbian themes: adventure, erotica, ethnic, feminist, mystery/suspense (amateur sleuth, private eye, police procedural), romance, science fiction (hard science, soft sociological), short story collection, thriller/espionage, western. Especially looking for lesbian romance." No horror. No gratuitous violence. Recently published *On the Road Again, The Further Adventures of Ramsey Sears*, by Amy Dean.

How to Contact: Query first. Include brief statement of name, address, phone, previous publication and a 1-2 page precis of the plot. SASE. Reports in 1 month. Simultaneous submissions OK.

Terms: Pays royalties of 8-15% "after recovery of publications costs." Provides 20 author's copies. Sends galleys to author. Publishes ms 1-2 years after acceptance. Writer's guidelines for #10 SAE and 1 first class stamp.

Advice: "We're looking to form long-term relationships with writers, so talented first novelists are ideal for us. We want to publish an author regularly over the years, build an audience for her and keep her in print. We're interested in books by, for and about lesbians. Books that are affirming for lesbian readers and authors. Would like to see more romances."

MAGE PUBLISHERS, (IV), 1032 29th St. NW, Washington DC 20007. (202)342-1642. Editorial Contact: Scott Ripley. Estab. 1985. "Small independent publisher." Publishes hardcover originals. Averages 4 total titles, 1 fiction title each year.

Needs: We publish *only* books on Iran. Ethnic (Iran) fiction.

How to Contact: Query first. SASE (IRC). Reports in 3 months on queries. Simultaneous submissions OK.

Terms: Pays royalties. Publishes ms 6-9 months after acceptance. Writer's guidelines for SASE. Book catalog free.

MANIC D PRESS, (II), P.O. Box 410804, San Francisco CA 94141. Editor: Jennifer Joseph. Estab. 1984. Small independent publisher. Publishes paperback originals. Books: 50 lb. paper; offset printing; perfect binding; average print order: 1,000. Averages 5 total titles, 2 fiction titles each year.

Needs: Literary. No military, western, religious, romance. Published *Bricks and Anchors*, by Jon Longhi (cyperpunk short stories); and *Graveyard Golf and Other Stories*, by Vampyre Mike Kassel (fantasy/horror short stories).

How to Contact: Accepts unsolicited mss. Query first. SASE. Reports in 1 month on queries; 1-2 months on mss. Simultaneous submissions OK.

Terms: Pays author's copies. Sends galleys to author. Publishes ms 6-24 months after acceptance. Writer's guidelines and book catalog for #10 SAE and 1 first class stamp.

Advice: "Don't send the whole novel. Always query first."

‡MARIE'S BOOKS, (II), Liberation Inc., Room 203C, 89 Robin Lane, Fairfield CT 06430-3939. (203)330-9596. Editor-in-Chief: Roberta Letendre. Estab. 1992. Publishes paperback originals. Books: perfect binding. Plans 3 first novels this year. Averages 3 total titles, all fiction.

• Liberation Inc.'s other imprints listed in this book are Lavender Press, Fire Island Press, McKnight Books and J & P Books.

Needs: Romance (contemporary, gothic, romantic suspense). No historical romances. Plans ongoing series.

How to Contact: Accepts unsolicited mss. Submit outline/synopsis and 6 sample chapters. Should include estimated word count.

Terms: Pays royalties of 10% minimum; 25% maximum and 10 author's copies. Sends galleys to author.

MARRON PUBLISHERS, INC., (II), Dark Secrets, Romance In Black, 229-28 129th Ave., Laurelton NY 11413. (718)481-9599. Co-owner: Marquita Guerra. Fiction Editor: Sharon A. Ortiz. Estab. 1988. "Marron Publishers is a small, growing independent publisher dedicated to printing quality works which celebrate ethnic and cultural diversity." Publishes paperback originals. Books: illustrations on newsletter (Dark Secrets); average print order: 10,000; first novel print order: 10,000. Plans 8 first novels this year. Averages 8-10 total titles each year (all fiction). Sometimes comments on rejected mss.
Needs: Adventure, contemporary, historical, mainstream, romance (contemporary, historical), mystery/suspense, young adult/teen (romance/ya). Looking for "romance for the *Romance In Black* line."
How to Contact: Accepts unsolicited mss (no queries). Submit outline/synopsis and 3 sample chapters, or complete ms with cover letter. SASE. Agented fiction 25%. Reports on queries in 2 weeks; on mss in 1 month. Accepts electronic submissions with prior approval.
Terms: Depends on experience of author and previous track record. "Individual arrangement with author depending on the book." Sends galleys to author. Publication time "depends on the book" (approximately 2 to 18 months). Writer's guidelines for 8½ × 11 SASE and 45¢ postage. Book catalog for SASE.
Advice: "Be honest and forthright in your cover letters without gushing. State your case – don't be shy about what you feel are your positive points. Always remember that you have to sell yourself to the publisher and don't back down on questions of quality – your name will appear on the book or the publication. Be open to criticism and flexible when it comes to certain changes. But be wary of changing your original concept to one that is foreign to your creative intent."

MERCURY HOUSE, (III), Suite 400, 201 Filbert St.,San Francisco CA 94133. Executive Editor: Thomas Christensen. Publisher: William Brinton. Submissions Editor: Sarah Malarkey. Small, independent publisher of quality fiction and nonfiction. Publishes hardcovers and some paperback originals and reprints. Averages 20 titles annually. 25% of books from first-time authors.
Needs: Literary adult fiction, nonfiction and translations. Recently published *Sylvia*, by Leonard Michaels; *Small Spaces Between Emergencies*, by Alison Moore; *The Harp and the Shadow*, by Alejo Carpentier.
How to Contact: No unsolicited mss. Submit query letter, 3 sample chapters, synopsis and SASE. Reports in 3 months. Book catalog for 8½ × 11 SAE and 65¢. No simultaneous submissions.

*MEY-HOUSE BOOKS, (II), Box 794, Stroudsburg PA 18360. (717)646-9556. Editorial contact person: Ted Meyer. Estab. 1983. One-person operation part-time with plans for at least 2 novels shortly. Publishes hardcover and paperback originals. Averages 1 title/year. Occasionally critiques or comments on rejected ms, "cost varies."
Needs: Adventure, contemporary, ethnic, science fiction. "No gay, erotic or lesbian fiction."
How to Contact: Accepts unsolicited mss. Query first. SASE. Reports in 1 month on queries. Simultaneous submissions OK.
Terms: Payment "varies." Sends galleys to author. *Subsidy publishes "on an individual basis."*

‡MID-LIST PRESS, (I, II), Jackson, Hart & Leslie, Inc., 4324-12th Ave., S., Minneapolis MN 55407. (612)822-3733. Associate Publisher: Marianne Nora. Editors Maria Ahrens, Jody Nolen, Lane Stiles. Estab. 1989. Small independent publisher. Publishes hardcover originals and paperback originals and hardcover reprints. Books: acid free paper; offset printing; perfect or smyth sewn binding; average print order: 1,000; first novel print order: 1,500. Plans 1 first novel this year. Averages 3 total titles, 1 fiction title each year. Often comments on rejected ms.
Needs: Adventure, erotica, ethnic/multicultural, experimental, family saga, fantasy, feminist, gay, historical (general), horror, humor/satire, lesbian, literary, mainstream/contemporary, military/war, mystery/suspense, new age/mystic/spiritual, psychic/supernatural/occult, regional, science fiction, short story collections, thriller/espionage, western. No childrens/juvenile, romance, young adult, religious. Recently published *Same Bed, Different Dreams*, by Hugh Gross (multicultural/literary). Publishes First Novel Series Award.
How to Contact: Accepts unsolicited mss. Query first (for general fiction) or submit complete ms with cover letter (for First Novel Series Award). Send SASE for reply, return of ms or send a disposable copy of the ms. Agented fiction 25%. Reports in 3 weeks on queries; 3 months on mss. Simultaneous submissions OK.
Terms: Pays royalty of 40% minimum; 50% maximum of profits. Average advance: $1,000 (for First Novel Series only). Sends galleys to author. Publishes ms 6-12 months after acceptance. Writer's guidelines for #10 SASE and 1 first class stamp or IRC.

MILKWEED EDITIONS, Suite 505, 528 Hennepin Ave., Minneapolis MN 55403. (612)332-3192. Editor: Emilie Buchwald. Estab. 1980 — *Milkweed Chronicle*/1984 — *Milkweed Editions*. Small press with emphasis on literary and visual arts work. Publishes hardcover and paperback originals. Books: book text quality — acid-free paper; offset printing; perfect or hardcover binding; illustrations in all books; average print order: 3,000; first novel print order depends on book. Averages 12 total titles/year. Number of fiction titles "depends on mss."

• For more on Milkweed, see the close-up interview with Editor Emilie Buchwald in the 1990 *Novel & Short Story Writer's Market*.

Needs: Contemporary, experimental, literary. Looking for excellent writing. No romance, mysteries, science fiction. Recently published *Aquaboogie*, by Susan Straight; *Cracking India*, by Bapsi Sidhwa; *The Boy Without a Flag*, by Abraham Rodriguez, Jr.

How to Contact: Accepts unsolicited mss, send to the attention of Elisabeth Fitz, First Reader. Submit outline/synopsis and 2 sample chapters. SASE. Reports in 1 month on queries; 2 months on mss. Simultaneous submissions OK. "Please send for guidelines. Must enclose SASE."

Terms: Authors are paid in royalties of 10%; advance is negotiable; 10 author's copies. Sends galleys to author. Book catalog for 3 first class stamps.

Advice: "Read good contemporary fiction; find your own voice. Do not send us pornographic work, or work in which violence is done to women or children or men."

‡MISTY HILL PRESS, (II), 5024 Turner Rd., Sebastopol, CA 95472. (707)823-7437. Managing Editor: Sally S. Karste. Estab. 1985. One person operation on a part-time basis. Publishes paperback originals. Books: illustrations; average print order: 2,000; first novel print order: 500-1,000. Plans 1 first novel this year. Publishes 1 title each year. Sometimes critiques rejected mss; *$15/hour charge for critiques*.

Needs: Juvenile (historical). Looking for "historical fiction for children, well researched for library market." Published *Trails to Poosey*, by Olive R. Cook (historical fiction); *Tales Fledgling Homestead*, by Joe Armstrong (nonfiction portraits).

How to Contact: Accepts unsolicited mss. Submit outline/synopsis and sample chapters. Reports within weeks. Simultaneous submissions OK.

Terms: Pays royalties of 5%. Sends prepublication galleys to author. Writer's guidelines and book catalog for SASE.

MOTHER COURAGE PRESS, (I, IV), 1533 Illinois St., Racine WI 53405. (414)634-1047. Executive Editor: Barbara Lindquist. Estab. 1981. Small feminist press. Publishes paperback originals. Books: perfect binding; sometimes illustrations; average print order: 3,000; first novel print order: 3,000. Plans 3 first novels 1991. Averages 4 total titles, 1 fiction title each year.

Needs: Lesbian adventure, lesbian feminist/humor/satire, lesbian romance, lesbian science fiction, lesbian suspense/mystery. "Need strongly feminist, lesbian or women oriented, nothing written by men." No short stories. Published *Mega*, by B.L. Holmes (science fiction lesbian); *Hodag Winter*, by Deborah Wiese.

How to Contact: Accepts unsolicited mss. Query first with outline/synopsis and 2 sample chapters. SAE. Reports in 6 weeks on queries; 3 months on mss. Simultaneous submissions OK.

Terms: Pays in royalties of 10-15%. Average advance: $250. Sends galleys to author. Book catalog for SAE.

Advice: "Write a good query letter, including, the plot of the novel, main characters, etc."

MOYER BELL LIMITED, Kymbolde Way, Wakefield RI 02879. (401)789-0074. President: Jennifer Moyer. Fiction Editor: Britt Bell. Estab. 1984. "Small publisher established to publish literature, reference and art books." Publishes hardcover and paperback originals and reprints. Books: Average print order 2,500; first novel print order: 2,500. Averages 14 total titles, 1 fiction title each year. Sometimes comments on rejected ms.

Needs: Serious literary fiction. No genre fiction. Published *The Other Garden*, by Francis Wyndham (literary).

How to Contact: Accepts unsolicited mss. Submit outline/synopsis and 2 sample chapters. SASE. Reports in 2 weeks on queries; 2 months on mss. Simultaneous and electronic submissions OK.

Terms: Pays royalties of 10% minimum. Average advance $1,000. Sends galleys to author. Publishes ms 9-18 months after acceptance. Book catalog free.

THE NAIAD PRESS, INC., (I, II, IV), Box 10543, Tallahassee FL 32302. (904)539-5965. Fax: (904)539-9731. Editorial Director: Barbara Grier. Estab. 1973. Books: 55 lb. offset paper; sheet-fed offset; perfect-bound; average print order: 12,000; first novel print order: 12,000. Published new writers within the last year. Publishes 24 total books/year.
 • The Naiad Press is one of the most successful and well-known lesbian publishers. Barbara Grier and Donna J. McBride recently received a Pubilsher's Service Award from the Lambda Literary Awards for 20 years of service.
Needs: Lesbian fiction, all genres. Recently published *Murder by Tradition* (a Kate Delafield mystery), by Katherine V. Forrest; *Love, Zena Beth*; *The Erotic Naiad*, edited by Katherine V. Forrest and Barbara Grier.
How to Contact: Query first only. SASE. Reports in 3 weeks on queries; 3 months on mss. No simultaneous submissions.
Terms: Pays 15% royalties using a standard recovery contract. Occasionally pays 7½% royalties against cover price. "Seldom gives advances and has never seen a first novel worthy of one. Believes authors are investments in their own and the company's future—that the best author is the author who produces a book every 12-18 months forever and knows that there is a *home* for that book." Publishes ms 1-2 years after acceptance. Book catalog for legal-sized SASE.
Advice: "We publish lesbian fiction primarily and prefer honest work (i.e., positive, upbeat lesbian characters). Lesbian content must be accurate . . . a lot of earlier lesbian novels were less than honest. No breast beating or complaining. Our fiction titles are becoming increasingly *genre* fiction, which we encourage. Original fiction in paperback is our main field, and its popularity increases. We publish books BY, FOR AND ABOUT lesbians. We are not interested in books that are unrealistic. You know and we know what the real world of lesbian interest is like. Don't even try to fool us. Short, well written books do best. Authors who want to succeed and will work to do so have the best shot."

THE NAUTICAL & AVIATION PUBLISHING CO. OF AMERICA INC., (IV), 8 W. Madison St., Baltimore MD 21201. (301)659-0220. President: Jan Snouck-Hurgronje. Estab. 1979. Small publisher interested in quality military history and literature. Publishes hardcover originals and reprints. Averages 10 total titles, 1-4 fiction titles each year. Sometimes comments on rejected mss.
Needs: Military/war (especially military history and Civil War). Looks for "novels with a strong military history orientation." Recently published *Pursuit of the Seawolf* and *Checkfire*, by VADM William P. Mack.
How to Contact: Accepts unsolicited mss. Query first or submit complete mss with cover letter. SASE necessary for return of mss. Agented fiction "miniscule." Reports on queries in 2-3 weeks; on mss in 3 weeks. Simultaneous submissions OK.
Terms: Pays royalties of 15%. Advance negotiable. After acceptance publishes ms "as quickly as possible—next season." Book catalog free on request.
Advice: Publishing more fiction. Encourages first novelists. "We're interested in good writing—first novel or last novel. Keep it historical, put characters in a historical context. Professionalism counts. Know your subject. *Convince us.*"

NEW DIRECTIONS, (I, II), 80 Eighth Ave., New York NY 10011. (212)255-0230. Editor-in-Chief: Peter Glassgold. Small independent publisher. Publishes hardcover and paperback originals and reprints. Average print order: 1,000 hardback; 3,000 paperback. Sometimes critiques rejected ms.
Needs: "Mostly avant-garde; will look at everything, including poetry."
How to Contact: Accepts unsolicited mss. Query first with outline/synopsis and sample chapters. SASE. Reports in 6-8 weeks on queries; 3-4 months on mss. No simultaneous submissions.
Terms: Pays royalties. Offers advance. Publishes ms at least 1 year after acceptance, "depends on type of book."
Advice: "Try to get published in a literary magazine first to establish a writing reputation and for the experience."

Market conditions are constantly changing! If you're still using this book and it is 1994 or later, buy the newest edition of Novel & Short Story Writer's Market *at your favorite bookstore or order directly from Writer's Digest Books.*

NEW RIVERS PRESS, Suite 910, 420 North 5th St., Minneapolis MN 55401. Publisher: C.W. Truesdale. Estab. 1968. Plans 5 fiction titles in 1992.
- See also the Minnesota Voices Project, sponsored by New Rivers Press, listing in the Contests and Awards section of this book.

Needs: Contemporary, literary, experimental, translations. "No popular fantasy/romance. Nothing pious, polemical (unless very good other redeeming qualities). We are interested in only quality literature and always have been (though our concentration in the past has been poetry)." Published *Out Far, in Deep*, by Alvin Handleman (short stories); *Borrowed Voices*, by Roger Sheffer (short stories); and *Suburban Metaphysics*, by Ronald J. Rindo (short stories).

How to Contact: Query. SASE. Reports in 4-6 months on queries; within 4-6 months of query approval on mss. "No multiple submissions tolerated."

Terms: Pays 100 author's copies; also pays royalties; no advance. Minnesota Voices Series pays authors $500 plus 15% royalties on list price for second and subsequent printings. Free book catalog.

Advice: "We are not really concerned with trends. We read for quality, which experience has taught can be very eclectic and can come sometimes from out of nowhere. We are interested in publishing short fiction (as well as poetry and translations) because it is and has been a great indigenous American form and is almost completely ignored by the commercial houses. Find a *real* subject, something that belongs to you and not what you think or surmise that you should be doing by current standards and fads."

NEW VICTORIA PUBLISHERS, Box 27, Norwich VT 05055. (802)649-5297. Editor: Claudia Lamperti. Publishes trade paperback originals. Averages 4-5 titles/year.

Needs: Adventure, fantasy, lesbian, historical, humor, feminist, mystery (amateur sleuth), romance, science fiction (soft sociological), thriller and western. Looking for "strong feminist characters, also strong plot and action. We will consider most anything if it is well written and appeals to a lesbian/feminist audience." Publishes anthologies or special editions. Recently published *Shadows of Aggar*, by Chris Anne Wolfe; *Death of Jocasta*, by J.M. Redmann; and *Falling Through the Cracks*, by Fritzie Rogers.

How to Contact: Submit outline/synopsis and sample chapters. SASE. Reports in 2 weeks on queries; 1 month on mss. Disk submissions OK.

Terms: Pays royalties of 10%.

Advice: "We would particularly enjoy a humorous novel."

NEWEST PUBLISHERS LTD., (IV), #310, 10359 Whyte Ave., Edmonton, Alberta T6E 1Z9 Canada. General Manager: Liz Grieve. Estab. 1977. Publishes paperback originals. Published new writers within the last year. Plans 1 first novel this year. Averages 8 total titles, 2 fiction titles each year. Sometimes offers brief comments on rejected ms.
- NeWest was chosen by the Alberta Book Industry Awards as Publisher of the Year in 1990. The publisher is continuing its Nunatak New Fiction Series featuring new western Canadian writers.

Needs: Literary. "Our press is most interested in western Canadian literature." Recently published *Grace Lake*, by Glen Huser; *Mostly Country*, by Rosemary Nixon; *Could I Have My Body Back Now, Please? Body-Fictions*, by Beth Goobie; *Lion's Granddaughter and Other Stories*, by Yasmin Ladha (all literary). Publishes anthologies; stories selected by the editors.

How to Contact: Accepts unsolicited mss. Query first or submit outline/synopsis and 3 sample chapters. SASE (IRC) necessary for return of manuscript. Reports in 2 weeks on queries; 3 months on mss. Accepts electronic submissions.

Terms: Pays royalties of 10% minimum. Sends galleys to author. Publishes ms at least 1 year after acceptance. Book catalog for 9 × 12 SASE or IRC.

NIGHTSHADE PRESS, (II), Ward Hill, Troy ME 04987. (207)948-3427. Contact: Carolyn Page or Ted Holmes. Estab. 1988. "Fulltime small press publishing literary magazine, poetry chapbooks, one short story reader and 2 short story collections per year. Short stories *only*, no novels please." Publishes paperback originals. Books: 60 lb. paper; offset printing; saddle-stitched or perfect-bound; illustrations; average print order: 400. Published new writers within the last year. Averages about 20 total titles, 2 or more fiction titles, short story reader each year, plus short history collection. Sometimes comments on rejected ms.
- Nightshade Press also publishes *Potato Eyes* listed in this book. For more see the close-up interview with the publishers in the 1991 *Novel & Short Story Writer's Market*.

Needs: Contemporary, humor/satire, literary, mainstream, regional. No religious, romance, preschool, juvenile, young adult, fantasy, faction, horror, psychic/occult. Recently published *The Nightshade Short Story Reader*, edited by Edward M. Holmes; *Wood Head: Stories from up North*, by Rebecca Rule.
How to Contact: Accepts unsolicited mss—short stories only. Tend not to read agented material. Reports in 3 weeks on queries; 2-4 months on mss. Accepts electronic submissions.
Terms: Pays 2 author's copies. Publishes ms about 1 year after acceptance. Writer's guidelines and book catalog for SASE. Individual contracts negotiated with short story collection authors.
Advice: "Would like to see more real humor; less gratuitous violence—the opposite of TV. We have over dosed on heavily dialected southern stories which treat country people with a mixture of ridicule and exaggeration. We prefer treatment of characterization which offers dignity and respect for folks who make do with little and who respect their environment."

‡NUAGE EDITIONS, (II), P. O. Box 8, Station "E", Montreal, Quebec H2T 3A5 Canada. (514)272-5226. Fax: (514)271-1218. Editor-in-Chief: Karen Haughian. Estab. 1986. One-person operation on fulltime basis. Publishes hardcover and paperback originals and reprints. Books: offset paper; offset printing; perfect binding; average print order: 100; first novel print order: 500. Plans 1 first novel this year. Averages 6-8 total titles, 3 fiction titles each year. Sometimes comments on rejected mss.
Needs: Literary, mystery/suspense (literary who-done-it), short story collections, translations. Especially seeking "literary fiction, preferably Canadian." Plans anthology (short fiction/poetry). Editors select stories. Recently published *Loneliness of Angels*, by Valmai Howe (novel); *The Formal Logic of Emotion*, by Michael Mirolla (short stories); *The Ecstacy Conspiracy*, by Lesley Choyce (novel). Publishes The Performance Series (drama).
How to Contact: Submit outline/synopsis and 2 sample chapters. Should include one-page bio and list of publishing credits. Send SASE (IRC) for reply, return of ms or send a disposable copy of the ms. Agented fiction 10%. Reports in 1 month on queries; 6 months on mss. Simultaneous submissions OK. Accepts electronic submissions (absolutely 3 1/2").
Terms: Pays royalties of 10%. Sends galleys to author. Publishes 1 year maximum after acceptance. Book catalog for 9×12 SASE.

OMMATION PRESS, (II, IV), 5548 N. Sawyer, Chicago IL 60625. Imprints include *Mati Magazine*, *Ditto Rations Chapbook Series*, *Offset Offshoot Series*, *Salome: A Journal for the Performing Arts*, *Dialogues on Dance Series*. Editorial Director: Effie Mihopoulos. Estab. 1975. Rarely comments on rejected mss.
• *Mati* and *Salome* are listed in the Literary/Small Circulation section of this book.
Needs: Contemporary, literary, experimental, feminist, prose poetry. "For the Dialogues on Dance Series, dance-related fiction; for the Offset Offshoot Series, poetry mss, including prose poems." Published *Victims Of The Latest Dance Craze*, by Cornelius Eady (1985 Lamont Selection by Academy of American Poets); *Invisible Mirror*, by Michael Cadnum.
How to Contact: Submit complete ms with SASE. Simultaneous submissions OK, if so indicated. Reports in 1 month.
Terms: Pays 50 author's copies (and $100 honorarium if grant money available). Book catalog for #10 SASE.

ORCA BOOK PUBLISHERS LTD., (I, IV), P.O. Box 5626, Sta. B, Victoria, British Columbia V8R 6S4 Canada. (604)380-1229. Publisher: R.J. Tyrrell. Estab. 1984. "Regional publisher of West Coast-oriented titles." Publishes hardcover and paperback originals. Books: quality 60 lb. book stock paper; illustrations; average print order: 3,000-5,000; first novel print order: 2,000-3,000. Plans 1-2 first novels this year. Averages 12 total titles, 2-3 fiction titles each year. Sometimes comments on rejected ms.
Needs: Contemporary, juvenile (5-9 years), literary, mainstream, young adult/teen (10-18 years). Looking for "contemporary fiction." No "romance, science fiction."
How to Contact: Publishes Canadian authors only. Query first, then submit outline/synopsis and 1 or 2 sample chapters. SASE. Agented fiction 20%. Reports in 2 weeks on queries; 1-2 months on mss.
Terms: Pays royalties of 10%; $500 average advance. Sends galleys to author. Publishes ms 6 months-1 year after acceptance. Writer's guidelines for SASE (IRC). Book catalog for 8½×11 SASE (IRC).
Advice: "We are looking to promote and publish new West Coast writers, especially Canadians."

OUR CHILD PRESS, 800 Maple Glen Lane, Wayne PA 19087. (215)964-0606. CEO: Carol Hallenbeck. Estab. 1984. Publishes hardcover and paperback originals and reprints. Published new writers within the last year. Plans 2 first novels this year. Plans 2 titles this year. Sometimes comments on rejected ms.

Needs: Adventure, contemporary, fantasy, juvenile (5-9 yrs.), preschool/picture book and young adult/ teen (10-18 years). Especially interested in books on adoption or learning disabilities. Published *Don't Call Me Marda*, by Sheila Welch (juvenile); and *Oliver—An Adoption Story*, by Lois Wickstrom.
How to Contact: Does not accept unsolicited mss. Query first. Reports in 2 weeks on queries; 2 months on mss. Simultaneous submissions OK.
Terms: Pays royalties of 5% minimum. Publishes ms up to 6 months after acceptance. Book catalog free.

THE OVERLOOK PRESS, 149 Wooster St., New York NY 10012. (212)477-7162. Estab. 1972. Small-staffed, full-time operation. Publishes hardcover and paperback originals and reprints. Averages 30 total titles; 7 fiction titles each year. Occasionally critiques rejected mss.
Needs: Fantasy, juvenile (fantasy, historical, sports, contemporary), literary, psychic/supernatural/ occult, regional (Hudson Valley), science fiction (hard science), thriller/espionage, translations. No romance or horror. Recently published *Divina Trace*, by Robert Antoni (novel); *The Diamond Lane*, by Karen Karbo (novel); *Cafe Berlin*, by Harold Nebenzal (novel).
How to Contact: Query first or submit outline/synopsis. SASE. Allow up to 6 months for reports on queries. Simultaneous submissions OK.
Terms: Vary.

‡OWL CREEK PRESS (III), 1620 N. 45th St., Seattle WA 98103. (206)633-5929. Editor: Rich Ives. Estab. 1979. Small independent literary publisher with plans to expand. Publishes hardcover and paperback originals. Books: photo offset printing; case or perfect binding; illustrations sometimes; average print order: 1,000; first novel print order: 1,000. Plans 3-4 short fiction collections/novels in next year or two. Averages 7 total titles, 0-3 fiction titles each year. Occasionally critiques rejected ms.
Needs: Contemporary, literary, short story collections, and translations. "Literary quality is our only criteria." No formula fiction.
How to Contact: Accepts unsolicited mss. "We recommend purchase of sample issue ($3 back issue, $5 current) of *The Montana Review* to determine our interests." Submit 1-3 sample chapters with SASE. Reports in 2 months. Simultaneous submissions OK (if stated). Publishes ms 3-18 months after acceptance.
Terms: Payment depends on grant/award money. Possible payment in royalties of 10% minimum, 20% maximum; author's copies, 10% of run minimum. Book catalog for SASE.
Advice: "We are expanding in all areas. The number of fiction titles in the next 2-3 years will depend on grants, sales and the quality of submissions. We ignore trends. Subject is irrelevant. Our *only* criterion is quality of the writing itself. Write to last—ignore fads and 'market advice'; good writers create their own markets."

PANDO PUBLICATIONS, (II), 5396 Laurie Lane, Memphis TN 38120. (901)682-8779. Editorial Contact Person: Andrew Bernstein. Estab. 1987. "Two person, full-time book publisher." Publishes hardcover and paperback originals. Books: 60 lb. paper; perfect-bound, Smythe-sewn or hardcover binding; average print order: 3,000-9,000. Averages 6-10 total titles each year. Rarely comments on rejected mss.
Needs: Adventure, historical, humor/satire, juvenile (animal, easy-to-read, historical, sports, spy/adventure, contemporary), mainstream, military/war, mystery/suspense, regional, science fiction, young adult/teen (easy-to-read, fantasy/science fiction, historical, problem novels, sports, spy/adventure).
How to Contact: Accepts unsolicited mss. Submit outline/synopsis and 3 sample chapters. SASE for ms. Reports in 1 month on queries; 3-4 months on ms. Simultaneous submissions OK. Accepts electronic submissions via WordPerfect.
Terms: Pays royalties of 6-12½%. Average advance is about ⅓ of royalty of 1st run; negotiable. Sends galleys to author. Publishes ms 6 months after acceptance.
Advice: Would like to see "more children's stories based on myth and legend, current happenings (world events, politics, demographic movements, social problems, ecological concerns, medical problems, growing up in a TV-VCR-cable-computer world, and so on)."

PAPIER-MACHE PRESS, (IV), 795 Via Manzana, Watsonville CA 95076. (408)726-2933. Editor/Publisher: Sandra Martz. Estab. 1984. Three-person operation on a full-time basis. Publishes anthologies and "poetry and fiction" originals. Books: 60-70 lb. offset paper; perfect-bound or case-bound; photographs; average print order: 3,000-6,000 copies. Published new writers within the last year. Publishes 4-6 total titles/year; 4-6 fiction/poetry titles/year.

Needs: Contemporary, feminist, short story collections, women's. Recently published fiction by Mary Ann Ashley, Molly Martin, Ruthann Robson; and *Merle's and Marilyn's Mink Ranch*, by Randeane Tetu.
How to Contact: Query first. SASE. Reports in 2 months on queries; 6 months on mss. Simultaneous and photocopied submissions OK. Accepts computer printouts.
Terms: Standard royalty agreements for novels/fiction collections. Complimentary copies for anthology contributors; honorarium for contributors when anthologies go into second printings.
Advice: "Indicate with your manuscript whether or not you are open to revision suggestions. Always indicate on original submission if this is a simultaneous submission or a previously published work. We can handle either, but only if we know in advance. Absolutely essential to query first."

‡PAPYRUS PUBLISHERS, (III), Box 466, Yonkers NY 10704. (914)664-0840. Editor-in-Chief: Geoffrey Hutchison-Cleaves. Fiction Editor: Jessie Rosé. Estab. London 1946; USA 1982. Small publisher. Publishes hardcover originals and reprints. Audio books; average print order 2,500. Averages 3 total titles each year (all fiction).
Needs: Mystery/suspense. "No erotica, gay, feminist, children's, spiritual, lesbian, political. Published *Wilderness*, by Tony Dawson (suspense); *Curse of the Painted Cats*, by Heather Latimer (romantic suspense); *Louis Wain — King of the Cat Artists 1860-1939*, by Heather Latimer (dramatized biography).
How to Contact: Does not accept unsolicited mss. Query first. SASE. Reports on queries in 6 weeks. "Not accepting right now."
Terms: Pays royalties of 10% minimum. Advance varies. Publishes ms 1 year after acceptance. Book catalog for SASE or IRC.

PATH PRESS, INC., (II), Suite 724, 53 W. Jackson, Chicago IL 60604. (312)663-0167. Fax: (312)663-0318. Editorial Director: Herman C. Gilbert. "Small independent publisher which specializes in books by, for and about Black Americans and Third World Peoples." Published new writers within the last year. Averages 6 total titles, 3 fiction titles each year. Occasionally critiques rejected ms.
Needs: Ethnic, historical, sports, and short story collections. Needs for novels include "black or minority-oriented novels of any genre, style or subject." Published *Brown Sky*, by David Covin (a novel of World War II); *Congo Crew*, by William Goodlett (a novel set in Africa during 1960-61).
How to Contact: Accepts unsolicited mss. Query first or submit outline/synopsis and 5 sample chapters with SASE. Reports in 2 months on queries; 4 months on mss. Simultaneous submissions OK.
Terms: Pays in royalties.
Advice: "Deal honestly with your subject matter and with your characters. Dig deeply into the motivations of your characters, regardless how painful it might be to you personally."

PAYCOCK PRESS, (II), Apt. #1, 5025 Bradley Blvd., Chevy Chase MD 20815. (301)656-5146. Editor/Publisher: Richard Peabody. Estab. 1976. Small independent publisher with international distribution. Publishes paperback originals and reprints. Books: 55 lb. natural paper; offset printing; perfect-bound; some illustrations; average print order: 1,000; first novel print order: 1,000. Encourages new writers. Averages 1 title each year. Occasionally comments on rejected mss. "Recently started producing audio tapes of music/spoken-word material."
Needs: Contemporary, literary, experimental, humor/satire and translations. "No tedious AWP résumé-conscious writing or NEA-funded minimalism. We'd be interested in a good first novel that deals with the musical changes of the past few years." Published *The Love Letter Hack*, by Michael Brondoli (contemporary/literary); *Natural History*, by George Myers, Jr. (poems and stories); and *The Walking Rain*, by Fortune Nagle (poems and stories).
How to Contact: Query with SASE. Reports in 1 week on queries; 1 month on mss.
Terms: Pays in author's copies — 10% of print run plus 50% of all sales "after/if we break even on book." No advance. Sends galleys to author.
Advice: "Keep trying. Many good writers simply quit. Many mediocre writers keep writing, eventually get published, and become better writers. If the big magazines won't publish you, try the small magazines, try the local newspaper. Always read your fiction aloud. If you think something is *silly*, no doubt we'd be embarrassed too. Write the kind of stories you'd like to read and can't seem to find. We are more concerned with *how* a novelist says what he/she says, than with *what* he/she says. We are more interested in *right now* than in books about the '50s, '60s, '70s, etc. We are publishing more in anthology format, and encourage first novelists."

PERMEABLE PRESS, (I), 900 Tennessee #15, San Francisco CA 94107-3014. (415)648-2175. Imprints are Xerotic Ephemera, Puck! Publisher: Brian Clark. Editor: Kurt Putnam. Estab. 1984. "Small literary press with inhouse design and typesetting." Publishes hardcover and paperback originals and paperback reprints. Books: 60 lb. paper; offset printing; perfect-bound; illustrations; average print order: 3,500. Published new writers within the last year. Plans 1 first novel this year. Averages 3 total titles, all fiction, each year. Sometimes comments on rejected ms.

Needs: Erotica, experimental, feminist, gay, historical, juvenile, lesbian, literary, preschool/picture book, psychic/supernatural/occult, science fiction (hard science, soft sociological), short story collections, thriller/espionage. Looking for "cyberpunk; conspiracy. Should be challenging to read." No romance. Recently published *Shaman*, by Hugh Fox (experimental memoir); and *The Royal Elephant*, by Lorraine Morrison (children's); *Shadow Self*, by Helen Duberstein (short stories).

How to Contact: Accepts unsolicited mss. Query first or submit outline/synopsis and 3 sample chapters. SASE. Reports in 4-6 weeks on queries; 3 months on mss. Accepts electronic submissions.

Terms: Pays royalties of 5-20%. Author's copies vary. Honorarium depends on grant/award money. Sends galleys to author. Writer's guidelines and book catalog for 9×12 SAE and 4 first class stamps.

Advice: "As a design firm our business has grown rapidly in several areas. Consequently we are currently looking for hot new titles as well as bargain reprint rights."

PIKESTAFF PUBLICATIONS, INC., (I, II), Box 127, Normal IL 61761. (309)452-4831. Imprints include The Pikestaff Press: Pikestaff Fiction Chapbooks; *The Pikestaff Forum*, general literary magazine. Editorial Directors: Robert D. Sutherland and James R. Scrimgeour. Estab. 1977. Small independent publisher with plans to expand gradually. Publishes hardcover and paperback originals. Books: paper varies; offset printing; b&w illustrations; average print order: 500-2,000. "One of the purposes of the press is to encourage new talent." Occasionally comments on rejected mss.

Needs: Contemporary, literary, and experimental. "No slick formula writing written with an eye to the commercial mass market or pure entertainment that does not provide insights into the human condition. Not interested in heroic fantasy (dungeons & dragons, swords & sorcery); science fiction of the space-opera variety; westerns; mysteries; love-romance; gothic adventure; or pornography (sexploitation)." Published fiction by Constance Pierce and Linnea Johnson.

How to Contact: Query or submit outline/synopsis and 1-2 sample chapters. "Anyone may inquire; affirmative responses may submit ms." SASE. Reports in 1 month on queries; 3 months on mss. No simultaneous submissions.

Terms: Negotiates terms with author. Sends galleys to author. Publishes ms within 1 year after acceptance.

Advice: "Have fictional characters we can really *care* about; we are tired of disembodied characters wandering about in their heads unable to relate to other people or the world about them. Avoid too much TELLING; let the reader participate by leaving something for him or her to do. Yet avoid vagueness, opaqueness, personal or 'private' symbolisms and allusions. Here we regard the relationship between the writer and editor as a cooperative relationship—we are colleagues in getting the book out. The writer has an obligation to do the best self-editing job of which he or she is capable; writers should not rely on editors to make their books presentable. Don't give up easily; understand your reasons for wanting the work published (personal satisfaction? money? fame? to 'prove' something? to 'be a novelist'? etc.). Ask yourself honestly, Should it be published? What can it provide for a reader that makes it worth part of that reader's *lifetime* to read? Be prepared for shocks and disappointments; study contracts carefully and retain as many rights and as much control over the book's appearance as possible. Be prepared to learn how to be your own best promoter and publicist."

PINEAPPLE PRESS, (II), P.O. Drawer 16008, Southside Station, Sarasota FL 34239. (813)952-1085. Executive Editor: June Cussen. Estab. 1982. Small independent trade publisher. Publishes hardcover and paperback originals and paperback reprints. Books: quality paper; offset printing; Smythe-sewn or perfect-bound; illustrations occasionally; average print order: 5,000; first novel print order: 2,000-5,000. Published new writers within the last year. Averages 12 total titles each year. Occasionally critiques rejected ms.

Needs: Contemporary, experimental, historical, environmental, regional, how-to and reference. Published *Princess of the Everglades*, by Charles Mink (novel).

How to Contact: Prefers query, outline or one-page synopsis with sample chapters (including the first) and SASE. Then if requested, submit complete ms with SASE. Reports in 2 months. Simultaneous submissions OK.

Terms: Pays royalties of 7½-15%. Advance is not usually offered. "Basically, it is an individual agreement with each author depending on the book." Sends galleys to author. Book catalog sent if label and 52¢ postage enclosed.

Advice: "We publish both Florida regional books and general trade fiction and nonfiction. Quality first novels will be published, though we usually only do one novel per year. We regard the author/editor relationship as a trusting relationship with communication open both ways. Learn all you can about the publishing process and about how to promote your book once it is published."

PIPPIN PRESS, 229 East 85th Street, Gracie Station Box 92, New York NY 10028. (212)288-4920. Publisher: Barbara Francis. Estab. 1987. "Small, independent children's book company, formed by the former editor-in-chief of Prentice Hall's juvenile division." Publishes hardcover originals. Books: 135-150 GSM offset-semi-matte paper (for picture books); offset, sheet-fed printing; Smythe-sewn binding; full color, black and white line illustrations and half tone, b&w and full color photographs. Averages 8-12 titles each year. Sometimes comments on rejected mss.

Needs: Juvenile only (5-9 yrs. including animal, easy-to-read, fantasy, science, humorous, spy/adventure). "I am interested in humorous novels for children of about 7-12 and in picture books with the focus on humor."

How to Contact: No unsolicited mss. Query first or submit outline/synopsis and 2 sample chapters. SASE. Reports in 2-3 weeks on queries; 3 months on mss. Simultaneous submissions OK.

Terms: Pays royalties. Sends galleys to author. Publication time after ms is accepted "depends on the amount of revision required, type of illustration, etc."

*POCAHONTAS PRESS, INC., (I, IV), Manuscript Memories, 832 Hulcheson Dr., Blacksburg VA 24060-3259. (703)951-0467. Editorial contact person: Mary C. Holliman. Estab. 1984. "One-person operation on part-time basis, with several part-time colleagues. Subjects not limited, but stories about real people are almost always required. Main intended audience is youth—young adults, ages 10-18." Books: 70 lb. white offset paper; offset litho printing; perfect binding; illustrations; average print order: 3,000-5,000. Averages 4 total titles, 2-3 fiction titles each year. Usually critiques or comments on rejected mss.

   • This press uses very little fiction. The publisher may consider making a short story into a short book, but does not generally publish novels or collections.

Needs: "Stories based on historical facts about real people." Contemporary, ethnic, historical, sports, regional, translations, western. "I will treat a short story as a book, with illustrations and a translation into Spanish or French and also Chinese someday." No fantasy or horror. Published *From Lions to Lincoln*, by Fran Hartman; and *Mountain Summer*, by Bill Mashburn.

How to Contact: Accepts unsolicited mss. Query first. "I don't expect to be considering any new material until mid-1993. I need to complete current projects first." Reports in 1 month on queries; 1-2 months on mss. "I try to meet these deadlines but seldom succeed." Simultaneous submissions OK. "If simultaneous, I would need to know up front what other options the author is considering."

Terms: Pays royalties of 10% maximum. $50 advance negotiable. Sends galleys to author. "I will subsidy publish—but expect book and author to meet the same qualifications as a regular author, and will pay royalties on all copies sold as well as pay back the author's investment as books are sold."

Advice: "Get an unbiased, non-friend editor and follow his or her suggestions. There's more good, publishable material out there than can ever all get published—don't get discouraged but keep trying—and keep revising."

POLESTAR BOOK PUBLISHERS, (I, II), P.O. Box 69382, Station K, Vancouver, British Columbia V5K 4W6 Canada. (604)251-9718. Publisher: Michelle Benjamin. Estab. 1983. "Small literary press with eclectic list of fiction, poetry, nonfiction and hockey books." Publishes paperback originals. Published new writers within the last year. Plans 2 first novels this year. Averages 10 total titles, 4-6 fiction titles each year. Sometimes comments on rejected ms.

Needs: Open. "No racist, sexist, violent themes/issues." Recently published *Rapid Transits*, by Holley Rubinsky (short stories); and *Disturbing the Peace*, by Caroline Woodward (short stories).

How to Contact: Accepts unsolicited mss. Submit outline/synopsis and 3 sample chapters. SASE. Agented fiction 10%. Reports in 1 month on queries; 6-8 weeks on mss. Simultaneous submissions OK.

Terms: Pays royalties of 10-12%; and 10 author's copies. Advance negotiable; $400 average. Sends galleys to author. Publication time after acceptance varies. Book catalog free.
Advice: "We have a Polestar First Fiction Series. We like the excitement of discovering new writers . . . feel *somewhat* that this is the role of the small press. We would like to see more passionate writing, less excess words."

THE PRAIRIE PUBLISHING COMPANY, Box 2997, Winnipeg, Manitoba R3C 4B5 Canada. (204)885-6496. Publisher: Ralph Watkins. Estab. 1969. Buys juvenile mss with illustrations. Books: 60 lb. high-bulk paper; offset printing; perfect-bound; line-drawings; average print order: 2,000; first novel print order: 2,000.
Needs: Open. Published: *The Homeplace*, (historical novel); *My Name is Marie Anne Gaboury*, (first French-Canadian woman in the Northwest); and *The Tale of Jonathan Thimblemouse*. Published work by previously unpublished writers within the last year.
How to Contact: Query with SASE or IRC. No simultaneous submissions. Reports in 1 month on queries, 6 weeks on mss. Publishes ms 4-6 months after acceptance. Free book catalog.
Terms: Pays 10% in royalties. No advance.
Advice: "We work on a manuscript with the intensity of a Max Perkins of Charles Scribner's Sons of New York. A clean, well-prepared manuscript can go a long way toward making an editor's job easier. On the other hand, the author should not attempt to anticipate the format of the book, which is a decision for the publisher to make. In order to succeed in today's market, the story must be tight, well written and to the point. Do not be discouraged by rejections."

PRESS GANG PUBLISHERS, (II, IV), 603 Powell St., Vancouver, British Columbia V6A 1H2 Canada. (604)253-2537. Estab. 1974. Feminist press, 3 full-time staff. Publishes paperback originals and reprints. Books: paperback; offset printing; perfect-bound; average print order: 3,500; first novel print order: 2,000. Plans 2 novels this year. Sometimes critiques rejected mss.
Needs: Looking for "feminist, mystery/suspense, short stories." Also accepts contemporary, erotica, ethnic (native women especially), humor/satire, lesbian, literary, science fiction. No children's/young adult/teen. Recently published *Paper, Scissors, Rock*, by Ann Decter (novel); *Sing Me No More*, by Lynette Dueck (novel); *Food & Spirits*, by Beth Brant (stories).
How to Contact: Accepts unsolicited mss. Query first. SASE (IRC). Reports in 2 months on queries; 3-4 months on mss. Simultaneous submissions OK. Accepts AT compatible discs.
Terms: Pays 8-10% royalties. Sends galleys to author. Book catalog free on request.

PUCKERBRUSH PRESS, (I,II), 76 Main St., Orono ME 04473. (207)581-3832. Publisher/Editor: Constance Hunting. Estab. 1979. One-person operation on part-time basis. Publishes paperback originals. Books: laser printing; perfect-bound; sometimes illustrations; average print order: 1,000. Published new writers within the last year. Averages 3 total titles (poetry) each year. Sometimes comments on rejected ms. *If detailed comment, $500.*
• An interview with Publisher Constance Hunting appeared in the 1992 *Writer's Market*. The publisher has been concentrating on poetry lately, but may consider fiction. See the listing for *Puckerbrush Review* in this book.
Needs: Contemporary, experimental, literary.
How to Contact: Accepts unsolicited mss. Submit complete ms with cover letter. SASE. Reports in 2 weeks on queries; 2 months on mss.
Terms: Pays royalties of 10%; 10 author's copies. Sends galleys to author. Publishes ms usually 1 year after acceptance. Writer's guidelines for #10 SAE and 1 first class stamp. "I have a book list and flyers."

*Q.E.D. PRESS, (II), 155 Cypress St., Ft. Bragg CA 95437. (707)964-9520. Senior Editor: John Fremont. Estab. 1985. "Small press publisher subsidiary of mid-size production house." Publishes hardcover and paperback originals. Books: acid free recycled 60 lb. paper; offset or Cameron Belt printing; perfect or Smythe-sewn binding; average print order: 3,000; first novel print order: 1,000. Plans 1 first novel this year. Averages 10 total titles, 2-3 fiction titles each year.
Needs: Experimental, faction, literary, mystery/suspense, translations. "Our needs are minimal, but we'll jump on something we think is hot. No formula anything." Recently published *The Lion and the Flame*, by Daniel Liebrwitz; *The Long Rench*, by Susan Davis; *The Itaole Substitute*, by Walt Novak.

How to Contact: Accepts unsolicited mss. Submit outline/synopsis with 3 sample chapters. SASE. Agented fiction 10%. Reports in 3 weeks on queries; 5 weeks on mss.
Terms: Pays royalties of 8-15%. *Subsidy publishes under another imprint.* Publishes ms 6 months to 2 years after acceptance. Writer's guidelines not available. Book catalog free.

QUARRY PRESS, (I,II), Box 1061, Kingston, Ontario, K7L 4Y5 Canada. (613)548-8429. Managing Editor: Melanie Dugan. Estab. 1965. Small independent publisher with plans to expand. Publishes paperback originals. Books: Rolland tint paper; offset printing; perfect-bound; illustrations; average print order: 1,200; first novel print order: 1,200. Published new writers within the past year. Plans 1 first novel this year. Averages 20 total titles, 4 fiction titles each year. Sometimes comments on rejected mss.
Needs: Experimental, feminist, historical, literary, short story collections. Published *Ritual Slaughter,* by Sharon Drache; *Engaged Elsewhere,* edited by Kent Thompson (includes work by Mavis Gallant, Margaret Laurence, Dougles Glover, Ray Smitz, Keath Fraser and others); published fiction by previously unpublished writers within the last year.
How to Contact: Accepts unsolicited mss. Query first. SASE for query and ms. Reports in 4 months. Simultaneous submissions OK.
Terms: Pays royalties of 7-10%. Advance: negotiable. Provides 5-10 author's copies. Sends galleys to author. Publishes ms 6-8 months after acceptance. Book catalog free on request.
Advice: "Publishing more fiction than in the past. Encourages first novelists. Canadian authors only for New Canadian Novelists Series. If mailing from US, need SAE with IRC (a must)."

*READ 'N RUN BOOKS (I), Subsidiary of Crumb Elbow Publishing, Box 294, Rhododendron OR 97049. (503)622-4798. Imprints are Elbow Books, Research Centrex, Wind Flow Press, Silhouette Imprints, Tyre Press, Oregon Fever Books and Trillium Art Productions. Publisher: Michael P. Jones. Estab. 1978. Small independent publisher with three on staff. Publishes hardcover and paperback originals and reprints. Books: special order paper; offset printing; "usually a lot" of illustrations; average print order: varies. Published new writers within the last year. Plans 1 first novel this year. Averages 10 titles, 2 fiction titles each year. Sometimes comments on rejected ms; *$75 charge for critiques depending upon length. May be less or more.*
Needs: Adventure, contemporary, ethnic, experimental, fantasy, feminist, historical, horror, humor/ satire, juvenile (animal, easy-to-read, fantasy, historical, sports, spy/adventure, contemporary), literary, mainstream, military/war, preschool/picture book, psychic/supernatural/occult, regional, religious/ inspirational, romance (contemporary, historical), science fiction, short story collections, spiritual, suspense/mystery, translations, western, young adult/teen (easy-to-read, fantasy/science fiction, historical, problem novels, romance, sports, spy/adventure). Looking for fiction on "historical and wildlife" subjects. "Also, some creative short stories would be nice to see for a change. No pornography." Recently published *Umpqua Agriculture, 1851,* by Jesse Applegate; *Life on the Oregon,* by Alfred Setan; *Samuel Kimbrough Barlow: A Pioneer Road Builder of Oregon,* by Mary Barlow Wilkins. This year starting anthology to give writers a chance to express themselves about nature and the environment.
How to Contact: Accepts unsolicited ms. Query first. Submit outline/synopsis and complete ms with cover letter. SASE. Reports in 1 month on queries; 1-2 months on mss. Simultaneous submissions OK.
Terms: Provides 5+ author's copies (negotiated). Sends galleys to author. Publishes ms 10-12 months after acceptance. *Subsidy publishes two books or more/year.* Terms vary from book to book. Writer's guidelines for 45¢ postage. Book catalog for SASE or IRC and $1.25 postage.
Advice: Publishing "more hardcover fiction books based on real-life events. They are in demand by libraries. Submit everything you have—even artwork. Also, if you have ideas for layout, provide those also. If you have an illustrator that you're working with, be sure to get them in touch with us. We are a great place for writers to get started if they have a professional working attitude and manner."

 The asterisk indicates a publisher who sometimes offers subsidy arrangements. Authors are asked to subsidize part of the cost of book production. See the introduction for more information.

RED DEER COLLEGE PRESS, (I, IV), Box 5005, Red Deer, Alberta T4N 5H5 Canada. (403)342-3321. Managing Editor: Dennis Johnson. Estab. 1975. Publishes hardcover and paperback originals. Books: offset paper; offset printing; hardcover/perfect-bound; average print order: 1,000-4,000; first novel print order: 2,500. Plans 2 first novels this year. Averages 10-12 total titles, 2 fiction titles each year. Sometimes comments on rejected mss.
Needs: Contemporary, experimental, literary, short story collections. No romance, sci-fi.
How to Contact: *Canadian authors only.* Does not accept unsolicited mss. Query first or submit outline/synopsis and 2 sample chapters. SASE. Agented fiction 10%. Reports in 1 month on queries; in 3 months on mss. Simultaneous submissions OK.
Terms: Pays royalties of 8-10%. Advance is negotiable. Sends galleys to author. Publishes ms 1 year after acceptance. Book catalog for 9 × 12 SASE (IRC).
Advice: "Final manuscripts must be submitted on Mac disk in MS Word. Absolutely *no* unsolicited mss. Query first."

REFERENCE PRESS, (IV), Box 70, Teeswater, Ontario N0G 2S0 Canada. (519)392-6634. Imprints are RP Large Print Books. Editor: Gordon Ripley. Estab. 1982. Small independent Canadian publisher of library reference material, computer software and large print books. Hardcover and paperback originals and hardcover reprints. Books: 70 lb. Zepher laid paper; offset printing; casebound, some perfect-bound; average print order: 1,000. Published new writers within the last year. Averages 10 total titles, 4 fiction titles each year. Always comments on rejected mss.
Needs: Sports. Published *Canadian Sports Stories* (fiction, anthology); *Dance Me Outside* and *Born Indian*, by W.P. Kinsella (large print).
Terms: Pays in royalties of 10%; 5 author's copies. Writer's guidelines and book catalog free. Accepts unsolicited mss. Accepts electronic submissions.

RIO GRANDE PRESS, (I), Imprints include *Se La Vie Writer's Journal*, P.O. Box 371371, El Paso TX 79937. (915)595-2625. Publisher: Rosalie Avara. Estab. 1989. "One person operation on a half-time basis. Planning to expand to story anthologies and/or novelettes in 1993." Publishes paperback originals. Books: offset printing; saddle stitching binding; average print order: 100. Published new writers within the last year. Plans 2-3 first novels this year. Averages 10 total titles, 2 fiction titles each year. Sometimes comments on rejected ms.
• Look for the *Se La Vie Writer's Journal* contest listing in this book.
Needs: Adventure, contemporary, ethnic, family saga, fantasy, humor/satire, literary, mystery/suspense (amateur sleuth, romantic suspense, private eye), regional, short story collections. Looking for "general interest, slice of life stories; good, clean, wholesome stories about everyday people. No sex, nor porn, no science fiction (although I may consider flights of fantasy, day dreams, etc.), no religious. Any subject within the 'wholesome' limits. No experimental styles, just good conventional plot, characters, dialogue."
How to Contact: Query first then submit outline/synopsis and 1st/last sample chapters or 2 stories in a collection. SASE. Reports in 2 weeks on queries; 3-4 weeks on mss.
Terms: Pays 1 author's copy, depends on grant/award money (if contest is involved, up to $25.) "Short story collections and/or novelettes—individual arrangements with author, depending on ms—probably a contributor's copy plus publication and review in *Se La Vie Writer's Journal*." Sends galleys to author (once only). Publishes ms 2-4 months after acceptance. Writer's guidelines for #10 SAE and 2 first class stamps. Book catalog for #10 SAE and 2 first class stamps.
Advice: "I enjoy working with writers new to fiction, especially when I see that they have really worked hard on their craft, i.e., cutting out all unnecessary words, using action dialogue, interesting descriptive scenes, thought-out plots and well rounded characters that are believable. Please read listing carefully noting what type and subject of fiction is desired. Don't send the entire ms (book) packed in a heavy (costly) book box. Please send me a short cover letter giving brief history of your writing experience or credits. If none, just say so. Or, send me the first and last chapters, and one central character description (a short synopsis, maybe). Would like to see more stories or novelettes with a Southwestern flavor; story collections centered around a central theme; novelettes that give a personal insight into age old problems of life."

RISING TIDE PRESS, (II), 5 Kivy St., Huntington Station NY 11746. (516)427-1289. Editor: Lee Boojamra. Estab. 1988. "Small, independent press, publishing lesbian fiction—novels only—no short stories." Publishes paperback trade originals. Books: 50-60 lb. offset paper; web printing; perfect-bound; average print order: 5,000; first novel print order: 4,000-6,000. Plans 4 first novels this year. Averages 4-6 total titles. Comments on rejected ms.

Needs: Lesbian adventure, contemporary, erotica, fantasy, feminist, lesbian, romance, science fiction, suspense/mystery, western. Looking for romance and mystery. "Nothing with heterosexual content." Published *Romancing The Dream*, by H.H. Johanna; *Edge of Passion*, by Shelley Smith.
How to Contact: Accept unsolicited mss. with SASE. Reports in 1 week on queries; 3-4 months on mss.
Terms: Pays 10-15% royalties. "We will assist writers who wish to self-publish for a nominal fee." Sends galleys to author. Publishes ms 6-18 months after acceptance. Writer's guidelines free for #10 SAE and 1 first class stamp.

‡SAND RIVER PRESS, (I), 1319 14th St., Los Osos CA 93402. (805)543-3591. Editor: Bruce Miller. Estab. 1987. "Small press." Publishes paperback originals. Books: offset printing; b&w or color illustrations; average print order: 3,000; first novel print order: 2,000. Averages 2-3 total titles, 1 fiction title each year. Sometimes comments on rejected ms.
Needs: Childrens/juvenile, erotica, ethnic/multicultural, horror (futuristic); lesbian, literary, mystery/suspense (private eye/hardboiled, amateur sleuth, malice domestic, police procedural); new age/mystic/spiritual; regional (west); science fiction (hard science). Publishes literary best anthology.
How to Contact: Accepts unsolicited mss. Submit outline/synopsis and 3 sample chapters. Include list of publishing credits. SASE for return of ms or a disposable copy of the ms. Reports in 3 weeks on queries; 6 weeks on mss. Simultaneous submissions OK.
Terms: Pays royalties of 8% minimum; 15% maximum. Average advance: $500-1,000. Provides 10 author's copies. Sends galleys to author. Publishes ms 1 year after acceptance. Book catalog for SASE.

SANDPIPER PRESS, (IV), Box 286, Brookings OR 97415. (503)469-5588. Owner: Marilyn Reed Riddle. Estab. 1979. One-person operation specializing in low-cost large-print 18 pt. books. Publishes paperback originals. Books: 70 lb. paper; saddle stitch binding, perfect-bound, 84 pages maximum; leatherette cover; b&w sketches or photos; average print order 2,000; no novels. Averages 1 title every 2 years. Occasionally critiques or comments on rejected mss.
Needs: From Native American "Indian" writers only, *true* visions and prophesies; from general public writers, unusual quotations, sayings.
How to Contact: Does not accept unsolicited mss. Query first or submit outline/synopsis. SASE. Reports in 1 month on queries; 1 month on mss. Simultaneous submissions OK.
Terms: Pays 2 author's copies and $10 Native American. Publisher buys true story and owns copyright. Author may buy any number of copies at 40% discount and postage. Book catalog for #10 SAE and 1 first class stamp.
Advice: Send SASE for more information.

THE SAVANT GARDE WORKSHOP, (I, II, IV), a privately-owned affiliate of The Savant Garde Institute, Ltd., P.O. Box 1650, Sag Harbor NY 11963. (516)725-1414. Publisher: Vilna Jorgen II. Estab. 1953. "Midsize multiple-media publisher." Publishes hardcover and paperback originals and reprints. Averages 2 total titles. Sometimes comments on rejected ms.
- Be sure to look at this publisher's guidelines first. Works could best be described as avant-garde/art-related, experimental.
Needs: Contemporary, family saga, fantasy, feminist, humanist, literary, mystery/suspense, philosophical, science fiction (soft sociological), spiritual, thriller/espionage. "We are open to the best, whatever it is." No "mediocrity, pot boilers, sadism or horror or erotica with no redeeming message." Recently published *01 or a Machine Called SKEETS*, by Artemis Smith (avant garde).
How to Contact: Query first with SASE. Agented fiction 50%. Reports in 1 week on queries; 3 weeks on mss. Simultaneous submissions OK. Accepts electronic submissions.
Terms: Average advance: $500, provides author's copies, honorarium (depends on grant/award money). Terms set by individual arrangement with author depending on the book and previous professional experience. Sends galleys to author. Publishes ms 18 months after acceptance. Writer's guidelines free.
Advice: "Most of the time we recommend authors to literary agents who can get better deals for them with other publishers, since we are looking for extremely rare offerings. We are not interested in the usual commercial submissions. Convince us you are a real artist, not a hacker." Would like to see more "thinking for the 21st Century of Nobel Prize calibre. We're expanding into multimedia CD-ROM copublishing and seek multitalented authors who can produce and perform their own multimedia work for CD-ROM release, primarily for the academic library market, later also for bookstores."

Close-up

Judith Shepard
Co-publisher
Second Chance Press
Permanent Press

© Martin Shepard

With Permanent Press and Second Chance Press you get just what the names imply. "Permanent Press takes original manuscripts," says Judith Shepard, half of the husband and wife publishing team who provide the guiding spirit for both presses, "while Second Chance Press takes once-published books we feel have been neglected or forgotten. And we never let our books go out of print.

"When we started out, some 120 titles ago, we did more Second Chance Press books, and fewer Permanent Press books. But as the years have gone on, we're doing more Permanent Press books."

In the beginning, they took books of every variety: humor, cookbooks, even political books. "After a while, we began to see that we did the best with literary fiction," she said.

Although they usually put out only 12 books a year, "we're willing to take a chance on a new writer," says Shepard, who reads all of the more than 3,000 submissions yearly.

"If I find something I really like, I pass it on to my husband [Martin Shepard]. If he also likes it, then we do the book. Given that, there has to be something in the submission letter or the first pages that really captures me. What won't capture me is an outline. And sometimes the submission letters read like simple plots. The plot doesn't engage me as much as the language. The best way to approach me," says Shepard, "is to write a cover letter and send the first two chapters."

Shepard cautions that writers won't get big author tours or big bucks distribution by working with her company. "What we can do for an author is give an enormous amount of individual attention. They never get a secretary," she says. "Plus, we have an excellent group of foreign agents who try to sell foreign country rights, and good film agents. We've been fairly successful at selling options. We also let the author have a lot of say so, if possible. We involve them, where at a larger publisher, it can happen that you don't see your book once it's accepted."

Publishing mostly fiction, "We don't look for books that are simply good for the marketplace. We look for books that we think are written very well and that we fall in love with as a piece of writing."

They don't publish mass market books, romance, science fiction, action/adventure ("unless it's written very well") or collections of short stories, but "we're open to the idea of a series. I would love to find a good idea for a series with a great detective," she says.

As to what makes good fiction, Shepard stresses, "The quality of language is what makes a manuscript stand out. I believe there are really no new stories to tell. So it's how the author tells it that intrigues me. I believe in Joseph Conrad's law, where he says that fiction must justify itself in every line. I like that as a concept."

—Linda L. Rome

SEAL PRESS, (IV), 3131 Western Ave., Seattle WA 98121. (206)283-7844. President: Faith Conlon. Estab. 1976. Publishes hardcover and paperback originals. Books: acid-free paper; offset printing; perfect or cloth binding; average print order: 4,000. Averages 8-12 total titles, including 5-6 fiction titles each year. Sometimes critiques rejected ms "very briefly."
Needs: Ethnic, feminist, lesbian, literary, mystery, young adult, short story collections. "We publish women only. Work must be feminist, non-racist, non-homophobic." Recently published *Disappearing Moon Cafe*, by Sky Lee (literary novel); *No Forwarding Address*, by Elisabeth Bowers (mystery novel); *No More Secrets*, by Nina Weinstein (young adult novel).
How to Contact: Query first. SASE. Reports in 1-2 months. Accepts "readable" computer printouts.
Terms: "Standard publishing practices; do not wish to disclose specifics." Sends galleys to author. Book catalog for SAE and 65¢ postage.

SECOND CHANCE PRESS AND THE PERMANENT PRESS, (II), Noyac Rd., Sag Harbor NY 11963. (516)725-1101. Co-publisher: Judith Shepard. Estab. 1977. Mid-size, independent publisher. Publishes hardcover originals and reprints. Books: hardcover; average print order: 1,500-2,000; first novel print order: 1,500-2,000. Published new writers within the last year. Plans 11 first novels this year. Averages 12 total titles; all fiction, each year.
  • See the close-up interview with Co-publisher Judith Shepard in this section.
Needs: Contemporary, humor/satire, literary, supsense/mystery. "I like novels that have a unique point of view and have a high quality of writing." No gothic, romance, horror, science fiction, pulp. Published *Dies Irae*, by Ruby Spinell (literary/mystery); *The Affair at Honey Hill*, by Berry Fleming (literary/historical); and *Zulus*, by Percival Everett (literary/futuristic).
How to Contact: Query first. Submit outline and no more than 2 chapters. SASE. Agented fiction 15%. Reports in 6 weeks on queries; 3 months on mss.
Terms: Pays royalties of 10-15%. Advance to $1,000. Sends galleys to author. Book catalog for $3.
Advice: "We are looking for good books, be they tenth novels or first novels, it makes little difference. The fiction is more important than the track record."

SEVEN BUFFALOES PRESS, (II), Box 249, Big Timber MT 59011. Editor/Publisher: Art Cuelho. Estab. 1975. Publishes paperback originals. Averages 4-5 total titles each year.
  • The Seven Buffaloes Press also publishes a number of magazines including *Azorean Express*, *Black Jack*, *Hill and Holler* and *Valley Grapevine*.
Needs: Contemporary, short story collections, "rural, American Hobo, Okies, American Indian, Southern Appalachia, Arkansas and the Ozarks. Wants farm- and ranch-based stories." Published *Rig Nine*, by William Rintoul (collection of oilfield short stories).
How to Contact: Query first with SASE. Reports in 1 week on queries; 2 weeks on mss.
Terms: Pays royalties of 10% minimum; 15% on second edition or in author's copies (10% of edition). No advance. Writer's guidelines and book catalog for SASE.
Advice: "There's too much influence from TV and Hollywood, media writing I call it. We need to get back to the people, to those who built and are still building this nation with sweat, blood, and brains. More people are into it for the money, instead of for the good writing that is still to be cranked out by isolated writers. Remember, I was a writer for 10 years before I became a publisher."

HAROLD SHAW PUBLISHERS, (II), Box 567, 388 Gundersen Dr., Wheaton IL 60189. (708)665-6700. Director of Editorial Services: Ramona Cramer Tucker. Estab. 1968. "Small, independent religious publisher with expanding fiction line." Publishes paperback originals and reprints. Books: 35 lb. Mando Supreme paper; sheet-fed printing; perfect-bound; average print order: 5,000. Published new writers within the last year. Plans 1 novel per year in Northcote Books (our literary/academic fiction subsidiary). Averages 30 total titles, 3-4 fiction titles each year. Sometimes critiques on rejected mss.
Needs: Literary, religious/inspirational, young adult/teen (13-18 years) problem novels. Looking for religious literary novels or young adult fiction (religious). No short stories, romances, children's fiction. Published *A Land of Heart's Desire*, *Lee William's Quest*, *A Waiting Legacy*, by Joy Pennock Gage (books one, two and three of the Seventh Child Series); *Absolutely Perfect Summer*, by Jeffrey Asher Nesbit (young adult fiction); *Hoverlight*, by Fay S. Lapka (young adult fiction).
How to Contact: Accepts unsolicited mss. Query first. Submit outline/synopsis and 2-3 sample chapters. SASE. Reports in 2 weeks on queries; 2-4 weeks on mss. Simultaneous submissions OK.
Terms: Pays royalties of 10%, Average advance $1,000. Provides 10 author's copies. Sends pages to author. Publishes ms 12-18 months after acceptance. Free writer's guidelines. Book catalog for 9 × 12 SAE and $1.25 postage.

Advice: "Character and plot development are important to us. We look for quality writing in word and in thought. 'Sappiness' and 'pop-writing' don't go over well at all with our editorial department."

*‡SHOESTRING PRESS, (I), Box 1223, Main Post Office, Edmonton, Alberta T5J 2M4 Canada. Fiction Editor: Lawrence Oliver. Estab. 1989. Publishes hardcover and paperback originals and paperback reprints. Published new writers within the last year. Plans 2 first novels this year. Averages 2 total titles (all fiction). Always comments on rejected ms; *$100 charge for critiques.*
Needs: Adventure, children's/juvenile (adventure, Indian), ethnic/multicultural (Indian), military/war, new age/mystic/spiritual, science fiction (hard science, soft/sociological), thriller/espionage, western (frontier saga). Publishes Indian, Exploration, Espionage series.
How to Contact: Accepts unsolicited mss. Query first. Include estimated word count, 500-word bio, Social Security number, list of publishing credits. SASE for a reply to query or return of ms. Reports in 4 months on queries; 6 months on mss. Simultaneous submissions OK.
Terms: Pays royalties of 5% minimum; 10% maximum. *Subsidy publishes 10%.* Sometimes sends galleys to author. Publishes ms 20 months after acceptance.

‡SLOUGH PRESS, (II), Box 1385, Austin TX 78767. Fiction Editor: Jim Cole. Estab. 1973. Publishes hardcover and paperback originals. Books: acid-free paper; offset printing; glue binding; average print order: 500-1,000. Averages 1-5 total titles, 0-2 fiction titles each year. Sometimes comments on rejected ms.
Needs: Erotica, ethnic, experimental, literary, mainstream and short story collections.
How to Contact: Accepts unsolicited mss. Submit outline/synopsis and sample chapters or complete ms with cover letter. SASE. Reports in 2 months on mss. Simultaneous submissions OK.
Terms: Pays royalties of 15% maximum. Sometimes sends pre-publication galleys to author. Publishes ms one year after acceptance.
Advice: "We never encourage anyone in the creative writing field. It's a religious calling, not a career or profession, with little monetary reward for most. Our last book of fiction was a literary collection of short stories mostly about the horse-racing world. It sold well to more enthusiasts of the sport. We like fiction with extra-literary appeal. I'd like to see some suggestions in the author cover letter that are concrete and specific on how the book could find readers and sell."

‡THE SMITH (III), 69 Joralemon St., Brooklyn NY 11201. Editor: Harry Smith. Estab. 1964. Books: 70 lb vellum paper for offset and 80 lb vellum for letterpress printing; perfect binding; often uses illustrations; average print order: 1,000; first novel print order: 1,000. Plans 2 fiction titles this year.
Needs: *Extremely* limited book publishing market—currently doing only 4-6 books annually, and these are of a literary nature, usually fiction or poetry. Recently published *The Cleveland Indian*, by Luke Salisbury.

SOHO PRESS, 853 Broadway, New York NY 10003. (212)260-1900. Publisher: Juris Jurjevics. Publishes hardcover originals and trade paperback reprints. Published new writers within the last year. Averages 20 titles/year.
Needs: Adventure, ethnic, historical, literary, mainstream, mystery/espionage, suspense. "We do novels that are the very best of their kind." Published *Shadow Catcher*, by Charles Fergus; *Meridian 144*, by Meg Files; and *Gerontius*, by James Hamilton-Paterson.
How to Contact: Submit query or complete ms with SASE. Reports in 1 month on queries; 6 weeks on mss. Simultaneous submissions OK.
Terms: Pays royalties of 10-15% on retail price. For trade paperbacks pays 7½% royalties to 10,000 copies; 10% after. Offers advance. Book catalog plus $1 for SASE.
Advice: "There aren't any tricks (to writing a good query letter)—just say what the book is. Don't analyze the market for it. Don't take writing courses too seriously, and *read* the best people in whatever genre you are working. We are looking for those who have taught themselves or otherwise mastered the craft."

SOLEIL PRESS, (IV), R.F.D. #1, Box 452, Lisbon Falls ME 04252. (207)353-5454. Editor: Denis Ledoux. Estab. 1988. "Soleil Press publishes writing by and/or about Franco-Americans (French-Canadian-American). SP has *no* interest in the European French experience." Publishes paperback originals. Average print order: 2,000. Published new writers within the last year. Averages 1-2 total titles, 0-1 fiction titles/year. Occasionally comments on rejected ms.

Needs: Ethnic (Franco-American). "No interest at all in exploring the French of France."
How to Contact: Does not accept unsolicited mss. Query. SASE. Reports in 1 month on queries; 1-2 months on mss. Simultaneous and photocopied submissions OK. Accepts computer printout submissions.
Terms: Pays in author's copies. Writer's guidelines and book catalog for SASE.

SOUTHERN METHODIST UNIVERSITY PRESS, (I), P.O. Box 415, Dallas TX 75275. (214)739-5959. Senior Editor: Kathryn M. Lang. Estab. 1936. "Small university press publishing in areas of film/theater, Southwest life and letters, religion/medical ethics and contemporary fiction." Publishes hardcover and paperback originals and reprints. Books: acid-free paper; perfect-bound; some illustrations; average print order 2,000. Published new writers within the last year. Plans 2 first novels this year. Averages 10-12 total titles; 5 fiction titles each year. Sometimes comments on rejected ms.
Needs: Contemporary, ethnic, historical, literary, mainstream, regional, short story collections. "We are booked for the next year or two; we always are willing to look at 'serious' or 'literary' fiction." No "mass market, sci fi, formula, thriller, romance." Recently published *Chasing Uncle Charley*, by Cruce Stark (first novel); *Things We Lost . . .*, by Deborah Navas (story collection); *The Tennessee Waltz and other Stories*, by Alan Cheuse.
How to Contact: Accepts unsolicited mss. Query first. Submit outline/synopsis and 3 sample chapters. SASE. Agented fiction 10%. Reports in 3 weeks on queries; 3 months on mss. No simultaneous submissions.
Terms: Pays royalties of 10% of net, negotiable advance, 10 author's copies. Publishes ms 1 year after acceptance. Book catalog free.
Advice: "We view encouraging first time authors as part of the mission of a university press. Send query describing the project and your own background." Looks for "quality fiction from new or established writers."

SPACE AND TIME, (IV), 138 W. 70th St. (4-B), New York NY 10023-4432. Book Editor: Jani Anderson. Estab. 1966—book line 1984. Two-person operation on part-time basis. Publishes paperback originals. Books: 50 lb. Lakewood white 512PPi paper; offset Litho printing; perfect-bound; illustrations on cover and frontispiece; average print order: 1,000; first novel print order: 1,000. Averages 8 total titles, 1 fiction title each year. Critiques or comments on rejected ms.
Needs: Fantasy, horror, psychic/supernatural/occult, science fiction. Wants "cross-genre material, such as horror-western, sf-mystery, occult-spy adventure, etc." Does not want "anything *without* some element of fantasy or sf (or at least the 'feel' of same)." Published *The Wall*, by Ardath Mayhar (horror-mystery); *Vanitas*, by Jeffrey Ford (sci-fantasy-horror); *The Gift*, by Scott Edelman (gay-horror).
How to Contact: *No unsolicited mss.* Query first or submit outline/synopsis and 2 sample chapters. Reports in 4-6 weeks on queries; 3-4 months on mss. Simultaneous submissions OK. "Prefer around 50,000 words."
Terms: Pays royalties of 10% based on cover price and print run, within 60 days of publication (additional royalties, if going back to press). Average advance $100, negotiable. Sends galleys to author. Book catalog free on request.

SPECTRUM PRESS, (I, II), Box 109, 3023 N. Clark St., Chicago IL 60657. (312)281-1419. Editor D.P. Agin. Estab. 1991. "Small independent electronic publisher." Publishes computer disks only. Published new writers within the last year. Plans 5 first novels this year. Averages 30 total titles, 25 fiction titles each year. Sometimes comments on rejected ms.
Needs: Contemporary, erotica, experimental, fantasy, feminist, gay, historical, lesbian, literary, mainstream, short story collections, translations. "Quality lesbian fiction of all kinds, feminist writing, literary novels." No juvenile or young adult. Recently published *The Tex-Mex Express*, by Ewing Campbell (novel); *On Sangamon*, by Tim Brown (novel); *Affinities*, by Rachel Perez (story collection). "We now have four lines: Spectrum Classics (classic literature and nonfiction); Contemporary Fiction and Poetry; Spectrum Obelisk Library (erotica)."
How to Contact: Accepts unsolicited mss. Query first. Submit outline/synopsis and sample chapters or complete ms with cover letter. Reports in 2 weeks on queries; 1 month on mss. Simultaneous submissions OK. Accepts electronic submissions on disk only. Prefer submission on IBM/MSDOS computer disk.

Terms: Pays royalties of 10-15%. Sends disk to author. Publishes within 2 months after acceptance. Writer's guidelines available. Book catalog free.
Advice: "We are interested in new voices and new attitudes. We prefer disk submissions in ASCII code or WordPerfect 5.1 format. Contact us first for other formats. Disks can be any size, any density, provided they are IBM/MSDOS."

THE SPEECH BIN, INC., (IV), 1766 20th Ave., Vero Beach FL 32960. (407)770-0007. Fax: (407)770-0006. Senior Editor: Jan J. Binney. Estab. 1984. Small independent publisher and major national and international distributor of books and material for speech-language pathologists, audiologists, special educators and caregivers. Publishes hardcover and paperback originals. Averages 6-10 total titles/year. "No fiction at present time, but we are very interested in publishing fiction relevant to our specialties."
Needs: "We are most interested in seeing fiction, including books for children, dealing with individuals experiencing communication disorders, other handicaps, and their families and caregivers, particularly their parents, or family members dealing with individuals who have strokes, physical disability, hearing loss, Alzheimer's and so forth."
How to Contact: Accepts unsolicited mss. Query first. SASE. Agented fiction 10%. Reports in 4-6 weeks on queries; 1-3 months on mss. Simultaneous submissions OK.
Terms: Pays royalties of 8%+. Sends galleys to author. Writer's guidelines for #10 SASE. Book catalog for 9×12 SAE with 3 first class stamps.
Advice: "We are most interested in publishing fiction about individuals who have speech, hearing and other handicaps."

SPINSTERS INK, (IV), (formerly Spinsters Book Co.), Minneapolis MN 55403. Managing Editor: Kelly Kager. Estab. 1978. Moderate size women's publishing company growing steadily. Publishes paperback originals and reprints. Books: 55 lb. acid-free natural paper; photo offset printing; perfect-bound; illustrations when appropriate; average print order: 5,000. Published new writers within the last year. Plans 3 first novels this year. Averages 6 total titles, 3-5 fiction titles each year. Occasionally critiques rejected ms.
Needs: Feminist, lesbian. Wants "full-length quality fiction—thoroughly revised novels which display deep characterization, theme and style. We *only* consider books by women. No books by men, or books with sexist, racist or ageist content." Recently published *Final Session*, by Mary Morell (mystery); *Being Someone*, by Ann MacLeod; and *Love and Memory*, by Amy Oleson.
How to Contact: Accepts unsolicited mss. Query or submit outline/synopsis and 3 sample chapters with SASE. Reports in 1 month on queries; 2 months on mss. Simultaneous submissions discouraged. Disk submissions OK (DOS format—MS Word or WP 5.0). Prefers hard copy with disk submission.
Terms: Pays royalties of 7-10%, plus 25 author's copies; unlimited extra copies at 45% discount. Free book catalog.
Advice: "In the past, lesbian fiction has been largely 'escape fiction' with sex and romance as the only required ingredients; however, we encourage more complex work that treats the lesbian lifestyle with the honesty it deserves. We run an annual Lesbian Fiction Contest designed to increase the body of quality literature about the lesbian lifestyle. The prize is $1,000."

‡THE SPIRIT THAT MOVES US PRESS, (II), P. O. Box 820-N, Jackson Heights NY 11372-0820. (718)426-8788. Editor/Publisher: Morty Sklar. Estab. 1974. Small independent literary publisher. Publishes hardcover and paperback originals. "We do, for the most part, simultaneous clothbound and trade paperbacks for the same title." Books: 60 lb. natural acid-free paper; mostly photo-offset, some letterpress; cloth and perfect binding; illustrations; average print order: 3,000; first novel print order: 3,000. Published new writers within the last year. Plans 1 first novel this year. Averages 2 fiction titles, mostly multi-author. Sometimes comments on rejected mss.
● The editor tells us that in 1983 he published the first collection in English in the U.S. of Jaroslav Seifert, who won the Nobel Prize for literature a year later, in 1984. Morty Sklar also

Stay informed! Keep up with changes in the market by using the latest edition of Novel & Short Story Writer's Market. *If this is 1994 or later, buy a new edition at your favorite bookstore or order directly from Writer's Digest Books.*

received the CCLM Editor's Grant Award (Coordinating Council of Literary Magazines) for excellence and vision in 1985. See the listing for his magazine, *The Spirit That Moves Us*, in this book.

Needs: Literary. "Our choice of 'literary' does not exclude almost any other category—as long as the writing communicates on an emotional level, and is involved with people more than things. Nothing sensational or academic; work that deals with things more than people. Publishes anthology *Phoenix: Stories from Former Drug Addicts* on an open basis; look for announcements or send SASE for time. Publishes *Free Parking*, edited by Morty Sklar (collection of previously unpublished stories) and *Editor's Choice III: Fiction, Poetry & Art from the U.S. Small Press*, edited by Morty Sklar (work nominated by other publishers). Publishes Editor's Choice, First Novel (new series; will call for open submissions in 1993).

How to Contact: Accepts unsolicited mss. Query letter only first "unless he/she sees an announcement that calls for manuscripts and gives a deadline." Should include estimated word count, bio and whether or not ms is a simultaneous submission. SASE (IRC) for reply or return of ms. Reports on mss "if rejected, soon; if under consideration, from 1-3 months."

Terms: Pays royalties of 10% net, $1,000 advance for first novel, and author's copies, also honorarium, depends on grant/award money. Sends galleys to author. Publishes up to 1 year after acceptance. Writer's Guidelines free for #10 SASE and 1 first class stamp or IRC "but the guidelines are only for certain books, like novels. We don't use general guidelines." Catalog for 6×9 SASE and 2 first class stamps.

Advice: "Our plans include the First Novel Series (it will have a more colorful name than that) which will publish a novel from the manuscripts that come to us by an open submission policy (our regular policy). Offers $1,000 award against royalties for the winner of first novel search through an open call for mss, plus a public reading. We also have made our *Editor's Choice* series a biennial (work selected from nominations by other editors, from work they published in their books and magazines). We are interested in work that is not only well written, but that gets the reader involved on an emotional level. In other words, no matter how skilled the writing is, or how interesting or exciting the story, if we don't care about the people in it, we won't consider it. Also, we are open to a great variety of styles, so just be yourself and don't try to second-guess the editor. You may have our 15th Anniversary collection, *Free Parking*, for $5.50 as a sample book."

*STARBOOKS PRESS, Subsidiary of Woldt Corp., P.O. Box 2737, Sarasota FL 34230-2737. (813)957-1281. President/Publisher: Patrick J. Powers. Estab. 1978. "Small press specializing in mature adult fiction and nonfiction, including mainly titles of gay orientation." Publishes paperback originals. Averages 10-12 total titles, 3 anthologies each year. Comments on rejected ms.

Needs: Gay fiction and nonfiction. Recently published *Angel: The Complete Quintet*, *The Kid* and *Legends*, all by John Patrick; and *Marty*, by William Barber.

How to Contact: Accepts unsolicited mss. Submit outline/synopsis and sample chapters. SASE. Reports in 1 month on queries; 6 weeks on mss. Simultaneous submissions OK.

Terms: Provides 5-25 contributor's copies on short stories or direct payment depending on author's pub credits. Individual arrangement with author depending on the book *Will consider subsidy publishing; offers co-op program.* Sends galleys to author. Publishes ms 6-8 months after acceptance. Writers guidelines for SASE. Book catalog free.

*STARBURST PUBLISHERS, (II), P.O. Box 4123, Lancaster PA 17604. (717)293-0939. Editorial Director: Ellen Hake. Estab. 1982. Publishes paperback and hardcover originals. Published new writers within the last year. Averages 12 total titles, 2 fiction titles per year.

Needs: Religious/inspirational: Adventure, contemporary, fantasy, historical, horror, military/war, psychic/supernatural/occult (with Judeo-Christian solution), romance (contemporary, historical), spiritual, suspense/mystery, western. Wants "inspirational material."

How to Contact: Submit outline/synopsis and 3 sample chapters. SASE. Agented fiction less than 10%. Reports in 6-8 weeks on manuscripts. Accepts electronic submissions via disk and modem, "but also wants clean double-spaced typewritten or computer printout manuscript."

Terms: Pays in variable royalties. "Individual arrangement with writer depending on the manuscript as well as writer's experience as a published author." *Subsidy publishes "occasionally."* Publishes ms up to one year after acceptance. Writer's guidelines for #10 SAE and 1 first class stamp. Book catalog for 9×12 SAE and 3 first class stamps.

*STATION HILL PRESS (II, III), Barrytown NY 12507. (914)758-5840. Imprint: Pulse. Publishers: George Quasha and Susan Quasha. Estab. 1978. Publishes paperback and cloth originals. Averages 20 total titles, 5-7 fiction titles each year.

Needs: Contemporary, experimental, literary, translations, and new age. Published *Operas and Plays*, by Gertrude Stein; *Narrative Unbound*, by Donald Ault.

How to Contact: Query first with SASE before sending ms. No unsolicited mss.

Terms: Pays in author's copies (10% of print run) or by standard royalty, depending on the nature of the material. *Occasional subsidy publishing.* "Co-venture arrangements are possible with higher royalty." Book catalog free on request.

‡STEMMER HOUSE PUBLISHERS, INC., (III), 2627 Caves Rd., Owings Mills MD 21117. (410)363-3690. Fax: (410)363-8459. President: Barbara Holdaidge. Estab. 1975. Small independent publisher. Publishes hardcover originals. Books: offset paper; offset printing; handbound; average print order: 10,000; first novel print order: 5,000. Averges 6 total titles, 1 fiction (if any).

Needs: Children's/juvenile (animal, historical), ethnic/multicultural, historical, mainstream/contemporary.

How to Contact: Accepts unsolicited mss. Submit outline/synopsis and sample chapters. Include estimated word count, one-page bio, list of publishing credits. Send SASE for reply, return of ms or send a disposable copy of the ms. Reports in 2 weeks on queries; 6 weeks on mss.

Terms: Pays royalties of 4% minimum; 10% maximum. Provides 6 author's copies. Sends galleys to author. Publishes ms 1 year after acceptance. Book catalog for 9 × 12 SAE and 3 first class stamps or IRC.

Advice: "We have become increasingly selective almost to the point of forgoing fiction while we concentrate on nonfiction."

STONE BRIDGE PRESS, (IV), P.O. Box 8208, Berkeley CA 94707. (510)524-8732. Fax: (510)524-8711. Publisher: Peter Goodman. Estab. 1989. "Small press focusing on books about Japan in English (business, language, culture, literature)." Publishes paperback originals and reprints. Books: 60-70 lb. offset paper; web and sheet paper; perfect-bound; some illustrations; average print order: 3,000; first novel print order: 2,000-2,500. Averages 6 total titles, 2 fiction titles, each year. Sometimes comments on rejected ms.

Needs: Japan-themed. If not translation, interested in the expatriate experience—all categories welcome: contemporary, erotica, ethnic, experimental, faction, literary, science fiction, short story collections, translations (from Japanese). "Primarily looking at material relating to Japan. Mostly translations, but we'd like to see samples of work dealing with the expatriate experience. Also Asian and Japanese-American. Published *Death March on Mount Hakkoda*, by Jiro Nitta (translation-faction); *Wind and Stone*, by Masaaki Tachihara (translation-literary); *Still Life and Other Stories*, by Junzo Shono (translation-literary).

How to Contact: Accepts unsolicited mss. Query first. Submit outline/synopsis and 3 sample chapters. SASE. Agented fiction 25%. Reports in 2 weeks on queries; 2 months on mss. Simultaneous submissions OK.

Terms: Pays royalties, offers negotiable advance. Publishes ms 18-24 months after acceptance. Book catalog for 2 first class stamps.

Advice: "As we focus on Japan-related material there is no point in approaching us unless you are very familiar with Japan. We'd especially like to see submissions dealing with the expatriate experience and fantasy and science fiction on Japanese themes as well, but with a decided literary tone, not mass market."

SUNSTONE PRESS, (IV), Box 2321, Santa Fe NM 87504-2321. (505)988-4418. Contact: James C. Smith, Jr. Estab. 1971. Midsize publisher. Publishes paperback originals. Average first novel print order: 2,000 copies. Published new writers within the last year. Plans 2 first novels this year. Averages 16 total titles, 2-3 fiction titles, each year.

Needs: Western. "We have a Southwestern theme emphasis. Sometimes buys juvenile mss with illustrations." No science fiction, romance or occult. Published *Apache: The Long Ride Home*, by Grant Gall (Indian/Western); *Border Patrol*, by Cmdr. Alvin E. Moore; and *The Last Narrow Gauge Train Robbery*, by Robert K. Swisher, Jr.

How to Contact: Accepts unsolicited mss. Query first or submit outline/synopsis and 2 sample chapters with SASE. Reports in 2 weeks. Simultaneous submissions OK. Publishes ms 9-12 months after acceptance.

Terms: Pays royalties, 10% maximum, and 10 author's copies.

‡TANAGER PRESS, (II), 145 Troy St., Mississauga Ontario L5G 1S8 Canada. (416)891-2502. Editorial Contact Persons: L. Hill, N. Ledwidge. Fiction Editor: J. Neveleff. Estab. 1977. Small publisher and mid-size distributor. Publishes hardcover originals and reprints and paperback originals. Books: H/3/pb; average print order: 3,000; first novel print order: 2,000-2,500. Plans 1 first novel this year. Averages 2 total titles, 1 fiction title.
Needs: Historical (general), humor/satire, mainstream/contemporary, mystery/suspense, religious/inspirational.
How to Contact: Does not accept unsolicited mss. Submit outline/synopsis and 1 sample chapter. Should include 50-word bio. SASE. Reports in 3-6 weeks on queries. Simultaneous submissions OK.
Terms: Pays royalties of 10% minimum; offers negotiable advance. Book catalog free.

TEXTILE BRIDGE PRESS, (II), Subsidiary of Moody Street Irregulars, Inc., Box 157, Clarence Center NY 14032. (716)741-3393. Imprints include The Jack Kerouac Living Writers Reading Series. President/Editor: Joy Walsh. Fiction Editor: Marion Perry. Estab. 1978. "We publish a magazine on and about the work of Jack Kerouac. We also publish book length manuscripts in the spirit of Kerouac when available." Publishes paperback originals. Books: bond paper; offset printing; saddle or perfect binding; average print order: 300-500; first novel print order: 500. Plans 1 first novel this year. Averages 5 total titles each year, 2 fiction titles each year. Sometimes comments on rejected ms; charges for critiques.
• The Moody Street Irregulars also publishes a newsletter dedicated to Jack Kerouac and the Beat writers.
Needs: Experimental, literary, short story collections. No romance, gothic. Published *Big Ben Hood*, by Emmanual Freed (literary); *Links of the Chain*, by William Harnock (short story collection); and *Walk With Me*, by Dorothy Smith (literary); published new writers within last year.
How to Contact: Accepts unsolicited mss. Submit complete ms with cover letter. SASE. Agented fiction 1%. Reports in 1 week on queries; 1 month on mss. Simultaneous submissions OK.
Terms: Pays in author's copies "if run 300, 30 copies/if 500, 50 copies." Sends galleys to author. Publishes ms 1 year after acceptance. Writers guidelines not available. Book catalog free, if available.

THIRD WORLD PRESS, 7524 S. Cottage Grove Ave., Chicago IL 60619. (312)651-0700. Assistant Editor: Haki Madhubuti. Estab. 1967. Small independent publisher with plans to expand. Publishes paperback originals. Plans 2 first novels this year. Averages 10 total titles, 3 fiction titles each year. Average first novel print order 15,000 copies.
Needs: Ethnic, historical, juvenile (animal, easy-to-read, fantasy, historical, contemporary), preschool/picture book, science fiction, short story collections, and young adult/teen (easy-to-read/teen, fantasy/science fiction, historical). "We primarily publish nonfiction, but will consider fiction by and about Blacks."
How to Contact: Accepts unsolicited mss. Query or submit outline/synopsis and 1 sample chapter with SASE. Reports in 6 weeks on queries; 5 months on mss. Simultaneous submissions OK. Accepts computer printout submissions.
Terms: Individual arrangement with author depending on the book, etc.

THISTLEDOWN PRESS, (II, IV), 668 East Place, Saskatoon, Saskatchewan S7J 2Z5 Canada. (306)244-1722. Editor-in-Chief: Patrick O'Rourke. Estab. 1975. Publishes paperback originals. Books: Quality stock paper; offset printing; perfect-bound; occasional illustrations; average print order 1,500-2,000; first novel print order: 1,000-1,500. Plans 1 first novel and 3 collections of stories. Publishes 12 titles/year, 6 or 7 fiction. Occasionally critiques rejected mss.
Needs: Literary, experimental, short story collections and novels.
How to Contact: "We *only* want to see Canadian-authored submissions. We will *not* consider multiple submissions." No unsolicited mss. Query first with SASE. Photocopied submissions OK. Reports in 2 months on queries. Recently published *Yuletide Blues*, by R.P. MacIntyre (young adult novel); *After Sixty: Going Home*, by Gertrude Story (short stories); *Sick Pigeon*, by M.A.C. Farrant (short fictions).
Advice: "We are primarily looking for quality writing that is original and innovative in its perspective and/or use of language. Thistledown would like to receive queries first before submission—perhaps with novel outline, some indication of previous publications, periodicals your work has appeared in."

Check the Category Indexes, located at the back of the book, for publishers interested in specific fiction subjects.

We publish Canadian authors only. We are continuing to publish more fiction and are looking for new fiction writers to add to our list. New Leaf Editions line is first books of poetry or fiction by emerging Western Canadian authors. Familiarize yourself with some of our books before submitting a query or manuscript to the press."

THREE CONTINENTS PRESS, (II, IV), 1901 Pennsylvania Ave. N.W., Suite 407, Washington DC 20006. (202)223-2554. Fiction Editor: Donald Herdeck. Estab. 1973. Small independent publisher with expanding list. Publishes hardcover and paperback originals and reprints. Books: library binding; illustrations; average print order: 1,000-1,500; first novel print order: 1,000. Averages 15 total titles, 6-8 fiction titles each year. Average first novel print order: 1,000 copies. Occasionally critiques ("a few sentences") rejected mss.
Needs: "We publish original fiction only by writers from Africa, the Caribbean, the Middle East, Asia and the Pacific. No fiction by writers from North America or Western Europe." Published *Fish House Secrets*, by Kathy Stinson; *The Blue Jean Collection, a Young Adult Short Story Anthology*; *Month's Mind*, by John V. Hicks (poetry). Also, short-story collections by established writers.
How to Contact: Query with outline/synopsis and sample pages and SAE, IRC. State "origins (non-Western), education and previous publications." Reports in 1 month on queries; 2 months on mss. Simultaneous submissions OK.
Terms: "We are not a subsidy publisher, but do a few specialized titles a year with subsidy. In those cases we accept grants or institutional subventions. Foundation or institution receives 20-30 copies of book and at times royalty on first printing. We pay royalties twice yearly (against advance) as a percentage of net paid receipts." Royalties of 5% minimum, 10% maximum; 10 author's copies; offers negotiable advance, $300 average. Depends on grant/award money. Sends galleys to author. Free book catalog.

THRESHOLD BOOKS, RD 4, Box 600, Dusty Ridge Rd., Putney VT 05346. (802)254-8300. Director: Edmund Helminski. Estab. 1981. Small independent publisher with plans for gradual expansion. Publishes paperback originals. Books: 60 lb. natural paper; offset litho printing; sew-wrap binding; average print order: 2,500. Averages 2-3 total titles each year. Occasionally critiques rejected ms.
Needs: Spiritual literature and translations of sacred texts. Published *Lineage*, by Bo Lozzoff (short stories); and *Toward the Fullness of Life, The Fullness of Love*, by Arnaud Desjardin (nonfiction on male-female relationships).
How to Contact: Accepts unsolicited mss. Query first, submit outline/synopsis and sample chapters or complete ms with SASE. Reports in 2 months. Simultaneous submissions OK. Publishes ms an average of 18 months after acceptance.
Terms: Pays in royalties of 10% of net. Sometimes sends galleys to author. Book catalog free on request.
Advice: "We are still small and publishing little fiction." Publishing "less fiction, more paperbacks due to our particular area of concentration and our size."

TIMES EAGLE BOOKS, (IV), Box 2441, Berkeley CA 94702. Fiction Editor: Mark Hurst. Estab. 1971. "Small operation on part-time basis." Specialized publisher limited to contributors from West Coast region. First novel print order: 2,500. Plans 2 first novels this year. Averages 2 titles/year, all fiction.
Needs: Contemporary. "Graphic descriptions of teenage life by West Coast youth, such as Bret Easton Ellis's *Less than Zero*." Published *Equator: The Story and the Letters*, by V.O. Blum (erotic/philosophical novel).
How to Contact: Does not accept or return unsolicited mss. Query first in one paragraph. Reports in 2 weeks.
Terms: Pays 10-15% royalties.

THE TRANSLATION CENTER, (II), 412 Dodge Hall, Columbia University, New York NY 10027. (212)854-2305. Editors: Frank MacShane, Lori Carlson. Estab. 1972. Publishes paperback originals. Books: 6×9; perfect bound; high-quality paper. Averages 2 total titles/year.
Needs: Translations.
How to Contact: Query first for upcoming anthologies. Recently published *Translation*, Vol. 26, "*Poetry Encore*", *Return Trip Tango & Other Stories From Abroad* (foreign poetry and fiction anthologies).
Terms: Pays in 2 translator's copies.

‡TUDOR PUBLISHERS, INC., (II), P.O. Box 38366, Greensboro NC 27438. (919)282-5907. Editor: Eugene Pfaff Jr.. Estab. 1986. Small independent press. Publishes hardcover and paperback originals. Book: offset; Smythe sewn hardcover/trade paperback; occasional illustrations; average print order: 3,000; first novel print order: 1,000-2,000. Plans 1 first novel this year. Averages 3-5 total titles, 1-2 fiction titles each year. Sometimes comments on rejected ms.
Needs: Literary, mystery/suspense, thriller/espionage (young adult), regional (Southeast), young adult/teen (10-18 years). "Especially needs suspense. No romance, western." Recently published *The Mean Lean Weightlifting Queen*, by Mark Emerson (YA novel); *Just Plane Murder*, by Dicey Thomas (suspense); published new writers within the last year.
How to Contact: Accepts unsolicited mss. "Outline and query first, please." Submit outline/synopsis and 3 sample chapters. SASE. Reports on queries in 2 weeks; 6 weeks on mss.
Terms: Pays royalties of 10%. Sends galleys to author. Publishes ms 1 year to 18 months after acceptance. Book catalog for # 10 SASE or IRC and one 1st class stamp.
Advice: "Tell us of any publishing done previously. Send a clear summary or outline of the book with a cover letter. Interested in suspense in both adult and young adult; also literary fiction of high quality. Send only your best work. No romance, science fiction, western; no multigenerational sagas unless of extremely high quality."

TURNSTONE PRESS, (II), 607-100 Arthur St., Winnipeg, Manitoba R3B 1H3 Canada. (204)947-1555. Managing Editor: Patricia Sanders. Estab. 1976. Books: Offset paper; perfect-bound; average first novel print order: 1,500. Published new writers within the last year. Averages 8 total titles/year. Occasionally critiques rejected ms.
Needs: Experimental and literary. "We will be doing only 2-3 fiction titles a year. Interested in new work exploring new narrative/fiction forms. We publish some anthologies (e.g. *Made in Manitoba*, edited by Wayne Tefs). Stories are nominated." Recently published *Raised by the River*, by Jake MacDonald; *Some Great Thing*, by Lawrence Hill; and *Touch the Dragon*, by Karen Connelly.
How to Contact: *Canadian authors only.* Send SASE or SAE and IRC. Reports in 1 month on queries; 2-4 months on mss.
Terms: Pays royalties of 10%; 10 author's copies. Book catalog free on request.
Advice: "Like most Canadian literary presses, we depend heavily on government grants which are not available for books by non-Canadians. Do some homework before submitting work to make sure your subject matter/genre/writing style falls within the publishers area of interest. Specializes in experimental literary, and prairie writing."

ULTRAMARINE PUBLISHING CO., INC., (III), Box 303, Hastings-on-the-Hudson NY 10706. (914)478-2522. Publisher: Christopher P. Stephens. Estab. 1973. Small publisher. "We have 150 titles in print. We also distribute for authors where a major publisher has dropped a title." Encourages new writers. Averages 15 total titles, 12 fiction titles each year. Buys 90% agented fiction. Occasionally critiques rejected ms.
Needs: Experimental, fantasy, mainstream, science fiction, and short story collections. No romance, westerns, mysteries.
How to Contact: Prefers agented ms. Does not accept unsolicited mss. Submit outline/synopsis and 2 sample chapters with SASE. Reports in 6 weeks. Simultaneous submissions OK.
Terms: Pays royalties of 10% minimum; advance is negotiable. Publishes ms an average of 8 months after acceptance. Free book catalog.

*UNIVERSITY EDITIONS, (I, II), 59 Oak Lane, Spring Valley, Huntington WV 25704. Imprint of Aegina Press. Managing Editor: Ira Herman. Estab. 1983. Independent publisher presently expanding. Publishes hardcover and paperback originals and reprints. Books: 50 lb. library-weight paper; litho offset printing; most are perfect-bound; illustrations; average print order: 500-1,000; first novel print order: 500-1,000. Plans 10 first novels this year. "We strongly encourage new writers." Averages 25 total titles, approximately 15 fiction titles each year. Often critiques rejected ms.
   ● See also the listing for Aegina Press in this section.
Needs: Adventure, contemporary, ethnic, experimental, fantasy, feminist, historical, romance (gothic), horror, humor/satire, juvenile (all types), literary, mainstream, mystery/suspense (private eye, romantic suspense, young adult), regional, science fiction (hard science, soft sociological), short story collections, translations and war. "Historical, literary, and regional fiction are our main areas of emphasis." Recently published *The May Day Incident*, by Jeff Myhre (spy novel); *Avatar of the Bowmaster*, by T. Lynn Neal (novel); and *The Milky Way Chronicle*, by Mark Castleberry (novel).

How to Contact: Accepts unsolicited mss. "We depend upon manuscripts that arrive unsolicited." Query or submit outline/synopsis and 3 or more sample chapters or complete ms. "We prefer to see entire manuscripts; we will consider queries and partials as well." SASE. Reports in 1 week on queries; 1 month on mss. Simultaneous submissions OK.

Terms: Payment is negotiated individually for each book. Depends upon author and subject. *Subsidy publishes most new titles.* Sends galleys to author.

Advice: "We attempt to encourage and establish new authors. Editorial tastes in fiction are eclectic. We try to be open to any type of fiction that is well written. We are publishing more fiction now that the very large publishers are getting harder to break into. We publish softcovers primarily, in order to keep books affordable."

THE UNIVERSITY OF ARKANSAS PRESS, (I), Fayetteville AR 72701. (501)575-3246. Director: Miller Williams. Acquisitions Editor: James Twiggs. Estab. 1980. Small university press. Publishes hardcover and paperback originals. Average print order 750 cloth and 2,000 paper copies. Averages 40 total titles, 2 short fiction titles (rarely a novel), each year.

• For more on this press, see the close-up interview with Director Miller Williams in the 1992 *Poet's Market.*

Needs: Literary, mainstream, novels, short story collections, and translations. Publishes anthologies or special editions. Stories are usually selected by the editor. Published *Writing for Love and Money,* by Katherin Perutz (novel); *Jonah and the Pink Whale,* by Jose Wolfango Montes Vannuci (novel), translated by Kay Pritchett; *Plato at Scratch Daniel's and Other Stories,* by Edward Falco.

How to Contact: Accepts unsolicited mss. Query first with SASE. Reports in 2 weeks. Simultaneous submissions OK.

Terms: Pays royalties of 10%; 10 author's copies. Publishes ms an average of 1 year after acceptance. Writer's guidelines and book catalog for 9×12 SASE.

Advice: "We are looking for fiction written with energy, clarity and economy. Apart from this, we have no predisposition concerning style or subject matter. The University of Arkansas Press does not respond to queries or proposals not accompanied by SASE."

UNIVERSITY OF IDAHO PRESS, (IV), 16 Brink Hall, University of Idaho, Moscow ID 83843. (208)885-7564. Director: James J. Heaney. Estab. 1972. "Small university press with combined scholarly and regional emphasis." Publishes hardcover and paperback originals and paperback reprints. Averages 8-10 total titles, 1-2 fiction titles each year. Sometimes comments on rejected ms.

Needs: Regional, short story collections. "We would like to publish some Western fictional works of suitable stylistic competence for a primarily regional market in Idaho and the inland Northwest. No fictionalized memoirs of pioneers, pony express riders, and so on." Published *Unearned Pleasures,* by Ursula Hegi (short story collection). Recently developed Northwest Folklife Series.

How to Contact: Accepts unsolicited mss. Query first. Reports in 1 month on queries; 4 months on mss. Accepts electronic submissions via disk.

Terms: Pays royalties. "Contracts are always negotiated individually. The small size of the regional fiction market makes less than luxurious terms a necessity for the publisher." Sends galleys to author. Writer's guidelines and book catalog free.

‡VANDAMERE PRESS, (II), AB Associates, P.O. Box 5243, Arlington VA 22205. Publisher/Editor-in-Chief: Art Brown. Estab. press 1984; firm 1976. "Small press, independent publisher of quality hard and soft cover books." Publishes hardcover and paperback originals. Published new writers within the last year. Averages 6+ total titles, 1 fiction title each year. Sometimes comments on rejected ms.

Needs: Adventure, erotica, historical, humor/satire, military/war, mystery/suspense (police procedural), science fiction (hard science, soft/sociological). No childrens/juvenile/young adult. Recently published *Hank Harrison for President,* by Fred T. Eckert (humor/satire).

How to Contact: Accepts unsolicited mss. Submit outline/synopsis and 3-4 sample chapters or complete ms with cover letter. Include bio (1-2 pages), list of publishing credits. Send SASE for reply, return of ms or send a disposable copy of the ms. Reporting time varies with work load. Simultaneous submissions OK.

Terms: Pays royalties; negotiable small advance. Sends galleys to author. Publishes ms 3 months-2 years after acceptance.

VÉHICULE PRESS, Box 125, Place du Parc Station, Montréal Québec H2W 2M9 Canada. Did not respond.

W.W. PUBLICATIONS, (IV), Subsidiary of A.T.S., Box 373, Highland MI 48357-0373. (813)585-0985. Also publishes *Minas Tirith Evening Star.* Editor: Philip Helms. Estab. 1967. One-man operation on part-time basis. Publishes paperback originals and reprints. Books: typing paper; offset printing; staple-bound; black ink illustrations; average print order: 500+; first novel print order: 500. Averages 1 title (fiction) each year. Occasionally critiques rejected ms.

● *Minas Tirith Evening Star* is also listed in this book. The publisher is an arm of the American Tolkein Society.

Needs: Fantasy, science fiction, and young adult/teen (fantasy/science fiction). "Specializes in Tolkien-related or middle-earth fiction." Recently published *Shaping of Middle-Earth's Maker*, by J.S. Ryan.

How to Contact: Accepts unsolicited mss. Submit complete ms with SASE. Reports in 1 month. Simultaneous submissions OK.

Terms: Individual arrangement with author depending on book, etc.; provides 5 author's copies. Free book catalog.

Advice: "We are publishing more fiction and more paperbacks. The author/editor relationship: a friend and helper."

‡WHITE PINE PRESS, (II), 76 Center St., Fredonia NY 14063. (716)672-5743. Fax: (716)672-5743. Director: Dennis Maloney. Fiction Editor: Elaine La Mattina. Estab. 1973. Independent literary publisher. Publishes paperback originals and reprints. Books: 60 lb. natural paper; offset; perfect binding; average print order: 2,000-3,000; first novel print order: 2,000. Plans 1 first novel this year. Averages 8-10 total titles, 6-7 fiction titles each year.

Needs: Ethnic/multicultural, literary, short story collections. Looking for "strong novels." No romance, science fiction or mystery. Plans anthology of Canadian short stories, Caribbean stories. Editors select stories. Recently published *An Occasion of Sin*, by John Montague (short stories); *This Time, This Place*, by Dennis Vannatta (short stories); *Secret Weavers: Stories of the Fantastic, by Latin American Women* (short stories).

How to Contact: Accepts unsolicited mss. Query letter with outline/synopsis and 2 sample chapters. Should include estimated word count and list of publishing credits. SASE for reply or return of ms. Agented fiction 10%. Reports in 2 weeks on queries; 3 months on mss. Simultaneous submissions OK.

Terms: Pays royalties of 5% minimum; 10% maximum. Offers negotiable advance. Pays in author's copies; payment depends on grant/award money. Sends galleys to author. Publishes 1-2 years after acceptance. Book catalog free for #10 SASE.

‡WILD EAST PUBLISHING CO-OPERATIVE LTD., 151 Ryan Court, Fredericton, New Brunswick B3A 2Y9 Canada. (506)472-9251. Fax: (506)472-9251. Fiction Editors: Margaret McLeod, Joe Blades. Estab. 1988. "Small book, chapbook and magazine publisher." Publishes paperback originals. Books: offset paper; offset printing; perfect binding; average print order: 100-1,000; first novel print order: 1,000. Published new writers within the last year. Plans 1 first novel this year. Averages 8 total titles, 3 fiction titles this year. Sometimes comments on rejected ms.

● See the listing for *Pottersfield Portfolio*, published by Wild East, also listed in this book.

Needs: Feminist, literary, regional (Atlantic), religious/inspirational; short story collections; young adult/teen ((fantasy/science fiction, problem novels). No erotica or westerns. Recently published *Years*, by Margaret McLeod; *A Day in the Life of a Warrior, or Safe in the Body of Goddes*, by Claudi Gahlinger; *Wages of Sin*, by Sylvia Morice. Publishes Salamanca Chapbook Series.

How to Contact: Accepts unsolicited mss. Submit outline/synopsis and 10% of chapters or complete ms with cover letter. Include 1-2 page bio and list of publishing credits. Reports in 2 weeks on queries; 2 months on mss. Accepts electronic submissions.

Terms: Pays royalties of 10% minimum; 15% maximum or author's copies (10% of run). Sends galleys to author. Published ms up to 2 years after acceptance. Writer's guidelines and book catalog free.

WILLOWISP PRESS, INC., (II), Subsidiary of SBF Services, Inc., 10100 SBF Dr., Pinellas Park FL 34666. (813)578-7600. Imprints include Worthington Press, Hamburger Press. Address material to Acquisitions Editor. Estab. 1984. Publishes paperback originals for children. Published new writers within the last year. Sometimes critiques rejected mss.

Needs: "Children's fiction and nonfiction, K-middle school." Adventure, contemporary and romance, for grades 5-8; preschool/picture book. No "violence, sex; romance must be very lightly treated." Published *Sister vs. Sister*, by Carol Perry; *So Much To Live For*, by Lurlene McDaniel; and *Dead Wrong*, by Alida E. Young.

How to Contact: Accepts unsolicited mss. Query (except picture books) with outline/synopsis and 2 sample chapters. Must send SASE. Report on queries varies; 2 months on mss. Simultaneous submissions OK. "Prefer hard copy for original submissions; prefer disk for publication."
Terms: Pay "varies." Publishes ms 6-12 months after acceptance. Writer's guidelines for #10 SAE and 1 first class stamp. Book catalog for 9×12 SAE with $1.25 postage.
Advice: "We publish what *kids* want to read, so tell your story in a straightforward way with 'kid-like' language that doesn't convey an adult tone or sentence structure."

WOMEN'S PRESS, (I, II, IV), Suite 233, 517 College St., Toronto, Ontario M6G 4A2 Canada. (416)921-2425. Estab. 1972. Publishes paperback originals. Books: Web coat paper; web printing; perfect-bound; average print order: 2,000; first novel print order: 1,500. Plans 2 first novels this year. Published new writers last year. Averages 8 total titles each year. Sometimes "briefly" critiques rejected ms.
Needs: Contemporary, feminist, lesbian, juvenile and adolescent (fantasy, historical, contemporary), literary, preschool/picture book, short story collections, mysteries, women's and young adult/teen (problem novels). Nothing sexist, pornographic, racist. Published *S.P. Likes A.D.*, by Catherine Brett; *Catherine, Catherine*, by Ingrid MacDonald; *Harriet's Daughter*, by Marlene Nourbese Philip.
How to Contact: Submit complete ms with SAE and "Canadian stamps or a check. Our mandate is to publish Canadian women or landed immigrants." Reports in 3 months. Simultaneous submissions OK.
Terms: Pays in royalties of 10% maximum; small advance. Sends galleys to author. Free book catalog.
Advice: "We publish feminist, lesbian and adolescent novels, anthologies of short stories and single-author story collections. We encourage women of all races and ethnicities to submit work and we have a particular interest in publishing writers of colour."

WOODLEY MEMORIAL PRESS, (IV), English Dept. Washburn University, Topeka KS 66621. (913)231-1010, Ext. 1448. Editor: Robert N. Lawson. Estab. 1980. "Woodley Memorial Press is a small press which publishes book-length poetry and fiction collections by Kansas writers only; by 'Kansas writers' we mean writers who reside in Kansas or have a Kansas connection." Publishes paperback originals. Averages 2 titles each year. Sometimes comments on rejected ms.
Needs: Contemporary, experimental, literary, mainstream, short story collection. "We do not want to see genre fiction, juvenile, or young adult." Publishes anthologies or special editions occasionally. "We have an annual contest for poetry and fiction in alternating years."
How to Contact: *Charges $5 reading fee.* Accepts unsolicited mss. Submit outline/synopsis and 2 sample chapters. SASE. Reports in 2 weeks on queries; 2 months on mss.
Terms: "Terms are individually arranged with author after acceptance of manuscript." Sends galleys to author. Publishes ms one year after acceptance. Writer's guidelines for #10 SAE and 1 first class stamp. Book catalog for #10 SAE and 2 first class stamps.
Advice: "We only publish one work of fiction a year, on average, and definitely want it to be by a Kansas author. We are more likely to do a collection of short stories by a single author."

WOODSONG GRAPHICS INC. (II), P.O. Box 304, Lahaska PA 18931-0304. (215)794-8321. Editor: Ellen Bordner. Estab. 1977. "Small publishing firm dedicated to printing quality books and marketing them creatively." Publishes paperback and hardcover originals. Books: Standard or coated stock paper; photo offset printing; GBC or standard binding; illustrations; average print order: 5,000; first novel print order; 2,500. Averages 6-8 total titles each year. "Sometimes" buys juvenile mss with illustrations. Occasionally critiques rejected mss.
Needs: Adventure, contemporary, gothic/historical and contemporary romance, historical (general), humor/satire, juvenile (animal, easy-to-read, fantasy, historical, picture book, spy/adventure, contemporary), literary, mainstream, mystery/suspense, psychic/supernatural/occult, science fiction, war, western, and young adult (easy-to-read/teen, fantasy/science fiction, historical, problem novels, spy/adventure). No deviant sex of any kind or pornography.
How to Contact: Accepts unsolicited mss. Query first or submit complete ms. SASE always. Simultaneous submissions OK. Reports in 3 weeks on queries, longer on mss. "We do everything possible to get replies out promptly, but do read everything we're sent . . . and that takes time." Publishes ms 6-12 months after acceptance.
Terms: Pays in royalties; negotiates advance. Sends galleys to author. "Arrangements will depend totally on the manuscript."
Advice: "If first novels are good, we have no problem with them, and we're always happy to look. Along with queries, send at least a few pages of actual ms text, since quality of writing is more important than topic where fiction is concerned. If you believe in what you've written, stick with it. There is so

much good material that we must reject simply because we can't afford to do everything. Others must have the same problem, and it's a matter of being on the right desk on the right day to finally succeed."

YITH PRESS, (I, IV), 1051 Wellington Rd., Lawrence KS 66049. (913)843-4341. Subsidiary: *Eldritch Tales Magazine*. Editor/Publisher: Crispin Burnham. Estab. 1984. One-man operation on part-time basis. Publishes paperback originals and reprints. Books: offset printing; perfect binding; illustrations; average print order: 500-1,000. Averages 1-2 titles each year. Average first novel print order: 500-1,000 (depending pre-publication orders). Occasionally critiques rejected ms.
Needs: Fantasy and horror. Accepts short stories for collections only. Novel needs include "anything in the supernatural horror category." No "mad slasher or sword and sorcery."
How to Contact: Accepts unsolicited mss. Submit complete ms with SASE. Reports in 2 months. Simultaneous submissions OK. Prefers letter-quality. Disk submissions OK with MacIntosh II system.
Terms: Individual arrangement with author depending on the book. Sends galleys to author. Pays in royalties of 25% minimum; 35% maximum.
Advice: "Be original, don't try to be the next Lovecraft or Stephen King. Currently, I plan to publish one or two books/year, along with *Eldritch Tales*. The author/editor relationship should be give and take on both sides. I will try *not* to rewrite the author's work. If I feel that it needs some changes then I'll suggest them to the author. We are currently on hold with the book line as we are trying to get *Eldritch Tales* out on a quarterly schedule. Any potential submitter should send a card to inquire as to status."

ZEPHYR PRESS, (III), 13 Robinson St., Somerville MA 02145. Subsidiary of Aspect, Inc. Editorial Directors: Ed Hogan and Leora Zeitlin. Estab. 1980. Publishes hardcover and paperback originals. Books: acid-free paper; offset printing; Smythe-sewn binding; some illustrations; average print order: 1,500-2,000; first novel print order: 1,000-1,500. Averages 5 total titles, 1-2 fiction titles each year.
Needs: Contemporary, ethnic, experimental, feminist/lesbian, gay, historical, humor/satire, literary, mainstream, regional, short story collections, also translations of French, Russian, Eastern European fiction. Published *Two Novels*, by Philip Whalen; and *The St. Veronica Gig Stories*, by Jack Pulaski.
How to Contact: "We no longer read unsolicited mss. We read small press and literary magazines to find promising writers. We accept queries from agents, and from authors whose previous publications and professional credits (you must include a summary of these), evince work of exceptional talent and vision. Queries should include vita, list of publications, and up to 10 samples pages, photocopies only. If we are interested, we will request the full manuscript. Otherwise, we will make no response."
Terms: Pays royalties approximately 12% of publisher's net for first edition. "There can be some flexibility of terms, based on mutual arrangements, if desired by author and publisher." Sends galleys to author. Book catalog for SASE.
Advice: "Seek well qualified feedback from literary magazine editors or agents and/or professionally established writers before submitting manuscripts to publishers. We regard the author/editor relationship as one of close cooperation, from editing through promotion."

ZOLAND BOOKS, INC., (II), 384 Huron Ave., Cambridge MA 02138. (617)864-6252. Publisher: Roland Pease. General Manager: Peter Nielsen. Marketing Director: Christine Alaimo. Estab. 1987. "We are a literary press, publishing poetry, fiction, photography, and other titles of literary interest." Publishes hardcover and paperback originals. Books: acid-free paper; sewn binding; some with illustrations; average print order: 2,000-5,000. Averages 7 total titles each year.
 ● For more on Zoland Books, see the close-up interview with Publisher Roland Pease in the 1991 *Novel & Short Story Writer's Market*.
Needs: Contemporary, feminist, literary, short story collections. Published *Small Victories*, by Sallie Bingham (novel); *Secret Words*, by Jonathan Strong (novel); and *Augusta Cotton*, by Margaret Erhart.
How to Contact: Accepts unsolicited mss. Query first, then send complete ms with cover letter. SASE. Reports in 2-4 weeks on queries; 4-6 weeks on mss.
Terms: Pays royalties of 5-8%. Average advance: $1,500; negotiable (also pays author's copies). Sends galleys to author. Publishes ms 1-2 years after acceptance. Book catalog for 6×9 SAE and 2 first class stamps.

International small press

The following small presses from countries outside the U.S. and Canada will consider novels or short stories in English. Some of the countries represented here include Australia,

England, India, Ireland, Italy, Malawi, New Zealand, Nigeria, Sweden, West Germany and Zimbabwe. Many of these markets do not pay in cash, but may provide author copies. Always include a self-addressed envelope with International Reply Coupons to ensure a response or the return of your manuscript. International Reply Coupons are available at the main branch of your local post office. To save the cost of return postage on your manuscript, you may want to send a copy of your manuscript for the publisher to keep or throw away and enclose a return postcard with one IRC for a reply.

AFRICA CHRISTIAN PRESS, P.O. Box 30, Achimota, Ghana, West Africa. Fiction Editor: Mr. Raymond Mills-Tetteh. Averages 6 fiction titles/year. "We are a Christian publishing house specializing in Christian fiction works by Africans or expariates with a long association with Africa." Length: 15,000 words minimum. Send: Cover letter, synopsis, brief summary, sample chapter/s and/or entire manuscript. Pays royalties. Mss should be "typewritten, double spaced, with generous margins." Send 2 copies and a SAE with IRCs for response/return. Write for catalog and/or writer's guidelines.

ANOWUO EDUCATIONAL PUBLICATIONS, P.O. Box 3918, 2R McCarthy Hill, Accra, Ghana. Fiction Editor: Samuel Asare Konadu. Average 5-10 fiction titles/year. "Publication development organization for Ghanaian, African and world literature: novels, workbooks, language development, etc." Length: 8-250 typed pages. Send brief summary and first and last chapter. Pays advance and royalties. Looks for cultural development, romance.

ASHTON SCHOLASTIC LTD., Private Bag 92801, Auckland, New Zealand. Fiction Editor: Penny Scown. Publishes 20-30 fiction titles annually. "Educational publishing with a focus on books for the teaching of language arts and children's literature for all ages from picture books to teen novels." Pays royalties. "Do not 'write down' to children—write the story you want to tell using the best language— i.e., most appropriate vocabulary, letting the story only dictate the length."

ATTIC PRESS, 4 Upper Mount St., Dublin, 2, Ireland. Managing Editor: Grainne Healy. Averages 6-8 fiction titles/year. "Attic Press is an independent, export-oriented, Irish-owned publishing house with a strong international profile. The press specializes in the publication of fiction and nonfiction books by and about women by Irish and international authors." Send cover letter, synopsis, brief summary, sample chapters. Pays advance on signing contract and royalties. "Please ensure that your book is by/about/for women; that it is properly laid out for reading—double-spaced typewritten etc." Write for catalog.

‡BELLEW PUBLISHING COMPANY LTD., Nightingale Centre, 8 Balham Hill, London WC1A 2DR England. Fiction Editor: Ib Bellew. Averages 30 fiction titles/year. "Literary." Length: 60,000-250,000 words. No longer interested in receiving freelance submissions.

BIBLIOTECA DI NOVA SF, FUTURO, GREAT WORKS OF SF, Perseo Libri srl, Box 1240, I-40100 Bologna Italy. Fiction Editor: Ugo Malaguti. "Science fiction and fantasy; novels and/or collections of stories." Pays 7% royalties on cover price; advance: $800-1,000 on signing contract. Buys Italian book rights; other rights remain with author. "While preferring published writers, we also consider new writers."

JONATHAN CAPE, 20 Vauxhall Bridge Rd., London SW1V 2SA England. Fiction Editor: David Godwin. Averages 20-25 fiction titles/year. Send a cover letter, synopsis, 2-3 sample chapters. Pays advance and royalties. "Send sample chapters first, not the whole ms." Our catalog is available on demand from our publicity dept.

CHRISTCHURCH PUBLISHERS LTD., 2 Caversham St., London S.W.3, 4AH UK. Fiction Editor: James Hughes. Averages 25 fiction titles/year. "Miscellaneous fiction, also poetry. More 'literary' style of fiction, but also thrillers, crime fiction etc." Length: 30,000 words minimum. Send a cover letter, synopsis, brief summary. "Preliminary letter and *brief* synopsis favored." Pays advance and royalties. "We have contacts and agents worldwide." Write for catalog.

AIDAN ELLIS PUBLISHING, Cobb House, Nuffield, Henley-on-Thames, Oxon RG9 5RT England. Fiction Editor: Aidan Ellis. Averages 12 fiction titles/year. "Founded in 1971, with an annual turnover of around £250,000 we are a small publishing house publishing fiction and general trade books."

Send a cover letter, synopsis, brief summary, sample chapter/s or entire manuscript. Pays advance on publication, royalties twice yearly. Write for catalog.

‡GMP PUBLISHER LTD., Box 247, London N17 9QR England. Editors: Lee Stacy, David Fernbach. Publishes 12-13 novels yearly and the occasional short story collection. "Principally publishing works of gay interest—both popular and literary." Pays royalties. Send synopsis and/or sample chapters first. "We're particularly interested in authors who use a word processor and can supply material on disk. This is particularly true with writers sending in work from abroad."

HEMKUNT, Publishers A-78 Naraina Industrial Area Ph.I, New Delhi India 110028. Managing Director: G.P. Singh. "We would be interested in novels, preferably by authors with a published work. Would like to have distribution rights for US, Canada and UK beside India." Send a cover letter, brief summary, 3 sample chapters (first, last and one other chapter). "Writer should have at least 1-2 published novels to his/her credit." Catalog on request.

HERITAGE BOOKS, 2-8 Calcutta Crescent, Gate 4, P.O. Box 610, Apapa, Lagos Nigeria. Fiction Editor: Bakin Kunama. "The type of fiction we are interested in: Must be from black writers; must be strongly Afrocentric; broadly Pan African; must enhance black image; must be trail blazing. Length: 40,000-60,000 words. Send a cover letter, brief summary, 1 sample chapter. Pays royalties.

‡KARNAK HOUSE, 300 Westbourne Park Road, London W11 1EH England. Fiction Editor: Amon Saba Saakana. Publishes 3-4 fiction titles annually. "An Afro-Caribbean publishing company concerned with global literary concerns of the Afrikan community, whether in North and South America, the Caribbean, Afrika or Europe. We rarely pay advances, and if so, very small, but pay a royalty rate of 8-10% on the published price of the book. We look for innovative work in the areas outlined above and work which attempts to express the culture, language, mythology—ethos—of the people. We look for work which tries to break away from standard English as the dominant narrative voice."

KAWABATA PRESS, (II), Knill Cross House, HR Anderton Rd., Millbrook, Torpoint, Cornwall PL10 1DX England. Fiction Editor: C. Webb. "Mostly poetry—but prose should be realistic, free of genre writing and clichés and above all original in ideas and content." Length: 200-4,000 words (for stories); 30,000-100,000 words (for novels). Send cover letter, synopsis and 1 sample chapter. "Don't forget return postage (IRCs)." Writers receive half of profits after print costs are covered. Write for guidelines and book list.

THE LITERATURE BUREAU, P.O. Box 8137 Causeway, Harare Zimbabwe. Fiction Editor: B.C. Chitsike. Averages 12 fiction titles/year. "All types of fiction from the old world novels to the modern ones with current issues. We publish these books in association with commercial publishers but we also publish in our own right." Length: 7,000-30,000 words. Send entire manuscript. Pays royalties. "Send the complete manuscript for assessment. If it is a good one it is either published by the Bureau or sponsored for publication. If it needs any correction a full report will be sent to the author." Obtain guidelines by writing to the Bureau. We have 'Hints to New Authors' a pamphlet for aspiring authors. These can be obtained on request.

‡THE MALVERN PUBLISHING CO. LTD., 32 Old Street, Upton-Upon-Severn, Worcs. WR8 OHW England. Fiction Editor: Cintia Stammers. Publishes 12 stories/year. "Full length adult fiction—60,000-80,000 words." Pays in royalties. "No science fiction or fantasy."

OBOBO BOOKS, 2-8 Calcutta Crescent, Gate 4, P.O. Box 610, APAPA, Lagos Nigeria. Fiction Editor: Ms. Obobo Osahon. "Positive image forming works for African kids." Length: 3,000-5,000 words maximum. Send a cover letter, brief summary, 1 sample chapter. Pays royalties.

PUBLISHERS GROUP SOUTH WEST (IRELAND), Allihies, Bantry, Country Cork IP2 91 Ireland. Executive Editor: Peter Haston. Averages 6-10 fiction titles/year. "Experimental fiction of all kinds, including audiobooks." Send synopsis and sample chapter, typed and posted registered airmail. Payment by agreement. Advice: "Contact publishers associations and research a publishing house that already produces work of the same kind. Determine which editor there has on his list the works most akin to yours. Do your research. Follow up." Send postcard of inquiry for catalog.

‡SHEBA FEMINIST PRESS, 10A Bradbury Street, London N16 8JN England. Fiction Editor: Michelle McKenzie. Tel: 071-254-1590. Fax: 071-249-1590. Averages 6 fiction titles/year. "Women's publishing collective. Priorities are working-class women, first-time writers, black women and lesbians. Women only." Length: 1,000-5,000 words. Send cover letter with synopsis and brief summary. Pays novels: advance and royalties; collections: fee from editor out of advance. "Obtain catalog by calling, faxing or writing. Guidelines, etc, available by request to the editor in writing."

THE VANITAS PRESS, Plaatslagarevägen 4 E 1, 22730 Lund Sweden. Fiction Editor: Mr. March Laumer. "One-person full-time operation publishing for prestige, not cash profit motives." Publishes fantasy, historical, satire, mainstream, romance (historical), short story collections. "At present exclusively interested in promising 'Oz' novels. Very actively interested in attracting writers/illustrators who would care to *collaborate* in the creation of 'latter-day' Oz novels. Best is for writers to send a first enquiry letter. They will be promptly notified whether to go on and submit work. Always send enquiry first, rather than the run up big postal charges on mss that will probably not be returned. We are glad to send advice on what/how to submit: a personal letter in and according to each particular case."

‡VIRAGO PRESS LIMITED, 20-23 Mandela St., London NWI OHQ England. Fiction Editors: Lennie Goodings, Ruth Petrie, Lynn Knight. Averages approximately 20 fiction titles/year. "Women's press—no humor, romance or sci-fi literary fiction wanted. Anything top quality." Length: 60,000-120,000 words. Send cover letter with brief summary and 3 sample chapters. Pays advance and royalty."Be original and interesting!"

Small press/'92-'93 changes

The following small presses appeared in the 1992 edition of *Novel & Short Story Writer's Market* but are not in the 1993 edition. Those presses whose editors did not respond to our request for an update are listed below without explanation. There are several reasons why a small press did not respond—they may be out of business, or overstocked with submissions. If an explanation was given, it is included next to the listing name.

Acadia Publishing Co. (asked to be deleted)
Alaska Native Language Center
Androgyne
Another Chicago Press
Arte Publico Press
The Authors Connection Press
Barlow Press
Center Press (asked to be deleted)
Child Welfare League of America (asked to be deleted)
China Books
Clothespin Fever Press (asked to be left out this year)
Esoterica Press
Frog In The Well
Fromm International Publishing Corporation (no outside fiction)
GMS Publications

Herbooks
Hermes House Press (asked to be left out this year)
Jayell Enterprises (out of business)
Knights Press
Libra Publishers, Inc.
Mosaic Press (asked to be deleted)
Open Hand Publishing, Inc. (no fiction)
The Paper Bag Press
Peachtree Publishers, Ltd.
The Post-Apollo Press
Prairie Journal Press
The Press Of MacDonald And Reinecke
Red Alder Books
Rydal Press
Samisdat (out of business)
Scare Ware Shoe Tree Press (sold)
Silverleaf Press, Inc.

Simon & Pierre Publishing Company Limited
Star Books, Inc.
Swamp Press
Tide Book Publishing Company
University of Illinois Press (asked to be left out this year)
Waterfront Press (out of business)
Watermark Press, Inc. (out of business)
Willowisp Press, Inc. (asked to be left out this year)
Woman In The Moon Publications
Wyrick & Company (asked to be deleted)
Yarrow Press (out of business)
York Press (inappropriate submissions)

Commercial Book Publishers

According to the Book Industry Study Group's annual report, *Book Industry Trends*, the commercial book publishing industry is expected to continue with slow, but steady growth. Considering the overall economy, this is good news for writers. The bad news, however, is that publishers and booksellers remain cautious and unlikely to take many risks with new novelists and short story writers.

On the other hand, some publishers, ignoring the odds, have added new fiction lines. Two years ago Dell launched its Abyss horror line which has since garnered critical acclaim (see the Close-up interview with Senior Editor Jean Cavelos on page 478). This year Chronicle Books added a fiction line and one of its first books, *Griffin and Sabine* has brought the publisher both success and attention.

Mergers, buy-outs and acquisitions within the commercial book publishing industry are no longer news. After the quick-dollar decade of the 1980s, it seems publishers are slowing down and taking a hard look at their lines and their overriding emphasis on the bottom line. As mentioned above, the word on all fronts continues to be "caution," but publishers appear to be responding to readers' demands for less emphasis on blockbusters and more on good, solid fiction. For specific trends in commercial publishing including various genres and subjects such as religious or children's fiction read the Commercial Fiction Trends Reporting on page 68.

Breaking into the commercial publishing market is a difficult but not impossible task. Each year, despite the competition, new writers are published. This year we've added a special section, First Bylines, starting on page 22, to draw attention to a few of these writers and have them share their experiences.

Hardcover, paperback, trade and mass market

It used to be the line between hardcover publishers and paperback publishers was clearly drawn. Today, this is very far from the truth. Many publishers of hardcover books also have trade paperback or mass market paperback imprints. It has become quite common for these publishers to try to secure both hardcover and paperback rights, known as hard-soft deals. For the most part these deals are offered to established authors, but occasionally they are offered to new writers whose work is expected to do well.

Trade paperbacks can be original or reprint titles and are marketed through bookstores. The paper quality is higher for these books than for mass market paperbacks. Many publishers are bringing new writers out in this format rather than in expensive hardcover editions. Literary novelists and short story authors are often published first in this form.

Mass market paperbacks have traditionally been cheaper editions (reprints) of hardbound books. Yet, some houses have become known for publishing paperbacks exclusively, including successful publishers of genre fiction such as Harlequin and TOR Books. While you'll find mass market racks in bookstores, they are also sold in grocery stores, department stores, drug stores and "super" store chains.

Returns have been a big problem for mass market publishers in recent years. Because of this, these publishers may not be publishing quite as many copies of books and may reduce or hold steady the number of different lines they publish. Mass market paperback publishers remain very open to new writers and rely more on the strength of their category lines than on "big names."

Choosing a commercial publisher

In addition to checking the bookstores and libraries for books by publishers that interest you, start by looking at the Category Index for this section. Check the Category Index for the subject or type of work you write. Each subject is followed by a list of publishers interested in that work. For more on using the indexes and on other ways to narrow your search, see How to Get the Most Out of This Book, starting on page 3.

The Roman numeral ranking codes appearing after the name of the publishing company will also help you determine which publishers to approach. The listings are ranked according to their openness to new writers. For the particulars on these codes, see the list at the end of this introduction.

As with our other listings, publishers new to this book are marked with a double dagger (‡). Book packagers are marked with a box (■) symbol. A packager creates books and then sells these to a publisher. Many produce fiction series written by one or several authors. Authors are generally paid a flat fee. Packagers are often very willing to work with new writers.

You may also see an asterisk (*) at the start of a listing. This lets you know the press sometimes funds the publication of its books through a subsidy arrangement. By our definition a subsidy press is one that requires a writer to financially subsidize the production of his or her books. Although this enables very small presses to publish more books, approach subsidy arrangements with caution. Find out exactly what type of production is involved and how many books will be produced. Check this figure with your local printer. If the press' figure is more, ask what type of marketing and distribution is planned and ask for proof.

Read the listings

Each listing contains information on the needs, terms and submission procedures. Within the "Needs" subcategory of a listing, you'll find a list of the types of fiction needed by the press. Some listings also include information on what types of fiction the press does not want to see. Following this is a list of books published. If the listing says "recently published," the list of books was updated this edition. If it just says "published," the press has provided this list of books more than one year in a row.

If a press asks for query first, make sure your letter is brief. If you are asked to send sample chapters, be sure to send the first three consecutive chapters. For more on submitting to publishers see the Business of Fiction Writing starting on page 76.

New to this edition

This year we've added a new feature that enables us to give you additional information. Our own editorial comments, set off by a bullet (●), appear in some listings. This is where we can tell you about awards or honors the press has received, whether we list other imprints by the same publisher, about any special interests or requirements and any information from our readers that will help you learn even more about the publisher. We've checked several sources, including the publishers themselves for information. Since this is a new feature, we do not claim to include every award or every press honored and we hope to increase the amount of this information in the future. Your input is welcome.

We've also added a number of subcategories to our Needs subhead. We've asked publishers to elaborate on the type of fiction they consider. For example, if a publisher publishes mysteries, we've asked what kind of mystery—police procedural, cozy, amateur sleuth, young adult or romantic suspense. With this additional information you can narrow your list of potential markets to those specifically interested in the type of fiction you write.

A note about agents

In this section more than any other, you will find publishers asking for "agented submissions only." Because the commercial fiction field has become so competitive, and publishers have such little time, some have found it easier to use agents as "first readers" to help cut down on the time it takes to go through unsolicited submissions. In the long run, they say, agents speed the publication process along, clearing the way for talented new writers.

Because it is getting almost as hard to find a good agent as it is to find a publisher, many writers see agents as just one more roadblock to publication. Yet those who have agents say they are invaluable. Not only can a good agent help make your work more marketable, they act as your business manager and advisor, keeping your interests upfront during contract negotiations.

For listings of agents and advice on how to find the best one for you, see the 1993 *Guide to Literary Agents and Art/Photo Reps*, published by Writer's Digest Books. The book separates nonfee- and fee-charging agents. While many agents do not charge any fees upfront, a few charge up to $100 to cover the cost of using outside readers. Be wary of those who charge large sums of money for reading. Reading fees do not guarantee representation. Think of an agent as a potential business partner and don't hesitate to ask tough questions about his or her credentials, experience and business practices.

Finding an agent can be very difficult for a new writer. Those published previously in journals and magazines have the best chance for serious consideration. Still many publishers do not require writers to have agents and new writers may submit directly.

For particulars on submitting work directly to commercial publishers, see the Business of Fiction Writing. If the publisher accepts complete manuscripts, send it with a brief cover letter and any other information outlined in the listing. If you want your manuscript returned, include a large self-addressed, stamped envelope. If you'd rather just send a disposable copy and save the postage, you may want to include a business-size SASE or postcard for a reply.

Both U.S. and Canadian publishers are listed in this section, followed by a section of International Commercial Publishers. When sending work to a country other than your own, include International Reply Coupons (IRCs) rather than stamps for return mail. These are available at the main branch of your local post office.

The ranking system for listings in this section is as follows:

I **Publisher encourages beginning or unpublished writers to submit work for consideration and publishes new writers frequently.**

II **Publisher accepts work by established writers and by new writers of exceptional talent.**

III **Publisher does not encourage beginning writers; publishes mostly writers with extensive previous publication credits or agented writers and very few new writers.**

IV **Special-interest or regional publisher, open only to writers on certain topics or from certain geographical areas.**

ACADEMY CHICAGO PUBLISHERS, (I), 213 W. Institute Place, Chicago IL 60610. (312)751-7302. Senior Editor: Anita Miller. Estab. 1975. Midsize independent publisher. Publishes hardcover and paperback originals and paperback reprints.

Needs: Biography, history, feminist, academic and anthologies. Only the most unusual mysteries, no private-eyes or thrillers. No explicit sex or violence. Serious fiction, not romance/adventure. "We will consider historical fiction that is well researched. No science fiction/fantasy, no religious/inspirational, no how-to, no cookbooks. In general, we are very conscious of women's roles. We publish very few children's books." Published *The Scarlet City: A Novel of 16th-Century Italy*, by Hella S. Haasse; *The Iron Gates of Santo Thomas: Interned by the Japanese, Manila 1942-1945*, by Emily Van Sickle.

How to Contact: Accepts unsolicited mss. Query and submit first three chapters, double spaced, with SASE. No simultaneous submissions. "Manuscripts without envelopes will be discarded. *Mailers* are a *must.*"

Terms: Pays 5-10% on net in royalties; no advance. Sends galleys to author.

Advice: "At the moment we are swamped with manuscripts and anything under consideration can be under consideration for months."

ALGONQUIN BOOKS OF CHAPEL HILL, 708 Broadway, New York NY 10003. Overstocked.

‡ARCADE PUBLISHING, (III), Distributed by Little, Brown & Co., 141 5th Ave., New York NY 10010. (212)475-2633. Fax: (212)353-8148. President, Editor-in-Chief: Richard Seaver. Fiction Editors: Richard Seaver, Jeannette Seaver, Cal Barksdale, Tim Bent. Estab. 1988. Independent publisher. Publishes hardcover originals and paperback reprints. Books: 50-55 lb. paper; Cameron Web press printing; notch, perfect binding; illustrations; average print order: 10,000; first novel print order: 3,000-5,000. Published new writers within the last year. Averages 40 total titles, 12 fiction titles each year. Does not comment on rejected ms.

Needs: Childrens/juvenile (preschool/picture book, animal, easy-to-read), literary, mainstream/contemporary, translations. No romance, sci fi, young adult. Recently published *Texas Summer*, by Terry Southern (literary); *Fields of Glory*, by Jean Rouaud (translation); *The Great Indian Novel*, by Shashi Tharoor (literary).

How to Contact: No unsolicited mss; unsolicited mss will be returned (SASE). Submit through an agent only. Agented fiction 100%. Reports in 2 weeks on queries; 3 months on mss.

Terms: Pays negotiable advances and royalties. 10 author's copies. Writer's guidelines and book catalog free.

ARCHWAY PAPERBACKS/MINSTREL BOOKS, 1230 Avenue of the Americas, New York NY 10020. (212)698-7268. Executive Editor: Patricia MacDonald. Published by Pocket Books. Imprints: Minstrel Books (ages 7-11); and Archway (ages 11 and up). Publishes paperback originals and reprints.

Needs: Young adult (mystery, suspense/adventure, thrillers, young readers (short, 64 pages and up), animals, friends, adventure, mystery, school, fantasy, family, etc.). No picture books. Recently published *Bury Me Deep*, by Christopher Pike; and *Dangerous Games*, by Peter Nelson. Published new writers this year.

How to Contact: Submit query first with outline; SASE "mandatory. If SASE not attached, query letter will not be answered."

ATHENEUM BOOKS FOR CHILDREN, (II), Imprint of the Macmillan Children's Book Group, 866 Third Ave., New York NY 10022. (212)702-7894. Vice President/Editorial Director: Jonathan J. Lanman. Fiction Editors: Gail Paris or Marcia Marshall (especially sf/fantasy). Second largest imprint of large publisher/corporation. Publishes hardcover originals. Books: Illustrations for picture books, some illustrated short novels; average print order: 6,000-7,500; first novel print order: 5,000. Averages 60 total titles, 30 middle grade and YA fiction titles each year. Very rarely critiques rejected mss.

• Books published by Atheneum Books for Children in 1992 have received the Newbury Medal (*Shiloh*, by Phyllis Reynolds Naylor) and the Christopher Award (*The Gold Coin*, by Alma Flor Ada, illustrated by Neal Waldman).

 The double dagger before a listing indicates that the listing is new in this edition. New Markets are often the most receptive to submissions by new writers.

Needs: Juvenile (animal, fantasy, historical, sports, adventure, contemporary), preschool/picture book, young adult/teen (fantasy/science fiction, historical, problem novels, sports, spy/adventure, mystery). No "paperback romance type" fiction. Published books include *Albert's Alphabet*, by Lesle Tryon (3-6, picture book); *Downriver*, by Will Hobbs (3-6, picture book); and *Shiloh*, by Phyllis Reynolds Naylor (8-12, middle grade novel); *Keep Laughing*, by Cynthia Grant (8-12 middle grade novel).

How to Contact: Accepts unsolicited mss "if novel length; we want outline and 3 sample chapters." SASE. Agented fiction 40%. Reports in 4-6 weeks on queries; 8-10 weeks on mss. Simultaneous submissions OK "if we are so informed and author is unpublished."

Terms: Pays in royalties of 10%. Average advance: $3,000 "along with advance and royalties, authors standardly receive ten free copies of their book and can purchase more at a special discount." Sends galleys to author. Writer's guidelines for #10 SAE and 1 first class stamp. Book catalog for 9×12 SAE and 6 first class stamps.

Advice: "We publish all hardcover originals, occasionally an American edition of a British publication. Our fiction needs have not varied in terms of quantity—of the 60-70 titles we do each year, 30 are fiction in different age levels. We are less interested in specific topics or subject matter than in overall quality of craftsmanship. First, know your market thoroughly. We publish only children's books, so caring for and *respecting* children is of utmost importance. Also, fad topics are dangerous, as are works you haven't polished to the best of your ability. (Why should we choose a 'jewel in the rough' when we can get a manuscript a professional has polished to be ready for publication.) The juvenile market is not one in which a writer can 'practice' to become an adult writer. In general, be professional. We appreciate the writers who take the time to find out what type of books we publish by visiting the libraries and reading the books. Neatness is a pleasure, too."

AVALON BOOKS, (I, II, IV), 401 Lafayette St., New York NY 10003. Vice President/Publisher: Barbara J. Brett. Imprint of Thomas Bouregy Company, Inc. Publishes hardcover originals. Average print order for all books (including first novels): 2,100. Averages 60 titles/year.

Needs: "Avalon Books publishes wholesome romances and westerns that are sold to libraries throughout the country. Intended for family reading, our books are read by adults as well as teenagers, and their characters are all adults: The heroines of the romances are all young (mid-twenties), single (no divorcees or widows, please!) women, and the heroes of the westerns range in age from late twenties to early thirties. There is no graphic sex in any of our novels; kisses and embraces are as far as our characters go. The heroines of the romances and the heroes of the westerns should all be looking forward to marriage at the end of the book. Currently, we publish five books a month: two romances, one mystery romance, one career romance and one western. All the romances are contemporary; all the westerns are historical. The important action in all our novels takes place over a short period of time, ranging from days to no longer than a year." Recently published *To Tame a Heart*, by Holly S. McClure (romance); *Country Blues*, by Marjorie Everitt (career romance); *Deadly Inheritance*, by Alice Sharpe (mystery romance); and *A Posse of Outlaws*, by Howard Pelham (western). Books range in length from a minimum of 40,000 words to a maximum of 50,000 words.

How to Contact: Submit the first chapter and a brief, but complete, summary of the book, or submit complete manuscript. Publishes many first novels and very little agented fiction. Enclose ms-size SASE. Reports in about 3 months. "Send SASE for a copy of our tip sheet."

Terms: $600 for the first book, $800 for the second, $1,000 thereafter, against the first 3,500 copies sold. (Initial run is 2,100.) A royalty of 10% is paid on any additional sales. The first half of the advance is paid upon signing of the contract; the second within 30 days after publication. Usually publishes within 6 to 8 months.

AVON BOOKS, (II), The Hearst Corporation, 1350 Avenue of the Americas, New York NY 10019. (212)261-6800. Imprints include Avon, Camelot and Flare. Associate Publisher Trade Division: Mark Gonpertz. Editor-in-Chief Avon Books: Robert Mecoy. Estab. 1941. Large paperback publisher. Publishes paperback originals and reprints. Averages 300 titles a year.

Needs: Fantasy, historical romance, mainstream, occult/horror, science fiction, medical thrillers, intrigue, war, western and young adult/teen. No poetry, mystery, short story collections, religious, limited literary or esoteric nonfiction. Published *Butterfly*, by Kathryn Harvey; *So Worthy My Love*, by Kathleen Woodiwiss.

How to Contact: Query letters only. SASE to insure response.

Terms: Vary. Book catalog for SASE. Sponsors Flare Novel competition.

BAEN BOOKS, (II), P.O. Box 1403, Riverdale NY 10471. (212)548-3100. Baen Science Fiction, Baen Fantasy. Publisher and Editor: Jim Baen. Executive Editor: Toni Weisskopf. Consulting Editor: Josepha Sherman. Estab. 1983. Independent publisher; books are distributed by Simon & Schuster. Publishes hardcover and paperback originals and paperback reprints. Published new writers within the last year. Plans 6-10 first novels this year. Averages 60 fiction titles each year. Occasionally critiques rejected mss.

Needs: Fantasy and science fiction. Interested in science fiction novels (generally "hard" science fiction) and fantasy novels "that are not rewrites of last year's bestsellers." Recently published *The Ship Who Searched*, by Anne McCaffrey and Mercedes Lackey (science fiction); *The Deeds of Paksenarrion*, by Elizabeth Moon (fantasy); and *Through the Ice*, by Piers Anthony and Robert Kornwise (fantasy).

How to Contact: Accepts unsolicited mss. Submit ms or outline/synopsis and 3 consecutive sample chapters with SASE. Reports in 2-3 weeks on partials; 4-8 weeks on mss. Will consider simultaneous submissions, "but grudgingly and not as seriously as exclusives."

Terms: Pays in royalties; offers advance. Sends galleys to author. Writer's guidelines for SASE.

Advice: "Keep an eye and a firm hand on the overall story you are telling. Style is important but less important than plot. We like to maintain long-term relationships with authors."

BAKER BOOK HOUSE, (II), P.O. Box 6287, Grand Rapids MI 49516. (616)676-9185. Assistant to Director of Publications: Jane Dekker. Estab. 1939. "Midsize Evangelical publisher." Publishes hardcover and paperback originals. Books: Web offset print; average print order: 5,000-10,000; first novel print order: 5,000. Plans 1 first novel this year. Averages 130 total titles. Sometimes comments on rejected ms.

Needs: "We are mainly seeking Christian fiction of two genres: Contemporary women's fiction and mystery." No fiction that is not written from a Christian perspective or of a genre not specified.

How to Contact: Does not accept unsolicited mss. Submit outline/synopsis and sample chapters. SASE. Agented fiction 100% (so far). Reports in 3-4 weeks on queries. Simultaneous submissions OK.

Terms: Pays royalties of 14% (of net). Sometimes offers advance. Sends galleys to author. Publishes ms 1 year after acceptance. Writer's guidelines for #10 SAE and 1 first class stamp. Book catalog for 9½×12½ SAE and 3 first class stamps.

Advice: "I would suggest that authors interested in writing contemporary women's fiction write us for more information regarding this genre."

BALLANTINE BOOKS, 201 E. 50th St., New York NY 10022. Subsidiary of Random House. Vice Pres. and Senior Editor: Pamela D. Strickler. Publishes originals (general fiction, mass-market, trade paperback and hardcover). Averages over 120 total titles each year.

Needs: Major historical fiction, women's mainstream and general contemporary fiction. Manuscripts can be submitted unsolicited to Pamela D. Strickler. Recently published *The Tokaido Road*, by Lucia St. Clair Robson; *The Expendables*, by Leonard Scott; and *For All Their Lives*, by Fern Michaels. Published new writers this year.

How to Contact: Submit brief outline/synopsis and complete ms. SASE required. Reports in 2 months on queries; 4-5 months on mss.

Terms: Pays in royalties and advance.

BANTAM SPECTRA BOOKS, (II, IV), Subsidiary of Bantam Doubleday Dell Publishing Group, 666 5th Ave., New York NY 10103. (212)765-6500. Vice-President and Publisher: Lou Aronica. Associate Publisher: Betsy Mitchell. Editor: Janna Silverstein. Associate Editor: Jennifer Hershey. Estab. 1985. Large science fiction, fantasy and speculative fiction line. Publishes hardcover originals, paperback originals and trade paperbacks. Averages 60 total titles each year, all fiction.

Needs: Fantasy, literary, science fiction. Needs include novels that attempt to broaden the traditional range of science fiction and fantasy. Strong emphasis on characterization. Especially well written traditional science fiction and fantasy will be considered. No fiction that doesn't have at least some element of speculation or the fantastic.

How to Contact: Does not accept unsolicited mss. Query first with 3 chapters and a short (no more than 3 pages) synopsis. SASE. Agented fiction 90%. Reports in 6-8 weeks on queries.

Terms: Pays in royalties; negotiable advance. Sends galleys to author.

‡BANTAM/DOUBLEDAY BOOKS, INC., (II), Division of Bantam Dell Doubleday Publishing Group, 666 5th Ave., New York NY 10103. (212)765-6500. Imprints include Skylark, New Age, Loveswept, Sweet Dreams, Sweet Valley High, Spectra, Crime Line, Domain, Fanfare and Starfire. Estab. 1945. Complete publishing: hard-cover, trade, mass market. Number of titles: Planned 400 for 1992.
Needs: Adventure, contemporary, ethnic, family saga, fantasy, feminist, gay/lesbian, glitz, gothic, historical, horror, humor/satire, literary, mystery, psychic/supernatural, religious/inspirational, romance, science fiction, spy, war, western and young adult. Recently published *Wilderness Tips*, by Margaret Atwood; *Rendezvous*, by Amanda Quick; *For the Sake of Elena*, by Elizabeth George.
How to Contact: Submit through agent. No unsolicited material accepted. Simultaneous submissions OK. Reports on queries as soon as possible.
Terms: Individually negotiated; offers advance.

THE BERKLEY PUBLISHING GROUP, (III), Subsidiary of G.P. Putnam's Sons, 200 Madison Ave., New York NY 10016. (212)951-8800. Imprints are Berkley, Jove, Diamond, Ace Science Fiction, Pacer. Editor-in-Chief: Leslie Gelbman. Senior Editor: Elizabeth Beier. Fiction Editors: Natalee Rosenstein, Judith Stern, John Talbot, Melinda Metz, Susan Allison, Ginger Buchanan, Carrie Feron, Gail Fortune and Hillary Cige. Nonfiction: Open. Large commercial category line. Publishes paperback originals, trade paperbacks and hardcover and paperback reprints. Books: Paperbound printing; perfect binding; average print order: "depends on position in list." Plans approx. 10 first novels this year. Averages 1,180 total titles, 1,000 fiction titles each year. Sometimes critiques rejected mss.
Needs: Fantasy, humor/satire, mainstream, mystery/suspense, psychic/supernatural/occult, romance (contemporary, historical), science fiction, war.
How to Contact: Accepts no unsolicited mss. Submit through agent only. Agented fiction 98%. Reports in 6-8 weeks on mss. Simultaneous submissions OK.
Terms: Pays royalties of 4-10%. Provides 25 author's copies. Writer's guidelines and book catalog not available.
Advice: "Aspiring novelists should keep abreast of the current trends in publishing by reading *The New York Times* Bestseller Lists, trade magazines for their desired genre and *Publishers Weekly*."

BERKLEY/ACE SCIENCE FICTION, (II), Berkley Publishing Group, 200 Madison Ave., New York NY 10016. (212)951-8800. Editor-in-Chief: Susan Allison. Estab. 1948. Publishes paperback originals and reprints. Number of titles: 10/month. Buys 85-95% agented fiction.
Needs: Science fiction and fantasy. No other genre accepted. No short stories. Published *The Cat Who Walks Through Walls*, by Robert Heinlein; *Neuromancer*, by William Gibson.
How to Contact: Submit outline/synopsis and 3 sample chapters with SASE. No simultaneous submissions. Reports in 2 months minimum on mss. "Queries answered immediately if SASE enclosed." Publishes ms an average of 18 months after acceptance.
Terms: Standard for the field. Sends galleys to author.
Advice: "Good science fiction and fantasy are almost always written by people who have read and loved a lot of it. We are looking for knowledgeable science or magic, as well as sympathetic characters with recognizable motivation. We need less fantasy and more science fiction. We are looking for solid, well-plotted SF: good action adventure, well-researched hard science with good characterization and books that emphasize characterization without sacrificing plot. In fantasy, again, we are looking for all types of work, from high fantasy to sword and sorcery." Submit fantasy and science fiction to Susan Allison, Ginjer Buchanan and Beth Fleisher.

JOHN F. BLAIR, PUBLISHER, (II, IV), 1406 Plaza Dr., Winston-Salem NC 27103. (919)768-1374. President: Margaret Couch. Editor: Stephen Kirk. Estab. 1954. Small independent publisher. Publishes hardcover and paperback originals. Books: Acid-free paper; offset printing; illustrations; average print order 2,500-5,000. Number of titles: 8 in 1992, 10 in 1993. Encourages new writers. Occasionally comments on rejected mss.
● For more on John F. Blair see the close-up interview with Stephen Kirk in the 1993 *Writer's Market*.
Needs: Contemporary, literary and regional. Generally prefers regional material dealing with southeastern U.S. No confessions or erotica. "We do not limit our consideration of manuscripts to those representing specific genres or styles. Our primary concern is that anything we publish be of high literary quality." Published works include *Blackbeard's Cup and Stories of the Outer Banks*, by Charles Harry Whedbee (folklore); and *The Legend of Nance Dude*, by Maurice Stanley (novel).

How would you like to get:

- up-to-the-minute reports on new markets for your writing
- professional advice from editors and writers on how to maximize your publishing opportunities
- in-depth interviews with leading authors who reveal their secrets of success
- expert opinion about writing and selling fiction, nonfiction, poetry and scripts
- all at a **$17.40 DISCOUNT!**

How to Contact: Query or submit with SASE. Simultaneous submissions OK. Reports in 1 month on queries, 3 months on mss. Publishes ms 1-2 years after acceptance. Free book catalog.
Terms: Negotiable.
Advice: "We are primarily interested in serious adult novels of high literary quality. Most of our titles have a tie-in with North Carolina or the southeastern United States. Please enclose a cover letter and outline with the manuscript. We prefer to review queries before we are sent complete manuscripts. Queries should include an approximate word count."

BOOKCRAFT, INC., (I), 1848 W. 2300 South, Salt Lake City UT 84119. (801)972-6180. Editorial Manager: Cory H. Maxwell. Publishes hardcover originals. Books: 60 lb. stock paper; sheet-fed and web press; average print order: 5,000-7,000; 3,000 for reprints. Published new writers within the last year. "We are always open for creative, fresh ideas."
● Books published by Bookcraft have received several awards from the Association of Mormon Letters.
Needs: Contemporary, family saga, historical, mystery/suspense (young adult, romantic suspense, private eye), romance (gothic), religious/inspirational, thriller/espionage and western (young adult, traditional frontier). Recently published *Cottonwood Summer*, by Jean Liebenthal; *Dominions of the Gadiantons*, by Robert Marcum; *The Work and the Glory: Like a Fire is Burning*, by Gerald N. Lund.
How to Contact: Query, submit outline/synopsis and sample chapters, or submit complete ms with SASE. Reports in 2 months.
Terms: Pays royalties; no advance. Sends galleys to author. Free book catalog and writer's guidelines.
Advice: "Our principal market is the membership fo The Church of Jesus Christ of Latter-Day Saints (Mormons) and manuscripts should relate to the background, doctrines or practices of that church. The tone should be fresh, positive and motivational, but not preachy. We do not publish anti-Mormon works. We publish both fiction and nonfiction, and publish in hardcover and softcover."

BOOKS IN MOTION, (I), Suite #501, 9212 E. Montgomery, Spokane WA 99206. (509)922-1646. President: Gary Challender. Estab. 1980. "Audiobook company, national marketer. Publishes novels, novellas and short stories in audiobook form *only*." Published new writers within the last year. Plans 12 first novels this year. Averages 70 total titles, 65 fiction titles each year.
Needs: "Our current priorities are business and self-help." Recently published *Cow County Law*, by M & M Lehman (western); *By A Promise Bound*, by Barbara Francis (historical drama/romance); and *Flight of the White Horse*, by Todd S. Moffett (fantasy).
How to Contact: Accepts unsolicited mss. Submit outline/synopsis and 4 sample chapters. SASE for ms. Reports within 3 weeks to 3 months. Simultaneous submissions OK.
Terms: Pays royalties of 10%. "We pay royalties every 6 months. Royalties that are received are based on the gross sales that any given title generates during the 6-month interval. Authors must be patient since it usually takes a minimum of one year before new titles will have significant sales." Publishes ms 6-12 months after acceptance. Book catalog free on request.
Advice: "We would like to see more short works, less than 700 pages. We are currently looking for works from 55 to 100 double-spaced, typed pages."

THOMAS BOUREGY & COMPANY, INC., 401 Lafayette St., New York NY 10003. Small category line. See Avalon Books.

BOYDS MILLS PRESS, (II), Subsidiary of Highlights for Children, 910 Church St., Honesdale PA 18431. (717)253-1164. Manuscript Coordinator: Beth Troop. Estab. 1990. "Independent publisher of quality books for children of all ages." Publishes hardcover. Books: Coated paper; offset printing; case binding; 4-color illustrations; average print order varies. Plans 4 fiction titles (novels).
● Boyd Mills Press is the publishing arm of *Highlights for Children*. See listings for the related magazine, a contest and a conference in this book.
Needs: Juvenile, young adult (adventure, contemporary, ethnic, historical, animal, sports. Recently published *Family Karate*, by Kathryn Ewing; *Walking the Rim*, by Susan Hart-Lindquist; *Pedro's Journal*, by Pam Conrad.
How to Contact: Accepts unsolicited mss. Send complete ms with cover letter. Reports in 1 month. Simultaneous submissions OK.
Terms: Pays standard rates. Sends pre-publication galleys to author. Time between acceptance and publication depends on "what season it is scheduled for." Writer's guidelines for #10 SAE and 1 first class stamp.

Advice: "We're interested in young adult novels of real literary quality as well as middle grade fiction that's imaginative with fresh ideas. Getting into the mode of thinking like a child is important."

BRADBURY PRESS, INC., (I, II), Affiliate of Macmillan, Inc., 866 3rd Ave., New York NY 10022. (212)702-9809. Vice President and Editorial Director: Barbara Lalicki. Publishes juvenile hardcover originals. Books: Excellent quality paper printing and binding; full-color or black-and-white illustrations—depends on what the book needs. Encourages new writers. Seldom comments on rejected mss.
Needs: Juvenile and young adult: contemporary, adventure, science fiction. Recently published *Woodsong*, by Gary Paulsen; *Windcatcher*, by Avi; and *Cricket and the Crackerbox Kid*, by Alane Ferguson.
How to Contact: Query first on novels. Send complete picture book ms with SASE. Specify simultaneous submissions. Reports in 3 months on mss.
Terms: Pays royalty based on retail price. Advance negotiable.

BRANDEN PUBLISHING CO., (I, II), Subsidiary of Branden Press, Box 843, 17 Station St., Brookline Village MA 02147. Imprint: I.P.L. Estab. 1967. Publishes hardcover and paperback originals and reprints. Books: 55-60 lb. acid-free paper; case- or perfect-bound; illustrations; average print order: 5,000. Plans 5 first novels this year. Averages 15 total titles, 5 fiction titles each year.
Needs: Adventure, contemporary, ethnic, historical, literary, mainstream, military/war, mystery/suspense, short story collections and translations. Looking for "contemporary, fast pace, modern society." No porno, experimental or horror. Published *Payola!*, by Gerry Cagle; *Miss Emily Martine*, by Lynn Thorsen; *Tales of Suicide*, by Luigi Pirandello; and *The Saving Rain*, by Elsie Webber.
How to Contact: Does not accept unsolicited mss. Query *only* with SASE. Reports in 1 week on queries.
Terms: Pays royalties of 5-10% minimum. Advance negotiable. Provides 10 author's copies. Sends galleys to author. Publishes ms "several months" after acceptance.
Advice: "Publishing more fiction because of demand. Do not make phone inquiries. Do not oversubmit; single submissions only; do not procrastinate if contract is offered."

*GEORGE BRAZILLER, INC., (III), 60 Madison Ave., New York NY 10010. (212)889-0909. President: George Braziller. Manuscript submissions: Lena Vayzman. Estab. 1955. Publishes hardcover originals and paperback reprints. Books: Cloth binding; illustrations sometimes; average print order: 4,000. Average first novel print order: 3,000. Buys 10% agented fiction. Averages 25 total titles, 6 fiction titles each year. Occasionally critiques rejected mss.
Needs: Art, feminist, literary, short story collections and translations. Recently published *You Don't Love Yourself*, by Nathalie Sarraute (literary); *The White Castle*, by Orhan Pamuk (literary); *And They Didn't Die*, by Lauretta Ngcobo (ethnic/feminist).
How to Contact: Query first with SASE. Reports in 2 weeks on queries. Publishes ms an average of 1 year after acceptance.
Terms: *Some subsidy publishing.* Negotiates advance. Must return advance if book is not completed or is not acceptable. Sends galleys to author. Free book catalog on request with oversized SASE.

*BRIDGE PUBLISHING, INC., (III, IV), 2500 Hamilton Blvd., South Plainfield NJ 07080. (201)754-0745. Editor: Kenneth Percy. Estab. 1981. Midsize independent publisher of Christian literature. Publishes cloth and paperback originals and reprints. Averages 35 total titles/year.
Needs: "We want quality, literary Christian fiction, written in the style of Frederick Buechner, John Cheever, and John Updike. No 'genre fiction' (romance, biblical novels, gothics, sci-fi, etc.). We want well written fiction that shows believable characters struggling to 'work out their salvations' in believable situations. Books that exhibit real human drama and stylistic craftsmanship." Published *Getting Them Sober*, by Toby Drews; *Help for the Battered Woman*, by Dr. Lydia Savina; and *The Teen Sex Survival Manual*, by Watkins.

 The asterisk indicates a publisher who sometimes offers subsidy arrangements. Authors are asked to subsidize part of the cost of book production. See the introduction for more information.

How to Contact: Accepts unsolicited mss. Submit complete ms with cover letter. SASE required. Reports in 2 months. Simultaneous submissions OK.

Terms: *Offers self/cooperative publishing services.* Writer's guidelines for #10 SAE and 1 first class stamp. Book catalog for $2.95.

Advice: "While we are not generally accepting fiction, we will consider manuscripts of exceptional merit. Authors must already have material published and/or other books published by reputable publishers. The work must be written from a biblical Christian worldview but does not necessarily need to be explicitly religious in nature. Only completed manuscripts will be considered."

BROADMAN PRESS, (II), 127 9th Ave. N., Nashville TN 37234. (615)251-2433. Editorial Director: Harold S. Smith. Religious publisher associated with the Southern Baptist Convention. Publishes hardcover and paperback originals. Books: Offset paper stock; offset printing; perfect or Smythe sewn binding; illustrations possible; average print order depends on forecast. Average number of titles: 3/year.

Needs: Adventure, historical, religious/inspirational, humor/satire, juvenile, and young adult. Will accept no other genre. Recently published: *Recovery of the Lost Sword*, L.L. Chaikin; *Mary of Magdala*, by Anne C. Williman; *Journey to Amanah: The Beginning*, by Colleen K. Snyder.

How to Contact: Query, but decision is not made until ms is reviewed. No simultaneous submissions. Reports in 2 months on queries and mss.

Terms: Pays 10% in royalties; no advance. Sends galleys to author if requested.

Advice: "We publish very few fiction works, but we encourage first novelists. We encourage a close working relationship with the author to develop the best possible product."

CAMELOT BOOKS, (II), Imprint of Avon Books, (Division of the Hearst Corporation), 1350 Avenue of the Americas, New York NY 10019. (212)261-6816. Editorial Director: Ellen E. Krieger. Estab. 1961. Publishes paperback originals and reprints for middle-grade juvenile list. Books: 6-10 line drawings in a few of the younger books. No color.

Needs: Juvenile (fantasy—"very selective," contemporary—"selective"). Looking for "contemporary, humorous books about real kids in real-life situations." No "science fiction, animal stories, picture books." Published *Haunting in Williamsburg*, by Lou Kassem; *The Return of the Plant that Ate Dirty Socks*, by Nancy McArthur; and *The Secret of the Indian*, by Lynne Reid Banks.

How to Contact: Accepts unsolicited mss. Submit complete ms with cover letter (preferred) or outline/synopsis and 3 sample chapters. Agented fiction 75%. Reports in 3-4 weeks on queries; 6-10 weeks on mss. Simultaneous submissions OK.

Terms: Royalties and advance negotiable. Sends galleys to author. Writer's guidelines for #10 SAE and 1 first class stamp. Book catalog for 9×11 SAE and 98¢ postage.

CARROLL & GRAF PUBLISHERS, INC., (III), 260 5th Ave., New York NY 10001. (212)889-8772. Contact: Editor. Estab. 1983. Publishes hardcover and paperback originals and paperback reprints. Plans 5 first novels this year. Averages 120 total titles, 75 fiction titles each year. Average first novel print order 7,500 copies. Occasionally critiques rejected mss.

Needs: Contemporary, erotica, fantasy, science fiction, literary, mainstream and mystery/suspense. No romance.

How to Contact: Does not accept unsolicited mss. Query first or submit outline/synopsis and sample chapters. SASE. Reports in 2 weeks.

Terms: Pays in royalties of 6% minimum; 15% maximum; advance negotiable. Sends galleys to author. Free book catalog on request.

‡CHRONICLE BOOKS, (I), 275 Fifth St., San Francisco CA 94103. (415)777-7240. Fiction Editor: Jay Schaefer. Estab. 1966. "Full-line publisher of 120 books per year." Publishes hardcover and paperback originals. Averages 120 total titles, 10 fiction this year. Sometimes comments on rejected ms.

Needs: Open. Looking for novellas, collections and novels. No romances, sci-fi, or any genre fiction: no category fiction. Publishes anthologies. Recently published *Griffin & Sabine*, by Bantok; *Parallel Life and Other Stories*, by Beeman; *New Orleans Stories*, edited by Miller.

How to Contact: Accepts unsolicited mss. Submit complete ms with cover letter. Send SASE for reply, return of ms or send a disposable copy of the ms. Agented fiction 50%. No simultaneous submissions.

Terms: Standard rates. Sends galleys to author. Publishes ms 9-12 months after acceptance.
Advice: "Send complete ms and wait for a response before sending more work. We do not have 'guidelines.' We are seeking quality fiction, not genre or commercial writing. Our fiction list is small but very well supported. Writers from west of the Rockies and new writers are particularly encouraged."

CITADEL PRESS, (II), Lyle Stuart Inc., 120 Enterprise Ave., Secaucus NJ 07094. (201)866-4199. Vice President: Allan J. Wilson. Estab. 1942. Publishes hardcover and paperback originals and paperback reprints. Averages 65 total titles, 4-7 fiction titles each year. Occasionally critiques rejected mss.
Needs: No religious, romantic or detective. Published *The Rain Maiden*, by Jill M. Phillips and *Human Oddities*, by Martin Monestiere.
How to Contact: Accepts unsolicited mss. Query first with SASE. Reports in 6 weeks on queries; 2 months on mss. Simultaneous submissions OK.
Terms: Pays in royalties of 10% minimum; 15% maximum; 12-25 author's copies. Advance is more for agented ms; depends on grant/award money.

■CLOVERDALE PRESS INC., (II), 109 West 17th St., New York NY 10011. (212)727-3370. Editorial Director: Jane Thornton. Estab. 1980. Book packager.
 ● For more on Cloverdale see the close-up with the editors in the 1990 *Novel & Short Story Writer's Market*.
Needs: "Needs vary greatly and frequently, depending on publishers' requirements." Currently producing *Sweet Dreams*, YA romances, *Nowhere High*, YA fiction, and adult nonfiction and how-to.
How to Contact: Does *not* accept unsolicited mss. Contact Marion Vaarn for guidelines. Include SASE.

CONTEMPORARY BOOKS, 180 N. Michigan Ave., Chicago IL 60601. Mostly nonfiction.

DAVID C. COOK PUBLISHING COMPANY, 850 N. Grove, Elgin IL 60120. (708)741-2400. Imprints: Chariot Books, Life Journey Books. Executive Editor: Catherine L. Davis. Estab. 1875. Publishes hardcover and paperback originals. Published new writers within the last year. Number of fiction titles: 35-40 juvenile, 4-6 adult. Encourages new writers.
Needs: Religious/inspirational, juvenile, young adult and adult; sports, animal, spy/adventure, historical, Biblical, fantasy/science fiction, picture book and easy-to-read. Recently published *With Wings as Eagles*, by Elaine Schulte; *Mystery of the Laughing Cat*, by Elspeth Campbell Murphy; *Mystery Rider at Thunder Ridge*, by David Gillett.
How to Contact: All unsolicited mss are returned unopened. Query with SASE. Simultaneous.submissions OK. Accepts computer printout submissions. Reports in 3 months.
Terms: Royalties vary ("depending on whether it is trade, mass market or cloth" and whether picture book or novel). Offers advance. Writer's guidelines with SASE.
Advice: "Chariot Books publishes books for toddlers through teens which help children better understand their relationship with God, and/or the message of God's book, the Bible. Interested in seeing contemporary novels (*not* Harlequin-type) adventure, romance, suspense with Christian perspective."

CROSSWAY BOOKS, (II, IV), Division of Good News Publishers, 1300 Crescent, Wheaton IL 60187. Estab. 1938. Midsize independent religious publisher with plans to expand. Publishes paperback originals. Average print order 5,000 copies. Buys 5% agented fiction. Averages 35 total titles, 8-10 fiction titles each year.
Needs: Contemporary, adventure, literary, religious/inspirational, science fiction and young adult (fantasy/science fiction). "All fiction published by Crossway Books must be written from the perspective of evangelical Christianity. It need not be *explicitly* Christian, but it must understand and view the world through Christian principle. For example, our books *Taliesin* and *Merlin* take place in a pre-Christian era, but Christian themes (e.g., sin, forgiveness, sacrifice, redemption) are present. We are *eager* to discover and nurture Christian novelists." No sentimental, didactic, "inspirational" religious fiction; heavy-handed allegorical or derivative (of C.S. Lewis or J.R.R. Tolkien) fantasy. Recently published *Glastonbury*, by Donna Fletcher Crow; *Lamper's Meadow*, by Barbra Minar.

Listings marked with a solid box are book packagers. See the introduction for more information.

How to Contact: Does not accept unsolicited mss. Send query with synopsis and sample chapters only. Reports in 4-6 months on queries. Publishes ms 1-2 years after acceptance.
Terms: Pays in royalties and negotiates advance. Book catalog for 9×12 SAE and $1.25.
Advice: "Publishing a higher quality of writing as we develop a wider reputation for excellent Christian fiction. Christian novelists—you must get your writing *up to standard*. The major reason novels informed by a Christian perspective do not have more presence in the market is because they are inferior. Sad but true. I believe Crossway can successfully publish and market *quality* Christian novelists. Also read John Gardner's *On Moral Fiction*. The market for fantasy/science fiction continues to expand (and genre fiction in general). There are more attempts lately at Christian science fiction and fantasy, though they generally fail from didacticism or from being overly derivative. We have a western adult and youth series, a mystery series."

THE CROWN PUBLISHING GROUP, (II), 201 E. 50th St., New York NY 10022. (212)572-6190. Imprints include Crown, Harmony Books, Orion Books, Clarkson N. Potter, Inc. Executive Vice Pres., Editor-in-Chief: Betty A. Prashker. Executive Editor, Crown: James O'Shea Wade. Editorial Director, Harmony Books: Peter Guzzardi. Editorial Director, Clarkson N. Potter: Carol Southern, Executive Editor: Lauren Shakely. Editorial Director, Orion Books: James O'Shea Wade. Executive Managing Editor: Laurie Stark. Estab. 1936. Large independent publisher of fiction and nonfiction. Publishes hardcover and paperback originals and reprints. Magazine: 50 lb. paper; offset printing; hardcover binding; sometimes illustrations; average print order: 15,000. Plans 4 first novels this year. Averages 250 total titles, 20 fiction titles each year. Average first novel print order: 15,000 copies. Occasionally critiques rejected mss.
Needs: Adventure, contemporary, historical, horror, humor/satire, literary, mainstream, science, war. Recently published *Plains of Passage*, by Jean Auel; *Dave Barry Talks Back*, by Dave Barry; *Russka*, by Edward Rutherfurd; *Zapp!*, by William Byam with Jeff Cox; and *Martha Stewart's Gardening*, by Martha Stewart.
How to Contact: Does not accept unsolicited mss. "Query letters only addressed to the Editorial Department. Complete mss are returned unread . . ." SASE. Reports in 3-4 months.
Terms: Pays advance against royalty; terms vary and are negotiated per book.

‡DARK HORSE COMICS, INC., (II, IV), 10956 Main St. S.E., Milwaukee OR 97222. (503)652-8815. Contact: Submissions Editor. Estab. 1986. "Dark Horse publishes all kinds of comics material, and we try not to limit ourselves to any one genre or any one philosophy. Most of our comics are intended for readers 15-40, though we also publish material that is accessible to younger readers." Comic books: newsprint or glossy paper, each title 24-28 pages. Averages 10-30 total titles each year.
Needs: Comics: adventure, children's/juvenile, fantasy (space fantasy, sword and sorcery, super hero), horror, humor/satire, mystery/suspense (private eye/hardboiled), psychic/supernatural, romance (contemporary), science fiction (hard science, soft/sociological), western (traditional). Proposals or scripts for comic books only. Plans anthology. Recently published comics by Andrew Vachss, Frank Miller, John Byrne, Chris Claremont, Clive Barker.
How to Contact: Does not accept unsolicited mss. Query letter first. Should include one-page bio, list of publishing credits. SASE (IRC) or disposable copy of ms. Reports in 2-3 weeks on queries; 1-2 months on mss. Simultaneous submissions OK.
Terms: Pays $25-100/page and 5-25 author's copies. "We usually buy first and second rights, other rights on publication." Writer's guidelines for #10 SASE and 1 first class stamp.
Advice: "Obtain copies of our Writer's Guidelines, Proposal Guidelines and Script Format Guidelines before making a submission." Looks for "originality, a sense of fun."

DAW BOOKS, INC., (I), 375 Hudson St., New York NY 10014. Publishers: Elizabeth R. Wollheim and Sheila Gilbert. Executive VP/Secretary-Treasurer: Elsie B. Wollheim. Submissions Editor: Peter Stampfel. Estab. 1971. Publishes paperback originals, hardcover reprints and hardcover originals. Books: Illustrations sometimes; average print and first novel order vary widely. May publish as many as 6 or more first novels a year. Averages 36 new titles plus 40 or more reissues, all fiction, each year. Occasionally critiques rejected mss.
- For more on DAW Books, see the close-up interview with Sheila Gilbert in the 1990 *Novel & Short Story Writer's Market*.
Needs: Science fiction (hard science, soft sociological) and fantasy only. Recently published *The Dragon Token*, by Melanie Rawn (novel); *Winds of Change*, by Mercedes Lackey (novel); *Chanur's Legacy*, by C.J. Cherryh; *Jaran*, by Kate Elliott. Publishes many original and reprint anthologies including *Sword & Sorceress* (edited by Marion Zimmer Bradley); *Cat Fantastic* (edited by Martin H. Green-

Close-up

Jeanne M. Cavelos
Senior Editor
Dell/Abyss

© Kathleen M. Heins

What makes a good horror writer? "I feel that everyone has something in them that really disturbs them, that they don't like to think about. The horror writer is willing to confront that in order to write a really good horror novel," says Jeanne Cavelos, senior editor at Dell.

Cavelos earned a bachelor's degree in astrophysics and worked at NASA before getting a master's in creative writing and entering the publishing field. "When I was in the creative writing program I really liked editing other people's stuff and realized I was pretty good at it," she says.

Cavelos, who oversees Abyss Books, a new line of mass market horror fiction introduced by Dell early in 1991, grew up reading horror and science fiction. "When I came to Dell there was no specific person doing this kind of stuff and nobody really liked it so gradually people started passing these manuscripts to me," she says. Dell's horror program at the time was on shaky ground. "We realized we had a really crummy horror program and we were going to discontinue publishing horror entirely unless we came up with a way that was different from what had been done in the past."

Dell was not alone. "Over the past five years, paperback horror publishers have glutted the market with poorly written, unoriginal horror and, in the process, have alienated a lot of loyal readers," says Cavelos. The Abyss line was formed with the intention of cleaning the slate and releasing only high-quality horror.

To that end, Cavelos is looking for books that offer different slants from traditional horror. Abyss' editorial guidelines instruct writers to focus, not on the monster in the closet, but how we as human beings react to it. Abyss has already received rave reviews, including an unsolicited letter of praise from horror giant Stephen King.

Books about the darker side of the human psyche are particularly appealing to Cavelos. "I really like books told in the first person where the person telling the story is going crazy and you don't know if what you're being told is real or fantasy," she says. "There's not enough of that type of book that's well done."

Cavelos says often a manuscript is rejected, not because it isn't well done, but because she's seen too many of the same type. "The thing I'm getting now, which I don't want to see much more of, is serial killer books," she says. "I would like to see people turn in other directions because there are a lot of other horrifying things in the world."

Writers interested in having horror novels published can get noticed by having their work appear in small horror magazines or anthologies first. "It's a good way to get noticed because you get people talking about you," says Cavelos, who is excited when she discovers new talent this way. "I'll give them a call and a lot of times they'll say 'I have three novels in my closet.'" Many of Abyss' authors are, in fact, first-time novelists.

Attending conventions, says Cavelos, helps writers make contacts by meeting other writers and getting to know what publishers are currently looking for and which publishers are overstocked. "You might send a book to somebody right at the time they've decided they're booked for three years and they'll just reject it without your ever knowing why," she says.

In a market that's been traditionally dominated by men, many of Abyss' authors are, just by coincidence, women. "I didn't plan it that way, but I do think women add fresh elements and extra life to horror that haven't existed before," says Cavelos.

Although she will read unagented manuscripts, Cavelos says it's in a writer's best interest to get representation. "I know a lot of editors who will not read unsolicited material or they will have someone else read it." An inexperienced writer also may not understand the intricacies of contract negotiations. "I try to give really fair terms to everyone I deal with but there are plenty of publishers who will push for all they can get if they think that you don't know what you're doing."

Cavelos recommends going to a bookstore to see who is publishing the types of novels that you are writing. Often, she says, the author will thank the editor and agent in the acknowledgment page, providing you with some good leads.

Of the approximately 30 manuscripts submitted to Abyss each week, about 10 are unsolicited. If you'd like to submit to Abyss keep your cover letter short (one page or less) and include a list of your previous publications. You should also enclose a plot outline of five pages or less, she says.

Cavelos likes to receive the entire manuscript at once. "If I read 50 pages and think it's promising I don't want to have to call somebody and ask them to send the rest because by the time they've sent it I'm reading something else." Cavelos stresses that you should only send one manuscript at a time. Abyss' preferred length is approximately 100,000 words.

Once you've sent your manuscript, don't expect a response for several months. "That's the downside of my reading so many of the submissions myself," says Cavelos. If you feel compelled to follow up, wait at least three months, and then don't call, write. "Some authors will call up once a week and ask 'Have you read it yet?' I wish I could read everything that fast but I can't. I might try to look at it quickly and make a very fast decision in order to get them out of my hair and that kind of decision usually isn't a yes."

Cavelos says that although rejections are frustrating, writers are advised to keep plugging away. "A lot of writers who are big now were rejected many, many times when they were starting out and just kept going. A lot of whether you're going to succeed or not is based on whether you're going to quit or keep trying because eventually you're going to get good at it and find somebody who's going to believe in you."

—Kathleen M. Heins

berg); *Tales From the Twilight Zone* (edited by Carol Serling). "You may write to the editors (after looking at the anthology) for guidelines % DAW."
How to Contact: Submit complete ms with SASE. Usually reports in 3-5 months on mss, but in special cases may take longer. "No agent required."
Terms: Pays an advance against royalties. Sends galleys to author (if there is time).
Advice: "We strongly encourage new writers. We are currently working with more than a dozen additional new authors whose first novels we plan to publish in 1991 and 1992. We like a close and friendly relationship with authors. We are publishing more fantasy than previously, but we are looking for more *serious* fantasy and especially need science fiction. To unpublished authors: Try to make an educated submission and don't give up."

DEL REY BOOKS, Subsidiary of Ballantine Books, 201 E. 50 St., New York NY 10022. (212)572-2677. Estab. 1977. Publishes hardcover originals and paperback originals and reprints. Plans 6-7 first novels this year. Publishes 60 titles each year, all fiction. Sometimes critiques rejected mss.
Needs: Fantasy and science fiction. Fantasy must have magic as an intrinsic element to the plot. No flying-saucer, Atlantis or occult novels. Recently published *Renegades of Pern*, by Anne McCaffrey (science fiction/hardcover original); *The Diamond Throne*, by David Eddings (fantasy/hardcover original); and *The Metaconcert*, by Julian May (science fiction/paperback reprint).
How to Contact: Accepts unsolicited mss. Submit complete manuscript with cover letter or outline/synopsis and first 3 chapters. Prefers complete ms. Address science fiction to SF editor; fantasy to fantasy editor. Reports in 2 weeks on queries; 10 months on ms.
Terms: Pays in royalties; "advance is competitive." Sends pre-publication galleys to author. Writer's guidelines for #10 SAE and 1 first class stamp.
Advice: Has been publishing "more fiction and more hardcovers, because the market is there for them. Read a lot of science fiction and fantasy, such as works by Anne McCaffrey, David Eddings, Larry Niven, Arthur C. Clarke, Terry Brooks, Frederik Pohl, Barbara Hambly. When writing, pay particular attention to plotting (and a satisfactory conclusion) and characters (sympathetic and well-rounded)—because those are what readers look for."

DELACORTE/DELL BOOKS FOR YOUNG READERS/DOUBLEDAY, (II, III, IV), Division of Bantam Doubleday Dell Publishing Group, Inc., 666 5th Ave., New York NY 10103. (212)765-6500. Imprints include Yearling and Laurel-Leaf Books and Yearling Classics. New imprint: Young Yearling Books, for readers 5-8 years old. Vice President/Publisher: Craig Virden. Large publisher specializing in young adult and middle-age fiction. Occasionally critiques or comments on rejected ms.
Needs: "First chapter books," juvenile, young adult. "We are looking for quality fiction—all categories possible." No romance of the formula type. Published *Fade*, by Robert Cormier; *Beans on the Roof*, by Betsy Byars; *Cal Cameron by Day, Spiderman by Night*, by Ann Cosum (winner of Delacorte fiction contest).
How to Contact: Query first. Unsolicited manuscripts not accepted. Fiction is agented. "Our contest is for first young adult novel. Deadline is December 31. Write for details."
Terms: Pays in royalties; advance is negotiable. Send galleys to author. Book catalog free on request.
Advice: "We are publishing more fiction than in the past. The market is good."

DELL PUBLISHING, 666 Fifth Avenue, New York NY 10103. (212)765-6500. Imprints include Delacorte Press, Delacorte Juvenile, Delta, Dell, Laurel, Laurel-Leaf and Yearling. Estab. 1922. Publishes hardcover and paperback originals and paperback reprints.
Needs: See below for individual imprint requirements.
How to Contact: Reports in 3 months. Simultaneous submissions OK. Please adhere strictly to the following procedures: 1. Send *only* a 4-page synopsis or outline with a cover letter stating previous work published or relevant experience. Enclose SASE. 2. *Do not* send ms, sample chapters or artwork. 3. *Do not* register, certify or insure your letter. Dell is comprised of several imprints, each with its own editorial department. Please review carefully the following information and direct your submissions to the appropriate department. Your envelope must be marked: Attention: (One of the following names of imprints), Editorial Department—Proposal.
DELACORTE: Publishes in hardcover; looks for top-notch commercial fiction and nonfiction; 35 titles/year.
DELTA: Publishes trade paperbacks including original fiction and nonfiction; 20 titles/year.
DELL: Publishes mass-market and trade paperbacks; looks for family sagas, historical romances, sexy modern romances, adventure and suspense thrillers, mysteries, psychic/supernatural, horror, war novels, fiction and nonfiction. 200 titles/year.

DELACORTE JUVENILE: Publishes in hardcover for children and young adults, grades K-12. 40 titles/year. "We prefer complete mss for fiction."

LAUREL-LEAF: Publishes originals and reprints in paperback for young adults, grades 7-12. 48 titles/year.

YOUNG YEARLING: pre K to 4th grade. Publishes originals and reprints in paperback for children.

YEARLING: Publishes originals and reprints in paperback for children, grades 1-6. 75 titles/year.

Terms: Pays 6-15% in royalties; offers advance. Sends galleys to author. Book catalog for 8½×11 SAE plus $1.30 postage (Attention: Customer Service).

Advice: "Don't get your hopes up. Query first only with 4-page synopsis plus SASE. Study the paperback racks in your local drugstore. We encourage first novelists. We also encourage all authors to seek agents."

DIAL BOOKS FOR YOUNG READERS, (II), Division of Penguin Books U.S.A. Inc., 375 Hudson St., New York NY 10014. (212)366-2000. Imprints include Pied Piper Books, Easy-to-Read Books. Editor-in-Chief/Pres./Publisher: Phyllis Fogelman. Estab. 1961. Trade children's book publisher, "looking for picture book mss and novels." Publishes hardcover originals. Plans 1 first novel this year. Averages 60-70 titles, mainly fiction. Occasionally critiques or comments on rejected ms.

Needs: Juvenile (1-9 yrs.) including: animal, fantasy, spy/adventure, contemporary and easy-to-read; young adult/teen (10-16 years) including: fantasy/science fiction, literary and commercial mystery and fiction. Published *Lionel in the Spring*, by Stephen Krensky (easy-to-read); *The Tale of Caliph Stork*, by Lenny Hort (picture book); and *Bailey's Bones*, by Victor Kelleher (novel).

How to Contact: Accepts unsolicited mss. Submit outline/synopsis and sample chapters or complete ms with cover letter. SASE. Agented fiction 50%. Reports in 3-4 weeks on queries. Simultaneous brief submissions OK.

Terms: Pays advance against royalties. Writer's guidelines free for #10 SAE and 1 first class stamp. Book catalog for 9×12 SAE and $1.92 postage.

Advice: "We are publishing more fiction books than in the past, and we publish only hardcover originals, most of which are fiction. At this time we are particularly interested in both fiction and nonfiction for the middle grades, and innovative picture book manuscripts. We also are looking for easy-to-reads for first and second graders. Plays, collections of games and riddles, and counting and alphabet books are generally discouraged. Before submitting a manuscript to a publisher, it is a good idea to request a catalog to see what the publisher is currently publishing. As the 'Sweet Valley High' phenomenon has loosened its stranglehold on YA fiction, we are seeing more writers able to translate traditional values of literary excellence and contemporary innovation into the genre. Make your cover letters read like jacket flaps—short and compelling. Don't spend a lot of time apologizing for a lack of qualifications. In fact, don't mention them at all unless you have publishing credits, or your background is directly relevant to the story. 'I found this folktale during a return trip to the Tibetan village where I spent the first ten years of my life.'"

DOUBLEDAY, (III), a division of Bantam Doubleday Dell Publishing Group, Inc., 666 Fifth Ave., New York NY 10103. (212)765-6500. Estab. 1897. Publishes hardcover and paperback originals and paperback reprints.

Needs: "Doubleday is not able to consider unsolicited queries, proposals or manuscripts unless submitted through a bona fide literary agent, except that we will consider fiction for Perfect Crime line, romance and western imprints."

How to Contact: Send copy of complete ms (60,000-80,000 words) to Perfect Crime Editor, Loveswept Editor or Western Editor as appropriate. Sufficient postage for return via fourth class mail must accompany ms. Reports in 2-6 months.

Terms: Pays in royalties; offers advance.

DOUBLEDAY CANADA LIMITED, 105 Bond St., Toronto, Ontario M5B 1Y3 Canada. No unsolicited submissions.

EAKIN PRESS, (II, IV), Box 90159, Austin TX 78709-0159. (512)288-1771. Imprint: Nortex. Editor: Edwin M. Eakin. Estab. 1978. Publishes hardcover originals. Books: Old style (acid-free); offset printing; case binding; illustrations; average print order 2,000; first novel print order 5,000. Plans 2 first novels this year. Averages 80 total titles each year.

Needs: Juvenile. Specifically needs historical fiction for school market, juveniles set in Texas for Texas grade schoolers. Published *Wall Street Wives*, by Ande Ellen Winkler; *Jericho Day*, by Warren Murphy; and *Blood Red Sun*, by Stephen Mertz. Published new writers within the last year.

How to Contact: Accepts unsolicited mss. First send query or submit outline/synopsis and 2 sample chapters. SASE. Agented fiction 5%. Simultaneous submissions OK. Reports in 3 months on queries. **Terms:** Pays royalties; average advance: $1,000. Sends galleys to author. Publishes ms 1-1½ years after acceptance. Writers guidelines for #10 SAE and 1 first class stamp. Book catalog for 75¢.
Advice: "Juvenile fiction only with strong Texas theme. Just beginning category of adult fiction. We receive around 600 queries or unsolicited mss a year."

ECLIPSE BOOKS/ECLIPSE COMICS, (II, IV), P.O. Box 1099, Forestville CA 95436. (707)887-1521. Editor-in-Chief: Catherine Yronwode. Estab. 1978. Books: White or coated stock, up to 200 pages, every page illustrated. "Publishes 10-20 titles—comics and graphic novels each month."
• For more on Eclipse, see "Off the Beaten Path" in the 1991 *Novel & Short Story Writer's Market.* Eclipse, in conjunction with HarperCollins, publishes the Harper-Eclipse line of graphic novels featuring work by Doris Lessing, Dean Koontz and Jonathan Carroll.
Needs: Comics and graphic novels: adventure, condensed/excerpted novel, contemporary, ethnic, experimental, fantasy, feminist, gay, historical, horror, juvenile, lesbian, literary, mainstream, mystery/suspense, psychic/supernatural/occult, romance, science fiction, serialized novel, thriller/espionage, translations, westerns, young adult. "No religious, nationalistic, racist material." Receives "hundreds" of unsolicited fiction mss/year. Recently published *Tecumsed*, by Allan Eckert and Tim Truman; *Dread*, by Clive Barker and Dan Brereton; and *Playing the Game*, by Doris Lessing and Daniel Vallely.
How to Contact: Send a cover letter, proposal, sample of script for artist to draw from. Reports in 3 months. SASE. Simultaneous and reprint submissions (especially adaptations of well-known prose fiction) OK. Sample copy for $3. Fiction guidelines for #10 SAE.
Terms: Pays $35-50/page (for a screenplay type of comics script, not a page of prose); advance against royalties (royalties are about 8%, but must be shared with the artist). Also pays 2-5 contributor's copies and discount on extras.
Advice: Looks for "interesting, original stories with in-depth characterization."

PAUL S. ERIKSSON, PUBLISHER, (II), Suite 208, Battell-on-the-Otter, Middlebury VT 05753. (802)388-7303. Editor: Paul S. Eriksson. Estab. 1960. Publishes hardcover and paperback originals.
Needs: Mainstream. Published *The Headmaster's Papers*, by Richard A. Hawley and *Hand in Hand*, by Tauno Yliruusi.
How to Contact: Query first. Publishes ms an average of 6 months after acceptance.
Terms: Pays 10-15% in royalties; advance offered if necessary. Free book catalog.
Advice: "Our taste runs to serious fiction."

M. EVANS & CO., INC., (II), 216 E. 49th St., New York NY 10017. (212)688-2810. Westerns Editor: Patrick Lo Brutto. Publishes hardcover and trade paper fiction and nonfiction. Publishes 40-50 titles each year.
Needs: Western.
How to Contact: Accepts unsolicited mss. Query first with outline/synopsis and 3 sample chapters. SASE. Agented fiction: 100%. Reports on queries in 3-5 weeks. Simultaneous submissions OK.
Terms: Pays in royalties and offers advance; amounts vary. Sends galleys to author. Publishes ms 6-12 months after acceptance.

FANTAGRAPHICS BOOKS, (II, IV), 7563 Lake City Way, Seattle WA 98115. (206)524-1967. Publisher: Gary Groth. Estab. 1976. Publishes comic books, comics series and graphic novels. Books: Offset printing; saddle-stitched periodicals and smythe-sewn books; heavily illustrated. Publishes originals and reprints. Publishes 10 titles each month.
• For more on Fantagraphics see "Off the Beaten Path" in the 1991 *Novel & Short Story Writer's Market.*
Needs: Comic books and graphic novels (adventure, fantasy, romance, mystery, horror, science, social parodies). "We look for subject matter that is more or less the same as you would find in mainstream fiction." Published *Blood of Palomar*, by Gilbert Hernandez; *The Dragon Bellows Saga*, by Stan Sakai; *Death of Speedy*; *Housebound With Rick Geary*; *Little Nemo in Slumberland*.
How to Contact: Send a plot summary, pages of completed art (photocopies only) and character sketches. May send completed script if the author is willing to work with an artist of the publisher's choosing. Include cover letter and SASE. Reports in 1 month.
Terms: Pays in royalties of 8% (but must be split with artist) and advance.

FARRAR, STRAUS & GIROUX, (III), 19 Union Sq. W., New York NY 10003. (212)741-6900. Imprints include Hill & Wang, The Noonday Press. Editor-in-Chief: Jonathan Galassi. Midsized, independent publisher of fiction, nonfiction, poetry. Publishes hardcover originals. Published new writers within the last year. Plans 2 first novels this year. Averages 100 total titles, 30 fiction titles each year.
Needs: Open. No genre material. Published *The Mambo Kings Play Songs of Love*, by Oscar Hijuelos; *My Son's Story*, by Nadine Gordimer; *The Burden of Proof*, by Scott Turow.
How to Contact: Does not accept unsolicited mss. Query first. "Vast majority of fiction is agented." Reports in 2 months. Simultaneous submissions OK.
Terms: Pays royalties (standard, subject to negotiation). Advance. Sends galleys to author. Publishes ms one year after acceptance. Writer's guidelines for #10 SAE and 1 first class stamp.

FARRAR, STRAUS & GIROUX/CHILDREN'S BOOKS, (II), 19 Union Sq. W., New York NY 10003. Imprint is Sunburst Books. Children's Books Publisher: Stephen Roxburgh. Editor-in-Chief: Margaret Ferguson. Number of titles: 40. Published new writers within the last year. Buys juvenile mss with illustrations. Buys 25% agented fiction.
Needs: Children's picture books, juvenile novels, nonfiction. Published *Celine*, by Brock Cole; *Carl's Afternoon in the Park*, by Alexandra Day; *Predator*, by Bruce Brooks.
How to Contact: Submit outline/synopsis and 3 sample chapters, summary of ms and any pertinent information about author, author's writing, etc. No simultaneous submissions. No unsolicited submissions during the month of August. Reports in 1 month on queries, 3 months on mss. Publishes ms 18 months to 2 years after acceptance.
Terms: Pays in royalties; offers advance. Book catalog with 6½ × 9½ SASE.
Advice: "Study our list before sending something inappropriate. Publishing more titles—our list has expanded."

‡FAWCETT (I, II, III), Division of Random House/Ballantine, 201 E. 50th St., New York NY 10022. (212)751-2600. Imprints include Ivy, Crest, Gold Medal, Columbine and Juniper. Executive Editor: Barbara Dicks. Editor-in-Chief: Leona Nevler. Estab. 1955. Major publisher of mass market and trade paperbacks. Publishes paperback originals and reprints. Prints 160 titles annually. Encourages new writers. "Always looking for *great* first novels."
Needs: Historical, suspense, occult, adventure, mysteries. Published *The Omega Command*, by John Land; *Mid-town South*, by Christopher O'Brian; *The Incense Tree*, by Jacqueline La Tourette.
How to Contact: Query with SASE. Send outline and sample chapters for adult mass market. If ms is requested, simultaneous submissions OK. Prefers letter-quality. Reports in 1 month on queries, 3 months on mss.
Terms: Pays usual advance and royalties.
Advice: "Gold Medal list consists of 5 original paperbacks per month—usually 4 are novels."

FEARON/JANUS/QUERCUS, (II), (formerly Fearon/Janus), Subsidiary of Simon & Schuster, Secondary Education Group, 500 Harbor Blvd., Belmont CA 94002. (415)592-7810. Publisher and Editorial Director: Kate Wilson. Estab. 1954. Special-education publishers with a junior high, high school, and adult basic education audience—publishing program includes high interest/low level fiction, vocational and life skills materials, and low reading level secondary textbooks in all academic areas. Publishes paperback originals and reprints. Books: 3 lb. book set paper; offset printing; perfect or saddle-wired binding; line art illustrations; average print order: 5,000.
Needs: "All materials are written to specification. It's a hard market to crack without some experience writing at low reading levels. Manuscripts for specific series of fiction are solicited from time to time, and unsolicited manuscripts are accepted occasionally." Published *A Question of Freedom*, by Lucy Jane Bledsoe (adventure novella—one of series of eight); *Just for Today*, by Tana Reiff (one novella of series of seven life-issues stories); and *The Everett Eyes*, by Bernard Jackson & Susie Quintanilla (one of twenty in a series of extra-short thrillers).
How to Contact: Submit outline/synopsis and sample chapters. SASE. Reports in 3 months. Simultaneous submissions OK.
Terms: Authors usually receive a predetermined project fee. Book catalog for 9 × 12 SAE with 4 first class stamps.

FLARE BOOKS, (II), Imprint of Avon Books, Div. of the Hearst Corp., 1350 Avenue of the Americas, New York NY 10019. (212)261-6816. Editorial Director: Ellen Krieger. Estab. 1981. Small, young adult line. Publishes paperback originals and reprints. Plans 2-3 first novels this year. Averages 30 titles, all fiction each year.

Needs: Young adult (easy-to-read [hi-lo], problem novels, romance, spy/adventure) "very selective." Looking for contemporary fiction. No historical, science fiction/fantasy, heavy problem novels. Published *Show Me the Evidence*, by Alane Ferguson; *One Step Short*, by Jane McFann; and *So Long at the Fair*, by Hadley Irwin.
How to Contact: Accepts unsolicited mss. Submit complete ms with cover letter (preferred) or outline/synopsis and 3 sample chapters. Agented fiction 75%. Reports in 3-4 weeks on queries; 6-10 weeks on mss. Simultaneous submissions OK.
Terms: Royalties and advance negotiable. Sends galleys to author. Writer's guidelines for #10 SAE and 1 first class stamp. Book catalog for 9×12 SAE with 98¢ postage. "We run a young adult novel competition each year."

FOUR WINDS PRESS, (II), Imprint of Macmillan Children's Book Group, 866 Third Ave., New York NY 10022. Editor-in-Chief: Virginia Duncan. Estab. 1966. A children's trade book imprint. Publishes hardcover originals. Books: 3 piece binding for older reading books, 1 piece binding for picture books. Books for children ages 3-12 usually illustrated; average print order 6,000-10,000; first novel print order: 6,000. Published new writers within the last year. Publishes 25 total titles each year. No longer publishing young adult fiction.
Needs: Picture book manuscripts for ages 2-4 and 5-8. Recently published *Mrs. Toggle's Zipper*, by Robin Pulver and *Crow Moon, Worm Moon*, by James Skofield (picture books).
How to Contact: Accepts unsolicited mss. SASE required. Reports in 8-12 weeks. No simultaneous submissions.
Terms: Pays royalties, negotiable advance and author's copies. Book catalogs *not* available. Manuscript guidelines and portfolio guidelines are available on request with #10 SAE and 1 first class stamp. "No calls, please."
Advice: "The majority of the fiction manuscripts accepted by Four Winds Press are picture book texts; we publish very little older fiction. Due to volume of submissions received, we cannot guarantee a quick response time or answer queries about manuscript status."

GARETH STEVENS, INC., (II, IV), 1555 N. River Center Dr., Milwaukee WI 53212. (414)225-0333. Editorial Director: Patricia Lantier-Sampon. Estab. 1984. "Midsize independent children's book publisher." Publishes hardcover originals. Books: Matte paper; sheet feed printing; reinforced binding; several 4-color illustrations; average print order: 5,000; first picture book print order: 4,000-5,000. Published new writers within the last year. Plans 3 first novels this year. Publishes total of 120 titles, 30 fiction titles/year.
• Gareth Stevens' books have won numerous awards including the Mid-American Publisher's Award, the New Zealand Children's Book of the Year and mention in the American Library Association's "notable books."
Needs: Picture books and very juvenile fiction.
How to Contact: Accepts unsolicited mss. Send outline/synopsis and sample chapters or complete ms with cover letter. SASE. Reports in 3 weeks on queries; 6 months on mss. Simultaneous submissions OK. Accepts electronic submissions (on Microsoft Word disks for Macs).
Terms: Pays outright fees or, sometimes royalties of 3% minimum, 5% maximum. Average advance: $750. Advance is negotiable. Sends pre-publication galleys to author. Publishes ms 1 year to 18 months after acceptance. Book catalog for 9×12 SAE and 1 first class stamp.

GESSLER PUBLISHING COMPANY, 55 W. 13th St., New York NY 10011. (212)627-0099. Editorial Contact Person: Seth C. Levin. Estab. 1932. "Publisher/distributor of foreign language educational materials (primary/secondary schools)." Publishes paperback originals and reprints. Averages 75 total titles each year. Sometimes comments on rejected ms.
Needs: "Foreign language or English as a Second Language." Needs juvenile, literary, preschool/picture book, short story collections, translations. Published *Don Quixote de la Mancha, (cartoon version of classic, in Spanish); El Cid*, (prose and poetry version of the classic in Spanish); and *Les Miserables* (simplified versions of Victor Hugo classic, in French).

Check the Category Indexes, located at the back of the book, for publishers interested in specific fiction subjects.

How to Contact: Query first, then send outline/synopsis and 2-3 sample chapters; complete ms with cover letter. Agented fiction 40%. Reports on queries in 1 month; on mss in 6 weeks. Simultaneous submissions OK.
Terms: Pay varies with each author and contract. Sends galleys to author. "Varies on time of submissions and acceptance relating to our catalogue publication date." Writer's guidelines not available. Book catalog free on request.
Advice: "We specialize in the foreign language market directed to teachers and schools—a book that would interest us has to be attractive to that market—a teacher would be most likely to create a book for us."

DAVID R. GODINE, PUBLISHER, INC., 300 Massachusetts Ave., Boston MA 02115. Presently overstocked.

GROSSET & DUNLAP, INC., (III), A Division of the Putnam & Grosset Group, 11th Floor, 200 Madison Ave., New York NY 10016. (212)951-8700. Publisher/Vice President: Jane O'Connor. Editor-in-Chief: Craig Walker.
Needs: Juvenile, preschool/picture book.
How to Contact: Queries only. "Include such details as length and intended age group and any other information that you think will help us to understand the nature of your material. Be sure to enclose a stamped, self-addressed envelope for our reply. We can no longer review manuscripts that we have not asked to see, and they will be returned unread."

HARCOURT BRACE JOVANOVICH, (III), 1250 Sixth Ave., San Diego CA 92101. (619)699-6810. Fax: (619)699-6777. Imprints include HBJ Children's Books, Gulliver Books, Jane Yolen Books and Browndeer Press. Director: Louise Howton. Senior Editors: Diane D'Andrade, Elizabeth Van Doren and Allyn Johnston. Editor: Karen Grove. Editorial Director of Browndeer Press: Linda Zuckerman. Publishes hardcover originals and paperback reprints. Averages 75 titles/year. Published new writers within the last year.
Needs: Young adult fiction, nonfiction for all ages, picture books for very young children, mystery. Recently published *Moon Rope*, by Lois Ehlert; *Drylongso*, by Virginia Hamilton; *Zomo*, by Gerald McDermott; and *A River Ran Wild*, by Lynne Cherry.
How to Contact: Unsolicited mss currently accepted *only* by HBJ Children's Books and Browndeer Press. Send to "Manuscript Submissions, HBJ Children's Books." SASE. For picture books, send complete ms; for novels, send outline/synopsis and 2-4 sample chapters. No simultaneous submissions. No phone calls. Responds in 6-8 weeks.
Terms: Terms vary according to individual books; pays on royalty basis. Writers' guidelines for #10 SASE; catalog for 9×12 SASE.
Advice: "Familiarize yourself with the type of book published by a company before submitting a manuscript; make sure your work is in line with the style of the publishing house. Research the market your work will reach; make yourself familiar with the current children's book field." New line: Environmental series "Gulliver Green Books."

HARLEQUIN ENTERPRISES, LTD., (II, IV), 225 Duncan Mill Rd., Don Mills, Ontario M3B 3K9 Canada. (416)445-5860. Imprints include Harlequin Romances, Harlequin Presents, Harlequin American Romances, Superromances, Temptation, Intrigue and Regency, Silhouette, Worldwide Mysteries, Gold Eagle. Editorial Director Harlequin: Karin Stoecker; Silhouette: Isabel Swift; Gold Eagle: Randall Toye. Estab. 1949. Publishes paperback originals and reprints. Books: Newsprint paper; web printing; perfect-bound. Published new writers within the last year. Number of titles: Averages 700/year. Buys agented and unagented fiction.
● Four books published by Harlequin in 1992 received Rita Awards.
Needs: Romance, glitz, heroic adventure, mystery/suspense (romantic suspense *only*). Will accept nothing that is not related to the desired categories. Recently published *Silence of Midnight*, by Karen Young (superromance); *Rafe's Revenge*, by Anne Stuart (Harlequin American Romance); *The Hood*, by Carin Ratterty (Harlequin Temptation).
Macomber, Leigh Michaels, Peggy Nicholson.
How to Contact: Send query letter or send outline and first 50 pages (2 or 3 chapters) or submit through agent with SAE and IRC or SASE (Canadian). Absolutely no simultaneous submissions. Reports in 1 month on queries; 2 months on mss.

Terms: Offers royalties, advance. Must return advance if book is not completed or is unacceptable. Sends galleys to author. Guidelines available.

Advice: "The quickest route to success is to follow directions for submissions: Query first. We encourage first novelists. Before sending a manuscript, read as many current Harlequin titles as you can. It's very important to know the genre and the series most appropriate for your submission." Authors may send manuscript for Romances and Presents to Paula Eykelhof, editor; Superromances: Marsha Zinberg, senior editor; Temptation: Birgit Davis-Todd, senior editor; Regencys: Marmie Charndoff, editor. American Romances and Intrigue: Debra Matteucci, senior editor and editorial coordinator, Harlequin Books, 6th Floor, 300 E. 42 Street, New York, NY 10017. Silhouette submissions should also be sent to the New York office, attention Isabel Swift. Gold Eagle query letters should be addressed to Feroze Mohammed, senior editor, at the Canada address. "The relationship between the novelist and editor is regarded highly and treated with professionalism."

HARMONY BOOKS, (II), Subsidiary of Crown Publishers, 201 E. 50th St., New York NY 10022. (212)572-6121. Contact: General Editorial Department. Publishes hardcover and paperback originals.
Needs: Literary fiction. Also publishes in serious nonfiction, history, biography, personal growth, media and music fields.
How to Contact: Accepts unsolicited mss. Query first with outline/synopsis and 2-3 sample chapters. SASE. Agented fiction: 75%. Simultaneous submissions OK.
Terms: Pays royalties and advance; amounts negotiable. Sends galleys to authors.

HARVEST HOUSE PUBLISHERS, (II, IV), 1075 Arrowsmith, Eugene OR 97402. (503)343-0123. Manuscript Coordinator: Mary Conner. Vice President of Editorial: Eileen L. Mason. Estab. 1974. Midsize independent publisher with plans to expand. Publishes hardcover and paperback originals and reprints. Books: 40 lb. ground wood paper; offset printing; perfect binding; average print order: 10,000; first novel print order: 10,000-15,000. Averages 80 total titles, 6 fiction titles each year.
Needs: Christian living, contemporary issues, family saga, humor, Christian preschool/picture books, mystery (romantic suspense, young adult), religious/inspirational and Christian romance (historical). Especially seeks inspirational, romance/historical and mystery. Recently published *As Time Goes By*, by Lori Wick; *Songs in the Whirlwind*, by June Masters Bacher; *Lady Rebel*, by Brenda Wilbee; and *Joshua*, by Ellen Gunderson Traylor. New fiction series for youth: "Addie McCormick Adventures," by Leanne Luca.
How to Contact: Accepts unsolicited mss. Query first or submit outline/synopsis and 2 sample chapters with SASE. Reports on queries in 2-8 weeks; on mss in 6-8 weeks. Simultaneous submissions OK.
Terms: Pays in royalties of 14-18%; 10 author's copies. Sends galleys to author. Writer's guidelines for SASE. Book catalog for 8½ × 11 SASE.

HERALD PRESS, (II), Division of Mennonite Publishing House, 616 Walnut Ave., Scottdale PA 15683. (412)887-8500. Imprints include Congregational Literature Division; Herald Press. Book Editor: S. David Garber. Fiction Editor: Michael A. King. Estab. 1908. "Church-related midsize publisher." Publishes paperback originals. Books: Recycled, acid-free Glatfelter thor paper; offset printing; adhesive binding; illustrations for children; average print order: 4,000; first novel print order: 3,500. Published new writers in the last year. Company publishes 30 titles/year. Number of fiction titles: 5/year. Sometimes critiques rejected mss.
Needs: Adventure, family saga, historical, juvenile (historical, spy/adventure, contemporary), literary, religious/inspirational, young adult/teen (historical, mystery, problem novels and spy/adventure). "Does not want to see fantasy, picture books." Recently published *Hagar*, by James R Shott; *Johnny Godshall*, by Glenn Lehman; and *Daniel*, by Mary Bornbarger.
How to Contact: Accepts unsolicited mss. Submit outline/synopsis and 2 sample chapters with SASE. Agented fiction 2%. Reports in 1 month on queries, 2 months on mss. Accepts electronics submissions (only *with* paper copy).
Terms: Pays 10-12% in royalties; 12 free author's copies. Pays after first 3 months, then once/year. Sends galleys to author. Publishes ms 1 year after acceptance. Writer's guidelines free. Book catalog for 50¢.
Advice: "Need more stories with Christian faith integrated smoothly and not as a tacked-on element."

HOLIDAY HOUSE, INC., (I, II), 425 Madison, New York NY 10017. (212)688-0085. Editor-in-Chief: Margery Cuyler. Estab. 1935. Independent publisher. Books: High quality printing; occasionally reinforced binding; illustrations sometimes. Publishes hardcover originals and paperback reprints. Published new writers within the last year. Number of titles: Approximately 50 hardcovers and 15 paperbacks each year.

Needs: Contemporary, Judaica and holiday, literary, adventure, humor and animal stories for young readers—preschool through middle grade. Recently published *Allergic to My Family*, by Liza Ketcham Murrow; *Out of Step*, by Mary Jane Auch. "We're not in a position to be too encouraging, as our list is tight, but we're always open to good 'family' novels and humor."

How to Contact: "We prefer query letters and three sample chapters for novels; complete manuscripts for shorter books and picture books." Simultaneous submissions OK as long as a cover letter mentions that other publishers are looking at the same material. Reports in 1 month on queries, 6-8 weeks on mss.

Terms: Advance and royalties are flexible, depending upon whether the book is illustrated.

Advice: "We have received an increasing number of manuscripts, but the quality has not improved vastly. This appears to be a decade in which publishers are interested in reviving the type of good, solid story that was popular in the '50s. Certainly there's a trend toward humor, family novels, novels with school settings, biographies and historical novels. Problem-type novels and romances seem to be on the wane. We are always open to well-written manuscripts, whether by a published or nonpublished author. Submit only one project at a time."

HENRY HOLT & COMPANY, (II), 6th Floor, 115 W. 18th St., New York NY 10011. (212)886-9200. Imprint includes Owl (paper). Publishes hardcover and paperback originals and reprints. Averages 50-60 total original titles, 20% of total is fiction each year.

Needs: Adventure, contemporary, feminist, historical, humor/satire, juvenile (5-9 years, including animal, easy-to-read, fantasy, historical, sports, spy/adventure and contemporary), literary, mainstream, suspense/mystery, translations and young adult/teen (10-18 years including easy-to-read, fantasy/science fiction, historical, problem novels, romance, sports and spy/adventure). Published *Fool's Progress*, by Edward Abbey; *Tracks*, by Louise Erdrich; *Trust*, by George V. Higgins; and *Frank Furbo*, by Wm. Wherton.

How to Contact: Accepts queries; no unsolicited mss. Agented fiction 95%.

Terms: Pays in royalties of 10% minimum; 15% maximum; advance. Sends galleys to author. Book catalog sent on request.

■HORIZON PUBLISHERS & DIST., INC., (III, IV), Box 490, 50 S. 500 West, Bountiful UT 84011-0490. (801)295-9451. President: Duane S. Crowther. Estab. 1971. "Midsize independent publisher with in-house printing facilities, staff of 30+." Publishes hardcover and paperback originals and reprints. Books: 60 lb. offset paper; hardbound, perfect and saddle-stitch binding; illustrations; average print order: 3,000; first novel print order: 3,000. Plans 2 first novels this year. Averages 25-30 total titles; 1-3 fiction titles each year.

Needs: Adventure, historical, humor/satire, juvenile, literary, mainstream, military/war, religious/inspirational, romance (contemporary and historical), science fiction, spiritual and young adult/teen (romance and spy/adventure). "Religious titles are directed only to the LDS (Latter-day Saints) market. General titles are marketed nationwide." Looking for "good quality writing in salable subject areas. Will also consider well-written books on social problems and issues, (divorce, abortion, child abuse, suicide, capital punishment and homosexuality)." Published *The Couchman and the Bells*, by Ted C. Hindmarsh.

How to Contact: Accepts unsolicited mss. Query first. SASE. Include Social Security number with submission. Reports in 2-4 weeks on queries; 10-12 weeks on mss. Simultaneous and electronic submissions OK if identified as such.

Terms: Pays royalties of 6% minimum; 12% maximum. Provides 10 author's copies. Sends page proofs to author. Publishes ms 3-9 months after acceptance. "We are not a subsidy publisher but we do job printing, book production for private authors and book packaging." Writer's guidelines for #10 SAE and 1 first class stamp.

Advice: Encourages "only those first novelists who write very well, with salable subjects. Please avoid the trite themes which are plaguing LDS fiction such as crossing the plains, conversion stories, and struggling courtships that always end in temple marriage. While these themes are important, they have been used so often that they are now frequently perceived as trite and are often ignored by those shopping for new books. In religious fiction we hope to see a process of moral, spiritual, or emotional growth presented. Some type of conflict is definitely essential for good plot development. Watch your vocabulary too—use appropriate words for the age group for which you are writing. We don't accept elementary children's mss for elementary grades."

HOUGHTON MIFFLIN COMPANY, (III), 2 Park St., Boston MA 02108. (617)725-5000. Subsidiary: Ticknor and Fields Inc. Publishes hardcover and paperback originals and paperback reprints. Averages 100 total titles, 50 fiction titles each year.
Needs: None at present. Published *The Translator*, by Ward Just.
How to Contact: Does not accept unsolicited mss. Buys virtually 100% agented fiction.

INTERLINK PUBLISHING GROUP, INC., (IV), 99 Seventh Ave., Brooklyn NY 11215. (718)797-4292. Imprints include: Interlink Books, Olive Branch Press and Crocodile Books USA. Publisher: Michel Moushabeck. Fiction Editor: Phyllis Bennis. Estab. 1987. "Midsize independent publisher." Publishes hardcover and paperback originals. Books: 55 lb. Warren Sebago Cream white paper; web offset printing; perfect binding; average print order: 5,000; first novel print order: 5,000. Published new writers within the last year. Plans 5-8 first novels this year. Averages 30 total titles, 5-8 fiction titles each year.
Needs: Needs adult fiction – relating to the Middle East, Africa or Latin America; translations accepted. Recently published *A Woman of Nazareth*, by Hala Deeb Jabbour; *The Children Who Sleep by the River*, by Debbie Taylor; *Prairies of Fever*, by Ibrahim/Nasrallah; and *The Silencer*, by Simon Louvish. Contemporary fiction in translation published under Emerging Voices: New International Fiction.
How to Contact: Does not accept unsolicited mss. Submit outline/synopsis only. SASE. Reports in 2 weeks on queries.
Terms: Pays royalties of 5% minimum; 8% maximum. Sends galleys to author. Publishes ms 1-1½ years after acceptance.

JAMESON BOOKS, (I, II, IV), Jameson Books, Inc., The Frontier Library, 722 Columbus St., Ottawa IL 61350. (815)434-7905. Editor: Jameson G. Campaigne, Jr. Estab. 1986. Publishes hardcover and paperback originals and reprints. Books: Free sheet paper; offset printing; average print order: 10,000; first novel print order: 5,000. Plans 6-8 novels this year. Averages 12-16 total titles, 4-8 fiction titles each year. Occasionally critiques or comments on rejected mss.
Needs: Very well-researched western (frontier pre-1850). No romance, sci-fi, mystery, et al. Published *Wister Trace*, by Loren Estelman; *Buckskin Brigades*, by L. Ron Hubbard; *One-Eyed Dream*, by Terry Johnston.
How to Contact: Does not accepted unsolicited mss. Submit outline/synopsis and 3 consecutive sample chapters. SASE. Agented fiction 50%. Reports in 2 weeks on queries; 2-5 months on mss. Simultaneous submissions OK.
Terms: Pays royalties of 5% minimum; 15% maximum. Average advance: $1,500. Sends galleys to author. Book catalog for 6×9 SASE.

JOY STREET BOOKS, 34 Beacon St., Boston MA 02108. (617)227-0730. Imprint of Little, Brown and Co. Children's Books Editor-in-chief: Melanie Kroupa. Publishes hardcover and quality paperback originals. Sometimes buys juvenile mss with illustrations.
Needs: General fiction, juvenile: sports, animal, mystery/adventure, realistic contemporary fiction, picture books and easy-to-read. Published *The Arizona Kid*, by Ron Koertge; *The Girl in the Box*, by Ouida Sebestyen; *Alias Madame Doubtfire*, by Anne Fine. Very interested in first novels.
How to Contact: Prefers query letter with sample chapters. SASE. Accepts simultaneous submissions.
Terms: Pays variable advances and royalties.

ALFRED A. KNOPF, (II), 201 E. 50th St., New York NY 10022. Contact: The Editors. Estab. 1915. Publishes hardcover originals. Number of titles: 45 in 1990. Buys 75% agented fiction. Published 11 new writers in 1991.
Needs: Contemporary, literary, suspense and spy. No western, gothic, romance, erotica, religious or science fiction. Recently published *Jazz* by Toni Morrison; *All The Pretty Horses*, by Cormac McCarthy; *Dreaming in Cuban* by Cristina Garcia. Published new writers within the last year.
How to Contact: Submit outline or synopsis with SASE. Reports within 1 month on mss. Publishes ms an average of 1 year after acceptance.
Terms: Pays 10-15% in royalties; offers advance. Must return advance if book is not completed or is unacceptable.
Advice: Publishes book-length fiction of literary merit by known and unknown writers.

KNOPF BOOKS FOR YOUNG READERS, (II), 225 Park Ave. South, New York NY 10003. Subsidiary of Random House, Inc. Editor-in-Chief: Janet Schulman. Publishes hardcover and paperback originals and reprints. New paperback imprints include Dragonfly Books (picture books), Bullseye (middle-grade fiction) and Borzoi Sprinters (Young Adult fiction). Averages 50 total titles, approximately 20 fiction titles each year.
Needs: "High-quality" contemporary, humor and nonfiction. "Young adult novels, picture books, middle group novels." Published *No Star Nights*, by Anna Smucker; *Mirandy and Brother Wind*, by Patricia McKissoch; *The Boy Who Lost His Face*, by Lewis Sachar.
How to Contact: Query with outline/synopsis and 2 sample chapters with SASE. Simultaneous submissions OK. Reports in 6-8 weeks on mss.
Terms: Sends galleys to author.

LEISURE BOOKS, (II), Division of Dorchester Publishing Co., Inc., Suite 1008, 276 Fifth Ave., New York NY 10001. (212)725-8811. Address submissions to Frank Walgren, editor. Mass-market paperback publisher—originals and reprints. Books: Newsprint paper; offset printing; perfect-bound; average print order: variable; first novel print order: variable. Plans 25 first novels this year. Averages 150 total titles, 145 fiction titles each year. Comments on rejected ms "only if requested ms requires it."
Needs: Romance (historical, futuristic, time travel), horror. Looking for "historical romance (115,000 words) and futuristic and time travel romance (90,000 words). Recently published *Terms of Love*, by Shirl Henke; *Comanche Flame*, by Madeline Baker.
How to Contact: Accepts unsolicited mss. Query first. SASE. Agented fiction 70%. Reports in 1 month on queries; 2 months on mss. "All mss must be typed, double-spaced on one side and left unbound."
Terms: Offers negotiable advance. Payment depends "on category and track record of author." Sends galleys to author. Publishes ms within 2 years after acceptance. Romance guidelines and book catalog for #10 SASE.
Advice: Encourages first novelists "if they are talented and willing to take direction, *and* write the kind of category fiction we publish. Please include a brief synopsis if sample chapters are requested."

LERNER PUBLICATIONS COMPANY, (II), 241 1st Ave. N., Minneapolis MN 55401. Imprints include First Avenue Editions. Editor: Jennifer Martin. Estab. 1959. "Midsize independent *children's* publisher." Publishes hardcover originals and paperback reprints. Books: Offset printing; reinforced library binding; perfect binding; average print order: 5,000-7,500; first novel print order: 5,000. Averages 70 total titles, 1-2 fiction titles each year. Sometimes comments on rejected ms.
● Lerner Publications' joke book series was recommended by "Reading Rainbow" (associated with the popular television show of the same name).
Needs: Young adult: Easy-to-read, problem novels, sports, adventure, mystery (young adult). Looking for "well-written middle grade and young adult. No *adult fiction* or single short stories." Recently published *Mystery in Miami Beach*, by Harriet K. Feder (middle grade mystery, age 9 and up).
How to Contact: Accepts unsolicited mss. Query first or submit outline/synopsis and 2 sample chapters. Reports in 1 month on queries; 2 months on mss. Simultaneous submissions OK.
Terms: Pays royalties. Offers advance. Provides author's copies. Sends galleys to author. Publishes ms 12-18 months after acceptance. Writer's guidelines for #10 SAE and 1 first class stamp. Book catalog for 9 × 12 SAE with $1.90 postage.
Advice: Would like to see "less gender and racial stereotyping; more protagonists from ethnic minority groups."

LION PUBLISHING CORPORATION, (II), 1705 Hubbard Ave., Batavia IL 60510. (708)879-0707. Editor: R.M. Bittner. Estab. 1984. "Christian book publisher publishing books for the *general* market." Publishes hardcover and paperback originals and paperback reprints. Books: Average print order 7,500; first novel print order 5,000. Plans 1-3 first novels this year. Averages 15 total titles, 2-5 fiction titles each year. Sometimes comments on rejected ms.
● Lion Publishing's book *The Paradise War*, by Stephen Lawhead, won the Critics' Choice Award from *Christianity Today* and Book of the Year from *Cornerstone* magazine. Another book, *Midnight Blue*, by Pauline Fisk, received England's Smarties Award, the largest cash prize for children's literature.
Needs: Open. "Because we are a Christian publisher, all books should be written from a Christian perspective." Recently published *Silver Hand*, by Stephen Lawhead (fantasy); *An Ordinary Exodus*, by Roger Bichelberger (literary); *Bury Her Sweetly*, by Linda Amey (mystery).

How to Contact: Accepts unsolicited mss. Submit complete ms with cover letter. SASE. Agented fiction 5%. Reports in 2-4 weeks on queries; 1-3 months on mss.
Terms: Pays negotiable royalties. Sends galleys to author. Publishes ms 1 year after acceptance. Writer's guidelines and book catalog free.
Advice: "Request our author guidelines."

LITTLE, BROWN AND COMPANY CHILDREN'S BOOKS, (II), Trade Division; Children's Books, 34 Beacon St., Boston MA 02108. Editorial Department. Contact: John G. Keller, publisher; Maria Modugno, editor-in-chief; Stephanie Owens Lurie, senior editor. Books: 70 lb. paper; sheet-fed printing; illustrations. Published new writers within the last year. Sometimes buys juvenile mss with illustrations "if by professional artist." Buys 60% agented fiction.
Needs: Middle grade fiction and young adult. Published *Maniac Magee*, by Jerry Spinelli; *The Day that Elvis Came to Town*, by Jan Marino.
How to Contact: Will accept unsolicited mss. "Query letters for novels are not necessary."
Terms: Pays on royalty basis. Sends galleys to author. Publishes ms 1-2 years after acceptance.
Advice: "We are looking for trade books with bookstore appeal. Young adult 'problem' novels are no longer in vogue, but there is now a dearth of good fiction for that age group. We are looking for young children's (ages 3-5) books and first chapter books. We encourage first novelists. New authors should be aware of what is currently being published. I recommend they spend time at the local library familiarizing themselves with new publications."

LITTLE, BROWN AND COMPANY, INC., (II, III), 34 Beacon St., Boston MA 02108. (617)227-0730. Imprints include Little, Brown, Joy Street, Bulfinch Press, Arcade Publishing. Medium-size house. Publishes adult and juvenile hardcover and paperback originals. Averages 200-225 total adult titles/year. Number of fiction titles varies.
Needs: Open. No science fiction. Published *Vineland*, by Thomas Pynchon; *Old Silent*, by Martha Grimes; *The Truth About Lorin Jones*, by Alison Lurie; published new writers within the last year.
How to Contact: Does not accept unsolicited mss. Query editorial department first; "we accept submissions from authors who have published before, in book form, magazines, newspapers or journals. No submissions from unpublished writers." Reports in 4-6 months on queries. Simultaneous and photocopied submissions OK.
Terms: "We publish on a royalty basis, with advance." Writer's guidelines free.

LODESTAR BOOKS, (II), An affiliate of Dutton Children's Books; A division of Penguin Books USA, Inc., 375 Hudson St., New York NY 10014. (212)366-2627. Editorial Director: Virginia Buckley. Senior Editor: Rosemary Brosnan. Books: 50 or 55 lb. antique cream paper; offset printing; hardcover binding; illustrations sometimes; average print order: 5,000-6,500; first novel print order 5,000. Published new writers within the last year. Number of titles: Approximately 25 annually, 12-15 fiction titles annually. Buys 50% agented fiction.

• Books published by Lodestar have won numerous awards including the American Library Association's "Notable Children's Books" and "Best Books for Young Adults" and the New England Book Award for Children's Books in 1992.

Needs: Contemporary, family saga, humorous, sports, mystery, adventure, for middle-grade and young adult. Recently published *Fear the Condor*, by David Nelson Blair (ages 12 up); *A Trial of Magic*, by Tom McGowen (ages 10-14); *To the Summit*, by Claire Rudolf Murphy (ages 12 up).
How to Contact: "Can query, but prefer complete ms." SASE. Simultaneous submissions OK. Reports in 2-4 months. Publishes ms an average of 1 year after acceptance.
Terms: Pays 8-10% in royalties; offers negotiable advance. Sends galleys to author. Free book catalog.
Advice: "We are looking to add to our list more books about black, Hispanic, Native American, and Asian children, in particular. We encourage first novelists. Publishing fewer young adult novels. Although they are difficult to find and difficult to sell reprint rights, we are doing well with our multicultural fiction, especially novels on Hispanic themes."

LOUISIANA STATE UNIVERSITY PRESS, (II), P.O. Box 25053, Baton Rouge LA 70894-5053. (504)388-6618. Fax: (504)388-6461. Editor-in-Chief: Margaret Fisher Dalrymple. Fiction Editor: Martha Lacy Hall. Estab. 1935. University press—medium size. Publishes hardcover originals. Average print order: 1,500-2,500; first novel print order: 2,000. Averages 60-70 total titles, 4 fiction titles each year.
Needs: Contemporary, literary, mainstream, short story collections. No genre fiction and/or juvenile material. Recently published *Marquis at Bay*, by Albert Belisle Davis (novel); *The Burning Glass*, by Helen Norris (stories); and *The Stars of Constantinople*, by Ólafur Jóhann Sigurdsson (stories). Pub-

lishes fiction anthologies. Author should submit proposal listing contents.

How to Contact: Does not accept unsolicited mss. Query first. "We provide a questionnaire to authors of mss we take under consideration." Send SASE (IRC) for reply, return of ms or send disposable copy of ms. Reports in 2-3 months on queries and mss. Simultaneous submissions OK.

Terms: Pays in royalties, which vary. Sends pre-publication galleys to the author.

LOVESWEPT, (I, II), Bantam Books, 666 5th Ave., New York NY 10103. (212)765-6500. Associate Publisher: Nita Taublib. Consulting Editors: Susann Brailey, Elizabeth Barrett. Senior Editors: Wendy McCurdy, Beth de Guzman. Imprint estab. 1982. Publishes paperback originals. Plans several first novels this year. Averages 72 total titles each year.

Needs: "Contemporary romance, highly sensual, believable primary characters, fresh and vibrant approaches to plot. No gothics, regencies or suspense."

How to Contact: Query with SASE; no unsolicited mss or partial mss. "Query letters should be no more than two to three pages. Content should be a brief description of the plot and the two main characters."

Terms: Pays in royalties of 6%; negotiates advance.

Advice: "Read extensively in the genre. Rewrite, polish and edit your own work until it is the best it can be – before submitting."

■LUCAS/EVANS BOOKS, (II), 1123 Broadway, New York NY 10010. (212)929-2583. Executive Director: Barbara Lucas. Projects Coordinator: Katherine Gleason. Editorial and Production Manager: Cassandra Conyers. Estab. 1984. "Book packager – specializes in children's books." Publishes hardcover and paperback originals. Published new writers within the last year. Averages 10-15 titles, all of which are children's picture books. Sometimes comments on rejected ms.

• *Sing for a Gentle Rain* won an IRA-CBC Young Adult Choice award in 1992.

Needs: "Looking for fiction and nonfiction series proposals and selected single juvenile books, preschool through high school. Published *Sing for a Gentle Rain*, by J. Alison James (Atheneum); *The Trouble with Buster*, by Janet Lorimer (Scholastic); and *The Glass Salamander*, by Ann Downer (Atheneum).

How to Contact: No unsolicited mss. Query first or submit outline/synopsis and 1 or 2 sample chapters. SASE. Agented fiction 15 to 25%. Reports in 2 months on mss.

Terms: Pays royalties; variable advance. Also makes work-for-hire assignments.

MARGARET K. McELDERRY BOOKS, (I, II), Imprint of the Macmillan Children's Book Group, 866 3rd Ave., New York NY 10022. (212)702-7855. Publisher: Margaret K. McElderry. Publishes hardcover originals. Books: High quality paper; offset printing; cloth and three-piece bindings; illustrations; average print order: 15,000; first novel print order: 6,000. Published new writers within the last year. Number of titles: 23/year. Buys juvenile and young adult mss, agented or non-agented.

• Books published by Margaret K. McElderry Books have received numerous awards including the Newbery and the Caldecott Awards.

Needs: All categories (fiction and nonfiction) for juvenile and young adult: picture books, early chapter books, contemporary, literary, adventure, mystery and fantasy. "We will consider any category. Results depend on the quality of the imagination, the artwork and the writing." Recently published *Hiawatha: Messenger of Peace*, by Dennis Fradin; *The Original Freddie Ackerman*, by Hadley Irwin; *The Animals: Selected Poems*, by Mado Michio, translated by the Empress Michiko of Japan, illustrated by Mitsumasa Anno.

How to Contact: Accepts unsolicited mss. Prefers complete ms. SASE for queries and mss. Simultaneous submissions OK if so indicated. Reports in 1 month on queries, 12-14 weeks on mss. Publishes ms an average of 1 year after acceptance.

Terms: Pays in royalties; offers advance.

Advice: "Imaginative writing of high quality is always in demand; also picture books that are original and unusual. Picture book manuscripts written in prose are totally acceptable. We are trying to publish more beginning chapter books – about 48 pages with text geared toward the 6-9 year old reader. Keep in mind that McElderry Books is a very small imprint which only publishes 12 or 13 books per season, so we are very selective about the books we will undertake for publication. Anyone hoping to become a children's book author should familiarize herself with the books (both good and bad) already on the market for children."

MACMILLAN CANADA, (II), A Division of Canada Publishing Corporation, 29 Birch Ave., Toronto, Ontario M4V 1E2 Canada. (416)963-8830. Senior Editor: Kristen Hansen. Estab. 1905. Publishes hardcover and trade paperback originals. Published new writers within the last year. Books: Average print order: 4,000-5,000; first novel print order: 1,500. Averages 35 total titles, 5-6 fiction titles each year. Rarely comments on rejected mss.
Needs: Literary, mainstream and mystery/suspense. Recently published *Last Rights*, by David Laing Dawson; *Tall Lives*, by Bill Gaston; *Swimming Toward the Light*, by Joan Clark; *The Nest Egg*, by S.L. Sparling; and *The Jacamar Nest*, by David Parry and Patrick Withrow.
How to Contact: No longer accepts unsolicited mss. Agented material only. SASE for return of ms. Reports in 1-2 months on mss. Simultaneous submissions OK.
Terms: Pays royalties of 8% minimum; 15% maximum; advance negotiable. Provides 10 author's copies. Sends galleys to author. Book catalog for 9 × 12 SASE.
Advice: "Canadian material only."

MACMILLAN CHILDREN'S BOOKS, (II), Macmillan Publishing Co., 866 Third Ave., New York NY 10022. (212)702-4299. Imprint of Macmillan Publishing/Children's Book Group. Contact: Submissions Editor. Estab. 1919. Large children's trade list. Publishes hardcover originals.
Needs: Juvenile submissions. Not interested in series. "We generally are not interested in short stories as such, unless intended as the basis for a picture book. As the YA market is weak, only extremely distinctive and well-written YA novels will be considered (and must be preceded by a query letter)." Published *Weasel*, by Cyntha De Felice; *Dynamite Dinah*, by Claudia Mills; *Borgel*, by Daniel Pinkwater.
How to Contact: Accepts unsolicited mss or for novel send query letter with outline, sample chapter and SASE. Response in 6-8 weeks. No simultaneous submissions.
Terms: Pays in royalties; negotiates advance. For catalog, send 9 × 12 envelope with 4 oz. postage.

MACMILLAN PUBLISHING CO, INC., 866 3rd Ave., New York NY 10022. Prefers not to share information.

METEOR PUBLISHING CORPORATION, (I, II), Kismet Romances, 3369 Progress Dr., Bensalem PA 19020. (215)245-1489. Editor-in-Chief: Kate Duffy. Senior Editor: Catherine Carpenter. "Category romance publisher distributed solely via direct mail." Publishes paperback originals. Published new writers within the last year. Plans 20 first novels this year. Averages 48 total titles, all fiction. Sometimes comments on rejected ms.
Needs: Romance (contemporary). Looking for "65,000-word contemporary romances." Recently published *Always*, by Catherine Sellers; *Silent Enchantment*, by Lacey Dancer; *Daddy's Girl*, by Janice Kaiser.
How to Contact: Accepts unsolicited mss. Submit outline/synopsis and 3 sample chapters, if previously published in same genre or complete ms with cover letter, if unpublished. Agented fiction 50%. Reports in 2 months on queries; 2-3 months on mss. Simultaneous submissions OK.
Terms: Pays royalties of 6-8%. Offers negotiable advance. Sends galleys to author. Publishes ms 6-12 months after acceptance.
Advice: "We receive approximately 25 mss/week. Most are previously unpublished. We buy the best that are submitted and promptly return those not of interest. All of our first novels acquired were reviewed as completed mss and all have been published."

MODERN PUBLISHING, A Division of Unisystems, Inc., (II), 155 East 55th St., New York NY 10022. (212)826-0850. Imprint: Honey Bear Books. Editorial Director: Kathy O'Hehir. Fiction Editor: Mandy Rubenstein. Estab. 1973. "Mass-market juvenile publisher; list mainly consists of picture, coloring and activity, and novelty books for ages 2-8 and board books." Publishes hardcover and paperback originals, and Americanized hardcover and paperback reprints from foreign markets. Average print order: 50,000-100,000 of each title within a series. "85% of our list first novels this year." Averages 100+ total titles each year. Sometimes comments on rejected mss.

Needs: Juvenile (5-9 yrs, including animal, easy-to-read, fantasy, historical, sports, spy/adventure and contemporary), preschool/picture book, young adult/teen (easy-to-read). Published new writers within the last year.

How to Contact: Accepts unsolicited mss. Submit complete ms. SASE. Agented fiction 5%. Simultaneous submissions OK. Reports in 2 months.

Terms: Pays by work-for-hire or royalty arrangements. Advance negotiable. Publishes ms 7-12 months after acceptance.

Advice: "We publish picture storybooks, board books, coloring and activity books, bath books, shape books and any other new and original ideas for the children's publishing arena. We gear our books for the preschool through third-grade market and publish series of four to six books at a time. Presently we are looking for new material as we are expanding our list and would appreciate receiving any new submissions. We will consider manuscripts with accompanying artwork or by themselves, and submissions from illustrators who would like to work in the juvenile books publishing genre and can adapt their style to fit our needs. However, we will only consider those projects that are written and illustrated for series of four to six books. Manuscripts must be neatly typed and submitted either as a synopsis of the series and broken-down plot summaries of the books within the series, or full manuscripts for review with a SASE."

WILLIAM MORROW AND COMPANY, INC., (II), 1350 Avenue of the Americas, New York NY 10019. Imprints include Hearst Books, Hearst Marine Books, Mulberry Books, Tambourine Books, Beech Tree Books, Quill Trade Paperbacks, Perigord, Greenwillow Books, Lothrop, Lee & Shepard and Fielding Publications (travel books), and Morrow Junior Books. Estab. 1926. Approximately one fourth of books published will be fiction.

Needs: "Morrow accepts only the highest quality submissions" in contemporary, literary, experimental, adventure, mystery/suspense, spy, historical, war, feminist, gay/lesbian, science fiction, horror, humor/satire and translations. Juvenile and young adult divisions are separate. Recently published *Gate of Rage*, by C.Y. Lee; *The Gold Bug Variations*, by Richard Powers; and *This Earth of Mankind*, by Pramoedya Ananta Toer. Published work by previously unpublished writers within the last year.

How to Contact: Submit through agent. All unsolicited mss are returned unopened. "We will accept queries, proposals or mss only when submitted through a literary agent." Simultaneous submissions OK. Reports in 2-3 months.

Terms: Pays in royalties; offers advance. Sends galleys to author. Free book catalog.

Advice: "The Morrow divisions of Morrow Junior Books, Greenwillow Books, Tambourine Books, Mulberry Books, Beech Tree Books, and Lothrop, Lee and Shepard handle juvenile books. We do five to ten first novels every year and about one-fourth of the titles are fiction. Having an agent helps to find a publisher."

MORROW JUNIOR BOOKS, (III), 1350 Avenue of the Americas, New York NY 10019. (212)261-6691. Editor-In-Chief: David L. Reuther. Plans 1 first novel this year. Averages 55 total titles each year.

Needs: Juvenile (5-9 years, including animal, easy-to-read, fantasy (little), spy/adventure (very little), preschool/picture book, young adult/teen (10-18 years, including historical, sports).

How to Contact: Does not accept unsolicited fiction mss.

Terms: Authors paid in royalties. Books published 12-18 months after acceptance. Book catalog free on request.

Advice: "Our list is very full at this time. No unsolicited manuscripts."

MULTNOMAH, 10209 Division SE, Portland OR 97266. Prefers not to share information.

THE MYSTERIOUS PRESS, (III), 1271 Ave. of the Americas, New York NY 10120. (212)522-7200. Imprint: Penzler Books. Editor-in-Chief: William Malloy. Editor: Sara Ann Freed and Kate Stine. Estab. 1976. Small independent publisher, publishing only mystery and suspense fiction. Publishes hardcover originals and paperback reprints. Books: Hardcover (some Smythe sewn) and paperback binding; illustrations rarely. Average first novel print order 5,000 copies. Critiques "only those rejected writers we wish particularly to encourage."

Needs: Mystery/suspense. Published *The Fourth Durango*, by Ross Thomas; *The Bridesmaid*, by Ruth Rendell; *Tomorrow's Crimes*, by Donald E. Westlake; published new writers within the last year.

How to Contact: Agented material only.

Terms: Pays in royalties of 10% minimum; offers negotiable advance. Sends galleys to author. Buys hard and softcover rights. Book catalog for SASE.

Advice: "We have a strong belief in the everlasting interest in and strength of mystery fiction. Don't talk about writing, do it. Don't ride bandwagons, create them. Our philosophy about publishing first novels is the same as our philosophy about publishing: The cream rises to the top. We are looking for writers with whom we can have a long-term relationship. A good editor is an angel, assisting according to the writer's needs. My job is to see to it that the writer writes the best book he/she is capable of, *not* to have the writer write *my* book. Don't worry, publishing will catch up to you; the cycles continue as they always have. If your work is good, keep it circulating and begin the next one, and keep the faith. Get an agent."

NAL/DUTTON, (III), A division of Penguin USA, 375 Hudson St., New York NY 10014. (212)366-2000. Imprints include Dutton, Onyx, Signet, Topaz, Mentor, Signet Classic, Plume, Plume Fiction, DAW, Meridian, Roc. Contact: Michaela Hamilton, editor-in-chief (Signet and Onyx); Arnold Dolin, associate publisher, Plume (trade paperback); Kevin Mulroy, editorial director, Dutton; Christopher Schelling, senior editor, Roc. Estab. 1948. Publishes hardcover and paperback originals and paperback reprints.

Needs: "All kinds of commercial and literary fiction, including mainstream, historical, Regency, New Age, western, thriller, science fiction, fantasy, gay. Full length novels and collections." Recently published *Needful Things*, by Stephen King; *Night Over Water*, by Ken Follett; *Against the Wind*, by J.F. Freedman. Published new writers within the last year.

How to Contact: Agented mss only. Queries accepted with SASE. "State type of book and past publishing projects." Simultaneous submissions OK. Reports in 3 months.

Terms: Pays in royalties and author's copies; offers advance. Sends galleys to author. Free book catalog.

Advice: "Write the complete manuscript and submit it to an agent or agents. We publish The Destroyer, The Trailsman, Battletech and other western and sf series — all by ongoing authors. Would be receptive to ideas for new series in commercial fiction."

NEW READERS PRESS, (IV), Publishing division of Laubach Literacy International, Box 131, Syracuse NY 13210. (315)422-9121. Directors of Acquisitions: Christina Jagger. Estab. 1959. Publishes paperback originals. Books: offset printing; paper binding; 6-12 illustrations per fiction book; average print order: 7,500; first novel print order: 5,000. Fiction titles may be published both in book form and as read-along audio tapes. Averages 30 total titles, 8-12 fiction titles each year.

Needs: High-interest, low-reading-level materials for adults with limited reading skills. Short novels of 12,000-15,000 words, written on 2nd-5th grade level. "Can be mystery, romance, adventure, science fiction, sports or humor. Characters are well-developed, situations realistic, and plot developments believable." Accepts short stories only in collections of 8-20 very short stories of same genre. Will accept collections of one-act plays that can be performed in a single class period (45-50 min.) with settings than can be created within a classroom. Short stories and plays can be at 3rd-5th grade reading level. All material must be suitable for classroom use in public education, i.e., little violence and no explicit sex. "We will not accept anything at all for readers under 16 years of age." Recently published *The Orange Grove & Other Stories*, by Rosanne Keller; *The Kite Flyer & Other Stories* by Rosanne Keller.

How to Contact: Accepts unsolicited mss. Query first or submit outline/synopsis and 3 sample chapters. SASE. Reports in 1 month on queries; 3 months on mss.

Terms: Pays royalties of 5% minimum, 7.5% maximum on gross sales. Average advance: $200. "We may offer authors a choice of a royalty or flat fee. The fee would vary depending on the type of work." Book catalog, authors' brochure and guidelines for short novels free.

Advice: "Many of our fiction authors are being published for the first time. It is necessary to have a sympathetic attitude toward adults with limited reading skills and an understanding of their life situation. Direct experience with them is helpful."

W.W. NORTON & COMPANY, INC., (II), 500 5th Ave., New York NY 10110. (212)354-5500. For unsolicited mss contact: Liz Malcolm. Estab. 1924. Midsize independent publisher of trade books and college textbooks. Publishes hardcover originals. Occasionally comments on rejected mss.

Close-up

Michaela Hamilton
Editorial Director
NAL/Dutton

"We're always looking for wonderful books of all kinds," says Michaela Hamilton, NAL/Dutton's editorial director for mass market books. She is interested in all kinds of commercial fiction — suspense, women's fiction, mysteries. She doesn't have any tip sheets or formula sheets, though. "It's writing that counts rather than format," she says. For the mass market, "the story should be so compelling that it appeals to a large number of people." In addition, the book must lend itself readily to a specific audience and fall into some recognizable area of publishing such as suspense, thriller, mystery, etc., with a defined audience. "Every writer should write to a specific audience," Hamilton says. "I think writers make a mistake when they say 'I'm just going to write what I like to write and it will find a market.' I think you do have to respect the audience and recognize the tastes of various areas of publishing. Writers should know their marketplace."

Concerning trends, Hamilton says she doesn't think that way about manuscripts. "I think good, solid storytelling is always in style." And she feels that concentrating on word length is "a pretty arbitrary way" of looking at books. "We don't buy them by the pound," she says. "We want full-length fiction but I wouldn't want to rule out something like *Black Water*, a fantastic book by Joyce Carol Oates which runs 154 pages long." On the other hand, an 800-page manuscript definitely would go back to the author for cutting.

Submissions for NAL/Dutton's mass market books are agented. Hamilton does accept queries by mail with SASE, but writers should *not* use the fax for that purpose.

She encourages writers to get involved in writers' groups, to attend writers' workshops and conferences. She feels that networking can be extremely important for a writer, not just in terms of finding contacts to help in getting published, but for the all-important moral support. "Writing is a lonely profession and writers need companionship." In addition to organizations such as Romance Writers of America and Mystery Writers of America that have chapters in many cities, she also suggests joining informal and unaffiliated writers' groups. "Before writers try out their material on a publisher or agent, they really should get feedback from a writers' group," she adds.

Above all, she advises writers to "sit down and write and write and write and never stop." As an editor, she hears about too many books that are "just a gleam in the author's eye," she says. "You wouldn't believe how many people approach me about books that they want me to get excited about but they haven't even written yet. If you're serious about being a writer, sit down and write and get something that you're happy with, that you think you're ready to show, because publishers absolutely are looking for fresh new writers, that new voice, that new excitement, that new name on their list."

— Pat Beusterien

Needs: High-quality fiction (preferably literary). No occult, science fiction, religious, gothic, romances, experimental, confession, erotica, psychic/supernatural, fantasy, horror, juvenile or young adult. Recently published *The Unquiet Earth*, by Denise Giardina; *Natural History*, by Maureen Howard; and *White Butterfly*, by Walter Mosely

How to Contact: Submit outline/synopsis and first 50 pages. Simultaneous submissions OK. Reports in 8-10 weeks. Packaging and postage must be enclosed to ensure safe return of materials.

Terms: Graduated royalty scale starting at 7½% or 10% of net invoice price, in addition to 15 author's copies; offers advance. Free book catalog.

Advice: "We will occasionally encourage writers of promise whom we do not immediately publish. We are principally interested in the literary quality of fiction manuscripts. A familiarity with our current list of titles will give you an idea of what we're looking for. Chances are, if your book is good and you have no agent you will eventually succeed; but the road to success will be easier and shorter if you have an agent backing the book. We encourage the submission of first novels."

PANTHEON BOOKS, (III), Subsidiary of Random House, 201 E. 50th St., New York NY 10022. (212)572-2404. Estab. 1942. "Small but well-established imprint of well-known large house." Publishes hardcover and trade paperback originals and trade paperback reprints. Averages 75 total titles, about one-third fiction, each year.

• A close-up interview with the senior editor appears in the 1992 *Writer's Market*.

Needs: Quality fiction.

How to Contact: Query letter and sample material. SASE. Attention: Editorial Department.

Advice: "We are beginning to publish more American fiction and fewer translations. We are also publishing more first novels."

PELICAN PUBLISHING COMPANY, (IV), Box 189, 1101 Monroe St., Gretna LA 70053. Editor: Nina Kooij. Estab. 1926. Publishes hardcover reprints and originals. Books: Hardcover and paperback binding; illustrations sometimes. Published new juvenile writers within the last year. Buys juvenile mss with illustrations. Comments on rejected mss "infrequently."

Needs: Juvenile fiction, especially with a regional and/or historical focus. "Our adult fiction is *very* limited." Recently published *Patrick's Corner*, by Seán Patrick and *Little Freddie at the Kentucky Derby*, by Kathryn Cocquyt.

How to Contact: Prefers query. May submit outline/synopsis and 2 sample chapters with SASE. No simultaneous submissions. "Not responsible if writer's only copy is sent." Reports in 1 month on queries; 3 months on mss. Publishes ms 12-18 months after acceptance.

Terms: Pays 10% in royalties; 10 contributor's copies; advance considered. Sends galleys to author. Catalog of titles and writer's guidelines for SASE.

Advice: "Research the market carefully. Order and look through publishing catalogs to see if your work is consistent with their lists."

PHILOMEL BOOKS, (II), The Putnam & Grosset Book Group, 200 Madison Ave., New York NY 10016. (212)951-8712. Editor-in-Chief: Paula Wiseman. Editorial Assistant: Laura Walsh. "A high-quality oriented imprint focused on stimulating picture books and young adult novels." Publishes hardcover originals and paperback reprints. Published new writers within the last year. Averages 50 total titles, 45 fiction titles/year. Sometimes comments on rejected ms.

• Books published by Philomel have won numerous awards. Most recently *I Am Regina*, by Sally Keehn (young adult) received the Carolyn Field Award.

Needs: Adventure, ethnic, family saga, fantasy, historical, juvenile (5-9 years), literary, mystery/suspense (romantic suspense), preschool/picture book, regional, short story collections, translations, western (young adult), young adult/teen (10-18 years). Looking for "ethnic novels with a strong cultural voice but which speak universally." No "generic, mass-market oriented fiction." Recently published *Feathers and Tails*, by David Kherdian; *The Leaving*, by Budge Wilson; *As Far As Mill Springs*, by Patricia Pendergraft.

How to Contact: Accepts unsolicited mss. Query first or submit outline/synopsis and 3 sample chapters. SASE. Agented fiction 40%. Reports in 6-8 weeks on queries; 6-10 weeks on mss. Simultaneous submissions OK.

Terms: Pays royalties, negotiable advance and author's copies. Sends galleys to author. Publishes ms anywhere from 1-3 years after acceptance. Writer's guidelines for #10 SAE and 1 first class stamp. Book catalog for 9 × 12 SASE.

Close-up

Julia Alvarez
Author

© Sara Eichner

Julia Alvarez concedes that she might not be a writer today had she remained in the Dominican Republic. As a 10-year-old girl arriving in America in 1960, she was exhilarated about the prospects of living in a new country, saddened at leaving her homeland behind and confused by the craziness of the time and this odd new language called English. "Suddenly, this was the language I was thrust into," says Alvarez, now a tenured professor of English at Middlebury College in Vermont. "I wanted to learn it so I could understand and so I could be understood. Early on I decided to become a writer because it was a way to make sense of things."

Alvarez immersed herself in writing poetry while an undergraduate and began focusing on fiction nearly 11 years ago. "Writing poetry was perfect training for me as a writer," she says. The transition did not happen overnight. "A lot of my poems were narrative poems. It was almost like my work led to writing stories. I still write poems. Sometimes I will start a piece as a poem, then realize it's a story. The point is to keep at it."

The stories Alvarez writes are mostly autobiographical and revolve around the memories of her youth in the Dominican Republic, her experiences adjusting to American culture and her coming to terms with the homeland she left behind. "Memory operates like a storyteller," she says. "You remember it in a way that's significant to you. I work out of my own life and I call it fiction. I'm not a journalist. I'm not interested in recording events, but in presenting the emotions behind the events."

Today, after publishing numerous short stories and poems, Alvarez has received acclaim for her first book, *How the Garcia Girls Lost Their Accents*, published by Algonquin Books in May 1991 and released in paperback by New American Library. The book is a compilation of short pieces presented in reverse chronology that tells the story of four well-to-do young girls who must flee the Dominican Republic with their family after a failed coup attempt. The stories are interspersed with Spanish. "I never thought you could use a Spanish word in a story written in English," she says. "But the first time I read [Maxine Hong Kingston's] *Woman Warrior* I knew use of foreign words would not be discouraged."

When Alvarez reached her thirties, she went through a period of self-doubt. "I thought that if I hadn't made a big splash by a certain age, I was not a good writer. But it's a process, and it has to be its own reward. Writing is difficult. If you want something easy, choose something else."

Her advice to beginning authors is to find a community of writers with whom you can exchange manuscripts, even if it means mailing stories to another part of the country. Take advantage of workshops and read your stories in front of a group of strangers to test material. Lastly, keep at it. "Stay with it and, if it matters to you enough, you'll get better."

—Dorothy Maxwell Goepel

POCKET BOOKS, (II), Division of Simon & Schuster, 1230 Avenue of the Americas, New York NY 10020. (212)698-7000. Imprints include Washington Square Press and Star Trek. Senior Vice President/Editorial Director: William Grose. Publishes paperback and hardcover originals and reprints. Averages 300 titles each year. Buys 90% agented fiction. Sometimes critiques rejected mss.
Needs: Contemporary, literary, faction, adventure, spy, historical, western, gothic, romance, military/war, mainstream, suspense/mystery, feminist, ethnic, erotica, psychic/supernatural, fantasy, horror and humor/satire. Recently published *To Dance with the White Dog*, by Terry Kay; *Boy's Life*, by Robert McCammon (hardcover); *Rules of Evidence*, by Jay Brandon (hardcover); published new writers within the last year.
How to Contact: Query with SASE. No unsolicited mss. Reports in 6 months on queries only. Publishes ms 12-18 months after acceptance.
Terms: Pays in royalties and offers advance. Sends galleys to author. Writer must return advance if book is not completed or is not acceptable. Free book catalog.

POSEIDON PRESS, (II), 1230 Avenue of the Americas, New York NY 10020. (212)698-7290. Distributed by Simon & Schuster. Publisher: Ann E. Patty. Executive Editor: Elaine Pfefferbilt. Estab. 1981. Hardcover and quality trade paper. Books: Paper varies; offset printing; illustrations; average print order varies; first novel print order: 5,000-7,500. Averages 20 total titles, 10-12 fiction titles (3 first novels) each year. Does "not critique rejected mss by unsolicited authors unless work merits it."
Needs: General fiction and nonfiction, commercial and literary. Recently published *First Wives Club*, by Olivia Goldsmith; and *Two Girls, Fat and Thin*, by Mary Gaitskill.
How to Contact: Query first. No unsolicited manuscripts or sample chapters. Reports in 3 months.
Terms: Payment varies, according to content of book.

‡PRESIDIO PRESS (IV), 505B San Marin Dr., Novato CA 94945. (415)898-1081. Editors: Dale Wilson, Joan Griffin and Robert Tate. Estab. 1976. Small independent general trade – specialist in military. Publishes hardcover originals. Books: 20 lb regular paper, average print order: 5,000. Published new writers within the last year. Publishes more than one military fiction book per list. Averages 20 total titles each year. Critiques or comments on rejected ms.
 • *Brules* by Harry Combs is a western, new for Presidio. They also may venture into mystery soon.
Needs: Historical with military background, war. Also mystery/suspense (police procedural, private eye), western (traditional, frontier saga, adult), thriller/espionage. Recently published *Brules*, by Harry Combs; *Coup*, by Alexander Grace; and *Grant's War*, by Ted Jones.
How to Contact: Accepts unsolicited mss. Query first or submit 3 sample chapters. SASE. Reports in 2 weeks on queries; 2 months on mss. Simultaneous submissions OK.
Terms: Pays in royalties of 15% of net minimum; advance: $1,000 average. Sends edited manuscripts and page proofs to author. Book catalog free on request.
Advice: "Think twice before entering any highly competitive genre; don't imitate; do your best. Have faith in your writing and don't let the market disappoint or discourage you."

G.P. PUTNAM'S SONS, The Putnam Publishing Group, 200 Madison Ave., New York NY 10016. Prefers not to share information.

‡QUILL, (III), William Morrow & Co., Inc., 1350 Avenue of the Americas, New York NY 10019. Editor: Andy Simpson. "Trade paperback line of William Morrow & Co. – Adult Trade – Midsize." Publishes paperback originals and reprints. Published new writers within the last year. Plans 1 first novel this year. Averages 50 total titles, 1 fiction title each year.
Needs: Experimental, feminist, gay, humor/satire, lesbian, literary, literary, mainstream/contemporary.
How to Contact: Does not accept unsolicited mss. Strongly suggest submitting outline/synopsis and 1 sample chapter through an agent. Include one-paragraph bio, list of publishing credits. SASE for a reply to query or send a disposable copy of the ms. Agented ficiton 99.5%. Reports in 2 months. Simultaneous submissions OK.
Terms: Standard rates. Sends galleys to author. Publishes ms 1 year after acceptance.
Advice: "Our parent company, William Morrow, publishes fiction in hardcover and sells the rights to other, larger paperback imprints and houses. We have done fiction in the past and do the occasional paperback original, but for the most part we do nonfiction. Write, re-write, and rewrite again. Then find an agent. Never be afraid to throw out a year's worth of work and start again – that's the sign of a writer on the way to becoming an author. No matter what the genre, write clearly and cut the fat."

Look at what the masters of the genre do that others don't and learn from that."

RANDOM HOUSE, INC., 201 E. 50th St., New York NY 10022. (212)751-2600. Imprints include Pantheon Books, Panache Press at Random House, Vintage Books, Times Books, Villard Books and Knopf. Contact: Adult Trade Division. Publishes hardcover and paperback originals. Encourages new writers. Rarely comments on rejected mss.
Needs: Adventure, contemporary, historical, literary, mainstream, short story collections, mystery/suspense. "We publish fiction of the highest standards." Authors include James Michener, Robert Ludlum, Mary Gordon.
How to Contact: Query with SASE. Simultaneous submissions OK. Reports in 4-6 weeks on queries, 2 months on mss.
Terms: Payment as per standard minimum book contracts. Free writer's guidelines.
Advice: "Please try to get an agent because of the large volume of manuscripts received, agented work is looked at first."

RESOURCE PUBLICATIONS, INC., (I, IV), Suite 290, 160 E. Virginia St., San Jose CA 95112. (408)286-8505. Book Editor: Kenneth Guentert. Estab. 1973. "Independent book and magazine publisher focusing on imaginative resources for professionals in ministry, education and counseling." Publishes paperback originals. Averages 12-14 total titles, 2-3 fiction titles each year.
Needs: Story collections for storytellers, "not short stories in the usual literary sense." No novels. Published *Jesus on the Mend: Healing Stories for Ordinary People*, by Andre Papineau; and *The Magic Stone: Stories for Your Faith Journey*, by James Henderschedt.
How to Contact: Query first or submit outline/synopsis and 1 sample chapter with SASE. Reports in 2 weeks on queries; 6 weeks on mss. No simultaneous submissions. Accepts disk submissions compatible with CP/M, IBM system. Prefers hard copy with disk submissions.
Terms: Pays in royalties of 8% minimum, 10% maximum; 10 author's copies. "We require first-time authors purchase a small portion of the press-run, but we do not subsidy publish under the Resource Publications imprint. However, our graphics department will help author's self-publish for a fee."

ST. MARTIN'S PRESS, 175 5th Ave., New York NY 10010. Did not respond.

CHARLES SCRIBNER'S SONS, 866 3rd Ave., New York NY 10022. Overstocked.

CHARLES SCRIBNER'S SONS, BOOKS FOR YOUNG READERS, Division of Macmillan Publishing Co., 866 Third Ave., New York NY 10022. (212)702-7885. Editorial Director: Clare Costello. Publishes hardcover originals. Averages 20-25 total titles, 8-13 fiction titles each year.
Needs: Juvenile (animal, easy-to-read, fantasy, historical, picture book, sports, spy/adventure, contemporary, ethnic and science fiction) and young adult (fantasy/science fiction, romance, historical, problem novels, sports and spy/adventure). Recently published *The Irish Piper*, by Jim Latimar (picture book); *Around the Table*, by Sholom Aleichem, translated by Aliza Shevrin (ages 10-13); *Cleaver & Company*, by James Duffy (ages 9-11).
How to Contact: Submit complete ms with SASE. Simultaneous submissions OK. Reports in 8-10 weeks on mss.
Terms: Free book catalog free on request. Sends galleys to author.

SIERRA CLUB BOOKS, 100 Bush St., San Francisco CA 94104. (415)291-1617. Fax: (415)291-1602. Editor-in-Chief: Jim Cohee. Estab. 1892. Midsize independent publisher. Publishes hardcover and paperback originals and paperback reprints. Averages 20-25 titles, 1-2 fiction titles each year.
Needs: Contemporary (conservation, environment).
How to Contact: Query only with SASE. "We will only deal with queries; we are not staffed to deal with mss." Simultaneous submissions OK. Reports in 6 weeks on queries.
Terms: Pays in royalties. Book catalog for SASE.
Advice: "Only rarely do we publish fiction. We will consider novels on their quality and on the basis of their relevance to our organization's environmentalist aims."

SILHOUETTE BOOKS, (II, IV), 6th Floor, 300 E. 42nd St., New York NY 10017. (212)682-6080. Imprints include Silhouette Romance, Silhouette Special Edition, Silhouette Desire, Silhouette Intimate Moments, Silhouette Shadows, Harlequin Historicals; also Silhouette Christmas Stories, Silhouette Summer Sizzlers, Harlequin Historical Christmas Stories. Editorial Director: Isabel Swift. Senior Editor & Editorial Coordinator (SIM, SS): Leslie J. Wainger. Seniors Editors: (SE) Tara Hughes Gavin,

(SD) Lucia Macro, (SR) Anne Canadeo. Editor: Melissa Senate, Gail Chasan. Historicals: Senior Editor: Tracy Farrell. Estab. 1979. Publishes paperback originals. Published 10-20 new writers within the last year. Buys agented and unagented adult romances. Number of titles: 316/year. Occasionally comments on rejected mss.
- Books published by Silhouette Books have received numerous awards including Romance Writers of America's Rita Award, awards from Romantic Times and best selling awards from Walden and B. Dalton bookstores.

Needs: Contemporary romances, historical romances. Recently published *Emmett*, by Diana Palmer (SR); *Hazards of the Heart*, by Dixie Browning (SD); *Falling for Rachel*, by Nora Roberts (SE); *Between Roc and a Hard Place*, by Heather Graham Pozzassere (IM); *Garters and Spurs*, by Deloras Scott, *Imminent Thunder*, by Rachel Lee (SS).

How to Contact: Submit query letter with brief synopsis and SASE. No unsolicited or simultaneous submissions. Publishes ms 9-24 months after acceptance.

Terms: Pays in royalties; offers advance (negotiated on an individual basis). Must return advance if book is not completed or is unacceptable.

Advice: "You are competing with writers that love the genre and know what our readers want—because many of them started as readers. Please note that the fact that our novels are fun to read doesn't make them easy to write. Storytelling ability, clean compelling writing and love of the genre are necessary."

SIMON & SCHUSTER, 1230 Avenue of the Americas, New York NY 10020. (212)698-7000. Imprints include Pocket Books, Linden Press.

Needs: General adult fiction, mostly commercial fiction.

How to Contact: Agented material 100%.

GIBBS SMITH, PUBLISHER, (II), Box 667, Layton UT 84041. (801)544-9800. Fax: (801)544-5582. Imprints: Peregrine Smith Books. Editorial Director: Madge Baird. Estab. 1969. Publishes hardcover and paperback originals and reprints. Books: Illustrations as needed; average print order: 5,000. Publishes 25+ total titles each year, 3-4 fiction titles.

Needs: Contemporary, literary, translations and nature. "Literary works exhibiting the social consciousness of our times." Published *Relative Distances*, by Victoria Jenkins; *Language in the Blood*, by Kent Nelson.

How to Contact: Query first. SASE. 60% of fiction is agented. Reports in 3 weeks on queries; 10 weeks on mss. Simultaneous submissions OK.

Terms: Pays 7-15% royalties. Sends galleys to author. Writer's guidelines for #10 SASE; book catalog for 9×6 SAE and 56¢ postage.

Advice: "Our foremost criteria is the literary merit of the work."

STANDARD PUBLISHING, (II, IV), 8121 Hamilton Ave., Cincinnati OH 45231. (513)931-4050. Director: Mark Plunkett. Estab. 1866. Independent religious publisher. Publishes paperback originals and reprints. Books: Offset printing; paper binding; b&w line art; average print order: 7,500; first novel print order: 5,000-7,500. Number of titles: 18/year. Rarely buys juvenile mss with illustrations. Occasionally comments on rejected mss.

Needs: Religious/inspirational and easy-to-read. "Should have some relation to moral values or Biblical concepts and principles." Katie Hooper Series, by Jane Sorenson; Julie McGregor Series, by Kristi Holl. Recently published *A Change of Heart* and *A Tangled Webb*, by Kristi Holl; *Jaws of Terror*, by Dayle Courtney.

How to Contact: Query or submit outline/synopsis and 2-3 sample chapters with SASE. "Query should include synopsis and general description of perceived market." Reports in 1 month on queries, 3 months on mss. Publishes ms 1-2 years after acceptance.

Terms: Pays varied royalties and by outright purchase; offers varied advance. Sends galleys to author. Catalog with SASE.

Advice: Publishes fiction with "strong moral and ethical implications." First novels "should be appropriate, fitting into new or existing series. We're dealing more with issues."

STODDART, 34 Lesmill Rd., Toronto, Ontario M3B 2T6 Canada. No American authors. Prefers not to share other information.

Close-up

Maureen F. McHugh
Author

© Betsy Cochrane

"Writing is a skill, like basketball," Maureen F. McHugh says, "not a body of information, like biology." According to McHugh, writing is not something you can study to become good. A writer needs constantly to practice. "Write a lot. Write anything; write every day, whether it's good or not."

McHugh follows her own advice rigorously. "I get up at four in the morning; I write for two hours, and then I go to work," she says. "I don't write when I get home, but I do write on weekends."

Just like everyone, however, McHugh has days when the words just won't come. "When I'm really stuck, I play solitaire until I can't stand it." She also finds things to do that she really dislikes, like scrubbing floors. "You know you don't like to do it and it needs to be done. You have to concentrate, but you don't have to concentrate hard." This, she says, gives your subconscious time to work out the problem.

She also says that it helps to have a job you hate. "If you can get a job which is not intellectually taxing and mildly demeaning, so much the better. Then you hate it so much it drives you to write."

Although McHugh's been driven to write for 15 years, she's only been published in the last six. She first published a short story in *Twilight Zone Magazine* in 1987, and that story, a modern day witch tale, won the "*Twilight Zone* First Reader's Poll." It went on to become an episode for a television show called "Monsters." Since then, she's been regularly publishing in *Asimov's Science Fiction Magazine* and *Twilight Zone Magazine*. She has recently published her first novel, *China Mountain Zhang*, and has another due out in 1993.

McHugh has the shortest publication story she knows of with her first novel. "Everyone talks about it taking years, but I was really lucky." She sold two short stories out of *China Mountain Zhang* to *Asimov's*. Then, when the novel was complete, she sent off a query letter to the editor of Tor Books. They bought the book six weeks later. "If I'd sent it to them the month before or the month after, they may not have taken it. It's all got to do with when they've got the money."

McHugh spent a year teaching in China, an experience she says was surprisingly normal. "It's just everyday life. You get up in the morning, eat your breakfast and go to work. You may go to work on a bicycle, but in a month you don't think about it." Her China experience helped her writing by allowing her to experience, first hand, life in another country. "In *China Mountain*, I wanted people to understand what it's like to live in a third world country, but I knew if I set it in China, it would be an exotic book. So I wanted to make the U.S. a third world country," she says.

"We tend to look at the world from our cultural perspective as middle Americans," says McHugh, "and I really would like to have people look at the world from different perspectives, particularly if I can do that without them realizing I've done it."

— David Borcherding

TAB BOOK CLUB (TEEN AGE BOOK CLUB), (II), Scholastic Inc., 730 Broadway, New York NY 10003. Contact: Greg Holch. Published new writers within the last year.
Needs: "TAB Book Club publishes novels for young teenagers in seventh through ninth grades. We do not publish short stories or standard teenage romances. A book has to be unique, different, and of high literary quality."
How to Contact: "Due to the extremely large number of submissions, we will not be looking at new manuscripts until January 1994. All submissions before that time will be returned unread." After that time, send "a query letter and the first 20 pages of the manuscript."
Advice: "I personally prefer humorous, light novels that revolve around a unique premise, such as *A Royal Pain,* by Ellen Conford. We publish mass-market entertainment reading, not educational books."

THORNDIKE PRESS, (IV), Division of Macmillan, Inc., Box 159, Thorndike ME 04986. (800)223-6121. Editorial Coordinator: Barbara Sholler. Estab. 1979. Midsize publisher of hardcover and paperback large print *reprints.* Books: Alkaline paper; offset printing; Smythe-sewn library binding; average print order: 4,000. Publishes 300 total titles each year.
Needs: *No fiction that has not been previously published.* Recently published *The Kitchen God's Wife,* by Amy Tan; *Hideaway,* by Dean R. Koontz; *A Bell for Adano,* by John Hersey.
How to Contact: Does not accept unsolicited mss. Query.
Terms: Pays 10% in royalties.
Advice: "Starting February, a young adult imprint (as yet, unnamed) large print line will begin. We do not accept unpublished works. With the exception of upcoming Young Adult Series, our audience is comprised, primarily, of seniors."

TOR BOOKS, (II), 175 Fifth Ave., New York NY 10010. Editor-in-Chief: Robert Gleason. Estab. 1980. Publishes hardcover and paperback originals, plus some paperback reprints. Books: 5 point Dombook paper; offset printing; Bursel and perfect binding; few illustrations. Averages 200 total titles, all fiction, each year. Some nonfiction titles.
Needs: Fantasy, mainstream, science fiction, suspense and westerns. Recently published *Xenocide,* by Orson Scott Card; *Midnight Sun,* by Ramsey Campbell; *The Nemesis Mission,* by Dean Ing; and *The Dragon Reborn,* by Robert Jordan.
How to Contact: Agented mss preferred. Buys 90% agented fiction. No simultaneous submissions. Address manuscripts to "editorial," *not* to the Managing Editor's office.
Terms: Pays in royalties and advance. Writer must return advance if book is not completed or is unacceptable. Sends galleys to author. Free book catalog on request.

TRILLIUM PRESS, (I, II), First Avenue, Unionville NY 10988. (914)726-4444. Vice President: Thomas Holland. Fiction Editor: William Neumann. Estab. 1978. "Independent educational publisher." Publishes hardcover and paperback originals and paperback reprints. Published new writers within the last year. Plans 40 first novels this year. Averages 150 total titles, 70 fiction titles each year.
Needs: Young adult/teen (10-18 years), fantasy/science fiction, historical, problem novels, romance (ya), sports and mystery/adventure, middle school/young adult (10-18) series. Recently published the following young adult series: Mystery & Adventure (including historical novels); Growing Up Right (values, relationships, adult development); science fiction. Also published *The Journal of Jenny September,* by Isaacsen-Bright; *The T-206 Honus Wagner Caper,* by Janet Amann; *A Matter of Choice,* by H. Henry Williams.
How to Contact: Accepts unsolicited mss. SASE. Reports in 3 months on mss.
Terms: Negotiated "as appropriate." Sends galleys to author. Writer's guidelines for #10 SAE and 1 first class stamp. Book catalog for 9×12 SAE and 3 first class stamps.

TROLL ASSOCIATES, (II), Watermill Press, 100 Corporate Drive, Mahwah NJ 07430. (201)529-4000. Editorial Contact Person: M. Frances. Estab. 1968. Midsize independent publisher. Publishes hardcover originals, paperback originals and reprints. Averages 100-300 total titles each year.
Needs: Adventure, historical, juvenile (5-9 yrs. including: animal, easy-to-read, fantasy), preschool/picture book, young adult/teen (10-18 years) including: easy-to-read, fantasy/science fiction, historical, romance (ya), sports, spy/adventure. Published new writers within the last year.
How to Contact: Accepts and returns unsolicited mss. Query first. Submit outline/synopsis and sample chapters. Reports in 2-3 weeks on queries.
Terms: Pays royalties. Sometimes sends galleys to author. Publishes ms 6-18 months after acceptance.

TSR, INC., Box 756, Lake Geneva WI 53147. (414)248-3625. Imprints include the Dragonlance® series, Forgotten Realms® series, Buck Rogers® Books, TSR® Books, Ravenloft® Books. Contact: Brian Thompson, Executive Editor. Estab. 1974. "We publish original paperback novels and 'shared world' books." TSR publishes games as well, including the Dungeons & Dragons® role-playing game. Books: Standard paperbacks; offset printing; perfect binding; b&w (usually) illustrations; average first novel print order: 75,000. Averages 20-30 fiction titles each year.

Needs: "We most often publish character-oriented fantasy and science fiction, and some horror. We work with authors who can deal in a serious fashion with the genres we concentrate on and can be creative within the confines of our work-for-hire contracts." Recently published *Sojourn*, by R.A. Salvatore; *The Kinslayer Wars*, by Douglas Niles; and *Sorcerer's Stone*, by L. Dean James.

How to Contact: "Because most of our books are strongly tied to our game products, we expect our writers to be very familiar with those products."

Terms: Pays royalties of 4% of cover price. Offers advances. Always sends galleys to authors. "Commissioned works, with the exception of our TSR® Books line, are written as work-for-hire, with TSR, Inc., holding all copyrights."

Advice: "With the huge success of our Dragonlance® series and Forgotten Realms® books, we expect to be working even more closely with TSR-owned fantasy worlds. Be familiar with our line and query us regarding a proposal."

TYNDALE HOUSE PUBLISHERS, (II, IV), P.O. Box 80, 351 Executive Drive, Wheaton IL 60189. (708)668-8300. Vice President of Editorial: Ron Beers. Estab. 1960. Privately owned religious press. Publishes hardcover and mass paperback originals and paperback reprints. Plans 4 first novels this year. Averages 100 total titles, 10 fiction titles each year. Average first novel print order: 5,000-10,000 copies.

Needs: Religious/inspirational. Recently published *Tourmaline*, by Jon Henderson (espionage); *Castle of Dreams*, by Donna Fletcher Crow (mystery romance); *Mark: Eyewitness*, by Ellen Traylor (biblical novel). Series include "Grace Livingston Hill," "Appomattox Sage" and "Reno Western" series.

How to Contact: Does not accept unsolicited mss. Queries only. Reports in 6-10 weeks. Publishes ms an average of 18 months after acceptance.

Terms: Pays in royalties of 10% minimum; negotiable advance. Must return advance if book is not completed or is unacceptable. Writer's guidelines and book catalog for 9 × 12 SAE and $2.40 for postage.

*VESTA PUBLICATIONS, LTD, (II), Box 1641, Cornwall, Ontario K6H 5V6 Canada. (613)932-2135. Editor: Stephen Gill. Estab. 1974. Midsize publisher with plans to expand. Publishes hardcover and paperback originals. Books: Bond paper; offset printing; paperback and sewn hardcover binding; illustrations; average print order: 1,200; first novel print order: 1,000. Plans 7 first novels this year. Averages 18 total titles, 5 fiction titles each year. Negotiable charge for critiquing rejected mss.

Needs: Adventure, contemporary, ethnic, experimental, faction, fantasy, feminist, historical, humor/satire, juvenile, literary, mainstream, mystery/suspense, preschool/picture book, psychic/supernatural/occult, regional, religious/inspirational, romance, science fiction, short story collections, translations, war and young adult/teen. Published *Sodom in her Heart*, by Donna Nevling (religious); *The Blessings of a Bird*, by Stephen Gill (juvenile); and *Whistle Stop and Other Stories*, by Ordrach.

How to Contact: Accepts unsolicited mss. Submit complete ms with SASE or SAE and IRC. Reports in 1 month. Simultaneous submissions OK. Disk submissions OK with CPM/Kaypro 2 system.

Terms: Pays in royalties of 10% minimum. Sends galleys to author. "For first novel we usually ask authors from outside of Canada to pay half of our printing cost." Free book catalog.

VILLARD BOOKS, (II, III), Random House, Inc., 201 E. 50th St., New York NY 10022. (212)572-2720. Editorial Director: Peter Gethers. Fiction Editors: Diane Reverand, Stephanie Long, Emily Bestler. Estab. 1983. Imprint specializes in commercial fiction and nonfiction. Publishes hardcover and trade paperback originals. Published new writers within the last year. Plans 2 first novels this year. Averages 40-45 total titles, approx. 10 fiction titles each year. Sometimes critiques rejected mss.

Needs: Strong commercial fiction and nonfiction. Adventure, contemporary, historical, horror, humor/satire, literary, mainstream, mystery/suspense, romance (contemporary and historical). Special interest in mystery, thriller, and literary novels. Recently published *How to Make an American Quilt*, by Whitney Otto (bestseller); *Domestic Pleasure*, by Beth Eutcheon; *First Hubby*, by Roy Blount.

How to Contact: Does not accept unsolicited mss. Submit outline/synopsis and 1-2 sample chapters to a specific editor. Agented fiction: 95%. Reports in 2-3 weeks. Simultaneous submissions OK.
Terms: "Depends upon contract negotiated." Sends galleys to author. Writer's guidelines for 8½×11 SAE with 1 first class stamp. Book catalog free on request.
Advice: "Most fiction published in hardcover."

WALKER AND COMPANY, (I), 720 5th Ave., New York NY 10019. Editors: Michael Seidman (mystery), J. Johnson (western), Mary Elizabeth Allen (regency), Peter Rubie (adventure), Emily Easton (young adult), Mary Kennan Herbert (trade nonfiction). Midsize independent publisher with plans to expand. Publishes hardcover and trade paperback. Average first novel print order: 4,000-5,000. Number of titles: 120/year. Published many new writers within the last year. Occasionally comments on rejected mss.
  • Books published by Walker and Company have received numerous awards including the Spur Award (for westerns) and nominations for the Shamus Awards for Best First Private Eye Novel (3 in 1991).
Needs: Nonfiction, sophisticated, quality mystery (cozy, amateur sleuth, private eye, police procedural), regency romance, quality thrillers and adventure, traditional western and children's and young adult nonfiction. Recently published *Suffer Little Children*, by Thomas D. Davis; *The Price of Victory*, by Vincent S. Green; *Throw Darts at a Cheesecake*, by Denise Dietz.
How to Contact: Submit outline and chapters as preliminary. Query letter should include "a concise description of the story line, including its outcome, word length of story, writing experience, publishing credits, particular expertise on this subject and in this genre. Common mistakes: Sounding unprofessional (i.e. too chatty, too braggardly). Forgetting SASE." Buys 50% agented fiction. Notify if multiple or simultaneous submissions. Reports in 3-5 months. Publishes ms an average of 1 year after acceptance.
Terms: Negotiable (usually advance against royalty). Must return advance if book is not completed or is unacceptable.
Advice: Publishing more fiction than previously, "exclusively hardcover. Manuscripts should be sophisticated. As for mysteries, we are open to all types, including suspense novels and offbeat, cross genre books. We are always looking for well-written western novels and thrillers that are offbeat and strong on characterization. Character development is most important in all Walker fiction. We have been actively soliciting submissions to all divisions."

WARNER BOOKS, (II), Subsidiary of Warner Publishing, Inc., 1271 Ave. of the Americas, Time Life Building, New York NY 10120. (212)522-7200. Imprints include Questor Science Fiction/Fantasy, Mysterious Press. Contact: Editorial dept. for specific editors. Estab. 1961. Publishes hardcover and paperback originals. Published new writers within the last year. Averages approx. 500 titles/year. Sometimes critiques rejected mss.
Needs: Adventure, contemporary, fantasy, horror, mainstream, mystery/suspense, preschool/picture book, romance (contemporary, historical, regency), science fiction, war, western. "We are continuing to publish romances, mainstream novels, science fiction, men's adventure, etc. No historicals that are not romances, Civil War novels, young adult." Recently published *Red Phoenix*, by Larry Bond (military thriller); *Mirror Image*, by Sandra Brown (commercial women's fiction).
How to Contact: Does not accept unsolicited mss. Query first. Agented fiction 85-90%. Reports in 6-8 weeks on mss. Simultaneous submissions accepted "but we prefer exclusive submissions".
Terms: Varies for each book.
Advice: "Continuing a strong, varied list of fiction titles. We encourage first novelists we feel have potential for more books and whose writing is extremely polished. Be able to explain your work clearly and succinctly in query or cover letter. Read books a publisher has done already—best way to get a feel for publisher's strengths. Read *Publishers Weekly* to keep in touch with trends and industry news."

WASHINGTON SQUARE PRESS, (III), Subsidiary of Pocket Books/Simon & Schuster, 1230 Ave. of the Americas, New York NY 10020. Senior Fiction Editor: Jane Rosenman. Estab. 1962. Quality imprint of mass-market publisher. Publishes paperback originals and reprints. Averages 15 titles, mostly fiction, each year.
Needs: Literary, high quality novels; serious nonfiction, journalistic nonfiction. Recently published *Pizza Face*, by Ken Siman; *Trouble the Water*, by Melvin Dixon; and *The World Around Midnight*, by Patricia Browning Griffith (all novels).

How to Contact: Query first. Agented fiction nearly all. Simultaneous submissions OK. "We cannot promise an individual response to unsolicited mss."

WESTERN PUBLISHING COMPANY, INC., 850 3rd Ave., New York NY 10022. (212)753-8500. Imprint: Golden Books. Juvenile Editors-in-Chief: Marilyn Solomon and Margo Lundell. Estab. 1907. High-volume mass market and trade publisher. Publishes hardcover and paperback originals. Number of titles: Averages 160/year. Buys 20-30% agented fiction.
Needs: Juvenile: Adventure, mystery, humor, sports, animal, easy-to-read picture books, and "a few" nonfiction titles. Published *Little Critter's Bedtime Story*, by Mercer Mayer; *Cyndy Szekeres' Mother Goose Rhymes*; and *Spaghetti Manners*, by Stephanie Calmenson, illustrated by Lisa MaCue Karsten.
How to Contact: Send a query letter with a description of the story and SASE. Unsolicited mss are returned unread. Publishes ms an average of 1 year after acceptance.
Terms: Pays by outright purchase or royalty.
Advice: "Read our books to see what we do. Call for appointment if you do illustrations, to show your work. Do not send illustrations. Illustrations are not necessary; if your book is what we are looking for, we can use one of our artists."

ALBERT WHITMAN & COMPANY, (I), 6340 Oakton St., Morton Grove IL 60053. (708)581-0033. Assistant Editor: Christy Grant. Associate Editor: Judith Mathews. Senior Editor: Abby Levine. Editor-in-Chief: Kathleen Tucker. Estab. 1919. Small independent juvenile publisher. Publishes hardcover originals and paperback reprints. Books: Paper varies; printing varies; library binding; most books illustrated; average print order: 7,500. Average 30 total titles/year. Number of fiction titles varies.
Needs: Juvenile (2-12 years including easy-to-read, fantasy, historical, adventure, contemporary, mysteries, picture-book stories). Primarily interested in picture book manuscripts and nonfiction for ages 2-8. Published *All About Asthma*, by William Ostrow and Vivian Ostrow; *You Push, I Ride*, by Abby Levine; *How the Ox Star Fell from Heaven*, by Lily Toy Hong; published new writers within the last year.
How to Contact: Accepts unsolicited mss. Submit complete ms, if not possible—3 sample chapters and outline; complete ms for picture books. "Queries don't seem to work for us." SASE. "Half or more fiction is not agented." Reports in 3 weeks on outline; 2 months average on mss. Simultaneous submissions OK. ("We prefer to be told.")
Terms: Payment varies. Royalties, advance; number of author's copies varies. Some flat fees. Sends galleys to author. Writer's guidelines for SASE. Book catalog for 9 × 12 SAE and $1.21 postage.
Advice: "Writers need only to send a manuscript; artwork does not need to be included. If we decide to buy the story, *we* will find an artist. Though it's *okay* to send a whole package, it's not necessary."

WINDSONG BOOKS, (II, IV), Subsidiary of St. Paul Books and Media, 50 St. Paul's Ave., Boston MA 02130. Children's Editor: Sister Anne Joan, fsp. Estab. 1932. "Midsize Roman Catholic publishing house." Publishes paperback originals. Plans 2 first novels this year. Publishes 20 total titles each year.
Needs: Juvenile (contemporary, religious/inspirational) and young adult (historical, problem novels, romance (Christian), religious/inspirational). Especially needs "young adult/teen novels with a Christian (and Catholic) focus. Religion should be vital in the plot and outcome."
How to Contact: Does not accept or return unsolicited mss. Send an outline/synopsis with 3 sample chapters. SASE. Reports in up to 2 months.
Terms: Pays in royalties of 4-8%. Also pays author's copies (amount varies). Publishes ms 2 years after acceptance. Writer's guidelines for #10 SAE and 1 first class stamp. Catalog for 9 × 12 SAE and 4 first class stamps.
Advice: Looks for "characters and plots in which religion, faith, convictions are not just written in, but essential to the person or story."

*WINSTON-DEREK PUBLISHERS, (II), Box 90883, Nashville TN 37209. (615)321-0535, 329-1319. Senior Editor: Marjorie Staton. Estab. 1978. Midsize publisher. Publishes hardcover and paperback originals and reprints. Books: 60 lb. old Warren style paper; litho press; perfect and/or sewn binding; illustrations sometimes; average print order: 3,000-5,000 copies; first novel print order: 2,000 copies. Published new writers within the last year. Plans 10 first novels this year. Averages 55-65 total titles, 20 fiction titles each year; "90% of material is from freelance writers; each year we add 15 more titles."
Needs: Historical, juvenile (historical), religious/inspirational, and young adult (easy-to-read, historical, romance) and programmed reading material for middle and high school students. "Must be 65,000 words or less. Novels strong with human interest. Characters overcoming a weakness or working

Close-up

William Kennedy
Author

William Kennedy was born in Albany, New York and still lives on the outskirts of the city. His newest book, *Very Old Bones* is the latest in his Albany-based series of books that include *Legs, Billy Phelan's Greatest Game* and the Pulitzer Prize-winning *Ironweed*.

Each book in the Albany cycle stands on its own as an interesting account of life and the struggle of man as he contends with his day-to-day existence. As a collection, the stories interweave and the characters interact from one book to the other. Yet the central character of one book may have only a background role in the following book. The protagonists in Kennedy's Albany cycle are members of the Phelan and Quinn families and each story unfolds from a different family member's perspective. This technique of chronicling a set of characters' lives has been employed successfully in genre fiction, especially science fiction, says Kennedy, and, of course, by William Faulkner and J.D. Salinger.

The possibilities for such a series seem virtually endless, he says, and he has at least four other books he wants to write in the Albany series. With each new book, the characters suggest many new directions in which to expand the family chronicles. One of the books, *Ironweed* also became a movie for which Kennedy wrote the screenplay. He says writing a screenplay is a big departure from his other work. "It's more like journalistic writing because you must be careful to get the story across concisely in each scene, much like writing a lead for every paragraph for a new story."

Kennedy began writing short stories in high school, but originally intended to become a journalist. He wrote for his college newspaper, but it wasn't until after a stint in the Army that he began to study literature seriously. *Angels and the Sparrows* was Kennedy's first book and it was a clear case for the need for perseverance as well as talent. After several rejections, he says, he set the book on the shelf for awhile. He never lost faith in the project, however, and after about 30 rejections, the book was published. Although Kennedy is proud of this first work, he says it was a book of its time and not the one he would write today. With each book, he says, a writer grows and, hopefully, improves.

Kennedy says he begins writing by sitting in front of his computer and "talking" to it, asking questions and solving problems until he is ready to write. He does a great deal of rewriting to get his work the way he wants it. "By the time I get into a book I know what the characters are going to do," says Kennedy. He says there are times when the story will take on a new direction without warning. In writing *Very Old Bones*, for example, he began the narration of the story with one character and ended by replacing it with another because, as the story progressed, it just made more sense to do so.

The sense of place in writing a novel is very important to Kennedy. He says he has published other books that were well received but when he focused on a particular setting, in this case Albany, the stories flowed more easily. "Albany is a city rich with history that is begging to be told." He's thinking of writing a political novel about the city during the times of Prohibition and the Depression. This period appeals to him, he says, because it was a colorful time of mobsters and gambling and political graft. People had to struggle to

© Mariana Cook

survive, he explains, and tramps and hobos lived from hand to mouth traveling the country by riding the rails.

In addition to *Very Old Bones* Kennedy has just finished *Charlie Malarkey and the Singing Moose* (Viking Children's Books), a sequel to a children's book, *Charlie Malarkey and the Belly Button* on which he collaborated with his son, Brendan. "It was a welcome change of pace from my other writing and, of course, I greatly enjoy working with my son."

Also this year, along with the paperback edition of *Very Old Bones* (Viking Paperbacks), Kennedy's nonfiction collection of essays, literary interviews and book reviews, *Riding the Trolley Car* (Viking-Penguin) is scheduled to be out Spring 1992. He says it's a collection of his life's work, "a rich mix from my point of view of the things I've done."

In addition to writing, Kennedy has taught creative writing at the State University of New York for several years and at Cornell University for one year. Although his publishing experiences have been very good, he says he's also had his share of rejections. Kennedy, who's been with the same agent for 14 years, says having an agent helps as does developing a good realtionship with an editor. The most important advice he can give a writer, he says, is to persevere even in the face of rejection and to write every day.

—Debbie Cinnamon

through a difficulty. Prefer plots related to a historical event but not necessary. No science fiction, explicit eroticism, minorities in conflict without working out a solution to the problem. Downplay on religious ideal and values." Recently published *The Train that Never Ran*, by George K. Bowers; *An Irregular Moon*, by Sara King; and *Lucy Lola's Come Next Year*, by Earnie Danat.

How to Contact: Submit outline/synopsis and 3-4 sample chapters with SASE. Simultaneous submissions OK. Reports in 4-6 weeks on queries; 6-8 weeks on mss. Must query first. Do not send complete ms.

Terms: Pays in royalties of 10% minimum, 15% maximum; negotiates advance. *Offers subsidy arrangements*. Book catalog on request for $1 postage.

Advice: "The public is reading contemplative literature. Authors should strive for originality and a clear writing style, depicting universal themes which portray character building and are beneficial to mankind. Consider the historical novel; there is always room for one more."

WORLDWIDE LIBRARY, (II), Division of Harlequin Books, 225 Duncan Mill Rd., Don Mills, Ontario M3B 3K9 Canada. (416)445-5860. Imprints are Worldwide Library Mystery; Gold Eagle Books. Senior Editor: Feroze Mohammed. Estab. 1979. Large commercial category line. Publishes paperback originals and reprints. Published new writers within the last year. Averages 60 titles, all fiction, each year. Sometimes critiques rejected ms. "Mystery program is largely reprint; no originals please."

Needs: "We are looking for action-adventure series and writers; future fiction." Recently published *Survival 2000; Soldiers of War; Time Warriors; Agents* – all action series. Soon to be published: *Hatchet, Code Zero, Time Raider, Cade, Nomad, Warkeep 2030.*

How to Contact: Query first or submit outline/synopsis/series concept or overview and sample chapters. SAE. U.S. stamps do not work in Canada; use International Reply Coupons or money order. Agented fiction 95%. Reports in 10 weeks on queries. Simultaneous submissions OK.

Terms: Advance and sometimes royalties; copyright buyout. Publishes ms 1-2 years after acceptance.

Advice: "Publishing fiction in very selective areas. As a genre publisher we are always on the lookout for new writing talent and innovative series ideas, especially in the men's adventure area."

YEARLING, (II, III), 666 5th Ave., New York NY 10103. (212)765-6500. Division of Bantam, Doubleday, Dell Publishing Co., Inc. Publishes originals and reprints for children grades K-6. Most interested in humorous upbeat novels, mysteries and family stories. 60 titles a year. "Will, regrettably, no longer consider unsolicited material at this time."

ZEBRA BOOKS, 475 Park Ave. S., New York NY 10016. Did not respond.

ZONDERVAN, 5300 Patterson SE, Grand Rapids MI 49530. (616)698-6900. Imprints include Academie Books, Daybreak Books, Francis Asbury Press, Lamplighter Books, Ministry Resources Library, Pyranee Books, Regency Reference Library, Youth Books and Zondervan Books. Publishers: Stan Gundry, Scott Bolinder. Estab. 1931. Large evangelical Christian publishing house. Publishes hardcover and paperback originals and reprints, though fiction is generally in paper only. Published new writers in the last year. Averages 150 total titles, 5-10 fiction titles each year. Average first novel: 5,000 copies.

Needs: Adult fiction, (mainstream, biblical, historical, adventure, sci-fi, fantasy, mystery), "Inklings-style" fiction of high literary quality and juvenile fiction (primarily mystery/adventure novels for 8-12-year-olds). Christian relevance necessary in all cases. Will *not* consider collections of short stories or inspirational romances. Recently published *Children in the Night* by Harold Myra; *Thorn in the Heart*, by Tim Stafford.

How to Contact: Accepts unsolicited mss. Write for writer's guidelines first. Include #10 SASE. Query or submit outline/synopsis and 2 sample chapters. Reports in 4-6 weeks on queries; 3-4 months on mss.

Terms: "Standard contract provides for a percentage of the net price received by publisher for each copy sold, usually 14-17% of net."

Advice: "Almost no unsolicited fiction is published. Send plot outline and one or two sample chapters. Most editors will *not* read entire mss. Your proposal and opening chapter will make or break you."

International commercial publishers

The following commercial publishers, all located outside the United States and Canada, also accept work from fiction writers. The majority are from England, a few are from India and one each is from Scotland and Ghana. As with other publishers, obtain catalogs and writer's guidelines from those that interest you to determine the types of fiction published and how well your work might fit alongside other offerings.

Remember to use self-addressed envelopes (SAEs) with International Reply Coupons (IRCs) in all correspondence with publishers outside your own country. IRCs may be purchased at the main branch of your local post office. In general, send IRCs in amounts roughly equivalent to return postage. When submitting work to international publishers, you may want to send a disposable copy of your manuscript and only one IRC along with a self-addressed postcard for a reply. This saves you the cost of having work returned.

‡THE BLACKSTAFF PRESS (I), 3 Galway Park, Dundonald BT16 0AN Northern Ireland. Editor: Hilary Bell. Midsize, independent publisher, wide range of subjects. Publishes hardcover and paperback originals and reprints. Contemporary, ethnic (Irish), historical, humor/satire, literary, short story collections, political thrillers and feminist.

MARION BOYARS PUBLISHERS INC., New York, Editorial Office: 24 Lacy Road, London SW15 1NL London. Fiction Editor: Marion Boyars. Publishes 15 novels or story collections/year. "A lot of American fiction. Authors include Ken Kesey, Eudora Welty, Stephen Koch, Samuel Charters, Page Edwards, Kenneth Gangemi, Tim O'Brien, Julian Green. British and Irish fiction. Translations from the French, German, Turkish, Arabic, Italian, Spanish." Send cover letter and entire manuscript "always with sufficient return postage by check." Pays advance against royalties. "Most fiction working *well* in one country does well in another. We usually have world rights, i.e. world English plus translation rights." Enclose return postage by check, minimum $3, for catalog.

ROBERT HALE LIMITED (II), Clerkenwell House, 45/47 Clerkenwell Green, London EC1R 0HT England. Publishes hardcover and trade paperback originals and hardcover reprints. Historical, mainstream and western. Length: 40,000-150,000 words. Send cover letter, synopsis or brief summary and 2 sample chapters.

‡HAMISH HAMILTON LTD., 27 Wrights Lane, London W8 5TZ England. Fiction Editors: Andrew Franklin, Kate Jones and Alexandra Pringle. General trade hardback publisher quality fiction — literary plus some crime and thrillers. Advance on delivery of accepted book or on accepted commission. Send first chapter with synopsis before submitting whole manuscript. SAE essential.

‡HARPERCOLLINS PUBLISHERS (NEW ZEALAND) LIMITED, P.O. Box 1, Auckland New Zealand. Publisher: Paul Bradwell. Averages 8-12 fiction titles/year (15-20 nonfiction). Teen fiction: 12 years plus: Tui imprint; Junior fiction: 8-11 years: Tui Junior imprint. Length: Tui: 30-40,000 words; Tui Junior: 15-17,000 words. Full ms preferred. Pays royalties. "It helps if the author and story have New Zealand connections/content. Write and ask for guidelines."

*HARSHA BOOK AGENCY, Hallmark Publishing Ltd., T.D. East Sannidhi Road, P.O. Box 3541, Kochi-682 035, Kerala, India. Managing and Editorial Director: C. I. Oommen. Publishers of trade paperbacks and educational books. Looking for adventure, novel and short fiction. Accepts unsolicited mss, simultaneous and photocopied submissions and computer printouts. Reports in 2 months. Pays in royalties of 10% maximum. No advance. "We also produce books for self publishers and small press with marketing and distribution support." No SASE/IRC required.

HEADLINE BOOK PUBLISHING PLC, 79 Great Titchfield St., London W1P 7FN England. Editorial Director: Jane Morpeth. Averages approximately 400 titles/year. Mainstream publisher of popular fiction and nonfiction in hardcover and mass-market paperback. Length: 120,000-200,000 words. "Study UK publishers' catalogs to see what is published in both the USA and the UK. Read the UK trade press: *The Bookseller* and *Publishing News* to get a feel for our market. *The Writers' & Artists' Yearbook* is useful." Pays advance against royalties. "Send a synopsis/5 consecutive chapters and *curriculum vitae* first, and return postage." Catalog available.

HODDER & STOUGHTON PUBLISHERS, 47 Bedford Square, London WC1B 3DP, England, U.K. Imprints: Coronet, NEL, Sceptre. Editorial Director: Clare Bristan. Fiction Editors: Humphrey Price (NEL); Anna Powell (Coronet); Carole Welch (Sceptre). Coronet: intelligent, mainstream romantic fiction; humour; historical novels/crime; Sceptre: literary—fiction and nonfiction; NEL: horror, SF, fantasy, humour, serious nonfiction. "We do not consider short stories." Length: 70,000-120,000 words. Payment is made "usually by an advance and then final payment on publication." Send a cover letter, synopsis and sample chapters. "If you can't get an agent to represent you, then do make enquiries to the editorial departments first, before sending off complete manuscripts."

JULIA MACRAE BOOKS, Random House, 20 Vauxhall Bridge Road, London SW1V 2SA England. Editors: Julia MacRae, Delia Huddy, Kate Petty. Children's books: Board books, picture books, fiction for juniors and teenagers, nonfiction. *Adult titles*: biography, history, music, religion. Send cover letter and entire manuscript. Writers are paid by royalties. Julia MacRae Books is an imprint of Random House.

‡MILLS & BOON, Eton House, 18-24 Paradise Road, Richmond, Surrey TW9 1SR England. Publishes 250 fiction titles/year. Modern romantic fiction, historical romances and medical romances. "We are happy to see the whole manuscript or 3 sample chapters and synopsis."

MY WEEKLY STORY LIBRARY, D.C. Thomson and Co., Ltd., 22 Meadowside, Dundee DD19QJ, Scotland. Fiction Editor: Mrs. D. Hunter. Publishes 48, 35,000-word romantic novels/year. "Cheap paperback story library with full-colour cover. Material should not be violent, controversial or sexually explicit." Length: 35,000-45,000 words. Writers are paid on acceptance. "Send the opening 3 chapters and a synopsis. Avoid too many colloquialisms/Americanisms. Stories can be set anywhere but local colour not too "local" as to be alien." Both contemporary and historical novels considered. Guidelines available on request.

‡PETER OWEN PUBLISHERS, 73 Kenway Rd., London SW5 ORE England. Fiction Editor: Gary Pulsifer. Averages 25 fiction titles/year. "Independent publishing house now 41 years old. Publish fiction from around the world, from Russia to Japan. Publishers of Shusuko Endo, Paul and Jane Bowles, Hermann Hesse, Octavio Paz, Colette etc." Send cover letter, synopsis, brief summary. Please include SASE (or IRCs). Pays advance and standard royalty. "Be concise. Always include SASE and/or international reply coupon. Do not send inappropriate material. Best to work through agent. Writers can obtain copy of our catalogue by SASE, and/or interntional reply coupon. No guidelines but it would help greatly if author was familiar with the list."

PICADOR, Pan MacMillan Ltd., 18-21 Cavaye Place, London SW10 9PG England. Publishing Director: Peter Straus. Publishes hardbound and paperback titles. "Picador is a literary imprint specializing in the best international fiction and nonfiction in recent years. Its authors include G. Garcia Marquez, Umberto Eco, Bruce Chatwin, Clive James, Julian Barnes, Graham Swift, Ian McEwan, Toni Morrison, Tom Wolfe." Length: 50,000-150,000 words. Send cover letter, synopsis, brief summary and 2 sample chapters. For catalog, send large addressed envelope and IRCs.

POPULAR PUBLICATIONS, P.O. Box 5592, Limbe, Malawi. Fiction Editor: Joseph-Claude Simwaka. Averages between 3-5 titles/year. "Popular Publications is probably the biggest publisher of Malawian fiction in the country. In order to boost and promote Malawian literary writers (creative works) the publishing house launched the Malawian Writers Series in 1974 to cater to fiction, short story collections and poetry. We also publish children's books on fiction." Length: 5,000-25,000 words. Send cover letter and entire manuscript. We pay 10% royalties by 31st December every year. "Submit a typewritten manuscript, double-spaced on A4 paper. It is also advisable for the writer to submit two copies of the same manuscript, one for us and the other for the Government Censorship Board. Writer too, should keep a triplicate copy." Write for catalog or guidelines.

QUARTET BOOKS LIMITED, 27-29 Goodge Street, London W1P1FD England. Chief Editor: Stephen Pickles. Publishes 50 stories/year. "Middle East fiction, European classics in translation, original novels." Payment is: advance—half on signature, half on delivery or publication. "Send brief synopsis and sample chapters. *No* romantic fiction, historical fiction, crime, science fiction or thrillers."

WEIDENFELD AND NICOLSON LTD., The Onion Publishing Group, Onion House, 5 Uppe St. Martin's Lane, London WC2H 9EA England. Fiction Editor: Allegra Huston. Publishes approx. 10 titles/year. "We are an independent publisher with a small fiction list. Authors include, or have included, V. Nabokov, J.G. Farrell, Olivia Manning, Edna O'Brien, Margaret Drabble, Richard Powers, John Hersey, Penelope Gilliatt, Charlotte Vale Allen. We publish literary and commercial fiction: sagas, historicals, crime." Pays by advance. Royalties are set against advances. "Send a covering letter, a detailed synopsis and some sample pages such as the first chapter. Do not send the whole typescript unless invited. Please enclose return postage and retain photocopies of all material sent. Very rare that we would publish a work by an author which had not previously been published in their own country."

Commercial publishers/'92-'93 changes

The following commercial publishers appeared in the 1992 edition of *Novel & Short Story Writer's Market* but do not appear in the 1993 edition. Those listings that did not respond to our request for an update are listed without further explanation below. There are several reasons why a publisher did not return an update—they could be overstocked, no longer taking taking fiction or have been recently sold—or they may have responded too late for inclusion. If a reason for the omission is known, it is included next to the publisher's name.

Accent Books (asked to be deleted)
Apple Books (no unsolicited material)
Bethany House Publishers (asked to be deleted)
Clarion Books (asked to be deleleted)
Diane Publishing Co. (no fiction)
Dorchester Publishing Co., Inc. (see Leisure Books)
Harpercollins Children's Books
Heartfire Romance

Holloway House Publishing Company (asked to be deleted)
Multnomah (asked to be deleted)
Point Books (no unsolicited material)
Clarkson N. Potter, Inc.
Price Stern Sloan, Inc. (no fiction)
Pulphouse Publishing, Inc. (no unsolicited material)
G.P. Putnam's Sons
St. Paul Books And Media

(asked to be left out this year)
Scholastic (no unsolicited material)
Stoddart (inappropriate submissions)
Summit Books (out of business)
Ticknor & Fields
Daniel Weiss Associates, Inc.
Wildstar Books/Empire Books (out of business)
Zebra Books

Contests and Awards

Contests and awards programs offer writers a number of benefits. In addition to honors and quite often cash awards, contests also offer writers the opportunity to be judged on the basis of quality alone without the outside factors that sometimes influence publishing decisions. New writers who win contests may be published for the first time, while more experienced writers may gain public recognition of an entire body of work.

There are contests for almost every type of fiction writing. Some focus on form, such as the Short Grain Contest, for postcard-length stories, and the *Quarterly West* Novella Competition, for novellas. Others feature writing on particular themes or topics including the Crime Writers Association Awards, the National Jewish Book Awards and the Spur Award Contest. Still others are prestigious prizes or awards for work that must be nominated such as National Endowment for the Arts Fellowship and Pulitzer Prize in Fiction. Chances are no matter what type of fiction you write, there is a contest or award program that may interest you.

Selecting and submitting to a contest

Use the same care in submitting to contests as you would sending your manuscript to a publication or book publisher. Deadlines are very important and where possible we've included this information. At times contest deadlines were only approximate at our press deadline, so be sure to write or call for complete information and additional rules.

Follow the rules to the letter. If, for instance, contest rules require you to put your name on a cover sheet only, you will be disqualified if you ignore this and put your name on every page. Find out how many copies to send. If you don't send the correct amount, by the time you are contacted to send more it may be past the submission deadline.

As with publishers, of course, your submission must be clean, neatly typed and professionally presented. Do not cost yourself points by sending a manuscript no one cares to handle or read.

One note of caution: Beware of contests that charge entry fees that are disproportionate to the amount of the prize. Contests offering a $10 prize, but charging $7 in entry fees, are a waste of your time and money.

If you are interested in a contest or award that requires your publisher to nominate your work, it's acceptable to make your interest known. Be sure to leave them plenty of time, however, to make the nomination deadline.

The Roman numeral coding we use to rank listings in this section is different than that used in previous sections. A new or unpublished writer is eligible to enter those marked **I** (and some **IV**s), while a writer with a published book (usually including self-published) may enter most contests ranked **II** (and, again, some **IV**s). Entrants for contests ranked **III** must be nominated by someone who is not the writer (usually the publisher or editor). The following is our ranking system:

    I Contest for unpublished fiction, usually open to both new and experienced writers.

    II Contest for published (usually including self-published) fiction, which may be entered by the author.

    III Contest for published fiction, which must be nominated by an editor, pub-

lisher or other nominating body.
IV Contest limited to residents of a certain region, of a certain age or to writing
on certain themes or subjects.

‡EDWARD ABBEY AWARD, (II, IV), *Buzzworm*/Patagonia Inc., Suite 206, 2305 Canyon Blvd., Boulder
CO 80302. (303)442-1969. Assistant Editor: Deborah Houy. "To honor the memory of Edward Abbey." Awarded to best published (or accepted for publication) novel in the previous year on environmental themes. Annual competition for novels. Award: $2,000. Judges: Editors of *Buzzworm*. Guide-
lines for SASE. Deadline March 1 (award given in July-August). Unpublished submissions.

‡JANE ADDAMS CHILDREN'S BOOK AWARD, (II), Jane Addams Peace Association/Women's International League for Peace and Freedom, 980 Lincoln Place, Boulder CO 80302-7234. Chair: Jean
Gore. "To honor the writer of the children's book that most effectively promotes peace, social justice,
world community and the equality of the sexes and all races." Annual competition for short stories,
novels and translations. Award: certificate. Competition receives approx. 200 submissions. Judges:
committee. Guidelines for SASE. Deadline April 1, for books published during previous year.

AIM MAGAZINE SHORT STORY CONTEST, (I), Box 20554, Chicago IL 60620. (312)874-6184. Contact:
Ruth Apilado and Mark Boone, publisher and fiction editor. Estab. 1984. Contest offered annually if
money available. "To encourage and reward good writing in the short story form. The contest is
particularly for new writers." Award: $100 plus publication in fall issue. "Judged by *Aim*'s editorial
staff." Sample copy for $3.50. Contest rules for SASE. Unpublished submissions. "We're looking for
compelling, well-written stories with lasting social significance."

ALABAMA STATE COUNCIL ON THE ARTS INDIVIDUAL ARTIST FELLOWSHIP, (II, IV), #1 Dexter
Ave., Montgomery AL 36130. (205)242-4076. Contact: Randy Shoults. "To provide assistance to an
individual artist." Semiannual awards: $5,000 and $10,000 grants. Competition receives approximately
30 submissions annually. Judges: Independent peer panel. Entry forms or rules for SASE. Deadline:
May 1. Two-year Alabama residency required.

ALASKA STATE COUNCIL ON THE ARTS LITERARY ARTS FELLOWSHIPS, (I, IV), Alaska State Council on the Arts, Suite 1E, 411 West 4th Ave., Anchorage AK 99501-2343. (907)279-1558. Contact:
Christine D'Arcy. "Open-ended grant award, non-matching, to enable creative writers to advance
their careers as they see it." Biennial. Award: $5,000. Judges: Peer panel review. Deadline: October
1. Alaskan writers only.

‡EDWARD F. ALBEE FOUNDATION FELLOWSHIP, (I), Edward F. Albee Foundation, Inc., 14 Harrison St., New York NY 10013. (212)226-2020. Contact: David Briggs. Provides one-month residencies
for writers and artists at the William Flanagan Memorial Creative Persons Center (better known as
"The Barn") in Montauk, on Long Island, New York. 24 residencies per year, June-September. Award
for writers of fiction, nonfiction, poetry and plays. Judges: several writers. Applications are accepted
from January 1 through April 1. Write for official guidelines.

‡ALBERTA NEW FICTION COMPETITION, (I, IV), Alberta Culture and Multiculturalism in cooperation with Doubleday Canada Ltd. of Toronto, 12th Floor, CN Tower, Edmonton, Alberta T5J 0K5
Canada. (403)427-6315. Contact: Director Of Arts Branch. Biennial award. To encourage the development of fiction writers living in the province of Alberta. The competition is open to all writers who
are residents of the province of Alberta. Deadline December 31. No SASE is necessary. Brochures
and further information available. Award: $4,000; of this, $2,500 is an outright award given by Alberta
Culture and $1,500 is an advance against royalties given by Doubleday. Three categories of submission:
full-length novel from 60,000-100,000 words; short story collection totaling approximately 60,000
words; novella/short story combination totaling 60,000 words.

 *The double dagger before a listing indicates that
the listing is new in this edition.*

‡**THE ALBERTA WRITING FOR YOUNG PEOPLE COMPETITION, (I, IV),** Alberta Culture and Multiculturalism in cooperation with Doubleday Canada Ltd. and Allarcom/Superchannel. 12th Floor, CN Tower, 10004-104 Avenue, Edmonton, Alberta T5J 0K5 Canada. (403)427-6315. Contact: Film and literature art branch director.Bienniel award (even years). The competition is designed to direct Alberta's writers to the challenging world of writing for juveniles. Unpublished submissions. Entry deadline: Dec. 31. The competition brochure and/or further information will be sent upon request. Award: $4,500 prize; an outright award of $2,000 from Alberta Culture and Multiculturalism, a $1,000 advance against royalties from Doubleday Canada Ltd. and a $1,500 12-month option for motion picture/television rights from Allarcom/Superchannel. "We have 2 categories: book mss for young adults (up to age 16) averaging 40,000 words in length; and book mss suitable for younger readers (8-12 years) running between 12,000 and 20,000 words."

THE NELSON ALGREN AWARD FOR SHORT FICTION, (I), *Chicago Tribune*, 435 N. Michigan Ave., Chicago IL 60611. (312)222-4540. Annual award to recognize an outstanding, unpublished short story, minimum 2,500 words, maximum 10,000 words. Awards: $5,000 first prize; three runners-up receive $1,000 awards. Publication of four winning stories in the *Chicago Tribune*. No entry fee. "All entries must be from "the Heartland," typed, double spaced and accompanied by SASE." A brochure bearing the rules of the contest will be sent to writers who inquire in writing. Deadline: Entries are accepted only from November 30-February 1.

ALLEGHENY REVIEW **AWARDS, (I, IV)),** Box 32, Allegheny College, Meadville PA 16335. Contact: John Burns and Vern Maczuzak, editors. Annual award for unpublished short stories. U.S. undergraduate students only. SASE for rules. Deadline: January 31.

AMBERGRIS **ANNUAL FICTION AWARD, (II),** *Ambergris* Magazine, Dept. N, P.O. Box 29919, Cincinnati OH 45229. Editor: Mark Kissling. Award "to recognize and reward excellence in short fiction." Annual competition for short stories. Award: $100 and nomination to *The Pushcart Prize*. Competition receives more than 1,000 mss/year. Judges: Editorial staff. Guidelines for #10 SASE. Unpublished submissions. "We give special but not exclusive consideration to works by Ohio writers or about the Midwest in general. Winner is chosen from all works submitted during the year. We prefer works under 5,000 words. Writers should review the results of previous contests. Current issue is $4.95 and sample copies are $3.95. See listing in Literary and Small Circulation Magazines for more details."

AMELIA MAGAZINE **AWARDS, (I),** 329 "E" St., Bakersfield CA 93304. (805)323-4064. Contact: Frederick A. Raborg, Jr., editor. The Reed Smith Fiction Prize; The Willie Lee Martin Short Story Award; The Cassie Wade Short Fiction Award; The Patrick T. T. Bradshaw Fiction Award; and four annual genre awards in science fiction, romance, western and fantasy/horror. Estab. 1984. Annually. "To publish the finest fiction possible and reward the writer; to allow good writers to earn some money in small press publication. *Amelia* strives to fill that gap between major circulation magazines and quality university journals." Unpublished submissions. Length: The Reed Smith—3,000 words max.; The Willie Lee Martin—3,500-5,000 words; The Cassie Wade—4,500 words max.; The Patrick T. T. Bradshaw—10,000 words; the genre awards—science fiction, 5,000 words; romance, 3,000 words; western, 5,000 words; fantasy/horror, 5,000 words. Award: "Each prize consists of $200 plus publication and two copies of issue containing winner's work." The Reed Smith Fiction Prize offers two additional awards when quality merits of $100 and $50, and publication; Bradshaw Book Award: $250 plus publication, 2 copies. Deadlines: The Reed Smith Prize—September 1; The Willie Lee Martin—March 1; The Cassie Wade—June 1; The Patrick T. T. Bradshaw—February 15; *Amelia* fantasy/horror—February 1; *Amelia* western—April 1; *Amelia* romance—October 1; *Amelia* science fiction—December 15. Entry fee: $5. Bradshaw Award fee: $7.50. Contest rules for SASE. Looking for "high quality work equal to finest fiction being published today."

AMERICAN ACADEMY AND INSTITUTE OF ARTS AND LETTERS LITERARY AWARDS, (III), 633 W. 155th St., New York NY 10032. (212)368-5900. Contact: Betsey Feeley, assistant to the executive director. Annual awards for previously published books. To honor authors for excellence in literature and encourage them in their creative work. Selection is by member of the Academy-Institute. *Applications not accepted*. Award: Prizes vary. Eight $7,500 Academy-Institute awards. Special awards include: The Richard & Hinda Rosenthal Foundation Award: $5,000 for "an American work of fiction published during the preceding 12 months"; The Sue Kaufman Prize for First Fiction: $2,500; and The William Dean Howells Medal for Fiction (every 5 years). Also the Award of Merit Medal for the Novel and $5,000 prize (every 6 years); the Award of Merit Medal for The Short Story and $5,000 prize (every 6 years); and The Gold Medal for Fiction (every 6 years). The Harold D. Vursell Memorial Award: $5,000 to single out recent writing in book form that merits recognition for the quality of its prose style. The Morton Dauwen Zabel Award: $2,500 for a writer of fiction of progressive, original and experimental tendencies (every 3 years). The Rome Fellowship in Literature (periodically) for a year's residence at the American Academy in Rome. The E.M. Forster Award ($12,500) for a young English writer to stay in the U.S. The Jean Stein Award ($5,000) given to a writer (nonfiction, fiction, poetry in succession) whose work takes risks expressing its commitment to the author's values and vision.

‡THE AMERICAN WAY FAUX FAULKNER CONTEST, (I), *American Way Magazine, Faulkner Newsletter of Yoknapatawpha Press* and University of Mississippi, P.O. Box 248, Oxford MS 38655. (601)234-0909. "To honor William Faulkner by imitating his style, themes and subject matter in a short parody." Annual competition for a 500-word (2-pages) parody. Award: 2 round-trip tickets to Memphis, plus 2 round-trip tickets anywhere in the world that American Airlines flies. Competition receives approx. 750-1,000 submissions. Judges: Willie Morris, Barry Hannah, Wallace Stegner (judges rotate every year or so—well-known authors). Guidelines for SASE. Deadline: February 1. Previously unpublished submissions. "*American Way* (in-flight courtesy magazine of American Airlines) runs an ad for their Faux Faulkner Contest in every other issue. Winner will be notified in May—announcement made Aug. 1, at Faulkner's home in Oxford, Mississippi. Contestants grant publication rights—and the right to release entries to other media—to the sponsors."

ANALECTA COLLEGE FICTION CONTEST, (I, IV), The Liberal Arts Council, FAC 19, Austin TX 78712. (512)471-6563. Awards Coordinator: Current Editor. Award to "give student writers, at the Univ. of Texas and universities across the country, a forum for publication. We believe that publication in a magazine with the quality and reputation of *Analecta* will benefit student writers." Annual competition for short stories. Award: $200. Competition receives approx. 80 submissions. Judges: Student editiorial board of approx. 15 people. No entry fee. Guidelines for SASE. Deadline: October 28. Unpublished submissions. Limited to college students. Length: 15 pages or less. "We also accept poetry, drama and art submissions."

SHERWOOD ANDERSON SHORT FICTION PRIZE, (I), *Mid-American Review*, Dept. of English, Bowling Green State University, Bowling Green OH 43403. (419)372-2725. Contact: Ellen Behrens, fiction editor. Award frequency is subject to availability of funds. "To encourage the writer of quality short fiction." No entry fee. No deadline. Unpublished material. "Winners are selected from stories published by the magazine, so submission for publication is the first step."

THE ANNUAL/ATLANTIC WRITING COMPETITIONS, (I, IV), Writers' Federation of Nova Scotia, Suite 203, 5516 Spring Garden Rd., Halifax, Nova Scotia B3J 1G6 Canada. (902)423-8116. Executive Director: Jane Buss. "To recognize and encourage unpublished writers in the region of Atlantic Canada. (Competition only open to residents of Nova Scotia, Newfoundland, Prince Edward Island and New Brunswick, the four Atlantic Provinces.)" Annual competition for short stories, novels, poetry, nonfiction, children's writing, drama, magazine feature/essay. Award: Various cash awards. Competition receives approximately 10-12 submissions for novels; 75 for poetry; 75 for children's; 75 for short stories; 10 for nonfiction. Judges: Professional writers, librarians, booksellers. Entry fee $15/entry. Guidelines for SASE. Unpublished submissions.

ANTIETAM REVIEW LITERARY AWARD, (I, IV), *Antietam Review*, 82 W. Washington St., Hagerstown MD 21740. (301)791-3132. Executive Editor: Susanne Kass. Annual award to encourage and give recognition to excellence in short fiction. Open to writers from Maryland, Pennsylvania, Virginia, West Virginia, Washington DC and Delaware. "We consider only previously unpublished work. We read manuscripts between October 1 and March 1." Award: $100 plus $100 for the story; the story is printed as lead in the magazine. "We consider all fiction mss sent to *Antietam Review* as entries for the prize. We look for well crafted, serious literary prose fiction under 5,000 words." Award dependent on funding situation. Send #10 SASE for guidelines.

ANVIL PRESS 3-DAY NOVEL WRITING CONTEST, (I), Anvil Press, Box 1575, Station A, Vancouver, British Columbia V6C 2P7 Canada. (604)876-8710. Contact: Editor. Contest to write the best novel in 3 days, held every Labor Day weekend. Annually, for unpublished novels. "Prize is publication." Receives approximately 500 entries for each award. Judged by Anvil Press editorial board. Entry fee

$10. Guidelines for SASE or SAE and IRC. Deadline: Friday before Labor Day weekend. "Entrants must register with Anvil Press. Winner is announced October 31."

ARIZONA AUTHORS' ASSOCIATION ANNUAL LITERARY CONTEST, (I), Suite 117, 3509 E. Shea Blvd., Phoenix AZ 85028. (602)996-9706. Contact: Gerry Benninger. Estab. 1981. Annually. "To encourage AAA members and all other writers in the country to write regularly for competition and publication." Award: "Cash prizes totalling $1,000 for winners and honorable mentions in short stories, essays and poetry. Winning entries are published in the *Arizona Literary Magazine.*" Entry fee: $6 for poetry, $8 for essays and short stories. Contest rules for SASE. Deadline: July 29. Unpublished submissions. Looking for "strong concept; good, effective writing, with emphasis on the subject/story."

ARIZONA COMMISSION ON THE ARTS CREATIVE WRITING FELLOWSHIPS, (I, IV), 417 W. Roosevelt St., Phoenix AZ 85003. (602)255-5882. Literature Director: Tonda Gorton. Fellowships awarded in alternate years to fiction writers and poets. Four awards of $5,000-7,500. Judges: Out-of-state writers/editors. Next deadline for fiction writers: September 1993. Arizona resident poets and writers over 18 years of age only.

ARTIST TRUST ARTIST FELLOWSHIPS; GAP GRANTS, (I, II, IV), Artist Trust, #415, 1402 Third Ave., Seattle WA 98101-2118. (206)467-8734. Awards Coordinator: Gabrielle Dean. Awards to "offer direct support to individual artists in all disciplines in Washington state: The Fellowship Program and the GAP (Grants for Artist Projects) Program. Our goal is to offer financial support for an artist's creative process, therefore grants are made to generative, rather than interpretive, artists." Annual fellowships and biannual grants for short stories, novels and story collections. Awards: $5,000 fellowship; up to $1,000 GAP. Competition receives approx. 200-300 submissions. Judges: Fellowship—Peer panel of 3 professional artists and arts professionals in each discipline; GAP—Interdisciplinary peer panel of 6-8 artists and arts professionals. Guidelines for SASE. Deadlines: Fellowship—Winter 1993; GAP—Spring and Fall 1993. Limited to Washington state artists only. Students not eligible.

ASF TRANSLATION PRIZE, (I, IV), American-Scandinavian Foundation, 725 Park Ave., New York NY 10021. (212)879-9779. Contact: Publishing office. Estab. 1980. Annual award "to encourage the translation and publication of the best of contemporary Scandinavian poetry and fiction and to make it available to a wider American audience." Competition includes submissions of poetry, drama, literary prose and fiction translations. Award: $2,000, a bronze medallion and publication in *Scandinavian Review*. Competition rules and entry forms available with SASE. Deadline: June 1. Submissions must have been previously published in the original Scandinavian language. No previously translated material. Original authors should have been born within past 100 years.

ASTED/GRAND PRIX DE LITTERATURE JEUNESSE DU QUEBEC-ALVINE-BELISLE, (III, IV), Association pour l'avancement des sciences et des techniques de la documentation, 1030 rue Cherrier, Bureau 505, Montréal, Québec Canada. (514)521-9561. President: Johanne Petel. "Prize granted for the best work in youth literature edited in French in the Quebec Province. Authors and editors can participate in the contest." Annual competition for fiction and nonfiction for children and young adults. Award: $500. Deadline: June 1. Contest entry limited to editors of books published during the preceding year. French translations of other languages are not accepted.

THE ATHENAEUM LITERARY AWARD, (II, IV), The Athenaeum of Philadelphia, 219 S. 6th St., Philadelphia PA 19106. Contact: Literary Award Committee. Annual award to recognize and encourage outstanding literary achievement in Philadelphia and its vicinity. Award: A bronze medal bearing the name of the award, the seal of the Athenaeum, the title of the book, the name of the author and the year. Judged by committee appointed by Board of Directors. Deadline: December. Submissions must have been published during the preceding year. Nominations shall be made in writing to the Literary Award Committee by the author, the publisher or a member of the Athenaeum, accompanied by a copy of the book. The Athenaeum Literary Award is granted for a work of general literature, not exclusively for fiction. Juvenile fiction is not included.

AWP AWARD SERIES IN THE NOVEL AND SHORT FICTION, (I), The Associated Writing Programs, c/o Old Dominion University, Norfolk VA 23529-0079. Annual award. The AWP Award Series was established in cooperation with several university presses in order to publish and make fine fiction available to a wide audience. Awards: $1,500 honorarium and publication with a university press. In addition, AWP tries to place mss of finalists with participating presses. Judges: Distinguished writers in each genre. Entry fee $10. Contest/award rules for SASE. Deadlines: Manuscript postmarked between January 1-February 29. Only book-length mss in the novel and short story collections are eligible. Manuscripts previously published in their entirety, including self-publishing, are not eligible. No mss returned.

AWP INTRO JOURNALS PROJECT, (IV), Old Dominion University, Norfolk VA 23529-0079. (804)683-3840. Contact: Maggie Anderson. "This is a prize for students in AWP member university creative writing programs only. Authors are nominated by the head of the creative writing department. Each school may send 2 nominated short stories." Annual competition for short stories. Award: $50 plus publication in participating journal. 1993 journals include *New England Review, Puerto del Sol, Indiana Review, Quarterly West, Mid-American Review, Willow Springs* and *Black Warrior Review.* Judges: AWP. Deadline: December 18. Unpublished submissions.

EMILY CLARK BALCH AWARDS, (I), *The Virginia Quarterly Review,* One West Range, Charlottesville VA 22903. Editor: Staige D. Blackford. Annual award "to recognize distinguished short fiction by American writers." For stories published in *The Virginia Quarterly Review* during the calendar year. Award: $500.

MILDRED L. BATCHELDER AWARD, (II), Association for Library Service to Children/American Library Association, 50 E. Huron St., Chicago IL 60611. (312)944-6780. To encourage international exchange of quality children's books by recognizing US publishers of such books in translation. Annual competition for translations. Award: Citation. Judge: Mildred L. Batchelder award committee. Guidelines for SASE. Deadline: December. Books should be US trade publications for which children, up to and including age 14, are potential audience.

GEORGE BENNETT FELLOWSHIP, (I), Phillips Exeter Academy, Exeter NH 03833. (603)772-4311. Coordinator, Selection Committee: Charles Pratt. "To provide time and freedom from monetary concerns to a person contemplating or pursuing a career as a professional writer." Annual award for writing residency. Award: A stipend ($5,000 at present), plus room and board for academic year. Competition receives approximately 130 submissions. Judges are a committee of the English department. Entry fee $5. SASE for application form and guidelines. Deadline: December 1.

BEST FIRST MALICE DOMESTIC NOVEL, (I, IV), Thomas Dunne Books, St. Martin's Press and Macmillan London Ltd., St. Martin's Press, 175 Fifth Ave., New York NY 10010. "To publish a writer's first 'malice domestic novel.'" Annual competition for novels. Award: Publication by St. Martin's Press in the US and Macmillan London in the UK. Advance: $10,000 (and standard royalties). Judges are selected by sponsors. Guidelines for SASE. Deadline: November 1. Unpublished submissions. "Open to any professional or nonprofessional writer who has never published a malice domestic novel and who is not under contract with a publisher to publish one. Malice domestic is a traditional mystery novel that is not hardboiled; emphasis is on the solution rather than the details of the crime. Suspects and victims know one another. In marginal cases, judges will decide whether entry qualifies."

BEST FIRST PRIVATE EYE NOVEL CONTEST, (I, IV), Private Eye Writers of America, St. Martin's Press and Macmillan London Ltd. Thomas Dunne Books, St. Martin's Press, 175 Fifth Ave., New York NY 10010. Annual award. To publish a writer's first "private eye" novel. Award: Publication of novel by St. Martin's Press in the US and Macmillan London in the UK. Advance: $10,000 against royalties (standard contract). Judges are selected by sponsors. Guidelines for SASE. Deadline: August 1. Unpublished submissions. "Open to any professional or nonprofessional writer who has never published a 'private eye' novel and who is not under contract with a publisher for the publication of a 'private eye' novel. As used in the rules, private eye novel means: a novel in which the main character is an independent investigator who is not a member of any law enforcement or government agency."

BEST SHORT STORY REJECTED BY REDBOOK (or other large market), (I), Housewife-Writer's Forum, P.O. Box 780, Lyman WY 82937. (307)786-4513. "To give new fiction writers a chance to have their work recognized." Annual contest for short stories. Awards: $30, $20, $10. Competition receives approx. 75 submissions. Judges: Fiction Editor Bob Haynie and Editor Diane Wolverton. Entry fee: $4. Guidelines for SASE. Unpublished submissions. Any genre except risqué; 2,000 words max. "The title of the contest is just to encourage writers who have found it difficult to break into large markets. Your story doesn't actually have to have been rejected."

IRMA S. AND JAMES H. BLACK CHILDREN'S BOOK AWARD, (II), Bank Street College, 610 W. 112th St., New York NY 10025. (212)663-7200, ext. 587. Children's Librarian: Linda Greengrass. Annual award "to honor the young children's book published in the preceding year judged the most outstanding in text as well as in art. Book must be published the year preceding the May award." Award: Press luncheon at Harvard Club, a scroll and seals by Maurice Sendak for attaching to award book's run. No entry fee. Deadline: January 15. "Write to address above. Usually publishers submit books they want considered, but individuals can too. No entries are returned."

THE BLACK WARRIOR REVIEW **LITERARY AWARD, (II, III),** Box 2936, Tuscaloosa AL 35486. (205)348-4518. Editor: James H.N. Martin. "Award is to recognize the best fiction published in *BWR* in a volume year. Only fiction accepted for publication is considered for the award." Competition is for short stories and novel chapters. Award: $500. Competition receives approximately 1,500 submissions. Prize awarded by an outside judge.

BOARDMAN TASKER PRIZE, (III, IV), 14 Pine Lodge, Dairyground Rd., Bramhall, Stockport, Cheshire SK7 2HS United Kingdom. Contact: Mrs. D. Boardman. "To reward a book which has made an outstanding contribution to mountain literature. A memorial to Peter Boardman and Joe Tasker, who disappeared on Everest in 1982." Award: £1,500. Competition receives approx. 15 submissions. Judges: A panel of 3 judges elected by trustees. Guidelines for SASE or SAE and IRC. Deadline: August 1. Limited to works published or distributed in the UK for the first time between November 1, 1992 and October 31, 1993. Publisher's entry only. "May be fiction, nonfiction, poetry or drama. Not an anthology. The prize is not primarily for fiction though that is not excluded. Subject must be concerned with mountain environment. Previous winners have been books on expeditions, climbing experiences; a biography of a mountaineer; novels."

BOSTON GLOBE-HORN BOOK AWARDS, (II), *Boston Globe* Newspaper, Horn Book Awards, *Horn Book Magazine*, 14 Beacon St., Boston MA 02108. Annual award. "To honor most outstanding children's fiction or poetry, picture and nonfiction books published within the US." Award: $500 first prize in each category; silver plate for the 2 honor books in each category. No entry fee. Entry forms or rules for SASE. Deadline: May 15. Previously published material from July 1-June 30 of previous year.

BRANDEIS UNIVERSITY CREATIVE ARTS AWARDS, (III), Brandeis University, Irving Enclave, Commission Office, Waltham MA 02254-9110. (617)736-3021 or 736-3010. Special Assistants to the President: Mary R. Anderson and Suzanne Yates. Awards "medal to an established artist in celebration of a lifetime of achievement, and a citation to an individual in an earlier stage of his or her career." Awards are made by internal selection only and may not be applied for.

BRAZOS BOOKSTORE (HOUSTON) AWARD (SINGLE SHORT STORY), (II, IV), The Texas Institute of Letters, P.O. Box 9032, Wichita Falls TX 76308. (817)689-4123. Awards Coordinator: James Hoggard. Award to "honor the writer of the best short story published for the first time during the calendar year before the award is given." Annual competition for short stories. Award: $500. Competition receives approx. 40-50 submissions. Judges: Panel selected by TIL Council. Guidelines for SASE. Deadline: January 4. Previously published submissions. Entries must have appeared in print between January 1 and December 31 of the year prior to the award. "Award available to writers who, at some time, have lived in Texas at least two years consecutively or whose work has a significant Texas theme. Entries must be sent directly to the three judges. Their names and addresses are available from the TIL office. Include SASE."

‡THE F.G. BRESSANI PRIZE, (II, IV), Italian Cultural Centre Society, 3075 Slocan Street, Vancouver, B.C. V5M 3E4 Canada. (604)430-3337. Contact: The Literary Committee. Prize "to promote excellence in writing from an ethnic minority viewpoint, to increase appreciation and understanding of Canada's cultural diversity, and to honor an important historical figure F.G. Bressani, the first Italian missionary in Canada." Award granted biannually. Competition for novels and story collections published between July 1, 1992 and June 30, 1994. Award: $500 in prose and poetry categories. Also offers prizes of $250 each for prose and poetry books written in Italian. (Prizes awarded in cooperation with the Istituto Italiano di Cultura.) Judges: "knowledgable people in our community." Guidelines for SASE. Deadline: June 1994. Published submissions. Prize "available to Canadian citizens or landed immigrants to Canada. Books must be written from a viewpoint of any of Canada's ethnic minority groups."

BREVILOQUENCE, (I, IV), *Writer's NW*, 24450 NW Hansen Rd., Hillsboro OR 97124. (503)621-3911. Contact: L. Stovall. "To create—with 99 words or less—a story with all the important elements of the form. Only open to writers in NW—OR, WA, AK, ID, MT and British Columbia." Annual competition for short stories. Award: Books—usually reference. Judges: Editors of newspaper. Entry fee $1. Deadline: May 1. Unpublished submissions.

BUMBERSHOOT WRITTEN WORKS COMPETITION, (I), Seattle's Arts Festival, Box 9750, Seattle WA 98109-0750. (206)622-5123. Editor: Judith Roche. Annual award for short stories. Award: 18 awards of $250 for poetry or literary prose. Winners published in Bumbershoot arts magazine, *Ergo!* and read at Bumbershoot Festival. Judges are professional writers/publishers. Entry forms or rules for SASE. Deadline: Mid-February.

BUNTING INSTITUTE FELLOWSHIP, (I), Mary Ingraham Bunting Institute of Radcliffe College, 34 Concord Ave., Cambridge MA 02138. (617)495-8212. Deadline: Inquire. Women scholars, creative writers, and visual and performing artists are eligible. Scholars must have held the Ph.D. or appropriate terminal degree at least two years prior to appointment (September 1). Non-academic applicants, such as artists, writers, social workers, lawyers, journalists, etc., need to have a significant record of accomplishment and professional experience equivalent to a doctorate and some post-doctoral work. For example, artists must have participated in some group and/or one-person shows; writers must have some published work; other professionals must have some years of work in their respective fields after the appropriate degree. Award: $28,500 stipend for a one-year appointment, September 1-August 31. Private office or studio space is provided, along with access to most Harvard/Radcliffe resources. Fellows are required to present a public lecture or reading in the Institute Colloquium Series or an exhibition in the Institute gallery. Bunting fellows are required to be in residence in the Cambridge/ Boston area for the entire term of appointment. "We do not provide housing." Number of fellowships awarded: 6-8. Applications go through three-stage selection process. In the first stage applications are reviewed by an individual reader in the applicant's field. (Creative writing and visual arts applications go to a relevant first stage committee—i.e., fiction, sculpture, etc.) All applications then go to a second stage committee in the applicant's field (i.e., psychology, literature, etc.), which chooses a small number of finalists. Fellows are chosen from the finalist group by an interdisciplinary final selection committee. Applications are judged on the significance and quality of the project proposal, the applicant's record of accomplishment, and on the difference the fellowship might make in advancing the applicant's career. Rejection letters are sent on a rolling basis, but should be received no later than the beginning of April. Finalists will be notified during the months of January and February. Fellows and alternates will be notified in the beginning of April. "We request that you provide us with the names of your three intended recommenders on the Summary Application Information sheet. We will send you the required forms with your letter of notification and you are requested to have your recommenders send their letters directly to us. We will not contact your recommenders."

BURNABY WRITERS' SOCIETY ANNUAL COMPETITION, (I, IV), 6450 Gilpin St., Burnaby, British Columbia V5G 2J3 Canada. (604)435-6500. Annual competition to encourage creative writing in British Columbia. "Category varies from year to year." Award: $100, $50 and $25 (Canadian) prizes. Receives 400-600 entries for each award. Judge: "Independent recognized professional in the field." Entry fee $5. Contest requirements for SASE. Deadline: May 31. Open to British Columbia authors only.

BUSH ARTIST FELLOWSHIPS, (I, IV), The Bush Foundation, E-900 First Nat'l Bank Building, 332 Minnesota St., St. Paul MN 55101. (612)227-5222. Contact: Sally Dixon, Program Director. "To provide artists of exemplary talent time to work in their chosen art forms." Annual grant. Award: Stipend maximum of $26,000 for 12-18 months, plus a production and travel allowance of $7,000. Competition receives approximately 550 submissions. Judges are writers, critics and editors from outside MN, SD, ND or WI. Applicants must be at least 25 years old, and Minnesota, South Dakota, North Dakota or Western Wisconsin residents. Students not eligible.

BYLINE **MAGAZINE LITERARY AWARDS, (I, IV),** Box 130596, Edmond OK 73013. (405)348-5591. Executive Editor/Publisher: Marcia Preston. "To encourage our subscribers in striving for high quality writing." Annual awards for short stories and poetry. Award: $250 in each category. Judges are published writers not on the *Byline* staff. Entry fee $5 for stories; $3 for poems. Postmark deadline: December 1. "Entries should be unpublished and not have won money in any previous contest. Winners announced in February issue and published in March issue with photo and short bio. Open to subscribers only."

CALIFORNIA WRITERS' CLUB CONTEST, (I, IV), California Writers' Club, 2214 Derby St., Berkeley CA 94705. (510)841-1217. Awards "to encourage writing." Prizes are free tuition to biennial writers' conference and cash. Competition receives varying number of submissions. Judges: Professional writers, members of California Writers' Club. Entry fee to be determined. For the contest rules, write to the Secretary. Deadline is mid-April. Next conference will be July 1993. Unpublished submissions. "Open to anyone who is not, nor has ever been, a member of California Writers' Club."

‡CALIFORNIA WRITERS' ROUNDTABLE ANNUAL WRITING CONTESTS, (I), The Los Angeles Chapter, Women's National Book Association, 11684 Ventura Blvd., Suite 807, Studio City CA 91604-2652. Contact: Lou Carter Keay. Annual competition for short stories. Award: $150 first prize; $75 second prize; $25 third prize. Entry fee $5 to nonmembers of Women's National Book Association. Guidelines for SASE. Deadline: September 30. Previously unpublished submissions. 3,000 word limit. "Manuscripts must be typed, on standard paper, 8½x11 inches. Margins of one inch on all sides. The title of short story must appear on each page, all pages numbered. Send 3 copies of the short story. Include a small envelope with a card containing the author's name, address and phone number, along with the title of short story. Do not put the name of author on the manuscript itself. If you wish one copy of your manuscript returned, include a SASE."

JOHN W. CAMPBELL MEMORIAL AWARD FOR THE BEST SCIENCE-FICTION NOVEL OF THE YEAR; THEODORE STURGEON MEMORIAL AWARD FOR THE BEST SF SHORT FICTION, (II, III), Center for the Study of Science Fiction, English Dept., University of Kansas, Lawrence KS 66045. (913)864-3380. Professor and Director: James Gunn. "To honor the best novel and short science fiction of the year." Annual competition for short stories and novels. Award: Certificate. "Winners' names are engraved on a trophy." Competition receives approx. 50-100 submissions. Judges: 2 separate juries. Deadline: May 1. For previously published submissions. "Ordinarily publishers should submit work, but authors have done so when publishers would not. Send for list of jurors."

CANADA COUNCIL AWARDS, (III, IV), Canada Council, Box 1047, 99 Metcalfe St., Ottawa, Ontario K1P 5V8 Canada. (613)598-4365. The Canada Council sponsors the following awards, for which no applications are accepted. *Canada-Australia Literary Prize*: 1 prize of $3,000, awarded in alternate years to an Australian or Canadian writer for the author's complete work; *Canada-French Community of Belgium Literary Prize*: 1 prize of $3,500, awarded in alternate years to a Canadian or Belgian writer on the basis of the complete works of the writer; *Canada-Switzerland Literary Prize*: 1 prize of $2,500, awarded in alternate years to a Canadian or Swiss writer for a work published in French during the preceding 8 years.

CANADA COUNCIL GOVERNOR GENERAL'S LITERARY AWARDS, (III, IV), Canada Council, Box 1047, 99 Metcalfe St., Ottawa, Ontario K1P 5V8 Canada. (613)598-4376. Contact: Writing and Publishing Section. "Awards of $10,000 each are given annually to the best English-language and best French-language Canadian work in each of seven categories: children's literature (text) and children's literature (illustration), drama, fiction, poetry, nonfiction and translation." All literary works published by Canadians between October 10 and September 30 the following year are considered. Canadian authors, illustrators and translators only. Books must be submitted by publishers and accompanied by a Publisher's Submission Form, available from the Writing and Publishing Section.

CANADIAN AUTHOR STUDENT'S CREATIVE WRITING CONTEST, (I, IV), Suite 500, 275 Slater St., Ottawa, Ontario K1P 5H9 Canada. (613)233-2846. Fax: (613)235-8237. Contact: Diane Kerner. "To encourage writing among secondary school students." Annual competition for short stories. Award: $100 plus $100 to the nominating teacher; $500 to pay for undergraduate education to a worthy student enrolled at a college. Receives 100-120 submissions. Judges: Magazine editors. "Entry form in Winter and Spring issues." Deadline: March. Unpublished submissions. Length: 2,500 words. Writer must be nominated by teacher.

CANADIAN AUTHORS ASSOCIATION LITERARY AWARDS (FICTION), (II, IV), Canadian Authors Association, Suite 500, 275 Slater St., Ottawa, Ontario K1P 5H9 Canada. (613)233-2846. Fax: (613)235-8237. National Director: Jeffrey Holmes. Annual award "to honor writing that achieves literary excellence without sacrificing popular appeal." For novels published during the previous calen-

Discover the Best New Fiction Published in America

"...firmly committed to discovering and showcasing the best new voices in American fiction."

— Richard Currey

Today STORY maintains its tradition of recognizing fresh new writing talent. Each handsomely-bound collection will introduce you to brilliant new authors who promise to be the literary greats of tomorrow, just as it introduced the world to the first works of Salinger, Capote, Mailer, Cheever and others.

Be on hand for the next STORY discovery, and start your subscription to the most widely circulated literary magazine published in America.

dar year. Award: $5,000 plus silver medal. No entry fee. Entry forms or rules for SASE. Deadline: December 15. Restricted to full-length English language novels. Author must be Canadian or Canadian landed immigrant. CAA also sponsors the Air Canada Award, literary awards as above in poetry, nonfiction and drama, and the Vicky Metcalf Awards for children's literature.

CANADIAN LIBRARY ASSOCIATION BOOK OF THE YEAR FOR CHILDREN AWARD, (III, IV), Canadian Library Association, 200 Elgin St., Ottawa, Ontario K2P 1L5 Canada. (613)232-9625. Contact: Membership Services Dept. "To encourage the writing in Canada of good books for children up to and including age 14." Annual competition for short stories and novels for children. Award: A specially designed medal. Competition receives approx. 10-20 submissions/year. Judges: CLA Book of the Year Award Committee. Guidelines for SASE. Deadline: February 1. Book must have been published in Canada during the last year and its author must be Canadian citizen or landed immigrant. Nominations are generally made by CLA membership—a call for nominations is posted in the Association's newsletter in October. "Although the award is sponsored by the Canadian Library Association, it is the Canadian Association of Children's Librarians (a section of Canadian Association of Public Libraries which in turn is a division of CLA) which staffs the Award Committee, selects the winner and administers the award."

‡CAPRICORN BOOK AWARD—FICTION, The Writer's Voice, 5 W. 63rd St., New York NY 10023. (212)875-4124. Annual competition for novels or story collections. Award: $500 and book published through New Rivers Press, plus featured reading. Entry fee $15. Deadline: December 31. Previously unpublished. Submit 100-200 double-spaced pages.

RAYMOND CARVER SHORT STORY CONTEST, (I), Dept. of English, Humboldt State University, Arcata CA 95521-4957. Contact: Coordinator. Annual award for previously unpublished short stories. First prize: $500 and publication in *Toyon*. Second Prize: $250. Entry fee $7.50/story. SASE for rules. Deadline: November. For authors living in United States only. Send 2 copies of story; author's name, address, phone number and title of story on separate cover page only. Story must be no more than 25 pages. Title must appear on first page. For notification of receipt of ms, include self-addressed stamped postcard. For Winners List include SASE.

‡WILLA CATHER FICTION PRIZE, Helicon Nine Editions, 9000 W. 64th Terrace, Merriam KS 66202. (913)722-2999. Contact: Gloria Vando Hickock. Annual competition for novels, story collections and novellas. Award: $1,000. Winners chosen by nationally recognised writers. Entry fee $15. Guidelines for SASE. Deadline December 1. Unpublished submissions. Open to all writers residing in the US and its territories.

THE *CHELSEA* AWARDS, (I), Box 5880, Grand Central Station, New York NY 10163. *Mail entries to*: Richard Foerster, Associate Editor, P.O. Box 1040, York Beach ME 03910. Annual competition for short stories. Prize: $500 and publication in *Chelsea* (all entries are considered for publication). Judges: The editors. Entry fee: $10 (for which entrants also receive a subscription). Guidelines for SASE. Deadline: June 15. Unpublished submissions. Manuscripts may not exceed 30 typed pages or about 7,500 words. The stories must not be under consideration elsewhere or scheduled for book publication within 6 months of the competition deadline.

‡CHILD STUDY CHILDREN'S BOOK AWARD (III, IV), Child Study Children's Book Committee at Bank St. College, 610 W. 112th St., New York NY 10025. Contact: Anita Wilkes Dore, Committee Chair. Annual award. "To honor a book for children or young people which deals realistically with problems in their world. It may concern social, individual and ethical problems." Only books sent by publishers for review are considered. No personal submissions. Books must have been published within current calendar year. Award: Certificate and cash prize.

THE CHILDREN'S BOOK AWARD, (II), Federation of Children's Book Groups, 30 Senneleys Park Rd., Northfield, Birmingham B31 1AL England. Award "to promote the publication of good quality books for children." Annual award for short stories, novels, story collections and translations. Award: "Portfolio of children's writing and drawings and a magnificent trophy of silver and oak." Judges: Thousands of children from all over the United Kingdom. Guidelines for SASE. Deadline: December 31. Published and previously unpublished submissions (first publication in UK). "The book should be suitable for children."

THE CHRISTOPHER AWARD, (II), The Christophers, 12 E. 48th St., New York NY 10017. (212)759-4050. Contact: Ms. Peggy Flanagan, awards coordinator. Annual award "to encourage creative people to continue to produce works which affirm the highest values of the human spirit in adult and children's books." Published submissions only. Award: Bronze medallion. "Award judged by a grassroots panel and a final panel of experts. Juvenile works are 'children tested.' " Examples of books awarded: *Dear Mr. Henshaw*, by Beverly Cleary (ages 8-10); *Sarah, Plain and Tall*, by Patricia MacLachlan (ages 10-12).

CINTAS FELLOWSHIP, (I, IV), Cintas Foundation/Arts International Program of I.I.E., 809 U.N. Plaza, New York NY 10017. (212)984-5564. Contact: Vanessa Palmer. "To foster and encourage the professional development and recognition of talented Cuban creative artists. *Not* intended for furtherance of academic or professional study, nor for research or writings of a scholarly nature." Annual competition for authors of short stories, novels, story collections and poetry. 12 awards of $10,000 each. Fellowship receives approx. 40 literature applicants/year. Judges: Selection committee. Guidelines for SASE. Deadline: March 2. Previously published or unpublished submissions. Limited to artists of Cuban lineage *only*. "Awards are given to artists in the following fields: visual arts, literature, music composition and architecture."

CITY OF REGINA WRITING AWARD, (I, IV), City of Regina Arts Commission, Saskatchewan Writers Guild, Box 3986, Regina, Saskatchewan S4P 3R9 Canada. (306)757-6310. "To enable a writer to work for 3 months on a specific writing project; to reward merit in writing." Annual competition for short stories, novels and story collections. Award: $3,300. Competition receives approx. 21 submissions. Judges: Selection committee of SWG. Guidelines for SASE. Deadline: Mid-March. Unpublished submissions. "Grant available only to residents of Regina for previous year."

COMMONWEALTH CLUB OF CALIFORNIA, (II, IV), California Book Awards, 595 Market St., San Francisco CA 94105. (415)543-3353. Contact: James D. Rosenthal, Executive Director. Main contest established in 1931. Annually. "To encourage California writers and honor literary merit." Awards: Gold and silver medals. Judges: Jury of literary experts. For books published during the year preceding the particular contest. Three copies of book and a completed entry form required. "Write or phone asking for the forms. Either an author or publisher may enter a book. We usually receive over 200 entries."

CONNECTICUT COMMISSION ON THE ARTS ARTIST GRANTS, (I, II, IV), 227 Lawrence St., Hartford CT 06106. (203)566-4770. Senior Program Associate: Linda Dente. "To support the creation of new work by a creative artist *living in Connecticut*." Biennial competition for the creation or completion of new works in literature, i.e. short stories, novels, story collections, poetry and playwriting. Award: $5,000. Judges: Peer professionals (writers, editors). Guidelines available in August. Deadline: January 1994. Writers may send either previously published or unpublished submissions—up to 10 pages of material. Connecticut residents only.

CONSEIL DE LA VIE FRANCAISE EN AMÉRIQUE/PRIX CHAMPLAIN (The Champlain Prize), (II, IV), Conseil de la vie française en amérique, 56 rue St-Pierre 1er étage, Québec G1K 4A1 Canada. Prix Champlain estab. 1957. Annual award to encourage literary work in novel or short story in French by Francophiles living outside Québec and in the US or Canada. "There is no restriction as to the subject matter. If the author lives in Quebec, the subject matter must be related to French-speaking people living outside of Quebec." Award: $1,500 in Canadian currency. The prize will be given alternately; one year for fiction, the next for nonfiction. Next fiction award in 1993. 3 different judges each year. Deadline: December 31. For previously published or contracted submissions, published no more than 3 years prior to award. Author must furnish 4 examples of work, curriculum vitae, address and phone number.

CRIME WRITERS' ASSOCIATION AWARDS, (III, IV), Box 172, Tring Herts HP23 5LP England. Six awards. Annual award for crime novels. Competition receives varied amount of submissions. Deadline: October 1. Published submissions in UK in current year. Book must be nominated by UK publishers.

‡*THE CRITIC* BIANNUAL SHORT STORY CONTEST, (I), *The CRITIC* magazine Thomas More Association, 205 W. Monroe, 6th Fl., Chicago IL 60606-5097. (312)609-8880. "To foster original fiction (short story) writing by new or established writers." Biannual competition for short stories. Award: $1,000. Competition receives approx. 250-300 submissions. Judges: Editorial staff of the Thomas More Association. Guidelines for SASE. Next contest in 1994. Deadline September 1 or 15, 1994. Previously unpublished. "No regional restrictions or word-length requirements, but entrants should be aware that *The CRITIC* is a Catholic, cultural and literary magazine."

THE *CRUCIBLE* POETRY AND FICTION COMPETITION, *Crucible*, Barton College, College Station, Wilson NC 27893. Annual competition for short stories. Award: $150 for first prize; $100 for second prize and publication in *Crucible*. Judges: The editors. Guidelines for SASE. Deadline April. Unpublished submissions. Fiction should be 8,000 words or less.

DALY CITY POETRY AND SHORT STORY CONTEST, (I), Daly City History, Arts, and Science Commission, % Serramonte Library, 40 Wembley Dr., Daly City CA 94015. (415)991-8025. Contest coordinator: Ruth Hoppin. "To encourage poets and writers and to recognize and reward excellence." Annual competition for short stories. Awards: $35, $20, $10 and $5. Competition receives 50 submissions. Judges are usually teachers of creative writing. Entry fee: $2/story. Guidelines for SASE. Deadline Jan. 2. Unpublished submissions. Length: 3,000 words maximum. "No profanity."

‡MARGUERITE DE ANGELI PRIZE, (I), Doubleday Books for Young Readers, 666 Fifth Ave., New York NY 10103. "To encourage the writing of fiction that examines the diversity of the American experience in the same spirit as the works of Marguerite de Angeli." Annual competition for first novels for middle-grade readers. Award: One Doubleday hardcover and Dell paperback book contract, with $1,500 cash prize and a $3,500 advance against royalties. Judges: Editors of Doubleday BFYR. Guidelines for SASE. Deadline: Submissions postmarked between April 1 and June 30. Previously unpublished (middle-grade) fiction.

DEEP SOUTH WRITERS CONFERENCE ANNUAL COMPETITION, (I), DSWC Inc., English Dept., University of Southwestern Louisiana, Box 44691, Lafayette LA 70504. (318)231-6908. Contact: Carl Wooton, director. Annual awards "to encourage aspiring, unpublished writers." Awards: Certificates and cash plus possible publication of shorter works. Contest rules for SASE and addition to mailing list. Deadline: July 15. Unpublished submissions.

DELACORTE PRESS ANNUAL PRIZE FOR A FIRST YOUNG ADULT NOVEL (I), Delacorte Press, Department BFYR, 666 Fifth Ave., New York NY 10103. (212)765-6500. Estab. 1983. Annual award "to encourage the writing of contemporary young adult fiction." Award: Contract for publication of book; $1,500 cash prize and a $6,000 advance against royalties. Judges are the editors of Delacorte Press Books for Young Readers. Contest rules for SASE. Unpublished submissions; fiction with a contemporary setting that will be suitable for ages 12-18. Deadline: December 31 (no submissions accepted prior to Labor Day). Writers may be previously published, but cannot have published a young adult novel before.

DELAWARE STATE ARTS COUNCIL, (I, IV), 820 N. French St., Wilmington DE 19801. (302)577-3540. Coordinator: Barbara R. King. "To help further careers of emerging and established professional artists." Annual awards for Delaware residents only. Awards: $5,000 for established professionals; $2,000 for emerging professionals. Judges are out-of-state professionals in each division. Entry forms or rules for SASE. Deadline: March 2.

JOHN DOS PASSOS PRIZE FOR LITERATURE, (III, IV), Longwood College, Farmville VA 23909. (804)395-2155. "The John Dos Passos Prize for Literature annually commemorates one of the greatest of 20th-century American authors by honoring other writers in his name." Award: A medal and $1,000. "The winner, announced each fall in ceremonies at the college, is chosen by an independent jury charged especially to seek out American creative writers in the middle stages of their careers—men and women who have established a substantial body of significant publication, and particularly those whose work demonstrates one or more of the following qualities, all characteristics of the art of the

Market categories: (I) Unpublished entries; (II) Published entries nominated by the author; (III) Published entries, nominated by the editor, publisher or nominating body; (IV) Specialized entries.

man for whom the prize is named: an intense and original exploration of specifically American themes; an experimental tone; and/or writing in a wide range of literature forms." Application for prize is by nomination only.

***DREAMS & VISIONS*: BEST SHORT STORY OF THE YEAR, (I, IV)**, Skysong Press, RR1, Washago, Ontario L0K 2B0 Canada. Contact: Steve Stanton. The "competition serves the dual purpose of rewarding literary excellence among the authors published in *Dreams & Visions*, and of providing feedback from subscribers as to the type of literature they prefer." Annual award for short stories. Award: $100. "Only the 21 stories published in *Dreams & Visions* each year are eligible for the award." Judges: Subscribers to *Dreams & Visions*. Guidelines for SASE. Unpublished submissions. Sample copy $3.95.

EATON LITERARY ASSOCIATES' LITERARY AWARDS PROGRAM, (I), Eaton Literary Associates, Box 49795, Sarasota FL 34230. (813)366-6589. Vice President: Richard Lawrence. Biannual award for short stories and novels. Award: $2,500 for best book-length ms, $500 for best short story. Competition receives approximately 2,000 submissions annually. Judges are 2 staff members in conjunction with an independent agency. Entry forms or rules for SASE. Deadline is March 31 for short stories; August 31 for book-length mss.

‡EPIPHANY SHORT FICTION CONTEST, *Epiphany A Journal of Literature*, P.O. Box 2699, University of Arkansas, Fayetteville AR 72701. Send entries to: Epiphany Short-Fiction Contest, 408 E. Tulsa Siloom Springs, AR 72761. "To recognize and award writers of fiction." Biannual award for short stories. Award: $250/1st, $150/2nd prize; $100 3rd prize. *Epiphany* staff judges the best 15. Creative writing professors from 5 schools judge the three best out of 15. Entry fee $5. Guidelines for SASE. Deadline: June 1 through December 30.

EYSTER PRIZES, (II), *The New Delta Review*, LSU/Dept. of English, Baton Rouge LA 70803. (504)388-5922. Editor: Janet Wondra. "To honor author and teacher Warren Eyster, who served as advisor to *New Delta Review* predecessors *Manchac* and *Delta*." Semiannual awards for best short story and best poem in each issue. Award: $50 and 2 free copies of publication. Competition receives approximately 400 submissions/issue. Judges are published authors. Deadline: September 1 for fall, February 15 for spring.

‡FANTASTIC FOUR SHORT STORY WRITING CONTESTS, *The Fiction Writer*, % Prudy Taylor Board, 1617 Francis St., North Ft. Meyers FL 33903. Annual competition for short stories. Judges: The editors of *The Fiction Writer*. Entry fee free for subscribers, $5 for non-subscribers. Guidelines for SASE. Deadline Contest 1: December; Contest 2: March 1; Contest 3: June; Contest 4: September. Previously unpublished submissions. Length: 1,500 words. Four contests: Contest #1: The A la Barbara Cartland Love Story. Entries must be love stories. Those written in the style of famed romance writer Barbara Cartland will be eligible for bonus awards; Contest #2: The Just Like James Herriott Animal Tales. Entries must be about animals. Those written in the style of English veterinarian James Herriott will be eligible for bonus awards. Contest #3: Crime Time a la John D. MacDonald. Entries must be crime/detection stories. Those written in the style of John D. MacDonald will be eligible for bonus awards. Contest #4: The Ghastly, Ghostly Journal of Poe. Entries must be ghost or horror tales. Those written in the style of Edgar Allan Poe will be eligible for bonus awards.

ROBERT L. FISH MEMORIAL AWARD, (II), Mystery Writers of America, Inc., 6th Floor, 17 E. 47th St., New York NY 10017. Estab. 1984. Annual award "to encourage new writers in the mystery/detective/suspense short story—and, subsequently, larger work in the genre." Award: $500. Judges: The MWA committee for best short story of the year in the mystery genre. Deadline: December 1. Previously published submissions published the year prior to the award. Looking for "a story with a crime that is central to the plot that is well written and distinctive."

DOROTHY CANFIELD FISHER AWARD, (III), Vermont Congress of Parents and Teachers, % Southwest Regional Library, Pierpoint Avenue, Rutland VT 05701. (802)828-3261. Contact: Grace Green, chairperson. Estab. 1957. Annual award. "To encourage Vermont schoolchildren to become enthusiastic and discriminating readers and to honor the memory of one of Vermont's most distinguished and beloved literary figures." Award: Illuminated scroll. Publishers send the committee review copies of books to consider. Only books of the current publishing year can be considered for next year's award. Master list of titles is drawn up in late February or March each year. Children vote each year in the spring and the award is given before the school year ends. Submissions must be "written by living American authors, be suitable for children in grades 4-8, and have literary merit. Can be nonfiction also."

FLORIDA ARTS COUNCIL/LITERATURE FELLOWSHIPS, (I, IV), Division of Cultural Affairs, Dept. of State, The Capitol, Tallahassee FL 32399-0250. (904)487-2980. Director: Ms. Peyton C. Fearington. "To allow Florida artists time to develop their artistic skills and enhance their careers." Annual award for fiction or poetry. Award: $5,000. Competition receives approximately 100 submissions/year. Judges are review panels made up of individuals with a demonstrated interest in literature. Entry forms for SASE. Deadline: January 17. Entry restricted to practicing, professional writers who are legal residents of Florida and have been living in the state for 12 consecutive months at the time of the deadline.

FLORIDA STATE WRITING COMPETITION, (I), Florida Freelance Writers Association, Box 9844, Fort Lauderdale FL 33310. (305)485-0795. "To offer additional opportunities for writers to earn income from their stories." Annual competition for short stories and novels. Award: Varies from $50-150. Competition receives approx. 300 short stories; 125 novels. Judges: Authors, editors and teachers. Entry fee from $5-15. Guidelines for SASE. Deadline: March 15. Unpublished submissions. Categories include literary, sf/fantasy, genre and novel chapter. Length: 7,500 words maximum. "Guidelines are revised each year and subject to change."

FOUNDATION FOR THE ADVANCEMENT OF CANADIAN LETTERS AUTHOR'S AWARDS, (II, IV), In conjunction with Periodical Marketers of Canada (PMC), Suite 503, 2 Berkeley St., Toronto, Ontario M5A 2W3 Canada. (416)363-8779. Award Coordinators: Ray Argyle, Janette Hatcher. "To recognize outstanding Canadian writing and design." Annual award for short stories, novels. Previous competition judged by an independent panel. Deadline: July 15. "Must be published in a Canadian 'mass market' publication."

MILES FRANKLIN LITERARY AWARD, (II, IV), Arts Management Pty. Ltd., 56 Kellett St., Potts Point, NSW 2011 Australia. Awards Coordinator: Hilary Shrubb. "For the advancement, improvement and betterment of Australian literature." Annual award for novels. Award: AUS $25,000, to the author. Guidelines for SASE. Deadline: Jan. 31. Previously published submissions. "The novel must have been published in the year of competition entry, and must present Australian life in any of its phases."

‡FRIENDS OF AMERICAN WRITERS AWARDS, (III, IV), #10A, 1440 N. Lakeshore Dr., Chicago IL 60610. Contact: President. "To encourage high standards and to promote literary ideals among American writers." Annual award for prose writing. Awards: $1,200 (1st prize) and $750 (2nd prize). Competition receives 50 entries. Judges: a committee of 14. Deadline: December 31. Manuscripts must have been published during current year. Limited to midwestern authors who have previously published no more than 3 books; or to authors of books set in the midwest and have not published more than 3 books previously. Two copies of the book are to be submitted to awards chairman by the publisher of the book. Young Peoples' books awards judged by committee of 9. Awards: $700 (1st prize); $400 (2nd prize). Same limitations.

GEORGIA COUNCIL FOR THE ARTS INDIVIDUAL ARTIST GRANTS, (I, IV), Suite 115, 530 Means Street, N.W., Atlanta GA 30318. (404)651-7920. Contact: Martha Evans. Annual award for "artist's option for creation of new work." Award: $5,000 maximum. Competition receives approx. 125 submissions. Judges: Professional advisory panel. Guidelines for SASE. Deadline April 1. "Support material must be current within past two years; application must be for new work. Artist must be resident of Georgia for at least one year prior to application date."

GOLD MEDALLION BOOK AWARDS, (III, IV), Evangelical Christian Publishers Association, Suite 101, 3225 S. Hardy Dr., Tempe AZ 85282. (602)966-3998. Executive Director of ECPA: Doug Ross. Annual award to "encourage excellence in evangelical Christian book publishing in 21 categories." Judges: "At least eight judges for each category chosen from among the ranks of evangelical leaders and book-review editors." Entry fee $100 for ECPA member publishers; $250 for non-member publishers. Deadline: December 1. For books published the previous year: Publishers submit entries.

THE WILLIAM GOYEN PRIZE FOR FICTION, (I), *TriQuarterly Magazine*, 2020 Ridge Ave., Evanston IL 60208-4302. (708)491-7614. Editorial Assistant: Gwenan Wilbur. "To award outstanding fiction; to bring recognition to newer/lesser-known writers." Biennial award for novels. Award: $3,000 and publication by TriQuarterly Books/Another Chicago Press. Competition receives approx. 250 submissions. Entry fee $15, includes 1-year subscription; $5 for current subscribers. Guidelines for SASE. Deadline: June 1-30. "Mss should be 150-400 pages in length, double-spaced. Original works in English and translations into English are eligible. Enclose SASE for return of your manuscript and our reply. Entry fee subject to change."

GREAT LAKES COLLEGES ASSOCIATION NEW WRITERS AWARDS, (III), Great Lakes Colleges Association, Wabash College, Crawfordsville IN 47933. Director: Marc Hudson. Annual award "to recognize new young writers; promote and encourage interest in good literature." For first books published "during the year preceding each year's February 28 deadline for entry, or the following spring." Award: "Invited tour of up to 12 Great Lakes Colleges (usually 7 or 8) with honoraria and expenses paid." Award judged by critics and writers in residence at Great Lakes Colleges Association colleges and universities. Entry form or rules for SASE. "Entries in fiction (there is also a poetry section) must be first novels or first volumes of short stories already published, and must be submitted (four copies) *by publishers only*—but this may include privately published books."

GREAT PLAINS STORYTELLING & POETRY READING CONTEST, (I,II), Box 438, Walnut IA 51577. (712)784-3001. Director: Robert Everhart. Estab. 1976. Annual award "to provide an outlet for writers to present not only their works, but also to provide a large audience for their presentation *live* by the writer. Attendance at the event, which takes place annually in Avoca, Iowa, is *required*." Award: 1st prize $75; 2nd prize $50; 3rd prize $25; 4th prize $15; and 5th prize $10. Entry fee: $5. Entry forms or rules for SASE. Deadline: Day of contest, which takes place over Labor Day Weekend. Previously published or unpublished submissions.

THE GREENSBORO REVIEW LITERARY AWARDS, (I), Dept. of English, UNC-Greensboro, Greensboro NC 27412. (919)334-5459. Editor: Jim Clark. Annual award. Award: $250. Contest rules for SASE. Deadline: September 15. Unpublished submissions.

HACKNEY LITERARY AWARDS, (I), Box A-3, Birmingham Southern College, Birmingham AL 35254. (205)226-4921. Contact: Special Events Office. Annual award for previously unpublished short stories, poetry and novels. Rules/entry form for SASE. Novel submissions must be postmarked on or before September 30. Short stories and poetry submissions must be postmarked on or before December 31.

‡HAMMETT PRIZE (NORTH AMERICAN), (II), International Association of Crime Writers, North American Branch, JAF Box 1500, New York NY 10116. (212)757-3915. Award to promote "excellence in the field of crime writing as reflected in a book published in the English language in the US and/or Canada." Annual competition for novels or nonfiction. Award: trophy. Competition receives approx. 150 submissions. Judges: Nominations committee made up of IACW members screens titles and selects 3-5 nominated books. These go to three outside judges, who choose the winner. Guidelines for SASE. Deadline December 1. Previously published submissions. Published entries must have appeared in print between January 1 and December 31 (of contest year). "Writers must be US or Canadian citizens or permanent residents working in the field of crime writing (either fiction or nonfiction). No word-length requirement."

BAXTER HATHAWAY PRIZE, (I), *Epoch Magazine*, 251 Goldwin Smith, Cornell University, Ithaca NY 14853-3201. (607)255-3385. Contact: Michael Koch. Award "to honor the memory of Baxter Hathaway, founder of *Epoch*, and to encourage new poets and fiction writers." Biennial award for a novella or long poem, depending on the year (1992, long poem; 1994, novella). Award: $1,000 and publication in *Epoch*. Competition receives 400+ submissions. Judge: A distinguished outsider. Guidelines for SASE. Sample copies with past winners for $4 each. Unpublished submissions. "Limited to writers who have published not more than one book of fiction or poetry (chapbooks excluded)."

DRUE HEINZ LITERATURE PRIZE, (II), University of Pittsburgh Press, 127 N. Bellefield Ave., Pittsburgh PA 15260. (412)624-4110. Annual award "to support the writer of short fiction at a time when the economics of commercial publishing make it more and more difficult for the serious literary artist working in the short story and novella to find publication." Award: $7,500 and publication by the University of Pittsburgh Press. Request complete rules of the competition before submitting a manuscript. Submissions will be received only during the months of July and August. Deadline: August 31. Manuscripts must be unpublished in book form. The award is open to writers who have published a book-length collection of fiction or a minimum of three short stories or novellas in commercial magazines or literary journals of national distribution.

HEMINGWAY DAYS SHORT STORY COMPETITION, (I), Hemingway Days Festival, Box 4045, Key West FL 33041. (305)294-4440. "To honor Nobel laureate Ernest Hemingway, who was often pursued during his lifetime by young writers hoping to learn the secrets of his success." Annual competition for short stories. Award: $1000—1st; $500—2nd; $500—3rd. Competition receives approx. 900 submissions. Judges: Panel lead by Lorian Hemingway, granddaughter of Ernest Hemingway and novelist based out of Seattle, WA. Entry fee $10/story. Deadline: July 1. "Open to anyone so long as the work is unpublished. No longer than 2,500 words." Send SASE for guidelines.

ERNEST HEMINGWAY FOUNDATION AWARD, (II), PEN American Center, 568 Broadway, New York NY 10012. Contact: John Morrone, coordinator of programs. Annual award "to give beginning writers recognition and encouragement and to stimulate interest in first novels among publishers and readers." Award: $7,500. Novels or short story collections must have been published during calendar year under consideration. Entry form or rules for SASE. Deadline: December 31. "The Ernest Hemingway Foundation Award is given to an American author of the best first-published book-length work of fiction published by an established publishing house in the US each calendar year."

THE O. HENRY AWARDS, (III), Doubleday, 666 Fifth Ave., New York NY 10103. Associate Editor: Arabella Meyer. Annual award "to honor the memory of O. Henry with a sampling of outstanding short stories and to make these stories better known to the public." These awards are published by Doubleday in hardcover and by Anchor Books in paperback every spring. Previously published submissions. "All selections are made by the editor of the volume, William Abrahams. No stories may be submitted."

HIGHLIGHTS FOR CHILDREN, **(I, IV)**, 803 Church St., Honesdale PA 18431. Editor: Kent L. Brown, Jr. "To honor quality stories (previously unpublished) for young readers." Three $1,000 awards. Stories: up to 600 words for beginning readers (to age 8) and 900 words for more advanced readers (ages 9 to 12). No minimum word length. No entry form necessary. To be submitted between January 1 and February 28 to "Fiction Contest" at address above. "No violence, crime or derogatory humor." Nonwinning entries returned in June if SASE is included with ms. "This year's category is sports stories for children." Send SASE for information.

THE ALFRED HODDER FELLOWSHIP, (II), The Council of the Humanities, Princeton University, 122 E. Pyne, Princeton NJ 08544. Executive Director: Carol Rigolot. "This fellowship is awarded for the pursuit of independent work in the humanities. The recipient is usually a writer or scholar in the early stages of his or her career, a person 'with more than ordinary learning' and with 'much more than ordinary intellectual and literary gifts.' " Traditionally, the Hodder Fellow has been a humanist outside of academia. Candidates for the Ph.D. are not eligible. Award: $38,000. The Hodder Fellow spends an academic year in residence at Princeton working independently. Judges: Princeton Committee on Humanistic studies. Guidelines for SASE. Deadline November 15. "Applicants must submit a résumé, a sample of previous work (10 page maximum, not returnable), and a project proposal of 2 to 3 pages. Letters of recommendation are not required."

THEODORE CHRISTIAN HOEPFNER AWARD, (I), *Southern Humanities Review*, 9088 Haley Center, Auburn University AL 36849. Contact: Dan R. Latimer or R.T. Smith, co-editors. Annual. "To award the authors of the best essay, the best short story and the best poem published in *SHR* each year." Award: $100 for the best short story. Judges: Editorial staff. Unpublished submissions to the magazine only. Only published work in the current volume (4 issues) will be judged.

HONOLULU **MAGAZINE/PARKER PEN COMPANY FICTION CONTEST, (I, IV)**, *Honolulu* Magazine, 36 Merchant St., Honolulu HI 96813. (808)524-7400. Editor: Ed Cassidy. "We do not accept fiction except during our annual contest, at which time we welcome it." Annual award for short stories. Award: $1,000 and publication in the April issue of *Honolulu* Magazine. Competition receives approximately 400 submissions. Judges: Panel of well-known Hawaii-based writers. Rules for SASE. Deadline: December 9. "Stories must have a Hawaii theme, setting and/or characters. Author should enclose name and address in separate small envelope. Do not put name on story."

L. RON HUBBARD'S WRITERS OF THE FUTURE CONTEST, (I, IV), P.O. Box 1630, Los Angeles CA 90078. Contest Administrator: Rachel Denk. Estab. 1984. Quarterly. "To find, reward and publicize new speculative fiction writers, so that they may more easily attain professional writing careers." Competition open to new and amateur writers of short stories or novelettes of science fiction or fantasy. Awards: 1st prize, $1,000; 2nd prize, $750; 3rd prize, $500. Annual grand prize $4,000. SASE for contest rules. Deadline: September 30. Unpublished submissions.

THE 'HUGO' AWARD (Science Fiction Achievement Award), (III, IV), The World Science Fiction Convention, c/o Howard DeVore, 4705 Weddel St., Dearborn Heights MI 48125. Temporary; address changes each year. "To recognize the best writing in various categories related to science fiction and fantasy." Award: Metal spaceship 15 inches high. "Winning the award almost always results in reprints of the original material and increased payment. Winning a 'Hugo' in the novel category frequently results in additional payment of $10,000-20,000 from future publishers." The award is voted on by ballot by the members of the World Science Fiction Convention from previously published material of professional publications. Writers may not nominate their own work.

ILLINOIS STATE UNIVERSITY NATIONAL FICTION COMPETITION, (I), Illinois State University/Fiction Collective, English Dept., Illinois State University, Normal IL 61761. (309)438-3025. Curtis White, series editor. Annual award for novels, novellas and story collections. Award: Publication. Competition receives approximately 150 submissions each year. Judges different each year. Entry fee $10. Deadline November 15. Entry forms or rules for SASE.

INTERNATIONAL JANUSZ KORCZAK LITERARY COMPETITION, (II, IV), Joseph H. and Belle R. Braun Center for Holocaust Studies Anti-Defamation League of B'nai B'rith, 823 United Nations Plaza, New York NY 10017. (212)490-2525. Contact: Dr. Dennis B. Klein, director. For published novels, novellas, translations, short story collections. "Books for or about children which best reflect the humanitarianism and leadership of Janusz Korczak, a Jewish and Polish physician, educator and author." Deadline: Inquire.

INTERNATIONAL READING ASSOCIATION CHILDREN'S BOOK AWARDS, (II), Sponsored by IRA/ Institute for Reading Research, Box 8139, 800 Barksdale Rd., Newark DE 19714-8139. (302)731-1600. Annual award to encourage an author who shows unusual promise in the field of children's books. Two awards will be given for a first or second book in two categories: one for literature for older children, 10-16 years old; one for literature for younger children, 4-10 years old. Award: $1,000 stipend. No entry fee. Contest/award rules and awards flyer available for IRA. Deadline: December 1. Submissions must have been published during the calendar year prior to the year in which the award is given. Send 10 copies of book to Eileen Burke, 48 Bayberry Rd., Trenton NJ 08618.

IOWA SCHOOL OF LETTERS AWARD FOR SHORT FICTION, THE JOHN SIMMONS SHORT FICTION AWARD, (I), Iowa Writers' Workshop, 436 English-Philosophy Building, The University of Iowa, Iowa City IA 52242. Annual awards for short story collections. To encourage writers of short fiction. Two awards of $1,000 each, plus publication of winning collections by University of Iowa Press the following fall. Entries must be at least 150 pages, typewritten, and submitted between Aug. 1 and Sept. 30. Stamped, self-addressed return packaging must accompany manuscript. Rules for SASE. Iowa Writer's Workshop does initial screening of entries; finalists (about 6) sent to outside judge for final selection. "A different well-known writer is chosen each year as judge. Any writer who has not previously published a volume of prose fiction is eligible to enter the competition for these prizes. Revised manuscripts which have been previously entered may be resubmitted."

‡IOWA WOMAN CONTEST, INTERNATIONAL WRITING CONTEST, P.O. Box 2938, Waterloo IA 50704. Annual award for short fiction, poetry and essays. Awards first place of $300; second place $150, in each category; $100 bonus if an Iowa writer wins. Judges: anonymous, women writers who have published work in the category. Entry fee: (Subscriber) — $5 for one story, essay or up to 3 poems; (Non-subscriber) — $10 for one story, essay, or up to 3 poems. Guidelines available for SASE. Deadline is December 31. Previously unpublished submissions *only*. Limited to women writers, with a 6,500 word limit on fiction and essays. "Submit typed or computer printed manuscripts with a cover sheet listing category, title, name, address and phone number. A single cover sheet per category is sufficient. Identify actual entry by title only. Do not identify author on the manuscript. Manuscripts cannot be returned; do not send SASE for return."

JOSEPH HENRY JACKSON AWARD, (I, IV), The San Francisco Foundation, Suite 910, 685 Market St., San Francisco CA 94105. Contact: Awards Program Coordinator. Annual competition "to award the author of an unpublished work-in-progress of fiction (novel or short stories), nonfiction or poetry." Award: $2,000 and award certificate. Entry form and rules available after November 1 for SASE. Deadline: January 15. Unpublished submissions only. Applicant must be resident of northern California or Nevada for 3 consecutive years immediately prior to the deadline date. Age of applicant must be 20 through 35.

JAPANOPHILE **SHORT STORY CONTEST, (I, IV),** *Japanophile*, Box 223, Okemos MI 48864. (517)669-2109. Contact: Earl R. Snodgrass, editor. Estab. 1972. Annual award "to encourage quality writing on Japan-America understanding." Award: $100 plus possible publication. Entry fee: $10. Send $4 for sample copy of magazine. Contest rules for SASE. Deadline: December 31. Prefers unpublished submissions. Stories should involve Japanese and non-Japanese characters.

JAPAN-UNITED STATES FRIENDSHIP COMMISSION PRIZE FOR THE TRANSLATION OF JAPANESE LITERATURE, (I, II, IV), The Donald Keene Center of Japanese Culture, 407 Kent Hall, Columbia University, New York NY 10027. (212)854-5036. Contact: Victoria Lyon-Bestor. "To encourage fine translations of Japanese literature and to award and encourage young translators to develop that craft." Annual competition for translations only. Award: $2,500 each for the best translation of a modern work of literature and for the best classical literary translation. Competition receives approx. 15 submissions. Judges: A jury of writers, literary agents, critics and scholar/translators. Guidelines for SASE. Deadline: December 31 postmark. Previously published or unpublished submissions. "Translators must be American citizens."

JESSE JONES AWARD FOR FICTION (BOOK), (I, IV), The Texas Institute of Letters, P.O. Box 9032, Wichita Falls TX 76308. (817)689-4123. Awards Coordinator: James Hoggard. "To honor the writer of the best novel or collection of short fiction published during the calendar year before the award is given." Annual award for novels or story collections. Award: $6,000. Competition receives approx. 30-40 entries per year. Judges: Panel selected by TIL Council. Guidelines for SASE. Deadline: January 4. Previously published fiction, which must have appeared in print between January 1 and December 31 of the prior year. "Award available to writers who, at some time, have lived in Texas at least two years consecutively or whose work has a significant Texas theme."

THE JANET HEIDINGER KAFKA PRIZE, (II, IV), University of Rochester, Susan B. Anthony Center and English Dept., 538 Lattimore Hall, Rochester NY 14627. (716)275-8318. Award for fiction by an American woman. Annual competition for short story collections and novels. Award: $1,000. Judges: Kafka Committee. Guidelines for SASE. Deadline: December 31. Recently published submissions. American women only.

KANSAS QUARTERLY/KANSAS ARTS COMMISSION AWARDS, (I),* *Kansas Quarterly*, 122 Denison Hall, Dept. of English, Kansas State University, Manhattan KS 66506-0703. Contact: Editors. Annual awards "to reward and recognize the best fiction published in *Kansas Quarterly* during the year from authors anywhere in the US or abroad. Anyone who submits unpublished material which is then accepted for publication becomes eligible for the awards." Award: Recognition and monetary sums of $250, $200, $100, $50. "Ours are not 'contests'; they are monetary awards and recognition given by persons of national literary stature." Fiction judges recently have included David Bradley, James B. Hall, Gordon Weaver and Mary Morris. No deadline; material simply may be submitted for consideration at any time. Include SASE.

ROBERT F. KENNEDY BOOK AWARDS, (II, IV), 1206 30th St., NW, Washington DC 20007. (202)333-1880. Endowed by Arthur Schlesinger, Jr., from proceeds of his biography, *Robert Kennedy and His Times*. Annual. "To award the author of a book which most faithfully and forcefully reflects Robert Kennedy's purposes." For books published during the calendar year. Award: $2,500 cash prize awarded in the spring. Deadline: January 4. Looking for "a work of literary merit in fact or fiction that shows compassion for the poor or powerless or those suffering from injustice." Four copies of each book submitted should be sent, along with a $25 entry fee.

KENTUCKY ARTS COUNCIL, KENTUCKY ARTISTS FELLOWSHIPS, (I, IV), 31 Fountain Place, Frankfort KY 40601. (502)564-3757. "To encourage and assist the professional development of Kentucky artists." Writing fellowships offered every other year in fiction, poetry, playwriting. Award: $5,000.

Competition received approximately "211 submissions in 1992 in all writing categories." Judges are out-of-state panelists (writers, editors, playwrights, etc.) of distinction. Open only to Kentucky residents (minimum one year). Entry forms available for *Kentucky residents.*" Deadline: September 15, 1994.

JACK KEROUAC LITERARY PRIZE, (I), Lowell Historic Preservation Commission, Suite 310, 222 Merrimack St., Lowell MA 01852. (508)458-7653. Award "to promote cultural activities in Lowell, a pivotal event in annual 'Lowell Celebrates Kerouac' festival." Annual award for short stories, poems and essays. Award: $500 honorarium and opportunity to perform reading of winning work at the "Kerouac Festival." Competition receives approximately 200 submissions. Judges: Professional authors. Guidelines available for SASE. Deadline is May 1. Unpublished submissions. Limited to: fiction – 30 pages or less; nonfiction – 30 pages or less; poetry – 15 pages or less.

AGA KHAN PRIZE, (I), Address entry to Aga Khan Prize, *Paris Review,* 541 E. 72nd St., New York NY 10021. Annual award. For the best short story received during the preceding year. Award $1,000 and publication. Award judged by the editors. Work should be submitted between May 1-June 1. Unpublished short story submissions (1,000-10,000 words). SASE required. Translations acceptable. Winners announced in the winter issue.

KILLER FROG CONTEST, (I, II), *Scavenger's Newsletter,* 519 Ellinwood, Osage City KS 66523. (913)528-3538. Contact: Janet Fox. Competition "to see who can write the funniest/most overdone horror story, or poem, or produce the most outrageous artwork on a horror theme." Annual award for short stories, poems and art. Award: $25 for each of 4 categories and "coveted froggie statuette." Winners also receive complimentary copies of *The Killer Frog* Anthology. Judge: Editor of *Scavenger,* Janet Fox. Guidelines available for SASE. Deadline is April 1 to July 1 (postmarked). Published or previously unpublished submissions. Limited to horror/humor. Length: up to 4,000 words.

LAWRENCE FELLOWSHIP, (I), Dept. of English Language and Literature, University of New Mexico, Albuquerque NM 87131. (505)277-6347. Contact: Prof. Scott Sanders, chairperson. Annual award. Fellowship for writers of unpublished or previously published fiction, poetry, drama. (June-August residency at D.H. Lawrence Ranch, $1,400 stipend). $10 processing fee. Deadline: January 31. Write for rules, application form. SASE for return of materials.

LES GRANDS PRIX DU *JOURNAL DE MONTRÉAL,* (I, IV), Union des écrivaines et écrivains Québécois, 3492, Rue Laval, Montréal, Québec H2X 3C8 Canada. (514)849-8540. "To support the development of the literature of Québec and assure the public recognition of its authors." Three annual awards, one each for prose, poetry and theater. Award: $1,500 each (Canadian). Judges: 5 judges, nominated by the *Journal de Montréal.* Deadline: June 10. For books published within the 12 months preceding June 1. For books published in Québec only. Writers must have published at least 3 books of literary creation including the one already submitted and must submit 6 copies of the work to be considered. Write for rules and entry form (in French).

LE PRIX MOLSON DE L'ACADÉMIE DES LETTRES DU QUÉBEC, (II, IV), Union des écrivaines et écrivains québécois, 3492, Rue Laval, Montréal, Québec H2X 3C8 Canada. (514)849-8540. Annual prize for a novel in French by a writer from Québec or another province in Canada. Award: $5,000 (Canadian). Judges: 5 persons, members of the Académie des Lettres du Québec. Guidelines for SASE. Deadline: June 10. Five copies of the work must be submitted. Write for guidelines and entry forms (in French).

STEPHEN LEACOCK MEDAL FOR HUMOUR, (II, IV), Stephen Leacock Associates, Box 854, Orillia, Ontario L3V 6K8 Canada. (705)325-6546. Award "to encourage writing of humour by Canadians." Annual competition for short stories, novels and story collections. Award: Stephen Leacock (silver) medal for humour and J.P. Wiser cash award of $3,500 (Canadian). Receives 25-40 entries. Five judges selected across Canada. Entry fee $25 (Canadian). Guidelines for SASE. Deadline: December 30. Submissions should have been published in the previous year. Open to Canadian citizens or landed immigrants only.

THE LEADING EDGE FICTION CONTEST, (I, IV), 3163 JKHB, Provo UT 84602. (801)378-2456. Competition "to generate interest in the magazine; to increase the quality of submissions to the magazine; to reward excellence in storytelling among new and upcoming authors." Annual award for short stories. Award: $100 first prize, $60 second prize, $40 third prize. Competition receives approximately 900 submissions each year. Judges: Editorial staff of *The Leading Edge*. Guidelines for SASE. Deadline: December 1. Previously unpublished fiction. "The contest is open to all writers of science fiction and fantasy, whether they be pro, semipro, or first timer. Word length should be under 20,000 words unless story absolutely requires more—whatever it takes to tell the story right. No novels. *The Leading Edge* is a semiprofessional magazine of science fiction and fantasy that caters to the new and upcoming author, artist and poet. It is our goal to be the magazine that the professionals look to to find the next generation of writers." Fiction contest winner will be chosen from the previous year's published stories.

LETRAS DE ORO **SPANISH LITERARY PRIZES, (I, IV)**, The Graduate School of International Studies, University of Miami, Box 248123, Coral Gables FL 33124. (305)284-3266. Director: Joaquin-Roy. "The *Letras de Oro* Spanish Literary Prizes were created in order to reward creative excellence in the Spanish language and to promote Spanish literary production in this country. *Letras de Oro* also serves to recognize the importance of Hispanic culture in the United States." Annual award for novels, story collections, drama, essays and poetry. The prizes are $2,500 cash. Deadline: October 12.

LITERATURE AND BELIEF WRITING CONTEST, (I, IV), Center for the Study of Christian Values in Literature, 3076-E JKHB, Brigham Young University, Provo UT 84602. (801)378-2304. Director: Jay Fox. Award to "encourage affirmative literature in the Judeo-Christian tradition." Annual competition for short stories. Award $150 (1st place); $100 (2nd place). Competition receives 200-300 entries. Judges: BYU faculty. Guidelines for SASE. Deadline: May 15. Unpublished submissions, up to 30 pages. All winning entries are considered for publication in the annual journal *Literature and Belief*.

LOFT-MCKNIGHT WRITERS AWARDS, (I, IV), The Loft, Pratt Community Center, 66 Malcolm Ave. SE, Minneapolis MN 55414. (612)379-8999. Program Director: Carolyn Holbrook-Montgomery. "To give Minnesota writers of demonstrated ability an opportunity to work for a concentrated period of time on their writing." Annual award for creative prose. 5 awards of $7,500; 2 awards of distinction of $10,500. Competition receives approximately 275 submissions/year. Judges are out-of-state judges. Entry forms or rules for SASE. "Applicants must be Minnesota residents and must send for and observe guidelines."

LOUISIANA LITERARY AWARD, (II, IV), Louisiana Library Association (LLA), Box 3058, Baton Rouge LA 70821. (504)342-4928. Contact: Chair, Louisiana Literary Award Committee. Annual award "to promote interest in books related to Louisiana and to encourage their production." Submissions must have been published during the calendar year prior to presentation of the award. (The award is presented in March or April.) Award: Bronze medallion and $250. No entry fee. Deadline: publication by December 31. "All Louisiana-related books which committee members can locate are considered, whether submitted or not. Interested parties may correspond with the committee chair at the address above. All books considered *must* be on subject(s) related to Louisiana or be written by a Louisiana author. Each year, there may be a fiction *and/or* nonfiction award. Most often, however, there is only one award recipient, and he or she is the author of a work of nonfiction."

THE JOHN H. MCGINNIS MEMORIAL AWARD, (I), *Southwest Review*, Box 4374, 307 Fondren Library West, Southern Methodist University, Dallas TX 75275. (214)373-7440. Contact: Elizabeth Mills, associate editor. Annual awards (fiction and nonfiction). Stories or essays must have been published in the *Southwest Review* prior to the announcement of the award. Awards: $1,000. Pieces are not submitted directly for the award, but simply for publication in the magazine.

THE ENID MCLEOD LITERARY PRIZE, (II, IV), Franco-British Society, Room 623, Linen Hall, 162-168 Regent St., London W1R 5TB England. Executive Secretary: Mrs. Marian Clarke. "To recognize the work of the author published in the UK which in the opinion of the judges has contributed most

Market conditions are constantly changing! If you're still using this book and it is 1994 or later, buy the newest edition of Novel & Short Story Writer's Market *at your favorite bookstore or order directly from Writer's Digest Books.*

to Franco-British understanding." Annual competition for short stories, novels and story collections. Award: Cheque and copy of Enid McLeod's memoirs. Competition receives approx. 6-12 submissions. Judges: The Marquis of Lansdowne (FBS President), Martyn Goff and Professor Douglas Johnson. Guidelines for SASE. Deadline: December 31. Previously published submissions. "Writers, or their publishers, may submit 4 copies to the London Office. No nominations are necessary."

MAGGIE AWARD, (I, IV), Georgia Romance Writers, Inc., Box 142, Acworth GA 30101. (404)974-6678. Contact: Marian Oaks. "To encourage and instruct unpublished writers in the romance genre." Annual competition for novels. Award: Silver pendant (1st place), certificates (2nd-4th). 4 categories—short contemporary romance, long contemporary romance, historical romance, mainstream. Judges: Published romance authors. Entry fee $25. Guidelines for SASE. Deadline: On or about June 1 (deadline not yet final). Unpublished submissions. Writers must be members of Romance Writers of America. Entries consist of 3 chapters plus synopsis.

MANITOBA ARTS COUNCIL SUPPORT TO INDIVIDUAL ARTISTS, (II, IV), Manitoba Arts Council, 525-93 Lombard Ave., Winnipeg, Manitoba R3B 3B1 Canada. (204)945-2237. Grants "to encourage and support Manitoba writers." Five awards: Major Arts Grant ($25,000 Canadian) for writers of national or international reputation. Writers Grants "A" ($10,000 Canadian) for writers who have published a book or had a full-length script produced. Writers Grants "B" for writers who have published. Writers Grants "C" for unpublished writers, research and travel, or self-publication. Deadlines: April 15 and September 15. Open only to Manitoba writers.

THE MARTEN BEQUEST AWARD, (I, IV), Arts Management Pty. Ltd., 56 Kellett St., Potts Point NSW 2011 Australia. Awards Coordinator: Hilary Shrubb. "For the furtherance of culture and the advancement of education in Australia by means of the provision of travelling scholarships as numerous as income will permit, to be awarded entrants who have been born in Australia, and awarded to candidates of either sex between the ages of 21 years and 35 years, who shall be adjudged of outstanding ability and promise." Award granted to writers every 2 years (next in 1994). Competition for writers of short stories, novels or story collections. Award: AUS $15,000 payable in two installments of $7,500 per annum. Guidelines for SASE. Deadline: Oct. 31, 1993.

WALTER RUMSEY MARVIN GRANT, (I, IV), Ohioana Library Association, 65 S. Front St. Room 1105, Columbus OH 43215. (614)466-3831. Contact: Linda Hengst. "To encourage young unpublished writers (under age 30)." Biennial competition for short stories. Award: $1,000. Guidelines for SASE. Deadline: January 31, 1994. Open to unpublished authors born in Ohio or who have lived in Ohio for a minimum of five years. Must be under 30 years of age. Up to six pieces of prose may be submitted; maximum 60 pages, minimum 10 pages.

MARYLAND STATE ARTS COUNCIL INDIVIDUAL ARTISTS AWARDS, (I, IV), 601 N. Howard St., Baltimore MD 21201. (301)333-8232. Contact: Charles Camp. Awards given to reward artistic excellence and to promote career development. Annual grant for writers of stories, novels, novellas and story collections. Several awards of $1,000, $3,000 and $6,000 given each year. Competition receives 200 applications for fellowships. Judge: Out-of-state selection panel. Further information available for SASE. Deadline: December 1. Applicants must be Maryland residents over 18. Students are not eligible. Writers are required to submit a body of work demonstrating artistic accomplishment and skill.

THE VICKY METCALF BODY OF WORK AWARD, (II, IV), Canadian Authors Association, Suite 500, 275 Slater St., Ottawa, Ontario K1P 5H9 Canada. (613)233-2846. National Director: Jeffrey Holmes. Annual award. "The prize is given solely to stimulate writing for children, written by Canadians, for a *number* of strictly children's books—fiction, nonfiction or even picture books. No set formula." To be considered, a writer must have published at least 4 books. Award: $10,000 for a body of work inspirational to Canadian youth. Deadline: December 31. No entry fee. "Nominations may be made by any individual or association by letter *in triplicate* listing the published works of the nominee and providing biographical information. The books are usually considered in regard to their inspirational value for children. Entry forms or rules for SASE."

VICKY METCALF SHORT STORY AWARD, (II, IV), Canadian Authors Association, Suite 500, 275 Slater St., Ottawa, Ontario K1P 5H9 Canada. (613)233-2846. Fax: (613)235-8237. National Director: Jeffrey Holmes. "To encourage Canadian writing for children (open only to Canadian citizens)."

Submissions must have been published during previous calendar year in Canadian children's magazine or anthology. Award: $3,000 (Canadian). Award of $1,000 to editor of winning story if published in a Canadian journal or anthology. No entry fee. Entry forms or rules for #10 SASE. Deadline: December 15. Looking for "stories with originality, literary quality for ages 7-17."

‡MICHIGAN ARTS AWARDS, (II, IV), Arts Foundation of Michigan, Suite 2164, 645 Griswold, Detroit MI 48227. (303)964-2244. "To recognize quality and dedication to the craft." Annual competition for short stories, novels, story collections, translations, body of work. Award: $5,000. Competition receives approx. 50 submissions. Judges: Board of Trustees and Advisors. Guidelines for SASE. Query for deadline. Previously published submissions or can be for work-in-progress. Michigan residents only.

‡MICHIGAN CREATIVE ARTIST GRANT, (II, IV), Arts Foundation of Michigan, Suite 2164 645 Griswold, Detroit MI 48226. (303)964-2244. Annual competition for short stories, novels, story collections, translations, body of work. Award: up to $10,000. Competition receives approx. 50 submissions. Judges: Board of Trustees and Advisors. Guidelines for SASE. Query for deadline. Previously published submissions but can be for work-in-progress. Michigan residents only.

‡MICHIGAN GENERAL GRANTS, (IV), Arts Foundation of Michigan, Suite 2164, 645 Griswold, Detroit MI 48226. (303)964-2244. "To support writers while creating new work." Deadlines change each year; inquire. Award: cash, amount varies. Competition receives approx. 50 submissions. Judges: Board of Trustees and Advisors. Guidelines available for SASE. Michigan residents only.

MIDLAND AUTHORS' AWARD, (II, IV), Society of Midland Authors, % Jim Bowman, 152 North Scoville, Oak Park IL 60302. (708)383-7568. "To honor outstanding books published during the previous year by Midwestern authors." Award: Monetary sum and plaque. Competition receives approximately 30-50 book submissions. Judges are usually members of Society of Midland Authors. Entry forms or rules for SASE. Authors must be residents of IL, IN, IA, KS, MI, MN, MO, NE, OH, SD, ND or WI. Send for entry form.

MILITARY LIFESTYLE SHORT STORY CONTEST, (I, IV), Suite 710, 4800 Montgomery Lane, Bethesda MD 20814-5341. (301)718-7600. "To publish the work of previously unpublished writers; to encourage those of our readers who are military to send us short stories about a lifestyle they know very well." Annual competition for short stories. First Prize: $500; Second Prize: $300; Third Prize: $200. "Also, all three are published in the July/August issue of *Military Lifestyle*." Competition receives 700 submissions. Judges: Editorial staff of *Military Lifestyle*. Guidelines for SASE. Deadline: March 31. Unpublished submissions. "Theme of contest changes annually. Contact magazine for details and contest rules."

MILKWEED EDITIONS NATIONAL FICTION PRIZE, (I), Milkweed Editions, Suite 505, 528 Hennepin Ave., Minneapolis MN 55403. (612)332-3192. Editor: Emilie Buchwald. Annual award for a novel, a short story collection, one or more novellas, or a combination of short stories and novellas. Award: Publication, $3,000 advance against royalties. Reading fee $5. Must request guidelines; send SASE. Begins: May 1. Deadline: August 15. "Please look at *Ganado Red* by Susan Lowell (our first winning NFP book), *Backbone* by Carol Bly, *The Country I Come From* by Maura Stanton, or *Larabi's Ox* by Tony Ardizzone (our 1992 winning NFP book)—this is the caliber of fiction we are searching for. Catalog available for 3 first class stamps, if people need a sense of our list."

THE MILNER AWARD, (III), Friends of the Atlanta-Fulton Public Library, 1 Margaret Mitchell Square, Atlanta GA 30303. (404)730-1710. Executive Director: Rennie Davant. Award to a living American author of children's books. Annual competition for novels and story collections. Award: $1,000 honorarium and specially commissioned glass sculpture by Hans Frabel. Judges: Children of Atlanta vote during children's book week. Prior winners not eligible. Children vote at will—no list from which to select. Winner must be able to appear personally in Atlanta to receive the award at a formal program.

MINNESOTA STATE ARTS BOARD/ARTISTS ASSISTANCE FELLOWSHIP, (I, IV), 432 Summit Ave., St. Paul MN 55102-2624. (612)297-2603. Artist Assistance Program Associate: Karen Mueller. "To provide support and recognition to Minnesota's outstanding literary artists." Annual award for fiction writers, creative nonfiction writers and poets. Award: Up to $6,000. Competition receives approx. 150 submissions/year. Deadline: October. Previously published or unpublished submissions. Send request or call the above number for application guidelines. Minnesota residents only.

MINNESOTA VOICES PROJECT, (IV), New Rivers Press, #910, 420 N. 5th St., Minneapolis MN 55401. Contact: C.W. Truesdale, editor/publisher. Annual award "to foster and encourage new and emerging regional writers of short fiction, novellas, personal essays and poetry." Requires bibliography of previous publications and residency statement. Awards: $500 to each author published in the series plus "a generous royalty agreement if book goes into second printing." No entry fee. Send request with SASE for guidelines in October. Deadline: April 1. Restricted to new and emerging writers from Minnesota, Wisconsin, North and South Dakota, and Iowa.

MISSISSIPPI ARTS COMMISSION ARTIST FELLOWSHIP GRANT, (I, IV), Suite 207, 239 N. Lamar St., Jackson MS 39201. (601)359-6030. Contact: Program Administrator. "To encourage and support the creation of new artwork, and to recognize the contribution that artists of exceptional talent make to the vitality of our environment. Awards are based upon the quality of previously created work." Award granted every 2 years on a rotating basis. Award for writers of short stories, novels and story collections. Grant: Up to $5,000. Judges: Peer panel. Guidelines for SASE. "The next available grants for creative writing, including fiction, nonfiction and poetry will be in 1993-94." Deadline: March 1. Applicants must be Mississippi residents. "The Mississippi Arts Commission's Art in Education Program contains a creative writing component. For more information, contact the AIE Coordinator. The Mississippi Touring Arts program offers writers the opportunity to give readings and workshops and have the Arts Commission pay part of the fee." For more information, contact the Program Administrator.

‡*THE MISSOURI REVIEW* EDITORS' PRIZE CONTEST 1993, 1507 Hillcrest Hall, Columbia MO 65211. (314)882-4474. Annual competition for short stories, poetry and essays. Award: Cash. Competition receives approx. 800-900 submissions. Judges: *The Missouri Review* staff. Entry fee $15. Guidelines for SASE. Deadline October 1. Previously unpublished submissions. Limit of 25 typed, double-spaced pages for fiction and essay, and limit of 10 for poetry.

MISSOURI WRITERS' BIENNIAL, (I, IV), Missouri Arts Council, Suite 105, 111 N. 7th St., St. Louis MO 63101-2188. (314)340-6845. Award to support and promote Missouri writers. Every 2 years competition for short stories, essays and poetry. Award: $5,000 each to 5 writers. Competition receives approx. 400 submissions. Judges: Panel of national judges. Guidelines for SASE. Deadline "approx." July 30. Unpublished submissions. "Writers must have lived in Missouri for at least 2 years immediately preceding submission. Writers *must* request complete written guidelines."

MONTANA ARTS COUNCIL FIRST BOOK AWARD, (IV), Room 252, 316 N. Park Ave., Helena MT 59620. (406)444-6430. Director of Artist Services-Programs: Martha Sprague. Biannual award for publication of a book of poetry or fiction—the best work in Montana. Submissions may be short stories, novellas, story collections or poetry. Award: Publication. Competition receives about 35 submissions/year. Judges are professional writers. Entry forms or rules for SASE. Deadline: Early April (1993). Restricted to residents of Montana; not open to degree-seeking students.

MONTANA ARTS COUNCIL INDIVIDUAL ARTIST FELLOWSHIP, (IV), Room 252, 316 N. Park Ave., Helena MT 59620. (406)444-6430. Director of Artist Services-Programs: Martha Sprague. Biannual award of $2,000. Competition receives about 35 submissions/year. Panelists are professional writers. Contest requirements available for SASE. Deadline: Spring, 1993. Restricted to residents of Montana; not open to degree-seeking students.

JENNY MOORE WRITER-IN-WASHINGTON, Jenny Moore Fund, English Department, George Washington University, Washington DC 20052. (202)994-8223. To provide a teaching residency. Annual competition. Award: $40,000 plus benefits. Receives approximately 150 applications. Judges: Committees from English department and board members of fund. Guidelines for SASE. Deadline: November 15. "Genre for 1993-94 position: poetry." Length: 10-15 pages of poetry.

NATIONAL BOOK COUNCIL/BANJO AWARDS, (III, IV), National Book Council, Suite 3, 21 Drummond Place, Carlton, Victoria 3053 Australia. "For a book of highest literary merit which makes an outstanding contribution to Australian literature." Annual competition for creative writing. Award: $15,000 each for a work of fiction and nonfiction. Competition receives approx. 100-140 submissions. Judges: 4 judges chosen by the National Book Council. Entry fee $30. Guidelines for SASE. Deadline: Mid-April. Previously published submissions. For works "written by Australian citizens or permanent residents and first published in Australia during the qualifying period." Books must be nominated by the publisher.

NATIONAL BOOK FOUNDATION, INC., (III), Rm. 904, 260 5th Ave., New York NY 10001. (212)685-0261. Executive Director: Neil Baldwin. Assistant: Liddy Detar. Annual award to honor distinguished literary achievement in three categories: nonfiction, fiction and poetry. Books published Dec. 1 through Nov. 30 are eligible. Award: $10,000 to each winner; $1,000 to four runners-up in each category. Awards judged by panels of critics and writers. Entry fee $100 per title. Deadline: July 15. November ceremony. Selections are submitted by publishers only, or may be called in by judges. Read *Publishers Weekly* for additional information.

NATIONAL ENDOWMENT FOR THE ARTS CREATIVE WRITING FELLOWSHIP, (I), Literature Program, Room 722 Pennsylvania Ave. NW, Washington DC 20506. (202)682-5451. "The mission of the NEA is to foster the excellence, diversity and vitality of the arts in the United States, and to help broaden the availability and appreciation of such excellence, diversity and vitality." The purpose of the fellowship is to enable creative writers "to set aside time for writing, research or travel and generally to advance their careers." Competition open to fiction writers who have published a novel or novella, a collection of stories or at least 5 stories in 2 or more magazines since Jan. 1, 1983. Annual award: $20,000. All mss are judged anonymously. Application and guidelines available upon request. Deadline: March 5.

NATIONAL JEWISH BOOK AWARDS, (II, IV), JWB Jewish Book Council, 15 E. 26th St., New York NY 10010. Contact: Paula Gottlieb, director. Annual awards "to promote greater awareness of Jewish-American literary creativity." Previously published submissions in English only by a US or Canadian author/translator. Awards judged by authors/scholars. Award: $750 to the author/translator plus citation to publisher. Over 100 entries received for each award. Contest requirements available for SASE. Awards made in these categories: Autobiography/Memoir (autobiography or memoir of life of Jewish person); Children's Literature (children's book on Jewish theme); Children's Picture Book (author and illustrator of a picture book on Jewish theme); Fiction (fiction of Jewish interest); Yiddish Literature (book of literary merit in Yiddish language); also nonfiction awards in Jewish Thought, Jewish History, the Holocaust, Israel, Scholarship, Sephardic Studies, Folklore/Anthropology and Visual Arts.

NATIONAL WRITERS CLUB ANNUAL NOVEL WRITING CONTEST, (I), National Writers Club, Suite 620, 1450 S. Havana, Aurora CO 80012. (303)751-7844. Contact: Sandy Whelchel, director. Annual award to "recognize and reward outstanding ability and to increase the opportunity for publication." Award: $500 first prize; $300 second prize; $100 third prize. Award judged by successful writers. Charges $25 entry fee. Contest rules and entry forms available with SASE. Opens November 1. Entry deadline: Feb. 28. Unpublished submissions, any genre or category. Length: 20,000-100,000 words.

NATIONAL WRITERS CLUB ANNUAL SHORT STORY CONTEST, (I), National Writers Club, Suite 620, 1450 S. Havana, Aurora CO 80012. (303)751-7844. Contact: Sandy Whelchel, Executive Director. Annual award to encourage and recognize writing by freelancers in the short story field. Award: $200 first prize; $100 second prize; $50 third prize. Opens March 1. Charges $10 entry fee. Write for entry form and rule sheet. All entries must be postmarked by July 1. Unpublished submissions. Length: No more than 5,000 words.

THE NATIONAL WRITTEN & ILLUSTRATED BY . . . AWARDS CONTEST FOR STUDENTS, (I, IV), Landmark Editions, Inc., Box 4469, Kansas City MO 64127. (816)241-4919. Contact: Nan Thatch. "Contest initiated to encourage students to write and illustrate original books and to inspire them to become published authors and illustrators." Annual competition. "Each student whose book is selected for publication will be offered a complete publishing contract. To insure that students benefit from the proceeds, royalties from the sale of their books will be placed in an individual trust fund, set up for each student by his or her parents or legal guardians, at a bank of their choice. Funds may be withdrawn when a student becomes of age, or withdrawn earlier (either in whole or in part) for educational purposes or in case of proof of specific needs due to unusual hardship. Reports of book sales and royalties will be sent to the student and the parents or guardians annually." Winners also receive an all-expense-paid trip to Kansas City to oversee final reproduction phases of their books. Books by students may be entered in one of three age categories: A—6 to 9 years old; B—10 to 13 years old; C—14 to 19 years old. Each book submitted must be both written and illustrated by the same student. "Any books that are written by one student and illustrated by another will be automatically disqualified." Book entries must be submitted by a teacher or librarian. Entry fee: $1. For rules and guidelines, send a #10 SAE stamped with 58¢ postage. Deadline: May 1 of each year.

NEBULA® AWARDS, (III, IV), Science Fiction and Fantasy Writers of America, Inc., 5 Winding Brook Dr. #1B, Guilderland NY 12084. (518)869-5361. Executive Secretary: Peter Dennis Pautz. Annual awards for previously published short stories, novels, novellas, novelettes. SF/fantasy only. "No submissions; nominees upon recommendation of members only." Deadline: December 31. "Works are nominated throughout the year by active members of the SFWA."

NEGATIVE CAPABILITY SHORT FICTION COMPETITION, (I), *Negative Capability,* 62 Ridgelawn Dr. E., Mobile AL 36608. (205)343-6163. Contact: Sue Walker. "To promote and publish excellent fiction and to promote the ideals of human rights and dignity." Annual award for short stories. Award: $1,000 best story award. Judge: Leon Driskell. Reading fee $10, "includes copy of journal publishing the award." Guidelines for SASE. Deadline: December 15. Length: 1,500-4,500 words. "Award honors an outstanding author each year, and the award is given his or her name."

THE NENE AWARD, (II), Hawaii Association of School Libraries and the Hawaii Library Association Children and Youth Section, % Jan Yap, chairperson, 2716 Woodlawn Dr., Honolulu HI 96822. (808)988-7208. Chairperson changes every year. Annual award "to help the children of Hawaii become acquainted with the best contemporary writers of fiction for children; to become aware of the qualities that make a good book; to choose the best rather than the mediocre; and to honor an author whose book has been enjoyed by the children of Hawaii." Award: Koa plaque. Judged by the children of Hawaii. No entry fee. A reading list of 48-52 books is compiled by the Selection Committee and submitted to children in schools across the state. Review copies may be sent for consideration to the Selection Committee.

NEUSTADT INTERNATIONAL PRIZE FOR LITERATURE, (III), *World Literature Today,* 110 Monnet Hall, University of Oklahoma, Norman OK 73019-0375. Contact: Dr. Djelal Kadir, director. Biennial award to recognize distinguished and continuing achievement in fiction, poetry or drama. Awards: $40,000, an eagle feather cast in silver, an award certificate and a special issue of *WLT.* "We are looking for outstanding accomplishment in world literature. The Neustadt Prize is not open to application. Nominations are made only by members of the international jury, which changes for each award. Jury meetings are held in February of even-numbered years. Unsolicited manuscripts, whether published or unpublished, cannot be considered."

THE NEW ERA WRITING, ART, PHOTOGRAPHY AND MUSIC CONTEST, (I, IV), *New Era Magazine* (LDS Church), 50 E. North Temple, Salt Lake City UT 84150. (801)240-2951. Managing Editor: Richard M. Romney. "To encourage young Mormon writers and artists." Annual competition for short stories. Award: Scholarship to Brigham Young University or Ricks College or cash awards. Competition receives approx. 300 submissions. Judges: *New Era* editors. Guidelines for SASE. Deadline: January 3. Unpublished submissions. Contest open only to 12-23-year-old members of the Church of Jesus Christ of Latter-Day Saints.

NEW HAMPSHIRE STATE COUNCIL ON THE ARTS INDIVIDUAL ARTIST FELLOWSHIP, (I, IV), 40 N. Main St., Concord NH 03301-4974. (603)271-2789. Artist Services Coordinator: Audrey V. Sylvester. Fellowship "for career development to professional artists who are legal/permanent residents of the state of New Hampshire." Annual award: Up to $3,000. Competition receives 150 entries for 15 awards in all disciplines. Judges: 7 panels of in-state and out-of-state experts (music, theater, dance, literature, film, etc.). Guidelines for SASE. Deadline: May 1. Submissions may be either previously published or unpublished. Applicants must be over 18 years of age; not enrolled as fulltime students; permanent, legal residents of New Hampshire 1 year prior to application. Application form required.

NEW LETTERS LITERARY AWARD, (I), *New Letters,* UMKC 5100 Rockhill, Kansas City MO 64110. (816)235-1168. Administrative Assistant: Glenda McCrary. Award to "discover and reward good writing." Annual competition for short stories. Award: $750. Competition receives 500 entries/year. Entry fee $10. Guidelines for SASE. Deadline May 15. Submissions must be unpublished. Length requirement: 5,000 words or less.

NEW VOICES IN POETRY AND PROSE SPRING AND FALL COMPETITION, (I), *New Voices in Poetry and Prose Magazine,* P.O. Box 52196, Shreveport LA 71135. (318)797-8243. Publisher: Cheryl White. "To recognize and publish a previously unpublished work of outstanding short fiction." Biannual award for short stories. Award: $100 (first place) and publication in *New Voices.* Competition receives approx. 50 submissions. Judges: Panel. Entry fee $10/short story. Guidelines for SASE. Deadlines:

April 30 and September 30. Unpublished submissions. "All writers welcome. There is no line limit, but as a general rule, works under 5,000 words are preferred."

NEW WRITING AWARD, (I), *New Writing Magazine,* Box 1812, Amherst NY 14226-1812. "We wish to seek out and reward *new* writing. Looking for originality in form and content. Awarding those who find the current literary scene a hard market because it is too confining." Annual open competition for prose (novel excerpt, short story, essay, humor, other) and poetry. Deadline: December 31. Award: Varies, but hope it to be $1,000. Additional awards for finalists. Possible publication. Judges: Panel of editors. Entry fee $10, $5 for each additional. Guidelines for SASE but no application form required—simply send submission with reading fee, SASE for manuscript return or notification, and 3×5 card for each entry, including: story name, author and address. Unpublished submissions only.

NEW YORK FOUNDATION FOR THE ARTS FELLOWSHIP, (I, IV), New York Foundation for the Arts, 14th Floor, 155 Avenue of Americas, New York NY 10013. Contact: Penelope Dannenberg. Biennial competition for short stories and novels. Approximately 15 awards of $7,000 each. Competition receives approx. 450 submissions. Judges: Fiction writers. Call for guidelines or send SASE. Deadline: September 1993. Previously published or unpublished submissions. "Applicants must have lived in New York state at least 2 years immediately prior to application deadline."

NEW YORK STATE EDITH WHARTON CITATION OF MERIT (State Author), (III, IV), NYS Writers Institute, Humanities 355, University at Albany/SUNY, Albany NY 12222. (518)442-5620. Contact: Thomas Smith, associate director. Awarded biennially to honor a New York State fiction writer for a lifetime of works of distinction. Fiction writers living in New York State are nominated by an advisory panel. Recipients receive an honorarium of $10,000 and must give two public readings a year.

JOHN NEWBERY AWARD, (III), American Library Association (ALA) Awards and Citations Program, Association for Library Service to Children, 50 E. Huron St., Chicago IL 60611. Executive Director: S. Roman. Annual award. Only books for children published during the preceding year are eligible. Award: Medal. Entry restricted to US citizens-residents.

CHARLES H. AND N. MILDRED NILON EXCELLENCE IN MINORITY FICTION AWARD, (I, IV), University of Colorado at Boulder and the Fiction Collective Two, English Dept. Publications Center, Campus Box 494, University of Colorado, Boulder CO 80309-0494. "We recognize excellence in new minority fiction." Annual competition for novels, story collections and novellas. Award: $1,000 cash prize; joint publications of mss by CU-Boulder and Fiction Collective Two. Competition receives approx. 60 submissions. Judges: Well-known minority writers. Guidelines for SASE. Deadline: November 30. Unpublished submissions. "Only specific recognized US racial and ethnic minorities are eligible. The definitions are in the submission guidelines. The ms must be book length (a minimum of 250 pages)."

THE NOMA AWARD FOR PUBLISHING IN AFRICA, (III, IV), % Hans Zell Associates, P.O. Box 56, Oxford OX1 2SJ England. Sponsored by Kodansha Ltd. Administered by *The African Book Publishing Record.* Award "to encourage publications of works by African writers and scholars in Africa, instead of abroad as is still too often the case at present." Annual competition for a new book in any of these categories: Scholarly or academic; books for children; literature and creative writing, including fiction, drama and poetry. Award: $5,000. Competition receives approx. 100 submissions. Judges: A committee of African scholars and book experts and representatives of the international book community. Chairman: Professor Abiola Irele. Guidelines for SASE. Previously published submissions. Submissions are through publishers only.

NORDMANNS-FORBUNDET TRANSLATION GRANT, (II, IV), Nordmann-Forbundet, Rädhusgt 23B, N-0158 Oslo 1 Norway. Fax: (02)425163. Contact: Dina Tolfsby, information officer. Annual award for translation of Norwegian poetry or fiction, preferably contemporary. Award: Maximum NOK 15,000. Competition receives approx. 10 submissions. Judges: A committee of three members. Deadline March 1. "The grants are awarded to foreign publishing houses that want to publish Norwegian literature in translation." Payment is made at the time of publication.

NORTH CAROLINA ARTS COUNCIL FELLOWSHIP, (IV), 221 E. Lane St., Raleigh NC 27611. (919)733-2111. Literature Director: Deborah McGill. Grants program "to recognize and encourage North Carolina's finest creative writers." Annual award: Up to $7,500 each for 4 writers. Council receives approximately 200 submissions. Judges are a panel of editors and published writers from outside the state. Writers must be over 18 years old, not currently enrolled in degree-granting program on undergraduate or graduate level, and must have been a resident of North Carolina for 1 full year prior to applying. Writers may apply in either poetry or fiction. Deadline: February 1.

NORTH CAROLINA ARTS COUNCIL RESIDENCIES, (IV), 221 E. Lane St., Raleigh NC 27611. (919)733-2111. Literature Director: Deborah McGill. "To recognize and encourage North Carolina's finest creative writers." Annual award. "We offer a two- to three-month residency at the LaNapoule Foundation in southern France and a two- to three-month residency at three other centers in the US subject to change each year." Judges: Editors and published writers from outside the state. Deadline for France, February 1; for US residencies, late August. Writers must be over 18 years old, not currently enrolled in degree-granting program on undergraduate or graduate level and must have been a resident of North Carolina for 1 full year prior to applying.

NORTH CAROLINA ARTS COUNCIL SCHOLARSHIPS, (IV), 221 E. Lane St., Raleigh NC 27611. (919)733-2111. Literature Director: Deborah McGill. "To provide writers of fiction, poetry, literacy and nonfiction with opportunities for research or enrichment. Available on a six-weeks basis throughout the year." Award up to $500 (with $1,500 budgeted for the category). "To be eligible writers must have lived in the state for at least a year and must have published a stipulated amount of work in his/her genre. Self-published or vanity press published work is ineligible." Call Council for details.

THE FLANNERY O'CONNOR AWARD FOR SHORT FICTION, (I), The University of Georgia Press, Terrell Hall, Athens GA 30602. (404)542-2830. Contact: Award coordinator. Annual award "to recognize outstanding collections of short fiction. Published and unpublished authors are welcome." Award: $1,000 and publication by the University of Georgia Press. Deadline: June 1-July 31. "Manuscripts cannot be accepted at any other time." Entry fee: $10. Contest rules for SASE. Ms will not be returned.

FRANK O'CONNOR FICTION AWARD, (I), *descant*, Dept. of English, Texas Christian University, Fort Worth TX 76129. (817)921-7240. Contact: Betsy Colquitt, Harry Opperman, Steve Sherwood or Stan Trachbenberg, Editors. Estab. 1979 with *descant*; earlier awarded through *Quartet*. Annual award to honor achievement in short fiction. Submissions must be published in the magazine during its current volume. Award: $500 prize. No entry fee. "About 12 to 15 stories are published annually in *descant*. Winning story is selected from this group."

THE SCOTT O'DELL AWARD FOR HISTORICAL FICTION, (II, IV), Scott O'Dell (personal donation), c/o Houghton Mifflin, 2 Park St., Boston MA 02108. (617)725-5000. Contact: Mrs. Zena Sutherland, professor, 1418 E. 57th St., Chicago IL 60637. Annual award "to encourage the writing of good historical fiction about the New World (Canada, South and Central America, and the United States) for children and young people." Award: $5,000. Entry forms or rules for SASE. Deadline: December 31. For books published during the year preceding the year in which the award is given. To be written in English by a U.S. citizen and published in the U.S. Looking for "accuracy in historical details, and all the standard literary criteria for excellence: style, setting, characterization, etc."

OHIO ARTS COUNCIL AID TO INDIVIDUAL ARTISTS FELLOWSHIP, (I, IV), 727 E. Main St., Columbus OH 43205-1796. (614)466-2613. "To recognize and support Ohio's outstanding creative artists." Annual grant/fellowship. Award: $5,000 or $10,000. Competition receives approx. 200-300 submissions/year. Judges: Panel of experts. Contact the OAC office for guidelines. Writers must be residents of Ohio and must not be students.

OHIOANA AWARD FOR CHILDREN'S LITERATURE, ALICE WOOD MEMORIAL, (IV), Ohioana Library Association, Room 1105, 65 S. Front St., Columbus OH 43215. (614)466-3831. Director: Linda Hengst. Competition "to honor an individual whose body of work has made, and continues to make, a significant contribution to literature for children or young adults." Annual award for body of work. Award: $1,000. Guidelines for SASE. Deadline: December 31 prior to year award is given. Published fiction. "Open to authors born in Ohio or who have lived in Ohio for a minimum of five years."

OHIOANA BOOK AWARD, (II, IV), Ohioana Library Association, Room 1105, 65 S. Front St. Columbus OH 43215. Contact: Linda R. Hengst, director. Annual award (only if the judges believe a book of sufficiently high quality has been submitted) to bring recognition to outstanding books by Ohioans or about Ohio. Criteria: Book written or edited by a native Ohioan or resident of the state for at least

5 years; two copies of the book MUST be received by the Ohioana Library by December 31 prior to the year the award is given; literary quality of the book must be outstanding. Award: Certificate and glass sculpture. Each spring a jury considers all books received since the previous jury. Award judged by a jury selected from librarians, book reviewers, writers and other knowledgeable people. No entry forms are needed, but they are available. "We will be glad to answer letters asking specific questions."

THE OKANAGAN SHORT FICTION AWARD, (I, IV), *Canadian Author,* Suite 500, 275 Slater St., Ottawa, Ontario K1P 5H9 Canada. Contact: Veronica Ross, fiction editor. Award offered 4 times a year. To present good fiction "in which the writing surpasses all else" to an appreciative literary readership, and in turn help Canadian writers retain an interest in good fiction. Award: $125 to each author whose story is accepted for publication. Entries are invited in each issue of the quarterly *CA.* Sample copy $5.50; guidelines printed in the magazine. "Our award regulations stipulate that writers must be Canadian, stories must not have been previously published, and be under 3,000 words. Mss should be typed double-spaced on 8½ × 11 bond. SASE with Canadian postage or mss will not be returned. Looking for superior writing ability, stories with good plot, movement, dialogue and characterization. A selection of winning stories has been anthologized as *Pure Fiction: The Okanagan Award Winners,* and is essential reading for prospective contributors."

OMMATION PRESS BOOK AWARD, (I, II), Ommation Press, 5548 N. Sawyer, Chicago IL 60625. (312)539-5745. Annual competition for short stories, novels, story collections and poetry. Award: Book publication, $50 and 50 copies of book. Competition receives approx. 60 submissions. Judge: Effie Mihopoulos (editor). Entry fee $12, includes copy of former award-winning book. Guidelines for SASE. Deadline: December 30. Either previously published or unpublished submissions. Submit no more than 50 pages.

OPEN VOICE AWARDS, (I), Westside YMCA—Writer's Voice, 5 W. 63rd St., New York NY 10023. (212)875-4124. Competition for short stories or poetry. Award: $500 honorarium and featured reading. Deadline: December 31. "Submit 10 double-spaced pages in a single genre. Enclose $10 entry fee."

OREGON INDIVIDUAL ARTIST FELLOWSHIP, (I, IV), Oregon Arts Commission, 550 Airport Rd. SE, Salem OR 97310. (503)387-3625. Artist Services Coordinator: Vincent Dunn. "Award enables professional artists to undertake projects to assist their professional development." Biennial competition for short stories, novels, poetry and story collections. Award: $3,000 and $10,000. (Please note: ten $3,000 awards and one $10,000 Master Fellowship Award are spread over 5 disciplines—literature, music/opera, media arts, dance and theatre awarded in even-numbered years.) Competition receives approx. 70 entries/year. Judges: Professional advisors from outside the state. Guidelines and application for SASE. Deadline: September 1. Competition limited to Oregon residents.

PACIFIC NORTHWEST WRITERS CONFERENCE LITERARY AWARD, Suite 804, 2033 6th Ave., Seattle WA 98121-2526. (206)443-3807. Annual competition for short stories and novels (adult and juvenile). Also for nonfiction articles and books, poetry and screenplays/scripts. First prize each category is $300. Entry fee $10 for members, $20 for nonmembers. Guidelines for 3 ounce postage. Deadline: Mid-April. Previously unpublished submissions.

DOBIE PAISANO FELLOWSHIPS, (IV), Office of Graduate Studies, University of Texas at Austin, Austin TX 78712. (512)471-7213. Coordinator: Audrey N. Slate. Annual fellowships for creative writing (includes short stories, novels and story collections). Award: 6 months residence at ranch; $7,200 stipend. Competition receives approx. 100 submissions. Judges: faculty of University of Texas and members of Texas Institute of Letters. Entry fee: $10. Application and guidelines on request. "Open to writers with a Texas connection—native Texans, people living in Texas now or writers whose work focuses on Texas and Southwest." Deadline: Third week in January.

PALM COUNCIL PHILIPPINE AMERICAN SHORT STORY CONTEST, (I, IV), Philippine Arts, Letters and Media Council, Washington DC, 10829 Split Oak Lane, Burke VA 22015. (703)503-9012. Competition "to encourage and recognize fiction writing talent in the Philippine American community and promote the writing of Philippine American fiction." Annual award for short stories (when money is available). Award: $300 for first prize, $200 for second, $100 for third. Competition receives approximately 25 submissions. Judges: Screening committee selects 10 best entries which are sent to a panel of judges (3) who select the winners. Guidelines available for SASE. Deadline is May 3. Previously unpublished fiction. Limited to Philippine American themes by writers of Philppine American ancestry. No more than 5,000 words.

‡PEARL SHORT STORY CONTEST, (I), *Pearl* Magazine, 3030 E. Second St., Long Beach CA 90803. (310)434-4523. Contact: Marilyn Johnson, editor. Award to "provide a larger forum and help widen publishing opportunities for fiction writers in the small press; and to help support the continuing publication of *Pearl*." Annual competition for short stories. Award: $50, publication in *Pearl* and 10 copies. Competition receives approx. 100 submissions. Judges: Editors of *Pearl* (Marilyn Johnson, Joan Jobe Smith, Barbara Hauk). Entry fee $5 per story. Guidelines for SASE. Deadline December 1-March 1. Unpublished submissions. Length: 4,000 words maximum. Include a brief biographical note and SASE for reply or return of manuscript. Accepts simultaneous submissions, but asks to be notified if story is accepted elsewhere. All submissions are considered for publication in *Pearl*. "Although we are open to all types of fiction, we look most favorably upon coherent, well-crafted narratives, containing interesting, believable characters and meaningful situations."

JUDITH SIEGEL PEARSON AWARD, (I), Wayne State University, Detroit MI 48202. Contact: Chair, English Dept. Competition "to honor writing about women." Annual award. Short stories up to 20 pages considered every third year (poetry and drama/nonfiction in alternate years). Award: Up to $400. Competition receives up to 100 submissions/year. Submissions are internally screened; then a noted writer does final reading. Entry forms for SASE.

WILLIAM PEDEN PRIZE IN FICTION, (I), *The Missouri Review*, 1507 Hillcrest Hall, University of Missouri, Columbia MO 65211. (314)882-4474. Contact: Speer Morgan, Greg Michalson, editors. Annual award "to honor the best short story published in *The Missouri Review* each year." Submissions are to be previously published in the volume year for which the prize is awarded. Award: $1,000. No entry deadline or fee. No rules; all fiction published in *MR* is automatically entered.

PEGASUS PRIZE, (III), Mobil Corporation, (Room 3C916), 3225 Gallows Rd., Fairfax VA 22037-0001. (703)846-2375. Director: Michael Morgan. To recognize distinguished works from literature not normally translated into English. Award for novels. "Prize is given on a country-by-country basis and does not involve submissions."

PEN/BOOK-OF-THE-MONTH CLUB TRANSLATION PRIZE, (II, IV), PEN American Center, 568 Broadway, New York NY 10012. (212)334-1660. Awards Coordinator: John Morrone. Award "to recognize the art of the literary translator." Annual competition for translations. Award: $3,000. Deadline: December 31. Previously published submissions within the calendar year. "Translators may be of any nationality, but book must have been published in the US and must be a book-length literary translation." Books may be submitted by publishers, agents or translators. No application form. Send three copies. "Early submissions are strongly recommended."

THE PEN/FAULKNER AWARD FOR FICTION, (II, III), c/o The Folger Shakespeare Library, 201 E. Capitol St. SE, Washington DC 20003. (202)544-7077. Attention: Janice Delaney, PEN/Faulkner Foundation Executive Director. Annual award. "To award the most distinguished book-length work of fiction published by an American writer." Award: $7,500 for winner; $2,500 for nominees. Judges: Three writers chosen by the Trustees of the Award. Deadline: December 31. Published submissions only. Writers and publishers submit four copies of eligible titles published the current year. No juvenile. Authors must be American citizens.

PENNSYLVANIA COUNCIL ON THE ARTS, FELLOWSHIP PROGRAM, (I, IV), 216 Finance Bldg., Harrisburg PA 17120. (717)787-6883. Annual awards to provide fellowships for creative writers. Award: Up to $5,000. Competition receives approx. 175 submissions for 12 to 15 awards/year. Six judges: Three poetry, three fiction, different each year. Guidelines mailed upon request. Deadline: October 1. Applicants must be Pennsylvania residents.

PENNY DREADFUL SHORT STORY CONTEST, (I), *sub-TERRAIN* Magazine, P.O. Box 1575, Station A, Vancouver, British Columbia V6C 2P7 Canada. (604)876-8710. Contact: B. Kaufman. "To inspire writers to get down to it and struggle with a form that is condensed and difficult. To encourage clean, powerful writing." Annual award for short stories. Prize: $100 and publication. Competition receives about 200 submissions. Judges: An editorial collective. Entry fee $8 (includes 4-issue subscription). Guidelines for SASE, or SAE and IRC, in November. "Contest kicks off in mid-November." Deadline:

April 15. Unpublished submissions. Length: 1,000 words. "We are looking for work that is trying to do something unique/new in form or content. Radical as opposed to the standard short story format. Experiment, take risks. That excites us. We are looking for work that expresses the experience of urban existence."

JAMES D. PHELAN AWARD, (I, IV), The San Francisco Foundation, Suite 910, 685 Market St., San Francisco CA 94105. Contact: Awards Program Coordinator. Annual award "to author of an unpublished work-in-progress of fiction (novel or short story), nonfictional prose, poetry or drama." Award: $2,000 and certificate. Rules and entry forms available after November 1 for SASE. Deadline: January 15. Unpublished submissions. Applicant must have been born in the state of California and be 20-35 years old.

PLAYBOY COLLEGE FICTION CONTEST, (I), *Playboy* Magazine, 680 North Lake Shore Dr., Chicago IL 60611. (312)751-8000. Fiction Editor: Alice K. Turner. Award "to foster young writing talent." Annual competition for short stories. Award: $3,000 plus publication in the magazine. Judges: Staff. Guidelines available for SASE. Deadline: January 1. Submissions should be unpublished. No age limit; college affiliation required. Stories should be 25 pages or fewer. "Manuscripts are not returned. Results of the contest will be sent via SASE."

EDGAR ALLAN POE AWARDS, (II), Mystery Writers of America, Inc., 6th Floor, 17 E. 47th St., New York NY 10017. Executive Director: Priscilla Ridgway. Annual awards to enhance the prestige of the mystery. For mystery works published or produced during the calendar year. Award: Ceramic bust of Poe. Awards for best mystery novel, best first novel by an American author, best softcover original novel, best short story, best critical/biographical work, best fact crime, best young adult, best juvenile novel, best screenplay, best television feature and best episode in a series. Contact above address for specifics. Deadline: December 1.

THE RENATO POGGIOLI TRANSLATION AWARD, (I, IV), PEN American Center, 568 Broadway, New York NY 10012. (212)334-1660. Awards Coordinator: John Morrone. Award "to encourage beginning and promising translator who is working on a book-length translation from Italian to English." Annual competition for translations. Award: $3,000. Competition receives approx. 30-50 submissions. Judges: A panel of three translators. Guidelines for SASE. Deadline: January 15. Unpublished submissions. "Letters of application should be accompanied by a curriculum vitae, including Italian studies and samples of translation-in-progress."

KATHERINE ANNE PORTER PRIZE FOR FICTION, (I), *Nimrod*, Arts and Humanities Council of Tulsa, 2210 S. Main St., Tulsa OK 74114. (918)584-3333. Editor: Francine Ringold. "To award promising young writers and to increase the quality of manuscripts submitted to *Nimrod*." Annual award for short stories. Award: $1,000 first prize; $500 second prize plus publication, two contributors copies and $5/page up to $25 total. Receives approx. 700 entries/year. Judge varies each year. Past judges: Ron Carlson, Rosellen Brown, Alison Lurie, Gordon Lish, George Garrett, Toby Olson, John Leonard and Gladys Swan. Entry fee: $10. Guidelines for #10 SASE. Deadline for submissions: April 15. Previously unpublished manuscripts. Length: 7,500 words maximum. "Must be typed, double-spaced. Our contest is judged anonymously, so we ask that writers take their names off of their manuscripts (need 2 copies total). Include a cover sheet containing your name, full address, phone and the title of your work. Include a SASE for notification of the results. We encourage writers to read *Nimrod* before submission to discern whether or not their work is compatible with the style of our journal. Back awards issues are $4.50 (book rate postage included)."

PRAIRIE SCHOONER THE LAWRENCE FOUNDATION AWARD, (I), 201 Andrews Hall, University of Nebraska, Lincoln NE 68588-0334. (402)472-1812. Contact: Hilda Raz, editor. Annual award "given to the author of the best short story published in *Prairie Schooner* during the preceding year." Award:

Market categories: (I) Unpublished entries; (II) Published entries nominated by the author; (III) Published entries, nominated by the editor, publisher or nominating body; (IV) Specialized entries.

$500. "Only short fiction published in *Prairie Schooner* is eligible for consideration."

PRISM INTERNATIONAL SHORT FICTION CONTEST, (I), *Prism International,* Dept. of Creative Writing, University of British Columbia, E455-1866 Main Mall, Vancouver, British Columbia V6T 1Z1 Canada. (604)822-2514. Contact: Publicity Manager. Award: $2,000 first prize and five $200 consolation prizes. Entry fee $15 plus $5 reading fee for each story (includes a 1 year subscription). SASE for rules/entry forms.

PULITZER PRIZE IN FICTION, (III), Graduate School of Journalism, 702 Journalism Bldg., Columbia University, New York NY 10027. Annual award for distinguished fiction *first* published in book form during the year by an American author, preferably dealing with American life. Award: $3,000. Deadline: Books published between January 1 and June 30 must be submitted by July 1. Books published between July 1 and December 31 must be submitted by November 1. Submit 4 copies of the book, entry form, biography and photo of author and $20 handling fee. Open to American authors.

PURE BRED DOGS/AMERICAN KENNEL GAZETTE, (I), 51 Madison Ave., New York NY 10010. (212)696-8331. Executive Editor: Elizabeth Bodner, DVM. Annual contest for short stories under 2,000 words. Award: Prizes of $500, $250 and $150 for top three entries. Top entry published in magazine. Judge: Panel. Contest requirements available for SASE. "The *Gazette* sponsors an annual fiction contest for short short stories on some subject relating to pure-bred dogs. Fiction for our magazine needs a slant toward the serious fancier with real insight into the human/dog bond and breed-specific pure-bred behavior."

PUSHCART PRIZE, (III), Pushcart Press, Box 380, Wainscott NY 11975. (516)324-9300. Contact: Bill Henderson, editor. Annual award "to publish and recognize the best of small press literary work." Previously published submissions, short stories, poetry or essays on any subject. Must have been published during the current calendar year. Award: Publication in *Pushcart Prize: Best of the Small Presses.* Deadline: Dec. 1. Nomination by small press publishers/editors only.

QUARTERLY WEST NOVELLA COMPETITION, (I), University of Utah, 317 Olpin Union, Salt Lake City UT 84112. (801)581-6168. Biennial award for novellas. Award: 2 prizes of $300+. Send SASE for contest rules. Deadline: Postmarked by December 31.

SIR WALTER RALEIGH AWARD, (II, IV), North Carolina Literary and Historical Association, 109 E. Jones St., Raleigh NC 27601-2807. (919)733-7305. Secretary-Treasurer: Jeffrey J. Crow. "To promote among the people of North Carolina an interest in their own literature." Annual award for novels. Award: Statue of Sir Walter Raleigh. Judges: University English and history professors. Guidelines for SASE. Book must be an original work published during the twelve months ending June 30 of the year for which the award is given. Writer must be a legal or physical resident of North Carolina for the three years preceding the close of the contest period. Authors or publishers may submit 3 copies of their book to the above address.

RHODE ISLAND STATE COUNCIL ON THE ARTS, (I, IV), Individual Artist's Fellowship in Literature, Suite 103, 95 Cedar St., Providence RI 02903-1034. (401)277-3880. Fellowship Program Director: Dawn Dunley Roch. Annual fellowship. Award: $6,000. Competition receives approximately 50 submissions. In-state panel makes recommendations to an out-of-state judge, who makes the final award. Entry forms for SASE. Deadline: April 1. Artists must be Rhode Island residents and not undergraduate or graduate students. "Program guidelines may change. Prospective applicants should contact RISCA prior to deadline."

HAROLD U. RIBALOW PRIZE, (II, IV), *Hadassah Magazine,* 50 W. 58th St., New York NY 10019. (212)333-59456. Contact: Alan M. Tigay, Executive Editor. Estab. 1983. Annual award "for a book of fiction on a Jewish theme. Harold U. Ribalow was a noted writer and editor who devoted his time to the discovery and encouragement of young Jewish writers." Book should have been published the year preceding the award. Award: $1,000 and excerpt of book in *Hadassah Magazine.* Deadline: December 31.

THE MARY ROBERTS RINEHART FUND, (III), George Mason University, 4400 University Dr., Fairfax VA 22030. (703)993-1185. Roger Lathbury, director. Biennial award for short stories, novels, novellas and story collections by unpublished writers (that is, writers ineligible to apply for NEA grants).

Award: Two grants whose amount varies depending upon income the fund generates. Competition receives approx. 75-100 submissions annually. Rules for SASE. Next fiction deadline: November 30, 1993. Writers must be nominated by a sponsoring writer, writing teacher, editor or agent.

SUMMERFIELD G. ROBERTS AWARD, (IV), The Sons of the Republic of Texas, Suite 222, 5942 Abrams Rd., Dallas TX 75231. Executive Secretary: Maydee J. Scurlock. "Given for the best book or manuscript of biography, essay, fiction, nonfiction, novel, poetry or short story that describes or represents the Republic of Texas, 1836-1846." Annual award of $2,500. Deadline: January 31. "The manuscripts must be written or published during the calendar year for which the award is given. Entries are to be submitted in quintuplicate and will not be returned."

ROBERTS WRITING AWARDS, (I), H. G. Roberts Foundation, Box 1868, Pittsburg KS 66762. (316)231-2998. Awards Coordinator: Stephen E. Meats. "To reward and recognize exceptional fiction writers with money and publication." Annual competition for short stories. Award: $500 (first place); $200 (second place); $100 (third place); publication for prize winners and honorable mention receipts. Competition receives approx. 600 submissions. Judge: Established fiction writer, different each year. Entry fee $6/story. Guidelines and entry form for SASE. Deadline: September 15. Previously unpublished submissions. "Open to any type of fiction, up to 15 typed pages."

ROCKY MOUNTAIN WOMEN'S INSTITUTE ASSOCIATESHIP, (I, II), Foote Hall 317, 7150 Montview Blvd., Denver CO 80220. (303)871-6923. Executive Director: Cheryl Bezio-Gorham. "Each year RMWI receives project proposals, selects those most promising and invites seven to ten to become Associates. These are artists, writers and scholars who are given office/studio space, stipends, support services and promotional events for one year." Competition receives approx. 150 submissions with selection based on excellence, project feasibility, group dynamics and need. Selection committees are composed of experts in arts/humanities. Entry fee $5. SASE for returns. Deadline: March 15 of each year for following September. Located at the University of Denver law campus, work space provided but not residence. Part-time commitment per week and Associates meet as group once each week.

ROMANCE WRITERS OF AMERICA GOLDEN HEART AND THE RITA AWARDS, (I, II, IV), #315, 13700 Veterans Memorial, Houston TX 77014. (713)440-6885. "To recognize best work in romantic fiction in 7 categories by members of RWA, both published and not-published." Annual award for novels. Golden Heart Award: Heart and certificate; The Rita Award: Etched plaque. Golden Heart Award receives 600+ submissions/year; The Rita Award receives 250+ submissions/year. Judges: Published writers, editors. Entry fee for Golden Heart is $25; The Rita fee is $15. Guidelines for SASE. Deadline: January 15. Previously published submissions for The Rita; unpublished for Golden Heart. Categories are "traditional, short and long contemporary, historical, single title (historical and contemporary), young adult."

SACRAMENTO PUBLIC LIBRARY FOCUS ON WRITERS CONTEST, (I, IV), 828 I St., Sacramento CA 95814. (916)440-5926. Contact: Debbie Runnels. Award presented by the Friends of the Sacramento Public Library "to support and encourage aspiring writers." Annual competition for short stories and novels. Awards: $100 (first place); $50 (second place); $25 (third place). Competition receives approx. 147 short story; 78 novel chapters; 71 children's stories plus poetry and nonfiction. Judges: Local teachers of English, authors and librarians. Entry fee $5/entry. Guidelines for SASE. Deadline: August 15. Unpublished submissions. Length: 2,500-word short story; 1,000-word story for children. Open to all writers in northern California.

***SAN JOSE STUDIES* BEST STORY AWARD, (I)**, Bill Casey Memorial Fund, 1 Washington Square, San Jose CA 95192. Contact: Fauneil J. Rinn. Winning author receives a year's complimentary subscription to journal, which prints notice of award, and is also considered for the Bill Casey Memorial Award of $100 for the best contribution in each year's volume of *San José Studies* in essay, fiction or poetry.

CARL SANDBURG AWARDS, (I, IV), Friends of the Chicago Public Library, Harold Washington Library Center, 400 S. State St., Chicago IL 60605. (312)747-4907. Annual. To honor excellence in Chicago or Chicago area authors (including 6 counties). Books published between May 31 and June 1 (the following year). $1,000 honorarium for fiction, nonfiction, poetry and children's literature. Medal awarded also. Deadline: September 1. All entries become the property of the Friends.

SASSY FICTION CONTEST, (I, IV), *Sassy,* 7th Floor, 230 Park Ave., New York NY 10169. (212)551-9500. Competition "to recognize promise in fiction writers aged 13-19 and to encourage teenagers to write." Annual award for short stories. Award: Scholarship. Competition receives approximately 5,000 submissions. Judges: Christina Kelly, Mary Kay Schilling, Jane Pratt. No entry fee. Guidelines available for SASE. Information in June issue of magazine; winners published in December issue. Unpublished fiction. Only for writers aged 13-19.

SCIENCE FICTION WRITERS OF EARTH (SFWoE) SHORT STORY CONTEST, (I, IV), Science Fiction Writers of Earth, Box 121293, Fort Worth TX 76121. (817)451-8674. SFWoE Administrator: Gilbert Gordon Reis. Purpose "to promote the art of science fiction/fantasy short story writing." Annual award for short stories. Award: $100 (1st prize); $50 (2nd prize); $25 (3rd prize). Competition receives approx. 75 submissions/year. Judge: Author Edward Bryant. Entry fee: $5 for 1st entry; $2 for additional entries. Guidelines for SASE. Deadline: October 30. Submissions must be unpublished. Stories should be science fiction or fantasy, 2,000-7,500 words. "Although many of our past winners are now published authors, there is still room for improvement. The odds are good for a well-written story."

SE LA VIE WRITER'S JOURNAL **CONTEST, (I, IV),** Rio Grande Press, P.O. Box 371371, El Paso TX 79937. (915)595-2625. Contact: Rosalie Avara, editor. Competition offered quarterly for short stories. Award: Publication in the *Se La Vie Writer's Journal* plus up to $10 and contributor's copy. Judge: Editor. Entry fee $4 for each or $7 for two. Guidelines for SASE. Deadlines: March 31, June 30, September 30, December 31. Unpublished submissions. Theme is "life" or "the writing life." Length: 500 words maximum.

THE SEATON AWARDS, (I, IV), *Kansas Quarterly,* 122 Denison Hall, Kansas State University KS 66506-0703. Annual awards to reward and recognize the best fiction published in *KQ* during the year from authors native to or resident in Kansas. Submissions must be previously unpublished. Anyone who submits unpublished material which is then accepted for publication becomes eligible for the awards. Award: Recognition and monetary sums of $250, $150, $100 and $50. No deadline. Material simply may be submitted for consideration at any time with SASE. "Ours are not contests. We give monetary awards and recognition to Kansas writers of national literary stature."

SEVENTEEN MAGAZINE **FICTION CONTEST, (I, IV),** *Seventeen Magazine,* 850 3rd Ave., New York NY 10022. Contact: Joe Bargmann. To honor best short fiction by a young writer. Rules are found in the November and December issues. Contest for 13-21 year olds. Deadline: April 31. Submissions judged by a panel of outside readers and *Seventeen*'s editors. Cash awarded to winners. First-place story considered for publication.

‡**SHORT AND SWEET CONTEST, (II, IV),** Perry Terrell Publishing, 1617 Newport Place, #24, Kenner LA 70065. (504)465-9412. "The purpose is to inspire and encourage creativity in humor. (My personal purpose is to see who has a sense of humor and who doesn't.)" Monthly competition, 1 to 2 months after deadline, for short stories. Award: $5. Receives approx. 15 to 47/month. Judges: Perry Terrell. Entry fee 50¢/entry. Guidelines for SASE. "Each month has a theme and begins with an open-ended sentence. Send SASE for details."

SHORT GRAIN CONTEST, (I), Box 1154, Regina, Saskatchewan S4P 3B4 Canada. Contact: Geoffrey Ursell. Annual competition for postcard stories and prose poems. Awards: $250 (1st prize), $150 (2nd prize) and $100 (third prize) in each category. "All winners and Honourable Mentions will also receive regular payment for publication in *Grain.*" Competition receives approximately 600 submissions. Judges: Canadian writers with national and international reputations. Entry fee $19.95 for 2 entries (includes one-year subscription); each additional entry $5. Guidelines for SASE or SAE and IRC. Deadline: April 30. Unpublished submissions. Contest entries must be either an original postcard story (a work of narrative fiction written in 500 words or less) or a prose poem (a lyric poem written as a prose paragraph or paragraphs in 500 words or less).

‡**SHORT STORY SCIENCE FICTION/FANTASY COMPETITION, (I, IV),** Maplecon SF/F Convention (O.F.I.), 2105 Thistle Crescent, Ottawa, Ontario K1H 5P4 Canada. Literary Coordinator: Madona Skaff. "To offer incentive and encouragement for amateur writers." Annual competition for short stories. Award: certificates and varying prizes. Competition receives approx. 20-25 submissions. Judges: professional authors. Guidelines for SASE. Deadline: August 30. Unpublished submissions. Available to any writer, anywhere, in amateur standing, i.e. has *not* had *more* than 3 short stories

published professionally in the SF/F field or not had a novel published in the SF/F field. Maximum word length: 7,000 words. "Name must not appear on ms itself—should be included on a separate sheet. Please include SASE. Use *Canadian* stamps or IRC's or include *loose* U.S. stamps as trade."

SIDE SHOW ANNUAL SHORT STORY CONTEST, (I), Somersault Press, P.O. Box 1428, El Cerrito CA 94530-1428. (510)215-2207. Editor: Shelly Anderson. "To attract quality writers for our 300-odd page paperback fiction annual." Awards: 1st: $30; 2nd: $25; 3rd: $20; $5/printed page paid to all accepted writers (on publication). Judges: The editors of *Side Show*. Entry fee $10 (includes subscription). Leaflet available. Sample copy for $12.50 plus $2.50 postage. Deadline: June 30. Multiple submissions encouraged (only one entry fee required for each writer). All mss with SASE critiqued.

CHARLIE MAY SIMON BOOK AWARD, (III, IV), Arkansas Department of Education, Elementary School Council, State Education Building, Capitol Mall, Division of Instruction, Room 301-B, Little Rock AR 72201. (501)682-4371. Contact: James A. Hester, Secretary/Treasurer, Arkansas Elementary School Council. Annual award "to encourage reading by children of Arkansas, to promote book discussions of books read, and to bring before children of Arkansas examples of quality children's literature they would not normally read or would have heard read." Award: Medallion. No entry fee. Previously published submissions. "The committee doesn't accept requests from authors. They will look at booklists of books produced during the previous year and check recommendations from the following sources: *Booklist, Bulletin of the Center for Children's Books, Children's Catalog, Elementary School Library Collection, Hornbook, Library of Congress Children's Books, School Library Journal.*"

SMITH BOOKS IN CANADA FIRST NOVELS AWARD, (III, IV), Books in Canada, 33 Draper St., Toronto, Ontario M5V 2M3 Canada. (416)340-9809. Contact: Paul Stuewe, editor. Annual award "to promote and recognize Canadian writing." Award: $5,000. No entry fee. Submissions are made by publishers. Contest is restricted to first novels in English, intended for adults, written by Canadian citizens or residents.

SNAKE NATION PRESS ANNUAL SUMMER CONTEST, (I), 110-#2 W. Force St., Valdosta GA 31601. (912)249-8334. Contact: Janice Daugharty. "Because we pay only in contributor's copy, this contest allows us to give some financial compensation." Annual award for short stories. Awards: $300, $200, $100. Competition receives approx. 500 submissions. Judge: Independent ("it varies"). Entry fee $5 (includes contest issue). Guidelines for SASE. Deadline: March 1 (for annual summer issue). Unpublished submissions only. Length: 5,000 words maximum.

KAY SNOW CONTEST, (I, IV), Willamette Writers, Suite 5-A, 9045 SW Barbur Blvd., Portland OR 97219. (503)452-1592. Contact: Contest Coordinator. Award "to create a showcase for writers of all fields of literature." Annual competition for short stories; also poetry (structured and nonstructured), nonfiction, juvenile, script and student writers. Award: $100 1st prize in each category, 2nd and 3rd prizes, honorable mentions. Competition receives approx. 500-1,000 submissions. Judges: Nationally recognized writers and teachers. Entry fee $10 nonmembers; $7 members. Guidelines for #10 SASE. Deadline: July 1 postmark. Unpublished submissions. Maximum 1,500 words. "This contest is held in association with our annual conference. Prizes are awarded at the banquet held during the conference in early August."

‡SOCIETY OF CHILDREN'S BOOK WRITERS AND ILLUSTRATORS GOLDEN KITE AWARDS (II), Society of Children's Book Writers and Illustrators, Box 66296, Mar Vista Station, Los Angeles CA 90066. Contact: Sue Alexander, chairperson. Annual award. "To recognize outstanding works of fiction, nonfiction and picture illustration for children by members of the Society of Children's Book Writers and published in the award year." Published submissions should be submitted from January to December of publication year. Deadline entry: December 15. Rules for SASE. Award: Statuette and plaque. Looking for quality material for children. Individual "must be member of the SCBWI to submit books."

SOCIETY OF CHILDREN'S BOOK WRITERS AND ILLUSTRATORS WORK-IN-PROGRESS GRANTS, (I, IV), Box 66296, Mar Vista Station, Los Angeles CA 90066. (818)347-2849. Contact: SCBWI. Annual grant for contemporary novel for young people; also nonfiction research grant and grant for work whose author has never been published. Award: 1st-$1,000; 2nd-$500 (work-in-progress); 1st-$1,000; 2nd-$400 (Judy Blume/SCBWI contemporary novel grant). Competition receives approx. 80 submissions. Judges: Members of children's book field—editors, authors, etc. Guidelines for SASE. Deadline:

Feb. 1-May 1. Unpublished submissions. Applicants must be SCBWI members only.

SOUTH DAKOTA ARTS COUNCIL, ARTIST FELLOWSHIP, (IV), Suite 204, 230 S. Phillips Ave., Sioux Falls SD 57102-0720. (605)339-6646. Award "to assist artists with career development. Grant can be used for supplies or to set aside time to work, but cannot be used for academic research or formal study toward a degree." Annual competition for writers. Award: Artist Career Development grant, $1,000; Artist Fellowship, $5,000. Competition receives approx. 80 submissions. "Grants are awarded on artists' work and *not* on financial need." Judges: Panels of in-state and out-of-state experts in each discipline. Guidelines for SASE. Deadline: February 1. Previously published or unpublished submissions. Fellowships are open only to residents of South Dakota.

‡SOUTHERN ARTS LITERATURE PRIZE, (II, IV), 13 St. Clement St., Winchester, Hampshire S023 9DQ England. Award "to recognize good works by authors (known or unknown) in the southern region (of the U.K.)." Annual competition for short stories, novels and poetry. Award £1,000 (plus winner commissions piece of work; value to £500). Competition receives approx. 20-30 submissions. Judges: 3 people (involved in literature or authors themselves), different each year. Guidelines for SASE. Southern arts region covers Hampshire, Berkshire, Wiltshire, Oxfordshire, Buckinghamshire, Isle of Wight and East Dorset. Write for information; fiction,poetry, nonfiction award alternate fiction award in 1993.

THE SOUTHERN REVIEW/LOUISIANA STATE UNIVERSITY ANNUAL SHORT FICTION AWARD, (II), *The Southern Review,* 43 Allen Hall, Louisiana State University, Baton Rouge LA 70803. (504)388-5108. Contact: Editors, *The Southern Review.* Annual award "to encourage publication of good fiction." For a first collection of short stories by an American writer appearing during calendar year. Award: $500 to author. Possible campus reading. Deadline: A month after close of each calendar year. The book of short stories must be released by a US publisher. Two copies to be submitted by publisher or author. Looking for "style, sense of craft, plot, in-depth characters."

SPUR AWARD CONTEST, (II, IV), Western Writers of America, 2800 N. Campbell, El Paso TX 79902. Secretary-treasurer: Francis L. Fugate. Annual award to encourage excellence in western writing. A spur is awarded for Best Historical Fiction, Best Juvenile Fiction and Best Short Fiction works. Entries are accepted only from the current calendar year for each year's award; that is, books can only be entered in the year they are published. Award: A wooden plaque shaped like a W with a bronze spur attached. Judges: A panel of experienced authors appointed by the current Spur Awards Chairman. Contest/award rules and entry forms available with SASE. Deadline: December 31. "A special Medicine Pipe Bearer Award, is offered in the Best First Western Novel competition. First novels may be entered in both Spur and Medicine Pipe Bearer competition. Works must be, in whole or in part, on settings, characters, conditions, or customs indigenous to the American West."

STAND MAGAZINE SHORT STORY COMPETITION, (I), *Stand Magazine,* 179 Wingrove Road, Newcastle upon Tyne NE4 9DA England. Biennial award for short stories. Award: 1st prize £1,250; 2nd prize £500; 3rd prize £250; 4th prize £150; 5th prize £100; 6th prize £75 (or US $ equivalent). Judges are Susan Hill and David Hughes. Entry fee $7. Guidelines and entry form on receipt of UK SAE or 2 IRCs. Deadline: March 31, 1993.

WALLACE E. STEGNER FELLOWSHIP, (I, IV), Creative Writing Program, Stanford University, Stanford CA 94305-2087. (415)723-2637. Contact: Gay Pierce, program coordinator. Annual award. Four two-year fellowships in fiction ($11,000 stipend plus required tuition of $4,000 annually). Entry fee $20. Deadline: January 2. For unpublished or previously published fiction writers. Residency required.

‡SUGAR MILL PRESS CONTESTS, (I, II), Perry Terrell Publishing, 1617 Newport Place, #24, Kenner LA 70065. (504)465-9412. "The purpose is to draw manuscripts from all writers, especially new writers, pay the winners first and reserve the right to print all (acceptable) material that is sent to Perry Terrell Publishing in *The Ultimate Writer, The Bracelet Charm, Amulet* or *The Veneration Quarterly*; also, to choose manuscripts of unique and outstanding quality to recommend to a small movie production company I have been invited to work with in California. (Writers will be notified before recommendation is made.)" Award is granted monthly, 4 to 6 months after contest deadlines. For short stories. Award: $100, $75, $50, $25 and 2 honorable mentions ($5). Competition receives approx. 25 to 75/ deadline. Judges: Perry Terrell, Editor; Jonathan Everett, Associate Editor; Julie D. Terrell, Features Editor. Entry fee $5. Guidelines for SASE. Deadlines are throughout each month. Previously published or unpublished submissions. "Please specify which deadline and/or contest being entered. If not specified, the editor will read, when time permits, and place the entry the next month." Send SASE for theme list.

SWG LITERARY AWARDS, (I, IV), Saskatchewan Writers Guild, Box 3986, Regina, Saskatchewan S4P 3R9 Canada. (306)757-6310. Awards "to recognize excellence in work by Saskatchewan writers." Annual competition for short stories, poetry, nonfiction and children's literature. Also a long manuscript category that rotates through poetry, nonfiction, drama and fiction. Awards: Manuscript awards (3) are $1,000; 3 awards of $150 in each of the short categories. Judges: Writers from outside the Province. Entry fee: $15 (one ms allowed); $4 for other categories (multiple submissions allowed). Guidelines for SASE. Deadline changes; write for guidelines. February 28. Unpublished submissions. Available only to Saskatchewan citizens.

‡TENNESSEE ARTS COMMISSION INDIVIDUAL ARTISTS FELLOWSHIP, (I,IV), Suite 100, 320 6th Ave. N, Nashville TN 37243-0780. (615)741-1701. Contact: Alice Swanson, director of literary arts. Competition "recognizes outstanding writers in the state." Annual award for fiction. Award: up to $5,000 ($2,500 minimum). Competition receives approximately 40 submissions. Judges are 2 out-of-state jurors. Entry forms available. Writers must be residents of Tennessee.

TEXAS-WIDE WRITERS CONTEST, (I, IV), Byliners, P.O. Box 6218, Corpus Christi TX 78413. (512)991-7969. Contest Committee Chairman: Patsy R. McCleery. "Contest to fund a scholarship in journalism or creative writing." Annual contest for adult and children's short stories, novels and poems. Award: Novels—1st $100, 2nd $75, 3rd $50; short stories—1st $75, 2nd $50, 3rd $25. Competition receives approximately 50 novel, 125 short story and 62 children's story submissions. Judges: Varies each year. Entry fee $5/story, $10/novel. Guidelines available for SASE. Deadline is March 1 (date remains same each year). Unpublished submissions. Limited to Texas residents and winter Texans. Length: Children's story limit 2,000 words; short story limit 3,000 words; novel 3 page synopsis plus chapter one. "Contest also has nostalgia, article and nonfiction book categories."

THURBER HOUSE RESIDENCIES, (II), The Thurber House, 77 Jefferson Ave., Columbus OH 43215. (614)464-1032. Literary Director: Michael J. Rosen. "Four writers/year are chosen as writers-in-residence, one for each quarter." Award for writers of novels and story collections. $5,000 stipend and housing for a quarter in the furnished third-floor apartment of James Thurber's boyhood home. Judges: Advisory panel. To apply send letter of interest and curriculum vitae. Deadline: December 15. "The James Thurber Writer-in-Residence will teach a class in the Creative Writing Program at The Ohio State University in either fiction or poetry, and will offer one public reading and a short workshop for writers in the community. Significant time outside of teaching is reserved for the writer's own work in progress. Candidates should have published at least one book with a major publisher, in any area of fiction, nonfiction or poetry, and should possess some experience in teaching."

TOWSON STATE UNIVERSITY PRIZE FOR LITERATURE, (II, IV), Towson State University Foundation, Towson State University, Towson MD 21204. (301)830-2128. Contact: Annette Chappell, dean, College of Liberal Arts. Annual award for novels or short story collections, previously published. Award: $1,200. Requirements: Writer must not be over 40; must be a Maryland resident. SASE for rules/entry forms. Deadline: May 15.

JOHN TRAIN HUMOR PRIZE, (I), *The Paris Review*, 541 E. 72nd St., New York NY 10021. Fiction Editor: George Plimpton. Award for the best previously unpublished work of humorous fiction, nonfiction or poetry. One submission per envelope. Award: $1,500 and publication in *The Paris Review*. Guidelines for SASE. Deadline: March 31. Manuscripts must be less than 10,000 words. No formal application form is required; regular submissions guidelines apply. For samples, send $7.50 to *The Paris Review*, 45-39171 Place, Flushing NY 11358.

TRANSLATION CENTER AWARDS, (I, II, IV), The Translation Center, 412 Dodge Hall, Columbia University, New York NY 10027. (212)854-2305. Contact: Award Secretary. Over a dozen annual awards "for outstanding translation of a substantial part of a book-length *literary* work." Language-specific awards for Dutch, French-Canadian, Portugese and Italian (fiction only), as well as open to all languages. Award: usually $1,000-2,500. No entry fee. Write for required application form. Deadline: January 15.

TRANSLATORS ASSOCIATION AWARDS, (III, IV), 84 Drayton Gardens, London SW10 9SB England. Scott Moncrieff Prize for best translation into English of 20th century French work; Schlegel-Tieck Prize for translations from German; John Florio Prize for translations from Italian into English; Bernard Shaw Prize for translations from Swedish; Portuguese Prize for translations, published or unpublished, from Portuguese (originals must be by Portuguese nationals). Award: Scott Moncrieff Prize: £1,500; Schlegel-Tieck Prize: £2,000; John Florio Prize (biannual): £900; Bernard Shaw Prize (every 3 years): £ 1,000; Portuguese Prize (every 3 years): £3,000. Judges: 3 translators. Deadline: December 31. Previously published submissions. Awards for translations published in UK during year of award. UK publishers submit books for consideration.

TRI-STATE FAIR LITERARY AWARDS, (I), %Marianne McNeil, 7003 Amarillo Blvd. E., Amarillo TX 79107. (806)379-5032. Annual competition for short stories. Award: Cash, Best of Show Awards for Prose and Poetry. Judges: Different judges each year. Entry fee $7-5 categories prose. Guidelines for SASE. Deadline: August 1. Unpublished submissions. Length: 3,000 words max. "Categories may change a bit from year to year. Guidelines required. At present: Prose—1. Short Story, 2. Articles, 3. Open. Entries are displayed at Literary Booth at Tri-State Fair during fair week."

UTAH ORIGINAL WRITING COMPETITION, (I,IV), Utah Arts Council, 617 East South Temple, Salt Lake City UT 84102. (801)533-5895. Literary Arts Coordinator: G. Barnes. Annual competition for poetry, essays, nonfiction books, short stories, novels and story collections. Awards: Vary; last year between $200-$1,000. Competition receives 700 entries. Judges: "Published and award-winning judges from across America." Guidelines available, no SASE necessary. Deadline: Mid-June or later. Submissions should be unpublished. Limited to Utah residents. "Some limitation on word-length. See guidelines for details."

VERMONT COUNCIL ON THE ARTS FELLOWSHIP, (I, II, IV), Vermont Council on the Arts, 133 State St., Montpelier VT 05633-6001. (802)828-3291. "To support creative development." Annual competition for short stories, novels, story collections and translations. Award: $3,500 with $500 Finalist Awards. The VCA awards approximately 17-20 Fellowships annually. There is no predetermined number of Fellowships by discipline. Judges: A peer panel makes recommendations to the VCA Board of Trustees. Guidelines for SASE after December 1. Previously published and unpublished submissions. Applicants must be legal residents of Vermont and must have lived in VT at least 6 months prior to date of application. Word length: 10-15 pages poetry, 10-20 pages fiction. Applicants may include a synopsis or summary of longer works in addition to submitted excerpts. Applicants must be 18 or older, may not be enrolled as fulltime students, and must have submitted all reports on past council grants. Grant money may not be used for foreign travel, tuition applied to academic programs, or purchase of permanent equipment. *Manuscripts should be unsigned and should indicate completion date.* Manuscripts must be sent with completed application.

VOGELSTEIN FOUNDATION GRANTS, (II), The Ludwig Vogelstein Foundation, Inc., Box 4924, Brooklyn NY 11240-4924. Executive Director: Frances Pishny. "A small foundation awarding grants to individuals in the arts and humanities. Criteria are merit and need. No student aid given." Send SASE for complete information after Jan. 31.

HAROLD D. VURSELL MEMORIAL AWARD, (III), American Academy and Institute of Arts and Letters, 633 W. 155th St., New York NY 10032. (212)368-5900. Annual award "to single out recent writing in book form that merits recognition for the quality of its prose style. It may be given for a work of fiction, biography, history, criticism, belles lettres, memoir, journal or a work of translation." Award: $5,000. Judged by 7-member jury composed of members of the Department of Literature of the American Academy and Institute of Arts and Letters. *No applications accepted.*

‡WALDEN FELLOWSHIP, (I, IV), Coodinated by: The Northwest Writing Institute, Lewis & Clark College, Campus Box 100, Portland OR 97219. (503)768-7745. Award "to give Oregon writers of fiction, poetry and creative nonfiction the opportunity to pursue their work at a quiet, beautiful farm in Southern Oregon." Annual competition for all types of writing. Award: 3-6 week residencies. Competition receives approx. 30 submissions. Judges: Committee judges selected by the sponsor. Guidelines for SASE. Deadline end of November. Oregon writers only. Word length: Maximum 30 pages prose, 8-10 poems.

EDWARD LEWIS WALLANT MEMORIAL BOOK AWARD, (II, IV), 3 Brighton Rd., West Hartford CT 06117. Sponsored by Dr. and Mrs. Irving Waltman. Contact: Mrs. Irving Waltman. Annual award. Memorial to Edward Lewis Wallant, which offers incentive and encouragement to beginning writers, for books published the year before the award is conferred in the spring. Award: $250 plus award certificate. Books may be submitted for consideration to Dr. Sanford Pinsker, Department of English, Franklin & Marshall College, P.O. Box 3003, Lancaster PA 17604-3003. "Looking for creative work of fiction by an American which has significance for the American Jew. The novel (or collection of short stories) should preferably bear a kinship to the writing of Wallant. The award will seek out the writer who has not yet achieved literary prominence."

WASHINGTON PRIZE FOR FICTION, (I), 1301 S. Scott St., Arlington VA 22204. (703)920-3771. Director: Larry Kaltman. Awards: $2,000 (1st prize), $1,000 (2nd prize), $500 (3rd prize). The judges are the English Department chairpersons of three Washington-area universities. The submission may be a novel, several novellas or a collection of short stories. There are no restrictions as to setting or theme. Contestants may reside anywhere. Length: 65,000 words minimum, previously unpublished. Entry fee: $25. Deadline: November 30 annually.

WASHINGTON STATE ARTS COMMISSION ARTIST FELLOWSHIP AWARD, (I, IV), 234 E. 8th Ave., P.O. Box 42675, Olympia WA 98504-2675. (206)753-3860. Arts Program Manager: Mary Frye. "Unrestricted award to a mid-career artist." Biannual award for writers of short stories, novels and literary criticism. Award: $5,000. Competition receives 100 entries. Judges: Peer panel. Guidelines upon request. Deadline: Spring/Summer. Literary arts award made in even-numbered years. Submissions can be either previously published or unpublished. Washington residents only. "Applicant must be 5 years out of school in field they're applying to and have 5 years of professional experience. No emerging artists."

‡WELLSPRING SHORT FICTION CONTEST, *Wellspring Magazine,* 770 Tonkawa Rd., Long Lake MN 55356. (612)471-9259. Award "to select well-crafted short fiction with interesting story lines." Biannual competition for short stories. Award: $100, $75, $25 and publication. Competition receives approx. 40 submissions. Judges: writers and readers. Entry fee $5. Guidelines for SASE. Deadline July 1, Jan. 1. Unpublished submissions. Word length: 2,000 words maximum.

WESTERN CANADIAN MAGAZINE AWARDS, (II, IV), 3898 Hillcrest Ave., North Vancouver, British Columbia V7R 4B6 Canada. (604)984-7525. "To honour and encourage excellence." Annual competition for short stories (fiction articles in magazines). Award: $500. Entry fee: $18-24 (depending on circulation of magazine). Deadline: January. Previously published submissions (between January and December). "Must be Canadian or have earned immigrant status and the fiction article must have appeared in a publication (magazine) that has its main editorial offices located in the 4 Western provinces, the Yukon or NW territories."

WESTERN HERITAGE AWARDS, (II, IV), National Cowboy Hall of Fame, 1700 NE 63rd St., Oklahoma City OK 73111. (405)478-2250. Contact: Dana Sullivant, public relations director. Annual award "to honor outstanding quality in fiction, nonfiction and art literature." Submissions are to have been published during the previous calendar year. Award: The Wrangler, a replica of a C.M. Russell Bronze. No entry fee. Entry forms and rules available October 1 for SASE. Deadline: December 31. Looking for "stories that best capture the spirit of the West."

WESTERN STATES BOOK AWARDS, Western States Arts Federation, 236 Montezuma, Santa Fe NM 87501. (505)988-1166. Literature Coordinator: Robert Sheldon. Estab. 1984. Annual award. "Recognition for writers living in the West; encouragement of effective production and marketing of quality books published in the West; increase of sales and critical attention." For unpublished manuscripts submitted by publisher. Award: $5,000 for authors; $5,000 for publishers. Contest rules for SASE. Write for information on deadline.

WILLIAM ALLEN WHITE CHILDREN'S BOOK AWARD, (III), Emporia State University, 1200 Commercial, Emporia KS 66801. (316)341-5037. Contact: Mary E. Bogan, executive secretary. Estab. 1952. Annual award to honor the memory of one of the state's most distinguished citizens by encouraging the boys and girls of Kansas to read and enjoy good books. "We do not accept submissions from authors or publishers." Award: Bronze medal. The White Award Book Selection Committee looks for excellence of literary quality in fiction, poetry and nonfiction appropriate for 4th through 8th graders.

All nominations to the annual White Award master list must be made by a member of the White Award Book Selection Committee.

WHITING WRITERS' AWARDS, (III), Mrs. Giles Whiting Foundation, Rm. 3500, 30 Rockefeller Pl., New York NY 10112. Director: Dr. Gerald Freund. Annual award for writers of fiction, poetry, nonfiction and plays with an emphasis on emerging writers. Award: $30,000 (10 awards). Writers are submitted by appointed nominators and chosen for awards by an appointed selection committee. Direct applications and informal nominations not accepted by the foundation.

LAURA INGALLS WILDER AWARD, (III), American Library Association/Association for Library Service to Children, 50 E. Huron St., Chicago IL 60611. Executive Director: S. Roman. Award offered every 3 years; next year 1995. "To honor a significant body of work for children, for illustration, fiction or nonfiction." Award: Bronze medal.

LAURENCE L. WINSHIP BOOK AWARD, (III, IV), *The Boston Globe*, P.O. Box 2378, Boston MA 02107-2378. (617)929-2649. Contact: Marianne Callahan, public affairs department. Annual award "to honor *The Globe*'s late editor who did much to encourage young talented New England authors." Award: $2,000. Contest rules for SASE. Deadline: June 30. Previously published submissions from July 1 to June 30 each year. Book must have some relation to New England – author, theme, plot or locale. To be submitted by publishers.

WISCONSIN ARTS BOARD INDIVIDUAL ARTIST PROGRAM, (II, IV), Suite 301, 131 W. Wilson St., Madison WI 53703. (608)266-0190. Contact: Elizabeth Malner. Annual awards for short stories, poetry, novels, novellas, drama, essay/criticism. Awards: 6 awards of $5,000; 4 awards of $3,500; 6 awards of $1,000. Competition receives approx. 175 submissions. Judges are 3 out-of-state jurors. Entry forms or rules upon request. Deadline: September 15. Wisconsin residents only. Students are ineligible.

WISCONSIN INSTITUTE FOR CREATIVE WRITING FELLOWSHIP, (I, II, IV), University of Wisconsin – Creative Writing, English Department, Madison WI 53705. Director: Ron Wallace. Competition "to provide time, space and an intellectual community for writers working on first books." Annual award for short stories, novels and story collections. Award: $20,000/9-month appointment. Competition receives approximately 300 submissions. Judges: English Department faculty. Guidelines available for SASE; write to Ron Kuka. Deadline is month of February. Published or unpublished submissions. Applicants must have received an M.F.A. or comparable graduate degree in creative writing. Limit one story up to 30 pages in length.

WORLD'S BEST SHORT SHORT STORY CONTEST, (I), English Department Writing Program, Florida State University, Tallahassee FL 32306. (904)644-4230. Contact: Jerome Stern, director. Annual award for short-short stories, unpublished, under 250 words. Prizewinning story gets $100, a box of Florida oranges and broadside publication; winner and finalists are published in *Sun Dog: The Southeast Review*. SASE for rules. Deadline: February 15. Open to all.

WRITER'S DIGEST ANNUAL WRITING COMPETITION (Short Story Division), (I), *Writer's Digest*, 1507 Dana Ave., Cincinnati OH 45207. (513)531-2222. Assistant Editor: Anne Hevener. Grand Prize is a trip to New York City with arrangements to meet editors in writer's field. Other awards include cash, reference books, plaques and certificates of recognition. Names of grand prize winner and top 100 winners are announced in the October issue of *Writer's Digest*. Top two entries published in booklet ($4.50). Send SASE to *WD* Writing Competition for rules or see January-May issues of *Writer's Digest*. Deadline: May 31. Entry fee: $5. All entries must be original, unpublished and not previously submitted to a *Writer's Digest* contest. Length: 2,000 words maximum, one entry only. No acknowledgment will be made of receipt of mss nor will mss be returned.

WRITERS GUILD OF ALBERTA LITERARY AWARD, (II, IV), Writers Guild of Alberta, 10523-100 Avenue, Edmonton, Alberta T5J 0A8 Canada. (403)426-5892. Executive Director: Lyle Weis. "To recognize, reward and foster writing excellence." Annual competition for novels and story collections. Award: $500, plus leather-bound copy of winning work. Short story competition receives 5-10 submissions; novel competition receives about 20; children's literature category up to 40. Judges: 3 published writers. Guidelines for SASE. Deadline: December 31. Previously published submissions (between January and December). Open to Alberta authors, resident for previous 18 months. Entries must be book-length and published within the current year.

WRITERS' JOURNAL ANNUAL FICTION CONTEST, (I), 27 Empire Dr., St. Paul MN 55103. (612)225-1306. Publisher/Managing Editor: Valerie Hockert. Annual award for short stories. Award: 1st place: $100; 2nd place: $50; 3rd place: $25. Also gives honorable mentions. Competition receives approximately 500 submissions/year. Judges are Valerie Hockert, Steven Petsch and others. Entry fee $5 each. Maximum of 3 entries/person. Entry forms or rules for SASE. Maximum length is 3,000 words. Two copies of each entry are required—one *without* name or address of writer.

THE WRITERS' WORKSHOP INTERNATIONAL FICTION CONTEST, (I), The Writers' Workshop, P.O. Box 696, Asheville NC 28802. (704)254-8111. Executive Director: Karen Tager. Annual award for fiction. Awards: $500 and submission to *The Paris Review* (1st prize), $250 (2nd prize), $100 (3rd prize). "Winners will also receive an autographed copy of one of E.L. Doctorow's highly acclaimed novels, *Billy Bathgate*; and one year's membership to The Writers' Workshop." Competition receives approximately 350 submissions. Past judges have been E.L. Doctrow, Reynolds Price, Peter Matthiessen and Nikki Giovanni. Entry fee $15/$12 members. Guidelines for SASE. Deadline: February. Unpublished submissions. Length: 30 typed, double-spaced pages. Multiple submissions OK.

WYOMING ARTS COUNCIL LITERARY FELLOWSHIPS, (I, IV), Wyoming Arts Council, 2320 Capitol Ave., Cheyenne WY 82002. (307)777-7742. Contact: Literature consultant. Award to "honor the most outstanding new work of Wyoming writers—fiction, nonfiction, drama, poetry." Annual competition for short stories, novels, story collections, translations, poetry. Award: 4 awards of $2,500 each. Competition receives approx. 120 submissions. Judges: Panel of writers selected each year from outside Wyoming. Guidelines for SASE. Deadline: August 1. Applicants "must be Wyoming resident for one year prior to application deadline. Must not be a full time student." No genre exclusions; combined genres acceptable. 25 pages double-spaced maximum; 10 pages maximum for poetry. Winners may not apply for 4 years after receiving fellowships.

YOUNG READER'S CHOICE AWARD, (III), Pacific Northwest Library Association, Graduate School of Library and Information Sciences, 133 Suzzallo Lib., FM-30, University of Washington, Seattle WA 98195. (206)543-1897. Contact: Carol A. Doll. Annual award "to promote reading as an enjoyable activity and to provide children an opportunity to endorse a book they consider an excellent story." Award: Silver medal. Judges: Children's librarians and teachers nominate; children in grades 4-8 vote for their favorite book on the list. Guidelines for SASE. Deadline: February 1. Previously published submissions. Writers must be nominated by children's librarians and teachers.

Contests/'92-'93 changes

The following contests, grants and awards appeared in the 1992 edition of *Novel & Short Story Writer's Market* but do not appear in the 1993 edition. Those contests, grants and awards that did not respond to our request for an update appear below without further explanation. If a reason for the omission is available, it is included next to the listing name.

American Fiction Vol III
James Tait Black Memorial Prizes
Boots Romantic Novel of the Year
Canadian Fiction Magazine Contributor's Prize
Colorado Council on the Arts & Humanities Creative Fellowship (program suspended)
Columbia Magazine Editors Awards (no longer awarded)
Edmonton Journal's Literary Awards (asked to be deleted)
Goodman Fielder Wattie Book Award
Guardian Children's Fiction Award

Hutton Fiction Contest (ceased publication)
Iowa Literary Awards (program discontinued)
Latino Literature Prize
Mademoiselle Fiction Writers Contest (discontinued)
Mind Book of the Year—The Allen Lane Award
National Book Council/Qantas New Writers Award (no longer awarded)
National Foundation for Advancement in the Arts/Arts Recognition and Talent Search (Arts)
New Jersey State Council on the Arts Prose Fellowship
Paper Bag Short Shorts
Published Short-Story Contest (no longer presented)

Rambunctious Review, Annual Fiction Contest
River City Writing Awards in Fiction
Sonora Review Fiction Contest
South Carolina Arts Commission and the State Newspaper South Carolina Fiction Project
South Carolina Arts Commission Literature Fellowship and Literature Grants
Story Time Short-Story Contest (ceased publication)
Mark Twain Award
Victorian Fellowship of Australian Writers Annual National Literary Awards
Young Adult Canadian Book Award (no longer awarded)

Resources

Resources

Conferences and Workshops

Over the years, it has become increasingly apparent that workshops and conferences can be an integral part of a writer's life. Indeed, the number of these events alone attests to their popularity. Even though we started this section last year, it has become by far the fastest growing section in the book.

In this section you will find a wide variety of both conferences and workshops for fiction writers—and even more are out there. A "typical" conference may have a number of workshop sessions, keynote speakers and perhaps even a panel or two. Topics may include everything from writing fiction, poetry or books for children to marketing work and locating an agent. Sometimes a theme will be the connecting factor.

Other conferences and workshops are more specific, catering to a certain type of writer or aspect of writing. The Eastern Writers' Conference, for example, is for writers with a connection to the Eastern U.S. The Florida Christian Writers Conference includes all aspects of Christian writing, and the SCBWI Conference in Children's Literature focuses on the writing and marketing of writing for children.

Each of the listings here includes information about the specific focus of an event as well as the planned panels or speakers. It is important to note, though, that some conference and workshop directors were still in the organizing stages when contacted. Consequently, some listings include last year's speakers and/or panels to simply give you an idea of what to expect. This holds true for the costs of many of these events as well. For more current information, it's best to send a self-addressed, stamped envelope to the director in question about three months before the date(s) listed.

Learning and networking

First and foremost, conferences and workshops provide writers with opportunities to learn more about their craft, whether it be the business or the writing side. Some even feature individual sessions with workshop leaders, allowing writers to specifically discuss their works-in-progress with people respected in their field. If these one-on-one sessions include critiques (generally for an additional fee), that, too, is included in the listings.

Besides learning from workshop leaders in formal sessions, writers may also benefit from conversations with other attendees. Writers on all levels enjoy sharing insights. Often a conversation over lunch can reveal a new market for your work or let you know which editors have changed houses. A casual chat while waiting for a session to begin can acquaint you with a new resource in your area or one available nationwide.

Another reason writers find conferences and workshops worthwhile is the opportunity to meet editors and agents. In fact, *The Writer's Book of Checklists* (Writer's Digest Books) indicates the best way to make business contacts is through workshops and conferences, followed by special-interest conventions, such as mystery or science fiction "cons." Be careful, however. Although some writers have been fortunate to sell manuscripts at such events, the availability of editors and agents does not usually mean these folks will want to read your six best short stories (unless, of course, you've scheduled an individual meeting with them). While editors and agents are glad to meet writers and discuss work in general terms, they cannot give extensive attention to everyone they meet.

To get the most out of your brief contact with an editor or agent, treat him or her as you would anyone you were meeting for the first time—be courteous and friendly. Ask specific questions about his or her job or, better yet, some point of his or her presentation. Let the conversation turn toward your writing naturally. If your time is up before you get the chance to mention your craft, don't worry. You can follow up later with a letter making reference to having met at such-and-such a conference.

Selecting a conference

To narrow down your options when it comes to finally selecting the right conference or workshop to attend, keep your goals in mind. If your goal is to learn how to improve your writing, for example, then consider the level of writers toward which the event is geared. A workshop focusing on the best ways to market work may hold valuable insight, but it may not help you learn how to determine what constitutes a good first chapter for a novel. If your goal is to network, then choose events where editors who focus on your type of writing will be in attendance.

Of course, writers should also take into consideration their own resources. If both your time and funds are limited, you may want to search for a conference or workshop in your city, state or province. Some conferences are actually regional events sponsored by branches of large organizations, such as the International Women's Writing Guild (IWWG) and the Society of Children's Book Writers and Illustrators (SCBWI). Many events are held during weekends and may be close enough that you can commute, so you don't have to take time off work and/or spend more than your budget allows.

On the other hand, you may want to combine your vacation with time spent meeting other writers and working on your craft. If this is the case, there are events such as the *Ploughshares* International Fiction Writing Seminar held in Holland or, if that's a little too far from home, Writing By the Sea in Cape May, New Jersey. It is important to at least consider the conference location and be aware of other activities to enjoy in the area. The listings in these pages describe both the location of the conference and the events or attractions available nearby.

Still other factors may influence your decision when selecting a certain workshop or conference. Those with contests allow writers to gain recognition and recoup some of their expenses. Similarly, some conferences and workshops have financial assistance or scholarships available. Finally, many are associated with colleges and/or universities and may offer continuing education credits. You will find all of these options included in the listings here. Again, send a self-addressed, stamped envelope for more details.

For more information about the wide range of conferences and workshops, you may want to consult *The Guide to Writers Conferences* (Shaw Associates, publishers, Suite 1406, 625 Biltmore Way, Coral Gables FL 33134) and the May issue of *Writer's Digest* magazine. Another source is *Author & Audience: A Readings and Workshops Guide*, both available from Poets & Writers, Inc. (72 Spring St., New York NY 10012).

ALABAMA WRITERS' CONCLAVE, 3225 Burning Tree Dr., Birmingham AL 35226. First Vice President Programs: Ann Moon Rabb. Estab. 1923. Annual. Conference held August 4 to August 6. Average attendance: 85-120. Conference to promote "all phases" of writing. Held at the Ramsay Conference Center (University of Montevallo). "We attempt to contain all workshops under this roof. Some functions take place at other campus buildings."

Costs: In 1992 fees for 3 days were $35 for members; $45 for nonmembers. Lower rates for one- or two-day attendence.
Accommodations: Accommodations available on campus (charged separately).
Additional Information: "We have had a works-in-progress group with members helping members." Sponsors a contest. Conference brochures/guidelines available for SASE. Membership dues are $15. Membership information from Harriette Dawkins, 117 Hanover Rd., Homewood AL 35209.

‡**ANNUAL WRITERS INSTITUTE,** 610 Langdon St., Madison WI 53703. (608)262-3447. Director: Christine DeSmet. Estab. 1990. Annual. Conference held in July. Conference duration: 2 days. Average attendance: 180. "Nonfiction on Day 1; Fiction on Day 2." Site is Wisconsin Center, 702 Langdon St. It sits on a large lake and is in the heart of campus and downtown of the Capitol. Theme is "Stories for the 90s: Changes in Readers and Markets for Writers." Guest speakers are several published writers, editors.
Costs: $75/day or $125 for both days. Inexpensive lunch options abound.
Accommodations: Lodging is nearby; information available through registration center or call director. University-run hotel lodging is approx. $45.
Additional Information: Critiques are optional. Cost is $15. Brochures are available for SASE.

ANTIOCH WRITERS' WORKSHOP, P.O. Box 494, Yellow Springs OH 45387. Director: Susan Carpenter. Estab. 1984. Annual. Average attendance: 80. Conference concentration: poetry, nonfiction and fiction. Conference located on Antioch College campus in the Village of Yellow Springs. Speakers planned for next conference include Joe David Bellamy, Mary Grimm, Ralph Keys and Stanley Plumly.
Costs: Tuition is $425 — lower for local and repeat — plus meals.
Accommodations: "We pick up free at airport." Accommodations made at dorms and area hotels. Cost is $10-17/night (for dorms).
Additional Information: Offers free critique sessions. Conference brochures/guidelines are available for SASE.

APPALACHIAN WRITERS CONFERENCE, Box 6935, Radford University, Radford VA 24142-6935. (703)831-5269; 639-0812. AWA President: Dr. R. Parks Lanier, Jr. Estab. 1980. Annual. Conference held from July 9 to July 11. Average attendance: 60. "Fiction, nonfiction, poetry, drama, story telling and grants writing are some of the topics discussed at each AWA Conference. Writers have some form of identification with the Appalachian region, either as the place from which they come, the place in which they live or the place about which they write." Radford University is located just off I-81 on the banks of the historic New River, 40 miles Southwest of Roanoke in Radford, Virginia. Participants may stay "in a newly renovated air-conditioned dormitory at very reasonable rates, cool, quiet, comfortable." The AWA is now regularly inviting editors to speak. Guest speakers. "Most of the AWA members are themselves authors with a national reputation."
Costs: AWA annual dues are $10. Meals in university cafeteria cost $5 or less.
Accommodations: Rooms are less than $50 for two nights, single occupancy.
Additional Information: There are contests for fiction, poetry, nonfiction and younger writers. AWA members are judges. Conference brochures/guidelines available for SASE.

ARIZONA CHRISTIAN WRITERS CONFERENCE, P.O. Box 5168, Phoenix AZ 85010. (602)838-4919. Director: Reg Forder. Estab. 1981. Annual. Conference held November 5 to November 7, 1993. Average attendance: 200. To promote all forms of Christian writing. Conference held in new Holiday Inn Hotel near airport in Phoenix. Panels planned for next conference include "Writing as a Ministry." Representatives from several publishing houses: Tyndale; Harvest House; Regal Books; *Christian Parenting Today Magazine*, are scheduled to speak at next conference.
Costs: Approx. $100 plus meals and accommodation.
Accommodations: Special price in our host hotel (Holiday Inn) $45 per night for 1 or 2 persons.
Additional Information: Conference brochures/guidelines are available for SASE. "This annual conference is held in Phoenix always on the first weekend in November."

 The double dagger before a listing indicates that the listing is new in this edition.

‡ARKANSAS WRITERS' CONFERENCE, 1115 Gillette Dr., Little Rock AR 72207. (501)225-0166. Director: Clovita Rice. Estab. 1944. Annual. Conference held: June 1993. Average attendance: 225. "We have a variety of subjects related to writing—we have some general sessions, some more specific, but try to vary each year's subjects."

Costs: Registration: $10; luncheon: $11; banquet: $13.

Accommodations: "We meet at a Holiday Inn—rooms available at reasonable rate." Holiday has a bus to bring anyone from airport. Rooms average $56/single.

Additional Information: "We have 36 contest categories. Some are open only to Arkansans, most are open to all writers. Our judges are not announced before conference, but are qualified, many out of state." Conference brochures are available for SASE after February 1. "We have had 226 attending from 12 states—over 2,200 contest entries from 43 states and New Zealand. We have a get acquainted party at my home on Thursday evening for early arrivers."

ARTS AT MENUCHA, P.O. Box 4958, Portland OR 97208. (503)234-6827. Board Member: Connie Cheifetz. Estab. 1966. Annual. Conference held August 7 to August 20. Conference duration: Each class lasts 1 week. Average attendance: 60 overall (6-10 per class). Conference held at a "residential private estate with dorm rooms, most with private bath. 100-acre wooded grounds overlooking the Columbia River. A beautiful, relaxing place with pool, tennis, volleyball and walking trails. Meals provided (family-style). 1993 will see us offering fiction and poetry workshops. Also we offer visual arts class."

Costs: '93 Rates $450/1 week; $800/2 weeks; includes room and board.

Accommodations: "We will pick folks up from Portland Airport, bus or train depot." Everyone, including instructors, stays at "Menucha" overnight Sun.-Sat. a.m.

Additional Information: Conference brochures/guidelines are available (no SASE needed).

AUSTIN WRITERS' LEAGUE FALL AND SPRING WORKSHOPS, E-2, 1501 W. 5th, Austin TX 78703. (512)499-8914. Executive Director: Angela Smith. Estab. 1982. Held each fall and spring (March, April, May, September, October, November). Conference duration: 1 day; Saturdays. Average attendance: at least 14 workshops in each series, each drawing from 15 to 150. To promote "all genres, fiction and nonfiction, poetry, writing for children, screenwriting, playwriting, legal and tax information for writers, also writing workshops for children and youth." Conference held at "St. Edward's University—classroom space and auditoriums. Located at 3001 S. Congress, Austin, Texas 78704." Workshops planned include: Finding and working with agents and publishers; writing and publishing short fiction; dialogue; characterization; voice of the fiction writer; basic and advanced fiction writing; book marketing and promotion; also workshops for genres. "Spring '93 series now being planned. Past speakers have included Dwight Swain, Natalie Goldberg, David Lindsey, D.F. Mills, Shelby Hearon."

Costs: Each three-hour workshop is $35-45 (members); $25 more for nonmembers. Six-hour labs are $75 (members); $25 more for nonmembers.

Accommodations: Austin Writers' League will provide assistance with transportation arrangements on request. List of hotels is available for SASE. Special rates given at some hotels for workshop participants.

Additional Information: Critique sessions offered. Individual presenters determine critique requirements. Those requirements are then made available through Austin Writers' League office and in workshop promotion. Contests and awards programs are offered separately from workshops. Conference brochures/guidelines are available on request. "In addition to regular series of workshops, Austin Writers' League sponsors ongoing informal classes in writing, plus weekend seminars and retreats throughout the year."

AUTUMN AUTHORS' AFFAIR, 1507 Burnham Ave., Calumet City IL 60409. (708)862-9797. President: Nancy McCann. Estab. 1983. Annual. Conference held in late October. Begins with Friday night buffet and ends with Sunday brunch. Average attendance: 300. "Focused on romance, contemporary and historical, but also features poetry, short story, mystery, young adult, childrens, screenplay writing and journalism." Site: Hyatt Regency, Oak Brook. Includes indoor parking, conference center, 425 guest rooms, 14 suites, indoor pool, exercise equipment, jacuzzi, and shopping center right across the street. Panels planned include "everything from the basics, to getting started, to how to handle the business aspects of your writing. Out of 25 workshops, 23 focus on 'fiction' writing."

Costs: 1992 cost was $100, which included Friday night buffet, Saturday continental breakfast and luncheon and Sunday brunch.
Accommodations: Information on overnight accommodations is made available with a "special" room rate for those attending conference. "Last year the rate for single, double or quad was $77. This year, this price may be slightly higher."
Additional Information: Brochures/guidelines available for SASE.

‡**BALTIMORE SCIENCE FICTION SOCIETY WRITER'S WORKSHOP**, P.O. Box 686, Baltimore MD 21203-0686. (301)563-2737. Contact: Steve Lubs. Estab. 1983. Conference/workshop held: roughly, 3 times/year. "Conference dates vary, please write for next date held and deadline information." Conference duration: 1 day. Average attendance: 7. Conference concentration is science fiction and fantasy. "Conference is held in a former movie theater (small) in the process of being renovated."
Costs: Manuscripts are submitted in advance—cost is 75¢/page.
Additional Information: "Manuscripts are submitted in advance, by a particular deadline. A copy of every submission is mailed to each participant, to read and critique before the workshop. We are an amateur writer's group, attempting to help anyone interested in writing better science fiction and/ or fantasy. This workshop is sponsored by a nonprofit group who promote science fiction and fantasy in the Baltimore-Washington D.C. area."

BAY AREA WRITERS WORKSHOP, P.O. Box 620327, Woodside CA 94062. (415)851-4568. Co-Directors: Laura Jason, Joyce Jenkins. Estab. 1988. Annual. Offers 4-5 separate weekend intensive workshops and a biennial 1-day conference, "Literary Publishing Day." Average attendance for 1-day conference: 250; each weekend workshop: 15. Workshops are offered in short story, novel and poetry, "both with a strong literary bent and a master class format." Sites: San Francisco, Berkeley and Palo Alto. "Literary Publishing & Resources features agents and editors from large and small presses. The 1992 conference included editors from Viking Penguin, *The New Yorker*, *American Poetry Review*, Copper Canyon and *Poetry Flash*. Workshop leaders for the last two years included Robert Hass, Li-Young Lee, Wanda Coleman, Olga Broumas, Larry Heinemann, Joy Williams, David Shields and Clarence Major."
Costs: $250/weekend workshop plus $15 application fee. Ten scholarships are available for writers based on the quality of the application manuscript. Cost for Literary Publishing & Resources: $45.
Additional Information: Weekend workshops include 15 hours of in-class time. No individual consultations. Brochures are available for SASE.

BE THE WRITER YOU WANT TO BE MANUSCRIPT CLINIC, 23350 Sereno Ct., Villa 30, Cupertino CA 95014. (415)691-0300. Contact: Louise Purwin Zobel. Estab. 1969. Workshop held irregularly—usually semiannually at several locations. Workshop duration: 1-2 days. Average attendance: 20-30. "This manuscript clinic enables writers of any type of material to turn in their work-in-progress—at any stage of development—to receive help with structure and style, as well as marketing advice." It is held on about 40 campuses at different times, including University of California and other university and college campuses throughout the west.
Costs: Usually $45-65/day, "depending on campus."
Additional Information: Brochures/guidelines available for SASE.

BLUE RIDGE WRITERS CONFERENCE, (NC), P.O. Box 188, Black Mountain NC 28711. (704)669-8421. Director: Yvonne Lehman. Estab. 1975. Annual. Conference held from August 6 to August 8. Conference duration: 2½ days. Average attendance: 70. Conference to promote "all" forms of writing. Conference held at Quality Inn, Biltmore in the mountains of North Carolina. Guest speakers *for 1992* were Thomas Clark, Virginia Muir, Dennis Hensley, Jeff Herman, Paricia Hagan, Liz Squires.
Costs: 1992 fees: $150 for full time tuition; part-time fees $10-30.
Accommodations: On-site facilities at Quality Inn, Biltmore. Rates: $32.50-65. Meals: Your choice— two QI restaurants or area eating places nearby.
Additional Information: Critique service available. Cost: $30. Work must be submitted by July 1. Conference brochures/guidelines are available for SASE.

BLUE RIDGE WRITERS CONFERENCE, (VA), 2840-C Hershberger Rd., Roanoke VA 24017. Chairman: Dr. Norman Peets. Estab. 1984. Annual. One-day conference held in October ("usually first Saturday, but this may change depending upon availability of speakers."). Average attendance: 120. Conference "to make available an opportunity for networking and exchange of ideas between writers, both aspiring and professional, in Virginia's Blue Ridge area. Also, to enhance the status of writers

and writing in this part of Virginia and to bring this artistic endeavor to the same level of public recognition, appreciation and pride in performance that is already enjoyed by music, the theater, dance and the fine arts." Site: Roanoke College, Salem, VA. Special bookstore features publications of speakers and books on writing. "Plans are incomplete for 1992, but we plan to include a session on poetry and another on screenwriting. We will also have fiction writing." Keynote not yet confirmed. Poet John Stone will participate in workshops.
Costs: $40; $20 for fulltime students. Includes luncheon and reception.
Additional Information: Brochures available for SASE.

‡BREAD LOAF WRITERS' CONFERENCE, Middlebury College, Middlebury VT 05753. (802)388-3711 ext. 5286. Administrative Coordinator: Carol Knauss. Estab. 1926. Annual. Conference held from August 17 to August 29. Conference duration: 12 days. Average attendance: 230. For fiction, nonfiction and poetry. Held at the summer campus in Ripton Vermont (belongs to Middlebury College).
Costs: $1,375 (includes room/board) (1992).
Accommodations: Accommodations are at Ripton. Onsite accommodations $475 (1992).

CANADIAN AUTHORS ASSOCIATION CONFERENCE, Suite 500, 275 Slater St., Ottawa, Ontario K1P 5H9 Canada. (613)233-2846. Fax: (613)235-8237. National Director: Jeffrey Holmes. Estab. 1921. Annual. Conference held June 18-20. Average attendance: 150. To promote "all genres—varies from year to year." University dormitory, air-conditioned—beautiful campus. On city bus line route. Topic for 1993 conference to be held at the Walter Gage Complex of the campus of the University of British Columbia is "Write Foot Forward."
Costs: Approx. $140 (Canadian); accommodation and meals extra, except for keynote breakfast and awards banquet. Special early-bird discounts.
Accommodations: Special accommodations available on request.
Additional Information: Conference brochures/registration forms are available for SAE and IRC.

‡CAPE COD WRITERS CONFERENCE, % Cape Cod Conservatory, Route 132, West Barnstable MA 02668. (508)775-4811. Executive Director: Marion Vuillenmier. Estab. 1963. Annual. Conference held: August 15-20. Conference duration: one week. Average attendance: 125. For fiction, nonfiction, poetry, juvenile writing and mystery/suspense. Held at Craigville Conference Center, a campus arrangement on shore of Cape's south side. Guest speakers and panelists for 1992 were Nancy Thayer, novelist; Chad Hoffman, Hollywood producer; Judson Hale, editor *Yankee* magazine; agent Alison Picard; editor Dana Isaacson of Pocket Books.
Costs: $80 registration and $50 per course; housing and meals separate, paid to the Conference Center.
Accommodations: Information on overnight accommodations made available. On-site accommodations at Craigville Conference Center plus 3 meals, approx. $70/day.
Additional Information: Conference brochures/guidelines are available for SASE. In addition to this conference, sponsors are planning a Writer's Conference in London (August 26-September 2). Total cost (including airfare) will be $1,995. Write or call for details.

‡CAPE LITERARY ARTS WORKSHOP, % Cape Cod Conservatory, Route 132, West Barnstable MA 02668. (508)775-4811. Executive Director: Marion Vuillenmier. Estab. 1985. Annual. Workshops held in 5 sessions, consecutive weeks in summer. Workshop duration: 6 days. Average attendance: limit to 10/workshop. Concentrations include mystery/suspense, scriptwriting, children's book writing and illustration. "Workshop site is an historic old colonial courthouse in a Cape Cod village."
Costs: $75 registration; $335 tuition.
Accommodations: Information on overnight accommodations is made available. Accommodations are made at nearby bed and breakfast establishments.
Additional Information: Brochures are available for SASE.

‡CHILDREN'S BOOK PUBLISHING: AN INTENSIVE WRITING & EDITING WORKSHOP, Rice University School of Continuing Studies, Box 1892, Houston TX 77251. (713)527-4803. Assistant Dean: Edie Carlson-Abbey. Estab. 1989. Annual. Conference held in summer. Conference duration: 5 days. Average attendance: 30. "Writing for children." Held in classrooms and meeting rooms in the Center for Continuing Studies, Rice University campus. "1992 workshop led by Mary Blount Christian, author of more than 100 books for children."

Costs: $695 plus $20 manuscript fee.

Accommodations: List of hotels available.

Additional Information: Critiques available if work submitted in advance, by deadline listed on brochure. Free conference brochures/guidelines.

‡**CHRISTIAN WRITERS CONFERENCE,** 177 E. Crystal Lake Ave., Lake Mary FL 32746. (407)324-5465. Fax: (407)324-0209. Conference Director: Dottie McBroom. Estab. 1948. Annual. Conference held from May 30 to June 2. Average attendance: 150. For fiction, writing for children, nonfiction. Held at Wheaton College, Wheaton, Illinois. Themes: Writing for broadcast media. In 1992 guest speakers were Len and Sandy LeSourd.

Costs: $295 single; $265 double (1992).

Accommodations: United Airlines conference rates available. Accommodations are dorms at Wheaton College. Onsite accommodations are included in cost.

Additional Information: Sponsors a contest: 1. Must register for entire conference; 2. Editors on staff judge the entries. Conference brochures/guidelines are available for SASE.

CHRISTOPHER NEWPORT UNIVERSITY WRITERS' CONFERENCE, 50 Shoe Lane, Newport News VA 23606-2998. (804)594-7158. Coordinator: Doris Gwaltney. Estab. 1981. Annual. Conference held April 2-3. Average attendance: 100. "Our workshop is for both published and unpublished writers in all genres. It provides a network for area writers, connecting them with markets, literary agents, editors and printers." The conference is held on the campus of Christopher Newport University in Newport News, Va. "We have a good food service, a bookstore, adequate meeting rooms and total access for the handicapped." Workshop presenters: Michael Mott — Poetry, Katie Letcher Lyle — Young people's fiction, Dorothy Weber — self publishing and other literary experts.

Costs: $65, includes wine-and-cheese reception on Friday evening in "Celebration of the Arts," coffee and pastries and lunch on Saturday.

Accommodations: Adequate parking available. "Our staff could help with arrangements for overnight accommodations."

Additional Information: "We have a literary contest in four areas: poetry, fiction, nonfiction and juvenile fiction. Each entry is critiqued by a judge who is a published writer in the field." Conference brochures/guidelines available for SASE.

COPYRIGHT WORKSHOP, 610 Langdon St., Madison WI 53703. (608)262-3447. Director: Christine DeSmet. Offered 2 times/year. Conference held March 26 (check with director for further dates). Average attendance: 50. "Copyright law for writers, publishers, teachers, designers." Conference held at Wisconsin Center, University of Wisconsin — Madison.

Costs: $115.

Additional Information: Conference brochures/guidelines are available.

CRAFT OF WRITING, UTD Box 839688, CN 1.1, Richardson TX 75083. (214)690-2204. Director: Janet Harris. Estab. 1983. Annual. Conference held September (check for exact dates). Average attendance: 150. "To provide information to accomplished and aspiring writers on how to write and how to get published. All genres are included. Areas of writing covered include characterization and dialogue to working with an agent." Conference held at the University of Texas-Dallas. The UTD Conference Center has an auditorium which seats 500, two lecture halls seating 160 each and several smaller classrooms. Workshops in 1992 included a panel of editors and agents (both national and local), "The Pleasure Motive," "The Profit Motive," "Your First Step Toward An Agent," and "A Step Beyond: Focusing on Point of View for Depth and Power of Story."

Costs: $175; includes 2 lunches and a banquet.

Accommodations: A block of rooms is held at the Richardson Hilton for $49/night. Call (214)644-4000 for reservations.

Additional Information: Critiques available. "There are no requirements. Participants may have manuscripts critiqued by members of the Greater Dallas Writers Association. Two manuscript critique sessions are scheduled. A manuscript contest is held prior to the conference. The deadline for submissions is August 1. Judges are specialists in the areas they are critiquing. There are nine categories with several cash prizes. Conference brochures/guidelines are available. Twenty-eight workshops are scheduled on a wide range of topics. Presenters include nationally known authors, agents, editors and publishers."

‡CUMBERLAND VALLEY WRITERS WORKSHOP, Dickinson College, Carlisle PA 17013-2896. (717)245-1291. Director: Judy Gill. Estab. 1990. Annual. Conference held from June 18 to June 25. Average attendance: 30-40. "2-day creative nonfiction (autobiography, personal essay, nature/science writing) and 5-day fiction. Workshop is held on the campus of Dickinson College, a small liberal arts college, in Carlisle, PA." Panel: "Writers Roundtable"—faculty respond to wide variety of questions submitted by participants. Guest speaker 1992: Jennifer Ash, editor at Random House.
Costs: Tuition for 5-day workshop: $280; room (optional): $100; board (optional): $100 (1992).
Accommodations: Special accommodations made. A residence hall on campus is reserved for workshop participants. Cost is $20 per night.
Additional Information: Applicants must submit a 10-page manuscript for evaluation prior to the workshop. Conference brochures/guidelines are available for SASE.

‡CUYAHOGA WRITERS' CONFERENCE, 4250 Richmond Rd., Highland Hills Village OH 44122-6195. Contact: Margo Bohanon, Assistant Professor of English. Estab. 1974. Annual. Conference held in May. Conference duration 2 days. Average attendance: 200. "We present workshops on all areas of writing. We normally present ten writers all of whom write in different genres." Site is the eastern campus of Cuyahoga Community College.
Costs: $25.
Accommodations: Information on overnight accommodations is made available; weekend rates at area hotels. Hotels are less than a mile from the conference site.
Additional Information: Writers may submit manuscripts for critique. There is a charge of $20. "Brochures describing the conference are available in April. No SASE necessary. We do maintain a mailing list."

DEEP SOUTH WRITERS CONFERENCE, P.O. Drawer 44691, Lafayette LA 70504. (318)231-6918. Contact: Director. Estab. 1960. Annual. Conference held third weekend in September. Average attendance: 200+. Conference focuses on "workshops and readings with an emphasis on poetry and fiction, secondarily on drama and nonfiction. Workshops may be how-to-do-it craft lectures, but they have varied tremendously over the years. The site has been a building housing the English department on the University of Southwestern Louisiana campus. Readers and workshop leaders have not yet been finalized. "Last year's conference featured Kelly Cherry, Tim O'Brien, Cheryl St. Germain, Peter Cooley, David Middleton, Jason Berry and Robert Olin Butler."
Costs: Pre-registration is $25; registration at the conference is $40, students pay $25 all times.
Accommodations: "We have provided a shuttle service for participants in the past. Some information about lodging is provided in our annual flyer. Information regarding local restaurants and local attractions is given out at the conference. Local per diem expenses in Lafayette for room and board range between $50 and $120."
Additional Information: Sponsors contest. Write for rules and entry requirements. Conference brochures/guidelines available for SASE.

‡DESERT WRITERS WORKSHOP/CANYONLANDS FIELD INSTITUTE, P.O. Box 68, Moab UT 84532. (801)259-7750. Special Program Coordinator: Linda Whitham. Estab. 1984. Annual. Held September 30-October 3. Conference duration: 3½ days. Average attendance: 29. Concentrations include fiction, nonfiction, poetry. Site is the Cunningham Ranch—an historic ranch recently purchased by the Nature Conservancy, 60 miles from Moab, Utah. "Theme is oriented towards understanding the vital connection between human beings and the natural world."
Costs: $300/person, which includes lunches Friday-Sunday, instruction, field trip, lodging.
Accommodations: At Cunningham Ranch, included in cost.
Additional Information: Critique work takes place during workshop. Participants are requested to send work to authors. Brochures are available for SASE. "Canyonlands Field Institute is a nonprofit educational organization that promotes a better understanding and respect for the unique cultural and natural history of the Colorado Plateau."

DUKE UNIVERSITY WRITERS' WORKSHOP, The Bishop's House, Durham NC 27708. (919)684-6259. Director: Marilyn Hartman. Estab. 1978. Annual. Conference held June 22 to June 26. Average attendance: 50. To promote "creative writing: beginning, intermediate and advanced fiction; short story; scriptwriting; children's writing; mystery; poetry; creative nonfiction." Conference held at "Duke University campus classrooms and meeting facilities. Gothic architecture, rolling green hills. Nationally recognized for its beauty and academic excellence, Duke sponsors this workshop annually for creative writers of various genres." Theme is creative writing ("that's our only song!").

Costs: $345 for conference (most meals not included).
Accommodations: On-campus hotel is $45/night, single occupancy (double occupancy @ $22.50). Includes "elegant service, afternoon tea, indoor pool and sauna, van transportation; writing desks in rooms."
Additional Information: Critiques available. "Works-in-progress requested 3 weeks before workshop. Each participant gets *private* consult plus small-group in-class critiques." Conference brochures/ guidelines are available. "No 'big' names, no mammoth lectures; simply *excellent*, concentrated instruction plus time to work. No glitz. Hard work. Great results."

EASTERN KENTUCKY UNIVERSITY CREATIVE WRITING CONFERENCE, Eastern Kentucky University, Richmond KY 40475. (606)622-5861. Conference Director: Harry Brown. Estab. 1962. Annual. Conference held June 14-18 (usually 3rd week in June). Average attendance: 12-15. Conference to promote poetry, fiction and creative nonfiction, including lectures, workshops, private conferences and peer group manuscript evaluation. The conference is held on the campus of Eastern Kentucky University "in the rolling hills of Eastern Kentucky, between the horse farms of the Bluegrass and the scenic mountains of the Appalachian chain." William Moseley and two other visiting writers will teach at the converence. Also helping with workshops will be EKU faculty Dorothy Sutton, Harry Brown, Hal Blythe, Charlie Sweet.
Costs: $55 for undergraduates ($153 if out-of-state); $79 for graduates ($224 if out-of-state). Cost includes 1 hour of credit in creative writing and is subject to change. Auditors welcome at same price. Dining in the cafeteria is approximately $6-8/day.
Accommodations: Air-conditioned dormitory rooms are available for $32 (double) or $46 (single) per week. "Linens furnished. Bring your own blankets, pillow and telephone."
Additional Information: "Participants are asked to submit manuscript in late May to be approved before June 1." For conference brochure, send SASE to English Department (attn: Creative Writing Conference).

EASTERN WRITERS' CONFERENCE, English Dept., Salem State College, Salem MA 01970. (508)741-6270. Conference Director: Rod Kessler. Estab. 1977. Annual. Conference held June 19-20. Average attendance: 60. Conferece to "provide a sense of community and support for area poets and fiction writers. We try to present speakers and programs of interest, changing our format from time to time. Conference-goers usually have an opportunity to read to an audience or have manuscripts professionally critiqued. We tend to draw regionally." Plans for next conference include "Breaking into Print: A Former Conference-Goer's Success Story." Previous speakers have included Marge Piercy, Audre Dubus and Dianne Benedict.
Costs: "under $100."
Accommodations: Information on overnight accommodations is made available.
Additional Information: "Optional ms critiques are available for an additional fee." Conference brochures/guidelines available for SASE.

‡FAIRVIEW SUMMIT WRITERS SANCTUARY WORKSHOPS, Route 9 Box 351, Cumberland MD 21502. (301)724-6842. Director: Petrina Aubol. Estab. 1991. Three held each year. Annually (March/April, June, October). Conference duration: 3 days (including weekend). Average attendance: 20-25. "March: nonfiction; June: fiction, including poetry and writing for children – also nonfiction; October: intense fiction workshop – novel segment, short story or childrens story. "We are located on top of a mountain at the end of a dead end road. Fairview Summit Sanctuary is a 100-acre wooded retreat fully equipped to provide meals, indoor swimming, informal meeting space and comfortable lodging from a newly renovated farm house and a modern luxury home." Will rotate visiting authors in different fields drawing on the vast Washington-Baltimore-Pittsburgh area. In 1992 we had children's writer Margarette Reid, romance writer Dorothy Wyatt, poet, novelist and creative writing professor Douglas DeMars, Edgar award winning novelist J. Madison Davis, science fiction author George Ewing is our workshop coordinator.
Costs: Three day workshop (Saturday, Sunday, Monday) $200 early registration, $250 late, includes 2 nights lodging, 8 meals (breakfast Saturday – lunch Monday); meals only, no lodging $150 early, $200 late.
Accommodations: Information on area lodging supplied on request – Fairview Summit can accommodate 20 overnight guests. $25 including breakfast per day for extra day lodging.
Additional Information: "For our fall fiction workshop we require novel segments, short stories or children's stories to be submitted for critique no later than two weeks before conference date. Fiction will be reworked at intense three day session. Conference brochure/guidelines are available for SASE.

We are investigating available grant money to bring writers to Fairview Summit."

‡CHARLENE FARIS SEMINARS FOR BEGINNERS, 9524 Guilford Dr. #A, Indianapolis IN 46240. (317)848-2634. Director: Charlene Faris. Estab. 1985. Held 2 or 3 times/year in various locations. Conference duration: 2 days. Average attendance: 10. Concentration on all areas of publishing and writing.
Costs: $125, tuition only.
Accommodations: "Can assist attendees with information on overnite accommodations."
Additional Information: Guidelines and conference dates available for SASE.

THE FESTIVAL OF THE WRITTEN ARTS, Box 2299, Sechelt, British Columbia V0N 3A0 Canada. (604)885-9631. Fax: (604)885-3967. Producer: Betty C. Keller. Estab. 1983. Annual. Festival held: August 12 to August 15. Average attendance: 2,500. To promote "all writing genres." Festival held at the Rockwood Centre. "The Centre overlooks the town of Sechelt on the Sunshine Coast. The lodge around which the Centre was organized was built in 1937 as a destination for holidayers arriving on the old Union Steamship Line; it has been preserved very much as it was in its heyday." A new twelve bedroom annex was added in 1982, and in 1989 the Festival of the Written Arts constructed a Pavilion for outdoor performances next to the annex. "The festival does not have a theme. Instead, it showcases 15 or more Canadian writers in a wide variety of genres each year."
Costs: In 1992, costs were $7.50 per event or $86 for weekend pass (Canadian funds.)
Accommodations: Lists of hotels and bed/breakfast available.
Additional Information: The festival runs contests during the 4 days of the event. Prizes are books donated by publishers. Brochures/guidelines are available.

‡FESTIVAL OF THE WRITTEN ARTS WRITERS-IN-RESIDENCE PROGRAM, Box 2299, Sechelt, British Columbia V0N 3A0 Canada. (604)885-9631. Secretary: Eleanor Kiefer. Estab. 1985. Three times/year (spring, summer, fall). Conference held April 15-19 and 22-29; May 6-9; August 6-11 and 16-21; November. Average attendance: 24. "Each set of workshops features different genres, but usually fiction at each season. All workshop leaders are qualified, published Canadian writers. Conference site is the "Rockwood Centre overlooking the town of Sechelt on the beautiful Sunshine Coast. The Lodge around which the Centre is organized was built in 1937 as a destination for holidayers arriving on the Old Union Steamship Line. A new twelve-bedroom annex was added in 1982, and in 1989 the Festival of the Written Arts constructed a pavilion for outdoor performances next to the annex. Writers-in-Residence participants are accommodated two (and in a few cases three) to a room with a private bathroom. Simple but nutritious meals are served in the dining room of the old Lodge."
Costs: In 1992 costs were $110 for tuition, $60 for accommodations, $65 for meals for 3-day workshop; $140 for tuition, $70 for accommodations, $75 for meals for 5-day workshop.
Accommodations: Students make their own transportation arrangements, including ferry transportation. Accommodation is provided as above.
Additional Information: "Students must submit a sample of their work before being accepted for the program—usually 2,000 words are asked for fiction classes. Each instructor has a chance to preview these submissions so that he/she may design the workshop appropriately." Conference brochures/ guidelines are available for SASE. "We keep our classes small for optimum benefit to the student. Many students return for further workshops but we are now getting applications from all over Canada and parts of the US."

FLORIDA CHRISTIAN WRITERS CONFERENCE, 2600 Park Ave., Titusville FL 32780. (407)269-6702. Conference Director: Billie Wilson. Estab. 1988. Annual. Conference is held: January 20 to January 24 (1994). Average attendance: 150. To promote "all areas of writing." Conference held at Park Avenue Retreat Center, a conference complex at a large church near Kennedy Space Center. Gloria Gaither and Sally Stuart are scheduled to speak at next conference.
Costs: Tuition $395, included tuition, room and board.
Accommodations: "We provide shuttle from the airport and from the hotel to retreat center. We make reservations at major hotel chain."
Additional Information: Critiques available. "Each writer may submit 3 works for critique. We have specialists in every area of writing to critique. We also provide line by line, written critique for a $30 fee." Conference brochures/guidelines are available for SASE.

‡**FLORIDA FIRST COAST WRITERS' FESTIVAL**, 3939 Roosevelt Blvd., FCCJ Kent Campus, Jacksonville FL 32205. (904)381-3433. Registrar: Fred Reynolds. Estab. 1985. Annual. Held 1st week of April (Fri. and Sat.) in various years (unless Good Friday interferes). Average attendance: 150-250. All areas: mainstream plus genre. Held on Kent Campus of Florida Community College at Jacksonville.
Costs: Maximum of $40 for 2 days.
Accommodations: The Marina Hotel at St. Johns Place has a special festival rate.
Additional Information: Conference brochures/guidelines are available for SASE.

FLORIDA ROMANCE WRITERS' FUN-IN-THE-SUN CONFERENCE, 1092 N.W. 10th Court, Boynton Beach FL 33426. Vice President/Conference Coordinator: Gail DeYoung. (407)734-5569. Estab. 1987. Annual. Conference held late February. "Predominately romance fiction, long and short, historical and contemporary, but each year we also emphasize another area—e.g. screenwriting, mystery-suspense, science fiction." Conference site is Ft. Lauderdale Hilton convenient to the airport. "We feature a variety of published romance authors as well as agents and editors in the field. 1993 keynote speaker is Heather Graham."
Costs: $115. Includes continental breakfast Saturday, lunch Saturday and welcome cocktail party Friday. Optional activities available at additional cost include Saturday dinner and Sunday "Brunch with the Experts."
Accommodations: "A special conference room rate is available at the hotel where the conference is held; $87/night single, double or triple occupancy."
Additional Information: "Some of our workshops involve critiques. The requirements are set by the individual speakers. Again this year an optional critique by professional reader Nalini Milne is available. Requirements are published with conference information." Conference brochures/guidelines are available for SASE in October.

‡**FLORIDA STATE WRITERS CONFERENCE**, P.O. Box 9844, Ft. Lauderdale FL 33310. (305)485-0795. Executive Director: Dana K. Cassell. Estab. 1983. Annual. Conference held from May 20 to May 23. Average attendance 300. Four tracks: fiction, nonfiction, general interest, specialty. Held at a hotel. (1993: Altamonte Hilton, Orlando). Theme for 1992 was mystery. Guest speakers and panelists in 1992 were Jane Haddam/Orania Papazaglou, William DeAndrea, agents, and editors.
Costs: Several packages with or without meals, single-day, 2-day, complete package, member/nonmember, early-bird specials. Range: $30-300.
Accommodations: Special hotel rate on-site. $60 single or double.
Additional Information: Critiques available for small extra fee depending upon length of material. Sponsors a contest. Judges: editors, authors, college professors. Conference brochures/guidelines are available for 9×12 SASE and 52¢ postage.

FORT CONCHO MUSEUM PRESS LITERARY FESTIVAL, 213 East Ave. D, San Angelo TX 76903. (915)657-4441. Contact: Cora Pugmire. Estab. 1988. Annual. Conference held the first weekend in August. Average attendance: 450. "The purposes of the festival are to showcase writers—from beginners to professionals—of Texas and the southwest through public readings, book displays and informal gatherings; to offer help for writers through writing workshops and informal gatherings with other writers, editors and publishers; and, generally, to support and encourage the literary arts in Texas and the Southwest." Location: A 22-building, 40-acre historic site. The festival is held in the oldest, fully restored building (1865). Several of the other buildings are also used for workshops. Free tours are offered to all participants. "Current festival plans include no special topic, but we will have at least one fiction workshop. Guest speakers will be published Texas writers and publishers/editors of Texas journals of books."
Costs: All events except the banquet are free. Banquet fee is between $8-12.
Accommodations: Transportation arrangements are made on an informal basis only. ("That is, people who need a ride can always find one.") Special accommodations are made at our motel; a list of other area motels and hotels is available.
Additional Information: Current contests are "literary performance" contests. Of those who read from their works during the festival, one poet and one prose writer receive an award. Conference brochures/guidelines are available for SASE.

FRANCIS MARION WRITERS' CONFERENCE, Francis Marion College, Florence SC 29501. (803)661-1500. Directors: Robert Parham, David Starkey. Estab. 1982. Conference held annually in June. Conference duration: 3 days. Average attendance: 40-50. Conference for "fiction, poetry, nonfiction and drama." Held in classrooms/college auditorium (at Francis Marion College).

Costs: $85.
Accommodations: Information on overnight accommodations made available through directors.
Additional Information: Some workshops for fiction writers are included. Sponsors a chapbook competition for participants. Brochures or guidelines available for SASE.

GREEN LAKE CHRISTIAN WRITERS CONFERENCE, American Baptist Assembly, Green Lake WI 54941-9589. (800)558-8898. Vice President of Program: Dr. Arlo R. Reichter. Estab. 1948. Annual. Conference held July 10 to July 17. Average attendance: 80. "The mission of the conference is to provide a setting and appropriate resource persons so Christian writers can further develop their writing skills—whether a beginner or seasoned writer. Held annually at the American Baptist Assembly which is a 1,000-acre conference center on Green Lake. The center offers lodging and meals as well as wide range of recreational opportunities. The Assembly is the national training center for American Baptist Churches. The conference is ecumenical." Gianfranco Pagnucci, Susan Pagnucci, Lenore Coberly, Jeri McCormick, Kristen Ingram, Jan White, Jeanne Donovan, Sally Stuart and others to be named are scheduled to speak at next conference.
Costs: Tuition is $80/person.
Accommodations: "We can provide ground transportation from Appleton and Oshkosh, Wisconsin airports; the Columbus, WI Amtrak station and Ripon, WI Greyhound Bus Stop—there is a charge and advance reservation is required." On-site facilities available. Costs: Rooms range (double occupancy) from $21 to $34/night; meals $18.75/day. Campground available as well as cottages, cabins and homes.
Additional Information: "Personal critique sessions with leaders may be scheduled. Major seminars include group critique. No advance submissions." Conference brochures/guidelines are available for SASE."Once a person has attended the writers conference they may return during specified fall, winter and spring weeks at a special low cost of $10/night—no instruction."

‡GREEN RIVER NOVELS-IN-PROGRESS WORKSHOP, 11906 Locust Rd., Louisville KY 40243. (502)245-4902. Director: Mary E. O'Dell. Estab. 1991. Annual. Conference held from January 3 to January 10. Average attendance: 35. "For novels; one instructor dealing with work for children/young people, other genres and mainstream handled by individual instructors. Short fiction collections, essay collections, misc. welcome. Each novelist instructor works with a small group (5-7 people) for five days; then agents/editors are there for panels and appointments on the weekend." Site is The University of Louisville's Shelby Campus, suburban setting, graduate dorm housing (private rooms available w/ shared bath for each 2 rooms). Meetings and classes held in nearby classroom building. Grounds available for walking, etc. Lovely setting, restaurants and shopping available nearby. Participants carpool to restaurants, etc." This year we are covering mystery, romance, thriller, young people's, fantasy/horror, sf, mainstream/literary. Guest speakers are Steve Womack (mystery); Gary Raisor (fantasy/horror); Martha Bennett Stiles (young people's); Karen Fields (romance); Bob Mayer (thriller); Betty Receveur (mainstream/literary).
Costs: Tuition—$250, housing $17 per night private, $12 shared. Meals on their own.
Accommodations: "We do meet participants' planes and see that participants without cars have transportation to meals, etc. If participants would rather stay in hotel, we will make that information available."
Additional Information: Participants send 60 pages/3 chapters upon application; these pages are turned over to instructors; each participant receives critique and, during Workshop Week, a private conference. Conference brochures/guidelines are available for SASE.

HEART OF AMERICA WRITERS' CONFERENCE, Johnson County Community College, 12345 College Blvd., Overland Park KS 66213. Program Coordinator: Judith Choice. Estab. 1984. Annual. Conference held March 26 to March 27. Average attendance: 150-200. "The conference features a choice of 12-20 sessions focusing on poetry, nonfiction, children's market, fiction, journaling, essay and genre writing." Conference held at the Cultural Education Center. "The new Cultural Education Center is a 163,000 sq. ft. facility featuring a large theater and concert hall, a recital hall, art gallery and multiple conference spaces. This site is located on the Johnson County Community College campus which serves suburban Kansas City, Missouri. Each year we offer 7-10 sessions of interest to fiction writers." Past guest speakers or panelists have included Natalie Goldberg, Linda Hogan, David Ray, Stanley Elkin.

Costs: $100, lunch, snacks, reception included.
Accommodations: "We provide lists of area hotels."
Additional Information: Manuscript critiques are offered for $20. First chapter for fiction; 5 pages for poetry. Conference brochures/guidelines are available for SASE.

HEMINGWAY DAYS WRITER'S WORKSHOP AND CONFERENCE, P.O. Box 4045, Key West FL 33041. (305)294-4440. Director of Workshop: Dr. James Plath. Festival Director: Michael Whalton. Estab. 1988. Annual. Conference/workshop held July 19 to July 21. Average attendance: 90. "The Hemingway Days Writer's Workshop and Conference focuses on fiction, poetry, stage and screenwriting, with one session per day concentrating on the craft as it relates to Ernest Hemingway and his work. Sessions are held in the Caribbean Spa Grand Cayman Room at the Pier House Resort, which has excellent audio visual facilities and seats 100." All sessions on day one deal with fiction writing; day two—poetry writing; day three—screen and playwriting.
Costs: $75. Guaranteed admission on a space-available basis includes admission to all sessions, workshop t-shirt and complementary snacks each day.
Accommodations: "As the time draws nearer, Hemingway Days packages will be available through Ocean Key House, Pier House, Southernmost Motel and Holiday Inn LaConcha. Last year the cost for 3 nights ranged from $60/2 in room per night plus tax; $160/3 in room per night suite, plus tax."
Additional Information: Brochures/guidelines are available for SASE. "The conference/workshop is unique in its daily emphasis on a different genre, but since it celebrates Hemingway the writer, the workshop will also uniquely include scholarly/critical sessions dealing with Hemingway's work."

HIGHLAND SUMMER CONFERENCE, Box 6935, Radford University, Radford VA 24142. (703)831-5366. Chair, Appalachian Studies Program: Dr. Grace Toney Edwards. Estab. 1978. Annual. Conference held June 14-25. Average attendance: 25. "The HSC features one (two weeks) or two (one week each) guest leaders each year. As a rule, our leaders are well known writers who have connections, either thematic, or personal, or both, to the Appalachian region. The genre(s) of emphasis depends upon the workshop leader(s). In 1992 we had as our leaders, for one week each: Bill Brown, poet, author, teacher and Wilma Dykemen, novelist, journalist, social critic, author of *Tall Woman* among others. The Highland Summer Conference is held at Radford University, a school of about 9,000 students. Radford is in the Blue Ridge Mountain of southwest Virginia about 45 miles west of Roanoke, VA."
Costs: "The cost is based on current Radford tuition for 3 credit hours plus an additional conference fee. On-campus meals and housing are available at additional cost. In 1992 conference tuition was $306 for undergraduates, $321 for graduate student."
Accommodations: We do not have special rate arrangements with local hotels. We do offer accommodations on the Radford University Campus in a recently refurbished residence hall. (In 1992 cost was $15.25-25 per night.)
Additional Information: "Conference leaders do typically critique work done during the two-week conference, but do not ask to have any writing submitted prior to the conference beginning." Conference brochures/guidelines are available for SASE.

HIGHLIGHTS FOUNDATION WRITERS WORKSHOP AT CHAUTAUQUA, Dept. NM, 711 Court St., Honesdale PA 18431. (717)253-1192. Conference Director: Jan Keen. Estab. 1985. Annual. Workshop held July 17 to July 24. Average attendance: 100. "Writer workshops geared toward beginner, intermediate, advanced levels. Small group workshops, one-to-one interaction between faculty and participants plus panel sessions, lectures and large group meetings. Workshop site is the picturesque community of Chautauqua, New York." Classes offered include Children's Interests, Writing Dialogue, Outline for the Novel, Conflict and Developing Plot. Past faculty has included James Cross Giblin, Chris Demarest, Laurence Pringle, Dayton Hyde, Eve Bunting, Lois Lowry, Walter Dean Myers and Pam Conrad.
Accommodations: "We coordinate ground transportation to and from airports, trains and bus stations in the Erie, PA and Jamestown/Buffalo, NY area. We also coordinate accommodations for conference attendees."
Additional Information: "We offer the opportunity for attendees to submit a manuscript for review at the conference." Workshop brochures/guidelines are available for SASE.

HOFSTRA UNIVERSITY SUMMER WRITERS' CONFERENCE, Hofstra UCCE, 205 Davison Hall, Hempstead NY 11550. (516)463-5016. Director, Liberal Arts: Lewis Shena. Estab. 1972. Annual (Every summer starting week after July 4). Conference to be held July 12 to July 23, 1993. Average attendance: 50. Conference offers workshops in fiction, nonfiction, poetry, juvenile fiction, stage/screenwriting and one other genre such as detective fiction or science fiction. Site is the university campus, a suburban setting, 25 miles from NYC. Guest speakers are not yet known. "We have had the likes of Oscar Hijuelos, Clive Barnes, Hilma and Meg Wolitzer, Budd Schulberg and Cynthia Ozick."

Costs: Non-credit (no meals, no room): approximately $600 for 3 workshops. Credit: Approximately $800/workshop (2 credits).

Accommodations: Free bus operates between Hempstead Train Station and campus for those commuting from NYC. Dormitory rooms are available for approximately $275. Those who request area hotels will receive a list. Hotels are approximately $75 and above/night.

Additional Information: "All workshops include critiquing. Each participant is given one-on-one time of ½ hour with workshop leader. Only credit students must submit manuscripts when registering. We submit work to the *Paris Review* when appropriate."

IOWA SUMMER WRITING FESTIVAL, 116 International Center, University of Iowa, Iowa City IA 52242. (319)335-2534. Director: Peggy Houston. Assistant Director: Karen Burgus Schootman. Estab. 1987. Annual. Festival held June 30 to July 13. Workshops are one week, two weeks or a weekend. Average attendance: limited to 12/class—over 900 participants throughout the summer. "We offer courses in most areas of writing: novel, fiction, essay, poetry, playwriting, screenwriting, freelance, nonfiction, writing for children, comedy, memoirs, women's writing and science fiction." Site is the University of Iowa campus. Guest speakers are undetermined at this time. Last year's guest readers were W.P. Kinsella, Michael Carey, Mona Van Duyn, Robert Olen Butler, Margot Livesay, Heather McHugh.

Costs: $265, one-week course; $530, two-week course and $125, weekend course (1992 rates). Housing and meals are separate.

Accommodations: Shuttle service from the Cedar Rapids airport to the university is available for a reasonable fee. "We offer participants a choice of accommodations, which we will book for them: Dormitory, $21/night; Iowa House, $43/night; Holiday Inn, $68/night (rates subject to changes)."

Additional Information: Brochure/guidelines are available.

I'VE ALWAYS WANTED TO WRITE BUT . . ., 23350 Sereno Ct., Villa 30, Cupertino CA 95014. (415)691-0300. Contact: Louise Purwin Zobel. Estab. 1969. Workshop held irregularly, several times a year at different locations. Workshop duration: 1-2 days. Average attendance: 30-50. Workshop "encourages real beginners to get started on a lifelong dream. Focuses on the basics of writing." Workshops held at about 40 college and university campuses in the west, including University of California.

Costs: Usually $45-65/day "depending on college or university."

Additional Information: Brochures/guidelines available for SASE.

IWWG EARLY SPRING IN CALIFORNIA CONFERENCE, International Women's Writing Guild, P.O. Box 810, Gracie Station, New York NY 10028. (212)737-7536. Executive Director: Hannelore Hahn. Estab. 1982. Annual. Conference held March 19 to March 21. Average attendance: 50. Conference to promote "creative writing, personal growth and empowerment." Site is "a 150-acre oasis located an hour from San Francisco in the wine country. Originally an Indian healing ground, it features tranquil meadows and streams, clear water springs, ancient oaks, almond trees, wood violets and decorative folk art. Nouvelle health cuisine is served in an original adobe dining room."

Costs: $100 for weekend program, plus room and board.

Accommodations: Accommodations are all at conference site; $110 for room and board.

Additional Information: Conference brochures/guidelines are available for SASE.

IWWG MEET THE AGENTS AND EDITORS: THE BIG APPLE WORKSHOPS, % International Women's Writing Guild, P.O. Box 810, Gracie Station, New York NY 10028. (212)737-7536. Executive Director: Hannelore Hahn. Estab. 1980. Biannual. Workshops held April 17 to April 18 and October 18 to October 19. Average attendance: 200. Workshops to promote creative writing and professional success. Site: Private meeting space of the New York Genealogical Society, mid-town New York City. Sunday afternoon openhouse with agents and editors.

Costs: $100.

Accommodations: Information on transportation arrangements and overnight accommodations made available.

Additional Information: Workshop brochures/guidelines are available for SASE.

IWWG MIDWESTERN CONFERENCE, % International Women's Writing Guild, P.O. Box 810, Gracie Station, New York NY 10028. (212)737-7536. Executive Director: Hannelore Hahn. Estab. 1990. Annual. Conference held May 1. Average attendance: 75. Conference to promote creative writing, personal growth and professional success. Site: "Elegant private Women's Athletic Club of Chicago." **Costs:** $75, includes lunch.
Additional Information: Conference brochures/guidelines are available for SASE.

IWWG NEW JERSEY CONFERENCE, % International Women's Writing Guild, P.O. Box 810, Gracie Station, New York NY 10028. (212)737-7536. Executive Director: Hannelore Hahn. Estab. 1988. Annual. Conference held November 6. Average attendance: 75. Conference to promote creative writing, personal growth and professional success. Site: "Former private mansion in residential part of Morristown, NJ."
Costs: $75, includes lunch.
Additional Information: Conference brochures/guidelines are available for SASE.

IWWG SUMMER CONFERENCE, % International Women's Writing Guild, P.O. Box 810, Gracie Station, New York NY 10028. (212)737-7536. Execuive Director: Hannelore Hahn. Estab. 1977. Annual. Conference held August 13 to August 20. Average attendance: 350. Conference to promote writing in all genres, personal growth and professional success. Conference is held "on the tranquil campus of Skidmore College in Saratoga Springs, NY, where the serene Hudson Valley meets the North Country of the Adirondacks." Fifty different workshops are offered. Overall theme: "Writing Towards Wholeness."
Costs: $300 for week-long program, plus room and board.
Accommodations: Transportation by air to Albany, New York or Amtrak train available from New York City. Conference attendees stay on campus.
Additional Information: "Lots of critiquing sessions. Contacts with literary agents." Conference brochures/guidelines available for SASE. "International attendance."

IWWG WRITE YOUR OWN STORY CONFERENCE, International Women's Writing Guild, P.O. Box 810, Gracie Station, New York NY 10028. (212)737-7536. Executive Director: Hannelore Hahn. Estab. 1992. Annual. Conference held October 30 to October 31, 1993. Average attendance: 75. Conference to promote all types of creative writing. Site: Agnes Scott Cullepe, Decatur GA, historic private southern women's college in residential neighborhood.
Costs: $100, plus room and board.
Accommodations: Information on overnight accommodations is available.
Additional Information: "We include critiques as often as possible." Conference brochures/guidelines are available for SASE.

‡**KEY WEST LITERARY SEMINAR,** 419 Petronia St., Key West FL 33040. (305)293-9291. Executive Director: Monica Haskell. Estab. 1983. Annual. Conference held second week in January. Conference duration: 3-5 days. Average attendance: 450. "Each year a different topic of literary interest is examined. Writers, scholars, editors, publishers, critics, and the public meet for panel discussions and dialogue. The agenda also includes readings, performances, question and answer sessions, book sales, a writers' workshop, social receptions, and a literary walking tour of Key West. The sessions are held at various locations in Key West, Florida, including the Tennessee Williams Fine Arts Center at the Florida Keys Community College and the Key West Art and Historical Society's East Martello Museum. Key West is the home of many well-known literary figures. The Key West Literary Seminar's theme varies from year to year. Past topics include travel and literature, mysteries, short stories, screenwriting and playwriting, as well as investigations into the work of Tennessee Williams, Ernest Hemingway, and Elizabeth Bishop. Call or write for details of upcoming events." Past speakers include William Goldman, Elmore Leonard, Jan Morris, Octavio Paz, Russell Banks, Mary Higgins Clark, James Merrill and John Wideman.
Costs: Seminar $275 and workshop $200 plus tax.
Accommodations: Tranportation from the hotel district to the main events is provided. Catalogs detailing the seminar schedule, guest speakers, registration, accommodations and local interest items are sent out upon request. Special room rates are available at participating hotels, motels, guest houses and inns. Room rates usually begin around $100.
Additional Information: Manuscript critique is an optional component of the writers' workshop. No more than 10 typewritten, double spaced pages may be submitted with workshop registration. Brochures are available for SASE.

‡**LDS WRITERS' WORKSHOP**, Box 1869 BYU-Hawaii, Laie HI 96762. (808)293-3633. Directors: Chris Crowe, John Bennion. Estab. 1991. Every 2 years. Conference held June 28-July 3, 1993. Concentration is "fiction and general writing—except for poetry, most other types are offered." Site is the campus of Brigham Young University-Hawaii, 40 miles from downtown Honolulu. "Our 1993 program includes Jack Weyland, Janice Kap Perry, Louise Plummer, Dean Hughes and other writers and editors."
Costs: Information not provided.
Accommodations: Information on overnight accommodations is made available; conference rates, on-site facilities.
Additional Information: "In addition to workshop sessions, our workshop offers an autograph session with authors, university credit, daily writing contests and a closing luau included with registration." Brochures available for SASE after November 1992.

MANHATTANVILLE COLLEGE WRITERS' WEEK, 2900 Purchase St., Purchase NY 10577. (914)694-3425. Dean of Adult and Special Programs: Ruth Dowd, R.S.C.J. Estab. 1982. Annual. Conference held June 28 to July 2. Average attendance: 50. "The Conference is designed not only for writers but for teachers of writing. Each workshop is attended by a Master teacher who works with the writers/teachers in the afternoon to help them to translate their writing skills for classroom use. For children's literature, journal writing, personal essay, poetry and fiction. Manhanttanville is a suburban campus 30 miles from New York City. The campus centers around Reid Castle, the administration building, the former home of Whitelaw Reid. Workshops are conducted in Reid Castle. We usually feature a major author as guest lecturer during the Conference. We have had such authors as Toni Morrison, Mary Gordon, Gail Godwin and Elizabeth Janeway.
Costs: Conference cost was $524 in 1992 which included 2 graduate credits plus $35 fee.
Accommodations: Students may rent rooms in the college residence halls. More luxurious accommodations are available at neighboring hotels. In the summer of 1991 the cost of renting a room in the residence halls was: $25 per night (single); $20 per night (double).
Additional Information: Conference brochures/guidelines are available for SASE.

‡**MAPLE WOODS COMMUNITY COLLEGE WRITER'S CONFERENCE**, 2601 NE Barry Rd., Kansas City MO 64156. (816)734-4878. Coordinator Continuing Education: Pattie Smith. Estab. 1983. Annual. Conference held October 2. Conference duration: 1 day. Average attendance: 100-125. Concentration varies from year to year. Conference site is at an area hotel.
Costs: $40 in past years for registration, lunch and entrance to conference.
Accommodations: Check for current costs.

‡**MARITIME WRITERS' WORKSHOP**, Extension & Summer Session, UNB Box 4400, Fredericton, New Brunswick E3B 5A3 Canada. (506)453-4646. Coordinator: Glenda Turner. Estab. 1976. Annual. Conference held in July. Conference duration: 1 week. Average attendance: 45. "Workshops in four areas: fiction, poetry, feature writing, writing for children." Site is University of New Brunswick, Fredericton campus.
Costs: $250, tuition; $125 meals; $100/double room; $125/single room (Canadian funds).
Accommodations: On-campus accommodations and meals.
Additional Information: "Participants must submit 10-20 manuscript pages which form a focus for workshop discussions." Brochures are available. No SASE necessary.

‡**MEDINA-WAYNE WRITERS CONFERENCE**, 311 W. Washington St., Medina OH 44256. (216)723-2633. Coordinator: Betty Wetzel. Estab. 1976. Held every two years. Conference to be held September, 1994. Conference duration: 2 days (Fri. evening and all day Sat.) Average attendance: 30-35. "To provide information on writing and publishing and to promote contacts between writers and speakers. Speakers are professionals in each area (fiction, nonfiction, poetry and juvenile). Sometimes editor is included. Six sessions are presented on Saturday. Since each speaker conducts only 3 sessions, opportu-

GET YOUR WORK INTO THE RIGHT BUYERS' HANDS!

You work hard... and your hard work deserves to be seen by the right buyers. With the constant changes in the industry, it's difficult to know who those buyers are. That's why you'll want to keep up-to-date with the most current edition of this indispensable market guide.

Keep ahead of the changes by ordering *1994 Novel & Short Story Writer's Market* today. You'll save yourself the frustration of getting manuscripts returned in the mail, stamped MOVED: ADDRESS UNKNOWN. And of NOT submitting your work to new listings because you don't know they exist. All you have to do to order the upcoming 1994 edition is complete the attached post card and return it with your payment or charge card information. Order now, and there's one thing that won't change from your *1993 Novel & Short Story Writer's Market* -- the price! That's right, we'll send you the 1994 edition for just $19.95. *1994 Novel & Short Story Writer's Market* will be published and ready for shipment in February 1994.

Don't let another opportunity slip by...get a jump on the industry with the help of *1994 Novel & Short Story Writer's Market*. Order today!
You deserve it!

More Books to Help You Get Published!

Practical Tips for Writing Popular Fiction
by Robyn Carr
This complete guide takes you step by step through each area of writing for specific genres, including romance, mystery, science fiction, fantasy, Westerns, suspense, historical, action/adventure and horror.
160 pages/$17.95/hardcover

Get That Novel Started! (And Keep It Going 'Til You Finish)
by Donna Levin
Here author/instructor Donna Levin offers practical, inspirational advice for getting the novel within underway, including how to get the idea, avoid being overwhelmed and dive into the writing.
176 pages/$17.95/hardcover

Scene of the Crime: A Writer's Guide to Crime-Scene Investigations
by Anne Wingate, Ph.D.
A factual, time saving reference book that gives you the facts and details of criminal investigations and police work.
240 pages/$15.95/paperback

Cause of Death: A Writer's Guide to Death, Murder & Forensic Medicine
by Keith D. Wilson, M.D.
This comprehensive guide for writers traces what happens to a body from trauma to burial — and all stops in between.
240 pages/$15.95/paperback

Use the coupon on the other side to order these books today!

nity is available for informal conversation with participants during the other sessions. We also offer a class in basics (how to get started, etc.) Conference is held at Wayne College of the University of Akron. The college is in Orrville, Ohio, in a rural area easily accessible from main highways. Individual classrooms are provided for classes and a main room for general meeting and for informal 'coffee and conversation' periods. The building is handicapped-accessible." Guest speakers or panelists in 1992: James E Martin (mystery), Lillian Cantleberry (biblical novels), Dandi Daley MacKall (nonfiction), Demetra Mihevic (Juvenile), David Hopes (poetry), David Kline (nonfiction: keynote).

Costs: In 1992: $40 pre-registration; $45 if paid at the door. Lunch is provided on Saturday, as well as cofee/tea and donuts in morning. Light reception on Friday evening, between keynote and panel discussion.

Accommodations: List of area motels is available.

Additional Information: Manuscripts submitted for contest are critiqued in writing by judges. Sponsors contest for each category. No restrictions except length. One ms may be submitted with registration; additional mss may be submitted for fee of $5 each. Cash prizes for 1st and 2nd place. Brochure and guidelines available for SASE.

‡MENDOCINO COAST WRITERS CONFERENCE, 1211 Del Mar Dr., Fort Bragg CA 95437. (707)961-1001. Director: Marlis Broadhead. Estab. 1990. Annual. Conference held May or June. Conference duration: 3 days. Average attendance: 70-80. "Inclusive — several genres, nonfiction, publishing and marketing, advertising, writing for children, self-publishing, women writers, etc." Held at "College of the Redwoods at the south edge of Fort Bragg, CA, a small mill town/tourist and retirees' center. The tiny campus overlooks the Pacific and is 8 miles north of Mendocino Village, a preserved Victorian town. Over 25 movies and TV shows have been filmed in this area."

Costs: $65, for Friday night through Sunday noon (sessions, readings, etc.) $10 extra per writing workshop (1992).

Accommodations: Information on overnight accommodations made available. "For 1993, I'm hoping to include a 2½ day stay at the nearby Mendocino Woodlands (rustic and inexpensive) where writers can work one-on-one with editors and agents. Local rooms go from $42 to $125 (elegant B&Bs)."

Additional Information: Conference brochures/guidelines are available for SASE. "The purpose of this conference is to study and celebrate writing in a supportive atmosphere. In the past, we've gotten high marks from attendees and presentors alike on the substance and atmosphere of the conferences."

MIDLAND WRITERS CONFERENCE, Grace A. Dow Memorial Library, 1710 W. St. Andrews, Midland MI 48640. (517)835-7151. Conference Co-Chairs: Eileen Finzel, Margaret Allen. Estab. 1980. Annual. Conference held June 12. Average attendance: 100. "The Conference is composed of a well-known keynote speaker and then, six workshops on a variety of subjects ranging from poetry, children's writing, freelancing, agents, etc. The attendees are both published and unpublished authors. The Conference is held at the Grace A. Dow Memorial Library in the auditorium and conference rooms. Keynoters in the past have included Andrew Greeley, Kurt Vonnegut, David Halberstam."

Costs: Adult - $45 before May 15, after May 15 the fee is $55; student, senior citizen and handicapped - $35 before May 15, after May 15 the fee is $45. A box lunch is available for $7.

Accommodations: A list of area hotels is available.

Additional Information: Conference brochures/guidelines are available for SASE.

MIDWEST WRITERS' CONFERENCE, 6000 Frank Ave. NW, Canton OH 44720 (216)499-9600. Conference Coordinator: Debbie Ruhe. Estab. 1968. Annual. Conference held October 1 and October 2. Average attendance: 250. "The conference provides an atmosphere in which aspiring writers can meet with and learn from experienced and established writers through lectures, workshops, competitive contest, personal interviews and informal group discussions. The areas of concentration include fiction, nonfiction, juvenile literature and poetry. The Midwest Writers' Conference is held on Kent State University Stark Campus in Canton, Ohio. This two-day conference is held in Main Hall, a four-story building and wheel chair accessible." Past topics have included "Increasing Your Productivity as a Writer," "Insider Tricks to Getting Published, A to Z," "Making the Poem: The Art and the Craft," "Can You Get There From Here," "Finding the Time to Write," "Children's Literature: The Story Behind the Story," "Fiction: In the Heart of the Heart of the Story," "Defined by What It Isn't: The Craft of Narrative Nonfiction." 1992 Presenters included: Dennis E. Hensley: author, lecturer, and adjunct professor, Indiana University; Jeffrey Herman: literary agent, The Jeff Herman Literary Agency, Inc.; David Citino: professor of English, director of creative writing, Ohio State University; Michael Heaton: columnist, feature writer, *The Plain Dealer*; Frank H. Weinstock: writer, lecturer, professor, M.D. of Opthalmology; Suzanne Thomas: director of publications, Malone College; Sue

Misheff: assistant professor of education and English, Malone College; Sheila Schwartz: professor of English, Cleveland State University; Mark Winegardner: professor of English, John Carroll University.
Costs: $65 includes Friday workshops, keynote address, Saturday workshops, box luncheon and manuscript entry fee (limited to two submissions); $40 for contest only (includes two manuscripts).
Accommodations: Arrangements are made with the Parke Hotel. The Parke Hotel is nearest Kent Stark, and offers a special reduced rate for conference attendees. Conferees must make their own reservations three weeks before the conference to be guaranteed this special conference rate.
Additional Information: Each manuscript entered in the contest will receive a critique. If the manuscript is selected for final judging, it will receive an additional critique from the final judge. Conference attendees are not required to submit manuscripts to the writing contest. Manuscript deadline is early August. For contest: A maximum of one entry for each category is permitted. Entries must be typed on 8½ × 11 paper, double-spaced. A separate page must accompany each entry bearing the author's name, address, phone, category and title of the work. Entries are not to exceed 3,000 words in length. Work must be original, unpublished and not a winner in any contest at the time of entry. Conference brochures and guidelines are available for SASE.

MIDWEST WRITERS WORKSHOP, Dept. of Journalism, Ball State University, Muncie IN 47306. (317)285-8200. Co-Director: Earl L. Conn. Estab. 1974. Annual. Workshop held August 4 to August 7. Average attendance: 100. For fiction, nonfiction, poetry. Conference held at Hotel Roberts in downtown Muncie.
Costs: In 1992, cost was $160 including opening reception, hospitality room and closing banquet.
Accommodations: Special hotel rates offered.
Additional Information: Critiques available. $25 for individual critiquing. Conference brochures/ guidelines are available for SASE.

MISSISSIPPI VALLEY WRITERS CONFERENCE, Augustana College, Rock Island IL 61201. (309)762-8985. Conference Founder/Director: David R. Collins. Estab. 1973. Annual. Conference held June 6 to June 11. Average attendance: 80. "Conference for all areas of writing for publication." Conference held at Augustana College, a liberal arts school along the Mississippi River. 1993 guest speakers include Evelyn Witter, Mel Boring, Max Collins, Kim Bush, H.E. Francis, Karl Largent, Jim Elledge, Roald Tweet, Rich Johnson.
Costs: In 1993 fees are $25 for registration; $35 for 1 workshop; $60 for two; plus $30 for each additional workshops; $20 to audit.
Accommodations: On-campus facitilites available. Accommodations are available at Westerlin Hall on the Augustana College campus. Cost for 6 nights is $75; cost for 15 meals is $75.
Additional Information: Conferees may submit manuscripts to workshop leaders for personal conferences during the week. Cash awards are given at the end of the conference week by workshop leaders based on manuscripts submitted. Conference brochures/guidelines are available for SASE. "Conference is open to the beginner as well as the polished professional—all are welcome."

MOUNT HERMON CHRISTIAN WRITERS CONFERENCE, P.O. Box 413, Mount Hermon CA 95041. (408)335-4466. Fax: (408)335-9218. Director of Public Affairs David R. Talbott. Estab. 1970. Annual. Conference held Friday-Tuesday over Palm Sunday weekend (April 2-6, 1993). Average attendance: 175. "We are a broad-ranging conference for all areas of Christian writing, including fiction, children's, poetry, nonfiction, magazines, books, educational curriculum and radio and TV script writing. This is a working, how-to conference, with many workshops within the conference involving on-site writing assignments. The Conference is sponsored by and held at the 440-acre Mount Hermon Christian Conference Center near San Jose, California, in the heart of the coastal redwoods. Registrants stay in hotel-style accommodations, and full board is provided as part of conference fees. Meals are taken family style, with faculty joining registrants. The faculty/student ratio is about 1:6 or 7. The bulk of our faculty are editors and publisher representatives from major Christian publishing houses nationwide."
Costs: Registration fees include tuition, conference sessions, resource notebook, refreshment breaks, room and board and vary from $420 economy to $520 deluxe, double occupancy.
Accommodations: Airport shuttles are available from the San Jose International Airport. Housing is not required of registrants, but about 95% of our registrants use Mount Hermon's own housing facilities (hotel style double-occupancy rooms). Meals with the conference are required, and are included in all fees.

Additional Information: Registrants may submit work for critique (2 works) in advance of the conference, then have personal interviews with critiquers during the conference. No advance work is required, however. Conference brochures/guidelines are available for SASE. "The residential nature of our conference makes this a unique setting for one-on-one interaction with faculty/staff. There is also a decided inspirational flavor to the conference, and general sessions with well-known speakers are a highlight."

NATIONAL LEAGUE OF AMERICAN PEN WOMEN CONFERENCE, P.O. Box 1707, Midlothian VA 23112. (804)744-6503. Conference Director: T.R. Hollingsworth. Estab. 1983. Conference held every two years. Conference duration: One day. Average attendance: 50-100. "For fiction, nonfiction, travel, regional, writing for children. Conference is usually held in a Richmond, Virginia hotel with banquet facilities. The day includes continental breakfast, lunch, book sales, autographing with well-known, published speakers."
Costs: $55 fee includes lunch, continental breakfast; $15 contest entry; $10 critique of contest entry.
Accommodations: Special rates for overnight stay the night before conference.
Additional Information: Critiques available. Sponsors contest: fiction or nonfiction, 1,500 word maximum, fee charged. Judges are professional writers in NLAPW. Conference brochures/guidelines are available for SASE.

NATIONAL WOMEN'S MUSIC FESTIVAL WRITERS CONFERENCE, P.O. Box 1427, Indianapolis IN 46206-1427. (317)636-7382. Estab. 1985. Annual. Conference held from June 3 to June 6. Average attendance: 2,500-3,000. To promote "feminist writing and publishing—fiction, poetry, journalism, drama." Conference held at Indiana University, Bloomington, IN.
Costs: Approx. $120 for program including all music performances.
Accommodations: Dorm housing available. Costs: Approx. $20/night/person double occupancy dorm room. Approx. $50 food for Fri.-Sun.
Additional Information: Conference brochures/guidelines are available for SASE. "Some workshops are open to women only."

‡**NATIONAL WRITERS CLUB WRITER'S CONFERENCE**, Suite 620, 1450 S. Havana, Aurora CO 80012. (303)751-7844. Executive Director: Sandy Whelchel. Estab. 1950s. Annual. Conference held in June. Conference duration: 3 days. Average attendance: 200-300. General writing and marketing. Hotel with conference facilities in suburban Denver. Theme "Write Today, Sell Tomorrow."
Costs: Approx. $250, will include meals.
Accommodations: Shuttle service from Stapleton International Airport will be available. Currently working on group air rates. Special hotel rates for attendees. On-site facilities at hotel.
Additional Information: Awards for previous contests will be presented at the conference. Conference brochures/guidelines are available for SASE.

‡**OAKLAND UNIVERSITY WRITERS' CONFERENCE**, 265 SFH, Rochester MI 48309-4401. (313)370-3120. Program Director: Nadine Jakoboswki. Estab. 1961. Annual. Conference held from October 15 to October 16. Average attendance: 400. "All areas; all purposes." Held at Oakland University Oakland Center: meetings rooms, dining area; O'Dowd Hall: lecture rooms; Meadow Brook Hall (on campus) evening reception. "Each annual conference covers all aspects and types of writing in 35 concurrent workshops on Saturday. Major writers from various genres are speakers at Friday evening reception and at the Saturday conference luncheon program. Individual critiques and hands-on writing workshops are conducted Friday." Areas: Poetry, articles, fiction, short stories, playwriting, nonfiction, young adult, children's literature. Guest speakers in 1992: Sue Harrison, young adult author, and James K. Morrow, science fiction author.
Costs: 1992: Conference registration: $53; luncheon, $8.50; Dinner reception program, $42; individual manuscript, $42; writing workshop, $32; writing ms audit, $22.
Accommodations: List is available.
Additional Information: Conference brochure/guidelines available for SASE.

‡**OHIO WRITERS' HOLIDAY**, 341 E. Schrock, Westerville OH 43081. Newsletter Editor/Treasurer: Judie Hershner. Estab. 1990. Annual. Conference held April 24. Average attendance: 80. "Womens' fiction, particularly romance fiction." Held in 1993 at the Radisson, Columbus, Ohio. Offers published authors roundtable—anyone can ask a questions of published author present. Guest speaker is Teresa Warfield (historical romance author) and Oscar Collier, Ohio agent.

Costs: $25 (includes meal/lunch and seminar).
Additional Information: Conference brochures/guidelines are available for SASE.

‡**OKLAHOMA FALL ARTS INSTITUTES,** P.O. Box 18154, Oklahoma City OK 73154. (405)842-0890.
Associate Director of Programs: Laura Anderson. Estab. 1983. Annual. Conference held from Oct.
28 to Oct. 31. Average attendance 100. "Fiction, poetry, nonfiction, writing for children and the art
of teaching writing are covered during the writing weekend." Held at "Quartz Mountain Arts and
Conference Center, an Oklahoma state lodge located in southwest Oklahoma at the edge of Lake
Altus/Lugert in the Quartz Mountains. Workshop participants are housed either in the lodge itself
(in hotel-room accommodations) or in cabins or duplexes with kitchens. Classes are held in special
pavilions built expressly for the Arts Institute. Pavilions offer a view of the lake and mountains.
Each year the Institute, as part of its 'Origins Oklahoma' humanities project, focuses on the cultural
contributions of a different ethnic or cultural group within the state. 1991 focused on Native Americans, 1992 on African-Americans, and 1993 will focus on Russian influences to our culture." No
featured panelists. Classes are taught by nationally recognized writers.
Costs: $350, which includes double-occupancy lodging, meals, tuition and a $25 application fee.
Accommodations: The Oklahoma Arts Institute leases all facilities at Quartz Mountain Arts and
Conference Center for the exclusive use of the Fall Arts Institutes participants. Lodging is included
in workshop cost.
Additional Information: Critique is usually done in class. Writers will need to bring completed works
with them. 1992 Course Catalog is available. Scholarships are available for a limited number of local
community artists. However, the Institutes are open to anyone.

OWFI ANNUAL CONFERENCE, 1304 McKinley Ave., Norman OK 73072. (405)321-4982. President:
Joye R. Swain. Estab. 1969. Annual. Conference held May 1-2 (always the first weekend in May).
Average attendance: 200-250. "The OWFI Annual Conference focuses on the nuts and bolts of writing
to sell. Speakers include writers of genre fiction (both book length and short), agents, publishers and
editors. This is a 'how to' program offering specific information for beginning writers and those who
are already selling. Friday night informal 'buzz sessions' are offered in hotel rooms where participants
discuss specialized and limited areas of writing." The conference is held at Days Inn South, in Oklahoma City. "We will have two large conference rooms with simultaneous presentations: one aimed at
beginning writers and one aimed at selling writers. In a book room we offer a wide variety of handouts
and guidelines as well as material written, edited or published by participants in the conference. A
director's suite is available for smaller groups which are organized spontaneously during the conference. A final awards banquet is held in a large dining area. We will have authors in the field speaking
on: mystery, science fiction, male action/adventure, women's mainstream, international intrigue. Other
topics are: What do agents do?; what happens to your baby (ms) when it gets to New York?; New
York markets; local markets; self-promotion – how to do it?; getting started as a writer; changing with
the changing markets during a writing career; what you need to know about contracts; plotting a novel;
developing characters." Guest speakers and panelists include Mel Odom and Jim Adair, authors, male
action/adventure; Michael Seidman, editor at Walker Books; Emma Merritt, past president, Romance
Writers of America; Dwight V. Swain, author of fact and fiction and nationally recognized teacher of
writing; Jyd Wall, mainstream author; Alice Orr, author and editor; and Robert L. Duncan, author,
international intrigue.
Costs: $50, including Friday dinner and Saturday night Awards Banquet. One day (not including
dinner): $35. Dinner tickets for spouses and guests: $15 for each evening.
Accommodations: Airport limousine service available for approximately $7. Rooms in the motel are
available for a special rate of $38 for conference attendees. The cost remains the same regardless of
the number of people in the room. Participants are welcome to make any other arrangements they
want on their own.
Additional Information: "Critique sessions are arranged at the conference between participants.
Speakers do not agree to critique manuscripts as a part of their appearance at the conference."
Organization sponsors annual contest. Send SASE for information. Conference brochures/guidelines
also available for SASE.

‡**OZARK CREATIVE WRITERS, INC.,** 6817 Gingerbread Lane, Little Rock AR 72204. (501)565-8889.
Director (Pres. of Board): Peggy Vining. Estab. 1973. Annual. Conference always held 2nd weekend
in October. Conference duration: 2½ days. Average attendance: 135-140. "All types of writing. Main
speaker for workshop in morning sessions – usually a novelist. Sattelite speakers – afternoon – various
types. Have included Songwriting Seminar last two years. Eureka Springs is a small resort town in the

foothills of the beautiful Ozarks. Conference site is the convention center. Very nice for a small group setting. Reserve early prior to Sept. 1 to insure place." Guest speaker in 1992 was Cherry Weiner, an agent from Manasplain, NJ.
Costs: $25, prior to Sept. 1st; $35 afterwards. Rooms are approx. $59/night and meals (2 banquets) $12 and 13.
Accommodations: Chamber of Commerce will send list; 50 rooms are blocked off for OCW prior to Sept. 1st. Accommodations vary at hotels. Many campsites also available.
Additional Information: We have approximately 20 various categories of writing contests. Selling writers are our judges. Entry fee is $25 full participation. Brochures are available for SASE.

PACIFIC NORTHWEST WRITERS SUMMER CONFERENCE, #804, 2033 6th Ave., Seattle WA 98121. (206)443-3807. Contact: Shirley Bishop. Estab. 1955. Annual. Conference held the last weekend in July. Average attendance: 500. Conference focuses on "fiction, nonfiction, poetry, film, drama, self-publishing, the creative process, critiques, core groups, advice from pros and networking." Site: Tyee Hotel, Olympia, WA. "Editors and agents come from both coasts. They bring lore from the world of publishing. The PNWC provides opportunities for writers to get to know editors and agents. The literary contest provides feedback from professionals and possible fame for the winners." The 1992 guest speaker was Al Young, author, poet, playwright.
Costs: $75-85/day. Meals and lodging are available at hotel or in nearby restaurants.
Accommodations: Buses take attendees to a surprise picnic. Lodging is available at Conference rates. Nearby hotels offer varying rates.
Additional Information: On-site critiques are available in small groups. Literary contest in these categories: science fiction, short stories/articles for children, multi-cultural, screenplay, adult genre short story, articles, nonfiction book, poetry, adult novel, picture books for children, juvenile novel and adult literary short stories. Send SASE for guidelines.

PACIFIC NORTHWEST WRITERS WINTER CONFERENCE, #804, 2033 6th Ave., Seattle WA 98121. (206)443-3807. Contact: Shirley Bishop. Estab. 1981. Annual. Weekend conference held in February. Average attendance: 200. "The conference is mostly hands-on workshops: novel, short story, nonfiction, film, poetry, getting started, keeping going." Site is the Greenwood Hotel, Bellevue, WA. "The winter conference is a good place to get started. Or a good place to recharge your batteries if your writing is stalled. If you're new in town, it's a good place to meet other writers." The 1991 guest speaker was Ann Rule, author of *The Stranger Beside Me* and *If You Really Loved Me*.
Costs: $87/day. Two days for $147. Meals are not included.
Accommodations: Lodging is available at the hotel or at surrounding motels.
Additional Information: On-site critiques are available in small groups. Literary contest in these categories: nonfiction books and articles, novels and short stories, playwriting. Brochures are available.

‡PASADENA WRITERS' FORUM, P.C.C. 1570 E. Colorado Blvd., Pasadena CA 91106-2003. (818)585-7602. Coordinator: Meredith Brucker. Estab. 1954. Annual. Conference held March 20. Conference duration: 1 day (Saturday). Average attendance: 225. "For the novice as well as the professional writer in any field of interest: fiction or nonfiction, including scripts, childrens, humor, poetry." Conference held on the campus of Pasadena City College. In 1992, a panel of literary agents, including Pat Teal, Gloria Stern, Sue Lasbury and Bart Andrews were in attendance.
Costs: $65, including box lunch and coffee hour.
Additional Information: Brochure upon request, no SASE necessary. "Pasadena City College also offers an eight-week Community Education class 'Writing For Publication' periodically."

‡PIMA WRITERS' WORKSHOP, 2202 W. Anklam Rd., Tucson AZ 85709. (602)884-6974. Director: Peg Files. Estab. 1988. Annual. Conference held in May. Conference duration 3 days. Average attendance: 150. "For anyone interested in writing—beginning or experienced writer. The workshop offers sessions on writing short stories, novels, nonfiction articles and books, children's and juvenile stories, poetry and screenplays." Sessions are held in the new Center for the Arts on Pima Community College's West Campus. Past speakers include Brian Garfield, Barbara Kingsolver, Mark Harris, Michael Collins, Nancy Mairs, Larry McMurtry, Lawrence Lieberman and Ron Powers. 1993 workshop will probably feature John Weston, Ron Powers, Allen Woodman and Nancy Mairs, among others.

Costs: $55. (Or participants may attend for college credit, in which case fees are $58 for Arizona residents and $283 for out-of-state residents). Meals and accommodations not included.
Accommodations: Information on local accommodations is made available, and special workshop rates are available at a specified motel close to the workshop site. The 1992 workshop motel's rate was $45/night, single or double.
Additional Information: Participants may have up to 20 pages critiqued by the author of their choice. Manuscripts must be submitted 2 weeks before the workshop. Conference brochure/guidelines available for SASE. "The workshop atmosphere is casual, friendly, and supportive, and guest authors are very accessible. Readings, films and panel discussions are offered as well as talks and manuscript sessions."

PLOUGHSHARES INTERNATIONAL FICTION WRITING SEMINAR, Emerson College, Division of Continuing Education, 100 Beacon St., Boston MA 02116. (617)578-8615. Contact person: Hank Zappala. Estab. 1990. Annual. Conference/workshop held: Summer, 1993. Conference duration: 2 weeks. Average attendance: 25. "Castle Well is not a classroom, but a community of practicing writers who breathe, think, discuss and debate fiction with their peers and a group of professional authors." Castle Well is a Renaissance Castle. Located in the Village of Well on the river Maas in southeastern Holland. Co-Directors are James Carroll and Robie Macauley.
Costs: In 1992, cost was $1,650 plus transportation. Tuition includes room and board, special events, workshops and excursions.
Accommodations: On-site accommodations.
Additional Information: Sample work required—1 short story or short segment of a longer work, no more than 15 pages. Brochures/guidelines available for SASE. "Seminar members may earn four credits toward graduate or undergraduate degrees."

PORT TOWNSEND WRITERS' CONFERENCE, Centrum, Box 1158, Port Townsend WA 98368. (206)385-3102. Director: Carol Jane Bangs. Estab. 1974. Annual. Conference held July 8-18. Average attendance: 180. Conference to promote poetry, fiction, creative nonfiction and writing for children. The conference is held at a 700-acre state park on the strait of Juan de Fuca. "The site is a Victorian-era military fort with miles of beaches, wooded trails and recreation facilities. The park is within the limits of Port Townsend, a historic seaport and arts community, approximately 80 miles northwest of Seattle, on the Olympic Peninsula." Panels include "Writing About Nature," "Journal Writing," "Literary Translation." There will be 5-10 guest speakers in addition to 10 full-time faculty.
Costs: $350 approx. tuition and $200 approx. room and board.
Accommodations: City bus transports ferry passengers to site. "Modest room and board facilities on site." Also list of hotels/motels/inns/bed & breakfasts/private rentals available.
Additional Information: "Admission to workshops is selective, based on manuscript submissions." Brochures/guidelines available for SASE. "The conference focus is on the craft of writing and the writing life, not on marketing."

PORTLAND STATE UNIVERSITY HAYSTACK PROGRAM IN THE ARTS & SCIENCES, PSU Summer Session, P.O. Box 751, Portland OR 97207. (503)725-4081. Contact: Maggie Herrington or Robert Mercer. Estab. 1968. Annual. Conference held from late June to early August generally in one-week sessions meeting Monday through Friday; some weekend workshops. Average attendance: 10-15/class. Conference offers "a selection of writing courses including fiction, nonfiction, poetry, essay and memoir—taught by well-known writers in small-group sessions, 6 hours/day." Classes are held in the local school with supplemental activities at the beach, pubs, lecture hall and other areas of the resort town.
Costs: $170 (weekend)-$305 (weeklong). Participants provide their own housing and meals.
Accommodations: "Housing costs are $50-400/week. Camping, bed and breakfasts and hotels are available."

‡PRAIRIE STATE COLLEGE WRITERS CONFERENCE, 202 S. Halsted St., Chicago Heights IL 60411. (708)709-3546. Conference Coordinator: Whitney Scott. Estab. 1990. Annual. Conference held in fall. Conference duration: 1 day. For fiction and poetry. Held at college conference center appropriate for teleconferencing. Theme for 1992 was "Visual inspiration for writing." Guest speakers for 1992 were Mary Jo Bang and James Andrew, Ph.D.
Costs: $8-25 (1992).
Additional Information: Conference brochures/guidelines are available for SASE.

‡PROFESSIONALISM IN WRITING SCHOOL, Suite 701, 4308 S. Peoria, Tulsa OK 74105. (918)PIW-5588. Coordinator: Norma Jean Lutz. Estab. 1982. Annual. Conference held from March 26 to March 27. Average attendance: 180. "A conference for Christians who write. Many areas are covered. From nuts and bolts of grammar, to book distribution, to play and script writing, to fiction! Always a strong emphasis on fiction." Held in a large spacious church in Tulsa, OK. 1993 theme: "Study to show thyself approved unto God" II Timothy 2:16. Guest speakers and panelists include V. Gil Beers, president Scripture Press Publ., Inc. (keynoter), Special Guest: Marjorie Decker, author of *The Christian Mother Goose* and many other well known authors and editors as well.
Costs: $120 advance $140 at door. (Meals, banquet, packet, all workshops for 2 days. Partials are available).
Accommodations: Shuttle from airport to selected hotel. Rides available from hotel to site at church. Nearby hotel offering PIW conferees special rates $39 per night.
Additional Information: "We have a critique service. $5 per submissions." Sponsors a contest: 5 categories w/cash prizes; $7 entry fee each. $30 max. for all 5 categories. Conference brochures/guidelines are available for SASE. "This is in conjunction with the Tulsa Christian Writers Club, in existence since 1977. Anyone can be an "At large" member of TCW and receive monthly newletter for $8/yr."

ROBERT QUACKENBUSH'S CHILDREN'S BOOK WRITING & ILLUSTRATING WORKSHOPS, 460 East 79th St., New York NY 10021. (212)744-3822. Instructor: Robert Quackenbush. Estab. 1982. Annual. Workshop held the second week in July. Average attendance: limited to 10. Workshops to promote writing and illustrating books for children. Held at the Manhattan studio of Robert Quackenbush, author and illustrator of over 150 books for young readers. "Focus is generally on picture books. All classes led by Robert Quackenbush."
Costs: $950 tuition covers all costs of the workshop, but does not include housing and meals. A $100 nonrefundable deposit is required with the $850 balance due one month prior to attendance.
Accommodations: A list of recommended hotels and restaurants is sent upon receipt of deposit.
Additional Information: Class is for beginners and professionals. Work submission required. Critiques during workshop. Conference brochures/guidelines are available for SASE.

‡RICE UNIVERSITY WRITERS' CONFERENCE, Rice University, Box 1892, Houston TX 77251. (713)527-4803. Assistant Dean, Rice School of Continuing Studies: Edie Carlson-Abbey. Estab. 1992. Annual. Conference held in June. Conference duration: 2 days. Average attendance: 170. For "fiction, writing for children, poetry, screenwriting, nonfiction articles." Held at an area hotel. Panels: "Finding an Agent"; "Getting Published"; "Screenwriting Q and A" (with professional screenwriters); other themes: writing techniques, all aspects of fiction writing. 1992 guest speakers included authors David Lindsey, Sharyn McCrumb, Susan Dunlap, Jay Brandon and others. Children's authors were Mary Blount Christian, Diane Stanley, Joan Lowery Nixon. Also a panel of literary agents.
Costs: $225.
Accommodations: Hotel list available. Special room rate from host hotel.
Additional Information: Conference brochures/guidelines are available.

‡ROCKY MT. FICTION WRITERS COLORADO GOLD, P.O. Box 260244, Denver CO 80226-0244. (303)697-1844. Conference Co-chair: Linda Herbert. Estab. 1983. Annual. Conference held in September. Conference duration: 3 days. Average attendance: 150. For novel length fiction. The conference will be held at the Sheraton Denver West in their conference facility. Themes include general novel length fiction, genre fiction, contemporary romance, mystery, sf/f, mainstream, history with possible horror and techno-thriller in 1993. Guest speakers and panelists are Ann McCaffrey, Dorothy Cannell, Phoebe Conn, Patricia Gardner Evans, Constance O'Day Flannery and Michael Palmer; 5 editors and 2 agents unknown at this time.
Costs: $130 (includes conference, reception, banquet). Editor workshop $20 additional.
Accommodations: Information on overnight accommodations made available of area hotels. The conference will be at the Sheraton Hotel. Room rates are $63/night.
Additional Information: Editor-conducted workshops are limited to 10 participants for critique with auditing available. First 10 pages to be brought alone. Workshops in science fiction, mainstream, mystery, historical, contemporary romance. Sponsors a contest. For 30-page mss and 10-page synopsis; 5 categories mentioned above. First rounds are done by qualified members, published and nonpublished, with editors doing the final ranking; 2 copies need to be submitted without author's name. $20 entry only, $30 entry and (one) critique. Guidelines available for SASE.

‡ROMANCE WRITERS OF AMERICA NATIONAL CONFERENCE, Suite 315, 13700 Veteran Memorial Dr., Houston TX 77014. (713)440-6885. Office Supervisor: Linda Fisher. Estab. 1980. Annual. Conference held from July 29 to August 1. Average attendance: 1,200. "Popular fiction, emphasis on all forms of romance and women's fiction. Held at Adams Mark Hotel, 4th and Chestnut, St. Louis, MO 63102. Our conference always focuses on selling romantic fiction with special workshops from publishers telling attendees how, specifically to sell to their houses." 1992 keynote and special speakers were: Sandra Canfield and Sandra Brown.
Costs: Fee for 1992 was $260 and included a reception, four meals plus two continental breakfasts. Room rates are separate.
Accommodations: Special conference rates at the Adams Mark Hotel are single: $99; double: $109.
Additional Information: Annual RITA awards are presented for romance authors. Annual Golden Heart awards are present for unpublished writers. Entry is restricted to RWA members. Conference brochures/guidelines are available for SASE.

‡ROPEWALK WRITERS' RETREAT, 8600 University Blvd., Evansville IN 47712. (812)464-1863. Conference Coordinator: Linda Cleek. Estab. 1989. Annual. Conference held June 13-19. Average attendance: 35. "The week-long RopeWalk Writers' Retreat gives participants an opportunity to attend workshops and to confer privately with one of five prominent writers. Historic New Harmony, Indiana, site of two nineteenth century utopian experiments, provides an ideal setting for this event with its retreat-like atmosphere and its history of creative and intellectual achievement. At RopeWalk you will be encouraged to write—not simply listen to others talks about writing. Each workshop will be limited to fifteen participants. The New Harmony Inn and Conference Center will be headquarters for the RopeWalk Writers' Retreat. Please note that reservations at the Inn should be confirmed by May 1." 1993 faculty are Lynn Emanuel, Andrew Hudgins, David St. John, Rust Hills and Ann Beattie.
Costs: $275 (1992), includes one dinner.
Accommodations: Information on overnight accommodations is made available. "Room-sharing assistance; some low-cost accommodations in private homes and/or park facilities."
Additional Information: For critiques submit mss approx. 6 weeks ahead. Brochures are available for SASE.

S.U.N.Y. COLLEGE FALL WRITING ARTS FESTIVAL, State University of New York at Oswego, Oswego NY 13126. (315)341-2602. Director of the Program in Writing Arts: Lewis Turco. Estab. 1968. Annual. Conference held October. Conference duration: 5 days, Monday-Thursday. Average attendance: 40-60. For fiction, poetry, drama writing. Conference held at the Student Union facilities. Past themes have included gay and lesbian writing, black writing.
Costs: All sessions free and open to public.
Accommodations: Attendees must make their own arrangements for board and accommodations. May be given information through the Office of Continuing Education at Swetmen Hall, State University College, Oswego NY 13126.
Additional Information: Information poster available for SASE.

‡SAGE HILL WRITING EXPERIENCE, Box 1731, Saskatoon, Saskatchewan S7K 3S1 Canada. Administrator: Steven Smith. Annual. Workshops in August. Workshop duration 7-14 days. Attendance: limited to 32-40. "Sage Hill Writing Experience offers a special working and learning opportunity to writers at different stages of development. Top quality instruction, low instructor-student ratio and the beautiful Sage Hill setting offer conditions ideal for the pursuit of excellence in the arts of fiction and poetry." The Sage Hill location features "individual accommodation, in-room writing area, lounges, meeting rooms, home-style cooking, gymnasium, bowling alley, swimming pool and walking woods and vistas in several directions." Five classes are held: Introduction to Creative Writing, Prose & Poetry; Fiction Workshop, Poetry Workshop, Intermediate; Fiction Colloquium, Advanced; Prose Colloquium, Advanced. 1992 faculty included Judith Krause, David Margoshes, Lorna Crozier, Guy Vanderhaeghe, Edna Alford, Dennis Cooley.
Costs: $400 (Canadian) includes instruction, accommodation, meals and all facilities.
Accommodations: Bus service from Saskatoon to Prud'hoome departs at 5:25 pm daily. Pre-arranged auto transportation also available. On-site accommodations located 75 kilometers outside Saskatoon.
Additional Information: For Introduction to Creative Writing: A five-page sample of your writing or a statement of your interest in creative writing; list of courses taken required. For intermediate and colloquium classes: A resume of your writing career and a 10-page sample of your work plus 5 pages of published work required. Guidelines are available for SASE. Scholarships and bursaries are available.

‡SAN DIEGO COUNTY CHRISTIAN WRITERS' GUILD, Box 1171, El Cajon CA 92022. Convener: Sherwood E. Wirt. Estab. 1977. Annual. Conference held in September. Conference duration one day. Average attendance: 125. Currently held at the Horizon Christian Fellowship. 1992 guest speakers included Carole Gift Page, Ernest E. Owen (retired publisher of Word Books), Ronald N. Haynes (senior acquisitions editor for Thomas Nelson) and others.
Costs: $65.
Additional Information: Conference brochures/guidelines are available for SASE.

SAN DIEGO STATE UNIVERSITY WRITERS CONFERENCE, SDSU-Aztec Center, San Diego CA 92182. (619)594-5152. Assistant to Director of Extension: Diane Dunaway. Estab. 1984. Annual. Conference held on weekend in January. Conference duration 2 days. Average attendance: Approx. 350. "This conference is held on the San Diego State University campus at the Aztec Center. The Aztec Center is conveniently located near parking. The meeting rooms are spacious and comfortable. All sessions meet in the same general area. Each year the SDSU Writers Conference offers a variety of workshops for the beginner and the advanced writer. This conference allows the individual writer to choose which workshop best suits his/her needs. In addition, office hours are provided so that attendees may meet with speakers, editors and agents in small, personal groups to discuss specific questions. Also, a wine-and-cheese reception is offered Saturday immediately following the workshops where attendees may socialize with the faculty in a relaxed atmosphere. Keynote speaker is to be determined."
Costs: Not to exceed $185. This includes all conference workshops and office hours, coffee and pastries in the morning, lunch and wine-and-cheese reception Saturday evening.
Accommodations: The Howard Johnson offers conference attendees a reduced rate, $45/night. Attendees must say they are with the SDSU Writers Conference.
Additional Information: A critique session will be offered. To receive a brochure, call or send a postcard with address to: SDSU Writers Conference, College of Extended Studies, San Diego State University, San Diego CA 92182. No SASE required.

‡SANTA FE WRITERS' CONFERENCE, 826 Camino de Monte Rey, Santa Fe NM 87501. (505)982-9301. Seminar Coordinator: Rae Taylor. Estab. 1984. Annual. Conference held in August. Conference duration: 6 days. Average attendance: 50. Concentrations are fiction and poetry. "Held at Plaza Resolane, a Ghost Ranch Study and Conference Center in downtown Santa Fe. Lodging, double rooms; dining room, cafeteria, meeting rooms."
Costs: $595 (1992 costs); lodging and food included.
Accommodations: On-site accommodations at Plaza Resolana.
Additional Information: Workshops for fiction and poetry require writers to submit 10 pages, submission fee $35. Brochures are available for SASE.

SCBWI CONFERENCE IN CHILDREN'S LITERATURE, NYC, P.O. Box 20233, Park West Finance Station, New York NY 10025-1511. Chairman: Kimberly Colen. Estab. 1975. Annual. Conference held "usually" 1st (or 2nd) Saturday in November. Average attendance: 350-400. Conference is to promote writing for children: Picture books, fiction, nonfiction, middle grade and young adult. "The past 3 years it has been at 3 different schools. In 1992 it was held at Bank Street College."
Costs: $55, members; $60 nonmembers; $5 additional on day of conference.
Accommodations: No accommodations available. Write for information; hotel names will be supplied.
Additional Information: Conference brochures/guidelines are available for SASE.

SCBWI/DRURY COLLEGE WRITING FOR CHILDREN WORKSHOP, 900 N. Benton, Springfield MO 65802. (417)865-8731. Directors: Lynn Doke or Sandy Asher. Estab. 1986. Annual. One-day workshop held in November. Average attendance: 60. Workshop to promote writing and illustrating fiction and nonfiction for young readers, held at Drury College. Panels planned for next workshop include Writing and Illustrating Picture Books, Marketing Your Work, and Writing for Middle Grade and Young Adult Readers. Faculty includes an editor from a major publishing house (i.e. Bantam, Scholastic) and invited authors. 1993 guest speakers include Barbara Sealing (author of *How to Write a Children's Book and Get it Published*) and Paula Morrow (editor, *Ladybug*).

Costs: $50, includes continental breakfast and luncheon. Discount for SCBWI members and early registrants.
Accommodations: Hotel information is made available.
Additional Information: Faculty will meet with individuals to discuss manuscripts and/or illustrations, $25 fee. Workshop brochures/guidelines are available for SASE.

SCBWI/HOFSTRA CHILDREN'S LITERATURE CONFERENCE, Hofstra University, University College of Continuing Education, 205 Davison Hall, Hempstead NY 11550. (516)463-5993. Co-organizers: Connie C. Epstein, Adrienne Betz, Lewis Shena. Estab. 1985. Annual. Conference to be held April 3. Average attendance: 160. Conference to promote writing for children. "Purpose is to bring together various professional groups—writers, illustrators, librarians, teachers—who are interested in writing for children. Each year we will organize program around a theme. Last year it was The American Experience, and this year it will be Style and Substance." The conference takes place at the Student Center Building of Hofstra University, located in Hempstead, Long Island. "We have two general sessions and five or six break-out groups that we hold in rooms in the Center or classrooms in nearby buildings. Lunch is provided." This year's conference will feature Walter Dean Myers and Richard Lewis as general speakers and offer special-interst groups in nonfiction (Russell Friedman) and contracts and copyright (Mary Flower) with others in picture books, fiction, folklore, etc. to be decided.
Cost: $47 (in previous years) for SCBWI members; $52 for nonmembers. Lunch included.

‡SCBWI/LOS ANGELES/WRITERS CONFERENCE IN CHILDREN'S LITERATURE, P.O. Box 66296, Mar Vista Station, Los Angeles CA 90066. (818)347-2849. Executive Director: Lin Oliver. Estab. 1972. Annual. Conference held in August. Conference duration 4 days. Average attendance: 350. Writing for children. Site: Doubletree Inn in the Marina Del Rey area (at the beach) in Los Angeles. Theme: "The Business of Writing."
Costs: $225 (does not include hotel room).
Accommodations: Information on overnight accommodations made available. Conference rates at the hotel about $100/night.
Additional Information: Ms critiques are available. Conference brochures/guidelines are available (after June 1993) for SASE.

‡SCBWI/MID-ATLANTIC, P.O. Box 1707, Midlothian VA 23112. (804)744-6503. Regional Advisor: T.R. Hollingsworth. Estab. 1984. Annual. Conference held in the fall. Conference duration: one day. Average attendance: 100. Writing for children. Usually held at a conference center of a well-knwon hotel chain. Themes in 1992 were "Marketing," fiction workshops for writers and "How-to" for illustrators. In 1992, guest speakers were Connie Epstein, Jim Giblin, Norm Bomor, editors and writers.
Costs: In 1992, $55 members, $60 non-members, includes continental breakfast and lunch.
Accommodations: Special conference rate on-site.
Additional Information: Sponsors writer's contest, illustrator's display and critique of contest entries. Entry requirements: Paid registration; 1,500 word ms, typed, double-spaced; limited to one manuscript per person. Conference brochures/guidelines are available for SASE.

‡SCBWI/NORTH CENTRAL TEXAS CHAPTER ANNUAL CONFERENCE, 2800 South Center St., Arlington TX 76013. (817)860-2702. Co-director Conference: Sue Ward. Estab. 1982. Annual. Conference held July 24 (Saturday). Average attendance: 100. Writing for children. Held at Arlington Community Center, large conference room with smaller rooms, if needed. In 1992 featured speakers were children's authors Dian Curtis Regan and Angela Shelf Medearis and Senior Editor at Lodestar Books, Rosemary Brosnan.
Costs: In 1992 costs were $40 for members; $45 for nonmembers.
Additional Information: Conference brochures/guidelines are available for SASE. Contact Person: Sue Ward: 717 Buttermilk, Arlington, TX 76006.

SCBWI/ROCKY MOUNTAIN CHAPTER FALL/WINTER WORKSHOPS, 8600 Firethorn Dr., Loveland CO 80538. (303)669-3755. Regional Advisor: Vivian Dubrovin. Annual. Fall Conference held 3rd Saturday of September; Winter Workshop held in February; Illustrators Workshop held in May. All last 1 day. Average attendance: 100-175. Fall conference features authors, editors and agents for children's work (picture book—YA). Winter workshop features headline authors. Also 3-day retreat in July, attendance 50-75. "Emphasis on small-group workshops on characterization, plotting, second level of writing, publishing etc." Illustrators workshop features illustrators of children's books and workshops on writing/illustrating and technical aspects particular to children's books. Conferences

rotate between college facilities, hotels and other meeting spaces. Brochures available approximately 3-4 weeks prior to event.
Costs: Generally around $50/day, less for SCBWI members. Lunch and snacks plus handouts included. 3-day retreat around $200.

‡SCBWI/ROCKY MOUNTAIN CHAPTER SUMMER RETREAT, 815 W. 5th, Loveland CO 80537. (303)667-5725. RMC/SCBW President: Ellen Javernick. Estab. 1981. Annual. Conference held from July 23 to July 25. Average attendance 50-60. Writing for children. Held at a retreat center near mountains outside of Colorado Springs, Colorado. Theme: "Writing for Different Age Groups." Presenters are Dian Curtus Regan, Lee Wardlow.
Costs: $150-175 (approx.).
Accommodations: On site double rooms (some singles available) single beds; accommodations included in price.
Additional Information: Critiques by speakers will be available at additional cost. Conference brochures/guidelines are available for SASE (after May 1993).

‡SCBWI/WISCONSIN FALL RETREAT, 26 Lancaster Ct., Madison WI 53719-1433. (608)271-0433. Regional Advisor: Sheri Cooper Sinykin. Estab. 1991. Annual. Conference held from November 5 to November 7. Average attendance: 60. Writing for children. In 1993 (and odd years) held at Siena Center in Racine, in even years, if available, held St. Benedict's Center in Madison. "Siena Center is on Lake Michigan and is a dorm-like, religious retreat house." Speakers in 1992 were Phyllis Reynolds Naylor, this year's Newbery winnter, and Susan Pearson, editor-in-chief of Lothrop, Lee & Shepard Books.
Costs: $175 for SCBWI members ($195 non-members), includes room, board, program and book (1992).
Accommodations: We try to have volunteers assist with airport transportation. Overnights are on-site and included. On-site housing runs about $25/night.
Additional Information: Critiques were offered in 1992 for an extra fee of $25. Conference brochures/guidelines are available in June for SASE.

‡SEATTLE PACIFIC UNIVERSITY CHRISTIAN WRITERS CONFERENCE, Seattle Pacific University School of Humanities, Seattle WA 98119. (206)281-2109. Director: Linda Wagner. Estab. 1980. Annual. Conference held in June. Conference duration: 3 days. Average attendance: 160. Concentration is both fiction and nonfiction writing for Christian writers. Site is on a college campus, dining room and dorms available for meals and boarding. 1992 guest speaker was Dr. Eugene Peterson (author of 13 books, including *Answering God*), several other writers and editors.
Costs: $175 (Pre-registration $160, meals and dorm separate).
Accommodations: Dorms available on campus. Cost: $25/night for room. Meals: $65/3 days.
Additional Information: Critiques available; send SASE for guidelines. "Available sessions include both lecture and writing workshops."

‡SEWANEE WRITERS' CONFERENCE, 310 St. Luke's Hall, Sewanee TN 37375. (615)598-1141. Contact: Cheri Peters. Estab. 1990. Annual. Conference held in July. Conference duration: 12 days. Average attendance: 90. "The purpose of the Sewanee Writers' Conference is to make it possible for serious, though not necessarily experienced, writers to work closely in a variety of contexts (workshop, individual conference, panel discussion, lecture, etc.) with a group of distinguished writers, critics, agents and editors. The conference takes place at the University of the South which, physically, is a collection of ivy-covered Gothic buildings located on the Cumberland Plateau, between Chattanooga and Nashville. The campus is rural and quiet, but the summer session of the College and the Sewanee Summer Music Center assure a full measure of films, lectures and concerts. Tennis courts, swimming pool and golf course, all within walking distance, are available to faculty and participants. The University domain (about 10,000 acres) is a perfect environment for swimming, jogging, hiking, rock climbing, horseback riding, or simple strolling and sunset watching." The 1992 faculty included John Casey, Amy Hempel, Stanley Elkin, Joe Ashby Porter, Ellen Douglas and Tim O'Brien, in fiction.
Costs: $1,000, a figure which includes tuition, room, board and activity fees.
Accommodations: "The Conference provides transportation to and from the Chattanooga and Nashville airports. Conference housing consists of single or double dormitory rooms with shared bathrooms (each bath joins two rooms). Interested persons may inquire at the Sewanee Writers' Conference office for a listing of area motels, inns, and bed-and-breakfast options. The cost of a dormitory room is included in the Conference fee."

Additional Information: "Our admission process is a competitive one, requiring a manuscript submission. If accepted to the Conference, a participant submits either a second copy of the manuscript that accompanied the application, or a different manuscript; the participant's choice serves as the basis of an hour-long one-on-one consultation (or critique) with a professional writer who works in the same genre as the participant." Brochures are available; SASE not necessary. "The cost of the Sewanee Writers' Conference in underwritten by the Walter E. Dakin Memorial Fund established through the estate of the late Tennessee Williams."

SHOOTING STAR WRITERS CONFERENCE, *Shooting Star Productions, Inc.,* (formerly Black Writers Conference), 7123 Race St., Pittsburgh PA 15208. (412)731-7464. Trustee/Publisher: Sandra Gould Ford. Estab. 1991. Annual. Conference held in late September. Conference duration: 1 day. Average attendance: 250. University setting. Themes relating to culture.
Costs: $50 early registration; $70 for late registration; individual sessions $15 each.
Accommodations: Discount at local hotel available ($69 for up to 4 adults).

SINIPEE WRITERS' WORKSHOP, P.O. Box 902, Dubuque IA 52004-0902. (319)556-0366. Director: John Tigges. Estab. 1985. Annual conference held April 24, 1993. Average attendance: 50-75. To promote "primarily fiction although we do include a poet and a nonfiction writer on each program. The two mentioned areas are treated in such a way that fiction writers can learn new ways to expand their abilities and writing techniques." The workshop is held on the campus of Clarke College in Dubuque. "This campus holds a unique atmosphere and everyone seems to love the relaxed and restful mood it inspires. This in turn carries over to the workshop and friendships are made that last in addition to learning and experiencing what other writers have gone through to attain success in their chosen field." 1993 guest speakers include Jo Horne Schmidt aka Ann Justice (best-selling romance novelist); Marshall Cook (nonfiction); Bill Pauly (poet); Mary Agria (writing grants for writing projects).
Costs: $60 early registration/$65 at the door. Includes all handouts, necessary materials for the workshop, coffee/snack break, lunch, drinks and snacks at autograph party following workshop.
Accommodations: Information is available for out-of-town participants, concerning motels etc. even though the workshop is one day long.
Additional Information: Fiction contest: Limit 1,500 words. In each category: 1st prize $50 plus publication in an area newspaper or magazine; 2nd prize 50% scholarship; 3rd 25% scholarship (scholarships for following year). Critique service available for contest entries. $10 additional. Conference brochures/guidelines are available for SASE. "We offer a 50% scholarship to full-time college and high school students as well as to Senior citizens 65 and older."

SOCIETY OF SOUTHWESTERN AUTHORS WRITERS' CONFERENCE, P.O. Box 30355, Tucson AZ 85751-0355. (602)299-3523. Conference Chair: Don Young. Estab. 1972. Annual. Conference held in January. Average attendance: 150-250. Conference "covers a spectrum of practical topics for writers. Each year varies, but there is a minimum of 12 different classes during the day, plus the keynote speaker." Conference held at Hotel Park Tucson.
Costs: $40 general ($50 walk-in); $30 students ($40 walk-in).
Additional Information: Conference brochures/guidelines are available for SASE.

‡SOUTHEASTERN WRITERS ASSOCIATION ANNUAL WORKSHOP, 4021 Gladesworth Lane, Decatur GA 30035. (404)288-2064. Director: Nancy Knight. Estab. 1976. Annual. Conference held from June 20 to June 26. Average attendance: 75. "For poetry, short story, mass market fiction, novel, playwriting, children's literature, nonfiction, inspiration. The conference is held at Epworth-by-the-Sea on St. Simon's Island, GA. The immaculate grounds are expansive and inspirational for writers. Several historical buildings are located on the site. Housing is reasonable and includes all meals."
Costs: $200 nonmembers, $170 members, $150 seniors.
Accommodations: 1992 rates – all on-site/handicap accessible, $234-274 (double), $319-391 (single), includes *all* meals including banquet.
Additional Information: Three mss may be submitted for critique and private consultation. Sponsors a contest. All categories of mss are judged for contests by the instructor. Conference attendance is the requirement. Conference brochures/guidelines are available for SASE. "We stress interaction between students and staff. Teachers are housed in the same area and available to students at almost any time. We are a hands-on kind of workshop – students are assigned work to be completed during free time which is usually read in class."

‡SOUTHEASTERN WRITERS CONFERENCE, Rt. 1, Box 102, Cuthbert GA 31740. (912)679-5445. Advertising Director: Pat Laye. Estab. 1975. Annual. Conference held in June. Conference duration: 1 week. Average attendance: 80 (Limited to 100 participants). Concentration is on fiction, poetry and juvenile—plus nonfiction and playwriting. Site: is "St. Simons Island, GA. Conference held at Epworth-by-the-Sea Conference Center—tropical setting, beaches. Each year we offer market advice, agent updates. All our instructors are professional writers presently selling in New York."
Costs: $150. Meals and lodging are separate. There is a senior citizen discount.
Accommodations: Air and bus attendees will be picked up at their arrival point and returned there. Information on overnight accommodations is made available. "On-site-facilities at a remarkably low cost. Facilities are motel style of excellent quality. Other hotels are available on the island."
Additional Information: Three manuscripts of 1 chapter each are allowed in three different categories. Sponsors a contest, many cash prizes. Brochures are available for SASE.

‡SOUTHERN CALIFORNIA WRITERS CONFERENCE/SAN DIEGO, 3745 Mt. Augustus Ave., San Diego CA 92111. (619)277-7302. Director: Betty Abell Jurus. Estab. 1987. Annual. Conference held January 15-18. Conference duration: 4 days. Average attendance: 200. "Our purpose is to help writers achieve their goals. Site is the Holiday Inn, Montgomery Field, San Diego, CA. Conference emphasis is on fiction and screen writing. Workshops also cover nonfiction, travel writing, the writing business, etc. and poetry. We also have 2 agents' panels and 1 editors' panel." 1993 speakers will include David Gerrold ("The Trouble With Tribbles"), Academy Award winner Michael Blake ("Dances With Wolves") and Victor Villaseñor ("Rain of Gold").
Costs: $195 for conference without lodging; full conference with lodging includes hotel, all conference events, and banquet: single room: $425, shared room: $350.
Accommodations: Hotel has shuttle service from airport. Special conference attendee accommodations made. Conferees register for hotel and conference through the conference.
Additional Information: "Work may be submitted for advance critique, followed by one-on-one discussion with the SCWC/SD reader during conference. Work may be read aloud and critiqued with designated workshops. No requirements for submission of work. Awards are given for work heard or read at conference. A special award is given for topic writing done at the conference. Judges are working, published writers or editors." Brochures are available, no SASE is necessary.

SOUTHWEST CHRISTIAN WRITERS ASSOCIATION, P.O. Box 2635, Farmington NM 87499. (505)327-1962. President: Kathy Cordell. Estab. 1980. Annual. Conference held September 18. Average attendance: 30. For "fiction (novel), short stories, writing for teens." Conference held at the First Presbyterian Church, 865 N. Dustin, Farmington, NM 87401. Panels include: Writing the teen novel; Marketing and dealing with editors; Writing for children. Guest speaker Carole Gift Page.
Costs: $39 (meals are "Dutch" at a local restaurant); $5 off early registration and additional $5 off for members.
Additional Information: Sponsors a contest. "One additional speaker invited (not decided yet). Freebies and a booktable available (authors may bring books to sell if attending conference)."

SOUTHWEST FLORIDA WRITERS' CONFERENCE, P.O. Box 06210, Ft. Myers FL 33906-6210. (813)489-9226. Conference Director: Joanne Hartke. Estab. 1980. Annual. Conference held Feb. 26-27 (always the 4th Friday night and Saturday of February). Average attendance: 150. "This year's conference will include fiction, poetry, nonfiction, an agent and others. The purpose is to serve the local writing community, whether they are novice or published writers." The conference is held on the Edison Community College campus. "We will have one final panel that will include several presenters from earlier in the day. It will be an open forum to ask questions, share ideas, say what works (and doesn't) for each. Last year's featured keynote address was given by Peter Matthiessen."
Costs: Friday, February 26—reception and keynote address: $15. Saturday February 27—full-day conference: $49 (continental breakfast and lunch included).
Additional Information: "We do sponsor a contest annually, with the prizes being gift certificates to local bookstores. Local, published writers offer volunteer critique/judging services." Conference brochures or guidelines available for SASE. "Every odd year the conference format is writing intensive rather than mainly presentations, with verbal and written critiques."

‡SPLIT ROCK ARTS PROGRAM, University of Minnesota, 306 Wesbrook Hall, 77 Pleasant St. SE, Minneapolis MN 55455. (612)624-6800. Estab. 1982. Annual. Workshops held in July and August. Over 45 one-week intensive residential workshops held. "The Split Rock Arts Program, now in its ninth season, is offered through the University of Minnesota on its Duluth campus. Over 45 one-week

intensive residential workshops in writing, visual arts, fine crafts and the process of creativity are held for six weeks in July and August. This unique arts community provides a nurturing environment in a beautiful setting overlooking Lake Superior and the cool summer port city of Duluth. Courses, which can be taken for credit, are offered in long and short fiction, nonfiction, poetry and children's literature." Instructors in 1992 were Paulette Bates Alden, Christina Baldwin, Carol Bly, Judith Ortiz Cofer, Carolyn Forché, Paul Gruchow, Will Weaver.

Costs: $300, tuition (may vary with options). Moderately priced housing available for additional cost.
Accommodations: Campus apartments available.
Additional Information: A limited number of scholarships are available based on qualification and need. Call for catalog.

‡STATE OF MAINE WRITERS' CONFERENCE, P.O. Box 296, Ocean Park ME 04063. (207)934-5034 June-August; (413)596-6734 September-May. Chairman: Richard F. Burns. Estab. 1941. Annual. Conference held: in August. Conference duration: 4 days. Average attendance: 70-75. "We try to present a balanced as well as eclectic conference. There is quite a bit of time and attention given to poetry but we also have children's literature, mystery writing, travel, novels/fiction and lots of items and issues of interest to writers such as speakers who are: publishers, editors, illustrators and the like. Our concentration is, by intention, a general view of writing to publish. We are located in Ocean Park, a small seashore village 14 miles south of Portland. Ours is a summer assembly center with many buildings from the Victorian Age. The conference meets in Porter Hall, one of the assembly buildings which is listed on the National Register of Historic Places. It is too early to give any line-up just yet, but within recent years our guest list has included: Lewis Turco, Bob Anderson, David McCord, Dorothy Clarke Wilson, Dennis LeDoux, Will Anderson, Christopher Keane and many others. We usually have about 10 guest presenters a year."
Costs: $59 (1992) includes the conference banquet. There is a reduced fee, $30, for students ages 21 and under. The fee does not include housing or meals which must be arranged separately by the conferees.
Accommodations: An accommodations list is available. "We are in a summer resort area and motels, guest houses and restaurants abound."
Additional Information: "We have a contest announcement which comes out in January-March and has about 17 contests on various genres. The prizes, all modest, are awarded at the end of the conference and only to those who are registered." Program guide comes out in April-June.

STEAMBOAT SPRINGS WRITERS GROUP, P.O. Box 774284, Steamboat Springs CO 80477. (303)879-9008. Chairperson: Harriet Freiberger. Estab. 1982. Annual. Conference held in Summer. Conference duration: 1 day. Average attendance: 40. "Our conference emphasizes instruction within the seminar format. Novices and polished professionals benefit from the individual attention and the camaraderie which can be established within small groups. A pleasurable and memorable learning experience is guaranteed by the relaxed and friendly atmosphere of the old train depot." Steamboat Arts Council sponsors the group at the restored Train Depot.
Costs: In 1991, tuition was $40 for members; $50 for nonmembers. Fee covers all conference activities, including lunch. Lodging available at Steamboat Resorts; 10% discount for participants."
Additional Information: "We are in the process of changing our format and will be featuring one instructor for a limited number of participants."

SUMMER IN FRANCE WRITING WORKSHOPS, HCOI, Box 102, Plainview TX 79072. (806)889-3533. Director: Bettye Givens. Annual. Conference: 27 days. Average attendance: 10-15. For fiction, poetry. The classrooms are in the Val de Grace 277 Rue St. Jacques in the heart of the Latin Quarter near Luxeumbourg Park in Paris. Guest speakers include Paris poets, professors and editors (sometimes lecture in English).
Costs: Costs not disclosed. Cost includes literature classes, art history and the writing workshop.
Accommodations: Apartments are available (begin at $300 with a roommate—each) or accommodations with a French family.
Additional Information: Conference brochures/guidelines are available for SASE. "Enroll early. Side trips out of Paris are planned as are poetry readings at the Paris American Academy and at Shakespeare & Co."

TEXAS WRITERS ASSOCIATION FALL, SPRING AND SUMMER WORKSHOPS, 219 Preston Royal, Shopping Center #3, Dallas TX 75230-3832. (214)363-9979. Executive Director: Jheri Fleet. Estab. 1989. Held 3 times/year. Conference held March/April, June and September/October. Conference

duration: ½ day—all day—2days (varies). Average attendance: From 15-200 depending on limitation. To promote all types of writing. "All workshop and conference speakers are successful published writers, agents, editors or producers who are lively, informative and congenial with attendees. The locations are selected with handicapped considered. No theme plan. Generally, about ½ our workshops are fiction related." Ongoing classes in both fiction and nonfiction.
Costs: "Cost is for members/nonmembers. Most half-day workshops are $60 or less for nonmembers. All day workshops generally are $80 or less for nonmembers."
Accommodations: Accommodations made available usually with discounts. Special hotel and airfare rates, on-site facility, in some cases rooms range from $45 a night to $90.
Additional Information: Critiques available. "Some critique sessions require prior submission, some do not. Must be no more than 20 pages—no poetry. TWA is one of the fastest growing statewide writers association with workshops and conferences in seven to ten Texas cities. TWA is the present home of the National Magazine Editors Conference which brings 20-40 major national magazines to Texas to meet with writers from all over the county." The official publication of TWA is *Writer's News*, a 24 page magazine. TWA is publication oriented.

THUNDER BAY LITERARY CONFERENCE, 211 N. First, Alpena MI 49707. (517)356-6188. Assistant Director: Judi Stillion. Estab. 1990. Annual. Two-day conference held in September or October. Average attendance: 100-150. "Our current area of concentration is Michigan writers. One objective is to heighten awareness and understanding of the heritage and current status of literature in the state." The conference is held at the Holiday Inn.
Costs: $25 (nonrefundable) $6.50 luncheon, $10 breakfast (1992).
Accommodations: Information on overnight accommodations is made available. Special rates are available at the Fletcher Motel for those who specify the conference.
Additional Information: Sponsors contest for adult short fiction and poetry. Michigan residents only. A panel of University of Michigan faculty will judge entries. Write for more information. Conference brochures/guidelines available for SASE.

‡MARK TWAIN WRITERS CONFERENCE, Suite A, 921 Center, Hannibal MO 63401. (314)221-1612. Contact: Jim Hefley. Estab. 1985. Annual. Conference held in June. Conference duration: 4 days. Average attendance: 50-70. "Concentration in fiction and nonfiction with specialization in children's writing, Mark Twain, photography, etc." Site is the "Hannibal-LaGrange College campus; women's residential hall for lodging. Excellent classroom and dining facilities near Mark Twain museum and other historical sites."
Costs: $349, includes meal, lodging, all program fees, trips to Mark Twain sites and pickup at area airport.
Accommodations: Free pickup at Quincy, IL airport and Amtrak station. Accommodations made available at women's residence hall.
Additional Information: Fiction or nonfiction critiques limited to two articles or short stories, or one book chapter with book outline. Brochures are available for SASE.

TŶ NEWYDD WRITER'S CENTRE, Llanystumdwy, Cricieth Gwynedd LL52 OLW, 0766-522811 United Kingdom. Administrator: Sally Baker. Estab. 1990. Regular courses held throughout the year. Every course held Monday-Saturday. Average attendance: 14. "To give people the opportunity to work side by side with professional writers. Site is Tŷ Newydd. Large manor house. Last home of the prime minister, David Lloyd George. Situated in North Wales, Great Britain—between mountains and sea." Featured tutors in 1992 were novelists Alice Thomas Ellis and Shelley Weiner.
Costs: £ 196 for Monday-Saturday (includes full board, tuition).
Accommodations: Transportation from railway stations arranged. Accommodation in Tŷ Newydd (onsite).
Additional Information: "Some courses require work to be submitted. Some do not. We have had several people from US on courses here in the past three years."

‡UCLA EXTENSION WRITERS' PROGRAM, 10995 Le Conte Ave., Los Angeles CA 90024. (310)825-9415 or (800)388-UCLA. Program Manager: Meryl Ginsberg. Estab. 1891. Courses held ongoingly, 4 quarters/year. New course line-up 4 times/year, with special intensive courses in summer. Program duration varies 12-week, 10-week, 6-week, 4-day and 2-day courses. Average attendance: 12-25 per class. "We cover fiction, nonfiction, poetry, playwriting, writing for young people, and we have the largest, most comprehensive screenwriting curriculum in the country, with special 4-day intensive courses every summer for people coming from out of town. Classes are held primarily on the UCLA campus in regular classrooms and conference rooms. We also hold classes in outlying areas around the city: Santa Monica, the San Fernando Valley, Pasadena." Guest speakers "are too numerous to mention: ongoing series such as Playwrights on Playwriting have featured Larry Gelbart, Terrence McNalley; Screenwriters on Screenwriting has featured Tom Schulman, Joe Eszterhas, Ray Bradbury; new speakers lined up every quarter."

Costs: Vary from $65-395. Intensive 4-day couses in summer cost $285.

Accommodations: Students make own arrangements. We can provide assistance in locating local accommodations.

Additional Information: "Some advanced-level classes have manuscript submittal requirements; instructions are always detailed in our quarterly publication, *The Writers' Program Quarterly*. The Writers' Program publishes a bi-annual literary journal. Work can be submitted by current and former Writers' Program students. An annual fiction prize, The James Kirkwood Prize in Creative Writing, has been established and is given annually to one fiction writer who was published that year in *WEST/WORD*, our literary journal. The prize is $500 and is judged by a New York literary agent and the contest's sponsors." Brochures are available.

‡**UNIVERSITY OF KENTUCKY WOMEN WRITERS CONFERENCE**, 106 Frazee Hall, UK, Lexington KY 40506-0031. (606)257-3295. Director: Betty Gabehart. Estab. 1979. Annual. Conference held in October. Conference duration: 4 days. Average attendance: 400 registrants. "Women writers, poets, novelists, short story writers, writers of children's literature, playwrights are selected each year to visit the UK campus and provide readings, panel discussions and workshops. Free for students showing ID; sliding scale fees for daily registration for non-students. The University of Kentucky is located in Lexington, Kentucky. All meeting rooms and facilities—mostly in the UK Student Center—are handicapped accessible. Near Keeneland racetrack and Shakertown at Pleasant Hill." Theme for 1992 was "family," especially the mother/daughter bond. Guest speakers and panelists in 1992 were Chrystos, Marianne Hirsch, J. California Cooper, Cynthia Kadohata, George Ella Lyon, Grace Paley, Jayne Anne Phillips.

Costs: In 1992, registration: $10/$15/$25 per day (self-selected), meals/lodging *not* provided.

Accommodations: List of accommodations available on request.

Additional Information: For workshops pre-submit mss with/$10 fee two months in advance; poetry, essay, children's literature, short fiction, plays. Write for details first. Conference brochures/guidelines are available for SASE.

UNIVERSITY OF MASSACHUSETTS AT LOWELL WRITERS' CONFERENCE, One University Ave., Lowell MA 01854. (508)934-2405. Program Coordinator: John Hurtado. Assistant Director: Dirk Messelaar. Estab. 1988. Annual. Conference held March 5-7. Average attendance: 85. Conference covers fiction, short stories, getting published, essays. Conference held at the University of Massachusetts at Lowell (formerly University of Lowell). The conference features readings and lectures in the O'Leary Library lecture room and seminars in the adjacent break-out rooms located in the library. Speakers, include Eleanor Lipman (fiction), Melanie Raethon (short story), Askold Melnycuk (poetry), D.K. Oklahoma (playwriting).

Costs: In 1993, $125/$75 full-time students $85/day plus $40 fee for individual conferences included light lunch and breaks.

Accommodations: Lists of hotels and special rates are available.

Additional Information: For a small additional fee, individual conferences with published authors are available on a limited basis. Ms must be submitted 3 weeks prior to the conference. Brochures/guidelines are available—no SASE required.

UNIVERSITY OF MASSACHUSETTS LOWELL WRITING PROGRAM, One University Ave., Lowell MA 01854. (508)934-2405. Program Coordinator: John Hurtado. Estab. 1989. Annual. Conference held July to mid-August. Conference duration: 6 weeks. Average attendance: 250 in 15 courses. Conference includes "credit courses in expository writing, fiction, poetry, playwriting, journalism, arts reporting, desktop publishing, writing children's literature and screenwriting in addition to free readings by nationally-known, award-winning, local writers. Courses are held at the University's Mogan Cultural Center, a renovated Millgirl Boardinghouse within the Lowell National Park and in various classrooms on both the North and South campuses."

Costs: In 1992, $285 per 3 credit undergraduate course, plus a one-time $25 registration fee.

Accommodations: Dormitory accommodations available on campus include board option.

Additional Information: Brochures available. "Audit option available at full tuition (pass/fail not available due to nature of courses and requirements)."

UNIVERSITY OF WISCONSIN AT MADISON SCHOOL OF THE ARTS AT RHINELANDER, 727 Lowell Hall, 610 Langdon St., Madison WI 53703. Administrative Coordinator: Kathy Berigan. Estab. 1964. Annual. Conference held from July 19-23. Average attendance: 280. Courses offered in writing, visual arts, drama, photography, music, folkarts, folk dancing. "1993 is our 30th anniversary." Conference held in junior high school in the city of Rhinelander in northern Wisconsin (James Williams Junior High School).
Costs: Tuition only—approximately $160. Some courses require materials or lab fee.
Accommodations: Information on overnight accommodations made available.
Additional Information: Ms critique workshop available. Request to be put on mailing list. "Courses offered in other 'arts' areas during week."

UNIVERSITY OF WISCONSIN AT MADISON WRITERS INSTITUTE, 610 Langdon St., Madison WI 53703. (608)262-3447. Director: Christine DeSmet. Estab. 1990. Annual. Conference held July 22 to July 23. Average attendance: 175. "Day 2 is fiction—genre writing; Day 1 is nonfiction—journalism freelance writing." Conference held at Wisconsin Center, University of Wisconsin at Madison. Themes: Mystery, suspense, sci fi, romance, mainstream for 1993 fiction. Guest speakers are published authors, editors and agents.
Costs: $75/day or $125 for 2 days; $15 critique fee.
Accommodations: Info on accommodations sent with registration confirmation. Critiques available Conference brochures/guidelines are available for SASE.

THE VANCOUVER INTERNATIONAL WRITERS FESTIVAL, 1243 Cartwright St., Vancouver, British Columbia V6H 4B7 Canada. (604)681-6330. Estab. 1988. Annual. Held during the 3rd week of October. Average attendance: 6,600. "This is a festival for readers and writers. The program of events is diverse and includes readings, panel discussions, workshops. Lots of opportunities to interact with the writers who attend." Held on Granville Island—in the heart of Vancouver. Three professional theaters are used as well as space in the Community Centre. "We try to avoid specific themes. Programming takes place between February and June each year and is by invitation."
Costs: Tickets are $8 and $12 (Canadian); some special events are a little more.
Accommodations: Local tourist info can be provided when necessary and requested.
Additional Information: Brochures/guidelines are available for SASE. "A reminder—this is a festival, a celebration, not a conference or workshop."

‡VASSAR COLLEGE INSTITUTE OF PUBLISHING AND WRITING: CHILDREN'S BOOKS IN THE MARKETPLACE, Vassar College, Box 300, Poughkeepsie NY 12601. (914)437-5903. Associate Director of College Relations: Maryann Bruno. Estab. 1983. Annual. Conference held in July. Conference duration: 1 week. Average attendance: 40. Writing and publishing children's literature. "The conference is held at Vassar College, a 1,000-acre campus located in the mid-Hudson valley. The campus is self-contained, with residence halls, dining facilities, and classroom and meeting facilities. Vassar is located 90 miles north of New York City, and is accessible by car, train and air. Participants have use of Vassar's athletic facilities, including swimming, squash, tennis and jogging. Vassar is known for the beauty of its campus." The panel theme for 1992 was "The Matchmaker: Choosing the Art for the Text." In 1992 guest speakers included the Dillons, Leonard Marucs, Nancy Willard, Rafe Martin, Margery Facklam, Jean Marzollo, Ed Young and others.
Costs: $700, includes full tuition, room and three meals a day.
Accommodations: There are special conference attendee accommodations on campus in a residence hall.
Additional Information: Writers may submit a 10-page sample of their writing for critique, which occurs during the week of the conference. Conference brochures/guidelines are available for SASE.

WELLS WRITERS' WORKSHOPS, 69 Broadway, Concord NH 03301. (603)225-9162. Director: Vic Levine. Estab. 1988. Held: 2 times/year in Wells, Maine. Conferences held from May 16 to May 21, 1993; September 12 to September 17, 1993. Maximum attendance: 6. "Workshop concentrates on short and long fiction, especially the novel. Focus is on the rational structuring of a story, using Aristotelian and scriptwriting insights. Throughout, the workshop balances direct instruction with the actual plotting and writing of the basic scenes of a novel or short story." Conference located in a "large, airy and light house overlooking the ocean with ample individual space for writers and group conferences. While the purposes of the workshop is to teach the process of plotting as it applies across the board—to all kinds of fiction, including novels, short stories, movies—it strives to meet the specific needs of participants, especially through individual conferences with the instructor."

Costs: "The cost of $550 covers tuition, room and basic board. Registration cost is $50 (nonrefundable). Payment may be in two or three installments."
Accommodations: Workshop supplies transportation from/to Portland International Airport—or other places, by arrangement. Workshop supplies accommodations.
Additional Information: Conference brochures/guidelines available for SASE. "Workshop has a scholarship fund which can, as it has in the past, defray part of the total expense of $550."

WESLEYAN WRITERS CONFERENCE, Wesleyan University, Middletown CT 06457. (203)347-9411, ext. 2448. Director: Anne Greene. Estab. 1956. Annual. 1993 Conference held from June 27 to July 2. Average attendance: 100. For novel, short story, poetry, nonfiction, literary journalism. The Conference is held on the campus of Wesleyan University, in the hills overlooking the Connecticut River. Meals and lodging are provided on campus. Readings of new fiction. Guest lectures on a range of topics including the art of memoir.
Costs: In 1992, tuition $415; meals $165; room $85.
Accommodations: "Participants can fly to Hartford or take Amtrak to Meriden, CT. We are happy to help participants make travel arrangements." Overnight participants stay on campus.
Additional Information: Ms critiques are available as part of the program but are not required. "We sponsor several scholarship competitions and award teaching fellowships. Application info is in conference brochure." Brochures/guidelines are available for SASE.

‡WILDACRES WRITERS WORKSHOP, 233 S. Elm St., Greensboro NC 27401. (919)273-4044. Director: Judith Hill. Estab. 1982. Annual. Conference held from July 10 to July 16. Average attendance: 100. For "short story, novel, sudden fiction, children's fiction, poetry, screenwriting, humor. Perched on a mountain-top, Wildacres' beautiful lodge-type buildings blend the comfort of modern life with the beauty of the Blue Ridge Mountains. The spacious two-bed rooms are carpeted, have maple furniture and private baths. Three family-style meals are served daily and there is a canteen where you can buy snacks, soft drinks, postcards and T-shirts. We usually have two agents in addition to our staff."
Costs: $340, includes room (double), meals and manuscript critique.
Accommodations: "If conferees fly into Asheville, NC, we will arrange for a van from the airport. Ours is a residential workshop. Everyone stays on the mountain for the full week." Accommodation cost included in the fee.
Additional Information: Includes one critique but all attendees must send in a sample of their writing prior to attending. Conference brochures/guidelines are available for SASE. "Wildacres is more than an excellent workshop. It is an experience our attendees never forget. 60% of our people have attended before. We make certain you have a good time! There are no cliques, no hierarchy—just writers having fun together."

‡WOODSTOCK PUBLISHING CONFERENCE AT BYRDCLIFFE, 34 Tinker St., Woodstock NY 12498. (914)679-2079. Program Director: Michael Perkins. Estab. 1986. Annual. Conference held in June. Conference duration: 1-2 days. Average attendance: 100. Concentration on fiction and publishing. "The Byrdcliffe Theater was built in 1902 and seats 100 people comfortably. The Villetta Inn, next door, is available for food and lodging." Planned theme is "The First Novel."
Costs: $75-100, includes lunch and reception.
Accommodations: Meets buses. A list of accommodations is made available.
Additional Information: Brochures or guidelines are available for SASE.

‡WRITE FOR SUCCESS WORKSHOP: CHILDREN'S BOOKS, 3748 Harbor Heights Dr., Largo FL 34644. (813)581-2484. Speaker/Coordinator: Theo Carroll. Estab. 1988. Held irregularly. Conference duration: 1 day. Average attendance: 80. Concentration is writing for children. "Site is the Belleview Mido Resort Hotel. Large conference room is promoted as the largest occupied wooden structure

in the world; a Victorian landmark built in 1896 in Clearwater, Florida." Workshop on writing for children.
Costs: $85 includes breakfast, lunch and materials. Limo available from Tampa airport. Information on overnight accommodations made available and special conference attendee accommodations are made.
Additional Information: Brochures for May seminar are available for SASE.

‡WRITE TO SELL WRITER'S CONFERENCE, 8465 Jane St., San Diego CA 92129. (619)484-8575. Director: Diane Dunaway. Estab. 1989. Annual. Conference held in May. Conference duration: 2 days. Average attendance: 300. Concentration includes general fiction and nonfiction; screenwriting to include mystery, romance, children's, television, movies; special novel writing workshop, contacts with top NY agents and editors. Site is the Irvine Marriott. Panelists include NY editors and agents, bestselling authors and screenwriters.
Costs: $195, includes lunch both days.
Accommodations: Special conference rate $68 per night in Irvine Marriott.

WRITE YOUR LIFE STORY FOR PAY, 23350 Sereno Ct., Villa 30, Cupertino CA 95014. (415)691-0300. Contact: Louise Purwin Zobel. Estab. 1969. Workshop held irregularly, usually semiannually at several locations. Workshop duration: 1-2 days. Average attendance: 30-50. "Because every adult has a story worth telling, this conference helps participants to write fiction and nonfiction in books and short forms, using their own life stories as a base." This workshop is held on about 40 campuses at different times, inluding University of California and other university and college campuses in the west.
Costs: Usually $45-65/day, "depending on campus."
Additional Information: Brochures/guidelines available for SASE.

‡THE WRITERS' CENTER AT CHAUTAUQUA, P.O. Box 408, Chautauqua NY 14722. (716)357-2445 or (717)872-8337. Director: Mary Jean Irion. Estab. 1987. Annual. Workshops held June 28 to August 27 "are offered in combination with a vacation at historic Chautauqua Institution, a large cultural resort in western New York for families and singles. Workshops are 2 hours, Monday-Friday; average attendance is 12." Guest speakers and panelists: Susan Rowan Masters will teach young writers section (July 26-30); Joan Millman (June 28-July 2) and Stanley W. Lindberg (July 26-30) will teach short story sessions; Zena Collier will teach novel session (August 2-6).
Costs: In 1992 $50/week. Meals, housing, gate ticket (about $135 per week), parking ($20) are in addition.
Accommodations: Information is available; but no special rates have been offered.
Additional Information: Each leader specifies the kind of workshop offered. Most accept submissions in advance; information is made available in March of each year, on request. Conference brochures/guidelines are available for SASE.

‡WRITERS CONNECTION SELLING TO HOLLYWOOD, Suite 180, 1601 Saratoga-Sunnyvale Rd., Cupertino CA 95014. (408)973-0227. Directors: Steve and Meera Lester. Estab. 1988. Annual. Conference held second week in August in L.A. area. Conference duration: 3 days. Average attendance: 200. "Conference targets scriptwriters and fiction writers, whose short stories, books, or plays have strong cinematic potential, and who want to make valuable contracts in the film industry. Full conference registrants receive a private consultation with the film industry producer or professional of his/her choice who make up the faculty. Panels, workshops, and 'Ask a Pro' discussion groups include agents, professional film and TV scriptwriters, and independent as well as studio and TV and feature film producers. In 1992: Private screening of *A Midnight Clear* and talk by the film's producer Marc Abraham. Film industry pros from 'Star Trek: The Next Generation,' 'Beverly Hills 90210,' Spielberg's Amblin Entertainment, Walt Disney Studios, NBC, Fox, Hanna Barbera, TNT, Children's Television Workshop, Dino De Laurentis, plus literary agents, reps from WGA and SAG, authors Syd Field, Richard Walter, Carl Sautter, and 'Hollywood's Script Doctor' Linda Seger."
Costs: In 1992: full conference: by July, $470 members, $495 nonmembers; after July 10 $495; $520 (included meals). Partial registration available.
Accommodations: Discount with designated conference airline. "We make hotel reservations—get a special rate. $100/night (in L.A.) private room; $50/shared room."
Additional Information: "This is the premiere screenwriting conference of its kind in the country, unique in its offering of an industry-wide perspective from pros working in all echelons of the film industry. Great for making contacts." Conference brochure/guidelines available for SASE.

‡**THE WRITER'S EDGE WORKSHOP,** University of Missouri, Journalism School, Box 838, Columbia MO 65205. (314)882-2880. Workshop Director: Dr. Lee Jolliffe. Estab. 1991. Held 3-4 times/year. Conference held June and July. Conference duration: 1 day. Average attendance: 35. "Concentrates on improving prose style and structure of fiction or 'literary' nonfiction. Selling what you've written." Held in "The Forum, a specially designed room at the Missouri Journalism School used for our many mid-career programs." Theme for 1993 is "improving your prose style." Guest speakers include Dr. Lee Jolliffe, Professor Byron Scott (Meredith Chair of Magazine Journalism).
Costs: $98 includes fee, breakfast, lunch, snacks and a conference notebook.
Accommodations: List of accommodations comes with conference packet.
Additional Information: Conference brochures/guidelines are available. "World-renowned Journalism School, top-flight faculty who are widely published and have close ties to editors."

‡**WRITERS ON WRITING AT BARNARD,** 3009 Broadway, New York NY 10027-6598. (212)854-7489. Director: Ann Birstein. Estab. 1988. Annual. Conference held in June. Conference duration: 1 month. Average attendance: 10-12. Includes 2 fiction workshops, 2 poetry workshops, 1 writing for children, 1 workshop for biography/memoir, 1 nonfiction. Held at "Barnard College, beautifully appointed lounge, comfortable classrooms, lovely rooms for readings and receptions." In 1992 guest speakers included Gwendolyn Brooks in honor of her 75th birthday; Virginia Barber, agent, Jill Bialosky, W.W. Norton editor, Michael Anderson, *New York Times Book Review* editor and others.
Costs: $950 non-credit, $1,050 credit (workshop fee only). Reduced fee for 2 workshops.
Accommodations: Campus housing is available. Information about hotels and parking garages will be sent to inquirers. Dorm rooms are approx. $100/week.
Additional Information: Conference brochures/guidelines are available for SASE.

‡**WRITER'S SEMINAR/ANOKA-RAMSEY COMMUNITY COLLEGE,** 11200 Mississippi Blvd. NW, Coon Rapids MN 55345. (612)422-3301. Director, Center for Business & Industry: Rosie Mortenson. Estab. 1987. Annual. Conference held in fall of 1993. Conference duration: 1 day. Average attendance: 30. "Goal is how to get published! Conference held in a seminar room in the College Development Center which is separate from the rest of the college."
Costs: In 1992 cost was $59.

‡**WRITERS TOUR OF GREECE,** Dept. of Philosophy, Western Washington University, Bellingham WA 98225. (206)676-3391. Contact: Professor Richard L. Purtill. Estab. 1984. Annual. Conference held late summer, early fall. Conference duration: 2 weeks. Average attendance: 10. Concentration is on fiction. Located in hotels in Greece: Athens Delphi, one island. "Theme is Greek mythology, archeology and history use in fiction and nonfiction."
Costs: $750, includes food only for a few meals, all lodging and travel inside Greece.
Accommodations: "We will help arrange airfare." Hotels are arranged and are part of the fee.
Additional Information: Prefer work to be submitted in advance. Writing assignments given on-site. Brochures are available for SASE.

‡**THE WRITERS' WORKSHOP,** P.O. Box 696, Asheville NC 28802. (800)627-0142. Executive Director: Karen Tager. Estab. 1984. Held 4 times/year. Conference duration: varies from 1 day to 20 weeks. Average attendance: 10. "All areas, for adults and children. We do not offer workshops dealing with romance or religion, however." Sites are throughout the South, especially North Carolina. Guest speaker was John Le Carré in 1992. Writer's retreat in the Florida Keys March 11-14 with Peter Matthiessen.
Costs: Vary. Financial assistance available to low-income writers. Information on overnight accommodations is made available.

WRITERS WORKSHOP IN SCIENCE FICTION, English Department/University of Kansas, Lawrence KS 66045. (913)864-3380. Professor: James Gunn. Estab. 1985. Annual. Conference held for two weeks in mid to late July. Average attendance: 8-10. Conference for writing and marketing science fiction. "Housing is provided and classes meet in Jayhawker Towers, an apartment complex on the University of Kansas campus. Workshop sessions operate informally in an apartment living room." Guest speaker: Frederik Pohl, SF writer and former editor and agent. We also expect to have an editor from Tor Books as critiquer.

Costs: Tuition: $400. Housing and meals are additional.

Accommodations: Several airport shuttle services offer reasonable transportation from the Kansas City International Airport to Lawrence. Apartments with cooking facilities are available in Jayhawker Towers; in 1992 the cost for two weeks was $160 per person.

Additional Information: "Admission to the workshop is by submission of an acceptable story. Two additional stories should be submitted by the end of June. These three stories are copied and distributed to other participants for critiquing and are the basis for the first week of the workshop; one story is rewritten for the second week." Brochures/guidelines are available for SASE. "The Writers Workshop in Science Fiction is intended for writers who have just started to sell their work or need that extra bit of understanding or skill to become a published writer."

WRITING BY THE SEA, 1511 New York Ave., Cape May NJ 08204. (609)884-7117, ext. 15. CMI Managing Director: Natalie Newton. Estab. 1990. Annual. Conference held November 1 to November 5. Conference duration: 4 days. Average attendance: 70. Conference offers "about 10 seminars on fiction and nonfiction writing in a retreat atmosphere at the Virginia Hotel." Conference held at "the Cape May Institute, an adult continuing education, nonprofit organization located in Victorian Cape May. Our modern facilities include a comfortable lecture hall and world class b&w photographic darkrooms. The Institute is noted for its support of the arts and hosts annual music and theater performances." Panels include "finding an agent" and "self-publishing." Guest speakers have included James Allen (agent), Esta Cassway (author), Page Edwards (author), Norma Leone (publisher), Margaret Mangum (author), David Poyer (author), Richard Rashke (author).

Costs: $295 for 5 days or $125/day—conference fee only.

Accommodations: For 1992, we have the entire Virginia Hotel, a luxuriously refurbished Victorian Inn from November 1-5. Cost is $65 (single) or $75 (double occupancy) per night.

Additional Information: Conference brochures/guidelines are available for SASE.

‡WRITING FOR PUBLICATION, Pittsburgh Theological Seminary, 616 N. Highland Ave., Pittsburgh PA 15206. Director of Continuing Education: The Rev. Mary Lee Talbot. Estab. 1983. Annual. Conference held May 5 to May 6. Average attendance: 120. To teach techniques for getting published. "Pittsburgh Theological Seminary is located in the East End of Pittsburgh. The 13-acre campus is in the middle of an urban center." Dr. Roland Tapp is the leader.

Costs: $75 registration plus room ($19 single, $13.50 double per person per night) and meals (breakfast and lunch served on campus).

Accommodations: On-campus housing is available.

Additional Information: Critiques are available. Manuscripts sent to Dr. Tapp one month before conference. Dr. Tapp also does individual sessions during the conference. Conference brochures/guidelines are available for SASE.

WRITING FOR PUBLICATION, Villanova University, Villanova PA 19085. (215)645-4620. Director: Wm. Ray Heitzmann, Ph.D. Estab. 1975. Semiannual. Conference dates vary, held fall, spring. Average attendance: 15-20 (seminar style). Conference covers marketing one's manuscript (fiction, nonfiction, book, article, etc.); strong emphasis on effective component of writing. Conference held in a seminar room at a university (easy access, parking, etc.). Panels include "Advanced Writing for Publication," "Part-time Writing," "Working With Editors." Panelists include Ray Heitzman, and others.

Costs: $295 (graduate credit); $195 (undergraduate credit); $100 (non-credit) plus $10 registration fee.

Accommodations: List of motels/hotels available, but most people live in area and commute. Special arrangements made on an individual basis.

Additional Information: Critiques available. Voluntary submission of manuscripts. Brochures/guidelines are available. "Workshop graduates have been very successful."

‡WRITING WORKSHOP, P.O. Box 65, Ellison Bay WI 54210. (414)854-4088. Resident Manager: Don Buchholz. Estab. 1935. Annual. Conference held from June 13 to June 19. Average attendance: 16. "General writing journal, poetry as well as fiction and nonfiction." Held in a "residential setting in deep woods on the shore of Green Bay. Housing, two to a room, private bath in rustic log and stone buildings. Great hall type of classroom for the conference, quiet and also in deep woods." Past guest speakers were Lowell B. Komie (short story), T.V. Olsen (novelist), Barbara Vroman (novelist).

Costs: In 1992 $465, includes board and room.

Additional Information: Catalog available upon request, size 8½ × 11 will not accommodate SASE.

YELLOW BAY WRITERS' WORKSHOP, Center for Continuing Education, University of Montana, Missoula MT 59812. (406)243-6486. Program Manager: Judy Jones. Estab. 1988. Annual. Conference held from mid to late August. Average attendance: 50-60. Includes four faculty: 2 fiction; 1 poetry; 1 creative nonfiction/personal essay. Conference "held at the University of Montana's Flathead Lake Biological Station, a research station with informal educational facilities and rustic cabin living. Located in northwestern Montana on Flathead Lake, the largest natural freshwater lake west of the Mississippi River. All faculty are requested to present a craft lecture—usually also have an editor leading a panel discussion." Past faculty: Carolyn Kizer, Thomas McGuane, Marilynne Robinson, Geoffrey Wolff, Mona Simpson, Blanche Boyd, James Tate, James Welch, Joy Williams, James Crumley, Carolyn Forche, William Kittredge, Linda Gregg, Robert Boswell, Antonya Nelson, Al Young. **Costs:** In 1992 $400 for tuition.
Accommodations: Shuttle is available from Missoula to Yellow Bay for those flying to Montana. Cost of shuttle is $40 (1992). On-site rates are $225 for room and board for the week (in 1992); commuter meal plans are available.
Additional Information: "We require a five-page writing sample to accompany the workshop application." Brochures/guidelines are available for SASE.

Other conferences and workshops

We had so many new listings for conferences and workshops this year that we ran out of room. Those who responded to our questionnaire too late to receive a full listing in this edition are listed below. We've included contact names, addresses and deadlines, however, so you may write for details. Remember to include self-addressed, stamped envelopes (or SAE with International Reply Coupons) with all requests for information.

‡**CLARION WEST WRITERS' WORKSHOP**, 340 15th Ave. E., Seattle WA 98112. (206)322-9083. Contact: Admissions Department. Conference held: June 20-July 30.

‡**COLUMBIA GORGE WRITER'S CONFERENCE**, 2470 Lichens Dr., Hood River OR 97031. (503)386-3112. Contact: Lana Fox. Conference held in April.

‡**FICTION FROM THE HEARTLAND CONFERENCE**, P.O. Box 32186, Kansas City MO 64111. Conference Coordinator: Carla Bracale. Conference held February 12-14.

‡**FICTION WRITING/ACAPULCO**, 3584 Kirkwood Pl., Boulder CO 80304. (303)444-0086. Conference Director: Barbara Steiner. Conference held November.

‡**GOLDEN LAKE WRITERS' WORKSHOPS**, 12708 2nd NW, Seattle WA 98177. (206)368-8054. Contact: Barbara Turner-Vesselago. Conference held June and August.

‡**LIGONIER VALLEY WRITERS CONFERENCE**, RR 4 Box 8, Ligonier PA 15658. (412)238-6397. Director: Tina Thoburn. Conference held July 9-11.

‡**JACK LONDON WRITERS' CONFERENCE**, 1500 Ralston Ave., Belmont CA 94403. (415)508-3708. Head, Dept. of English, College of Notre Dame: Dr. Marc Wolter Beek. Conference held March 13.

‡**RAIN FOREST WRITERS CONFERENCE**, P.O. Box 22889, Juneau AK 99802. (907)789-5179. Conference Chairman: Stoney Compton. Conference held in June.

‡**SCBWI/MICHIGAN WORKING WRITERS RETREAT**, %2011 Waite Ave., Kalamazoo MI 49008. (616)345-6906. Contact: Ellen Howard. Held late summer/early fall.

‡**SCBWI/MICHIGAN WORKSHOP**, %2011 Waite Ave., Kalamazoo MI 49008. (616)345-6906. Contact: Ellen Howard. Held May 1.

‡**SCBWI/MINNESOTA WORKSHOP**, 4042 24th Ave., Minneapolis MN 55406. (612)724-2097. Held in spring.

‡SOUTHWEST WRITERS WORKSHOP CONFERENCE, Suite C, 1336 Wyoming NE, Albuquerque NM 87112. (505)293-0303. Office Manager: Suzanne Spletzer. Conference held September 10-12.

‡SQUAW VALLEY COMMUNITY OF WRITERS, P.O. Box 2352, Olympic Valley CA 96146. (916)583-5200. Executive Director, Creative Arts Society: Maria Ferensowicz. Conference held July 17 (Art of the Wild), July 24 (Poetry), August 7 (Fiction).

‡PARIS WRITERS' WORKSHOP/WICE, 20 Bd du Montparnasse, Paris France 75015. (33-1)45-66-75-50. Director: Carol Allen. Conference held June 28-July 2.

‡TRENTON STATE COLLEGE WRITERS' CONFERENCE, English Department, Trenton State College, Hillwood Lakes CN 4700, Trenton NJ 08650-4700. (609)771-3254. Director: Jean Hollander. Conference held in April.

‡WASHINGTON INDEPENDENT WRITERS (WIW) SPRING WRITERS CONFERENCE, #200, 733 15th St. NW, Washington DC 20005. Executive Director: Isolde Chapin. Conference held in May.

‡THE WRITE MAGIC, 1140 Waverly St., Eugene OR 97401. (503)485-0583 (eves). Publicity Chair: Ann Simas. Conference held May 22, 23.

‡THE WRITERS' SUMMER SCHOOL, Swanwick, The Red House, Mardens Hill, Crowborough, East Sussex TN6 1XN England. Contact: Philippa Boland. Conference held August 14-20.

‡WRITING WITH YOUR WHOLE SELF, P.O. Box 1310, Boston MA 02117. (617)266-1613. Director: Marcia Yudkin. Conference held one Saturday in April, June, September, November, February.

Conferences and workshops/changes '92-'93

The following conferences and workshops appeared in the 1992 edition of *Novel & Short Story Writer's Market* but do not appear in the 1993 edition. Those conferences and workshops that did not respond to our request for an update appear below without further explanation. If a reason for the omission is available, it is included next to the listing name. There are several reasons why a conference or workshop may not appear—it may not be an annual event, for example, or it may no longer be held.

Auburn Writers Conference
Flight of the Mind - Summer Writing Workshop for Women
Florida International University South Beach Writers Workshop
Florida Romance Writers
Florida Suncoast Writers' Conference
International Black Writers
The International Film Workshops
Kingston School of Writing Summer Workshop
Mississippi Writers' Club Conference
NAPA Valley Writers' Conference
North Carolina Writers' Network Fall Conference
The Ozarks Writers Conference
Palm Springs Writers Guild Annual Conference
Pennwriters Conference
Philadelphia Writers' Conference
Publishing and Writing: Children's Books in the Marketplace
Shenandoah Valley Writers Guild
Sinclair Community College's Annual Writers' Conference
Third Coast Writers Conference
Westchester Writers' Conference
Writers in Residence Programs
Writing Workshop for People Over 57

Retreats and Colonies

Retreats and colonies deserve a section all their own because they function quite differently from conferences and workshops. Whereas the latter events are bustling with people meeting people and attending scheduled activities, folks at the former places don't "bustle" at all. Retreats and colonies are places for writers to find solitude and concentrated time to focus solely on their writing. Communal meals may be the only scheduled activities. Also, a writer's stay at a retreat or colony is typically anywhere from one to 12 weeks (sometimes longer), while time spent at a conference or workshop is generally anywhere from one day to two weeks (perhaps a month at most).

Like conferences and workshops, however, retreats and colonies span a wide range. Some, such as the Djerassi Program, are open only to individuals "with a record of solid achievement but who are not very well-known" and those with established reputations while others, such as the The Clearing are open to "any adult 18 to 81 (and we'll relax the 81 requirement)." And you'll find retreats and colonies everywhere from Hattiesburg, Mississippi, to rural Hawaii to a national park in Burgundy, France.

Despite different focuses and/or locations, all retreats and colonies have one thing in common: They are places where writers may work undisturbed, usually in very nature-oriented and secluded settings. A retreat or colony serves as a place for rejuvenation; a writer can find new ideas, rework old ones or put the finishing touches to works-in-progress.

Determine your work habits

Arrangements at retreats and colonies differ dramatically so it may help to determine your own work habits before you begin your search. While some retreats house writers in one main building, others provide separate cottages. In both cases, residents are generally given private work space, although they usually must bring along their own typewriters or personal computers. Meals are another factor. Some colonies offer communal, family-style meals at set times; some prepare meals for each resident individually and still others require residents to prepare meals themselves. If you tend to work straight through meals now, you might want to consider a retreat or colony that offers the last option.

A related consideration for most folks is cost. Again, the types of arrangements vary. A good number of residencies are available at no cost or only a minimal daily cost, sometimes including the cost of meals, sometimes not. The MacDowell Colony, for example, asks artists to contribute "according to their financial resources." Other residencies, such as those through the Ucross Foundation, are "awards," resulting from competitive applications. Some retreats and colonies provide residencies as well as stipends for personal expenses. Finally, for those residencies that are fairly expensive, scholarships or fee waivers are often available.

Plan ahead

In general, residencies at retreats and colonies are competitive because only a handful of spots are available at each place. Writers must often apply at least six months in advance for the time period they desire. While some locations are open year-round, others are available only during certain seasons. Planning to go during the "off-season" may lessen your competition. Also, most places will want to see a writing sample with your application, so be prepared to show your best work—whether you are a beginning writer or an established one. In addition, it will help to have an idea of the project you'll work on while in residence, since some places request this information with their applications as well.

Each listing in this section provides information about the type of writers accepted; the location, accommodations and meal plan available; the costs; and, finally, the application process. As with markets and conferences and workshops, changes in policies may be made after this edition has gone to press. Send a self-addressed, stamped envelope to the places that interest you to receive the most up-to-date details.

For other listings of retreats and colonies, you may want to see *The Guide to Writers Conferences* (Shaw Associates, Publishers, Suite 1406, 625 Biltmore Way, Coral Gables FL 33134), which not only provides information on conferences, workshops and seminars but also residencies, retreats and organizations. Another resource is *100 Havens for Creatives*, from ACTS Institute, Inc. (P.O. Box 10153, Kansas City MO 64111).

ACT I CREATIVITY CENTER, PO Box 10153, Kansas City MO 64111. Administrator: Char Plotsky. Estab. 1984. For all disciplines *on an invitational basis only*. Time offered each year varies, as does location at Lake of the Ozarks and in Kansas City, Missouri.
Costs: Costs vary.
To Apply: Invitation only. Send SASE to get on list for next invitation notice.

‡EDWARD F. ALBEE FOUNDATION (THE BARN), 14 Harrison St., New York NY 10013. (212)226-2020. Contact: Foundation Secretary: David Briggs. For writers (fiction, nonfiction, playwrights, etc.) and visual artists (painters, sculptors, etc.). " 'The Barn' is located in Montauk, NY." Available for 1 month residencies from June-September. Provisions for the writer include private rooms. Accommodates 4 writers at one time.
Costs: No cost, but residents are responsible for their food, travel and supplies.
To Apply: Write or call for information and applications. Brochures or guidelines are available for SASE.

ATLANTIC CENTER FOR THE ARTS, 1414 Art Center Ave., New Smyrna Beach FL 32168. (904)427-6975. Program Director: James J. Murphy. Estab. 1980. "Residencies at Atlantic Center are open to all who meet selection requirements. Master Artists, who are selected in consultation with the Advisory Council, set the structure of the residency, determine what will be accomplished and set criteria for selection of Associates. Associates, who are typically artists at mid-career, are selected by Master Artists through portfolio review (in this case, examples of writing résumés, etc.) Atlantic Center is located on 67-acres of hammockland on Turnbull Bay, a tidal estuary in New Smyrna Beach, Florida. Buildings include the Administration Building, Workshop, Fieldhouse, 3 Master Artists' Cottages and 28 units of Associate Housing. All buildings are air-conditioned and connected by raised wooden walkways. Associate units have private bath, desk and refrigerator. Writers often meet in Fieldhouse, which has copy machine, kitchen, bath, typewriters, tables and chairs." The Center usually offers 6 residencies each year, usually three weeks in length. Residencies occur throughout the year, but may not always offer opportunities to writers. Accommodates up to 28 Associates (including all disciplines).
Costs: $600 including private room/bath; $200, tuition only and Associates provide their own accommodations, and transportation. Depending on the many factors involved, costs for the 3-week residency may vary from $900 to $1,500. Scholarships are available in selected disciplines for some residencies.
To Apply: Application requirements are different for each residency. Send for information. Application deadlines are generally 4-5 months before start of a residency; notification usually occurs 3-4 weeks after application deadline. Brochure/guidelines available for SASE. Some college credit available.

The double dagger before a listing indicates that the listing is new in this edition.

BELLAGIO STUDY AND CONFERENCE CENTER, Rockefeller Foundation, 1133 Avenue of the Americas, New York NY 10036. (212)852-8431. Manager: Susan Garfield. Estab. 1960. "Scholars and artists from any country and in any discipline are invited to apply. Successful applicants will be individuals of achievement with significant publications, exhibitions or shows to their credit. Bellagio Study and Conference Center, also known as Villa Serbelloni, occupies a wooded promontory . . . Includes main house and seven other buildings. Set in the foothills of the Italian Alps." Residencies are approximately 5 weeks long. Offered February through mid-December. Each scholar and artist is provided with a private room and bath and with a study in which to work. IBM and Apple PCs and printers available on sign-up basis. Accommodates 145 residents chosen annually.
Costs: "The Center does not provide financial assistance to scholars in residence nor does it ordinarily contribute to travel expenses. Once at the center, all scholars and spouses are guests of the foundation."
To Apply: Send for application. Application includes form, half-page abstract describing purpose of project, detailed project description, brief curriculum vitae, one sample of published work, reviews. Brochure/guidelines available. Do not send SASE.

THE BLUE MOUNTAIN CENTER, Blue Mountain Lake, New York NY 12812. (518)352-7391. Director: Harriet Barlow. Residencies for established writers. "Provides a peaceful environment where residents may work free from distractions and demands of normal daily life." Residencies awarded for 1 month between June and October. For provisions, costs, other information, send SASE for brochure.
To Apply: Application deadline: February 1.

‡CAMARGO FOUNDATION, 64 Main St., P.O. Box 32, East Haddam CT 06423. Administrative Assistant: Jane M. Viggiani. Estab. 1971. For one artist, one writer, one musician; and graduate students and scholars working on projects relating to French culture. There are facilities for 12 grantees each semester. "Grantees are given a furnished apartment, rent free, on an estate on the Mediterranean about 20 miles east of Marseilles. Families may accompany grantee, but must remain the entire period of the grant." Grant period is from early September to mid-December or from mid-January to May 31. Minimum residency is three months. "A workroom is available and computer facilities, though it is suggested that writers bring their own equipment, space and scheduling may be tight."
Costs: None. There is no stipend.
To Apply: "There is no fee. Write to Administrative Assistant giving name and address to request application materials. Packet will be mailed upon request. All materials requested must be received in this ofice by March 1 of the year previous to the one for which application is being made. Applicant will be notified of selection decisions by April 15 of that year."

CHÂTEAU DE LESVAULT, Onlay 58370 France, Director: Bibbi Lee. Estab. 1984. Open to writers of fiction and nonfiction, poets, playwrights, researchers. Located in "Burgundy within the National Park 'Le Morvan,' the Château de Lesvault is a classic French manor with fully furnished rooms including a salon, dining room and library. The château is surrounded by a large private park and there is a lake on the property." Available in 4-week sessions from October through April. Provisions for the writer include a large private room for sleeping and working, three meals a day (5 days a week), complete use of the château facility. Accommodates 5.
Costs: Cost for a 4-week session is 4,500 French francs. Included is all lodging and all meals.
To Apply: Send a letter to the Selection Committee briefly describing the writing project, two references and a sample of work (max. 3 pages). Specify the 4-week session requested. No application fee required. Brochure/guidelines available for SASE.

THE CLEARING, P.O. Box 65, Ellison Bay WI 54210. (414)854-4088. Resident Manager: Louise or Don Buchholz. Estab. 1935. Open to "any adult 18 to 81 (and we'll relax the 81 requirement)." Located in "historic native log and stone buildings on 128-acres of native forest on the shore of Green Bay. Hiking trails, beach swimming, enjoyable countryside for bicycling. Housed in twin bedded private bath facility. Meals served family style. Classroom is large hall in wooded setting. Clearing open mid-May to mid-Oct. for week-long sessions beginning Sunday night with supper, ending Saturday morning with breakfast — usually 2 or 3 writing weeks per year." Provisions for the writer include options of sharing a twin bedroom or 6-bed dorm, meals furnished, workspace in bedroom, living room, school building or quiet nooks on the grounds. Accommodates 20-24 writers.
Costs: $425-465/person per week includes board, room and tuition. (No Thursday night supper.) Scholarships are available. Brochure/guidelines available.

CUMMINGTON COMMUNITY OF THE ARTS, R.R. 1, Box 145, Cummington MA 01026. (413)634-2172. Contact: Rick Reiken. Estab. 1923. Open to all artists. "Land is rural; 110 acres of rolling hills in Berkshires, western Massachusetts. Buildings vary from large old-style homes to individual cabins. Private." Offered year-round for 2 weeks to 3 months. Provisions for the writer include private room/studio (one room total), meals included. Accommodates up to 20 writers. Workshop space also available.
Costs: $600, all inclusive. Send $15 with application. Brochure/guidelines available for SASE.

CURRY HILL PLANTATION WRITER'S RETREAT, 404 Cresmont Ave., Hattiesburg MS 39401. (601)264-7034. Director: Elizabeth Bowne. Estab. 1977. Open to all fiction and nonfiction writing, except poetry and technical writing. This workshop is held at an antebellum home, located on 400-acres of land. It is limited to only eight guests who live in, all of whom receive individual help with their writing, plus a 3-hour workshop each evening when the group meets together. The location is six miles east of Bainbridge, Georgia. Offered April 4-10. Provisions for the writer include room and board. Accommodates 8 writers.
Costs: $400 for the week; includes room and board and individual help, one hour per guest each day.
To Apply: Interested persons should apply *early* January. Brochure/guidelines available for SASE.

DJERASSI RESIDENT ARTISTS PROGRAM, (formerly Djerassi Foundation), 2325 Bear Gulch Rd., Woodside CA 94062. "The Djerassi Program appoints approximately 30 artists a year to spend 1 to 3 months working on independent or collaborative projects in a setting of unusual beauty and privacy. We are seeking applications at two levels. One is the level of great promise: artists who have a record of solid achievement but are not yet very well known, for whom appointments as resident artists might make a difference. The other is the level of national or international distinction: artists with established reputations, for whom a change of scene might offer refreshment and inspiration." Provisions for the writer include living/studio accommodations as well as meals. Accommodates 30 writers and other artists/year.
Costs: "The Djerassi Program award is strictly a residential grant." All accommodations are provided at no cost.
To Apply: Request application form. Return with $15 application fee, writing sample (short fiction or chapter/s from a book) and publication information on each work. Application period: February 1-March 31. Brochure/guidelines available for SASE.

‡DORSET COLONY HOUSE FOR WRITERS, Box 519, Dorset VT 05251. (802)867-2223. Director: John Nassivera. Estab. 1980. Colony is open to all writers. Facility and grounds include large 19th century house in New England village setting; national historic landmark house and village. Available 2 months in spring and 2 months in fall. Accommodates 8 writers.
Costs: $75/week; meals not included; fully functional kitchen in house and restaurants easy walk away.
To Apply: No fees to apply; send inquiry anytime. Brochures are available for SASE.

FINE ARTS WORK CENTER IN PROVINCETOWN, P.O. Box 565, Provincetown MA 02657. (508)487-9960. Contact: Writing Coordinator. Estab. 1968. Open to emerging writers and visual artists. "Located on the grounds of the former Days Lumberyard complex, the facility has offered studio space to artists and writers since 1914. Renovated coal bins provide artist studios; several houses and a refurbished Victorian Barn offer apartments for writers. The complex encircles the Stanley Kunitz Common Room where fellows and visiting artists offer readings to the public." A seven-month residency offered from October 1 to May 1 each year. "Each writer is awarded his/her own apartment with kitchen and bath. All apartments are furnished and equipped with kitchen supplies. A monthly stipend of $375 is also provided." Accommodates 10 writers (four fiction, four poets).
Costs: No fees other than application fee ($20).
To Apply: Application deadline: February 1. Writing sample: Send 1 or 2 short stories. If novel, excerpt including opening section and synopsis. Limit: 40 pages. Send up to 20 pages of poetry. Send six copies. Check guidelines for details. Brochure/guidelines available for SASE.

THE TYRONE GUTHRIE CENTRE AT ANNAGHMAKERRIG, New Bliss, County Monaghan, Ireland. Tel: 047-54003. Resident Director: Bernard Loughlin. Estab. 1981. Open to writers, painters, sculptors, composers, directors, artists. There are "11 work rooms in house, generally with private bathroom. Also 5 new houses which are self-catering. 400-acres, large lake and gardens. Sitting room, library, kitchen, diningroom." Closed for 2-week period at Christmas only. Provisions for the writer include private room and meals. Accommodates 16 writers and other artists.

Costs: IR £1,500/month for big house, meals included. IR £150/week for self-contained houses – also have to pay food, heating, electricity and outgoings.
To Apply: Write for application form. Considered at bimonthly board meeting. Brochure/guidelines available for SASE.

THE HAMBIDGE CENTER, P.O. Box 339, Rabun Gap GA 30568. Estab. 1934. Open to artists from all fields. Includes "600 acres of wooded, rural property serenely set in north Georgia mountains; traversed by streams and waterfalls." 2-week to 2-month stays from May to October. Provisions for writers include private cottages and studios. Accommodates 7 writers.
Costs: $125/week with dinner provided Monday-Friday. Some scholarships available, (very limited and reviewed individually.)
To Apply: Schedule is set during March. Application fee is $20. Application form mailed upon request. Brochure/guidelines available for SASE.

KALANI HONUA, RR2, Box 4500, Pahoa HI 96778. (808)965-7828. Director: Richard Koob. Estab. 1980. Open to all education interests. "Kalani Honua, the 'harmony of heaven and earth,' provides an environment where the spirit of aloha flourishes. Located on twenty secluded acres bordered by lush jungle and rugged coastline forged by ancient lava flows, Kalani Honua offers an authentic experience of rural Hawaii. The surrounding area, including sacred sites and state and national parks, is rich with the island's history and magic." Available year-round, although greatest availability is May and June and September, October, November, December. Provisions for the writer include "comfortable, private room and workspace. 3 meals offered/day, beautiful coastal surroundings and recreation facilities (pool, sauna, jacuzzi, tennis, valleyball, biking) near beaches and Volcano National Park. (Qualifying writers receive stipend to help with costs.)" Accommodates usually 1-5 as artists-in-residence.
Costs: $24-80/night depending on choice of lodging (varying from private room with shared bath to private cottage with private bath) and depending on stipend amount. Meals are approx. $24/day or may be self-provided in kitchen available. Scholarships available. Professional career documentation and assurance the residency will be successfully completed.
To Apply: Application fee $10. Brochure/guidelines available for SASE. College credit may be arranged through University of Hawaii.

‡LEIGHTON ARTIST COLONY, THE BANFF CENTRE, Box 1020 Station 22, Banff, Alberta T0L 0C0 Canada. (403)762-6180. Registrar: Annie Hillis. Estab. 1984. "The Leighton Artist Colony provides time and space for professional artists to produce new work. The colony is situated in a pine grove on the side of a mountain and consists of eight specially designed studios set apart from one another. Available for one week to three month residencies. Apply at anytime. Juries are held three times a year. Space is limited and artists are encouraged to apply at least six months in advance of start date. Provisions include private room, studio and choice of meal plan. Accommodates 3 professional artists at one time.
Costs: Approximately $72-81/day (Canadian). Financial subsidy for those who demonstrate need is offered in the form of a discount. Maximum discount for Canadians $36/day; for others $25/day.
To Apply: Send completed application form, resume, press releases, reviews and a selection of published work or manuscripts in progress. Brochures or guidelines available for free.

THE MACDOWELL COLONY, 100 High St., Peterborough NH 03458. (603)924-3886 or (212)966-4860. Admissions Coordinator: Pat Dodge. Estab. 1907. Open to writers, composers, visual artists, film/video artists, interdisciplinary artists and architects. Includes "main building, library, 3 residence halls and 31 individual studios on over 400 mostly wooded acres, one mile from center of small town in southern New Hampshire." Available up to 8 weeks year-round. Provisions for the writer include meals, private sleeping room, individual secluded studio. Accommodates variable number of writers, averaging 10 at a time.
Costs: Artists are asked to contribute toward the cost of their residency according to their financial resources.
To Apply: Application forms available. Application deadline: January 15 for summer; April 15 for fall/winter, September 15 for winter/spring. Writing sample required. For novel, send a chapter or section. For short stories, send 2-3. Send 6 copies. Brochure/guidelines available for SASE.

MILLAY COLONY FOR THE ARTS, Steepletop, P.O. Box 3, Austerlitz NY 12017-0003. (518)392-3103. Executive Director: Ann-Ellen Lesser. Assistant Director: Gail Giles. Estab. 1973. Open to professional writers, composers, visual artists. Includes "600-acres – mostly wooded, fields, old farm. Two

buildings house artists — separate studios (14' × 20') and bedrooms." Available year round. Accommodates 5 people at a time for one month residencies.
Costs: No fees.
To Apply: Requires sample of work and 1 professional reference. Application deadlines: February 1 for June-September; May 1 for October-January; September 1 for February-May. Brochure/guidelines available for SASE.

PALENVILLE INTERARTS COLONY, P.O. Box 59, Palenville NY 12463. (518)678-3332. Contact: Admissions Director. "Artists residencies for professional/and emerging literary artists." Located at base of Catskill Mountains at an old summer campground. Main house has 8 rooms, kitchen and dining hall. Cabins for studios and some living space. Trails, fields, dance studio, theater. Available June-September. Accommodates up to 12-15 writers or other artists.
Costs: Write for details.
To Apply: Application fee: $10. Writing samples required. Applications are considered on a competition basis; judges are a panel of 8 distinguished artists. Deadline: April 1. Brochure/guidelines available for SASE.

RAGDALE FOUNDATION, 1260 N. Green Bay Rd., Lake Forest IL 60045. (708)234-1063. Director: Michael Wilkerson. Estab. 1976. For qualified writers, artists and composers. Ragdale, located 30 miles north of Chicago near Lake Michigan, is "the grounds of acclaimed Chicago architect Howard Van Doren Shaw's historic family home." Accommodations include the Ragdale House, the Barnhouse and the new Friends Studio. Available in 2-week to 2-month sessions year-round, except for the last 2 weeks in summer and 2 weeks in December. Provisions for the writer include room; linens, laundered by Ragdale and meals. "Breakfast and lunch supplies are stocked in communal kitchens, enabling residents to work throughout the day uninterrupted by scheduled meals. The evening meal is the only exception: wholesome, well-prepared dinners are served six nights a week. The Ragdale House and Barnhouse both contain informal libraries, and the property overlooks a large nature preserve." Accommodates 10.
Costs: $10/day. Scholarships based on financial need are available. "Fee waiver application and decision process is separate from artistic admission process."
To Apply: "Residents are chosen by a selection committee composed of professionals in their artistic discipline. Applicants are required to submit an application, project description, slides or a writing sample and three references." Application fee: $20. Deadlines: September 15 for January-April, January 15 for May-August and April 15 for September-December. Brochure/guidelines available for SASE.

THE SYVENNA FOUNDATION WRITERS-IN-RESIDENCE, Route 1, Box 193, Linden TX 75563. (903)835-8252. Associate Director: Barbara Carroll. Estab. 1987; first resident in 1989. For beginning and intermediate women writers, all genres. "Two private cottages in rural, wooded area of Northeast Texas, 6½ miles from nearest town. Cottages are within walking distance of main house and administrative offices. Cottages are self-sufficient and equipped with all modern conveniences." Available in four 2- or 3-month terms, January through November. Provisions for the writer include rent- and utilities-free private cottage with workspace. "Residents are responsible for their own meals, laundry and other personal needs. Pick-up truck available once a week for residents without their own transportation." Accommodates 2 at one time (1/cottage).
Costs: "No charge for application or residency. Monthly stipend provided to help offset living expenses."
To Apply: Send SASE to Syvenna Foundation for application materials. Deadlines: April 1 for September-November; August 1 for January-March, October 1 for April-May and December 1 for June-August.

UCROSS FOUNDATION, 2836 U.S. Hwy. 14-16 East, Clearmont WY 82835. (307)737-2291. Program Coordinator: Ruth Adams. Estab. 1982. For "Artists of *all* disciplines. We are in a rural setting of Wyoming, in a town with a very small population. The facilities are part of a renovated ranch." Available for 2 weeks to 2 months. "Each artist is provided a private studio, private bedroom, common living area and meals. We have the potential of accommodating 4 writers at one time."
Costs: Ucross Foundation awards residencies.
To Apply: Residents are selected through biannual competition, judged by a 3-member committee. Deadlines: March 1 for August-December, October 1 for January-May. Brochure/guidelines available for SASE.

VERMONT STUDIO CENTER, P.O. Box 613, Johnson VT 05656. (802)635-2727. Registrar: Susan Kowalsky. Estab. 1984. "The Vermont Studio Center now offers 2 week Writing Studio Sessions led by prominent writers/teachers focusing on the craft of writing. Independent Writers' Retreats are also available year-round for those wishing more solitude. Room, working studio and excellent meals are included in all our programs. Generous work-exchange Fellowships are available. For information/ application write: Vermont Studio Center, PO Box 613, Johnson, VT 05656 – or call (802)635-2727."
Costs: No information given. Write for information.

‡VILLA MONTALVO ARTIST RESIDENCY PROGRAM, P.O. Box 158, Saratoga CA 95071. Artist Residency Coordinator: Lori A. Wood. Estab. 1942. For "writers, visual artists, musicians and composers. Villa Montalvo is a 1912 Mediterranean-style villa on 176 acres. There are extensive formal gardens and miles of redwood trails. Residencies are from 1-3 months, year-round. Each writer is given a private apartment with kitchen. Apartments for writers have either 2 rooms or a unique balcony or veranda. All apartments are fully-stocked (dishes, linens, etc.), except for food. Artists provide their own food." Accommodates 3 writers (5 artists in total).
Costs: "There are no costs for residency. We require a $100 security deposit, which is returned at end of residency. There are 4 fellowships available each year. These are awarded on the basis of merit to the 4 most highly-rated applicants. One of these must be a writer, and one a woman artist or writer."
To Apply: Application form, resumé, statement of proposed project, 3 professional recommendations, $20 application fee. Brochure/guidelines available for SASE.

VIRGINIA CENTER FOR THE CREATIVE ARTS, Mt. San Angelo, Box VCCA, Sweet Briar VA 24595. (804)946-7236. Director: William Smart. Estab. 1971. For writers, visual artists and composers. "Located in a rural setting, within sight of the Blue Ridge Mountains. 450-acre estate, with a herd of Holsteins. Fellows live in a 10-year-old residence; there are 22 bedrooms, dining room, living rooms, library, laundry room, etc. Studios are located some 5 minutes away by foot. There are a few other small buildings, outdoor swimming pool and year-round swimming available across the road at Sweet Briar College." Available year-round for residencies from 2 weeks to 3 months. Provisions for the writer include private bedroom, private soundproof studio and all meals. Accommodates 13 writers.
Costs: "The standard fee is $20/day, which includes everything." Scholarships are available.
To Apply: $15 application fee. Write or call for application form. Deadlines: Jan. 25, May 25, Sept. 25. Brochure/guidelines available for SASE.

THE WOODSTOCK GUILD'S BYRDCLIFFE ARTS COLONY, 34 Tinker St., Woodstock NY 12498. (914)679-2079. Executive Director: Sondra Howell. Estab. 1902. For writers, playwrights and visual artists. "The historic 600-acre Byrdcliffe Arts Colony is in Woodstock, one and a half miles from the village center. The residency program takes place in the Villetta Inn and Annex and includes a large community living room and common kitchen." Available for four one-month periods starting June 1. Provisions for writer include a private room and studio space. "Meals are not provided; residents share a large fully equipped communal kitchen." Accommodates 10 writers.
Costs: $500 per month. Fee reductions available for writers staying for more than one period. Financial aid is available. "Potential residents are asked to include a list of savings and holdings, a list of income from the last two years (photocopied tax forms), and a projection of income and expenses for the current year."
To Apply: Submit application with $5 handling fee. Literary artists must submit no more than 12 pages of poetry, one chapter or story-length prose piece, professional resume, reviews of articles (if available) and 2 references. Residents are selected by a committee of professionals in the arts. Brochure and application available for SASE.

‡**HELENE WURLITZER FOUNDATION OF NEW MEXICO,** Box 545, Taos NM 87571. (505)758-2413. President: Henry A. Sauerwein, Jr. Estab. 1953. "No restrictions. 12 separate houses, studios." Available April 1-September 30 annually. Provisions for the writer include single house/studio dwelling. **Costs:** No charge. (Must supply own food.)
To Apply: Write to the Foundation.

Retreats and colonies/changes '92-'93

The following retreats and colonies appeared in the 1992 edition of *Novel & Short Story Writer's Market* but do not appear in the 1993 edition. Those that did not respond to our request for an update appear below without further explanation. If a reason for the omission is available, it is included next to the listing name. There are several reasons why a retreat or colony may not appear—it may not have room for fiction writers this year or it may no longer be open.

Centrium Artist-In-Residence
Cottages at Hedgebrook
Dorland Mountain Arts Colony
Hilai Residencies
Northwood Institute Alden B.

Dow Creativity Center
Saskatchewan Writers'/Artists' Colonies
West Virginia Division of Culture And History, Arts and

Humanities Section, Artist-In-Residence Program
Wolf Pen Women Writers Colony (asked to be deleted)
Yaddo

Organizations and Resources

When you write, you write alone. It's just you and the typewriter or computer screen. Yet the writing life does not need to be a lonely one. Joining a writing group or organization can be an important step in your writing career. By meeting other writers, discussing your common problems and sharing ideas, you can enrich your writing and increase your understanding of this sometimes difficult, but rewarding life.

The variety of writers' organizations seems endless—encompassing every type of writing and writer—from small, informal groups that gather at a local coffeehouse to critique each others' work to regional groups that hold annual conferences to share marketing tips. National organizations and unions fight for writers' rights and higher wages for freelancers and international groups monitor the treatment of writers around the world.

In this section you will find state-, province- and region-based groups such as the California Writers' Club, The Nebraska Writers Guild and the Federation of British Columbia Writers. You'll also find national organizations including the National Writers Club and the Canadian Authors Association. The Mystery Writers of America and the Western Writers of America are examples of groups devoted to a particular type of writing. Whatever your needs or goals, you're likely to find a group listed here to interest you.

A few organizations helpful to writers are not clubs or groups and they do not fit neatly into any one category. We've included a few of these, too, as "resources." These are gathering places or helpful services available to writers. The Writers Room in New York City and the Writers HelpLine are two examples of those featured here.

Selecting a writers' organization

To help you make an informed decision, we've provided information on the scope, membership and goals of the organizations listed on these pages. We asked groups to outline the types of memberships available and the benefits members can expect. Most groups will provide additional information for a self-addressed, stamped envelope and you may be able to get a sample copy of their newsletter for a modest fee.

Keep in mind joining a writers' organization is a two-way street. When you join an organization, you become a part of it and, in addition to membership fees, most groups need and want your help. If you want to get involved, opportunities can include everything from chairing a committee to writing for the newsletter to helping set up an annual conference. The level of your involvement is up to you.

The group you select to join depends on a number of factors. First, you must determine what you want from membership in a writers' organization. Then send for more information on the groups that seem to fit your needs. Start, however, by asking yourself:

● Would I like to meet writers in my city? Am I more interested in making contacts with other writers across the country or around the world?

● Am I interested in a group that will critique my work and give me feedback on my work-in-progress?

● Do I want marketing information and tips on dealing with editors?

● Would I like to meet other writers who write the same type of work I do or am I interested in meeting writers from a variety of fields?

● How much time can I devote to meetings and are regular meetings important to me? How much can I afford to pay in dues?

- Would I like to get involved in running the group, working on the group's newsletters, planning a conference?
- Am I interested in a group devoted to writers' rights and treatment or would I rather concentrate on the business of writing?

For more information

Because they do not usually have the resources or inclination to promote themselves widely, finding a local writers' group is usually a word-of-mouth process. If you think you'd like to join a local writers' group and do not know of any in your area, check notices at your library or contact a local college English department. You might also try contacting a group based in your state, province or region listed here for information on smaller area groups.

For more information on writers' organizations, check *The Writer's Essential Desk Reference* (Writer's Digest Books, 1507 Dana Ave., Cincinnati OH 45207). Other directories listing organizations for writers include the *Literary Market Place* and *International Literary Market Place* (R.R. Bowker, 245 W. 17th St., New York NY 10011). The National Writers Club also has a list of writers' organizations. For more writers resources see *Literary/Writing Resources Lists*, (Poets and Writers, 72 Spring St., New York NY 10012.) This series of publications lists organizations, publications, bookstores and reading venues by region.

ARIZONA AUTHORS ASSOCIATION, Suite 117, 3509 E. Shea Blvd., Phoenix AZ 85028. (602)996-9706. President: Gerry Benninger. Estab. 1978. Number of Members: 500. Type of Memberships: Professional, writers with published work; associate, writers working toward publication; affiliate, professionals in the publishing industry. "Primarily an Arizona organization but open to writers nationally." Benefits include bimonthly newsletter, discount rates on seminars, workshops and newsletter ads, use of AAA reference library, discounts on writing books, discounts at bookstores, copy shops, critique groups and networking events. "Sponsors workshops on a variety of topics of interest to writers (e.g. publishing, marketing, structure, genres)." Publishes *Authors Newsletter*, bimonthly ($40/yr.). Dues: Professional and associate, $40/year; affiliate: $45/year; student: $20/year. Holds monthly critique group and quarterly networking events. Send SASE for information.

ASSOCIATED WRITING PROGRAMS, Old Dominion University, Norfolk VA 23529-0079. (804)683-3839. Publications Editor: D.W. Fenza. Estab. 1967. Number of Members: 1,300 (individual members). Types of Membership: Institutional (universities); graduate students; *Chronicle* subscribers. Open to any person interested in writing; most members are students or faculty of university writing programs (worldwide). Benefits include information on creative writing programs; grants and awards to writers; a job placement service for writers in academe and beyond. "We hold an Annual Conference/Meeting in a different US city every spring; also an annual Award Series in poetry, short story collections, novel and creative nonfiction, in which winner receives $1,500 honorarium and automatic publication with a participating press. We act as agent for finalists in Award Series—try to place their manuscript with publishers throughout the year." Manuscripts accepted January 1-February 28 only. SASE for guidelines. Publishes *AWP Chronicle* 6 times/year; 3 times/academic semester. Available to members for free. Nonmembers may order a subscription $18/yr. Also publishes the *AWP Official Guide to Writing Programs* which lists about 330 creative writing programs in universities across the country and in Canada. *Guide* is updated every 2 years; cost is $15.95 plus $2 for library rate shipping or $4 for 1st class. Dues: $45 for individual membership and an additional $37 for our placement service. We keep dossiers on file and send them to school or organization of person's request. You must be a member to be a part of the placement service. Holds two meetings per year for the Board of Directors. Send SASE for information.

AUSTIN WRITERS' LEAGUE RESOURCE CENTER, Austin Writers' League, 1501 W. 5th, E-2, Austin TX 78703. (512)499-8914. Executive Director: Angela Smith. Estab. 1981. Number of Members: 1,600. Types of Memberships: Regular, student/senior citizen, organization, corporate. Monthly meetings and use of resource center/library is open to the public. "Membership includes both aspiring and professional writers, all ages and all ethnic groups." Job bank is also open to the public. Public also has access to technical assistance. Partial and full scholarships offered for some programs. Of 1,500 members, 800 reside in Austin. Remaining 700 live all over the US and in other countries. Benefits include monthly newsletter, monthly meetings, study groups, resource center/library-checkout privileges, discounts on workshops, seminars, classes, job bank, access to insurance information, discounts on books and tapes, participation in awards programs, technical/marketing assistance, copyright forms and information, access to computers and printers. Center has four rooms plus two offices and storage area. Public space includes reception and job bank area; conference/classroom; library/computer room; and copy/mail room. Library includes 400 titles. Two computers and printers are available for member use. Sponsors fall and spring workshops, weekend seminars, informal classes, sponsorships for special events such as readings, production of original plays, media conferences; Violet Crown Book Awards, newsletter writing awards, poetry contest for annual anthology. Publishes *Austin Writer* (monthly newsletter), membership/subscription: $40, $35-students, senior citizens. Monthly meetings. Study groups set their own regular meeting schedules. Send SASE for information.

THE AUTHORS GUILD, 330 West 42nd St., New York NY 10036. (212)563-5904. Executive Director: Helen Stephenson. Estab. 1921. Number of Members: 6,500. Membership dues based on income scale from writing. Open to published authors or those with firm contract offers. "The Authors Guild is a national society of professional authors." Benefits through "collective power and voice," achieving many direct economic benefits from improvement of contracts and royalty statement to the protection of authors' First Amendment rights. Other benefits: Contract advice, surveys and reports and assistance, group insurance available. Publishes the *Authors Guild Bulletin*, containing information on matters of interest to writers. Also publishes *Your Book Contract*, a 35-page pamphlet analyzing publishing contracts and *The Authors Guild Recommended Trade Book Contract and Guide*. Dues: $90 for first year; then dues are based on income scale from $90-500, depending on writing income. Send SASE for information.

CALIFORNIA WRITERS' CLUB, 2214 Derby St., Berkeley CA 94705. (510)841-1217. Estab. 1909. Number of Members: 900. Type of Memberships: Associate and active. Open to: "All published writers and those deemed able to publish within five years." Benefits include speakers—authors, editors, agents, anyone connected with writing—heard at monthly meetings, marketing information, workshops, camaraderie of fellow writers. Sponsors workshops, conferences, awards programs/contests. Publishes a monthly newsletter at state level, monthly newsletter at branch level. Available to members only. Dues: $25/year. Meets monthly. Send SASE for information.

CANADIAN AUTHORS ASSOCIATION, #500, 275 Slater St., Ottawa, Ontario K1P 5H9 Canada. (613)233-2846. Fax: (613)235-8237. National Director: Jeffrey Holmes. Estab. 1921. Number of Members: 800. Type of Memberships: Member (voting); associate (non-voting). "Member must have minimum sales to commercial publications. Associates need not have published yet." National scope (Canada) with 18 regional branches. Benefits include networking, marketing advice, legal advice, several publications, annual conference, awards programs. Sponsors workshops, conferences, awards programs/contests. Publishes *Canadian Author*, quarterly $15 (Canadian)/year; $20 (Canadian) for foreign and *National Newsline* (to members only). Dues: $107 (Canadian). "Each branch meets monthly." Send SASE for information.

‡FAIRBANKS ARTS ASSOCIATION, P.O. Box 72786, Fairbanks AK 99707-2786. (907)456-6485. Executive Director: Janel Thompson. Estab. 1966. Members: 400. "Membership is open to anyone interested in supporting Fairbanks' arts and cultural community." Scope: Regional (interior Alaska) although a number of members are scattered throughout Alaska and the lower 48 states. Benefits include reduced fees for technical and professional workshops; assistance in all of art (or technique, great writing, resumes, etc.); invitations to all association events (including gallery openings, political forums, workshops, etc.); group medical insurance (including studio insurance); discount on all items purchased through gallery store; subscription to *Fairbanks Arts*. Sponsors several art-related events. "We publish *Fairbanks Arts*, a bimonthly magazine that is also sent to 100+ subscribers and sold in local retail outlets throughout interior Alaska." Subscriptions are $15/year. Membership $25/year (includes magazine, etc.). Board of Directors meets 1st Thursday every month, plus monthly visual, literary and community arts meetings. Send SASE for information.

FEDERATION OF BRITISH COLUMBIA WRITERS, MPO Box 2206, Vancouver, British Columbia V6B 3W2 Canada. Manager: Corey Van't Haaff. Estab. 1982. Number of Members: 865. Types of Membership: regular and subsidized for those with limited income. "Open to established and emerging writers in any genre, provincial-wide." Benefits include newsletter, liaison with funding bodies, publications, workshops, readings, literary contest. Sponsors readings and workshops. Publishes a newsletter 4 times/year, included in membership. Dues: $50 Canadian (regional) regular; $25 limited income. Send SASE for information.

HORROR WRITERS OF AMERICA (HWA), Box 1077, Eden NC 27288. Did not respond to questionnaire, but information available.

INTERNATIONAL ASSOCIATION OF CRIME WRITERS (NORTH AMERICAN BRANCH), JAF Box 1500, New York NY 10116. (212)757-3915. Executive Director: Mary A. Frisque. Estab. 1987. Number of Members: 225. Open to: "Published authors of crime fiction, nonfiction, screenplays and professionals in the mystery field (agents, editors, booksellers). Our branch covers the US and Canada, there are other branches world-wide." Benefits include information about crime-writing world-wide and publishing opportunities in other countries. "We sponsor annual members' receptions during the Edgar awards week in New York and in the spring and in the fall we host a reception at the Bouchercon. We also have occasional receptions for visiting authors/publishers. We give an annual award, the North American Hammett Prize, for the best work (fiction or nonfiction) of literary excellence in the crime writing field. We publish a quarterly newsletter, *Border Patrol*, available to members only." Dues: $50 year. Send SASE for information.

‡MYSTERY WRITERS OF AMERICA (MWA), 17 E. 47th St., 6th Floor, New York NY 10017. Executive Director: Priscilla Ridgway. Estab. 1945. Number of Members: 2,500. Type of memberships: Active members (professional, published writers of fiction or nonfiction crime/mystery/suspense; Associate members (professionals in allied fields, i.e. editor, publisher, writer, critic, news reporter, publicist, librarian, bookseller, etc.); Corresponding members (writers qualified for active membership who live outside the US). Unpublished writers, students and mystery fans may petition for Affiliate member status. Benefits include promotion and protection of writers' rights and interests, including counsel and advice on contracts, MWA courses and workshops, a national office with an extensive library, an annual conference featuring the Edgar Allan Poe Awards, the *MWA Mystery Writer's Handbook*, the *MWA Anthology*, a national newsletter, regional conferences, meetings and newsletters. Newsletter, *The Third Degree*, is published 10 times/year for members. Annual dues: $65 for US members; $32.50 for Corresponding members.

THE NATIONAL LEAGUE OF AMERICAN PEN WOMEN, INC., Headquarters: Pen Arts Building, 1300 17th St., NW, Washington DC 20036. (202)785-1997. Contact: National President. Estab. 1897. Number of Members: 5,000. Type of Memberships: Three classifications: Arts, letters, music composition. Open to: Professional women. "Professional to us means our membership is only open to women who sell their art, writings or music compositions. We have 200 branches in the continental US, Hawaii and the Republic of Panama. Some branches have as many as 100 members, some as few as 10 or 12. It is necessary to have 5 members to form a new branch." Benefits include marketing advice, use of a facility, critiques and competitions. Our facility is national headquarters which has a few rooms available for Pen Women visiting the D.C. area, and for Board members in session four times a year. Branch and State Association competitions, as well as biennial convention competitions. Offers a research library of books and histories of our organization only. Sponsors awards biennially to Pen Women in each classification: Art, letters, music and $1,000 award biennially to nonPen Women in each classification for women over 35 years of age who wish to pursue special work in her field. *The Pen Woman* is our membership magazine, published from five to nine times a year, free to members, $7 a year for nonmember subscribers. Dues: $25/year for national organization, from $5-10/year for branch membership and from $1-5 for state association dues. Branches hold regular meeting each month, September through May except in northern states which meet usually March through September (for travel convenience). Send SASE for information.

NATIONAL WRITERS CLUB, Suite 620, 1450 S. Havana, Aurora CO 80012. (303)751-7844. Executive Director: Sandy Whelchel. Estab. 1937. Number of Members: 4,000. Types of Memberships: Regular membership for those without published credits; professional membership for those with published credits. Open to: Any interested writer. National/International plus we have 16 chapters in various states. Benefits include critiques, marketing advice, editing, literary agency, complaint service, chapbook publishing service, research reports on various aspects of writing, five contests, National Writers Press—self-publishing operation, computer bulletin board service, regular newsletter with updates on marketing, bimonthly magazine on writing related subjects, discounts on supplies, magazines and some services. Sponsors periodic conferences and workshops: short story contest opens March, closes July 1; novel contest opens November, closes February 28. Publishes *Flash Market News* (monthly publication for professional members only); *NWC Newsletter* (monthly publication for members only); *Authorship Magazine* (bimonthly publication available by subscription $18 to nonmembers). Dues: $50 regular; $60 professional. For professional membership requirement is equivalent of 3 articles or stories in a national or regional magazine; a book published by a royalty publisher, a play, TV script, or movie produced. An initial $15 set up fee is required for first time members. Send SASE for information. Chapters hold meetings on a monthly basis.

THE NEBRASKA WRITERS GUILD, P.O. Box 30341, Lincoln NE 68503-0341. President: Diane L. Kirkle. Estab. 1925. Number of Members: 166. Type of Memberships: Active, associate, youth. Open to: Professional and aspiring writers and poets, editors, publishers, librarians, educators and others allied to the writing/publishing industry. Statewide scope. Benefits include marketing advice, critiques, moral support. Sponsors 2 conferences/year. Publishes the *NWG Bulletin* once a year; *The Broadside* (newsletter) twice/year for members only. Dues: $15/year (active and associate members); $7/year (youth members). Meets twice/year. Send SASE for information.

NEW HAMPSHIRE WRITERS AND PUBLISHERS PROJECT, P.O. Box 150, Portsmouth NH 03802-0150. (603)436-6331. Executive Director: Barbara Tsairis. Estab. 1988. Number of Members: 395. Type of Memberships: Senior/student; individual; business; institutional. Open to anyone interested in the literary arts—writers (fiction, nonfiction, journalists, poets, scriptwriters, etc.), teachers, librarians, publishers and *readers*. Statewide scope. Benefits include a bimonthly publication featuring articles about NH writers and publishers; leads for writers, new books listings; and NH literary news. Also—use of resource library and discounts on workshops, readings, conferences. Dues: $25 for individuals; $15 for seniors, students; $50 for businesses; $35 for libraries and other institutions. Send SASE for information.

OZARKS WRITERS LEAGUE, P.O. Box 152, Branson MO 65616. (417)334-6016. Board Member: Debbie Redford. Estab. 1983. Number of Members: 250. Open to: Anyone interested in writing, photography and art. Regional Scope: Missouri, Arkansas, Oklahoma, Kansas—"Greater Ozarks" area. Benefits include mutual inspiration and support; information exchange. Sponsors quarterly seminars/workshops, two annual writing competitions, one annual photography competition, special conferences. Publishes quarterly newsletter, the *Owls Hoot*, available to nonmembers for limited receipt. Dues: $10/year. Meets quarterly—February, May, August, November. Send SASE for information.

PHILADELPHIA WRITERS ORGANIZATION, P.O. Box 42497, Philadelphia PA 19101. (215)387-4950. Administrative Coordinator: Jane Brooks. Estab. 1981. Number of members: 250. Types of membership: full (voting), associate, student. Open to any writer, published or unpublished. Scope is tri-state area—Pennsylvania, Delaware, New Jersey, but mostly Philadelphia area. Benefits include medical insurance (for full members only), disability insurance, monthly meetings with guest panelists, Spring workshop (in full day) plus Editors Marketplace. Sponsors Spring workshop, Writers Meeting Editors Marketplace. Publishes a monthly newsletter for members only. Dues: $50 (full and associate); $25-student. Proof of publication required (minimum of 2,000 words-full members). Meets monthly throughout year except August. Send SASE for information.

ROMANCE WRITERS OF AMERICA (RWA), #315, 13700 Veterans Memorial Drive,. Houston TX 77014. Did not respond to questionnaire. Write for information.

SCIENCE FICTION AND FANTASY WORKSHOP, 1193 South 1900 East, Salt Lake City UT 84108. (801)582-2090. Director/Editor: Kathleen D. Woodbury. Estab. 1980. Number of members: 400. Types of membership: "Active" is listed in the membership roster and so is accessible to all other members;

"inactive" is not listed in the roster. Open to "anyone, anywhere. Our scope is international although over 96% of our members are in the US." Benefits include "several different critique groups: short stories, novels, articles, screenplays, poetry, etc. We also offer services such as copyediting, working out the numbers in planet building (give us the kind of planet you want and we'll tell you how far it is from the sun, etc.—or tell us what kind of sun you have and we'll tell you what your planet is like), brainstorming story, fragments or cultures or aliens, a clearing house for information on groups who write/critique science fiction and fantasy in your area, etc. We sponsored a writing contest at a science fiction convention last year and plan to do so this year." Publishes *SF and Fantasy Workshop* (monthly); non-members subscribe for $10/year; samples are $1 and trial subscription: $6/6 issues. "We also publish a fiction booklet on an irregular basis. It contains one short story and three critiques by professional writers. Cost to anyone is $5/5 issues or $8/10 issues." Dues: Members pay a one-time fee of $5 (to cover the cost of the roster and the new-member information packet) and the annual $10 subscription fee. To renew membership, members simply renew their subscriptions. Our organization is strictly by mail. Send SASE for information.

SCIENCE FICTION AND FANTASY WRITERS OF AMERICA, INC., 5 Winding Brook Drive #1B, Guilderland NY 12084. (518)869-5361. Executive Secretary: Peter Dennis Pautz. Estab. 1965. Number of Members: 1,200. Type of Memberships: Active, associate, affiliate, institutional, estate. Open to: "Professional writers, editors, anthologists, artists in the SF/fantasy genres and allied professional individuals and institutions. Our membership is international; we currently have members throughout Europe, Australia, Central and South America, Canada and some in Asia." We produce a variety of journals for our members, annual membership directory and provide a grievance committee, publicity committee, circulating book plan and access to TEIGIT medical/life/disability insurance. We award the SFWA Nebula Awards each year for outstanding achievement in the genre at novel, novella, novelet and short story lengths." Quarterly *SFWA Bulletin* to members; nonmembers may subscribe at $15/4 issues within US/Canada; $18.50 overseas. Bimonthly *SFWA Forum* for active members only. Annual *SFWA Membership Directory* for members; available to professional organizations for $60. Active membership requires professional sale in the US of at least three short stories or one full-length book. Affiliate membership requires at least one professional sale in the US or other professional sale in the US or other professional involvement in the field. Dues are pro-rated quarterly; info available upon request. Business meetings are held during Annual Nebula Awards weekend and usually during the annual World SF Convention. Send SASE for information.

‡SCIENCE FICTION WRITERS OF EARTH, P.O. Box 121293, Fort Worth TX 76121. (817)451-8674. Administrator: Gilbert Gordon Reis. Estab. 1980. Number of Members: 64-100. Open to: Unpublished writers of SF and fantasy short stories. "We have a few writers in Europe, Canada and Australia, but the majority are from the US. Writers compete in our annual contest. This allows the writer to find out where he/she stands in writing ability. Winners often receive requests for their story from publishers. Many winners have told us that they believe that placing in the top ten of our contest gives them recognition and has assisted in getting their first story published." Dues: One must submit a SF or fantasy short story to our annual contest to be a member. Cost is $5 for membership and first story. $2 for each additional ms. The nominating committee meets several times a year to select the ten stories of the annual contest. Information about the organization is available for SASE.

SMALL PRESS WRITERS AND ARTISTS ORGANIZATION (SPWAO), 309 N. Humphrey Circle, Shawano WI 54166. (715)524-2750. SPWAO President: Mike Olson. Estab. 1977. Number of members: 300-400. Open to all members (anyone who paid dues for current year). Scope is international. "A service organization dedicated to the promotion of excellence in the small press fields of science fiction, fantasy and horror." Benefits include market news, critiquing services (art, poetry, fiction), grievance arbitration, reviews, nonfiction articles and essays, editor-mentor program, info-swap/collaboration service, etc. "We've added two new benefits for members: publisher's clearance, and newsletters on tape for the blind or visually impaired." Facilities include SPWAO library/archives. Sponsors awards and contests; have held conventions in conjunction with known cons—NECON, BUBONICON. Publishes *SPWAO Newsletter* (monthly), available to nonmembers for $4 postage; *Showcase* (yearly or as funding allows), $8.95; *Alpha Gallery* (funding allows) $7.50. Dues: US: $17.50 initial, $15 renew; 2 year new member option $28.50; *rebate available new members joining under current year plan after May 1*; Canadian: $20 new, $17.50 renew; International: $20 new and renew. Send SASE for information.

‡SOCIETY OF MIDLAND AUTHORS, 152 N. Scoville, Oak Park IL 60302-2642. (708)383-7568. President: Jim Bowman. Estab. 1915. Number of Members: 160. Type of memberships: Regular, published authors and performed playwrights; Associate, librarians, editors, etc., others involved in publishing. Open to: Residents or natives of 12 midland states: Illinois, Iowa, Indiana, Michigan, Wisconsin, Nebraska, S. Dakota, N. Dakota, Ohio, Kansas, Missouri and Minnesota. Benefits include newsletter, listing in directory. Sponsors annual awards in 7 categories, with upwards of $300 prizes. Awards dinner in May at Drake Hotel, Chicago. Publishes newsletter several times/year. Dues: $15/year. Holds "5 program meetings/year, open to public at Newberry Library, Chicago, featuring writers, editors, etc. on bookwriting subjects, setlling, etc." Brochures are available for SASE.

‡WASHINGTON CHRISTIAN WRITERS FELLOWSHIP, P.O. Box 11337, Bainbridge Island WA 98110. (206)842-9103. Director: Elaine Wright Colvin. Estab. 1982. Number of Members: 300. Open to: All writers. Scope is state-wide. Benefits include meetings, speakers, how-to critiques, private consultation. Sponsors a monthly seminar second Saturday each month 9:30 am-2 pm. Publishes a bimonthly newsletter, *W.I.N.* Dues: $15. Meetings $3 (members), $6 (non members). Meets monthly—second Saturday. Brochures are available for SASE.

WASHINGTON INDEPENDENT WRITERS, #220, 733 15th St. NW, Washington DC 20005. (202)347-4973. Executive Director: Isolde Chapin. Estab. 1975. Number of Members: 2,500. Type of Memberships: Full, associate, senior, student, dual. Open to any writer or person who has an interest in writing. Regional scope. Benefits include group health insurance, grievance committee, job bank, social events, workshops, small groups, networking, etc. Sponsors monthly workshops, spring conference. Publishes *The Independent Writer* newsletter, published 11 times/year. Newsletter subscription $35/year, must live outside metropolitan area. Dues: $75/year full and associate members; $45 senior and student members; $120 dual members (2 writers living at the same address). Holds monthly workshops and small group meetings. Send SASE for information.

‡WESTERN WRITERS OF AMERICA, Office of the Secretary Treasurer, 2800 N. Campbell, El Paso TX 79902-2522. (915)532-3222. Secretary-Treasurer: Francis L. Fugate. Estab. 1953. Number of Members: 528. Type of Membership: Active, Associate, Patron. Open to: Professional, published writers who have multiple publications of fiction or nonfiction (usually at least three) about the West. Associate membership open to those with one book, a lesser number of short stories or publications or participation in the field such as editors, agents, reviewers, librarians, television producers, directors (dealing with the West). Patron memberships open to corporations, organizations and individuals with an interest in the West. Scope is international. Benefits: "By way of publications and conventions, members are kept abreast of developments in the field of Western literature and the publishing field, marketing requirements, income tax problems, copyright law, research facilities and techniques, and new publications. At conventions members have the opportunity for one-on-one conferences with editors, publishers and agents." Sponsors an annual four-day conference during fourth week of June featuring panels, lectures and seminars on publishing, writing and research. Includes the Spur Awards to honor authors of the best Western literature of the previous year. Publishes a newsletter six times/year for members. Also publishes *The Roundup Quarterly* (reviews of Western fiction and works by Western writers) available to nonmembers for $30. Publishes membership directory. Dues; $60 for active membership, $60 for associate membership, $250 for patron. For information on Spur Awards, send SASE.

THE WRITERS ALLIANCE, Box 2014, Setauket NY 11733. Executive Director: Kiel Stuart. Estab. 1979. Number of Members: 125. Open to all writers: Professional, aspiring, those who have to write business memos or brochures; those interested in desktop publishing. National scope. Benefits: Members can run one classified or display ad in each issue of membership newsletter, *Keystrokes*; which also provides software and hardware reviews, how-to articles, market information and general support. Sponsors local writer's workshops. Publishes *Keystrokes*, quarterly, $15/year (payable to Exec. Dir. Kiel Stuart) covers both the cost of membership and newsletter. Local writer's critique group meets every two weeks. Send SASE for information.

THE WRITER'S CENTER, 7815 Old Georgetown Rd., Bethesda MD 20814. (301)654-8664. Director: Jane Fox. Estab. 1977. Number of Members: 2,200. Open to: Anyone interested in writing. Scope is regional DC, Maryland, Virginia, West Virginia, Pennsylvania. Benefits include newsletter, discounts in bookstore, workshops, public events, subscriptions to *Poet Lore*, use of equipment and library. Center offers workshops, reading series, research library, equipment, newsletter and limited workspace. Sponsors workshops, conferences, award for narrative poem. Publishes *Carousel*, bimonthly. Nonmembers can pick it up at the Center. Dues: $30/year. Fees vary with service, see publications. Brochures are available for SASE.

WRITERS CONNECTION, Suite 180, 1601 Saratoga-Sunnyvale Rd., Cupertino CA 95014. Executive Director: Mardeene Mitchell. Estab. 1983. Number of Members: 1,500. Open to: Anyone interested in writing or publishing. Mainly northern California scope, but we have members nationwide. Benefits include job placement service, seminars, referral network, newsletter, bookstore, resource library, meeting facility, mailing lists, advertising. Offers grammar help-line and research library. Sponsors workshops, conferences, annual Selling to Hollywood conference. Publishes *Writers Connection* monthly newsletter. One-year subscription is $18. Dues: $40/year. Newsletter/catalog available for 9 × 12 SAE and 3 first class stamps.

WRITERS' FEDERATION OF NEW BRUNSWICK, P.O. Box 37, Station A, Fredericton, New Brunswick E3B 4Y2 Canada. Project Coordinator: Anna Mae Snider. Estab. 1983. Number of Members: 180. Membership is open to anyone interested in writing. "This a provincial organization. Benefits include promotion of members' works through newsletter announcements and readings and launchings held at fall festival and annual general meeting, participation in a Writers-in-Schools Program, manuscript reading service, workshops held at fall and spring events. The WFNB sponsors a fall festival and an annual general meeting which features workshops, readings and book launchings." There is also an annual literary competition, open to residents of New Brunswick only, which has prizes of $200, $100 and $30 in four categories: Fiction, nonfiction, children's literature and poetry and $400 prize for the best manuscript of poems (48 pgs.) Publishes a quarterly newsletter. Dues: $15/year. Board of Directors meets approximately 5 times a year. Annual General Meeting is held in April of each year. Send SASE for information.

WRITERS' FEDERATION OF NOVA SCOTIA, 203-5516 Spring Garden Rd., Halifax, Nova Scotia B3J 1G6 Canada. Executive Director: Jane Buss. Estab. 1976. Number of Members: 500. Type of Memberships: General membership, student membership, Nova Scotia Writers' Council membership (professional), Nova Scotia Dramatists' Co-op membership (for playwrights), Honorary Life Membership. Open to: Anyone who writes, and is a resident or native of Nova Scotia. Provincial scope, with a few members living elsewhere in the country or the world. Benefits include advocacy of all kinds for writers, plus such regular programs as workshops and regular publications, including directories and a newsletter. Sponsors workshops, two annual conferences (one for general membership, the other for the professional wing), two book awards, one annual competition for unpublished manuscripts in seven categories; a writers in the schools program, a manuscript reading service, reduced photocopying and typing rates, a typing referral service. Publishes *Eastword*, six issues annually, available by subscription for $30 (Canadian) to nonmembers. Dues: $30/year (Canadian). Holds an annual general meeting, an annual meeting of the Nova Scotia Writers' Council, several board meetings annually. Send 5 × 7 SASE for information.

WRITERS GUILD OF ALBERTA, WordWorks Building, 10523 - 100 Avenue, Edmonton, Alberta T5J 0A8 Canada. (403)426-5892. Executive Director: Lyle Weis. Estab. 1980. Number of Members: 700. Membership open to current and past residents of Alberta. Regional (provincial) scope. Benefits include discounts on programs offered; manuscript evaluation service available; bimonthly newsletter; contacts; use of photocopier at discount; info on workshops, retreats, readings, etc. Sponsors workshops 2 times/year, retreats 3 times/year, annual conference, annual book awards program (Alberta residents only). Publishes *WestWord* 6 times/year; available for $25/year (Canadian) to nonmembers. Dues: $55/year for regular membership; $20/year senior/students/limited income; $100/year donating membership—charitable receipt issued (Canadian funds). Organized monthly meetings. Send SASE for information.

‡WRITER'S HELPLINE, Craigville Press, P.O. Box 86, Centerville MA 02632. Proprietor: Marion Vuilleumier. Estab. 1991. Writers' Helpline number is 1-900-988-1838 ext. 549. Cost is $2/minute. Must be 18 years or older. "For the latest market needs and writing tips dial the Writer's Helpline on your Touchtone phone—available 24 hrs., 7 days, messages changed as new information is received from agents, editors, publishers, etc. Messages are brief, so for the price of a long distance phone call, the latest news is available."

‡WRITERS INFORMATION NETWORK, P.O. Box 11337, Bainbridge Island WA 98110. (206)842-9103. Director: Elaine Wright Colvin. Estab. 1980. Number of Members: 750. Open to: All interested in writing for religious publications/publishers. Scope is national and several foreign countries. Benefits include bimonthly newsletter, market news, advocacy/grievance procedures, professional advice, writers conferences, press cards, author referral, free consultation. Sponsors workshops, conferences throughout the country each year—mailing list and advertised in *W.I.N.* newsletter. Bimonthly newsletter: $15/year. Dues: $15 (newsletter subscription included). Holds monthly meetings in Seattle, WA. Brochures are available for SASE.

THE WRITERS ROOM, INC., 5th Floor, 153 Waverly Place, New York NY 10014. (212)807-9519. Executive Director: Renata Rizzo. Estab. 1978. Number of Members: 150. Open to: Any writer who shows a serious commitment to writing. "We serve a diverse population of writers, but most of our residents live in or around the NYC area. We encourage writers from around the country (and world!) to apply for residency if they plan to visit NYC for a while." Benefits include 24-hour access to the facility. "We provide desk space, storage areas for computers, typewriters, etc., a kitchen where coffee and tea are always available, bathrooms, a library and lounge. We also offer in-house workshops on topics of practical importance to writers and monthly readings of work-in-progress." Dues: $165 per quarter/year. Send SASE for application and background information.

‡THE WRITERS' WORKSHOP, P.O. Box 696, Asheville NC 28802. (800)627-0142. Executive Director: Karen Tager. Estab. 1984. Number of Members: 1,250. Type of Memberships: Student/low income $15; family/organization $40; individual $25; friend $50. Open to all writers. Scope is national. Benefits include discounts on workshops, quarterly newsletter, admission to Annual Celebration every summer, critiquing services through the mail. Center offers reading room, assistance with editing your work, contacts with NY writers and agents. Publishes a newsletter. Available to nonmembers. Published 4 times/year. $15 low income; $25 other. Dues: $15 low income/student, $25 individual (includes newsletter). Meets several times a year. Annual meeting is in July. Brochures are available for SASE.

Organizations and resources/changes '92-'93

The following organizations and resources appeared in the 1992 edition of *Novel & Short Story Writer's Market* but do not appear in the 1993 edition. Those that did not respond to our request for an update appear below without further explanation. If a reason for the omission is available, it is included next to the listing name. There are several reasons why an organization may not appear—its membership may be too full or the group may have disbanded.

Canadian Society of Children's Authors, Illustrators and Performers
Council of Author & Journal ists
Island Writers Association
Just Buffalo Literary Center, Inc.
North Carolina Writers' Network

Publications of Interest to Fiction Writers

This section features listings for magazines and newsletters that focus on writing or the publishing industry. While many of these are not markets for fiction, they do offer articles, marketing advice or other information valuable to the fiction writer. Several magazines in this section offer actual market listings while others feature reviews of books in the field and news on the industry.

Changes in publishing happen very quickly and magazines can help you keep up with the latest news. Some magazines listed here, including *Writer's Digest* and the *Canadian Writer's Journal*, cover the entire field of writing, while others such as *Children's Book Insider* and *Locus* focus on a particular type of writing.

You will also find information on some publications for writers in the introductions to other sections in this book. Many literary and commercial magazines for writers listed in the markets sections are also helpful to the fiction writer. Keep an eye on the newsstands and library shelves for others and let us know if you've found a publication particularly useful.

‡AWP CHRONICLE, Assoc. Writing Programs, Old Dominion University, Norfolk VA 23529. (804)683-3839. Editor: D.W. Fenza. 6 times/year. "Articles on the teaching of creative writing." Lists fiction markets (back pages for "submit"). Sample copies available; single copy price $3.50. Subscription: $18/year; $25/year overseas.

‡CANADIAN CHILDREN'S LITERATURE/LITTÉRATURE CANADIENNE POUR LA JEUNESSE, Department of English, University of Guelph, Guelph, Ontario N1G 2W1 Canada. (519)824-4120, ext. 3189. Editors: Mary Rubio, Elizabeth Waterston, Daniel Chouinard. Bimonthly. "In-depth criticism of English and French Canadian literature for young people. Scholarly articles and reviews are supplemented by illustrations, photographs, and interviews with authors of children's books. The main themes and genres of children's literature are covered in special issues." Reviews novels and short story collections. Send review copies to the editors. Sample copies available; single copy price is $6 (Canadian) plus postage $2. Subscriptions: $25 (Canadian), plus $8 for non-Canadian addresses.

CANADIAN WRITER'S JOURNAL, Box 6618, Depot 1, Victoria, British Columbia V8P 5N7 Canada. (604)477-8807. Editor: Gordon M. Smart. Quarterly. "Mainly short how-to and motivational articles related to all types of writing and of interest to both new and established writers. Sponsors annual short fiction contest." Lists markets for fiction. Sample copies available for $4 ($C for Canadian orders, $US for US orders). Subscription price: $15/year; $25/2 years ($C for Canadian orders, $US for US orders).

‡CAROUSEL, The Writer's Center, 4508 Walsh St., Bethesda MD 20815. (301)654-8664. Editors: Allan Lefcowitz and Mitch Roberson. Bimonthly. "*Carousel* is the newsletter for The Writer's Center. We publish book reviews and articles about writing and the writing scene." Lists fiction markets. Reviews novels and short story collections. Sample copies available. Subscriptions: $30 Writer's Center Membership.

CHILDREN'S BOOK INSIDER, %Backes, 4077 S. Ponderosa Dr., Evergreen CO 80439. Editor: Laura Backes. Monthly. "Publication is devoted solely to children's book writers and illustrators. 'At Presstime' section gives current market information each month for submissions to publishers. Other articles include information on the publishing contract and how to negotiate, how to write a cover letter, how to assemble a strong portfolio, writing tips, and interviews with published authors and illustrators. Aimed at people just starting out in publishing." Lists markets for fiction, nonfiction and illustration. Reviews novels and short story collections. Review copies should be sent to Laura Backes (only if person has 2 or more books published). Sample copies for SASE (no charge). Single copy price: $2.75. Subscription price: $33/year (US); $38/year (Canadian).

‡**FAIRBANKS ARTS**, P.O. Box 72786, Fairbanks AK 99707. (907)456-6485. Editor: Al Geist. Bimonthly. *"Fairbanks Arts*, a publication of the Fairbanks Arts Association, is designed to promote excellence in Alaskan contemporary and traditional arts. Publishes fiction (2,000 words)." Sample copies available; single copy price is $2.75. Subscriptions: $15/year.

‡**FEMINIST BOOKSTORE NEWS**, P.O. Box 882554, San Francisco CA 94188. (415)626-1556. Fax (415)626-8970. Editor: Carol Seajay. Bimonthly. *"FBN* is a 100+ page bimonthly magazine with reviews of more than 250 new feminist and lesbian titles and articles on the world of women and books. Regular columns include a 'Writing Wanted' section featuring calls for submission." Reviews novels and short story collections. Send review copies to Ann Morse. Sample copies available; single copy price is $6. Subscriptions: $60/year ($9 Canadian postage/$19 international postage).

‡**THE FICTION WRITER**, P.O. Box 9844, Ft. Lauderdale FL 33310. (305)485-0795. Editor: Prudy Taylor Board. Quarterly. *"The Fiction Writer* is primarily interested in practical, how-to articles concerning writing and selling fiction. Our readers include both beginning and selling fiction writers." Includes "interviews with successful writers focused on how they write and sell their fiction; articles dealing with the publishing business as it relates to the writer." Lists fiction markets. Reviews novels and short story collections. Send review copies to Editor, 1617 Francis St., North Ft. Myers FL 33903. Sample copies available for $3.95. Subscriptions: $12/year in US; add $4/year Canada and Mexico; add $8/year other foreign delivery.

GILA QUEEN'S GUIDE TO MARKETS, P.O. Box 97, Newton NJ 07860-0097. Editor: Kathy Ptacek. "Includes *complete* guidelines for fiction (different genres), poetry, nonfiction, greeting cards, etc." Also includes "theme section" each month – science fiction/fantasy/horror, mystery/suspense, romance, outdoor/sports, etc., and "mini-markets." Regular departments include new address listings, dead/suspended markets, moving editors, anthologies, markets to be wary of, publishing news, etc. Every issue contains updates (of material listed in previous issues) new markets, conferences, contests. Publishes articles on writing topics, self-promotion, reviews of software and books of interest to writers." Sample copy: $4. Subscriptions: $24/year (US); $28/year (Canada); $40/year (overseas).

‡**LAMBDA BOOK REPORT**, 1625 Connecticut Ave., NW, Washington DC 20009-1013. (202)462-7924. Editor: Jane L. Troxell. Bimonthly. "This review journal of contemporary gay and lesbian literature appeals to both readers and writers. Fiction queries published regularly." Lists fiction markets. Reviews novels and short story collections. Send review copies to Attn: Book Review Editor. Single copy price is $3.95/US. Subscriptions: $19.95/year (US); international rate: $31.95 (US $).

‡**LOCUS, The Newspaper of the Science Fiction Field**, P.O. Box 13305, Oakland CA 94661. (510)339-9196. Editor: Charles N. Brown. Monthly. "Professional newsletter of science fiction, fantasy and horror; has news, interviews of authors, book reviews, column on electronic publishing, forthcoming books listings, monthly books-received listings, etc." Occasionally lists markets for fiction. Reviews novels or short story collections. Sample copies available. Single copy price is $3.95. Subscription price: $38/year, (2nd class mail) for US, $43 (US)/year, (2nd class) for Canada; $43 (US)/year (2nd class) for overseas.

MYSTERY SCENE, Mystery Enterprises, 3840 Clark Rd., SE, Cedar Rapids IA 52403. Mystery and horror reviews and articles. Write for more information.

‡**NEW WRITER'S MAGAZINE**, P.O. Box 5976, Sarasota FL 34277. (813)953-7903. Editor: George J. Haborak. Bimonthly. *"New Writer's Magazine* is a publication for aspiring writers. It features 'how-to' articles, news and interviews with published and recently published authors. Will use fiction that has a tie-in with the world of the writer." Lists markets for fiction. Reviews novels and short story collections. Send review copies to Editor. Sample copies available; single copy price is $3. Subscriptions: $14/year, $25/two years. Canadian $20 (US funds). International $30/year (US funds).

‡**OHIO WRITER**, P.O. Box 528, Willoughby OH 44094. (216)257-6410. Editor: Linda Rome. Bimonthly. "Interviews with Ohio writers of fiction and nonfiction; current fiction markets in Ohio." Lists fiction markets. Reviews novels and short story collections. Sample copies available for $2. Subscriptions: $12/year; $30/3 years; $18/institutional rate.

POETS & WRITERS, 72 Spring St., New York NY 10012. Covers all types of writing. Bimonthly. "Keeps writers in touch with the news they need. Reports on grants and awards, including deadlines for applications; publishes manuscript requests from editors and publishers; covers topics such as book contracts, taxes, writers' colonies and publishing trends; features essays by and interviews with poets and fiction writers. Lists markets for fiction. Sample copies available; single copy price is $3.95. Subscriptions: $18/year; $32/2 years; $46/3 years.

‡**QUANTUM—Science Fiction and Fantasy Review**, 8217 Langport, Gaithersburg MD 20877. (301)948-2514. Editor: D. Douglas Fratz. Triannually. "*QUANTUM* features articles and columns by, and interviews with, the field's top authors, as well as book reviews, and is a 5-time Hugo Award nominee." Reviews novels and short story collections. Send review copies to Editor. Sample copies available; single copy price is $3. Subscriptions: 3/$7 (US); 3/$10 (foreign).

RISING STAR, 47 Byledge Rd., Manchester NH 03104. (603)623-9796. Editor: Scott E. Green. Published every 5-7 weeks. "A newsletter which covers new markets for writers and artists in the science fiction/fantasy/horror genres." Lists markets for fiction. Reviews novels and short story collections. Send review copies to Scott E. Green. Sample copies available. Single copy price: $1.50. Subscription price: $7.50 for 6 issues (checks payable to Scott E. Green) $10 for overseas subscribers.

SCAVENGER'S NEWSLETTER, 519 Ellinwood, Osage City KS 66523. (913)528-3538. Editor: Janet Fox. Monthly. "A market newsletter for SF/fantasy/horror writers with an interest in the small press. Articles about SF/fantasy/horror writing/marketing." Lists markets for fiction. Sample copies available. Single copy price: $2. Subscription price: $12.50/year, $6.25/6 months. Canada: $16, $8; overseas $22, $11 (US funds only).

SCIENCE FICTION CHRONICLE, P.O. Box 2730, Brooklyn NY 11202-0056. (718)643-9011. Editor: Andrew Porter. Monthly. "Monthly newsmagazine for professional writers, editors, readers of SF, fantasy, horror." Lists markets for fiction "updated every 4 months." Reviews novels and short story collections. Send review copies to Don D'Ammagagi, 323 Dodge St. E. Providence RI 02914. Sample copies available with 9 × 12 SASE with $1.21 postage; single copy price is $2.75 (US) or £3 (UK). Subscriptions: $30 bulk, $36 first class US and Canada; £25 UK, DM69 in Germany.

‡**SCIENCE FICTION CONVENTION REGISTER**, Box 3343, Fairfax VA 22038. (703)273-3297. Editor: Erwin S. Strauss. Quarterly. "Directory of over 500 upcoming science fiction and related conventions." Sample copies available; single copy price is $2.50. Subscriptions: $10/year.

‡**THE SMALL PRESS BOOK REVIEW**, P.O. Box 176, Southport CT 06490. (203)268-4878. Editor: Henry Berry. Bimonthly. "Brief reviews of all sorts of books from small presses/independent publishers." Addresses of publishers are given in reviews. Reviews novels and short story collections. Send review copies to editor. Sample copies available for $4; single copy price is $5. Subscriptions: $28/year, six-issue subscription.

SMALL PRESS REVIEW, P.O. Box 100, Paradise CA 95967. (916)877-6110. Editor: Len Fulton. Quarterly. "Publishes news and reviews about small publishers, books, magazines." Lists markets for fiction. Reviews novels and short story collections. Sample copies available. Subscription price: $23/year.

THE WRITER, 120 Boylston St., Boston MA 02116-4615. Editor: Sylvia K. Burack. Monthly. Lists markets for fiction (March and October issues have special fiction lists annually. July lists book publishers). Single copy price: $2.25. Subscription price: $27/year, $50/2 years. Special introductory offer: 5 issues $10. Canadian and foreign at additional $8 (US) per year.

WRITERS CONNECTION, Suite 180, 1601 Saratoga-Sunnyvale Rd., Cupertino CA 95014. (408)973-0227. Editor: Jan Stiles. Monthly. "How-to articles for writers, editors and self-publishers. Topics cover all types of writing, from fiction to technical writing. Columns include markets, contests and writing events and conferences for fiction, nonfiction and occasionally poetry." Lists markets for fiction. Sample copies available. Single copy price: $2. Subscription price: $18 ($24 in Canada/U.S. dollars). "We do not publish fiction or poetry."

WRITER'S DIGEST, 1507 Dana Ave., Cincinnati OH 45207. (513)531-2222. Editor: Bruce Woods. Monthly. "*Writer's Digest* is a magazine of techniques and markets. We *inspire* the writer to write, *instruct* him or her on how to improve that work, and *direct* it toward appropriate markets." Lists markets for fiction, nonfiction, poetry. Single copy price: $2.75. Subscription price: $21.

WRITER'S GUIDELINES, HC77 Box 608, Pittsburg MO 65724. Editor: Susan Salaki. Bimonthly. "Fiction writers are welcome to submit material for our Roundtable Discussions, a section devoted to the grassroots approach of revealing and/or developing a workable submission and acceptance system for writers. Our magazine also assists writers in obtaining guidelines from over two hundred different magazine and book editors through our Guidelines Service. We also offer a Adopt-A-Writer program whereby the managing editor of WGM 'adopts' up to 10 writers and works with each writer on a one-on-one basis for six months." Lists markets for fiction. Reviews novels and short story collections of subscribers. Send SASE for guidelines. Single copy price: $4. Subscription price: $16; Canada, $26; Overseas, $42.

WRITERS' JOURNAL, (Minnesota Ink section), 27 Empire Dr., St. Paul MN 55103. (612)225-1306. Managing Editor: Valerie Hockert. Bimonthly. "Provides a creative outlet for writers of fiction." Sample copies available. Single copy price: $3; $3.75 (Canadian). Subscription price: $14.97; $18.97 Canada.

‡WRITERS NEWS, Hainault Road, Little Heath, Romford RM6 5NP England. "Practical advice for established and aspiring writers. How-to articles, news, markets and competitions." Lists markets for fiction. Free trial issue available. Subscriptions: £31.90 (UK), £49.90 (US/Canada) on direct debit or credit card; or £36.90 (UK), £54.90 (US/Canada) if paying cash.

WRITER'S YEARBOOK, 1507 Dana Ave., Cincinnati OH 45207. (513)531-2222. Editor: Bruce Woods. Annual. "An annual collection of the best writing *about* writing, with a survey of the year's 100 top markets for freelancers." Single copy price: $3.95.

‡THE WRITING SELF, P.O. Box 245 Lenox Hill Station, New York NY 10021. (212)662-8849. Edirtor: Scot Nourok. Quarterly. "*The Writing Self* is devoted to the act of writing. The goal of this publication is to create a network and support for creative writers, i.e. poets, novelists, short story writers, as well as playwrights and journalists. We publish personal essays that describe what it is like to be a writer. Each issue includes an interview, book review, contest, inner voice column and short fiction. Sometimes lists markets for fiction. Reviews novels and short story collections. Send review copies to editor. Sample copies available; single copy price is $2.50. Subscriptions: $9.95 (US), $14.95 in Canada and $21.95 overseas.

Publications of interest to fiction writers/ changes '92-'93

The following publications appeared in the 1992 edition of *Novel & Short Story Writer's Market* but do not appear in the 1993 edition. Those that did not respond to our request for an update appear below without further explanation. If a reason for the omission is available, it is included next to the listing name.

Factsheet Five
The Nightmare Express
The Nook News Conferences &
   Klatches Bulletin
The Nook News Contests &

Awards Bulletin
The Nook News Market Bulletin
The Nook News Review of
   Writer's Publications

Writer's Info (ceased publication)
The Writer's Nook News

Glossary

Advance. Payment by a publisher to an author prior to the publication of a book to be deducted from the author's future royalties.

All rights. The rights contracted to a publisher permitting a manuscript's use anywhere and in any form, including movie and book-club sales, without additional payment to the writer.

Anthology. A collection of selected writings by various authors.

Auction. Publishers sometimes bid against each other for the acquisition of a manuscript that has excellent sales prospects.

Backlist. A publisher's books not published during the current season but still in print.

Belles lettres. A term used to describe fine or literary writing more to entertain than to inform or instruct.

Book producer/packager. An organization that may develop a book for a publisher based upon the publisher's idea or may plan all elements of a book, from its initial concept to writing and marketing strategies, and then sell the package to a book publisher and/or movie producer.

Category fiction. See Genre.

Chapbook. A booklet of 15-30 pages of fiction or poetry.

Cliffhanger. Fictional event in which the reader is left in suspense at the end of a chapter or episode, so that interest in the story's outcome will be sustained.

Clip. Sample, usually from newspaper or magazine, of a writer's published work.

Cloak-and-dagger. A melodramatic, romantic type of fiction dealing with espionage and intrigue.

Commercial. Publishers whose concern is salability, profit and success with a large readership.

Contemporary. Material dealing with popular current trends, themes or topics.

Contributor's copy. Copy of an issue of a magazine or published book sent to an author whose work is included.

Copublishing. An arrangement in which the author and publisher share costs and profits.

Copyediting. Editing a manuscript for writing style, grammar, punctuation and factual accuracy.

Copyright. The legal right to exclusive publication, sale or distribution of a literary work.

Cover letter. A brief letter sent with a complete manuscript submitted to an editor.

"Cozy" (or "teacup") mystery. Mystery usually set in a small British town, in a bygone era, featuring a somewhat genteel, intellectual protagonist.

Cyberpunk. Type of science fiction, usually concerned with computer networks and human-computer combinations, involving young, sophisticated protagonists.

Division. An unincorporated branch of a company (e.g. Viking Penguin, a division of Penguin USA).

Experimental fiction. Fiction that is innovative in subject matter and style; avant-garde, non-formulaic, usually literary material.

Exposition. The portion of the storyline, usually the beginning, where background information about character and setting is related.

Fair use. A provision in the copyright law that says short passages from copyrighted material may be used without infringing on the owner's rights.

Fanzine. A noncommercial, small-circulation magazine usually dealing with fantasy, horror or science-fiction literature and art.

First North American serial rights. The right to publish material in a periodical before it appears in book form, for the first time, in the United States or Canada.

Formula. A fixed and conventional method of plot development, which varies little from one book to another in a particular genre.

Frontier novel. Novel that has all the basic elements of a traditional western but is based upon the frontier history of "unwestern" places like Florida or East Tennessee.

Galleys. The first typeset version of a manuscript that has not yet been divided into pages.

Genre. A formulaic type of fiction such as romance, western or horror.

Gothic. A genre in which the central character is usually a beautiful young woman and the setting an old mansion or castle, involving a handsome hero and real danger, either natural or supernatural.

Graphic novel. An adaptation of a novel into a long comic strip or heavily illustrated story of 40 pages or more, produced in paperback.

Hard-boiled detective novel. Mystery novel featuring a private eye or police detective as the protagonist; usually involves a murder. The emphasis is on the details of the crime.

Honorarium. A small, token payment for published work.

Horror. A genre stressing fear, death and other aspects of the macabre.

Imprint. Name applied to a publisher's specific line (e.g. Owl, an imprint of Henry Holt).

Interactive fiction. Fiction in book or computer-software format where the reader determines the path the story will take by choosing from several alternatives at the end of each chapter or episode.

International Reply Coupon (IRC). A form purchased at a post office and enclosed with a letter or manuscript to a international publisher, to cover return postage costs.

Juvenile. Fiction intended for children 2-12.

Libel. Written or printed words that defame, malign or damagingly misrepresent a living person.

Literary. The general category of serious, non-formulaic, intelligent fiction, sometimes experimental, that most frequently appears in little magazines.

Literary agent. A person who acts for an author in finding a publisher or arranging contract terms on a literary project.

Mainstream. Traditionally written fiction on subjects or trends that transcend experimental or genre fiction categories.

Malice domestic novel. A traditional mystery novel that is not hard-boiled; emphasis is on the solution. Suspects and victims know one another.

Manuscript. The author's unpublished copy of a work, usually typewritten, used as the basis for typesetting.

Mass market paperback. Softcover book on a popular subject, usually around 4 × 7, directed to a general audience and sold in drugstores and groceries as well as in bookstores.

Ms(s). Abbreviation for manuscript(s).

Multiple submission. Submission of more than one short story at a time to the same editor. Do not make a multiple submission unless requested.

Narration. The account of events in a story's plot as related by the speaker or the voice of the author.

Narrator. The person who tells the story, either someone involved in the action or the voice of the writer.

New Age. A term including categories such as astrology, psychic phenomena, spiritual healing, UFOs, mysticism and other aspects of the occult.

Nom de plume. French for "pen name"; a pseudonym.

Novella (also novelette). A short novel or long story, approximately 7,000-15,000 words.

#10 envelope. 4 × 9½ envelope, used for queries and other business letters.

Novels of the West. Novels that have elements of the western but contain more complex characters and subjects such as fur trading, cattle raising and coal mining.

Offprint. Copy of a story taken from a magazine before it is bound.

One-time rights. Permission to publish a story in periodical or book form one time only.

Outline. A summary of a book's contents, often in the form of chapter headings with a few sentences outlining the action of the story under each one; sometimes part of a book proposal.

Over the transom. Slang for the path of an unsolicited manuscript into the slush pile.

Page rate. A fixed rate paid to an author per published page of fiction.

Payment on acceptance. Payment from the magazine or publishing house as soon as the decision to print a manuscript is made.

Payment on publication. Payment from the publisher after a manuscript is printed.

Pen name. A pseudonym used to conceal a writer's real name.

Periodical. A magazine or journal published at regular intervals.

Plot. The carefully devised series of events through which the characters progress in a work of fiction.

Proofreading. Close reading and correction of a manuscript's typographical errors.

Proofs. A typeset version of a manuscript used for correcting errors and making changes, often a photocopy of the galleys.

Proposal. An offer to write a specific work, usually consisting of an outline of the work and one or two completed chapters.

Prose poem. Short piece of prose with the language and expression of poetry.

Protagonist. The principal or leading character in a literary work.

Public domain. Material that either was never copyrighted or whose copyright term has expired.

Pulp magazine. A periodical printed on inexpensive paper, usually containing lurid, sensational stories or articles.

Purple prose. Ornate writing using exaggerated and excessive literary devices.

Query. A letter written to an editor to elicit interest in a story the writer wants to submit.

Reader. A person hired by a publisher to read unsolicited manuscripts.

Reading fee. An arbitrary amount of money charged by some agents and publishers to read a submitted manuscript.

Regency romance. A genre romance, usually set in England between 1811-1820.

Remainders. Leftover copies of an out-of-print book, sold by the publisher at a reduced price.

Reporting time. The number of weeks or months it takes an editor to report back on an author's query or manuscript.

Reprint rights. Permission to print an already published work whose rights have been sold to another magazine or book publisher.

Roman à clef. French "novel with a key." A novel that represents actual living or historical characters and events in fictionalized form.

Romance. The genre relating accounts of passionate love and fictional heroic achievements.

Royalties. A percentage of the retail price paid to an author for each copy of the book that is sold.

SASE. Self-addressed stamped envelope.

Science fiction. Genre in which scientific facts and hypotheses form the basis of actions and events.

Second serial rights. Permission for the reprinting of a work in another periodical after its first publication in book or magazine form.

Self-publishing. In this arrangement, the author keeps all income derived from the book, but he pays for its manufacturing, production and marketing.

Sequel. A literary work that continues the narrative of a previous, related story or novel.

Serial rights. The rights given by an author to a publisher to print a piece in one or more periodicals.

Serialized novel. A book-length work of fiction published in sequential issues of a periodical.

Setting. The environment and time period during which the action of a story takes place.

Short short story. A condensed piece of fiction, usually under 700 words.

Simultaneous submission. The practice of sending copies of the same manuscript to several editors or publishers at the same time. Some people refuse to consider such submissions.

Slant. A story's particular approach or style, designed to appeal to the readers of a specific magazine.

Slice of life. A presentation of characters in a seemingly mundane situation which offers the reader a flash of illumination about the characters or their situation.

Slush pile. A stack of unsolicited manuscripts in the editorial offices of a publisher.

Speculation (or Spec). An editor's agreement to look at an author's manuscript with no promise to purchase.

Splatterpunk. Type of horror fiction known for its very violent and graphic content.

Subsidiary. An incorporated branch of a company or conglomerate (e.g. Alfred Knopf, Inc., a subsidiary of Random House, Inc.).

Subsidiary rights. All rights other than book publishing rights included in a book contract, such as paperback, book-club and movie rights.

Subsidy publisher. A book publisher who charges the author for the cost of typesetting, printing and promoting a book. Also Vanity publisher.

Suspense. A genre of fiction where the plot's primary function is to build a feeling of anticipation and fear in the reader over its possible outcome.

Synopsis. A brief summary of a story, novel or play. As part of a book proposal, it is a comprehensive summary condensed in a page or page and a half.

Tabloid. Publication printed on paper about half the size of a regular newspaper page (e.g. *The National Enquirer*).

Tearsheet. Page from a magazine containing a published story.

Theme. The dominant or central idea in a literary work; its message, moral or main thread.

Trade paperback. A softbound volume, usually around 5×8, published and designed for the general public, available mainly in bookstores.

Unsolicited manuscript. A story or novel manuscript that an editor did not specifically ask to see.

Vanity publisher. See Subsidy publisher.

Viewpoint. The position or attitude of the first- or third-person narrator or multiple narrators, which determines how a story's action is seen and evaluated.

Western. Genre with a setting in the West, usually between 1860-1890, with a formula plot about cowboys or other aspects of frontier life.

Whodunit. Genre dealing with murder, suspense and the detection of criminals.

Work-for-hire. Work that another party commissions you to do, generally for a flat fee. The creator does not own the copyright and therefore can not sell any rights.

Young adult. The general classification of books written for readers 12-18.

Category Index

The category index is a good place to begin searching for a market for your fiction. Below is an alphabetical list of subjects of particular interest to the editors listed in *Novel & Short Story Writer's Market.* The index is divided into sections: literary and small circulation magazines, commercial periodicals, small press and commercial publishers. Some of the markets listed in the book do not appear in the Category Index, because they have not indicated specific subject preferences. Most of these said they accept "all categories." Listings that were very specific also do not appear here. An example of this might be a magazine accepting "fiction about trout fishing only." If you'd like to market your romance novel, check the Commercial Publishers subhead under Romance. There you will find a list of those publishers interested in the subject. To find the page numbers for the ones you select, check the Markets Index. Then read the listings *carefully* to find the romance publishers best suited to your work.

Literary and Small Circulation Magazines

Adventure. Abyss Magazine 88; Advocate, The 90; Aguilar Expression, The 91; Amateur Writers Journal 93; Amelia 94; Amherst Review, The 96; Ansuda Magazine 97; Arnazella 100; Atalantik 102; Atlantean Press Review, The 103; Barrelhouse, The 106; Belletrist Review, The 108; Black Jack 112; Blizzard Rambler, The 114; Blue Water Review, The 115; Blueline 115; Breakthrough! 118; Carousel Literary Arts Magazine 122; Chapter One 123; Chrysalis 126; Cochran's Corner 128; Collections 129; Crime Club 135; Dagger of the Mind 136; Diffusions 140; Dream International/Quarterly 140; Eldritch Science 143; ELF: Eclectic Literary Forum 144; Event 145; Fighting Woman News 150; Fugue 154; Gotta Write Network Litmag 158; Grasslands Review 159; Green Mountains Review 160; Green's Magazine 160; Hawaii Pacific Review 165; Hob-Nob 169; Hyperbole Studios 173; Iconoclast, The 174; Indian Youth of America Newsletter 174; Infinity Limited 175; Innisfree 175; ipsissima verba/the very words 177; Jeopardy 178; Journal of Regional Criticism 180; Just A Moment 181; Kumquat Meringue 185; Lactuca 186; Leading Edge, The 187; Legend 189; Lighthouse 190; Lines In The Sand 191; Llamas Magazine 193; Long Shot 194; MacGuffin, The 196; Merlyn's Pen 199; Milwaukee Undergraduate Review, The 202; Mindscapes 204; Monocacy Valley Review, The 206; Monthly Independent Tribune Times, The 206; Nahant Bay 209; New Press Literary Quarterly, The 214; New Voices in Poetry and Prose 216; Nimrod 218; No Idea Magazine 219; Noisy Concept 219; Oak, The 223; Ouroboros 226; Oxalis 227; P.I. Magazine 228; Palace Corbie 230; Paper Bag, The 231; Perceptions (Montana) 235; Pirate Writings 238; Portable Wall, The 241; Post, The 242; Potpourri 242; Queen's Quarterly 250; Rag Mag 251; Re Arts & Letters 253; Renegade 255; Renovated Lighthouse Publications 255; Riverwind 257; Salome: A Journal for the Performing Arts 259; San Gabriel Valley Magazine 260; San Miguel Writer 260; Scream of the Buddha 261; Sensations Magazine 263; Shift Magazine 265; Short Story Digest, The 266; Short Stuff Magazine for Grown-ups 266; Slate and Style 270; Sozoryoku 275; SPSM&H 278; Thema 285; Tickled By Thunder 287; Timberlines 287; Tucumcari Literary Review 289; Ultimate Writer, The 290; Vandeloecht's Fiction Magazine 293; VeriTales 293; Villager, The 296; Vincent Brothers Review, The 296; Vintage Northwest 297; Virginia Quarterly Review 297; Wagons of Steel Magazine 298; Whisper 301; Wisconsin Restaurateur, The 304; Words of Wisdom 305; Wordsmith 306; Writers' Open Forum 308

Canadian. Antigonish Review, The 98; Atavachron and All Our Yesterdays 102; Atlantis (Nova Scotia) 103; Bardic Runes 106; Blood & Aphorisms 114; Breakthrough! 118; Capilano Review, The 121; Carousel Literary Arts Magazine 122; Chalk Talk 122; Dal-

From the publishers of <u>Writer's</u> <u>Digest</u> and *<u>Writer's</u> <u>Market</u>*

Go One-On-One
With a Published Author

Are you serious about learning to write better? Getting published? Getting paid for what you write? If you're dedicated to your writing, **Writer's Digest School** can put you on the fast track to writing success.

You'll Study With A Professional

Writer's Digest School offers you more than textbooks and assignments. As a student you'll correspond <u>directly with a professional writer</u> who is currently writing **and selling** the kind of material you want to write. You'll learn from a pro who knows from personal experience what it takes to get a manuscript written and published. A writer who can guide you as you work to achieve the same thing. A true mentor.

Work On Your Novel, Short Story,
Nonfiction Book, Or Article

Writer's Digest School offers six courses: The Novel Writing Workshop, the Nonfiction Book Workshop, Writing to Sell Fiction (Short Stories), Writing to Sell Nonfiction (Articles), the Science Fiction and Fantasy Workshops and the Mystery Writing Workshops. Each course is described on the reverse side.

If you're serious about your writing, you owe it to yourself to check out **Writer's Digest School**. Mail the coupon below today for FREE information! Or call **1-800-759-0963**. (Outside the U.S., call (513) 531-2222.) Writer's Digest School, 1507 Dana Avenue, Cincinnati, Ohio 45207-1005.

Reg. #73-0409H

- -

Send Me Free Information!

I want to write and sell with the help of the professionals at **Writer's Digest School**. Send me free information about the course I've checked below:

☐ Novel Writing Workshop   ☐ Writing to Sell Fiction (Short Stories)
☐ Nonfiction Book Workshop   ☐ Writing to Sell Nonfiction (Articles)
☐ Science Fiction & Fantasy Workshops   ☐ Mystery Writing Workshops

Name _____

Address _____

City _____ State _____ Zip + 4 _____

Phone: (Home) (___) _____ (Bus.) (_____) _____

Mail this card today! No postage needed.
Or Call **1-800-759-0963** for free information today.

INSXXX3

There are six **Writer's Digest School** courses to help you write better and sell more:

Novel Writing Workshop. A professional novelist helps you iron out your plot, develop your main characters, write the background for your novel, and complete the opening scene and a summary of your novel's complete story. You'll even identify potential publishers and write a query letter.

Nonfiction Book Workshop. You'll work with your mentor to create a book proposal that you can send directly to a publisher. You'll develop and refine your book idea, write a chapter-by-chapter outline of your subject, line up your sources of information, write sample chapters, and complete your query letter.

Writing to Sell Fiction. Learn the basics of writing/selling short stories: plotting, characterization, dialogue, theme, conflict, and other elements of a marketable short story. Course includes writing assignments and one complete short story.

Writing to Sell Nonfiction. Master the fundamentals of writing/selling nonfiction articles: finding article ideas, conducting interviews, writing effective query letters and attention-getting leads, targeting your articles to the right publication, and other important elements of a salable article. Course includes writing assignments and one complete article manuscript (and its revision).

Science Fiction and Fantasy Workshops. Explore the exciting world of science fiction and fantasy with one of our professional science fiction writers as your guide. Besides improving your general writing skills, you'll learn the special techniques of creating worlds, science and magic, shaping time and place. And how to get published in this world. Choose Short Story or Novel Writing.

Mystery Writing Workshops. With the personal attention, experience and advice from a professional, published mystery writer, you'll uncover the secrets of writing suspenseful, involving mysteries. In addition to learning the genre's special techniques like how to drop red herrings, when and where to plant critical clues and what to keep hidden from your reader, you'll continue to improve your general writing skills that will lay a critical foundation for your story. Choose Short Story or Novel Writing.

Mail this card today for **FREE** information!

BUSINESS REPLY MAIL
FIRST CLASS MAIL   PERMIT NO. 17   CINCINNATI, OHIO

POSTAGE WILL BE PAID BY ADDRESSEE

Writer's Digest School
1507 DANA AVENUE
CINCINNATI OH 45207-9965

housie Review, The 137; Dance Connection 137; Dandelion Magazine 137; Descant (Ontario) 139; Dreams & Visions 141; Event 145; Fiddlehead, The 150; Fireweed 151; Grain 158; Green's Magazine 160; Herspectives 167; Kola 185; Legend 189; Lost 194; New Quarterly, The 215; NeWest Review 216; Peckerwood 233; Plowman, The 239; Pottersfield Portfolio, The 243; Prairie Fire 243; Prism International 244; Quarry 249; Queen's Quarterly 250; Shift Magazine 265; Sidetrekked 267; Sub-Terrain 281; This Magazine 286; Tickled By Thunder 287; Underpass 290; Whetstone 300; White Wall Review 301; Writ Magazine 307

Children's/Juvenile. Acorn, The 89; Advocate, The 90; Atalantik 102; Black Scholar, The 113; Brilliant Star 119; Chalk Talk 122; Chapter One 123; Cochran's Corner 128; Hob-Nob 169; Hopscotch: The Magazine for Girls 170; Hunted News, The 172; Lighthouse 190; Lines In The Sand 191; Mimsy Musing 203; Otterwise 226; Shattered Wig Review 264; Spoofing! 277; Ultimate Writer, The 290; Wisconsin Restaurateur, The 304; Writers' Open Forum 308; Young Voices Magazine 309

Condensed Novel. Ararat Quarterly 99; Art:Mag 101; Atalantik 102; Bahlasti Paper 105; Brownbag Press 119; Chaminade Literary Review 123; Chapter One 123; Diffusions 140; Fireweed 151; Forbidden Lines 153; G.W. Review, The 155; Gulf Coast 161; Hob-Nob 169; Hopewell Review, The 170; Hyperbole Studios 173; Immanent Face Magazine 174; Indian Youth of America Newsletter 174; Kennesaw Review 183; Kenyon Review, The 184; Lactuca 186; Language Bridges Quarterly 187; Libido 189; Limestone: A Literary Journal 190; Manoa 198; Moody Street Review, The 206; Nahant Bay 209; NCASA Journal 210; Night Owl's Newsletter 218; Perceptions (Montana) 235; Poetry Motel 240; Primal Voices 244; Psychotrain 246; Puck! 247; Renegade 255; River Styx 257; Ruby's Pearls 258; Shift Magazine 265; Short Fiction By Women 266; Snake Nation Review 271; Tamaqua 283; VeriTales 293; Vincent Brothers Review, The 296; Vintage Northwest 297; West 299; Witness 304; Wordsmith 306

Erotica. Aberations 88; Adrift 89; Alabama Literary Review 91; Alpha Beat Soup 93; Amelia 94; Anarchy 96; Anything That Moves 98; Arnazella 100; Art:Mag 101; Asylum Annual 101; Baby Sue 105; Bahlasti Paper 105; Bakunin 105; Barrelhouse, The 106; Belletrist Review, The 108; Brownbag Press 119; Changing Men 123; Chapter One 123; Clifton Magazine 127; Coe Review, The 129; Diffusions 140; Dream International/ Quarterly 140; Eidos 142; Erotic Fiction Quarterly 145; Fat Tuesday 148; Fireweed 151; Fish Drum Magazine 151; Fritz 154; Gay Chicago Magazine 156; Graffiti Off The Asylum Walls 158; Heart Attack Magazine 165; Hunted News, The 172; Hyperbole Studios 173; Hyphen Magazine 173; Kumquat Meringue 185; Lactuca 186; Libido 189; Long Shot 194; Magic Changes 197; Meshuggah 200; Nahant Bay 209; Noisy Concept 219; Oxalis 227; Palace Corbie 230; Paper Bag, The 231; Paper Radio 231; Perceptions (Ohio) 235; Poetic Space 239; Poetry Motel 240; Portable Lower East Side 241; Poskisnolt Press 241; Psychotrain 246; Puck! 247; Rag Mag 251; Riverwind 257; Salmon Magazine 259; Salt Lick Press 260; Sanskrit 261; Scream of the Buddha 261; Semiotext(e) 263; Shattered Wig Review 264; Shift Magazine 265; Sign of the Times 268; Slipstream 270; Snake Nation Review 271; Spit: A Journal of the Arts 276; SPSM&H 278; Starry Nights 279; Sub-Terrain 281; Urbanus/Raizirr 292; Wagons of Steel Magazine 298; West 299; Wicked Mystic 302; Words of Wisdom 305; Worm 306; Yellow Silk 309; Zero Hour 309

Ethnic/Multicultural. ACM, (Another Chicago Magazine) 89; Acorn, The 89; Adrift 89; Advocate, The 90; Agora 91; Aguilar Expression, The 91; Alabama Literary Review 91; Amelia 94; American Dane 95; Americas Review, The 96; Amherst Review, The 96; Anarchy 96; Antietam Review 98; Ararat Quarterly 99; Arnazella 100; Art:Mag 101; Atalantik 102; Aura Literary/Arts Review 104; Azorean Express, The 104; Bahlasti Paper 105; Bakunin 105; Bamboo Ridge 106; Barrelhouse, The 106; Bella Figura, La

107; Bilingual Review 110; Black Hammock Review, The 110; Black Jack 112; Black Scholar, The 113; Black Writer Magazine 113; Blood & Aphorisms 114; Blue Water Review, The 115; Bridge, The 118; Brownbag Press 119; Callaloo 120; Caribbean Writer, The 121; Carousel Literary Arts Magazine 122; Chaminade Literary Review 123; Chapter One 123; Chiricú 126; Cicada 127; Clifton Magazine 127; Coe Review, The 129; Collages and Bricolages 129; Concho River Review 131; Cottonwood 133; Crazyquilt 134; Cream City Review, The 134; Crucible 135; Diffusions 140; Dream International/Quarterly 140; ELF: Eclectic Literary Forum 144; Epoch Magazine 144; Feminist Studies 149; Fireweed 151; Fish Drum Magazine 151; Five Fingers Review 151; Footwork 153; Four Directions, The 153; Fritz 154; Fugue 154; Grasslands Review 159; Gulf Coast 161; Hawaii Pacific Review 165; Hawaii Review 165; Hayden's Ferry Review 165; Heartlands Today, The 166; Hill and Holler 168; Home Planet News 170; Hyphen Magazine 173; Iconoclast, The 174; Infinity Limited 175; Innisfree 175; ipsissima verba/the very words 177; Italian Americana 178; Japanophile 178; Jeopardy 178; Jewish Currents Magazine 179; Journal of Regional Criticism 180; Just A Moment 181; Kennesaw Review 183; Kenyon Review, The 184; Kestrel 184; Kola 185; Kumquat Meringue 185; Left Bank 188; Left Curve 189; Linden Lane Magazine 191; Little Magazine, The 192; Lizard's Eyelid Magazine 193; Long Shot 194; Long Story, The 194; MacGuffin, The 196; Mark 198; Maryland Review, The 198; Metropolitain 200; Middle Eastern Dancer 201; Midland 201; Milwaukee Undergraduate Review, The 202; Miorita, a Journal of Romanian Studies 204; Mobius 205; Moody Street Review, The 206; mOOn 207; Muse Portfolio 207; Nahant Bay 209; NCASA Journal 210; New Letters Magazine 214; New Press Literary Quarterly, The 214; Nimrod 218; North Dakota Quarterly 220; North East ARTS Magazine 221; Now & Then 222; Nuez, La 222; Onionhead 225; Owen Wister Review 227; Oxalis 227; Oxford Magazine 228; Painted Bride Quarterly 229; Painted Hills Review 229; Palace Corbie 230; Panhandler, The 231; Paper Bag, The 231; Pennsylvania Review 235; Phoebe (New York) 236; Plowman, The 239; Poetic Space 239; Poetry Forum Short Stories 239; Poetry Motel 240; Pointed Circle, The 240; Portable Lower East Side 241; Portable Wall, The 241; Poskisnolt Press 241; Potpourri 242; Primal Voices 244; Psychotrain 246; Puck! 247; Puerto Del Sol 248; Rafale 251; Rag Mag 251; Raven Chronicles, The 253; Reconstructionist 253; Response 256; River Styx 257; Riverwind 257; Rockford Review, The 258; Rohwedder 258; Ruby's Pearls 258; Salmon Magazine 259; Salt Lick Press 260; San Jose Studies 260; San Miguel Writer 260; Sanskrit 261; Seattle Review, The 262; Semiotext(e) 263; Shattered Wig Review 264; Shift Magazine 265; Short Fiction By Women 266; Side Show 267; Sing Heavenly Muse! 268; Skylark 269; Slipstream 270; Snake Nation Review 271; Sonoma Mandala 272; South Dakota Review 273; Southern California Anthology 273; Southern Exposure 274; Sozoryoku 275; Spindrift 276; Spit: A Journal of the Arts 276; Spoofing! 277; SPSM&H 278; Struggle 280; Studio One 281; TAL 283; Tamaqua 283; Tampa Review 283; This Magazine 286; Timberlines 287; Tributary 288; Tucumcari Literary Review 289; Ultimate Writer, The 290; Urbanus/Raizirr 292; Valley Grapevine 292; Valley Women's Voice 293; VeriTales 293; Viet Nam Generation 296; Vincent Brothers Review, The 296; Virginia Quarterly Review 297; West 299; Willow Review 303; Words of Wisdom 305; Wordsmith 306; Working Classics 306; Worm 306; Writers' Forum 307; Xavier Review 309; Zero Hour 309

Experimental. Aberations 88; ACM, (Another Chicago Magazine) 89; Adrift 89; Advocate, The 90; Aguilar Expression, The 91; Alabama Literary Review 91; Alaska Quarterly Review 92; Alpha Beat Soup 93; Amaranth Review, The 93; Ambergris 94; Amelia 94; Amherst Review, The 96; Anarchy 96; Antietam Review 98; Antioch Review 98; Archae 99; Arnazella 100; Artful Dodge 101; Art:Mag 101; Asylum Annual 101; Asymptotical World, The 102; Atalantik 102; Azorean Express, The 104; Baby Sue 105; Bad Haircut 105; Bahlasti Paper 105; Bakunin 105; Barrelhouse, The 106; Black Hammock Review, The 110; Black Ice 111; Black River Review 112; Blood & Aphorisms 114; Blue

Water Review, The 115; Bluff City 116; Blur 116; Bogg 116; Bottomfish Magazine 117; Boulevard 117; Brownbag Press 119; Calliope 121; Capilano Review, The 121; Carousel Literary Arts Magazine 122; Chaminade Literary Review 123; Changing Men 123; Chapter One 123; Chicago Review 125; Chiron Review 126; Chrysalis 126; Clockwatch Review 128; Collages and Bricolages 129; Collections 129; Compost Newsletter 131; Conjunctions 132; Corona 132; Cottonwood 133; Cream City Review, The 134; Crime Club 135; Crucible 135; Dagger of the Mind 136; Deathrealm 138; Denver Quarterly 138; Deuterium 139; Diffusions 140; Dream International/Quarterly 140; Dreams & Nightmares 141; eXpErImENtAL (bAsEemEnT) 146; Explorations '93 146; Eyes 147; Fat Tuesday 148; Feminist Baseball 149; Fiction 149; Fine Madness 151; Fireweed 151; Fish Drum Magazine 151; Five Fingers Review 151; Flipside 152; Florida Review, The 152; Footwork 153; Forbidden Lines 153; Fritz 154; Fugue 154; G.W. Review, The 155; Gaslight 155; Georgia Review, The 156; Gettysburg Review, The 156; Graffiti Off The Asylum Walls 158; Grain 158; Grand Street 159; Grasslands Review 159; Green Mountains Review 160; Greensboro Review 160; Gulf Coast 161; Gypsy 162; Habersham Review 162; Hawaii Pacific Review 165; Hawaii Review 165; Hayden's Ferry Review 165; Heaven Bone 166; Home Planet News 170; Hopewell Review, The 170; Housewife-Writer's Forum 171; Howling Dog 172; Hunted News, The 172; Hyperbole Studios 173; Hyphen Magazine 173; Immanent Face Magazine 174; Indiana Review 175; Infinity Limited 175; Interim 176; ipsissima verba/the very words 177; Iris 177; Jeopardy 178; Journal of Regional Criticism 180; Just A Moment 181; Kennesaw Review 183; Kenyon Review, The 184; Kestrel 184; Kumquat Meringue 185; Leading Edge, The 187; Left Curve 189; Limberlost Review, The 190; Limestone: A Literary Journal 190; Linden Lane Magazine 191; Lines In The Sand 191; Lite Magazine 192; Little Magazine, The 192; Lizard's Eyelid Magazine 193; Long Shot 194; Lost 194; Lost and Found Times 195; Lost Worlds 195; Louisville Review, The 196; Lynx 196; MacGuffin, The 196; Madison Review, The 197; Magic Realism 197; Merlyn's Pen 199; Mid-American Review 201; Midland 201; Milwaukee Undergraduate Review, The 202; Mind in Motion 203; Mindscapes 204; Minnesota Review, The 204; Mississippi Review 205; Mobius 205; Monocacy Valley Review, The 206; Monthly Independent Tribune Times, The 206; mOOn 207; Nahant Bay 209; NCASA Journal 210; New Delta Review 212; New Letters Magazine 214; New Press Literary Quarterly, The 214; new renaissance, the 215; New Virginia Review 216; Next Phase 216; Night Owl's Newsletter 218; Nimrod 218; No Idea Magazine 219; Nocturnal Lyric, The 219; Noisy Concept 219; North Dakota Quarterly 220; Northwest Review 221; Oak, The 223; Office Number One 223; Ohio Review, The 223; Old Hickory Review 224; Onionhead 225; Other Voices 225; Ouroboros 226; Owen Wister Review 227; Oxalis 227; Oxford Magazine 228; Painted Bride Quarterly 229; Painted Hills Review 229; Palace Corbie 230; Panhandler, The 231; Paper Bag, The 231; Paper Radio 231; Partisan Review 232; Pennsylvania Review 235; Perceptions (Montana) 235; Perceptions (Ohio) 235; Phoebe (New York) 236; Phoebe (Virginia) 236; Pinehurst Journal, The 238; Poetic Space 239; Poetry Forum Short Stories 239; Portable Wall, The 241; Porter International, Bern 241; Poskisnolt Press 241; Potpourri 242; Prairie Fire 243; Primal Voices 244; Psychotrain 246; Puck! 247; Puckerbrush Review 247; Puerto Del Sol 248; Pulsar 248; Quarry 249; Quarry West 249; Queen's Quarterly 250; Rag Mag 251; Re Arts & Letters 253; Renegade 255; Renovated Lighthouse Publications 255; Response 256; River Styx 257; Rockford Review, The 258; Rohwedder 258; Ruby's Pearls 258; Salad 259; Salmon Magazine 259; Salt Lick Press 260; San Miguel Writer 260; Sanskrit 261; Scream of the Buddha 261; Seattle Review, The 262; Semiotext(e) 263; Shattered Wig Review 264; Shift Magazine 265; Shockbox 265; Shooting Star Review 265; Short Fiction By Women 266; Sidewalks 267; Sign of the Times 268; Single Scene, The 269; Skylark 269; Slipstream 270; Snake Nation Review 271; Sonoma Mandala 272; South Dakota Review 273; Southern California Anthology 273; Sozoryoku 275; Spectrum (Massachusetts) 275; Spindrift 276; Spit: A Journal of the Arts 276; SPSM&H 278; Story 280; Struggle 280; Sub-Terrain 281; Sycamore Review

282; Tamaqua 283; Tampa Review 283; Temporary Culture 284; Theatre of the Night 284; Thema 285; Thin Ice 285; 13th Moon 286; This Magazine 286; Thrust 286; Tributary 288; Turnstile 289; 2 AM Magazine 290; Twopenny Porringer, The 290; Ultimate Writer, The 290; Underpass 291; Unsilenced Voice, The 292; Urbanus/Raizirr 292; Vandeloecht's Fiction Magazine 293; VeriTales 293; Verve 294; Videomania 294; Viet Nam Generation 296; Vincent Brothers Review, The 296; Wagons of Steel Magazine 298; West 299; Westview 300; Whetstone 300; Widener Review, The 302; Willow Review 303; Wisconsin Academy Review 303; Wisconsin Review 304; Witness 304; Wordsmith 306; Working Classics 306; Worm 306; Xavier Review 309; Yellow Silk 309; Zero Hour 309; Zoiks! 310; Zyzzyva 311

Fantasy. Aberations 88; Abyss Magazine 88; Advocate, The 90; Alabama Literary Review 91; Amateur Writers Journal 93; Amelia 94; Amherst Review, The 96; Ansuda Magazine 97; Argonaut 100; Arnazella 100; Art:Mag 101; Asymptotical World, The 102; Bahlasti Paper 105; Bardic Runes 106; Barrelhouse, The 106; Being 107; Beyond 110; Black Hammock Review, The 110; Blizzard Rambler, The 114; Bradley's Fantasy Magazine, Marion Zimmer 117; Bravo Mundo Nuevo 118; Carousel Literary Arts Magazine 122; Chapter One 123; Clifton Magazine 127; Coe Review, The 129; Collections 129; Companion in Zeor, A 130; Compost Newsletter 131; Corona 132; Crazyquilt 134; Crime Club 135; Dagger of the Mind 136; Deathrealm 138; Deuterium 139; Diffusions 140; Dream International/Quarterly 140; Dreams & Nightmares 141; Eldritch Science 143; ELF: Eclectic Literary Forum 144; Eyes 147; Feminist Baseball 149; Fighting Woman News 150; Figment Magazine 150; Fireweed 151; Fish Drum Magazine 151; Forbidden Lines 153; Fugue 154; Gaslight 155; Golden Isis Magazine 157; Gotta Write Network Litmag 158; Grasslands Review 159; Green Egg/How About Magic? 159; Green's Magazine 160; Haunts 164; Hawaii Pacific Review 165; Hayden's Ferry Review 165; Heart Attack Magazine 165; Heaven Bone 166; Hob-Nob 169; Hobson's Choice 169; HorTasy 171; Hyperbole Studios 173; Immanent Face Magazine 174; Infinity Limited 175; Innisfree 175; ipsissima verba/the very words 177; Jeopardy 178; Journal of Regional Criticism 180; Just A Moment 181; Kennesaw Review 183; Language Bridges Quarterly 187; Leading Edge, The 187; Legend 189; Lines In The Sand 191; Lite Magazine 192; Long Shot 194; Lost Worlds 195; MacGuffin, The 196; Magic Changes 197; Magic Realism 197; Merlyn's Pen 199; Meshuggah 200; Midnight Zoo 202; Milwaukee Undergraduate Review, The 202; Minas Tirith Evening-Star 203; Mind in Motion 203; Mississippi Review 205; Mobius 205; Mythic Circle, The 209; Nahant Bay 209; Nassau Review 210; New Laurel Review 213; New Press Literary Quarterly, The 214; New Voices in Poetry and Prose 216; Next Phase 216; Night Owl's Newsletter 218; No Idea Magazine 219; Nocturnal Lyric, The 219; Noisy Concept 219; Nuclear Fiction 222; Office Number One 223; Old Hickory Review 224; Once Upon A World 224; Ouroboros 226; Oxalis 227; Pablo Lennis 229; Palace Corbie 230; Pandora 230; Paper Bag, The 231; Paper Radio 231; Perceptions (Montana) 235; Pirate Writings 238; Pléiades Magazine/Philae 238; Poetic Space 239; Poetry Forum Short Stories 239; Poetry Motel 240; Poskisnolt Press 241; Potpourri 242; Primal Voices 244; Primavera 244; Processed World 245; Puck! 247; Pulphouse 248; Pulsar 248; Quanta 249; Quarry 249; Queen's Quarterly 250; Rag Mag 251; Random Realities 252; Redcat Magazine 254; Rejects 255; Renegade 255; Renovated Lighthouse Publications 255; Riverside Quarterly 257; Rockford Review, The 258; Salmon Magazine 259; Salome: A Journal for the Performing Arts 259; San Miguel Writer 260; Seattle Review, The 262; Semiotext(e) 263; Sensations Magazine 263; Short Story Digest, The 266; Sidetrekked 267; Single Scene, The 269; Skylark 269; Slate and Style 270; Snake Nation Review 271; Southern Humanities Review 274; Sozoryoku 275; Spit: A Journal of the Arts 276; SPSM&H 278; Square One 278; Tampa Review 283; Theatre of the Night 284; Thin Ice 285; This Magazine 286; Tickled By Thunder 287; Tomorrow 287; Tributary 288; Twisted 289; 2 AM Magazine 290; Ultimate Writer, The 290; Unreality 291; Vandeloecht's Fiction Magazine 293; VeriTales 293;

Verve 294; Videomania 294; Vintage Northwest 297; Wagons of Steel Magazine 298; Weirdbook 300; Whisper 301; Witness 304; Wordsmith 306; Writers' Open Forum 308; Yellow Silk 309

Feminist. ACM, (Another Chicago Magazine) 89; Adrift 89; Advocate, The 90; Alabama Literary Review 91; Amelia 94; American Voice, The 96; Americas Review, The 96; Amherst Review, The 96; Anarchy 96; Antietam Review 98; Arnazella 100; Art:Mag 101; Atlantis (Nova Scotia) 103; Aura Literary/Arts Review 104; Bahlasti Paper 105; Bakunin 105; Bella Figura, La 107; Blood & Aphorisms 114; Broomstick 119; Brownbag Press 119; Callaloo 120; Calyx 121; Carousel Literary Arts Magazine 122; Changing Men 123; Chapter One 123; Clifton Magazine 127; Coe Review, The 129; Collages and Bricolages 129; Communities: Journal of Cooperation 130; Compost Newsletter 131; Corona 132; Crucible 135; Daughters of Sarah 138; Diffusions 140; Earth's Daughters 142; ELF: Eclectic Literary Forum 144; Event 145; Farmer's Market, The 147; Feminist Studies 149; Fiction 149; Fighting Woman News 150; Five Fingers Review 151; Fritz 154; Graffiti Off The Asylum Walls 158; Gypsy 162; Hayden's Ferry Review 165; Heresies 167; Herspectives 167; Home Planet News 170; Hurricane Alice 172; Iowa Woman 177; ipsissima verba/the very words 177; Iris 177; Jeopardy 178; Kennesaw Review 183; Kenyon Review, The 184; Kestrel 184; Kumquat Meringue 185; Left Bank 188; Limestone: A Literary Journal 190; Little Magazine, The 192; Lizard's Eyelid Magazine 193; Long Shot 194; Long Story, The 194; Mati 199; Midland 201; Milwaukee Undergraduate Review, The 202; Minnesota Review, The 204; Mobius 205; mOOn 207; Muse Portfolio 207; Nahant Bay 209; NCASA Journal 210; Noisy Concept 219; North Dakota Quarterly 220; Northwest Review 221; Onionhead 225; Owen Wister Review 227; Oxalis 227; Oxford Magazine 228; Painted Bride Quarterly 229; Palace Corbie 230; Paper Bag, The 231; Pennsylvania Review 235; Perceptions (Montana) 235; Phoebe (New York) 236; Pinehurst Journal, The 238; Poetic Space 239; Poetry Forum Short Stories 239; Poetry Motel 240; Portable Wall, The 241; Poskisnolt Press 241; Primal Voices 244; Primavera 244; Psychotrain 246; Puck! 247; Rag Mag 251; Rainbow City Express 251; Re Arts & Letters 253; Red Cedar Review 253; Renegade 255; Response 256; River Styx 257; Riverwind 257; Rohwedder 258; Salmon Magazine 259; Salome: A Journal for the Performing Arts 259; Salt Lick Press 260; San Miguel Writer 260; Sanskrit 261; Seattle Review, The 262; Semiotext(e) 263; Shattered Wig Review 264; Shift Magazine 265; Short Fiction By Women 266; Side Show 267; Sing Heavenly Muse! 268; Sinister Wisdom 269; Skylark 269; Snake Nation Review 271; Sonoma Mandala 272; Southern California Anthology 273; Southern Exposure 274; Southern Humanities Review 274; Sozoryoku 275; Spit: A Journal of the Arts 276; SPSM&H 278; Struggle 280; Studio One 281; Tamaqua 283; 13th Moon 286; This Magazine 286; Urbanus/Raizirr 292; Valley Women's Voice 293; VeriTales 293; Videomania 294; Viet Nam Generation 296; Vincent Brothers Review, The 296; Virginia Quarterly Review 297; West 299; Willow Review 303; Wisconsin Restaurateur, The 304; Witness 304; Words of Wisdom 305; Working Classics 306; Yellow Silk 309; Zero Hour 309

Gay. ACM, (Another Chicago Magazine) 89; Adrift 89; Amelia 94; Amherst Review, The 96; Anarchy 96; Anything That Moves 98; Arnazella 100; Art:Mag 101; Bahlasti Paper 105; Bakunin 105; Brownbag Press 119; Carousel Literary Arts Magazine 122; Changing Men 123; Coe Review, The 129; Compost Newsletter 131; Corona 132; Crazyquilt 134; Crucible 135; Deuterium 139; Diffusions 140; Evergreen Chronicles, The 145; Fag Rag 147; Feminist Baseball 149; Feminist Studies 149; Fish Drum Magazine 151; Five Fingers Review 151; Fritz 154; Gay Chicago Magazine 156; Hayden's Ferry Review 165; Home Planet News 170; Hunted News, The 172; Hyphen Magazine 173; Kennesaw Review 183; Kenyon Review, The 184; Kumquat Meringue 185; Left Bank 188; Libido 189; Little Magazine, The 192; Long Shot 194; Milwaukee Undergraduate Review, The 202; Minnesota Review, The 204; mOOn 207; Nahant Bay 209; NCASA Journal 210; North East ARTS Magazine 221; Northwest Gay & Lesbian Reader, The 221; Onionhead 225; Owen Wister Review 227; Oxalis 227; Oxford Magazine 228; Painted Bride Quarterly 229; Palace Corbie 230; Pennsylvania Review 235; Perceptions (Ohio) 235; Phoebe (New York) 236; Pinehurst Journal, The 238; Poetic Space 239; Poetry Motel 240; Portable Lower East Side 241; Poskisnolt Press 241; Primal Voices 244; Primavera 244; Psychotrain 246; Puck! 247; Puckerbrush Review 247; RFD 256; River Styx 257; Salmon Magazine 259; Salt Lick Press 260; San Miguel Writer 260; Sanskrit 261; Seattle Review, The 262; Semiotext(e) 263; Sensations Magazine 263; Shattered Wig Review 264; Shift Magazine 265; Short Fiction By Women 266; Side Show 267; Sign of the Times 268; Snake Nation Review 271; Southern Exposure 274; Spit: A Journal of the Arts 276; SPSM&H 278; Tamaqua 283; This Magazine 286; Urbanus/Raizirr 292; Veri-Tales 293; Viet Nam Generation 296; West 299; White Review, The James 301; Working Classics 306; Worm 306; Yellow Silk 309; Zero Hour 309

Historical. Advocate, The 90; Agora 91; Alabama Literary Review 91; Amelia 94; Amherst Review, The 96; Appalachian Heritage 99; Ararat Quarterly 99; Archae 99; Arnazella 100; Art:Mag 101; Atalantik 102; Barrelhouse, The 106; Black Writer Magazine 113; Breakthrough! 118; Callaloo 120; Caribbean Writer, The 121; Chapter One 123; Chrysalis 126; Cochran's Corner 128; Concho River Review 131; Crazyquilt 134; Crime Club 135; Daughters of Sarah 138; Deuterium 139; Dream International/Quarterly 140; ELF: Eclectic Literary Forum 144; Fireweed 151; Fritz 154; Fugue 154; Gettysburg Review, The 156; Gotta Write Network Litmag 158; Hayden's Ferry Review 165; Home Planet News 170; Housewife-Writer's Forum 171; Hyperbole Studios 173; Hyphen Magazine 173; Indian Youth of America Newsletter 174; Infinity Limited 175; Iowa Woman 177; ipsissima verba/the very words 177; Journal of Regional Criticism 180; Just A Moment 181; Kenyon Review, The 184; Lamplight, The 186; Language Bridges Quarterly 187; Left Curve 189; Legend 189; Lighthouse 190; Linington Lineup 191; Lite Magazine 192; Llamas Magazine 193; MacGuffin, The 196; Merlyn's Pen 199; Midland 201; Milwaukee Undergraduate Review, The 202; Mind Matters Review 203; Minnesota Review, The 204; Miorita, a Journal of Romanian Studies 204; Mobius 205; Monocacy Valley Review, The 206; Mountain Laurel, The 207; Muse Portfolio 207; Nahant Bay 209; Nassau Review 210; New Voices in Poetry and Prose 216; Nomos 220; North Atlantic Review 220; North Dakota Quarterly 220; North East ARTS Magazine 221; Oak, The 223; Ouroboros 226; Oxalis 227; Painted Hills Review 229; Palace Corbie 230; Pinehurst Journal, The 238; Poetry Forum Short Stories 239; Portable Wall, The 241; Potpourri 242; Primal Voices 244; Prophetic Voices 246; Puck! 247; Queen's Quarterly 250; Re Arts & Letters 253; Renegade 255; Renovated Lighthouse Publications 255; Response 256; Riverwind 257; San Miguel Writer 260; Seattle Review, The 262; Sensations Magazine 263; Shift Magazine 265; Short Stuff Magazine for Grown-ups 266; Southern California Anthology 273; Sozoryoku 275; Spectrum (Massachusetts) 275; Spindrift 276; Spit: A Journal of the Arts 276; SPSM&H 278; Struggle 280; Sycamore Review 282; Tampa Review 283; Timberlines 287; Tucumcari Literary Review 289; Ultimate Writer, The 290; VeriTales 293; Villager, The 296; Vincent Brothers Review, The 296; Vintage Northwest 297; West 299; Westview 300; Willow Review 303; Wisconsin Academy Review 303; Words of Wisdom 305; Wordsmith 306; Working Classics 306; Worm 306; Writers' Open Forum 308; Xavier Review 309

Horror. Aberations 88; Abyss Magazine 88; Advocate, The 90; Aguilar Expression, The 91; Amherst Review, The 96; Ansuda Magazine 97; Art:Mag 101; Asymptotical World, The 102; Bahlasti Paper 105; Barrelhouse, The 106; Being 107; Belletrist Review, The 108; Bloodreams 114; Brownbag Press 119; Carousel Literary Arts Magazine 122; Chapter One 123; Clifton Magazine 127; Cochran's Corner 128; Collections 129; D.C. 136; Dagger of the Mind 136; Dark Tome 137; Deathrealm 138; Diffusions 140; Dream International/Quarterly 140; Dreams & Nightmares 141; Eldritch Tales 143; Eyes 147; Feminist Baseball 149; Forbidden Lines 153; Fugue 154; Gaslight 155; Graffiti Off The Asylum Walls 158; Grasslands Review 159; Grue Magazine 161; Haunts 164; Heart

Humor/Satire.

Prose 216; Night Owl's Newsletter 218; No Idea Magazine 219; Nocturnal Lyric, The 219; Noisy Concept 219; Nomos 220; North Dakota Quarterly 220; Oak, The 223; Office Number One 223; Onionhead 225; Oregon East 225; Other Voices 225; Ouroboros 226; Owen Wister Review 227; Oxalis 227; Oxford Magazine 228; P.I. Magazine 228; P.U.N. (Play on Words), The 228; Painted Hills Review 229; Panhandler, The 231; Pearl 233; Pegasus Review, The 234; Pennsylvania Review 235; Perceptions (Ohio) 235; Phoebe (New York) 236; Pinehurst Journal, The 238; Poetic Space 239; Poetry Magic Publications 240; Poetry Motel 240; Portable Wall, The 241; Poskisnolt Press 241; Potato Eyes 242; Potpourri 242; Primal Voices 244; Primavera 244; Processed World 245; Psychotrain 246; Puck! 247; Queen's Quarterly 250; Red Cedar Review 253; Renegade 255; Response 256; River Styx 257; Riverwind 257; Rockford Review, The 258; Ruby's Pearls 258; Salad 259; Salome: A Journal for the Performing Arts 259; San Gabriel Valley Magazine 260; San Jose Studies 260; San Miguel Writer 260; Sanskrit 261; Seattle Review, The 262; Secret Alameda, The 262; Sensations Magazine 263; Shattered Wig Review 264; Shift Magazine 265; Shockbox 265; Short Story Digest, The 266; Short Stuff Magazine for Grown-ups 266; Side Show 267; Sidewalks 267; Single Scene, The 269; Skylark 269; Slate and Style 270; Slipstream 270; Snake Nation Review 271; Sonoma Mandala 272; Snake River Reflections 271; Southern California Anthology 273; Southern Exposure 274; Southern Humanities Review 274; Spit: A Journal of the Arts 276; Spoofing! 277; SPSM&H 278; Story 280; Struggle 280; Studio One 281; Sub-Terrain 281; Sycamore Review 282; Tamaqua 283; Tampa Review 283; Thema 285; Thin Ice 285; Tickled By Thunder 287; Timberlines 287; Tributary 288; Tucumcari Literary Review 289; Turnstile 289; 2 AM Magazine 290; Ultimate Writer, The 290; Unsilenced Voice, The 292; Urbanus/Raizirr 292; Vandeloecht's Fiction Magazine 293; VeriTales 293; Verve 294; Videomania 294; Villager, The 296; Vincent Brothers Review, The 296; Vintage Northwest 297; Virginia Quarterly Review 297; Wagons of Steel Magazine 298; West 299; Whisper 301; Willow Review 303; Wisconsin Academy Review 303; Wisconsin Restaurateur, The 304; Words of Wisdom 305; Wordsmith 306; Working Classics 306; Writers' Open Forum 308; Yellow Silk 309; Zero Hour 309; Zoiks! 310

Lesbian. ACM, (Another Chicago Magazine) 89; Adrift 89; Amelia 94; Amherst Review, The 96; Anything That Moves 98; Arnazella 100; Art:Mag 101; Bahlasti Paper 105; Bakunin 105; Bella Figura, La 107; Brownbag Press 119; Carousel Literary Arts Magazine 122; Changing Men 123; Coe Review, The 129; Compost Newsletter 131; Corona 132; Crucible 135; Diffusions 140; Evergreen Chronicles, The 145; Feminist Baseball 149; Feminist Studies 149; Fireweed 151; Fish Drum Magazine 151; Five Fingers Review 151; Fritz 154; Gay Chicago Magazine 156; Heresies 167; Herspectives 167; Home Planet News 170; Hunted News, The 172; Hurricane Alice 172; Hyphen Magazine 173; Iris 177; Kenyon Review, The 184; Kumquat Meringue 185; Left Bank 188; Libido 189; Little Magazine, The 192; Long Shot 194; Milwaukee Undergraduate Review, The 202; Minnesota Review, The 204; Mobius 205; mOOn 207; Nahant Bay 209; Northwest Gay & Lesbian Reader, The 221; Onionhead 225; Owen Wister Review 227; Oxalis 227; Oxford Magazine 228; Painted Bride Quarterly 229; Palace Corbie 230; Pennsylvania Review 235; Perceptions (Ohio) 235; Phoebe (New York) 236; Pinehurst Journal, The 238; Poetic Space 239; Poetry Motel 240; Portable Lower East Side 241; Poskisnolt Press 241; Primavera 244; Psychotrain 246; Puck! 247; River Styx 257; Salmon Magazine 259; Salt Lick Press 260; San Miguel Writer 260; Sanskrit 261; Seattle Review, The 262; Sensations Magazine 263; Shattered Wig Review 264; Shift Magazine 265; Short Fiction By Women 266; Side Show 267; Sign of the Times 268; Sinister Wisdom 269; Snake Nation Review 271; Sonoma Mandala 272; Southern Exposure 274; Spit: A Journal of the Arts 276; SPSM&H 278; 13th Moon 286; This Magazine 286; Urbanus/Raizirr 292; Valley Women's Voice 293; VeriTales 293; Videomania 294; Viet Nam Generation 296; West 299; Working Classics 306; Worm 306; Yellow Silk 309

Literary. Adrift 89; Advocate, The 90; Agora 91; Alabama Literary Review 91; Alaska

Nahant Bay 209; Nassau Review 210; NCASA Journal 210; Nebo 210; Nebraska Review, The 211; New Delta Review 212; New England Review 213; New Laurel Review 213; New Letters Magazine 214; New Mexico Humanities Review 214; New Orleans Review 214; New Press Literary Quarterly, The 214; New Quarterly, The 215; new renaissance, the 215; New Virginia Review 216; New Voices in Poetry and Prose 216; Night Owl's Newsletter 218; Noisy Concept 219; North American Review, The 220; North Dakota Quarterly 220; North East ARTS Magazine 221; Northwest Review 221; Now & Then 222; Nuez, La 223; Office Number One 223; Ohio Review, The 223; Old Hickory Review 224; Old Red Kimono, The 224; Onionhead 225; Oregon East 225; Other Voices 225; Ouroboros 226; Outerbridge 226; Owen Wister Review 227; Oxalis 227; Oxford Magazine 228; Painted Bride Quarterly 229; Painted Hills Review 229; Palace Corbie 230; Panhandler, The 231; Paper Bag, The 231; Paper Radio 231; Paris Review, The 232; Partisan Review 232; Pearl 233; Peckerwood 234; Pegasus Review, The 234; Pennsylvania English 234; Phoebe (New York) 236; Phoebe (Virginia) 236; Pikestaff Forum, The 237; Pinehurst Journal, The 238; Pirate Writings 238; Pléiades Magazine/Philae 238; Ploughshares 238; Poetic Space 239; Poetry Forum Short Stories 239; Poetry Motel 240; Pointed Circle, The 240; Portable Lower East Side 241; Portable Wall, The 241; Porter International, Bern 241; Poskisnolt Press 241; Potato Eyes 242; Potpourri 242; Primal Voices 244; Primavera 244; Prism International 245; Processed World 245; Psychotrain 246; Puck! 247; Puckerbrush Review 247; Puerto Del Sol 248; Quarry 249; Quarterly West 250; Queen's Quarterly 250; Radio Void 250; Rag Mag 251; Rainbow City Express 251; Raven Chronicles, The 253; Red Cedar Review 253; Renegade 255; Renovated Lighthouse Publications 255; Response 256; Review, Latin American Literature and Arts 256; River Styx 257; Riverwind 257; Rockford Review, The 258; Rohwedder 258; Salad 259; Salmon Magazine 259; Salome: A Journal for the Performing Arts 259; Salt Lick Press 260; San Jose Studies 260; San Miguel Writer 260; Sanskrit 261; Santa Monica Review 261; Scream of the Buddha 261; Secret Alameda, The 262; Seems 263; Semiotext(e) 263; Sensations Magazine 263; Sewanee Review, The 264; Shattered Wig Review 264; Shift Magazine 265; Shockbox 265; Shooting Star Review 265; Short Fiction By Women 266; Side Show 267; Sidewalks 267; Signal, The 268; Silverfish Review 268; Sing Heavenly Muse! 268; Skylark 269; Slipstream 270; Snake Nation Review 271; Snake River Reflections 271; Sonoma Mandala 272; Sonora Review 272; South Dakota Review 273; Southern Exposure 274; Southern Review, The 274; Southwest Review 275; Sozoryoku 275; Spirit That Moves Us, The 276; Spit: A Journal of the Arts 276; SPSM&H 278; Story 280; Stroker Magazine 280; Struggle 280; Studio One 281; Sub-Terrain 281; Sycamore Review 282; Tamaqua 283; Tampa Review 283; Texas Review, The 284; Thema 285; 13th Moon 286; This Magazine 286; Threepenny Review, The 286; Tickled By Thunder 287; Timberlines 287; Triquarterly 288; Tucumcari Literary Review 289; Turnstile 289; Twopenny Porringer, The 290; Underpass 291; Unmuzzled Ox 291; Valley Grapevine 292; Vandeloecht's Fiction Magazine 293; VeriTales 293; Verve 294; Viet Nam Generation 296; Villager, The 296; Vincent Brothers Review, The 296; Virginia Quarterly Review 297; Washington Review 298; Webster Review 298; West 299; West Branch 299; Westview 300; Widener Review, The 302; Willow Review 303; Willow Springs 303; Wisconsin Academy Review 303; Wisconsin Restaurateur, The 304; Wisconsin Review 304; Witness 304; Worcester Review, The 305; Wordsmith 306; Working Classics 306; Worm 306; Writ Magazine 307; Writers' Forum 307; Xavier Review 309; Yellow Silk 309; Zyzzyva 311

Mainstream/Contemporary. ACM, (Another Chicago Magazine) 89; Acorn, The 89; Adrift 89; Advocate, The 90; Aguilar Expression, The 91; Alabama Literary Review 91; Amaranth Review, The 93; Amateur Writers Journal 93; Amelia 94; American Literary Review 95; Americas Review, The 96; Amherst Review, The 96; Antaeus 97; Antietam Review 98; Antigonish Review, The 98; Antioch Review 98; Ararat Quarterly 99; Archae 99; Arnazella 100; Art:Mag 101; Asylum Annual 101; Atalantik 102; Atlan-

view, The 264; Shift Magazine 265; Shooting Star Review 265; Short Fiction By Women 266; Short Story Digest, The 266; Short Stuff Magazine for Grown-ups 266; Side Show 267; Sidewalks 267; Single Scene, The 269; Skylark 269; Slate and Style 270; Slipstream 270; Snake Nation Review 271; Sonoma Mandala 272; Soundings East 272; South Dakota Review 273; Southern California Anthology 273; Southern Exposure 274; Southern Review, The 274; Sozoryoku 275; Spectrum 275; Spindrift 276; Spirit That Moves Us, The 276; Spit: A Journal of the Arts 276; SPSM&H 278; Square One 278; Story 280; Stroker Magazine 280; Studio One 281; Sycamore Review 282; Tampa Review 283; Texas Review, The 284; Thema 285; This Magazine 286; Tickled By Thunder 287; Timberlines 287; Triquarterly 288; Tucumcari Literary Review 289; Turnstile 289; Ultimate Writer, The 290; Underpass 291; University of Portland Review 291; Unmuzzled Ox 291; Vandeloecht's Fiction Magazine 293; VeriTales 293; Verve 294; Videomania 294; Vincent Brothers Review, The 296; Webster Review 298; West 299; Westview 300; Whetstone 300; Whisper 301; Widener Review, The 302; Willow Review 303; Wisconsin Academy Review 303; Wisconsin Restaurateur, The 304; Witness 304; Words of Wisdom 305; Wordsmith 306; Worm 306; Writers' Forum 307; Writers' Open Forum 308; Xavier Review 309

Mystery/Suspense. Acorn, The 89; Advocate, The 90; Aguilar Expression, The 91; Alabama Literary Review 91; Amateur Writers Journal 93; Amelia 94; Amherst Review, The 96; Ansuda Magazine 97; Arnazella 100; Art:Mag 101; Atalantik 102; Atlantean Press Review, The 103; Barrelhouse, The 106; Belletrist Review, The 108; Blizzard Rambler, The 114; Blue Water Review, The 115; Breakthrough! 118; Carousel Literary Arts Magazine 122; Chapter One 123; Chrysalis 126; Cochran's Corner 128; Crazyquilt 134; Crime Club 135; Dagger of the Mind 136; Deuterium 139; Diffusions 140; Eagle's Flight 141; ELF: Eclectic Literary Forum 144; Fighting Woman News 150; Fugue 154; Gaslight 155; Gotta Write Network Litmag 158; Grasslands Review 159; Green's Magazine 160; Gulf Stream Magazine 161; Hardboiled 164; Hawaii Pacific Review 165; Heart Attack Magazine 165; Hob-Nob 169; Housewife-Writer's Forum 171; Hyperbole Studios 173; Infinity Limited 175; Innisfree 175; ipsissima verba/the very words 177; Just A Moment 181; Lamplight, The 186; Lighthouse 190; Lines In The Sand 191; Linington Lineup 191; Lite Magazine 192; Long Shot 194; Merlyn's Pen 199; Milwaukee Undergraduate Review, The 202; Monthly Independent Tribune Times, The 206; Muse Portfolio 207; Mystery Notebook 208; Mystery Street 208; Mystery Time 209; Nahant Bay 209; New Voices in Poetry and Prose 216; No Idea Magazine 219; Noisy Concept 219; Nomos 220; North East ARTS Magazine 221; Oak, The 223; Ouroboros 226; Oxalis 227; P.I. Magazine 228; Paper Bag, The 231; Perceptions (Montana) 235; Pinehurst Journal, The 238; Pirate Writings 238; Pléiades Magazine/Philae 238; Poetry Forum Short Stories 239; Post, The 242; Potpourri 242; PSI 246; Renegade 255; Ruby's Pearls 258; Salmon Magazine 259; Salome: A Journal for the Performing Arts 259; San Miguel Writer 260; Seattle Review, The 262; Sensations Magazine 263; Short Story Digest, The 266; Short Stuff Magazine for Grown-ups 266; Single Scene, The 269; Skylark 269; Snake Nation Review 271; Snake River Reflections 271; Sozoryoku 275; Spit: A Journal of the Arts 276; Spoofing! 277; SPSM&H 278; Square One 278; Struggle 280; Thema 285; Tickled By Thunder 287; Tucumcari Literary Review 289; 2 AM Magazine 290; Ultimate Writer, The 290; Unsilenced Voice, The 292; Vandeloecht's Fiction Magazine 293; VeriTales 293; Villager, The 296; Vincent Brothers Review, The 296; Vintage Northwest 297; Wisconsin Restaurateur, The 304; Words of Wisdom 305; Wordsmith 306; Writers' Open Forum 308

New Age/Mystic/Spiritual. Being 107; New Frontier 213; Rainbow City Express 251; Renovated Lighthouse Publications 255

Psychic/Supernatural/Occult. Abyss Magazine 88; Amherst Review, The 96; Ansuda Magazine 97; Art:Mag 101; Asymptotical World, The 102; Atalantik 102; Bahlasti

Paper 105; Barrelhouse, The 106; Being 107; Black Hammock Review, The 110; Bloo-dreams 114; Brownbag Press 119; Chapter One 123; Coe Review, The 129; Compost Newsletter 131; Corona 132; Crime Club 135; D.C. 136; Dark Tome 137; Deathrealm 138; Diffusions 140; Dream International/Quarterly 140; Eldritch Tales 143; Fat Tuesday 148; Forbidden Lines 153; Golden Isis Magazine 157; Graffiti Off The Asylum Walls 158; Green Egg/How About Magic? 159; Grue Magazine 161; Haunts 164; Hayden's Ferry Review 165; Heart Attack Magazine 165; Heaven Bone 166; Hob-Nob 169; Hyphen Magazine 173; Infinity Limited 175; ipsissima verba/the very words 177; Journal of Regional Criticism 180; Just A Moment 181; Kennesaw Review 183; Lite Magazine 192; Lizard's Eyelid Magazine 193; Long Shot 194; Lost 194; Lost Worlds 195; MacGuffin, The 196; Meshuggah 200; Midnight Zoo 202; Milwaukee Undergraduate Review, The 202; Monthly Independent Tribune Times, The 206; mOOn 207; Nahant Bay 209; New Voices in Poetry and Prose 216; Nocturnal Lyric, The 219; Noisy Concept 219; Office Number One 223; Ouroboros 226; Pablo Lennis 229; Palace Corbie 230; Perceptions (Montana) 235; Perceptions (Ohio) 235; Poskisnolt Press 241; Psychotrain 246; Puck! 247; Quanta 249; Random Realities 252; Rejects 255; Renegade 255; San Gabriel Valley Magazine 260; San Miguel Writer 260; Scream of the Buddha 261; Seattle Review, The 262; Semiotext(e) 263; Shattered Wig Review 264; Short Story Digest, The 266; Snake Nation Review 271; Sozoryoku 275; Spit: A Journal of the Arts 276; Thema 285; Thin Ice 285; Tickled By Thunder 287; Twisted 289; 2 AM Magazine 290; Unreality 291; Unsilenced Voice, The 292; Vandeloecht's Fiction Magazine 293; VeriTales 293; Wagons of Steel Magazine 298; Weirdbook 299; Wicked Mystic 302; Wordsmith 306; Writers' Open Forum 308; Zero Hour 309; Zoiks! 310

Regional. Acorn, The 89; Advocate, The 90; Agora 91; Alabama Literary Review 91; Amherst Review, The 96; Appalachian Heritage 99; Arnazella 100; Artemis 100; Art:-Mag 101; Aura Literary/Arts Review 104; Belletrist Review, The 108; Black Hammock Review, The 110; Blue Water Review, The 115; Blueline 115; Breakthrough! 118; Bridge, The 118; Callaloo 120; Chapter One 123; Cicada 127; Clifton Magazine 127; Clockwatch Review 128; Coe Review, The 129; Concho River Review 131; Confrontation 132; Cornfield Review 132; Corona 132; Cottonwood 133; Cream City Review, The 134; Crime Club 135; Crucible 135; Descant (Texas) 139; Diffusions 140; Door County Almanak 140; ELF: Eclectic Literary Forum 144; Event 145; Farmer's Market, The 147; Fish Drum Magazine 151; Five Fingers Review 151; Fugue 154; Gettysburg Review, The 156; Grasslands Review 159; Gulf Coast 161; Gulf Stream Magazine 161; Habersham Review 162; Hawaii Pacific Review 165; Hawaii Review 165; Hayden's Ferry Review 165; Heartlands Today, The 166; Heaven Bone 166; High Plains Literary Review 168; Hill and Holler 168; Hob-Nob 169; Hopewell Review, The 170; Hyphen Magazine 173; Infinity Limited 175; Innisfree 175; Iowa Woman 177; ipsissima verba/the very words 177; Japanophile 178; Jeopardy 178; Journal of Regional Criticism 180; Just A Moment 181; Kennesaw Review 183; Kestrel 184; Kumquat Meringue 185; Lactuca 186; Left Bank 188; Left Curve 189; Lighthouse 190; Loonfeather 194; Louisiana Literature 195; Manoa 198; Mark 198; Merlyn's Pen 199; Metropolitain 200; Middle Eastern Dancer 201; Midland 201; Milwaukee Undergraduate Review, The 202; Miorita, a Journal of Romanian Studies 204; Monocacy Valley Review, The 206; Moody Street Review, The 206; Mountain Laurel, The 207; Muse Portfolio 207; Nahant Bay 209; NCASA Journal 210; New Mexico Humanities Review 214; New Voices in Poetry and Prose 216; NeWest Review 216; Now & Then 222; Oak, The 223; Onionhead 225; Oregon East 225; Oxalis 227; Painted Hills Review 229; Partisan Review 232; Peckerwood 234; Pennsylvania Review 235; Phoebe (Virginia) 236; Poetic Space 239; Pointed Circle, The 240; Portable Lower East Side 241; Portable Wall, The 241; Potato Eyes 242; Primal Voices 244; Puck! 247; Rag Mag 251; Raven Chronicles, The 253; Re Arts & Letters 253; Red Cedar Review 253; Renovated Lighthouse Publications 255; Response 256; Riverwind 257; Rockford Review, The 258; Rohwedder 258; Salad 259; Salmon Magazine 259;

San Jose Studies 260; San Miguel Writer 260; Sanskrit 261; Seattle Review, The 262; Sensations Magazine 263; Shattered Wig Review 264; Shift Magazine 265; Shooting Star Review 265; Short Stuff Magazine for Grown-ups 266; Sidewalks 267; Skylark 269; Snake Nation Review 271; Snake River Reflections 271; Sonoma Mandala 272; South Dakota Review 273; Southern California Anthology 273; Southern Exposure 274; Southern Humanities Review 274; Sozoryoku 275; Spindrift 276; Spit: A Journal of the Arts 276; Spoofing! 277; SPSM&H 278; Struggle 280; Studio One 281; Sycamore Review 282; Tamaqua 283; Thema 285; This Magazine 286; Timberlines 287; Tucumcari Literary Review 289; Turnstile 289; Vandeloecht's Fiction Magazine 293; VeriTales 293; Vincent Brothers Review, The 296; Washington Review 298; West 299; Widener Review, The 302; Willow Review 303; Wisconsin Academy Review 303; Wisconsin Restaurateur, The 304; Words of Wisdom 305; Working Classics 306; Writers' Forum 307; Writers' Open Forum 308; Xavier Review 308; Zyzzyva 311

Religious/Inspirational. Acorn, The 89; Agora 91; Amateur Writers Journal 93; Ararat Quarterly 99; Arnazella 100; Being 107; Beloit Fiction Journal 108; Black Writer Magazine 113; Breakthrough! 118; Carousel Literary Arts Magazine 122; Chaminade Literary Review 123; Chapter One 123; Cochran's Corner 128; Crime Club 135; Daughters of Sarah 138; Diffusions 140; Dreams & Visions 141; Explorer Magazine 147; Heaven Bone 166; Hob-Nob 169; Journal of Regional Criticism 180; Language Bridges Quarterly 187; Living Water Magazine 193; Milwaukee Undergraduate Review, The 202; New Anglican Review 211; New Catholic Review 212; New Press Literary Quarterly, The 214; New Voices in Poetry and Prose 216; Now & Then 222; Pablo Lennis 229; Painted Hills Review 229; Palace Corbie 230; Pegasus Review, The 234; Perceptions (Montana) 235; Poetry Forum Short Stories 239; Puck! 247; Queen of All Hearts 250; Rainbow City Express 251; Reconstructionist 253; Renegade 255; Response 256; Riverwind 257; Skylark 269; Starlight 279; TAL 283; Tickled By Thunder 287; Ultimate Writer, The 290; Valley Women's Voice 293; VeriTales 293; Vintage Northwest 297; Wordsmith 306; Xavier Review 309

Romance. Acorn, The 89; Advocate, The 90; Aguilar Expression, The 91; Amateur Writers Journal 93; Amherst Review, The 96; Atalantik 102; Aura Literary/Arts Review 104; Black Hammock Review, The 110; Breakthrough! 118; Carousel Literary Arts Magazine 122; Chapter One 123; Cochran's Corner 128; Corona 132; Deuterium 139; Diffusions 140; Dream International/Quarterly 140; Eagle's Flight 141; Explorer Magazine 147; Fugue 154; Gay Chicago Magazine 156; Gotta Write Network Litmag 158; Hayden's Ferry Review 165; Heart Attack Magazine 165; Hob-Nob 169; Housewife-Writer's Forum 171; Infinity Limited 175; ipsissima verba/the very words 177; Jeopardy 178; Journal of Regional Criticism 180; Just A Moment 181; Lamplight, The 186; Lighthouse 190; Merlyn's Pen 199; Milwaukee Undergraduate Review, The 202; Muse Portfolio 207; New Voices in Poetry and Prose 216; Oak, The 223; Oxalis 227; Peoplenet 235; Poetry Forum Short Stories 239; Poskisnolt Press 241; Post, The 242; Potpourri 242; PSI 246; Renegade 255; Salome: A Journal for the Performing Arts 259; San Miguel Writer 260; Sensations Magazine 263; Short Stuff Magazine for Grown-ups 266; Skylark 269; SPSM&H 278; 2 AM Magazine 290; Ultimate Writer, The 290; Vandeloecht's Fiction Magazine 293; VeriTales 293; Villager, The 296; Virginia Quarterly Review 297; Wordsmith 306; Writers' Open Forum 308

Science Fiction. Aberations 88; Abyss Magazine 88; Acorn, The 89; Advocate, The 90; Agora 91; Alabama Literary Review 91; Amaranth Review, The 93; Amateur Writers Journal 93; Amelia 94; Amherst Review, The 96; Anarchy 96; Argonaut 100; Arnazella 100; Art:Mag 101; Atalantik 102; Atavachron and All Our Yesterdays 102; Atlantean Press Review, The 103; Aura Literary/Arts Review 104; Bahlasti Paper 105; Barrelhouse, The 106; Belletrist Review, The 108; Beyond 110; Black Hammock Review, The 110; Blizzard Rambler, The 114; Blue Water Review, The 115; Bravo Mundo Nuevo

118; Callaloo 120; Carousel Literary Arts Magazine 122; Chapter One 123; Chrysalis 126; Clifton Magazine 127; Cochran's Corner 128; Coe Review, The 129; Collections 129; Communities: Journal of Cooperation 130; Companion in Zeor, A 130; Compost Newsletter 131; Cosmic Landscapes 133; Cottonwood 133; Crazyquilt 134; Crime Club 135; Dagger of the Mind 136; Deathrealm 138; Deuterium 139; Diffusions 140; Dream International/Quarterly 140; Dreams & Nightmares 141; Eldritch Science 143; ELF: Eclectic Literary Forum 144; Explorer Magazine 147; Feminist Baseball 149; Fighting Woman News 150; Figment Magazine 150; Fish Drum Magazine 151; Forbidden Lines 153; Fugue 154; Gaslight 155; Gotta Write Network Litmag 158; Grasslands Review 159; Green's Magazine 160; Hawaii Pacific Review 165; Hayden's Ferry Review 165; Heart Attack Magazine 165; Hob-Nob 169; Hobson's Choice 169; Home Planet News 170; Hyperbole Studios 173; Hyphen Magazine 173; Iconoclast, The 174 Immanent Face Magazine 174; Infinity Limited 175; Innisfree 175; ipsissima verba/the very words 177; Jeopardy 178; Journal of Regional Criticism 180; Just A Moment 181; Leading Edge, The 187; Left Curve 189; Lines In The Sand 191; Lite Magazine 192; Long Shot 194; Lost Worlds 195; MacGuffin, The 196; Magic Changes 197; Mark 198; Mati 199; Merlyn's Pen 199; Meshuggah 200; Midnight Zoo 202; Milwaukee Undergraduate Review, The 202; Mind in Motion 203; Minnesota Review, The 204; Mobius 205; Nahant Bay 209; Neophyte 211; New Voices in Poetry and Prose 216; Nimrod 218; No Idea Magazine 219; Nocturnal Lyric, The 219; Noisy Concept 219; Nomos 220; Nuclear Fiction 222; Once Upon A World 224; Other Worlds 226; Ouroboros 226; Oxalis 227; Pablo Lennis 229; Palace Corbie 230; Pandora 230; Paper Radio 231; Perceptions (Montana) 235; Perceptions (Ohio) 235; Pirate Writings 238; Poetry Forum Short Stories 239; Poetry Motel 240; Portable Wall, The 241; Potpourri 242; Primavera 244; Processed World 245; Puck! 247; Pulphouse 248; Pulsar 248; Quanta 249; Queen's Quarterly 250; Random Realities 252; Re Arts & Letters 253; Rejects 255; Renegade 255; Renovated Lighthouse Publications 255; Riverside Quarterly 257; Salmon Magazine 259; Salome: A Journal for the Performing Arts 259; San Miguel Writer 260; Sanskrit 261; Scream of the Buddha 261; Seattle Review, The 262; Semiotext(e) 263; Sensations Magazine 263; Short Story Digest, The 266; Sidetrekked 267; Skylark 269; Snake Nation Review 271; Spindrift 276; Spit: A Journal of the Arts 276; SPSM&H 278; Square One 278; Struggle 280; Temporary Culture 284; Thema 285; 13th Moon 286; Tickled By Thunder 287; Tomorrow 287; Tributary 288; 2 AM Magazine 290; Twopenny Porringer, The 290; Ultimate Writer, The 290; Urbanus/Raizirr 292; Vandeloecht's Fiction Magazine 293; VeriTales 293; Videomania 294; Vincent Brothers Review, The 296; Vision 297; Whisper 301; Wisconsin Restaurateur, The 304; Wordsmith 306; Worm 306; Writers' Open Forum 308

Senior Citizen/Retirement. Advocate, The 90; Amelia 94; Chapter One 123; Corona 132; Diffusions 140; Hayden's Ferry Review 165; Hob-Nob 169; ipsissima verba/the very words 177; Just A Moment 181; Lighthouse 190; Lines In The Sand 191; Muse Portfolio 207; Oxalis 227; Pléiades Magazine/Philae 238; Poetry Forum Short Stories 239; Portable Wall, The 241; Poskisnolt Press 241; Primal Voices 244; Salmon Magazine 259; San Miguel Writer 260; Shattered Wig Review 264; Snake Nation Review 271; Spit: A Journal of the Arts 276; SPSM&H 278; Struggle 280; Timberlines 287; Tucumcari Literary Review 289; VeriTales 293; Vincent Brothers Review, The 296; Vintage Northwest 297; Wordsmith 306; Writers' Open Forum 308

Serialized/Excerpted Novel. Agni 90; Alabama Literary Review 91; Antaeus 97; Art:Mag 101; Bahlasti Paper 105; Bakunin 105; Bellowing Ark 108; Black Hammock Review, The 110; Black Jack 112; Callaloo 120; Coe Review, The 129; Compost Newsletter 131; Crazyquilt 134; Crime Club 135; Diffusions 140; Farmer's Market, The 147; Fat Tuesday 148; Forbidden Lines 153; Gettysburg Review, The 156; Green Mountains Review 160; Gypsy 162; Hob-Nob 169; Hunted News, The 172; Hyperbole Studios 173; Hyphen Magazine 173; Immanent Face Magazine 174; ipsissima verba/the very words

177; Lost Worlds 195; Madison Review, The 197; Mid-American Review 201; Mystery Notebook 208; Nassau Review 210; NCASA Journal 210; New Press Literary Quarterly, The 214; New Virginia Review 216; Now & Then 222; Other Voices 225; Painted Hills Review 229; Phoebe (Virginia) 236; Pikestaff Forum, The 237; Pléiades Magazine/Philae 238; Poetic Space 239; Puerto Del Sol 248; Quanta 249; Quarry 249; Salmon Magazine 259; Salome: A Journal for the Performing Arts 259; San Miguel Writer 260; Seattle Review, The 262; Shattered Wig Review 264; Shift Magazine 265; Skylark 269; South Dakota Review 272; Southern California Anthology 273; Spindrift 276; Spit: A Journal of the Arts 276; Vincent Brothers Review, The 296; Virginia Quarterly Review 297; Widener Review, The 302; Willow Springs 303; Witness (Michigan) 304; Wordsmith 306; Writ Magazine 307; Xavier Review 308

Short Story Collections. Ararat Quarterly 99; Aura Literary/Arts Review 104; Daughters of Sarah 138; New Laurel Review 213; North Dakota Quarterly 220; Nuclear Fiction 222; Painted Bride Quarterly 229; Valley Women's Voice 293

Sports. Advocate, The 90; Aethlon 90; Amelia 94; Atlantean Press Review, The 103; Beloit Fiction Journal 108; Blue Water Review, The 115; Carousel Literary Arts Magazine 122; Changing Men 123; Chapter One 123; Chrysalis 126; Diffusions 140; ELF: Eclectic Literary Forum 144; Fugue 154; Hob-Nob 169; Iconoclast, The 174 ipsissima verba/the very words 177; Just A Moment 181; Lighthouse 190; Magic Changes 197; Milwaukee Undergraduate Review, The 202; New Press Literary Quarterly, The 214; Now & Then 222; Oxalis 227; Portable Wall, The 241; Primal Voices 244; Riverwind 257; Skylark 269; Spit: A Journal of the Arts 276; Spitball 277; Sycamore Review 282; Thema 285; Valley Women's Voice 293; Vandeloecht's Fiction Magazine 293; VeriTales 293; Witness 304; Wordsmith 306; Writers' Open Forum 308

Thriller/Espionage. ACM, (Another Chicago Magazine) 89; Adrift 89; Agni 90; Alabama Literary Review 91; Alaska Quarterly Review 92; Amelia 94; Amherst Review, The 96; Antaeus 97; Antigonish Review, The 98; Antioch Review 98; Ararat Quarterly 99; Archae 99; Arnazella 100; Artful Dodge 101; Art:Mag 101; Asylum Annual 101; Atalantik 102; Atlantean Press Review, The 103; Bad Haircut 105; Bakunin 105; Barrelhouse, The 106; Bella Figura, La 107; Black Hammock Review, The 110; Black Ice 111; Brownbag Press 119; Callaloo 120; Chaminade Literary Review 123; Chariton Review, The 124; Chelsea 124; Cicada 127; Coe Review, The 129; Columbia: A Magazine of Poetry & Prose 130; Confrontation 132; Conjunctions 132; Crab Creek Review 133; Cream City Review, The 134; Descant (Ontario) 139; Diffusions 140; Dream International/Quarterly 140; Fiction 149; Fighting Woman News 150; Fine Madness 151; Fireweed 151; Folio: A Literary Journal 152; G.W. Review, The 155; Grand Street 159; Green Mountains Review 160; Gulf Coast 161; Gypsy 162; Hawaii Pacific Review 165; Hawaii Review 165; Hopewell Review, The 170; Hunted News, The 172; Hyperbole Studios 173; Hyphen Magazine 173; Immanent Face Magazine 174; Infinity Limited 175; ipsissima verba/the very words 177; Jeopardy 178; Jewish Currents Magazine 179; Kenyon Review, The 184; Kestrel 184; Language Bridges Quarterly 187; Left Curve 189; Lynx 196; MacGuffin, The 196; Manoa 198; Mati 199; Metropolitain 200; Mid-American Review 201; Midland 201; Miorita, a Journal of Romanian Studies 204; Mississippi Review 205; Moody Street Review, The 206; mOOn 207; Nahant Bay 209; NCASA Journal 210; New Delta Review 212; New Laurel Review 213; New Letters Magazine 214; New Orleans Review 214; New Press Literary Quarterly, The 214; new renaissance, the 215; Nimrod 218; Northwest Review 221; Oregon East 225; Owen Wister Review 227; Oxford Magazine 228; Painted Bride Quarterly 229; Painted Hills Review 229; Palace Corbie 230; Partisan Review 232; Peckerwood 234; Pennsylvania Review 235; Phoebe (New York) 236; Phoebe (Virginia) 236; Pinehurst Journal, The 238; Poetic Space 239; Portable Wall, The 241; Porter International, Bern 241; Primal Voices 244; Prism International 245; Psychotrain 246; Puck! 247; Puerto Del Sol 248;

Commercial Periodicals

Treasure Hunter 368; Pockets 375; Radiance 378; Ranger Rick Magazine 380; Road King Magazine 381; Shofar 383; Sports Afield 384

Canadian. Atlantic Salmon Journal 329; Bowbender 333; Canadian Messenger 335; Chickadee 337; Companion of Saint Francis and St. Anthony, The 339; Indian Life Magazine 356; Lethbridge Magazine 363; Messenger of the Sacred Heart 367; Out Magazine 374; Vancouver Child, The 391

Childrens/Juvenile. Associate Reformed Presbyterian, The 328; Chickadee 337; Child Life 337; Children's Digest 337; Children's Playmate 338; Clubhouse 338; Creative Kids 341; Cricket Magazine 342; Crusader Magazine 342; Discoveries 343; Friend Magazine, The 347; GUIDE Magazine 350; Highlights for Children 352; Home Altar, The 353; Humpty Dumpty's Magazine 355; Jack and Jill 358; Junior Trails 359; Kid City 359; Kindergarten Listen 360; Ladybug 362; Lollipops Magazine 364; My Friend 369; Noah's Ark 371; On the Line 372; Pockets 375; R-A-D-A-R 378; Ranger Rick Magazine 380; Shofar 383; Single Parent, The 384; Story Friends 385; Street News 385; Sunshine Magazine 387; Touch 390; Turtle Magazine for Preschool Kids 391; Vancouver Child, The 391; Wonder Time 394; Young Crusader, The 395

Condensed Novel. Arizona Coast 327; Campus Life Magazine 334; Career Focus; College Preview; Direct Aim; Journey; Visions 335; Common Touch Magazine 339; Grit 350; Tikkun 390; Virtue 392; Women's American ORT Reporter 394;

Erotica. Chic 336; Contact Advertising 340; First Hand 346; Gallery Magazine 347; Gent 348; Hot 'N' Nasty 354; Hustler 355; Hustler Busty Beauties 355; Options 373; Pillow Talk 375; Private Letters 376; Radiance 378; Swank Magazine 387; Texas Connection Magazine 389;

Etnic/Multicultural. American Citizen Italian Press, The 326; Art Times 327; Baltimore Jewish Times 330; Bomb Magazine 332; Boston Review 332; Buffalo Spree Magazine 334; Career Focus; College Preview; Direct Aim; Journey; Visions 335; Detroit Jewish News 342; Emerge Magazine 344; Hadassah Magazine 351; India Currents 356; Indian Life Magazine 356; Inside 357; Jive, Black Confessions, Black Romance, Bronze Thrills, Black Secrets 358; Lilith Magazine 364; Live 364; Midstream 367; Moment Magazine 368; Organica Quarterly 373; Other Side, The 374; Pockets 375; Radiance 378; Reform Judaism 380; Sassy Magazine 382; Shofar 383; Street News 385; Tikkun 390; Women's American ORT Reporter 394

Experimental. Bomb Magazine 332; Boston Review 332; Career Focus; College Preview; Direct Aim; Journey; Visions 335; Common Touch Magazine 339; Modern Gold Miner and Treasure Hunter 368; Organica Quarterly 373; Other Side, The 374; Sassy Magazine 382

Fantasy. AMAZING® Stories 325; Art Times 327; Asimov's Science Fiction 327; Common Touch Magazine 339; Contact Advertising 340; Dragon Magazine 343; Emerge Magazine 344; Magazine of Fantasy and Science Fiction 366; Omni 371; Oui Magazine 374; Playboy Magazine 375; Pockets 375; Radiance 378; Ranger Rick Magazine 380; Shofar 383; Weird Tales 392

Feminist. American Atheist 326; Art Times 327; Buffalo Spree Magazine 334; Common Touch Magazine 339; Contact Advertising 340; Lilith Magazine 364; Other Side, The 374; Radiance 378; Sassy Magazine 382; Sojourner 384; Tikkun 390; Vancouver Child, The 391; Women's American ORT Reporter 394; Women's Glib 394

Gay. Art Times 327; Bear 330; Contact Advertising 340; Drummer 344; First Hand 346; Guide, The 350; Hot Shots 355; Options 373; Out Magazine 374; Powerplay Magazine 376; Sassy Magazine 382; Tikkun 390; Xtra Magazine 395

Mystery/Suspense. bePuzzled 331; Boys' Life 333; Buffalo Spree Magazine 334; Career Focus; College Preview; Direct Aim; Journey; Visions 335; Common Touch Magazine 339; Cosmopolitan Magazine 341; Dialogue 343; Emerge Magazine 344; Gallery Magazine 347; Grit 350; Hitchcock Mystery Magazine, Alfred 353; Modern Gold Miner and Treasure Hunter 368; New Mystery 370; Other Side, The 374; Oui Magazine 374; Pockets 375; Portland Magazine 376; Queen's Mystery Magazine, Ellery 377; Radiance 378; Ranger Rick Magazine 380; Road King Magazine 381; Shofar 383; Street News 385; Woman's World Magazine 393

Psychic/Supernatural/Occult. Emerge Magazine 344; Iniquities 357; Lilith Magazine 364; Weird Tales 392

Regional. Aloha 325; Atlantic Salmon Journal 329; Boston Review 332; Buzz 334; Dialogue 343; First 346; Georgia Sportsman 348; Lady's Circle 362; Lethbridge Magazine 363; Northeast 371; Portland Magazine 376; Sassy Magazine 382; Street News 385; Sunday Journal Magazine 387; Vancouver Child, The 391; Washingtonian, The 392; Wy'East Historical Journal 394; Yankee Magazine 395

Religious/Inspirational. Alive Now! 325; Associate Reformed Presbyterian, The 328; Baltimore Jewish Times 330; Campus Life Magazine 334; Canadian Messenger 335; Christian Single 338; Clubhouse 338; Common Touch Magazine 339; Companion of Saint Francis and St. Anthony, The 339; Crusader Magazine 342; Detroit Jewish News 342; Discoveries 343; Evangel 344; Family, The 345; Freeway 347; Friend Magazine, The 347; Gem, The 347; Grit 350; GUIDE Magazine 350; Hi-call 352; High Adventure 352; Home Altar, The 353; Home Life 353; Home Times 354; I.D. 356; Ideals Magazine 356; Indian Life Magazine 356; Inside 357; Junior Trails 359; Kindergarten Listen 360; Lady's Circle 362; Liguorian 363; Lilith Magazine 364; Live 364; Living with Teenagers 364; Lookout, The 365; Lutheran Journal, The 365; Magazine for Christian Youth! 365; Mature Living 366; Mature Years 366; Messenger of the Sacred Heart 367; Metro Singles Lifestyles 367; Midstream 367; Moment Magazine 368; My Friend 369; New Era Magazine 370; Noah's Ark 371; On the Line 372; Other Side, The 374; Pockets 375; Purpose 377; R-A-D-A-R 378; Reform Judaism 380; St. Anthony Messenger 381; St. Joseph's Messenger and Advocate of the Blind 381; Seek 382; Shofar 383; Standard 384; Story Friends 385; Straight 385; Student Leadership Journal 386; Student, The 386; Teen Power 388; Teens Today 389; Touch 390; TQ (Teenquest) 390; Virtue 392; Vista 392; With Magazine 393; Wonder Time 394; Young Salvationist/Young Soldier 396

Romance. Baby Connection News Journal, The 329; Career Focus; College Preview; Direct Aim; Journey; Visions 335; Common Touch Magazine 339; Cosmopolitan Magazine 341; Fifty Something Magazine 345; Good Housekeeping 349; Grit 350; Jive, Black Confessions, Black Romance, Bronze Thrills, Black Secrets 358; Metro Singles Lifestyles 367; St. Anthony Messenger 381; St. Joseph's Messenger and Advocate of the Blind 381; Virtue 392; Woman's World Magazine 393

Science Fiction. Aboriginal Science Fiction 324; AMAZING® Stories 325; Analog Science Fiction & Fact 326; Art Times 327; Asimov's Science Fiction 327; Boys' Life 333; Career Focus; College Preview; Direct Aim; Journey; Visions 335; Emerge Magazine 344; Grit 350; Iniquities 357; Juggler's World 359; Magazine of Fantasy and Science Fiction 366; Omni 371; Playboy Magazine 375; Radiance 378; Ranger Rick Magazine 380

Senior Citizen/Retirement. Arizona Coast 327; Dialogue 343; Fifty Something Magazine 345; Lady's Circle 362; Lilith Magazine 364; Mature Living 366; Mature Years 366; Modern Gold Miner and Treasure Hunter 368; Montana Senior Citizens News 369; St. Anthony Messenger 381; St. Joseph's Messenger and Advocate of the Blind

Small Press

Children's/Juvenile. Advocacy Press 402; Annick Press Ltd. 404; Arjuna Library Press 405; Atlantean Press, The 405; Black Moss Press 408; Blind Beggar Press 408; Borealis Press 409; Carolina Wren Press 412; Colonial Press 415; Coteau Books 416; Creative with Words Publications 417; Cross-Cultural Communications 417; Crystal River Press 418; E.M. Press, Inc. 421; Homestead Publishing 428; Jesperson Press Ltd. 430; Jordan Enterprizes Publishing Company 430; Kar-Ben Copies, Inc. 430; Kruza Kaleidoscopix, Inc. 431; Lee & Low Books 432; Lester Publishing Limited 432; Lollipop Power Books 432; Long Publishing Co., Hendrick 432; Misty Hill Press 437; Orca Book Publishers Ltd. 440; Our Child Press 440; Overlook Press, The 441; Pando Publications 441; Permeable Press 443; Pippin Press 444; Prairie Publishing Company, The 445; Read 'n Run Books 446; Shoestring Press 451; Stemmer House Publishers, Inc. 455; Third World Press 456; University Editions 458; Willowisp Press, Inc. 460; Women's Press 461; Woodsong Graphics Inc. 461

Erotica. Arjuna Library Press 405; Asylum Arts 405; British American Publishing, Ltd. 409; Creative Arts Book Co. 417; Dragonsbreath Press, The 420; Guyasuta Publisher 426; HMS Press 428; Infinite Savant Publishing 428; Mid-List Press 436; Permeable Press 443; Press Gang Publishers 445; Sand River Press 448; Slough Press 451; Vandamere Press 459

Ethnic/Multicultural. Authors Unlimited 406; Bamboo Ridge Press 406; Barn Owl Books 406; Bilingual Press/Editorial Bilingüe 407; Blind Beggar Press 408; British American Publishing, Ltd. 409; Carolina Wren Press 412; Coffee House Press 415; Council for Indian Education 416; Cross-Cultural Communications 417; Eighth Mt. Press, The 421; Feminist Press at the City University of New York, The 422; Fifth House Publishers 423; Griffon House Publications 425; Guernica Editions 425; Haypenny Press 426; Helicon Nine Editions 427; Heritage Press 427; Island House 429; Jordan Enterprizes Publishing Company 430; Kitchen Table: Women of Color Press 431; Mage Publishers 435; Mey-House Books 436; Mid-List Press 436; Path Press, Inc. 442; Pocahontas Press, Inc. 444; Press Gang Publishers 445; Read 'n Run Books 446; Sand River Press 448; Sandpiper Press 448; Seal Press 450; Seven Buffaloes Press 450; Shoestring Press 451; Slough Press 451; Soho Press 451; Soleil Press 451; Southern Methodist University Press 452; Stemmer House Publishers, Inc. 455; Stone Bridge Press 455; Third World Press 456; Three Continents Press 457; University Editions 458; White Pine Press 460; Zephyr Press 462

Experimental. Aegina Press, Inc. 403; Applezaba Press 404; Arjuna Library Press 405; Asylum Arts 405; Black Heron Press 407; Black Tie Press 408; Blind Beggar Press 408; Cacanadadada 410; Carolina Wren Press 412; Carpenter Press 413; Coffee House Press 415; Cross-Cultural Communications 417; Dan River Press 419; Dragonsbreath Press, The 420; Griffon House Publications 425; Gryphon Publications 425; Haypenny Press 426; Heaven Bone Press 426; Helicon Nine Editions 427; Independence Publishers of Georgia Inc. 428; Island House 429; Jordan Enterprizes Publishing Company 430; Mid-List Press 436; Milkweed Editions 437; New Directions 438; New Rivers Press 439; Ommation Press 440; Paycock Press 442; Permeable Press 443; Pikestaff Publications, Inc. 443; Pineapple Press 443; Puckerbrush Press 445; Q.E.D. Press 445; Quarry Press 446; Read 'n Run Books 446; Red Deer College Press 447; Slough Press 451; Station Hill Press 455; Textile Bridge Press 456; Thistledown Press 456; Turnstone Press 458; Ultramarine Publishing Co., Inc. 458; University Editions 458; Zephyr Press 462

Family Saga. E.M. Press, Inc. 421; Mid-List Press 436; Savant Garde Workshop, The 448

Fantasy. Aegina Press, Inc. 403; Applezaba Press 404; Ariadne Press 404; Arjuna Library Press 405; Authors Unlimited 406; British American Publishing, Ltd. 409; Carpenter Press 413; Clear Light Publishers 414; Dan River Press 419; Dragonsbreath Press, The

Romance. Aegina Press, Inc. 403; Arjuna Library Press 405; Authors Unlimited 406; Bryans & Bryans 410; E.M. Press, Inc. 421; Jordan Enterprizes Publishing Company 430; Marie's Books 435; Marron Publishers, Inc. 436; Read 'n Run Books 446; University Editions 458; Woodsong Graphics Inc. 461

Science Fiction. Aegina Press, Inc. 403; Aegina Press, Inc. 403; Arjuna Library Press 405; Authors Unlimited 406; Black Heron Press 407; British American Publishing, Ltd. 409; Dan River Press 419; Dayspring Press, Inc. 420; Dragonsbreath Press, The 420; Fasa Corporation 422; Feminist Press at the City University of New York, The 422; Gryphon Publications 425; Haypenny Press 426; Heaven Bone Press 426; Infinite Savant Publishing 428; Jordan Enterprizes Publishing Company 430; McKnight Books 434; Mey-House Books 436; Mid-List Press 436; Overlook Press, The 441; Pando Publications 441; Permeable Press 443; Press Gang Publishers 445; Read 'n Run Books 446; Sand River Press 448; Savant Garde Workshop, The 448; Shoestring Press 451; Space and Time 452; Third World Press 456; Ultramarine Publishing Co., Inc. 458; University Editions 458; Vandamere Press 459; W.W. Publications 459; Woodsong Graphics Inc. 461

Short Story Collections. Aegina Press, Inc. 403; Applezaba Press 404; Asylum Arts 405; Atlantean Press, The 405; Bamboo Ridge Press 406; Beil, Publisher, Inc., Frederic C. 406; Bilingual Press/Editorial Bilingüe 407; Black Moss Press 408; Blind Beggar Press 408; Books for All Times, Inc. 408; Calyx Books 410; Cane Hill Press 412; Carolina Wren Press 412; Clockwatch Review Press 415; Coffee House Press 415; Colonial Press 415; Confluence Press Inc. 416; Coteau Books 416; Council for Indian Education 416; Creative Arts Book Co. 417; Cross-Cultural Communications 417; Dan River Press 419; Daniel and Company, Publishers, John 419; Dragonsbreath Press, The 420; Ecco Press, The 421; Eighth Mt. Press, The 421; Goose Lane Editions 424; Graywolf Press 425; Gryphon Publications 425; Guyasuta Publisher 426; Haypenny Press 426; Helicon Nine Editions 427; Homestead Publishing 428; Independence Publishers of Georgia Inc. 428; Island House 429; Kitchen Table: Women of Color Press 431; Lester Publishing Limited 432; Mid-List Press 436; New Rivers Press 438; NuAge Editions 440; Papier-Mache 441; Path Press, Inc. 442; Permeable Press 443; Press Gang Publishers 445; Quarry Press 446; Read 'n Run Books 446; Red Deer College Press 447; Rio Grande Press 447; Seal Press 450; Seven Buffaloes Press 450; Slough Press 451; Southern Methodist University Press 452; Spectrum Press 452; Textile Bridge Press 456; Third World Press 456; Thistledown Press 456; Three Continents Press 457; Ultramarine Publishing Co., Inc. 458; University Editions 458; University of Arkansas Press, The 459; University of Idaho Press 459; White Pine Press 460; Wild East Publishing Co-operative Ltd. 460; Women's Press 461; Zephyr Press 462; Zoland Books, Inc. 462

Sports. Authors Unlimited 406; Path Press, Inc. 442; Pocahontas Press, Inc. 444; Reference Press 447

Thriller/Espionage. Aegina Press, Inc. 403; Atlantean Press, The 405; Authors Unlimited 406; E.M. Press, Inc. 421; Gryphon Publications 425; Independence Publishers of Georgia Inc. 428; Mid-List Press 436; Overlook Press, The 441; Permeable Press 443; Savant Garde Workshop, The 448; Shoestring Press 451; Tudor Publishers, Inc. 458

Translations. Applezaba Press 404; Asylum Arts 405; Atlantean Press, The 405; Beil, Publisher, Inc., Frederic C. 406; Bilingual Press/Editorial Bilingüe 407; Blind Beggar Press 408; British American Publishing, Ltd. 409; Calyx Books 410; Carolina Wren Press 412; Catbird Press 413; Creative Arts Book Co. 417; Cross-Cultural Communications 417; Feminist Press at the City University of New York, The 422; Griffon House Publications 425; Helicon Nine Editions 427; Independence Publishers of Georgia Inc. 428; Italica Press 429; Mercury House 436; New Rivers Press 439; NuAge Editions 440; Overlook Press, The 441; Paycock Press 442; Pocahontas Press, Inc. 444; Q.E.D. Press

445; Read 'n Run Books 446; Station Hill Press 455; Stone Bridge Press 455; Three Continents Press 457; Translation Center, The 457; University Editions 458; University of Arkansas Press, The 459; Women's Press 461; Zephyr Press 462; Zoland Books, Inc. 462

Western. Atlantean Press, The 405; Authors Unlimited 406; British American Publishing, Ltd. 409; Clear Light Publishers 414; Coteau Books 416; Creative Arts Book Co. 417; Dan River Press 419; Homestead Publishing 428; J & P Books 430; Mid-List Press 436; Pocahontas Press, Inc. 444; Read 'n Run Books 446; Shoestring Press 451; Sunstone Press 455; Woodsong Graphics Inc. 461

Young Adult/Teen. Arjuna Library Press 405; Bethel Publishing 407; Blind Beggar Press 408; Borealis Press 409; British American Publishing, Ltd. 409; Colonial Press 415; Cross-Cultural Communications 417; Crystal River Press 418; Davenport Publishers, May 419; Evergreen Publications, Inc. 422; Haypenny Press 426; Homestead Publishing 428; J & P Books 430; Jordan Enterprizes Publishing Company 430; Lester Publishing Limited 432; Long Publishing Co., Hendrick 432; Marron Publishers, Inc. 436; Orca Book Publishers Ltd. 440; Our Child Press 440; Pando Publications 441; Pocahontas Press, Inc. 444; Read 'n Run Books 446; Seal Press 450; Shaw Publishers, Harold 450; Shaw Publishers, Harold 450; Third World Press 456; Tudor Publishers, Inc. 458; W.W. Publications 459; Wild East Publishing Co-operative Ltd. 460; Women's Press 461; Woodsong Graphics Inc. 461

Commercial Publishers

Adventure. Avalon Books 470; Bantam/Doubleday Books, Inc. 472; Books In Motion 473; Bouregy & Company, Inc., Thomas 473; Branden Publishing Co. 474; Broadman Press 475; Cloverdale Press Inc. 476; Crown Publishing Group, The 477; Dell Publishing 480; Fawcett 483; Harlequin Enterprises, Ltd. 485; Herald Press 486; Holiday House, Inc. 486; Holt & Company, Henry 487; Horizon Publishers and Dist., Inc. 487; Morrow And Company, Inc., William 493; Philomel Books 496; Pocket Books 498; Random House, Inc. 499; Vesta Publications, Ltd 503; Villard Books 503; Walker and Company 504; Warner Books 504; Worldwide Library 508; Zondervan 508

Canadian. Harlequin Enterprises, Ltd. 485; Macmillan Canada 492; Vesta Publications, Ltd 503; Worldwide Library 508

Children's/Juvenile. Arcade Publishing 469; Atheneum Books for Children 469; Boyds Mills Press 473; Bradbury Press, Inc. 474; Broadman Press 475; Camelot Books 475; Dell Publishing 480; Dial Books for Young Readers 481; Eakin Press 481; Farrar, Straus & Giroux/Children's Books 483; Four Winds Press 484; Gareth Stevens, Inc. 484; Gessler Publishing Company 484; Grosset & Dunlap, Inc. 485; Harcourt Brace Jovanovich 485; Herald Press 486; Holiday House, Inc. 486; Holt & Company, Henry 487; Horizon Publishers and Dist., Inc. 487; Interlink Publishing Group, Inc. 488; Joy Street Books 488; Knopf Books for Young Readers 488; Little, Brown and Company Children's Books 490; Lodestar Books 490; Lucas/Evans Books 491; McElderry Books, Margaret K. 491; Macmillan Children's Books 492; Modern Publishing 492; Morrow Junior Books 493; Pelican Publishing Company 496; Philomel Books 496; Scribners Sons Books for Young Readers, Charles 499; Troll Associates 502; Vesta Publications, Ltd 503; Warner Books 504; Western Publishing Company, Inc. 505; Whitman & Company, Albert 505; WindSong Books 505; Winston-Derek Publishers 505; Yearling 508

Erotica. Carroll & Graf Publishers, Inc. 475; Pocket Books 496

Ethnic/Multicultural. Bantam/Doubleday Books, Inc. 472; Branden Publishing Co.

474; Philomel Books 496; Pocket Books 496; Vesta Publications, Ltd 503

Experimental. Morrow And Company, Inc., William 493; Quill 498; Vesta Publications, Ltd 503

Family Saga. Bantam/Doubleday Books, Inc. 472; Bookcraft, Inc. 473; Harvest House Publishers 486; Herald Press 486; Philomel Books 496

Fantasy. Avon Books 470; Baen Books 471; Bantam Spectra Books 471; Bantam/Doubleday Books, Inc. 472; Berkley Publishing Group, The 472; Berkley/Ace Science Fiction 472; Carroll & Graf Publishers, Inc. 475; Cloverdale Press Inc. 476; Daw Books, Inc. 477; Del Rey Books 480; Delecorte/Dell Books for Young Readers 480; NAL/Dutton 494; Philomel Books 496; Pocket Books 498; Tor Books 502; TSR, Inc. 503; Vesta Publications, Ltd 503; Warner Books 504; Zondervan 508

Feminist. Academy Chicago Publishers 468; Ballantine Books 471; Bantam/Doubleday Books, Inc. 472; Braziller, Inc., George 474; Holt & Company, Henry 487; Morrow And Company, Inc., William 493; Pocket Books 498; Quill 498; Vesta Publications, Ltd 503

Gay. Bantam/Doubleday Books, Inc. 472; Morrow And Company, Inc., William 493; NAL/ Dutton 494; Quill 498

Glitz. Bantam/Doubleday Books, Inc. 472; Harlequin Enterprises, Ltd. 485

Historical. Academy Chicago Publishers 468; Avon Books 470; Ballantine Books 471; Bantam/Doubleday Books, Inc. 472; Bookcraft, Inc. 473; Branden Publishing Co. 474; Broadman Press 475; Cloverdale Press Inc. 476; Crown Publishing Group, The 477; Dell Publishing 480; Fawcett 483; Harvest House Publishers 486; Herald Press 486; Holt & Company, Henry 487; Horizon Publishers and Dist., Inc. 487; Morrow And Company, Inc., William 493; NAL/Dutton 494; Pelican Publishing Company 496; Philomel Books 496; Pocket Books 498; Presidio Press 498; Random House, Inc. 499; Vesta Publications, Ltd 503; Villard Books 503; Winston-Derek Publishers 505; Zondervan 508

Horror. Avon Books 470; Bantam/Doubleday Books, Inc. 472; Cloverdale Press Inc. 476; Crown Publishing Group, The 477; Daw Books, Inc. 477; Dell Publishing 480; Leisure Books 489; Morrow And Company, Inc., William 493; NAL/Dutton 494; Pocket Books 496; TSR, Inc. 503; Villard Books 503; Walker and Company 504; Warner Books 504

Humor/Satire. Bantam/Doubleday Books, Inc. 472; Berkley Publishing Group, The 472; Books In Motion 473; Broadman Press 475; Crown Publishing Group, The 477; Harvest House Publishers 486; Holt & Company, Henry 487; Horizon Publishers and Dist., Inc. 487; Knopf Books for Young Readers 489; Morrow And Company, Inc., William 493; Pocket Books 498; Quill 498; Vesta Publications, Ltd 503; Villard Books 503

Lesbian. Morrow And Company, Inc., William 493; Quill 498

Literary. Arcade Publishing 469; Bantam Spectra Books 471; Blair, Publisher, John F. 472; Branden Publishing Co. 474; Carroll & Graf Publishers, Inc. 475; Crown Publishing Group, The 477; Gessler Publishing Company 484; Herald Press 486; Knopf, Alfred A. 488; Louisiana State University Press 490; Macmillan Canada 492; Morrow And Company, Inc., William 493; Norton & Company, Inc., W.W. 494; Philomel Books 496; Pocket Books 498; Quill 498; Smith, Publisher, Gibbs 500; Washington Square Press 504

Mainstream/Contemporary. Arcade Publishing 469; Avon Books 470; Ballantine Books 471; Berkley Publishing Group, The 472; Blair, Publisher, John F. 472; Bookcraft, Inc. 473; Branden Publishing Co. 474; Carroll & Graf Publishers, Inc. 475; Crown Pub-

496; Random House, Inc. 499; Resource Publications, Inc. 499; Vesta Publications, Ltd 503

Thriller/Espionage. Bookcraft, Inc. 473; Presidio Press 498; Walker and Company 504

Translations. Arcade Publishing 469; Branden Publishing Co. 474; Braziller, Inc., George 474; Gessler Publishing Company 484; Holt & Company, Henry 487; Interlink Publishing Group, Inc. 488; Morrow And Company, Inc., William 493; Philomel Books 496; Smith, Publisher, Gibbs 500; Vesta Publications, Ltd 503

Western. Avalon Books 470; Avon Books 470; Bookcraft, Inc. 473; Bouregy & Company, Inc., Thomas 473; Cloverdale Press Inc. 476; Doubleday 481; Evans & Co., Inc., M. 482; Jameson Books 488; NAL/Dutton 494; Philomel Books 496; Pocket Books 498; Presidio Press 498; Tor Books 502; Walker and Company 504; Warner Books 504

Young Adult/Teen. Archway Paperbacks/Minstrel Books 469; Atheneum Books for Children 469; Avon Books 470; Bantam/Doubleday Books, Inc. 472; Bookcraft, Inc. 473; Boyds Mills Press 473; Bradbury Press, Inc. 474; Broadman Press 475; Cloverdale Press Inc. 476; Crossway Books 476; Delecorte/Dell Books for Young Readers 480; Dell Publishing 480; Harcourt Brace Jovanovich 485; Herald Press 486; Holiday House, Inc. 486; Holt & Company, Henry 487; Horizon Publishers and Dist., Inc. 487; Knopf Books for Young Readers 489; Lerner Publications Company 489; Little, Brown and Company Children's Books 490; Lodestar Books 490; Lucas/Evans Books 491; McElderry Books, Margaret K. 491; Morrow Junior Books 493; Philomel Books 496; Scribners Sons Books for Young Readers, Charles 499; Tab Book Club 502; Trillium Press 502; Troll Associates 502; Vesta Publications, Ltd 503; Walker and Company 504; WindSong Books 505; Winston-Derek Publishers 505

Markets Index

Can't find a listing? Check pages 320-321 for Literary and Small Circulation Magazines/ '92-'93 Changes, page 399 for Commercial Periodicals/'92-'93 Changes, page 465 for Small Presses, page 511 for Commercial Publishers/'92-'93 Changes, page 551 for Contests/'92-'93 Changes, page 591 for Conferences and Workshops, page 599 for Retreats and Colonies/'92-'93 Changes or page 608 for Organizations/'92-'93 Changes.

Can't find a listing? Check pages 320-321 for Literary and Small Circulation Magazines/ '92-'93 Changes, page 399 for Commercial Periodicals/'92-'93 Changes, page 465 for Small Presses, page 511 for Commercial Publishers/'92-'93 Changes, page 551 for Contests/'92-'93 Changes, page 591 for Conferences and Workshops, page 599 for Retreats and Colonies/'92-'93 Changes or page 608 for Organizations/'92-'93 Changes.

Can't find a listing? Check pages 320-321 for Literary and Small Circulation Magazines/ '92-'93 Changes, page 399 for Commercial Periodicals/'92-'93 Changes, page 465 for Small Presses, page 511 for Commercial Publishers/'92-'93 Changes, page 551 for Contests/'92-'93 Changes, page 591 for Conferences and Workshops, page 599 for Retreats and Colonies/'92-'93 Changes or page 608 for Organizations/'92-'93 Changes.

**Can't find a listing? Check pages 320-321 for Literary and Small Circulation Magazines/
'92-'93 Changes, page 399 for Commercial Periodicals/'92-'93 Changes, page 465 for
Small Presses, page 511 for Commercial Publishers/'92-'93 Changes, page 551 for Contests/'92-'93 Changes, page 591 for Conferences and Workshops, page 599 for Retreats
and Colonies/'92-'93 Changes or page 608 for Organizations/'92-'93 Changes.**

Can't find a listing? Check pages 320-321 for Literary and Small Circulation Magazines/ '92-'93 Changes, page 399 for Commercial Periodicals/'92-'93 Changes, page 465 for Small Presses, page 511 for Commercial Publishers/'92-'93 Changes, page 551 for Contests/'92-'93 Changes, page 591 for Conferences and Workshops, page 599 for Retreats and Colonies/'92-'93 Changes or page 608 for Organizations/'92-'93 Changes.

Can't find a listing? Check pages 320-321 for Literary and Small Circulation Magazines/'92-'93 Changes, page 399 for Commercial Periodicals/'92-'93 Changes, page 465 for Small Presses, page 511 for Commercial Publishers/'92-'93 Changes, page 551 for Contests/'92-'93 Changes, page 591 for Conferences and Workshops, page 599 for Retreats and Colonies/'92-'93 Changes or page 608 for Organizations/'92-'93 Changes.

Can't find a listing? Check pages 320-321 for Literary and Small Circulation Magazines/ '92-'93 Changes, page 399 for Commercial Periodicals/'92-'93 Changes, page 465 for Small Presses, page 511 for Commercial Publishers/'92-'93 Changes, page 551 for Contests/'92-'93 Changes, page 591 for Conferences and Workshops, page 599 for Retreats and Colonies/'92-'93 Changes or page 608 for Organizations/'92-'93 Changes.

Can't find a listing? Check pages 320-321 for Literary and Small Circulation Magazines/ '92-'93 Changes, page 399 for Commercial Periodicals/'92-'93 Changes, page 465 for Small Presses, page 511 for Commercial Publishers/'92-'93 Changes, page 551 for Contests/'92-'93 Changes, page 591 for Conferences and Workshops, page 599 for Retreats and Colonies/'92-'93 Changes or page 608 for Organizations/'92-'93 Changes.

Other Books of Interest

General Writing Books

Beginning Writer's Answer Book, edited by Kirk Polking (paper) $13.95
Dare to Be a Great Writer, by Leonard Bishop (paper) $14.95
Discovering the Writer Within, by Bruce Ballenger & Barry Lane $17.95
Freeing Your Creativity, by Marshall Cook $17.95
Getting the Words Right: How to Rewrite, Edit and Revise, by Theodore A. Rees Cheney (paper) $12.95
How to Write a Book Proposal, by Michael Larsen (paper) $11.95
How to Write Fast While Writing Well, by David Fryxell $17.95
How to Write with the Skill of a Master and the Genius of a Child, by Marshall J. Cook $18.95
Knowing Where to Look: The Ultimate Guide to Research, by Lois Horowitz (paper) $18.95
Make Your Words Work, by Gary Provost $17.95
On Being a Writer, edited by Bill Strickland (paper) $16.95
Pinckert's Practical Grammar, by Robert C. Pinckert (paper) $11.95
12 Keys to Writing Books That Sell, by Kathleen Krull (paper) $12.95
The 28 Biggest Writing Blunders, by William Noble $12.95
The 29 Most Common Writing Mistakes & How to Avoid Them, by Judy Delton (paper) $9.95
The Wordwatcher's Guide to Good Writing & Grammar, by Morton S. Freeman (paper) $15.95
Word Processing Secrets for Writers, by Michael A. Banks & Ansen Dibell (paper) $14.95
The Writer's Book of Checklists, by Scott Edelstein $16.95
The Writer's Digest Guide to Manuscript Formats, by Buchman & Groves $18.95
The Writer's Essential Desk Reference, edited by Glenda Neff $19.95

Nonfiction Writing

The Complete Guide to Writing Biographies, by Ted Schwarz $6.99
Creative Conversations: The Writer's Guide to Conducting Interviews, by Michael Schumacher $16.95
How to Do Leaflets, Newsletters, & Newspapers, by Nancy Brigham (paper) $14.95
How to Write Irresistible Query Letters, by Lisa Collier Cool (paper) $10.95
The Writer's Digest Handbook of Magazine Article Writing, edited by Jean M. Fredette (paper) $11.95

Fiction Writing

The Art & Craft of Novel Writing, by Oakley Hall $17.95
Characters & Viewpoint, by Orson Scott Card $13.95
The Complete Guide to Writing Fiction, by Barnaby Conrad $18.95
Creating Characters: How to Build Story People, by Dwight V. Swain $16.95
Creating Short Fiction, by Damon Knight (paper) $10.95
Dialogue, by Lewis Turco $13.95
The Fiction Writer's Silent Partner, by Martin Roth $19.95
Get That Novel Started! (And Keep Going 'Til You Finish), by Donna Levin $17.95
Handbook of Short Story Writing: Vol. I, by Dickson and Smythe (paper) $12.95
Handbook of Short Story Writing: Vol. II, edited by Jean Fredette (paper) $12.95

How to Write & Sell Your First Novel, by Collier & Leighton (paper) $12.95

Manuscript Submission, by Scott Edelstein $13.95

Mastering Fiction Writing, by Kit Reed $18.95

Plot, by Ansen Dibell $13.95

Practical Tips for Writing Popular Fiction, by Robyn Carr $17.95

Spider Spin Me a Web: Lawrence Block on Writing Fiction, by Lawrence Block $16.95

Theme & Strategy, by Ronald B. Tobias $13.95

The 38 Most Common Writing Mistakes, by Jack M. Bickham $12.95

Writer's Digest Handbook of Novel Writing, $18.95

Writing the Novel: From Plot to Print, by Lawrence Block (paper) $11.95

Special Interest Writing Books

Armed & Dangerous: A Writer's Guide to Weapons, by Michael Newton (paper) $14.95

Cause of Death: A Writer's Guide to Death, Murder & Forensic Medicine, by Keith D. Wilson, M.D. $15.95

The Children's Picture Book: How to Write It, How to Sell It, by Ellen E.M. Roberts (paper) $19.95

Children's Writer's Word Book, by Alijandra Mogliner $19.95

Comedy Writing Secrets, by Mel Helitzer (paper) $15.95

The Complete Book of Feature Writing, by Leonard Witt $18.95

Creating Poetry, by John Drury $18.95

Deadly Doses: A Writer's Guide to Poisons, by Serita Deborah Stevens with Anne Klarner (paper) $16.95

Editing Your Newsletter, by Mark Beach (paper) $18.50

Families Writing, by Peter Stillman (paper) $12.95

A Guide to Travel Writing & Photography, by Ann & Carl Purcell (paper) $22.95

Hillary Waugh's Guide to Mysteries & Mystery Writing, by Hillary Waugh $19.95

How to Pitch & Sell Your TV Script, by David Silver $17.95

How to Write & Sell Greeting Cards, Bumper Stickers, T-Shirts and Other Fun Stuff, by Molly Wigand (paper) 15.95

How to Write & Sell True Crime, by Gary Provost $17.95

How to Write Horror Fiction, by William F. Nolan $15.95

How to Write Mysteries, by Shannon OCork $13.95

How to Write Romances, by Phyllis Taylor Pianka $15.95

How to Write Science Fiction & Fantasy, by Orson Scott Card $13.95

How to Write Tales of Horror, Fantasy & Science Fiction, edited by J.N. Williamson (paper) $12.95

How to Write the Story of Your Life, by Frank P. Thomas (paper) $11.95

How to Write Western Novels, by Matt Braun $1.00

The Magazine Article: How To Think It, Plan It, Write It, by Peter Jacobi $17.95

Mystery Writer's Handbook, by The Mystery Writers of America (paper) $11.95

Powerful Business Writing, by Tom McKeown $12.95

Scene of the Crime: A Writer's Guide to Crime-Scene Investigation, by Anne Wingate, Ph.D. $15.95

Successful Scriptwriting, by Jurgen Wolff & Kerry Cox (paper) $14.95

The Writer's Complete Crime Reference Book, by Martin Roth $19.95

The Writer's Guide to Conquering the Magazine Market, by Connie Emerson $17.95

Writing for Children & Teenagers, 3rd Edition, by Lee Wyndham & Arnold Madison (paper) $12.95

Writing Mysteries: A Handbook by the Mystery Writers of America, Edited by Sue Grafton, $18.95

Writing the Modern Mystery, by Barbara Norville (paper) $12.95

The Writing Business

A Beginner's Guide to Getting Published, edited by Kirk Polking (paper) $11.95

Business & Legal Forms for Authors & Self-Publishers, by Tad Crawford (paper) $4.99

The Complete Guide to Self-Publishing, by Tom & Marilyn Ross (paper) $16.95

How to Write with a Collaborator, by Hal Bennett with Michael Larsen $1.00

This Business of Writing, by Gregg Levoy $19.95

Writer's Guide to Self-Promotion & Publicity, by Elane Feldman $16.95

A Writer's Guide to Contract Negotiations, by Richard Balkin (paper) $4.25

Writing A to Z, edited by Kirk Polking $24.95

To order directly from the publisher, include $3.00 postage and handling for 1 book and $1.00 for each additional book. Allow 30 days for delivery.